HABITAT MANAGEMENT FOR MIGRATING AND WINTERING WATERFOWL IN NORTH AMERICA

HABITAT MANAGEMENT FOR MIGRATING AND WINTERING WATERFOWL IN NORTH AMERICA

Edited by

LOREN M. SMITH
Texas Tech University

ROGER L. PEDERSON
Ducks Unlimited, Inc.

RICHARD M. KAMINSKI
Mississippi State University

Texas Tech University Press

Library of Congress Cataloging-in-Publication Data

Habitat management for migrating and wintering waterfowl in North
  America / edited by Loren M. Smith . . . [et al.].
        p.   cm.
     ISBN 0-89672-204-X (alk. paper). — ISBN 0-89672-205-8 (pbk. :
  alk. paper)
        1. Waterfowl—North America—Habitat.   2. Wildlife habitat
  improvement—North America.   I. Smith, Loren M.   II. Pederson,
  Roger L. III. Kaminski, Richard M.
  QL696.A52H32   1989   89-5113
  639.9′78—dc20   CIP

92 93 94 95 96 97 98 99 / 9 8 7 6 5 4 3 2

Texas Tech University Press
Lubbock, Texas 79409-1037 USA

This book is dedicated to:

Frank C. Bellrose, Jr.
and
Jessop B. Low

For their pioneering efforts in
the management of migrating and wintering waterfowl habitat
in North America.

CONTENTS

Foreword ix

Preface xi

ATLANTIC FLYWAY

Tidal and Nontidal Wetlands of Northern Atlantic States
Dennis G. Jorde, Jerry R. Longcore, and Patrick W. Brown......................1
Chesapeake Bay and North Carolina Sounds
Larry J. Hindman and Vernon D. Stotts 27
South Atlantic Coastal Wetlands
David H. Gordon, Brian T. Gray, Robert D. Perry, Michael B. Prevost,
Thomas H. Strange, and R. Kenneth Williams 57
Southern Reservoirs and Lakes
Fred A. Johnson and Frank Montalbano III 93
Beaver Pond Wetlands: A Southern Perspective
Dale H. Arner and Gary R. Hepp 117

MISSISSIPPI FLYWAY

The Great Lakes Marshes
Theodore A. Bookhout, Karl E. Bednarik, and Roy W. Kroll 131
Riverine and Deepwater Habitats for Diving Ducks
Carl E. Korschgen 157
Upper Mississippi Valley Wetlands—Refuges and Moist-Soil Impoundments
Frederic A. Reid, James R. Kelley, Jr., T. Scott Taylor,
and Leigh H. Fredrickson 181
Mississippi Alluvial Valley
Kenneth J. Reinecke, Richard M. Kaminski, David J. Moorhead,
John D. Hodges, and James R. Nassar....................................203
Southern Coastal Marshes and Lakes
Robert H. Chabreck, Ted Joanen, and Stuart L. Paulus 249

CENTRAL FLYWAY

Northern Great Plains
Roger L. Pederson, Dennis G. Jorde, and S. Gay Simpson 281
High Plains Reservoirs and Sloughs
James K. Ringelman, William R. Eddleman, and Harvey W. Miller............311
Playa Lakes
Eric G. Bolen, Guy A. Baldassarre, and Fred S. Guthery 341
The Rice Prairies
William C. Hobaugh, Charles D. Stutzenbaker,
and Edward L. Flickinger 367
The Texas Coast
Charles D. Stutzenbaker and Milton W. Weller............................385
The East Coast of Mexico
Guy A. Baldassarre, Arthur R. Brazda, and Emilio Rangel Woodyard 407

PACIFIC FLYWAY
Northwest Riverine and Pacific Coast
  I. Joseph Ball, Richard D. Bauer, Kees Vermeer,
    and Michael J. Rabenberg 429
The Great Basin Marshes
  John A. Kadlec and Loren M. Smith 451
The Central, Imperial, and Coachella Valleys of California
  Mickey E. Heitmeyer, Daniel P. Connelly, and Roger L. Pederson 475
The Pacific Coast of Mexico
  Gary W. Kramer and Rodrigo Migoya 507

BIOPOLITICAL STRATEGIES
Biopolitical Strategies for Waterfowl Habitat Preservation and Enhancement
  Rollin D. Sparrowe, Thomas J. Dwyer, Peter G. Poulos,
    Laurence R. Jahn, David M. Smith, and Robert J. Misso 531

FOREWORD

As the twentieth century nears its final decade, the North American duck population is in trouble. Prolonged drought over much of the duck nesting grounds, which has curtailed production, is a major cause of the current depression of duck numbers. But there have been many other contributors, such as acid rain in the Northeast, lead poisoning in heavily shot areas, selenium poisoning in irrigation sumps of the West, botulism and algal poisoning in drought-stricken marshes, avian cholera in the High Plains, lost and degraded habitats throughout the flyways, and overshooting of some species. Some of these decimators are localized or temporary, but others, like drainage and filling of wetlands, are permanent and irreversible.

However, this gloomy picture is brightened by recent developments. The adoption of the North American Waterfowl Management Plan (NAWMP) by Canada and the United States in 1986 marks the beginning of a new era in waterfowl management, one featuring a degree of cooperation never before envisioned. The (NAWMP) calls for the integrated efforts of those working directly with waterfowl management, but seeks, in addition, to enlist the support of those impacting waterfowl habitat indirectly, such as agriculturists, foresters, and developers. It states clearly that "in all waterfowl management decisions and actions, first priority should be given to perpetuate waterfowl populations and their supporting habitats," a policy statement "dependent on the protection, restoration, and management of habitat." The authors of the NAWMP recognized that without adequate habitat for production, molting, staging, migration, wintering, and recreational use of the resource, management has little purpose and is doomed. The NAWMP has set population goals by species, and has specified the minimum habitat needs to accomplish these goals. Thus, there is now a "blueprint" accepted by the management fraternity challenging fulfillment.

Necessarily brief (encompassing only 32 pages), the Plan lacks the details that administrators and managers will need to support and conduct a successful program. It calls for sufficient habitat to meet the requirements of 62 million breeding ducks, at least 100 million migrating ducks, and 6 million wintering geese. Moreover, it specifies the habitat areas of highest priorities for meeting these goals, but leaves the details to be worked out.

Just when needed most, along comes this book on the management of migration and wintering habitat to help flesh-out the Plan. *Habitat Management for Migrating and Wintering Waterfowl in North America* provides the details about each priority area and others nearly as important in all four flyways. Whether your interest is in tidal basins, interior marshes, artificial impoundments, and/or river bottomlands, you will find answers to many of your questions, written by experts within each habitat area. Nowhere can you find a comparable assimilation of information.

Over 60 biologists, managers, and administrators have contributed their expertise in writing this book. The 21 chapters not only project the knowledge of each author, but also draw extensively from the literature regarding pertinent waterfowl biology and habitat management.

Besides supplementing the NAWMP, this book will provide support for a number of emerging federal, provincial, state, and private programs that show promise of enhancing the habitat base. In Canada, each province with the Canadian Wildlife Service is finalizing a waterfowl management plan as Canada's contribution toward the overall plan. Local municipalities, Ducks Unlimited Canada, and individual landowners are an integral part of the process. In the United States the 1985 Farm Bill, designed to reduce soil erosion and decrease production of surplus crops, helps maintain and enhance waterfowl habitat through its Sodbuster and Swampbuster provisions and the Conservation Reserve Program. Some state programs, with direct or indirect benefits to waterfowl, are also being brought into the overall plan. Ducks Unlimited's new policy of developing wetlands for migrating and wintering waterfowl in the United States, Mexico, and Canada is another major contribution to the total program. And so is the work of The Nature Conservancy in acquiring threatened natural areas. In short, the machinery for protecting the habitat that North American waterfowl need to maintain desired numbers is grinding away at an increasing rate. But protection is not enough! Intensive management will be required, which must be based on the kind of information contained in this book.

Arthur S. Hawkins
Hugo, Minnesota

PREFACE

During the 1980s, more research emphasis than previously expended has been placed on the ecology and management of nonbreeding waterfowl. This effort has resulted from the realization that, to manage waterfowl poulations effectively, we must understand the annual cycle of waterfowl requirements. Reviews of past research on breeding waterfowl indicate that studies concerning waterfowl habitat and its management did not receive serious investigation until after many studies on the birds themselves were conducted (e.g., behavior, reproductive biology). Indeed, breeding habitat studies have been conducted earnestly only since the 1960s, although intensive waterfowl research on the breeding grounds has occurred for more than 50 years. After witnessing the recent flurry of wintering waterfowl studies, it became apparent that the emphasis again was being placed on waterfowl biology rather than on habitat and its management for waterfowl. Moreover, more extensive wetlands research has been conducted by ecologists in southerly locations than in northern breeding regions. Therefore, habitat management is emphasized in this book because (1) habitat ultimately determines the numbers and composition of the waterfowl present, (2) information from few wetland ecology studies has been applied by waterfowl habitat managers, and (3) habitat management for migrating and wintering waterfowl in North America has not been consolidated and assembled.

The various geographic areas presented in the chapters were determined by their importance as migrating and/or wintering areas, based on the relative numbers of waterfowl using them. Certainly, not all areas important to migrating waterfowl could be included here. Many important habitats during migration (e.g., James Bay [Canada]) occur in the breeding grounds; these are not considered because they are best managed for breeding waterfowl or simply are protected from outside influences. We limit our consideration essentially to areas within the conterminous United States, near-border regions of Canada, and east and west coastal Mexico. We chose to organize the book chapters by flyway rather than by ecoregions because waterfowl are managed on the former basis. However, this approach also leads to questions as to which flyway a particular chapter might belong. For example, the chapter on beaver ponds logically applies to the Atlantic and Mississippi flyways; however, it appears only in the Atlantic Flyway to prevent redundancy. Repetition occurs across chapters in management strategies and waterfowl requirements presented, regardless of the way in which chapters are organized, because many techniques used in habitat management are common to all regions.

As the various authors began preparing their respective chapters, it became apparent that what was perceived to be a readily available source of published literature on habitat management was not available or available only in unpublished reports. To the surprise of many authors, the strategies used for habitat management were seldom in written form. Thus, this book should provide a consolidation of the published literature, unpublished reports, and previously undocumented strategies, and may provide the impetus for habitat managers to document their own efforts in written form.

The audiences we hope to reach with this book are the biologists responsible for the management of waterfowl habitat, students studying waterfowl ecology and management, and researchers embarking on studies of nonbreeding waterfowl.

ACKNOWLEDGMENTS

Costs for publication of the book were defrayed by the initiating sponsors: the Caesar Kleberg Foundation for Wildlife Conservation, Delta Waterfowl and Wetlands Research Station, and the Mississippi Department of Wildlife Conservation. Additional financial support was provided by the College of Agricultural Sciences, Texas Tech University; Ducks Unlimited Inc.; the School of Forest Resources, Mississippi State University; the United States Fish and Wildlife Service; and the W. E. Walker Wildlife Conservation Foundation.

We express our sincere thanks to the following individuals for various types of assistance with the chapters: C. Allen, C. Ankney, S. Atkins, T. Bahti, R. Baskett, T. Bell, F. Bellrose, R. Berry, J. Boland, G. Bond, Jr., J. Boyles, M. Brinson, D. Carroll, J. Clem, N. Collins, B. Conant, C. Cordes, P. Corr, P. Covington, R. Craig, R. Crawford, B. Crenshaw, P. Currier, A. de la Cruz, D. Dennis, R. Dimmick, L. Ditto, R. Drobney, H. Duebbert, T. Eberhardt, R. Erickson, N. Euliss, K. Ewel, L. Fredrickson, L. George, D. Gilmer, V. Glooshenko, J. Gosselink, D. Graber, W. Green, G. Grodhaus, G. Haarmeyer, D. Hall, W. Haller, S. Havera, H. W. Heusman, W. Hubert, J. Huener, D. Humburg, R. Jarvis, M. Josselyn, P. Keddy, F. Knopf, M. Kraft, G. Kramer, J. Lamendola, R. Linder, K. Lines, J. Lokemoen, W. Lovering, J. Lovvorn, C. Madsen, R. Malecki, G. Martz, T. McCabe, E. McCollum, G. McCullough, C. MacInnes, M. McLandress, G. Mensik, P. Merola, T. Michot, A. Miller, M. Miller, M. Mitchell, J. Moser, D. Moulton, J. Myers, T. Myers, O. Pehrsson, E. Pendleton, M. Percival, R. Phillips, A. Prochowicz, H. Raffaele, D. Rano, D. Rathke, D. Raveling, R. Rhoades, D. Rundle, C. Ryan, M. Ryan, J. Singleton, M. Smale, P. Smith, J. Snyder, P. Springer, W. Stiles, F. Strand, M. Strong, G. Swanson, M. Szymczak, J. Takekawa, M. Tansy, J. Teal, D. Thornburg, A. van der Valk, L. Vangilder, P. Vohs, J. Ware, J. Weeks, J. Wetzel, S. Wheeler, D. Woodruff, and S. Young. Thanks are also extended to K. Arellano, C. Stogner, C. Hampton, T. Kight, and C. Wasson for the technical and editorial assistance provided.

L. M. Smith
R. L. Pederson
R. M. Kaminski
December, 1988

ATLANTIC FLYWAY

Brackish marsh managed for saltmarsh bulrush, widgeongrass, and dwarf spikerush in the foreground, with prescribed marsh burning occurring in the background, Santee Coastal Reserve, South Carolina (photo taken by B. T. Gray).

TIDAL AND NONTIDAL WETLANDS OF NORTHERN ATLANTIC STATES

DENNIS G. JORDE, U.S. Fish and Wildlife Service, Patuxent Wildlife Research Center, Laurel, MD 20708

JERRY R. LONGCORE, U.S. Fish and Wildlife Service, Patuxent Wildlife Research Center, Laurel, MD 20708

PATRICK W. BROWN, U.S. Fish and Wildlife Service, West Virginia Cooperative Fish and Wildlife Research Unit, 333 Percival Hall, West Virginia University, Morgantown 26506-6125

Tidal and nontidal wetlands of importance to waterfowl in Maine, Vermont, New Hampshire, Massachusetts, Rhode Island, Connecticut, and New York will be the focus of this chapter. These Northern Atlantic states (NAS) are located in the Atlantic Flyway south of eastern Canada and north of New Jersey and Pennsylvania (Fig. 1). Waterfowl habitat in the NAS consists of saline tidal, marine and estuarine systems; and freshwater tidal and nontidal riverine, lacustrine, and palustrine systems. These habitats are used extensively by migrating waterfowl, but only coastal and large inland areas of open water receive significant use during winter (Bellrose 1980).

Estimates of the total area of wetland habitat in the NAS vary (Table 1) (Sanderson and Bellrose 1969, Alexander et al. 1986). Coastal wetlands are estimated to cover 151,579 ha (Alexander et al. 1986), and are the most important habitats. However, only 12% of wetlands along the Atlantic Coast are considered to have moderate to high value to waterfowl (Bellrose 1980). The south shore of Long Island, New York, has abundant coastal marshes and estuaries, and is the northern-most important wintering area for waterfowl on the Atlantic coast (J. D. Moser, pers. commun.).

Inland habitats include >400,000 ha of forested wetlands, about 24,291 ha of lakes and wetlands (excluding the Great Lakes), and an additional 36,437 ha of bogs of limited value to waterfowl (Bellrose 1980). Generally, these inland habitats are not considered important to

FROM ALEXANDER (1986)

Fig. 1. States of the Northern Atlantic region (from Alexander et al 1986)

wintering waterfowl. However, coastal wetlands in the NAS attract a significant proportion of brant (*Branta bernicla*), snow geese (*Chen caerulescens atlantica*),

Table 1. Coastal wetland areas (thousands of ha) of the Northern Atlantic States compiled by the National Oceanic and Atmospheric Administration (Alexander et al. 1986).

State	Salt marsh	Fresh marsh	Tidal flats	Swamp	Total
Maine	6.7	10.4	23.6	10.2	50.9
New Hampshire	3.0	-	-	-	3.0
Massachusetts	19.5	6.1	16.8	10.1	52.5
Rhode Island	3.2	-	-	23.1	26.3
Connecticut	6.7	-	-	-	6.7
New York	10.8	1.4	-	-	12.2
Totals	49.9	17.9	40.4	43.4	151.6

Canada geese (*B. canadensis*), common
eiders (*Somateria mollissima*), mallards
(*Anas platyrhynchos*), and black ducks
(*A. rubripes*) during migration and winter.

The objective of this chapter is to
review habitat requirements and management for migrating and wintering waterfowl in the NAS. Our review includes (1)
location and characterization of major
waterfowl habitats, (2) diversity and
abundance of waterfowl, (3) ecological
aspects of waterfowl habitats, and (4)
assessment of current and future habitat
management in the NAS.

NORTHERN TIDAL AND NONTIDAL WETLANDS

Physical Description

Most of Maine, New Hampshire, New
York, western Massachusetts, and all of
Vermont (Bailey 1976) are included
within the Laurentian Mixed Forest Province (Bailey 1980). This area generally
has low relief, rolling hills, and low
mountains (300-900 m). Lakes, poorly
drained depressions, moraines, drumlins,
eskers, outwash plains, and other glacial
features are characteristic of the area.

The climate of the province includes
moderately long and somewhat severe
winters, but with at least 120 days each
year with average temperatures >10 C.
The frost-free season lasts 100-140 days.
Average annual temperatures range from
2-10 C. Annual precipitation ranges from
60-115 cm and occurs mostly in summer.

Vegetation in the NAS is characteristic
of the Laurentian Mixed Forest and is
transitional between the deciduous forest
to the south and the northern boreal
forest. Soils vary greatly, including combinations of peat, muck, marl, clay, silt,
sand, gravel, and boulders. Spodosols
(Buol et al. 1973) produced in cool,
relatively humid climates under coniferous forests in northern temperate areas
dominate in New England, but are
relatively infertile. Inceptisols and alfisols
are soils under northern deciduous forests.

Most of Connecticut, Rhode Island,
eastern Massachusetts, coastal New
Hampshire, and the southern tip of
Maine fall within the Eastern Deciduous
Forest Province (Bailey 1980). Elevations
range from sea level to 760 m; most of
this province in the NAS has rolling
topography. The climate includes warm
summers and cold winters, with an
average annual temperature ranging
between 4-15 C. Precipitation is greatest
in the summer months, ranging between
90-150 cm each year. Alfisols are characteristic soils.

WATERFOWL HABITATS OF THE NAS

The major wetland habitats used by
waterfowl follow the classification of
Cowardin et al. (1979). Plant nomenclature follows Gleason (1952).

Marine

Marine habitats of the NAS attract sea
ducks (Mergini) and bay ducks (Aythyini).
Marine habitats include saline subtidal
and intertidal areas directly exposed to
wave action and tides of the Atlantic
Ocean. Salinities are >30 ppt. Subtidal
habitats are continuously submerged,
whereas intertidal habitats are alternately
exposed and flooded by tides. Marine
substrates have rocky to sandy shorelines
and bottoms, bars and reefs, and scattered
beds of aquatic vegetation such as sea
lettuce (*Ulva lactuca*), kelp (*Macrocystis*
spp.), and knotted wrack (*Ascophyllum
nodosum*). American lobster (*Homarus
americanus*), beds of blue mussels (*Mytilis
edulis*) and scallops (*Pecten* spp.), and
clam worms (*Nereis* spp.) are examples of
dominant animals.

Estuarine

Estuaries of the NAS provide habitat
for sea ducks (Mergini), bay ducks

Fig. 2. Estuarine habitat of the Jordan River, Maine. Rockweed (*Fucus* spp.) ledges at high tide and exposed mudflats at low tide are prime winter waterfowl habitat in the NAS.

(Aythyini), and dabbling ducks (Anatini). Estuaries are tidal, saltwater habitats partly enclosed by land that may receive freshwater run-off. Salinity is 0.5 to 30.0 ppt. Estuaries in the northern NAS have rocky shorelines intermixed with salt marshes, tidal mud flats, and sandy beaches; they are intermingled with forests that often extend to the high-tide line (Fig. 2). The adjacent low salt marshes are regularly flooded by tides (<4m) (Nixon 1982) and drained by narrow (<2m) and deep (<4m) tidal channels. Habitats in estuaries of the NAS south of Boston, Massachusetts, have more expansive salt marshes than north of Boston, especially in New York (Teal 1986), and are less rocky. These salt marshes are flooded by tides (<2m) and often are drained by shallow (<2m), meandering tidal creeks. Estuarine wetlands include submergent (e.g., eelgrass *Zostera marina*, rockweed) and emergent (e.g., *Spartina* spp.) vegetation, shrub, and forested wetlands. Eelgrass is the dominant submerged aquatic plant (Thayer et al. 1984), whereas *Spartina* is the dominant emergent plant (Nixon 1982, Teal 1986). Periwinkles (*Littorina* spp.) and fiddler crabs (*Uca pugnax*) are abundant in intertidal zones, whereas soft-shelled clams (*Mya arenaria*), blue mussels and clam worms are dominant in subtidal areas. Ice forms along shorelines and on tidal flats for several days or weeks annually, which limits use of aquatic foods by waterfowl.

Riverine

Major groups of waterfowl using riverine habitat include dabbling ducks and bay ducks. Riverine habitats are either tidal or nontidal, with some nontidal subsystems extending long distances (>50km) inland depending on elevation and gradient. Inland, nontidal rivers are high gradient and have gravel bottoms, whereas tidal rivers are predominantly low gradient and have mud or sand bottoms. Salinity is usually <0.5 ppt, but some tidal habitats may exceed this level (Cowardin et al. 1979). Riverine habitats provide a variety of aquatic plants (e.g., pickerelweed [*Pontederia cordata*], sedge [*Carex* spp.], smartweeds [*Polygonums* spp.]) and invertebrates (e.g., snails [*Lymnaea* spp.], fingernail clams [*Pisidium abditum*]) used by waterfowl. In tidal areas, freshwater seeps and streams that drain into tidal mudflats provide fresh drinking water and year-round foraging habitat for several species of dabbling ducks, except during periods of extreme cold and ice (Albright 1981, Jorde 1986). Availability and abundance of foods are dependent on time of year and location of the habitat (Albright 1981, Jorde 1986).

Lacustrine and Palustrine

Lacustrine and palustrine habitats generally attract geese and dabbling ducks. Lacustrine habitats are >2 m deep tidal or nontidal wetlands and are >8 ha. They lack trees and shrubs, but often are surrounded by upland or forest habitats. Palustrine habitats differ from lacustrine by being <2 m in depth, <8 ha, and usually nontidal. Salinity is low (0.5 ppt) in tidal areas of both wetland types; hence, they become ice-bound during cold winters. Wetland habitats in tidal areas can be difficult to classify because of variability within wetland classification modifiers (e.g., salinity, tidal influence, soil types, vegetation). Lacustrine marshes are generally located in areas having a major inflow of freshwater, but experiencing daily tidal cycles (<0.5m); whereas palustrine tidal marshes are high back marshes with persistent vegetation and occasional tidal flooding (Odum et al. 1984). Low marshes along river edges should be classified as riverine (Odum et al. 1984). Flora of palustrine habitats

includes cattails (*Typha* spp.), water lily (*Nymphaea odorata*), peat moss (*Sphagnum fuscum*), and deciduous and evergreen trees and shrubs. Cordgrass, spike grass (*Distichlis* spp.), and reeds (*Phragmites communis*) are dominant species in high salt marshes (Nixon 1982). Common invertebrates include freshwater mollusk (*Elliptio dariensis*), back swimmer (*Notonecta lunata*), mosquito (*Aedes* spp.), and spiders (e.g., *Cornicularia* spp.). Gastropods are the most common invertebrates (>40%) in some high salt marshes (Tiner cited in Nixon 1982).

Widgeongrass (*Ruppia maritima*), duckweed (*Lemna minor*), cattails, and deciduous trees and shrubs are examples of dominant vegetation in freshwater lacustrine habitats (Cowardin et al. 1979). However, in tidal freshwater marshes, the flora includes broad-leaved emergent perennial macrophytes (e.g., pickerelweed), herbaceous annuals (e.g., smartweed), annual and perennial plants (e.g., cutgrass [*Leersia* spp.]), and hyrophytic shrubs (e.g., button bush [*Cephalanthus occidentalis*]) (Odum et al. 1984). Invertebrates include copepods, chironomids, oligochaetes, amphipods, snails, and crabs. In comparison, regularly flooded lacustrine salt marshes (low marshes) are dominated by cordgrass, whose abundance and distribution greatly affects the occurrence of other species such as glassworts (*Salicornia* spp.) and spike grass (Teal 1986). Widgeongrass is a submerged aquatic plant in irregularly flooded wetlands. Examples of common invertebrates of low salt marshes include long-horned grasshoppers (*Conocephalus spartinae*), mosquitos, snails, and crabs (Teal 1986). Palustrine and lacustrine mudflats and tidal salt marshes support abundant food resources often used by foraging waterfowl during winter.

Lakes and Reservoirs

Major waterfowl using lakes and reservoirs include geese, dabbling ducks, and diving ducks. Lakes and reservoirs generally are classified as lacustrine habitats. Salinity is usually <0.5 ppt. Plant communities often are composed of freshwater species such as wild rice (*Zizania aquatica*), pondweeds (*Potamogeton* spp.), and bulrush (*Scirpus* spp.). These habitats influence fall migration of waterfowl, especially when located near agricultural fields. Some waterfowl overwinter on lakes and reservoirs during mild winters.

Uplands

Upland habitats are used mostly by geese, dabbling ducks, and wood ducks (*Aix sponsa*). Uplands consist primarily of forested land and farmland. Forested wetlands, beaver (*Castor canadensis*) flowages, and bogs are used by breeding wood ducks, ring-necked ducks (*Aythya collaris*), and black ducks, but these habitats are little-used by migrating and wintering waterfowl (Bellrose 1980). Waterfowl use cropland during migration where waste grain is available. Like other regions in North America, cornfields adjacent to large bodies of water are attractive to waterfowl.

Urban

Mallards and geese are the major waterfowl species using urban habitats. Urban wetlands are not described by Cowardin et al. (1979), but can be classified as palustrine or lacustrine. However, we delineate these habitats because of their human influences and their use by increasing numbers of ducks and geese wintering in the NAS (Heusmann 1988) Many urban wetlands are man-made or extensively altered natural habitats that include pools, ponds, and lakes used for recreation or municipal water supply reservoirs, flood control, sewage lagoons, industrial cooling, wastewater ponds, and other uses. Development of urban wetlands focuses on human needs for water supplies, open

spaces, and quality living environments near cities. Consequently, conflicting attitudes of private citizens based on economic and political considerations may supersede management of these habitats for waterfowl.

IMPORTANCE OF NAS HABITATS TO WATERFOWL
Migration and Wintering Areas

In the NAS, major migration routes of waterfowl are associated with rivers and lakes that guide waterfowl south and southeast toward wintering areas along the Atlantic coast. Waterfowl usually concentrate at specific locations where food is available, but also show habitat affinities influenced by previous use. For example, geese seem to migrate inland along routes that encompass large lakes and reservoirs, especially those adjacent to agricultural fields.

Most inland wetlands in the NAS freeze during winter. Therefore, major waterfowl wintering areas are located along the coast where a variety of dabbling ducks, diving ducks, and sea ducks use coastal wetlands and estuaries. Exceptions occur in the Great Lakes and other large lakes and rivers where open water provides important wintering areas for relatively large populations of geese, black ducks, mallards, and redheads (*Aythya americana*) (Bookhout et al. 1989). For the remainder of inland areas, scattered urban wetlands and small areas below reservoirs and electric power plants provide open water, but limited food resources, for small numbers of waterfowl.

Migration corridors across Maine are mainly along the coast for dabbling ducks, sea ducks, and geese (Bellrose 1968). There are no major migration corridors for diving ducks. The Penobscot River (Fig. 3) is especially important in central Maine. Farther south the Kennebec and Androscoggin rivers join with 4 smaller rivers to form Merrymeeting

1 LAKE ERIE
2 NIAGARA RIVER
3 LAKE ONTARIO
4 ST. LAWRENCE RIVER
5 FINGER LAKES
6 MOHAWK RIVER VALLEY
7 LONG ISLAND SOUND
8 QUINNIPIAC RIVER
9 CONNECTICUT RIVER
10 THAMES RIVER
11 POINT JUDITH
12 NARRAGANSETT BAY
13 MASSACHUSETTS' BAYS

14 CONNECTICUT RIVER VALLEY
15 MUD CREEK WILDLIFE MANAGEMENT AREA
16 LAKE CHAMPLAIN
17 DEAD CREEK WILDLIFE MANAGEMENT AREA
18 UMBAGOG LAKE
19 CONNECTICUT RIVER VALLEY
20 MERRIMACK RIVER
21 SEABROOK MARSHES
22 GREAT BAY ESTUARIES
23 MERRYMEETING BAY
24 PENOBSCOT RIVER
25 FRENCHMAN BAY

Fig. 3. Major migration and wintering areas of waterfowl in the Northern Atlantic States, based on personal communications with state waterfowl biologists.

Bay near Richmond, Maine (Fig. 3). This 4,000-ha tidal freshwater marsh supports up to 40,000 waterfowl (Spencer et al. 1980). Black ducks, green-winged teal (*Anas crecca*), blue-winged teal (*A. discors*), and Canada geese are the most common species. The attractiveness of Merrymeeting Bay is related to wild rice and other plant foods (Spencer et al. 1980) (Fig. 4).

Because most inland wetlands freeze, estuarine habitats along Maine's 5,970-km coastline (Jacobson et al. 1987) provide resting and feeding areas in winter. Black ducks, common eiders, and scoters (*Melanitta* spp.) occur in sheltered bays, where rivers enter the ocean, and in the lee of islands along the coast (Longcore and Gibbs 1988).

Waterfowl migrating through Vermont concentrate on Lake Champlain, Missiquoi National Wildlife Refuge (NWR), Mud Creek and Dead Creek State Wildlife Refuges (T. R. Myers, pers. commun.) (Figs. 3 and 5). Lake Champlain (Fig. 3) is most attractive to diving ducks, espe-

cially lesser scaups (*Aythya affinis*) and canvasbacks (*A. valisineria*), because of the available aquatic plant foods at the northern end of the lake. Missiquoi NWR (Fig. 5) is noted for its fall concentrations of ring-necked ducks. Mud Creek and Dead Creek State Wildlife Refuges (Fig. 3) attract migrating geese. Canada geese winter in the Champlain Valley in years of little snow.

The Great Bay estuary of New Hampshire (Fig. 3) is an important migrating and wintering area for black ducks and geese (S. H. Wheeler, pers. commun.). Scaup and other waterfowl use this area until freeze-up. Although heavily developed, the Seabrook coastal marshes continue to attract black ducks and teal during fall. Inland, the Connecticut River Valley, Merrimack River Valley, and Umbagog Lake are important to migrating waterfowl. Umbagog Lake is a shallow 607-810 ha lake and marsh with wild rice production. Urban ponds provide habitat for more than 2,000 mallards, when natural inland wetlands freeze during winter.

Wetland habitats most important to waterfowl in Massachusetts are mudflats and saltmarshes along the coast in the Northeastern Coastal Plain and New England seaboard lowland region (U.S. Department of Interior 1959). The Connecticut River (Fig. 3) is an important migration corridor in the western part of the state during fall and spring (H W Heusmann, pers. commun.). Waterfowl use Parker River NWR (Fig. 5) during fall and spring. Reservoirs are important to waterfowl during migration, but these habitats freeze during winter. Urban, suburban, and rural ponds are receiving increasing use by waterfowl during winter (Heusmann 1984). Waterfowl move to open water in rivers below dams, river bends, and coastal segments of rivers when inland ponds and lakes freeze. Habitats with open water during winter attract buffleheads (*Bucephala albeola*) in

Fig. 4. Tidally influenced freshwater, emergent wetlands of Merrymeeting Bay, Maine. Extensive beds of wild rice attract migrant black ducks, mallards, green-winged and blue-winged teal, and Canada geese.

southeastern Massachusetts (H W Heusmann, pers. commun.).

Habitats most used by waterfowl migrating through Rhode Island include coastal saltwater ponds at Point Judith and freshwater ponds located close to the Atlantic Ocean (J. E. Myers, pers. commun.) (Fig. 3). Areas around Point Judith are noted for concentrations of common goldeneye (*Bucephala clangula*). Narragansett Bay attracts buffleheads, oldsquaw (*Clangula hyemalis*), mergansers (*Mergus* spp.), and other waterfowl during spring migration. Inland, canvasbacks concentrate on the Bristol River during late fall; redheads and canvasbacks also use Worden Pond. Freshwater ponds attract waterfowl, especially ring-necked ducks, during spring. Because inland wetlands freeze during winter, coastal habitats are important to wintering waterfowl. For example, Prudence Island is considered

the best wintering area for scaup in Rhode Island (J. E. Myers, pers. commun.).

The most valuable habitats in Connecticut for migratory and wintering waterfowl are tidal brackish and saline marshes, tidal rivers, mud flats, and coastal bays (P. R. Merola, pers. commun.). However, banding data reveal that the Connecticut River also is used heavily by mallards, black ducks, wood ducks, and green-winged teal migrating from New England and Quebec, Canada. The Quinnipiac and Thames Rivers also are important during migration (Fig. 3). Inland, palustrine emergent and lacustrine wetlands attract waterfowl during September and October. During winter, inland wetlands freeze and are not available to waterfowl. Some reservoirs attract waterfowl where open water is adjacent to agricultural fields or where supplemental

1	IROQUOIS	13	NANTUCKET
2	MONTEZUMA	14	MONOMOY
3	MISSISQUOI	15	MASSASOIT
4	WAPACK	16	THACHER ISLAND
5	OXBOW	17	PARKER RIVER
6	GREAT MEADOWS	18	RACHEL CARSON
7	SALT MEADOW	19	POND ISLAND
8	TRUSTOM POND	20	FRANKLIN ISLAND
9	NINIGRET	21	SEAL ISLAND
10	BLOCK ISLAND	22	PETIT MANAN
11	SACHUEST POINT	23	CROSS ISLAND
12	NOMANS LAND ISLAND	24	MOOSEHORN

Fig. 5. Location of National Wildlife Refuges in the Northern Atlantic States.

food is available. Urban ponds attract mallards during winter (P. R. Merola, pers. commun.).

The most valuable wetlands to waterfowl in New York are adjacent to the Atlantic Ocean, Long Island Sound, the Hudson, Niagara, and St. Lawrence Rivers, Lakes Champlain and Ontario, and the Finger Lakes (U.S. Department of Interior 1955) (Fig. 3). Canada geese migrate across central and western New York enroute to the Delmarva Peninsula in North Carolina. A migration corridor for canvasbacks, redheads, and other divers is found in the Central Lakes region of New York, including the Finger Lakes, Oneida Lake, Montezuma NWR (Fig. 5), and the Mohawk River Valley (Fig. 3) (Benson et al. 1957, Bellrose 1968). The Finger Lakes also are important staging areas for geese. Greater scaup (Aythya marila) also migrate from the Lake Ontario-St. Lawrence River area across New York to Long Island Sound.

One of the most important corridors for migrating black ducks in the region extends from eastern Ontario across central New York to the Chesapeake Bay. Probably 75% of the black ducks winter-

ing from the Chesapeake Bay to Pamlico Sound arrive by this corridor. About 33% of the black ducks wintering in New Jersey arrive via this corridor that extends from western Quebec down the Lake Champlain and Hudson River valleys.

Marshes, shallow-water areas, barrier beaches, and bays along the shore of Long Island Sound from Shinnecock to Jamaica Bays are among the most valuable migration and wintering grounds along the Atlantic Coast (U.S. Department of Interior 1955). Oneida Lake and marshes associated with the St. Lawrence River valley, Lake Ontario, and Lake Erie (Fig. 3) are recognized as important wintering areas for mergansers, buffleheads, and common goldeneyes (Benson et al. 1957). Also, the Niagara River provides winter habitat for canvasbacks and scaup. In the Finger Lakes region, geese and mallards are attracted to remaining open water in Canandaigua, Seneca, and Cayuga Lakes adjacent to cornfields. Montezuma NWR and Cayuga Lake have attracted cumulatively as many as 500,000 Canada geese, snow geese, and various ducks. Greatest use occurs in April; however, several hundred thousand geese and ducks may use the area during fall. At Iroquois NWR (Fig. 5), up to 100,000 geese and 25,000 ducks congregate in April.

Diversity and Abundance of Waterfowl

Migration.—Thirty-four waterfowl species comprising 1-3 million birds either migrate through or winter in the NAS (Table 2). Among the Anserini, Canada geese, brant, and snow goose are numerically most important. Wood ducks contribute substantially to the fall flight in the NAS. Black ducks, green-winged teal, and blue-winged teal are the most numerous dabbling ducks, with fewer northern pintail, American wigeon, gadwall, and northern shoveler. Among the diving ducks, the ring-necked duck and the lesser

Table 2. Numbers[a] of waterfowl migrating to or through the Northern Atlantic States each year.

Tribe/species	Range
Anserini	
Mute swan (*Cygnus olor*)	2,000-4,000
Tundra swan (*C. columbianus*)	tr[b]
Greater snow goose (*Chen caerulescens atlantica*)	70,000-180,000
Lesser snow goose (*C. c. carulescens*)	tr
Canada goose	30,000-500,000
Brant	70,000-150,000
Cairinini	
Wood duck	140,000-210,000
Anatini	
Mallard	20,000-50,000
American black duck	150,000-170,000
Gadwall (*Anas strepera*)	5,000-10,000
American wigeon (*A. americana*)	30,000-50,000
Green-winged teal	190,000-350,000
Blue-winged teal	175,000-375,000
Northern shoveler (*A. clypeata*)	2,000-15,000
Northern pintail (*A. acuta*)	2,000-8,000
Aythyini	
Redhead	10,000-50,000
Canvasback	8,000-20,000
Greater scaup	77,000-290,000
Lesser scaup	5,000-100,000
Ring-necked duck	45,000-540,000
Oxyurini	
Ruddy duck (*Oxyura jamaicensis*)	1,000-2,000
Mergini	
Common merganser (*Mergus merganser*)	6,000-7,000
Red-breasted merganser (*M. serrator*)	63,000-84,000
Hooded merganser (*M. cucullatus*)	10,000-15,000
Bufflehead	30,000-39,000
Common goldeneye	6,000-39,000
Barrow's goldeneye (*Bucephala islandica*)	tr
King eider (*Somateria spectabilis*)	tr
Common eider	59,000-163,000
Harlequin duck (*Histrionicus histrionicus*)	tr
Oldsquaw	4,000-21,000
Black scoter (*Melanita nigra*)	1,000-3,000
White-winged scoter (*M. fusca*)	3,000-33,000
Surf scoter (*M. perspicillata*)	2,000-3,000

[a]Based on unpublished data from the Migratory Bird Management Office, U.S. Fish and Wildlife Service; Bellrose (1976, 1980); Corr (1985); Erskine (1987).

[b]tr = <100.

scaup dominate, but redheads and canvasback are numerous some years. Of the sea ducks, red-breasted mergansers and hooded mergansers, common goldeneyes, buffleheads, and white-winged scoters are most important.

Winter.—Twenty species of waterfowl, averaging 0.5 million birds, winter annually in the NAS (Table 3). Canada geese, brant, American black ducks, and increasing numbers of mallards use the NAS during winter. In descending order of abundance, greater scaup, lesser scaup, redhead, and canvasback winter in the lower NAS.

HABITAT AND WATERFOWL REQUIREMENTS
Important Foods and Foraging Habitats

Food is probably the most important variable influencing winter habitat use by waterfowl in the NAS. Although plant foods dominate the diet of dabbling ducks and diving ducks during fall and winter on freshwater wetlands (Bellrose 1980), invertebrate foods are used in coastal wetlands. Aquatic invertebrates of riverine habitats are used by waterfowl year round, except when ice cover is present. In tidal areas, mud flats provide year-round foraging habitat for several species of dabbling ducks (Albright 1981, Jorde 1986).

For black ducks wintering in the NAS, mollusks account for ≥65% of all foods eaten (Mendall 1949, Hartman 1963, Grandy 1972, Lewis and Garrison 1984). Black ducks also supplement their diet with eelgrass and widgeongrass in marshes, and, when available, agricultural grains. Canvasbacks traditionally have eaten >80% plant foods such as wild celery (*Vallisneria americana*), pondweeds, and widgeongrass, but shift to predominantly animal foods where aquatic plant foods have decreased or disappeared. Greater scaup eat plant and

Table 3. Numbers[a] ($\bar{X}$ and range) of waterfowl wintering in the Northern Atlantic States, 1980-1986.

Tribe/species	$\bar{X}$	Range
Anserini		
Mute swan	3,000	2,000-4,000
Tundra swan	tr[b]	-
Greater snow goose	tr	-
Lesser snow goose	tr	-
Canada goose	73,000	58,000-107,000
Brant	14,000	5,000-22,000
Cairinini		
Wood duck	tr	-
Anatini		
Mallard	18,000	5,000-39,000
American black duck	60,000	52,000-70,000
Gadwall	tr	-
American wigeon	334	0-1,000
Green-winged teal	tr	-
Blue-winged teal	tr	-
Northern shoveler	tr	-
Northern pintail	tr	-
Aythyini		
Redhead	6,000	2,000-12,000
Canvasback	11,000	12,000-16,000
Greater scaup	55,000	35,000-88,000
Lesser scaup	19,000	12,000-30,000
Oxyurini		
Ruddy duck	233	0-500
Mergini		
Common merganser	4,000	3,000-5,000
Red-breasted merganser	36,000	29,000-43,000
Hooded merganser	tr	-
Bufflehead	9,000	6,000-12,000
Common goldeneye	27,000	22,000-36,000
Barrow's goldeneye	tr	-
King eider	tr	-
Common eider	125,000	59,000-163,000
Harlequin duck	tr	-
Oldsquaw	7,000	4,000-10,000
Black scoter	7,000	1,000-22,000
White-winged scoter	17,000	3,000-53,000
Surf scoter	1,000	2,000-32,000

[a]Based on data for 1980-1986 from unpublished records of the Migratory Bird Management Office, U.S. Fish and Wildlife Service.
[b]tr = <100.

animal foods, but seemingly favor clams and other mollusks. Blue mussels are preferred along the coast of Connecticut and sea lettuce is eaten when available (Bellrose 1980).

Coastal habitats are the most important wintering areas for sea ducks. Stott and Olson (1973) believed that food availabil-

ity and the physical structure of the substrate were major determinants of habitat selection. They observed white-winged, surf, and black scoters concentrated near the mouths of estuaries, where bivalves were abundant. These sea ducks selected areas of sandy substrate primarily containing Atlantic razor (*Siliqua coastata*) and arctic wedge clams (*Mesodesma arctatum*). Most of the winter diet of eiders, white-winged scoters, and buffleheads is animal matter (>90%), especially mollusks and crustaceans. Along the Maine coast, eiders often feed in deep water on invertebrates and are known to depredate commercial beds of blue mussels and other shellfish.

Oldsquaw also forage in deep water and consume bivalves, gastropods, isopods, shrimp (*Crangon septemspinsosus*), fish, and a variety of plant foods. Goldeneyes use areas with rocky substrates, and feed mainly on amphipods, isopods, crabs, gastropods, plant tubers, seeds, and leafy vegetation. These foods commonly cling to Irish moss (*Chondrus crispus*) that covers rocky sublittoral areas. The winter diet of mergansers consists mostly of marine fish, but is supplemented with crustaceans and invertebrates. Red-breasted mergansers feed on small fish present amidst Irish moss and rocky crevices.

Waste grains in the NAS are important foods for migrating and wintering geese and mallards. Corn is preferred, but wheat and other agricultural foods are readily eaten. Waterfowl are particularly dependent on agricultural and supplemental sources of corn during winter, which directly influence their geographic distribution and behavioral patterns.

Eelgrass is an important marine plant food for waterfowl (McRoy 1966, Ogilvie and St. Joseph 1976, Jacobs et al. 1981) because of its direct and indirect role in providing plant and animal foods, a relationship important enough to influence waterfowl survival and distribution

(Tubbs and Tubbs 1983). Populations of brant collapsed after an eelgrass die-off in the early 1930s (Cottam 1934, Cottam et al. 1944, Cottam and Munro 1954, den Hartog 1977). A more limited decline in Canada geese also was related to the demise of eelgrass. Brant numbers increased again in the early 1950s, perhaps because of a change in diet to widgeongrass and sea lettuce. After eelgrass communities recovered, some brant returned to their diet of eelgrass (Palmer 1976). However, brant along Long Island still forage primarily on sea lettuce (J. D. Moser, pers. commun.), but they also forage on cultivated grasses in New York (Smith et al. 1985).

Waterfowl tend to remain close to foraging areas during winter in the NAS. For example, during the severe winter of 1980-81, black ducks in Maine loafed within 0.5 km from ice-free clam and blue mussel beds (Longcore and Gibbs 1988). These areas are near low tide zones where strong currents prevent icing (Hartman 1963).

In urban habitats, where natural vegetation is scarce, waterfowl depend on supplemental feeding. Nearby grain fields and salt marshes also are used when available. Supplemental foods most often fed include bread, corn, and bird seed (Figley and VanDruff 1982).

Recent studies indicate that different species of waterfowl obtain similar energy and nutrients from the same foods (Miller 1984, Buchsbaum et al. 1986), but that the amount of true metabolized energy obtained varies by food type and rate of intake (Jorde and Owen 1988). Waterfowl do not select foods based only on gross metabolizable energy content (Hoffman and Bookhout 1985); therefore, waterfowl managers must have information about other food characteristics (e.g., nutrient content and density) to manage waterfowl habitat effectively. Unfortunately, very little is known about the diets of migrating and wintering waterfowl in the NAS, and most of the preferred natural food and habitats are not easily manipulated by waterfowl managers.

Habitat Use and Behavior

Nutritional and thermodynamic characteristics of different habitats in the NAS influence habitat use by waterfowl during winter. For example, black ducks on the Maine coast rest on shorelines during the day (Jorde 1986, Longcore and Gibbs 1988), probably to absorb solar radiation (Jorde 1986). However, black ducks use open water sites at night and on cloudy days. When temperatures are <0 C, black ducks seek shelter in the lee of landforms, especially islands and coves protected from prevailing winds (Longcore and Gibbs 1988). Winter severity forces black ducks to group tightly (Grandy 1972, Longcore and Gibbs 1988), reduce activity, and vie for thermally optimal sites (Albright 1981). Hickey (1980) reported that thermoregulatory costs for black ducks increased 186% in response to wind-chill decrease from −5 to −20 C on Prince Edward Island, Canada. Similarly, a variety of environmental and social factors influenced distribution and habitat use of brant and geese at Long Island, New York (Burger et al. 1983), and common goldeneye in coastal central Maine (Eggeman 1986). These included wind speed and direction, tide stage, type of substrate, time-of-day, pair status, age, sex, and previous use of a site.

Winter-Ice Conditions

Ice cover strongly affects the winter distribution of waterfowl in coastal wetlands (Spencer et al. 1980). Estuaries freeze progressively outward from the shore during winter. Tidal flats often freeze during the ebb tide, and temperatures are often too low between tides to thaw flats (Fig. 6). When tidal flats freeze, dabbling ducks disperse to the zone between the low-water mark and the

Fig. 6. Estuarine habitat temporarily unavailable to waterfowl because of extensive ice cover at high and low tides.

maximum feeding depth (about 60 cm). Food may be readily available at other sites within 16 km, but black ducks often remain in their traditional wintering habitats (Hagar 1950, Hartman 1963). When temperatures drop below −5 C, widespread icing of mudflats is common. If icing occurs in areas where mudflats are being used by waterfowl, the presence of small, ice-free sites (often <100 m^2) may be extremely important for foraging. These areas often are near the low-tide line where currents are strong. When other mudflats are frozen, these open areas may be the only places where black ducks can feed. Foraging opportunities may be restricted to a short time just before and after low tide. Consequently, these areas may be vital for black duck survival during cold weather (Hartman 1963).

Causes of Mortality

Disease and Parasites.—Outbreaks of disease occur sporadically throughout the NAS. Disease and parasites of waterfowl may account for the majority of non-hunting mortality (Stout and Cornwell 1976). Generally, the response by managers is to restrict movements of birds into infected areas.

Duck Virus Enteritis (DVE) was first identified in North America during an outbreak at a commercial duck farm on Long Island in 1967. Although efforts were made to confine the disease, it eventually spread to other commercial duck farms and into the wild duck population (Leibovitz 1971). By 1969, mallards, black ducks, greater scaup, bufflehead, and Canada geese died from disease (Leibovitz 1969). Subsequently, DVE has occurred only sporadically.

Although avian cholera (*Pasteurella multocida*) outbreaks have been common since first reported in 1963, the disease has not been widespread. Outbreaks of avian cholera kill common eiders of an insular nesting island colony, whereas birds on other islands within a few kilometers may be unaffected. The disease evidently is not an important variable that limits eider populations in Maine; outbreaks have not been reported outside of the breeding season.

Disease outbreaks also are a major source of mortality among waterfowl using urban wetlands. Figley and Van-Druff (1982) reported that avian botulism (*Clostridium botulinium*), DVE, and avian cholera are common. Their mail survey indicated that most wildlife agencies do not respond to disease outbreaks occurring in urban habitats. However, botulism has become such a serious problem in some urban habitats that public feeding of waterfowl has been banned.

Parasites have been known to cause death of individual birds, but their overall effect on populations is difficult to assess. *Polymorphus botulis* is a common intestinal parasite in Maine eiders, which has caused mortality (Grenquist 1970). Protozoan blood parasites (*Leucocytozoan*, *Haemoproteus*, and *Plasmodium*) are common in waterfowl in central Maine (O'Meara 1954). In a sample of wood ducks, *Haemoproteus nettionis* and *Leucocytozoan simondi* were found in 80% of the birds (Thul 1977), and also were common among other breeding waterfowl. However, their occurrence and significance in spring or fall migrants are unknown.

Contaminants.—Pesticides and pollution cause mortality in urban and agricultural environments (Figley and VanDruff 1982). Diazinon caused mortality of brant on Long Island golf courses and sod farms. Fenthion, parathion, and other organophosphates also have poisoned waterfowl (Grue et al. 1983). Concentrations of some persistent pesticides (e.g. DDT, DDE) in the body tissues of waterfowl have decreased since their ban by the Environmental Protection Agency (White et al. 1981). Longcore and Stendell (1982) reported that DDE residues in black ducks have decreased since the 1960s when high levels of DDE residues in females may have reduced reproductive success. Generally, organochloride contaminations of waterfowl in the NAS does not seem to be a major problem, although exceptions have occurred (Fleming et al. 1983, Hunter et al. 1984).

The frequency of occurrence of lead in gizzards of waterfowl is high enough to cause concern about lead poisoning throughout the NAS (White and Stendell 1977, Longcore et al. 1982, Feierabend 1984). Programs to phase out lead shot are currently being implemented.

Predators.—Bald eagles (*Haliaeetus leucocephalus*) (Todd et al. 1982) and gulls (*Larus* spp.) (Albright 1981) are probably the most important predators of migrating and wintering waterfowl, but they do not cause extensive mortality (Hartman 1960). Unlike predators in coastal habitats, mammals (especially domestic cats) are the most frequent predators of waterfowl using urban wetlands; however, gulls also kill urban waterfowl (Figley and VanDruff 1982).

Weather.—The effects of weather on mortality among waterfowl during winter are not well known in the NAS. Mortality often results from starvation associated with severe weather (Hagar 1950). Weight loss during successive periods of extreme cold probably causes high mortality in black ducks. Grandy (1972) predicted that major mortality of black ducks would occur 1 in 5 years depending on weather conditions and food availability. The effect of weather-related mortality in winter is difficult to quantity because scavengers quickly consume dead birds.

HABITAT MANAGEMENT

Wetlands As Environmental Indicators

Redistribution of waterfowl is usually a subtle indicator of changing habitat quality and availability in the NAS. However, reduced habitat use also may reflect mortality that is caused by hunting (Raveling 1978). Redistribution of geese often results from development of agricultural row crops. Local, regional, and continental changes in waterfowl numbers also may influence waterfowl use of an area. Redistribution of Canada geese in the NAS poses important management questions concerning management of subpopulations, reassessment of banding programs, and regulation of harvest (Trost and Malecki 1985).

Habitat Changes

Loss of wetland habitat in the NAS has been caused by draining, dredging and filling, pollution, acid rain, agricultural practices, siltation, timber harvest, commercial use of coastal areas, and urbanization. Loss of estuaries to dredging and filling alone was 8% in 10 Atlantic Coast states (Cottam in Bellrose 1980). The rate of loss of estuarine habitat in New York has been estimated as 300 ha/year (O'Connor and Terry in Tiner 1984).

Inland wetland losses in the NAS undoubtedly have been greatest in the agricultural region of central New York and in urban areas. These declines may have been great enough to partly contribute to population declines of several species, especially black ducks (Rogers and Patterson 1984). Specifically, the breeding range of mallards has expanded eastward concomitant with a decline of the black duck population (Ankney et al. 1987). Conversely, black ducks have expanded their range westward in northern U.S. and Canada. Johnsgard (1960) believed that deforestation and land-use changes have caused a redistribution and

population increase of mallards, and have caused a decrease of black ducks in the eastern U.S. No conclusive information is available to indicate whether these range expansions are beneficial or detrimental to these species, and current opinions among wildlife professionals remain divided (Ankney et al. 1987).

Pollution caused by industrial discharges continues to degrade and destroy wetlands, rivers, and estuaries, and may be the biggest threat to habitat in industrial areas of the NAS. A long-standing practice that is developing into a major concern in the NAS is the illegal dumping of toxic chemicals and other industrial wastes into aquatic habitats. Besides loss of habitat, these activities contaminate environments that predispose birds to chemical toxicoses. Combating this problem requires wildlife management agencies to increase cooperative efforts among government agencies, waste producers, and the general public. Far-ranging public awareness programs and aggressive enforcement of environment protection laws provide the most effective action (Morse 1987).

Acid rain has become a major concern in recent years. Acid rain affects aquatic invertebrate food resources used by breeding waterfowl (Haines and Hunter 1981, Haramis and Chu 1987, Longcore et al. 1987). Low wetland pH influences duckling survival and the diet of ring-necked ducks (McAuley and Longcore 1988a,b). Acidification from mining occurs in some areas, but the effects seem small in comparison to acid rain.

Housing and commercial development of farmlands will eventually reduce available agricultural foods for waterfowl, especially migrant geese (P. R. Merola, pers. commun.). Approximately 25% of the 20,000-30,000 migrant geese that stop in Connecticut use farm ponds as roosting and loafing sites during fall. Waterfowl use of farm ponds and wetlands for breeding and migration may be substantial over the NAS, but these habitats probably have little importance during winter. Protecting existing wetlands, creating additional ponds, and planting agricultural crops adjacent to ponds would offset the loss of habitat important to migrating waterfowl.

Siltation and erosion resulting from farming degrade wetlands, rivers, and estuaries. Excessive nutrients are a major concern around cattle feedlots and poultry farms, where algal blooms degrade habitat of breeding and migrating waterfowl. Because many wetlands in the NAS are nutrient poor, a rest-rotation grazing strategy along a portion of the wetland margin may increase the productivity of some wetlands and attract waterfowl.

Regulations requiring buffer timber strips around wetlands and along permanent rivers and streams have greatly reduced erosion and sedimentation (Fig. 7). However, small, seasonal, temporary, and semipermanent wetlands often are cleared of timber and filled with sediment. Restoring damaged wetlands and enforcement of wetland protection laws would reverse this loss of waterfowl habitat.

Construction of urban ponds has increased throughout the NAS since 1960. Golf courses, sewage lagoons, ponds, and other urban aquatic habitats have attracted increasing numbers of ducks and geese. In some areas, waterfowl densities have complicated waterfowl management. Conflicts are most acute when large numbers of waterfowl are attracted to urban areas located near reservoirs developed for recreation, public water supply, and flood protection. Restoring wetlands, constructing new wetlands, manipulating the availability of food resources, and educating the public may be effective management solutions.

Mallards are the dominant species in urban areas year-round (Adams et al. 1985), whereas other waterfowl use urban wetlands only during fall and winter. Increased use of urban habitats by waterfowl is probably influenced more by availability of suitable habitat than by disturbance during the hunting season (Figley and VanDruff 1982).

Habitat Management For Waterfowl

Management of waterfowl habitat in the NAS often relies on manipulating water levels to provide breeding habitat, but benefits may extend to migrating and wintering waterfowl. For example, Connecticut has 60 freshwater impoundments ranging from 4-40 ha that are used by migrating dabbling ducks even though these areas are managed mostly for breeding waterfowl. Management practices include (1) manipulating water levels to provide food and nesting cover, (2) controlling encroachment of undesirable species, (3) providing agricultural foods, and (4) managing beaver populations.

Many dams and control structures built since 1940 are currently used for drawdowns to encourage growth of waterfowl food plants such as rice cutgrass (*Leersia oryzoides*), duck potato (*Sagittaria* spp.), and millet (*Echinochloa* spp.). Also, some mill ponds have water-control structures that can be used to manage adjacent wetlands. These wetlands are reflooded during the summer and fall for waterfowl use. Water-control structures were constructed to stabilize water levels because flooding during summer is a common cause of nest failure among some overwater nesting waterfowl. Unfortunately, the water level in many wetlands is not managed after the impoundment is established, which may limit food production (Weller 1981). Opportunities for intensive management of these areas are limited by unfavorable cost-benefit ratios. However, an option is moist-soil plant management (Fredrickson and Taylor 1982). This type of management regulates water levels and allows wetland managers to take advantage of natural seed banks to produce waterfowl food. Periodic drawdowns of

Fig. 7. Buffer strips of mature trees protect some wetlands in harvested forests throughout the NAS.

impoundments aerate marsh soils (Cook and Powers 1958) and rejuvenate plant growth and production of invertebrates. Also, drawdowns can be an effective management technique for brackish impoundments and salt marshes, especially when combined with other management techniques such as burning, mowing, disking, and applying herbicides (Bellrose and Low 1978).

Another management option is seeding aquatic food plants, such as wild rice (Emerson 1961), and reestablishing beds of submerged aquatic vegetation (Thorhaug 1980). Other management techniques to provide natural foods and habitat for waterfowl include blasting potholes to create or open up existing wetlands, and reducing dense stands of cattail with cutting and flooding treatments. Some wetlands that lack nutrients require different habitat management (MacNamara 1957). For example, nutrient "implants" in sterile wetlands in Nova

Scotia are being evaluated (F. Payne, pers. commun.).

Upland soil management also is a possibility. Liming and fertilizing dikes and wheat fields at Moosehorn NWR (Fig. 8) has increased use of these areas by Canada geese (D. M. Mullen, pers. commun.) and raised pH values to 6-7 in impoundments, ameliorating effects of acid rain.

An option for managing aquatic habitat is cooperative projects. For example, Connecticut has a cooperative program with the U.S. Army Corps of Engineers to retain water on selected flood-control areas during fall and to drain them in late spring. These areas function similarly to green-tree impoundments.

Purple loosestrife (Lythrum salicaria) is a hardy, exotic perennial that is a problem where wetlands are periodically drained. Purple loosestrife thrives in moist-soil and shallow-water wetlands (Smith 1964). Dense stands of this species

Fig. 8. Inland, freshwater impoundments of Moosehorn NWR, Maine. Staging area for local black ducks and wood ducks, and migrant green-winged teal and Canada geese.

invade and dominate other wetland vegetation and reduce the quality of the wetland for wildlife (Malecki and Rawinski 1979). This species is a prolific seed producer and is extremely difficult to control after plants begin producing seed (Gagnon 1953). This species has infested major portions of New York, tidal and freshwater wetlands of the Connecticut River, and some wildlife refuges in Massachusetts. Purple loosestrife also occurs in Rhode Island, New Hampshire, Vermont, and Maine, but currently is not considered a major pest.

Generally, chemical control with Roundup (N-[phosphono-methyl] glycine) is most cost effective, but Roundup also kills other vegetation that is desirable (Thompson et al. 1987). Water manipulation is a successful method to control purple loosestrife in cattail stands, whereas fire is not effective. Because this species thrives under drawdown management regimes, managers applying moist-soil methods in the NAS should become familiar with this species before beginning drawdowns.

Phragmites also has become a nuisance throughout coastal areas. This species now dominates many tidal wetlands in New York, Connecticut, and Rhode Island, and is increasing in Massachusetts. Although none of these states currently have programs to control phragmites, future management is planned. In Rhode Island, managers are considering water-level manipulation and use of chemicals. Chemical control with glyphosate (e.g., Rodeo and Roundup) dispensed from a helicopter and followed by burning the dead canes, may be the most cost-effective method (Jones and Lehman 1987).

Open-marsh water management in coastal areas is being developed and implemented by several states. These methods are modeled after mosquito control techniques devloped during the early- to mid-1900s (Daiber 1987), but now include more planning for wetland hydrology and quality (Portnoy et al. 1987). Currently, Massachusetts has a pilot program on the Cape Cod marshes, and Connecticut has a mosquito ditching program administered by the Department of Health.

Open-marsh water management programs include pond construction and ditching in areas of a salt marsh where mosquito breeding sites are a major concern. Construction includes removal of excess surface water by excavating soil or filling with soil. A mosaic of ditches are connected to excavated ponds to allow mosquito-eating fish access to mosquito-breeding areas (Candeletti 1979). Excavated ponds provide resting and foraging habitat for migrating and wintering waterfowl. If properly planned and administered, open-marsh water management is considered a cost-effective method of control for mosquitoes (Shisler and Schulze 1985) that increases waterfowl habitat.

Cultivation of grains on selected federal and state-owned areas has become a necessity to provide food for migrating and wintering waterfowl, especially mallards and geese (Bellrose and Low 1978). During winter, several species of waterfowl, including swans, are attracted to areas along the coast where corn is supplied by landowners and private organizations. Although feeding programs are not common, waterfowl may become dependent on these food resources.

Throughout the NAS, beaver populations and how they are managed influence waterfowl habitat. Beaver populations were reduced during the mid-1800s but have increased greatly since the mid-1900s. Throughout the NAS, especially in Connecticut and New York, beaver have a positive influence on increasing habitat for waterfowl and in supporting high densities of migrating dabbling ducks (P. R. Merola, pers. commun.). Although there is wide recognition of the value of beaver ponds to waterfowl, management of beaver in the region focuses mainly on sustaining yields of beaver or reducing damage complaints. Most research on the value of beaver flowages to waterfowl has emphasized their usefulness during spring. Older impoundments attract fewer waterfowl than newly created impoundments (Beard 1953, Benson and Foley 1956, Renouf 1972, Brown and Parsons 1979). Beaver management is not considered important to managing winter habitat for waterfowl because wetlands are inland and freeze during November.

Protection From Disturbance

In many areas, waterfowl have become dependent on refuges for protection from hunting. Telemetry studies with black ducks at the Moosehorn NWR in Maine (Longcore, unpubl. data) have revealed that, following the opening of the hunting season in adjacent New Brunswick, Canada, radio-marked ducks would return to the NWR. Mortality of urban mallards from hunting is lower than for natural populations (Heusmann 1983). Therefore, the "refuge effect" (Raveling 1978) of urban habitats and management of urban wetlands by local governments may substantially increase urban waterfowl populations. Establishing more refuges would provide protection from hunting to a larger segment of the waterfowl population.

Disease and Environmental Contaminants

In areas that are foci of repeated occurrences of avian botulism, impoundments and wetlands could be renovated to minimize shallow shoreline and to increase water depth (Bellrose and Low 1978). Although extensive immunization of wild waterfowl is not practical, immunization of local populations at sites where repeated outbreaks occur may be beneficial. Vaccine can be administered to wild birds during banding programs to control avian cholera (Price 1985). Recently, new vaccines and immunization techniques have enhanced the possibilities for control of disease (Price 1985).

Lead poisoning in the NAS can be eliminated by educating the public and by enforcing existing regulations. Similarly, the only effective way to reduce contaminants and pollution is stronger, more effective enforcement of environmental laws that provide a legal basis to protect habitat.

Assessment of Regional Management

Management of winter habitat in the NAS does not receive high regional or national priority because management needs have not been identified, programs may be too costly, and numbers of waterfowl are relatively small. The Atlantic Flyway accounts for only 8% of the U.S. mallard harvest and winters only 3% of the mallard population. However, the increase in harvest of mallards among flyways was greatest (94%) in the Atlantic Flyway (Bartonek et al. 1984). Similarly, 74% of the black duck population winters along the Atlantic coast but <20% are found in the NAS.

Probably the most common management effort in the NAS is either protection or acquisition of important waterfowl habitats. In some situations (e.g., many coastal habitats), this is the only practical approach. The greatest priority of waterfowl managers in New York is to acquire all remaining wetlands north of Montezuma NWR, habitats that used to be the prime waterfowl areas in the state because of their central location. New York has acquired >15 refuges along the shoreline of Lake Ontario and plans to purchase more land. In addition,

wetlands and waterfowl along the St. Lawrence Seaway are an important component of the North American Waterfowl Management Plan (U.S. Fish and Wildlife Service and Canadian Wildlife Service 1986). Connecticut has acquired 60 state management areas to protect wildlife, including waterfowl.

Constructing ponds for waterfowl on purchased land is difficult in Rhode Island because of current state laws. The state must first obtain easements and development rights and then set aside the wetland for construction. Therefore, waterfowl habitat programs in Rhode Island are focused on protecting and managing state-owned wetlands. Massachusetts has 162 state-park ponds and many small, municipal ponds in urban areas that attract waterfowl, especially mallards, black ducks, and geese. The number of these small ponds and the number of waterfowl using them are increasing. New Hampshire expects major changes in waterfowl habitat in the southern part of the state, an area of increasing urban and industrial development. State wetland managers plan to acquire wetlands using Duck Stamp and Ducks Unlimited revenues. In Vermont, >3,600 ha of wetlands have been acquired for state waterfowl management areas. In addition, Vermont conducted an extensive wetland inventory, surveyed public opinion about wetland protection, and is compiling a master list of wetlands to acquire using Land and Water Conservation funds. Maine has a program to protect more than 200 coastal islands and has numerous state waterfowl management areas.

The U.S. Fish and Wildlife Service continues to identify and acquire wetlands and adjacent upland habitats for waterfowl and to place them under federal wildlife management programs (Barton 1986). Personnel administering these programs at the field level are available to advise landowners concerning management of wetlands for waterfowl. The Small Wetlands Program for refuges, waterfowl production areas, and easements require habitat to be restored, including previously degraded wetlands. Predator management also is included in this program. Additional extension personnel and cooperation among federal and state agencies are needed to expand this program.

The U.S. Fish and Wildlife Service has acquired coastal habitats important to breeding and wintering waterfowl throughout the NAS (Riley and Riley 1979). For example, 42 of 55 NWRs in the NAS are located in coastal areas (Andrews 1987). However, <10,121 ha of additional waterfowl habitat have been identified for purchase by the year 2000. In eastern Canada, similar efforts have been made by the Canadian Wildlife Service to preserve 40% of developed coastal wetlands important to waterfowl (Barkhouse 1987).

Waterfowl habitats are protected, to some extent, by laws governing land and water use. Effective laws to protect wetlands were enacted during the 1970s throughout the NAS. In New York, coastal habitat changes have stabilized because of the Tidal Wetland Act. Some wetlands (e.g., Long Island bays) have started to recover since these laws were passed. In Connecticut, clearing vegetation to the upper water zone is still permitted adjacent to wetlands. The resulting habitats are more favorable for geese and mallards, but less so for black ducks and wood ducks than were the original habitats. Wetland laws protect the most important marshes in Connecticut, but other inland wetlands are not adequately protected.

Laws to protect wetlands in Rhode Island provide for a 183-m buffer zone, 46 m of which must remain undisturbed. However, industrial and urban development continue to threaten wetlands in Rhode Island where the seemingly small, annual loss of habitat is a significant part of total remaining wetlands. Like New York, wetland protection laws in Massachusetts have reduced losses of coastal habitat. However, because development is permitted within a 30-m buffer zone, urbanization continues to cause many losses, especially small habitat areas used by black ducks. Laws to protect inland wetlands in Massachusetts are limited in scope and enforced by towns and cities. Unfortunately, enforcement efforts vary and wetlands continue to be lost. Laws in New Hampshire, Vermont, and Maine also afford some protection to wetlands, but losses caused by urban development, agriculture, and forestry continue to occur. For example, Vermont's Wetland Act enacted in 1986 protects large wetlands from direct and indirect effects, but does not provide complete protection for small wetlands. In addition, exemptions from the law are granted to agricultural and forestry interests. Maine has several laws that protect wetlands (e.g., Alteration of Coastal Wetlands Law, Freshwater Wetlands Law) by regulating activities in or adjacent to wetlands, ponds, rivers, and streams.

Future Management and Research Needs

Because most wildlife habitat and potential hunting areas in the NAS are privately owned, wildlife managers are faced with the challenge of integrating management of private areas with programs on federal and state lands. For example, Brown et al. (1984) stated that successful wildlife management in the eastern U.S. depends on hunting access to private lands. Management of waterfowl also must include programs that address public access concerns and encourage waterfowl management by private landowners. Education programs are the best approach, including expanded availability of extension services.

Wetland laws are protecting waterfowl habitat throughout the NAS, but losses continue to influence waterfowl numbers and distribution. Therefore, the challenge faced by federal and state agencies is to determine how effectively laws are now protecting wetlands. Protection and management of wetlands in the NAS must be a cooperative effort among federal, state, and private interests.

Regarding the decline of black ducks, research and management efforts should not focus on and be guided by a single species or factor (e.g., hunting, breeding habitat, geographic range) because of complexities and interactions between waterfowl and human interest. Waterfowl harvests should not be used simply to manage waterfowl, but rather should be a function of continuously updated assessments of habitat quality and availability (Rogers and Patterson 1984).

Research must focus on interactions between each species of waterfowl and the habitats they use at local staging and wintering areas. Much more information is needed to manage coastal habitats effectively for waterfowl. Particular attention must be given to nutritional and microclimate aspects of these habitats to determine how much habitat is actually available for waterfowl to use.

Nutritional demands are keystones to understanding waterfowl distribution, habitat use, behavior, and survival during winter. There is no information concerning the influence of shifts in diet on the ability of waterfowl species to survive severe winters in the NAS.

Relatively little is known about the ecological conditions that constitute suitable habitat for waterfowl in this region. Also, the effect of pollutants and contaminants is not well studied. Understanding these relationships is important for determining how changes in habitat may affect waterfowl populations.

Mid-winter inventories of waterfowl populations are currently conducted as a cooperative effort by federal and state agencies, but no concurrent effort is being made to survey availability and quality of winter habitats. A coordinated and extensive initiative should be undertaken to delineate apparent habitat availability (habitat that seems to be available to waterfowl) from true habitat availability (habitat that waterfowl can actually use). Only when true habitat availability is known and information is periodically updated can realistic estimates of waterfowl populations be calculated. Thereafter, reasonable plans to monitor changes in populations, to establish harvest levels, and to manage habitats on local or regional scales can be more appropriately developed.

SUMMARY

Estimated total area of wetland habitat in the NAS region varies, but currently is >600,000 ha of coastal and inland wetlands. Habitat types include marine, estuarine, riverine, lacustrine and palustrine, lakes and reservoirs, uplands, and urban wetlands. Major migration and wintering areas are comprised of these habitats, mostly along the coast during winter, but also inland where ice is not prevalent. An estimated 1.2 to 3 million waterfowl, represented by 34 species, migrate to or through the NAS. Of these, 20 species, averaging 0.5 million birds, winter annually in the NAS.

Food is probably the most important variable influencing habitat use by waterfowl in the NAS during winter. Diets are highly variable within and among waterfowl species, ranging from plant-dominated to animal-dominated foods depending on habitat type and geographic location. However, little detail is known about the diets of most migrating and wintering waterfowl in the NAS, and most of the preferred natural foods and habitats cannot be easily manipulated by waterfowl managers.

Mortality caused by disease, contaminants, and weather are a major concern
throughout the NAS. Although mortality
from these causes occurs sporadically, the
number of waterfowl lost can be high.
Mortality caused by some pesticides has
decreased during the past 20 years, but
toxic environmental contaminants still
are a major concern throughout the NAS.

Wetlands are environmental indicators
of waterfowl abundance and distribution.
Subsequently, wetland loss and habitat
changes caused by draining, dredging and
filling, pollution, acid rain, agricultural
practices, siltation, timber harvest, urbanization, and commercialization of coastal
areas are the greatest concern in the NAS.
Effective management of waterfowl in the
NAS requires manipulating habitats by
regulating water levels, controlling undesirable plants, providing agricultural
foods, and managing beaver populations.

Management of winter habitat in the
NAS has not received high regional or
national priority because management
needs have not been identified, programs
are too costly, and numbers of waterfowl
are relatively small. Either protection or
acquisition of important waterfowl habitats is the most extensive management
effort. Stronger laws afford more protection to wetlands, but losses caused by
urban development, agriculture, and forestry continue to occur. Management of
waterfowl must include programs that
encourage management by private landowners. Protection and management of
wetlands also must be a cooperative effort
among federal, state, and private interests.

Research must focus on interactions
between waterfowl and their habitats at
local migration and wintering areas.
More information is needed to understand
ecological conditions, especially nutritional demands, which constitute suitable
habitat for waterfowl wintering in the
NAS.

LITERATURE CITED

Adams, L. W., L. E. Dove, and T. M. Franklin. 1985. Mallard pair and brood use of urban stormwater-control impoundments. Wildl. Soc. Bull. 13:46-51.

Albright, J. J. 1981. Behavioral and physiological responses of coastal-wintering black ducks (*Anas rubripes*) to changing weather in Maine. M.S. Thesis, Univ. Maine, Orono. 72 pp.

Alexander, C. E., M. A. Broutman, and D. W. Field. 1986. An inventory of coastal wetlands of the USA. Natl. Oceanic and Atmospheric Admin., Washington, D.C. 14 pp.

Andrews, R. 1987. Other waterbirds and their use of coastal wetlands in the northeastern United States. Pages 71-80 *in* W. R. Whitman and W. H. Meredith, eds. Waterfowl and wetlands symp.: proc. of a symp. on waterfowl and wetlands management in the coastal zone of the Atlantic Flyway. Del. Coast. Manage. Prog., Dep. Nat. Res. and Environ. Control, Dover.

Ankney, C. D., D. G. Dennis, and R. O. Bailey. 1987. Increasing mallards, declining American black ducks: coincidence or cause and effect? J. Wildl. Manage. 51:523-529.

Bailey, R. G. 1976. Ecoregions of the United States. U.S.D.A. For. Serv., Ogden, Utah. 100 pp.

———. 1980. Description of the ecoregions of the United States. U.S.D.A. For. Serv. Intermoun-tain Reg. Misc. Publ. 1319. 77 pp.

Barkhouse, H. P. 1987. Management related study of man-made wetlands located in coastal regions of the maritime provinces, Canada. Pages 82-97 *in* W. R. Whitman and W. H. Meredith, eds. Waterfowl and wetlands symp.: proc. of a symp. on waterfowl and wetlands management in the coastal zone of the Atlantic Flyway. Del. Coast. Manage. Prog., Dep. Nat. Res. and Environ. Control, Dover.

Barton, K. 1986. Federal wetlands protection pro-grams. Pages 373-411 *in* F. Ditri, ed. Audubon Wildl. Rep. New York, N.Y. 1,094 pp.

Bartonek, J. C., R. J. Blohm, R. K. Brace, F. D. Caswell, K. E. Gamble, H. W. Miller, R. S. Pospahala, and M. M. Smith. 1984. Status and needs of the mallard. Trans. North Am. Wildl. and Nat. Resour. Conf. 49:501-526.

Beard, E. B. 1953. The importance of beaver in waterfowl management at the Seney National Wildlife Refuge. J. Wildl. Manage. 17:398-436.

Bellrose, F. C. 1968. Waterfowl migration corridors east of the Rocky Mountains. Ill. Nat. Hist. Surv., Biol. Note Number 61, Urbana. 24 pp.

———. 1976. The comeback of the wood duck. Wildl. Soc. Bull. 4:107-110.

———. 1980. Ducks, geese and swans of North America. Third ed. Stackpole Books, Harris-burg, Pa. 540 pp.

——, and J. B. Low. 1978. Advances in waterfowl management research. Wildl. Soc. Bull. 6:63-72.

Benson, D., and D. Foley. 1956. Waterfowl use of small, man-made wildlife marshes in New York State. N.Y. Fish and Game J. 3:217-224.

——, ——, and D. L. Schierbaum. 1957. The problem of setting duck hunting seasons in New York. N.Y. Fish and Game J. 4:194-202.

Bookhout, T. A., K. E. Bednarik, and R. W. Kroll. 1989. The Great Lakes Marshes. Pages 131-156 *in* L. M. Smith, R. L. Pederson, and R. M. Kaminski, eds. Habitat management for migrating and wintering waterfowl in North America. Texas Tech Univ. Press, Lubbock.

Brown, M. K., and G. R. Parsons. 1979. Waterfowl production on beaver flowages in a part of northern New York. N.Y. Fish and Game J. 26:142-153.

Brown, T. L., D. J. Decker, and J. W. Kelly. 1984. Access to private land for hunting in New York: 1963-1980. Wildl. Soc. Bull. 12:344-349.

Buchsbaum, R., J. Wilson, and I. Valiela. 1986. Digestibility of plant constituents by Canada geese and Atlantic brant. Ecology 67:386-393.

Buol, S. W., F. D. Hale, and R. J. McCracken. 1973. Soil genesis and classification. Iowa State Univ. Press, Ames. 360 pp.

Burger, J., R. Trout, W. Wander, and G. Ritter. 1983. Jamaica Bay studies: IV. Abiotic factors affecting abundance of brant and Canada geese on an east coast estuary. Wilson Bull. 95:384-403.

Candeletti, R. 1979. Naturalistic techniques for open water marsh management with the latest style rotary ditcher. Proc. N.J. Mosquito Control Assoc. 66:74-78.

Cook, A. H., and C. F. Powers. 1958. Early biochemical changes in the soils and waters of artificially created marshes in New York. N.Y. Fish and Game J. 5:9-65.

Corr, P. O. 1985. Waterfowl management plan—1985. Maine Dep. Inland Fish and Wildl., Orono. 96 pp.

Cottam, C. 1934. Past periods of eel-grass scarcity. Rhodora 36:261-264.

——, J. F. Lynch, and A. L. Nelson. 1944. Food habits and management of American sea brant. J. Wildl. Manage. 8:36-56.

——, and D. A. Munro. 1954. Eelgrass status and environmental relations. J. Wildl. Manage. 18:449-460.

Cowardin, L. M., V. Carter, F. C. Golet, and E. T. LaRoe. 1979. Classification of wetlands and deepwater habitats of the United States. U.S. Fish and Wildl. Serv. FWS/OBS-79/31. Washington, D.C. 103 pp.

Daiber, F. C. 1987. A brief history of tidal marsh mosquito control. Pages 234-252 *in* W. R. Whitman and W. H. Meredith, eds. Waterfowl and wetlands symp.: proc. of a symp. on waterfowl and wetlands management in the coastal zone of the Atlantic flyway. Del. Coast. Manage. Prog., Dep. Nat. Resour. and Environ. Control, Dover.

den Hartog, C. 1977. Structure, function and classification in seagrass communities. Pages 89-122 *in* C. P. McRoy and C. Helfferinch, eds. Seagrass ecosystems, a scientific perspective. Marcel Dekker, New York, N.Y.

Eggeman, D. R. 1986. Influence of environmental conditions on distribution and behavior of common goldeneyes wintering in Maine. M.S. Thesis, Univ. of Maine, Orono. 117 pp.

Emerson, F. B., Jr. 1961. Experimental establishment of food and cover plants in marshes created for wildlife in New York state. N.Y. Fish and Game J. 8:130-144.

Erskine, A. J. 1987. A preliminary waterfowl population budget for the Atlantic Provinces, 1978-85. Pages 65-72 *in* A. J. Erskine, ed. Waterfowl breeding population surveys, Atlantic Provinces. Can. Wildl. Serv. Occas. Pap. Number 60.

Feierabend, J. S. 1984. A national summary of lead poisoning in bald eagles and waterfowl. Nat. Wildl. Fed., Washington, D.C. 54 pp.

Figley, W. K., and L. W. VanDruff. 1982. The ecology of urban mallards. Wildl. Monogr. 81. 40 pp.

Fleming, W. J., D. R. Clark, Jr., and C. J. Henny. 1983. Organochlorine pesticides and PCB's: a continuing problem for the 1980's. Trans. North Am. Wildl. and Nat. Resour. Conf. 48:186-199.

Fredrickson, L. H., and T. S. Taylor. 1982. Management of seasonally flooded impoundments for wildlife. U.S. Fish and Wildl. Serv. Res. Publ. 148. 28 pp.

Gagnon, L. P. 1953. The control of purple loosestrife in La Commune at Baie du Febvre—1952. Pages 135-136 *in* Proc. Eastern Section, Nat. Weed Commission, Canada.

Gleason, H. A. 1952. The new Britton and Brown illustrated flora of the northeastern United States and adjacent Canada. 3 Vols. Hafner, New York, N.Y. 800 pp.

Grandy, J. W., IV. 1972. Winter ecology of maritime black ducks (*Anas rubripes*) in Massachusetts, with special reference to Nauset Marsh, Orleans, and Eastham. Ph.D. Dissertation, Univ. Massachusetts, Amherst. 110 pp.

Grenquist, P. 1970. On mortality of the eider duck (*Somateria mollissima*) caused by acanthocephalan parasites. Suomen Rissta 22:24-34.

Grue, C. E., W. J. Fleming, D. C. Busby, and E. F. Hill. 1983. Assessing hazards of organophosphate pesticides to wildlife. Trans. North Am. Wildl. and Nat. Resour. Conf. 48:200-220.

Hagar, J. A. 1950. Black duck mortality in the Parker River region, winter of 1949-1950. Mass. Div. Fish and Game, Amherst. 14 pp.

Haines, T. A., and M. L. Hunter. 1981. Waterfowl and their habitat: threatened by acid rain? Int. Waterfowl Symp. 4:177-190.

Haramis, G. M., and D. J. Chu. 1987. Acid rain effects on waterfowl: use of black duck broods to assess food resources of experimentally acidified wetlands. Pages 173-181 in A. W. Diamond and F. L. Filion, eds. The value of birds. Int. Counc. for Bird Preservation. Tech. Publ. Number 6.

Hartman, F. E. 1963. Estuarine wintering habitat for black ducks. J. Wildl. Manage. 27:339-347.

———. 1960. Ecology of black ducks wintering in the Penobscot estuary. M.S. Thesis, Univ. Maine, Orono. 142 pp.

Heusmann, H. W. 1983. Mallards in the park: contribution to the harvest. Wildl. Soc. Bull. 11:169-171.

———. 1984. Park waterfowl populations in Massachusetts. J. Field Ornithol. 55:89-96.

———. 1988. The role of parks in the range expansion of the mallard in the northeast. Pages 405-412 in M. W. Weller, ed. Waterfowl in winter. Univ. of Minnesota Press, Minneapolis.

Hickey, T. E., Jr. 1980. Activity budgets and movements of black ducks Anas rubripes in Prince Edward Island. M.S. Thesis, McGill Univ., Montreal. 94 pp.

Hoffman, R. D., and T. A. Bookhout. 1985. Metabolizable energy of seeds consumed by ducks in Lake Erie marshes. Trans. North Am. Wildl. and Nat. Resour. Conf. 50:557-565.

Hunter, M. L., Jr., J. W. Witham, and H. Dow. 1984. Effects of a carbaryl-induced depression in invertebrate abundance on the growth and behavior of American black duck and mallard ducklings. Can. J. Zool. 62:452-456.

Jacobs, R. P., C. den Hartog, B. F. Braster, and F. C. Carriere. 1981. Grazing of the seagrass Zostera noitii by birds at Terschelling (Dutch Wadden Sea). Aquatic Bot. 10:241-259.

Jacobson, H. A., G. L. Jacobson, Jr., and J. T. Kelly. 1987. Distribution and abundance of tidal marshes along the coast of Maine. Estuaries 10:126-131.

Johnsgard, P. A. 1960. Wintering distribution changes in mallard and black ducks. Am. Midl. Nat. 66:477-484.

Jones, W. L., and W. C. Lehman. 1987. Phragmites control and revegetation following aerial applications of glyphosate in Delaware. Pages 185-196 in W. R. Whitman and W. H. Meredith, eds. Waterfowl and wetlands symp.: proc. of a symp. on waterfowl and wetlands management in the coastal zone of the Atlantic Flyway. Del. Coast. Manage. Prog., Dep. Nat. Resour. and Environ. Control, Dover.

Jorde, D. G. 1986. Nutritional and thermodynamic aspects of the ecology of black ducks wintering in Maine. Ph.D. Dissertation, Univ. Maine, Orono. 114 pp.

———, and R. B. Owen, Jr. 1988. Efficiency of nutrient use by black ducks wintering in Maine. J. Wildl. Manage. 52:209-211.

Leibovitz, L. 1969. The comparative pathology of duck plague in wild Anseriformes. J. Wildl. Manage. 33:294-303.

———. 1971. Duck plague. Pages 22-32 in J. W. Davis, R. C. Anderson, L. Karstad, and D. O. Trainer, eds. Infectious and parasitic diseases of wild birds. Iowa State Univ. Press, Ames.

Lewis, J. C., and R. L. Garrison. 1984. Habitat suitability index models: American black duck (wintering). U.S. Fish and Wildl. Serv. FWS/OBS-82/10/18. 16 pp.

Longcore, J. R., P. O. Corr, and H. E. Spencer, Jr. 1982. Lead shot incidence in sediments and waterfowl gizzards from Merrymeeting Bay, Maine. Wildl. Soc. Bull. 10:3-10.

———, and J. P. Gibbs. 1988. Distribution and numbers of American black ducks along the Maine coast during the severe winter of 1980-1981. Pages 377-389 in M. W. Weller, ed. Waterfowl in winter. Univ. of Minnesota Press, Minneapolis.

———, R. K. Ross, and K. L. Fisher. 1987. Wildlife resources at risk through acidification of wetlands. Trans. North Am. Wildl. and Nat. Resour. Conf. 52:608-618.

———, and R. C. Stendell. 1982. Black ducks and DDE: review and status. Trans. Northeast. Sect. Wildl. Soc. 39:68-75.

MacNamara, L. G. 1957. Potentials of small waterfowl areas. Trans. North Am. Wildl. and Nat. Resour. Conf. 22:92-96.

Malecki, R. A., and T. J. Rawinski. 1979. Purple loosestrife: a need for concern. Cornell Univ. Conserv. Circ. 17:1-5.

McAuley, D. G., and J. R. Longcore. 1988a. Survival of juvenile ring-necked ducks on wetlands of different pH. J. Wildl. Manage. 52:169-176.

———. 1988b. Foods of juvenile ring-necked ducks: relationship to wetland pH. J. Wildl. Manage. 52:177-185.

McRoy, C. P. 1966. The standing stock and ecology of eelgrass (Zostera marina L.) in Izembek Lagoon, Alaska. M.S. Thesis, Univ. of Washington, Seattle. 137 pp.

Mendall, H. L. 1949. Food habits in relation to black duck management in Maine. J. Wildl. Manage. 13:64-101.

Miller, M. R. 1984. Comparative ability of northern pintails, gadwalls, and northern shovelers to metabolize foods. J. Wildl. Manage. 48:362-370.

Morse, W. B. 1987. Conservation law enforcement: a new profession is forming. Trans. North Am. Wildl. and Nat. Resour. Conf. 52:169-175.

Nixon, S. W. 1982. The ecology of New England high salt marshes: a community profile. U.S. Fish and Wildl. Serv. FWS/OBS-81/55. 70 pp.

Odum, W. E., T. J. Smith, III, J. K. Hoover, and C. C. McIvor. 1984. The ecology of tidal freshwater marshes of the United States east coast: a community profile. U.S. Fish and Wildl. Serv. FWS/OBS-83/17. 177 pp.

Ogilvie, M. A., and A. K. M. St. Joseph. 1976. Dark-bellied brant geese in Britain and Europe, 1956-76. British Birds 69:422-439.

O'Meara, D. C. 1954. Brood parasites in Maine waterfowl—especially *Leucocytozoan* spp. M.S. Thesis, Univ. of Maine, Orono. 55 pp.

Palmer, R. S. 1976. Handbook of North American birds. Vol. 3. Yale University Press, New Haven, Conn. 560 pp.

Portnoy, J. W., C. T. Roman, and M. A. Soukup. 1987. Hydrologic and chemical impacts of diking and drainage of a small estuary (Cape Cod National Seashore): effects on wildlife and fisheries. Pages 254-265 *in* W. R. Whitman and W. H. Meredith, eds. Waterfowl and wetlands symp.: proc. of a symp. on waterfowl and wetlands management in the coastal zone of the Atlantic Flyway. Del. Coastal Manage. Prog., Dep. Nat. Resour. and Environ. Control, Dover.

Price, J. I. 1985. Immunizing Canada geese against avian cholera. Wildl. Soc. Bull. 13:508-515.

Raveling, D. G. 1978. Dynamics of distribution of Canada geese in winter. Trans. North Am. Wildl. and Nat. Resour. Conf. 43:206-225.

Renouf, R. N. 1972. Waterfowl utilization of beaver ponds in New Brunswick. J. Wildl. Manage. 36:740-744.

Riley, L., and W. Riley. 1979. Guide to the National Wildlife Refuges. Anchor Press/Doubleday, Garden City, N.J. 653 pp.

Rogers, J. P., and J. H. Patterson. 1984. The black duck population and its managment. Trans. North Am. Wildl. and Nat. Res. Conf. 49:527-534.

Sanderson, G. C., and F. C. Bellrose. 1969. Wildlife habitat management of wetlands. Suppl. dos An. Acad. Brasil. Cienc. 41:153-204.

Shisler, J. K., and T. L. Schulze. 1985. Methods for evaluation of costs associated with permanent and temporary control methods for salt marsh mosquito abatement. J. Am. Mosquito Control Assoc. 1:164-168.

Smith, L. M., L. D. Vangilder, and R. A. Kennamer. 1985. Foods of wintering brant in eastern North America. J. Field Ornithol. 56:286-289.

Smith, R. H. 1964. Experimental control of purple loosestrife (*Lythrum salicaria*). N.Y. Fish and Game J. 11:35-46.

Spencer, H., Jr., J. Parsons, and K. J. Reinecke. 1980. Waterfowl. Pages 15-50 *in* S. I. Fefer and P. A. Schettig, eds. An ecological characteriza-tion of coastal Maine. Biol. Serv. Prog. U.S. Fish and Wildl. Serv. Vol. 3. FWS/OBS-80/29.

Stott, R. S., and D. P. Olson. 1973. Food-habitat relationships of sea ducks on the New Hampshire coastline. Ecology 54:996-1007.

Stout, I. J., and G. W. Cornwell. 1976. Nonhunting mortality of fledged North American waterfowl. J. Wildl. Manage. 40:681-693.

Teal, J. M. 1986. The ecology of regularly flooded salt marshes of New England: a community profile. U.S. Fish and Wildl. Serv., Biol. Rep. 85(7.4). 61 pp.

Thayer, G. W., W. J. Kenworthy, and M. S. Fonseca. 1984. The ecology of eelgrass meadows of the Atlantic coast: a community profile. U.S. Fish and Wildl. Serv. FWS/OBS-84/02. 147 pp.

Thompson, D. Q., R. L. Stuckey, and E. B. Thompson. 1987. Spread, impact, and control of purple loosestrife (*Lythrum salicaria*) in North American wetlands. U.S. Fish and Wildl. Serv., Fish Wildl. Res. 2. 55 pp.

Thorhaug, A. 1980. Techniques for creating seagrass meadows in damaged areas along the east coast of the U.S.A. Pages 105-116 *in* J. C. Lewis and E. W. Bunce, eds. Rehabilitation and creation of selected coastal habitats: proc. of a workshop. U.S. Fish and Wildl. Serv. FWS/OBS-80/27. 162 pp.

Thul, J. 1977. A parasitological and morphological study of migratory and non-migratory wood ducks (*Aix sponsa*) of the Atlantic Flyway. Wildl. Dis. Res. Prog. Rep. Dec. 7, 1977. Coll. of Veterinary Medicine, Univ. of Florida, Gainesville. 20 pp.

Tiner, R. W., Jr. 1984. Wetlands of the United States: current status and recent trends. National Wetlands Inventory, U.S. Fish and Wildl. Serv. 59 pp.

Todd, C. S., L. S. Young, R. B. Owen, Jr., and F. J. Gramlich. 1982. Food habits of bald eagles in Maine. J. Wildl. Manage. 46:636-645.

Trost, R. E., and R. A. Malecki. 1985. Population trends in Atlantic flyway Canada geese: implications for management. Wildl. Soc. Bull. 13:502-508.

Tubbs, C. R., and J. M. Tubbs. 1983. The distribution of *Zostera* and its exploitation by waterfowl in the Solent, southern England. Aquatic Bot. 15:223-239.

U.S. Department of Interior. 1955. Wetlands of New York. Fish and Wildl. Serv., Off. River Basin Stud. Boston, Mass. 18 pp.

———. 1959. Wetlands of Massachusetts. Fish and Wildl. Serv., Off. River Basin Studies. Boston, Mass. 17 pp.

United States Fish and Wildlife Service and Canadian Wildlife Service. 1986. North American waterfowl management plan. U.S. Fish and Wildl. Serv., Washington, D.C. 31 pp.

Weller, M. W. 1981. Freshwater marshes: ecology and wildlife management. Univ. Minnesota Press, Minneapolis. 146 pp.

White, D. H., K. A. King, C. A. Mitchell, and A. J. Krynitsky. 1981. Body lipids and pesticide burdens of migrant blue-winged teal. J. Field Ornithol. 52:23-28.

——, and R. C. Stendell. 1977. Waterfowl exposure to lead and steel shot on selected hunting areas. J. Wildl. Manage. 41:469-475.

CHESAPEAKE BAY AND NORTH CAROLINA SOUNDS

LARRY J. HINDMAN, Maryland Forest, Park and Wildlife Service, P.O. Box 68, Wye Mills, MD 21679
VERNON D. STOTTS, Route 1, Box 124, Queenstown, MD 21658

The Chesapeake Bay in Maryland and Virginia and the sounds of North Carolina with their extensive and varied wetland habitats historically have been a major wintering area for waterfowl. An estimated 1.3 million waterfowl winter in this region, comprising 40% of the wintering waterfowl in the Atlantic Flyway. This region is the wintering area for the entire eastern population of tundra swans (*Cygnus columbianus*), 71% of the Atlantic population of Canada geese (*Branta canadensis*), and 75% of the canvasbacks (*Aythya valisineria*) in the Atlantic Flyway (Bellrose 1980).

Our objectives in this chapter are to (1) define the changes that have occurred in waterfowl populations of the Maryland-Virginia-North Carolina area, (2) discuss what affects their occurrence, and (3) describe the habitat management practices that are being used to manage these populations.

CLIMATE

The humid, temperate climate is modified by the Atlantic Ocean. The coldest period of the year is late January and early February. The average daily temperature in winter is 2 C in the vicinity of Chestertown, Maryland, and 4 C near Cape Hatteras, North Carolina. Precipitation ranges from about 115 cm in the north to about 140 cm in the south and occurs mainly as rain. Tropical storms of hurricane force strike this region occasionally, but the intensity of rainfall is generally moderate. Snowfall occurs infrequently in late winter, but can be of great enough magnitude to cause a southward shift in waterfowl species dependent upon availability of agricultural foods. The prevailing wind is west to northwest during winter. Winds of 80-100 km/hr can accompany winter storms, but average much less.

CHESAPEAKE BAY

Chesapeake Bay (Fig. 1) is the largest estuary in the conterminous United States (U.S.). It was created during the last 15,000 years by the flooding of the lower valley of the Susquehanna River (Lippson 1973). As a drowned valley, it has hundreds of peripheral rivers, bays, and creeks, a long convoluted shoreline, and extensive areas of shallow waters.

The eastern shore is the Delmarva Peninsula (Delaware, eastern Maryland, and Virginia) that lies between the bay and the Atlantic Ocean and Delaware Bay. The Susquehanna River originates in New York and Pennsylvania, splits the Appalachian Range, and becomes tidal about 700 km before it enters the Chesapeake Bay at its head. The western shore is rough and deeply incised by the tributary estuaries of the Patuxent, Potomac, Rappahannoch, James, and York rivers.

Chesapeake Bay is about 290 km long and 8-48 km wide, with depths to 53 m. Average depth of the open bay is 8.4 m, but average depth of the total system (including tributaries) is 6.5 m. The open bay has a surface area of about 6,500 km^2, but the total estuarine system (including tributaries) covers about 11,500 km^2. The total shoreline of the bay and its tributaries is an estimated 13,033 km, with 6,400 km and 6,600 km in Maryland and Virginia, respectively (Lippson 1973). Marshes fringe the Chesapeake and its tributaries, encompassing 172,000 ha, with 85,800 ha in Maryland and 86,200 ha in Virginia.

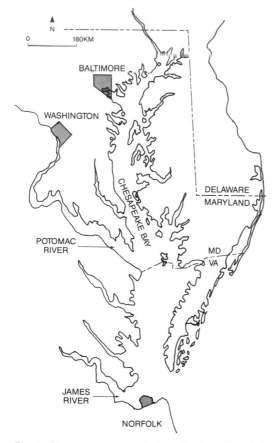

Fig. 1. Cheasapeake Bay in Maryland and Virginia

there (0-5 ppt salinity) increases along the length of the bay, reaching 25-30 ppt at the mouth. Salinity also varies across the bay from lower salinities on the western side of the bay to higher salinities along the Eastern Shore.

CURRITUCK-ALBEMARLE-PAMLICO SOUNDS

The series of barrier islands, known as the Outer Banks, along the North Carolina coast from the Virginia border to just south of Cape Lookout, separate the Atlantic Ocean from the inner portion of the North Carolina Coastal Plain known as the Currituck-Albemarle-Pamlico Sound complex. This complex (Fig. 2) is the second largest estuarine system (809,000 ha) along the east coast of the U.S. and extends for a length of about 274 km, with a maximum width of 48 km (National Estuary Study 1970). The waters are generally shallow, ranging from 2 m in Currituck Sound to 6 m in Pamlico Sound. Due to the restricted tidal flow between the Atlantic Ocean and Albemarle and Pamlico sounds, the mean tidal range is about 15.2 cm (Bumpus et al. 1973).

Tidal marshes occur at the landward sides of the barrier beaches, as a fringe to the small islands in the sounds, and commonly along the mainland shore. Regular tidal pulses occur only in those areas adjacent to the inlets. The marshes, in response to this type of tidal activity, show a mosaic pattern involving salt- and freshwater marsh (Wells 1928). The mainland shore along the western edge of the sounds is low, with many river marshes and swamps.

Currituck Sound is fresh to slightly brackish, 4.8-14.5 km wide and 64.4 km long. The waters of the open sound are 0.9-2.4 m deep, but the areas fringed by marshes in the central and eastern parts range from 0.3-0.9 m deep. The total water surface is about 185,322 ha (Quay and Critcher 1962).

Although the bay lies totally within the Atlantic Coastal Plain, it drains water from a 165,760 km² drainage basin, which includes part of the Piedmont and the Allegheny plateaus. More than 50 tributaries contribute water to the Chesapeake, providing a mixture of waters with a broad geochemical range. Tides move up the bay from the ocean twice every 24.8 hours. The tidal range is greatest at the mouth of the bay (0.76 m) and at the end of most of the large rivers, and is about 0.6 m at the head of the bay (Lippson 1973).

Water salinity throughout Chesapeake Bay and its tributaries is an important factor that affects the distribution of animal and plant species. From the site of freshwater inflow of the Susquehanna River at the head of the bay, the salinity

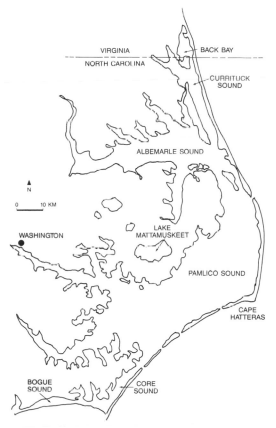

Fig. 2. Sounds and bays in Virginia and North Carolina.

Pamlico Sound, a very shallow body of water that extends 130 km south to southeastwardly from Roanoke Island, is 12.9-48.3 km wide. The sound has had large expanses of submerged aquatic plants in wide sandy areas along the shore (Halvorson and Dawson 1973). Other important estuaries extending beyond this vast complex are Back Bay, Virginia, at the north end and Core and Bogue sounds to the south.

HABITAT IMPORTANCE
Important Wetlands and Uplands

Wetlands that fringe the bays and sounds of Maryland, Virginia, and North Carolina vary in plant composition and habitat structure according to salinity, tidal fluctuations, water depth, and type of dominant vegetation. Accordingly, there exists a variety of wetlands, descriptions of which follow.

Estuarine River-Marsh.—These wetlands extend inland along the narrow valley floors of tributary streams. One of the longest, along the Nanticoke River (Maryland), is in some places 3 km wide. River marshes are located upstream of freshwater estuarine river-marshes and brackish estuarine river-marshes downstream (Stewart 1962).

Freshwater estuarine river-marsh occurs in fresh to slightly brackish water. Diversity of emergent plants is high and varies with water depth. Common plants are pickerelweed (*Pontederia cordata*), spatterdock cowlily (*Nuphar advena*), river bulrush (*Scirpus fluviatilis*), swamp rosemallow (*Hibiscus palustris*), common reed (*Phragmites communis*), and wildrice (*Zizania aquatica*) (Stewart 1962). Plant names follow Scott and Wasser (1980).

Brackish estuarine river-marsh occurs downstream in waters of increased salinity (5-15 ppt). Big cordgrass (*Spartina cynosuroides*) is dominant. However, cordgrass may be interspersed with narrowleaf cattail (*Typha angustifolia*), switchgrass panicum (*Panicum virgatum*), dotted smartweed (*Polygonum punctatum*), and swamp rosemallow. These marshes are especially attractive to dabbling ducks in the fall because of these plant foods. Waterfowl use of this habitat type is lower during winter because the marshes frequently freeze.

Fresh Estuarine Bay-Marsh.—This habitat attracts comparatively smaller populations of wintering waterfowl than riverine marshes. These marshes develop on broad, shallow estuarine flats that are flooded by fresh or slightly brackish tidal water. Tidal streams in this habitat are usually broad, poorly defined, and often merge into a complex of connecting ponds. Olney bulrush (*Scirpus olneyi*) is dominant in most freshwater estuarine bay-marshes, especially close to drainage channels. American bulrush (*S. americana*) usually dominates along the higher margins of the marsh. Other plants that typify this habitat are narrowleaf cattail, dwarf spikerush (*Eleocharis parvula*), white waterlily (*Nymphaea odorata*), and swamp rosemallow (Stewart 1962). Canada geese and black ducks (*Anas rubripes*) are common migrants. Canada geese use shallow ponds that occur in this habitat, particularly those that contain stands of Olney bulrush.

Salt Estuarine Bay-Marsh.—These wetlands include large offshore islands, as well as the outer fringe of marsh along the bayshores of the lower eastern shore of Maryland and Virginia. Salinity is high (>15 ppt) and tidal range narrow (21-24 cm). Characteristic plant species include smooth cordgrass (*Spartina alterniflora*), which occurs in a narrow zone along tidal streams inundated on high tides; marshhay cordgrass (*S. patens*), which is found in larger areas above the normal high-tide mark; saltmarsh bulrush (*Scirpus robustus*) and seashore saltgrass (*Distichlis spicata*), which grow in patches of poorly drained areas. Bigleaf sumpweed (*Iva frutescens*) forms narrow strips along natural levees (Stewart 1962). Common widgeonweed (*Ruppia maritima*) is abundant throughout most ponds and creeks where tidal waters are clear. Black ducks are widely distributed throughout this habitat during the year.

Fresh Estuarine Bay.—These bays have declined in importance to waterfowl due to reduced water quality and the subsequent decline of submerged aquatic vegetation (SAV) (Bayley et al. 1978, Stevenson and Confer 1978, Orth and Moore 1981). In Chesapeake Bay, gradually increased turbidity and nutrient levels, due to agricultural runoff and urbanization, have contributed to this decline (Kemp et al. 1983). The Susquehanna Flats, once renowned for its abundance of rooted SAV and concentrations of canvasbacks and other diving ducks, presently supports only remnant populations of native plant species and spiked watermilfoil (*Myriophyllum spictatum*). Since tropical storm Agnes in 1972, which restructured bottom sediments and caused extensive damage to submerged plant communities, the flats have been used only as a resting area by a few thousand Canada geese and a few hundred ducks.

Common submerged plants in fresh estuarine bays include American wildcelery (*Vallisneria americana*), southern naiad (*Najas guadalupensis*), muskgrass (*Chara* sp.), pondweeds (*Potamogeton* spp.), waterstar mudplantain (*Heteranathera dubia*), and nitella (*Nitella* sp.) (Stewart 1962). Spiked watermilfoil is the dominant submerged aquatic plant in some areas.

Use of the fresh estuarine bays by waterfowl has declined where habitats have deteriorated. In areas where fresh estuarine bays adjoin extensive upland agricultural lands, thousands of Canada geese, mallards, (*Anas platyrhynchos*) and black ducks use these bays as resting sites. However, ice conditions restrict use of these areas by waterfowl (Lovvorn 1987). In recent years, thousands of common mergansers (*Mergus merganser*) have been displaced temporarily by ice in freshwater streams into the Susquehanna Flats region of the Chesapeake Bay.

Slightly Brackish Estuarine Bay.— Increasingly brackish areas provide a transition between fresh and brackish estuarine bays; it is here that diversity of SAV is greatest. Historically, the predominant species were thorowort pondweed (*Potamogeton perfoliatus*), American wildcelery, and common widgeonweed (Stewart 1962). Wildcelery has become sparse in most habitats in the upper Chesapeake (Stevenson and Confer 1978). Thorowort pondweed, like other submerged aquatic species in the Bay, has declined in abundance. Hydrilla (*Hydrilla verticillata*), an important waterfowl food in Florida (Johnson and Montalbano

1984), was reported growing in the Potomac River in 1982 (Steward et al. 1984). This species has increased in abundance and now dominates other submerged plants along a 10 km portion of this habitat (Orth et al. 1987). Common species found in this habitat are fennelleaf pondweed (*P. pectinatus*), baby pondweed (*P. pusillus*), horned poolmat (*Zannichellia palustris*), Canadian waterweed (*Elodea canadensis*), and muskgrass (Stewart 1962).

Canvasback, lesser scaup (*Aythya affinis*), American wigeon (*Anas americana*), ruddy duck (*Oxyura jamaicensis*), and redhead (*Aythya americana*) are the primary species found in this habitat. In the Chesapeake Bay, waterfowl use of this habitat is limited due to human disturbances and pollution.

Brackish Estuarine Bay.—This habitat is the most important waterfowl habitat in the Chesapeake Bay and North Carolina Sounds. Biomass of SAV is probably greatest in this habitat. Widgeonweed is the dominant species, followed by thorowort and fennelleaf pondweeds. Species which are common include common eelgrass (*Zostera marina*), horned poolmat, spiked watermilfoil, Canadian waterweed, and hollow-green algae (*Enteromorpha* spp.). American shoalweed (*Halodule beaudettei*) is locally common in some North Carolina sounds, where it is especially important to redheads.

Wintering and transient waterfowl include Canada geese, mallard, black duck, tundra swan, canvasback, common goldeneye (*Buchephala clangula*), and lesser scaup. Large concentrations of Canada geese winter in the brackish estuarine bays along the eastern shore of Chesapeake Bay in the Chester and Choptank rivers and Eastern Bay (Stewart 1962). Geese and swans use adjacent agricultural fields and shoals of this habitat type for feeding. Brackish estuarine bays and interior impoundments are

used as roost areas by Canada geese and tundra swans. Dabbling ducks use this habitat type as sanctuary when hunting pressure and ice force them out of adjacent marshes.

Salt Estuarine Bay.—These openwater bays cover an extensive portion of the Chesapeake Bay. Common eelgrass, common widgeonweed, and sea lettuce (*Ulva lactuca*) are dominant; fennelleaf pondweed and horned poolmat occur in some areas (Stewart 1962).

Waterfowl use is highest in this habitat during cold winters, when many waterfowl are forced from areas of low salinity due to ice formation. Conversely, waterfowl use is lowest during mild winters. Common transient and wintering waterfowl include lesser and greater scaup (*Aythya marila*), common goldeneye, bufflehead (*Bucephala albeola*), oldsquaw (*Clangula hyemalis*), and scoters (*Melanitta* spp.). Canada geese and black ducks occur regularly in shoal water areas adjacent to extensive marshes of the salt estuarine bays or near upland agricultural fields.

Wooded Bottomlands.—This habitat borders various streams of the coastal plain interior. Principal migrants include wood ducks (*Aix sponsa*), mallards, black ducks, and hooded mergansers (*Lophodytes cucullatus*). Use by migrant waterfowl varies yearly and may be influenced by the abundance of mast of American beech (*Fagus grandifolia*) and pin oak (*Quercus palustris*).

Man-made Impoundments.—These wetlands are scattered throughout the coastal plain interior of Maryland, Virginia, and North Carolina, reaching greatest density in Kent County, Maryland, where they occur at a density of 1-2/km² (Harvey 1987). Stotts (1983) reported 6,918 ponds on Delmarva Peninsula; most (6,412) were less than 1.4 ha. Many of these ponds are managed by private landowners as sanctuary ponds to attract wintering geese. Harvey (1987) found that these ponds occurred at a density of 1/7 km². This abundance of farm ponds and sanctuaries combined with abundant agricultural foods, has greatly influenced the distribution of Canada geese. Most of the Atlantic Population of Canada geese winter in this region. Mallards, black ducks, and, to a lesser extent, northern pintails (*Anas acuta*) and tundra swans use interior impoundments for resting when they are adjacent to important feeding areas. Recently, greater snow geese (*Chen caerulescens atlantica*) have used a few of these impoundments as roosts in areas where field-feeding by this species now occurs.

Agricultural Fields and Pastureland.— Uplands throughout the coastal plain have become increasingly valuable for a number of waterfowl species. Winter wheat, barley, corn, and soybeans are major crops. Waste corn and soybeans available after harvest provided an alternative food source for waterfowl at the same time that traditional foods of emergent and submergent plants were declining. Unharvested corn is used by private landowners and state and federal agencies to provide winter foods for field-feeding ducks and geese. Winter wheat, barley, and rye are used by Canada geese, snow geese, and tundra swans throughout the Maryland-Virginia-North Carolina region. Tundra swans began to feed in agricultural fields in this region in the late 1960s. Tundra swans wintering in North Carolina continue use of agricultural foods despite availability of emergent and submergent foods in adjacent wetlands (Bortner 1985).

MAJOR WATERFOWL SPECIES AND ABUNDANCES

Numbers of Wintering Waterfowl

Steiner (1984) compiled waterfowl population data in the Atlantic Flyway as indicated by the mid-winter waterfowl inventory (MWI). Since 1954, all but a

Table 1 Prominent species (Stewart 1962) and peak waterfowl numbers (Hindman 1978a) in Maryland's Chesapeake Bay.

Month	Prominent species, 1958-59	Peak numbers, 1973-78
October	American wigeon, black duck	American wigeon, northern pintail, total dabbling ducks
November	Canada goose, American wigeon	Canada goose, total waterfowl
December	Canada goose, black duck	Mallard
January	Canada goose, black duck	Redhead, canvasback, scaups, goldeneye, ruddy duck, total diving ducks
February	No survey	Ring-necked duck (*Aythya collaris*), bufflehead, oldsquaw, scoters, mergansers, swans
March	Canada goose, black duck	No survey
April	No survey	Black duck, gadwall, blue-winged teal, northern shoveler (*Anas clypeata*)

few species in the flyway have shown downward trends. Because of the importance of the Maryland-Virginia-North Carolina bays and sounds, populations seen here affect flyway estimates.

Total wintering waterfowl have declined from 2,036,300 in 1954-56 to 1,168,200 in 1982-84 (Steiner 1984). Dabbling duck numbers dropped from 663,600 to 177,500; only gadwall (*Anas strepera*) have exhibited increases. Diving duck numbers fell from 887,100 to 380,800, with only bufflehead and oldsquaw increasing. Geese went up from 435,400 to 631,500, but Atlantic brant (*Branta bernicla hrota*) decreased. Tundra swans also increased from 60,500 to 78,200.

Peak and Staging Populations

Early fall migrants include blue-winged and green-winged teal (*Anas discors, A. crecca*), northern pintail, and American wigeon in August and September. Large numbers of scoters and scaups begin migration by early November. Stewart (1962) made monthly counts from October 1958 through March 1959, showing peak populations in early December for the upper Chesapeake Bay. Stewart (1962) and Hindman (1978a) recorded arrival and departure times of the various species in the Chesapeake Bay (Table 1). Sincock et al. (1966) surveyed Back Bay and Currituck Sound and its use by waterfowl, and recorded the passage of waterfowl through Virginia and North Carolina from 1958-64 (Table 2).

Weekly surveys made by National Wildlife Refuges showed that black ducks, gadwalls, green-winged teals, pintails, wigeons, canvasbacks, ruddy ducks, brant, all geese, and tundra swans appeared to make orderly progressions southward in the fall and winter. Hindman (1978b), using ground and aerial surveys in unison throughout Maryland's tidewater bays and the oceanfront between 1973 and 1977, indicated that scoters moved down the coast by mid-September, with many following the shoreline into and back out of Chesapeake Bay, with peak numbers occurring the first 3 weeks in October. Oldsquaw, however, appeared to arrive in Chesapeake Bay from an overland northwesterly route during the middle of October, with peaks in early November.

Two of the most spectacular staging areas are the extensive open-water shoals at the mouth of the Chester River and the Susquehanna Flats. The most visible staging occurred in Canada geese, tundra swan, and the diving ducks, principally canvasbacks, scaups, and redheads. Dabblers were more secretive, tending to stage in large marshes, and moving northward in smaller groups.

WATERFOWL SPECIES DIVERSITY
Dabbling Ducks

The black duck is declining and the

Table 2. Occurrence of peak waterfowl numbers in Back Bay and Currituck Sound, 1958-64 (Sincock et al. 1966).

Species	Period
Mallard	Early Dec-early Jan
Black duck	Late Nov-early Feb
Gadwall	Late Nov-mid Mar
American wigeon	Oct-early December
Green-winged teal	Late Nov-mid-Feb
Blue-winged teal	Mid-Mar-early Apr; mid-Sept at times
Northern shoveler	Mid-Mar-early Apr; mid-Sept; early Jan at times
Northern pintail	Mid-Dec-early Jan; mid-Oct at times
Wood duck	Mid-Sep-early Jan
Redhead	Mid-Dec-mid-Feb
Canvasback	Early Jan-mid-Mar
Scaups	Early Dec-early Jan; mid-Oct at times
Ring-necked duck	Mid-Nov-early Jan
American goldeneye	Late Nov-early Jan
Bufflehead	Mid-Nov-early Dec
Scoters	Early Dec-mid-Mar
Oldsquaw	Mid-Nov-early Apr
Mergansers	Late Nov-early Feb
Atlantic brant	Early Jan-early Feb
Snow geese	Early Jan-mid-Mar
Canada geese	Early Dec-early Jan; mid-Oct at times
Tundra swan	Mid-Dec-early Jan

mallard increasing as breeding birds in this region (Nicholson 1955, Stotts 1987). One primary reason for this has been the release of hand-reared mallards by private and state conservation agencies since the late 1940s (Stewart and Robbins 1958, Stewart 1962, Stotts 1971, 1987). Other surveys indicated that proliferation of ponds here and elsewhere in the flyway also was contributing to the spread of mallards (Robbins 1982, Robbins et al. 1986).

The dabbling duck species with the largest populations have declined the most since the 1950s. The smaller, more secretive species have shown the same rate of decline, but they are poorly surveyed.

Overall, dabbling ducks had a wintering index of 663,600 in the mid-1950s, falling to 177,500 in the mid-1980s, (Steiner 1984). Some species declines parallel that of SAV in Chesapeake Bay (Perry 1987). Populations of American wigeon were most closely associated with these declines in vegetation.

Diving Ducks

Diving ducks range through all habitats of the region from fresh to saline, but the greatest populations are associated with salinities of 0-15 ppt. These habitats were the hardest hit by SAV declines, which resulted eventually in deterioration of the invertebrate faunal structure of such areas (Perry et al. 1981). The large number of diving ducks on the Susquehanna Flats in the 1950s were reduced to a few hundred after the decline of American wildcelery in the 1960s; continental populations of ducks declined also at that time (Perry et al. 1981).

After reduction of vegetation on Susquehanna Flats, it was still common to see thousands of rafted divers off Westmoreland Park in the Potomac River. With further declines of water quality from the late 1960s-1980s, many of these diving ducks have left Chesapeake Bay and have increased in the bays and sounds of North Carolina, especially Core Sound. Because of the importance of SAV in the diet of redheads, this species has almost disappeared from the Chesapeake Bay. In contrast, some species (e.g., bufflehead), which consume animal foods, have increased. (Perry et al. 1981).

Long-term trends in numbers of wintering divers has been downward. From a 3-year high of 801,500 in the mid-1950s, populations declined to 237,900 in 1984 (Steiner 1984).

Mergansers

The red-breasted merganser (*Mergus serrator*) is common throughout the region, especially in salt and brackish habitats during winter. Common and hooded mergansers winter primarily in freshwater habitats, but the latter often frequents brackish creeks and marshes. The mid-winter count for mergansers was about 32,300 in the mid-1950s and has fallen to about 23,900 (Steiner 1984).

Seaducks

Oldsquaw and scoters are more transient than most other ducks in this region. Brackish or saline waters over 3 m deep among oyster bars and other shellfish beds are important habitats. Wintering populations declined from 43,300 in the mid-1950s to 19,000 in the early 1980s (Steiner 1984).

Geese

Resident Canada geese make up a significant part of wintering populations along the eastern seaboard. Atlantic brant, lesser (*Chen c. caerulescens*) snow geese and greater snow geese and 4 races of Canada geese (*Branta c. interior, B. c. moffitti, B. c. maxima*, and *B. c. hutchinsii*) are the main components of the region's geese (Stotts 1983).

Although all geese in this region continue to use the shoots and roots of emergent and submersed aquatic plants, they no longer are totally dependent on these foods during migration and winter. Geese, except for brant, intensively use agricultural forages, harvested grains, lawns, and pastures. Large bodies of water are used for roosting. Additionally, they are attracted to ponds constructed for agricultural, recreational, and sewage purposes.

Frequently, these changes in food habits have been associated with severe winters that prevented access to aquatic habitats (Stotts 1972, Ferrigno 1978, Nelson 1978, Myers et al. 1982). Brant fed on lawns, golf courses, pastures, and hayfields during extensive ice cover, and the habit was perpetuated in ensuing winters.

Goose populations have increased in the flyway, but the increase has not always included southern areas or coastal flocks. In the Maryland-Virginia-North

Carolina region, wintering geese have increased from 435,300 in the mid-1950s to 631,500 (Steiner 1984). Brant decreased from 53,300 to 27,600. Snow geese (mostly greater snow geese) have increased from 37,100 to 64,500 since the mid-1950s. During that period, however, Canada geese have nearly disappeared from South Carolina, Georgia, and Florida, while populations have fallen from 149,800 to 33,300 in North Carolina. Similarly, coastal flocks of Canada geese in the mid-Atlantic region have decreased (Stotts 1983).

Swans

Swans found in this region are the mute (*Cygnus olor*), tundra, and trumpeter (*C. buccinator*). The exotic mute swan has been expanding its breeding range within Maryland and has invaded Virginia during winter. The trumpeter, reintroduced in the Central Flyway in Canada, has occurred during winter counts. The tundra swan has its primary wintering ground in this region (Bellrose 1980).

Tundra swans in this region were shoal-water feeders (Stewart and Manning 1958, Stewart 1962) before the winter of 1969-70. During that winter, a 6 week freeze in the Chesapeake resulted in field-feeding, which was reinforced in ensuing years following declines in SAV (Maryland For., Park, and Wildl. Serv., unpubl. rep.) Recently, wintering tundra swans have decreased in Chesapeake Bay but increased in Back Bay-Currituck Sound, where SAV still thrives. Overall, the wintering tundra swan population has increased from 60,500 to 78,200 between the mid-1950s and mid 1980s. Wintering mute and trumpeter swans now number slightly over 100 birds.

HABITAT CHANGES AND IMPACTS

Wetland Habitats

Wetlands along the U.S. east coast continue to disappear or deteriorate at a faster rate than they are created or enhanced, although many planning programs have begun to reduce wetland losses. Virginia had an average wetland loss of 243 ha/yr before enactment of restrictive regulations; losses after enactment dropped to 8 ha/yr (Cook 1985). By 1968, Maryland had lost 7.2% of its emergent wetlands present in 1942 (Metzgar 1973). Legislation reduced that loss from 405 to 8 ha/yr after 1970 (Redelfs in Tiner 1984, Whitman and Meredith 1987). In the U.S., estuarine wetland losses averaged 7,287 ha/yr from the mid-1950s to the mid-1970s (Tiner 1984).

Agriculture continues to be one of the greatest factors in wetland loss in the mid-Atlantic region. Shrub wetlands, especially pocosins, have been converted to agricultural fields, pine plantations, and peat mines in North Carolina. Bottomland hardwoods have been cut for timber or bottomlands cleared and drained for agriculture in North Carolina, Virginia, and Maryland (Tiner 1984).

However, farm pond construction adds waterfowl habitat. The USDA District (B. E. Nichols, pers. commun.) reported that there were 3,622 ponds totaling 5,668 ha in the Delmarva Peninsula in 1982. Stotts (1956) reported 1,329 ponds totaling 1,775 ha in Maryland's tidewater counties.

Impoundments have been a major tool in marsh management for waterfowl, muskrats (*Ondatra zibethicus*), and mosquitoes (Whitman and Meredith 1987). Recently, however, other management interests such as marine fisheries have slowed the construction of structures (Montague et al. 1987). Furthermore, some studies of black duck habitat use (Conroy et al. 1987, Morton et al. 1987) have indicated that tidal marsh may be more critical than impoundments to waterfowl during stress periods.

Dredge and fill operations continue to change or destroy estuarine wetlands. Parallel-grid ditching for mosquito control was used extensively during the 1930s, and many coastal marshes were treated this way in the 1970s. Almost 4,049 ha of Maryland's Chesapeake Bay marshes were drained by this method between 1958 and 1975 (C. R. Lesser, pers. commun.). In September 1975, open marsh water management (OMWM) techniques (a system of tidal and limited tidal ponds and ditches) were initiated. Since then, 7,814 ha have been treated with OMWM methods; 5,516 ha in previously ditched marshes (2,834 ha in Chesapeake Bay and 2,601 ha along Maryland's ocean bays) and 1,749 ha in previously unditched Chesapeake marshes. North Carolina is beginning to use OMWM methods, but Virginia is not. Both have been using parallel-grid ditching methods for mosquito control, which generally causes excessive drying and negative changes in marsh ecology.

Boat ownership and attendant effects on coastal wetlands have increased dramatically since 1960. In Maryland's tidal areas, boat registration has increased from 43,541 in 1960 to 111,322 in 1976 to 123,985 in 1986.

Effects of a rise in sea level were addressed in the International Conference on Health and Environmental Effects of Ozone Modification and Climate Change (Hull and Titus 1986, Titus 1986*a*, *b*). A substantial rise in sea level could ". . . inundate wetlands and lowlands, accelerate coastal erosion, exacerbate coastal flooding, and increase the salinity of estuaries . . ." (Titus 1986*c*).

Agricultural Changes

Agricultural lands have become an important component of waterfowl habitat since wetland destruction accelerated in the 1940s. Geese, swans, and dabbling ducks have increased their use of waste grain, green wheat and barley, and pastures. However, grain-harvest methods have improved (e.g., fields with an average of 405 kg/ha of waste corn with cob harvest are now leaving less with picker-shellers).

Waste grains have been the main winter food of Canada geese, mallards, northern pintails, and black ducks during recent years. Wheat, barley, and some garden crops (e.g., spinach) are important to Canada geese. Since the 1970s, tundra swans and snow geese have greatly increased use of these crops.

Factors involved in the switch to agricultural foods by waterfowl include increased field size since 1940. Average farm size has increased from 32 to 57 ha in Maryland, Virginia and North Carolina. The respective increases for soybeans between 1948 and 1978 have been 431%, 139%, and 244%. Winter barley has increased in all 3 states (36, 35, and 80%, respectively). However, winter wheat has decreased in all 3 states (72, 61, and 42%, respectively), as has hay and pasture (U.S. Dep. Agric. 1950, 1980).

Garden crops have increased about 6% annually in the 1980s in Maryland's Chesapeake area (C. D. Homann, pers. commun.). Poultry farming also has increased; thus, grain farming has increased to supply that industry. Overall, however, agricultural lands in estuarine areas have been extensively converted to housing and industrial development since the 1940s.

HABITAT IMPORTANCE RELATIVE TO WATERFOWL REQUIREMENTS

Important Plant and Animal Food Resources

Stewart (1962) examined the gizzard contents of harvested waterfowl in the upper Chesapeake Bay (Maryland) between 1945 and 1959. For the majority of waterfowl, common widgeonweed and thorowort pondweed were the most important foods in the upper Chesapeake. Corn also was important to many species. Other food plants important locally included American wildcelery, Olney bulrush, and dotted smartweed. The more important animal foods were Baltic clams (*Macoma balthica*), saltmarsh snails

(*Melampus bidentalis*), various gastropods (e.g., *Littoridinops* spp., *Bittium* spp., and *Acteocina canaliculata*), amphipods (*Gammaridae*), mud crabs (*Xanthidae*), and midge larve (*Chironomidae*) (Stewart 1962).

Since Stewart's (1962) study, many changes have occurred in the quality, quantity, and distribution of the biota of Chesapeake Bay. Consequently, several waterfowl species have changed their diets. Canada geese changed their diet from aquatic plants to agricultural crops and weeds in the 1940s and 1950s. Subsequent to these changes has been a deterioration of the water quality of the bay causing a decrease in SAV and an increase in pollution-tolerant invertebrates (e.g., *Rangia* and *Corbicula* spp.). However, decreases in SAV have resulted in reductions of invertebrates. Several snail species, abundant on Susquehanna Flats in 1960, were essentially gone by 1969 (Stotts 1970). Demise of SAV beds in the early 1970s contributed to the high mortality of soft-shelled clams (*Mya arenaria*). Widespread agricultural development provided alternative foods for field-feeding species. Greater snow geese switched from marsh-plant shoots and rhizomes to feeding on agricultural crops in the 1970s.

Rawls (1978) examined the food contents of harvested waterfowl in the upper Chesapeake Bay (Maryland) between 1959 and 1968. Plant material represented 78% of all foods consumed by waterfowl. Corn was eaten to a greater extent than any other upland plant by Canada geese, mallards, and northern pintails. Corn also was found in canvasbacks, lesser scaup, and redheads, suggesting illegal baiting in some areas. Important plant foods were thorowort pondweed, common widgeonweed, spiked watermilfoil, southern naiad, and sea lettuce. Rawls (1978) found that soft-shelled clams and the Baltic clam contributed most to the total volume of animal food. Perry and Uhler

(1976) determined that the Baltic clam was extremely important in the diet of canvasbacks from 11 wintering areas in the Chesapeake Bay. Thorowort pondweed was the most important plant food consumed by canvasbacks (Perry and Uhler 1976).

Harvey (1987) found that Canada geese in Kent County, Maryland, preferred hay pasture and corn stubble in early fall, but shifted to feeding primarily on corn during winter. Standing corn was a preferred food only when snow cover was present. Harvested soybean fields were avoided until late winter when they were frequented by about 20% of the foraging flocks.

Tundra swans had been dependent upon SAV and, to a lesser extent, invertebrates in Chesapeake Bay during winter. Swans were forced to abandon these foods because of prolonged freezes in 1969-70 and because of large-scale SAV mortality in 1972 and 1973 (Stotts 1973). Reduced SAV resources in 1970-72 caused swans to use agricultural crops. Perhaps as a result of the decline in SAV, tundra swan numbers have declined in Maryland and increased in North Carolina where SAV has been better.

Quay and Critcher (1962) found that diving ducks (except buffleheads) in Currituck Sound predominately consumed aquatic vegetation (gizzard studies). Florschutz (1972) found that spiked watermilfoil was an important food item of waterfowl from Back Bay, Virginia, and Currituck Sound, North Carolina, during 1968-71. Data revealed that 72% of the digestive tracts of Canada geese, 10 duck species, and American coots (*Fulica americana*) contained spiked watermilfoil. Highest milfoil use was by scaups, followed by gadwall, American wigeon, Canada geese, redhead, northern pintail, green-winged teal, ruddy duck, black duck, coot, mallard, and canvasback. Other natural foods used by waterfowl in this area included common widgeonweed, southern naiad, American wildcelery, and flatsedges (*Cyperus* spp.) (Florschutz 1972).

Perry and Uhler (1982) determined that the Baltic clam was the predominant food of canvasbacks in the Pamlico River area, whereas fennelleaf pondweed predominated in birds from impoundments on the Outer Banks. Shoalweed formed 100% of the esophageal food in redheads from Pamlico Sound (Perry and Uhler 1982). Lesser scaup fed predominantly on mollusks (*Mulinia lateralis, Rangia cuneata*). Ring-necked ducks fed mainly on SAV, and greater scaup, bufflehead, and ruddy ducks fed mainly on surf clams. Most diving ducks fed more on invertebrates and less on SAV than in the past (Perry and Uhler 1982).

Prior to widespread agricultural development, Yelverton and Quay (1959) found 63% of Canada goose gizzards collected at Lake Mattamuskeet, North Carolina, during the fall and winter hunting season contained spikerush and American bulrush. Native grasses and corn accounted for 11% and 22%, respectively, of the food volume. In Currituck Sound, Florschutz (1972) found that spiked watermilfoil comprised 25%, other foods 24%, and grit 50% of the contents of Canada goose gizzards. Other foods were largely pondweeds, common widgeonweed, southern naiad, and American wildcelery.

Bortner (1985) studied the feeding ecology and energy balance of tundra swans at Mattamuskeet. Food items from swans included 32% marsh emergents, 60% agricultural foods, and 4% submerged aquatic plants. Agricultural items included soybean seeds (28%) and hulls (14%), wheat leaves (7%), and corn (11%). In November-December, marsh vegetation was most important, whereas wheat became increasingly important in late winter and spring. Corn was used only in January, probably because of availability and cold temperatures. Soybeans were most important in February, and SAV was most important in mid-winter.

Relationship of Important Foods and Nutritional Requirements

Whether the nutritional requirements and energy demands of waterfowl wintering in Chesapeake Bay and North Carolina sounds are being satisfied by available waterfowl foods is not known. In Chesapeake Bay where SAV beds have declined, canvasbacks were found to obtain alternate food sources and now feed predominately on mollusks (Perry et al. 1981). Perry et al. (1986) concluded that this food source is not as nutritionally complete as the high-energy plant tubers upon which it formerly fed. Canvasbacks now may have to obtain greater volumes of low-energy invertebrates rather than high-energy plants to meet energy needs. Thus, the availability of food in Chesapeake Bay may be critical to canvasback distribution (Perry et al. 1986). Other areas, such as North Carolina, now may be providing large quantities of preferred foods, especially for redheads (Perry and Uhler 1982). The increased use of animal foods by canvasbacks and other diving ducks in Chesapeake Bay also may increase their exposure to pesticides and heavy metals, affecting survival and reproductive success.

At Lake Mattamuskeet, North Carolina, Bortner (1985) found that tundra swans could meet energy demands by foraging on agricultural foods, but was unclear whether swans could satisfy energy requirements feeding on available bulrush rhizomes alone. He concluded that the large areas of crops provide adequate food throughout the winter, which supplement native foods. Field-feeding by geese may increase winter survival due to the abundance and availability of high-energy agricultural foods.

Available Water

The Chesapeake Bay and its tributaries include approximately 641,106 ha of open tidal waters (Metzgar 1973). The most important to waterfowl are the depths

<2.2 m (mean low water) (161,774 ha) and 2.2–3.7 m (114,144 ha). Back Bay, Virginia, and the North Carolina sounds provide extensive shallow water for waterfowl in that area.

Availability of open water and waterfowl habitat use is influenced by ice cover (Lovvorn 1987). Ponds, reservoirs, and shallow impoundments begin to freeze in December in the northern part of the region. During prolonged freezes, tidal marshes and creeks are ice-covered, which forces waterfowl to open leads in ice-covered rivers and bays. Because of strong currents, tidal and freshwater creeks often remain open during severe cold periods.

In Chesapeake Bay, ice generally builds up along the Delmarva Peninsula due to prevailing northwest winds, leaving the deeper waters of the western shore relatively ice-free. However, during extremely cold periods, ice accumulates in this zone and only major shipping channels are maintained. At Back Bay, Virginia, and Currituck Sound, North Carolina, freeze-up occurs frequently forcing waterfowl to Pamlico Sound and areas farther south.

In Maryland, some sanctuary ponds used by waterfowl during winter remain ice-free because of their size, the use of artificial circulators, and/or high numbers of birds. Mallards, black ducks, Canada geese, and swans use alternative roost sites in tidal creeks and rivers, where they can successfully maintain open water.

Canada geese and other field-feeding waterfowl will often be displaced to move to southerly wintering areas following a snowfall of >16 cm and the failure of winds to open agricultural fields (files Maryland Dep. Nat. Resour.). Large numbers of Canada geese have been observed to move from Maryland to Virginia and North Carolina under these circumstances. Two or more weeks of prolonged snow cover can cause this redistribution. The displaced geese return northward during milder weather.

Protection and Cover

Protection from hunting and disturbance is an important aspect of waterfowl habitat. In this region, protection of migrating and wintering waterfowl is provided by 14 National Wildlife Refuges (NWR) and large estuaries. Waterfowl hunting is permitted only on Assateague National Seashore and Mattamuskeet NWR. Before 1973, waterfowl hunting on Lake Mattamuskeet was allowed on 40% of the refuge. Hunting on this area was closed beginning in 1973, but has been open since 1984 for 20 days/year. In 1984, North Carolina opened an experimental hunting season for tundra swans.

Refuges are maintained on several state wildlife management areas throughout this region, but regulated public waterfowl hunting is allowed on most. There are numerous other federal, state, county, municipal, corporate, and private areas where waterfowl are afforded protection. Ponds constructed to attract Canada geese on Maryland's upper Eastern Shore often are managed as sanctuaries, whereas hunting is regulated on surrounding uplands.

Shelter from strong winds and storms is probably not a problem for waterfowl using the tributaries of Chesapeake Bay, Back Bay, Lake Mattamuskeet, and Currituck Sound due to the variety of shoreline exposures, surrounding tree belts, and islands. On the Chesapeake Bay, Albemarle Sound, and Pamlico Sound, however, shelter is not always available. In rough weather inland ponds adjacent to these areas provide shelter as night-time roosts . However, some inland ponds used by waterfowl in this region are not protected from wind, and mortality has occurred in rare instances.

Waterfowl in this region use exposed tidal mudflats and sand bars for loafing. Chesapeake Bay in Maryland and its tributaries provide about 980 ha of this habitat (Metzgar 1973). Loafing areas are especially important to puddle ducks.

Additional loafing sites are pond edges, dikes, hummocks, muskrat lodges, partly submerged trees, floating logs, lawns, and small islands with low cover where waterfowl are safe or can easily observe potential predators. Harvey (1987) found that Canada geese in Maryland used agricultural fields for loafing between feeding periods.

DISEASE

The most significant disease outbreaks in the region have been caused by avian cholera (*Pasteurella multocida*). In 1970, an estimated 88,000 waterfowl (primarily diving ducks) died from cholera (Locke et al. 1970). Perhaps the largest die-off recorded in North America occurred on Chesapeake Bay during March-April 1978 (Montgomery et al. 1979). Mortality was heavy among diving ducks (90%), especially oldsquaw (80%). Losses ranged between 26,200 and 209,600 waterfowl. Control measures included collection and proper disposal of carcasses. Waterfowl losses to avian cholera may occur in Chesapeake Bay annually, but are undetected. In Back Bay, Virginia, a flock of coots infected with the disease were killed using an aerial application of tergitol (Pursglove et al. 1976).

Duck viral enteritus has been recorded from several locations throughout the region, but in nearly all instances has involved captive flocks of mallards, black ducks, Canada geese, and lesser numbers of gadwall, northern pintail, and domestic fowl (Montgomery et al. 1981). Small numbers of Canada geese, greater snow geese, and tundra swans are lost each year to visceral gout and aspergillosis.

ENVIRONMENTAL CONTAMINANTS

Lead poisoning is a source of mortality among some waterfowl in this region. In Maryland, high lead levels have been detected in the wing bones of Canada geese (Stotts 1980). In addition, elevated lead levels in liver tissue and increasing ingestion rates were detected in black ducks, scaup, and pintails collected in Maryland in the 1970s (Stotts 1973, 1980, Scanlon et al. 1980). Estimated losses of waterfowl to lead poisoning in Maryland were 16,000 annually in the 1970s (Stotts 1973). Lead ingestion has been a chronic problem at Mattamuskeet NWR, causing annual mortality in tundra swans and other waterfowl (L. Ditto, pers. commun.).

Birds of Chesapeake Bay have been exposed to synthetic organochlorine insecticides and polychlorinated biphenyls (PCBs) (Ohlendorf 1981). Some of these pollutants are highly toxic and can cause direct mortality, whereas others reduce reproductive success. Tissues of canvasbacks collected from Chesapeake Bay during 1972-76 generally contained low concentrations of organochlorine pesticides and PCBs Dieter et al. 1976, White et al. 1979). Experimental studies with other waterfowl species suggest that these residues were below levels known to affect reproduction and survival (Ohlendorf 1981). A few samples, however, contained detrimental concentrations of DDE or PCBs.

Chesapeake Bay is not considered to be highly contaminated with heavy metals, but aquatic plants and clams can accumulate significant quantities of metals. Certain heavy metals were found being assimilated at low levels by some diving ducks through an unknown part of their food chain (Di Giulio and Scanlon 1984). Di Giulio and Scanlon (1985) found that cadmium and lead concentrations were generally greater in whole plants than in soft tissues of clams. They concluded that the changes occurring in the food habits of some Chesapeake waterfowl toward increased clam consumption, as a result of declining SAV, are not increasing ingestion of cadmium and lead.

Inorganic fertilizers used by the agricultural community have been implicated as one of the causes of eutrophication in

Chesapeake Bay and the decline in SAV (Kemp et al. 1983). Excessive amounts of nitrogen and phosphorus have encouraged algae blooms and the proliferation of epiphytes upon the stems and leaves of important plants (which cause a decrease in photosynthetic activity and increase SAV mortality). Other sources of nutrients entering the bay include effluent from waste-water treatment plants and residential lawns.

Herbicides used in small-grain agriculture were once blamed for the decline in bay water quality and SAV loss. However, recent research has shown that levels of atrazine and linuron (<10.0 ppm) do not reach levels in the bay which could cause plant stress (>25.0 ppm) (Macalaster et al. 1982). However, the effects upon invertebrates and other waterfowl foods are unknown.

Waterfowl die-offs due to toxic levels of pesticides to control cutworm infestation of corn crops have been implicated in causing mortality of dabbling ducks (Hindman 1983) and bald eagles (*Haliaeetus leucocephalus*) (G. D. Therres, pers. commun.) in the Chesapeake Bay. Diazanon is considered to be a potential threat to Canada geese and brant that feed upon lawns and turf farms. Although mortality from diazanon ingestion has not been documented in this geographical area, this pesticide has caused losses of American wigeon, Canada geese, and brant in other areas of the flyway (Stone 1979).

One of the worst oil spills in recent history occurred in the lower Chesapeake Bay in February 1976. Approximately 946 kl of No. 6 oil were discharged after a barge sank near the mouth of the Potomac River (Roland et al. 1977). Estimated numbers of waterfowl killed ranged from 20,000-50,000 birds. Environmental impacts on adjacent marshes fringed with saltmarsh cordgrass were judged to be minimal. Contingency plans for reducing environmental damage caused by toxic spills in this region have been prepared by state agencies.

HABITAT MANAGEMENT
Wetlands

Mosquito Control.—Some of the most active marsh management practices in the Maryland-Virginia-North Carolina coastal plain are done by mosquito control agencies. During the 1930s, extensive parallel-grid ditch networks were installed by the Civilian Conservation Corps. Currently, control of mosquitoes is accomplished by spraying chemical insecticides and by physically altering the mosquito breeding habitat. OMWM the newest technique of water management for salt-marsh mosquito control, attempts to reduce mosquito breeding by altering or eliminating ovipositioning and larval-rearing sites (Fig. 3). It also enhances predation by larvivorous fishes through selective ponding and ditching (Ferrigno and Jobbins 1966, Ferrigno et al. 1967). A corollary goal of OMWM is to restore or enhance wildlife habitat on the salt marsh, primarily through creation of standing bodies of water on the marsh surface with no impedance of surface-flooding tides (Whitman and Meredith 1987)

OMWM has been implemented in Chesapeake Bay (Maryland) salt marshes since 1976. North Carolina mosquito control agencies do not practice OMWM, but have plans to initiate it on an experimental basis (O. Florschutz Jr., pers. commun.). Use of OMWM relies heavily on closed ponds (nontidal) with radial ditches and semi-tidal ditches (still ditches). Ponds are located in marshes dominated by marshhay cordgrass and seashore saltgrass where density of mosquito breeding depressions are high. Ponds are excavated to a depth of 30 cm, with a narrow fish reservoir 76-91 cm deep on 1 or 2 sides of the pond edge. Ponds are sometimes installed in expansive areas of smooth cordgrass. Pond size

Fig. 3. Mosquito control agencies can use open marsh water management techniques to maintain water levels for dabbling ducks and other marsh animals (Photo by C. R. Lesser).

averages 0.04 ha. Other mosquito breeding depressions are connected to the ponds by radial ditches (Fig. 4). Pond radial ditches are 46-91 cm deep and 61-91 cm wide, and are connected to pond-reservoir ditches. Pond radials are often extended from natural ponds. Spoil excavated from both ponds and radial ditches is deposited on the adjacent marsh for a width of 15.2 m and heights ranging 2-10 cm. Within 2 growing seasons following OMWM installation most of the spoil-banks are covered by indigenous plant species (C. R. Lesser, pers. commun.). Ponds created by OMWM often are revegetated with desirable SAV, such as common widgeonweed, fennelleaf pond-weed, and muskgrass.

In addition to pond creation, non tidal ditch systems incorporating either a 15.2- or 30.5-m earthen water-control structure or sill are installed as part of an OMWM project. A sill system is designed to remove sheet water without lowering the subsurface water table (kept to <15 cm of the marsh surface). A sill system allows tidal exchange and passage of larvivorous fish. Water exchange might occur on 25% of all high tides. The sill system provides a stable environment for growing SAV.

Although tidal ditches are used in some OMWM projects in coastal Maryland and Virginia, open tidal ditching has been shown to cause water table depression and increase the probability of shrub invasion (e.g., *Iva frutescens, Baccharis halmifolia*) in brackish, high marsh zones in Delaware (Meredith et al. 1983) and Maryland's Eastern Shore (Lesser and Saveikis 1979). As a result, only closed or semiclosed ditch systems are employed on state-owned wetlands in Maryland. Maryland's Department of Natural Resources (DNR) also requires additional pond construction by the state's mosquito control agency to increase marsh surface

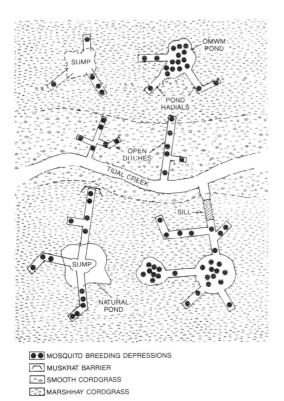

MOSQUITO BREEDING DEPRESSIONS
MUSKRAT BARRIER
SMOOTH CORDGRASS
MARSHHAY CORDGRASS

Fig. 4. Schematic diagram of open marsh water management alterations (from Meredith et al. 1983).

water on DNR wetlands as a mitigation feature to allowing OMWM on their lands.

Evaluation of OMWM's impact on Chesapeake Bay marshes has been underway since 1978. General observations indicate that the increase of marsh surface water has increased the use of these marshes by dabbling ducks and other waterbirds. Since the establishment of OMWM in the 1960s, Daiber (1987) reported on the continued reduction of mosquito breeding, the increase in marsh productivity and wildlife numbers, and the enhancement of the tidal marsh food web.

Wildlife agencies often block old mosquito grid ditches with flash-board structures to maintain late fall and winter water levels at the marsh surface. Many of these ditches bisected natural ponds. Par-

tial drawdown to maintain water at 20 cm below marsh level between 15 April and 1 October allows production of SAV and provides food and cover for duck broods.

A primary objective of wetland alteration for waterfowl is to improve the interspersion of emergent cover and open water. The importance to waterfowl of a desirable combination of emergent cover and surface water in freshwater marshes is well documented (Weller and Spatcher 1965, Weller and Frederickson 1974). However, the addition of ponds to high brackish marshes as a management technique to enhance the habitat quality of marshes for waterfowl and other marsh fauna has not been fully explored.

Blasted Potholes and Dugouts.— Potholes blasted with ammonium nitrate/fuel oil (ANFO) mixtures in high-phase tidal marsh has been a technique used by conservation agencies and private landowners in the region to increase the amount of surface water (Fig. 5). Blasted potholes were the principal waterfowl management technique used at Swan Quarter NWR. Potholes were used to enhance 6,073 ha of marsh dominated by needlerush (*Juncus romerianus*). Blasted potholes that have been used in freshwater marshes and in sumps with dense vegetation and highly organic soil are generally short-lived. Those located in firm soils of high-phase marshes have an average longevity of about 15 years. Potholes in freshwater marshes average 1.2 to 1.5 m deep and 9.1 to 10.7 m in diameter upon construction. Those blasted in high-phase brackish marshes averaged 1.9 m deep and ranged in size from 4.3 to 38.1 m when ANFO charges were placed in irregular lines (Warren and Bandel 1968).

Emergent plants, such as smartweed, coast barnyardgrass (*Echinochloa walteri*), and spikerushes, usually invade the spoil around the edge of the potholes in freshwater marshes. Japanese millet (*E. crusgalli frumentacea*) broadcasted on the

Fig. 5. Potholes blasted in high marshes provide permanent waters for resident and migrant ducks and other wetland animals.

spoil of potholes blasted in freshwater marshes in April has germinated well.

The spoil and shallow edges of potholes blasted in the saline marshes are generally revegetated with marshhay cordgrass, seashore saltgrass, and saltmarsh bulrush. Clusters of 5-15 potholes of various sizes within a radius of 61 m were used by Maryland DNR to increase surface water in high-phase brackish marshes for waterfowl. Another group of potholes was placed 152 to 305 m away to create clusters of ponds attractive to a greater variety of ducks. Stotts (1971) indicated that potholes blasted at the heads of old mosquito ditches, especially at the marsh-upland interphase, when used in combination with flashboard structures near the ditch outlet, would be more beneficial to waterfowl and provide better control of mosquitoes than ditches alone. This combination provided additional water surface, SAV growth, and deep reservoirs for fish with drawdown capabilities.

Since the mid-1970s, pothole blasting has been largely replaced by pond excavation as a technique to improve the ratio of surface water to emergent cover. At Deal Island and Fishing Bay on Maryland's lower Eastern Shore, about 45 ponds of 0.2-0.4 ha each have been excavated in high-phase, brackish marsh. This area previously contained few natural ponds. In similar habitat at Monie Bay Wildlife Management Area (WMA) adjacent to Deal Island WMA, surveys conducted by R. D. Drobney (unpubl. data) indicated a low diversity and density of birds. An adjacent 1,137 ha impoundment held exceptionally high densities and diversity of waterfowl and other marsh birds. The apparent differences between the two areas before pond construction were the amount of open water and the degree of interspersion between open water and emergent vegetation.

Following excavation of ponds, increased use by dabbling ducks and wading birds has been apparent. Shallow

(<38 cm) dugout ponds were constructed with deeper (0.8-0.9 m) fish reservoirs along 1 or 2 sides. The substrate was composed of a shallow (10 cm) organic layer over a firm layer of inorganic soils (S. A. Dawson, pers. commun.). The rectangular shape of these ponds facilitated equipment operation and provided more shoreline edge than circular ponds.

After 1-2 growing seasons, many of these ponds supported widgeonweed, muskgrass, and fennelleaf pondweed. An additional 75 ponds of similar size and configuration have been completed by the Maryland Department of Agriculture Mosquito Control as part of their OMWM program. These alterations to the salt marsh appear to benefit waterfowl and other wildlife, but the long-term consequences are unknown.

Shallow Impoundments.—One of the primary objectives of impoundment management by wildlife agencies is to provide an abundance of desirable waterfowl foods and open water for resting. In many areas of Maryland, mosquito control is a secondary objective. In North Carolina and other areas of the Atlantic Flyway, many impoundments were constructed to serve as an alternative method of water-level management to control mosquitoes. Tidal impoundments in this region have been managed to encourage common widgeonweed, fennelleaf pondweed, and muskgrass while maintaining emergent cover.

Managing shallow impoundments for SAV and mosquito control requires maintaining permanent water levels during the growing season at 10-25 cm deep. During drought, water levels within impoundments have been maintained by pumping. If necessary, these impoundments are drawn down during the growing season every 1-3 years to allow the reestablishment of emergent plants and to flush the system of excess salts. Drawdown is initiated in late March and is completed by early April. Reflooding is initiated in

mid-May. Common widgeonweed and muskgrass are the dominant SAV in tidal impoundments managed in this region. Fennelleaf pondweed appears during wet years when salinity declines (<10-15 ppt). Area of impoundments managed as permanent water under state and federal control in Maryland is 1,660 ha; the largest (1,134 ha) is at Deal Island WMA. Approximately 3,671 ha of tidal impoundments have been planned for construction at Cedar Island NWR and Alligator River NWR in North Carolina and Fishing Bay WMA in Maryland.

Moist-Soil Plant Management.—Shallow impoundments in this region also are managed to encourage moist-soil plants as foods for migrating and wintering waterfowl. Currently, several NWRs (primarily in North Carolina) have been using moist-soil management along with other traditional management practices to enhance waterfowl habitat. Moist-soil management uses water manipulations to encourage the growth of native wetland plants from soils when moisture is at or slightly below field capacity (Fredrickson and Taylor 1982). Following drawdown and subsequent germination and early plant growth (plant height at least 10-15 cm), the impoundment is gradually reflooded to a depth suitable for desired seed-producing plants and the target wildlife species (Fredrickson and Taylor 1982, Prevost 1987).

Impoundments managed for moist soils in North Carolina are drawn down in April to encourage annuals including barnyardgrasses, panicums (*Panicum* spp.), American bulrush, squarestem spikerush (*Eleocharis quadrangulata*), smartweeds, redroot flatsedge (*Cyperus erythrorhizos*), and beggarticks (*Bidens* spp.). Following desired plant growth, impoundments are reflooded in October-November making food resources available to waterfowl.

Mattamuskeet NWR in North Carolina manages 1,215 ha of moist soil impoundments. These impoundments are divided into 243-ha cells, which allow rotation of management regimes among different cells. About every 5 years, control of undesirable herbaceous vegetation is needed after successive years of moist-soil management. In coastal North Carolina, cattails and woolgrass bulrush (*Scirpus cyperinus*) are considered undesirable (O. Florschutz Jr., pers. commun.). Control of cattail is accomplished by conducting a drawdown of the impoundment in March, followed by a prescribed burn as soon as conditions permit. Following the burn, the impoundment soils are either plowed or disked. The mechanical cultivation helps to eliminate any undesirable woody vegetation, such as hardwood seedlings. In impoundments at Mattamuskeet NWR, annuals (primarily barnyardgrasses) revegetate the soils following this treatment (O. Florschutz Jr., pers. commun.). The impoundments are reflooded between early October to late November, and water levels are maintained through the winter until an April drawdown.

Moist-soil impoundments are also part of habitat management at Mackay Island NWR (12 ha), Pungo NWR (202 ha), and Blackwater NWR (49 ha). At Pungo NWR, fall flooding of a 194-ha, moist-soil impoundment is conducted in November-December. Spring drawdown is in mid-April. At Pungo NWR, woolgrass bulrush requires control every 3-4 years by an early-spring drawdown and deep plowing of the soils, followed by fall flooding. Moist-soil management has not been used extensively, however, in this region.

Flooded Timber and Green-Tree Impoundments.—Hundreds of impoundments with inundated timber have been developed in this region. Most have been constructed by private landowners and have not been managed as green-tree impoundments; consequently, timber mortality has resulted. These wooded impoundments are dominated by emergent plants and common hornwort (*Ceratophyllum demersum*). Managed green-tree impoundments within the mid-Atlantic coastal region are located on a few state WMAs and on NWRs. These areas are dominated by red maple (*Acer rubrum*) and blackgum tupelo (*Nyssa sylvatica*) at Mackay Island NWR and by willow oak (*Quercus phellos*), American sweetgum (*Liquidambar styraciflua*), bitternut hickory (*Carya cordiformis*), and red maple at Eastern Neck NWR. Sedges (*Carex* spp.) and smartweeds dominate the shallows.

Normal water management for green-tree impoundments in the upper Chesapeake Region requires a late February to early March drawdown with reflooding in mid-October (H. O. Olsen, pers. commun.). In coastal North Carolina, green-tree impoundments are de-watered in mid-March and flooded in late October to early November (O. Florschutz, Jr., pers. commun.)

Prescribed Burning.—Except for water-level manipulations, prescribed burning is the most effective practice used in this region. Burning helps maintain successional stages of desirable annuals, discourages undesirable herbaceous perennials and woody species, removes matted vegetation, releases nutrients, increases seed availability in dense vegetation, and improves effectiveness of mechanical or chemical manipulation.

Most marshes of the Eastern Shore of the Chesapeake Bay are burned annually in late winter to encourage stands of Olney bulrush and discourage saltgrass and marshhay cordgrass. Burning reduces the level of brackish high marsh so that desirable bulrushes (*S. olneyi, S. americanus, S. robustus*) can re-invade. In the brackish marshes of Chesapeake Bay, burning to encourage bulrushes should not be done during drought periods when the marsh is flooded with salt tides (salinity >15 ppt) (G. S. Willey, pers. commun.). A prescribed burn conducted during periods of high salinity can cause "scalded" areas, which may become unproductive mud flats. An area void of all vegetation probably will be invaded by less desirable, salt-tolerant species, such as saltwort (*Salicornia* spp.). The preferred salinity range for winter burning of Olney three-square is 7-12 ppt.

Burning is used at Mackay Island NWR to encourage bulrush for greater snow geese. Prescribed burning is done every 3 years following a hard frost between mid-November to mid-March. Late winter burns also have been used at Blackwater NWR to promote growth of Olney bulrush for lesser snow geese. Burning also makes seeds of saltmarsh bulrush available to feeding ducks.

Tidal marshes also are burned in December-January to facilitate the trapping of muskrat and nutria (*Myocastor coypus*). Harvesting muskrats minimizes burrowing damage to dikes. Early spring burns, however, are detrimental to nesting dabbling ducks and marsh birds. Burning should not be done after March 1 in the Chesapeake Region. Fire lanes should be constructed just within upland borders of the marsh-upland interphase to protect upland food and cover plants.

Control of Undesirable Plants.—Most undesirable herbaceous and woody plant species can be controlled by using water-level manipulation, mechanical control, and prescribed burning. Only rarely is chemical control necessary. Common reed grows everywhere. It seeds profusely and spreads vegetatively (Woodhouse and Knutson 1982). Once established, the plant forms dense stands and may invade adjacent areas, crowding out more desirable wetland plants. Invasion of common reed into wetlands reduces food and cover value of the wetland for waterfowl. Most efforts to control common reed have met with little success. Certain sites have been controlled with a winter burn, followed by prolonged flooding. However, many sites cannot be treated in this manner.

Extensive experimentation to control common reed has been conducted in Delaware (Jones and Lehman 1987). Glyphosate, a systemic herbicide, provided control without producing harmful effects to other aquatic organisms. Currently, this herbicide is being used to control common reed on a limited scale in the Maryland Virginia-North Carolina region on WMAs and NWRs.

Glyphosate is diluted with clean water and mixed with a nontoxic surfactant prior to application and is applied to common reed between mid-September to mid-October prior to any killing frost. In the Chesapeake Region, these dates correspond to the period when the plant is translocating food reserves from the leaves and stem downward to the rhizomes. The herbicide is applied to the plant leaves by aerial application (helicopter) on large acreages or by backpack sprayer when treating small stands. The herbicide is absorbed by the plant foliage and translocated into the root system causing cellular disruption, cessation of growth, and eventually death (Jones and Lehman 1987).

Recommended helicopter application rate for glyphosate is 7 l/ha, but concentrations as low as 4.7 l/ha have produced control and provided substantial monetary savings. Two annual treatments are required at most sites to achieve 58-99% control (Jones and Lehman 1987). A late-winter burn following the first spraying also may improve growing conditions for other vegetation. Revegetation by native wetland plants on treated areas has resulted in increased use of the wetland by migrating and wintering waterfowl. In addition, muskrat populations may increase. Presently, glyphosate herbicide can be used only in upland sites and nontidal wetlands. Use in tidal wetlands has not been approved by the Environmental Protection Agency. Current common reed control projects in tidal wetlands are done on an experimental basis.

Agricultural Uplands

Cropping Practices.—Agricultural lands in this region are primarily in private or corporate ownership. They are managed for corn, soybean, rye, winter wheat, and barley. Following a fall corn harvest, a cover crop of wheat, barley, or rye is planted and allowed to mature. Cover crops are harvested in June followed by soybean planting.

Many landowners do not follow corn harvest with a small grain crop, but prefer to leave the corn stubble and waste grain for wintering geese. Others will aerially broadcast either winter wheat or rye into standing corn immediately prior to harvest to promote germination and to enhance agricultural fields for waterfowl. National Wildlife Refuges in Maryland and North Carolina also use this technique to provide food for geese. Strips of wheat (drilled) are often incorporated into stubble fields for the same purpose.

The practice of leaving standing corn is common. This technique is widespread throughout the major Canada goose wintering range on Maryland's Eastern Shore, where goose hunting is a $50 million industry annually (Stotts 1985). Unharvested corn is left in strips 6-25 rows wide or in bands around upland edges of ponds. Private landowners and waterfowl outfitters rely on this practice to enhance their recreational or commercial hunting opportunities. National Wildlife Refuges and state WMAs in coastal North Carolina and Remington Farms in Maryland provide unharvested corn.

Green-cover crops and pastures are abundant on private lands adjacent to Chesapeake Bay and North Carolina sounds. Cover crops include winter wheat, barley, rye, and Ladino clover. On private lands, pastures and lawns adjacent to Canada goose roost sites are used extensively by foraging geese, but are not managed for this purpose.

Crop Leases.—Leasing private agricultural lands adjacent to Canada goose roost sites is used by the North Carolina Wildlife Resources Commission to enhance wintering goose habitat (T. D. Monschein, pers. commun.). Hunting and public access are prohibited. Lands planted to corn are leased for approximately $66/ha. On each 405-ha tract leased, approximately 81 ha are planted to winter wheat following the corn harvest with 10 ha of corn left standing. The remaining area remains in corn stubble. In Maryland, revenues raised by the Easton Waterfowl Festival, Inc., are used to reimburse landowners for leaving unharvested corn or soybeans on farms serving as sanctuaries for Canada geese. Aerial seeding of winter wheat into standing corn also is done. Approximately 2,429 ha are being managed (J. E. Gerber, pers. commun.).

Farm Ponds.—Inland impoundments in Kent County, Maryland, have created a unique habitat for Canada geese (Fig. 6). These ponds differ from other farm ponds mainly in the protection they afford geese from hunting (Harvery 1987). Landowners provide sanctuary ponds where geese can rest and roost undisturbed. Landowners or lessees also may control hunting pressure and leave unharvested crops for late-winter use by geese (Harvey 1987). Goose management practiced in Maryland could be viewed as many small refuges (Harvey 1987).

Other grains such as sorghum and millets are used by private landowners, hunting clubs, state wildlife agencies, and NWRs in the Mid-Atlantic Coastal region to provide foods for migrating and wintering waterfowl. Controlled, low-level impoundments constructed to flood millets or grain crops to a depth of 10-25 cm are attractive as feeding and resting areas for dabbling ducks and Canada geese.

Critical Area Legislation

A major change which is affecting current and future management of upland habitats adjacent to Chesapeake Bay is

Fig. 6. Upland ponds are popular for attracting and holding geese during fall and winter.

known as "Critical-Area" legislation, an integral part of the current effort to clean up the bay (Chesapeake Bay Critical Area Commission 1986). The objective of this legislation is to slow the degradation of the Chesapeake Bay, restore water quality, and enhance natural resources. Provisions of this legislation that benefit waterfowl include (1) development of guidelines to protect waterfowl-concentration areas from industrial and urban development, (2) establishment of a 305-m-wide buffer zone around tidal waters of the bay in which development is limited, (3) development of wildlife habitat (with emphasis on black ducks) on all lands within a 31-m buffer around tidal bay waters, (4) implementation of soil management practices to reduce agricultural runoff, (5) reduction of toxic and hazardous substances and wastes, (6) reduction of nitrogen and phosphorus levels, and (7) increased control of shore erosion.

Refuge and Disturbance Management

Wintering waterfowl require disturbance-free areas for resting and feeding. Disturbance occurs largely in the form of hunting, commercial and recreational boating, aircraft traffic, and military maneuvers. Refuges from hunting are provided on state and federal lands, corporations, and private land.

Human access to waterfowl habitats on NWRs is limited. Only Assateague National Seashore and Mattamuskeet NWR permit waterfowl hunting. Other NWRs limit human access to regulated vehicular traffic, muskrat trapping, and approved research projects. At some NWRs, vehicle traffic, walking trails, and recreational fishing are restricted annually between 1 November and 31 March. Deer hunting seasons are held in the early fall prior to arrival of peak numbers of wintering waterfowl. If permitted, upland game hunting is limited to the last few days of statewide seasons. Research projects often are permitted only during summer. Many areas are closed to public access. Vertical airspace up to 457 m over NWRs is restricted by the Federal Aviation Authority to minimize waterfowl disturbance from aircraft.

On state WMAs, waterfowl are provided refuge areas adjacent to public hunting areas. North Carolina leases upland feeding sites for geese adjacent to traditional roost sites. Human access to these fields is prohibited from fall harvest until spring planting. Military bombing activity is curtailed between 1 October and 15 March on Bloodsworth Island in Chesapeake Bay.

Waterfowl hunting from sneakboats and other types of gunning rigs is prohibited in some public waters. In Maryland, the use of sneakboats is permitted only on WMAs and the upper Potomac River. Duck-blind regulations that limit the offshore distance and maximize the interval between blinds also provide resting areas for waterfowl.

Some privately owned lands provide waterfowl sanctuary and limit hunting to a small portion of the habitat. Many properties are hunted only 1 to 2 times per week, providing safe feeding, roosting, and loafing areas on nonhunting days.

Disease and Environmental Contaminant Management

Waterfowl mortality from disease and toxic pollutants is monitored by government wildlife agencies through surveillance. Sick or dead waterfowl are submitted to diagnostic laboratories in this region as part of state disease contingency plans and the National Disease Contingency Plan of the U.S. Fish and Wildlife Service (FWS). Control of disease outbreaks usually involves a cooperative effort between the state and the FWS National Wildlife Disease Laboratory. In Maryland, measures are used to minimize the transmission of avian diseases to wild waterfowl from game-farm mallards released into natural habitats. However, carrier birds of such avian diseases as DVE are released without detection. Lead poisoning and other heavy metals in the body tissues are monitored annually by state and federal agencies. Pesticide exposure in waterfowl is monitored through examination of waterfowl tissues from the FWS Waterfowl Parts Collection Survey. Critical Area Legislation and programs associated with bay cleanup effort should reduce levels of contaminants, nutrients, and suspended sediments. Implementation of nontoxic shot zones will reduce lethal and sublethal effects of lead shot ingestion. Implementation of OMWM projects should reduce levels of pesticides used to control mosquitoes in waterfowl habitats of this region.

RESEARCH NEEDS AND MANAGEMENT RECOMMENDATIONS

Black duck population and mortality studies are being continued to understand problems with this declining species. Research has included the need to understand the conflicts between black ducks and wild or released mallards. Redheads, canvasbacks, and all diving ducks dependent on estuarine invertebrates (which have taken on added importance with SAV reductions) need to be monitored.

The effects of insecticides upon plant and animal foods used by migrating and wintering waterfowl need to be determined. Effects of OMWM projects upon plant associations and wetland hydrology also need to be determined. Cost-benefits of increased surface water (ponds and ditches) in high-phase marsh with few natural ponds need to be quantified and weighed against any identifiable adverse effects.

The invasion of hydrilla in the Potomac River and upper Chesapeake Bay should be monitored closely. Possible competition between native SAV species needs to be investigated. Nutritional requirements of wintering waterfowl from this region need to be determined, particularly for important game species with low population levels. We need to know how various foods affect winter survival, distribution, and physical condition of certain species.

The effect of acid precipitation on the abundance and distribution of important waterfowl foods needs to be studied. Moist-soil management is relatively new to this region. Research is needed to determine water-level regimes that promote desirable seed-producing plants and waterfowl use. The effects of glyphosate herbicide applications used to control common reed in nontidal wetlands also deserve further study.

Management agencies should work with private landowners to provide additional waterfowl habitat and to assist them in the restoration and enhancement of existing habitats under their ownership.

SUMMARY

The Chesapeake Bay, Currituck-Albermarle-Pamlico sounds, and other important sounds and bays from Maryland, Virginia, and North Carolina have the most important habitats for wintering waterfowl in the Atlantic Flyway. The important habitats include freshwater and brackish estuarine river-marshes, and freshwater and salt estuarine bay-marshes. Important open-bay habitats are fresh, slightly brackish, and brackish estuarine bays. Slightly brackish estuarine bays, which usually have the greatest diversity of submerged aquatic plant and animal foods, are the most important habitat for migrant waterfowl. Other areas that provide additional habitat for waterfowl areas are wooded bottomlands, agricultural fields, and man-made ponds and impoundments.

Numbers have been declining for many duck species. Populations of geese and swans have maintained or increased their size and distribution. Movement of these birds to and from this region vary by species and weather factors. Many species are becoming more dependent on upland habitats. Some, such as the redhead and American wigeon, are decreasing in numbers and distribution because of deteriorating conditions of estuarine plant and animal foods.

Major changes have occurred in all habitats, especially with regard to human influences. Some wetland losses are recovered through construction of upland ponds and impoundments. Mosquito drainage projects have been modified to reduce severe problems that had resulted from parallel and direct ditching. Changes in waterfowl feeding habits have increased the importance of grains, pastures, and garden crops for dabbling ducks, Canada and snow geese, and tundra swans. Generally, ice conditions have not been a factor in winter survival of these waterfowl; they readily disperse to avoid ice.

Diseases (e.g., avian cholera) and environmental contaminants (e.g., oil spills, lead shot) have been implicated in waterfowl mortality in this region. Inorganic fertilizers have been implicated in reduction of submerged aquatic vegetation.

Habitat management techniques have included open-marsh water management to control mosquitoes and improve marshes for dabbling ducks. Blasted potholes and dugouts have also been used to create permanent water in dense marshes. Impoundments have been used to modify emergent marshes into shallow pools supporting submerged aquatic plants and invertebrates. Moist-soil management is being used in sites previously little used by waterfowl. Prescribed burning is often used in marshes to maintain annual seed plants and green shoots for ducks, geese, and muskrats. Chemical controls, especially for common reed, have been recommended and used to improve wetland plant communities.

In upland areas, management tech niques used include standing grain crops left for wintering waterfowl. Numbers of farm ponds for waterfowl have proliferated. Inviolate refuges have been established in upland and estuarine waters to provide sanctuaries from disturbance factors. Critical shoreline areas are being preserved and managed through regulation to provide protection of bay waters from development and local toxic contamination. Waterfowl and their habitats are constantly under surveillance for disease outbreaks and occurrence of toxic pollutants.

Research and management needs include studies of populations and mortality in black ducks. Other species of interest are canvasback and redhead and the environmental factors that influence their health and survival in this region.

LITERATURE CITED

Bayley, S., V. D. Stotts, P. F. Springer, and J. H. Steenis. 1978. Changes in submerged aquatic macrophyte populations at the head of the Chesapeake Bay, 1958-1975. Estuaries 1:73-84.

Bellrose, F. C. 1980. Ducks, geese and swans of North America. Third ed. Stackpole Books, Harrisburg, Pa. 540 pp.

Bortner, J.B. 1985. Bioenergetics of wintering tundra swans in the Mattamuskeet Region of North Carolina. M.S. Thesis, Univ. Maryland, College Park. 69 pp.

Bumpus, D. F., R. E. Lynde, and D. M. Shan. 1973. Physical oceanography. Pages 1-68 in S. B. Saila, coord. Coastal and offshore environmental inventory: Cape Hatteras to Nantucket Shoals. Mar. Publ. Ser. No. 2, Univ. Rhode Island, Kingston.

Chesapeake Bay Critical Area Commission. 1986. A guide to the Chesapeake Bay critical area criteria. State of Maryland, Annapolis. 73 pp.

Conroy, M. J., G. R. Costanzo, and D. B. Stotts. 1987. Winter movements of American black ducks in relation to natural and impounded wetlands in New Jersey. Pages 31-43 in W. R. Whitman and W. H. Meredith, eds. Waterfowl and wetlands symp: proc. of a symp. on waterfowl and wetlands management in the coastal zone of the Atlantic Flyway. Del. Coast. Manage. Progr., Dep. Nat. Resour. and Environ. Control, Dover.

Cook, R. J. 1985. How is federal, state, local partnership working in Virginia? Pages 360-352 in H. A. Groman, T. R. Henderson, E.J. Moyers, D. M. Burke, and J. A. Kusler, eds. Proc. Wetlands of the Chesapeake. Environ. Law Inst., Washington, D.C.

Daiber, F. C. 1987. A brief history of tidal marsh mosquito control. Pages 234-252 in W. R. Whitman and W. H. Meredith, eds. Waterfowl and wetlands symp: proc. of a symp. on waterfowl and wetlands management in the coastal zone of the Atlantic Flyway. Del. Coast. Manage. Prog., Dep. Nat. Resour. and Environ. Control, Dover.

Dieter, M. P., M. C. Perry, and B. M. Mulhern. 1976. Lead and PCBs in canvasback ducks: relationships between enzyme levels and residues in blood. Arch. Environ. Contam. Toxicol. 5:1-13.

Di Giulio, R. T., and P. F. Scanlon. 1984. Heavy metals in tissues of waterfowl from the Chesapeake Bay, U.S.A. Environ. Pollut. Ser. A. 35:29-48.

——, and ——. 1985. Heavy metals in aquatic plants, clams, and sediments from the Chesapeake Bay, U.S.A., implications for waterfowl. Sci. of the Total Environ. 41:259-274.

Ferrigno, F., 1978. Snow goose, brant, swan committee report. Pages 29-40 in Proc. Atlantic. Waterfowl Counc., Williamsburg, Va.

——, and D. M. Jobbins. 1966. A summary of nine years of applied mosquito-wildlife research in Cumberland County, N.J. salt marshes. Proc. N.J. Mosquito Control Assoc. 71:98-106.

——, ——, and M. P. Shinkle. 1967. Coordinated mosquito control and wildlife management for the Delaware Bay coastal marshes. Proc. N.J. Mosquito Extermin. Assoc. 54:80-94.

Florschutz, O., Jr. 1972. The importance of Eurasian milfoil (Myriophyllum spicatum) as a waterfowl food. Proc. Annu. Conf. Southeast. Assoc. Game and Fish Comm. 26:189-194.

Frederickson, L. H., and T. S. Taylor. 1982. Management of seasonally flooded impoundments for wildlife. U.S. Fish and Wildl. Serv. Resour. Publ. 148. 29 pp.

Halvorson, W. L., and C. G. Dawson. 1973. Coastal vegetation. Pages 91-92 in S. B. Saila, ed. Coastal and offshore environmental inventory: Cape Hatteras to Nantucket Shoals. Univ. Rhode Island Mar. Publ. Ser. No. 3, Kingston.

Harvey, W. F., IV. 1987. Winter movements and resource use by Canada geese affiliated with Kent County, Maryland. M.S. Thesis. Cornell Univ., Ithaca, N.Y. 96 pp.

Hindman, L. J. 1978a. Survey of waterfowl populations on state wildlife management areas. Md. Wildl. Admin., Fed. Aid in Fish and Wildl.

Restor. Prog. Rep., Proj. W-45-R-10, Job. No. I-1. Annapolis. 24 pp.

——. 1978b. Seaduck survey. Md. Wildl. Admin., Fed. Aid in Fish and Wildl. Restor. Prog. Rep., Proj. W-45-R-10, Job. No. I-2. Annapolis. 13 pp.

——. 1983. Nonconsumptive waterfowl mortality. Md. For. Park and Wildl. Ser., Fed. Aid in Fish and Wildl. Restor. Prog. Rep., Proj. W-45-15. Annapolis. 14 pp.

Hull, C., and J. Titus. 1986. Greenhouse effect, sea level rise and salinity in the Delaware estuary. U.S. Environ. Protect. Agency. 230-05-86-010. Washington, D.C. 88 pp.

Johnson, F. A., and F. Montalbano III. 1984. Selection of plant communities by wintering waterfowl on Lake Okeechobee, Florida. J. Wildl. Manage. 48:174-178.

Jones, W. L., and W. C. Lehman. 1987. Phragmites control and revegetation following aerial applications of glyphosate in Delaware. Pages 185-196 *in* W. R. Whitman and W. H. Meredith, eds. Waterfowl and wetlands symp.: proc. of a symp. on the waterfowl and wetlands management in the coastal zone of the Atlantic Flyway. Del. Coast. Manage. Prog., Dep. Nat. Resour. and Environ. Control, Dover.

Kemp, W. M., R. R. Twilley, J. C. Stevenson, W. R. Boynton, and J. C. Means. 1983. The decline of submerged vascular plants in upper Chesapeake Bay: summary of results concerning possible causes. Mar. Tech. Soc. J. 17:78-89.

Lesser, C. R., and D. E. Saveikis. 1979. A study of the impacts of a mosquito control, integrated pest management program on selected parameters of the ecology of Chesapeake Bay high marsh communities in Maryland. Final Rep., EPA Grant No. X003147-01, Md. Dep. Agric., Plant Industries and Pest Manage., Mosquito Control, Annapolis. 194 pp.

Lippson, A. J. 1973. The Chesapeake Bay in Maryland: an atlas of natural resources. The Johns Hopkins Univ. Press, Baltimore, Md. 55 pp.

Locke, L. N., V. D. Stotts, and G. Wolfhard. 1970. An outbreak of fowl cholera in waterfowl on the Chesapeake Bay. J. Wildl. Dis. 6:404-407.

Lovvorn, J. R. 1987. Behavior, energetics, and habitat relations of canvasback ducks during winter and early spring migration. Ph.D. Thesis, Univ. Wisconsin, Madison. 173 pp.

Macalester, E. G., D. A. Barker, and M. Kasper, editors. 1982. Chesapeake Bay program technical studies: synthesis. U.S. Environ. Protect. Agency, Washington, D.C. 634 pp.

Meredith, W. H., D. E. Saveikis, and C. J. Stachecki. 1983. Delaware's open marsh management research program: an overview and update. Proc. N.J. Mosquito Control Assoc. 70:42-47.

Metzgar, R. G. 1973. Wetlands in Maryland. Md. Dep. State Planning Pub. No. 157. Baltimore. 158 pp.

Montague, C. L., A. V. Zale, and H. F. Percival. 1987. The nature of export from fringing marshes, with reference to the production of estuarine animals and the effect of impoundments. Pages 438-448 *in* W. R. Whitman and W. H. Meredith, eds. Waterfowl and wetlands symp.: proc. of a symp. on the waterfowl and wetlands management in the coastal zone of the Atlantic Flyway. Del. Coast. Manage. Prog., Dep. Nat. Resour. and Environ. Control, Dover.

Montgomery, R. D., G. Stein, Jr., V. D. Stotts, and F. H. Settle. 1979. The 1978 epornitic of avian cholera on the Chesapeake Bay. Avian Dis. 23:966-978.

——, ——, M. N. Novilla, S. Hurley, and R. J. Fink. 1981. Case report—an outbreak of duck virus enteritis (duck plaque) in a captive flock of mixed waterfowl. Avian Dis. 25:207-213.

Morton, J. M., R. L. Kirkpatrick, and M. R. Vaughn. 1987. Wetland use by black ducks wintering at Chincoteague, Virginia. Pages 27-29 *in* W. R. Whitman and W. H. Meredith, eds. Waterfowl and wetlands symp.: proc. of a symp. on the waterfowl and wetlands management in the coastal zone of the Atlantic Flyway. Del. Coast. Manage. Prog., Dep. Nat. Resour. and Environ. Control, Dover.

Myers, J., W. Hesselton, L. Alexander, M. Dureau, and M. Lepage. 1982. Waterfowl feeding in the Atlantic Flyway, 1976-1977. Wildl. Soc. Bull. 10:381-384.

National Estuary Study. 1970. Appendix B. Management studies in specific estuaries, Vol. 3. U.S. Bur. Sport Fish. and Wildl., Washington, D.C. 326 pp.

Nelson, H. K. 1978. Effects of the winter of 1976-77 on waterfowl. Int. Waterfowl Symp. 3:39-44.

Nicholson, W. R. 1955. Waterfowl studies. Md. Game Inland. Fish Comm., Fed. Aid in Fish and Wild. Restor. Prog. Rep. Proj. W-30-R-3, Job 3. Baltimore. 13 pp.

Ohlendorf, H. M. 1981. The Chesapeake Bay's birds and organochlorine pollutants. Trans. North Am. Wildl. and Nat. Resour. Conf. 46:259-270.

Orth, R. J., and K. A. Moore. 1981. Submerged aquatic vegetation of the Chesapeake Bay: past, present, and future. Trans. North Am. Wildl. and Nat. Resour. Conf. 46:271-283.

——, J. Simmons, J. Capelli, V. Carter, A. Frisch, L. J. Hindman, S. Hodges, K. A. Moore, and N. Rybicki. 1987. Distribution of submerged aquatic vegetation in the Chesapeake Bay and tributaries and Chincoteague Bay—1986. Va. Inst. Mar. Sci., Gloucester. 180 pp.

Perry, M. C. 1987. Waterfowl of Chesapeake Bay. Pages 94-115 *in* S. K. Majumdar, L. W. Hall,

Jr., and H. M. Austin, eds. Contaminant problems and management of living Chesapeake Bay resources. Pa. Acad. Sci., Easton, Md.

——, and F. M. Uhler. 1976. Availability and utilization of canvasback food organisms in Chesapeake Bay. Atl. Estuarine Res. Soc., Rehobeth Beach, Del. 25 pp.

——, and ——. 1982. Food habits of diving ducks in the Carolinas. Proc. Annu. Conf. Southeast. Assoc. Fish and Wildl. Agencies 36:492-504.

——, R. E. Munro, and G. M. Haramis. 1981. Twenty-five year trends in diving duck populations in Chesapeake Bay. Trans. North Am. Wildl. and Nat. Resour. Conf. 46:229-310.

——, W. J. Kuenzel, B. K. Williams, and J. A. Serafin. 1986. Influence of nutrients on feed intake and condition of captive canvasbacks in winter. J. Wildl. Manage. 50:427-434.

Prevost, M. B. 1987. Management of plant communities for waterfowl in coastal South Carolina. Pages 168-181 in W. R. Whitman and W. H. meredith, eds. Waterfowl and wetlands symp.: proc. of a symp. on the waterfowl and wetlands management in the coastal zone of the Atlantic Flyway. Del. Coast. Manage. Prog., Dep. Nat. Resour. and Environ. Control, Dover.

Pursglove, S. R., D. R. Holland, F. H. Settle, and D. C. Gnegy. 1976. Control of a fowl cholera outbreak among coots in Virginia. Proc. Annu. Conf. Southeast. Fish and Wildl. Agencies 30:602-609.

Quay, T. L., and T. S. Critcher. 1962. Food habits of waterfowl in Currituck Sound, North Carolina. Proc. Annu. Conf. Southeast. Assoc. Game and Fish Comm. 16:200-209.

Rawls, C. K. 1978. Food habits of waterfowl in the Upper Chesapeake Bay, Maryland. Univ. Maryland Center for Environ. Estua. Stud., Solomons. 140 pp.

Redelfs, A. E. 1980. Wetland values and losses in the United States. M.S. Thesis, Oklahoma State Univ., Stillwater. 143 pp.

Robbins, C. S. 1982. Recent changes in the ranges of North American birds. Int. Ornithol. Congr. 18:737-742.

——, D. Bystrak, and P. Geissler. 1986. The breeding bird survey: its first fifteen years, 1965-1979. U.S. Fish and Wildl. Serv. Res. Publ. 157. 196 pp.

Roland, J. V., G. E. Moore, and M. A. Bellanca. 1977. The Chesapeake Bay oil spill February 2, 1976: case history. Pages 523-527 in J. O. Ludwigson, ed. 1977 Oil spill conf. Am. Petroleum Inst., Washington, D.C.

Scanlon, P. F., V. D. Stotts, R. G. Oderwald, T. J. Deitrick, and R. J. Kendall. 1980. Lead concentrations in livers of Maryland waterfowl with and without lead shot present in gizzards. Bull. Environ. Contam. and Toxic. 25:855-860.

Scott, T. G., and G. H. Wasser. 1980. Checklist of North American plants for wildlife biologists. The Wildl. Soc., Washington, D.C. 58 pp.

Sincock, J. L., J. A. Kerwin, J. L. Coggin, A. W. Dickson, K. H. Johnston, and R. E. Wollitz. 1966. Back Bay-Currituck Sound report: waterfowl studies. U.S. Bur. Sport Fish. and Wildl. Washington, D.C. 63 pp.

Steiner, A. J. 1984. Mid-winter waterfowl inventory, Atlantic Flyway, 1954-1984 trend analysis. U.S. Fish and Wildl. Serv. Newton Corner, Mass. 284 pp.

Stevenson, J. C., and N. M. Confer. 1978. Summary of available information of Chesapeake Bay submerged aquatic vegetation. U.S. Dep. Int. FWS/OBS-78/66. NITS, Springfield, Va. 333 pp.

Steward, K. K., T. K. Van, V. Carter, and A. H. Pieterse. 1984. Hydrilla invades Washington, D.C. and the Potomac. Am. J. Bot. 71:162-163.

Stewart, R. E., 1962. Waterfowl populations in the upper Chesapeake region. U.S. Fish and Wildl. Serv. Sci. Rep., Wildl. No. 65. 208 pp.

——, and J. Manning. 1958. Distribution and ecology of whistling swans in the Chesapeake Bay region. Auk 75:203-212.

——, and C. Robbins. 1958. Birds of Maryland and the District of Columbia. Bur. Sports Fish. and Wildl., North Am. Fauna No. 62. 401 pp.

Stone, W. B. 1979. Poisoning of wild birds by organophosphate and carbamate pesticides. N.Y. Fish and Game J. 26:37-47.

Stotts, V. D. 1956. Wetlands of Maryland. Maryland Game and Inland and Fish Comm., Fed. Aid in Fish and Wildl. Restor., Prog. Rep., Proj. W-30-R-4, Job No. 1, Annapolis. 68 pp.

——. 1970. Susquehanna Flats vegetative survey. Md. Fish and Wildl. Adm., Fed. Aid in Fish Wildl. Restor. Rep. Annapolis. 8 pp.

——. 1971. Improving (changing) wetlands for waterfowl and other wildlife. Proc. Md. Mosquito Wildl. Conf., Annapolis. 8 pp.

——. 1972. Periodic Canada Goose survey. Md. Wildl. Adm., Fed. Aid in Fish and Wildl. Restor. Prog. Rep., Proj. W-45-R-4, Job I-3, Annapolis. 17 pp.

——. 1973. Non-consumptive waterfowl surveys (Lead poisoning supplement). Md. Wildl. Adm., Fed. Aid in Fish and Wildl. Restor. Proj. W-54-R-4, Job No. 4, Annapolis. 17 pp.

——. 1980. Incidence of ingested shot pellets in harvested waterfowl. Md. Wildl. Adm., Fed. Aid in Fish and Wildl. Restor. Proj. W-45-R-12. Job No. III-5, Annapolis. 22 pp.

——. 1983. Canada goose management plan for the Atlantic Flyway, 1983-1995, part II: history and current status. Atlantic Waterfowl Counc., Patuxent Wildl. Res. Center., Laurel, Md. 189 pp.

———. 1985. Values and functions of Chesapeake wetlands for waterfowl. Pages 129-142 *in* H. Groman, T. Henderson, E. Meyers, D. Burke, and J. Kusler, eds. Proc. conf. wetlands of the Chesapeake. Environ. Law Inst., Washington, D.C.

———. 1987. A survey of breeding American black ducks in the Eastern Bay region of Maryland in 1986. U.S. Fish and Wildl. Serv., Contract No. 14-16-005-86-017. Annapolis, Md. 103 pp.

Tiner, R. W., Jr. 1984. Wetlands of the United States: current status and recent trends. U.S. Fish and Wildl. Serv., Washington, D.C. 59 pp.

Titus, J. G., editor. 1986a. Effects of changes in stratospheric ozone and global climate. Vol. 1. Environ. Protect. Agency, Washington, D.C. 379 pp.

———, editor. 1986b. Effects of changes in stratospheric ozone and global climate. Vol. 4. Environ. Protect. Agency, Washington, D.C. 193 pp.

———. 1986c. The causes and effects of sea level rise. Pages 219-248 *in* J. G. Titus, ed. Effects of changes in stratospheric ozone and global climate. Vol. 1. Environ. Protect. Agency, Washington, D.C.

U.S. Dep. Agric. 1950. Agricultural statistics. U.S. Gov. Print. Off., Washington, D.C. 591 pp.

———. 1980. Agricultural statistics. U.S. Gov. Print. Off., Washington, D.C. 603 pp.

Warren, J., and D. Bandel. 1968. Pothole blasting in Maryland wetlands. Proc. Annu. Conf. Southeast. Assoc. Game and Fish Comm. 22:58-68.

Weller, M. W., and C. E. Spatcher. 1965. Role of habitat in the distribution of marsh birds. Iowa Agric. Home Econ. Exp. Stn. Spec. Rep. No. 43. 31 pp.

———, and L. H. Frederickson. 1974. Avian ecology of a managed glacial marsh. Living Bird 12:269-291.

Wells, B. W. 1928. Plant communities of the coastal plain of North Carolina and their successional relations. Ecology 9:23-242.

White, D. H., R. C. Stendell, and B. M. Mulhern. 1979. Relations of wintering canvasbacks to environmental pollutants—Chesapeake Bay, Maryland. Wilson Bull. 91:279-287.

Whitman, W. R., and W. H. Meredith, editors. 1987. Waterfowl and wetlands symp.: proc. of a symp. on waterfowl and wetlands management in the coastal zone of the Atlantic Flyway. Del. Coast. Manage. Prog., Dep. Nat. Resour. and Environ. Control, Dover.

Woodhouse, W. W., and T. L. Knutson. 1982. Atlantic coastal marshes. Pages 45-70 *in* R. L. Lewis III, ed. Creation and restoration of wetland plant communities. CRC Press, Boca Raton, Fla.

Yelverton, C. S., and T. L. Quay. 1959. Food habits of the Canada goose at Lake Mattamuskeet, North Carolina. Wildl. Res. Comm., Raleigh, N.C. 44 pp.

SOUTH ATLANTIC COASTAL WETLANDS

DAVID H. GORDON,[1] Delta Waterfowl and Wetlands Research Station, Atlantic Flyway Substation, Star Route 1, Box 226, Georgetown, SC 29440 and Department of Wildlife and Fisheries, Mississippi State University, Mississippi State, MS 39762

BRIAN T. GRAY, Delta Waterfowl and Wetlands Research Station, Atlantic Flyway Substation, Star Route 1, Box 226, Georgetown, SC 29440 and Department of Wildlife and Fisheries, Mississippi State University, Mississippi State, MS 39762

ROBERT D. PERRY, South Carolina Wildlife and Marine Resources Department, Star Route 1, Box 226, Georgetown, SC 29440

MICHAEL B. PREVOST, South Carolina Wildlife and Marine Resources Department, P.O. Box 398, McClellanville, SC 29458

THOMAS H. STRANGE, South Carolina Wildlife and Marine Resources Department, P.O. Box 37, McClellanville, SC 29458

R. KENNETH WILLIAMS, Kinloch Plantation, Route 2, Box 195, Georgetown, SC 29440

Wetland management in the South Atlantic Coastal Zone (SACZ) had its origin in the 18th- and 19th-century rice industry of South Carolina and Georgia. The need for an economy to support settlements and the discovery that rice could be grown in the SACZ led to the development of water-manipulation systems for rice production in tidal freshwater wetlands. Today, wetland managers use a modification of these systems to provide habitat for waterfowl.

This chapter focuses on wetland management in coastal areas of South Carolina and Georgia for migrating and wintering waterfowl. Although waterfowl management is the primary objective of many impoundment owners (Morgan 1974, Tiner 1977, Gresham and Hook 1982, Tompkins 1986), other management objectives include providing habitat for nongame, mosquito control, aquaculture, fishing, and aesthetics (Strange 1987). An adequate portrayal of SACZ waterfowl habitat management requires a basic understanding of regional coastal wetland ecosystems and the historical interaction of human culture with these environments.

ECOLOGICAL CHARACTERIZATION

Geological Description

The coastal zone of South Carolina and Georgia (Fig. 1) is situated within the Atlantic Coastal Plain (Vankat 1979). Detailed historical and recent descriptions of the region's complex geomorphology are provided by Johnson et al. (1974) and Mathews et al. (1980). The SACZ can be divided into 3 geomorphological zones: (1) the arcuate strand, a relatively straight coast incised by few tidal inlets extending approximately 100 km from the North Carolina border to Winyah Bay, South Carolina; (2) the cuspate delta area, composed of sediments supplied by the Santee River system between Winyah Bay and Bulls Bay; and (3) the barrier island-tidal inlet zone, which includes the southern 160 km of the South Carolina coast and all of the Georgia coast (Johnson et al. 1974, Brown 1976).

The coastal region is comprised of a series of distinct, shore-parallel terrace complexes, composed of linear sand ridges and back-barrier broad, clayey plains (Cooke 1936, Colquhoun 1969, Barry 1980, Mathews et al. 1980). Sediments deposited during the present high sea level form the river bottoms, deltas, swamps, marshes, barrier islands, tidal flats, and estuarine bottoms (Barry 1980, Davis et al. 1980). Sediment deposits have

---

[1]Present university affiliation: Department of Aquaculture, Fisheries and Wildlife, Clemson University, Clemson, SC 29634.

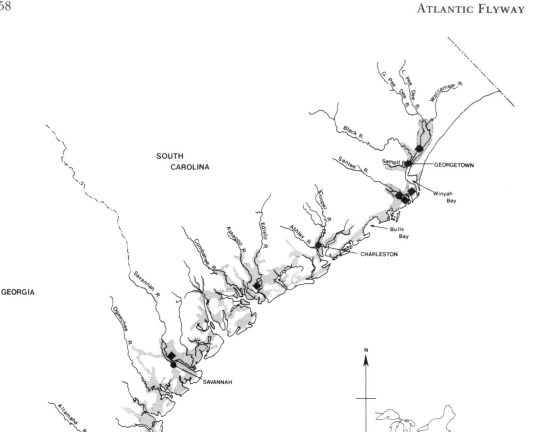

Fig. 1. South Atlantic Coastal Zone with locations of major river systems, associated tidal marsh, and waterfowl management areas.

given rise to 5 coastal soil types of which loamy and clayey soils of wet lowlands and clayey tidal marsh soils rank first and second in areal importance. Soils in brackish and salt marsh zones (i.e., sulfaquents) have a clay loam texture and an accumulation of >1% sulfur as sulfides. They are permanently wet and frequently flooded by brackish to saline water (Craddock and Wells 1973).

Climate

The SACZ has a temperate climate influenced by the Atlantic Ocean, a southerly latitude (30°-33° N), and low elevation (Purvis 1987). The northward-flowing Gulf Stream provides a warming effect, whereas the Appalachian Mountains block cold air masses arriving from the northwest. Average maximum July temperatures range between 30-33 C and average minimum temperatures range between 21-24 C. Mean minimum January temperatures for South Carolina are 2-5 C and for Georgia are 5-7 C. Average monthly relative humidity ranges between 50% and 65%. The growing season (about 280 days) is limited by spring (mid-March) and fall (mid-November) freezes.

Mean annual precipitation in the coastal zone of both states ranges between 114-139 cm. Rainfall is most abundant in summer and early fall, with dry periods in October and November. Precipitation in late fall and winter is associated with frontal movements, whereas spring and summer precipitation typically results from convective afternoon thunderstorms.

Wind patterns differ somewhat between South Carolina and Georgia (Mathews et al. 1980). Prevailing wind directions for South Carolina are: January—SW, April—SSW, July—SW, October—NNE. Prevailing wind directions for Georgia are: January—WNW, April—SSE, July—SSW, and October—NNE.

Coastal Wetlands

The South Carolina-Georgia coast is classified as a mixed-energy coast impacted by a combination of wave and tidal energy (Hayes 1976). Mean tidal range increases from north to south, from approximately 1.4 m on the north coast of South Carolina to 2.2 m on the Georgia coast. The complex geomorphology and hydrology have produced 4 coastal ecological systems: tidal rivers, sedimentary deltas, tidal marshes, and bays. Although each system can be separately identified, they often are functionally interrelated components within major estuaries (Pritchard 1967).

Estuarine hydrography is influenced by tides, precipitation, freshwater runoff from land, evaporation, wind, river flow, meteorological pressure centers, and the area and shape of the estuary (Cowardin et al. 1979, Mathews et al. 1980). SACZ estuaries can be classified as either drowned river valleys or bar-built estuaries (Pritchard 1967), having a 2-layer flow with vertical mixing (partially mixed) characterized by river-flow and tidal mixing, or vertically homogeneous with tidal currents predominating. Water circulation patterns in many estuaries are largely influenced by volume and rate of freshwater inflow (Mathews et al. 1980), and consequently consist of a gradient from tidal fresh water near the head of the estuary to near-marine conditions in the mouth of the estuary (Odum et al. 1984). These factors interact to affect water quality, specifically salinity, and ultimately affect the distribution and composition of resident biota.

Cowardin et al. (1979) classified SACZ wetlands as Estuarine and Riverine Systems. Wetlands within the Estuarine System fall within the Intertidal Subsystem, defined as the area from extreme low spring water to extreme high water and associated splash zone. Wetlands within the Riverine System fall within the Tidal Subsystem, extending from the upper boundary of the Estuarine System (where ocean-derived salts measure <0.5 ppt during the period of average annual flow) to the extreme upper limit of tidal fluctuations. In this chapter, however, we use a widely accepted regional wetland classification scheme that identifies 3 wetland types: (1) tidal freshwater marsh (Riverine/Tidal), (2) salt marsh (Estuarine/Intertidal), and (3) brackish marsh (Estuarine/Intertidal), a transitional type between tidal freshwater and salt marshes (Havel 1976, Tiner 1977). Plant species diversity is highest in the tidal freshwater marshes located at the upper reaches of the estuary, and decreases progressively in brackish and salt marshes. Plant nomenclature follows Radford et al. (1964) and Tiner (1977).

Tidal Freshwater Marsh

Extensive tidal freshwater marshes are located in the SACZ (Table 1). South

Table 1. Estimated surface area and percent of total coastal marsh for various wetland types found in South Carolina and Georgia.

Wetland type	South Carolina		Georgia	
	ha[a]	%	ha	%
Salt marsh	135,425	66	154,755[b,c]	87
Brackish marsh	14,155	7	—	—
Tidal freshwater marsh	26,125	13	19,047[b]	11
Remnant impoundments[d]	25,860	13	4,637[e]	3
Total tidal marsh	175,705	86	173,803[b,e]	98
Coastal impoundments[f]	28,522	14	3,235[e]	2
Total coastal marsh[g]	204,227	100	177,037	100

[a]Tiner 1977 or Aichele 1984.
[b]Wilkes 1976.
[c]Includes brackish marsh.
[d]Included in salt marsh, brackish marsh, and freshwater marsh estimates.
[e]C. V. Waters, unpubl. data.
[f]Diked and managed wetlands.
[g]Includes coastal impoundments.

Carolina and Georgia contain 28% of the tidal freshwater marsh on the Atlantic Coast (Wilkes 1976, Mathews et al. 1980). Tidal freshwater marshes exhibit temporal and spatial variation due to the interaction of dynamic hydrological conditions and wetland morphology (Odum et al. 1984). Tidal freshwater marshes are predominantly influenced by inflowing riverine fresh water, although ocean tides markedly affect the hydroperiod causing 2 tidal cycles daily. Consequently, tidal freshwater marshes are characterized by high plant species and community diversities and a pronounced seasonal sequence of vegetation different from brackish and salt marshes (Tiner 1977, Odum et al. 1984). Zonation is not sharply defined as in salt and brackish marshes.

Dominant plants in tidal freshwater marshes include yellow pond lily (*Nuphar luteum*), Canadian waterweed (*Anacharis canadensis*), southern wildrice (*Zizaniopsis miliacea*), wild rice (*Zizania aquatica*), Virginia arrowarum (*Peltandra virginica*), pickerelweed (*Pontederia cordata*), golden club (*Orontium aquaticum*), lizard's tail (*Saururus cernuus*), arrowheads (*Sagittaria* spp.), smartweeds and tearthumbs (*Polygonum* spp.), cattail (*Typha* spp.), and sedges (*Cyperus* spp. and *Carex* spp.) (Fig. 2). Codominants include common rush (*Juncus effusus*),

softstem bulrush (*Scirpus validus*), square-stem spikerush (*Eleocharis quadrangulata*), giant cordgrass (*Spartina cynosuroides*), climbing hempweed (*Mikania scandens*), water-hemp (*Amaranthus cannabinus*), compact dotter (*Cuscuta compacta*), tag alder (*Alnus serrulata*), swamp dogwood (*Cornus stricta*), button bush (*Cephalanthus occidentalis*), willows (*Salix* spp.), common bald cypress (*Taxodium distichum*), red maple (*Acer rubrum*), and tupelo-gums (*Nyssa* spp.).

Salt Marsh

The majority of SACZ coastal wetlands has been classified as salt marsh (Table 1). Plant species composition in salt marsh is influenced primarily by salinity and frequency and length of inundation. Two zones within salt marsh are typically identified, low and high marsh (Tiner 1977). Distinct plant assemblages characterize these zones due to differences in elevation, submergence, exposure, and soil salinity (Adams 1963, Waisel 1972). Low marsh is flooded by tides twice daily and extends from near mean sea level to the approximate mean high water level. High marsh occurs above this zone and is irregularly flooded, generally by higher than average tides (Tiner 1977, Mitsch

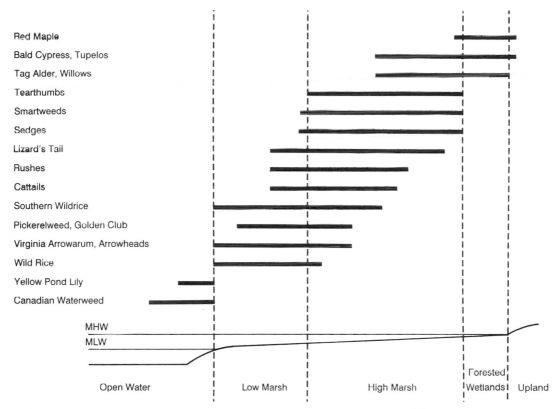

Fig. 2. Vegetation distributions relative to water levels in South Carolina and Georgia tidal freshwater marsh. MHW = mean high water; MSL = mean sea level; MLW = mean low water.

and Gosselink 1986). Low marsh is dominated by smooth cordgrass (*Spartina alterniflora*) with a tall (100-300 cm) form occurring along creek banks and a short (17-80 cm) form occurring in the interior low marsh (Mitsch and Gosselink 1986) (Fig. 3). Soil salinities in low marsh rarely exceed water salinities (Daiber 1986). The high marsh zone is characterized by greater plant diversity than the low marsh and is typified by salt grass (*Distichlis spicata*), black needle rush (*Juncus roemerianus*), glassworts (*Salicornia* spp.), sea ox-eye (*Borrichia frutescens*), sea lavender (*Limonium carolinianum*), and marsh-hay cordgrass (*Spartina patens*) (Tiner 1977). Wax myrtle (*Myrica cerifera*), sea myrtle (*Baccharis halimifolia*), and marsh elder (*Iva frutescens*) are typical of the high marsh-upland transition zone. Soil salinities in

high marsh can often exceed those of the tidal waters due to evaporation during extended periods of exposure (Ranwell 1972).

Brackish Marsh

Brackish marsh comprises <10% of SACZ coastal marsh (Table 1). It represents a transition zone between tidal freshwater marshes and salt marshes and is influenced by marine and riverine systems. Brackish marshes have salinity ranges between 1-20 ppt and share vegetative characteristics with both tidal freshwater and salt marsh (Tiner 1977). Elevation of the marsh floor in relation to mean high tide as well as other site-specific variables such as soil pH and soil moisture affect plant distribution. Plants inhabiting brackish marsh are subject to wide variances in tidal range and salinity,

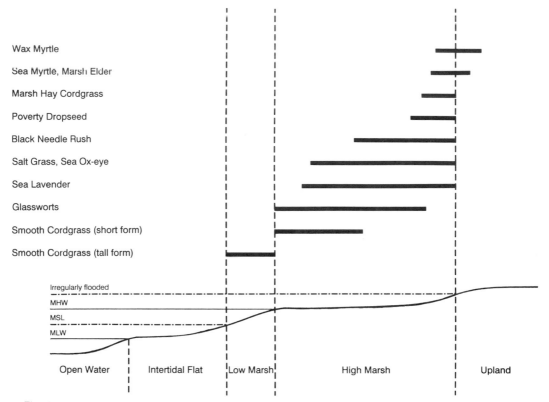

Fig. 3. Vegetation distributions relative to water level in South Carolina and Georgia tidal salt marsh. MHW = mean high water; MSL = mean sea level; MLW = mean low water.

conditions that preclude establishment of less tolerant vegetation and reduce species diversity.

Dominant plant species in brackish marshes include giant cordgrass and black needle rush (Fig. 4). Black needle rush is dominant in more seaward brackish marshes. Codominant species include wax myrtle, sea myrtle, marsh elder, and saltmarsh aster (*Aster subulatus*) at higher elevations, salt grass at intermediate elevations, and saltmarsh bulrush (*Scirpus robustus*) and smooth cordgrass at lower elevations. Brackish marshes located closer to the head of the estuary become vegetatively heterogeneous with the local occurrence of cattails, sedges, southern wildrice, American bulrush (*Scirpus americanus*), and softstem bulrush.

Remnant Impoundments

Remnant or abandoned impoundments are located throughout tidal freshwater and brackish zones in wetlands used for rice cultivation during the 18th and 19th centuries. Less than 15% of South Carolina's coastal marshes are included in this category, but South Carolina has about 4 times more remnant impoundments than Georgia (Table 1). These marshes are subject to tidal influence as dike systems and water-control structures have deteriorated with age. As opposed to unaltered tidal marsh in the same wetland zones, remnant impoundments often have modified creek systems that were incorporated into canals or blocked by dikes. Linear drainage and access canals were constructed throughout these systems and continue to function much as was intended when these areas were managed for rice production. Plant species composition in these wetlands is generally similar to that described for tidal freshwater and brackish marshes.

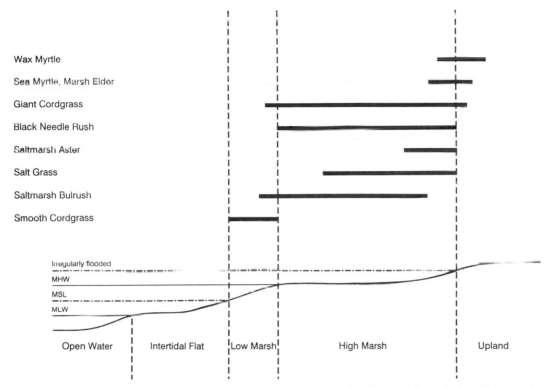

Fig. 4. Vegetation distributions relative to water level in South Carolina and Georgia brackish marsh. MHW = mean high water; MSL = mean sea level; MLW – mean low water.

Tidal Forested Wetlands

Forested wetlands subject to tidal influence typically occur in the upper reaches of estuaries and range inland to the point of negligible tidal influence. There are few areal estimates of tidal forested wetlands for South Carolina and Georgia. Penfound (1952) described these areas as being dominated by slow-growth cypress-tupelo communities. Much of this wetland type was cleared for rice culture during the 19th century (Heyward 1937, Hilliard 1975). Commercial logging during the 20th century has removed almost all large cypress trees; however, a nearly closed canopy of medium-growth cypress-tupelo remains. Understory development is limited by low light penetration and stress from waterlogging. Shrubs include red bay (*Persea borbonia*), tag alder, wax myrtle, sweet bay magnolia (*Magnolia virginia*), and swamp dogwood.

HISTORY OF LAND USE AND WATERFOWL HABITAT MANAGEMENT

Agrarian Rice Era

Man made extensive use of SACZ wetlands for growing rice. This industry resulted in extreme modifications of the coastal environment and produced a unique set of technologies, both of which played an integral role in development of waterfowl habitat management. Rice culture also spawned a cultural and socio-economic philosophy that embraces private ownership and use of wetlands. The rice industry is still embroiled in decisions and policy concerning SACZ wetlands (Latimer 1968, Banks 1987, Devoe et al. 1987).

Rice was introduced into Charleston, South Carolina, around 1680 (Salley 1936, Hilliard 1975, Kovacik 1979). Initially,

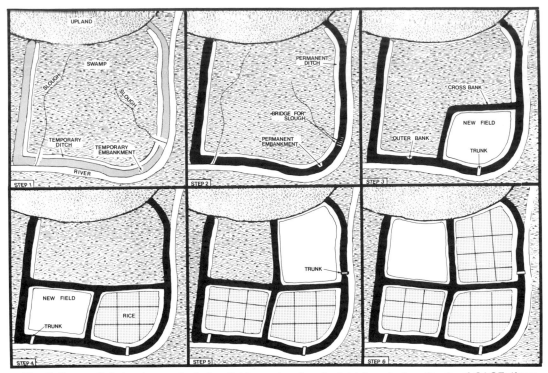

Fig. 5. Sequential development of rice field construction in tidal forested wetlands of SACZ (from Hilliard 1975).

rice was grown inland as an upland crop without irrigation, but the benefits of field flooding were quickly recognized, and rice cultivation became associated with floodplains of inland swamps (Hilliard 1975). Small impoundments (usually <12 ha) were constructed adjacent to small freshwater streams where cypress, gum, and tupelo trees had been cleared (Hilliard 1975, Rowland 1987), and water from streams was used for irrigation. Drought sometimes limited water availability, and rains frequently broke dams and washed out fields (Hilliard 1975). The inland swamp method of rice cultivation dominated the industry until shortly before the American Revolution (Rowland 1987), when rice planters began to use tidal zones of the larger South Carolina river systems (Fig. 1).

Rice cultivation in the tidal zone was advantageous due to a predictable supply of fresh water and water control (Hilliard 1975). Diel variation in water levels, due

to tides, facilitated gravity-flow flooding of fields. Nevertheless, the required conditions of fresh water and sufficient tidal amplitude (1-2 m) limited the areas within estuaries where rice could be grown. Sites having suitable features were found in forested tidal swamps dominated by cypress and gum. Decades of innovation resulted in construction of extensive systems of dikes, canals, ditches, and tide-operated, gravity-flow water-control structures (Fig. 5). By the early 1800s, tidal rice culture was considered a perfected process (Rogers 1970).

The SACZ rice era ended shortly after the Civil War (Kovacik 1979). Between 1870 and 1900, the SACZ was hit by numerous tropical storms and hurricanes causing damage to dikes and canals (Kovacik 1979, Rowland 1987), and reconstruction was impossible (Rogers 1970, Purvis et al. 1986). Attempts to grow rice commercially in the region persisted until the early 1900s.

Rice planting required considerable alteration of the natural wetland environment (Rowland 1987). The first major impact was extensive clearing of forested, tidal swamps (Doar 1936, Heyward 1937, Hilliard 1975, Joyner 1984). Ditch and dike construction permanently modified natural drainage patterns and caused large-scale changes in wetland plant communities. As the demise of the rice industry occurred, most diked fields were abandoned and rapidly became vegetated by naturally occurring wetland species. Tidewater rice culture had transformed extensive forested wetlands into coastal freshwater marshes. Intact and remnant rice plantation wetland impoundments provided waterfowl habitat.

Post-Agrarian Rice Era

Major purchases of rice plantations by wealthy sportsmen began in the 1890s and continued until the 1930s (Rogers 1970). Plantation owners repaired and maintained existing dikes and water-control structures to develop waterfowl hunting areas (Kovacik 1979, Miglarese and Sandifer 1982, Porcher 1985, Strange 1987). However, waterfowl habitat management in the sense of intensive environmental manipulations to improve wetland habitats did not exist. Habitat management simply consisted of supplying fresh water to diked fields during the growing season to propagate natural vegetation and keeping areas constantly flooded during the hunting season. Also, openings in the marsh vegetation were sometimes created.

Large-scale dike construction in coastal marsh began again during the late 1930s and 1940s in South Carolina (P. M. Wilkinson, pers. commun.), primarily in anticipation of, and in response to, the Santee-Cooper Diversion Project (Anonymous 1942). The Santee-Cooper Diversion Project, completed in 1942, was designed to generate hydroelectric power (Mathews et al. 1980). This project resulted in the diversion of 88% of the Santee River's mean annual discharge into the Cooper River (Kjerfve 1976). The Lower Santee River's annual mean discharge decreased from 525 to 62 m^3/s and the Cooper River's discharge increased from 2 to 422 m^3/s (U.S. Army Corps of Engineers 1966, U.S. Geological Survey 1975). As a result of decreased water flow into the Santee River system, the Santee Delta experienced an increase in average salinity at the mouth of the estuary from <1 ppt (Kjerfve 1976) to 20-24 ppt (Mathews et al. 1981). Increased salinities resulted in extensive changes in wetland plant communities. Areal coverage of tidal freshwater marsh in the Santee Delta was reduced and became confined to the uppermost reaches of the estuary. Salt and brackish marshes became dominant. The increased discharge into the Cooper River resulted in an annual mean decrease in salinity from 31 ppt to 16 ppt in the lower regions of the river 8 km from the open ocean (Zetler 1953). Decreased salinities resulted in the expansion of fresh marsh in the upper region of the Cooper River Estuary (Tiner 1977).

Over the next 20 years, new dikes and water-control structures were added in the Santee Delta to prevent salt water intrusion. Remnant rice field dikes were small in cross-section, about 30 cm above mean high tide, and in many cases, not water tight (Anonymous 1942). New dikes were required to prevent salt water from entering fields so freshwater plants could still grow. However, the extent to which salt water penetrated the estuary made it nearly impossible to obtain fresh water from the river at many sites. Consequently, many sites could be flooded only with brackish water.

Fields flooded with brackish water produced salt-tolerant vegetation dominated by species of low food value to waterfowl (e.g., giant cordgrass), but growth of desirable waterfowl food plants [e.g., widgeon grass (*Ruppia maritima*)] occurred at scattered sites. During the

Table 2. Important federal and state waterfowl areas located in the coastal zone of South Carolina and Georgia.

State	Waterfowl area	River/estuarine system	Wetland area (ha)	
			Managed	Unmanaged
South Carolina	Samworth WMA[a]	Pee Dee/Waccamaw	325	19
	Yawkey Wildlife Center	Winyah Bay/Santee	953	1,258
	Santee Delta WMA	Santee	459	148
	Santee Coastal Reserve	Santee	4,719	1,970
	Bear Island WMA	South Edisto/Ashepoo	1,789	2,026
	Cape Romain NWR[b]	Bulls Bay	411	12,125
	Savannah NWR Complex	Savannah; Port Royal and Calibogue Sounds	1,114	5,773
	Total		9,770	23,319
Georgia	Savannah NWR Complex	Savannah; Wassaw, Ossabaw, Sapelo, and Altamaha Sounds	431	10,995
	Altamaha WMA	Altamaha	1,821	6,667
	Total		2,252	17,672

[a]Wildlife Management Area.
[b]National Wildlife Refuge.

1950s and 1960s, wetland management became more sophisticated, and practical management procedures involving water and mechanical manipulations were developed to encourage growth of freshwater and brackish plants (Baldwin 1950, 1956, Neely 1958, Davison and Neely 1959, Neely 1960, Baldwin 1968, Neely 1968, Wilkinson 1970). The preceding events, plus the growing information base pertaining to waterfowl habitat management in the southeastern U.S., helped refine management procedures during the 1970s to present-day standards.

Other significant impacts on SACZ wetlands and waterfowl habitat include construction of the Atlantic Intracoastal Waterway (AIW) in 1941; residential, urban, and industrial development; and recreational activities. Effects of these impacts on waterfowl habitats have been less obvious, and, in many instances, not fully understood. The AIW and associated navigation projects have destroyed marsh by dredging and filling and have affected water circulation and quality in estuaries. Increased commercial and recreational boat traffic into or adjacent to marshes has influenced water quality and erosion. Human encroachment on wetlands of the

SACZ has increased tremendously since 1960 and is expected to continue. Recreational use of coastal wetlands for hunting, fishing, and boating has grown proportionately to population growth. Other impacts on wetlands include resort and recreational development of adjacent and upstream uplands, with the primary effects being water-quality degradation from sewage and industrial discharges and nonpoint runoff.

Along the major river systems of the SACZ, federal, state, and private waterfowl management areas and refuges have been established (Table 2). Government acquisition of wetlands to benefit wildlife began in the late 1930s. In South Carolina, the area of managed coastal waterfowl habitat in private ownership exceeds that of governmental agencies (Tompkins 1986). An estimated 65% of 28,522 ha of managed coastal wetlands are privately owned. Comparable data are not available for privately managed coastal wetlands in Georgia. However, several small, privately managed waterfowl areas are located on the Savannah, Ogeechee, and Satilla rivers (R. H. Folk, III and M. L. Morrison, pers. commun.).

IMPORTANCE TO MIGRATING AND WINTERING WATERFOWL

Populations

United States Fish and Wildlife Service (USFWS) mid-winter waterfowl surveys conducted in the Atlantic Flyway since 1954 represent the most reliable index of wintering populations within the SACZ. From 1954 through 1987, South Carolina wintered an average of 30% of the dabbling ducks within the flyway (Fig. 6). Since 1970, South Carolina has wintered an average of 54% of the American green-winged teal (*Anas crecca*), 50% of the northern shovelers (*A. clypeata*), 35% of the mallards (*A. platyrhynchos*), 32% of the northern pintails (*A. acuta*) and American wigeon (*A. americana*), and 31% of the gadwall (*A. strepera*) in the flyway (Gordon et al. 1987). Managed coastal wetlands, especially on the Santee River Estuary, are very important to these species (Gordon et al. 1987, Prevost 1987, Strange 1987). Georgia winters considerably fewer dabbling ducks, averaging about 2% of the flyway total since 1954 (Fig. 6). Both states winter <100,000 diving ducks, averaging about 3% of the flyway population since 1954 (Fig. 7). Ring-necked ducks (*Aythya collaris*) and lesser scaup (*A. affinis*) are the most abundant species.

Historically, SACZ wintering goose populations have been small. Since 1954, South Carolina and Georgia have wintered an average of 3% and 0.1% of the Atlantic Flyway Canada goose (*Branta canadensis*) flock, respectively. Murphy Island, in the Santee River Estuary, is the only location in the Southeast that has consistently wintered snow geese (*Chen caerulescens*) since 1960 (Carney et al. 1983, South Carolina Wildl. and Mar. Resour. Dep., unpubl. data).

The geographic location of the SACZ helps explain the area's importance to migrating waterfowl. In addition to serving as an important wintering area,

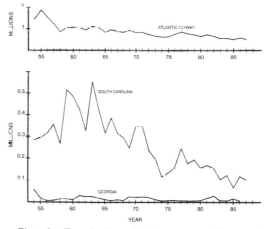

Fig. 6. Trends in wintering populations of dabbling ducks in South Carolina, Georgia, and the Atlantic Flyway.

these wetlands also serve as staging areas for migrating waterfowl that winter in Florida, the Caribbean Islands, and South America (Bellrose 1980). Important staging and wintering areas include the Pee Dee-Waccamaw-Black rivers area, north of Georgetown, S.C.; the Santee River Estuary, south of Georgetown; the Ashepoo-Combahee-Edisto river basin in southern South Carolina; the lower Savannah River, north of Savannah, Ga.; and the lower Altamaha River, south of Darien, Ga. (Fig. 1). The majority of migrant

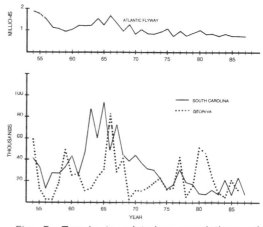

Fig. 7. Trends in wintering populations of diving ducks in South Carolina, Georgia, and the Atlantic Flyway.

waterfowl begin passing through the
SACZ in October, although large
numbers of blue-winged teal (*Anas discors*) move through as early as late
August. The majority of waterfowl wintering in the SACZ do not arrive until
mid-November and reach peak numbers
in mid-December. Spring migration of
winter residents may begin as early as
mid-February in warm winters and most
have left by the first full moon in March.
Migrants returning from latitudes south
of the SACZ (e.g., blue-winged teal,
gadwall, northern pintail, and American
wigeon) move through the region in
March. Migrant blue-winged teal may
remain in SACZ wetlands as long as late
April.

Generally, the common waterfowl species (listed in decreasing order of abundance) associated with freshwater management areas are wood duck, (*Aix sponsa*)
green-winged teal, mallard, northern pintail, ring-necked duck, black duck (*Anas
rubripes*), northern shoveler, and blue-
winged teal. Managed areas within the
brackish zone generally attract green-
winged teal, northern pintail, American
wigeon, mallard, gadwall, northern shoveler, blue-winged teal, ring-necked duck,
and black duck. Managed areas within
the salt marsh zone generally attract
green-winged and blue-winged teal,
American wigeon, northern pintail,
northern shoveler, and gadwall.

Species composition of the SACZ waterfowl harvest indicates the relative importance of species to hunters. Harvest
records of coastal counties in the SACZ
from 1961-1980 indicate wood ducks comprise the major proportion of the harvest,
followed by green-winged teal, mallard,
American wigeon, ring-necked duck,
northern pintail, and gadwall (Carney et
al. 1975, 1983). However, harvest records
from state management areas from 1977-
87 document green-winged teal as the
species most harvested, followed by mallard, blue-winged teal, northern pintail,

and American wigeon (Georgia Dep. Nat.
Resour., unpubl. data; South Carolina
Wildl. and Mar. Resour. Dep., unpubl.
data).

Ecological Importance of SACZ Wetlands

The migration and wintering period
experienced by waterfowl is a behavior-
ally and physiologically important period
that not only influences the immediate
welfare of waterfowl but also subsequent
reproductive output (Heitmeyer and Fredrickson 1981, Krapu 1981, Hepp et al.
1986, Kaminski and Gluesing 1987).
Waterfowl shift from low densities on
breeding grounds to large, gregarious
groups during migration and the wintering period (Weller 1975, Tamisier 1985).
This behavioral change leads to greater
densities of waterfowl on generally
smaller wintering areas and necessitates a
strong shift in both selection of habitats
and consumer level (Weller 1975). The
nutritional and energetic requirements of
molt, pairing, migration, and thermoregulation experienced by nonbreeding
waterfowl further influence habitat and
food selection.

Management of southern wetlands for
waterfowl has traditionally emphasized
plant species that provide food for
migrating and wintering waterfowl. A
modern perspective of waterfowl habitat
management recognizes that habitat selection by waterfowl is a complex phenomenon and is based on the biological
needs of each species. Thus, the primary
objective of SACZ waterfowl habitat management is to provide functional wetland
habitats that accommodate the needs of
migrating and wintering waterfowl (Gray
et al. 1987). Management aims to provide
habitats that include an abundance and
diversity of nutritious foods, vegetative
structure, and resting areas.

Food.—Waterfowl food habits studies
in the SACZ have been based either
wholly (Conrad 1965, Kerwin and Webb

1972) or in part (Landers et al. 1976, Prevost et al. 1978, Swiderek 1982) on gizzard contents. These results are biased in favor of hard food items that are most difficult to digest (Swanson and Bartonek 1970). Also, all but one study (Swiderek 1982) used the aggregate volume method, not the preferred weighted aggregate percent method (Swanson et al. 1974), potentially biasing the relative importance of foods recorded.

In managed tidal freshwaterr wetlands, seeds of bulrushes, flat sedges, and spikerushes, when available, are consumed by all dabbling ducks common to the SACZ as well as ring-necked duck and scaup (Conrad 1966, Kerwin and Webb 1972, Landers et al. 1976). Smartweed seeds receive relatively high use by teal, mallard, black duck, northern pintail, wood duck, and ring-necked duck, but low use by American wigeon and gadwall (Conrad 1966, Kerwin and Webb 1972, Landers et al. 1976). Asiatic dayflower (*Aneilema keisak*) seeds are consumed by mallard, northern shoveler, teal, and occasionally by ring-necked duck and lesser scaup (Conrad 1966, Kerwin and Webb 1972). Redroot (*Lachnanthes caroliniana*) rhizomes are consumed by mallard, northern pintail, American wigeon, and occasionally by gadwall, black duck, northern shoveler, and green-winged teal (Landers et al. 1976). The foliage and seeds of bushy pondweed (*Najas quadalupensis*) are used by American wigeon and gadwall. Water-shield seeds (*Brasenia schreberi*) are consumed extensively by ring-necked duck (Kerwin and Webb 1972).

In managed brackish wetlands, seeds of saltmarsh millet (*Echinochloa walteri*), fall panic grass (*Panicum dichotomiflorum*), and saltmarsh bulrush are readily consumed by all dabbling duck species as well as lesser scaup and ring-necked duck. Mallard, black duck, teal, and northern pintail use the seeds most, with occasional use by American wigeon, gadwall,

scaup, wood duck, ring-necked duck, and northern shoveler (Kerwin and Webb 1972, Landers et al. 1976, Prevost et al. 1978). Foliage and seeds of widgeon grass, and foliage, seeds, and tubers of dwarf spikerush (*Eleocharis parvula*) also are consumed by the species listed above with most frequent use by American wigeon, gadwall, northern pintail, and teal (Kerwin and Webb 1972, Landers et al. 1976, Prevost et al. 1978).

Gulf Coast muskgrass (*Chara hornemannii*), sea purslane (*Sesuvium maritimum*), and widgeon grass are the most commonly used plant species occurring in managed wetlands within the salt marsh zone. Use of Gulf Coast muskgrass tubers and vegetation has been reported for northern pintail, American wigeon, gadwall, ruddy duck (*Oxyura jamaicensis*), and northern shoveler (Swiderek 1982). Sea purslane seeds appear to be consumed mostly by northern pintail and teal (Swiderek 1982). Cely (1979) reported that canvasbacks (*Aythya valisineria*) preferred banana waterlily (*Nymphaea mexicana*) over widgeon grass and muskgrass in managed certain wetlands within the salt marsh zone.

Mallard (Heitmeyer 1985), northern pintail, and green-winged teal (Euliss and Harris 1987) have been documented to increase consumption of invertebrates in late winter. Most likely, certain SACZ duck species use invertebrates, but studies are limited.

A diversified diet of natural foods and invertebrates provides the needed balance of energy, protein, and minerals required by waterfowl (Table 3). Seeds, tubers, and foliage of target plant species within managed impoundments contain important nutrients. Seeds of sedge, smartweed, and pondweed (*Potamogeton* spp.) and tubers of muskgrass are relatively poor sources of protein but good sources of energy. Seeds and tubers are important to waterfowl during periods of increased energy intake such as cold weather or

Table 3. Nutrient composition of watorfowl foods associated with managed wetlands in coastal South Carolina.

Family species	% dry weight					Energy (kcal/kg)	Source
	Crude protein	Crude fat	Crude fiber	NFE	Ash		
Cyperaceae							
Scirpus robustus (seeds)	8.5	4.3	14.2	69.9	3.2		Spinner and Bishop (1950)
	8.3	3.2	16.2	65.8	6.4		Bardwell et al. (1962)
S. americanus (seeds)	8.0	5.2	13.7	70.6	2.5		Spinner and Bishop (1950)
S. validus (seeds)	6.7	3.5	39.7	47.0	2.5	4,870 (GE)[a]	Sugden 1973
Eleocharis parvula (foliage)	12.1		41.9			3,440 (GE)	Paulus 1980
E. quadrangulata (seeds)	4.8	2.3	50.6	36.6	5.5		Bardwell et al. (1962)
E. sp. (seeds)	6.8	2.1	38.9	40.2	11.9		Bardwell et al. (1962)
Carex spp. (seeds)	10.1	6.2	19.2		7.6		Fredrickson and Taylor (1982)—2 spp. av.
	11.9	4.7	26.9	51.2	5.3		Spinner and Bishop (1950)—4 spp. av.
						4,788 (GE)	Kendeigh and West (1965)—1 spp.
Cyperus spp. (seeds)	8.9	3.4	17.2	63.9	7.4		Bardwell et al. (1962)—2 spp. av.
						3,686 (GE)	Fredrickson and Taylor (1982)—1 spp.
						5,196 (GE)	Kendeigh and West (1965)—1 spp.
Polygonaceae							
Polygonum pennsylvanicum (seeds)	10.5	2.3	21.3	62.4	3.4		Spinner and Bishop (1950)
						4,183 (GE)	Fredrickson and Taylor (1982)
						4,514 (GE)	Kendeigh and West (1965)
P. hydropiperoides (seeds)	8.4	1.9	20.1	57.9	2.0		Landers et al. (1976)
P. spp. (seeds)	9.1	2.7	17.2	58.5	2.8		Landers et al. (1976)—2 spp. av.
	9.5	2.2	18.3	66.5	3.5		Bardwell et al. (1962)—1 spp.
						4,715 (GE)	Kendeigh and West (1965)—2 spp. av.
Gramineae							
Panicum dichotomiflorum (seeds)	14.4	1.7	21.1	48.4	8.1		Landers et al. (1976)
	15.2	4.1	19.9	51.7	9.4		Bardwell et al. (1962)
						4,647 (GE)	Kendeigh and West (1965)
Echinochloa walteri (seeds)	17.2	4.2	13.2	49.9	7.2		Landers et al. (1976)
	16.3	3.6	14.2	61.4	4.4		Bardwell et al. (1962)
Najadaceae							
Ruppia maritima (foliage)	16.9		41.1			3,580 (GE)	Paulus (1980)
	15.1	1.9	22.8	46.5	14.4		Spinner and Bishop (1950)
	21.9	1.5	16.5	35.1	25.2		Swiderek (1982)
	16.6	2.5	15.0	41.8	24.1	3,410 (GE)	Sugden (1973)
						850 (ME)[b]	Sugden (1973)
(seeds)	7.8	2.9	35.2	51.0	3.1		Swiderek et al. (1988)
Characeae							
Chara hornemanii (foliage)	17.8	1.3	17.7	30.8	32.6		Swiderek (1982)
(tubercles)	2.1	0.7	1.0	95.8	0.4		Swiderek (1982)
Commelinaceae							
Aneilema keisak (seeds)	21.3	0.5	10.8	49.0	8.1		Landers et al. (1976)
Aizoaceae							
Sesuvium maritmum (seeds)	17.9	8.2	31.9	38.2	4.0		Swiderek (1982)
Invertebrates	31-80				3-71	3,700-6,970[c] (GE)	Driver et al. (1974)

[a]Gross energy.
[b]Metabolizable energy.
[c]Ash-free dry weight.

premigratory fat deposition. Widgeon grass, muskgrass foliage, fall panic grass, saltmarsh millet, Asiatic dayflower, and sea purslane seeds appear to have adequate levels of protein. Invertebrates are high in the essential amino acids (Driver et al. 1974) that are needed for molt as well as for replenishing protein reserves resulting from daily activities. Drobney (1977) suggested foraging time decreases when foods of high energy and low fiber content are selected, allowing more time for other activities. Paulus (1980) supported this hypothesis with evidence that feeding activity in gadwall decreased, and locomotor, comfort, and alert activities increased as levels of gross energy intake increased. Feeding activity, however, was negatively correlated with fiber content. An abundance of high quality foods in managed areas facilitates the acquisition of energy and other essential nutrients in a relatively short period of time.

Vegetative Structure.—White and James (1978) identified emergent vegetation as an important physical component separating wintering waterfowl species along a cline from heavily vegetated areas to open water. Mallard and wood duck, for example, are more secretive in behavior than most dabbling ducks and prefer flooded timber or dense emergent vegetation. In intermediate coastal marshes, mallard use small openings in dense stands of tall annual grasses, but prefer stands of saltmarsh bulrush in brackish zones. Gadwall and American wigeon are generally attracted to open areas with submergent vegetation. Teal and northern pintail seem intermediate in preference, occurring in open areas and in moderately dense stands of emergent vegetation.

Emergent vegetation provides concealment, loafing sites, and windbreaks. Salt grass mats are important resting sites for dabbling ducks in coastal South Carolina (Gray et al. 1987), especially in the lee of tall emergent vegetation. Additionally, these loafing areas allow ducks to rest out of water, facilitating energy conserving postures (Tamisier 1974, 1976). Mudflats or sandbars, if available, also serve as good loafing areas.

Water Depth.—Water depth regulates food availability and consequently dictates the occurrence of different waterfowl species (White and James 1978). In the SACZ, teal usually feed from exposed mudflats to depths of about 5-15 cm. Mallard and northern pintail use intermediate depths ranging from 15-35 cm, whereas American wigeon and gadwall feed in deeper water, provided submergent plants (e.g., widgeon grass) are <25 cm below the surface. Ring-necked duck and lesser scaup generally feed in areas over a wide range of water depths (i.e., >35 cm). Managers in coastal South Carolina have long recognized water depth as an effective management tool in controlling waterfowl use; fluctuations of 5-10 cm can influence waterfowl use of an area. Managers can either deeply flood or drawdown specific management areas to affect waterfowl use.

Drawdown of wetlands during late winter in preparation for the next growing season usually benefits dabbling ducks, wading birds, and shorebirds, because foods become available during drawdown. Additionally, aquatic invertebrates are concentrated as water levels recede.

Wetland Size and Juxtaposition.— Wetland size and location are important factors influencing waterfowl use. Related to these factors is disturbance. Presence of avian predators in the area does not appear to affect wetland use by waterfowl (D. H. Gordon, unpubl. data). However, human activity (e.g., excessive hunting pressure, heavy boat traffic) causes disturbance and will displace waterfowl. In the Pee Dee-Waccamaw river system of South Carolina, waterfowl heavily use small (<40 ha), managed freshwater wetlands diurnally before and after the waterfowl hunting season, but only nocturnally during the hunting season. This behavior is attributed to the high density of hunters in the area. Larger managed wetlands (>100 ha), with equal disturbance around the perimeter, hold ducks throughout the diurnal period if hunter density within the unit is properly managed. Waterfowl hunts on most managed wetlands in coastal South Carolina are limited to ≤2/week during mornings only, and the density of hunters is kept low. By minimizing disturbance, managers allow waterfowl more opportunity to meet physiological and behavioral needs.

Juxtaposition of managed wetlands relative to other important wetlands influences waterfowl use. Small, well-managed wetlands adjacent to large wintering areas are more likely to hold waterfowl than small, well-managed wetlands a long distance from large, important wintering areas. Additionally, having several managed wetlands in close proximity provides a diversity of habitats to waterfowl, better enabling them to meet their physiological needs.

HABITAT MANAGEMENT

Overview

Waterfowl habitat management in the SACZ is primarily limited to tidal freshwater and brackish marshes that have been diked for water-level control and is directed at enhancing the growth of natural wetland vegetation. Advantages of natural vegetation management include: (1) increased habitat diversity, (2) improved nutritional quality because of the variety of foods available, (3) cost-effective management, (4) the ability to manage larger areas, and (5) benefits to other wildlife and fish. Basically, wetland management in the SACZ endeavors to be complementary to the adaptations and life histories of plant species valuable to waterfowl.

Although transition zones between tidal freshwater, brackish, and salt marshes exist (Penfound and Hathaway 1938,

Gresham and Hook 1982), management procedures have been described for biota associated with 4 or 5 distinct marsh types (Palmisano 1972a, Wilkinson 1984). Along the south Atlantic coast, tidal freshwater, brackish, and salt marsh often are dominated by a single emergent species (southern wildrice, giant cordgrass, and smooth cordgrass, respectively); however, transitional types (intermediate and brackish salt marsh) are composed of species endemic to marshes of both lower and higher salinities (Penfound and Hathaway 1938, Palmisano 1972b). Certain species serve as indicators of transitional communities, such as American bulrush, which occurs in intermediate marshes (Penfound 1952). Indicator species are useful in the characterization of marsh types for waterfowl habitat management. Because plant communities in unmanaged marshes provide a direct indication of management potential for specific sites (Table 4), knowledge of transitional marsh types insures predictable responses to specific management procedures.

Water-level manipulation is the most important wetland management technique used. However, several hydrologic and seasonal variables govern water-level manipulation schedules. Important hydrologic variables include duration and frequency of flooding, water depth, salinity, turbidity, water temperature, and dissolved oxygen within and outside the impoundment. Seasonal factors include variations in local weather patterns, tide schedules, and lunar phases.

Wind direction and velocity influence tidal amplitudes affecting water-management capabilities and schedules. For example, salinity concentrations between 1 and 20 ppt normally affect management in brackish areas, but extreme variations in water salinity can occur due to annual and seasonal variations in weather. Strong northeasterly winds with new-moon and full-moon tides tend to

Table 4. Recognized coastal wetland types and dominant flora in the Santee River Estuary, South Carolina.

Wetland type	Water salinity (ppt)	Dominant plant species	
		Unmanaged marsh	Managed marsh
Fresh marsh	<1	*Zizaniopsis miliacea* *Alternanthera philoxeroides* *Polygonum* spp. *Pontederia cordata* *Sagittaria* spp. *Peltandra virginica* *Taxodium distichum* *Nyssa* spp.	*Polygonum punctatum* *Polygonum arifolium* *Panicum dichotomiflorum* *Aneilema keisak* *Cyperus* spp.
Intermediate marsh	1-5	*Zizaniopsis miliacea* *Spartina cynosuroides* *Typha angustifolia* *Scirpus validus* *Scirpus americanus* *Scirpus robustus*	*Panicum dichotomiflorum* *Echinochloa walteri* *Scirpus robustus* *Setaria magna* *Polygonum punctatum* *Cyperus* spp.
Brackish marsh	5-20	*Spartina cynosuroides* *Scirpus robustus* *Spartina alterniflora*	*Scirpus robustus* *Eleocharis parvula* *Ruppia maritima* *Leptochloa fascicularis*
Brackish/salt marsh	20-30	*Spartina alterniflora* *Spartina cynosuroides* *Juncus roemerianus*	*Ruppia maritima* *Eleocharis parvula* *Sesuvium maritimum*
Salt marsh	30-35	*Spartina alterniflora*	*Ruppia maritima* *Sesuvium maritimum*

increase estuarine and river salinities. Decreased river flows during drought periods allow salt water intrusion farther upstream, resulting in increased salinity in estuarine waters. Conversely, excessive rainfalls during the growing season and freshets can dilute salinities in managed areas and the adjacent tidewaters. Thus, managers must respond to these dynamic habitat conditions and implement appropriate management tactics.

Management Techniques

Management objectives determine where dike and ditch construction should occur and the required number and optimal placement of water-control structures. The potential for water-level manipulation and mixing of tidewaters of varying salinity for flooding a particular area are integral to effective wetland management. Salinity gradients vary with the amount of fresh water entering a system due to river flow, rainfall, and amplitude of lunar tides. Monthly variation in tidal amplitudes, which range from below mean low water to above mean high water, enhance water circulation and mixing and facilitate complete flooding and drainage of an area.

Dikes constructed and maintained by dragline dredges or hydraulic trackhoes are frequently constructed atop remnant ricefield dikes. The tops of dikes are generally at least 1 m above mean high water to withstand all but storm surges during hurricanes and catastrophic floods. Williams (1987) provided a detailed description of dike specifications and construction procedures.

Although a variety of metal and wood water-control structures are used in the SACZ (Williams 1987), unique to the SACZ is a structure known as a "trunk" (Doar 1936, Heyward 1937) that connects impoundments with surrounding tidal

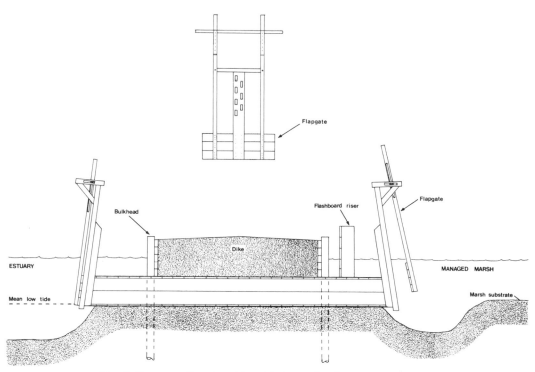

Fig. 8. Cross-sectional and frontal views of a rice trunk in a dike.

wetlands (Fig. 8). This structure was designed specifically for water manipulation in tidal wetlands. The device permits a variety or combination of incremental settings of doors and flash-board-riser heights so as to manage or circulate water levels within an impoundment. Spillways or flash-board-riser boxes serve as automatic metering devices that discharge excess headwater on each low tide. Properly adjusted trunks will control water levels automatically as the tide rises and ebbs. Rigid trunk-monitoring schedules (including water-salinity checks) must be maintained so adjustments can be made in response to daily and seasonal variations in tidal amplitude and site-specific hydrologic situations. During intensive periods of water manipulation, trunks may need to be checked or adjusted daily; otherwise, a minimum weekly schedule can be maintained.

Trunks should be installed with the bottom of the structure at/or 10-15 cm below the mean low water mark to facilitate complete drainage and maximum reflooding potential. Trunks should be well sealed into dikes with clay soils and secured with a bulkhead (Williams 1987). Proper trunk location is crucial. Consideration must be given to the varying freshness or salinity of tidal waters that may occur along the tidal perimeter of the dike. At least one water-control structure should be installed for each 61 ha under management for optimum flooding and draining (P. M. Wilkinson, pers. commun.).

The potential for drainage also allows for burning, mowing, mechanical disturbance, and/or herbicide application. Of these techniques, burning is most important and widely used. Burning is desirable for several reasons (Yancey 1964): (1) plant succession is affected, and growth of herbaceous plants that are good seed producers is promoted; (2) extensive stands of dense vegetation are broken up, creating open water areas after flooding; (3) seeds are released to the marsh floor where they become available for water-fowl; (4) seed germination may be enhanced (Martin and Cushwa 1966, Landers 1981); and (5) burning eliminates "sour marsh" conditions caused when rank, green vegetation is flooded and decomposed.

Fall burning is most frequent and is generally a scheduled step in the annual management scenario for tidal freshwater and intermediate marshes. Fall burns prepare the marsh for flooding by creating a desirable interspersion of cover and water. Hot, clean burns should be avoided as they remove emergent cover and create too much open water. During warm, wet fall months, burning should not be attempted until after a "killing" frost. First frost along the South Carolina and Georgia coast usually occurs in late November or early December. If October and early November are cool and dry, plant maturity and senescence may occur earlier, permitting burning prior to frost.

Spring burns are prescribed only in specific situations, primarily to control plants competing with target species. Marshes burned in the spring are typically drained in late February or early March for several weeks. A hot, clean burn over a very dry marsh bed may be desirable in spring. "Root burns" at this time of year can help eliminate competing plants.

Usually 3-5 days with low to moderate humidity are recommended before burning. Winds should not exceed 18.5 km/hr on the day of burning. Fires are typically set using a drip torch. A patchy or streaky burn can be accomplished by setting fires in 20-40 m strips, skipping strips of equal length. There are advantages and disadvantages to using either a headfire or backfire, but their relevance varies with specific site and situational factors. In dense vegetation, backfires may be preferred because of the high fuel load and potential for a clean burn using a headfire. Headfires are effective in sparse

vegetation (low fuel load) that is not capable of carrying a backfire. Large areas can be burned in less time using head-fires, but unless weather and site conditions are right, more vegetation than desired can be burned. The key elements in achieving successful marsh burns with predictable results are caution, experience, and evaluation of results.

Tidal Freshwater Marsh

Target Plant Species/Communities.—Generally 4-5 plant species codominate managed tidal freshwater wetlands (Tiner 1977). Smartweeds, Asiatic dayflower, spikerushes, and various grasses and sedges can be successfully managed in tidal freshwater wetlands (Baldwin 1956, Morgan 1974). These species respond best to moist-soil management in wetlands having soils of moderate acidity (pH 4-5) and moderate to high mineral content (Percival 1968). Redroot is adapted to soils of high organic matter and acidity where soil moisture is high throughout the growing season. Dominant species in managed deepwater, or semipermanently flooded situations include white water-lily (*Nymphaea odorata*), yellow pond lily, water-shield and coontail (*Ceratophyllum demersum*).

Typical Annual Management.—Moist-soil management in tidal freshwater wetlands begins in late winter or early spring as most waterfowl begin to leave the region (Table 5). At this time, the marsh is dewatered and allowed to dry. Spring drawdown prevents persistent emergents (e.g., Virginia arrowarum and golden club) from becoming established or competing with target species. Delaying drawdown until early summer (June) may encourage an undesirable, highly competitive growth of southern wildrice (Larimer 1982). Late February drawdown promotes optimum smartweed and Asiatic dayflower production. Generally, the marsh bed is irrigated during the last week of April, and desired soil moisture

Table 5 Water management regimes and associated plant communities in southeastern coastal impoundments.

Marsh zone	Water management	Food plants	Competing/cover plants
Fresh marsh (<1 ppt)	Early-spring drawdown with saturated alluvial soils; late-fall flooding to $\bar{x}$ depth of 22 cm.	Polygonum punctatum P. hydropiperoides P. arifolium P. sagittatum Aneilema keisak Eleocharis quadrangulata Scirpus validus Peltandra virginica	Zizaniopsis miliacea Typha latifolia Scirpus cyperinus Juncus effusus Alternanthera philoxeroides
	Early-spring drawdown with moist-dry alluvial soils; late-fall flooding to $\bar{x}$ depth of 22 cm.	Panicum dichotomiflorum Echinochloa crusgalli Cyperus spp.	Erianthus giganteus Eupatorium capillifolium Sesbania exalta Erechtites hieracifolia Ambrosia artemisiifolia
	Early-spring drawdown with moist-saturated organic soils; late-fall flooding to $\bar{x}$ depth of 22 cm.	Lacnanthes caroliniana Panicum verrucosum Polygonum spp. Cyperus spp. Panicum spp.	Cladium jamaicense Centella asiatica Liquidambar styraciflua Persea borbonia Acer rubrum Cyrilla racemiflora
	Semipermanently flooded to depths of 15-122 cm.	Eleocharis quadrangulata E. equisetoides Brasenia schreberi Nymphaea odorata Ceratophyllum demersum Najas spp. Chara spp. Potamogeton spp.	Panicum hemitomon Zizaniopsis miliacea Typha latifolia Alternanthera philoxeroides Ludwigia spp. Nuphar spp. Nelumbo lutea Nymphoides spp. Cabomba carolina Utricularia spp. Myriophyllum heterophyllum
Intermediate marsh (1-5 ppt)	Early-spring drawdown with saturated alluvial soils; late-fall flooding to $\bar{x}$ depth of 22 cm.	Scirpus robustus Scirpus validus Echinochloa walteri Polygonum punctatum	Spartina cynosuroides Typha angustifolia Alternanthera philoxeroides
	Early-spring drawdown with moist-dry alluvial soils; late-fall flooding to $\bar{x}$ depth of 22 cm.	Panicum dichotomiflorum Setaria magna Cyperus spp.	Aster spp. Erechtites hieracifolia Spartina cynosuroides Sesbania exalta Baccharis halimifolia
	Early-spring drawdown with moist-saturated organic soils; late-fall flooding to $\bar{x}$ depth of 22 cm.	Lacnanthes caroliniana Scirpus robustus Panicum spp. Cyperus spp. Echinochloa walteri Setaria magna	Cladium jamaicense Typha angustifolia Spartina cynosuroides
Brackish marsh (5-20 ppt)	Early-spring drawdown with saturated alluvial and/or organic soils; late-spring/early-summer complete drawdown; early-/midsummer reflooding with gradual increase in water depth, fall lowering of water levels to 22 cm.	Scirpus robustus Ruppia maritima Eleocharis parvula Leptochloa fascicularis Sesuvium maritimum	Spartina cynosuroides Spartina bakeri Spartina patens Typha angustifolia Typha domingensis Distichlis spicata Juncus roemerianus Scirpus olneyi

Table 5.—Continued

Marsh zone	Water management	Food plants	Competing/cover plants
Brackish/salt marsh (20-30 ppt)	Early-spring drawdown with saturated alluvial and/or organic soils; late-spring/early-summer complete drawdown; early/midsummer reflooding with gradual increase in water depth; fall lowering of water levels to 22 cm.	*Ruppia maritima* *Eleocharis parvula* *Sesuvium maritimum*	*Spartina alterniflora* *Juncus roemerianus* *Distichlis spicata*
Salt marsh (30-35 ppt)	Semipermanently flooded to depths of 15-122 cm. Flooded with water salinity <5 ppt.	*Nymphaea mexicana* *Potamogeton pectinatus* *Najas quadalupensis* *Chara* spp.	*Typha domingensis* *Typha angustifolia* *Scirpus californicus* *Nelumbo lutea*
	Early-spring complete drawdown with alluvial soils; midspring reflooding to sustained depths of 61 cm; fall lowering of water levels to $\bar{x}$ depth of 22 cm.	*Ruppia maritima* *Eleocharis parvula*	*Spartina alterniflora* *Juncus roemerianus* *Distichlis spicata*
	Early-spring complete draw down with muck soils; midspring reflooding to sustained depths of 61 cm; fall lowering of water levels to $\bar{x}$ depth of 22 cm.	*Chara hornemannii* *Ruppia maritima*	*Spartina alterniflora*
	Early-spring drawdown with moist organic soils; late-summer/early-fall reflooding to $\bar{x}$ depth of 22 cm.	*Sesuvium maritimum* *Ruppia maritima*	*Spartina alterniflora* *Distichlis spicata* *Salicornia* spp. *Pluchea purpurascens* *Aster subulatus* *Aster tenuifolius*

is maintained throughout the growing season. Grasses and sedges can be encouraged by maintaining relatively drier soils. Smartweeds and spikerushes are encouraged by high soil moisture.

Water circulation, accomplished by twice daily exchange of tidal water in and out of an impoundment, is preferred for managing tidal freshwater wetlands (Fig. 9). Moist-soil management employing water circulation requires careful adjustment of trunk doors and flash-board risers for proper water management. Water exchange in and out of an impoundment enhances water quality and dissolved nutrient and detrital export. Soil moisture can be regulated by static water-level maintenance (no water exchange)

throughout the growing season, but continual degradation of impoundment water quality and more rapid growth of emergent vegetation (which obstructs water flow in perimeter ditches and drainage networks) will occur.

Occasionally, a few cm of sheet water may cover the impoundment bed for a few days because of heavy rainfall, unusually high tides, or improperly adjusted or malfunctioning water-control structures. Normally this is not a problem unless flooding occurs in early spring when young plants can be killed. If shallowly flooded in summer, vegetation can be killed when direct sunlight and high ambient temperatures cause high water temperatures and "blanch" plants. In

Fig. 9. Water circulation in managed tidal fresh marsh. Inside flapgate of trunk is pushed open by water flow associated with morning high tide in April.

either case, plant production over extensive areas can be lost; although with subsequent drawdown, there may be time for germination and growth of other annuals.

In early September, moist-soil impoundments are drained (water level about 10 cm below marsh bed) to remove surface water and hasten plant senescence in preparation for burning. The marsh bed should not be excessively dried or a root burn may result. Once the desirable interspersion of cover and water is created by burning, impoundments are immediately flooded and maintained at an average depth of 22 cm, the optimum depth for attracting ducks.

If moist-soil conditions are maintained for several years, common cattail (*Typha latifolia*), woolgrass bulrush (*Scirpus cyperinus*), and southern wildrice can become established. If drier soils are maintained for several years, plume grass (*Erianthus giganteus*), dog-fennel (*Eupatorium capillifolium*), goldenrod (*Solidago* spp.), and asters (*Aster* spp.) can become dominant. Moist and dry soils should be alternated to reduce the abundance of these species and to maintain a more desirable plant community.

Tidal freshwater wetlands having organic, acidic soils can be managed for redroot. Redroot production requires moderate soil moisture throughout the growing season. Redroot often grows in association with smartweed and warty panicum (*Panicum verrucosum*), although smartweed production in organic soils is often insignificant. A redroot management scenario (Table 5) follows a late-February or early-March drawdown to allow oxidation for several weeks. Rotary cultivation or disking is usually recommended for certain portions of impounded acreage on at least a 3-year rotation. Rotary cultivation spreads rhizomes and also releases previously unavailable nutrients. Stands that are not subjected to soil disturbance lose vigor and become dominated by less desirable plant species. If rotary cultivation is not planned, soils can be moistened in middle to late April. Saw grass (*Cladium jamaicense*) is often the principal competing species in fresh wetlands with organic soil. Saw grass can be retarded by avoiding standing water and saturated soil.

The alternative to moist-soil management in tidal freshwater marshes is deepwater (0.6-1.0 m) or semipermanently flooded management (Table 5). Wetlands managed in this manner must have dikes capable of holding deep water and adequate control structures. Moist-soil impoundments can be converted to deepwater management. Initially, such wetlands are burned in late winter and flooded to maximum depth. Trunks are maintained in the flooding position at all times during spring through fall to accumulate all possible tidewater inflow. Flash-board risers are set to retain all rainfall. Golden club and Virginia arrowarum usually become established in early spring and dominate throughout the growing season. Late in the growing season in deeper areas and ditches, white water-lily, yellow pondlily, water-shield, coontail, bushypondweed, and curly-leaf pondweed (*Potamogeton crispus*) become established. Water depths >61 cm tend to discourage establishment of common cattail and southern wildrice.

Advantages to converting freshwater wetlands to deepwater management include (1) increased wetland habitat diversity; (2) provision of production habitat for wood ducks, common moorhens (*Gallinula chloropus*), and mottled ducks (*Anas fulvigula*); and (3) benefits to other wildlife dependent on permanent water. A disadvantage of deepwater management is the increase of organic accumulations. In highly productive wetlands systems, this can promote eutrophication. Organic matter can float to the surface in areas that remain flooded for several successive years. This problem can be avoided by keeping impoundments dry from February through June every 3 to 4 years and implementing moist-soil management for at least 1 growing season. Prior to returning to deepwater management such areas should be burned in late winter.

Management Variations.—Each impoundment has unique characteristics that dictate management variations. Some target species in tidal freshwater wetlands respond well to and tend to be most productive after disturbance. Burning is the most commonly prescribed technique for disturbance (Conrad 1966, Morgan 1974), but it is not recommended for management of redroot due to risk of a peat fire, subsequent loss of organic matter, and eventual subsidence of the marsh bed. Because elevation is often critical in marsh management, every effort should be made to prevent bed subsidence. Other disturbance techniques include mowing (Neely 1968), livestock grazing (Neely 1968, Morgan et al. 1975), and disking (Baldwin 1968, Neely 1968, Percival et al. 1970, Morgan 1974).

Generally, management of competing vegetation is met by water management designed for target species. However, hemp sesbania (*Sesbania exaltata*) often invades and tends to be stimulated by spring burning and late (April-May) drawdown. Control methods include mowing immediately prior to seed maturation (Prevost 1987).

Brackish Marsh

Target Plant Species/Communities.—In the brackish zone, 3 salinity regimes and associated plant communities should be identified for management purposes. Where salinities are between 1-5 ppt (intermediate marsh), the focus should be on moist-soil management (Table 5). In the 5-20 ppt zone (brackish marsh) and 20-30 ppt zone (brackish-salt marsh), management should focus on submersed aquatics and certain persistent emergents.

Intermediate marshes support vegetation characteristic of the fresh-brackish marsh transition zone. Managed intermediate marsh usually supports fall panic grass, saltmarsh millet, saltmarsh bulrush, flatsedges, dotted smartweed (*Polygonum punctatum*), and giant foxtail (*Setaria magna*).

In brackish marshes, widgeon grass, saltmarsh bulrush, and dwarf spikerush are the principal species. Sprangletop (*Leptochloa fascicularis*) may occur sporadically. Widgeon grass, dwarf spikerush, and sea purslane are the principal plants encouraged in brackish-saline wetlands.

Typical Annual Management.—Water levels in managed intermediate marsh are lowered gradually during late winter (late February) and early spring, and moist-soil conditions are maintained through September (Table 5). Water levels in perimeter ditches 10 cm below the marsh floor are adequate to maintain moist-soil conditions. Water-control structures are adjusted to maintain water circulation in ditches providing tidewater salinities do not exceed 5-7 ppt.

During spring drawdown, saltmarsh bulrush often exhibits vernal dominance. Later, stands of saltmarsh millet, fall panic grass, dotted smartweed, flat sedges, and giant foxtail become established (Fig. 10). Drawdowns with excessive soil drying

Fig. 10. Intermediate marsh in early June. After burning and flooding in late November, sites dominated by dense flatsedge stands (foreground) will be openwater areas separated by tall emergents such as giant cordgrass (background).

favor growth of giant cordgrass, fireweed (*Erechtites hieracifolia*), and asters. Conversely, excessive soil moisture or shallow flooding may promote undesirable species including alligator-weed (*Alternanthera philoxeroides*), narrow-leaved cattail (*Typha angustifolia*), southern cattail (*T. domingensis*), and southern wildrice.

After the growing season, water levels in managed intermediate marsh are lowered, and the marsh bed is dried. Following vegetation senescence, the marsh is burned and flooded to a depth of 20-30 cm. When burning is incomplete or where dense vegetation persists, it may be desirable to flood the area with as much as 50 cm of water and gradually decrease water levels to 20-30 cm as waterfowl use increases. Deeper flooding and gradual lowering of water levels causes standing vegetation to weaken and fall, thereby increasing food availability.

Annual water management in brackish marsh begins with a drawdown in March or April until a saturated soil condition is achieved (Table 5). During this period, saltmarsh bulrush usually becomes established. Brackish marsh soils are kept saturated and are not allowed to dry to prevent acidification or cat-clay formation (Edelman and Von Staveren 1958, Neely 1958, Czyscinski 1975). Periodic rains in April prevent excessive drying, although occasional flushing of tidal waters through the area is necessary. Draining for 1-2 weeks in April allows marsh soils to stabilize and will minimize water turbidity when the area is reflooded.

Twice daily flushing (or circulating) of tidal waters through the area begins in May and continues until June. The marsh should be flooded to a depth of 15-20 cm with water in the salinity range of 5-15 ppt. Until mid-October, water levels

Fig. 11. Managed brackish marsh in mid-July. Raising water levels slowly throughout the growing season enhances growth of the emergent salt marsh bulrush and, in openwater areas, widgeon grass and dwarf spikerush.

are raised in 10-15 cm increments during new-moon and full-moon tides of each month to enhance the growth of widgeon grass, dwarf spikerush, and saltmarsh bulrush (Fig. 11). Scattered stands of sprangletop may occur in open areas at a lower elevation than where saltmarsh bulrush exists. Sprangletop and salt-marsh bulrush continue to grow after reflooding.

Water-control structures must be care-fully manipulated during the growing season. Salinity is monitored carefully during flooding, because levels >15 ppt will affect growth and seed production of saltmarsh bulrush adversely. Widgeon grass and dwarf spikerush, which grow best in open areas, tolerate higher salini-ties. Water circulation retards infestation of widgeon grass beds by filamentous algae (*Cladophora* spp.), which can shade and kill widgeon grass.

Excessive rainfall during the growing season may dilute salinity concentrations. Flash-board risers may be used to remove excess rainwaters during ebb tides. Con versely, retention of rainwater following drought, can offset high salinities that may have developed. After mid-October, water levels are gradually decreased to a mean depth of 22 cm.

Management Variations.—In interme-diate and brackish marshes, eradication of giant cordgrass is often necessary. Man-aged areas are drained and allowed to dry during February and March. When dry, giant cordgrass stands are burned with a hot fire. Burning of giant cordgrass, followed by flooding to depths of 30-60 cm from March to October, is an effective control measure (Prevost 1987). Coordina-tion of late-winter burning with a period of high tides facilitates rapid, deep flood-ing of cordgrass. Deep flooding following

burning or mechanical cutting of vegetation eliminates the exchange of oxygen to
rhizomes and kills the plant (Murkin and
Ward 1980, Kaminski et al. 1985). Control
of giant cordgrass necessitates the sacrifice
of the growing season.

Another method used to control giant
cordgrass involves deep flooding (30-60
cm) without burning. Although oxygen
exchange from the previous year's growth
to the rhizomes is not eliminated, cordgrass stands are reduced. Salinities >12
ppt also will inhibit giant cordgrass.
Other methods employed to eradicate
giant cordgrass include mowing and
compaction using an all-terrain marsh
masher, followed by deep flooding (Prevost 1987). Dense stands of saltmarsh
bulrush frequently become established
following burning or mechanical treatments (Palmisano 1967, Palmisano and
Newsom 1967).

Where water salinities range between 20
and 30 ppt, efforts are directed towards
production of widgeon grass and dwarf
spikerush. Water management regimes are
similar to those described for brackish
marshes with salinities of 5-20 ppt, but
high salinities severely limit growth of
desirable (e.g., saltmarsh bulrush) and
undesirable species (e.g., cattail, giant
cordgrass). Small stands of saltmarsh
bulrush that persist may increase temporarily in size during seasons of abundant
rainfall and accompanying lower salinities. The principal competing plant species in brackish-salt marshes are smooth
cordgrass and black needle rush. However, these 2 plants provide important
emergent structure around openwater
areas with widgeon grass and dwarf
spikerush.

Good seed production by saltmarsh
bulrush occurs in marshes with salinities
of 3-7 ppt (Neely 1962), but growth is
severely restricted at salinities >20 ppt
(Palmisano 1972a). Prolonged growing-
season droughts can interfere with brackish marsh management. Summer flooding

may be delayed for extended periods
because of high tidewater salinities during droughts. Soil salinities within
impoundments can increase as a result of
evaporative concentration of soluble salts.
Saltmarsh bulrush becomes stressed in
this situation, and culm and leaf production is greatly reduced or eliminated.
Under these conditions, sea purslane may
flourish in higher marsh zones normally
vegetated by saltmarsh bulrush. Managers
alert to these circumstances can adjust
management procedures to capitalize on
the production of sea purslane.

Management of brackish marshes <40
ha by typical management schedules often
results in extensive, dense stands of
saltmarsh bulrush lacking openwater
areas, which are not attractive to waterfowl. Flooding to depths of 46-61 cm for
an entire growing season will reduce
saltmarsh bulrush density, create openings, promote the growth of widgeon
grass and dwarf spikerush, and thereby
enhance waterfowl use.

Water temperature influences flooding
schedules for impoundments managed for
widgeon grass. Widgeon grass requires a
temperature range of 15-20 C for germination and seedling development and 20-25
C for vegetative growth and reproduction
(Setchell 1924). Joanen and Glasgow
(1965) noted that widgeon grass growth
began in February when water temperatures reached 18-19 C. Flowering and
fruiting were first observed in May when
water temperatures were 29-30 C. Growth
rate declined during summer, but growth
was noted again in September and ceased
in November. However, Swiderek (1982)
noted a resurgence of widgeon grass
growth in late August when water
temperatures were as high as 35 C.

In South Carolina, various reflooding
schedules ranging from March to early
October have yielded good widgeon grass
production. When reflooding was
initiated during March through May,
widgeon grass stands often would be

destroyed by filamentous algae or would die-off in late summer to early fall. Although widgeon grass seeds were produced when impoundments were flooded in the spring, vegetative parts were weak, and standing crops deteriorated in fall. However, when reflooding was delayed until late June or early July, excellent widgeon grass production occurred.

Salt grass may be controlled by using burning and deep-flooding techniques similar to those described for giant cordgrass control. Thompson (1981) reported common reed (*Phragmites communis*) may be controlled by burning and mowing followed by flooding to depths of 12-13 cm. Compaction and subsequent flooding of common reed stands also have been identified as effective control methods (Clay and Suprenant 1987). In coastal South Carolina, common reed has been effectively controlled by cutting it down to the marsh floor followed by flooding to depths of 45-60 cm for a single growing season (Prevost 1987). If water-level manipulation and/or mechanical methods are not proving effective for controlling common reed, herbicide applications (Rodeo or Amitrol-T) during early-flowering stages can control the species, but with varying success.

In brackish-salt marshes with salinities of 20-30 ppt, open ponds often are invaded by extensive stands of sea purslane during extended spring drawdowns. In such instances, saturated soils should be maintained until sea purslane has matured (late July to early August) before flooding for widgeon grass and dwarf spikerush production. Flooding as late as August or September may still produce good crops of widgeon grass and dwarf spikerush (Neely 1962, Prevost 1987). However, smooth cordgrass gradually increases in successive years regardless of specific water-management regimes. Complete drawdown for an entire growing season will effectively control smooth cordgrass, and dead stems may be

removed by burning. Such prolonged drawdowns, however, often result in reduced soil pH, temporarily precluding plant growth.

Efforts to correct soil conditions in brackish marshes that have been drained for 5 years indicate that repeated flooding and drawdown can be successful in elevating soil pH to levels supporting desirable plants (Neely 1962). Neely (1962) concluded pHs of about 4 or 5, respectively, were necessary for growth of dwarf spikerush and widgeon grass; however, he cautioned that a rapid transition to alkaline conditions may result in precipitation of ferric hydroxide. Joanen and Glasgow (1965) found that soils with pH values averaging 5.8-7.0 supported good stands of widgeon grass. These results are consistent with numerous field observations of plant responses to various water-management schedules throughout the SACZ. They suggest that a gradual exchange of water is the most desirable method to encourage dwarf spikerush and widgeon grass in marshes that have been subjected to prolonged drawdowns. A continuous partial exchange or 2-3 complete changes of water at 4- to 6-week intervals during the growing season generally produces satisfactory results. However, the rate of water exchange will vary according to physical and chemical factors associated with individual situations.

SALT MARSH

The value of salt marshes as migration and wintering habitat for most waterfowl species has been considered to be minimal in the southeastern United States (Palmisano 1972a, Johnson et al. 1974, Chabreck 1979). In South Carolina, however, well-defined management procedures have been developed to encourage plant communities providing food and cover for waterfowl.

Target Plant Species/Communities.— Widgeon grass may be grown on mineral or organic soils in marshes that can be flooded to depths of 46 cm. Although widgeon grass will tolerate water salinities >35 ppt, vegetative growth and seed production are reduced in high salinities (Martin and Uhler 1939, Mayer and Low 1970, Swiderek 1982). Gulf Coast muskgrass may be encouraged on muck soils. In marshes containing organic soils, sea purslane can be grown through summer drawdown management as discussed in the previous section. Sea purslane is the only seed-producing plant in southeastern marshes that can be encouraged by drawdown in marshes of high soil salinity. Semipermanently flooded salt marsh sloughs with remnant creek channels containing soft mud produce banana waterlily and certain desirable species of submersed aquatics [e.g., sago pondweed (*Potamogeton pectinatus*), bushy pondweed, and muskgrass].

Typical Annual Management.—Management procedures for widgeon grass in salt marsh zones are similar to those in brackish marshes (Table 5). However, certain modifications are required to maintain water salinities between 10 and 20 ppt for optimum biomass production (Neely 1960, Baldwin 1968, Morgan et al. 1975). Following annual or biennial spring drawdown, reflooding is initiated in late March to mid-April when salinities are generally lower in tidal creeks. Water levels are maintained at 30-60 cm. Large (≥40 ha) impoundments or impoundment complexes with multiple control structures can be reflooded from structures located up the estuary where salinities typically are less. In late spring and summer, adjusting water-control structures to dilute salinity following rainfall assists in maintaining desired salinity levels. During spring, summer, and early fall, water-control structures are adjusted to circulate tidal water through the marsh to minimize high water temperatures and algal blooms.

Salt marsh impoundments often are characterized by unstable soils and high water turbidity associated with sediments rich in reduced organic materials. Joanen and Glasgow (1965) stressed the importance of properly timed drawdowns to stabilize soils, minimize water turbidity to enhance widgeon grass germination and growth, and to minimize uprooting of widgeon grass seedlings by wave action. In South Carolina, a complete drawdown of 2-4 weeks in early spring generally achieves substrate oxidation without resulting in excessive acidification, which temporarily precludes plant growth (Edelman and Van Staveren 1958, Neely 1958). A late-summer or early-fall drawdown also may be practiced when widgeon grass is destroyed by filamentous algae (Prevost et al. 1978) or succumbs to late-summer die-offs (Percival et al. 1970, Swiderek 1982). In several instances involving fall reflooding, salinities have been reduced by rainfall from tropical storms and excellent widgeon grass production has resulted. As prolonged periods of sustained flooding reduce emergent growth, drawdowns of proper duration also perpetuate the desired interspersion of open water and emergents (e.g., smooth cordgrass and black needle rush).

Gulf Coast muskgrass thrives in certain salt marshes with muck soils and salinities favorable for widgeon grass (Table 5). In South Carolina, water temperature, pH, and hardness are similar in both Gulf Coast muskgrass and widgeon grass impoundments (Swiderek 1982); both plants coexist in coastal impoundments (R. L. Joyner and P. M. Wilkinson, pers. commun.). Muskgrass exhibits a greater tolerance to periods of high salinity, the ability to better withstand wave action and turbidity, and to compete more successfully with filamentous algae than widgeon grass. However, consistent, successful management of this species is limited by a lack of specific information concerning its life history (Swiderek 1982).

Optimum establishment and growth of sea purslane occurs on soils of high

Fig. 12. Managed salt marsh in mid-April. Sea purslane, dwarf spikerush, and saltmarsh bulrush can occur and be managed as codominants (foreground) given the occurrence of abundant rainfall during a mid-spring drawdown.

organic matter, whereas attempts to manage for sea purslane on heavy clay soils have resulted in cat-clay conditions (Swiderek 1982). The typical management schedule involves an early to mid-spring drawdown for germination and growth and early-fall flooding to make seeds available for waterfowl. In years of abundant rainfall, desirable brackish marsh plants, including saltmarsh bulrush, sprangletop, and dwarf spikerush may also become codominant (Fig. 12). However, this management strategy, if practiced for several successive growing seasons, results in a gradual increase in saltmarsh asters, sand spurrey (*Spergularia marina*), glassworts (*Salicornia europaea, S. bigelovii*), camphorweed (*Pluchea purpurascens*), salt grass, and smooth cordgrass. Efforts to minimize growth of these species by varying drawdown dates suggest that delaying drawdown until late May retards growth

of competing vegetation and allows for excellent sea purslane production.

Management Variations.—Although non food producing emergents such as salt grass and smooth cordgrass enhance habitat diversity, resting sites, and cover, such species may increase and limit food production. Therefore, after several seasons of drawdown for sea purslane management, marshes should be flooded for several growing seasons to reduce coverage of non food producing emergents and promote widgeon grass. Salt grass may be effectively controlled by late-fall or winter burning followed by flooding to depths of 30-60 cm for an entire growing season.

Another option involves early-spring drawdown for sea purslane, followed by late-summer or fall flooding for widgeon grass production (Table 5). This procedure results in a double-cropping of plant foods and diversified nutritional resources within a single management unit.

Depending on the timing of flooding and water salinity, widgeon grass biomass and seed production may be reduced due to an abbreviated growing season. However, filamentous algae competition and summer die-offs generally are avoided.

Banana waterlily grows in certain managed salt marshes that have been flooded and maintained as deepwater areas with water salinities <5 ppt (Table 5). Salinities are maintained within tolerance limits by rainfall, runoff, and late-winter tidal flooding when salinities may be compatible for banana waterlily growth. This management is most often associated with barrier islands having diked salt marsh creek channels and sloughs with soft mud soils and alkaline waters. Desirable submersed aquatics commonly growing in association with banana waterlily include sago pondweed, bushy pondweed, and muskgrass. Banana waterlily rootstocks will survive occasional inundation with saline water; consequently, competing vegetation such as southern and narrow-leaved cattail and bullwhip bulrush (*Scirpus californicus*) may be effectively controlled by periodic flooding with high salinity water (Baldwin 1968, Cely 1979).

RESEARCH NEEDS

Intensive wetland management requires impounding wetlands so wetland hydrology can be manipulated. When done properly, wetland manipulations result in functional and productive wetlands, but often with plant and animal communities different from the preimpoundment state. Coastal wetland impoundments are perceived by some groups as unnecessary modifications to existing wetlands that impose substantial harm to wildlife, fin fish, and shellfish resources. Although these ''harmful'' effects are largely unsubstantiated with scientific evidence, the widespread perception of their existence has led to conservative government policies and regulations that essentially prohibit

wetland impoundment and subsequent management in the region. Research is needed to provide a more comprehensive understanding of the structure and function of tidal freshwater and brackish wetland ecosystems and to evaluate the effects of existing wetland management practices on these systems. This information will promote the design of wetland impoundment systems and development of management practices that will insure wise use of SACZ wetlands, minimizing adverse impacts to wetlands dependent species.

A better understanding of migrating and wintering waterfowl habitat requirements is needed. Accurate descriptions of preferred habitats and their functional significance (i.e., use for feeding, resting, pairing, etc.) to various species should be developed. Fundamental descriptive habitat-use studies are needed for certain species. Studies that elucidate the role of microhabitat features in waterfowl habitat selection and their relevance to wetland management will promote a continual refinement of management practices, enhancing the overall quality of available wetland habitats.

Although plant seed production was the initial emphasis in waterfowl habitat management, the importance of foliage, tubers, shoots, and invertebrates is recognized in a modern approach. However, there is a need for well-designed food habits studies in the SACZ to determine the relative importance of food resources available to migrating and wintering waterfowl. At present, due to the methodology of previous food habits studies, the importance of invertebrate and other soft food items to SACZ waterfowl is not well understood. Studies of the ecology of invertebrate communities in managed wetland systems also are needed.

Plant ecology studies are needed to better understand the life histories of wetland plant species and ecotypic variations that may exist. Both descriptive and experimental studies are required to better determine the influence of environmental factors on the germination, growth, and distribution of plants in managed wetlands, particularly those factors manipulated by wetland management.

SUMMARY

A modern perspective of waterfowl habitat management recognizes that habitat selection by waterfowl is a complex phenomenon, based on the fulfillment of biological needs of each species. The primary objective of SACZ waterfowl habitat management is to provide wetland habitats to accommodate the needs of migrating and wintering waterfowl. Management manipulations aim to provide spatially and temporally heterogeneous habitats that include a diversity of food resources in a mosaic of desirable physical habitat features.

Waterfowl habitat management in the SACZ has evolved to a level of sophistication that recognizes the value of wetland function and diversity. Inherent differences among wetland types have led to the development of management procedures that benefit diverse plant and animal communities. When practiced correctly, waterfowl habitat management is multiple-objective wildlife enhancement.

SACZ wetland management is predicated upon the enhancement of natural wetland vegetation communities, specifically the response of target plant species to environmental manipulations. Hydrologic manipulations are most important and are facilitated by tide-operated water-control structures unique to the region. Waterfowl habitat management in the SACZ primarily occurs in tidal freshwater and brackish marshes that have been diked for water-level control.

Tidal freshwater marsh typically is managed in 2 ways. Moist-soil management is most common and entails a growing season drawdown where moist to saturated soils are maintained to encourage growth of smartweeds, spikerushes, Asiatic day-flower, and various sedges and grasses. Fall burning followed by winter flooding creates an interspersion of cover and water attractive to ducks. The alternative approach is deepwater or semipermanently flooded management. Marshes maintained under this water regime encourage growth of various floating-leaved and submersed aquatic plants.

Brackish marsh management is more complex. Combinations of seasonally timed water-level and water salinity manipulations are used to promote growth of salt-tolerant plant communities attractive to waterfowl in 3 salinity zones. Fresh-brackish or intermediate marsh (1-5 ppt) is managed for various annual grasses and sedges under a moist soil management regime similar to tidal freshwater marsh. Management in brackish marsh (5-20 ppt) and brackish-salt marsh (20-30 ppt) involves an early-spring drawdown during which saturated soils are maintained for several weeks. Water levels are then incrementally raised throughout the growing season, promoting growth of certain submersed aquatic (e.g., widgeon grass and dwarf spikerush) and emergent (e.g., saltmarsh bulrush) plants.

Management of salt marsh is limited in the SACZ, but some well-defined management procedures have been developed where opportunities exist. Management procedures to promote widgeon grass in salt marsh zones are similar to those in brackish marshes. Gulf Coast muskgrass can be encouraged in certain situations where muck soils exist. Growth of sea purslane can be promoted by a mid-spring drawdown on specific sites having highly organic soils. Fall flooding makes the seeds of this plant available to waterfowl.

The extensive coastal wetlands of the SACZ have been subject to intensive management since the late 18th century. Man's initial, large-scale alteration and manipulation of wetlands for rice production established a regional tradition of wetland ownership and management, and created the sites and technology for waterfowl habitat management procedures. These events, coupled with historically abundant SACZ waterfowl populations, have provided the impetus for property owners and resource agencies to acquire, maintain, and create managed wetlands for waterfowl.

Although a high value is currently placed on SACZ wetlands, they are increasingly threatened by residential, urban, and industrial development, navigational projects, recreational activities, pollution, and commercialization of wetland resources. Continued government and private ownership of SACZ wetlands coupled with a holistic perspective of wetland ecology and management are key elements to the future existence of quality habitat for SACZ waterfowl populations.

LITERATURE CITED

Adams, D. A. 1963. Factors influencing vascular plant zonation in North Carolina salt marshes. Ecology 44:445-456.

Aichele, R. 1984. An addendum to "an inventory of South Carolina's coastal marshes." S.C. Coastal Council, Charleston. 4 pp.

Anonymous. 1942. Lower Santee River, South Carolina: survey report to determine the effects of diversion on navigation, irrigation and wildlife. U.S. Eng. Off., Charleston, S.C. 45 pp.

Baldwin, W. P. 1950. Recent advances in managing coastal plain impoundments for waterfowl. Proc. Annu. Conf. Southeast. Assoc. Game and Fish Comm. (Mimeogr. Rep.). 11 pp.

———. 1956. Food supply key to attracting ducks. S.C. Wildl. 3:5-12.

———. 1968. Impoundments for waterfowl on South Atlantic and Gulf coastal marshes. Pages 127-133 in J. D. Newsom, ed. Proc. marsh and estuary manage. symp. Louisiana State Univ., Baton Rouge.

Banks, R. L. 1987. Coastal impoundments in South Carolina: environmental parameters considered in the regulatory review process. Pages 480-485 in W. R. Whitman and W. H. Meredith, eds. Waterfowl and wetlands symp.: proc. of a symp. on waterfowl and wetlands management in the coastal zone of the Atlantic Flyway. Del. Coast. Manage. Prog., Dep. Nat. Resour. and Environ. Control, Dover.

Bardwell, J. L., L. L. Glasgow, and E. A. Epps. 1962. Nutritional analyses of foods eaten by pintails and teal in south Louisiana. Proc. Annu. Southeast. Assoc. Game and Fish Comm. 16:209-217.

Barry, J. M. 1980. Natural vegetation of South Carolina. Univ. South Carolina Press, Columbia. 214 pp.

Bellrose, F. C. 1980. Ducks, geese and swans of North America. Third ed. Stackpole Books, Harrisburg, Pa. 540 pp.

Brown, J. P. 1976. Variations in South Carolina coastal morphology. Pages II-2 - II-15 in M. O. Hayes and T. W. Kana, eds. Terrigenous clastic depositional environments. Univ. South Carolina Dep. Geol. Coastal Res. Div. Tech. Rep. 11-CRD, Columbia.

Carney, S. M., M. F. Sorensen, and E. M. Martin. 1975. Distribution in states and counties of waterfowl species harvested during 1961-70 hunting seasons. U.S. Fish and Wildl. Serv. Spec. Sci. Rep. Wildl. 187. 132 pp.

———, ———, and ———. 1983. Distribution of waterfowl species harvested in states and counties during 1971-80 hunting seasons. U.S. Fish and Wildl. Serv. Spec. Sci. Rep. 254. 114 pp.

Cely, J. E. 1979. The ecology and distribution of banana waterlily and its utilization by canvasback ducks. Proc. Annu. Conf. Southeast. Assoc. Fish and Wildl. Agencies 33:43-47.

Chabreck, R. H. 1979. Winter habitat of dabbling ducks—physical, chemical, and biological aspects. Pages 133-142 in T. A. Bookhout, ed. Waterfowl and wetlands—an integrated review. North Cent. Sect. Wildl. Soc., Madison, Wis.

Clay, R. T., and M. Suprenant. 1987. Effects of burning and mechanical manipulation on Phragmites australis in Quebec. Final Rep., Ducks Unlimited Canada, Winnipeg, Man. 27 pp.

Colquhoun, D. J. 1969. Geomorphology of the lower coastal plain of South Carolina. S.C. State Develop. Bd., Div. Geol., Columbia. 36 pp.

Conrad, W. B., Jr. 1965. A study of the food habits of ducks wintering on the lower Pee Dee and Waccamaw Rivers, Georgetown, South Carolina. M.S. Thesis, Auburn Univ., Auburn, Ala. 100 pp.

———. 1966. A food habits study of ducks wintering on the lower Pee Dee and Waccamaw Rivers, Georgetown, South Carolina. Proc. Annu. Conf. Southeast. Assoc. Fish and Wildl. Comm. 19:93-98.

Cooke, C. W. 1936. Geology of the coastal plain of South Carolina. U.S. Geol. Surv. Bull. 867. 196 pp.

Cowardin, L. M., V. Carter, F. C. Golet, and E. T. LaRoe. 1979. Classification of wetlands and deepwater habitats of the United States. U.S. Fish and Wildl. Serv. Pub. FWS/OBS-79/31. 103 pp.

Craddock, G. R., and R. D. Wells. 1973. Entisols—soils that show no profile development. Pages 24-28 *in* S. W. Buol, ed. Soils of the southern states and Puerto Rico. U.S. Dep. Agric. Southern Coop. Ser. Bull. 174.

Czyscinski, K. S. 1975. The development of acid sulfate soils ("cat clays") on the Annandale Plantation, Georgetown County, South Carolina. Ph.D. Dissertation, Univ. South Carolina, Columbia. 153 pp.

Daiber, F. C. 1986. Conservation of tidal marshes. Van Nostrand Reinhold Co., New York, N.Y. 341 pp.

Davis, J. S., M. D. McKenzie, J. V. Miglarese, R. H. Dunlap, J. J. Manzi, and L. A. Barclay. 1980. Ecological characterization of the sea island coastal region of South Carolina and Georgia, resource atlas. U.S. Fish and Wildl. Serv. FWS/OBS-79/43. 56 pp.

Davison, V. E., and W. W. Neely. 1959. Managing farm fields, wetlands and waters for wild ducks in the South. U.S. Dep. Agric. Farmers' Bull. 2144. 14 pp.

Devoe, M. R., D. S. Baughman, and J. M. Dean. 1987. South Carolina's wetland impoundments: a summary of research and policy issues. Pages 187-498 in W. R. Whitman and W. H. Meredith, eds. Waterfowl and wetlands symp.: proc. of a symp. on waterfowl and wetlands management in the coastal zone of the Atlantic Flyway. Del. Coast. Manage. Prog., Dep. Nat. Resour. and Environ. Control, Dover.

Doar, D. 1936. Rice and rice planting in the South Carolina lowcountry. Contrib. Charleston Museum VIII. 70 pp.

Driver, E. A., L. G. Sugden, and R. J. Kovach. 1974. Calorific, chemical and physical values of potential duck foods. Freshwater Biol. 4:281-292.

Drobney, R. D. 1977. The feeding ecology, nutrition, and reproductive bioenergetics of wood ducks. Ph.D. Thesis, Univ. Missouri, Columbia. 170 pp.

Edelman, C. H., and J. M. Van Staveren. 1958. Marsh soils in the United States and in the Netherlands. Soil and Water Conserv. 13:5-17.

Euliss, N. H., Jr., and S. W. Harris. 1987. Feeding ecology of northern pintails and green-winged teal wintering in California. J. Wildl. Manage. 51:724-732.

Fredrickson, L. H., and T. S. Taylor. 1982. Management of seasonally flooded impoundments for wildlife. U.S. Fish and Wildl. Serv. Res. Publ. 148. 29 pp.

Gordon, D. H., B. T. Gray, and R. M. Kaminski. 1987. A preliminary analysis of habitat use by dabbling ducks wintering in coastal wetlands of South Carolina. Pages 13-24 *in* W. R. Whitman

and W. H. Meredith, eds. Waterfowl and wetlands symp.: proc. of a symp. on waterfowl and wetlands management in the coastal zone of the Atlantic Flyway. Del. Coast. Manage. Prog., Dep. Nat. Resour. and Environ. Control, Dover.

Gray, B. T., D. H. Gordon, and R. M. Kaminski. 1987. Functional attributes of coastal wetlands for waterfowl: perspectives for research and management. Pages 205-222 *in* W. R. Whitman and W. H. Meredith, eds. Waterfowl and wetlands symp.: proc. of a symp. on waterfowl and wetlands management in the coastal zone of the Atlantic Flyway. Del. Coast. Manage. Prog., Dep. Nat. Resour. and Environ. Control, Dover.

Gresham, C. E., and D. D. Hook. 1982. Rice fields of South Carolina: a resource inventory and management policy evaluation. Coastal Zone Manage. J. 9:183-203.

Havel, J. F. 1976. Vascular plant survey of the lower Santee River floodplain. Pages 23-32 *in* T. P. Nelson, ed. Lower Santee River environmental quality study. S.C. Water Resour. Comm. Rep. 122, Columbia.

Hayes, M. O. 1976. Lecture notes. Pages I-1 - I-37 *in* M. O. Hayes and T. W. Kana, eds. Terrigenous clastic depositional environments. Univ. South Carolina Dep. Geol. Coastal Res. Div. Tech. Rep. 11-CRD, Columbia.

Heitmeyer, M. E. 1985. Wintering strategies of female mallards related to dynamics of lowland hardwood wetlands in the Upper Mississippi Delta. Ph.D. Thesis, Univ. Missouri, Columbia. 378 pp.

———, and L. H. Fredrickson. 1981. Do wetland conditions in the Mississippi Delta hardwoods influence mallard recruitment? Trans. North Am. Wildl. and Nat. Resour. Conf. 46:44-57.

Hepp, G. R., R. J. Blohm, R. E. Reynolds, J. E. Hines, and J. D. Nichols. 1986. Physiological condition of autumn-banded mallards and its relationship to hunting vulnerability. J. Wildl. Manage. 50:177-183.

Heyward, D. C. 1937. Seed from Madagascar. Univ. North Carolina Press, Chapel Hill. 256 pp.

Hilliard, S. B. 1975. The tidewater rice plantation: an ingenious adaptation to nature. Pages 57-66 *in* H. J. Walker, ed. Geoscience and man. Vol. 12. Louisiana State Univ., Baton Rouge.

Joanen, T., and L. L. Glasgow. 1965. Factors influencing the establishment of widgeon grass stands in Louisiana. Proc. Annu. Conf. Southeast. Assoc. Game and Fish Comm. 19:78-92.

Johnson, A. S., H. O. Hillestad, S. F. Shanholtzer, and G. F. Shanholtzer. 1974. An ecological survey of the coastal region of Georgia. Natl. Park Serv. Sci. Manage. Ser. 3, Washington, D.C. 233 pp.

Joyner, C. W. 1984. Down by the riverside: A South Carolina slave community. Univ. Illinois Press, Chicago. 345 pp.

Kaminski, R. M., and E. A. Gluesing. 1987. Density- and habitat-related recruitment in mallards. J. Wildl. Manage. 51:141-148.

————, H. R. Murkin, and C. E. Smith. 1985. Control of cattail and bulrush by cutting and flooding. Pages 253-254 in H. Prince and F. D'Itri, eds. Coastal wetlands. Lewis Publishers, Inc., Chelsea, Mich.

Kendeigh, S.C., and G. C. West. 1965. Calorific values of plant seeds eaten by birds. Ecology 46:553-555.

Kerwin, J. A., and L. G. Webb. 1972. Foods of ducks wintering in coastal South Carolina, 1965-1967. Proc. Annu. Conf. Southeast. Assoc. Fish and Wildl. Comm. 25:223-245.

Kjerfve, B. 1976. The Santee-Cooper: a study of estuarine manipulations. Pages 44-56 in M. Wiley, ed. Estuarine processes. Vol. 1. Uses, stresses and adaptation to the estuary. Academic Press, New York, N.Y.

Kovacik, C. F. 1979. South Carolina rice coast landscape changes. Proc. Tall Timbers Ecol. Manage. Conf. 16:47-65.

Krapu, G. L. 1981. The role of nutrient reserves in mallard reproduction. Auk 98:29-38.

Landers, J. L. 1981. The role of fire in bobwhite quail management. Pages 73-80 in G. W. Wood, ed. Prescribed fire and wildlife in southern forests. Belle W. Baruch For. Sci. Inst., Clemson Univ., Georgetown, S.C.

————, A. S. Johnson, P. H. Morgan, and W. P. Baldwin. 1976. Duck foods in managed tidal impoundments in South Carolina. J. Wildl. Manage. 40:721-728.

Larimer, T. C. 1982. Integration of wood duck production with attraction of migratory waterfowl in coastal fresh marsh. M.S. Thesis., Univ. Georgia, Athens. 59 pp.

Latimer, E. 1968. Jurisdiction and ownership of marshes and estuaries of the South Atlantic and Gulf Coasts. Pages 33-40 in J. D. Newsom, ed. Proc. marsh and estuary manage. symp. Louisiana State Univ., Baton Rouge.

Martin, A. C., and F. M. Uhler. 1939. Food of game ducks in the United States and Canada. U.S. Dep. Agric. Tech. Bull. 634. 308 pp.

Martin, R. E., and C. T. Cushwa. 1966. Effects of heat and moisture on leguminous seed. Proc. Tall Timbers Fire Ecol. Conf. 5:159-175.

Mathews, T. D., F. W. Stapor, Jr., C. R. Richter, J. V. Miglarese, M. D. McKenzie, and L. A. Barclay, editors. 1980. The ecological characterization of the sea island coastal region of South Carolina and Georgia. Vol. 1. Physical features of the characterization area. U.S. Fish and Wildl. Serv. FWS/OBS-79/40. 212 pp.

————, M. H. Shealy, and N. Cummings. 1981. Hydrography of South Carolina Estuaries, with emphasis on the North and South Santee and Charleston Harbor-Cooper River Estuaries. S.C. Mar. Resour. Cent. Tech. Rep. 47, Columbia. 128 pp.

Mayer, F. L., Jr, and J. B. Low. 1970. The effect of salinity on widgeon grass. J. Wildl. Manage. 34:658-661.

Miglarese, J. V., and P. A. Sandifer, editors. 1982. An ecological characterization of South Carolina wetland impoundments. S.C. Mar. Resour. Cent. Tech. Rep. 51, Columbia. 132 pp.

Mitsch, W. J., and J. G. Gosselink. 1986. Wetlands. Van Nostrand Reinhold Co., New York, N.Y. 537 pp.

Morgan, P. H. 1974. A study of tidelands and impoundments within a three-river delta system—the South Edisto, Ashepoo, and Combahee rivers of South Carolina. M.S. Thesis, Univ. Georgia, Athens. 92 pp.

————, A. S. Johnson, W. P. Baldwin, and J. L. Landers. 1975. Characteristics and management of tidal impoundments for wildlife in a South Carolina estuary. Proc. Annu. Conf. Southeast. Assoc. Game and Fish Comm. 29:526-539.

Murkin, H. and P. Ward. 1980. Early spring cutting to control cattail in a northern marsh. Wildl. Soc. Bull. 8:254-256.

Neely, W. W. 1958. Irreversible drainage—a new factor in waterfowl management. Trans. North Am. Wildl. Conf. 14:30-34.

————. 1960. Managing Scirpus robustus for ducks. Proc. Annu. Conf. Southeast. Assoc. Game and Fish Comm. 14:30-34.

————. 1962. Saline soils and brackish waters in management of wildlife, fish, and shrimp. Trans. North Am. Wildl. and Nat. Resour. Conf. 27:321-335.

————. 1968. Planting, disking, mowing, and grazing. Pages 212-221 in J. D. Newsom, ed. Proc. marsh and estuary manage. symp. Louisiana State Univ., Baton Rouge.

Odum, W. E., T. J. Smith III, J. K. Hoover, and C. C. McIvor. 1984. The ecology of tidal freshwater marshes of the United States east coast: a community profile. U.S. Fish and Wildl. Serv. FWS/OBS-83/17. 177 pp.

Palmisano, A. W. 1967. Ecology of Scirpus olneyi and Scirpus robustus in Louisiana coastal marshes. M.S. Thesis, Louisiana State Univ., Baton Rouge. 145 pp.

————. 1972a. Habitat preference of waterfowl and fur animals in the northern Gulf Coast marshes. Pages 163-190 in R. H. Chabreck, ed. Coastal marsh and estuary manage. symp. Louisiana State Univ., Baton Rouge.

————. 1972b. The effect of salinity on the germination and growth of plants important to wildlife in the Gulf Coast Marshes. Proc. Annu. Conf. Southeast. Assoc. Game and Fish Comm. 25:215-223.

——, and J. D. Newsom. 1967. Ecological factors affecting occurrence of *Scirpus olneyi* and *Scirpus robustus* in the Louisiana coastal marshes. Proc. Annu. Conf. Southeast. Assoc. Game and Fish Comm. 21:171-173.

Paulus, S. L. 1980. The winter ecology of the gadwall in Louisiana. M.S. Thesis, Univ. North Dakota, Grand Forks. 357 pp.

Penfound, W. T. 1952. Southern swamps and marshes. Bot. Rev. 18:413-446.

——, and E. S. Hathaway. 1938. Plant communities in the marshlands of southeastern Louisiana. Ecol. Monogr. 8:1-56.

Percival, H. F. 1968. Ecological study of selected waterfowl food plants: some ecological conditions under which selected waterfowl food plants grow in South Carolina. S.C. Wildl. Resour. Dep. Job Completion Rep., Proj. W-38-R-5, Columbia. 109 pp.

——, L. G. Webb, and N. R. Page. 1970. Some ecological conditions under which selected waterfowl food plants grow in South Carolina. Proc. Annu. Conf. Southeast. Assoc. Game and Fish Comm. 24:121-126.

Porcher, R. D. 1985. A teacher's field guide to the natural history of the Bluff Plantation Wildlife Sanctuary. Kathleen O'Brian Foundation, New Orleans, La. 291 pp.

Prevost, M. B. 1987. Management of plant communities for waterfowl in coastal South Carolina. Pages 167-183 *in* W. R. Whitman and W. H. Meredith, eds. Waterfowl and wetlands symp.: proc. of a symp. on waterfowl and wetlands management in the coastal zone of the Atlantic Flyway. Del. Coast. Manage. Prog., Dep. Nat. Resour. and Environ. Control, Dover.

——, A. S. Johnson, and J. L. Landers. 1978. Production and utilization of waterfowl foods in brackish impoundments in South Carolina. Proc. Annu. Conf. Southeast. Assoc. Game and Fish Comm. 32:60-70.

Pritchard, D. W. 1967. What is an estuary: physical viewpoint. Pages 3-5 *in* G. H. Lauff, ed. Estuaries. Am. Assoc. Adv. Sci. Publ. 83, Washington, D.C.

Purvis, J. C. 1987. General characteristics of South Carolina's climate. S.C. State Climatology Off., Columbia. 21 pp.

——, W. Tyler, and S. Sidlow. 1986. Hurricanes affecting South Carolina. S.C. State Climatology Off., Columbia. 21 pp.

Radford, A. E., H. E. Ahles, and C. R. Bell. 1964. Manual of the vascular flora of the Carolinas. Univ. North Carolina Press, Chapel Hill. 1,183 pp.

Ranwell, D. S. 1972. Ecology of salt marshes and sand dunes. Chapman and Hall, London. 258 pp.

Rogers, G. C. 1970. The history of Georgetown County, South Carolina. Univ. of South Carolina Press, Columbia. 565 pp.

Rowland, L. S. 1987. Alone on the river: The rise and fall of the Savannah River rice plantations of St. Peter's Parish, South Carolina. S.C. Historical Mag. 88:121-150.

Salley, A. S. 1936. The true story of how the Madagascar Gold seed rice was introduced into South Carolina. Pages 51-58 *in* D. Doar, ed. Rice and rice planting in the South Carolina low country. Contrib. Charleston Museum VIII.

Setchell, W. A. 1924. *Ruppia* and its environmental factors. Proc. Natl. Acad. Sci. 10:286-288.

Spinner, G. P., and J. S. Bishop. 1950. Chemical analysis of some wildlife foods in Connecticut. J. Wildl. Manage. 14:175-180.

Strange, T. H. 1987. Goals and objectives of waterlevel manipulations in impounded wetlands in South Carolina. Pages 130-137 *in* W. R. Whitman and W. H. Meredith, eds. Waterfowl and wetlands symp.: proc. of a symp. on waterfowl and wetlands management in the coastal zone of the Atlantic Flyway. Del. Coast. Manage. Prog., Dep. Nat. Resour. and Environ. Control, Dover.

Sugden, L. G. 1973. Feeding ecology of pintail, gadwall, American wigeon and lesser scaup ducklings in southern Alberta. Can. Wildl. Serv. Rep. Ser. 24. 45 pp.

Swanson, G. A., and J. C. Bartonek. 1970. Bias associated with food analysis in gizzards of blue-winged teal. J. Wildl. Manage. 34:739-746.

——, G. L. Krapu, J. C. Bartonek, J. R. Serie, and D. H. Johnson. 1974. Advantages in mathematically weighting waterfowl food habits data. J. Wildl. Manage. 38:302-307.

Swiderek, P. K. 1982. Production, management, and waterfowl use of sea purslane, Gulf Coast muskgrass, and widgeon grass in brackish impoundments. M.S. Thesis, Univ. Georgia, Athens. 103 pp.

——, A. S. Johnson, P. E. Hale, and R. L. Joyner. 1988. Production, management, and waterfowl use of sea purslane, gulf coast muskgrass, and widgeongrass in brackish impoundments. Pages 441-457 *in* M. W. Weller, ed. Waterfowl in winter. Univ. Minnesota Press, Minneapolis.

Tamisier, A. 1974. Etho-ecological studies of teal wintering in the Camargue (Rhone Delta, France). Wildfowl 27:123-133.

——. 1976. Diurnal activities of green-winged teal and pintail wintering in Louisiana. Wildfowl 27:19-32.

——. 1985. Some considerations on the social requirements of ducks in winter. Wildfowl 36:104-108.

Thompson, D. J. 1981. Effects of fire on *Phragmites australis* and associated species at Delta Marsh,

Manitoba, M.S. Thesis, Univ. Manitoba, Winnipeg. 180 pp.

Tiner, R. W., Jr. 1977. An inventory of South Carolina's coastal marshes, S.C. Mar. Resour. Cent. Tech. Rep. 23, Columbia. 33 pp.

Tompkins, M. E. 1986. Scope and status of coastal wetland impoundments in South Carolina. Pages 31-57 *in* M. R. Devoe and D. S. Baughman, eds. South Carolina coastal wetland impoundments: ecological characterization, management, status, and use. Vol. II. Technical synthesis. S.C. Sea Grant Consortium Tech. Rep. SC-56-tr-86-2, Charleston.

U.S. Army Corps of Engineers 1966. Survey report on Cooper River, S.C. (shoaling in Charleston Harbor). Appendix D: model studies. U.S. Army Eng. District, Charleston, S. C. 31 pp.

U.S. Geological Survey. 1975. Water resources data for South Carolina for Water Year 1974. U.S.G.S. Water Data Rep. SL-74-1. 190 pp.

Vankat, J. L. 1979. The natural vegetation of North America. John Wiley and Sons, New York, N.Y. 262 pp.

Waisel, Y. 1972. Biology of halophytes. Academic Press, New York, N.Y. 395 pp.

Weller, M. W. 1975. Migratory waterfowl: a hemispheric perspective. Publ. Biologicas Instituto de Investigaciones Cien., U.A.N.L. 1:89-130.

White, D. H., and D. James. 1978. Differential use of fresh water environments by wintering waterfowl of coastal Texas. Wilson Bull. **90**:99-111.

Wilkes, R. L. 1976. Tidal marsh and swamp extent in Georgia. U.S. Dep. Agric. Soil Conserv. Serv. Hinesville, Ga. 5 pp.

Wilkinson, P. M. 1970. Vegetative succession in newly controlled marshes. S.C. Wildl. and Mar. Resour. Dep., Job Completion Rep., Columbia. 37 pp.

——. 1984. Nesting ecology of the American alligator in coastal South Carolina. S.C. Wildl. and Mar. Resour. Dep., Study Completion Rep., Columbia. 113 pp.

Williams, R. K. 1987. Construction, maintenance and water control structures of tidal impoundments in South Carolina. Pages 138-166 *in* W. R. Whitman and W. H. Meredith, eds. Waterfowl and wetlands symp.: proc. of a symp. on waterfowl and wetlands management in the coastal zone of the Atlantic Flyway. Del. Coast. Manage. Prog., Dep. Nat. Resour. and Environ. Control, Dover.

Yancey, R. K. 1964. Matches and marshes. Pages 619-626 *in* J. P. Linduska, ed. Waterfowl tomorrow. U.S. Fish and Wildl. Serv., Washington, D.C.

Zetler, B. D. 1953. Some effects of the diversion of the Santee River on the waters of Charleston Harbor. Trans. Am. Geophys. Union 34:729-732.

SOUTHERN RESERVOIRS AND LAKES

FRED A. JOHNSON, Game and Fresh Water Fish Commission, 3991 S.E. 27th Court, Okeechobee, FL 34974
FRANK MONTALBANO III, Game and Fresh Water Fish Commission, 620 S. Meridian Street, Tallahassee, FL 32399-1600

The southeastern coastal plain of the United States (U.S.) is well suited for the formation of wetlands. Twenty-seven percent (10,923,482 ha) of all the wetlands in the lower 48 states lie within North Carolina, South Carolina, Georgia, and Florida (National Wetlands Inventory, unpubl. data). However, only about 9% of these wetlands are of high or moderate value to waterfowl (Shaw and Fredine 1956). Among the best are the coastal wetlands which dominate major wintering areas (Addy 1964, Johnsgard 1975, Bellrose 1980). Although of lesser importance, the interior reservoirs and natural lakes of the southern Atlantic Flyway (Fig. 1) also provide important migrating and wintering habitats for ducks and geese (Chamberlain 1960, Addy 1964, Bellrose 1980).

We define reservoirs as man-made lakes or ponds in which water is collected or stored for some specific purpose(s), such as flood control, navigation, or water supply. Within the southern Atlantic Flyway, reservoirs occur in a wide array of sizes and configurations, providing a diversity of waterfowl habitats of widely varying quality. Included are the major multipurpose reservoirs of the U.S. Army Corps of Engineers (COE), hydroelectric reservoirs constructed by public utility companies, flood-control reservoirs typically constructed by the U.S. Soil Conservation Service (SCS), and farm ponds constructed under various programs of the U.S. Department of Agriculture (USDA).

In the 1950s, Shaw and Fredine (1956) reported that there were less than 220,000 ha of inland open water in the southern Atlantic Flyway. Today, 26 major reservoirs constructed principally by the COE or by various regional power companies total over 280,000 ha of potential waterfowl habitat (file data, COE). Some 370,000 farm ponds and small reservoirs comprise another 250,000 ha of surface water (file data, SCS).

Reservoirs may provide new or additional waterfowl habitat, especially in regions largely devoid of open water (White and Malaher 1964, Chabreck 1979). The benefits can be substantial, particularly when local food supplies are adequate and readily available (Wiebe 1946, Wiebe et al. 1950, White and Malaher 1964, Neely and Davison 1971, Chabreck 1979). However, reservoirs can

Fig. 1. Reservoirs and lakes in the southern Atlantic Flyway providing important habitat for migrating and wintering waterfowl.

adversely impact waterfowl habitat if marshes and bottomland hardwoods are eliminated or detrimentally altered due to impoundment (White and Malaher 1964). Bottomland hardwoods are important as wintering habitat for ducks (Harris 1984, Tiner 1984) and as important production areas for wood ducks (*Aix sponsa*) (Harris 1984).

Natural lakes are rare in the southern Atlantic Flyway except in Florida, where there are approximately 7,800 basins ≥4 ha in size (Fernald 1984). These lakes comprise approximately 550,600 ha (Edmiston and Myers 1983, Palmer 1984), representing about 13% of Florida's freshwater wetlands (National Wetlands Inventory, unpubl. data). Although natural lakes are located throughout the state, they occur more frequently in peninsular Florida (Palmer 1984).

Most lakes in Florida originated as solution basins, formed when percolating groundwater dissolved subsurface limestone (Palmer 1984). These basins are usually circular, conically-shaped in cross-section, and are filled with water from rivers, runoff, or underground sources (Edmiston and Myers 1983). Other lake basins are relict sea-bottom depressions, exposed by tectonic movement or falling sea levels. These shallow lakes, although generally small in size individually, form an extensive area in southern Florida (Chamberlain 1960). Still other lakes were formed by erosion and sedimentation processes in river floodplains (Edmiston and Myers 1983).

Only those permanent lakes with extensive littoral zones of emergent, floating-leaved, or submersed macrophytes provide high-quality habitat (Chamberlain 1960). These lakes can originate from any of the processes described above, but most often are associated with major river systems. Many of the sinkhole lakes lack extensive marshes and do not support sizable waterfowl populations. Most relict sea-bottom depressions are intermittently or seasonally flooded and are not used extensively by wintering waterfowl except in wet years.

Our objectives in the following review are (1) to provide a brief account of those reservoirs and lakes in the southern Atlantic Flyway that are important to waterfowl, (2) to discuss existing and recommended techniques for improving those habitats, and (3) to provide guidance for future management and research. Throughout our review we emphasize Florida lakes because they generally provide better waterfowl habitat and offer greater management potential than reservoirs.

MAJOR MIGRATION AND WINTERING AREAS
Reservoirs

Reservoirs in the southern Atlantic Flyway serve as important resting areas for migrating waterfowl. Bellrose (1968) described several significant waterfowl migration corridors that intercept major reservoir developments. The South Carolina corridor is a migration route for 400,000 dabbling ducks, including mallards (*Anas platyrhynchos*), northern pintails (*A. acuta*), American wigeon (*A. americana*), gadwalls (*A. strepera*), and northern shovelers (*A. clypeata*), which winter primarily along the Atlantic Coast (Bellrose 1968). This corridor crosses most of the large reservoir projects in South Carolina, including Hartwell, Russell, and Clarks Hill Lakes in the Savannah River basin, and Lakes Greenwood, Murray, Marion, and Moultrie in the Santee River basin. Another migration corridor for 65,000 dabbling ducks terminates in coastal North Carolina and traverses the J. H. Kerr and Gaston reservoirs in that state (Bellrose 1968). The mid-Florida corridor extends across central Tennessee, northeastern Alabama, and southwestern Georgia, and terminates in Florida (Bellrose 1968). This migration route is used by mallards, northern pintails, and American wigeon and crosses the Walter F. George Reservoir on the Georgia-Alabama border.

An important migration route for ring-necked ducks (*Aythya collaris*) and lesser scaup (*A. affinis*) crosses western North Carolina and extends to coastal South Carolina (Bellrose 1968). This corridor crosses Lake Wylie, Wateree Lake, and Lakes Marion and Moultrie. Brisbin (1974) also noted use of Par Pond (a 1,120-ha reservoir on the Savannah River) by these two species. Bellrose (1968) depicted at least four other major diving-duck migration corridors, each used by 76,000–250,000 ducks. Lesser scaup, ring-necked ducks, canvasbacks (*A. valisineria*), and approximately 75,000 redheads (*A. americana*) move into southern Georgia and Florida along these routes (Bellrose 1968). At least 11 major reservoirs provide more than 121,000 ha of potential resting habitat.

Phosphate Mines

Small reservoirs used for storage and settling of phosphatic ores (Farmer and Blue 1978) provide attractive habitat in the southern Atlantic Flyway for a variety of wintering (Montalbano et al. 1978, King et al. 1980) and resident (Montalbano 1980, Wenner and Marion 1981, Montalbano et al. 1983) waterfowl. Phosphate mining has affected over 74,000 ha in Florida alone (C. W. Hendry, unpubl. rep., Governor's Office, Tallahassee, Fla., 1978) and resulted in the creation of 24,000 ha of settling pond habitat (Environmental Protection Agency 1978) deemed attractive to waterfowl. Much of the remaining lands affected by mining are included in a mosaic of flooded mine pits (Maehr 1981), many of which provide sheltered deepwater habitat for waterfowl.

At least 19 species of wintering waterfowl have been recorded in phosphate settling-ponds in Florida, including dabbling and diving ducks, Canada (*Branta*

canadensis) and snow geese (*Chen caerulescens*), and tundra swans (*Cygnus columbianus*) (Montalbano et al. 1978, Stafford 1979, King et al. 1980, Maehr 1981). About 8,500 ducks, primarily northern shovelers, blue-winged teal (*Anas discors*), mottled ducks (*A. fulviqula*), ring-necked ducks, and lesser scaup, winter in the 2 major phosphate-mining regions in Florida (F. Johnson, unpubl. data).

Natural Lakes

Among southern lakes, Mattamuskeet, Pungo, Phelps, and Alligator Lakes in eastern North Carolina provide important habitats for wintering waterfowl. Historically, Lake Mattamuskeet was the primary wintering area for the mid-Atlantic population of Canada geese (Addy and Heyland 1968), with populations often exceeding 100,000 birds (Florshutz 1968). However, large components of this population were "short-stopped" in the 1950s (Florshutz 1968), and current populations generally do not exceed 20,000 (D. Luscz, pers. commun.). Other important wintering species include northern pintail, canvasback, lesser scaup, mallard, black duck (*Anas rubripes*), American wigeon, and lesser (*C. c. caerulescens*) and greater (*C. c. atlanticus*) snow geese (L. R. Ditto, pers. commun.). Lake Mattamuskeet is the most important wintering area for tundra swans in North Carolina, with a peak population of 38,000 birds (L. R. Ditto, pers. commun.).

In the Tallahassee area of northern Florida, Lakes Miccosukee, Iamonia, and Jackson provide relatively small, but important habitats (Chamberlain 1960). Formed by sinkholes in natural valleys (Edmiston and Myers 1983), these lakes are major wintering sites for ring-necked ducks (Chamberlain 1960). Ring-necked ducks first arrive around mid-October, peak in late November at over 20,000 birds, and are essentially gone by mid-March (T. S. Taylor, unpubl. data).

Midwinter survey data suggests that these lakes also provide important wintering habitat for lesser scaup and wood ducks.

Bellrose (1968) described a duck migration corridor extending through central Florida, where the Kissimmee River system is the major surface-water feature (Fig. 2). The upper Kissimmee Valley is comprised of a chain of lakes that were connected by natural sloughs before being modified for navigation and flood control (Van Arman et al. 1984). Prior to extensive wetland alterations, the Kissimmee Valley wintered populations of 20,000 to 25,000 ducks (Sincock et al. 1957). Most (80%) waterfowl used the upper chain-of-lakes (Perrin et al. 1982), with Lakes Kissimmee, Tohopekaliga, Cypress, Hatchineha, and Istokpoga supporting the largest populations (Sincock et al. 1957). Historically, ring-necked ducks, mallards, mottled ducks, canvasbacks, northern pintails, American wigeon, and blue-winged teal were abundant (Sincock et al. 1957). Recent surveys suggest that ring-necked ducks, blue-winged teal, and mottled ducks greatly outnumber other species with peak populations occurring in February (Perrin et al. 1982). Lake Istokpoga continues to be a traditional wintering site for canvasbacks, with an average of 3,000 birds (F. Johnson, unpubl. data).

The Kissimmee River system is the major tributary for Lake Okeechobee, the second largest freshwater lake in the conterminous U.S. (Van Arman et al. 1984). This lake provides some of the best waterfowl habitat in Florida (Chamberlain 1960), with wintering duck populations numbering about 170,000 (Johnson 1987). The most common duck in open water is the lesser scaup, whose winter population averages 97,000 birds (Turnbull et al. 1986). The ring-necked duck is the most common species inhabiting the extensive lake marshes (Johnson and Montalbano 1984); 35,000 (Bellrose 1968) to 50,000 (Johnson 1987) overwinter there.

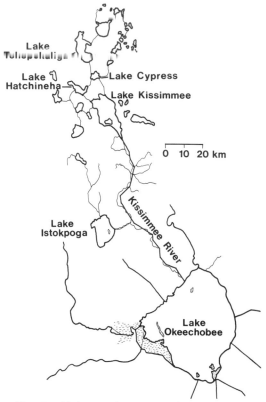

Fig. 2. Major surface-water features of the Kissimmee River system and Lake Okeechobee in south-central Florida.

American wigeon, blue-winged teal, and mottled ducks are also common (Chamberlain 1960, Johnson and Montalbano 1984). Recently, fulvous whistling-ducks (*Dendrocygna bicolor*) have wintered on the lake in large numbers; flocks of 1,000-4,000 birds are not uncommon. Wintering duck populations sharply increase in November, peak in December, and gradually decline through March (Chamberlain 1960).

The lakes and marshes of the St. Johns River Valley have long been recognized as among the best waterfowl habitat in Florida (Sincock 1958, Chamberlain 1960). In the 1950s, the upper St. Johns River Valley (Fig. 3) supported peak populations of 15,000 ducks (Sincock 1958). Significant numbers of waterfowl first arrive in mid-November, followed by fairly stable populations until mid-Febru-

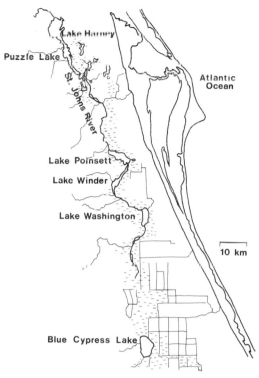

Fig. 3. The upper St. Johns River basin in east-central Florida.

ary (Sincock 1958). Historically, ring-necked duck, northern pintail, American wigeon, blue-winged teal, and northern shoveler were the most abundant species. Recent midwinter surveys suggest decreased numbers, with lesser scaup, ring-necked duck, and blue-winged teal predominating.

Habitat Changes

Between the 1950s and 1970s the loss of wetlands was greater in the southeastern U.S. than in any other region of the country (National Wetlands Inventory, unpubl. data). The greatest losses were of palustrine forested wetlands, and some of these losses can be attributed to reservoir construction (Brinson et al. 1981). Man-made reservoirs in the eastern half of the U.S. largely account for a nationwide increase in open water habitat (Tiner 1984). White and Malaher (1964) concluded that reservoirs that eliminate bot-

tomlands are potentially detrimental to waterfowl populations. However, Tiner (1984) reported that these new reservoirs were created mostly from uplands and therefore provide new habitats for waterfowl. Unfortunately, reservoirs built and operated for navigation, flood control, and power supply, without specific development and changes in mode of operation, do not offer good waterfowl habitat (Wiebe et al. 1950).

Strip-mining for phosphate has had a tremendous impact on water resources, especially in central Florida (Betz 1984). The USDA (1979) reports that only 3 states have had more land disturbed by surface mining than Florida. Approximately 20,000-24,000 ha are currently occupied by settling ponds, and another 2,400 ha are disturbed by mining each year (Swihart et al. 1984). In addition to the destruction of surface wetlands and the depletion of groundwater (Swihart et al. 1984), phosphate mining releases radioactive isotopes and toxic trace elements into the environment (Montalbano et al. 1983).

Because of pressure to alter wetlands for agricultural and urban development, Florida has been subject to extensive drainage, flood control, and navigation projects. Large-scale wetland destruction began in 1882, when businessman Hamilton Disston began channelization in the upper Kissimmee Valley and near Lake Okeechobee to promote development of southern Florida (Huber and Heaney 1984). Extensive efforts followed to drain the Everglades marshes adjacent to Lake Okeechobee for agricultural purposes (Betz 1984). Several hurricanes during the 1920s forced the federal government to begin a major program of flood control throughout southern Florida (Huber and Heaney 1984). Today, the Everglades basin (including the Kissimmee River system and Lake Okeechobee) contains a network of nearly 1,300 km of levees and 800 km of canals (Tiner 1984). Construc-

Fig. 4. Flood control projects, including the channelization of the Kissimmee River, drained over 56,000 ha of wetlands in the Everglades basin.

tion of this water-control system destroyed 16,000 ha of marsh and facilitated drainage of over 40,000 ha of adjacent wetlands (Thompson 1983, Fig. 4). Degradation of aquatic habitats continues due to stabilization of water levels, proliferation of certain exotic plants, and agricultural and urban runoff (Estevez et al. 1984).

The St. Johns River basin has had a similar, but more recent, history of drainage and flood control projects. Prior to development in the upper basin, approximately 117,000 ha of marsh were inundated during years of normal rainfall (Campbell et al. 1984). Since the turn of the century, over 90,000 ha of the floodplain have been diked and drained for agriculture (Cox and Moody 1976). These largely unregulated developments decreased water supply during the winter dry season, increased flood peaks, and created critical water-quality problems (Campbell et al. 1984).

Artificial regulation of water levels probably poses the greatest continuing threat to the quality of waterfowl habitat in Florida lakes. Water level fluctuation is necessary for maintaining productive wetland ecosystems (Weller 1978), and historically was an important characteristic of Florida's lakes and marshes (Estevez et al. 1984). The levels of most Florida lakes have been stabilized to prevent flooding and to insure adequate water supplies during dry periods (Estevez et al. 1984). Stabilization of water levels reduces the extent of emergent plants and increases the inundation frequency in much of the littoral zone (Fig. 5). Because hydrosoils are exposed less frequently, organic sediments accumulate and the substrate becomes less suitable for plant growth (Holcomb and Wegener 1971, Estevez et al. 1984). Diversity and production of waterfowl food plants usually declines (Weller 1978, Fredrickson and Taylor 1982).

Lake Okeechobee provides an example of how flood-control and water-supply projects have jeopardized waterfowl habi-

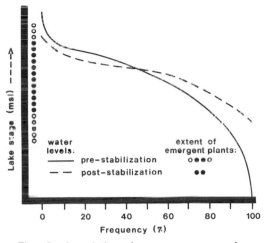

Fig. 5. Inundation frequency curves for a hypothetical lake prior to and after water level stabilization.

tat on many Florida lakes. Sincock (1957) studied the littoral vegetation of Lake Okeechobee and predicted habitat changes likely to occur with construction of a flood-control levee. Subsequent water level stabilization resulted in perennials replacing annuals and in a decrease in plant species richness (Ager and Kerce 1970). Prompted by concerns of declining habitat quality, Pesnell and Brown (1977) studied the inundation characteristics of the major emergent plant communities to provide baseline data for assessing the impacts of future water management policies. Since 1978, the artificial maintenance of higher water levels to meet water-supply demands has virtually eliminated the spikerush (*Eleocharis cellulosa*) community, has promoted expansion of cattail (*Typha* spp.), and has encouraged domination of the moist-soil zone by torpedo grass (*Panicum repens*) (Milleson 1987). Plant nomenclature follows Godfrey and Wooten (1979, 1981).

HABITAT MANAGEMENT

Reservoir and Lake Habitats

Wetland and deepwater habitats associated with reservoirs and lakes are classified as palustrine or lacustrine (Cowardin et al. 1979). Lacustrine habitat generally lacks extensive vegetation (<30% areal coverage), and in reservoirs is bounded by a contour approximating normal pool elevation. Palustrine wetlands are typically heavily vegetated, and occur shoreward of the lacustrine system. In the southeastern U.S., palustrine wetlands are better developed in lake basins than in reservoirs because the topography is less severe and because water-level fluctuations are less frequent and drastic. Within reservoirs, palustrine wetlands often are confined to alluvial deposits or shallow coves (Stanford 1979, Harvey et al. 1987).

Wetland classes represented on southern reservoirs and lakes include unconsolidated bottom, aquatic bed, and emergent, scrub-shrub, and forested wetlands (see Cowardin et al. 1979 for detailed descriptions of these wetland classes). Shaw and Fredine (1956) described the major habitats occurring on lakes and reservoirs as seasonally flooded basins, inland fresh meadows, shallow and deep marshes, open water, and shrub and wooded swamps (Types 1-7, respectively). Penfound (1952) provided the most comprehensive description of these habitats as they occur in the southeastern U.S., but good descriptions of some habitats were also given by Hunt (1943) and Chamberlain (1960). A list of major plant species occupying wetlands in southeastern reservoirs and lakes is provided in Table 1.

Management Practices

Reservoirs.—The Fish and Wildlife Coordination Act of 1934 gave the U.S. Fish and Wildlife Service the opportunity to use reservoir projects constructed or licensed by the federal government for migratory bird habitat development (White and Malaher 1964). Subsequent revisions to the act in 1946 and 1958 required consideration of measures to protect, develop, and improve fish and wildlife habitat in the planning, construction, and operation of reservoirs (Shaw and Fredine 1956, White and

Table 1. Major plant species occurring in the wetlands of southern reservoirs and lakes.[a]

Wetland class	Species
Aquatic bed	Coontail (*Ceratophyllum demersum*)
	Fanwort (*Cabomba caroliniana*)
	Watermilfoil (*Myriophyllum* spp.)
	Southern naiad (*Najas quadalupensis*)
	Watershield (*Brasenia shreberii*)
	Wildcelery (*Vallisneria americana*)
	Illinois pondweed (*Potamogeton illinoensis*)
	Spatterdock (*Nuphar luteum*)
	Fragrant waterlily (*Nymphaea odorata*)
	American lotus (*Nelumbo lutea*)
	Hydrilla (*Hydrilla verticillata*)
	Water hyacinth (*Eichhornia crassipes*)
	Alligatorweed (*Alternanthera philoxeroides*)
Emergent	Giant cutgrass (*Zizaniopsis miliacea*)
	Cattail
	Bulrush (*Scirpus* spp.)
	Maidencane (*Panicum hematomon*)
	Torpedograss
	Smartweed (*Polygonum* spp.)
	Arrowhead (*Sagittaria* spp.)
	Pickerelweed (*Pontederia cordata*)
Scrub-shrub	Buttonbush (*Cephalanthus occidentalis*)
	Wax myrtle (*Myrica cerifera*)
	Willow (*Salix* spp.)
Forested	Bald cypress (*Taxodium distichum*)
	Tupelo (*Nyssa* spp.)
	Water oak (*Quercus nigra*)
	Overcup oak (*Quercus lyrata*)

[a]Sources: Hunt (1943), Penfound (1952), Shaw and Fredine (1956), Sincock and Powell (1957), Chamberlain (1960), Johnson and Montalbano (1984), and Harvey et al. (1987).

Malaher 1964, Zallen 1979). The Eufaula National Wildlife Refuge (NWR), located on the Georgia/Alabama border and the Santee NWR in South Carolina are examples of major waterfowl habitat projects developed under the provisions of the Coordination Act.

Despite some successes attributable to the Coordination Act, reservoirs in the southern Atlantic Flyway generally provide poor habitat for wintering waterfowl. Inadequate food is frequently the major limiting factor (Wiebe 1946, Wiebe et al. 1950, Givens et al. 1964, Neely and Davison 1971, Chabreck 1979) because frequent water level fluctuations restrict establishment of aquatic plants (Taylor

and Taylor 1976). On large reservoirs, extreme water depth and turbidity restrict light penetration, further inhibiting the production of submersed plants (Wiebe 1946, Wiebe et al. 1950, Givens et al. 1964). Even when conditions are more conducive for aquatic plant growth, extreme water-level fluctuations can limit access to plant communities by waterfowl (Wiebe 1946, Wiebe et al. 1950, Chabreck 1979).

Managers have employed a number of strategies to enhance food production or otherwise mitigate a shortage of food on southern reservoirs. Subimpoundments within reservoir basins (Fig. 6) are used successfully to produce and make available submersed and emergent vegetation (Wiebe 1946, Barstow 1963, White and Malaher 1964). On Lake Marion in South Carolina, shallow bays and adjacent low-lying areas were enclosed with dikes to mitigate the loss of wetlands resulting from reservoir development (G. W. Bond Jr., pers. commun.). Part of the Santee NWR, these impoundments are managed for moist-soil plants or planted to corn, milo, or browntop millet and flooded. Several hectares of hardwood bottomland also are artificially flooded to make mast available to wintering ducks. At Clarks Hill Lake on the Savannah River, the COE constructed an 8-ha impoundment that can be drained, planted, and reflooded for wintering ducks (U.S. Army Corps of Engineers 1985c). At Eufaula NWR on the Walter F. George Reservoir, 3 subimpoundments totaling 200 ha are managed for moist-soil and submersed plants (Turnbull 1985).

Annual drawdowns are necessary on those impoundments managed for annual seed-bearing plants. On the southeastern coastal plain, early spring and summer drawdowns are usually recommended for good production of millets (*Echinochloa* spp.), panic grasses (*Panicum* spp.), and smartweeds (Table 2). Reflooding should be complete by September or early

Fig. 6.   Subimpoundments at Santee NWR on Lake Marion Reservoir, South Carolina.

October to make foods available to early migrants (Atlantic Waterfowl Council 1972).

The growth of undesirable plant species (e.g., cattail, saltmeadow cordgrass [*Spartina patens*], common reed [*Phragmites communis*], alligatorweed) can be problematic in freshwater impoundments (Baldwin 1967, Carney and Chabreck 1977, Heitzman 1978, Prevost 1986, T. Carroll, unpubl. data, L. R. Ditto, pers. commun.). Control of these plants is successfully accomplished through burning, grazing, herbiciding, or by mechanical manipulations (e.g., disking), usually in conjunction with a drawdown. These practices often provide additional benefits such as improved germination and growth of desirable plants, and increased availability of foods to waterfowl (Neely 1967, Heitzman 1978, Prevost 1986).

Unflooded agricultural crops can provide a supplemental food source near those reservoirs lacking sufficient natural foods (Wiebe 1946, Wiebe et al. 1950, Givens et al. 1964, Chabreck 1979). The benefits of such programs are largely limited to dabbling ducks (Givens et al. 1964, Chabreck 1979) and geese (Givens et al. 1964, McGilvrey 1966) because diving ducks are less able to forage in unflooded fields. In the southern Atlantic Flyway, mallards, wood ducks, northern pintails, black ducks, American green-winged (*Anas crecca*) and blue-winged teal, American wigeon, and Canada geese use agricultural crops produced by NWR farming programs (McGilvrey 1966, Turnbull 1985, G. W. Bond Jr., pers. commun.). A variety of crops, including corn, soybeans, and oats are cultivated (McGilvrey 1966, Chabreck 1979). At Santee NWR, corn and winter wheat are planted through cooperative agreements with private farmers (G. W. Bond Jr., pers. commun.). Corn, rye, peanuts, sorghum, and wheat are grown on Eufaula NWR to provide food for a variety of wildlife species (Combs 1982).

Table 2. Waterfowl food plants encouraged by drawdown in freshwater wetlands in the southeastern U.S.

Location	Time of drawdown	Food plants	Reference
Tennessee	Late April-early May	Smartweed, millet	Barstow 1963
South Atlantic and Gulf Coasts	February-March	Smartweed	Baldwin 1967
	Late summer	Dwarf spikerush (*Eleocharis parvula*)	
Lake Mattamuskeet NWR, North Carolina	April	Dwarf spikerush, smartweed, fall panic grass (*Panicum dichotomiflorum*)	L. R. Ditto, pers. commun.
South Carolina	February-March	Redroot (*Lachnanthes caroliniana*), smartweed, panic grass, flatsedge (*Cyperus* spp.)	Prevost (1986)
	Spring	Smartweed, panic grass, millet, flatsedge	Morgan et al. (1975)
	Summer	Smartweed, millet	Landers et al. (1976)
Georgia	January, May, and June	Panic grass, spikerush, smartweed	Larimer (1982)
Louisiana	May	Spikerush, paspalum (*Paspalum* spp.)	Carney and Chabreck (1977)
Florida	February	Watershield	Tarver (1980)
	February	Spikerush, smartweed, millet	Holcomb and Wegener (1971)
	March	Spikerush	Worth (1983)

Agricultural crops provide a high-energy, readily available food source. However, most agricultural crops are low in protein and cannot meet all of the nutritional demands of wintering waterfowl (Fredrickson and Taylor 1982, Baldassarre et al. 1983, Fredrickson and Ried 1987). Jorde et al. (1983) observed that wintering mallards supplemented corn intake with natural foods, and Bossenmaier and Marshall (1958) reported that waterfowl fed in aquatic habitats even when waste grain was readily available. Arthur (1968) also observed preferences for native foods. These observations led Baldassarre and Bolen (1984) to suggest that field-feeding on agricultural crops is a response to a shortage of natural foods resulting from the degradation and loss of wetlands. Although agricultural programs on reservoir uplands may be necessary to insure sufficient food resources, we recommend management of nearby aquatic habitats for nutritionally complete native foods. In recognition of the nutritional limitations of cultivated crops, some impoundments have been converted from row crops to moist-soil plants (L. R. Ditto, pers. commun.).

A lack of shelter, particularly on large reservoirs, also can limit the quality of habitat. Wind and wave action frequently restrict use by dabbling ducks to sheltered coves that offer protection (Chabreck 1979). Shelter also can be important in providing protection from human harassment. Thompson (1973) and Thornburg (1973) reported alteration in use patterns by diving ducks at Keokuk Pool on the Mississippi River in response to disturbance. We have noted similar responses by ring-necked ducks wintering on large lakes in Florida. In light of the tremendous public use of multipurpose reservoirs (U.S. Army Corps of Engineers 1985*a*, *b*, *c*), designation of sanctuaries may be advisable on those reservoirs situated along important migration corridors.

The proliferation of exotic plants may play a significant role in the use of reservoirs by waterfowl. Addy (1964) viewed exotics, including Eurasian watermilfoil (*Myriophyllum spicatum*), as threats to waterfowl habitat. However, several authors (Florschutz 1972, Gasaway et al. 1977, Montalbano et al. 1978, Montalbano et al. 1979, Hardin et al. 1984, Hohman 1984, Johnson and Montalbano 1984, 1987) suggested that certain exotics may be valuable in enhancing habitat quality. Florschutz (1972) determined that 72% of a sample of 170 waterfowl, including Canada geese, 6 species of dabbling ducks, and 4 species of diving ducks used Eurasian watermilfoil as food. Turnbull (1985) noted the presence of Eurasian watermilfoil on Eufaula NWR and suggested that this habitat was used by wintering American wigeon. A variety of waterfowl species used habitat dominated by Eurasian watermilfoil on the Jim Woodruff Reservoir in Florida (L. A. Ager, pers. commun.).

Recent evidence suggests that hydrilla (Fig. 7), an exotic submersed plant (Haller 1978), also provides attractive habitat for wintering waterfowl (Gasaway et al. 1977, Johnson and Montalbano 1984). Although widely regarded as a pest plant (Haller 1978), hydrilla is an important duck food in Florida (Montalbano et al. 1978, Montalbano et al. 1979, Hardin et al. 1984) and was preferred over native plants by wintering ducks on Lake Okeechobee (Johnson and Montalbano 1984). Hydrilla supports a higher diversity of duck species than many other plant communities, and because of its ability to produce food over a great range of water depths, accommodates the foraging strategies of both dabbling and diving ducks in deep water (Johnson and Montalbano 1984). Hydrilla also supports a greater number of macroinvertebrates than aquatic plants with more open growth forms (Watkins et al. 1983).

Hydrilla's ability to dominate a body of water rapidly (Haller and Sutton 1975) and to thrive under a wide range of environmental conditions (Tarver et al.

Fig. 7. The exotic hydrilla is an important waterfowl food on many southern reservoirs and lakes.

1978) renders it especially noteworthy from the standpoint of waterfowl habitat on large reservoirs. Hydrilla occurs in all 4 southern Atlantic Flyway states (Johnson and Montalbano 1987) and could provide food for both dabbling and diving ducks on those reservoirs lacking sufficient native foods. Waterfowl make extensive use of hydrilla beds in the Lake Marion Reservoir in South Carolina (T. Strange, pers. commun.) and in the Jim Woodruff Reservoir in Florida (D. H. Brakhage, pers. commun.).

Phosphate Mines.—Phosphate settling ponds are developed by constructing a retaining levee around a complex of old mine cuts (King et al. 1980). Clay slurry, a by-product of the phosphate extraction process, is then pumped into the reservoir and the excess water is decanted. The clay substrate produces a variety of plants and animals which are consumed by waterfowl. In one study, primrose willow (*Ludwigia peruviana*), flatsedge, and hydrilla were the most important plant foods for wintering ducks (Montalbano et al. 1978). Invertebrates were also an important food source, with midges (Chironomidae) and snails (Gastropoda) accounting for 23% of waterfowl diets (Montalbano et al. 1978).

Although the attractiveness of phosphate settling ponds to waterfowl is considerable, these man-made wetlands have limitations regarding their long-

term contribution to wintering habitat.
Early successional settling ponds have
greater habitat diversity (Maehr and Marion 1984) and produce a greater variety of
plant and animal foods for waterfowl
than older ponds (Montalbano et al. 1978,
Montalbano 1980, Montalbano et al.
1983). However, the value of settling
ponds diminishes through time because
open water and exposed mudflats become
choked with dense stands of vegetation
(Montalbano et al. 1978, King et al. 1980).
Proliferation of undesirable plants (e.g.,
cattail and willow) is further accelerated
when substrates are dewatered pursuant to
industrial objectives.

Several authors have suggested the
possibility of managing settling ponds for
enhanced or sustained benefits to waterfowl (Montalbano et al. 1978, King et al.
1980, Montalbano 1980, Wenner and
Marion 1981). An extensive system of
water control structures is placed in levees
during settling pond construction to
facilitate segregation of water from particulate materials. These structures are adequate for regulating discharges to
accomplish both industrial and waterfowl
management objectives (Montalbano et al.
1978). However, settling pond substrates
are typically higher in elevation than
surrounding lands. Consequently, it may
be difficult to provide adequate water
supplies for these elevated wetlands following cessation of mining activities
(Gilbert et al. 1981). It should be possible
to maintain desirable habitat on these
wetlands through water-level manipulation, use of herbicides, prescribed burns,
and/or mechanical practices if water
sources adequate to meet management
needs can be developed.

Despite management opportunities,
environmental conditions in phosphate
settling ponds appear conducive to avian
botulism (*Clostridium botulinum* Type
C) outbreaks (Forrester et al. 1980, Marion et al. 1983, Fig. 8). Dynamic water
levels, abundant vegetation, high ambient

Fig. 8. Conditions in phosphate settling ponds
are conducive to outbreaks of avian botulism.

temperatures, and the abundance of birds
contribute to the potential for epizootics
of the disease (Forrester et al. 1980). *C.
botulinum* Type C occurs less frequently
in phosphate substrates during winter
than in other seasons (Marion et al. 1983),
suggesting that the threat is greatest to
resident waterfowl. Nevertheless, managers must be aware of the possibility of
avian botulism outbreaks, and must be
prepared to take remedial action (Jensen
and Williams 1964). Deep flooding can
successfully discourage waterfowl use of a
settling pond if an outbreak occurs
(Forrester et al. 1980, G. L. Holder, pers.
commun.).

Radioactive isotopes released during
mining also have caused concern among
waterfowl managers. Montalbano et al.
(1983) determined that ^{226}Ra concentrations in mottled ducks using phosphate
settling ponds were greater than those
from natural wetlands. However, ^{226}Ra
concentrations and a variety of physical
condition indices were not correlated,
suggesting minimal adverse impact.
Bone/substrate ^{226}Ra ratios were similarly
higher for birds collected on settling
ponds than for those taken from natural
wetlands (O'Meara et al. 1986). However,
the ^{226}Ra levels detected probably did not
constitute a significant health hazard for
waterfowl. Concentrations of ^{226}Ra in the
muscle of waterfowl collected from set-

tling ponds were not believed sufficient to pose a health threat to humans (Montalbano et al. 1983, O'Meara et al. 1986).

Natural Lakes.—Lake Mattamuskeet is one of the few natural lakes in the southern Atlantic Flyway where waterfowl habitat is intensively managed. Although little or no habitat management is conducted in the lake proper, Lake Mattamuskeet NWR personnel manage moist-soil impoundments, a green-tree reservoir, and agricultural crops on adjacent sites (L. R. Ditto, pers. commun.).

Most refuge impoundments are managed for moist-soil plants such as dwarf spikerush, millet, and three-square bulrush (*Scirpus americanus*) (L. R. Ditto, pers. commun.). Drawdowns begin in April or May and continue through July. All moist-soil impoundments are reflooded by rainfall and/or pumping by late November. Undesirable plants such as cattail and saltmeadow cordgrass are controlled by plowing and/or burning on 3-5 year intervals. Impoundments are dewatered in February or March in those years when control is necessary. Plowing and/or disking is conducted prior to 30 June, when possible, to permit growth of annual food plants prior to flooding in fall. In heavy stands of cattail and saltmeadow cordgrass, early-fall fires have provided the most effective control.

Few of the impoundments at Lake Mattamuskeet NWR are managed for submersed plants because of their abundance in the lake proper (L. R. Ditto, pers. commun.). The growth of wildcelery, naiad (*Najas* spp.), and redhead grass (*Potamogeton perfoliatus*) in impoundments is encouraged by dropping water levels to 15-30 cm in January. Once the shoots have reached the surface in midsummer, water levels are raised to 35-56 cm to optimize seed production and waterfowl use. Impoundments managed for submersed plants require a drawdown during the growing season every 3-5 years to restore productivity.

In Florida, wintering waterfowl populations must rely largely on wetlands whose managers are not particularly concerned with waterfowl habitat (Chamberlain 1960). Basic management techniques designed to benefit waterfowl habitat are seldom practiced, except on limited areas set aside specifically for waterfowl (Goodwin 1979). The abundance of Florida's wetlands probably has contributed to a sense of complacency about the ability of the state's wetlands to provide adequate wintering habitat (Chamberlain 1960, Goodwin 1979). However, the majority of Florida's 4,589,000 ha of wetlands (National Wetlands Inventory, unpubl. data) are of low to negligible value to waterfowl (Shaw and Fredine 1956).

Although wetland protection and enhancement for the benefit of wildlife are receiving more attention in Florida (McCormack et al. 1984), waterfowl managers are still constrained by land-use conflicts. Multipurpose lake management is necessary in order to meet demands for consumptive water use, recreation, navigation, and flood control (Edmiston and Myers 1983). As Florida's human population expands, the increasing demands placed on lakes will place severe limitations on implementation of large-scale waterfowl habitat programs.

Within the constraints imposed by multipurpose management, there are approaches available to waterfowl managers other than direct manipulation of habitat. For example, restoration of degraded lake ecosystems can be beneficial to waterfowl regardless of the objectives of those restoration efforts. Lakes degraded by eutrophication sometimes lose their attractiveness to waterfowl because of: (1) decreased diversity in plant and animal communities (Uttormark 1979), (2) the development of organic sediments, (3) algal blooms which shade out submersed macrophytes (Estevez et al. 1984), and (4) excessive growth of undesirable plants (Edmiston and Myers 1983).

Those lake restoration techniques most directly affecting waterfowl habitat include dredging, aquatic plant control, and drawdowns (Edmiston and Myers 1983).

Dredging, more than any other technique, has the potential for returning entire lake basins to preeutrophic conditions (Peterson 1979). The primary objectives in dredging for lake restoration are (1) physical improvement of the basin by removing excess vegetation and sediments (Peterson 1979), and (2) reduction in the significance of sediments as an internal nutrient source (Uttormark 1979). Dredging is not without potential adverse environmental impacts, however. Of particular concern to the waterfowl manager are (1) destruction of benthic and vegetative communities, (2) reduced primary production resulting from increases in turbidity, and (3) release of toxic substances such as pesticides to the water column (Peterson 1979, Edmiston and Myers 1983). However, these impacts appear to be relatively short-lived, and when the longer-term benefits are considered, dredging is among the more effective lake restoration techniques (Peterson 1979).

The potential environmental and sociological impacts of excessive aquatic plant growth should be an important concern for waterfowl managers (Johnson and Montalbano 1987). Of the techniques available for dealing with problems of hypereutrophication, aquatic plant control is the most widely used. In Florida, the Department of Natural Resources is the lead agency in managing aquatic vegetation, and its primary emphasis is on the control of exotic plants (Schardt 1986). Aquatic plant control techniques currently include the use of herbicides, mechanical harvesters, biological controls, and drawdowns (Chestnut 1982).

Whereas many aquatic plant control programs either have a beneficial or neutral effect on waterfowl habitat, some policies and techniques have great potential for harm. The use of grass carp (Ctenopharyngodon idella) to control submersed plants has increased dramatically in Florida in recent years (Valin 1985). Further, production of sterile triploid grass carp and the relaxation of state and federal restrictions on their stocking are expected to result in widespread use of these fish for aquatic plant control (Leslie et al. 1987). Grass carp have a preference for certain important waterfowl food plants (Van Dyke et al. 1984, Clugston and Shireman 1987, Wiley et al. 1987), have caused increases in turbidity (Leslie et al. 1983), and, in hypereutrophic waters, can transform the lake into a phytoplankton-based system (Leslie et al. 1987). At Lake Wales, Florida, declines in waterfowl populations were attributed, in part, to the stocking of grass carp (Gasaway et al. 1977). The potential threat posed to waterfowl habitat by grass carp introductions cannot be overstated (Gasaway and Drda 1977). Close scrutiny and oversight of stocking programs are necessary to insure that grass carp are not introduced into aquatic systems providing important waterfowl habitat.

Mechanical harvesting and drawdowns offer the most promise for accomplishing the dual objectives of nuisance aquatic plant control and waterfowl habitat enhancement in Florida lakes. Mechanical harvesting has advantages over chemical control because nutrients are removed from the system and impacts on nontarget plants are minimized (Edmiston and Myers 1983). However, target species for harvesting should not be limited to exotic plants if the interests of waterfowl habitat are to be served (Johnson 1987). The harvesting of plants that compete with waterfowl food plants (e.g., cattail, water hyacinth) could reduce nutrient loads while enhancing waterfowl habitat (Fig. 9). Unfortunately, conventional harvesting machines are slow and cannot work in water depths less than 30-60 cm (Dunst

Fig. 9. Mechanical harvester clearing water hyacinth and cattail.

et al. 1974). Operating costs range from $50-$100/ha, but can run as high as $280-$560/km of canal in Florida (Anonymous 1972). The effectiveness and costs of aquatic plant harvesting vary and the reader is referred to Burton et al (1979) and Bagnall (1982) for details.

Artificial drawdowns have been long recognized as one of the best techniques for improving waterfowl habitat (Griffith 1948, Uhler 1956, Meeks 1969, Carney and Chabreck 1977, Fredrickson and Taylor 1982). Drawdowns also are receiving attention as a tool for nuisance aquatic plant control (Haller et al. 1982, Leslie 1988) and as a means for mitigating undesirable effects of water level stabilization (Worth 1983, Milleson 1987, Leslie 1988). The extensive system of canals, pumps, and water-control structures associated with most public lakes in Florida provides the means to implement drawdowns for a variety of benefits, including enhancement of waterfowl habitat.

Typically, drawdowns on Florida lakes have been conducted during the growing season to improve fisheries habitat (Wegener and Williams 1974), and during the winter to control undesirable aquatic vegetation (Hestand and Carter 1975, Haller et al. 1982). A spring-summer drawdown is generally recommended for improving waterfowl habitat. On Lake Miccosukee, a February-September drawdown resulted in a 70% reduction in unconsolidated organic matter and stimulated watershield germination (Tarver 1980). A summer drawdown on Lake Tohopekaliga rejuvenated the substrate, stimulated production of desirable aquatic plants (Wegener and Williams 1974), and increased the standing crop of aquatic macroinvertebrates (Wegener and McCall 1974). Holcomb and Wegener (1971) reported that the drawdown of Lake Tohopekaliga increased the production of important waterfowl food plants such as spikerushes, flatsedges, swamp smartweed (*Polygonum hydropiperoides*), and millet (*Echinochloa walteri*). However, the drawdown reduced or eliminated desirable submersed macrophytes such as southern naiad and wildcelery (Holcomb and Wegener 1971).

Winter drawdowns have been used on Florida lakes primarily to control undesirable submersed vegetation. Hestand and Carter (1974, 1975) reported that a September-February drawdown on Lake Oklawaha gave excellent control for coontail, hydrilla, southern naiad, and Brazilian elodea (*Egaria densa*). Haller et al. (1982) recommended a winter drawdown for hydrilla control. We do not recommend a winter drawdown in Florida lakes where waterfowl depend heavily on submersed plants for food.

Because the frequency of water level manipulations will be limited by water-supply and other land-use constraints, other techniques will be necessary to maintain and enhance waterfowl habitat. These practices include manipulation of plant communities by grazing or burning.

The effects of livestock grazing on waterfowl breeding habitat have been studied (Bue et al. 1952, Bossenmaier 1964, Kirsch 1969, Gjersing 1975, Mudinger 1976), but impacts on wintering habitat have received little attention. Chabreck (1968) reported that moderate grazing on Louisiana coastal marshes had few serious impacts on wildlife, and that in some cases it encouraged the growth of waterfowl food plants. In freshwater marshes in South Carolina, cattle grazed on undesirable plants such as alligator-weed and avoided smartweeds (Morgan et al. 1975). Neely (1967) believed that moderate spring and summer grazing in marshes where smartweeds occur can be beneficial because cattle control competing plants. Managers in South Carolina sometimes combine intensive grazing and a summer drawdown to encourage panic grasses (Landers et al. 1976). Whyte and Silvy (1981) concluded that a rest period

should coincide with the beginning of the growing season and extend through the seed dispersal season for maximum benefit to waterfowl. Prevost (1986) also suggested that cattle be removed in late summer to permit panic grasses to produce seed. Range for livestock is an important land use in southern Florida (Van Arman et al. 1984), and lake managers are seeking ways to incorporate grazing into lake restoration and wildlife habitat enhancement practices (unpubl. rep., Dep. Environ. Regul., Tallahassee, Fla., 1986).

Fire is an important force in the ecology of the southeastern coastal plain (Boyce 1971). Prescribed burning in uplands has an extensive history in the southeast (Bacon 1971), but little effort has been made to evaluate its applicability for improving habitat for wintering waterfowl. Marsh burning can be beneficial by increasing food plant production and providing improved waterfowl access (Daiber 1986). Burning prevents invasion of grasslands by woody plants, and is therefore important in maintaining the wet prairies and marshes of southern Florida (Hofstetter 1974). Davison and Neely (1959) considered burning a valuable tool for reducing coarse perennial plants and duff, thereby creating more favorable conditions for growing waterfowl food plants.

Marsh fires are generally classified as cover, root, or peat burns (Yancey 1964, Hoffpauer 1967, Daiber 1986). Cover or wet burns are conducted in fall or winter when soil moisture is sufficient to prevent the roots from burning. The purpose of these burns is to reduce the density of vegetation, thereby providing better access for waterfowl. Cover burns are not effective for changing plant species composition unless the root system can be flooded after the fire (Heitzman 1978). Root burns during periods of low soil moisture are useful for retarding plant succession (Prevost 1986). During very dry periods, peat burns can produce open-water ponds, which are attractive to ducks (Yancey 1964). Peat burns in Everglades sawgrass (*Cladium jamaicensis*) communities have created ponds that produce and make available valuable food plants (e.g., fragrant waterlily) (R. W. Ellis, pers. commun.).

CONCLUSIONS AND RECOMMENDATIONS

Although a great many techniques are potentially available for managing waterfowl habitat in the southeastern U.S., the multipurpose use of reservoirs and lakes severely restricts the use of these techniques. In this review, we have documented those practices useful for intensive habitat management on selected sites and have suggested how the waterfowl manager may reap the benefits of programs which are designed to restore and manage limnetic systems for a broader array of purposes. Often, the presence of wintering waterfowl and the economic benefits of associated hunting opportunities can be used as part of the justification for restoring and managing lake ecosystems. Although the maximum potential of the habitat to support wintering waterfowl may not be realized, nonetheless, the benefits can be substantial.

In our review of the literature, we were dismayed by the paucity of published studies relating to the role of southern reservoirs and natural lakes as waterfowl habitat. Apparently, much of the knowledge possessed by managers remains in internal reports and, therefore, is not readily available. Information regarding numbers and phenology of migrating and wintering waterfowl, their habitat use and preferences, diets, and the extent of consumptive and nonconsumptive use of the waterfowl resource should be published or made available through workshops. Otherwise, we believe that it will be difficult to make an effective case for habitat enhancement projects when the potential benefits to waterfowl only can be explained in either a general or esoteric way. The needed exchange of information would allow biologists to better evaluate the appropriateness of incorporating waterfowl habitat-enhancement programs into multipurpose management plans.

The opportunities and needs for future research in the southern Atlantic Flyway are considerable. Typically, waterfowl managers have been more concerned with wetland loss and degradation than with an understanding of habitat use and resource allocation in relation to the requirements of waterfowl in winter (Fredrickson and Drobney 1979, Fredrickson 1982). Much of the management on southern reservoirs and lakes is directed at providing adequate food resources, only one item in a complex matrix of wintering requirements. This approach may attract more ducks to a specific site but may alter species composition, potentially at the expense of species with more specific habitat requirements. Additionally, the value of wetland complexes on the wintering grounds has been recognized (Fredrickson 1982), implying that the effects of modifying a given wetland may reach beyond the site in question. Many of the questions regarding the interaction of waterfowl and their habitats will be answered from research throughout the wintering range, but the need for studies in the southeastern U.S. is particularly critical because wetland destruction continues at a rapid pace.

A fuller understanding of waterfowl requirements is but the first step. Many of the most basic techniques for managing waterfowl habitats have not been critically evaluated in southern freshwater wetlands. Drawdowns, certain aquatic plant control practices, burning, and grazing offer considerable promise but must be tested and developed before optimum management recommendations can be made. Further, we believe that the waterfowl manager can no longer afford to confine his efforts to those rare sites where waterfowl habitat is the primary focus. Innovative techniques for improving habitat within the constraints of existing land use must be developed. This approach will be extremely challenging, but we believe that it offers the best chance for providing adequate wintering habitat.

SUMMARY

Reservoirs and lakes in the southern Atlantic Flyway provide about 1.1 million ha of potential waterfowl habitat. Large reservoirs (280,000 ha total) serve as important resting areas for ducks en route to coastal wintering sites in North and South Carolina. Natural lakes are rare in the region except in Florida, where there are about 7,800 basins comprising 550,600 ha. Lake complexes in the Tallahassee area and in the Kissimmee and St. Johns River basins provide important wintering habitat, especially for diving ducks.

Between the 1950s and 1970s, the loss of wetlands was greater in the southeastern U.S. than in any other region of the country. The greatest losses were of palustrine forested wetlands, and some of these losses can be attributed to reservoir construction. Reservoirs can provide new habitats for waterfowl, but reservoirs built and operated for navigation, flood control, and power supply generally do not offer good waterfowl habitat. Florida's lakes have been subject to extensive drainage, flood-control, and navigation projects. Large-scale structural modifications in the Kissimmee and St. Johns River basins destroyed over 100,000 ha of palustrine wetlands. Artificial regulation of water levels in the remaining wetlands has diminished production and diversity of waterfowl food plants.

Managers have employed a number of strategies to enhance food production or otherwise mitigate a shortage of food on southern reservoirs. Impoundments within reservoir basins are used to produce moist-soil or submersed food plants. Agricultural crops provide a supplemental food source near reservoirs lacking sufficient natural foods. Exotic plants such as Eurasian watermilfoil and hydrilla have become established in many reservoirs and are often important foods.

Newly constructed phosphate settling ponds attract large concentrations of wintering ducks in Florida, but their value diminishes over time. If water sources are available, it should be possible to maintain desirable habitat through water-level manipulations, use of herbicides, prescribed burns, and/or mechanical practices. Despite management opportunities, the presence of *Clostridium botulinum* Type C and elevated levels of radioactive isotopes in settling pond substrates are cause for concern.

In Florida, wintering waterfowl must rely on wetlands whose managers are not particularly concerned with waterfowl habitat. Demands placed on lakes for water supply, recreation, navigation, and flood control place limitations on efforts to enhance waterfowl habitat. However, restoration of hypereutrophic lakes can improve habitat conditions regardless of the objectives of those restoration efforts. Lake restoration techniques most directly affecting waterfowl habitat include dredging, aquatic plant control, and drawdowns.

Aquatic plant control is the most widely used technique for dealing with problems stemming from hypereutrophication. Mechanical harvesting has advantages over chemical control because nutrients are removed from the system, and impacts on nontarget plants are minimized. Other aquatic plant control policies have potential for great harm. The use of grass carp to control submersed plants has increased dramatically in recent years. Scrutiny and oversight of stocking programs is necessary to protect waterfowl habitat.

Drawdowns are receiving more attention as a tool for nuisance aquatic plant control and as a means for mitigating undesirable effects of water-level stabilization. Spring and summer drawdowns in Florida have rejuvenated substrates, stimulated production of waterfowl food plants, and increased the standing crop of macroinvertebrates. Winter drawdowns are not recommended where waterfowl depend heavily on submersed vegetation.

Because the frequency of water-level manipulations is limited by water-supply constraints, grazing and prescribed burning might also be used to manipulate plant communities. Limited data suggest moderate grazing can be beneficial because cattle control undesirable plants. Marsh burning can be beneficial by increasing food plant production and improving access.

Opportunities to improve waterfowl habitat depend largely on managers' ability to implement habitat enhancement techniques within the constraints of existing land use. Unfortunately, many of the tools needed to accomplish this task are unavailable. Managers have been constrained to a superficial approach to habitat management because: (1) there are few published accounts of southern reservoirs and lakes as waterfowl habitat, (2) wintering waterfowl requirements are poorly understood, and (3) basic management techniques have not been critically evaluated in southern freshwater wetlands.

LITERATURE CITED

Addy, C. E. 1964. Atlantic Flyway. Pages 167-184 *in* J. P. Linduska, ed. Waterfowl tomorrow. U.S. Gov. Print. Off., Washington, D.C.

——, and J. D. Heyland. 1968. Canada goose management in eastern Canada and the Atlantic Flyway. Pages 10-23 *in* R. L. Hine and C. Schoenfeld, eds. Canada goose management: current continental problems and programs. Dembar Educ. Res. Serv., Madison, Wis.

Ager, L. A., and K. E. Kerce. 1970. Vegetational changes associated with water level stabilization on Lake Okeechobee, Florida. Proc. Annu. Conf. Southeast. Assoc. Game and Fish Comm. 24:338-351.

Anonymous. 1972. Steady advances in aquatic weed control. Weeds Today 3(3):6-7.

Arthur, G. C. 1968. Farming for Canada geese. Pages 113-115 *in* R. L. Hine and C. Schoenfeld, eds. Canada goose management: current continental problems and programs. Dembar Educ. Res. Serv., Madison, Wis.

Atlantic Waterfowl Council. 1972. Techniques handbook of waterfowl habitat development and management. Atlantic Waterfowl Counc., Bethany Beach, Del. 218 pp.

Bacon, E. M. 1971. Keynote address. Pages 7-10 *in* Prescribed burning symp. proc. U.S. For. Serv., Southeast For. Exp. Stn., Asheville, N.C.

Bagnall, L. O. 1982. Aquatic plant harvesting and harvesters. Pages 37-41 *in* T. L. Chestnut, ed. Proc. conf. on strategies for aquatic weed manage. Univ. Florida, Gainesville.

Baldassare, G. A., and E. G. Bolen. 1984. Field-feeding ecology of waterfowl wintering on the southern high plains of Texas. J. Wildl. Manage. 48:63-71.

——, R. J. Whyte, E. E. Quinlan, and E. G. Bolen. 1983. Dynamics and quality of waste corn available to postbreeding waterfowl in Texas. Wildl. Soc. Bull. 11:25-31.

Baldwin, W. P. 1967. Impoundments for waterfowl on South Atlantic and Gulf coastal marshes. Pages 127-133 *in* J. D. Newsom, ed. Proc. marsh and estuary manage. symp. Louisiana State Univ., Baton Rouge.

Barstow, C. J. 1963. Waterfowl management on two U.S. Army Corps of Engineers multipurpose reservoirs in mid-Tennessee. Proc. Annu. Conf. Southeast. Assoc. Game and Fish Comm. 17:50-60.

Bellrose, F. C. 1968. Waterfowl migration corridors east of the Rocky Mountains in the United States. Ill. Nat. Hist. Survey Biol. Notes No. 61. 23 pp.

——. 1980. Ducks, geese and swans of North America. Stackpole Books, Harrisburg, Pa. 540 pp.

Betz, J. V. 1984. Water use. Pages 108-115 *in* E. A. Fernald and D. J. Patton, eds. Water resources atlas of Florida. Florida State Univ., Tallahassee.

Bossenmaier, E. F. 1964. Cows and cutter bars. Pages 627-634 *in* J. P. Linduska, ed. Waterfowl tomorrow. U.S. Gov. Print. Off., Washington, D.C.

——, and W. H. Marshall. 1958. Field-feeding by waterfowl in southeastern Manitoba. Wildl. Monogr. 1. 32 pp.

Boyce, S. G. 1971. Foreword. Pages 5-6 *in* Prescribed burning symp. proc. U.S. For. Serv., Southeast For. Exp. Stn., Asheville, N.C.

Brinson, M. M., R. J. Swift, R. C. Plantico, and J.
    S. Barclay. 1981. Riparian ecosystems: their
    ecology and status. U.S. Fish and Wildl. Serv.
    FWS/OBS-81/17. 154 pp.

Brisbin, I. L., Jr. 1974. Abundance and diversity of
    waterfowl inhabiting heated and unheated por-
    tions of a reactor cooling reservoir. Pages 579-
    593 in J. W. Gibbons and R. R. Sharitz, eds.
    Thermal ecology. Atomic Energy Comm. Symp.
    Ser. CONF-730505.

Bue, I. G., L. Blankenship, and W. H. Marshall.
    1952. The relationship of grazing practices to
    waterfowl breeding populations and production
    on stock ponds in western South Dakota. Trans.
    North Am. Wildl. and Nat. Resour. Conf.
    17:396-414.

Burton, T. M., D. L. King, and J. L. Ervin. 1979.
    Aquatic plant harvesting as a lake restoration
    technique. Pages 177-185 in Lake restoration:
    proc. natl. conf. U.S. Environ. Protect. Agency,
    Washington, D.C.

Campbell, D., D. A. Munch, R. Johnson, M. P.
    Parker, B. Parker, D. V. Rao, R. Marella, and
    E. Albanesi. 1984. St. Johns River Water
    Management District. Pages 158-177 in E. A.
    Fernald and D. J. Patton, eds. Water resources
    atlas of Florida. Florida State Univ., Tallahas-
    see.

Carney, D. F., and R. H. Chabreck. 1977. Spring
    drawdown as a waterfowl management practice
    in a floating fresh marsh. Proc. Annu. Conf.
    Southeast. Assoc. Fish and Wildl. Agencies
    31:266-271.

Chabreck, R. H. 1968. The relation of cattle and
    cattle grazing to marsh wildlife and plants in
    Louisiana. Proc. Annu. Conf. Southeast. Assoc.
    Game and Fish Comm. 22:55-58.

——. 1979. Winter habitat of dabbling ducks—
    physical, chemical, and biological aspects.
    Pages 133-142 in T. A. Bookhout, ed. Waterfowl
    and wetlands—an integrated review. North
    Cent. Sect., Wildl. Soc., Madison, Wis.

Chamberlain, E. B., Jr. 1960. Florida waterfowl
    populations, habitats and management. Fla.
    Game and Fresh Water Fish Comm. Tech. Bull.
    No. 7. 62 pp.

Chestnut, T. L., editor. 1982. Proc. conference on
    strategies for aquatic weed management. Univ.
    Florida, Gainesville. 86 pp.

Clugston, J. P., and J. V. Shireman. 1987. Triploid
    grass carp for aquatic plant control. U.S. Fish
    and Wildl. Serv. Fish and Wildl. Leafl. 8. 3 pp.

Combs, D. L. 1982. Social organization in a flock of
    resident Canada geese at Eufaula National
    Wildlife Refuge. M.S. Thesis, Auburn Univ.,
    Auburn, Ala. 118 pp.

Cowardin, L. M., V. Carter, F. C. Golet, and E. T.
    LaRoe. 1979. Classification of wetlands and
    deepwater habitats in the United States. U.S.
    Fish and Wildl. Serv. FWS/OBS-70/31. 103 pp.

Cox, D. T., and H. L. Moody. 1976. Upper St.
    Johns River study. Game and Fresh Water Fish
    Comm., Dingell-Johnson Proj. F-25. Tallahas-
    see, Fla. 887 pp.

Daiber, F. C. 1986. Conservation of tidal marshes.
    Van Nostrand Reinhold Co., Inc., New York,
    N.Y. 341 pp.

Davison, V. E., and W. W. Neely. 1959. Managing
    farm fields, wetlands, and waters for wild ducks
    in the south. U.S. Dep. Agric. Farmer's Bull.
    No. 2144. 14 pp.

Dunst, R. C., S. M. Born, P. D. Uttormark, S. A.
    Smith, S. A. Nichols, J. O. Peterson, D. R.
    Knauer, S. L. Serns, D. R. Winter, and T. L.
    Wirth. 1974. Survey of lake rehabilitation
    techniques and experiences. Wis. Dep. Nat.
    Resour. Tech. Bull. No. 75. 179 pp.

Edmiston, H. L., and V. B. Myers. 1983. Florida
    lakes—a description of lakes, their processes,
    and means of protection. Dep. Environ. Regul.,
    Tallahassee, Fla. 30 pp.

Environmental Protection Agency. 1978. Environ-
    mental impact statement: central Florida phos-
    phate industry. Vol. 2. U.S. Environ. Protect.
    Agency, Atlanta, Ga. 572 pp.

Estevez, E. D., B. J. Hartman, R. Kautz, and E. D.
    Purdum. 1984. Ecosystems of surface waters.
    Pages 92-107 in E. A. Fernald and D. J. Patton,
    eds. Water resources atlas of Florida. Florida
    State Univ., Tallahassee.

Farmer, E. E., and W. G. Blue. 1978. Reclamation of
    lands mined for phosphate. Pages 585-608 in F.
    W. Schaller and P. Sutton, eds. Reclamation of
    drastically disturbed lands. Am. Soc. Agron.,
    Crop Sci., and Soil Sci., Madison, Wis.

Fernald, E. A. 1984. Summary and recommenda-
    tions. Pages 278-281 in E. A. Fernald and D. J.
    Patton, eds. Water resources atlas of Florida.
    Florida State Univ., Tallahassee.

Florshutz, O., Jr. 1968. Canada goose populations,
    hunting pressure, kill, crippling loss, and age
    ratios at Mattamuskett, North Carolina. Pages
    53-57 in R. L. Hine and C. Schoenfield, eds.
    Canada goose management: current continental
    problems and programs. Dembar Educ. Res.
    Serv., Inc., Madison, Wis.

——. 1972. The importance of Eurasian milfoil as
    a waterfowl food. Proc. Annu. Conf. Southeast.
    Assoc. Game and Fish Comm., 26:189-194.

Forrester, D. J., K. C. Wenner, F. H. White, E. C.
    Greiner, W. R. Marion, J. E. Thul, and G. A.
    Berkoff. 1980. An epizootic of avian botulism in
    a phosphate mine settling pond in northern
    Florida. J. Wildl. Dis. 16:323-327.

Fredrickson, L. H. 1982. Habitat. Pages 34-41 in
    Workshop on the ecology of wintering water-
    fowl. Delta Waterfowl Res. Stn., Portage la
    Prairie, Manitoba.

——, and R. D. Drobney. 1979. Habitat utilization
    by postbreeding waterfowl. Pages 119-131 in T.

A. Bookhout, ed. Waterfowl and wetlands—an integrated review. North Cent. Sect., Wildl. Soc., Madison, Wis.

——, and F. A. Reid. 1987. Nutritional values of waterfowl foods. *In* Prototype handbook—managing waterfowl habitats: breeding, migrating, wintering. U.S. Fish and Wildl. Serv., Off. Inform Transfer, Fort Collins, Colo. 6 pp.

——, and T. S. Taylor. 1982. Management of seasonally flooded impoundments for wildlife. U.S. Fish and Wildl. Serv. Resour. Publ. 148. 29 pp.

Gasaway, R. D., and T. F. Drda. 1977. Effects of grass carp introduction on waterfowl habitat. Trans. North Am. Wildl. and Nat. Resour. Conf. 42:73-85.

——, S. Hardin, and J. Howard. 1977. Factors influencing wintering waterfowl abundance in Lake Wales, Florida. Proc. Annu. Conf. Southeast. Assoc. Fish and Wildl. Agencies 31:77-83.

Gilbert, T., T. King, and B. Barnett. 1981. An assessment of wetland habitat establishment at a central Florida phosphate mine site. U.S. Fish and Wildl. Serv. FWS/OBS-81/38. 96 pp.

Givens, L. S., M. C. Nelson, and V. Ekedahl. 1964. Farming for waterfowl. Pages 599-610 *in* J. P. Linduska, ed. Waterfowl tomorrow. U.S. Gov. Print. Off., Washington, D.C.

Gjersing, F. M. 1975. Waterfowl production in relation to rest-rotation grazing. J. Range Manage. 28:37-42.

Godfrey, R. K., and J. W. Wooten. 1979. Aquatic and wetland plants of the southeastern United States: monocotyledons. Univ. Georgia Press, Athens. 712 pp.

——, and ——. 1981. Aquatic and wetland plants of the southeastern United States: dicotyledons. Univ. Georgia Press, Athens. 933 pp.

Goodwin, T. M. 1979. Waterfowl management practices employed in Florida and their effectiveness on native and migratory waterfowl populations. Fla. Sci. 42:123-129.

Griffith, R. 1948. Improving waterfowl habitat. Trans. North Am. Wildl. Conf. 13:609-617.

Haller, W. T. 1978. Hydrilla: a new and rapidly spreading aquatic weed problem. Univ. Florida Inst. Food and Agric. Sci. Circ. S-245. 13 pp.

——, J. V. Shireman, and D. E. Canfield. 1982. Physical control. Pages 42-43 *in* T. L. Chestnut, ed. Proc. conf. on strategies for aquatic weed manage. Univ. Florida, Gainesville.

——, and D. L. Sutton. 1975. Community structure and competition between *Hydrilla* and *Vallisneria*. Hyacinth Control J. 13:48-50.

Hardin, S., R. Land, M. Spelman, and G. Morse. 1984. Food items of grass carp, American coots, and ring-necked ducks from a central Florida lake. Proc. Annu. Conf. Southeast. Assoc. Fish and Wildl. Agencies 38:313-318.

Harris, L. D. 1984. Bottomland hardwoods: valuable, vanishing, vulnerable. Coop. Ext. Serv., Univ. Florida, Gainesville. 16 pp.

Harvey, R. M., J. R. Pickett, and R. D. Bates. 1987. Environmental factors controlling the growth and distribution of submersed aquatic macrophytes in two South Carolina reservoirs. Lake and Reservoir Manage. 3:243-255.

Heitzman, B. 1978. Management of salt marsh impoundments for waterfowl in North Carolina. Wildl. Resour. Comm., Raleigh, N.C. 35 pp.

Hestand, R. S., and C. C. Carter. 1974. The effects of a winter drawdown on aquatic vegetation in a shallow water reservoir. Hyacinth Control J. 12:9-12.

——, and ——. 1975. Succession of aquatic vegetation in Lake Ocklawaha two growing seasons following a winter drawdown. Hyacinth Control J. 13:43-47.

Hoffpauer, C. M. 1967. Burning for coastal marsh management. Pages 134-139 *in* J. D. Newsom, ed. Proc. marsh and estuary manage. symp. Louisiana State Univ., Baton Rouge.

Hofstetter, R. H. 1974. The effect of fire on the pineland and sawgrass communities of southern Florida. Pages 256-286 *in* P. J. Gleason, ed. Environments of South Florida: past and present. Miami Geol. Soc. Memoir 2.

Hohman, W. L. 1984. Diurnal time-activity budgets for ring-necked ducks wintering in central Florida. Proc. Annu. Conf. Southeast. Assoc. Fish and Wildl. Agencies 38:158-164.

Holcomb, D., and W. Wegener. 1971. Hydrophytic changes related to lake fluctuations as measured by point transect. Proc. Annu. Conf. Southeast. Assoc. Game and Fish Comm. 25:570-583.

Huber, W. C., and J. P. Heaney. 1984. Drainage, flood control, and navigation. Pages 116-121 *in* E. A. Fernald and D. J. Patton, eds. Water resources atlas of Florida. Florida State Univ., Tallahassee.

Hunt, K. W. 1943. Floating mats on a southern coastal plain reservoir. Bull. Torrey Bot. Club 70:481-488.

Jensen, W. I., and C. S. Williams. 1964. Botulism and fowl cholera. Pages 333-341 *in* J. P. Linduska, ed. Waterfowl tomorrow. U.S. Gov. Print. Off., Washington, D.C.

Johnsgard, P. A. 1975. Waterfowl of North America. Indiana Univ. Press, Bloomington. 575 pp.

Johnson, F. A. 1987. Lake Okeechobee's waterfowl habitat: problems and possibilities. Aquatics 9(3):20-21.

——, and F. Montalbano III. 1984. Selection of plant communities by wintering waterfowl on Lake Okeechobee, Florida. J. Wildl. Manage. 48:174-178.

——, and ——. 1987. In my opinion . . . considering waterfowl habitat in hydrilla control policies. Wildl. Soc. Bull. 15:466-469.

Jorde, D. G., G. L. Krapu, and R. D. Crawford. 1983. Feeding ecology of mallards wintering in Nebraska. J. Wildl. Manage. 47:1044-1053.

King, T., L. Hord, T. Gilbert, and F. Montalbano III. 1980. An evaluation of wetland habitat establishment and wildlife utilization in phosphate clay settling areas. Proc. Annu. Conf. Restor. and Creation of Wetlands 7:35-49.

Kirsch, L. M. 1969. Waterfowl production in relation to grazing. J. Wildl. Manage. 33:821-828.

Landers, J. L., A. S. Johnson, P. H. Morgan, and W. P. Baldwin. 1976. Duck foods in managed tidal impoundments in South Carolina. J. Wildl. Manage. 40:721-728.

Larimer, T. C. 1982. Integration of wood duck production with attraction of migratory waterfowl in coastal fresh marsh. M.S. Thesis, Univ. Georgia, Athens. 59 pp.

Leslie, A. J., Jr. 1988. Literature review of drawdown for aquatic plant control. Aquatics 10:12-18.

——, L. E. Nall, and J. M. Van Dyke. 1983. Effects of vegetation control by grass carp on selected water-quality variables in four Florida lakes. Trans. Am. Fish. Soc. 112:777-787.

——, J. M. Van Dyke, R. S. Hestand III, and B. Z. Thompson. 1987. Management of aquatic plants in multi-use lakes with grass carp (Ctenopharyngodon idella). Lake and Reservoir Manage. 3:266-276.

Maehr, D. S. 1981. Bird use of a north-central Florida phosphate mine. Fla. Field Nat. 9:28-32.

——, and W. R. Marion. 1984. Bird abundance and distribution in a north Florida phosphate mine. Proc. Annu. Conf. Southeast. Assoc. Fish and Wildl. Agencies 38:111-120.

Marion, W. R., T. E. O'Meara, G. D. Riddle, and H. A. Berkoff. 1983. Prevalence of Clostridium botulinum Type C in substrates of phosphate-mine settling ponds and implications for epizootics of avian botulism. J. Wildl. Manage. 19:302-307.

McCormack, F. A., J. K. Lewis, T. Swihart, W. Hinkley, and G. W. Wilson Jr. 1984. Emerging issues and conflicts. Pages 252-269 in E. A. Fernald and D. J. Patton, eds. Water resources atlas of Florida. Florida State Univ., Tallahassee.

McGilvrey, F. B. 1966. Fall food habits of ducks near Santee Refuge, South Carolina. J. Wildl. Manage. 30:577-580.

Meeks, R. L. 1969. The effect of drawdown date on wetland plant succession. J. Wildl. Manage. 33:817-821.

Milleson, J. F. 1987. Vegetation changes in the Lake Okeechobee littoral zone 1972 to 1982. South

Fla. Water Manage. Dist. Tech. Publ. 87-3. West Palm Beach. 33 pp.

Montalbano, F., III. 1980. Summer use of two central Florida phosphate settling ponds by Florida ducks. Proc. Annu. Conf. Southeast. Assoc. Fish and Wildl. Agencies 34:584-590.

——, S. Hardin, and W. M. Hetrick. 1979. Utilization of hydrilla by ducks and coots in central Florida. Proc. Annu. Conf. Southeast. Assoc. Game and Fish Comm. 33:36-42.

——, W. M. Hetrick, and T. C. Hines. 1978. Duck foods in central Florida phosphate settling ponds. Pages 247-255 in D. E. Samuel, J. R. Stauffer, C. H. Hocutt, and W. T. Mason, eds. Surface mining and fish/wildlife needs in the eastern U.S. U.S. Fish and Wildl. Serv. FWS/OBS-78/81.

——, J. E. Thul, and W. E. Bolch. 1983. Radium 226 and trace elements in mottled ducks. J. Wildl. Manage. 47:327-333.

Morgan, P. H., A. S. Johnson, W. P. Baldwin, and J. L. Landers. 1975. Characteristics and management of tidal impoundments for wildlife in a South Carolina estuary. Proc. Annu. Conf. Southeast. Assoc. Game and Fish Comm. 25:526-539.

Mudinger, J. G. 1976. Waterfowl response to rest-rotation grazing. J. Wildl. Manage. 40:60-68.

Neely, W. M. 1967. Planting, disking, mowing and grazing. Pages 212-221 in J. D. Newsom, ed. Proc. marsh and estuary manage. symp. Louisiana State Univ., Baton Rouge.

——, and V. E. Davison. 1971. Wild ducks on farmland in the south. U.S. Dep. Agric. Farmer's Bull. 2218. 14 pp.

O'Meara, T. E., W. R. Marion, C. E. Roessler, G. S. Roessler, H. A. Van Rinsvelt, and O. B. Myers. 1986. Environmental contaminants in birds: phosphate-mine and natural wetlands. Fla. Inst. Phosphate Res. Publ. No. 05-003-045. 77 pp.

Palmer, S. L. 1984. Surface water. Pages 54-67 in E. A. Fernald and D. J. Patton, eds. Water resources atlas of Florida. Florida State Univ., Tallahassee.

Penfound, W. T. 1952. Southern swamps and marshes. Bot. Review 18:413-445.

Perrin, L. S., M. J. Allen, L. A. Rowse, F. Montalbano III, K. J. Foote, and M. W. Olinde. 1982. A report on fish and wildlife studies in the Kissimmee River basin and recommendations for restoration. Game and Fresh Water Fish Comm., Off. Environ. Serv., Tallahassee, Fla. 260 pp.

Pesnell, G. L., and R. T. Brown III. 1977. The major plant communities of Lake Okeechobee, Florida, and their associated inundation characteristics as determined by gradient analysis. South Fla. Water Manage. Dis. Tech. Publ. 77-1. West Palm Beach. 68 pp.

Peterson, S. A. 1979. Dredging and lake restoration. Pages 105-114 *in* Lake restoration: proc. natl. conf. U.S. Environ. Protect. Agency, Washington, D.C.

Prevost, M. B. 1986. Management of plant communities for waterfowl in coastal South Carolina. Pages 168-183 *in* W. R. Whitman and W. H. Meredith, eds. Proc. symp. waterfowl and wetlands manage. in the coastal zone of the Atlantic Flyway. Del. Coast. Manage. Prog., Dep. Nat. Resour., Dover.

Schardt, J. D. 1986. Florida aquatic plant survey. Dep. Nat. Resour., Bur. Aquatic Plant Manage., Tallahassee, Fla. 124 pp.

Shaw, S. P., and C. G. Fredine. 1956. Wetlands of the United States; their extent and their value to waterfowl and other wildlife. U.S. Fish and Wildl. Serv. Circ. 39. 67 pp.

Sincock, J. L. 1957. A study of the vegetation on the northwest shore of Lake Okeechobee; its frequency, distribution, ecology, wildlife values, and predicted distribution by elevation with proposed water control measures. Game and Fresh Water Fish Comm., Pittman-Robertson Proj. W-19-R. Tallahassee, Fla. 52 pp.

———. 1958. Waterfowl ecology in the St. Johns River Valley as related to the proposed conservation areas and changes in the hydrology from Lake Harney to Ft. Pierce, Florida. Game and Fresh Water Fish Comm., Pittman-Robertson Proj. W-19-R. Tallahassee, Fla. 122 pp.

———, and J. A. Powell. 1957. An ecological study of waterfowl areas in central Florida. Trans. North Am. Wildl. Conf. 22:220-236.

———, ———, R. K. Hyde, and H. E. Wallace. 1957. The relationship of the wintering waterfowl population of the Kissimmee River Valley to the hydrology, topography, distribution of the vegetation and the proposed hydrological regulations. Game and Fresh Water Fish Comm., Pittman-Robertson Proj. W-19-R. Tallahassee, Fla. 72 pp.

Stafford, S. K. 1979. Inland records of oldsquaws and surf scoters from North Florida. Fla. Field Nat. 7:25-26.

Stanford, J. A. 1979. Proliferation of river deltas in reservoirs: a "natural" mitigative process? Pages 193-195 *in* The mitigation symposium: national workshop on mitigating losses of fish and wildlife habitat. Rocky Mt. For. and Range Exp. Stn. Gen. Tech. Rep. RM-65. 684 pp.

Swihart, T., J. Hand, D. Barker, L. Bell, J. Carnes, C. Cosper, R. Deuerling, W. Hinkley, R. Leins, F. Livingston, D. York, and C. Gluckman. 1984. Water quality. Pages 68-91 *in* E. A. Fernald and D. J. Patton, eds. Water resources atlas of Florida. Florida State Univ., Tallahassee.

Tarver, D. P. 1980. Water fluctuation and the aquatic flora of Lake Miccosukee. J. Aquat. Plant Manage. 18:19-23.

———, J. A. Rogers, M. J. Malaher, and R. L. Lazor. 1978. Aquatic and wetland plants of Florida. Dep. Nat. Resour., Tallahassee, Fla. 127 pp.

Taylor, R. J., and C. Taylor. 1976. Multipurpose use of reservoirs. Ann. Okla. Acad. Sci. 5:106-112.

Thompson, D. 1973. Feeding ecology of diving ducks on Keokuk Pool, Mississippi River. J. Wildl. Manage. 37:367-381.

Thompson, R. 1983. America's disappearing wetlands. Congr. Q. Editorial Res. Rep. (19 August):615-631.

Thornburg, D. D. 1973. Diving duck movements on Keokuk Pool, Mississippi River. J. Wildl. Manage. 37:382-389.

Tiner, R. W., Jr. 1984. Wetlands of the United States: current status and recent trends. U.S. Gov. Print. Off., Washington, D.C. 59 pp.

Turnbull, R. E. 1985. Activity budgets of mallards and American wigeon wintering at Eufaula National Wildlife Refuge, Alabama-Georgia. M.S. Thesis, Auburn Univ., Auburn, Ala. 37 pp.

———, D. H. Brakhage, and F. A. Johnson. 1986. Mortality of wintering lesser scaup from commercial trotlines on Lake Okeechobee, Florida. Proc. Annu. Conf. Southeast. Assoc. Fish and Wildl. Agencies 40:465-469.

Uhler, F. M. 1956. New habitats for waterfowl. Trans. North Am. Wildl. Conf. 21:453-469.

U.S. Army Corps of Engineers. 1985a. Water resources development by the U.S. Army Corps of Engineers in Georgia. U.S. Army Eng. Div., South Atl., Atlanta, Ga. 104 pp.

———. 1985b. Water resources development by the U.S. Army Corps of Engineers in North Carolina. U.S. Army Eng. Div., South Atl., Atlanta., Ga. 111 pp.

———. 1985c. Water resources development: State of South Carolina. U.S. Army Eng. Div., South Atl., Atlanta, Ga. 77 pp.

U.S. Department of Agriculture. 1979. The status of land disturbed by surface mining in the United States: basic statistics by state and county as of July 1, 1977. U.S. Gov. Print. Off., Washington, D.C. 100 pp.

Uttormark, P. D. 1979. General concepts of lake degradation and lake restoration. Pages 65-70 *in* Lake restoration: proc. natl. conf. Environ. Protect. Agency, Washington, D.C.

Valin, D. J. 1985. Herbivorous fish permitting update. Aquatics 7(4):13-14, 21.

Van Arman, J., D. Nealon, S. Burns, B. Jones, L. Smith, T. MacVicar, M. Yansura, A. Federico, J. Bucca, M. Knapp, and P. Gleason. 1984. South Florida Water Management District. Pages 138-

157 *in* E. A. Fernald and D. J. Patton, eds, Water resources atlas of Florida. Florida State Univ., Tallahassee.

Van Dyke, J. M., A. J. Leslie Jr., and J. E. Nall 1984. The effects of grass carp on the aquatic macrophytes of four Florida lakes. J. Aquatic Plant Manage. 22:87-95.

Watkins, C. E., II, J. V. Shireman, and W. T. Haller. 1983. The influence of aquatic vegetation upon zooplankton and benthic macroinvertebrates in Orange Lake, Florida. J. Aquatic Plant Manage. 21:78-83.

Wegener, W., and T. D. McCall. 1974. Aquatic macroinvertebrate responses to an extreme drawdown. Proc. Annu. Conf. Southeast. Assoc. Game and Fish Comm. 28:126-144.

——, and V. Williams. 1974. Fish population responses to improved lake habitat utilizing extreme drawdown. Proc. Annu. Conf. Southeast. Assoc. Game and Fish Comm. 28:144-161.

Weller, M. W. 1978. Management of freshwater marshes for wildlife. Pages 267-284 *in* R. E. Good, D. F. Whigham, and R. L. Simpson, eds. Freshwater wetlands. Academic Press, New York, N.Y.

Wenner, K. C., and W. R. Marion. 1981. Wood duck production on a North Florida phosphate mine. J. Wildl. Manage. 45:1037-1042.

White, W. M., and G. W. Malaher. 1964. Reservoirs. Pages 381-389 *in* J. P. Linduska, ed. Waterfowl tomorrow. U.S. Gov. Print. Off., Washington, D.C.

Whyte, R. J., and N. J. Silvy. 1981. Effects of cattle on duck food plants in southern Texas. J. Wildl. Manage. 45:512-515.

Wiebe, A. H. 1946. Improving conditions for migratory waterfowl on TVA impoundments. J. Wildl. Manage. 10:4-8.

——, E. R. Cady, and P. Bryan. 1950. Waterfowl on the Tennessee River impounds. Trans. North Am. Wildl. Conf. 15:111-117.

Wiley, M. J., P. P. Tazik, and S. T. Sobaski. 1987. Controlling aquatic vegetation with triploid grass carp. Ill. Nat. His. Surv. Circ. 57. 16 pp.

Worth, D. 1983. Preliminary environmental responses to marsh dewatering and reduction in water regulation schedule in Water Conservation Area 2A. South Fla. Water Manage. Dist. Tech. Publ. 83-6. West Palm Beach. 63 pp.

Yancey, R. K. 1964. Matches and marshes. Pages 619-626 *in* J. P. Linduska, ed. Waterfowl tomorrow. U.S. Gov. Print. Off., Washington, D. C.

Zallen, M. 1979. An analysis of the proposed rules to implement the Coordination Act. Pages 527-531 *in* The mitigation symposium: national workshop on mitigating losses of fish and wildlife habitat. Rocky Mt. For. and Range Exp. Stn. Gen. Tech. Rep. RM-65. 684 pp.

BEAVER POND WETLANDS: A SOUTHERN PERSPECTIVE

DALE H. ARNER, Department of Wildlife and Fisheries, Mississippi State University, Mississippi State, MS 39762
GARY R. HEPP[1], Savannah River Ecology Laboratory, Drawer E, Aiken, SC 29801

Over 50% of the 87 million ha of original wetlands in the conterminous United States (U.S.) have been destroyed (Frayer et al. 1983). From 1954 to 1974, wetland habitats disappeared at a rate of approximately 185,000 ha annually (Frayer et al. 1983). Most of this loss can be attributed to agricultural development, with the greatest loss occurring in the southern U.S. Approximately 95% of the wetlands remaining in the lower 48 states are inland, freshwater, palustrine wetlands (Tiner 1984). However, palustrine wetlands are being lost at a faster rate than any others (Mitsch and Gosselink 1986). Turner et al. (1981) estimated that hardwood bottomlands disappeared at a rate of 175,000 ha/yr from 1960 to 1975. Even today, inland wetlands do not share the same degree of protection as coastal wetlands. Inland wetlands are in jeopardy, particularly in the southern U.S. In the Mississippi Alluvial Valley (MAV), only about 20% of the original bottomland hardwood forests remains (MacDonald et al. 1979).

Concomitant with the loss of wetland habitat is the loss of ecological values associated with these habitats (Wharton 1979). Wetlands can be extremely productive ecosystems that function as sinks, helping to filter nutrients and reduce sedimentation, thereby maintaining the quality of nearby water systems (Tiner 1984). They also provide critical habitat for many species of fish and wildlife. Bottomland hardwoods are considered one of the most important habitats for fish and wildlife in the U.S. (Fredrickson 1978, Forsythe and Gard 1980).

The following discussion is devoted to beaver (*Castor canadensis*) pond habitats; palustrine wetlands that are actually increasing in area in the southern U.S. Our objectives are to: (1) assess the current status of beaver ponds in the southern U.S., (2) describe the general characteristics of these wetlands, (3) discuss the importance of beaver ponds in relation to meeting needs of wintering and migrating waterfowl, and (4) describe management of these habitats for waterfowl.

STATUS OF BEAVERS

Before the Europeans settled North America, beavers ranged from the arctic tundra to the deserts of northern Mexico (Jenkins and Busher 1979). Beginning in the 17th century, beavers were harvested extensively, but in the early 1900s, they were almost extirpated. Restocking programs, strict harvest regulations, and natural expansion of remnant populations have helped beavers return to much of their former range. The present beaver population in North America, however, probably represents only a small fraction of original numbers (Naiman et al. 1986).

Many southeastern states relocated beavers beginning about 1940. These efforts generally were successful. Golley (1966) estimated that beavers were present in 12 of 46 counties in South Carolina by the mid-1960s; just a decade later they were present in at least 28 of 46 counties (Woodward et al. 1976). In Mississippi, beaver ponds increased in area from 9,469 ha in 1966 to approximately 29,000 ha in 1976 (Arner and DuBose 1978). Similar expansion has taken place in North Carolina. A 1983 survey in North Carolina showed that beavers were present in

[1]Present address: Department of Zoology and Wildlife Science, Auburn University, Auburn, AL 36849-5414.

80 of 100 counties, and they affected a minimum of 35,858 ha of bottomland habitat (Woodward et al. 1985). Beaver populations continue to grow throughout the southeastern U.S. They presently are distributed in all southeastern states (Fig. 1) and affect a minimum of 288,000 ha (Table 1).

In many areas, beavers cause significant damage to forestry and agricultural production, and effective management programs are needed (Arner and DuBose 1978, Woodward 1983, Spencer 1985). Much emphasis has been placed on the damage that beavers cause, but little attention has been given to the beneficial aspects of beaver ponds. Some workers, however, consider beaver to be essential components of the landscape and suggest that beavers should be integrated into most resource management programs (Naiman et al. 1986). Beavers increase habitat diversity by flooding and opening forested habitats, which ultimately causes greater interspersion of successional stages. This increased habitat complexity is beneficial because it leads to the establishment of a more diverse wildlife community (Reese and Hair 1976, Hair et al. 1978). Waterfowl in particular use beaver pond wetlands extensively (Speake 1955, Arner 1964). As the loss of palustrine bottomland wetlands continues, the importance of beaver pond habitats to waterfowl throughout the annual cycle will probably increase.

CHARACTERISTICS OF BEAVER PONDS

Beavers normally are associated with riparian ecosystems. In the southeastern U.S., these are typically hardwood bottomlands or floodplain forests. There are very few studies that document the physical and vegetative characteristics of beaver ponds in the southeastern U.S. Most studies simply have described the general relationships between beaver ponds and the fish or wildlife populations. Pullen

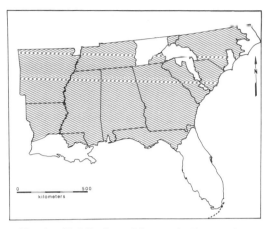

Fig. 1. Distribution of beaver in the southeastern U.S. A modification of the range map presented by Hill (1982).

(1971) described 2 general classes of beaver impoundments: stream-channel ponds and floodplain ponds. Beaver ponds in stream channels usually are small (<1 ha) and narrow. Floodplain ponds are generally shallow and sometimes inundate extensive areas. A single beaver colony usually has a mixture of pond types, with differing physical and biological characteristics.

Hepp (1977) developed a wetland classification system for beaver ponds in the Piedmont region of South Carolina. Results of Hepp's (1977) study illustrated the diversity of beaver pond wetlands occurring within a single watershed. Beaver ponds were separated into 7 wetland types depending on characteris-

Table 1. Minimum area impacted by beavers in 8 southeastern states.

State	Area affected (ha)	Reference
Alabama	35,560	Beshears (1967)
Arkansas	66,200	Wigley and Garner (1987)
Georgia	116,500	Godbee and Price (1975)
Louisiana	a	
Mississippi	29,000	Arner and DuBose (1978)
N. Carolina	35,900	Woodward et al. (1985)
S. Carolina	4,400	Woodward et al. (1976)
Tennessee	a	

[a] No estimates of the area are available for Louisiana and Tennessee.

Table 2. Classification of beaver pond wetlands in the Piedmont region of South Carolina.

Wetland types[a]	Dominant vegetation[b]	Water depth (cm)
Deciduous forest	water oak (*Quercus nigra*), sweet gum (*Liquidambar styracilfua*), and red maple (*Acer rubrum*)	40
Deciduous shrub	tag alder (*Alnus serralata),* buttonbush (*Cephalanthus occidentalis),* and swamp privit (*Ligustrum sinese*)	22
Emergent vegetation	Asiatic dayflower (*Aneilema keisak),* rice cutgrass (*Leersia oryzoides),* and soft rush (*Juncus effusus*)	22
Bur-reed	bur-reed (*Sparganium americanum*) and beggar ticks (*Bidens frondosa*)	12
Rice cutgrass	rice cutgrass and tearthumb (*Polygonum satittatum*)	23
Floating-leaved	pondweeds (*Potamogeton* spp.)	26
Open water	< 30% vegetated	52

[a]Wetland type was based on the areal coverage of the dominant vegetation.

[b]A dominant was the uppermost layer of vegetation that had an areal coverage >30% (plant nomenclature follows Radford et al. 1968 and Hotchkiss 1972).

tics of the dominant vegetation (Table 2), which is largely influenced by factors such as age of the pond, topography, and soil characteristics. Plant nomenclature follows Radford et al. (1968) and Hotchkiss (1972).

Beaver ponds are transitional habitats. The individual plant species or groups of species that become established may differ regionally, but the successional processes are similar. Soon after beavers impound a bottomland area, many of the trees are killed, which opens the canopy and makes conditions more suitable for growth of herbaceous aquatic or semi-aquatic vegetation. Next, because beaver ponds trap sediments from runoff, water depth decreases with pond age (Naiman et al. 1986). Shallow water (<30 cm) is necessary for development of many aquatic plants that are important to waterfowl. It may take several years for deepwater beaver ponds to acquire optimal development of aquatic vegetation. Emergent vegetation (e.g., rice cutgrass, Asiatic dayflower, and bur-reed) gradually becomes established on the pond's perimeter and in the shallow zones of ponds. Floating-leaved plants (e.g., pondweeds and watershield (*Brasenia schreberi*]) grow well along the margins of the wetland in water that is usually <1 m deep. Deciduous shrubs (e.g., buttonbush and tag alder) become established in

older beaver ponds with shallow, slow-moving water. Vegetation provides both food and cover and is a key factor that determines the suitability of beaver ponds to migratory and wintering waterfowl.

WATERFOWL USE OF BEAVER PONDS

The southeastern U.S. is an important wintering area for waterfowl. Many species are distributed in coastal habitats, but wood ducks (*Aix sponsa*) and mallards (*Anas platyrhynchos*) extensively use inland freshwater wetlands in fall and winter. Beaver ponds are an important component of inland freshwater habitats for waterfowl. In addition to wood ducks and mallards, beaver ponds are used by many other species of waterfowl during the nonbreeding season. For example, 10 species of waterfowl occur from October-March in a swamp system along the Savannah River in South Carolina where beavers are an integral component of the wetland system (Table 3). Blue-winged teal use the wetland in autumn and spring, whereas the other species occur throughout the fall and winter. Similar data are lacking for other southeastern locations, but these species of ducks are usually the principal users of beaver ponds in fall and winter.

Mallards and wood ducks are the key species found in a swamp system at the

Table 3. Seasonal occurrence of waterfowl using a beaver-influenced swamp system at the Savannah River Plant in South Carolina (Mayer et al. 1986)

Species	October-November	December January	February-March
Wood duck	X	X	X
American wigeon (*Anas americana*)	X	X	X
Green-winged teal (*A. crecca*)	X	X	X
Mallard	X	X	X
Black duck (*A. rubripes*)	X	X	X
Northern pintail (*A. acuta*)	X	X	X
Blue-winged teal (*A. discors*)	X		X
Northern shoveler (*A. clypeata*)	X	X	X
Ring-necked duck (*Aythya collaris*)	X	X	X
Hooded merganser (*Mergus cucullatus*)	X	X	X

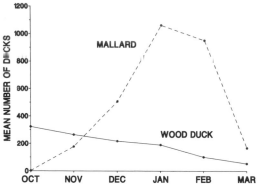

Fig. 2. Relative abundances of mallards and wood ducks using a beaver-influenced swamp system on the Savannah River Plant, South Carolina.

Savannah River Plant (SRP) (Mayer et al. 1986), and, with few exceptions (e.g., black ducks), should be the main species using beaver ponds in the southeastern U.S. Beaver ponds, with dead, standing timber and a well-developed shrub layer, provide excellent roosting habitats for wood ducks and other species of waterfowl during fall and winter (Speake 1955, Almand 1965, Taberrer 1971, Luckett 1977).

Wood ducks used the SRP swamp throughout the winter, and their abundance was fairly constant during October, November, and December (Fig. 2). A decrease in numbers in January and February probably reflected the start of spring migration by individuals from northern breeding areas and/or possibly a dispersal of birds to breeding sites on the SRP. Wood ducks begin nesting at the SRP in late January (Kennamer and Hepp 1987).

Mallards first arrived in the SRP swamp in early November, but peak numbers occurred during January and February (Fig. 2). Most mallards winter-

ing in this region of the country migrate along the Savannah River drainage and use coastal areas of South Carolina (Bellrose 1980). They spend little time in the inland wetlands during fall migration, but use increases as they begin their migration to breeding areas.

Food-habits studies show that acorns (*Quercus* spp.) are used extensively by wintering wood ducks (Landers et al. 1977, Drobney and Fredrickson 1979, Delnicki and Reinecke 1986). When mast crops fail, however, wood ducks must depend on seeds from herbaceous aquatic vegetation to meet nutrient requirements (Landers et al. 1977). Beaver pond wetlands produce a variety of natural foods that are used by wood ducks and other wintering waterfowl (Johnson et al. 1975). Asiatic dayflower, a common plant in many southern beaver ponds (Hepp 1977), was ranked second in importance only to acorns in the diet of wood ducks on the SRP (Landers et al. 1977). Beaver pond systems with a network of diverse wetlands can provide the necessary food requirements for wood ducks during their annual cycle.

In the past, mallards wintering in hardwood bottomlands foraged extensively on acorns (Wright 1961). However, this has changed in areas like the MAV where wetlands have been drained and the land has been converted to agricultural production. Mallards in the MAV now feed heavily on agricultural grains (Delnicki and Reinecke 1986). Several workers (Fredrickson and Taylor 1982) suggest that seeds from moist-soil plants may serve as an alternative food source for mallards, and consideration should be given to managing such plants (Delnicki and Reinecke 1986). In many cases, beaver ponds produce an abundant supply of foods important to waterfowl. Drawdowns can enhance the growth of naturally occurring emergent vegetation that is attractive to waterfowl. When beaver ponds have little desirable vegetative growth, plantings may be necessary to increase the production of food.

MANAGEMENT OF BEAVER PONDS

Discussion of beaver pond management for waterfowl will be directed at the following impoundment conditions: (1) beaver ponds with shallow water areas having few emergent plants, and where water level can be manipulated; (2) beaver ponds with shallow water dominated by emergent plants, and where water level can be manipulated; and (3) beaver ponds with no possibilities for drainage.

Shallow Water With Few Emergent Plants

Arner et al. (1969) reported that 58% of the beaver ponds sampled in Mississippi had shallow water, but little or no emergent vegetation. In these wetlands, germination and growth of naturally occurring emergent plants can be encouraged by simply installing drains (Fig. 3) to reduce the water level and expose the substrate. Arner (1963) introduced the 3-log drain that can be made from green logs or water-soaked logs from the pond; standing snags are too buoyant. Perforated drainpipe or a box drain also can be used (Fig. 4). For beaver dams that are

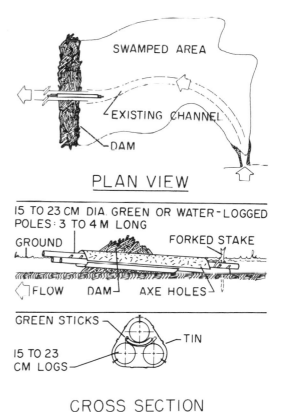

Fig. 3. Design and placement of the 3-log drain for manipulating water level in beaver ponds.

constructed in the stream channel, the drain should be placed with the upstream portion of the logs submerged and staked down (Fig. 3). If the dam is large, several breaks at various places in the dam may be needed to expedite movement of water from the impounded area. Use of a drain to expose shallow areas would not be practical if the terrain is flat.

Management techniques and goals for beaver ponds are similar to moist-soil management procedures described by Fredrickson and Taylor (1982). Soils in many wetland areas already contain seeds of desirable emergent vegetation. Arner (1963) reported that 2 of 3 beaver ponds that were drained in Alabama produced plants traditionally valued as waterfowl food. Studies of plant life history may be a useful starting point for evaluating

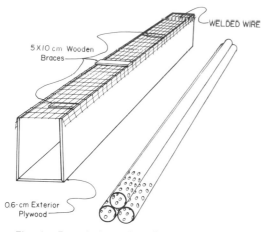

Fig. 4. Box drain and perforated drainpipe for beaver ponds.

management strategies for particular wetlands (van der Valk and Davis 1978, Leck and Graveline 1979, Smith and Kadlec 1983). Knowledge of the seed bank can provide useful information for scheduling initial water-level manipulation, because growth of plants can be controlled by the timing and speed of drawdowns (Meeks 1969, Fredrickson and Taylor 1982). For example, Radford et al. (1968) notes that sesbania (*Sesbania exaltata*), an undesirable plant, flowers from July to September. Preacher (1975) reported that this plant can be inhibited by delaying drainage in beaver ponds until late summer.

In beaver ponds that have minimal coverage of desirable aquatic vegetation and where the seed bank is depauperate, it may be necessary to plant commercially available seed if immediate use of beaver ponds by wintering waterfowl is desired. Arner (1963) recommended the planting of Japanese millet (*Echinochloa crusgalli var. frumentacea*) under these wetland conditions. Drains were installed from mid-July to mid-August, and seeds were planted at the rate of 3.7 kg/ha without fertilizer. After the millet seed heads fully developed (usually 55-60 days), the drain was removed unless the beaver had previously plugged it.

Yields of Japanese millet from 1,572-2,694 kg/ha have been measured on beaver ponds (Fig. 5) in Alabama (Arner 1963, Preacher 1975). Although these yields are greater than those reported for other native wetland plant species in the southeastern U.S., sprangletops (*Leptochloa* spp.), smartweeds (*Polygonum* spp.), and panic grasses (*Panicum* spp.) produce substantial quantities of seed (Fredrickson and Taylor 1982). Managing for a variety of native plants that have a wide range of moisture tolerances can reduce the probability of crop failure, and will probably attract a greater diversity of waterfowl species. This might be accomplished best by sowing Japanese millet over 1/2 - 2/3 of the dewatered beaver pond and leaving the remainder to develop into native wetland species.

Shallow Water With Many Emergent Plants

Areas with abundant emergent plants are usually older beaver ponds. The species of emergent plants occupying the shallow areas will dictate the type of management necessary for improving the habitat for waterfowl. Valuable emergent plant species are those known to be consistent producers of seeds and/or underground vegetative structures that are used as food by waterfowl. Such plants commonly found in beaver ponds in the southeastern U.S. are stout smartweed (*Polygonum densiflorum*) (Arner et al. 1974, Brock 1987), Asiatic dayflower (Landers et al. 1977), red-rooted sedge (*Cyperus erythororhizos*) (Arner 1963, Preacher 1975), and nodding smartweed (*P. lapathifolium*) (Arner et al. 1974). Wild millet (*Echinochloa* spp.) ranks as one of the best duck food plants of shallow wetland areas (Martin and Uhler 1939). Beak rush (*Rhynchospora corniculata*) is also a good producer of seed in Mississippi with yields of 494-813 kg/ha (Brock 1987).

Fig. 5. Fifty-day-old Japanese millet planted on mantachie soil. Seed yield was 2,072 kg/ha (photo by H. Huffstatler).

Several wetland plant species grow in shallow-water areas of beaver ponds but are poor producers of seeds. Swamp smartweed (*P. hydropiperoides*) and rice cutgrass commonly invade shallow areas of seasonally dewatered beaver ponds. Seeds of these plants are frequently used by waterfowl, but these species are poor producers of seed in Alabama and Mississippi. Studies of swamp smartweed, for example, showed yields ranging from 7-53 kg/ha in Alabama (Arner 1963) and 21-85 kg/ha in Mississippi (Arner et al. 1974, Brock 1987). Seed yields for stout smartweed were 5-31 times higher than for swamp smartweed (Brock 1987). Seed production of rice cutgrass is below that of many other species such as wild millet and stout smartweed. Low and Bellrose (1944) reported yields of 117 kg/ha for rice cutgrass in the Illinois River valley, and in Mississippi, Arner recorded yields of 139 kg/ha. However, Fredrickson and Taylor (1982) reported yields of 340 kg/ha for rice cutgrass in Missouri, and sug-

gested that rice cutgrass had the best seed production when drawdowns occurred mid- to late-summer and the soil was kept saturated. Other plant species of little food value to waterfowl that are commonly found in older beaver ponds are cattail (*Typha* spp.), wool grass (*Scirpus cyperinus*), and alder.

Wetland vegetation should not be evaluated solely on its ability to produce seeds. Perennial plants provide cover, which is important to many species of wintering waterfowl, as well as habitat for aquatic invertebrates. Aquatic invertebrates are an important protein source for breeding wood ducks (Drobney and Fredrickson 1979). Wood ducks use beaver ponds extensively during the breeding season (Luckett 1977). Manipulation of water level and other management procedures must be carefully planned, so that breeding wood ducks are not affected adversely. A good management plan for waterfowl enhancement in beaver ponds should take into consideration the necessity of providing large quantities of palatable seed, invertebrates, and protective cover for feeding waterfowl.

Data are lacking for many southeastern wetland plants; however, available data reveal that such plants as stout smartweed harbor twice as many invertebrates (R. Smith, pers. commun.) and produce >5 times as much seed as swamp smartweed (Arner 1963). The standing crops of a number of aquatic plants were investigated in winter and early spring by Teels et al. (1976). Their findings showed that eastern wolffiella *(Wolffiella floridana)* and pennywort *(Hydrocotyle ranunculoides)* persisted through winter or early spring, providing a substrate for invertebrates. Some other persistent aquatic plants were bur-reed, snail seed pondweed *(Potamogeton diversifolius)*, and parrotfeather *(Myriophyllum brasilinse)*; the former two are fair to good producers of seed. In evaluating emergent and submergent plants for invertebrate production, persistency during winter and early spring should be ascertained, and the leafy component of the plants should be noted. Studies of submerged aquatics have indicated that the largest crops of invertebrates are associated with those plants possessing finely dissected leaves (Moyle 1961, Krull 1970).

If undesirable vegetation is a problem, it can be controlled by using one or more of the following: (1) water-level manipulation, (2) burning, (3) mechanical disturbance, and (4) herbicides. Timing of drawdowns and reflooding of the beaver ponds can have a major influence on vegetative growth. Fredrickson and Taylor (1982) recommended that reflooding should begin as soon as desirable emergents are established so that undesirable plants such as cockleburs *(Xanthium strumarium)* will be stunted or killed. This assumes that water level in beaver ponds can be controlled in a timely fashion.

Burning is used in many southern freshwater marsh impoundments to retard succession and open dense stands of vegetation. It could be used similarly in beaver pond wetlands and should increase germination and growth of aquatic plants. Burning is usually done in late winter or very early spring after water is drawn down. A clean cover burn removes all standing vegetation, but changes in the vegetation type usually do not occur. Burns that occur when marsh soils are dry damage the roots of plants and may change the vegetation type. This type of burn is useful for eliminating undesirable vegetation.

Herbicides also can control growth of undesirable plants. Baker (1966) reported the control of soft-rush, wool-grass, cattail, and rice cutgrass using Dalapon (2-dichloropropionic acid), a herbicide composed of 85% Dalapon sodium salt and 15% inert ingredients, with 0.5 kg of Dalapon dissolved in 12 l of water. Baker (1966) used 17 kg of Dalapon per 188 l of water per ha. The chemical, 2,4,5-T, was most effective on alder using 12 l of 2,4,5-T ester per 1,309 l of water per ha. The use of a backpack mist blower proved to be far superior to a backpack sprayer in applying herbicides. The herbicide applications were made in May; the dams were broken and millet planted in mid-July with millet producing a yield of 2,321 kg/ha.

Swamp smartweed has proved to be far more resistant to herbicides than the above-mentioned plant species. Banvel 720 is recommended for swamp smartweed control (W. Houston, pers. commun.). Banvel 720 is the trade name for a mixture of 2,4-D and Dicamba. It should be sprayed when smartweed is blooming, then followed with a second application in 2-3 weeks. Suggested application mixture is 1 l Banvel for 100 l water. Control would be more effective with a drawdown before spraying. Frequently when plants are sprayed in standing water, they are not killed below the water's surface.

Impounded Areas with No Drainage

Beaver commonly inhabit areas that are dominated by a cypress-tupelo (*Taxodium distichum Nyssa aquatica*) overstory. Although beaver frequently construct dams at some outlets in such areas, there is usually insufficient elevation change at any point for the use of hidden drains, and management practices will have to be oriented toward developing aquatic plant communities of food value to waterfowl. Most of these areas have some floating plants, such as duck weeds (*Spirodela* spp., *Lemna* spp.) and water-meal (*Wolffia* spp., *Wolffiella* spp.). All are high in nutrients and palatable to dabbling ducks (Mbagwu and Adeniji 1988). If the pond is deficient in these plants, it might be worthwhile to introduce them. Big duckweed (*Spirodela* spp.) does best in water with a neutral pH, whereas duckweed (*Lemna* spp.) does well in acidic and highly organic water. In acidic cypress-tupelo areas in Mississippi, frogbit (*Limnobium spongia*) and the pondweeds were successfully introduced by transplanting the entire plants (Arner, unpubl. data). Bur-reed is frequently found in cypress-tupelo swamps. Young rooted specimens of this species also can be transplanted (Martin and Uhler 1939). Watershield is a common component of swamp areas and provides seeds palatable to waterfowl. It can be propagated by seed or rootstock and planted in the fall (Martin and Uhler 1939). Najas (*Najas quadalupensis*) is a palatable waterfowl food, and growing parts of plants can be transplanted (Martin and Uhler 1939). Pennywort (*Hydrotoyle ranunculoides*) harbored the greatest number of invertebrates in late winter and early spring when compared to other plant species present in Mississippi (Arner et al. 1974). This plant can be established by seeds or parts of rooted stems.

Aquatic plants that might become problem plants by choking out more desirable aquatic plants include bladderwort (*Utricularia* spp.), coontail (*Ceratophyllum demersum*), and fanwort (*Cabomba caroliniana*). If these plants become dominant, herbicide control could be tried, but the cost of total control may be prohibitive.

Many cypress-tupelo sloughs have been cut over, and frequently a dense young growth of cypress or tupelo dominates. When this occurs, extensive shade prohibits establishment of many desirable aquatics. It may be advisable to clear-cut a number of small areas to produce scattered openings before an attempt is made to establish desirable aquatics.

RESEARCH NEEDS

We know very little about the abundance and species composition of waterfowl that use beaver ponds in the southeastern U.S. Future research should document the use of beaver pond habitats by migrating and wintering waterfowl during wet, dry, and average years of precipitation; however, effective techniques must be developed to census waterfowl in flooded forestlands. In addition, studies should be initiated to determine characteristics of beaver pond wetlands that are important to waterfowl. Basic studies of habitat use and food habits, for example, will provide information to guide future management decisions. Seed and invertebrate yields should be determined for some of the plants commonly found in beaver impoundments such as beak rush, frogbit, panic grasses, wild millets, bur-reed, and thalia (*Thalia dealbata*).

Management techniques such as prescribed burning and water-level manipulation should be evaluated for their cost effectiveness and ability to make significant changes in the composition and structure of beaver pond vegetation.

Management of beaver ponds for wintering waterfowl should always consider potential effects on the reproduction of resident wood ducks. Beaver ponds provide excellent habitats for wood ducks throughout their breeding cycle. In the South, wood ducks begin nesting as early as January. Water-level management of beaver ponds should be scheduled so as not to interfere with reproduction. Management plans that reduce aquatic invertebrates also should be avoided because female wood ducks depend on invertebrates as a source of protein for egg production.

SUMMARY

Beaver populations have returned to much of their former range and now affect a minimum of 288,000 ha in the southeastern U.S. With continuing losses of palustrine habitats in the southeast, the importance of beaver pond wetlands to waterfowl may increase. Beaver pond systems usually are diverse wetlands that support a wide array of plants and animals. Dabbling ducks, particularly mallards and wood ducks, use beaver ponds extensively during the fall and winter. These wetland complexes are excellent natural habitats for wintering waterfowl, but managing them (e.g., water level, burning) frequently can help to produce better habitat conditions. Beaver ponds often have been overlooked, but their widespread occurrence throughout the southeastern U.S. dictates that they should receive greater attention by wetland and waterfowl managers in the future.

Management actions designed for beaver ponds depend on whether the ponds can be drained. Three-log drains and box-drains are described for use in draining beaver ponds. Where a diverse seed bank is present, moist-soil management is a viable management technique for promoting waterfowl use of beaver ponds. If the seed bank is depauperate, it may be necessary to plant commercially available seed such as Japanese millet. Where dense emergents dominate the vegetation, it may be necessary to control the emergents with fire or herbicides in an attempt to promote high-seed-producing moist-soil species. In beaver ponds where it is not possible to drawdown the area, it might be possible to transplant submergent species.

LITERATURE CITED

Almand, J. D. 1965. A contribution to the management requirements of the wood duck (*Aix sponsa*) in the Piedmont of Georgia. M.S. Thesis, Univ. Georgia, Athens. 78 pp.

Arner, D. H. 1963. Production of duck food in beaver ponds. J. Wildl. Manage. 27:76-81.

———. 1964. Research and a practical approach needed in management of beaver habitat in the southeastern United States. Trans. North Am. Wildl. and Nat. Resour. Conf. 29:150-158.

———, J. Baker, D. Wesley, and B. Herring. 1969. An inventory and study of beaver impounded water in Mississippi. Proc. Annu. Conf. Southeast. Assoc. Game and Fish Comm. 23:110-128.

———, E. D. Norwood, and B. M. Teels. 1974. Comparison of aquatic ecosystems in two national waterfowl refuges. Proc. Annu. Conf. Southeast. Assoc. Game and Fish Comm. 28:456-467.

———, and J. S. DuBose. 1978. Increase in beaver impounded water in Mississippi over a ten year period. Proc. Annu. Conf. Southeast. Assoc. Fish and Wildl. Agencies 32:150-153.

Baker, J. L. 1966. The renovation of beaver ponds for the production of duck food. M.S. Thesis, Mississippi State Univ., Mississippi State. 36 pp.

Bellrose, F. C. 1980. Ducks, geese and swans of North America. Third ed. Stackpole Books, Harrisburg, Pa. 540 pp.

Beshears, W. W. 1967. Status of beaver in Alabama. Pages 2-6, *in* Proc. first Alabama beaver symp. Game and Fish Div., Ala. Dep. Conserv. and Ala. For. Prod. Assoc., Montgomery, Ala.

Brock, S. C. 1987. Seed yields of four moist-soil plants on Noxubee National Wildlife Refuge. M.S. Thesis, Mississippi State Univ., Mississippi State. 35 pp.

Delnicki, D., and K. J. Reinecke. 1986. Mid-winter food use and body weights of mallards and wood ducks in Mississippi. J. Wildl. Manage. 50:43-51.

Drobney, R. D., and L. H. Fredrickson. 1979. Food selection by wood ducks in relation to breeding status. J. Wildl. Manage. 43:109-120.

Forsythe, S. W., and S. W. Gard. 1980. Status of bottomland hardwoods along the lower Mississippi River. Trans. North Am. Wildl. and Nat. Resour. Conf. 45:333-340.

Frayer, W. E., T. J. Monahan, D. C. Bowden, and F. A. Grayhill. 1983. Status and trends of wetlands and deepwater habitats in the conterminous United States, 1950s to 1970s. Dep. For. and Wood Sci., Colorado State Univ., Fort Collins. 32 pp.

Fredrickson, L. H. 1978. Lowland hardwood wetlands: current status and habitat values for wildlife. Pages 296-306 *in* P. E. Greeson, J. R. Clark, and J. E. Clark, eds. Wetland functions and values: the state of our understanding. Am. Water Resour. Assoc., Minneapolis, Minn.

———, and T. S. Taylor. 1982. Management of seasonally flooded impoundments for wildlife. U.S. Fish and Wildl. Serv. Resour. Publ. 148. 29 pp.

Godbee, J., and T. Price. 1975. Beaver damage survey. Ga. For. Comm., Macon, Ga. 24 pp.

Golley, F. B. 1966. South Carolina mammals. Univ. Georgia Press, Athens. 181 pp.

Hair, J. D., G. R. Hepp, L. M. Luckett, K. P. Reese, and D. K. Woodward. 1978. Beaver pond ecosystems and their relationships to multi-use natural resource management. Pages 80-92 *in* R. R. Johnson and J. F. McCormick, eds. Strategies for protection and management of floodplain wetlands and other riparian ecosystems. U.S. Dep. Agric. For. Serv., GTR-WO-12. 409 pp.

Hepp, G. R. 1977. The ecology of wood duck (*Aix sponsa*) broods in the Piedmont Region of South Carolina. M.S. Thesis, Clemson Univ., Clemson, S.C. 113 pp.

Hill, F. P. 1982. Beaver. Pages 256-281 *in* J. A. Chapman and G. A. Feldhamer, eds. Wild mammals of North America: biology, management, and economics. John Hopkins Univ. Press, Baltimore, Md.

Hotchkiss, N. 1972. Common marsh, underwater and floating-leaved plants of the United States and Canada. Dover Publications, New York, N.Y. 223 pp.

Jenkins, S. H., and P. E. Busher. 1979. *Castor canadensis*. Mammalian Species 120:1-8.

Johnson, R. C., J. W. Preacher, J. R. Gwaltney, and J. E. Kennamer. 1975. Evaluation of habitat manipulation for ducks in an Alabama beaver pond complex. Proc. Annu. Conf. Southeast. Assoc. Game and Fish Comm. 29:512-518.

Kennamer, R. A., and G. R. Hepp. 1987. Frequency and timing of second broods in wood ducks Wilson Bull. 99:655-662.

Krull, J. N. 1970. Aquatic plant macroinvertebrate associations and waterfowl. J. Wildl. Manage. 34:707-718.

Landers, J. L., T. T. Fendley, and A. S. Johnson. 1977. Feeding ecology of wood ducks in South Carolina. J. Wildl. Manage. 41:118-127.

Leck, M. A., and K. J. Graveline. 1979. The seed bank of a freshwater tidal marsh. Am. J. Bot. 66:1006-1015.

Low, J. B., and F. C. Bellrose. 1944. The seed and vegetative yields of waterfowl food plants in the Illinois River Valley. J. Wildl. Manage. 8:7-22.

Luckett, L. M. 1977. Ecology and management of the wood duck, *Aix sponsa*, in the Piedmont region of South Carolina. M.S. Thesis, Clemson Univ., Clemson, S.C. 99 pp.

MacDonald, P. O., W. E. Frazer, and J. K. Clauser. 1979. Documentation, chronology, and future projections of bottomland hardwood habitat loss in the Lower Mississippi Alluvial Plain. Vol. 1. Basic rep. U.S. Fish and Wildl. Serv., Ecol. Serv., Vicksburg, Miss. 133 pp.

Martin, A. C., and F. M. Uhler. 1939. Food of game and ducks in the United States and Canada. U.S. Dep. Agric. Tech. Bull. 634. 157 pp.

Mayer, J. J., R. A. Kennamer, and R. T. Hoppe. 1986. Waterfowl of the Savannah River Plant. Comprehensive Cooling Water Stud. Final Rep. Savannah River Plant, U.S. Dep. Energy, Aiken, S.C. 189 pp.

Mbagwn, I. G., and H. A. Adeniji. 1988. The nutritional content of duckweed (*Lemna paucicostata* Hegelm) in the Kainji Lake area, Nigeria. Aquatic Bot. 29:357-366.

Meeks, R. L. 1969. The effect of drawdown on wetland plant succession. J. Wildl. Manage. 33:817-821.

Mitsch, W. J., and J. G. Gosselink. 1986. Wetlands. Van Nostrand Reinhold Co., New York, N.Y. 539 pp.

Moyle, J. B. 1961. Aquatic invertebrates as related to larger water plants and waterfowl. Minn. Dep. Conserv. Res. Planning Invest. Rep. No. 233. 24 pp.

Naiman, R. J., J. M. Melillo, and J. E. Hobbie. 1986. Ecosystem alteration of boreal forest streams by beaver (*Castor canadensis*). Ecology 67:1254-1269.

Preacher, J. W. 1975. An evaluation of duck food plants produced in a beaver pond in Marion County, Alabama. M.S. Thesis, Auburn Univ., Auburn, Ala. 52 pp.

Pullen, T. M. 1971. Some effects of beaver (*Castor canadensis*) and beaver pond management on the ecology and utilization of fish populations along warm-water streams in Georgia and South Carolina. Ph.D. Thesis, Univ. Georgia, Athens. 84 pp.

Radford, A. E., H. E. Ahles, and C. R. Bell. 1968. Manual of the vascular flora of the Carolinas. Univ. North Carolina Press, Chapel Hill. 1,183 pp.

Reese, K. P., and J. D. Hair. 1976. Avian species diversity in relation to beaver pond habitats in the Piedmont Region of South Carolina. Proc. Annu. Conf. Southeast. Assoc. Fish and Wildl. Agencies 30:437-447.

Smith, L. M., and J. A. Kadlec. 1983. Seed banks and their role during drawdown of a North American marsh. J. Appl. Ecol. 20:673-684.

Speake, D. W. 1955. Waterfowl use of creeks, beaver swamps, and small impoundments in Lee County, Alabama. Proc. Annu. Conf. Southeast. Assoc. Game and Fish Comm. 9:178-185.

Spencer, J. 1985. A plague of beavers. Am. For. 91:22-27, 62-63.

Taberrer, D. K. 1971. The wood duck roost as an index to wood duck abundance in Louisiana. M.S. Thesis, Louisiana State Univ., Baton Rouge. 77 pp.

Teels, B. M., B. Anding, D. H. Arner, E. Norwood, and D. E. Wesley. 1976. Aquatic plant invertebrates and waterfowl associations in Mississippi. Proc. Annu. Southeast. Assoc. Fish and Wildl. Agencies 30:610-616.

Tiner, R. W. 1984. Wetlands of the United States: current status and recent trends. U.S. Fish and Wildl. Serv., National Wetlands Inventory, Washington, D.C. 59 pp.

Turner, R. E., S. W. Forsythe, and N. J. Craig. 1981. Bottomland hardwood forest and land resources of the southeastern United States. Pages 13-28 in J. R. Clark and J. Benforado, eds. Wetlands of bottomland hardwood forests. Elsevier, Amsterdam.

van der Valk, A. G., and C. B. Davis. 1978. The role of seed banks in the vegetation dynamics of prairie glacial marshes. Ecology 59:322-335.

Wharton, C. H. 1979. Values and functions of bottomland hardwoods. Trans. North Am. Wildl. and Nat. Resour. Conf. 45:341-353.

Wigley, T. B., and M. E. Garner. 1987. Impact of beavers in the Arkansas Ozarks. Ark. Agric. Exp. Sta., Rep. Ser. 298. 12 pp.

Woodward, D. K. 1983. Beaver management in the southeastern United States: a review and update. Pages 163-165 in D. A. Decker, ed. Proc. first eastern wildl. damage control conf. Ithaca, N.Y.

———, J. D. Hair, and B. P. Gaffney. 1976. Status of beaver in South Carolina as determined by a postal survey of landowners. Proc. Annu. Conf. Southeast. Assoc. Fish and Wildl. Agencies 30:448-454.

———, R. B. Hazel, and B. P. Gaffney. 1985. Economic and environmental impacts of beavers in North Carolina. Pages 89-96 in P. T. Bromley, ed. Proc. second eastern wildl. damage control conf., Raleigh, N.C.

Wright, T. W. 1961. Winter foods of mallards in Arkansas. Proc. Annu. Conf. Southeast. Assoc. Game and Fish Comm. 13:291-296.

MISSISSIPPI FLYWAY

Managed green-tree reservoir showing flooded bottomland hardwoods, Noxubee National Wildlife Refuge, Mississippi (photo by R. W. Alexander).

THE GREAT LAKES MARSHES

THEODORE A. BOOKHOUT, Ohio Cooperative Fish and Wildlife Research Unit, The Ohio State University, Columbus, OH 43210
KARL E. BEDNARIK, Ohio Division of Wildlife, Crane Creek Wildlife Experiment Station, Oak Harbor, OH 43449
ROY W. KROLL, Winous Point Shooting Club, Port Clinton, OH 43452

Our objectives in this paper are to provide an overview of the physical setting of the Great Lakes, to describe the distribution and characteristics of their coastal marshes, to provide information on waterfowl use of these marshes, and to describe practices used to manage and retain Great Lakes marshes. We include those marshes contiguous with one of the Great Lakes, Lake St. Clair, and the St. Marys, St. Clair, Detroit, and Niagara rivers. Although the term *marsh* is not used in the wetland classification system that will be followed here (Cowardin et al. 1979), we include emergent wetlands and aquatic beds of the palustrine, lacustrine, and riverine systems in our use of the word. This decision is complicated by the fact that waterfowl, particularly diving ducks, use open water adjacent to Great Lakes marshes. We included use of these open waters by ducks and geese when data were available.

THE PHYSICAL SETTING

The Great Lakes coastal marshes are associated with the greatest reservoir of fresh water on earth; the 5 lakes have a coastline of >15,100 km, cover 246,568 km², and contain an estimated 25,000 km³ of water. The bedrock formations of the Great Lakes region comprise a large area of Precambrian rocks that form the Precambrian shield, which lies north of the Lakes and extends southward into central Wisconsin (Hough 1958) (Fig 1).

Lake Superior lies almost entirely within the Precambrian shield. It is nearly surrounded by an escarpment 122-244 m high that descends into water 152-274 m deep. These features contrast with

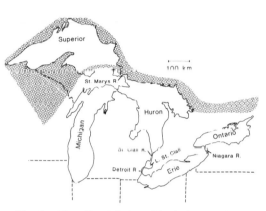

Fig. 1. The Great Lakes. Shaded area depicts area of shoreline within the Precambrian shield.

coastal wetlands of most other Great Lakes, which have low-angle, offshore profiles (Herdendorf and Hartley 1980). The northern shore of Lake Huron, along the North Channel and northeastern shore of Georgian Bay, is on the edge of the Precambrian shield. The lake basin otherwise is within the Paleozoic rock province of the region, as are the entire basins of Lakes Michigan, Erie, and Ontario. Glacial till, composed of boulders to clay-sized material, receives the brunt of wave action on the beaches. If only clay is present, it is carried away in suspension, and waves continue to erode the land. The latter has caused problems in maintaining the outer dikes of the southwestern Lake Erie marshes.

Freezing of the lakes closes ports and most of the connecting waters to navigation in mid-December (Hough 1962), and they remain closed until mid-April over most of the lakes. Solid ice generally forms in protected embayments and channels that might extend 16 km into the larger lakes. Lakes Erie and Ontario may have 80-95% of their surfaces ice-covered in severe winters (Becton and Chandler 1963). Ice breakup in spring can scour barrier beaches, reducing the value of backwaters to spring-migrating water-fowl.

The Great Lakes are subject to tempor-ary, coastal seiches that occur commonly in Lakes Erie and St. Clair and in Green Bay of Lake Michigan (Herdendorf and Hartley 1980). In Lake Erie, for example, water levels rise as much as 2.6 m, while lowering at the windward end of the lake. Seiches can be troublesome to the mainte-nance of diking systems.

Mean levels of the Great Lakes also fluctuate annually, largely caused by precipitation, which ranges from about 74 cm around Lake Superior to 86 cm around Lake Ontario. Lake levels were above normal from 1973 to 1987, reaching an all-time high in 1986 (U.S. Army Corps of Engineers 1987). These high levels caused breaching and destruction of many outer-marsh dikes. However, the Great Lakes Basin has received near average rainfall since 1986, which has alleviated some problems of marsh main-tenance.

More than 13% of the United States (U.S.) population and about 33% of Canada's population live in the Great Lakes Drainage Basin (Powers and Robertson 1966); declining water quality has been a consequence. Recently, 42 "Areas of Concern" were identified by the Water Quality Board of the International Joint Commission (The Center for the Great Lakes 1986). The concern is for inputs into the system, such as phospho-rus, contaminants (e.g., toxaphene, chlor-inated dioxins), municipal and industrial discharges, sewer overflow, urban and agricultural land runoff, and in-place pollutants (Great Lakes Water Quality Board 1982). Additionally, the demand for lakefront property for private, municipal, and industrial development creates a constant threat to retention of Great Lakes marshes.

DISTRIBUTION OF GREAT LAKES MARSHES

Lake Superior has only about 3,500 ha of coastal marshes. In its western area, about 3,300 ha of emergent marshes occur in Kakagon and Fish Creek sloughs near Chequamegon Bay, Wisconsin, and Allouez Bay near Duluth, Minnesota (Table 1). Michigan's largest Lake Super-ior marsh is the Portage Entry marsh in Keweenaw Bay.

Green Bay contains the most important marshes of Lake Michigan's nearly 3,500 ha; these 508 ha are essentially the only marshes that remain along the west side (T. M. Bahti, pers. commun.). Few marshes

Table 1. Estimated area (ha) of coastal marshes in Lakes Superior, Michigan, and Huron, 1987.

Marsh	Controlled	Uncontrolled	Farmed
LAKE SUPERIOR			
Wisconsin			
Kakagon Sloughs		2,867	
Fish Creek Sloughs		339	
Allouez Bay		95	
Michigan			
Portage Entry		243	
Total		3,544	
LAKE MICHIGAN			
Wisconsin			
Green Bay West Shore		508	
Michigan			
Grand Haven		445	
Pere Marquette		263	
Manistee	74	1,821	
Betsie		121	
Pentwater		81	
Muskegon State Game Area		202	
Total	74	3,441	
LAKE HURON			
Ontario			
Bruce Peninsula (6 marshes)		356	
Georgian Bay		12,600	
Michigan			
Munuscong Bay		809	
Wigwam Bay		81	
Nayanquing Point	130	142	225
Tobico	194	162	
Quanicassee		243	
Fish Point	405	356	534
Wildfowl Bay		769	
Total	729	15,518	759

occur along the east shore of Lake Michigan, and most are located in lakes, rivers, and estuaries, such as the Grand, Pentwater, and Manistee rivers, and Muskegon Lake. Marshes that once existed on the 97-km Illinois coastline have been almost entirely converted for economic development (D. D. Thornburg, pers. commun.).

The largest area of Lake Huron marshes lies along the shoreline of Georgian Bay; about 8,500 of the total 12,600 ha occur in the Parry Sound District. These are some of the deepest marshes in the Great Lakes, approaching 4 m in water depth (R. E. Craig, pers. commun.). Saginaw Bay contains the greatest concentration of Michigan's coastal marshes (about 2,500 ha). Most remaining wetlands within the U.S. border occur between the Straits of Mackinac and Drummond Island. On the Ontario shores of Lake Huron, about 350 ha of marsh exist on the west side of Bruce Peninsula. The only other marsh listed by Glooschenko et al. (Provincially and regionally significant wetlands in southern Ontario, Wildlife Branch, Ontario Ministry of Natural Resources Interim Report, 1987 [unpublished]) is the 42-ha portion of the 123-ha Port Franks wetland, which is about 40 km northeast of Sarnia.

The southern Great Lakes, including Lake St. Clair, contain the greatest amount of coastal marshes in proportion to total surface area (Table 2). Lake St. Clair is an expansive, shallow basin with a surface area of 1,110 km^2, a mean depth of 3.0 m, and a maximum depth of 6.4 m (Herdendorf et al. 1986). The largest marsh area is the St. Clair Delta (about 17,500 ha), but marsh fragments are present around the perimeter of the lake.

The shallow western end of Lake Erie (average depth 7.4 m, maximum depth 18.9 m) from the mouth of the Detroit River to Sandusky Bay, Ohio, has most of the Lake's marshes on the U.S. side. Nearly 90% of Ohio's 5,300 ha are

controlled marshes, another 604 ha are farmed and flooded wetlands (Table 2). The remaining 162 ha of U.S. marshes occur at Presque Isle, Pennsylvania (Table 2). On the Ontario side, major marshes from west to east are Point Pelee, Rondeau Bay, and Long Point-Turkey Point. Together, these comprise about 12,000 ha of marshes (Glooschenko et al. 1987, unpubl. rep.).

Most of New York's Lake Ontario marshes are between Rochester on the west and the Sandy Pond area northeast of Oswego on the east; the largest (1,376 ha) is South Sodus Marsh. All New York lakeshore marshes, except for East Bay and Beaver Creek, are uncontrolled marshes (Table 2). Most of Ontario's more than 8,000 ha of marshes on Lake Ontario are concentrated in the peninsula that comprises Prince Edward County (Table 2).

HABITAT IMPORTANCE TO WATERFOWL

Probably 3 million waterfowl migrate annually through the Great Lakes region (Great Lakes Basin Commission 1975, Figs. 2-4). The spring and autumn migrations consist of large numbers of diving and sea ducks (Aythyini and Mergini), dabbling ducks (Anatini), Canada geese (*Branta canadensis*), and some snow geese (*Chen caerulescens*), tundra swans (*Cygnus columbianus*), and American coots (*Fulica americana*).

Lake Superior

Lake Superior coastal marshes are of minor importance to waterfowl because of their relative scarcity. However, Portage Marsh (#2, Fig. 5) is a high density breeding area for mallards (*Anas platyrhynchos*), blue-winged teals (*A. discors*), and American coots (G. F. Martz, pers. commun.). Shoal areas of the Apostle Islands, Isle Royale, Whitefish Bay, and the upper St. Marys River are important

Table 2. Estimated area (ha) of the coastal marshes of Lakes St. Clair, Erie, and Ontario, 1987.

Marsh	Controlled	Uncontrolled	Farmed
LAKE ST. CLAIR			
Ontario			
Walpole Island	4,172	6,788	
Other Lake St. Clair	734	1,160	
St. Clair River		96	
Detroit River	256	332	
Michigan			
St. Clair Flats		2,023	
St. Johns		445	
Harsen's Island	486		567
Total	5,648	10,844	567
LAKE ERIE			
Ontario			
Big Creek	70	405	
Big Creek NWA, Lee Brown & Flight Club	770	526	
Point Pelee		1,050	
Rondeau Park/Bay		792	
Long Point/Turkey Point		6,780	
Grand River		522	
Other Lake Erie	17	819	
Michigan			
Point Mouillee	130	194	18
Erie Club	324	81	71
Erie State Game Area		769	
Ohio			
Ottawa NWR	1,902	283	121
Magee Marsh/Crane Creek	648		
Winous Point Club	617	20	30
Bay View	293	10	20
Ottawa Club	526	20	162
Toussaint Club	445		
Other private clubs	162	24	330
Other public areas	67	337	
Pennsylvania			
Presque Isle		162	
Total	5,971	12,794	752
LAKE ONTARIO			
Ontario			
Prince Edward Co.	121	782	
Bloomfield Creek		383	
Presqu'ile Prov.			
Park & Bay		216	
Sawguin Creek		1,010	
Big Island		732	
Little & Wilton creeks		244	
Other Lake Ontario (N=292)	76	4,355	
New York			
Lakeview WMA		809	
Dexter Marsh WMA		275	
Deer Creek		219	
Stony Creek		109	
Other Jefferson & Oswego Co. (N=24)		612	
South Sodus		1,376	
East Bay	101	182	
Beaver Creek	57	85	
Port Bay		142	
Irondequoit Bay		142	
Braddock Bay		567	
Niagara County		57	
Other west end Lake Ontario (N=7)		255	
Total	355	12,552	

to migrating waterfowl (Great Lakes Basin Commission 1975). Most dabbling ducks are gone from the St. Marys River by the end of October, and by early November several areas on the river are heavily used by rafting greater and lesser scaups (*Aythya marila, A. affinis*) and redheads (*A. americana*) (Duffy et al. 1987).

Lake Michigan

Green Bay (#3, Fig. 5) contains Lake Michigan's most important coastal marshes. Some duck nesting occurs along the Fox and Wolf rivers (Great Lakes Basin Commission 1975). During the 1930s, the deltas at the mouths of the Fox, Duck Creek, and Suamico rivers attracted large numbers of waterfowl, but human and industrial pollution caused ecological problems. Subsequent efforts to preserve marsh habitat culminated in the development of the Green Bay West Shores Master Plan (Roznik et al. 1979). A primary objective of the plan was to conserve, manage, and enhance the littoral zone and adjacent uplands that provide habitat for breeding and migratory waterfowl.

Green Bay marshes are important autumn areas for ducks, primarily divers. Aerial surveys in October 1977 revealed 29,600 divers in lower Green Bay (Roznik et al. 1979). Species included greater and lesser scaups, mergansers (*Mergus mer-*

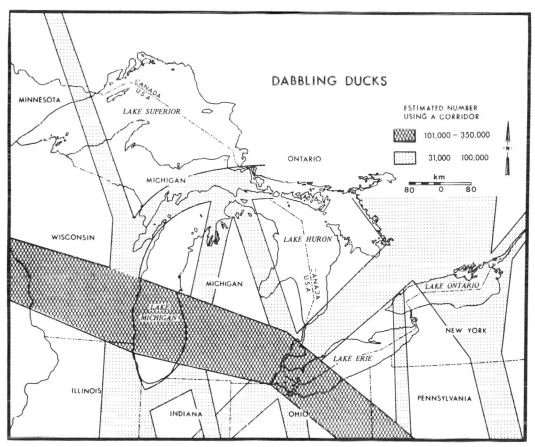

Fig. 2.   Autumn migration corridors of dabbling ducks across the Great Lakes (after Bellrose 1968).

ganser, M. serrator), ring-necked ducks (*A collaris*), common goldeneyes (*Bucephala clangula*), redheads, canvasbacks (*A. valisineria*), oldsquaws (*Clangula hyemalis*), buffleheads (*B. albeola*), and ruddy ducks (*Oxyura jamaicensis*). Canada geese often rest along the shoreline before migrating to Illinois and Kentucky (Ishmael 1986). In the north end of Lake Michigan, important coastal areas for autumn migration concentrations are Little Bay de Noc and Portage Bay.

Greatest waterfowl use is in autumn when migrant and local ducks and geese congregate in staging areas. Buffleheads, greater scaups, and ruddy ducks that winter on the Atlantic coast migrate across Lake Michigan. Lesser scaups, common mergansers, and Canada geese follow the shoreline.

Few species of waterfowl are present in winter, but up to 12,000 oldsquaws occur in deep water off Milwaukee, Wisconsin. However, large flocks of oldsquaws are not as common as are flocks of wintering red-breasted mergansers and common goldeneyes that frequent shallow bays, river mouths, and power plant outlets.

Lake Huron

Dennis et al. (1984) assessed migrant waterfowl use of the Ontario shorelines of Lake Huron and the southern Great Lakes. They ranked 17 waterfowl areas in descending order by waterfowl use during spring and autumn migration (Table 3). Seven areas were associated with Lake Erie lower Detroit River, 4 with Lake Ontario, 3 with Lake St. Clair and the St. Clair and Detroit rivers, 2 with Lake Huron, and 1 with the Niagara River.

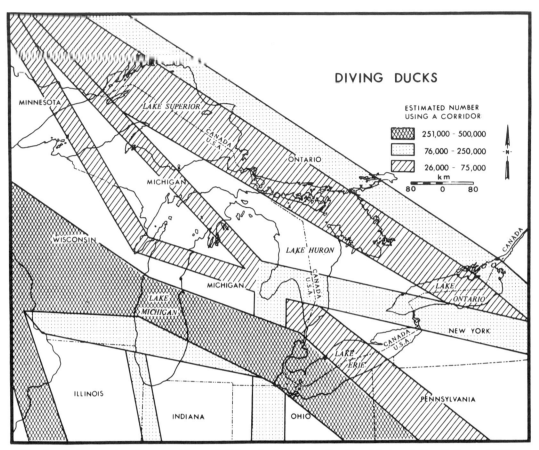

Fig. 3.   Autumn migration corridors of diving ducks across the Great Lakes (after Bellrose 1968).

The west shore of Bruce Peninsula (Fig. 5), ranked 17th, has scarce aquatic vegetation and limited waterfowl use during autumn migration. The shoreline is irregular, with expanses of exposed limestone bedrock, sheltered bays, and inlets with islands. Common mergansers are most abundant.

Waterfowl use the southeastern shore of Lake Huron (ranked 14th) along a 0.5-km-wide coastal zone from Sauble Beach to the St. Clair River. The sand bottom supports little aquatic vegetation, and waterfowl use is low. In autumn, common species are common mergansers, buffleheads, mallards, and greater scaups.

Saginaw Bay marshes (Fig. 5) are important staging areas for dabbling and diving ducks during autumn migrations. G. F. Martz (pers. commun., 1987) gave

peak 1-day autumn estimates of 78,000-122,000 ducks and 16,600-18,700 geese for Michigan's intensively managed waterfowl areas. Main concentration areas for ducks were Harsen's Island (30,000-40,000, largely mallards and black ducks [*Anas rubripes*]), Fish Point (15,000-20,000, mostly mallards), Point Mouillee (4,000-10,000, mostly mallards), and Erie Club (2,000-10,000, mostly mallards and black ducks). Farther north, the Tawas Bay area near the mouth of Saginaw Bay, the Les Cheneaux Islands area (northeast of Mackinac Island), and the St. Marys River including Munuscong Bay had 120,000, 151,000, and 455,000 estimated waterfowl use-days, respectively (Jaworski and Raphael 1978). During the 1940s, major concentrations of canvasbacks and other divers occurred at the mouth of the

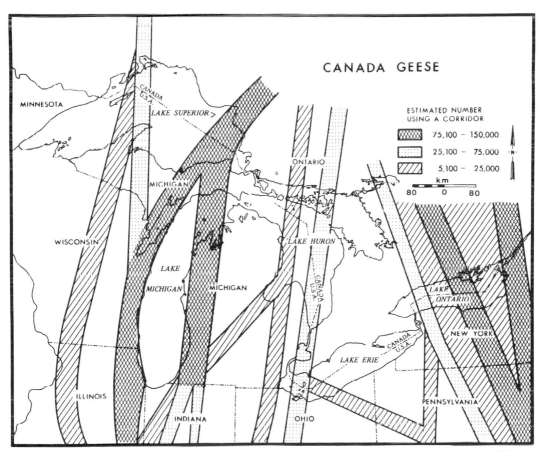

Fig. 4. Autumn migration corridors of Canada geese across the Great Lakes (after Bellrose 1968).

Saginaw River (Miller 1943), but this area no longer attracts large numbers of migrants because of water pollution, siltation, and scarcity of waterfowl foods (U.S. Department of the Interior 1967). About 21% of Michigan's annual duck harvest (85,990) occurs in Saginaw Bay.

Lake St. Clair and St. Clair River

The St. Clair River from Lake Huron to Walpole Island holds little aquatic vegetation because of fast current and depth, and wave forces generated by the passage of large, commercial vessels (Edsall et al. 1988). Sheltered areas are scarce. Autumn waterfowl numbers exceed 1,000 when nearby marsh areas with less current are frozen. Common species are common mergansers, red-

heads, canvasbacks, American wigeons (*Anas americana*), mallards, and scaups.

Waterfowl use during migration, duck harvest, and production of young all indicate that the marshes and associated open waters of Lake St. Clair (Fig. 5) might be the most important wetland system in the Great Lakes region, with the possible exception of Long Point in Lake Erie (Herdendorf et al. 1986). The Lake St. Clair marshes ranked second in importance among Ontario's major waterfowl areas (Table 3).

Lake St. Clair's east-shore marshes, including Walpole Island, contain habitat types attractive to dabbling and diving ducks, Canada geese, and tundra swans (Dennis and North 1984). About 39% of the marshes are diked, and the entire area is maintained mainly for waterfowl hunt-

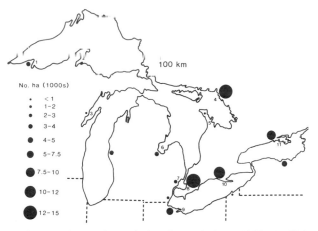

Fig. 5. Distribution of coastal marshes of the Great Lakes, 1987. 1—Kakagon and Fish Creek sloughs; 2—Portage Entry; 3—Green Bay; 4—Georgian Bay; 5—Bruce Peninsula; 6—Saginaw Bay; 7—St. Clair Flats; 8—Walpole Island; 9—Sandusky Bay; 10—Long Point/Turkey Point; 11—Prince Edward County.

ing, except for a 240-ha area operated as a National Wildlife Area (Dennis and North 1984). In autumn, this area has the highest Canada goose use and second highest redhead and canvasback use.

Hunting pressure and disturbance by boaters and fishermen force most diving ducks to leave the U.S. waters of Lake St. Clair before food supplies are consumed (Jaworski and Raphael 1978). In the 1930s-40s, as many as 750,000 ducks congregated on Lake St. Clair during autumn migration (Miller 1943), when the lake was renowned as a concentration area for migrating canvasbacks, redheads, scaups, and buffleheads. It remains so today (Table 4), although numbers have declined (Dennis and Chandler 1974, Jaworski and Raphael 1978, Dennis and North 1984).

Much of Ontario's south shore of Lake St. Clair and all of the north Detroit River shoreline are developed for industry and residences. With the exception of an island, waterfowl habitat is generally limited to open water. Mallards, canvasbacks, redheads, and mergansers use the area in spring and autumn (Table 3). The situation is similar on the Michigan side of the river, which no longer freezes. Waterfowl wintering here are threatened by the heat- and oil-polluted waters (Great Lakes Basin Commission 1975).

Lake Erie and Detroit River

Today, the Detroit River is the busiest port in the Great Lakes, and its sediments are seriously polluted with a variety of toxic organic substances and heavy metals (Manny et al. 1988). Nevertheless, it is an important resting and feeding ground for migrating waterfowl, especially diving ducks. Since the 1930s, industrial effluents have kept the river ice-free for nearly all of its 51-km length. In 1980 and 1981, about 11,700 and 4,500 ducks, respectively, wintered there. The largest of about 22 wetlands containing marsh habitat is the 250-ha marsh near the mouth of the Canard River (Manny et al. 1988).

Early Ohio records indicate that the western Lake Erie marshes, extending from present-day Vermillion, Ohio, to the mouth of the Detroit River in Michigan, bordered a wilderness encompassing nearly 122,000 ha of marsh and swamp. Located at a crosspoint of the Mississippi and Atlantic flyways, the marshes attracted waterfowl from both flyways (Robey 1949) that winter along the Atlantic Coast. Trautman's (1981) many references to waterfowl abundance in Portage,

Table 3. Waterfowl use of Ontario's shoreline habitats of the southern Great Lakes, autumn–winter 1968-73. Numbers are thousands of waterfowl days (adapted from Dennis et al. 1984). Areas are listed from uppermost to lowest position in the Great Lakes drainage system. Rank denotes relative importance to waterfowl as measured in use-days.

Rank	Area	Ducks	Geese	Swans	Total identified waterfowl
17	West Bruce Peninsula	9			9
14	East Lake Huron	57	1		59
16	St. Clair River	34			34
2	St. Clair marshes	6,368	673	12	7,052
13	South Lake St. Clair & North Detroit River	111	1		112
4	Lower Detroit River marshes	1,199	160	Tr	1,360
10	Point Pelee	54	3		57
9	West & central Lake Erie	92	45		137
7	Rondeau Bay marshes	302	3	2	307
1	Long Point marshes	7,016	926	24	7,655
6	Outer Long Point bay	969	3		1,053
8	Northeast Lake Erie	888	14		905
12	Niagara River	973			981
10	South Lake Ontario	509	3		516
5	Toronto shoreline	1,357	165		1,636
11	North Lake Ontario	259	1		262
3	Prince Edward County marshes	2,662	9		2,711
	Total	22,858	1,407	38	24,303

Toussaint, Swan, and other creeks and rivers imply an abundance of aquatic vegetation upon which the waterfowl fed. Beds of wild celery (*Vallisneria americana*) (scientific names of plants follow Fassett 1969) were particularly attractive to great numbers of canvasbacks, redheads, and scaups migrating southeastwardly.

Few of the present-day marshes have retained their original characteristics. By 1951, only about 12,140 of the original 121,407 ha remained. Drainage, siltation, land-fill, introduction of exotic plants, and control of water levels by diking systems contributed to the changes. About 6,600 ha of Ohio's marshes were destroyed between 1972 and 1987. Today, Ohio's marshes along the southwest shore comprise about 5,300 ha (Weeks 1975). Nearly all are diked, controlled marshes. Most ducks migrating through Ohio in autumn pass through the Lake Erie marsh region and western Ohio. The

migration usually occurs as a series of flights, peaking in late November-early December (Table 5). Mallards and black ducks comprise about 88% of the total.

The significance of Ohio's Lake Erie marshes to waterfowl, particularly to black ducks, might be increasing. In December 1986, 48,400 black ducks were counted here, representing perhaps 65% of the black ducks inventoried in the Mississippi Flyway's midwinter waterfowl count conducted 1 month later. On 1 December 1988, 63,400 black ducks were observed, before the midwinter inventory had been made. Clearly, Ohio's Lake Erie marshes have importance to migrating ducks greater than that indicated by size (5,600 ha) alone.

The lower Detroit River marshes and the marshes associated with Ontario's Lake Erie shore to Holiday Beach Provincial Park have high numbers of Canada geese in autumn. The favorable climate and the river currents enable birds to use

Table 4. Numbers of identified waterfowl on areas within Lake St. Clair, Michigan and Canada, 7 Oct-3 Dec 1974 (file data, Wildlife Div., Michigan Dep. Nat. Resour.).

| Species | Michigan | | | | | |
	Harsens Island	Dickinson Island	St. Johns Marsh	Anchor Bay	Lake St. Clair (Canada)	Total
Mallard	19,550	137	1,354	647	4,598	26,286
Black duck	4,900	20	35	460	2,937	8,352
Baldpate				17	1,830	1,847
Northern pintail	650		31	45		726
Blue-winged teal			247			247
Green-winged teal	95		27			122
Total dabblers	25,195	157	1,739	1,169	9,665	37,925
Canvasback		950		8,064	56,305	65,319
Redhead		10		6,509	3,896	10,415
Scaups				6,098	7,956	14,054
Goldeneye		865		3,496	382	4,743
Bufflehead		205	1	10	24	240
Total divers		2,030	1	25,252	69,407	96,690
Coots	90	12	360	258	612	1,332
Swans					402	402
Total	25,285	2,199	2,100	26,679	80,086	136,349

the area later in autumn than in most other areas. The funneling effect of the Great Lakes shoreline, baited sanctuaries, and nearby grainfields result in heavy waterfowl use. Several of the shoreline marshes are managed primarily for waterfowl hunting. Dennis et al. (1984) reported that, although waterfowl use in 1974-81 had not changed when compared to data reported for 1968-73 by Dennis and Chandler (1974), autumn numbers of mergansers and black ducks had declined but numbers of canvasbacks and redheads

Table 5. Average numbers of migrating ducks in Ohio's Lake Erie marshes, 1980-84 (file data, Div. Wildlife, Ohio Dep. Nat. Resour.).

Date	Total ducks	% of total flight
1 Sep	13,731	3
15 Sep	14,645	3
1 Oct	32,009	6
15 Oct	51,558	10
1 Nov	73,902	15
15 Nov	87,530	17
1 Dec	105,030	21
15 Dec	92,703	18
1 Jan	20,804	4
15 Jan	12,187	2
Total	504,099	99

had increased. They postulated that the loss of emergent aquatics that occurred as a result of higher water levels in the Great Lakes decreased dabbling duck use.

The west end of Lake Erie in Ontario consists primarily of shoreline devoid of marsh vegetation, with steep clay cliffs extending directly to Lake Erie. Small flocks of goldeneyes and buffleheads and large flocks of common and red-breasted mergansers used the area during autumns, 1969-73 (Dennis and Chandler 1974). Smaller numbers of dabbling ducks, geese, and swans used the shoreline as a resting area and fed in grainfields or in baited sanctuaries (Table 3). Autumn waterfowl use-days decreased during the above period from 272,400 to 136,800, largely because of decreased merganser use.

The Point Pelee National Park-Hillman Creek marshes are an autumn staging site for large numbers of common mergansers. Human disturbance from waterfowl hunting and muskrat (*Ondatra zibethicus*) trapping and lack of suitable sanctuaries result in low waterfowl use. Dennis et al. (1984) attributed a decline in waterfowl use-days from the early 1970s to a decline in waterfowl food plants.

During the autumns of 1968-73, large numbers of greater and lesser scaups, canvasbacks, and redheads used the Rondeau Bay marshes and the Lake Erie waters adjacent to Rondeau Provincial Park. Artificial feeding and cornfields contribute to holding dabbling ducks in the area. Powerboat traffic affects diving ducks; they rest on the open waters of Lake Erie during times of peak disturbance and feed in Rondeau Bay in early morning and late evening. Recent major decreases in aquatic vegetation in Rondeau Bay resulted in a dramatic reduction in waterfowl use (380,000 to 306,700 days), particularly for diving ducks (Table 3). However, mallard use-days increased in autumn from 33,600 to 143,700 because of baited sanctuaries managed by the Ontario Ministry of Natural Resources (Dennis et al. 1984).

The Long Point and Turkey Point marshes and Long Point Bay waters (Fig. 5, #10) have the greatest numbers of canvasbacks and redheads of any area along Ontario's Great Lakes shoreline during autumn migrations, the highest number of diving duck use days, and the second highest number of total waterfowl use-days. Much of the marshland is managed for waterfowl hunting and muskrat trapping. Large numbers of waterfowl are held on sanctuaries, some with abundant natural foods, whereas others are baited. In the years when the corn harvest is late and reduced amounts of waste grain are available, dabbling duck numbers in the marshes are reduced. Powerboat disturbance is a problem here, too, and birds have adjusted similarly to those at Rondeau Bay. Autumn waterfowl use-days totaled 7,655,000 (Table 3); mallard use comprised 20%, black ducks 9%, canvasbacks and redheads 35%, other dabbling ducks 20%, other diving and sea ducks 8%, and geese 4%.

Limestone bedrock is exposed along sections of the shoreline at the east end of Lake Erie, and steep cliffs extend into the Lake. Dabbling duck habitat is of low quality (Dennis and Chandler 1974), except for the Grand River marshes, where heavy hunting pressure and lack of suitable sanctuaries cause most ducks to leave early. Along the Lake Erie shoreline, large numbers of greater and lesser scaups, common goldeneyes, and common mergansers are present in autumn. Surveys in 1980-81 showed that peak waterfowl numbers were about 14,000. Currently, the area has the second highest number of scaup use-days in autumn. Little management of waterfowl habitat is done in this area. The Nanticoke generating station's thermal discharge prevents water from freezing, enabling ducks to remain late in autumn (McCullough 1984).

On the U.S. side of Lake Erie, no important marshes are present east of Sandusky Bay to the Ohio-Pennsylvania border. In Pennsylvania, Presque Isle State Park and associated Presque Isle Bay attract considerable numbers of migrating waterfowl, but contain little marsh area. New York biologists reported no marshes along their eastern Lake Erie shoreline.

Lake Ontario

The Canadian side of the Niagara River, from Lake Erie to Lake Ontario, receives about 127,000 waterfowl use-days from scaups, goldeneyes, canvasbacks, and common and red-breasted mergansers in autumn. Numbers increase as winter approaches and other wetlands freeze. Little marsh habitat is present, but submerged aquatics occur in certain stretches of the river (Dennis and Chandler 1974). By 1982, the area had the highest autumn diving duck use-days (376 days/ha) (Dennis et al. 1984). Autumn use-days (981,000 days, Table 3) by diving ducks increased from the 1968-73 period, perhaps resulting from a concurrent increase in submergent aquatics and other waterfowl foods. Mergansers comprised 50% of the total, canvasbacks and redheads 13%, other diving ducks 32%, and mallards and black ducks 4%.

Clay cliffs make up much of the shoreline from Hamilton Harbour, Ontario, to the mouth of the Niagara River. No marshland is present, so dabbling duck use is low. Scaup concentrations, the second highest of any area surveyed, occurred off the confluence of the Welland Canal with Lake Ontario, probably a result of suitable offshore feeding areas (Dennis and Chandler 1974). The birds are relatively undisturbed by powerboats, and the waters are protected from prevailing winds.

Much of the original marsh habitat along the Toronto, Ontario, shoreline has been eliminated, but concentrations of dabbling ducks, diving ducks, and Canada geese occur there in autumn. In 1974-81, autumn use was 1,635,000 days, 51% of which was by mallards and black ducks, and 16% was by Canada geese. It is the only area where a significant proportion of waterfowl use the area for nesting (e.g., mallards, black ducks, and Canada geese). The proximity of cities, an increase in the number of nearby cornfields, and much artificial feeding contribute to their survival (Dennis and Chandler 1974). Mallards and black ducks have shown minor increases because of restrictive firearms-discharge laws.

The north shore of Lake Ontario has limited waterfowl use. Much of the shoreline is steep, little marsh habitat exists, and little artificial feeding takes place. Waterfowl use-days are similar to those of the Hamilton-Toronto, Ontario, harbor area. Mallards, black ducks, scaups, and goldeneyes are the most important numerically. Dabbling ducks feed on grain crops inland, but hunting pressure causes most of them to leave the area after opening day of hunting season (Dennis and Chandler 1974).

Prince Edward County's southwestern and southeastern shorelines and marshes (Fig. 5) are the third most important waterfowl area in Ontario. This area has the highest concentrations of scaups and mergansers in autumn. Birds are attracted to the shelter of various bays, in the absence of boat traffic. Some artificial feeding is done in the marshes during autumn. Because of heavy hunting pressure and lack of adequate sanctuaries, however, most dabbling ducks leave the area soon after opening day of hunting season (Dennis and Chandler 1974). Of the 271,000 autumn waterfowl use-days, scaup use comprised 66%, merganser use was 10%, and other diving duck and dabbler use was 7% each; use by geese was insignificant. Some brant (*Branta bernicla*) stop here and along the more eastern shoreline, though less regularly than in spring (Erskine 1988).

New York's Lake Ontario marshes are concentrated east of the city of Rochester. Wilson (1969) identified about 7,463 ha of wetlands along the eastern Lake Ontario-St. Lawrence River shoreline, about 5,000 of which lie along Lake Ontario proper. All New York marshes on the lakeshore are uncontrolled marshes except for about 160 ha at the East Bay and Beaver Creek marshes.

T. D. Carroll (pers. commun.) estimated numbers of dabblers, divers, and Canada geese in New York's central Lake Ontario marshes to be 10,800, 13,000, and 5,500, respectively, in 1986-87. Primary use is by dabblers until the marshes freeze in December or January. Common species are mallards, black ducks, wood ducks (*Aix sponsa*), and blue- and green-winged teals. Diving duck use is primarily in the east branch of 18-Mile Creek and Tuscarara Bay wetlands. Small flocks (10-20 birds) of scaups, common goldeneyes, buffleheads, and common mergansers use these wetlands. Most diving ducks use the open water of Lake Ontario and the lower Niagara River (T. D. Carroll, pers. commun.). Several thousand scaups are present in November and December on these areas, which are also used by oldsquaws from January through March.

PHYSIOLOGICAL REQUIREMENTS OF MIGRATING WATERFOWL

Although substantial waterfowl production occurs on some areas, the primary importance of Great Lakes marshes is replenishment of energy expended during migration (Hoffman and Bookhout 1985). Prince (1979) stated that the energy needed for maintenance during migration might approach energetic demands of breeding. Prince (1979) suggested that the daily energy expenditure for free-living mallards at 0-20 C during the postbreeding period is 280-290 kcal/bird/day, excluding the cost of migration. Fredrickson and Drobney (1979) estimated energy costs and time for replenishment of endogenous fat reserves for migratory waterfowl for various flight intervals (2-14 h) and distances flown (128-895 km). Birds in flight 2 hours used 120 kcal and required 0.8 to 1.7 days for replenishment; those in flight 14 hours used 840 kcal and required 5.3 to 12.1 days for replenishment.

Fredrickson and Drobney (1979) discussed the problem of how to estimate the food requirements of migratory waterfowl. Complicating factors include annual changes in numbers of waterfowl using the area, temperature, water conditions, food availability, condition and physiologic requirements of birds, number of days on migrational areas, and hunting pressure or other harassment. Still another important factor is how efficiently waterfowl can metabolize energy (i.e., the difference between gross energy [GE] and true metabolizable energy [TME] of the foods). Hoffman and Bookhout (1985) and Fredrickson and Taylor (1982) gave GE values for seeds of several species of plants on moist-soil impoundments. Hoffman and Bookhout (1985) estimated that energy requirements of mallards and pintails arriving on

southwestern Lake Erie marshes are about 290 and 243 kcal/day, respectively, and Sugden (1979) predicted that field-feeding mallards require 294 kcal/day. Neither estimate included costs of migration. Hoffman and Bookhout (1985) estimated that daily consumption rates for mallards and pintails were 115 and 91 g, respectively; their values were based on Sincock's (1962) conclusion that the average consumption of food per duck per day could be estimated as 10% of the body weight. At those rates, mallards and pintails could exist on seeds of rice-cutgrass *(Leersia oryzoides)* and walters millet *(Echinochloa walteri)*, with a limited amount of energy left for fat storage, but not on large-seeded smartweed *(Polygonum pensylvanicum)* or softstem bulrush *(Scirpus validus)* seeds.

Fredrickson and Taylor (1982) pointed out that little information is available on the TME in naturally occurring foods. More work is needed in this area, but one fact seems clear: in the face of declining amounts of marsh, with concomitant concentration of waterfowl, the quality of the remaining Great Lakes marshes is of critical importance to migrating waterfowl. The less energy required for foraging, the greater the significance of even low-energy foods for energy accumulation (Hoffman and Bookhout 1985). Provision of corn, whether by cropping or baiting, delivers adequate energy (ca. 4.70 kcal/g dry matter), but some essential nutrients are lacking (Fredrickson and Taylor 1982), which must be acquired from natural foods in migrational staging areas.

HABITAT MANAGEMENT OF GREAT LAKES MARSHES

We define natural marsh as marsh relying on naturally occurring seed-tuber banks of aquatic macrophytes for production of vegetation. This category excludes those managed wetlands that are agriculturally cultivated and flooded for waterfowl use. Natural marshes of the Great

Lakes are of 2 types: those in which control of water levels is used for habitat management (controlled marsh), and those in which it is not (uncontrolled marsh), although many supplemental management practices might be applied on a limited scale on the latter areas to affect vegetation.

Characteristics of the Vegetation

Fredrickson and Taylor (1982) discussed vegetation management on moist-soil areas, including available nutritive content of selected plant species and plant response to rapid or slow drawdowns conducted in early or late spring. Of the many species of aquatic plants that affect habitat quality of Great Lakes marshes, several are targeted by managers who have capability for water-level control. These include the emergent plants: cattail (*Typha latifolia*), bulrush (*Scirpus* spp.), burreed (*Sparganium* spp.), smartweeds (*Polygonum* spp.), chufa or nutsedge (*Cyperus* spp.), walters millet, wild rice, rice cut-grass, panic-grasses (*Panicum* spp.), bluejoint (*Calamagrostis canadensis*), and reed canary grass (*Phalaris arundinacea*); the submergent plants: coontail (*Ceratophyllum demersum*), pondweeds (*Potamogeton* spp.), water milfoil (*Myriophyllum* spp.), wild celery, and naiads (*Najas* spp.); and the floating-leaved plants: arrowhead (*Sagittaria* spp.), pickerelweed (*Pontederia cordata*), water lilies (*Nuphar* spp., *Nymphaea* spp.), water lotus (*Nelumbo lutea*), and duckweeds (*Spirodela* spp., *Lemna* spp.). The density, location, and interspersion of aquatic plant communities can be of equal or greater importance than species composition in determining desirability to waterfowl (see discussion of shallow marsh management).

Habitat Management of Uncontrolled Marshes

Most (74%) Great Lakes marshes are uncontrolled (Table 1), and capabilities for habitat management are limited. Management of uncontrolled marshes is largely passive (i.e., influenced primarily by natural forces). Long-term and storm-induced water levels of the Great Lakes largely determine the amounts, locations, and habitat conditions of these marshes. Most uncontrolled marshes that once were established with the ebb and flow of Great Lakes water levels are now excluded from landward advance by drainage or diking for agriculture and development. Thus, during high water levels, the uncontrolled marshes lose area unlikely to be regained. The most notable habitat loss has occurred in southwest Lake Erie where uncontrolled marshes in Michigan and Ohio are almost nonexistent. Before 1982, much of Ontario's Lake St. Clair marshes and many of New York's Lake Ontario marshes were overgrown with cattail. These areas benefitted from high water levels by increased interspersion of vegetation and open water. Since 1983, however, the sustained inundation has destroyed large cattail stands, and net losses in Canada currently far outnumber gains (G. B. McCullough, pers. commun.). Unprecedented decreases in Great Lakes water levels that occurred in 1987 (0.52 m) should provide short-term relief to widespread destruction of uncontrolled marshes. In addition, attempts to restore aquatic vegetation (e.g., transplanting tubers of *Potamogeton pectinatus* in Rondeau Bay on Lake Erie) have been proposed (Hanna 1984).

In the few Great Lakes marshes where the landward advance of marsh is not restricted by agriculture, development, or topography, sustained (>2 years) high lake levels can be beneficial. In these marshes, natural processes of wetland establishment can occur on flooded uplands during years of high water. Additionally, short-term (<2 years) or seasonal fluctuation of water levels can cause desirable changes in marsh vegetation (e.g., from monotypic cattail to submergent species, Keddy and Reznicek

1986). In 1987, some small marshes in Lake Ontario (New York) and in Lake Erie at Presque Isle (Pennsylvania) continued to benefit from higher waters (J. E. Lamendola, G. T. Volgstadt, pers. commun.). Stuckey (1981) reviewed available literature for the lower Great Lakes region and documented drastic losses ($\bar{x} -$ 44%) in submergent vegetation since 1940 for 15 studies of aquatic vascular plants. Stuckey (1978) also reported on the cause of the decline of submergent species, the most water tolerant of rooted aquatic plants. High water, increased turbidity, and increased recreational use of waters by humans were principal causes of the decline.

Most management for migrating and wintering waterfowl in uncontrolled marshes generally focuses on elimination of undesirable vegetation. Unwanted vegetation includes noxious plants of little value for wildlife, such as purple loosestrife (*Lythrum salicaria*), willow (*Salix* spp.), swamp loosestrife *(Decodon verticillatus)*, and buttonbush *(Cephalanthus occidentalis)*, or unfavorable growth characteristics of desired species such as cattail, bulrush, reed canary grass, and numerous submergent species. In addition to wildlife use and preference, considerations for boat and hunter access are important.

Management techniques for uncontrolled marshes include crushing, mowing, burning, blasting, and spraying of excessively dense stands of emergents, which are less attractive to birds (Weller and Fredrickson 1973). These techniques generally are selected on the basis of cost and access to the control site. Beule (1979) reviewed techniques used in Wisconsin marshes. Control of submergent plants is usually accomplished by cutting with underwater mowing or chopping implements. New York marsh managers have used "cookie cutters" and blasting to open cattail stands and to retard growth of submergents. Both techniques have limited effectiveness and short (1-3 years) duration. Water chestnut (*Trapa natans*) has been a problem in New York marshes for more than 20 years, but continued intensive removal, including hand pulling, has resulted in acceptable control (D. C. Woodruff, pers. commun.). Additional concerns in New York include invasion of purple loosestrife and pesticide accumulations from nearby fruit farming.

In Wisconsin, Michigan, Ohio, and southeastern Ontario, invasion of purple loosestrife is a serious threat to all wetlands. Because of its strong competition with, and replacement of, other more desirable aquatic emergents, purple loosestrife has had a disastrous impact on native vegetation, and more than 50% of the biomass of some wetland communities has been displaced (Thompson et al. 1987). Marshes that have been washed out during high water have a high incidence of loosestrife invasion when water levels recede. Additional problem plants include: willow, reed canary grass, buttonbush, and rose mallow (*Hibiscus palustris*). Management of these undesirable species often is difficult because access by equipment usually is restricted to thick ice conditions of midwinter, and treatment by a person on foot is limited in effectiveness. Private marshes in Ohio have achieved short-term control of purple loosestrife with aerial applications of glyphosate-based herbicides (G. R. Balogh, pers. commun.).

Management of Ontario's southern marshes for migrating and wintering waterfowl is directed toward maintaining well-interspersed cattail communities by typical methods, i.e., crushing, mowing, and burning. Controlled marshes of eastern and northern Lake Ontario (including New York and Ontario) differ from those of Michigan, Ohio, and Wisconsin. Water-level control in Lake Ontario marshes is partial, provided by barrier beaches or sand-gravel bars that might percolate water under head pressure or erode completely during storm activity. These natural levees later reestablish through deposition. Management of these partially controlled marshes is similar to that of uncontrolled marshes, because access problems exist. Although these inside marshes are separated from direct lake-level fluctuations, few of them are managed via water-level control.

Habitat Management and Legal Baiting

In Ontario's 12,750 ha of marshes along Lake St. Clair, the primary management goal is to maintain well-interspersed stands of cattail and open water. Also, legal baiting (distributing supplemental food) is practiced extensively in Ontario. Bait (chiefly cereal grains) can be deposited by permit anywhere and in any amount in the marsh, but no hunting can occur within 400 m of the bait site. Use of legal baiting has increased since 1976 and now is a significant management practice in Ontario's Lake St. Clair and Lake Erie, because baited areas are a cost-effective way to improve hunting success (Dennis and North 1984).

One point of view is that legal baiting, by increasing hunter success, is crucial to maintaining marshes. If the marsh cannot support quality duck hunting and receive that income, it likely will be converted to agriculture. This is particularly true for diked areas with drainage capability (McCullough 1981). Costs of intensive drawdown management as practiced in the U.S. are substantially greater than that of baiting and are viewed as prohibitive.

From a management perspective, legal baiting creates an ironic situation. Both American and Canadian marsh managers attempt to preserve existing marshes via maintaining quality duck hunting. To compensate for what was once a rapid migration, Ontario marsh managers have employed legal baiting. The U.S. enjoys a much longer migration chronology but is restricted to much less alluring habitat-management practices. As a result, along the U.S. Great Lakes, intensive management of marshes for food production by water-level control has received increased emphasis. This method is the best available option for providing an attractive food resource to migrating waterfowl, but compared to legal baiting it is incredibly expensive.

Management of Controlled Marshes

Water-level control is the basis of natural marsh management in the Great Lakes region. Control is accomplished by obstructing or enhancing natural drainage with a variety of structures. These range from a board jammed into a muskrat run to an engineer-designed spillway and pumping station constructed of concrete and steel. Controlled marshes usually require systems of dikes or levees combined with pumping of water to control levels. Stationary pumps between 15.2 and 91.4 cm diameter (Fig. 6) or portable PTO-drive pumps between 20.3 and 40.6 cm are used commonly. Stationary pumps are more efficient to operate but are more expensive to install. Portable pumps are more versatile and are best used for smaller marsh units (perhaps < 100 ha). Linde (1969), Beule (1979), and Piehl (1986) described applications and installation of water-level-control devices.

Among the deviations from standard controlled marsh management in the Great Lakes are the eastern Lake Ontario marshes of New York and Ontario. There, temporary sand- and gravel bars preclude annual water-level control. Thus, these areas are managed similarly to uncontrolled marshes. New York has a unique management problem with fisherman-induced drawdowns. Persons fishing for salmonids dig through narrow sandbars to create their own warmer water "feeder

Fig. 6. A diesel pump with a 50-cm intake and 60-cm discharge (32,000 l/min) is useful in manipulating water levels in a Lake Erie marsh.

streams" to Lake Ontario to attract the fish, thereby dewatering marshes.

Three stages of a controlled, natural marsh are discussed (1) mudflats, or moist-soil areas; (2) shallow marsh, or hemimarsh; and (3) deep marsh, or open-water marsh. Management of these marsh stages are examined by comparing (1) characteristics (vegetation types, diversity, interspersion), (2) water-level control (levels, timing, problems), and (3) importance to migrating waterfowl (relative use, food, seed, cover).

Mudflat management.—Managed mudflats are characterized by dense stands of annual emergents, high seed production, and intensive use by migrating waterfowl. Germination of these plants occurs on moist soil after complete water removal and mudflat exposure (Martin et al. 1957). Common plant species include smartweeds, millets, nutsedges, beggarticks (*Bidens* spp.), and rice cut-grass (Meeks 1969). These plants often grow robustly, and seed production can be high in quantity and metabolizable energy

(Sugden 1973, Hoffman and Bookhout 1985). Monotypic stands of mudflat plants often establish in zones that correspond to soil moisture during germination periods (Kadlec 1962). When zonation is absent and species overlap, 3 or 4 plant species of different mature heights might grow on the same area, producing multiple life-forms of vegetation. However, we have observed that overall plant diversity and community interspersion are low in moist-soil units in southwestern Lake Erie. Water is essentially absent from the area during the growing season, generally restricted to adjacent canals or mudflat fringes.

Several researchers initially demonstrated the effectiveness of water-level control for marsh management in Great Lakes states (Hartman 1949, Hopkins 1962 [Wisconsin]; DiAngelo 1953, Kadlec 1962 [Michigan]; Bednarik 1963, Meeks 1969 [Ohio]; Harris 1957 [Minnesota]). Fredrickson and Taylor (1982) provided a comprehensive listing of 166 marsh management references within 11 categories of wetland ecology. Research and case-history management information have demonstrated that seed banks, soil and water chemistry, plant succession, and the timing, duration, and magnitude of water-level control are principal factors influencing aquatic plant growth. Harris and Marshall (1963) and Weller (1978) reviewed these factors as they are influenced by environmental variables.

An early May to early June timing for mudflat exposure promotes germination of moist-soil annuals. An actual mudflat condition is the desired condition for spring and early summer. Water levels should not be permitted to flood small seedlings, although irrigation of established plants is beneficial to prevent dried mudflats and invasion by unwanted upland plants. Water levels maintained within 10-20 cm of the mudflat elevation usually will provide the required soil moisture. Residual seed sources (van der Valk and Davis 1978, Smith and Kadlec 1983) directly influence plant species occurrence.

The highly desirable mudflat condition can be prolonged for several management seasons and, if closely monitored, can be maintained for more than a decade. The benefits of mudflat management do not come without drawbacks, however. In addition to plant successional advance from annual drawdowns, most undesirable plant species (e.g., willow and purple loosestrife) invade and prosper under the spring drawdown regime used for mudflat management (Harris and Marshall 1963, Thompson et al. 1987). These plants usually invade gradually, and managers have several growing seasons to respond with higher water levels (Fig. 7) and mechanical or chemical control. If seed banks are ignored, sudden invasions of problem species can occur. Intensive management of problem species might be required for 4-5 years or longer to recover a desirable condition.

The obvious and most effective method of returning a substandard mudflat to its productive potential is by setting back plant succession (Harris and Marshall 1963). This goal can be accomplished through 1-2 years of deep water management, drying and disking, or, as a last resort, application of herbicide. Residual seed sources or rootstocks from undesirable vegetation may persist, however, and must be eliminated during successive years of management (Linde 1969, Rawinski 1982).

The capacity of properly managed mudflat vegetation to attract fall migrating waterfowl is easily underestimated. Waterfowl use can approach that of a baited area. In most Great Lakes marshes, the vegetation association of nodding smartweed (Polygonum lapathifolium), walters millet, and nutsedge is the most common and attractive food source. Moist-soil plants attract and harbor the largest numbers of waterfowl of all natural habitat types. Waterfowl use can be dispersed on some managed mudflats if capabilities exist to reflood the area gradually. Waterfowl will not feed extensively on these seeds unless water covers the mudflat.

Shallow marsh (hemimarsh) management.—A shallow marsh is best represented by a typical cattail marsh in the Great Lakes region. Generally, emergent perennials like cattail and bulrush prevail. Submergent species such as sago pondweed (Potamogeton pectinatus), curly pondweed (P. crispus), water milfoil, coontail, and bladderwort (Utricularia spp.) are common in shallow marshes and provide a substantial component of the food resource in foliage, tuber, and seeds, as well as harboring invertebrates. Moist-soil annual plants are less common, because few will germinate under water.

Shallow marshes also have been termed hemimarshes, because they exhibit an interspersed coverage of 50% open water and 50% emergent vegetation. The coverages of vegetation and water can be managed by water-level control and by

Fig. 7. After several growing seasons of mudflat management, undesirable plant species such as the cottonwoods (*Populus* spp.) pictured here often invade and prosper. They were controlled by raising water levels.

control of muskrat populations to achieve maximal interspersion of vegetation and open water (Weller 1978).

Water level control in a shallow marsh requires maintenance of 10-30 cm of water across the main basin through the growing season. A partial drawdown beginning immediately after the spring thaw will encourage regrowth of perennials from rootstocks (Beule 1979). Conversely, increased water levels from winter and spring precipitation can be left unchanged to suppress plant community expansion. As temperatures increase in shallow waters, tubers and seeds of submergent plants begin growing.

If carp (*Cyprinus carpio*) numbers are low and clear water consequently can be maintained, dense mats of submergents might cover the water surface by August. Submergent plant foliage and seeds are primary waterfowl foods in shallow marshes, so carp control should be attempted. Reduced aquatic plant germination and growth resulting from carp activity are well-documented (Anderson 1950, King and Hunt 1967, Perry 1982). Although it is manpower intensive, some success with carp control has been demonstrated. Complete dewatering of the marsh and subsequent fish kill, combined with reflooding through steel or wire grating to prevent reintroduction of carp, will enable desired plants to become established. Small fish cannot be excluded, however, and a return to fish eradication might be required in 6-8 years. Changes in marsh management goals can help alleviate that problem, however. One solution is to cycle back into deep marsh management; another is to dewater and advance to mudflat management. Either option will effectively lessen impacts of carp.

Carp control negatively impacts other fish species, either by use of grates that exclude adults from spawning areas or by direct mortality from rotenone treatment. Establishment of submergent plants and subsequent high quality fish spawning habitat is desirable. However, if incidence of game fish breeding (e.g., northern pike [*Esox lucius*]) is low (Chubb and Liston 1986), the importance of fisheries management must remain secondary to providing quality wetland habitat.

Shallow marsh is the easiest stage to prolong, because partial spring drawdowns might be all that is required. Monitored closely, shallow marsh can be maintained for 4-8 years before changes are warranted; however, the incidence and cost of these problems, e.g., undesirable vegetation control and dike repair, are minimal. Other factors including benefits to resident wetland wildlife (Weller and Fredrickson 1973), sustained muskrat harvest (Bednarik 1956, Bishop et al. 1979), and good hunting make this a highly desirable management stage.

Hemimarshes are of maximum benefit to the greatest number of wetland wildlife species (Weller and Spatcher 1965). Correspondingly, almost all species of waterfowl common to the region use shallow marshes. Waterfowl use during autumn migration is substantial, but foods of submergent and perennial emergent plants are seldom preferred over seeds of mudflat plants.

Shallow marshes distribute migratory waterfowl use effectively. The diversity and interspersion of plant communities permit waterfowl use over the entire area. This distribution tends to provide sustained use of the area throughout migration, as opposed to managed mudflats, where vegetation can be decimated by large flocks of ducks in 1-2 weeks. The combination of food and refuge is provided best by shallow marshes, for both components are readily available and suit the needs of a wide range of waterfowl.

Deep Marsh.—Deep marsh is typified by open water and scattered clumps of perennial, emergent vegetation. Com-

munities of floating-leaved plants are common, but few mudflat species exist. Submergent vegetation (generally of sporadic occurrence because of increased turbidity and carp populations), aquatic macroinvertebrates, and muskrat "cuttings" are principal waterfowl foods. In terms of providing food, deep marshes are the least attractive stage to waterfowl.

Water levels during the growing season range from about 30 to 106 cm ($\bar{x} = 46$ cm) across the main basin. Maintaining existing vegetation and minimizing erosion of dikes from high water levels are principal challenges to deep marsh management. Water accumulated from autumn and winter precipitation must be removed rapidly by partial drawdown in spring. Waves incorporating $\geq$30 cm of water can uproot vegetation, increase turbidity, erode dikes, and reduce plant growth. Underharvested muskrat populations can have similar impacts.

Our experience in Ohio's Lake Erie marshes indicate that few undesirable plant species will establish or survive 2-3 years of flooding with 76 cm of water; thus, deep marsh management has been used effectively for their control. Dike erosion under these conditions will be substantial unless dikes are protected by rip-rap or other barriers (Linde 1969). Exceptions to control by flooding include purple and swamp loosestrife, and occasionally willow and rose mallow. Muskrat populations can reach high densities in deep marsh if cattail stands predominate (Bednarik 1956), and muskrat damage to interior dikes generally increases over successive years of deep-water management. Once emergent, perennial plants exhibit signs of depletion, muskrat emigration increases. A return to moist-soil or shallow marsh management will stimulate a rapid recolonization of the area even after complete eradication of vegetation (Kroll and Meeks 1985).

In ideal situations when carp control produces low turbidity, the deep marsh stage can be maintained $\geq$2 years. One of the most desirable habitats for migrating and wintering canvasbacks and redheads is deep marsh with dense growths of preferred submergent vegetation (wild celery, water milfoil). Maintenance of deep marsh under ideal conditions, as above, enhances wetland habitat diversity.

Numbers of migrating waterfowl using deep-marsh habitats are generally smaller than those of other marsh stages, and deep marshes tend to have the lowest hunter success of the 3 marsh types. Partly for this reason, some managers prohibit hunting on deep-marsh units and use them as seasonal refuges. Deep marsh is generally most attractive to diving ducks and some dabblers such as American wigeons, gadwalls, and northern shovelers. All species of waterfowl wintering in Great Lakes marshes use deep marshes during freeze-up, however. Densities of waterfowl may be so great that their activities prevent remaining openings from freezing, even during brief periods of sub-zero temperatures.

Wetland Farming

More than 1,600 ha of cropland, usually in areas of ≥40 ha, are managed for waterfowl in the Great Lakes marshes of Michigan, Ohio, Ontario, and Wisconsin (Tables 1, 2). These areas are managed mainly for waterfowl hunting with standard agricultural practices, followed by autumn flooding. If farming conditions are adequate or better, and if autumn water is available, flooded crops can attract and harbor waterfowl in large numbers. Flooded croplands in Michigan's Lake St. Clair region exhibit among the highest waterfowl use-days of the Great Lakes marshes.

Principal crops grown are corn, soybeans, wheat, buckwheat, Japanese and proso millet, and sorghum (milo). Farming techniques and dates of activity usually follow local patterns, although corn crops often are planted up to 1 month earlier to allow for drying and

harvesting before or during the waterfowl hunting season. Corn stubble often is mowed to remove impediments to waterfowl attempting to land.

Principal management concerns in cultivated wetlands include (1) timing of seed maturity with hunting seasons, (2) pre-season blackbird (*Quiscalus, Agelaius, Molothrus*) or waterfowl crop depredation, (3) frost damage to immature crops, and (4) availability of water in autumn. Progressive flooding of cropland is commonly used to distribute use over time. Crop fields left dry receive substantially more use by geese than by ducks.

The "boom or bust" phenomenon applies readily to cultivated wetlands, particularly for crops such as buckwheat and millet. Immature buckwheat is highly susceptible to drowning in sheetwater from a heavy rainstorm, and Japanese millet can be ravaged by thousands of blackbirds, some feeding within a few meters of a propane exploder gun. Costs of farming in wetlands are generally greater than those in uplands. The additional costs of water-level control (including structures) and increased operating costs on wet ground can make this form of waterfowl-habitat management prohibitively expensive. Once managers see the high attraction of flooded crops to waterfowl, however, many of them are tempted to try to repeat it annually, often eliminating marshes in the process.

An ideally managed marsh complex should include components of the 3 marsh types discussed above. If management objectives are for duck hunting, probably less area should be allocated to deep marsh. If the objective is for refuge and resident wildlife, however, a greater proportion should be committed to hemi-marsh and deep marsh.

RESEARCH NEEDS

The magnitude of the effect of loss of Great Lakes marshes on migrating waterfowl has not been specifically defined and should be investigated. This suggests formation of a regional state-provincial committee, or establishment of Great Lakes Marsh Technical Committees within the Mississippi and Atlantic flyways, or some other type of body with U.S. and Canadian representation. The objective should be to develop new mechanisms for protecting and restoring Great Lakes marshes. These methods must include effective legislation, inasmuch as previous regulations have permitted a continued loss of marshes. If the amount of existing marsh is to be stabilized, creation or reestablishment of Great Lakes marshes is indicated.

We know relatively little about energy needs of migrating waterfowl and what wild foods yield in TME to waterfowl. More research should be directed to total nutritional analysis (including macro- and micronutrient content in addition to GE) of natural marsh foods (seeds, stems, leaves, tubers, invertebrates) and how efficiently waterfowl metabolize them. Most work has been done with tame mallards. Methods must be developed to measure accurately the energy demands of many species of migrating waterfowl, what they derive from the foods eaten on stopover areas, whether these areas are adequate nutritionally, and, if not, what marsh management techniques can be developed to optimize food quality on managed marshes. For example, Hoffman and Bookhout (1985) suggested that manipulating water levels in Lake Erie marshes to produce more rice cut-grass and walters millet would provide seeds of higher TME. It would then be essential to learn whether waterfowl responded positively to such manipulations and whether the effect was nutritionally beneficial.

Emphasis here has been on autumn migrating waterfowl, but Great Lakes marshes are important to spring migrants as well. Can procedures be developed to improve the value of these marshes to spring migrants? Much recent research has focused on the value of invertebrates to breeding waterfowl. In the southern Great Lakes marshes, particularly, relatively little waterfowl production takes place. For the most part birds use these marshes as stopover sites on their way to more northerly breeding areas. Invertebrates probably are the principal food source at this time. Preliminary work in Ohio indicates that dewatering in late March to the 50% water level, rather than in the usual mid-May period, results in significant increases in invertebrate biomass, and that ducks respond positively to this increase in spring. The applicability of this procedure to other Great Lakes marshes should be studied.

Stuber and Sather (1984) pointed out the paradox of lacking information to understand fully a complex environmental system (wetlands), while needing to generalize and make predictions so that rapidly vanishing resources can be protected. They categorized research gaps into hydrology, water quality, food-chain support, and habitat. In discussing habitat, they underscored the problem of making generalizations based on studies at specific sites and stressed that regional hypotheses on habitat requirements need to be based on typical wetlands in that region. Weller (1978:280) stated, "What is needed most to advance marsh management theory and practice are experimental data gathered concurrently by a team of specialists in marsh plants, limnology, hydrology, invertebrates, and vertebrates." He listed 11 topics that need to be addressed, including habitat stimuli that attract wildlife to marshes, germination conditions that make marsh drawdowns or other water manipulations more effective and predictable, and the relationship of invertebrates to marsh dynamics. Those, and the other topics, have relevance to research on the Great Lakes marshes.

CONCLUSIONS

Retention of the remaining Great Lakes marshes is the greatest challenge for providing essential habitat for migrating waterfowl. Jaworski and Raphael (1978) suggested that, with limited exception, only publicly owned marshes were reasonably safe from foreseeable development by the private sector.

Great Lakes marshes are unique because of their proximity to human populations. This makes them more available for human use, but more susceptible to destruction and development. Waterfowl use is greatest on the nearly 34,000 ha of marsh in Lake St. Clair and in Lake Erie from Ontario's Long Point west and south to Ohio's Sandusky Bay. We believe that the significance of these marshes to waterfowl has been underestimated.

The continued existence of Great Lakes marshes is tied directly to maintaining huntable numbers of waterfowl, for it is largely the waterfowl hunter who is subsidizing the restoration and protection of wetlands (National Shooting Sports Foundation 1973, Wildlife Management Institute 1984). Although the future of publicly owned marshes seems secure, that of privately owned marshes does not. Whether they will remain as marshes will depend on sentiment, in part (e.g., some current hunting club members represent fourth-generation association), but the decision will be an economic one. Managing controlled marshes as we have described in this paper is one of the most intensive and expensive forms of waterfowl management on the continent. For example, the current U.S. Government cost estimate of dike construction, including rip-rapping, is about \$400/linear meter. The reward for supporting this endeavor is, and must be, quality hunting opportunity.

SUMMARY

The more than 15,100 km of Great Lakes shoreline suggest an abundance of marshes that directly abut the lakes and connecting rivers. Within the Precambrian shield, however, which underlies nearly all of Lake Superior and much of eastern Lake Huron, the shorelines are characterized by steep escarpments and few marshes. Coastal marshes usually are associated with low-angle offshore profiles. The southern Great Lakes and Lake St. Clair contain the greatest amount of coastal marshes.

Because of their scarcity, Lake Superior coastal marshes are not significant to the autumn migrating waterfowl that use the Great Lakes. The Green Bay marshes of Lake Michigan are important autumn staging areas for divers. The Ontario shoreline of Lake Huron is relatively lightly used by autumn migrants, but Saginaw Bay marshes receive significant use.

The Lake St. Clair marshes had Ontario's highest number of Canada goose use-days and second highest redhead and canvasback use-days in 1968-73; use was similar in 1976-82. Overall, the area ranked second of Ontario's 17 major waterfowl use-areas on the Great Lakes shoreline.

Ontario's Long Point-Turkey Point marshes on Lake Erie have the greatest numbers of canvasbacks and redheads for any area along Ontario's Great Lakes shoreline. Disturbance by powerboats is common for several Lake Erie shoreline areas. Ducks have adapted by resting most of the day in the open waters and feeding in the marshes in early morning and late evening.

Ontario's north shore area of Lake Ontario has limited waterfowl use. Farther east, Prince Edward County's shoreline marshes are the third most important waterfowl area along Ontario's Great Lakes shoreline.

Most (74%) Great Lakes marshes are naturally existing and uncontrolled, and capabilities for managing them are limited. Management generally concerns elimination of unwanted vegetation—either plants of low wildlife value, or unfavorable growth characteristics of desired species.

Legal baiting as practiced in Canada might compensate the need for food production management to attract and hold migrating ducks. In the U.S., controlled marshes are managed for natural food production by water-level control. Controlled marshes usually require systems of dikes or levees combined with pumping of water to control water levels. Three stages of controlled marshes are: mudflats or moist-soil areas, shallow-marsh or hemimarsh, and deep marsh or open-water marsh.

Managed mudflats are characterized by dense stands of annual emergents, high seed production, and intensive use by migrating waterfowl. Common species produced include smartweeds, millets, nutsedge, and rice cut-grass. Overall plant diversity and community interspersion are low. Water is removed in early May to early June, to expose mudflats through the growing season, and is replaced by early September.

Shallow marsh is best represented by emergent, perennial species. Vegetation and water can be managed to provide the highest degree of interspersion of any marsh stage. Submergent plants are a primary duck food, but they will not persist if carp are present. The diversity and interspersion of plant communities enhance waterfowl use over managed areas.

Deep marsh is typified by open water (depth 30-106 cm) and scattered clumps of perennial, emergent vegetation. In terms of providing food, they are the least attractive stage to migratory waterfowl. Duration of the deep marsh stage seldom exceeds 3 years because of decreased attractiveness to waterfowl and high costs of erosion. Waterfowl often use the large expanses of open water for resting, and effective management of deep marshes may include use as a refuge area.

More than 1,600 ha of cropland are managed for waterfowl in the Great Lakes marshes, principally for hunting. Major crops grown are corn, soybeans, buckwheat, and Japanese millet. A principal management concern is timing of seed maturity with hunting seasons. Progressive flooding of cropland is used to distribute waterfowl use over time.

Retention of the remaining Great Lakes marshes is the greatest challenge for providing essential habitat for migrating waterfowl in the future. Because these marshes are close to relatively high human population densities, they are more available for use, but more susceptible to destruction. The future of publicly owned marshes seems secure, but that of private marshes does not. Managing controlled marshes by water-level control is quite expensive, and the reward must be quality hunting. Financial support is needed from other marsh user groups, particularly from nongame programs.

LITERATURE CITED

Anderson, J. M. 1950. Some aquatic vegetation changes following fish removal. J. Wildl. Manage. 14:206-209.

Bednarik, K. E. 1956. Muskrat in Ohio Lake Erie marshes. Ohio Dep. Nat. Resour., Columbus. 67 pp.

————. 1963. Marsh management techniques. Game Res. Ohio 1:91-96.

Beeton, A. M., and D. C. Chandler. 1963. The St. Lawrence Great Lakes. Pages 535-558 in D. G. Frey, ed. Limnology in North America. Univ. Wisconsin Press, Madison.

Bellrose, F. C. 1968. Waterfowl migration corridors, east of the Rocky Mountains in the United States. Ill. Nat. Hist. Surv. Biol. Note 61. 24 pp.

Berry, C. R. 1982. Behavior and ecology of carp in the Bear River Migratory Bird Refuge. Final Rep., Utah Coop. Fish. Res. Unit, Utah State Univ., Logan. 48 pp.

Beule, J. D. 1979. Control and management of cattails in southeastern Wisconsin wetlands. Wis. Dep. Nat. Resour. Tech. Bull. 112. 39 pp.

Bishop, R. A., R. D. Andrews, and J. Rockney. 1979. Marsh management and its relationship to vegetation, waterfowl, and muskrats. Proc. Iowa Acad. Sci. 86:50-56.

Chubb, S. L., and C. R. Liston. 1986. Density and distribution of larval fishes in Pentwater Marsh, a coastal wetland on Lake Michigan. J. Great Lakes Res. 12:332-343.

Cowardin, L. M., V. Carter, F. C. Golet, and E. T. LaRoe. 1979. Classification of wetlands and deepwater habitats of the United States. U.S. Dep. Int., Fish and Wildl. Serv. FWS/OBS-79-31. 131 pp.

Dennis, D. G., and R. E. Chandler. 1974. Waterfowl use of the Ontario shorelines of the southern Great Lakes during migration. Pages 58-65 *in* H. Boyd, ed. Canadian Wildlife Service waterfowl studies in eastern Canada, 1969-73. Can. Wildl. Serv. Rep. Ser. 29.

———, and N. R. North. 1984. Waterfowl use of the Lake St. Clair marshes during migration in 1968-69, 1976-77, and 1982. Pages 43-52 *in* S. G. Curtis, D. G. Dennis, and H. Boyd, eds. Waterfowl studies in Ontario, 1973-81. Can. Wildl. Serv. Occas. Pap. 54.

———, G. B. McCullough, N. R. North, and R. K. Ross. 1984. An updated assessment of migrant waterfowl use of the Ontario shorelines of the southern Great Lakes. Pages 37-42 *in* S. G. Curtis, D. G. Dennis, and H. Boyd, eds. Waterfowl studies in Ontario, 1973-81. Can. Wildl. Serv. Occas. Pap. 54.

DiAngelo, S. 1953. Aquatic plant succession at certain waterfowl flooding projects in Michigan. M.S. Thesis, Univ. Michigan, Ann Arbor. 112 pp.

Duffy, W. G., T. R. Batterson, and C. D. McNabb. 1987. The St. Marys River, Michigan: an ecological profile. U.S. Dep. Int., Fish and Wildl. Serv. Biol. Rep. 85(7.10). 138 pp.

Edsall, T. A., B. A. Manny, and C. N. Raphael. 1988. The St. Clair River and Lake St. Clair, Michigan: an ecological profile. U.S. Dep. Int., Fish and Wildl. Serv. Biol. Rep. 85(7.3). 130 pp.

Erskine, A. J. 1988. The changing patterns of brant migration in eastern North America. J. Field Ornithol. 59:110-119.

Fassett, N. C. 1969. A manual of aquatic plants. Univ. Wisconsin Press, Madison. 405 pp.

Fredrickson, L. H., and R. D. Drobney. 1979. Habitat utilization by postbreeding waterfowl. Pages 119-131 *in* T. A. Bookhout, ed. Waterfowl and wetlands—an integrated review. North Cent. Sect., Wildl. Soc., Madison, Wis.

———, and T. S. Taylor. 1982. Management of seasonally flooded impoundments for wildlife. U.S. Dep. Int. Fish and Wildl. Serv. Resour. Publ. 148. 29 pp.

Great Lakes Basin Commission. 1975. Great Lakes Basin framework study. Appendix 17. Wildlife. U.S. Dep. Int., Bur. Sport Fish. and Wildl., Ann Arbor, Mich. 140 pp.

Great Lakes Water Quality Board. 1982. 1982 report on Great Lakes water quality. Report to the International Joint Commission, Windsor, Ont. 153 pp.

Hanna, J. E. 1984. A management strategy for the restoration of aquatic vegetation in Rondeau Bay, Lake Erie. Prepared for Southwestern Region, Ontario Ministry of the Environment. (irreg. pagin.)

Harris, S. W. 1957. Ecological effects of drawdown operations for the purpose of improving waterfowl habitat. Ph.D. Thesis, Univ. Minnesota, St. Paul. 209 pp.

———, and W. H. Marshall. 1963. Ecology of water level manipulations on a northern marsh. Ecology 44:331-343.

Hartman, G. F. 1949. Management of central Wisconsin flowages. Wis. Conserv. Bull. 14:19-22.

Herdendorf, C. E., and S. M. Hartley, editors. 1980. Fish and wildlife resources of the Great Lakes coastal wetlands within the United States. Vol. 1. Overview. Ohio State Univ. CLEAR Tech. Rep 170:1. 471 pp.

———, C. N. Raphael, and E. Jaworski. 1986. The ecology of Lake St. Clair wetlands: a community profile. U.S. Dep. Int., Fish and Wildl. Serv. Biol. Rep. 85(7.7). 187 pp.

Hoffman, R. D., and T. A. Bookhout. 1985. Metabolizable energy of seeds consumed by ducks in Lake Erie marshes. Trans. North Am. Wildl. and Nat. Resour. Conf. 50:557-565.

Hopkins, R. C. 1962. Drawdown for ducks. Wis. Conserv. Bull. 27:18-19.

Hough, J. L. 1958. Geology of the Great Lakes. University of Illinois Press, Urbana. 313 pp.

———. 1962. Geologic framework. Pages 3-27 *in* H. J. Pincus, ed. Great Lakes basin. Am. Assoc. Adv. Sci. Publ. 71.

Ishmael, W. E. 1986. Lake Michigan is alive with ducks. Page 27 *in* Wisconsin: grateful for the Great Lakes. Coastal Zone Manage., Wis. Dep. Nat. Resour., Madison.

Jaworski, E., and C. N. Raphael. 1978. Coastal wetlands value study in Michigan. Phase I. Fish, wildlife, and recreational values of Michigan's coastal wetlands. Div. Land Resour. Prog., Mich. Dep. Nat. Resour., Lansing. 98 pp.

Kadlec, J. A. 1962. Effects of a drawdown on a waterfowl impoundment. Ecology 43:267-281.

Keddy, P. A., and A. A. Reznicek. 1986. Great Lakes vegetation dynamics: the role of fluctuating water levels and buried seeds. J. Great Lakes Res. 12:25-36.

King, D. R., and G. S. Hunt. 1967. Effect of carp on vegetation in a Lake Erie marsh. J. Wildl. Manage. 31:181-188.

Kroll, R. W., and R. L. Meeks. 1985. Muskrat population recovery following habitat re-establishment near southwestern Lake Erie. Wildl. Soc. Bull. 13:483-486.

Linde, A. F. 1969. Techniques for wetland management. Wis. Dep. Nat. Resour. Res. Rep. 45. 156 pp.

Manny, B. A., T. A. Edsall, and E. Jaworski. 1988. The Detroit River, Michigan: an ecological profile. U.S. Dep. Int., Fish and Wildl. Serv. Biol. Rep. 85(7.17). 86 pp.

Martin, A. C., R. C. Erickson, and J. H. Steenis. 1957. Improving duck marshes by weed control. U.S. Fish and Wildl. Serv. Circ. 19. 60 pp.

McCullough, G. B. 1981. Wetland losses in Lake St. Clair and Lake Ontario. Pages 81-89 in A. Champagne, ed. Proc. Ontario wetland conf., 18-19 Sept., Toronto.

————. 1984. Overwintering of waterfowl adjacent to the Nanticoke Generating Station, Lake Erie, Ontario, 1978 and 1979. Pages 32-36 in S. G. Curtis, D. G. Dennis, and H. Boyd, eds. Waterfowl studies in Ontario, 1973-81. Can. Wildl. Serv. Occas. Pap. 54.

Meeks, R. L. 1969. Effect of drawdown date on wetland plant succession. J. Wildl. Manage. 33:817-821.

Miller, H. 1943. Waterfowl survey, Saginaw Bay-Lake St. Clair-Lake Erie. Mich. Dep. Conserv., Div. Wildl. P-R. Proj. 13-R. 132 pp.

National Shooting Sports Foundation. 1973. What they say about hunting. Nat. Shooting Sports Found., Riverside, Conn. 22 pp.

Piehl, J. L., ed. 1986. Wetland restoration: a techniques workshop. Minn. Chap., The Wildl. Soc., Fergus Falls. 48 pp.

Powers, C. F., and A. Robertson. 1966. The aging Great Lakes. Sci. Am. 215:94-104.

Prince, H. H. 1979. Bioenergetics of postbreeding dabbling ducks. Pages 103-117 in T. A. Bookhout, ed. Waterfowl and wetlands—an integrated review. North Cent. Sect., Wildl. Soc., Madison, Wis.

Rawinski, T. J. 1982. The ecology and management of purple loosestrife (Lythrum salicaria L.) in central New York. M.S. Thesis, Cornell Univ., Ithaca, N.Y. 88 pp.

Robey, G. D. 1949. Ohio. Pages 178-192 in E. V. Connett, ed. Wildfowling in the Mississippi Flyway. D. Van Nostrand Co., Inc., New York, N.Y.

Roznik, F., J. Raber, D. Olson, L. Lintereur, L. Kernen, J. Korotev, and R. Cook. 1979. Green Bay West Shores master plan concept element. Wis. Dep. Nat. Resour., Madison. 54 pp.

Sincock, J. 1962. Estimating consumption of food by wintering waterfowl populations. Proc. Annu. Conf. Southeast. Assoc. Game and Fish Comm. 16:217-221.

Smith, L. M., and J. A. Kadlec. 1983. Seed banks and their role during drawdown of a North American marsh. J. Appl. Ecol. 20:673-684.

Stuber, P. R., and J. H. Sather. 1984. Research gaps in assessing wetland function. Trans. North Am. Wildl. and Nat. Resour. Conf. 49:304-311.

Stuckey, R. L. 1978. The decline of lake plants. Nat. Hist. 87:66-69.

————. 1981. Disappearance of submersed aquatic vascular plants from the lower Great Lakes region. Proc. Conf. Great Lakes Res. 24:25.

Sugden, L. G. 1973. Metabolizable energy of wild duck foods. Can. Wildl. Serv. Prog. Notes 35. 4 pp.

————. 1979. Grain consumption by mallards. Wildl. Soc. Bull. 7:35-39.

The Center for the Great Lakes. 1986. Areas of concern. Great Lakes Reporter 3(4):5.

Thompson, D. Q., R. L. Stuckey, and E. B. Thompson. 1987. Spread, impact, and control of purple loosestrife (Lythrum salicaria) in North American wetlands. U.S. Dep. Int., Fish and Wildl. Serv. Res. 2. 55 pp.

Trautman, M. C. 1981. The fishes of Ohio with illustrated keys. Rev. ed. Ohio State Univ. Press, Columbus. 782 pp.

U.S. Army Corps of Engineers. 1987. Great Lakes levels update no. 27, 5 October 1987. Dep. Army, Detroit Dist., Detroit, Mich. 1 pp.

U.S. Department of the Interior. 1967. Fish and wildlife as related to water quality of the Lake Erie Basin. U.S. Dep. Int., Washington, D.C. 170 pp.

van der Valk, A. G., and C. B. Davis. 1978. The role of seed banks in the vegetation dynamics of prairie glacial marshes. Ecology 59:322-335.

Weeks, J. L. 1975. Ohio wetlands inventory, 1972-74. Ohio Dep. Nat. Resour., Div. Wildl. Inservice Docum. 17. 24 pp.

Weller, M. W. 1978. Management of freshwater marshes for wildlife. Pages 267-284 in R. Good, D. Whigham, and R. Simpson, eds. Freshwater wetlands. Academic Press, New York, N.Y.

————, and L. H. Fredrickson. 1973. Avian ecology of a managed glacial marsh. Living Bird 12:269-291.

————, and C. S. Spatcher. 1965. Role of habitat in the distribution and abundance of marsh birds. Iowa State Univ. Agric. Home Econ. Exp. Stn. Spec. Rep. 43. 31 pp.

Wildlife Management Institute. 1984. Placing wildlife management in perspective. Wildl. Manage. Inst., Washington, D.C. 27 pp.

Wilson, J. E. 1969. Wetlands of eastern Lake Ontario and the St. Lawrence River. Div. Fish Wildl., N.Y. Dep. Environ. Conserv., Albany. 65 pp.

RIVERINE AND DEEPWATER HABITATS FOR DIVING DUCKS

CARL E. KORSCHGEN, U.S. Fish and Wildlife Service, Northern Prairie Wildlife Research Center, La Crosse Field Station, La Crosse, WI 54601

Most populations of diving ducks depend on large lakes and riverine impoundments in the Upper Mississippi Flyway of the United States (U.S.) for feeding and resting during fall and spring migration. Historically, wetlands in Minnesota, Wisconsin, Iowa, and Illinois covered millions of hectares. Wetland losses have been 6.7 million ha in these states (Tiner 1984). Most of the riverine and deepwater wetlands remain, but few are useful to waterfowl, due to anthropogenic and natural causes. Nevertheless, they still may have management potential in the future.

The most numerous diving ducks using riverine and deepwater habitats in the Mississippi Flyway include canvasback (*Aythya valisineria*), lesser scaup (*A. affinis*), redhead (*A. americana*), and ring-necked duck (*A. collaris*). Greater scaup (*A. marila*), bufflehead (*Bucephala albeola*), common goldeneye (*B. clangula*), hooded merganser (*Lophodytes cucullatus*), common merganser (*Mergus merganser*), and ruddy duck (*Oxyura jamaicensis*) also use riverine and deepwater wetlands, but peak counts during migration are relatively small. Between 1955 and 1980, the breeding population of diving ducks in North America has numbered around 10 million. This level is about 25% of the total breeding duck population in North America and contributes approximately 17 million birds to the fall flight (Jessen 1981).

The geographical areas to be discussed in this paper are part of the Central U.S. named the Central Lowland Province (Hunt 1967). This province is distinguished chiefly on the basis of geologic structure and history, but, in part, on the basis of climatic differences. Most of the Central Lowland Province was glaciated, and the sections of the province are distinguished chiefly by their glacial histories. The Central Lowland is divided by Hunt (1967) into the Small Lakes Section, Driftless Section, Great Lakes Section, and Till Plain.

The Small Lakes Section covers most of Minnesota and northern Iowa, consisting of a plain with hummocky moraines. Much of the surface is knob and kettle topography, except that ponds and marshes are smaller and fewer here than marshes farther east, probably because the annual rainfall here is about 50 cm. The Driftless Section comprises the southwestern quarter of Wisconsin and the adjoining 400 km of the Mississippi River. Valleys contain deposits discharged by glacial meltwaters and deep deposits of loess. In the north is the Great Lakes Section, a plain of glacial till attributable to the Wisconsin glaciation, which encompasses parts of Wisconsin and Michigan. Parts of the till plains are hummocky with knobs and kettle holes containing lakes, ponds, or swamps.

Compared to other parts of the U.S., the climate of the Central Lowland Province is continental. Temperature differences between seasons are extreme: winters are cold and blizzards frequent; summers are warm. Most of the precipitation takes place during the growing season, and average annual temperatures range from 9 C in the north to 15 C in the south. Temperatures temporally limit waterfowl use of wetland habitats at these latitudes. For example, the average date of occurrence of the first permanent 2.5 cm of snow in Minnesota relates closely to the dates that ice will form on most of the wetlands and preclude waterfowl use (Fig. 1).

The wetlands addressed in this chapter

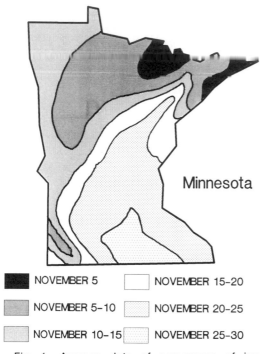

NOVEMBER 5 NOVEMBER 15–20

NOVEMBER 5–10 NOVEMBER 20–25

NOVEMBER 10–15 NOVEMBER 25–30

Fig. 1. Average date of occurrence of ice cover on Minnesota wetlands (adapted from Kuehnast et al. 1982).

are classified as riverine and lacustrine (Cowardin et al. 1979). Deepwater habitats are permanently flooded and are too deep (> 2 m) to support emergent plants. The Riverine System includes all wetlands and deepwater habitats contained within a channel, with 2 exceptions: (1) wetlands dominated by trees, shrubs, persistent emergents, emergent mosses, or lichens, and (2) wetlands with water containing ocean-derived salts in excess of 0.5%. Most of the wetlands and deepwater habitats discussed in this chapter can be further characterized into the Lower Perennial Subsystem of the Riverine System, in which the topographic gradient is low and water velocity is slow. Water is usually, but not always, flowing, and the substrate consists mainly of sand and mud. Oxygen deficits may sometimes occur. Aquatic fauna is composed mostly of species that reach their maximum abundance in still water. The Lacustrine

System includes wetlands and deepwater habitats with all of the following characteristics: (1) situated in a topographic depression or a dammed river channel, (2) lack trees, shrubs, persistent emergents, emergent mosses or lichens with > 30% areal coverage, and (3) are > 8 ha in size. The Lacustrine System is further characterized by the Limnetic and Littoral subsystems. The Limnetic Subsystem includes all deepwater habitats within the Lacustrine System. The Littoral Subsystem is all wetland habitats from the shore to a depth of 2 m below low-water level or to the maximum extent of nonpersistent emergents, if these grow at depths greater than 2 m.

The objectives of this paper are to describe the associations between migrating waterfowl in the Mississippi Flyway and riverine and deepwater habitats, especially those along the Mississippi River, and to discuss their management. Emphasis will be on 4 species of diving ducks (canvasback, redhead, lesser scaup, and ring-necked duck) due to their importance to the continental waterfowl population and their use of these habitats during fall and spring migration. Management of these habitats will benefit most other waterfowl because their habitat distributions overlap. For example, tundra swans (*Cygnus columbianus*) frequently use habitats similar to diving ducks; therefore, many of the management practices to promote the production of aquatic food plants would benefit them. Management practices (e.g., fish control, water control, and plant management) for the Mississippi Flyway inland wetlands, moist-soil impoundments and refuges (Reid et al. 1989), Central Flyway High Plains reservoirs and sloughs (Ringelman et al. 1989), and Pacific Flyway Great Basin intermountain marshes (Kadlec and Smith 1989) may be applicable to deepwater and riverine wetlands. Plant names in this chapter follow Fassett (1972).

HABITAT IMPORTANCE

The concept of fall migration corridors (Bellrose 1968, 1980) best describes the importance of the Upper Midwest, Great Lakes, and Midwest regions to migrating diving ducks. The Prairie Corridor (Fig. 2) lies between the Missouri and the Mississippi rivers and is used perhaps by only 20,000 lesser scaup and 5,000 ring-necked ducks. The Mississippi River Corridor, the major corridor for diving ducks, divides in Minnesota; one branch takes an east-southeast direction, whereas the other takes a south-southeast turn. This chapter focuses on the Mississippi River Corridor. Many of the wetlands referred to as "lakes" are actually riverine impoundments (e.g., most of the Wisconsin lakes and National Wildlife Refuges [NWR]). Table 1 contains migrational habitats by location, size, and major diving duck species. These wetlands comprise the major wetlands in the Mississippi River Corridor (Figs. 3 and 4).

Minnesota lakes have been inventoried by the Minnesota Department of Natural Resources (DNR) (unpubl. data) as part of their game lakes surveys. The surveys were occasionally repeated over a number of years and qualitatively describe vegetation species composition and relative abundance. Similar surveys in Wisconsin were conducted by Zimmerman (1953) that show food and cover resources of the wetlands and the physical, biological, and economic factors affecting aquatic life.

Trumbull Lake in Iowa is a shallow lake with maximum depth of 1.5 m. Water depth can be managed, and water level has been observed to control establishment of emergent and submersed aquatic plants (A. Hayden, unpubl. data). In low-water years, pondweeds (*Potamogeton* spp.), wildcelery (*Vallisneria americana*), waterweed (*Elodea canadensis*), arrowhead (*Sagittaria* spp.), and other species of plants proliferate. Red

MISSOURI RIVER CORRIDOR

PRAIRIE CORRIDOR

MISSISSIPPI RIVER CORRIDOR

Fig. 2. Location of diving duck migration corridors in the upper portion of the Mississippi Flyway (Bellrose 1968).

Rock Lake and Rathbun Lake are U.S. Army Corps of Engineers flood control reservoirs on the Des Moines and Chariton rivers, respectively, completed in 1969. As flood-control reservoirs, they are subject to great fluctuations (6+ m) in water levels and consequently do not support stable beds of aquatic vegetation. Iowa lakes are used primarily by lesser scaup.

The most important areas for migrating diving ducks along the Mississippi River Corridor are Navigation Pools 5, 7, 8, 9, and Keokuk Pool (Pool 19) on the Mississippi River (Fig. 4). Navigation Pools 5, 7, 8, and 9 extend for about 150 km and contain large open-water areas and shallow marsh zones with luxuriant growths of submersed and emergent aquatic vegetation. Keokuk Pool extends from Keokuk, Iowa, to Oquawka, Illinois, but the most important area for diving ducks

Table 1 Summary of diving duck (use indicated by *) migration habitats (primarily used during the fall) in the U.S.—upper portion of the Mississippi Flyway[a].

State	Name of area	Ha	Canvasback	Redhead	Lesser scaup	Ring-necked
Minnesota	Lake Christina	1,599	*			
	Leech Lake	44,245	*	*		
	Aspinwall Lake	160	*			
	Bear Lake	632	*			
	Cross Lake	142	*			*
	Dead Lake	3,169	*		*	*
	French Lake	143	*			
	Jennie Lake	128	*			
	Lake of the Woods	384,615	*			
	Mineral Lake	311	*			
	Nett Lake	2,983	*			*
	Ocheda Lake	720	*			
	Lake Orwell	160	*			
	Patterson Lake	226	*			
	Red Rock Lake	316	*			
	Sandhill Lake	242	*			
	Schilling Lake	315	*			
	Swan Lake	3,783	*			
	Ten Mile Lake	585	*			
	Thief Lake	3,008	*		*	
	Upper Rice Lake	753	*			
	Tamarac NWR	17,408	*	*	*	*
	Rice Lake NWR	7,310	*		*	*
	Pool 5, Upper Miss. River NWR	1,417	*		*	*
	Sallie Lake	487			*	
	Lower Red Lake	73,279			*	*
	Height of Land lake	1,596			*	
	Big Flat Lake	798				*
	Mud Lake	583			*	*
	Agassiz NWR	11,943			*	*
	Lake Winnebigosh	21,630			*	
	Drumbeater Lake	152			*	*
	Osakis Lake	2,538			*	
	Roseau River State Wildlife Area	4,858			*	
	Shell Lake	1,367			*	
	Squaw Lake	1,168				*
	Carlos Avery Refuge	810				*
	Sherburne NWR	3,644				*
	Mesabainnigma Lake	—				*
	Leech Lake	44,245			*	
	Turtle Lake	245			*	
Wisconsin	Lake Poygan	5,709	*	*	*	*
	Lake Butte Des Mortes	3,603	*	*	*	*
	Lake Puckaway	2,186	*	*		*
	Lake Winneconne	1,822	*			
	Rush Lake	1,255	*			
	Fox Lake	850	*			
	Lake Koshkonong	4,251	*			
	Lake Mendota	3,927	*			
	Beaver Dam Lake	2,186	*			
	Pool 4, Upper Miss. River NWFR[b]	486	*			
	Pool 5, Upper Miss. River NWFR	486	*	*	*	
	Pool 7, Upper Miss. River NWFR	7,000	*	*	*	*
	Pool 8, Upper Miss. River NWFR	8,000	*	*	*	*
	Big Green Lake	2,966				*
	Necedah NWFR	4,049				*
Iowa	Red Rock Reservoir	3,603	*			
	Rathbun Reservoir	4,453	*			
	Trumbull Lake	495			*	*
Iowa/Wisconsin	Pool 9, Upper Miss. River NWFR	2,591	*	*	*	*

Table 1. Continued

State	Name of area	Ha	Canvasback	Redhead	Lesser scaup	Ring-necked duck
Iowa/Illinois	Pool 19, Upper Miss. River (Keokuk Pool)	8,907	*	*	*	*
Illinois	Pool 13, Upper Miss. River (Spring Lake)	1,417	*	*		
	Pool 25, Upper Miss. River, Batchtown area	911		*		
	Pool 26, Upper Miss. River	10,510			*	*
	Spring Lake	486		*		
	Lake Michigan	—			*	

[a]Information in this table was derived from M. Reeves (unpublished U.S. Fish and Wildl. Serv.), F. Bellrose (unpubl. data), and personal communication with waterfowl biologists in Minnesota, Wisconsin, Iowa, and Illinois.

[b]NWFR = National Wildlife and Fish Refuge.

encompasses the 32-km stretch from Keokuk to Fort Madison, Iowa. The Illinois River and large lakes in Minnesota and Wisconsin formerly were important to diving ducks and other waterfowl. In the mid-1980s, their overall importance, especially for canvasbacks, was negligible compared to the Mississippi River.

Wetland habitats on the Mississippi River are similar in many respects because they were formed by construction of locks and dams in the 1930s. Each pool has 3 relatively distinct longitudinal zones based upon distance from the dam. The area immediately above a dam is normally a deep pool with open water and little marsh habitat (Eckblad 1986). These are the areas used by diving ducks. Because of the extensive planning efforts and academic interests on the Upper Mississippi River, the biological, chemical, and physical components of these habitats have been characterized. For information on Navigation Pool 5, see Nielsen et al. (1978) and Fremling et al. (1976); Pool 7, see Korschgen et al. (1988); Pool 8, see Sefton (1976), Elstad (1977), and Swanson and Sohmer (1978), Pool 9, see Donnermeyer (1982); Pool 13, see Eckblad (1986); and Pool 19, see Steffeck et al. (1985) and Jahn and Anderson (1986). Jackson et al. (1981) summarized sources of literature on the resource components of all Mississippi River pools. Mohlenbrock (1983) prepared an annotated bibliography of the aquatic macrophytes of the Upper Mississippi River from Cairo, Illinois, to St. Paul, Minnesota. This bibliography covers ecological requirements, distribution, and use of the dominant emersed, floating, and submersed macrophytes in navigation pools used by diving ducks. Hagen et al. (1977), Olson and Meyer (1976), and Minor et al. (1977) classified and compared the changes over time in aquatic and terrestrial habitats of the Upper Mississippi River from Hastings, Minnesota (Pool 3), to Cairo, Illinois (below Pool 26).

Population survey data in the upper midwest have been collected by the U.S. Fish and Wildlife Service and the Illinois Natural History Survey. Populations fluctuate widely among years in response to changes in flyway populations, the food base, and weather conditions. Surveys on the Mississippi River in the Keokuk Pool area in fall 1941 revealed only moderate numbers of diving ducks (F. C. Bellrose, unpubl. data). By 1946, the number of lesser scaup had greatly increased, but canvasbacks numbers were low, peaking at only 5,500. Serie et al. (1983) compiled annual (1961-1977) survey data for canvasbacks on Mississippi River pools 7, 8 (combined), and Keokuk Pool. A peak of 147,000 canvasbacks was observed in 1975 on Pools 7 and 8 (combined) and 169,000 in 1970 on Keokuk Pool. During the 1978-1984 period, a peak of 195,000 canvasbacks (Fig. 5) was observed on

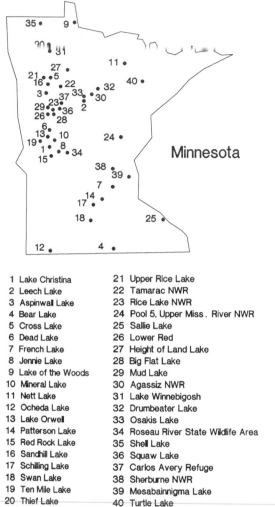

Fig. 3. Distribution of migration habitats for diving ducks in Minnesota.

1 Lake Christina
2 Leech Lake
3 Aspinwall Lake
4 Bear Lake
5 Cross Lake
6 Dead Lake
7 French Lake
8 Jennie Lake
9 Lake of the Woods
10 Mineral Lake
11 Nett Lake
12 Ocheda Lake
13 Lake Orwell
14 Patterson Lake
15 Red Rock Lake
16 Sandhill Lake
17 Schilling Lake
18 Swan Lake
19 Ten Mile Lake
20 Thief Lake

21 Upper Rice Lake
22 Tamarac NWR
23 Rice Lake NWR
24 Pool 5, Upper Miss. River NWR
25 Sallie Lake
26 Lower Red
27 Height of Land Lake
28 Big Flat Lake
29 Mud Lake
30 Agassiz NWR
31 Lake Winnebigosh
32 Drumbeater Lake
33 Osakis Lake
34 Roseau River State Wildlife Area
35 Shell Lake
36 Squaw Lake
37 Carlos Avery Refuge
38 Sherburne NWR
39 Mesabainnigma Lake
40 Turtle Lake

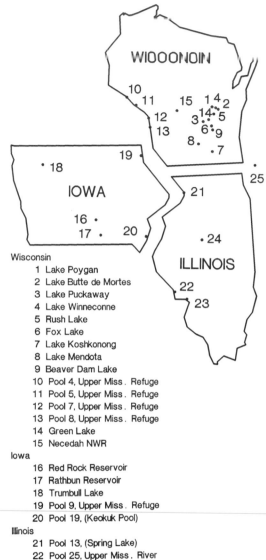

Wisconsin
1 Lake Poygan
2 Lake Butte de Mortes
3 Lake Puckaway
4 Lake Winneconne
5 Rush Lake
6 Fox Lake
7 Lake Koshkonong
8 Lake Mendota
9 Beaver Dam Lake
10 Pool 4, Upper Miss. Refuge
11 Pool 5, Upper Miss. Refuge
12 Pool 7, Upper Miss. Refuge
13 Pool 8, Upper Miss. Refuge
14 Green Lake
15 Necedah NWR
Iowa
16 Red Rock Reservoir
17 Rathbun Reservoir
18 Trumbull Lake
19 Pool 9, Upper Miss. Refuge
20 Pool 19, (Keokuk Pool)
Illinois
21 Pool 13, (Spring Lake)
22 Pool 25, Upper Miss. River
23 Pool 26, Upper Miss. River
24 Spring Lake
25 Lake Michigan

Fig. 4. Distribution of migration habitats for diving ducks in Wisconsin, Iowa, and Illinois.

Navigation Pools 7, 8, and 9 (combined). Many ring-necked ducks and lesser scaup also used these pools during this latter time period (Fig. 5). A maximum of 875,000 diving ducks was estimated on Keokuk Pool in 1969. On Keokuk Pool, waterfowl surveys during the falls of 1948-1984 made by the Illinois Natural History Survey revealed a yearly mean peak of 345,000 diving ducks (F. C. Bellrose, unpubl. data). The composition (%) of the population was lesser scaup 71, canvasback 18, ring-necked ducks 10, and redheads 1. Peak populations during the last 10 years have been lower (Fig. 6).

The Minnesota DNR compiles waterfowl population data in fall from a variety of sources in periodic reports. During 1980-1987, wetlands with lesser scaup numbers over 5,000 birds (excluding the Mississippi River) included Agassiz NWR, Thief Lake, Tamarac NWR, Lake Geneva, Lake Winnibigoshish, Osakis Lake, Dead Lake, Shell Lake, Roseau River Wildlife Management Area (WMA),

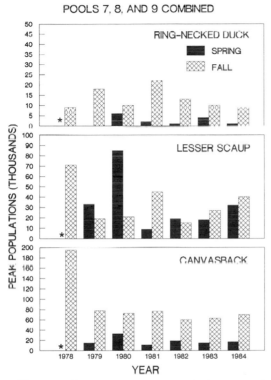

Fig. 5. Peak survey counts of ring-necked duck, lesser scaup, and canvasbacks on Navigation Pools 7, 8, and 9 of the Upper Mississippi River, 1979-1984. An asterisk indicates that no surveys were conducted.

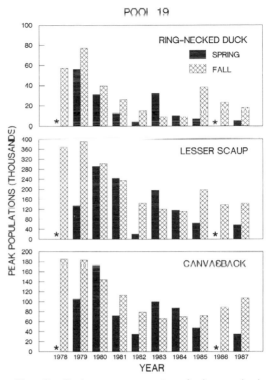

Fig. 6. Peak survey counts of ring-necked duck, lesser scaup, and canvasbacks on Navigation Pool 19 of the Upper Mississippi River, 1978-1987 (S. Havera, Ill. Nat. Hist. Surv., unpubl. data). An asterisk indicates that no surveys were conducted.

Sherburne NWR, and Lower Red Lake. Lakes with ring-necked duck populations over 5,000 included Tamarac NWR, Rice Lake NWR, Drumbeater Lake, Nett Lake, Hole-in-the-Bog Lake, Mesabaininigama Lake, Squaw Lake, Bowstring Lake, Lower Rice Lake, Round Lake, Leech Lake, Carlos Avery WMA, Mud/Goose WMA, Mud/Bray, and Fiske-Blue Rocks Lake Refuge. Only 3 lakes (Leech Lake, Sallie Lake, Dead Lake) had redhead duck populations over 5,000 birds. No lakes had over 5,000 canvasbacks.

The Wisconsin DNR conducted diving duck population surveys from 1984 to 1986 on 15 lakes (Beaver Dam Lake, Fox Lake, Lake Maria, Lake Puckaway, Big Green Lake, Rush Lake, Lake Winnebago, Lake Poygan, Lake Winneconne, Lake Butte Des Morts, Green Bay, Lake Mendota, Lake Kegonsa, Lake Koshko-

nong, Buffalo Lake, and Lake Wisconsin), which historically were important to diving ducks in east-central Wisconsin. Canvasback numbers were 0-149 birds, lesser scaup < 8,000, ring-necked duck < 200, and redhead duck < 500 (R. Kahl, unpubl. data).

The chronology of fall migration across the various regions of the Midwest is depicted for each species in Bellrose (1980). Generally, Minnesota wetlands are used in October, the Wisconsin areas from 15 October to 15 November, Iowa areas in late October through December, and Illinois areas in November and December. Some diving ducks winter on the Mississippi River in Keokuk Pool and Pool 26 if weather is mild and feeding areas are not ice-covered.

Most changes in the distribution of

migrating diving ducks in the Upper Midwest over the past several decades have been attributed to changes in land and water use. The relationship between changes in the aquatic plant communities and invertebrate and vertebrate animal populations in the Illinois River Valley have been documented for a 75-year period (Mills et al. 1966, Bellrose et al. 1979, Sparks 1984). Losses of the invertebrate and plant food components of the habitat between 1946 and 1964 seriously impacted the numbers and distribution of lesser scaup, ring-necked ducks, and canvasbacks. Factors that directly affected the species composition and abundance of the wetland plants were (1) fluctuating water levels, (2) water turbidity, (3) water depth, and (4) competition among plant species. The fundamental food item for diving ducks at Keokuk Pool has been fingernail clams *(Musculium transversum)* (Thompson 1973). High populations of fingernail clams may not have developed until the early 1950s.

Degradation from sedimentation threatens riverine and deepwater habitats by either eliminating them or making them unsuitable for aquatic life. The Illinois River illustrates a situation in which modification by man has resulted in severe changes in the habitat. Drainage and levee districts drained almost half the existing bottomland lakes between 1909 and 1922, which increased flood heights and the deposition of sediments on the remaining lakes and floodplains (Bellrose et al. 1983). Erosion from uplands and tributary stream banks has resulted in high sedimentation rates that are rapidly filling bottomland lakes.

The role of organic and inorganic chemical contaminants in degradation of wetland habitats on the Illinois and Mississippi rivers has been difficult to substantiate because of the myriad of interacting water-quality, sediment, and contaminant factors. Large metropolitan areas on the upstream end of these rivers are known to have contributed to increased levels of trace metals and compounds such as polychlorinated biphenyls (PCBs) (Metropolitan Waste Control Commission 1982, Sprafka 1981, Bailey and Rada 1984, Sparks 1984).

HABITAT IMPORTANCE RELATIVE TO WATERFOWL REQUIREMENTS

Diving ducks feed mostly in large bodies of water. Generally, they obtain their food beneath the surface of the water and away from shore. During fall migration, these species are predominantly herbivorous, except for lesser scaup that consume animal foods (Table 2). Geographic variation exists in the diet based upon the availability of preferred foods. In general, diving ducks take more of the subterranean parts of the plant such as winter buds, tubers, rootstalks, and green vegetative parts than seeds (Cottam 1939).

Most diving duck food-habit studies have been summarized in detail by Bellrose (1980) and Palmer (1976). The common plant foods (includes seeds, tuber, and foliage) (Table 3) represent the most important species to manage in deepwater and riverine wetlands. Animal foods are primarily benthic invertebrates, which can be managed to some extent by management of water and sediment quality and the vegetation complex.

Korschgen et al. (1988) investigated the feeding ecology of canvasbacks on Lake Onalaska of Pool 7. In fall 1980, canvasbacks harvested 40% (152,000 kg dry) of the standing crop of wildcelery winterbuds. On the same area, Takekawa (1987) studied the time-activity budgets and energetics of migrating canvasbacks during October and November 1983 and 1984. Canvasbacks fed 19% of the time and spent most of the remaining time in energy-conserving behaviors such as resting and sleeping. Migrating canvasbacks gained 2,570 kJ/day (Takekawa 1987) on the Upper Mississippi River, which

Table 2. Percent volume of plant and animal foods in the diet of migrating diving ducks.

Food	Species				Location	Season	Reference
	Canvasback	Redhead	Lesser scaup	Ring-necked duck			
Plant	84.8	90.7	60.0	93.2	Entire		
Animal	15.2	9.2	40.0	6.7	U.S.	Fall	Kubicheck (1933)
Plant	80.6	89.7	59.6	81.5	Entire		
Animal	19.4	10.3	40.4	18.5	U.S.	Fall	Cottam (1939)
Plant	95.4	98.8	89.7	98.4			
Animal	4.4	1.2	11.3	1.6	Missouri	Fall	Korschgen (1955)
Plant	65.0	77.9	9.7	65.9			
Animal	35.0	22.1	90.4	34.1	Illinois	Fall	Anderson (1959)
Plant	100.0		1.2	100.0			
Animal			98.8		Ill./Iowa	Fall	D. Steffeck and F. Paveglio (unpubl. data)
Plant[a]	98.8						
Animal[a]	1.2				Wisconsin	Fall	Korschgen et al. (1988)
Plant[a]	70.9						
Animal[a]	29.0				Wisconsin (Pools 7,8,9)	Spring	J. Barzen and C. Korschgen (unpubl. data)
Plant[a]	56.2						
Animal[a]	43.9				Ill./Iowa (Pool 19)	Spring	J. Barzen and C. Korschgen (unpubl. data)

[a]Percent aggregate volume.

resulted in a gain of 170 g of fat and a 10-15% increase in body weight (J. R. Serie, unpubl. data). For canvasbacks to gain that much weight, food resources must be abundant and available, and the birds must have time to exploit the resource.

Day (1984) studied the behavior of diving ducks on Keokuk Pool of the Upper Mississippi River during the fall and found that male and female canvasbacks fed 25% and 21% of each day, respectively. Compared to the Lake Onalaska data, canvasbacks spent slightly more time (not statistically tested) foraging on Keokuk Pool where they were feeding primarily upon fingernail clams. Winterbuds of wildcelery contain 14 times more metabolizable energy than fingernail clams (J. Y. Takekawa, unpubl. data), which may explain partly why canvasbacks spend slightly more time foraging on Keokuk Pool than on Lake Onalaska. No time-activity budget information is available for canvasbacks using the Mississippi River during spring migration.

Wetlands >100 ha with abundant food resources are important to diving ducks. Because of their physical size, these wetlands afford protection from most predators, and even provide some protection from hunting activities due to regulations in Minnesota and Wisconsin, which limit open-water hunting. On the Upper Mississippi River, 16,500 ha of the major concentration areas are closed to hunting. In 1988, the "closed areas" were closed only to hunting and trapping during the waterfowl hunting season. People fishing, sightseeing, and boating can cause considerable disturbance to the ducks within the "closed areas."

ENVIRONMENTAL PROBLEMS

Diving ducks using large riverine and deepwater habitats are susceptible to pollution, such as oil spills and contaminants. Oil spills can result in direct

Table 3. Composite list of fall foods (use indicated by *) making up the bulk of the diet of migrating diving ducks in the Mississippi Flyway[a].

	Canvasback	Redhead	Lesser scaup	Ring-necked duck
Submersed plants				
Sago pondweed (Potamogeton pectinatus)	*	*		
Pondweeds (P. spp.)	*	*	*	*
Wildcelery	*			
Coontail (Ceratophyllum demersum)				*
Widgeon grass (Ruppia maritima)		*		
Emergent plants				
Sedge (Scirpus spp.)		*		
Arrowhead (Sagittaria spp.)	*			
Wild rice (Zizania aquatica)	*			*
Yellow water lily (Nuphar spp.)				*
Bur reed (Sparganium spp.)	*			
Smartweed (Polygonum spp.)				*
Sedges (Cyperus spp.)				*
Benthic Invertebrates				
Dragonflies (Odanata)			*	
Fingernail clams (Sphaeriidae)	*		*	*
Snails (Gastropoda)	*		*	*
Beetles (Coleoptera)			*	*
Mayfly (Hexagenia spp.)	*	*	*	*
Caddis flies (Trichoptera)			*	*
Midges (Chironomidae)	*	*		*
Flies (Diptera)			*	
Bugs (Hemiptera)			*	*

[a]See Table 2 for sources of the information.

mortality of ducks due to the effects of hypothermia. Fortunately, in the habitats discussed in this chapter, there has been no major loss of diving ducks to oil pollution during the last 10 years, but the possibility remains, especially along the Illinois and Mississippi rivers where commercial barge and train traffic transport oil and other toxic materials. Many wetlands in the industrialized watersheds have become contaminated to some degree by municipal and industrial discharges. On the Upper Mississippi River, levels of PCBs in fish from some pools are too high to permit commercial marketing (Hora 1984) and invertebrates such as mayflies, snails, and clams are known to concentrate PCBs 10 to 300 times sediment levels (Mauck and Olson 1977, Sparks and Smith 1979). PCBs could bioaccumulate in diving ducks if consumption of contaminated invertebrates continued for a prolonged time.

Lead poisoning also is a problem for diving ducks. Minnesota, Wisconsin, Iowa, and Illinois are known to have frequent waterfowl mortalities due to lead poisoning (Friend 1987). Several of the lakes and riverine pools used by diving ducks have been hunted with lead shot for a century or more. The incidence of lead poisoning should decrease with the mandatory use of steel shot.

The invasion of waterfowl habitat by exotic plant species such as Eurasian milfoil (Myriophyllum spicatum) also can cause habitat degradation. Eurasian milfoil has impacted diving duck habitats in Lake Mendota, Wisconsin, where the milfoil apparently replaced wildcelery (Titus 1977). Milfoil also may be a threat to the extensive plant beds in the Mississippi River as it becomes more common.

HABITAT MANAGEMENT

Nearly all wetlands used traditionally

by diving ducks during migration are quite large (Table 1). Managing large wetlands requires major planning and involves the manipulation of water quality, depth, and flow, and surrounding uplands to promote the establishment of desired habitats. In contrast to wetland management for breeding waterfowl, in which cover is a primary concern, wetland management for migrating and wintering diving ducks involves production of preferred plant and animal foods. Water availability is rarely a problem for diving ducks in fall and winter. The most important consideration is water quality. Management of the water regime is accomplished by controlling water quality, water depth, water flow, and plant and animal communities. Loss of wetland habitats due to sedimentation is an extremely serious problem and can be controlled by reducing erosion on upland areas. Reducing sediments in the aquatic system is expensive, difficult to engineer, and the impacts can only be mitigated. Schnick et al. (1982) summarized many of the structural, hydrological, biological, and regulatory management techniques that are applicable to lakes and riverine wetlands. Literature references and detailed explanations are given for such management techniques as dredging, bank stabilization, water-level regulation, riprap revetments, bulkheads, groins, wing dam and dikes, fixed breakwater structures, floating breakwater structures, revegetation, soil stabilizers, erosion-control mattings, island creation, fish screens and barriers, water-control structures, and control of nuisance plants.

Water Quality Tolerance of Aquatic Plants

Various components of turbidity can affect submersed aquatic vegetation in several ways. Particulates in the water can physically block the penetration of light through the water column. Stained or colored waters differentially absorb various wavelengths of sunlight, and plankton can cause mats or blooms that block sunlight or use red and blue wavelengths of sunlight that are used for photosynthesis (Stevenson and Confer 1978, Muncy et al. 1979). Suspended solids may be harmful to submersed aquatic vegetation when deposited on leaf surfaces, thereby reducing light transmission to photosynthetically-active leaf surfaces and possibly altering gas and nutrient exchange (Davis and Brinson 1980). Edwards (1969) postulated that suspended solids at high flows could have an abrasive effect on submersed aquatic vegetation. Thick layers of suspended solids deposited on the riverbed could make it difficult for submersed aquatic vegetation to become rooted (Mills et al. 1966). If turbidity is extreme, the resulting sedimentation may physically bury some macrophytes. Wetzel and McGregor (1968) found that low light intensity inhibits germination of bushy pondweed *(Najas flexilis)* and muskgrass *(Chara* spp.). Seeds of other submersed aquatic vegetation species may exhibit a similar limitation.

Several investigators have studied the distribution of submersed aquatic plants in systems that have plant communities similar to those in the Midwest. A survival index (0-1) for submersed plants (Table 4) (based on data from lakes in northern Iowa) was developed by Davis and Brinson (1980)—a high index number is indicative of better survival under adverse water quality. Studies and observations of the submersed plant communities of several pools of the Upper Mississippi River indicate that only plants with a survival index >0.8 are represented by large standing crops or biomass; long-leaf pondweed being the only exception (Pools 2-12 [Minor et al. 1977]; Pools 10-26 [Hagen et al. 1977]; Pool 8 [Sefton 1976]; Pool 19 [Steffeck et al. 1985]) (Fig. 4). Further increases in the turbidity levels will likely eliminate additional species from a dominant status. The dominant

Table 4. Survival index (0-1) for submersed aquatic plants based on data from northern Iowa lakes (Davis and Brinson 1980). A high index number is indicative of better survival under adverse conditions.

Species	Index
Coontail (*Ceratophyllum demersum*)	1.0
Sago pondweed	1.0
Clasping-leaf pondweed (*Potamogeton richardsonii*)	1.0
Horned pondweed (*Zannichellia palustris*)	1.0
Waterweed	0.8
Mud plantain (*Heteranthera dubia*)	0.8
Wildcelery	0.8
Bushy pondweed	0.7
Flat-stemmed pondweed (*P. zosteriformis*)	0.6
Leafy pondweed (*P. foliosus*)	0.3
Variable pondweed (*P. gramineus*)	0.3
Floating-leaf pondweed (*P. natans*)	0.3
Large-leaf pondweed(*P. amplifolius*)	0.2
Long-leaf pondweed (*P. nodosus*)	0.0
Whitestem pondweed (*P. praelongus*)	0.0

species in the Mississippi River at the present time are those that reproduce asexually from rootstalks or tubers, and apparently reproduce sexually from seeds only during periods of extraordinary water clarity that arise during times of drought (C. E. Korschgen, unpubl. data).

Drawdown Effects on Submersed Aquatic Plants

Drawdowns are a valuable technique for deepwater marsh management but must be used with care. Basin morphometry, soil characteristics, existing plant communities, waterfowl use, productivity, and seasonal water supplies are factors that affect the decision to use drawdowns (Yoakum et al. 1980). Benefits of drawdowns include (1) consolidation of loose sediment, and possible control of turbidity generated by waves and boat wakes; (2) provision of and opportunity to improve, construct, or maintain water-control structures; (3) decomposition of organic material; and (4) release of nutrients.

Stable water levels during the growing season sometimes are preferable in impoundments suitable for the continued production of submersed plants (Kadlec 1962, Green et al. 1964, Yoakum et al. 1980). Studies in the Mississippi River Valley (Anderson 1940, Low and Bellrose 1944) have shown that certain species of submersed aquatics (e.g., sago pondweed and wildcelery) make their best growth under stabilized water levels. However, water areas often are reduced in value for waterfowl if the level is stable or if water levels change (Green et al. 1964).

During drawdowns, submersed aquatics are eliminated on exposed substrates. Seeds of some species, especially sago pondweed, can withstand extended periods of drying in pool bottoms and then germinate after flooding (Steenis 1939, Sharp 1939, 1951). Harris (1957) found that submersed aquatics in portions of drawdown units, which remained wet at Agassiz NWR, thrived and generally produced heavy to excellent seed crops during the period of lowered water levels. According to Agassiz NWR personnel, there was a noticeable increase in the number and size of sago beds during the years of drawdown. During the summer of 1953, the second year of drawdown, Harris (1957) observed excellent seed crops on many beds of sago and clasping-leaf pondweed.

Keith (1961) observed that slowly dropping water levels during July and early August exposed extensive beds of pondweeds, which responded with heavy seeding. A rise in water level from 43 to 51 cm on a Utah marsh increased the weight of sago pondweed in shallow areas but decreased the weight at deeper sites (Robel 1962). Lowering water levels at the time of seeding stimulates seed production where there is already a good crop of pondweeds (Linde 1969). Sharp (1951) suggested that too much water stabilized at depths >91 cm >10 years is more detrimental to submersed plants than periodic low water levels that occur about once every 5 years.

Winter drawdowns apparently improve the germination of seeds and encourage submersed aquatics to regenerate with vigor (Green et al. 1964). During the early 1940s, winter water levels were maintained at low levels in pools of the Upper Mississippi River. Water levels were then increased in the spring to normal pool levels. Aquatic plant growth was among the best ever recorded, and seed production increased during the following year. According to Green et al. (1964), drawdowns to encourage aquatic growth should be started late enough in the fall so that seed germination of emergent plants is inhibited, but early enough to permit drying of the top soil layer so as to stimulate germination of aquatic seeds the following spring.

The use of winter drawdowns should be used with caution considering the lack of research in this area. Plants such as wildcelery and sago pondweed that are propagating from winterbuds, tubers, or rhizomes could be adversely affected by severe freezing during the winter.

Drawdown Effects on Emergent Plants

Attention has been given to the possibility of using drawdowns to establish perennial emergent food and cover plants (Errington 1948). Linde (1969) reported that early drawdowns in May tend to give emergent seedlings a longer period of growth that undoubtedly increases their number and survival rate. A drawdown in late June favors moist-soil plants, but survival of emergents may be poorer than in early drawdowns. The effectiveness of early drawdowns is reduced because undesirable plant species such as cattails (*Typha* spp.) become established before conditions are suitable for the germination of excellent waterfowl food plants such as the smartweeds (Hopkins 1962). Schmidt (1951) suggested that late drawdowns (June or July) favor the production of annuals, and early drawdowns

favor the production of perennials. Various authors have reported the detrimental effects that prolonged stabilized water levels have on most species of emergent aquatics (Uhler 1944, Penfound and Schneidau 1945, Martin 1953).

Management of Invertebrate Populations

Most of the information on invertebrate populations of riverine or deepwater habitats has been provided by aquatic ecologists studying the influence of environmental factors and plant community composition and structure on invertebrate diversity and abundance. Aquatic vascular plants greatly influence invertebrate communities. Increasing plant biomass increases habitat complexity and is well correlated with increasing size and diversity of aquatic invertebrate associations (Heck and Wetstone 1977, Stoner 1980, Wiley et al. 1984, Bell and Westoby 1986). All diving duck species take advantage of abundant invertebrate populations when they are available.

Various macrophyte species might be used differentially by invertebrates (Andrews and Hasler 1943, McGaha 1952, Collias and Collias 1963, Krull 1970, Dvorak and Best 1982, Keast 1984, Rooke 1984). Krecker (1939) suggested that the reason for such differences might be related to morphological differences among plants. Plants such as milfoil with dissected leaves offer a more protected space and easier attachment, and have the highest density of invertebrates; whereas plants with long, flat leaves such as wildcelery have lower invertebrate densities. Chilton (1986) suggested that other mechanisms such as predation might also explain why plants have different invertebrate communities.

Sago pondweed and wildcelery have been the subject of several comparative studies with other plants. Gastropods often compose a larger percentage of the invertebrate groups in a wildcelery community than in the coontail or milfoil communities (Mackie and Quadri 1971, Gerrish and Bristow 1979, Keast 1984, Chilton 1986). Chilton (1986), studying similar plant communities on the Upper Mississippi River, found that the most abundant taxonomic groups were Trichoptera, Hemiptera, Chironomidae, Odonata, Amphipoda, and Gastropoda.

Sago pondweed communities in Delta Marsh, Manitoba, were found to be the habitat of the snail (*Physa gyrina*) (Pip and Stewart 1976). Krull (1970) also found that sago pondweed harbored several invertebrate species. It is unknown whether invertebrates associated with plants are available to migrating and wintering ducks. Krull (1970) presented data on the seasonality of some nonbenthic species.

Benthic invertebrates are common in the diet of diving ducks. Some of the species are fingernail clams, mayflies, and midges. Life-history studies have been conducted on these species, but little is known about managing for them. However, invertebrate populations are sensitive to environmental contaminants—organic and inorganic. Mills et al. (1966) found that the majority of invertebrate species were eliminated from the Illinois River by the discharge of water from the Chicago Sanitary and Ship Canal. Sparks (1984), Sparks and Sandusky (1983), and Sandusky and Sparks (1979) indicated that fingernail clams in the Illinois River are potentially very sensitive to contaminants. Mayflies are also sensitive to contaminant levels (Mauck and Olson 1977). Therefore, management of invertebrate communities implies that rivers and lakes be maintained as contaminant-free as possible. Changes in the texture of the sediment also can influence invertebrates such as mayflies (Fremling 1970).

Planting of Selected Plant Food Species

Vegetation establishment is usually accomplished by natural plant invasion, by planting selected species, or by a combination of natural invasion and planting (Hunt et al. 1970). Under special circumstances, it can be beneficial and informative to attempt plantings of selected plant species where habitat conditions are favorable (i.e., light transparency, water depth, soil quality). This is particularly applicable in new impoundments or where prevalent conditions have been altered.

In the upper Midwest region, several transplants of wildcelery (C. E. Korschgen, unpubl. data) and sago pondweed tubers (Hanna Associates 1984) have been attempted with relatively good success. Wildcelery plantings on Lake Poygan, Lake Winneconne, and Lake Butte Des Morts, Wisconsin (R. Kahl, pers. commun), Lake Puckaway, Wisconsin (D. Brege, pers commun.), and Sherburne NWR, Minnesota (J. Johnson, pers. commun.), became established and have continued to persist for several years. Propagation techniques for wildcelery have been summarized by Korschgen and Green (1988) and for sago pondweed (H. A. Kantrud, U.S. Fish and Wildl. Serv., Northern Prairie Wildl. Res. Cent., unpubl. data).

If commercial sources of propagules are not available, wild propagules must be collected and stored. The collection, storage, and handling of the seeds of upland and wetland plants were discussed by McAtee (1939), Martin and Uhler (1939), Moyle and Hotchkiss (1945), Kadlec and Wentz (1974), Hunt et al. (1978), and the U.S. Army Engineer Waterways Experiment Station (1978).

Control of Fish

In North America, much effort also has been placed on carp (*Cyprinus carpio*) control to preserve aquatic vegetation for waterfowl (Weier and Starr 1950). Although many fish-control projects have been implemented on waterfowl areas in the Mississippi Flyway, documentation of the results of such efforts is scarce. Therefore, some of the following information has been extracted from a broader geographical source.

Carp affect the growth of submersed plants by consuming vegetative and reproductive portions and by causing increased water turbidity, with a consequent reduction in light penetration (Jackson and Starrett 1959). Robel (1962) found that enclosures in which no carp were confined had a 100% vegetative cover. The relation between carp population levels and increased water turbidity is greatly influenced by soil type.

In many instances, large increases of vegetation and waterfowl use have resulted after the removal of carp from a marsh (Anderson 1950, Cahoon 1953, Smith 1957). Reductions of carp populations, without total elimination, also have resulted in increased vegetation in Lake Mattamuskeet, North Carolina, and Lake Puckaway, Wisconsin (Cahoon 1953; D. Brege, pers. commun.). Another reported advantage of the removal of carp is that the presence of the fish can disturb waterfowl (Weier and Starr 1950).

Chemical toxicants provide the primary economical and effective way to control or remove undesirable fish populations from large wetlands that cannot be drained. This is particularly true if complete removal of the fish population is desired. Attempts to remove rough fish with fishing gear or by other physical methods generally have been unsuccessful (Prévost 1960).

Only 2 chemicals were registered in 1988 for use as fish toxicants: rotenone and antimycin. For a detailed description of these compounds, see Lennon et al. (1970) and Schnick et al. (1982). The toxicity of rotenone to fish is affected by light, temperature, oxygen concentration, alkalinity, and turbidity (Almquist 1959). Rotenone toxicity is reversible, which is a disadvantage at times. Fish that move out of a toxic concentration of rotenone into areas such as springs or inflowing streams might recover. Lennon and Parker (1959) observed that many fish affected by the chemical sank to the bottom and appeared dead, but recovered if currents or seeps exposed them to fresh water.

Barrier dams prevent fish passage, as a result of either having an elevated spillway or having an apron that produces shallow, fast, turbulent flow. Minimum head differential required as a barrier to carp and other rough fish is 1 m. Designs and techniques for constructing barrier dams are function- and site-specific. Designs range in complexity from concrete buttresses with elaborate aprons to timber cribs and earthen dams fitted with weirs. Electrified weirs are used on many waterfowl areas to prevent reinvasion by rough fish. Lake Christina, Minnesota, Trempealeau NWR, and headwaters of Lake Puckaway, Wisconsin, have electrified weirs for such a purpose.

Human Disturbance

Management of migration and wintering areas for diving ducks must include a human element. Jahn and Hunt (1964) suggested that even the best habitats will be used lightly by migrant ducks if human disturbance is excessive. Diving ducks, perhaps, are more intolerant of disturbances than other waterfowl. Jessen (1981) believed that the largely unrecognized wariness of lesser scaup to all kinds of disturbances, especially hunting, reduced their use of many tall habitats in the lake region of the Upper Midwest. Diving ducks also have been found to alter their daily activity patterns in response to disturbances by feeding more at night than during the day (Thornburg 1973, Pedroli 1982). Hunting has been identified as one of the major activities that results in disturbance to birds.

The few quantitative studies that have been conducted (Evenson et al. 1974, Korschgen et al. 1985) indicated that the frequency of disturbances and the number of birds involved can be quite substantial on some staging areas. The exact energetic costs of the disturbances remain unknown; however, it is suspected that under some circumstances the energetic costs can be significant. It is evident that diving ducks are disturbed not only by the presence of a boat, but also by the noise from outboard motors.

Several management techniques have been employed to curtail disturbances on wetlands important to waterfowl. These techniques basically involve establishment of local, statewide, or flyway hunting regulations to limit the time and space in which hunting can occur. Jahn and Hunt (1964) summarized guidelines for the establishment of closed areas and hunting regulations for waterfowl in Wisconsin. Most of their points pertain to areas in other locales. Their guidelines are not specific to diving ducks and probably require modification to serve the needs of canvasbacks, redheads, lesser scaup, and ring-necked ducks.

Diving ducks also can be provided additional protection from disturbances in areas that are hunted by limiting the size of outboard motors, which would effectively curtail the speed and noise of boats. Legal hunting hours can be modified, such as in Minnesota, where daily hunting ends at 1600 hours. The La Crosse District of the Upper Mississippi River National Wildlife and Fish Refuge (NWFR) has been active in providing educational material to the public regarding the importance of Pool 7 to diving ducks and the affect of boating disturbances upon the birds. The refuge has erected information panels at all of the landings adjacent to the Pool explaining the ecology of migrating canvasbacks in the area. In 1986, the refuge conducted a pilot program requesting the public to voluntarily avoid an area of Pool 7 that had been delineated as the most important habitat for all diving ducks. Based upon 2 years of data, it appeared that the public voluntarily reduced activity in the area (R. Steinbach, pers. commun.).

EXAMPLES OF MAJOR LAKE AND RIVERINE MANAGEMENT PROJECTS

Lake Christina, Minnesota

Lake Christina is a 1,600-ha lake that averages about 1.5 m in depth and is located in west-central Minnesota. Until 1950, Lake Christina supported dense beds of aquatic plants preferred by diving ducks, including sago pondweed and widgeon grass. Historically, Lake Christina was one of the Mississippi Flyway's most heavily used feeding and resting area for canvasbacks on their spring and fall migrations. The lake's best years were in the late 1930s and 1940s. Numbers of canvasbacks varied from 40,000 to 60,000 birds. Total numbers of waterfowl using the lake were estimated at 300,000 to 400,000. Following the peak of 60,000 canvasbacks in 1942, the population using the lake decreased until 1949. That year, an estimated 800,000 birds were present. Of this number, 80% were American coots (*Fulica americana*). About 160,000 ducks were present, consisting of 100,000 to 150,000 canvasbacks. At the time, this concentration represented approximately 20% of the total continental population of canvasbacks.

Since the 1950s, deteriorating water quality, primarily from high turbidity, has precluded the growth of rooted aquatic plants, and use by diving ducks has diminished. This turbidity seems to be caused by wind and fish (black bullheads [*Ictalurus melas*] and carp), which generate resuspension of sediments, phytoplankton, and other particulate organic matter, and direct precipitation of calcite (Butler and Hanson 1988).

Lake Christina potentially can be restored as migration habitat, but it is of little value to waterfowl in its present, deteriorated state. Until vegetation conditions improve, use of Lake Christina by waterfowl will remain minimal. The solution was to clarify water to improve light penetration to sufficient depth for aquatic growth. The most-desired management technique would be to decrease water levels to simulate a natural drawdown. A drawdown, however, is impractical because adjacent Pelican Lake is a fishing and resort lake.

Lake Christina's habitat was improved following periods of severe reductions in its rough fish populations. In order to reduce turbidity and enhance aquatic plant growth, the Minnesota DNR treated the lake with a fish toxicant (no longer registered by the U.S. Environmental Protection Agency) in November 1965. It was partially successful in eliminating the rough fish population. This fish removal effort was followed by 2 winterkills in 1968-69 and 1969-70, in which the major portion of the fish population was removed. In the following years, the lake's waters cleared and submergent plants flourished with an associated increase in waterfowl use.

These improvements in water clarity, vegetation production, and increased use by waterfowl were short-lived. By 1980, rough fish numbers had increased dramatically, and high turbidity was again restricting the growth of submerged aquatic plants.

The first phase of the reclamation effort was completed in October 1987 when Lake Christina, Lake Anka, and 3 adjacent wetlands were treated with rotenone. Several helicopters equipped with spraying booms treated 1,723 ha with 61,200 l of rotenone. An electric weir fish barrier on the outlet of Lake Christina prevents fish from moving into the lake. In 1988, predatory game fish were stocked in Lake Christina. The cost ranged from $300,000 to $400,000.

Weaver Bottoms, Pool 5

Weaver Bottoms (1,620 ha) is a migra- tion area above Lock and Dam 5 on the Upper Mississippi River. It is one of the most heavily hunted areas along the Mississippi River and attracts diving ducks, puddle ducks, and tundra swans.

A series of locks and dams were placed in the Upper Mississippi River in the 1930s to provide a 3 m deep navigation channel. That action created a vast backwater complex for fish and wildlife. In recent years, the habitat quality of many of these backwater areas has been declining.

The area is part of the Upper Mississippi River NWFR. From shortly after impoundment in the 1930s until the middle to late 1960s, approximately 75% (1,100 ha) of Weaver Bottoms contained marsh vegetation. During that time, Weaver Bottoms contained a diversity of plant and animal species. However, during the late 1960s and early 1970s, marsh vegetation decreased. In 1982, emergent and floating-leaf aquatic plants covered only 33% (540 ha) of the area. This decrease in vegetation and the area's inability to recover have been attributed to a variety of reasons, including 2 major floods in the late 1960s, uprooting and removal of vegetation by ice, changed flow and sedimentation, and reduced water clarity caused by wind-induced wave erosion. In addition to the problem of the degraded aquatic plant community, Weaver Bottoms was accumulating sediment that was projected to fill the area by 2048 (Nielsen et al. 1978).

This rehabilitation project, which in 1988 was in the construction phase, is highlighted here because its scope is immense and it centers around major changes in the hydrology of a large river to increase the quality of the water regime. In a joint effort between the St. Paul District of the Army Corps of Engineers and the U.S. Fish and Wildlife Service's Upper Mississippi NWFR, a management plan was developed for Weaver Bottoms that included the construction of 6 barrier islands and the

Fig. 7. Side channel modifications and island construction in Weaver Bottoms, Navigation Pool 5 of the Upper Mississippi River.

modification of 14 side channels entering Weaver Bottoms (Berry and Anderson 1987). The major design objective of the islands was to reduce wind fetch, thus preventing wind-induced wave erosion. Other factors considered were construction, stability, aesthetics, and waterfowl nesting. Fine sediments within Weaver Bottoms were deposited on the islands to provide soil suitable for vegetation. Because most of the Weaver Bottoms backwater is <2 m deep, the dredging provided the added advantage of deeper habitat for fish.

The side-channel modifications (Fig. 7) were intended to reduce flows substantially, but not totally eliminate them. Therefore, the selected plan has a variety of side-channel modifications including 2 rock closures, 5 dredged-material closures, 3 rock stabilization closures, and 4 partial closures. The rock closing structures were designed to eliminate normal flow yet allow overflow during seasonal high water. The dredged-material closures will eliminate normal flow and flow during seasonal high waters. The partial closing structures were designed to reduce flow through these side channels under all river discharges except major floods.

The project was scheduled to be constructed in 2 phases. In Phase 1, all the side channel modifications and 2 of the barrier islands were constructed. Phase 1 construction was completed by 1 October 1987. In Phase 2, scheduled for 1991, the remaining 4 islands and other project features determined to be necessary from the results of monitoring the effects of the Phase 1 construction would be constructed, within authority and funding limitations.

The project is expected to have many positive environmental benefits for Weaver Bottoms. A main benefit is that the project will reduce the introduction of sediment into backwater areas, thereby increasing the quality of the water and the quantity of submersed vegetation such as wildcelery and sago pondweed.

The proposed management techniques are experimental; therefore, a 10-year monitoring program has been developed. The purpose of the monitoring program is to assess the effectiveness of the project in reaching its stated goals and objectives and to identify any unforeseen and unacceptable affects on the environment, public use, or navigation.

CONCLUSIONS

Management options for lakes and riverine impoundments are frequently limited by state and federal statutes that mandate that water levels be maintained at stated elevations. Management of deepwater and riverine wetlands usually requires manipulation of the water regime to enhance the productivity of selected plant and invertebrate communities. Management of the watershed to reduce sedimentation and to improve water quality in the wetlands is the most effective means to accomplish this goal. Most other management practices such as drawdown, plantings, and fish control usually have short-term benefits.

Nearly all of the deepwater and riverine wetlands discussed in this chapter are owned by federal or state governments. Management of these habitats for waterfowl has been difficult because these wetlands are complex hydrological systems with diverse physical, chemical, and biological components. Because all environmental influences are not known and are difficult to control, management outcomes are not highly predictable. Furthermore, most large wetlands require multi-ple-use management plans because of the diverse recreational and economic uses required by the public. The most important habitats for diving ducks in the Upper Midwest are the navigation pools on the Upper Mississippi River, some of which are included in the Upper Mississippi River NWFR. Refuge management activities are required by federal law to be subservient to the commercial navigation interests also authorized by Congress. Most of the traditional diving ducks areas in Wisconsin are impoundments on the the Fox River, which are now managed primarily for recreational activities. However, examples of successful habitat management for diving ducks under these constraints are few. Water-level control and carp control are 2 techniques most frequently employed by waterfowl managers in the Upper Midwest.

RESEARCH NEEDS

Research for development of habitat management techniques should focus on the following:

1. The autecology of important food-producing organisms within the wetland in relation to hydrology, water quality, and sediment quality. Highest priority should be given to studies of submersed and emergent plant species.
2. Long-term studies to provide information of the rate and direction of succession in aquatic systems.
3. Seed-bank studies to indicate the number, species composition, and viability of aquatic plant seeds.
4. Better methods of controlling rough fish populations.
5. Sociological studies so that effective methods can be used to educate the public regarding disturbances to migrating and wintering waterfowl.
6. The nutritional and energetic requirements of waterfowl during spring migration.

Weller (1988) noted additional research needs. Many of these relate the use and selection of habitat to the biology and physiology of migrating and wintering waterfowl. When managers have a thorough understanding of the habitat components and bird biology, strategies can be developed for effective conservation of the waterfowl resource.

SUMMARY

Several species of diving ducks are very dependent on large lakes and riverine impoundments in the upper portions of the Mississippi Flyway of the U.S. as feeding and resting areas during migration. Historically, the numbers of such areas were well over 100, but only a few of these remain significant due to anthropogenic and natural causes; however, many still have management potential. Management of deepwater and riverine wetlands requires an understanding of complex hydrological and biological systems. Management plans will have to focus on multiple-use benefits that will provide favorable habitat for diving ducks.

Management of habitat focuses on preferred diving duck foods. Water availability is rarely a problem; the most important consideration is water quality. Controlling rough fish and planting of selected plant species has met with success. Human disturbance is also an important consideration in this area. Research should center on autecological studies of key plants and long-term studies of the communities.

LITERATURE CITED

Almquist, E. 1959. Observations on the effect of rotenone emulsives on fish food organisms. Inst. Freshwater Res., Dottningholm, Rep. 40:146-160.

Anderson, H. G. 1940. Studies preliminary to a waterfowl habitat restoration program along the Illinois River. Trans. North Am. Wildl. and Nat. Resour. Conf. 5:369-372.

———. 1959. Food habits of migratory ducks in Illinois. Ill. Nat. Hist. Surv. Bull. 27:289-344.

Anderson, J. M. 1950. Some aquatic vegetation changes following fish removal. J. Wildl. Manage. 14:206-209.

Andrews, J. D., and A. D. Hasler. 1943. Fluctuations in the populations of the littoral zone in Lake Mendota. Wis. Acad. Sci., Arts, and Letters 35:175-185.

Bailey, P. A., and R. G. Rada. 1984. Distribution and enrichment of trace metals (Cd, Cr, Cu, Ni, Pb, Zn) in bottom sediments of Navigation Pools 4 (Lake Pepin), 5, and 9 of the Upper Mississippi River. Pages 119-138 in J. G. Wiener, R. V. Anderson, and D. R. McConville, eds. Contaminants in the Upper Mississippi River. Proc. 15th Annu. Mtg. Mississippi River Res. Consortium.

Bell, J. D., and M. Westoby. 1986. Abundance of macrofauna in dense seagrass is due to habitat preference, not predation. Oecolgia 68:205-209.

Bellrose, F. C. 1968. Waterfowl migration corridors east of the Rocky Mountains in the United States. Ill. Nat. Hist. Surv. Biol. Notes 61. 23 pp.

———. 1980. Ducks, geese and swans of North America. Stackpole Books, Harrisburg, Pa. 540 pp.

———, S. P. Havera, F. L. Paveglio, Jr., and D. S. Steffeck. 1983. The fate of lakes in the Illinois River Valley. Ill. Nat. Hist Surv. Biol. Notes 119. 27 pp.

———, F. L. Paveglio, Jr., and D. S. Steffeck. 1979. Waterfowl populations and the changing environment of the Illinois River Valley. Ill. Nat. Hist. Surv. Bull. 32. 54 pp.

Berry, R. F., and D. D. Anderson. 1987. Habitat development applications: Lower Pool 5 channel maintenance/Weaver Bottoms rehabilitation plan. Pages 134-139 in M. C. Landin and H. K. Smith, eds. Beneficial use of dredge material—proc. of the first interagency workshop, 7-9 October 1986, Pensacola, Fla.

Butler, M. G., and M. A. Hanson. 1988. Final summary of pre-treatment limnological studies on Lake Christina. Mimeogr. Rep., North Dakota State Univ., Fargo. 30 pp.

Cahoon, W. G. 1953. Commercial carp removal at Lake Mattamuskeet, North Carolina. J. Wildl. Manage. 17:312-317.

Chilton, E. W. 1986. Macroinvertebrate communities associated with selected macrophytes in Lake Onalaska: effects of plant type, predation, and selective feeding. Ph.D. Thesis, Ohio State Univ., Columbus. 166 pp.

Collias, N. E., and E. C. Collias. 1963. Selective feeding by wild ducklings of different species. Wilson Bull. 75:6-14.

Cottam, C. 1939. Food habits of North American diving ducks. U.S. Dep. Agric. Tech. Bull. 643. 140 pp.

Cowardin, L. M., V. Carter, F. C. Golet, and E. T. LaRoe. 1979. Classification of wetlands and deepwater habitats of the United States. U.S. Fish and Wildl. Serv. FWS/OBS-79/31. 130 pp.

Davis, J. G., and M. M. Brinson. 1980. Responses of submersed vascular plant communities to environmental change. U.S. Fish and Wildl. Serv. FWS/OBS-79/33. 79 pp.

Day, D. M. 1984. Use of diving duck activity patterns to examine seasonal and habitat utilization of lower reaches of Pool 19, Mississippi River. M.S. Thesis, Western Illinois Univ., Macomb. 117 pp.

Donnermeyer, G. N. 1982. The quantity and nutritive quality of *Vallisneria americana* biomass, in Navigation Pool No. 9 of the Upper Mississippi River. M.S. Thesis, Univ. of Wisconsin-La Crosse, LaCrosse. 93 pp.

Dvorak, J., and E. P. H. Best. 1982. Macroinvertebrate communities associated with macrophytes of Lake Vechten: structural and functional relationships. Hydrobiologia 95:115-126.

Eckblad, J. W. 1986. The ecology of pools 11-13 of the Upper Mississippi River. a community profile. Nat. Wetlands Res. Center, Biol. Rep. 85(7.8). 88 pp.

Edwards, D. 1969. Some effects of siltation upon aquatic macrophyte vegetation in rivers. Hydrobiologia 34:29-37.

Elstad, C. A. 1977. Macrobenthic survey of Navigation Pool Number 8 of the Upper Mississippi River, with special reference to ecological relationships. M.S. Thesis, Univ. of Wisconsin-La Crosse, La Crosse. 231 pp.

Errington, P. L. 1948. Environmental control for increasing muskrat production. Trans. North Am. Wildl. and Nat. Resour. Conf. 13:596-605.

Evenson, D., C. Hopkins, and G. Martz. 1974. Waterfowl and waterfowl hunting at Houghton Lake Mich. Dep. Nat. Resour. Wildl. Div. Info. Circ. 171. Lansing. 7 pp.

Fassett, N. C. 1972. A manual of aquatic plants. Univ. of Wisconsin Press, Madison. 405 pp.

Fremling, C. R. 1970. Factors influencing the distribution of burrowing mayflies along the Mississippi River. Proc. Int. Conf. on Ephemeroptera 1:12-25.

——, D. N. Nielsen, D. R. McConville, R. N. Vose. 1976. The Weaver Bottoms: a field model for the rehabilitation of backwater areas of the Upper Mississippi River by modification of standard channel maintenance practices. Prepared for U.S. Army Corps of Eng., St. Paul District, St. Paul, Minn., Contract No. DACW37-75-C-0193, 0194.

Friend, M. 1987. Lead poisoning. Pages 175-189 *in* M. Friend, ed. Field guide to wildlife diseases. U.S. Fish and Wildl. Serv. Resour. Publ. 167. 225 pp.

Gerrish, N., and J. M. Bristow. 1979. Macroinvertebrate associations with aquatic macrophytes and artificial substrates. J. Great Lakes Res. 5:69-72.

Green, W. E., L. G. MacNamara, and F. M. Uhler. 1964. Water off and on. Pages 468-557 *in* J. P.

Linduska, ed. Waterfowl tomorrow. U.S. Dep. Int., Bur. Sport Fish. and Wildl., Washington, D.C.

Hagen, R., L. Werth, and M. Meyer. 1977. Upper Mississippi River habitat inventory. Res. Rep. 77-5. Remote Sensing Lab. Inst. of Agric., For., and Home Econ., Univ. Minnesota. U.S. Fish and Wildl. Serv. Contract No. 14-16-0003-30,686. 18 pp.

Hanna Associates. 1984. A management strategy for the restoration of aquatic vegetation in Rondeau Bay, Lake Erie. Southwestern Region, Ontario Ministry of the Environ., Ottawa.

Harris, S. W. 1957. Ecological effects of drawdown operations for the purpose of improving waterfowl habitat. Ph.D. Thesis, Univ. of Minnesota, St. Paul. 209 pp.

Heck, K. L., and G. S. Wetstone. 1977. Habitat complexity and invertebrate species richness and abundance in tropical seagrass meadows. J. Biogeogr. 4:135-142.

Hopkins, R. C. 1962. Drawdown for ducks. Wis. Conserv. Bull. 27:18-19.

Hora, M. E. 1984. Polychlorinated biphenyls (PCBs) in common carp (*Cyprinus carpio*) of the Upper Mississippi River. Pages 231-239 *in* J. G. Wiener, R. V. Anderson, and D. R. McConville, eds. Contaminants in the Upper Mississippi River. Proc. 15th Annu. Mtg. Mississippi River Res. Consort., La Crosse, Wis.

Hunt, C. B. 1967. Physiography of the United States. W. H. Freeman and Company, San Francisco, Calif. 480 pp.

Hunt, L. J., A. W. Ford, M. C. Landin, and B. R. Wells. 1978. Upland habitat development with dredged material: Engineering and plant propagation. U.S. Army Corps of Eng. Waterways Exp. Stn., Vicksburg, Miss. Tech. Rep. DS-78-17, Washington, D.C. 160 pp.

Jackson, G. A., C. E. Korschgen, P. A. Thiel, J. M. Besser, D. W. Steffeck, and M. H. Bockenhauer. 1981. A long-term resource monitoring plan for the Upper Mississippi River System. Upper Mississippi River Basin Comm., Comprehensive Master Plan for the Manage. of the Upper Mississippi River System, Tech. Rep. F, Vol. I and II, Minneapolis, Minn. 966 pp.

Jackson, H. O., and W. C. Starrett. 1959. Turbidity and sedimentation at Lake Chautauqua, Illinois. J. Wildl. Manage. 23:157-168.

Jahn, L. A., and R. V. Anderson. 1986. The ecology of Pools 19 and 20, Upper Mississippi River: a community profile. Natl. Wetlands Res. Center, Biol. Rep. 85(7.6). 142 pp.

Jahn, L. R., and R. A. Hunt. 1964. Duck and coot ecology and management in Wisconsin. Wis. Conserv. Dep. Tech. Bull. 33. 212 pp.

Jessen, R. L. 1981. Special problems with diving ducks. Proc. Int. Waterfowl Symp. 4:139-149.

Kadler, J. A. 1962. Effects of drawdown on a waterfowl impoundment. Ecology 43:267-281.

———, and L. M. Smith. 1989. The Great Basin marshes. Pages 451-474 in L. M. Smith, R. L. Pederson, and R. M. Kaminski, eds. Habitat management for migrating and wintering waterfowl in North America. Texas Tech Univ. Press, Lubbock.

———, and W. A. Wentz. 1974. State-of-the-art survey and evaluation of marsh plant establishment techniques: induced and natural. Volume 1. Report of research. U.S. Army Corps of Eng., Waterways Exp. Stn., Environ. Effects Lab., Ft. Belvoir, Va. DACW72-74-C-0010. 231 pp.

Keast, A. 1984. The introduced macrophyte, *Myriophyllum spicatum*, as habitat for fish and their prey. Can. J. Zool. 62:1289-1303.

Keith, L. B. 1961. A study of waterfowl ecology on small impoundments in southeastern Alberta. Wildl. Monogr. 6. 88 pp.

Korschgen, C. E., L. S. George, and W. L. Green. 1985. Disturbance of diving ducks by boaters on a migrational staging area. Wildl. Soc. Bull. 13:290-296.

———, and L. S. George, and W. L. Green. 1988. Feeding ecology of canvasbacks staging on Pool 7 of the Upper Mississippi River. Pages 237-250 in M. W. Weller, ed. Waterfowl in winter. Univ. Minnesota Press, Minneapolis.

———, and W. L. Green. 1988. American wildcelery (*Vallisneria americana*): ecological considerations for restoration work. U.S. Fish and Wildl. Serv., Fish Wildl. Tech. Rep. No. 19. 24 pp.

Korschgen, L. J. 1955. Fall foods of waterfowl in Missouri. Mo. Dep. Conserv., P-R Ser. 14. Jefferson City, Mo. 41 pp.

Krecker, F. H. 1939. Animal population of submerged aquatic plants. Ecology 20:553-562.

Krull, J. M. 1970. Aquatic plant-macroinvertebrate associations and waterfowl. J. Wildl. Manage. 34:707-718.

Kubichek, W. F. 1933. Report on the food of five of our most important game ducks. Iowa State Coll. J. Sci. 8:107-126.

Kuehnast, E. L., D. G. Baker, and J. A. Zandlo. 1982. Climate of Minnesota: part XIII—duration and depth of snowcover. Univ. Minnesota Agric. Exp. Stn. Tech. Bull. 333. 11 pp.

Lennon, R. E., and P. S. Parker. 1959. The reclamation of Indian and Abrams Creeks in Great Smoky Mountains National Park. U.S. Fish and Wildl. Serv. Special. Sci. Rep.—Fish. 306. 22 pp.

———, J. B. Hunn, R. A. Schnick, and R. M. Burress. 1970. Reclamation of ponds, lakes, and streams with fish toxicants: a review. Food and Agric. Organ. of the United Nations, FAO Fish. Tech. Pap. 100. 99 pp.

Linde, A. F. 1969. Techniques for wetland management. Wis. Dep. Nat. Resour., Res. Rep. No. 45, 156 pp.

Low, J. B., and F. C. Bellrose. 1944. The seed and vegetative yield of waterfowl food plants in the Illinois River Valley. J. Wildl. Manage. 8:7-22.

Mackie, G. L., and S. U. Quadri. 1971. A quantitative sampler for aquatic phytomacrofauna. J. Fish. Res. Board Can. 28:1322-1324.

Martin, A. C. 1953. Improving duck marshes by weed control. U.S. Fish and Wildl. Serv. Circ. 19. 49 pp.

———, and F. M. Uhler. 1939. Food of game ducks in the United States and Canada. U.S. Dep. Agric. Tech. Bull. 634. Washington, D.C. 308 pp.

Mauck, W., and L. Olson. 1977. Polychlorinated biphenyls in adult mayflies (*Hexagenia bilineata*) from the Upper Mississippi River, 1977. Bull. Environ. Contam. and Toxicol. 17:387-390.

McAtee, W. L. 1939. Wildlife food plants. Their value, propagation, and management. Collegiate Press, Ames, Iowa. 141 pp.

McGaha, Y. J. 1952. The limnological relations of insects to certain aquatic flowering plants. Trans. Am. Microsc. Soc. 71:355-381.

Metropolitan Waste Control Commission. 1982. 1981 river quality report, summary volume. Metropolitan Waste Control Comm., Quality Control Dep., Minneapolis, Minn. Rep. 81-048.

Mills, H. B., W. C. Starrett, and F. C. Bellrose. 1966. Man's effect on the fish and wildlife of the Illinois River. Ill. Nat. Hist. Surv. Biol. Notes 57. 24 pp.

Minor, J. M., L. M. Caron, and M. P. Meyer. 1977. Upper Mississippi River habitat inventory between Hastings, Minnesota, and Guttenberg, Iowa. Res. Rep. 77-7 Remote Sensing Lab., Univ. of Minnesota. U.S. Fish and Wildl. Serv. Contract No. 14-16-0003,686. 18 pp.

Mohlenbrock, R. H. 1983. Annotated bibliography of the aquatic macrophytes of the Upper Mississippi River covering the area from Cairo, Illinois to St. Paul, Minnesota. U.S. Fish and Wildl. Serv., Rock Island, Ill., Contract No. 14-16-0003-83-041. 239 pp.

Moyle, J. B., and N. Hotchkiss. 1945. The aquatic and marsh vegetation of Minnesota and its value to waterfowl. Minn. Dep. Conserv. Tech. Bull. 3. 122 pp.

Muncy, R. J., G. J. Atchison, R. V. Bulkley, B. W. Menzel, L. G. Perry, and R. C. Summerfelt. 1979. Effects of suspended solids and sedimentation on reproduction and early life of warmwater fishes: a review. Environ. Protect. Agency, Corvallis, Ore. EPA-600/3-79-042. 101 pp.

Nielsen, D. N., C. R. Fremling, R. N. Vose, and D. R. McConville. 1978. Phase I study of the Weaver-Belvidere area, Upper Mississippi River.

U.S. Fish and Wildl. Serv., St. Paul, Minn., Contract No. 14-16-0003-77-060. 25 pp.

Olson, K. N., and M. P. Meyer. 1976. Vegetation, land, and water surfaces changes in the upper navigable portion of the Mississippi River basin over the period 1939 1973. Univ. of Minnesota, Remote Sensing Lab., Res. Rep. No. 76-4. 225 pp.

Palmer, R. S., editor. 1976. Handbook of North American birds. Volume 3. Yale Univ. Press, New Haven, Conn. 560 pp.

Pedroli, J. C. 1982. Activity and time budget of tufted ducks on Swiss lakes in winter. Wildfowl 33:105-112.

Penfound, W. T., and J. D. Schneidau. 1945. The relation of land reclamation to aquatic wildlife resources in southeastern Louisiana. Trans. North Am. Wildl. and Nat. Resour. Conf. 10:308-318.

Pip, E., and I. M. Stewart. 1976. The dynamics of two aquatic plant-snail associations. Can. J. Zool. 54:1192-1205.

Prévost, G. 1960. Use of fish toxicants in the Province of Quebec. Can. Fish. Cult. 25:37-39.

Reid, F., S. Taylor, J. Kelley, and L. H. Fredrickson. 1989. Upper Mississippi Valley wetlands—refuges and moist-soil impoundments. Pages 181-202 *in* L. M. Smith, R. L. Pederson, and R. M. Kaminski, eds. Habitat management for migrating and wintering waterfowls in North America. Texas Tech Univ. Press, Lubbock.

Ringelman, J., W. Eddleman, and H. W. Miller. 1989. High plains reservoirs and sloughs. Pages 311-340 *in* L. M. Smith, R. L. Pederson, and R. M. Kaminski, eds. Habitat management for migrating and wintering waterfowl in North America. Texas Tech Univ. Press, Lubbock.

Robel, R. J. 1962. The relationship of carp to waterfowl food plants on a western marsh. Dep. Info. Bull. 62-4, Federal Aid Completion Rep., Project W-29-R, Job I-1, Utah Dep. Fish and Game, Salt Lake City. 103 pp.

Rooke, J. B. 1984. The invertebrate fauna of three species of plants and rock surfaces in a small stream. Hydrobiologia 134:81-87.

Sandusky, M. J., and R. E. Sparks. 1979. Investigations of declines in fingernail clam (*Musculium transversum*) populations in the Illinois River and Pool 19 of the Mississippi River. Bull. Am. Malacological Union Inc. 1979:11-15.

Schmidt, F. V. 1951. Planned water level control and the resultant effect on vegetation. Northeast. Game Conf., 7 pp.

Schnick, R. A., J. M. Morton, J. C. Mochalski, and J. T. Beall. 1982. Mitigation and enhancement techniques for the Upper Mississippi River and other large river systems. U.S. Fish and Wildl. Serv., Resour. Publ. 149. Washington, D.C. 714 pp.

Sefton, D. F. 1976. The biomass and productivity of aquatic macrophytes in Navigation Pool 8 of the Upper Mississippi River. M.S. Thesis, Univ. of Wisconsin—La Crosse, La Crosse. 179 pp.

Seric, J. R., D. L. Trauger, and D. E. Sharp. 1983. Migration and winter distributions of canvasbacks staging on the Upper Mississippi River. J. Wildl. Manage. 47:741-753.

Sharp, W. M. 1939. Propagation of *Potamogeton* and *Sagittaria* from seeds. Trans. North Am. Wildl. and Nat. Resour. Conf. 4:351-358.

——. 1951. Environmental requirements of a fresh water marsh and the ecology of some aquatic plants. Northeast. Game Conf. 6 pp.

Smith, D. J. 1957. Carp in relation to waterfowl. Pages 26-28 *in* Managing our fish and wildlife resources. Univ. of Minnesota Press, Minneapolis.

Sparks, R. E. 1984. The role of contaminants in the decline of the Illinois River: implications for the upper Mississippi. Pages 25-66 *in* J. E. Weiner, R. V. Anderson, and D. R. McConville, eds. Contaminants in the Upper Mississippi River. Butterworth Publishers, Stoneham, Mass.

——, and M. J. Sandusky. 1983. Identification of the water quality factors which prevent fingernail clams from recolonizing the Illinois River, Phase III. Univ. of Illinois, Champaign Water Resour. Center Res. Rep. 179. 55 pp.

——, and K. E. Smith. 1979. Contaminants in fish food organisms and duck food organisms from Keokuk Pool, Mississippi River. Unpubl. Rep. U.S. Fish and Wildl. Serv., Environ. Contam. Evaluation Prog. St. Paul, Minn. 39 pp.

Sprafka, M. J. 1981. Evaluation of heavy metal loadings at the metro wastewater treatment plant. M.S. Thesis, Univ. of Minnesota., Minneapolis. 54 pp.

Steenis, J. H. 1939. Marsh management on the Great Plains waterfowl refuges. Trans. North Am. Wildl. and Nat. Resour. Conf. 4:400-405.

Steffeck, D. S., F. L. Paveglio, and C. E. Korschgen. 1985. Distribution of aquatic plants in Keokuk Pool (Navigation Pool 19) of the Upper Mississippi River. Proc. Iowa Acad. Sci. 92:111-114.

Stevenson, J. C., and N. M. Confer. 1978. Summary of available information on Chesapeake Bay submerged vegetation. U.S. Fish and Wildl. Serv., FWS/OBS-78/66. 335 pp.

Stoner, A. W. 1980. The role of seagrass biomass in the organization of benthic macrofaunal assemblages. Bull. Mar. Sci. 30:537-551.

Swanson, S. D., and S. H. Sohmer. 1978. The vascular flora of navigation Pool 8 of the Upper Mississippi River. Proc. Iowa Acad. Sci. 85:45-61.

Takekawa, J. Y. 1987. Energetics of canvasbacks staging on an Upper Mississippi River pool during fall migration. Ph.D. Thesis, Iowa State Univ., Ames. 189 pp.

Thompson, D. 1973. Feeding ecology of diving ducks on Keokuk Pool. J. Wildl. Manage. 37:367-381.

Thornburg, D. D. 1973. Diving duck movements on Keokuk Pool, Mississippi River. J. Wildl. Manage. 37:382-389.

Tiner, R. W., Jr. 1984. Wetlands of the United States: current status and trends. National Wetlands Inventory, Newton Corner, Mass. 59 pp.

Titus, J. E. 1977. The comparative physiological ecology of three submersed macrophytes. Ph.D. Thesis, Univ. of Wisconsin, Madison. 195 pp.

Uhler, F. M. 1944. Control of undesirable plants in waterfowl habitats. Trans. North Am. Wildl. and Nat. Resour. Conf. 9:295-303.

U.S. Army Corp of Engineers Waterways Experiment Station. 1978. Wetland habitat development with dredged material; engineering and plant propagation. Waterways Exp. Stn., Vicksburg, Miss. Tech. Rep. DS-78-16. 158 pp.

Weier, J. L., and D. F. Starr. 1950. The use of rotenone to remove rough fish for the purpose of improving waterfowl refuge areas. J. Wildl. Manage. 14:203-205.

Weller, M. W., editor. 1988. Waterfowl in winter. Univ. Minnesota Press, Minneapolis. 624 pp.

Wetzel, R. G., and D. L. McGregor. 1968. Apenic culture and nutritional studies of aquatic macrophytes. Am. Midl. Nat. 80:52-63.

Wiley, M. J., R. W. Gorden, S. W. Waite, and T. Powless. 1984. The relationship between aquatic macrophytes and sport fish production in Illinois ponds; a simple model. North Am. J. Fish. Manage. 4:111-119.

Yoakum, J., W. P. Dasmann, H. R. Sanderson, C. M. Nixon, and H. S. Crawford. 1980. Habitat improvement techniques. Pages 329-403 in S. D. Schemnitz, ed. Wildlife management techniques manual. Fourth Ed. The Wildl. Soc., Washington, D.C.

Zimmerman, J. R. 1953. Waterfowl habitat surveys and food habit studies, 1940-1943. Game Manage. Div., Wis. Dep. Nat. Resour., Madison. 176 pp.

UPPER MISSISSIPPI VALLEY WETLANDS—REFUGES AND MOIST-SOIL IMPOUNDMENTS[1]

FREDERIC A. REID, Gaylord Memorial Laboratory, School of Forestry, Fisheries and Wildlife, University of Missouri-Columbia, Puxico, MO 63960

JAMES R. KELLEY, JR., Gaylord Memorial Laboratory, School of Forestry, Fisheries and Wildlife, University of Missouri-Columbia, Puxico, MO 63960

T. SCOTT TAYLOR, Gaylord Memorial Laboratory, School of Forestry, Fisheries and Wildlife, University of Missouri-Columbia, Puxico, MO 63960

LEIGH H. FREDRICKSON, Gaylord Memorial Laboratory, School of Forestry, Fisheries and Wildlife, University of Missouri-Columbia, Puxico, MO 63960

The floodplains of the Mississippi River and its network of tributaries have been traditional migration and wintering habitats for millions of North American waterfowl. The great passages of ducks, geese, and swans of just 150 years ago have been replaced by increasingly scarce flocks of most species. Reasons for declines in waterfowl numbers are complex and include habitat degradation throughout breeding, migration, and wintering ranges. Habitat modifications in the Upper Mississippi Valley (UMV), general trends in waterfowl use, and the present habitat management challenges are the foci of this chapter. We also identify specific management practices related to seasonally flooded wetlands that have proven effective in the UMV.

For purposes of this chapter, our discussion of UMV wetlands—refuges and moist-soil impoundments—concentrates on the area from Minneapolis, Minnesota, to Memphis, Tennessee (45°-35°, N-S lat.), and from Sioux City, Iowa, to Nashville, Tennessee (97°-87°, W-E long.) (Fig. 1). The hydrology of this region is dominated by the Mississippi River and its tributaries, including the Missouri,

[1]Financial support was provided by Gaylord Memorial Laboratory (Univ. Missouri-Columbia and Missouri Dep. of Conserv. cooperating), Fed. Aid Proj. W-13-R, Missouri Coop. Fish and Wildl. Res. Unit, USFWS Contracts No. USDI-14-16-0009-(801-029), -(1509-3), -(1509-4), -(1556-11), the W. J. Rucker and Edward K. Love Fellowships (Univ. Missouri), Sigma-Xi, and the Missouri Agric. Exp. Stn., Proj. 183, J. Ser. #10,604.

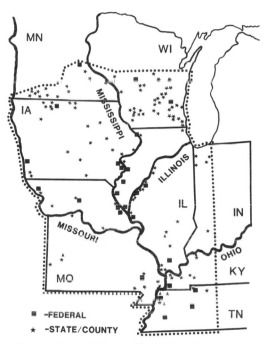

Fig. 1. Map of Upper Mississippi Valley showing public wetlands >400 ha for federal National Wildlife Refuges (boxes) and state/county areas (stars) within dotted area (after Bellrose 1980).

Ohio, and Illinois rivers. Glacial activity shaped the topography of the northern third of the area, and continental moraines impacted hydrology. Three wetland systems are common throughout the region: (1) riverine, (2) lacustrine, and (3) palustrine (Cowardin et al. 1979).

Riverine habitats in this area are extremely important to diving ducks, especially lesser scaup (*Aythya affinis*) and canvasback (*A. valisineria*), but these are discussed in greater detail by Korschgen (1989). However, the impacts of riverine flooding

cycles on palustrine floodplains are discussed. Lacustrine wetlands are the only
freshwater wetland to increase in area
during the last 30 years (Tiner 1984).
These gains, however, have resulted from
the creation of farm ponds and reservoirs.
Ducks principally loaf and roost on large,
open, lacustrine sites (Heitmeyer and
Vohs 1984). Lacustrine wetlands, both
natural and man-made, are discussed in
greater detail by Bookhout et al. (1989)
and Ringleman et al. (1989).

Palustrine wetlands are the dominant
wetland type throughout North America
(Tiner 1984). Three classes of palustrine
wetlands are recognized in the UMV: (1)
forested, (2) scrub-shrub, and (3) emergent. Forested wetlands in the UMV are
dominated by bottomland hardwoods. In
the northern portion of this region, red
maple (*Acer rubrum*), green ash (*Fraxinus
pennsylvanica*), and American elm
(*Ulmus americana*) are common (plant
nomenclature follows Steyermark 1963).
In the south, bald cypress (*Taxodium
distichum*), water tupelo (*Nyssa aquatica*), and overcup oak (*Quercus lyrata*)
are present on wetter sites, whereas drier
sites are dominated by pin oak (*Q.
palustris*), sycamore (*Platanus occidentalis*), and sweet gum (*Liquidambar stryra-
ciflua*). Cottonwood (*Populus deltoides*),
black willow (*Salix nigra*), and silver
maple (*A. saccharinum*) are common in
riparian corridors. Scrub-shrub wetlands
are transitional, dominated by buttonbush (*Cephalanthus occidentalis*) and willow (*Salix* spp.). These forested habitats
and their relationship to waterfowl use
are discussed elsewhere (Fredrickson 1979,
Fredrickson and Heitmeyer 1988, Reinecke et al. 1989). Emergent palustrine
wetlands include seasonally and semipermanently flooded marshes. These herbaceous wetlands occur as openings in
bottomland forests, backwater channels in
floodplains, and depressional areas in
glacial moraines. Man-made emergent
wetlands may exist in former palustrine

wetland sites that were drained for agriculture and then converted to managed
wetlands. Agricultural fields (e.g., corn,
soybean, rice, wheat, and milo) also may
be used by waterfowl in the UMV from
fall to early spring.

WETLAND DEGRADATIONS

The abundance and diversity of
wetlands that existed in North America
have been radically degraded by agriculture, industry, and urbanization. Approximately 54% of the original wetlands in
the conterminous United States (U.S.)
have been lost (Tiner 1984). Agriculture
accounted for 87% of wetland losses from
the mid-1950s to mid-1970s (Frayer et al.
1983). Palustrine wetlands, the most
important wetlands in the UMV, suffered
the greatest recent declines. Approximately 2.4 million ha of forested
wetlands, 0.2 million ha of scrub-shrub,
and 1.1 million ha of emergent wetlands
account for nearly 3.7 million ha of
palustrine wetlands that were lost
between the 1950s and 1970s. These losses
represent about 10% of all existing continental palustrine wetlands.

Specific losses in the UMV include
substantial conversion to agriculture in
western and southern Minnesota and
Wisconsin. Although nearly 4 million ha
of wetlands once existed in Wisconsin,
only about 1 million ha remain, with 64%
in private ownership in the mid-1970s
(Johnson 1976). Of the original 0.8-1.6
million ha of natural wetlands in Iowa,
most have disappeared, so that less than
10,900 ha exist today (Bishop 1981).
Losses in some portions of Missouri,
Illinois, and western Indiana have been
nearly as severe, but are poorly documented. The 50,000-ha Sny Bottoms of
west-central Illinois, that had long histories of traditional waterfowl use, have
been completely drained for agriculture.
Bottomland hardwood forests have been
drained and cleared throughout the
region. Less than 4% of original swamp

habitat exists in Missouri or Illinois (Korte and Fredrickson 1977, Tiner 1984). Kentucky has lost 37% of its original wetland area along the Mississippi and Ohio rivers in a recent 20-year period (Tiner 1984). Agricultural subsidies, flood insurance, technological advances in farming equipment (allowing tillage of wet and large, unbroken tracts), and high grain yields during drought periods may continue to encourage conversion of existing wetlands and intensified drainage of wet agricultural lands. Although the Swamp Buster provisions of the 1985 Farm Bill have slowed wetland loss in some areas, drainage continues at a rapid rate in many other areas (Eddleman et al. 1988).

CLIMATE AND RIVERINE HYDROLOGY

Waterfowl use of UMV wetlands is dependent upon climatic conditions that influence the length of the growing season and the number of ice-free days, as well as riverine hydrology that influences the timing and duration of floodplain inundation. Temperature and precipitation exhibit a wide range of conditions in a north-south cline over the UMV (Fig. 2). The northern portions have 4–5 months (November/December to March) when mean monthly temperatures rarely rise above freezing. In the southern portion, mean monthly temperatures rarely fall to 0 C, and are >15 C for 7 months. However, variations among years are such that, in some years, freezing temperatures do not occur in the south or high temperatures occur for considerable periods in the north. Precipitation levels range annually from 67 cm at Minneapolis, Minnesota, to 131 cm at Memphis, Tennessee. Peak rainfall occurs in late spring and early summer in the north, whereas winter precipitation and early spring rains are more common in the south (U.S. National Climatic Center 1983). Early winter precipitation is critical in the south because as water accumulates, wintering habitats are flooded gradually. As latitude increases, so does total annual snowfall, but total precipitation and growing season decline. Freezing temperatures from November through March make water availability low in the north.

Precipitation and ice-melt typically produce high flow and high water levels in spring throughout the UMV. Seasonal stage peaks are typical in spring along the large river systems. Although low flows normally occur in late summer or early fall, flooding events are possible during any month. Surface freezing of even the largest rivers occurs in the northern region in winter, and limits available open water. The Mississippi River typically is frozen from 10 December to 20 March in Minneapolis (U.S. National Climatic Center 1983).

Constriction of large riverine floodplains by mainstem levees and wing dike construction has occurred systematically over the last 150 years. Federal dike and levee construction was implemented after the Civil War. Development of the dipper dredge in the late 19th century provided the technological means to ditch, channel, and clear floodplain forests and marshes. As levee districts initiated drainage projects, floodplains were converted to agriculture, and increasing demands for higher mainstream levees were common (Nolen 1913). The lock and dam system of the Upper Mississippi River was initiated in the late 1920s as a federal response to the 1927 flood and as a means to promote barge traffic.

Prevention of natural river flow by channel constriction and navigational works such as wing dikes, side channel dikes, and revetments into floodplains resulted in higher flood peaks despite reduced discharge (Belt 1975). Although the 1973 flood had a peak discharge approximately 35% less than the estimated flow for 1844, the flood stage at St. Louis,

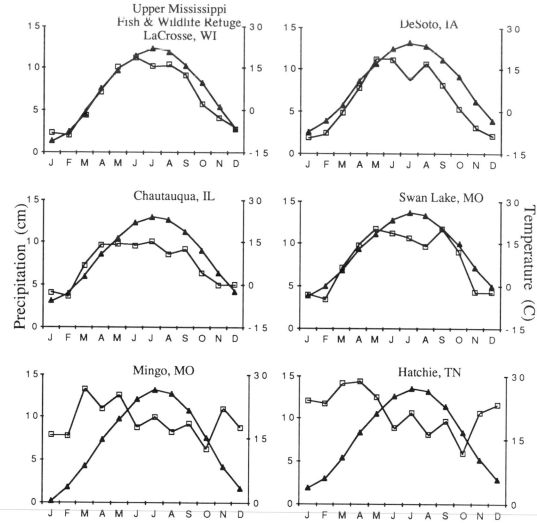

Fig. 2. Mean monthly precipitation and temperature for several National Wildife Refuges in the Midwest (period covers 1951-1980). Solid triangles represent temperature means, whereas open boxes represent precipitation means.

Missouri, was 0.3 m higher (Table 1). Under natural flooding conditions, the Mississippi River eroded both banks and bottom and then spilled over into its natural reservoir, the floodplain (Belt 1975). Record floods have become increasingly common since the 1930s (Fig. 3), and the floods of 1973 and 1983 reached the highest stages ever recorded. Man-made navigational works and channel constricting levees have produced large floods from only moderate river flows, and forced the Mississippi River out of its the natural dynamic regime (Belt 1975).

Man's modifications to the other large river systems in the region are equally as devastating to floodplain habitats and riverine flow dynamics. From 1879 to 1972, the Missouri River was shortened by 73.4 km between Rulo, Nebraska, and St. Louis, Missouri (Funk and Robinson 1974). About 93% of the emergent wetlands, backwaters, and sloughs along the Missouri River have been converted to agriculture or dredged for navigational channels (U.S. Fish and Wildlife Service 1980). Recent peak floods of the Missouri River reached all-time highs in October

Table 1. Flooding events of the Mississippi River, St. Louis, Missouri[a]

Year	Consecutive days	River crest (m)	Peak discharge (m³/sec)
1844	58[b]	12.88[c]	37,100
1908	?	10.67	24,100
1973	77	13.18	24,100

[a]Adapted from Belt (1975).
[b]During entire year.
[c]Official flood stage is 9.15 m at St. Louis.

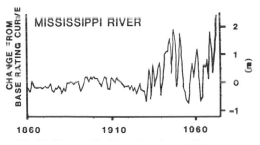

ST. LOUIS GAUGE, MISSOURI

Fig. 3. Long-term flooding events of the Mississippi River-St. Louis, Missouri, 1861-1973. Relation of change in river stage from base rating curve (computed from discharge/gauge height of yearly flood maxima) to time (from Belt 1975).

1986 and resulted in 146 breaks in mainstem levees from Kansas City to St. Louis, Missouri. A recent change in policy by the U.S. Army Corps of Engineers, which mandates a 10% financial commitment from local levee districts for levee repairs, may result in more floodplain area being subjected to river fluctuations. Consumptive water uses, principally irrigation for agriculture, presently utilize >8.6% (6 x 10⁹ m³) of the total annual discharge of the Missouri River (Schmulbach et al. 1989). Nonpoint contaminants (e.g., chlordane, dieldrin, and PCBs) currently present hazards to fish and wildlife in the floodplains, as well as directly to the river channels.

One of the best-documented case histories of riverine changes related to man's activities is that of the Illinois River Valley (Mills et al. 1966, Havera and Bellrose 1985). Cropland (principally corn and soybeans) increased 67% in the drainage basin from 1945-1976 (Bellrose et al. 1979). Such large-scale shifts in land use resulted in extensive increases in turbidity and sedimentation rates. These degradations, combined with increases in contaminant runoff from croplands, precipitated losses of aquatic vegetation and decreases in invertebrate, fish, and waterfowl resources. Mallard use-days declined from 25-55 million in the early 1950s to 14-40 million in the 1980s (Havera and Bellrose 1985). Whereas some of this decline could be related to a reduced continental mallard population, similar analysis for the Mississippi River bordering Illinois demonstrated an increasing

trend in mallard use (Havera and Bellrose 1985). Sedimentation modified once diverse lake bottoms to uniform flats of silt, reducing water storage and increasing downstream flooding.

Tributary systems throughout the UMV have lost their floodplains, which buffer flooding events (Fig. 4) and control erosion. Wherever loess soils are farmed, topsoil losses are great. Such losses are tremendous in the UMV, where Tennessee, Missouri, Iowa, and Illinois lead the nation in sheet and rill erosion (USDA 1977). Examples of erosional losses in Missouri range from 29 metric tons/ha/yr for Pike County in the northeastern portion of the state to 49 mt/ha/yr in St. Genevieve County in the southeast (M. Smale, pers. commun.). Local erosion rates may reach as high as 168 mt/ha/yr in gully stretches to 448 mt/ha/yr in stream channels bordered by intensive row cropping (M. Smale, pers. commun.). Other common modifications of floodplains by man include impoundment of riverine systems for hydroelectric power (Fig. 4), which eliminates the potential for seasonal drying of floodplain habitats and the germination of emergent plants.

HABITAT VALUES FOR WATERFOWL

Despite major degradations of important habitats, waterfowl continue to use

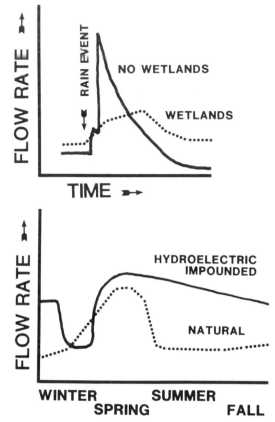

Fig. 4. Impacts of flooding regimes with: (a) rain event and loss of floodplain wetlands (after Odum 1979), and (b) impoundment for hydroelectric power.

Table 2. Waterfowl species for which the Upper Mississippi Valley is a critical migration corridor.[a]

Primary	Secondary
Tundra swan	American wigeon
(*Cygnus columbianus*)	(*Anas americana*)
Lesser snow goose	Gadwall
(*Chen caerulescens*)	(*Anas strepera*)
Canada goose	Green-winged teal
(*Branta canadensis*)	(*Anas crecca*)
Wood duck	Black duck
(*Aix sponsa*)	(*Anas rubripes*)
Mallard	Northern pintail
(*Anas platyrhynchos*)	(*Anas acuta*)
Blue-winged teal	Northern shoveler
(*Anas discors*)	(*Anas clypeata*)
Canvasback	Redhead
(*Aythya valisineria*)	(*Aythya americana*)
Ring-necked duck	Ruddy duck
(*Aythya collaris*)	(*Oxyura jamaicensis*)
Lesser scaup	
(*Aythya affinis*)	
Hooded merganser	
(*Lophodytes cucullatus*)	

[a]Primary importance is assigned to species for which the UMV is the single or 1 of 2 major corridors in North America. Secondary is assigned to species for which the UMV is a major corridor, but not the most important migration pathway in North America.

major river corridors of the UMV. The UMV is the primary migrational corridor for 10 species of waterfowl in North America, and is a secondary migrational corridor of considerable importance to 8 other species (Table 2). In addition, 13 other waterfowl species can be found regularly in small numbers during migration in the UMV (Bellrose 1980).

Migration is an adaptive trait that allows waterfowl to exploit seasonal resources in fluctuating temperate and arctic environments (Weller 1975). For waterfowl, the timing of migration (and associated biological activities such as pair formation, molt, and lipid deposition) is related to the availability of seasonally fluctuating foods and water. Annual variations in wetland conditions

seemingly provide proximate cues that influence the timing of specific biological events, whereas long-term environmental variations are the ultimate factors yielding morphological and social organizational differences among waterfowl groups (Nudds and Kaminski 1984, Fredrickson and Heitmeyer 1988).

Whereas the annual cycle for waterfowl is typically divided into 4 periods (breeding, fall migration, wintering, and spring migration) for research and management purposes, the complex process of gathering energy and nutrients for maintenance, survival, and reproduction crosses seasonal boundaries. For example, winter wetland conditions in the Mississippi Alluvial Valley (MAV) may influence mallard recruitment rates (Heitmeyer and Fredrickson 1981, Kaminski and Gluesing 1987). Fall migration habitats provide key resources that may be important for satisfying physiological and behavioral demands during winter (Fredrickson and Drobney 1979). Quality foraging habitats along migration routes may reduce the demand for food on wintering habitats and may enable birds to arrive on wintering grounds in good body condition (Bellrose 1954, Fredrickson and Drobney 1979). Water conditions and ice cover influence the distribution of migrating and wintering waterfowl. As such, the division between migration and wintering habitats is not obvious. What may be regarded as "migrational" habitat one year may be important "wintering" habitat another year. Thus, managers should consider providing resources to waterfowl for broad physiological and behavioral events rather than specific time periods.

Staging

Most puddle and diving ducks complete the wing and much of the body molt on staging areas before fall migration (Bergman 1973). Staging areas are typically large lakes or semipermanently flooded wetlands, which often are north of natal areas (Salomonsen 1968). Although large concentrations of waterfowl may use a specific staging area, competition for food resources may be reduced by niche partitioning. Isolation is a key requirement for most molting areas and is illustrated by the lack of molting ducks on southwestern Manitoba lakes where considerable human disturbance occurs (Bergman 1973). Many important staging sites for migrants in the Upper Midwest exist in Manitoba, Ontario, Minnesota, and Wisconsin.

Early-Fall Migration

Fall migration appears to be related, among other factors, to the drying or freezing of northern wetlands and the commencement of late fall-winter rains in more southerly wetlands (Bellrose et al. 1979, Heitmeyer 1985). Historically, the drying of floodplains stimulated germination of moist-soil plants and concentrated invertebrate prey. In the Midwest, blue-winged teal and northern pintail are

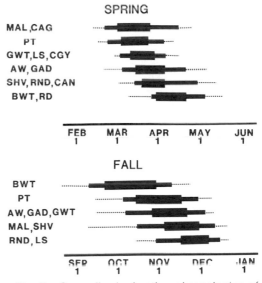

Fig. 5. Generalized migration chronologies of selected waterfowl species in the Upper Midwest. Dates based on 12 years of data from a mid-region location (Ted Shanks Wildlife Area [WA], Missouri). (MAL = mallard; CAG = Canada geese; PT = northern pintail, GWT = green-winged teal; LS = lesser scaup; CGY = common. goldeneye; AW = American wigeon; GAD = gadwall; SHV = northern shoveler, RND = ring-necked duck, CAN = canvasback; BWT = blue-winged teal; RD = ruddy duck).

among the first southward migrants to exploit these shallow water conditions (Fig. 5). As fall rains flood new areas, other waterfowl continue to exploit high-energy foods such as seeds, tubers, and, to a lesser degree, invertebrates, which are produced in these floodplains.

Late-Fall to Early-Winter Migration

Migration and wintering wetlands within river floodplains are typically flooded along a gradient (Fredrickson and Heitmeyer 1988), and this gradient is critical for acquisition of recently flooded food resources by waterfowl. With late fall rains, a continuum of zones become inundated including the lower scrub-shrub or buttonbush-willow areas, then overcup oak zones, and finally, the higher sites such as pin oak-sweetgum flats. Several duck species, including mallard, gadwall, and American wigeon, readily exploit scrub-shrub habitats to gain isolation for courting pairs and to acquire food resources. Ducks, such as the mallard, gain body and lipid mass quickly by feeding on mast crops. Where wetland degradation has occurred, waterfowl, especially mallards and Canada geese, exploit waste grain in agricultural fields (MacDonald et al. 1979, Reinecke et al. 1989). Grains and soybeans are used by mallards when natural mast crops fail, ice cover precludes use of natural habitats, or natural wetlands are absent (Heitmeyer 1985, Combs 1987). Cereal grains are an important source of energy for some dabbling ducks and geese, but native foods are necessary to offset the protein and mineral deficiencies in grains. Cereal grains may be an important component of a refuge complex even in intensively farmed areas, as off-refuge sites often are not available to waterfowl because they are heavily hunted or harvested (Austin 1988).

Late-Winter to Spring

During late winter, female mallards enter prebasic molt and consume crustacean prey (Heitmeyer 1987, 1988). These prey are rich in essential amino acids and occur along flooding gradients. Specific patterns of exploitation within these gradients by other waterfowl species are unknown, but similarities during winter may exist. As the molt is completed, the females shift to high-caloric foods for the energetically expensive spring migration. Local and regional movements occur in all directions from a focal center during winter (Delnicki and Reinecke 1986), and the movements may be related to availability of traditional wetland sites.

Spring Migration

For early migrants, the onset of spring migration (Fig. 5) is related to ice-out. Waterfowl exploit newly flooded seasonal wetlands (Heitmeyer 1985, LaGrange 1985, Gruenhagen 1987), and many, espe-

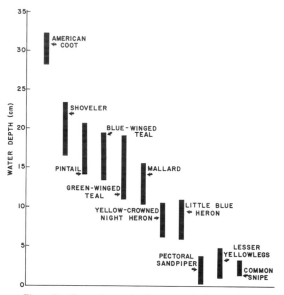

Fig. 6. Foraging depths used by migrant dabbling ducks and 6 common waterbirds—Mingo NWR, Missouri (Fredrickson and Taylor 1982).

cially females, feed extensively on invertebrate resources. Forested and emergent palustrine wetlands are used during spring migration. Several species, including wood duck, hooded merganser, and giant Canada goose, breed throughout the UMV. Mallard, blue-winged teal, redhead, ruddy duck, and American coot (*Fulica americana*) breed in the UMV, but their distribution is primarily restricted to glaciated portions of the region.

MEETING HABITAT NEEDS

One of the greatest challenges facing wetland managers today is to provide the resources required for different waterfowl, including individuals of varying physical condition and social status, that utilize a single wetland complex. For example, in western Tennessee, courting hooded mergansers, premigratory green-winged teal, and immature black ducks that have just entered prebasic molt may be present simultaneously on an area. Each of these species would require somewhat different resources during early spring. Niche separation of wintering waterfowl occurs via differences in temporal usage of resources (Fredrickson and Heitmeyer 1988) and spatial usage of microhabitats, such as water depth and structural features (White and James 1978, Thomas 1982). Migrating waterfowl display some of the same patterns of microhabitat use, but a common denominator is that dabbling ducks forage in shallow water depths (10-25 cm) (Fig. 6). Unfortunately, as attempts are made to maximize managed flooded area, many wetlands often are flooded too deeply to facilitate foraging. When sites are gradually flooded or drained, conditions mimic natural floodplain events.

Although the UMV is considered important because of migrational habitats, it is also important because it contains critical wintering habitat for waterfowl (Table 3). As much as 40% of the continental populations of mallards and black ducks winter throughout the MAV. Of this total, 50% of the birds may winter in the UMV. Mallards in the MAV exhibit flexible homing to specific localities (Bellrose and Crompton 1970), which are influenced by temperature, water and food conditions, and population size (Nichols et al. 1983). Tennessee and Cross Creeks National Wildlife Refuges (NWRs), in western Tennessee, are especially important for wintering mallards and black ducks. Population levels may reach as high as 0.5 million birds on the Tennessee NWR. The most common diving duck wintering in the region is the ring-necked duck, which selects somewhat more open habitats than those preferred by forest-adapted species like mallards and wood ducks.

Four wintering populations of Canada geese are present in the UMV (Bellrose 1980). Approximately 30% of the Western Prairie Population (WPP) winters between Swan Lake NWR, Missouri, and Schell Osage Wildlife Area (WA), Missouri; whereas 50% of the Tennessee Valley Population (TVP) of Canada geese winters in western Tennessee and Ken-

Table 3. Percent of North American waterfowl wintering in Mississippi corridor.[a]

Species	Upper Mississippi Valley	Total MAV[b]
Mallard	10-20	30-40
Black duck	5-20	20-40
Ring-necked duck	5-10	
Canada goose		
Western Prairie Population	~30	
Tennessee Valley Population	~50	
Eastern Prairie Population	~90	
Mississippi Valley Population	~100	

[a]After Bellrose (1980) and U.S. Fish and Wildlife Service midwinter inventory data.
[b]MAV = Mississippi Alluvial Valley.

tucky. About 90% of the Eastern Prairie Population (EPP) winters between Rochester, Minnesota, and Swan Lake NWR, Missouri; whereas the Mississippi Valley Population (MVP) winters almost exclusively in southern Illinois, Missouri, western Kentucky, and Tennessee. Eight other waterfowl species, including snow goose, white-fronted goose, American wigeon, gadwall, northern pintail, green-winged teal, common goldeneye, and wood duck, regularly winter in the UMV, whereas another 14 species occur in small numbers (Bellrose 1980).

Five-year trends in U.S. Fish and Wildlife Service midwinter inventories for the entire Mississippi Flyway from 1955-87 provide indices of declining duck numbers from peak levels in the late 1960s. Mallard numbers declined from a peak of >4 million birds in the late 1950s to just over 2 million birds in 1987 (Fig. 7). Although the region still winters >2 million mallards and >4.5 million ducks of all species, recent declines are alarming. When conditions are dry in eastern Texas, eastern Oklahoma, and western Louisiana, duck numbers in the MAV, during wet winters, increase substantially, especially species such as northern pintail and gadwall (C. W. Shaiffer, pers. commun.).

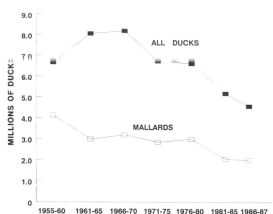

Fig. 7. Five-year trends in midwinter inventory of all ducks and mallards for the Mississippi Flyway 1955-87.

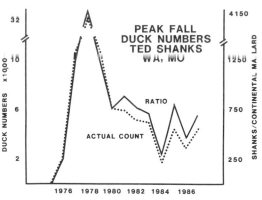

Fig. 8. Fall peaks of waterfowl populations in the 1,015-ha moist-soil/agriculture refuge at Ted Shanks WA, Missouri, 1975-87 (Ill. Nat. Hist. Surv.). Trend of actual peak counts each year in dotted line. Ratio ($\times10^{-6}$) of peak counts/annual continental mallard populations in solid line.

Certain sites have attracted increasing numbers of birds despite declining continental populations. Drawdowns of impounded water created improved habitats for mallards and snow geese at Squaw Creek NWR (Burgess 1969). Acquisition and development of the Ted Shanks Wildlife Area (WA) in northeastern Missouri is another example. Peak fall counts in a 1,015-ha moist-soil-agriculture complex suggest a rapid response of waterfowl to restoration of traditional wetlands (Fig. 8). The decrease in peak duck numbers in the early 1980s at the Shanks WA was a result of the decline in continental duck populations and the development of other nearby waterfowl refuges and habitat (Clarence Cannon NWR and U.S. Army Corps of Engineers' Mark Twain Reservoir).

HISTORY AND ROLE OF PUBLIC REFUGES

The Migratory Bird Treaty Act of 1918 eliminated market hunting, but it put forth no specific provision or mechanisms for federal habitat acquisition. Because the treaty obligated federal protection to migratory waterfowl, the need for federal waterfowl refuges was established. In 1924, the U.S. Congress authorized the appropriation of $1.5 million to purchase bottomlands along the Upper Mississippi River to establish a refuge for migratory birds (Gabrielson 1943). This first appropriation of money by Congress for the purchase of a wildlife reserve was principally for migrational habitat.

By 1932, 0.36 million ha of NWR lands existed in the U.S. In the 1930s, legislation such as the Migratory Bird Hunting Stamp Act (of which 90% of the funds were to be used for migratory waterfowl refuges), the 1936 authorization of $6 million for waterfowl restoration programs, and the Federal Aid in Wildlife Restoration (Pittman/Robertson) Act were passed. Important UMV refuges acquired included Swan Lake and Squaw Creek NWRs, Missouri, and Chautauqua NWR, Illinois. By 1941, 3.9 million ha of NWR lands existed in the U.S.—a 10-fold increase in a 9-year period. At the time, however, conservationists argued that many were merely "paper" refuges—areas lacking dynamic water regimes, protection from aggressive timber practices, and freedom from human disturbances (Gabrielson 1943). Acquisition emphasis shifted to breeding areas in the late 1950s and early 1960s, whereas management practices on migrational and wintering areas shifted to flooding of row crops. Today, nearly 0.5 million ha of public wetlands exist in the UMV (Table 4).

Table 4. Area (ha) of wetlands in public ownership in the Upper Mississippi Valley.[a]

Location	Federal NWR	State/county
Southern Minnesota	16,848	12,958
Southern Wisconsin	60,412	114,037
Iowa	26,980	55,298
Missouri	17,388	31,375
Illinois	35,587	44,041
Western Indiana	0	14,077
Western Kentucky	825	9,290
Western Tennessee	32,933	16,914
Midwest total	190,971	297,290
Federal + State	488,361	

[a]Modified after Bellrose (1980).

Regional distribution of large refuges (>400 ha) reveals the importance of glacial wetlands and major floodplain habitats (Fig. 1).

Refuges are important in providing sanctuaries free from disturbance and in providing food resources that enable migrating birds to replenish depleted energy reserves (Bellrose 1954). Refuges also provide habitats for social and behavioral interactions. Private ownership of wetlands by duck hunting clubs is probably most important in the Illinois River Valley, in the Reelfoot Lake area of Tennessee, and at the confluence of the Mississippi and Missouri Rivers in St. Charles County, Missouri. A recent inventory of wetlands in Missouri (Humburg 1987) indicated that 15,500 ha are managed by private duck hunting clubs, with approximately 38% (5,870 ha) located in St. Charles County.

An understanding of key legal and judicial actions related to wetlands can enable resource personnel to better implement mechanisms for protection and acquisition. The first test of the Migratory Bird Treaty Act came to the U.S. Supreme Court in Missouri vs. Holland (1920), where Missouri's state attorney general was arrested during spring waterfowl shooting. The court held that the taking of any migratory bird species was prohibited, unless done pursuant to federal permit or regulation. Regional conflicts over spring shooting ended after this case. Conflicts over dam construction and dredge projects have ended in federal courts in Minnesota and Indiana, involving cases such as U.S. vs. Byrd (USCA 1979). This case was based on deposition of fill in a lacustrine marsh by a private citizen. The court decided such action constituted pollution under the Federal Clean Water Act. State courts often have decided permit cases related to the "taking" issue. Just vs. Marinette County (WIDC 1972) upheld a local zoning ordinance that required a permit prior to filling of any wetland. The Minnesota Supreme Court unanimously affirmed a state agency's authority to block a private citizen from draining a marsh on his own land in Christenson vs. Minnesota (MNSC 1987). The court based its decision on 1976 and 1978 state laws that gave the Minnesota Department of Natural Resources authority to inventory and protect state waters. By 1987, 1.5 million ha including over 12,000 lakes, 6,600 streams, and over 10,000 wetlands had been classified in protected status throughout Minnesota.

HABITAT MANAGEMENT

The desire to improve nature is a common perspective held by much of society, including some waterfowl managers. The pricelessness of untampered nature (Errington 1963) should be considered where undisturbed wetlands are present. The dynamic processes of natural systems cannot be improved upon by man, and protection, rather than manipulation, should be the management goal. In most of the UMV, however, degradations to wetlands are great. Active management, including manipulations of water, soil, and vegetation, is essential where hydrology has been modified or habitats have been degraded. Restoration on former wetlands degraded by agriculture should include reforestation and management of emergent wetlands.

Prescriptions for management of forested or riparian wetlands of the UMV are available (Fredrickson 1979, Fredrickson and Reid 1986, Batema 1987). Management of marsh and seasonally flooded emergent (moist-soil) wetlands produce native foods and cover for migrant waterfowl. In northern areas, managers have attempted to attain a 50:50 cover-water interspersion in semipermanent marshes (Weller and Spatcher 1965), but an understanding of the impacts of 5- to 7-year hydrologic cycles is essential (Weller and Fredrickson 1974, Nelson and Kadlec 1984).

Moist-soil management was first described for the Illinois River Valley (Low and Bellrose 1944), but had been practiced on a smaller scale by private duck hunting club managers in the UMV and southeastern U.S. Moist-soil management offers tremendous potential in restored and some natural wetlands. This management practice emulates natural drying conditions through artificial drawdown of impoundments. Exposure of soils allows germination of plants, which produce abundant seeds, tubers, and browse for wildlife. Substrate for aquatic invertebrates also is provided, and these organisms are important prey for waterfowl. Some 129 of 153 bird species which use moist-soil impoundments in eastern Missouri consume invertebrates (Fredrickson and Reid 1986). Naturally occurring areas of mudflats still exist in floodplains of the UMV, but as agricultural practices have become more intensive these remaining mudflat sites have become smaller and less numerous. When crops cannot be planted in a given year, sites often naturally dewater during the growing season, and moist-soil plants germinate. However, many farmers disk or mow sites in late summer to reduce unwanted "weeds," thus eliminating waterfowl food resources.

Moist-soil management is a common technique throughout the UMV on state wetland areas and on over 80% of NWRs.

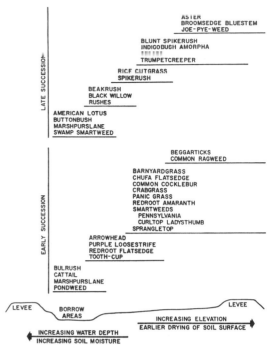

Fig. 9. Distribution of common moist-soil plants along a flooding gradient (Fredrickson and Taylor 1982). Scientific names of plants follow Fredrickson and Taylor (1982).

Successful moist-soil management is based on a conceptual understanding of habitat characteristics and life requisites of wildlife. In natural wetland sites, propagule (seed and bud) banks typically are sufficient to produce lush herbaceous stands if drawdown allows germination. For moist-soil manipulations, plants respond to the timing of annual drawdowns and the stage of wetland succession (Fig. 9). For example, barnyardgrass (*Echinochloa* spp.) and chufa (*Cyperus esculentus*) germinate after mid-season drawdowns. However, these species are less likely to germinate, or generally produce fewer seeds, during each successive growing season than when similar management is practiced among years. Once seed production has dropped to low levels, a physical disturbance (such as disking) may be necessary to shift plant response to early successional stages, and in this case, also to increase seed and tuber production (Fredrickson and Taylor

1982). An integrated management program requires soil and water manipulations for a complex of impoundments, but must be tempered by a manager's experience in a specific locale.

Development and Operational Considerations

Development of moist-soil wetlands requires preliminary site considerations such as floodwater source, dewatering network, levees, size of units, and juxtaposition of wetland complex. Biological aspects of the target species should be considered as well (Fredrickson and Reid 1986). Among the most important considerations in development is source of floodwater, which may determine quantity, quality, and predictability of wetland waters. Four sources of water for management include (1) rainfall, (2) river-stream, (3) reservoir, and (4) ground water. Whereas rainfall is least costly, it is also the least dependable source, and specific amounts and timing of water are unpredictable. Some pumping to dewater may even be necessary if rain events are too heavy. Rainfall may increase turbidity, and potential problems with acid rain as a flooding source are increasing. Predictability of river-stream sources are dependent on watershed rainfall patterns, which dictate stream flow. Sediments and agricultural or industrial toxicants may severely impact the quality of river or groundwater sources. Monitoring may be necessary to reduce the potential for poisoning of waterfowl on refuge sites. Reservoirs provide generally predictable sources, dependent on size of impoundment, but severe siltation can occur over time. Reservoir construction modifies natural wetlands and can change downstream flow patterns. Groundwater is useful in arid regions with high evapotranspiration and few sources of surface water, but is expensive to pump. Groundwater is cold and may be deficient in

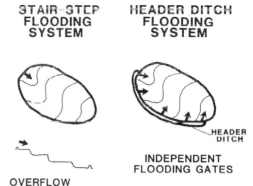

Fig. 10. Stair-step versus header ditch flooding system design in waterfowl impoundments.

some nutrients, yielding reduced plant growth.

Development of the flooding-drawdown network requires engineering and wetland managerial input. Although a stair-step flooding system, which allows sequential overflow across several contours, may be initially less costly to construct, this configuration does not provide independent flooding potential for units within the system. A header-ditch flooding system must be developed for independent control of units (Fig. 10). Use of former floodplain sloughs or existing drainage ditches as part of the header ditch system may reduce construction costs and impacts on natural contours (Baskett 1988).

Decisions on pump type or design often are made with only initial costs as a consideration. Diesel engines typically cost less to install, but cost more to maintain over time, require regular monitoring, and are noisy. Electric pumps typically cost more to purchase and may require a line fee for initial hook-up and an annual fee from the utility company for start-up charges. However, electric pumps require less maintenance over time, do not require constant monitoring, and run quietly.

To compare long-term pumping costs among 3 pump types, a 25-year scenario was developed (Fig. 11). Estimates were

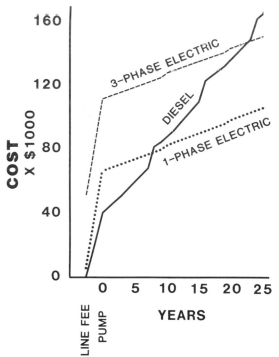

Fig. 11. Twenty-five year cost comparison—3-phase electric, 1-phase electric, and diesel power. Based on trends from 10 years of economic data—1 electric and 8 diesel pumps (Missouri Dep. of Conservation) and 20 years of data—4 electric pumps (TVA) (P. Covington and S. Atkins, pers. commun.). The 1-phase electric pumps have not been tested for more than several years, and early evidence suggests that the design may require extensive repair or replacement.

based on documented maintenance, energy, and repair analyses of 10-year trends from 1 electric and 8 diesel pumps (Missouri Dep. of Conservation) and 20 years of data from 4 electric pumps (Tennessee Valley Authority) on large (>800 ha) areas (P. Covington and S. Atkins, pers. commun.). We estimated diesel costs at $0.30/1, whereas electric costs were approximately 50% of that amount for comparable energy use. The 3-phase electric pump is initially the most costly. If annual start-up charges are required, 3-phase electric pumps will always remain the most costly design. The 1-phase electric pump does not require an initial line fee, and the slope of the maintenance cost curve is low.

Long-term life expectancies of 1-phase engines are not known; thus, the figures are only estimates. The average purchase price of the diesel pump is least expensive, but the slope of maintenance costs is steepest. Complete overhaul of diesel engines is required approximately every 4 years or 4,500 hours of use. A skilled mechanic in residence, who can service diesel pumps when problems develop, is mandatory. Long-term costs will vary with changing fuel prices, repair demands, and individual situations, but long-term economic assessment should be part of the decision-making process for pump type selection.

Levee construction for moist-soil areas is one of the most costly aspects of development. In the UMV, large levees 6,969 m^3/km, 0.6 m above full pool level, 3.2-m across top, 3(or 4):1 slopes are desirable (Fredrickson and Taylor 1982). Gradually sloping levees maintain their structure despite heavy equipment and frequent traffic and are less easily damaged by furbearers and ice movement. Siting of water-control structures and configuration of borrow areas is critical to ensure complete drainage for future manipulations. Placement of borrow areas outside of units can substantially reduce initial pumping costs when flooding units. The configuration of 2 moist-soil units at Mingo NWR, Missouri, represents an example of pumping costs for shorebirds and waterfowl where borrow areas are within and outside the units. Although a unit lacking deep borrow areas inside the levees was small (8.1 ha), only $50 was required to provide good foraging conditions. In contrast, after expending $500 for pumping a large area (14.5 ha) with deep borrow areas within the levees, no surface water was present.

On intensively managed sites, contour levees assure effective use of entire units by waterfowl and provide more precise water-level control for vegetation management. If levees are not located on contours, bird use of traditional swales and sloughs will be reduced or lost. To demonstrate the long term benefits derived from contour levees, we compared different development strategies, with and without contour levees, on a hypothetical 400-ha managed wetland (Table 5). The initial cost of contour levees was 320% greater than the construction of a single bisecting levee when construction costs were equivalent ($1.15/m³) for levee construction with areas of relatively steep slope (contours >0.5m) (Table 5). The entire area with contour levees can be managed effectively (providing optimal foraging depths and for control and production of vegetation). The area lacking contour levees has only 45% of the surface areas available for optimum foraging depths (otherwise too deep or dry) or effective vegetation management at any given time. Over a 20-year period, the unit with contour levees would provide 8,000 ha of habitat that can be effectively managed. In contrast, the area lacking contour levees only would provide 3,600 ha of habitat that could be effectively managed. Thus, during the course of 20 years, contour levees provide an additional 4,400 ha of habitat (Table 5). Intensively managed moist-soil impoundments of the UMV can consistently produce 1,344 kg/ha of seeds. Assuming that the site maintains this production over a 20-year period, the area with contour levees would yield an additional 5.9 million kg of moist-soil seeds. Even with relatively low averages of 900 kg/ha for intensively managed sites, the yield would be an additional 4.0 million kg.

Production of 5.9 million kg of seeds has the potential to provide mallard-sized birds with over 65 million potential use-days of food over a 20-year period. These estimates are based on seed production alone, but moist-soil areas also provide abundant tuber, browse, and invertebrate resources that are readily consumed by

Table 5. Cost comparison in development of a hypothetical 400 ha impoundment with levees on contours and with levees not on contours.

Parameter	On contours	Not on contours
Cost of interior levees	$40,651	$12,704
($1.15/m³)	(35,349 m³)	11,047 m³)
Initial levee cost/ha	$102	$32
Area effectively managed (%)	100%	45%
20-year cost ($/effective ha)	$5.08	$3.53
20-year effectively managed area (ha)	8,000	3,600
Difference (ha/20 years)	4,400	
Additional seed production is (1344 kg/ha)	− 5.9 million kg moist-soil seeds	
Additional waterfowl use-days is (0.09 kg food/day for for mallard-sized bird)	= 65.7 million use-days in 20-year period	

waterfowl (McKenzie 1987). For example, below-ground biomass of chufa alone may add 360 kg/ha to the food base of a site (Kelley 1986). Addition of these resources to the food base would increase potential waterfowl use. The long-term benefits achieved from contour levees may warrant the initial cost of development. Given the limited funds available for acquisition and development of public lands, investments for contour levees may outweigh additional land purchases where habitats may have limited waterfowl potential.

Moist-soil units should not be leveled, because small undulations within units are desirable for varied habitat conditions for a number of wetland species. Laser technology (that can accurately and quickly locate contours) used with a rice-levee plow provide good potential for relatively inexpensive construction of low levees for intensive management. These small levees may be adequate for up to 2 years. Once such levees are breached, however, they are difficult to repair.

Size of individual moist-soil impound-

Table 6. Operational costs for moist-soil management.[a,b]

Item	Costs/ha
Land manager	$5.11
Water control	4.87
Mow dikes	1.43
Levees	3.81
Pumps	13.57
Modify succession (mow & disc)	4.65
Total cost/year	$33.44
Corn cost/year	$716.58

[a]Costs from Mingo NWR, Mo., adjusted to 1988 costs.
[b]After Fredrickson and Taylor (1982).

Table 7. Physical disturbances for vegetation control and their estimated costs.

Types	Characteristics	Cost
Mow	Chops above-ground vegetation Quick and inexpensive	$14.80/ha
Disc	Disturbs both above- and below-ground vegetation Modifies perennials Loss of soil nitrogen over time	$19.76/ha
Doze	Modifies all vegetation and top soil May be necessary for flood debris Increases depth and pumping costs Erosional problems Soil compaction Destruction of natural swales Expensive	$679.50/ha

ments may range from 1 to 1,500 ha. Small units have the advantage of greater potential to maintain precise water levels. Large units generally have a greater diversity and are less susceptible to disturbance. A minimum of 6 units can provide a complex for waterfowl use (Fredrickson and Taylor 1982). As the number of units increases, many more management options become available as manipulations can be timed to match plant life-history strategies to satisfy cover and food requirements of target animal species (Fredrickson and Reid 1986).

Capital investment for large moist-soil complexes can be large, but levee construction to flood row-crops also entails extensive development. The high annual costs of row-crop production are well-known to wildlife managers, yet moist-soil management provides an alternative with economic and biological benefits. Operational costs for moist-soil management are minimal when compared to row-crop investments (as low as 5% of corn investments) (Table 6). The major cost difference is related to the fertilizer, lime, herbicides, insecticides, fuel, and machinery required for successful row-crop production (Fredrickson and Taylor 1982).

Manipulation of vegetation is one of the major costs for moist-soil management. As seed-producing annuals are replaced by perennial plants, or as monocultures develop, water manipulation, burning, and chemical or physical

manipulations may be necessary to maintain high seed yields (Reid and Fredrickson 1987). Mowing, disking, crushing, and bulldozing are typical physical procedures to set back succession (Table 7). Costs of these procedures vary, but are typically greater than for farming operations because machinery is easily damaged in wet, clay soils. Experienced equipment operators and mechanics are valuable during the short dry period when manipulations are possible. When equipment or time is unavailable, lessee farmers can perform physical disturbances in exchange for farming rights. However, individuals who do not understand the goals of a habitat program can destroy valuable vegetation, introduce toxicants into the refuge system, and modify water regime schedules.

Plants that quickly develop monocultures are difficult to reduce in abundance, have minimal values for wetland wildlife, outcompete plants with greater value, and should be considered undesirable (Reid and Fredrickson 1987). Most undesirable plants are perennials or woody vegetation. Controlling annuals is easier than controlling perennials, and control of undesirables often requires the same manipulations that are used to encourage

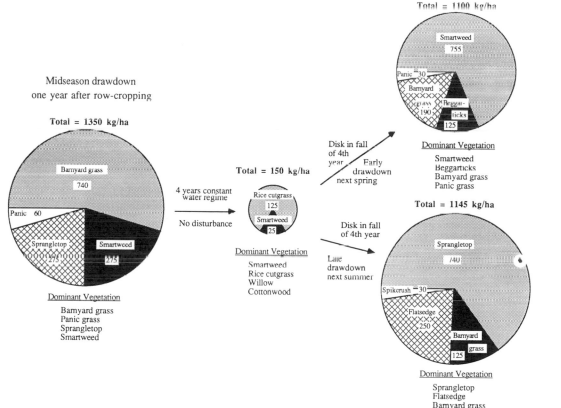

Fig. 12. Modification of seed production in moist-soil management. Based on seed production at Mingo NWR, Missouri (scientific names follow Fredrickson and Taylor 1982), and vegetation response at Ted Shanks WA, Missouri.

desirable vegetation. Timing of irrigation may be critical in the control of undesired herbaceous growth, such as common cocklebur (*Xanthium strumarium*). If shallow flooding inundates newly established cocklebur seedlings for a period of 24-48 h, these plants will either die or be stunted; whereas more desirable species, such as annual grasses, smartweeds (*Polygonum* spp.), or sedges (*Carex* spp.) will increase growth in response to the spate. Such manipulations emphasize the importance of water control. Control of undesirable perennial and woody growth also requires the potential for drying impoundments and for precise water control. Removal of woody vegetation, such as willow, can be difficult and varies considerably with latitude. At northern latitudes, newly established seedlings can

be controlled by shallow flooding, whereas shallow flooding usually promotes woody growth and invasion in more southerly latitudes (Fredrickson and Taylor 1982). In southern regions, moist-soil impoundments must be dewatered, dried, and disked to remove unwanted woody seedlings and small saplings. Periodic physical manipulations may be necessary in a 3- to 7-year rotation of woody control.

Maintenance of good seed production, while providing other food resources on intensively managed areas, requires a balance between soil disturbance and water manipulations. A potential scenario, based on seed production at Mingo NWR (Fredrickson and Taylor 1982) and vegetation response at Ted Shanks WA, is presented in Figure 12. High production during the early stages of succession

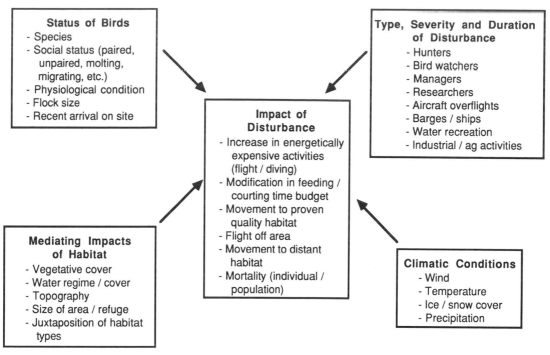

Fig. 13.   Major factors that influence disturbance (human) impacts on waterbirds.

(1,350 kg/ha) can be reduced (over 4 years) to 11% of original seed production where soils are not disturbed and water management is similar among years. Two common alternatives to increase food production result in differences in plant species composition based on time of dewatering during the next growing season, but seed yield is about the same (1,100 kg/ha). As moist-soil areas develop, waterfowl use associated with certain foraging modes appears to produce effects similar to disking. This is especially true for geese that grub for tubers or new browse (Smith and Odum 1981).

HUMAN DISTURBANCES OF WATERBIRDS

As quality wetland habitats become smaller and scarcer in North America, and continental populations of waterfowl decline, the issue of human disturbance becomes increasingly important. These disturbances not only lead to obvious

movements of birds from quality habitats, but also result in more subtle effects on foraging or behavioral interactions. The type, severity, and duration of a disturbance, traditionally, have been identified. However, the status of the birds and the climatic and habitat conditions also influence behavioral response and must be monitored to determine the impact of disturbance on waterfowl (Fig. 13). The subtle influences that result from disturbances by bird watchers or research personnel may have a greater impact on specific birds in a given area than more obvious disturbances from hunting or water-related recreation in other areas. Climatic conditions can influence the impacts of disturbance. For instance, ducks are less likely to take flight after a disturbance during severe winds or heavy precipitation than during calm periods. Not only are there variations in responses among species (Tuite et al. 1984), but flock size, social status, and age of birds also can influence impacts of disturbance. Mediating habitat considerations that reduce the effects of disturbance include the percent and type of vegetative cover, water regime, and percent of the basin flooded.

As waterfowl concentrate on quality habitats, public pressure for hunting increases. Harassment by hunters can lead to an increase in flight or diving activities, a corresponding reduction in time available for foraging, and prevention of waterfowl access to limited food resources. Feeding patterns may be modified, including shifts to night feeding (Tamisier 1985). Under severe conditions, a reduction of caloric intake can result in the need for additional foraging time (Fredrickson and Drobney 1979, Fredrickson and Reid 1987). Disturbance of roosting sites also can yield increases in hunting mortality (Raveling 1979), flight time (energetic costs), and foraging time.

The synergistic effects of several simultaneous disturbances can be severe but are little known. Sport fishing caused more disturbance to diving ducks during fall than hunting on the Upper Mississippi River (Korschgen et al. 1985), and caused approximately 50% as much disturbance as hunting boats during fall on Lake Poygan, Wisconsin (R. Kahl, pers. commun.). The priority needs of the waterfowl resource must be recognized on quality habitats. The fallacy of "multiple use" having little impact on waterfowl habitat use cannot be ignored. Areas with minimal disturbance are necessary during migration, molt, and pairing processes. Spatial and temporal sanctuaries throughout the UMV are critical, and a series of refuges 10-30 km apart should exist (Bellrose 1954, Delnicki and Reinecke 1986). Too often, sanctuaries include marginal habitats that are subjected to high public use. Effective sanctuaries must include a complex of habitat types that provide important food and cover resources.

RESEARCH NEEDS

The pattern of habitat use for all waterfowl species should be identified across the annual cycle. This information will be crucial for acquisition, development, and intensified management throughout the Mississippi River migrational corridor and entire continent. Plant production (seed, browse, and tuber) should be assessed under various management regimes. Likewise, zooplankton, macroinvertebrate, and fish populations should be monitored in relation to standard wetland management strategies. The nutrient quality and metabolizable energy of various native and cereal foods should be carefully analyzed in relation to time of year, soil nutrients, and water regime. Values of vegetation structure should be measured, such as the thermal protective contribution of timber breaks and robust herbaceous vegetation. Impacts of intensive management on soil nutrients should be examined. For example, little is understood of long-term nitrogen losses or the potential for fertilization of sites. The synergistic effects of human disturbances on waterfowl survival and reproduction must be quantified.

SUMMARY

Wetlands of the UMV are dominated by palustrine types (forested, scrub-shrub, and emergent) shaped by glacial moraine in the northern UMV and the Mississippi River watershed throughout the region. These natural wetlands have been altered or lost in the last 150 years by man's activities, principally agriculture. Despite such degradations, this region is a major migration corridor for 18 species of waterfowl. Wintering habitats also are available, and 5-20% of the continental populations of mallard and black duck may winter in the UMV. Ring-necked duck and Canada goose (MVP, TVP, EPP, and WPP) are the most common wintering diving duck and goose species. Wintering duck populations in the entire Mississippi Flyway have declined since the late 1950s, but the region still winters

>2 million mallard and >4.5 million total ducks. Public wetlands (0.5 million ha) are extremely important in the UMV in providing some areas free from human disturbances and in providing resources for physiological and behavioral waterfowl needs. Although these public lands comprise a relatively small percentage of original wetlands, intensive management can increase the carrying capacity to mitigate some of the habitat loss in the UMV. Habitat management for emergent wetlands include marsh and moist-soil techniques. Development considerations include (1) floodwater source, (2) flooding-dewatering network, (3) pumps and levees, (4) size and number of impoundments, and (5) juxtaposition of habitat types. For intensively developed sites, contour levees may be one of the most cost-effective investments. Sanctuaries, free from human disturbance, must include a mosiac of habitat types that provide important food and cover resources.

LITERATURE CITED

Austin, J. 1988. Wintering ecology of Canada geese, Swan Lake National Wildlife Refuge. Ph.D. Thesis, Univ. Missouri, Columbia. 90 pp.

Baskett, R. K. 1988. Grand Pass Wildlife Area: modern wetland restoration strategies at work. Pages 220-224 in J. M. Zelazny and J. S. Feierabend, eds. Proc. symp. on increasing our wetland resource. Natl. Wildl. Fed., Washington, D.C.

Batema, D. L. 1987. Relations among wetland invertebrate abundance, litter decomposition and nutrient dynamics in a bottomland hardwood ecosystem. Ph.D. Thesis, Univ. Missouri, Columbia. 191 pp.

Bellrose, F. C., Jr. 1954. The value of waterfowl refuges in Illinois. J. Wildl. Manage. 18:160-169.

——. 1980. Ducks, geese and swans of North America. Third ed. Stackpole Books, Harrisburg, Pa. 540 pp.

——, and R. D. Crompton. 1970. Migrational behavior of mallards and black ducks as determined from banding. Ill. Nat. Hist. Surv. Bull. 30:167-234.

——, F. L. Paveglio, Jr., and D. W. Steffeck. 1979. Waterfowl populations and the changing environment of the Illinois River valley. Ill. Nat. Hist. Surv. Bull. 32:1-54.

Belt, C. B., Jr. 1975. The 1973 flood and man's constriction of the Mississippi River. Science 189:681-684.

Bergman, R. D. 1973. Use of southern boreal lakes by post-breeding canvasbacks and redheads. J. Wildl. Manage. 37:160-170.

Bishop, R. A. 1981. Iowa's wetlands. Proc. Iowa Acad. Sci. 88:11-16.

Bookhout, T. A., K. E. Bednarik, and R. W. Kroll. 1989. The Great Lakes marshes, Pages 131-156 in L. M. Smith, R. L. Pederson and R. M. Kaminski, eds. Habitat management for migrating and wintering waterfowl in North America. Texas Tech Univ. Press, Lubbock.

Burgess, H. 1969. Habitat management on a mid-continent waterfowl refuge. J. Wildl. Manage. 33:843-847.

Combs, D. L. 1987. Ecology of male mallards during winter in the Upper Mississippi Alluvial Valley. Ph.D. Thesis, Univ. Missouri, Columbia, 223 pp.

Cowardin, L. M., V. Carter, F. C. Golet, and E. T. LaRoe. 1979. Classification of wetlands and deepwater habitats of the United States. U.S. Fish and Wildl. Serv. FWS/OBS-79/31. 103 pp.

Delnicki, D., and K. J. Reinecke. 1986. Midwinter food use and body weights of mallards and wood ducks in Mississippi. J. Wildl. Manage. 50:43-51.

Eddleman, W. R., F. L. Knopf, B. Meanley, F. A. Reid, and R. Zembal. 1988. Conservation of North American Rallids. Wilson Bull. 100:458-475.

Errington, P. L. 1963. The pricelessness of untampered nature. J. Wildl. Manage. 27:313-320.

Frayer, W. E., T. J. Monahan, D. C. Bowden, and F. A. Graybill. 1983. Status and trends of wetlands and deepwater habitats in the conterminous United States, 1950s to 1970s. Colorado State Univ. Rep., Fort Collins, 32 pp.

Fredrickson, L. H. 1979. Lowland hardwood wetlands: current status and habitat values for wildlife. Pages 296-306 in P. E. Greeson, J. R. Clark, and J. E. Clark, eds. Wetland function and values: the state of our understanding. Am. Water Resour. Assoc., Minneapolis, Minn. 674 pp.

——, and R. D. Drobney. 1979. Habitat utilization by postbreeding waterfowl. Pages 119-131 in T. A. Bookhout, ed. Waterfowl and wetlands—an integrated review. North Cent. Sect. Wildl. Soc., Madison, Wis. 147 pp.

——, and M. E. Heitmeyer. 1988. Wetland use of southern forested wetlands by waterfowl. Pages 307-323 in M. W. Weller, ed. Waterfowl in winter—a symposium and workshop. Univ. Minnesota Press, Minneapolis.

——, and F. A. Reid. 1986. Wetland and riparian habitats: a nongame management overview.

Pages 59-96 *in* J. B. Hale, L. B. Best, and R. L. Clawson, eds. Management of nongame wildlife in the midwest: a developing art. North Cent. Sect. Wildl. Soc., Chelsea, Mich. 171 pp.

———, and ———. 1987. Waterfowl use of wetland complexes *in* Managing waterfowl habitats: breeding, migration, wintering. U.S. Fish Wildl. Serv.-OIT, Fort Collins, Colo./Gaylord Lab., Puxico, Mo. 6 pp.

———, and T. S. Taylor. 1982. Management of seasonally flooded impoundments for wildlife. U.S. Dep. Int., Fish and Wildl. Serv. Resour. Publ. 148. 29 pp.

Funk, J. L., and J. W. Robinson. 1974. Changes in the channel of the lower Missouri River and effects on fish and wildlife. Mo. Dep. Conserv. Aquatic Ser. 11:1-52.

Gabrielson, I. N. 1943. Wildlife refuges. MacMillan Co., New York, N.Y. 257 pp.

Gruenhagen, N. M. 1987. Feeding ecology, behavior and carcass dynamics of migratory female mallards. M.S. Thesis, Univ. Missouri, Columbia. 158 pp.

Havera, S. P., and F. C. Bellrose. 1985. The Illinois River: a lesson to be learned. Wetlands 4:29-41.

Heitmeyer, M. E. 1985. Wintering strategies of female mallards related to dynamics of lowland hardwood wetlands in the Upper Mississippi Delta. Ph.D. Thesis, Univ. Missouri, Columbia. 378 pp.

———. 1987. The prebasic moult and basic plumage of female mallards (*Anas platyrhynchos*). Can. J. Zool. 65:2248-2261.

———. 1988. Protein costs of the prebasic molt of female mallards. Condor 90:263-266.

———, and L. H. Fredrickson. 1981. Do wetland conditions in the Mississippi Delta hardwoods influence mallard recruitment? Trans. North Am. Wildl. and Nat. Resour. Conf. 46:44-57.

———, and P. A. Vohs, Jr. 1984. Characteristics of wetlands used by migrant dabbling ducks in Oklahoma, USA. Wildfowl 35:61-70.

Humburg, D. D. 1987. A survey of protected wetlands in Missouri. Mo. Dep. Conserv., Columbia. 5 pp.

Johnson, C. D. 1976. Wetland use in Wisconsin; historical perspective and present picture. Wis. Dep. Nat. Resour. Water Quality Planning Sect., Madison. 48 pp.

Kaminski, R. M., and E. A. Gluesing. 1987. Density- and habitat-related recruitment in mallards. J. Wildl. Manage. 51:141-148.

Kelley, J. R., Jr. 1986. Management and biomass production of selected moist-soil plants. M.S. Thesis, Univ. Missouri, Columbia. 68 pp.

Korschgen, C. E. 1989. Riverine and deepwater habitats for diving ducks. Pages 157-180 *in* L. M. Smith, R. L. Pederson, and R. M. Kaminski, eds. Habitat management for migrating and

wintering waterfowl in North America. Texas Tech Univ. Press, Lubbock.

———, L. S. George, and W. L. Green. 1985. Disturbance of diving ducks by boaters on a migrational area. Wildl. Soc. Bull. 13:290-296.

Korte, P. L., and L. H. Fredrickson. 1977. Loss of Missouri's lowland hardwood ecosystem. Trans. North Am. Wildl. and Nat. Resour. Conf. 42:31-46.

LaGrange, T. G. 1985. Habitat use and nutrient reserve dynamics of spring migratory mallards in central Iowa. M.S. Thesis, Iowa State Univ., Ames. 81 pp.

Low, J. B., and F. C. Bellrose, Jr. 1944. The seed and vegetative yield of waterfowl food plants in the Illinois River Valley. J. Wildl. Manage. 8:7-22.

MacDonald, P. O., W. E. Frayer, and J. K. Clauser. 1979. Documentation, chronology, and future projections of bottomland hardwood habitat loss in the lower Mississippi Alluvial Plain. Vol. I: Basic Rep. U.S. Fish and Wildl. Serv., Ecol. Serv., Vicksburg, Miss. 133 pp.

McKenzie, D. F. 1987. Utilization of rootstocks and browse by waterfowl on moist-soil impoundments in Missouri. M.S. Thesis, Univ. Missouri, Columbia. 93 pp.

Mills, H. B., W. C. Starrett, and F. C. Bellrose. 1966. Man's effect on the fish and wildlife of the Illinois River. Ill. Nat. Hist. Surv. Biol. Notes 57:1-24.

Nelson, J. W., and J. A. Kadlec. 1984. A conceptual approach to relating habitat structure and macroinvertebrate production in freshwater wetlands. Trans. North Am. Wildl. and Nat. Resour. Conf. 49:262-270.

Nichols, J. D., K. J. Reinecke, and J. E. Hines. 1983. Factors affecting the distribution of mallards wintering in the Mississippi alluvial valley. Auk 100:932-946.

Nolen, J. H. 1913. Missouri's swamp and overflow lands and their reclamation. Report to the 47th Missouri General Assembly. Hugh Stephens Printing Co., Jefferson City, Mo. 141 pp.

Nudds, T. D., and R. M. Kaminski. 1984. Sexual size dimorphism in relation to resource partitioning in North American dabbling ducks. Can. J. Zool. 62:2009-2012.

Odum, E. P. 1979. The value of wetlands: a hierarchical approach. Pages 16-25 *in* P. E. Greeson, J. R. Clark, and J. E. Clark, eds. Wetland function and value: the state of our understanding. Am. Water Resour. Assoc. Minneapolis, Minn. 674 pp.

Raveling, D. G. 1979. Traditional use of migration and winter roost sites by Canada geese. J. Wildl. Manage. 43:229-235.

Reid, F. A., and L. H. Fredrickson. 1987. Wetland management: preliminary considerations for manipulating vegetation. *In* Managing water-fowl habitats: breeding, migration, wintering, U.S. Fish and Wildl. Serv.-OIT, Fort Collins, Colo./Gaylord Lab., Puxico, Mo. 5 pp.

Reinecke, K. J., R. M. Kaminski, D. J. Moorhead, J. D. Hodges, and J. R. Nassar. 1989. Mississippi Alluvial Valley. Pages 203-247 *in* L. M. Smith, R. L. Pederson, and R. M. Kaminski, eds. Habitat management for migrating and wintering waterfowl in North America. Texas Tech Univ. Press, Lubbock.

Ringelman, J. K., W. R. Eddleman, and H. W. Miller. 1989. High plains reservoirs and sloughs. Pages 311-340 *in* L. M. Smith, R. L. Pederson, and R. M. Kaminski, eds. Habitat management for migrating and wintering waterfowl in North America. Texas Tech Univ. Press, Lubbock.

Salomonsen, F. 1968. The moult-migration. Wild-fowl 19:5-24.

Schmulbach, J. C., L. W. Hesse, and J. E. Bush. 1989. Missouri River—Great Plains thread of life. In Press *in* D. A. Neitzel, ed. Water quality of North American river systems. U. S. Environ. Protect. Agency, Washington, D.C.

Smith, T. J., and W. E. Odum. 1981. The effects of grazing by snow geese on coastal salt marshes. Ecology 62:98-106.

Steyermark, J. A. 1963. Flora of Missouri. Iowa State Univ. Press, Ames. 1,725 pp.

Tamisier, A. 1985. Hunting as a key environmental parameter for the western Palearctic duck populations. Wildfowl 36:95-103.

Thomas, C. 1982. Wintering ecology of dabbling ducks in central Florida. M.S. Thesis, Univ. Missouri, Columbia. 60 pp.

Tiner, R. W., Jr. 1984. Wetlands of the United States: current status and recent trends. U.S. Fish and Wildl. Serv. Wetlands Inventory, Washington, D.C. 59 pp.

Tuite, C. H., P. R. Hanson, and M. Owen. 1984. Some ecological factors affecting winter wildfowl distribution on inland waters in England and Wales, and the influence of water-based recreation. J. Appl. Ecol. 21:41-62.

United States Department of Agriculture. 1977. Basic statistics 1977. National resources inventory. Soil Conserv. Serv., Iowa State Univ., Ames, Stat. Lab. Bull. 686. 200 pp.

United States Fish and Wildlife Service. 1980. Fish and wildlife coordination act report for the Missouri River stabilization and navigation project. Kansas City, Mo. 77 pp.

United States National Climatic Center. 1983. Climate normals for the U.S. (Base: 1951-80). Asheville, N.C. 712 pp.

Weller, M. W. 1975. Migratory waterfowl: a hemispheric perspective. Publ. Biol. Inst. Inv. Cienc., U.A.N.L., Mexico 1:89-130.

———, and L. H. Fredrickson. 1974. Avian ecology of a managed glacial marsh. Living Bird 12:269-291.

———, and C. E. Spatcher. 1965. Role of habitat in the distribution and abundance of marsh birds. Spec. Rep. 43, Iowa State Univ. Agric. and Home Econ. Exp. Stn., Ames. 31 pp.

White, D. H., and D. James. 1978. Differential use of freshwater environments by wintering waterfowl of coastal Texas. Wilson Bull. 90:99-111.

MISSISSIPPI ALLUVIAL VALLEY

KENNETH J. REINECKE, U.S. Fish and Wildlife Service, Patuxent Wildlife Research Center, Rm 236, 900 Clay Street, Vicksburg, MS 39180

RICHARD M. KAMINSKI, Department of Wildlife and Fisheries, P.O. Drawer LW, Mississippi State University, Mississippi State, MS 39762

DAVID J. MOORHEAD, Extension Forest Resources Department, University of Georgia, P.O. Box 1209, Tifton, GA 31793

JOHN D. HODGES, Department of Forestry, P.O. Drawer FR, Mississippi State University, Mississippi State, MS 39762

JAMES R. NASSAR, U.S. Fish and Wildlife Service, National Wetlands Research Center, Rm 206, 900 Clay Street, Vicksburg, MS 39180

For many years, availability of migration and wintering habitat was thought to have little effect on waterfowl populations (e.g., Hawkins 1964). However, continuing losses of wintering habitat (Tiner 1984, Forsythe 1985) and a better appreciation of the interdependence of waterfowl requirements throughout the annual cycle (Anderson and Batt 1983) have led to a more balanced concern for the conservation of breeding, migration, and wintering habitats. For example, the North American Waterfowl Management Plan (NAWMP) (Canadian Wildlife Service and U.S. Fish and Wildlife Service [CWS and FWS] 1986) proposes to restore prairie nesting areas and protect 277,624 ha of migration and wintering habitat for mallards (*Anas platyrhynchos*) and northern pintails (*A. acuta*) in the lower Mississippi River and Gulf Coast regions by the year 2000. In this chapter, we review habitat management in the Mississippi Alluvial Valley (MAV), 1 of 2 major wintering areas in the lower Mississippi River-Gulf Coast region.

Most habitats of waterfowl wintering in the MAV are croplands, moist-soil areas, or forested wetlands (Fig. 1). Farming has been an important management practice in the MAV since the first waterfowl refuges were established during the 1930s. In this review, any area that is seeded annually is considered cropland. Moist-soil habitats are natural, or managed, seasonally flooded wetlands dominated by grasses, sedges, or other herbaceous plants. The principle of increasing seed production of annual plants with seasonal drawdowns of moist-soil sites was recognized in the 1940s (Low and Bellrose 1944), but it was not until the 1970s (Fredrickson and Taylor 1982) that moist-soil management was widely applied. Forested wetlands are a complex of habitats including temporarily and seasonally flooded bottomland hardwoods, and permanently and semipermanently flooded shrub and wooded swamps. The practice of constructing impoundments or greentree reservoirs (GTRs) to flood live hardwood timber during the dormant season began in the MAV during the 1930s (Rudolph and Hunter 1964). Management of croplands and moist-soil areas is common in other flyways, whereas interest in bottomland hardwoods is greatest in the MAV.

Our review comprises 6 sections. In the first, we characterize the MAV. The second and third sections summarize information regarding waterfowl populations in the MAV and their biological requirements during migration and winter. The fourth section describes the 3 principal habitats managed for waterfowl and their integration into habitat management complexes. In the fifth section, we describe a method for classifying habitats and use the proposed classification to illustrate qualitatively the status and trends of wintering habitat in the

Fig. 1. Principal habitats of waterfowl wintering in the Mississippi Alluvial Valley (MAV) are public and private croplands, moist-soil areas, and forested wetlands subject to natural flooding (A), or controlled water levels (B).

MAV. The last section considers implications to future waterfowl management and research.

CHARACTERISTICS OF THE MAV

Physiography

The MAV is >800 km long, varies in width from 32-128 km, and comprises approximately 10 million ha in 7 states (Fig. 2). The eastern boundary of the MAV is marked by well-defined loess hills; the western boundary is less distinct, because it is interrupted by valleys of major tributaries such as the Arkansas, Ouachita, and Red Rivers.

The Mississippi River alternately eroded and filled the MAV with alluvium during the Pleistocene as glaciers advanced and retreated, and the Gulf Coast sea level rose and fell (Saucier

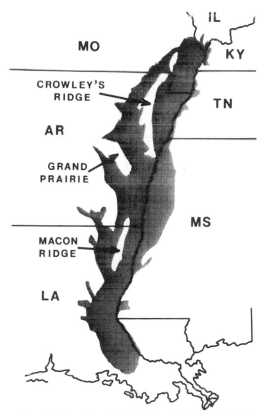

Fig. 2. The Mississippi Alluvial Valley (MAV), a major waterfowl migration and wintering area in the lower Mississippi River-Gulf Coast region.

1974). The present floor of the MAV rises gradually northward at about 0.1 m/km from near sea level in southern Louisiana to approximately 100 m in southeastern Missouri. Most local topographic relief in the MAV results from meandering of stream and river channels and rarely exceeds 5 to 10 m. Areas of the MAV that are elevated above the present valley floor and not subject to flooding include (1) Crowley's Ridge in northeastern Arkansas and southeastern Missouri, (2) the Grand Prairie of eastcentral Arkansas, and (3) Macon Ridge in southeastern Arkansas and northeastern Louisiana (Fig. 2). Of the three, only the Grand Prairie is important to waterfowl.

Climate

The climate of the MAV is characterized as humid subtropical (Lower Mississippi Region Comprehensive Study Coordinating Committee [LMRCSCC] 1974a). The growing season ranges from 210 days in southeastern Missouri to 270 days in southern Louisiana. Average annual rainfall varies from 115 cm in the northern MAV to 150 cm in the southern MAV, and generally exceeds evapotranspiration. Although peak seasonal rainfall occurs during winter or spring in the northern MAV and during summer in the southern MAV, winter precipitation is similar throughout the region. Late summer and early fall are the driest periods of the year in the MAV, and habitat conditions in natural wetlands often are unfavorable for early-migrating waterfowl. By late autumn, however, rains become more frequent, and winters are generally wet and mild.

Average maximum temperatures during January range from 7 C in the north to 18 C in the south, and average minima range from −1 to 13 C. Because average minimum temperatures are near freezing at the northern limit of the MAV, ice frequently covers wetlands and concentrates waterfowl wintering farther north, whereas shallow waters generally remain ice-free and waterfowl are more widely dispersed to the south. Winter snowfall averages 15 to 30 cm in the northern MAV but <2 cm in southern Louisiana.

Hydrology

Historically, most of the MAV was subject to periodic flooding by the Mississippi River and its tributaries. Hydrologic relationships in the MAV have been altered, however, by federally funded water resource developments for flood control and agriculture (Reinecke et al. 1988b). In western Mississippi, for example, the 2-year flood (i.e., a water level that would be reached or exceeded on average 1 in every 2 years) originally inundated >1.8 million ha (Galloway 1980). Construction of the mainstem Mississippi River levee system reduced the 2-

year flood to approximately 415,000 ha (Galloway 1980). Additional development of interior river basins in western Mississippi has restricted the 2-year flood to portions of the upper Yazoo River basin, the lower Yazoo basin or backwater, and the batture lands lying between the Mississippi River and its levee to the east. Current estimates are that the 2-year flood inundates approximately 52,000 ha in the upper Yazoo basin, 21,000 ha in the lower Yazoo basin, and 143,000 ha of batture lands (U.S. Fish and Wildl. Serv., Vicksburg, Miss., unpubl. data). Thus, the cumulative reduction of the 2-year flood in western Mississippi is approximately 88%.

Most analyses of hydrologic data for the MAV concern annual rather than seasonal events, and consequently emphasize spring floods, which generally occur during March and April (e.g., Klimas 1988) after most wintering waterfowl have departed. The occurrence of water conditions favorable for waterfowl wintering in the MAV is determined primarily by winter rainfall in tributary basins. For example, Heitmeyer (1985) showed that winter rainfall caused seasonal flooding that attracted mallards to Mingo Swamp in southeastern Missouri.

Groundwater resources also contribute to the management of habitat for waterfowl wintering in the MAV. The Mississippi River Valley alluvial aquifer underlying the MAV may be the largest source of fresh groundwater in the U.S. (LMRCSCC 1974a). It has facilitated development of irrigated agriculture in the MAV and has provided a costly but reliable source of water for managing public and private wetlands during dry years.

Vegetation

Hydrology directly and indirectly influences the distribution of natural vegetation in the MAV. Depth, timing, duration, and frequency of flooding, especially during the growing season, directly affect plant survival and reproduction (Fredrickson 1978). Flooding also indirectly influences water relationships in plant communities through its role in sediment distribution and soil formation. Thus, forest stands with a similar frequency and duration of flooding may vary in species composition because of differences in soil texture and drainage (Klimas 1987).

Typical distributions of woody plant species along moisture gradients in the MAV have been described (Fig. 3) (Fredrickson 1978, Larson et al. 1981). Common baldcypress (plant names follow Scott and Wasser 1980) and water tupelo predominate in the overstory where flooding or soil saturation is relatively permanent. Overcup oak and water hickory occur where saturation generally persists more than a quarter of the growing season; and American sweetgum, sugar hackberry, and several species of oak occupy sites where dormant season flooding is common but saturation during the growing season is brief and irregular. Habitat managers are particularly interested in red oaks (subgenus *Erythrobalanus*), such as pin, Nuttall (*Q. nuttallii*), willow, water (*Q. nigra*), cherrybark, and Shumard (*Q. shumardii*) oak, because they produce most of the acorns eaten by wintering waterfowl.

WATERFOWL POPULATIONS IN THE MAV

Mallards and Other Dabbling Ducks

The MAV is best known as a wintering area for mallards. Winter mallard populations formerly averaged about 1.5 million (Bellrose 1980, Bartonek et al. 1984), but have declined recently because of poor recruitment in prairie and parkland nesting areas (Reynolds 1987). The greatest number of mallards generally is found in Arkansas, which is also the leading harvest area in the United States (Munro and Kimball 1982). If harvest estimates

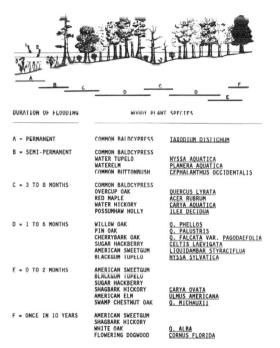

DURATION OF FLOODING	WOODY PLANT SPECIES	
A = PERMANENT	COMMON BALDCYPRESS	TAXODIUM DISTICHUM
B = SEMI-PERMANENT	COMMON BALDCYPRESS WATER TUPELO WATERELM COMMON BUTTONBUSH	 NYSSA AQUATICA PLANERA AQUATICA CEPHALANTHUS OCCIDENTALIS
C = 3 TO 8 MONTHS	COMMON BALDCYPRESS OVERCUP OAK RED MAPLE WATER HICKORY POSSUMHAW HOLLY	 QUERCUS LYRATA ACER RUBRUM CARYA AQUATICA ILEX DECIDUA
D = 1 TO 6 MONTHS	WILLOW OAK PIN OAK CHERRYBARK OAK SUGAR HACKBERRY AMERICAN SWEETGUM BLACKGUM TUPELO	Q. PHELLOS Q. PALUSTRIS Q. FALCATA VAR. PAGODAEFOLIA CELTIS LAEVIGATA LIQUIDAMBAR STYRACIFLUA NYSSA SYLVATICA
E = 0 TO 2 MONTHS	AMERICAN SWEETGUM BLACKGUM TUPELO SUGAR HACKBERRY SHAGBARK HICKORY AMERICAN ELM SWAMP CHESTNUT OAK	 CARYA OVATA ULMUS AMERICANA Q. MICHAUXII
F = ONCE IN 10 YEARS	AMERICAN SWEETGUM SHAGBARK HICKORY WHITE OAK FLOWERING DOGWOOD	 Q. ALBA CORNUS FLORIDA

Fig. 3. Schematic cross-section of forested wetlands in the Mississippi Alluvial Valley (MAV) showing the distribution of woody plant species relative to depth and duration of flooding. 1 = 10-year flood; 2 = mean annual high water; 3 = mean annual low water; A = permanently flooded; B = semipermanently flooded; C = flooded 3 to 8 months; D = flooded 1 to 6 months; E = flooded 0 to 2 months; and, F = flooded 1 in 10 years (after Fredrickson 1978).

are valid indices of relative abundance, mallards are the most numerous species of waterfowl migrating through or wintering in all states of the MAV (Table 1).

Analyses of band returns indicate that states in the MAV derive mallard harvests from similar breeding populations, and that harvest derivation varies little during the hunting season (Munro and Kimball 1982). From 60-70% of the mallards harvested in the MAV are produced in prairie wetlands of southern Saskatchewan, southwestern Manitoba, and the Missouri River basin; another 20-30% are from boreal and subarctic river deltas, lakes, and ponds of northern Alberta, Saskatchewan, and Manitoba, the Northwest Territories, and western Ontario.

Data for other dabbling ducks are limited. American black ducks rank high only in the harvests of Kentucky and Tennessee, states located at the northern end of the MAV and east of the Mississippi River (Table 1). Dabbling duck diversity is greatest in the southern MAV. Harvest of dabbling ducks other than mallards is <25% of the estimated mallard harvest in Arkansas, whereas the corresponding harvests are approximately equal in the MAV parishes of Louisiana (Carney et al. 1975, 1983).

Louisiana is the only state where winter population surveys are available for comparison with waterfowl harvest data. The relative abundance of dabbling ducks estimated with aerial surveys in southcentral Louisiana during the winters of 1985-86 and 1986-87 (Strader 1987), and a survey in northeastern Louisiana during 1985-86 (Dell et al. 1987), are consistent with their average rank in the harvest (Table 1). All 3 sources of data indicate that mallards, pintails, gadwalls, and green-winged teal are the most abundant dabbling ducks in Louisiana.

Wood Ducks

The status of wood ducks in the MAV is difficult to assess because population estimates are not available. However, harvest statistics indicate that wood ducks are probably second in abundance only to mallards, at least in states of the southern MAV (Table 1). Both the rank of wood ducks in the harvest and the size of annual harvests in the MAV (Carney et al. 1975, 1983) support Fredrickson and Heitmeyer's (1988) conclusion that more wood ducks winter in the southern than northern MAV. If the derivation of wood ducks harvested in the MAV is similar to that of the southern reference area of Bowers and Martin (1975), then about 40% of the wintering population are residents of the MAV, 40% are migrants from the north-central states of Missouri, Illinois, Iowa, Minnesota, and Wisconsin, and 10-15%

Table 1 Rank of various species of waterfowl in the harvest of states comprising the Mississippi Alluvial Valley (MAV). Ranks were based on harvest estimates for counties or parishes in the MAV (Carney et al. 1975, 1983).

State	Time period	Mallard	Wood duck Aix sponsa	Gadwall Anas strepera	Green-winged teal Anas crecca	American wigeon Anas americana	Ring-necked duck Aythya collaris	Lesser scaup Aythya affinis	Black duck Anas rubripes	Northern pintail	Canada goose Branta canadensis
KY	1961-70	1	7	8	5	4	9	6	3	-[a]	2
	1971-80	2	3	6	7	5	8	11	4	-[a]	1
MO	1961-70	1	2	3	5	8	10	9	11	6	4
	1971-80	1	3	6	5	8	7	9	13	11	2
TN	1961-70	1	2	3	8	7	4	10	5	6	12
	1971-80	1	3	2	10	5	7	11	6	9	4
AR	1961-70	1	2	3	4	5	9	10	8	6	-[a]
	1971-80	1	2	3	4	5	7	6	11	8	15
MS	1961-70	1	2	4	3	6	5	8	7	11	17
	1971-80	1	2	3	4	5	6	7	8	11	16
LA	1961-70	1	2	5	3	10	7	8	15	4	19
	1971-80	1	2	4	3	9	8	7	14	5	-[a]

[a]Insufficient data for computing a rank.

are from the lake states of Michigan, Indiana, and Ohio (Bowers and Martin 1975, Bowers and Hamilton 1977).

Diving Ducks and the Ruddy Duck

The status of most diving ducks in the MAV is not well known. Winter surveys traditionally have focused on dabbling ducks, and harvest estimates for diving ducks are difficult to interpret because some habitats (e.g., catfish ponds) are inaccessible to hunters, and some species (e.g., ruddy ducks [Oxyura jamaicensis]) may be avoided. Nevertheless, harvest estimates (Table 1) and aerial surveys in northeastern Louisiana (Dell et al. 1987) and western Mississippi (Wells 1982) indicate that ring-necked ducks and lesser scaup are relatively abundant and well-distributed in the MAV. During the winters of 1983-87, ruddy ducks and lesser scaup were 2 of the most abundant species among 50,000-150,000 waterfowl and American coots (Fulica americana) using catfish ponds in western Mississippi (Dubovsky and Kaminski 1987a, Christopher et al. 1988). Canvasbacks (Aythya valisineria) are less widely distributed than ring-necked ducks, lesser scaup, or ruddy ducks, but may be present in substantial numbers (e.g., 20,000-30,000) at traditional wintering areas such as Catahoula Lake, Louisiana (St. Amant 1959, Dell et al. 1987).

Geese

In addition to resident giant Canada geese (Branta canadensis maxima), Mississippi Valley and Eastern Prairie Population (MVP and EPP) Canada geese (B. c. interior), and midcontinent snow geese (Chen caerulescens) and white-fronted geese (Anser albifrons) winter in the MAV (Trost et al. 1980, 1981, Leslie 1983, Bateman et al. 1988). Although the numerical status of these populations generally is favorable (CWS and FWS 1986), the distribution of Canada geese has been a concern of managers in the Mississippi Flyway for >25 years (Rusch et al. 1985).

Prior to 1944, MVP Canada geese wintered primarily in southeastern Louisiana and along the lower Mississippi River (Hanson and Smith 1950, Hankla and Rudolph 1967). Most EPP Canada geese wintered in southwestern Louisiana or eastcentral Arkansas (Vaught and Kirsch 1966). By the 1960s, however, most

MVP and EPP geese wintered at refuges in southern Illinois (Reeves et al. 1968) and northcentral Missouri (Vaught and Kirsch 1966), respectively. Relocation of >20,000 MVP and EPP geese from northern to southern refuges during 1953-1965 (Hankla 1968), and hazing and altered management practices on northern refuges during the 1960s and 1970s (Rusch et al. 1985), failed to encourage geese to migrate farther south. Current efforts to restore migratory traditions of Canada geese emphasize identification and protection of remnant populations that still use southern wintering areas (Trost et al. 1980).

Most midcontinent snow geese wintered in brackish coastal marshes south of the MAV until the 1960s (Bateman et al. 1988). Since then, from 2,000-18,000 snow geese have been observed in central and northeastern Louisiana during winter aerial surveys (Bateman et al. 1988). Surveys in eastern Arkansas also indicate a substantial increase in the number of snow geese wintering there (S. Yaich, pers. commun.).

White-fronted geese are less abundant in the MAV than snow geese (Dell et al. 1987). Leslie (1983) observed about 6,000 white-fronted geese on a survey in northeastern Louisiana, and smaller numbers are usually present in Arkansas and Mississippi.

BIOLOGICAL REQUIREMENTS OF WATERFOWL WINTERING IN THE MAV

Food Use and Nutrition

Mallards and Other Dabbling Ducks.— The principal foods of mallards vary among locations and among years within locations, but generally include agricultural grains, seeds and tubers of moist-soil plants, acorns, and invertebrates such as isopods, snails, and fingernail clams. In southeastern Missouri, pin oak and cherrybark oak acorns dominate the diet during years of good mast production and favorable water conditions (Heitmeyer 1985, Combs 1987). In eastern Arkansas and western Mississippi, however, large areas of cropland are flooded naturally or artificially, and rice and soybeans are important (Wright 1959, Delnicki and Reinecke 1986). Seeds and tubers of grasses, sedges, and other moist-soil plants growing in managed and natural wetlands are an important component of the diet at all sites (Wright 1959, Wills 1971, Heitmeyer 1985, Delnicki and Reinecke 1986, Combs 1987). Invertebrates generally provide <10% of the diet in agricultural (Delnicki and Reinecke 1986) and moist-soil (McKenzie 1987) habitats, but may be more important in forested wetlands (Heitmeyer 1985).

Food habits data for other dabbling ducks are limited. A small sample of green-winged teal from Mississippi ate primarily grass and sedge seeds (D. Delnicki, pers. commun.), whereas tubers of chufa flatsedge (*Cyperus esculentus*) and seeds of barnyardgrass (*Echinochloa crusgalli*) were the most important foods of northern pintails at Catahoula Lake (Wills 1971). Mallards and other dabbling ducks often feed together in flooded croplands and moist-soil areas, and probably eat similar foods.

Wood Ducks.—Data regarding winter foods of wood ducks are limited. Acorns from Nuttall, water, willow, and other bottomland oaks are the primary source of energy, and agricultural grains are secondary (Delnicki and Reinecke 1986). Invertebrates probably contribute a significant proportion of the diet to offset the low protein content of acorns.

Diving Ducks and the Ruddy Duck.— At Catahoula Lake, Louisiana, most diving ducks eat tubers of chufa flatsedge (Wills 1971). In other habitats, ring-necked ducks eat seeds of moist-soil and aquatic plants, and some invertebrates (Bellrose 1980). Lesser scaup generally eat a greater proportion of benthic invertebrates, especially mollusks (Thompson 1973), than ruddy ducks that filter small invertebrates such as midge (Chironomidae) larvae from soft sediments. Foods that attract ruddy ducks and lesser scaup to catfish ponds in Mississippi may include commercial fish rations (Christopher 1985).

Geese.—Historically, Canada geese that wintered in the MAV probably ate shoots of grasses, sedges, and willows (*Salix* spp.) growing on islands and sandbars in the Mississippi River (Hanson and Smith 1950). Although grains such as corn and milo, and green browse from wheat and clovers, now dominate their diet (Bellrose 1980), Canada geese also readily forage in moist-soil impoundments. In southeastern Missouri, fleshy roots of buttonweed (*Diodia virginiana*), shoots and rhizomes of swamp smartweed (*Polygonum hydropiperoides*), and spikerushes (*Eleocharis obtusa, E. smallii*) were important foods (McKenzie 1987).

Foods of snow geese and white-fronted geese have not been studied in the MAV. However, in southeastern Texas and southwestern Louisiana, these geese mainly eat rice during fall and early winter, then switch to grasses and sedges during January when the rice is depleted and new vegetative growth is available (Hobaugh 1984, Leslie and Chabreck 1984).

The nutrition of wintering waterfowl has received little study (Reinecke et al. 1988*a*). Although activities of wintering waterfowl such as flight, thermoregulation, and courtship depend primarily on dietary energy, molt requires increased protein intake. Acorns, seeds of moist-soil plants, and agricultural grains are probably interchangeable as sources of dietary energy, but not as sources of protein. Invertebrates and moist-soil seeds provide a greater quantity and better quality of protein than acorns or agricultural grains (Fredrickson and Taylor 1982).

Heitmeyer (1987) described the prebasic molt of female mallards, and estimated (Heitmeyer 1988) that feather growth during the peak of molt increased daily

protein requirements by 3 g. Heitmeyer (1985) also noted that female mallards increased the proportion of invertebrates in their diet during molt, and were able to initiate prebasic molt earlier during the wet winter of 1982-83 than during 1980-81 or 1981-82 when water conditions were less favorable. There was no increase of invertebrates in food samples from female gadwalls molting during late winter in Louisiana (Paulus 1980, 1984), however, and the rate of replacement of molted flight feathers by captive wild-strain mallards fed only oats was nearly as great as the rate of replacement among mallards fed oats supplemented with turkey pellets containing 22% protein (Pehrsson 1987). In an experiment with captive wild-strain mallards in Mississippi during the winter of 1987-88, females fed *ad libitum* a commercial ration containing 12% crude protein initiated prebasic molt earlier than females fed restricted amounts of the same food (D. M. Richardson and R. M. Kaminski, unpubl. data). Thus, availability of adequate food may affect the initiation and completion of prebasic molt, but the need for a substantial increase of invertebrates in the diet remains an untested hypothesis.

Nutrition also affects body weights of wintering mallards. In Mississippi, mallard body weights increased during the wet winter of 1982-83 and decreased during the dry winter of 1980-81 (Delnicki and Reinecke 1986). Similarly, field studies in Missouri during 1980-86 indicated that mallard body weights increased when water conditions and mast production were favorable, or when rainfall was sufficient to flood low-lying cropland (Heitmeyer 1985, Combs 1987). Rainfall provides a good index to food availability in the MAV, because use of most natural and agricultural foods by dabbling ducks requires surface water.

Habitat Use and Distribution

Mallards and Other Dabbling Ducks.—Habitats used by mallards have been studied at several MAV wintering areas, including southeastern Missouri (Heitmeyer 1985, Combs 1987), western Mississippi and eastern Arkansas (Reinecke et al. 1987), and northeastern Louisiana (Dell et al. 1987). Primary foraging habitats at these sites include GTRs and naturally flooded bottomland hardwoods, moist-soil areas, and flooded cropland. Other habitats such as marshes, reservoirs, shrub swamps, beaver (*Castor canadensis*) ponds, and oxbow lakes are used as resting or roosting areas and provide isolation from human disturbance, protection from predators, and a location for courtship and other social activities. A variety or complex of habitats is needed to satisfy the biological requirements of wintering mallards because members of the population may differ in their habitat needs at any particular time. For example, juvenile or unpaired mallards may be more likely to feed in croplands than adults, pairs may seek the isolation of shrub swamps to avoid harassment from courting parties using open marshes, and molting females may forage in flooded forests to obtain invertebrates (Heitmeyer 1985).

Efforts to understand factors affecting the winter distribution of dabbling ducks in the MAV have focused primarily on mallards. Recent analyses of band recoveries have shown that: (1) proportionately more mallards are attracted to the MAV during winters with greater rainfall and, presumably, better food resources (Nichols et al. 1983); (2) mallards winter farther south in the MAV during cold winters (Nichols et al. 1983); (3) differences in the winter distribution of males and females are relatively small (Nichols and Hines 1987); and, (4) adults show greater fidelity to wintering areas than juveniles (Nichols and Hines 1987).

Precipitation and temperature also affect the distribution of mallards after arrival in the MAV. Seventy-nine (94%) of 84 radio-marked female mallards departed the area of White River National Wildlife Refuge (NWR) in Arkansas during 17 consecutive days of freezing temperatures in late December 1983 (Reinecke et al. 1987). By early January, the average location of marked females was nearly 100 km to the south. During the winter of 1984–85, however, another sample of marked females moved an average of 50 km north following heavy rains and flooding along the White, Cache, and Bayou DeView Rivers.

Dabbling ducks other than mallards generally use flooded croplands, moist-soil areas, and openings in forested wetlands. During aerial surveys in northeastern Louisiana, most dabbling duck species were observed in flooded soybean and rice fields during early winter, and in flooded pastures during late winter (Dell et al. 1987). Moist-soil areas such as Catahoula Lake in Louisiana traditionally attract large numbers of pintails and other dabbling ducks (Wills 1971). During migration, green-winged teal often use shallow dead-timber swamps and slough margins, whereas gadwalls prefer deeper wooded sloughs and dead-timber swamps with submerged aquatics (Fredrickson and Heitmeyer 1988). Northern shovelers (*Anas clypeata*) are the exception among dabbling ducks; they are more abundant in open water habitats, especially aquaculture ponds (Dubovsky and Kaminski 1987b, Christopher et al. 1988). Factors affecting the distribution of dabbling ducks other than mallards have received little study in the MAV, but patterns of natural and managed flooding probably influence distribution the most (Dell et al. 1987).

Wood Ducks.—Forested wetlands in the MAV satisfy the habitat requirements of resident wood ducks throughout the annual cycle, and the requirements of northern migrants during winter (Fredrickson and Heitmeyer 1988). Wood ducks often are observed in agricultural or other open areas (Nassar et al. 1988), but the majority use forested wetlands during winter (Dell et al. 1987). In western Missisippi, radio-marked wood ducks restricted their activities to forested wetlands (K. J. Reinecke, unpubl. data). At night, they roosted in shrub swamps with dense overhead cover, and during the day dispersed into surrounding wooded sloughs and flooded bottomland hardwoods.

Diving Ducks and the Ruddy Duck.— Habitats of diving ducks and ruddy ducks include the deeper zones of moist-soil habitats and croplands, and a variety of other wetlands such as aquaculture ponds, oxbow lakes, wooded sloughs, rivers, and reservoirs. The value of moist-soil habitat for diving ducks is illustrated by the abundance of ring-necked ducks, lesser scaup, canvasbacks, and redheads (*Aythya americana*) at Catahoula Lake, Louisiana (St. Amant 1959, Wills 1971, Dell et al. 1987). Ring-necked ducks also use deeply flooded cropland (Dell et al. 1987), and are the only diving duck to frequent wooded sloughs (Fredrickson and Heitmeyer 1988).

Recent studies in Mississippi have documented the importance of catfish ponds and identified some of the factors correlated with their use. The abundance and diversity of waterfowl associated with catfish pond complexes were positively related to the size of pond complexes and area of adjacent ponds, and negatively related to latitude and distance from the Mississippi River (Dubovsky 1987, Dubovsky and Kaminski 1987b). Indices of food resources, such as invertebrate densities and crops grown on adjacent land, had little effect on use of catfish ponds, perhaps because waterfowl exploit commercial rations fed to the catfish.

Geese.—In southern Illinois, Canada geese roost in lakes, ponds, and reservoirs, and feed primarily in croplands (Bell and Klimstra 1970, Anderson and Joyner 1985). Refuges generally are used as roosting areas, and freedom from

disturbance is an important factor affecting roost selection (Anderson and Joyner 1985). Foraging habitats include managed pastures, moist-soil impoundments, and fields of corn and small grains (Bell and Klimstra 1970, McKenzie 1987).

After arriving at wintering areas in southeastern Texas and southwestern Louisiana, white-fronted geese and snow geese feed in harvested rice fields until the rice seed is depleted or deteriorates in late December or January (Hobaugh 1984, Leslie and Chabreck 1984). Thereafter, if rainfall is adequate, geese graze in rice fields and in tilled, soybean, and fallow fields. During dry years, growth of natural vegetation is sparse, and most foraging occurs in improved pastures of wheat, ryegrass, or oats. Similar foraging habitats are available in the MAV, and irrigation reservoirs, aquaculture ponds, lakes, and flooded fields are used as roost sites.

Social Behavior

Mallards and Other Dabbling Ducks.— Courtship and pair formation dominate the social behavior of dabbling ducks during winter. Heitmeyer (1985) studied the chronology of pair formation of mallards wintering in the MAV, and found that the proportion of paired females increased from <20% during October to >80% during February. More importantly, he showed that progress of pair formation is related to habitat conditions. Females paired earliest during the winter of 1982-83 when food availability and body weights were greatest.

Black ducks, gadwalls, and American wigeon generally pair during late autumn and early winter, whereas northern shovelers, northern pintails, and green-winged teal acquire alternate plumage later and pair during middle to late winter (Hepp and Hair 1983). Food availability is probably the most important influence of habitat on the social behavior of these species, as it is among mallards. Field and experimental studies of black ducks have shown that greater food availability or body weights can advance the chronology of courtship (Brodsky and Weatherhead 1985) and pair formation (Hepp 1986).

Wood Ducks.—In southeastern Missouri, courtship among wood ducks begins during September, and by November 60% of the females were paired (Armbruster 1982). Although few wood ducks remain in Missouri throughout winter, courtship undoubtedly continues among migrants in the southern MAV, as the majority of females are paired by late January (Armbruster 1982). Little information is available on habitats used by wood ducks during courtship and pair formation.

Diving Ducks and the Ruddy Duck.— Courtship and pair formation among diving ducks generally begin in late winter, and continue during spring migration and after arrival on the breeding grounds (Weller 1965). Habitats important to diving ducks for social behavior have not been identified in the MAV.

Geese.—Among wintering geese, access to food and roost sites is related to family size (Raveling 1969). Thus, it is advantageous for juvenile geese to remain with their parents until the family returns to the breeding area. Subadult geese probably do not establish pair bonds during autumn or winter, but may engage in courtship during the final phases of spring migration (Prevett and MacInnes 1980). Managing habitat to promote family unity of geese requires controlling hunting and other disturbances that disrupt families during fall and winter (Prevett and MacInnes 1980, Bartelt 1987).

Population Dynamics

Mallards and Other Dabbling Ducks.— Heitmeyer and Fredrickson (1981) were the first to suggest that some of the variation of mallard age ratios in the Mississippi Flyway harvest could be explained by habitat conditions in the MAV, especially winter rainfall. Kaminski and Gluesing (1987) conducted a similar analysis, and reported that an index of winter habitat (i.e., water) conditions in the MAV correlated positively with mallard age ratios; however, winter habitat conditions accounted for less variation in mallard age ratios than either population density or habitat conditions on the breeding grounds. Cross-seasonal effects of winter habitat on breeding success of mallards presumably result from positive relationships between female body weights and favorable winter habitat conditions (Heitmeyer 1985, Delnicki and Reinecke 1986), and from relationships between female body weights and clutch size (Krapu 1981).

Relationships between winter habitat conditions and mallard survival rates received considerable study during the recent Stabilized Duck Hunting Regulations Evaluation. Reinecke et al. (1987) showed that seasonal survival rates of radio-marked female mallards were greatest during the winter of 1982-83 when rainfall and habitat availability increased. Band recovery rates, and presumably hunting mortality, decreased during wet winters when more feeding and resting areas were available (Blohm et al. 1987), and were negatively related to body weights of mallards banded prior to hunting seasons in the MAV (Hepp et al. 1986, Blohm et al. 1987). Differences in recovery rates between mallards banded on and off refuges indicated that refuges provide some protection from hunting mortality (Blohm et al. 1987).

Wood Ducks.—Southern wood ducks generally have higher annual survival and lower hunting mortality rates than their northern counterparts (Bowers and Martin 1975). It is unlikely, however, that winter habitat conditions in the MAV are responsible for differences in these population parameters because northern and southern wood ducks winter together.

Habitat conditions in the MAV could influence reproductive success of wood ducks, because winter body weights of wood ducks vary among years (Delnicki and Reinecke 1986). However, available data indicate that nutrient reserves deposited by female wood ducks in preparation for nesting are acquired after arrival at breeding areas (Drobney 1982).

Diving Ducks and the Ruddy Duck.— Cross-seasonal effects of winter and migration habitats on recruitment rates of diving ducks have not been studied, but are most likely to occur in early-nesting species (Alisauskas and Ankney 1990).

Geese.— Hunting is often the dominant source of mortality among geese, and may be the primary limiting factor for certain populations (Raveling and Lumsden 1977). Consequently, management of winter habitat for geese generally emphasizes control of hunting on resting and/or feeding areas. Vaught and Kirsch (1966) found that harvest of EPP Canada geese near Swan Lake NWR, Missouri, was inversely related to food production on refuge lands. In Wisconsin, mortality rates of MVP Canada geese increased during the late 1970s when goose managers reduced agricultural programs and hazed geese from refuges. Food production for geese on southern refuges probably benefits survival more than reproduction because most of the nutrient reserves important for the breeding success of midcontinent snow, white-fronted, and Canada geese are deposited on temperate and subarctic staging areas (Krapu and Reinecke 1990).

Diseases and Environmental Contaminants

The MAV is fortunate in being less subject to disease problems than wintering areas in the Central or Pacific flyways. Duck virus enteritis, fowl cholera, and botulism have been reported in the MAV, or in waterfowl populations using this area during migration or winter (Friend 1987), but extensive mortalities have not occurred.

Soil texture and rainfall patterns in the MAV facilitate the movement of agricultural chemicals to aquatic habitats, and contamination of these systems with persistent organochlorine compounds was common in the past (Schmitt and Winger 1980). Large quantities of agricultural chemicals are still applied in the MAV, but exposure to persistent organochlorines has decreased nationwide (Fleming et al. 1983) and, with the exception of local sources of continuing contamination (e.g., White et al. 1988), pesticides are not thought to be a threat to waterfowl populations in the MAV.

Lead poisoning is the most serious environmental contaminant affecting waterfowl in the MAV. The classic studies of Bellrose (1959) indicated that lead shot ingestion rates and incidents of lead poisoning mortality were greatest in the Mississippi Flyway, and suggested that 4% of Mississippi Flyway mallards and 2-3% of continental waterfowl died each year as a result of lead poisoning. Lead shot ingestion rates of mallards in the Mississippi Flyway changed relatively little between 1938-54 (8.4%) and 1977-79 (7.8%) (Anderson et al. 1987), and were greater (9.2%) in the southern (including the MAV) than in the middle (6.9%) or northern (7.4%) portions of the Mississippi Flyway during 1977-79. Lead poisoning mortality is not limited to dramatic die-offs, because Zwank et al. (1985) showed that lead poisoning was the probable cause of death of 76% of the "sick" mallards collected at Catahoula Lake, Louisiana, during a period when no outbreak was reported. Fortunately, nontoxic steel shot replaces rather than increases the quantity of shot ingested by waterfowl (Anderson et al. 1987), and a commitment has been made to progressively eliminate the use of toxic lead shot for waterfowl hunting in the U.S. (FWS 1988).

HABITAT MANAGEMENT

Cropland

Clearing of bottomland forests for farming began during the early 1700s in the southern MAV and during the middle 1700s farther north (LMRCSCC 1974b). By 1937, 3.7 million ha of the MAV were in crop production, the principal commodities being cotton (33%), corn (27%), and "other crops" (31%) (MacDonald et al. 1979). Between 1937 and 1977, there was a substantial decrease of corn production, moderate increases of wheat and rice, and a substantial increase of soybeans. By 1977, total cropland in the MAV exceeded 5.7 million ha.

Current Management Practices.—Rice, corn, grain sorghum, and soybeans are the crops most often used to provide food for waterfowl on private and public lands in the MAV. Most private croplands that are managed for waterfowl during winter are used during summer to grow cash crops of rice or soybeans, or less commonly, corn or grain sorghum. Interviews with refuge managers in the MAV indicated that corn was planted on more public waterfowl management areas than grain sorghum, rice, or soybeans.

Because rice, soybeans, grain sorghum, and corn are important cash crops in the MAV, technical assistance with production methods is available from local U.S. Department of Agriculture personnel. Management of private cropland for waterfowl generally occurs after normal agricultural harvests and consists primarily of impounding shallow water on harvested fields. Preparation of rice fields in Louisiana to attract waterfowl was described by Wesley (1979). After rice is harvested with a combine, fields are disked to loosen and mix soil with grain and straw, or rolled with a water-filled drum to create openings in the dense stubble. Then, irrigation levees are repaired and fields are flooded to a depth of approximately 20 cm. Costs of preparing fields range from $25-50/ha and depend primarily on costs for water management, which vary with initial soil moisture conditions and subsequent rainfall.

Methods of managing crops for waterfowl are more variable on public lands because refuges can use practices that would be considered baiting elsewhere. Corn may be harvested, left standing, or gradually knocked down during winter to stimulate use by waterfowl. Grain sorghum and soybeans may be harvested or left for waterfowl, and may or may not be flooded, whereas rice is always flooded.

Another group of potential foods, which may be considered agricultural crops because they are seeded each year, includes the "millets" and buckwheat (*Fagopyrum sagittatum*). Millets are grasses of the genera *Pennisetum, Panicum, Echinochloa, Setaria, Paspalum, Eleusine, Eragrostis,* and *Digitaria* (Martin et al. 1976) that are closely related to natural moist-soil species. Use of these species on MAV refuges is limited. The total area under management probably is <500 ha, most of which is planted to Japanese millet (*Echinochloa crusgalli* var. *frumentacea*). Smaller areas are managed for branched panicum (or browntop millet [*Panicum ramosum*]) or buckwheat.

Among the advantages of planting these species as food for waterfowl are low cost, rapid growth, and less susceptibility to depredations by wildlife. Although few detailed evaluations have been conducted by waterfowl researchers, general management practices have been described (Neely and Davison 1971, Martin et al. 1976, Denton 1987). Seeds of these species can be broadcast or drilled, and usually mature in about 60 days. Seeding rates are 40-70 kg/ha for buckwheat and 15-25 kg/ha for Japanese millet and branched panicum. Buckwheat and branched panicum require well-drained soils, whereas Japanese millet tolerates saturated soils and shallow flooding.

Table 2. Area planted (ha), yield (kg/ha), and production costs ($/ha) for rice, corn, grain sorghum, and soybeans in Arkansas, Louisiana, and Mississippi during 1986.

Production statistics and commodities	State		
	Arkansas[a]	Louisiana[b]	Mississippi[c]
Area planted			
Rice	413,320	48,301	80,972
Corn	27,206	146,999	4,541
Grain sorghum	237,085	90,906	45,672
Soybeans	1,269,150	550,727	533,333
Yield			
Rice	5,955	5,526	6,052
Corn	6,899	7,161	4,736
Grain sorghum	3,873	4,558	3,957
Soybeans	1,405	1,087	1,190
Production costs			
Rice	112-121	136-139	142
Corn	101	69	79
Grain sorghum	44-61	43	59-62
Soybeans	28-43	36-45	38-44

[a]Arkansas Cooperative Extension Service (unpubl. reps.).
[b]Paxton et al. (1986).
[c]Mississippi Cooperative Extension Service (1986a,b,c).

Contribution to Biological Requirements.—Croplands are primarily feeding sites for waterfowl. Under intensive management, soybean, grain sorghum, rice, and corn yields in the MAV exceed 1,000, 4,000, 5,000, and 6,000 kg/ha, respectively (Table 2). Reported yields for buckwheat, branched panicum, and Japanese millet are 1,000, 1,600-1,700, and 2,000-3,000 kg/ha (Low and Bellrose 1944, Arner 1963, Martin et al. 1976, Denton 1987). Farming on waterfowl management areas often results in low yields, however, because of limited cultivation, irrigation, and chemical applications. Fredrickson and Taylor (1982) estimated that corn production at Mingo NWR in Missouri was 62% of the national average. Food production from croplands on management areas in the MAV should be documented periodically to ensure farming programs are consistent with local and regional waterfowl management objectives. Production can be estimated directly if a cooperative farmer harvests part of a field, or determined subjectively by a manager familiar with the site.

For private croplands, food availability after harvest is more relevant to waterfowl than estimates of yield. Reinecke (unpubl. data) sampled 9 harvested rice fields in the Grand Prairie region of Arkansas during early winter in 1983-84 and 8 fields in 1984-85, and estimated that 223 and 140 kg/ha, respectively, of rice were available when migrating mallards arrived. These values are similar to an estimate of 164 kg/ha obtained in the same area during the late 1940s (McNeal 1950). Soybean losses during harvest are approximately 5% in the MAV (Mayeaux et al. 1980). Applying this rate of loss to estimated soybean yields in the MAV (Table 2) suggests that the amount of soybeans available to ducks after harvest is probably 50-70 kg/ha, which is similar to estimates of 48 and 63 kg/ha reported from Illinois (Warner et al. 1985). Soybeans deteriorate rapidly when flooded, however, and are of little value to waterfowl after 30 days under water (Shearer et al. 1969).

Another potential source of food in rice and soybean fields is seeds of grasses, sedges, and other plant species, which averaged 12 and 37 kg/ha in Arkansas rice fields during the winters of 1983-84

Table 3. Apparent and true metabolizable energy (AME and TME[a]) (kcal/g) of selected agricultural grains for mallards or Canada geese.

Common name	Mallard		Canada goose	Reference
	AME	TME	AME	
Barley	3.17			Sugden (1971)
Corn			3.97	Joyner et al. (1987)
		3.67		K. J. Reinecke (unpubl. data)
Grain sorghum			3.96	Joyner et al. (1987)
Proso millet	3.57			Purol (1975)
Rice		3.34		K. J. Reinecke (unpubl. data)
Rye	3.34			Sugden (1971)
Soybeans		2.65		K. J. Reinecke (unpubl. data)
Wheat			3.85	Joyner et al. (1987)
	3.53			Sugden (1971)
		3.38		K. J. Reinecke (unpubl. data)

[a]See Miller and Reinecke (1984) for distinction between AME and TME.

and 1984-85, respectively (K. J. Reinecke, unpubl. data). Food availability in harvested corn and grain sorghum fields has not been studied in the MAV, but average corn availability ranged from 203-447 kg/ha in Illinois (Warner et al. 1985), Iowa (Frederick and Klaas 1982), Nebraska (Reinecke and Krapu 1986), and Texas (Baldassarre et al. 1983); and grain sorghum availability ranged from 148-436 kg/ha in western Texas (Iverson et al. 1985). Small numbers of snails often are present in food samples from ducks that feed in rice fields (Delnicki and Reinecke 1986), but the biomass of invertebrates available in flooded croplands is probably small.

Decreasing foraging efficiency probably prevents waterfowl from using all the food available in croplands and other habitats. Mallards feeding by sight in dry fields in Texas reduced corn densities to 15 kg/ha (Baldassarre and Bolen 1984), but ducks that use tactile cues to feed in water probably cannot exploit food densities much less than 50 kg/ha. This hypothesis is supported by circumstantial evidence from a study in Arkansas, where samples of rice collected from fields after several weeks of feeding by dabbling ducks averaged 40-60 kg/ha (K. Reinecke, unpubl. data), and in Missouri, where mallards ate few tubers of chufa flatsedge

when their biomass in a moist soil impoundment was 71 kg/ha (McKenzie 1987).

With the exception of soybeans, metabolizable energy values of grains are consistently high, ranging from 3.17-3.97 kcal/g (Table 3). Soybeans provide less energy than other grains because they contain biochemicals that interfere with digestive enzymes and prevent assimilation of nutrients. No estimates of the metabolizable energy of Japanese millet, branched panicum, or buckwheat are available. They probably provide less energy than rice, corn, or grain sorghum, however, because small seeds have proportionally larger seed coats and more crude fiber than larger seeds.

The protein content of rice, corn, and grain sorghum is only about 10% (Natl. Res. Counc. 1977), but digestibility of the protein is relatively high. Joyner et al. (1987) estimated that approximately 80% of the protein in corn and grain sorghum was digested by Canada geese. Baldassarre et al. (1983) suggested that agricultural seeds do not contain enough protein or an adequate distribution of amino acids to provide a complete diet for wintering waterfowl. Observational data indicating that mallards feeding in agricultural fields consistently include a small percentage of invertebrates in their diet support this conclusion (Delnicki and Reinecke 1986). Moreover, recent experimental data indicate that female mallards fed only soybeans during winter are unable to maintain body weight (Loesch 1988).

Other Management Considerations.— An advantage of using cropland to produce food for waterfowl is that management methods are well known and can be delegated to staff members or cooperative farmers. Another advantage is that upland sites can be used to produce corn, grain sorghum, and soybeans. In most of the MAV, however, mallards only feed in dry fields when flooded foraging sites are unavailable because of drought or cold weather. Croplands also can be used to create opportunities for viewing waterfowl, and can be integrated with moist-soil management. Tilling and planting sections of moist-soil impoundments every few years can retard plant succession and promote moist-soil seed production without depleting natural seedbanks.

The principal disadvantages of farming are high costs and limited benefits to waterfowl other than the provision of high-energy food. Costs of producing cash crops on private lands in Arkansas, Louisiana, and Mississippi (Table 2) may not reflect costs of farming on wildlife management areas, but should indicate relative costs of providing selected foods. Ratios of yield to cost for grain sorghum and corn are similar, and both are greater than those for rice and soybeans (Table 2). If metabolizable energy (Table 3) also is considered, the ratio of yield to cost for soybeans is even less. Row crops are important for geese and several species of dabbling ducks, but provide little food for other wetland wildlife species.

Moist-Soil Impoundments

Moist-soil management relies on spring or summer drawdowns to stimulate growth of food-producing herbaceous plants from seeds and tubers present in the soil. After stands of desirable species are established, impoundments are flooded from late summer or autumn through spring to provide migration and winter habitat for waterfowl and other wetland wildlife.

Moist-soil management is well suited for use in the MAV. Natural seeds that germinate under moist-soil conditions are abundant in fertile alluvial soils (Low and Bellrose 1944, Green et al. 1964), and floodplains that have been developed for agriculture generally have good potential for creating moist-soil habitat (Fredrickson 1985, Fredrickson and Reid 1986). With proper water management, waterfowl food plants are easily established because many moist-soil plant species persist in croplands despite annual tillage.

Current Management Practices.— Moist-soil management has been described by Fredrickson and Taylor (1982) and by Reid et al. (1989). Management strategies described in these publications have resulted, in part, from research conducted in southeastern Missouri. Therefore, most plant and animal responses described in these studies should be applicable in the MAV. To avoid duplication, our review emphasizes contributions of moist-soil management to the biological requirements of migrating and wintering waterfowl, and general advantages and disadvantages of moist-soil methods.

The most effective application of moist-soil management involves complexes of impoundments, each with the capability for independent operation. Fredrickson and Reid (1986) described strategies for integrating habitat and wildlife management on such complexes to attract waterfowl and other wetland birds. Key elements of the proposed management scheme involve manipulating water levels on 5 units in the complex to make food and other habitat resources available to birds during appropriate phases of their annual cycles (Table 4). The scheme described produces habitat conditions that

Table 4. Integrated habitat manipulations recommended by Fredrickson and Reid (1986) for a hypothetical complex of 5 moist-soil impoundments.

Impoundment	Season		
	Spring	Summer	Fall
1	Late partial drawdown	Complete drawdown	Late shallow flood
2	Mid-season complete drawdown	Disc and irrigate	Late shallow flood
3	Early partial drawdown	Early complete drawdown	Early shallow flood
4	Early complete drawdown	None	Early shallow flood
5	Late complete drawdown	None	Shallow disc and flood

attract ducks, geese, passerines, and raptors during winter; and ducks, rails, waders, and shorebirds during spring and autumn (Fredrickson and Reid 1986). Although these habitat manipulations may not apply everywhere, the general concept of developing complexes of several impoundments capable of independent operation is important for enhancing habitat and wildlife diversity.

Contribution to Biological Requirements.—Seeds provide the greatest biomass of food in moist-soil habitats, but tubers, roots, rhizomes, stems, leaves, and invertebrates also can be important. Seed production varies substantially within and among plant species, and among study sites (Table 5). Data suggest that barnyardgrasses, flatsedges, beakrushes, some smartweeds, and sprangletop produce more seed than do other species for which estimates exist (Fredrickson and Taylor 1982). Water regimes also affect seed production. Fredrickson and Taylor (1982) concluded that total seed production usually is greater on impoundments after early drawdowns, and that late drawdowns result in higher plant stem densities and species diversity. Studies in the Mississippi River floodplain north of the MAV indicated that species richness and densities of invertebrates were greater in seasonally flooded moist-soil than in permanently flooded marsh impoundments (Reid 1983).

Food production in moist-soil impoundments in the MAV is difficult to assess, because most studies present estimates for samples collected randomly within stands of selected plant species rather than randomly within management units. Consequently, average food production cannot be determined unless the distribution of each species in the impoundment is known. Three studies provide data on average seed availability for entire management units (Table 6). Estimates range from 364 kg/ha for a fallow rice field in southern Louisiana to 1,629 kg/ha for intensively managed moist-soil impoundments in southeastern Missouri (Table 6). The lower estimate is probably indicative of seed yields when management efforts are limited, whereas the higher estimate illustrates potential yields (i.e., 4 times greater) with intensive management. We consider 450 kg/ha a reasonable estimate of average seed production for evaluating the carrying capacity of moist-soil impoundments in the MAV, because: (1) most moist-soil units currently under management have only partial control of water levels, (2) data regarding food production over entire management units are limited, and (3) little is known about deterioration of seeds prior to arrival of waterfowl.

Although densities, distribution, and seasonal abundance of invertebrates have been investigated in moist-soil habitats,

Table 5. Estimated biomass (kg/ha) of dry seeds or tubers produced by selected species of moist-soil plants.

Common name	Scientific name	Biomass	Reference
Pondweed	*Potamogeton americanus*	940	Low and Bellrose (1944)
Signalgrass	*Brachiaria extensa*	15	Davis et al. (1961)
Brownseed paspalum	*Paspalum plicatulum*	3	Harmon et al. (1960)
		104	Davis et al. (1961)
Warty panicum	*P. verrucosum*	274	Arner (1963)
Fall panicum	*Panicum dichotomiflorum*	55	Davis et al. (1961)
Wild millets		140	Davis et al. (1961)
Barnyardgrass	*Echinochloa crusgalli*	17	Harmon et al. (1960)
		993	Arner et al. (1974)
		2,925	Low and Bellrose (1944)
Coast barnyardgrass	*E. walteri*	14	Jemison and Chabreck (1962)
		913	Singleton (1951)
		1,499	Low and Bellrose (1944)
Giant bristlegrass	*Setaria magna*	1	Jemison and Chabreck (1962)
Lovegrass	*Eragrostis hypnoides*	396	Low and Bellrose (1944)
Red sprangletop	*Leptochloa filiformis*	1	Jemison and Chabreck (1962)
Red rice	*Oryza sativa* var.	4	Davis et al. (1961)
Rice cutgrass	*Leersia oryzoides*	154	Singleton (1951)
Flatsedge	*Cyperus albomarginatus*	1	Harmon et al. (1960)
Fragrant flatsedge	*C. odoratus*	121	Jemison and Chabreck (1962)
Rice flatsedge	*C. iria*	2	Harmon et al. (1960)
Chufa flatsedge			
(akenes)		115	Low and Bellrose (1944)
(tubers)		37	Kelley (1986)
		2,046[a]	Wills (1970)
Straw-colored flatsedge	*C. strigosus*	333	Low and Bellrose (1944)
Redroot flatsedge	*C. erythrorhizos*	293	Arner (1963)
		673	Low and Bellrose (1944)
Squarestem spikerush	*Eleocharis quadrangulata*	1	Harmon et al. (1960)
		9	Singleton (1951)
Bullwhip bulrush	*Scirpus californicus*	49	Singleton (1951)
		62	Harmon et al. (1960)
Horned beakrush	*Rhynchospora corniculata*	876	Brock (1987)
		1,022	Singleton (1951)
Sawgrass	*Cladium jamaicensis*	386	Jemison and Chabreck (1962)
Smartweeds	*Polygonum* spp.	50	Davis et al. (1961)
Marsh knotweed	*P. coccineum*	49	Low and Bellrose (1944)
Stout smartweed	*P. densiflorum*	503	Brock (1987)
		540	Arner et al. (1974)
Curltop ladysthumb	*P. lapathifolium*	519	Arner et. al. (1974)
		772	Low and Bellrose (1944)
Pennsylvania smartweed	*P. pensylvanicum*	528	Arner et al. (1974)
		1,000	Low and Bellrose (1944)
Dotted smartweed	*P. punctatum*	150	Low and Bellrose (1944)
		166	Olinde et al. (1985)
Swamp smartweed		18	Toth et al. (1972)
		53	Brock (1987)
		79	Arner et al. (1974)
		172	Arner (1963)
		653	Singleton (1951)
Marshpurslane	*Ludwigia glandulosa*	927	Brock (1987)
Dodder	*Cuscuta* sp.	7	Jemison and Chabreck (1962)

[a]Assumes that dry weight is 36.4% of wet weight (J. R. Kelley, unpubl. data).

Table 6. Estimated biomass (kg/ha) of dry plant seeds available in moist-soil habitats in southern Louisiana and southeastern Missouri.

Location	Habitat	Species	Biomass	Reference
Louisiana	Fallow ricefield	Millets	140	Davis et al. (1961)
		Paspalums	104	
		Fall panicum	55	
		Smartweeds	50	
		Signalgrass	15	
		Total	364	
Louisiana	Seasonally flooded coastal marsh	Sawgrass	386	Jemison and Chabreck (1962)
		Flatsedges	121	
		Bullwhip bulrush	62	
		Coast barnyardgrass	14	
		Giant bristlegrass	1	
		Sprangletop	1	
		Total 585		
Missouri	Moist-soil impoundments	All species combined	Total 1,629	Fredrickson and Taylor (1982)

few data on biomass are available. In one study, however, estimates of the seasonal biomass of invertebrates associated with emergent and submersed aquatics averaged about 50 kg (wet)/ha or 10-20 kg (dry)/ha (Arner et al. 1974). Thus, the contribution of invertebrates to food availability in moist-soil impoundments is probably more important qualitatively than quantitatively. Also, many moist-soil impoundments in the MAV are not flooded as early in autumn as originally recommended (Fredrickson and Taylor 1982). This delay probably decreases deterioration of seeds, but may also inhibit development of invertebrate populations.

Nutritional characteristics of foods produced in moist-soil impoundments generally are good. The gross energy of seeds of moist-soil plants is similar to that of agricultural grains (Fredrickson and Taylor 1982). Not all of the gross energy is available to waterfowl, however, because moist-soil seeds contain more indigestible crude fiber than agricultural grains. The proportion of crude fiber in moist-soil seeds generally varies from 10-20% (Fredrickson and Taylor 1982), whereas most grains are <10% (Natl. Res. Counc. 1977). Direct estimates of the metabolizable energy of selected natural seeds for mallards and northern pintails (Hoffman and

Bookhout 1985) varied from 1.08 and 1.25 kcal/g, respectively, for Pennsylvania smartweed, to 3.00 and 2.82 kcal/g for rice cutgrass (Table 7). Given available data, 2.5 kcal/g is a reasonable estimate of the average metabolizable energy of seeds produced in moist-soil impoundments.

Foods available in moist-soil habitats provide good sources of protein and minerals. The crude protein content of most natural seeds ranges from 10-20%, and is nearly 25% for beggarticks (*Bidens* spp.) (Fredrickson and Taylor 1982). The protein content of invertebrates often exceeds 50% (dry) (Krapu and Swanson 1975), and even small quantities of invertebrates substantially increase the percentage of protein in diets dominated by agricultural grains (Reinecke and Krapu 1986). Invertebrates and natural seeds provide, at least collectively, a better distribution of amino acids and more minerals than agricultural grains (Baldassarre et al. 1983, Heitmeyer 1985).

Moist-soil impoundments also provide an interspersion of open water and vegetation, and a diversity of water depths attractive to various species of waterfowl. Water depth and presence of emergent vegetation are factors associated with niche partitioning among wintering duck

Table 7. Apparent and true metabolizable energy (AME and TME[a]) (kcal/g) of selected moist-soil seeds and an aquatic invertebrate for mallards and/or northern pintails.

Common name	Mallard		Pintail		Reference
	AME	TME	AME	TME	
Barnyardgrass			2.89		Miller (1987)
Junglerice barnyardgrass (*Echinochloa colonum*)		2.54			K. J. Reinecke (unpubl. data)
Coast barnyardgrass		2.86		2.82	Hoffman and Bookhout (1985)
Rice cutgrass		3.00		2.82	Hoffman and Bookhout (1985)
Pennsylvania smartweed		1.08		1.25	Hoffman and Bookhout (1985)
Soldierfly (Stratiomyiidae) larvae	2.39				Purol (1975)

[a]See Miller and Reinecke (1984) for distinction between AME and TME.

species (White and James 1978). Open water provides access to food resources and sites for courtship and other social behavior, whereas vegetation contributes thermal cover, isolation, and loafing sites.

Other Management Considerations.— Moist-soil management is relatively economical (Fredrickson and Taylor 1982). Costs for constructing and maintaining levees and manipulating water levels are similar for moist-soil and cropland impoundments, but moist-soil management eliminates all of the costs of seeding and fertilizing, and some of the costs for tillage and chemicals used to control undesirable vegetation. Principal costs of moist-soil management result from flooding, disking, burning, and application of chemicals to maintain productive plant communities.

Moist-soil management also is less susceptible to adverse weather than farming. Drought is probably equally damaging to both habitats, but flooding has a greater negative effect on crops than on moist-soil vegetation. Floods that eliminate annual agricultural production only alter the species composition of moist-soil impoundments. Smartweeds respond to spring drawdowns, whereas early and late summer drawdowns favor barnyardgrasses and sprangletop, respectively (Fredrickson and Taylor 1982).

Another advantage of moist-soil management is the ability to provide habitat for upland and wetland wildlife other than waterfowl. During long-term studies in Missouri, Fredrickson and Reid (1986) observed >150 species of birds, including ducks, geese, herons, rails, and shorebirds, as well as mammals, amphibians, and reptiles in moist-soil impoundments.

Moist-soil management has relatively few shortcomings. Frequent inspections of moist-soil impoundments by wetland managers are necessary, especially during drawdowns, to monitor development of desirable or initiate control of undesirable plant species (Fredrickson and Taylor 1982). Biological expertise needed to evaluate plant responses may limit the number of staff members to whom management responsibilities can be delegated. Also, the degree of water control required for consistently good seed production is currently available at only a few sites in the MAV. Most existing moist-soil impoundments have gravity drainage capabilities, but few have dependable sources of ground or surface water for irrigation. Another potential problem is that waterfowl using moist-soil impoundments or impoundment complexes are susceptible to disturbance. Impoundments often are developed in clusters for efficient levee construction and water management. If disturbance is not controlled, frequent maintenance, research, and public use activities can affect waterfowl use of management units. Nevertheless, the wide applicability, relative economy, and benefits of moist-soil habitat to waterfowl and other wildlife greatly outweigh disadvantages.

Bottomland Hardwoods and GTRs

Waterfowl managers are interested in the entire forested wetland complex, but direct most of their management efforts toward the species of oaks that produce acorns for waterfowl. Fortunately, these species also are valuable for timber production, and management practices designed to enhance growth and quality of timber stands generally promote acorn production. The most intensively managed bottomland hardwood sites are GTRs, which use levees and water-control structures to provide dependable flooding of forested wetlands for migrating and wintering waterfowl (see Mitchell and Newling 1986, for guidelines regarding GTR development). More than 100 GTRs are currently under management in the MAV (Wigley and Filer 1989).

GTRs have been the subject of a number of investigations, because managed water regimes modify soil moisture and nutrient relationships, and have the potential for altering plant and animal communities (Fredrickson 1979). General perceptions among managers are that GTRs decrease reproduction and increase mortality of desirable tree species, but that they have little effect on acorn production or tree growth (Wigley and Filer 1989). Unfortunately, studies of GTR and bottomland hardwood management, like most large-scale field ecological studies (Hurlbert 1984), generally lack true replication of treatments. Thus, results must be interpreted cautiously, and the generality of findings judged by the consistency of treatment effects among independent studies.

Current Management Practices

Water Regimes.—Most bottomland hardwood stands are subject to natural or uncontrolled flooding; the remainder are in GTRs that have partial or complete control of water levels. Natural flooding in the MAV results from surface ponding of rainfall or overflow from rivers and streams (Fredrickson and Heitmeyer 1988), and is variable from year to year. Reinecke (unpubl. data) determined that water depths favorable for feeding by mallards occurred in bottomland forests at White River NWR in Arkansas during 31 (58%) of 53 winters from 1932-85. By comparison, winter flooding of GTRs is highly predictable. A recent survey of GTR managers indicated that 95% of GTRs are flooded every year (Wigley and Filer 1989).

GTRs and natural sites also differ regarding the timing of flooding, which generally begins and ends earlier in GTRs than in natural areas (White 1985). Theoretically, GTRs should be flooded after tree growth has ended in autumn, and should be drained before growth resumes in spring (Rudolph and Hunter 1964). In recent years, the median dates that managers located north and south of 36 degrees latitude planned to flood GTRs were 15 October and 1 November, respectively (Wigley and Filer 1989). Most southern managers tried to flood GTRs in November, whereas equal numbers of northern managers flooded GTRs in September, October, and November. The median dates southern and northern managers intended to drain GTRs during spring were 10 March and 1 April. Southern GTRs were drained most frequently in March, and northern GTRs in April. GTR managers generally completed fall flooding on schedule, but often had difficulty completing spring drainage because of interference from beavers, natural flooding, and vandals (Wigley and Filer 1989).

Natural Succession and the Role of Timber Harvesting.—Succession in bottomland hardwoods generally results in the dominance of shade-tolerant species such as elms, red ash (*Fraxinus pennsylvanica*), red maple, and sugar hackberry, and a decrease of shade-intolerant red oaks (Hodges and Switzer 1979, Lea 1988). Smith (1984), for example, noted that pin oak seedlings were abundant in forest openings in Missouri when conditions for germination were favorable, yet few seedlings survived beneath closed canopies for >1 or 2 years. Similarly, Johnson (1975) reported that Nuttall oak seedlings in Mississippi survived 5-15 years in shade, but were only 1 m tall. Experiments demonstrating that photosynthetic rates of 1- and 2-year-old pin oak seedlings growing in flooded and control plots were limited primarily by availability of light in the understory (D. J. Moorhead, unpubl. data) also support the hypothesis that red oaks require the increased light available in forest openings to ensure growth and survival. Thus, active management may be necessary to maintain a substantial component of mast-producing oaks in bottomland hardwood forests.

Timber harvests can be used to influence the species composition of future forest stands. The success of harvesting methods in regenerating, or ensuring the replacement of, shade-intolerant bottomland hardwoods varies with the species composition of the previous stand and harvesting method applied (Kennedy and Johnson 1984).

The most effective harvesting method for regenerating red oaks is small clearcuts, which combine some of the features of shelterwood, clearcutting, and coppice silvicultural methods to create an uneven-aged forest of even-aged patches (Lea 1988). A prerequisite for successful regeneration of red oaks and other shade-intolerant hardwoods is the establishment of seedlings (or advance regeneration) of the desired species in the understory before harvest. Partial or shelterwood cuts are then used to create the openings necessary for seedling development, the adequacy of which can be assessed before the clearcut is completed (Sander et al. 1976, Ashley 1979, Marquis and Bjorkhom 1982). After the final harvest, competition among herbaceous plants, vines, and seedlings is intense, and development

of the new forest stand often appears disappointing. Less desirable species such as American hornbeam (*Carpinus caroliniana*) initially dominate some stands, but these species become suppressed over time (Bowling and Kellison 1983, Johnson and Krinard 1988). Nuttall oaks may require 15 to 20 years to attain competitive positions in the developing forest canopy (Krinard and Kennedy 1987).

Openings created to encourage reproduction of oaks should be >0.5 ha. Clearcuts of 1-4 ha are sometimes referred to as "group selection" cuts, but should not be confused with the smaller group selection cuts used in the uneven-aged silvicultural system. Small clearcuts that minimize aesthetic problems while providing openings for development of oaks are currently the most effective method for integrating timber and waterfowl management.

In the shelterwood harvesting method, trees are removed during a series of partial cuts, similar to thinnings, which gradually open the overstory and increase light levels at the forest floor (Loftis 1983). This method has often been recommended as an effective way to encourage reproduction of shade-intolerant species before the final harvest, but results have been inconsistent (Sander 1979, Loftis 1983, Smith et al. 1983). Modifications such as control of understory and midstory competition (Janzen and Hodges 1985, Hodges and Janzen 1987), or enrichment or underplanting (Nix et al. 1985), may improve results.

Selection harvesting methods are designed to create and maintain uneven-aged stands. Trees in all diameter classes are harvested or otherwise removed to achieve a balanced size or age distribution of seedlings, saplings, and larger trees. Unfortunately, the intended distribution is seldom attained. There are 2 basic variations of the selection method, single-tree and group selection. In single-tree selection, individual mature trees are harvested and seedlings develop in the resulting openings. Single-tree selection is not often used to manage bottomland hardwoods for timber production because it favors shade-tolerant species and is the least efficient of all harvesting methods. Regeneration of oaks and other shade-intolerant species can be achieved by group selection harvesting of trees from sites <0.5 ha in area, but periodic stand improvement cutting must be done to ensure the growth and survival of desirable species, and regulation of treatments to accomplish this is difficult. Like single-tree selection, harvesting operations in group selection methods are less efficient than those in even-aged management.

Effects of GTRs on Tree Growth and Species Composition.—Recent studies have suggested that gradual changes in species composition are occurring in GTRs in Missouri and Mississippi, with the abundance of pin oaks and Nuttall oaks decreasing, at least in the understory, and water-tolerant species such as water hickory, overcup oak, and red maple increasing (Newling 1981, Smith 1984). Thus, it is important to understand effects of GTR water management practices on seed production, germination, growth, and survival of oaks and other bottomland hardwood species.

Acorn production in GTRs seems adequate for the regeneration of oaks (McQuilkin and Musbach 1977), and it is unlikely that flooding prevents germination of acorns or seeds of other bottomland hardwoods (Briscoe 1961, DuBarry 1963). Responses of seedlings to flooding vary among species relative to the timing and duration of flooding (Hosner 1958, 1960; Krinard and Johnson 1981), and include closure of leaf stomatae, reduction of photosynthesis, alteration of hormonal balances, and decreased nutrient uptake (Kozlowski and Pallardy 1984). When prolonged flooding occurs during the growing season, cherrybark oak and

other species that are sensitive to saturated soils recover slowly and incompletely (Pezeshki and Chambers 1985), whereas seedlings of red ash and other water tolerant species recover completely (Kozlowski and Pallardy 1979). Red ash, water hickory, and overcup oak also avoid stresses that result from floods occurring early in the growing season by initiating leaf development as much as a month later than other species (Broadfoot and Williston 1973).

Winter flooding and temporary flooding during the growing season have little short-term detrimental effect on mature bottomland hardwoods. Black (1984) studied the phenology and water relationships of 40- to 45-year-old pin oaks subjected to winter flooding, temporary flooding during the growing season, and continuous flooding. Annual winter flooding for >20 years did not affect water relationships or leaf development of pin oaks. Short-term flooding during the growing season resulted in a temporary loss of stomatal control and advanced the onset of autumn leaf senescence by 2 weeks compared to trees on naturally flooded control plots. During the first year of continuous flooding, water relationships of pin oaks were normal, but autumn leaf senescence began 2 weeks earlier than in control plots. Leaf development and water relationships were normal during the second year of continuous flooding, but flower production decreased, developing acorns aborted, and leaves became chlorotic in August. Broadfoot (1958) observed similar responses in cherrybark oaks and willow oaks during the second year of continuous flooding.

Results of research on the long-term effects of GTRs on growth and survival rates of mature trees have been inconsistent. Early studies in Mississippi (Broadfoot 1958, 1967) noted increased tree and stand growth during years immediately following initiation of GTR management, and attributed the positive response to increased availability of soil moisture during the growing season. In more recent studies, Newling (1981) reported that a Mississippi GTR had no effect on diameter growth of Nuttall oak or sugar hackberry, and positive and negative effects, respectively, on overcup oak and red ash, whereas Schlaegel (1984) concluded that 17 years of winter flooding decreased volume growth and increased mortality of Nuttall oaks in the same GTR. Fredrickson (1979) reported that a Missouri GTR increased growth of overcup oaks, but had no effect on growth of pin oaks or willow oaks. In the same study area, Smith (1984) and Rogers and Sander (1989) found that growth of pin oaks from GTRs and control sites were similar, but also noted that growth of pin oaks in GTRs did not respond positively to thinning treatments. Inconsistent or negative long-term effects of GTRs on growth and survival of pin oaks and Nuttall oaks, and positive effects on overcup oaks, suggest that current management practices favor species that are more tolerant of flooding.

Acorn Production.—The most important sources of variation in acorn production probably are annual variation and spatial variation among forest stands having different proportions of red oaks in the canopy. Variation of acorn production with stand composition has not been investigated, but data from a 14-year study in southeastern Missouri (McQuilkin and Musbach 1977) indicated that average acorn production ranged from 7 kg(wet)/ha in 1967 to 405 kg(wet)/ha in 1957, and appeared to cycle at intervals of 4-5 years.

Other factors affecting acorn production are environmental conditions, and the size, crown development, and individual characteristics of trees. Freezing temperatures during flowering, for example, can substantially decrease subsequent acorn production (Gysel 1956). In Missouri, stands of pin oaks and willow oaks

with trees >27.9 cm diameter at breast height (DBH) produced 10-20% more acorns than stands with comparable basal areas of trees <25.4 cm DBH (McQuilkin and Musbach 1977). Studies in Arkansas and Mississippi (Cypert and Webster 1948, Francis 1983) showed that some individual oaks were consistently good acorn producers, and indicated that trees with crowns in a dominant position in the canopy, receiving full sunlight from the sides as well as above, were better acorn producers than codominant trees receiving light only from above.

The effect of GTRs on acorn production was investigated in Missouri (McQuilkin and Musbach 1977) where availability of fully developed acorns to waterfowl was comparable in a GTR and adjacent naturally flooded sites over 14 years. Total acorn production in the control plots was greater, but dormant season flooding in the GTR apparently killed weevil (*Curculio* spp.) pupae wintering in the soil, and the resulting decrease in acorn damage by weevil larvae compensated for differences in total acorn production. Nuttall oaks on naturally flooded plots in Mississippi produced nearly twice as many acorns as those in a GTR over a 5-year period (Francis 1983). The effect of delayed spring drainage of GTRs on acorn production has not been studied, but probably is similar to that of continuous flooding, which generally results in decreased flower production and aborted acorn development during the second growing season (Broadfoot 1958, Black 1984).

Restoration of Bottomland Hardwoods.—Since 1981, >1,500 ha have been manually or mechanically seeded with acorns to restore selected species of oaks on former farmland in the MAV (Johnson and Krinard 1987). Collecting acorns for seeding required substantial effort, with costs for labor averaging $50/ha. Fortunately, red oak acorns collected during a year of good production provide viable seed for 2 or 3 years. Recommendations are to plant acorns 5-10 cm deep and at least 1 m apart in rows separated by 3 to 4 m. Seeding can be done manually without site preparation or with a modified soybean planter following disking or other treatments. Preliminary results indicate that about 35% of the acorns planted produce seedlings at a cost of $80-125/ha. Success of plantings, like timber-stand development following clearcuts, is difficult to assess initially because of the presence of competing vegetation, but by 15-20 years, oaks should be well represented in the developing canopy.

Management Guidelines for GTRs

Water management and control of timber harvesting are the most useful tools for maintaining productivity of GTRs. Flooding of GTRs during fall should not begin until trees become dormant, as indicated by the onset of autumn coloration and leaf fall. Water depths should be <30-40 cm to facilitate feeding by ducks (Heitmeyer 1985). Drainage during spring should be completed by the time new leaves begin to develop, unless GTRs are dominated by water-tolerant species such as overcup oak and water hickory. Spring drawdowns should be gradual to concentrate aquatic invertebrates for migrating waterfowl and to retain nutrients in GTRs. Fluctuating water levels and occasional winters without flooding simulate natural water regimes better than stable water levels, and may be necessary for decomposition of detritus and cycling of nutrients. Drainage of beaver ponds and other sites that retain water should be facilitated; otherwise, overcup oak, water hickory, and red ash will gradually replace less water-tolerant species such as pin, Nuttall, willow, and cherrybark oaks.

Application of traditional timber-stand improvement practices in GTRs and naturally flooded bottomland hardwood stands is often limited by the manpower and funds available at wildlife management areas. If resources are available, periodic thinning and improvement cuttings can be used to control stand density and to improve the composition and quality of remaining trees. Intervals between treatments are about 10 years, but depend on age, density, and vigor of the timber stand. Cutting cycles usually are shortest in young vigorous stands on good sites. Trees removed at each cutting are selected from species that are less desirable for timber or mast production, trees of poor quality, or those removed for density control. Oaks that are >25 cm DBH and in dominant or codominant positions in the forest canopy should be retained for current acorn production. To ensure future acorn production, stands containing oaks that are <25 cm DBH should be thinned to maintain or increase growth rates and promote crown development.

Good seed crops can be infrequent in red oaks (Johnson 1975), and flooding of GTRs should be withheld for 2 or 3 winters following a year of exceptional acorn production to encourage seedling establishment. If natural seed sources are unavailable, acorns can be planted in limited areas to establish desirable species before the overstory is harvested. Reduced transmission of sunlight to the forest floor limits the growth of red oak seedlings in GTRs with closed canopies, and thinning of the forest overstory is necessary to provide sufficient light for seedling development. Occasionally, local application of herbicides may be necessary to release seedlings from competition with less desirable species. Small clearcuts are currently the recommended method of harvesting bottomland hardwoods to create the openings necessary for growth of shade-intolerant red oaks.

Contribution to Biological Requirements

The only quantitative data regarding

Table 8. Observed biomass (kg[dry]/ha[a]) of acorns in bottomland hardwood stands in Missouri at 3 levels of production (McQuilkin and Musbach 1977), and biomass predicted for other stands assuming acorn production is proportional to the percent basal area of red oaks among trees >25 cm diameter at breast height.

% basal area of red oaks	Observed or predicted	Annual acorn production		
		Low	Average	High
20	Predicted	1	18	51
40	Predicted	2	36	102
80	Observed	4	71	204

[a]Assumes dry weight of edible part of acorns = 0.5 × wet weight of whole acorns (K. J. Reinecke, unpubl. data).

food availability in bottomland hardwoods are from the series of studies at Mingo Swamp in Missouri (Minckler and McDermott 1960, Minckler and Janes 1965, McQuilkin and Musbach 1977), in which pin oaks and willow oaks together comprised 79-88% of the basal area of stands sampled. Mean annual biomass of acorns collected in elevated baskets ranged from 7-405 kg(wet)/ha, and averaged 142 kg/ha. Because shell and water contribute about 50% of the fresh weight of acorns (K. J. Reinecke, unpubl. data), production of potential food in the Missouri studies averaged approximately 71 kg(dry)/ha. Thus, average acorn production in bottomland hardwood stands in the Missouri studies was less than the average availability of food in moist-soil impoundments, and probably less than that of most harvested croplands other than soybeans. Maximum acorn production was, however, comparable to food availability in harvested croplands. The metabolizable energy of the dry, edible portion of acorns (about 3.5 kcal/g [K. J. Reinecke, unpubl. data]) is greater than that of moist-soil seeds, but less than that of cereal grains.

If acorn production is proportional to the percent basal area of red oaks among the larger trees (e.g., >25 cm DBH) in a timber stand, then average acorn production of stands containing various percentages of oaks can be approximated using the Missouri data (Table 8). Assuming 50 kg (dry)/ha of food is necessary to attract feeding waterfowl, as discussed earlier, we can make general predictions regarding the probability or frequency of mallards feeding in bottomland hardwood stands relative to stand composition and acorn production (Fig. 4). Limited field observations are consistent with the predicted responses (Fig. 4). Mallards did not feed in bottomland hardwoods at Mingo Swamp during a year of poor acorn production (Combs 1987). However, mallards did feed in flooded hardwood stands at Mingo Swamp during 4 of 6 winters from 1980-86 (Heitmeyer 1985, Combs 1987), suggesting that availability of acorns was adequate in stands containing a large proportion of red oaks during years when production was average or better (Fig. 4). At White River NWR in Arkansas, few bottomland hardwood stands contain >20-30% red oaks (U.S. Fish and Wildl. Serv., unpubl. data, White River NWR, DeWitt, Ark.). Intensive feeding by mallards in bottomland hardwoods occurred only once at White River NWR during the winters of 1982-88 (C. W. Shaiffer, pers. commun.), and that was during a year of particularly good acorn production. No data are available to interpret responses for other combinations of stand characteristics and acorn production rates.

Data regarding biomass of aquatic invertebrates in bottomland hardwoods are limited. In Missouri, White (1985) sampled invertebrates during the winter of 1979-80 and estimated a mean biomass of 13.7 kg(dry)/ha. Invertebrate biomass may underestimate production, but mal-

ACORN PRODUCTION

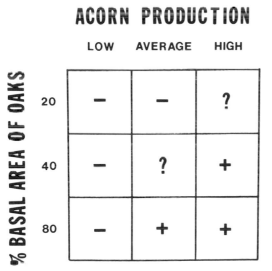

Fig. 4. Hypothetical responses of mallards to opportunities for feeding on acorns in flooded bottomland forests at 3 levels of acorn production and forest stand composition. + = positive response; − = limited or no response; ? = response unknown.

lards are unlikely to exploit invertebrates at these densities unless other foods such as acorns are available or invertebrates are concentrated by declining water levels.

Forested wetlands provide important habitat values other than food. In Mississippi, radio-marked mallards returned from feeding on private croplands to roost in shrub and wooded swamps on refuges, apparently to obtain security from human and natural predators (K. J. Reinecke, unpubl. data). Forested wetlands also provide mallards with sites for loafing and maintenance activities, protection from predators during courtship, and opportunities for isolation following pair formation (Heitmeyer 1985).

The overall role of forested wetlands in the population dynamics of mallards wintering in the MAV is difficult to determine, because the influences of natural and agricultural habitats are confounded. When water and habitat conditions in forested wetlands are favorable, low-lying croplands also are flooded.

Other Management Considerations

Management of forested wetlands for waterfowl ensures the availability of habitat for many other wildlife species. Flooding of forested wetlands increases habitat for the reproduction and growth of many fish. Semiaquatic and aquatic mammals, including mink (*Mustela vison*), otter (*Lutra canadensis*), nutria (*Myocastor coypu*), and beaver are abundant in forested wetlands, whereas large omnivores and carnivores such as the black bear (*Ursus americanus*), cougar (*Felis concolor*), and red wolf (*Canis rufus*) now are restricted in range or are locally extinct. Bottomland hardwoods typically support greater densities of breeding and wintering forest birds than adjacent upland forests (Dickson 1978).

Because of their extent and functional characteristics, forested wetlands provide important ecosystem values as well as wildlife habitat. Storage of floodwaters is one of the most important ecological functions of forested wetlands in the MAV. It has been estimated, for example, that clearing and draining of bottomland forests have reduced flood storage capacity of the MAV from the equivalent of 60-days discharge of the Mississippi River to about 12 days (Mitsch and Gosselink 1986).

Unlike croplands and moist-soil impoundments, forested wetlands on wildlife management areas can generate revenues. In the late 1970s, estimates of net annual income from bottomland hardwoods in the MAV ranged from $10-160/ha, depending on stand composition and site characteristics (MacDonald et al. 1979). Bottomland forests also provide most of the opportunities available on public lands for waterfowl hunting.

Disadvantages of managing forested wetlands for waterfowl include (1) mean food production is relatively low, and temporal and spatial variation of production is great, (2) site characteristics often limit options for increasing food production, and (3) long-term commitments are needed to solve research and management problems. Variation of food production and water conditions periodically limit food availability in forested wetlands. Acorn production in Missouri failed during at least 4 years from 1956-69 (McQuilkin and Musbach 1977), and acorn production in Mississippi failed 2 years from 1975-79 (Francis 1983). Water conditions during these years are unknown, but probably further reduced food availability in certain winters.

Site characteristics often limit the extent to which managers can increase mast production in existing forest stands because red oaks occur primarily on temporarily and seasonally flooded sites, most of which already have been cleared for crop production (Klimas 1988). Forest stands dominated by overcup oak and other water-tolerant species cannot be managed for red oaks because of excessive flooding or soil saturation. Poor soil drainage also limits crop production as an alternative on these sites, but may be compatible with moist-soil management unless flooding is severe enough to damage levees and water control structures.

The length of time needed to restore or alter the species composition of forested wetlands is a problem because public agencies often acquire bottomland hardwood tracts that have been managed with little concern for future stand composition. A minimum of 20-30 years is needed to restore acorn production on these sites (McQuilkin and Musbach 1977), assuming adequate seed sources are available and efforts are made to encourage the growth of oaks. Researchers face similar problems. Studies on the effects of environmental conditions or management practices on the growth, fruit production, or survival of important tree species may require decades to complete (e.g., McQuilkin and Musbach 1977, Krinard

and Kennedy 1987), whereas responses to treatments applied in croplands or moist-soil impoundments generally can be observed in <1 year.

Habitat Complexes

The importance of complexes or functional groups of different wetland habitat types was first recognized in prairie breeding areas where complexes of prairie wetlands of varying water permanence and salinity satisfy the requirements of a diverse community of breeding waterfowl (Krapu and Duebbert 1989). The value of wetland complexes to wintering waterfowl was recognized by Fredrickson and Heitmeyer (1988). In the MAV, habitat complexes are important locally and regionally. At the local level, forested wetland habitat complexes include oxbow lakes, shrub and wooded swamps, and seasonally flooded bottomland hardwoods, whereas waterfowl-habitat management complexes include croplands, moist-soil impoundments, and forested wetlands. Regional habitat complexes involve combinations of artificially and naturally flooded public and private land.

Forested Wetland Habitat Complexes.— Historically, mallards wintering in the MAV satisfied most of their habitat requirements in forested wetlands. Given the original extent of bottomland forests, mallards probably found abundant food, especially acorns, and favorable water conditions somewhere in the MAV during most winters. The behavior of mallards prior to development of the MAV was probably not much different than that observed at Mingo Swamp during recent years (Heitmeyer 1985, Combs 1987). A complex of natural habitats enabled mallards to feed on acorns and invertebrates in flooded forests or on seeds of moist-soil plants in beaver swamps and slough margins, to roost and court in more open marshes and sloughs, and to escape predation and social harassment in shrub swamps.

Continued management of forested wetland complexes provides valuable habitat for waterfowl and a variety of other wildlife species. However, forested wetlands no longer afford complete winter habitat for mallards. When mast production fails locally, there are not enough alternative bottomland hardwood sites remaining for mallards to find sufficient food elsewhere. Consequently, management of forested wetlands should be integrated with other management methods that provide alternative foods.

Waterfowl Habitat Management Complexes.—The objectives of many waterfowl management areas in the MAV are to provide habitat for migrating and wintering waterfowl, maintain a diversity of wildlife species, and operate within a reasonable budget. Habitat complexes can satisfy these objectives more effectively than individual habitats, because the strengths of one management method compensate for the weaknesses of another. Forested wetlands provide excellent wildlife habitat with low management costs, but food production for waterfowl is limited. Moist-soil impoundments are intermediate in management costs and food production, and provide habitat for a diversity of wetland and upland wildlife species. Crop production provides the greatest yield of waterfowl food per unit area, but management costs are high and benefits to other wildlife generally are low. Habitat complexes also are complementary regarding quality of waterfowl foods produced. Croplands primarily provide energy, whereas natural foods contribute energy, protein, and other nutrients.

Although the advantages of habitat complexes are clear, the best ratio of habitat types is less obvious. Farming probably should be limited to the minimum area necessary to satisfy food production objectives that are not attainable with moist-soil impoundments and forested wetlands. Moist-soil impound-

ments generally produce more food and are more consistently productive than bottomland forests. Moist-soil management should be increased in the MAV consistent with the availability of adequate sites and funds for development and operation. Forested wetlands should remain an important habitat on refuges in the MAV because of their low management costs and general wildlife habitat values.

Regional Complexes of Public and Private Land.—Just as habitat management complexes provide different benefits to waterfowl than individual habitats, habitats on public and private land function differently at the regional level. Public lands provide waterfowl with important food resources, diverse natural habitats, and refuges, and provide people with hunting and viewing opportunities. Although limited in number, public management areas also contribute to the maintenance of historic patterns of waterfowl distribution.

Private lands that are actively managed for waterfowl provide important food resources and hunting opportunities, but often have limited habitat diversity and food quality. Unmanaged private lands become attractive to waterfowl with seasonal flooding. Both categories of private land are important to the maintenance of waterfowl distribution patterns because of their great number and wide distribution.

CLASSIFICATION, STATUS, AND TRENDS OF WINTER HABITAT
Classifying Winter Habitat for Regional Planning

Assessing the status of winter habitat in the MAV and measuring progress toward goals of the NAWMP can be facilitated by adopting an effective habitat classification system. A classification system comprising 4 habitat types and 3 land ownership and management categories (Fig. 5) is sufficiently general, yet flexible enough to

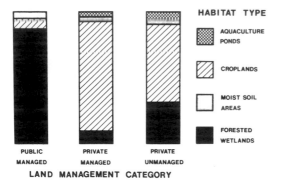

Fig. 5. Relative habitat composition of 3 land ownership and management categories in the Mississippi Alluvial Valley (MAV).

accommodate further refinements, such as separation of seasonally and semipermanently flooded forested wetlands. Most of the habitat types occur in each landownership category, and, with the exception of aquaculture ponds, correspond to habitat management practices described in preceding sections. Aquaculture ponds provide winter habitat, but have no corresponding management methods because ponds that produce bait or food fish generally are not managed for waterfowl (Dubovsky 1987), and ponds that produce crayfish are managed as croplands or moist-soil impoundments (Nassar et al. 1988).

Land ownership and management categories separate habitats into private and public lands, and indicate whether the objectives of the land manager include providing winter habitat for waterfowl. This distinction is important to make because options for protecting habitat differ among ownership categories. Public lands managed for waterfowl include primarily state and federal wildlife management areas. Lands that are owned or leased by individuals or clubs, and managed to provide winter habitat, are classified as private lands managed for waterfowl. The third category, private lands not managed for waterfowl, includes private lands that provide winter habitat but are not managed for that purpose.

Habitat availability in the latter category is unpredictable and depends on the extent of winter flooding.

Differences in relative habitat composition among land ownership categories are apparent (Fig. 5). Public lands include a large proportion of forested wetlands and smaller areas of croplands and moist-soil impoundments. Most actively managed private lands are flooded rice or soybean fields. The second largest area of private lands managed for waterfowl probably is in GTRs. Other management efforts on private land include a few experiments with moist-soil management and a small, but increasing, area of aquaculture ponds in southern Louisiana managed for crayfish and waterfowl.

Private lands that benefit, but are not managed for waterfowl, include primarily cropland and bottomland forests subject to natural flooding. However, croplands in the MAV also include substantial areas of wet soils that are marginal for crop production and function as unmanaged moist-soil areas. Aquaculture ponds are the remaining component of habitat in the unmanaged category.

Status and Trends of Winter Habitat

Public Lands Managed for Waterfowl.—Migration and wintering habitat on public lands in the MAV have increased during recent years (Fig. 6A) through acquisitions such as Panther Swamp, Tensas River, Cache River, and Chickasaw NWRs, and through improved management of existing lands. The total area of natural resource lands in the MAV was approximately 315,000 ha during the early 1980s (Forsythe 1985), but only a portion of that amount, probably <100,000 ha, was important waterfowl habitat. Data regarding the current status of habitat in this category could be obtained from records of state and federal management areas, but have not been summarized.

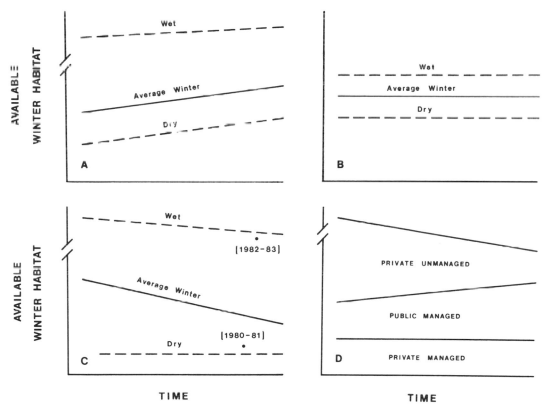

Fig. 6. Graphic models of the status, trends, and variation of winter habitat availability in the Mississippi Alluvial Valley (MAV) under selected water conditions. A = public lands managed for waterfowl; B = private lands managed for waterfowl; C = private lands not managed for waterfowl; and D = habitat availability on 3 land ownership and management categories under average water conditions.

The dynamic hydrology of wetlands in the MAV complicates determination of the status and trends of habitat on public lands. Habitat availability increases dramatically, as indicated by the split axis in Figure 6A, when rainfall causes ponding of surface water and overbank flooding of rivers and streams. Conversely, only permanent wetlands and management units with controlled water levels are available during dry years. Habitat availability during dry and average winters probably has increased at a greater rate than during wet winters (Fig. 6A) because capabilities for controlling water levels have improved on many management areas. Estimates of habitat availability during dry winters could be calculated from existing data on the area of permanent

wetlands and area of management units with controlled water levels, but assessing habitat availability during average or wet winters will be more difficult.

Private Lands Managed for Waterfowl.—Attempts were made during the 1960s to inventory habitat on private hunting clubs in the Mississippi Flyway, but the results were incomplete. Anderson and Kozlik (1964) estimated that 25 hunting clubs in Mississippi and 350 clubs in Arkansas managed >10,000 and 40,000 ha, respectively. In Louisiana, 1,000 clubs controlled approximately 600,000 ha, most of which were coastal wetlands south of the MAV. Although incomplete, these data suggest that 50,000-100,000 ha of private lands are managed for waterfowl in the MAV.

Furthermore, food availability on these lands may exceed that on public wildlife management areas because most private land is managed as cropland (Fig. 5).

Figure 6B reflects the current lack of information regarding this habitat category. We know the area of habitat is substantial, but have little data regarding changes over time. Habitat availability in this category is less variable than in other land ownership categories because most of the area is cropland that can be flooded independent of rainfall. Nevertheless, small yearly changes in habitat availability undoubtedly occur, because some managers only flood fields or GTRs when rainfall is sufficient to saturate soils and reduce water management costs.

Private Lands not Managed for Waterfowl.—Habitat availability in this category probably has exhibited more short- and long-term variation than either category of managed habitat (Fig. 6C). Most short-term variation is associated with yearly differences in winter rainfall, whereas long-term trends have resulted primarily from changes in land use.

Relationships between short-term variation of water conditions and availability of wintering habitat in the MAV have been recognized previously. St. Amant (1959) reported that availability of waterfowl habitat in northeastern Louisiana varied from 80,940-404,700 ha, depending on the extent of winter flooding. More recently, Dell et al. (1987) estimated that >200,000 ha of flooded cropland were available in northeastern Louisiana during December 1985 following heavy rains, but only 20,000 ha were available in January 1986 after the flooding receded. During dry years, winter habitat on private unmanaged land is limited to permanent wetlands and aquaculture ponds. Habitat availability during average or wet winters is unknown.

There has been a negative long-term trend for average habitat availability on unmanaged private land (Fig. 6C).

National wetland inventories conducted during the 1950s and 1970s indicated that the greatest habitat losses during the interim were of forested wetlands in the MAV (Tiner 1984). Although waste grain from crops grown in former forested wetlands is a large potential food resource, waterfowl use of agricultural fields in the MAV generally requires flooding (e.g., Combs 1987), and improving drainage of existing cropland is the primary objective of current flood control projects (Reinecke et al. 1988b).

Habitat availability during winters of average precipitation has declined at a greater rate than habitat availability during wet winters (Fig. 6C) because most drainage projects are designed to control floods that occur frequently (e.g., every 2, 3, or 5 years) rather than major floods that occur every 25, 50, or 100 years. Unfortunately, waterfowl populations have limited mechanisms for responding numerically to infrequent but dramatic increases in available winter habitat. The long-term trend of habitat availability during dry winters is difficult to determine, because losses of relatively permanent wooded and shrub swamps have been offset to an unknown degree by construction of aquaculture ponds. Aquaculture ponds are the only source of winter habitat on unmanaged private land that has increased during recent years (Table 9). In aggregate, aquaculture ponds currently provide >80,000 ha of potential waterfowl habitat in the MAV. As noted by Dubovsky and Kaminski (1987b), however, catfish ponds cannot substitute for natural wetlands, and receive little use by dabbling ducks other than northern shovelers.

IMPLICATIONS FOR MANAGEMENT AND RESEARCH

One of the primary objectives of applied waterfowl research is to determine effects of changes in habitat availability on waterfowl populations. Understanding

Table 9. Area (ha) of aquaculture ponds producing channel catfish, bait fish, and crayfish in the Mississippi Alluvial Valley (MAV) of Arkansas, Louisiana, and Mississippi during 1986.

State	Channel catfish	Bait fish	Crayfish	Reference
Arkansas	5,225	10,522	399	Farwick (1987)
Louisiana	2,275	1,020	25,630	Louisiana Cooperative Extension Service (1986)
Mississippi	33,164	364	47	Wellborn et al. (1987)

variation of winter habitat availability in the MAV (Fig. 6A-C) is essential for relating results of recent research to regional habitat protection programs, because waterfowl responses to short-term natural variation of winter water conditions probably are representative of responses to long-term trends in habitat availability. In this context, recent studies suggest that, during winters such as 1982-83 (Fig. 6C) when rainfall is above normal and habitat on unmanaged private land increases substantially, greater proportions of Mississippi Flyway mallards are attracted to the MAV (Nichols et al. 1983), mallard body weights increase (Heitmeyer 1985, Delnicki and Reinecke 1986), pair formation and molting occur sooner (Heitmeyer 1987), seasonal mortality rates decrease (Hepp et al. 1986, Blohm et al. 1987, Reinecke et al. 1987), and subsequent recruitment rates may increase (Heitmeyer and Fredrickson 1981, Kaminski and Gluesing 1987). Thus, short-term variation of habitat availability provides insights regarding the costs of losing or benefits of gaining winter habitat in the MAV.

Past habitat-protection efforts in the MAV can be characterized as an attempt to offset losses of habitat on unmanaged private lands through acquisition and development of public lands (Fig. 6D). However, habitats in the 3 land ownership categories are not entirely interchangeable. Managers of public lands can increase food production, but cannot meet demands for waterfowl hunting or maintain historic patterns of distribution as well as a complex of public and private lands can. To be successful, the

NAWMP must complement acquisition and development of habitat complexes on public lands with effective programs for maintaining and enhancing winter habitat on private lands. If wildlife extension and federal farm programs provide adequate incentives, private landowners have the necessary water management capabilities to substantially increase winter habitat in the MAV (Zekor and Kaminski 1987). Habitat values of private lands subject to natural flooding can be protected with wildlife extension activities, flood easements, and interagency agreements regarding operation of flood control and water resource development projects.

A major objective of the NAWMP is to protect migration and wintering habitat of dabbling ducks in the MAV (CWS and FWS 1986). Implementation of the NAWMP can be viewed as an experiment in which habitat-protection measures are applied to the MAV to effect changes in habitat availability and waterfowl populations. Essential components of any experiment are establishing appropriate goals and monitoring progress toward them. Data and ideas reviewed in this paper suggest 2 ways of contributing to the information needs of the NAWMP in the MAV.

Assessing Food Production as an Index of Carrying Capacity

Sufficient data are available to use food production for evaluating habitat-protection and management efforts in the MAV. Agricultural grains, moist-soil seeds, acorns, and invertebrates, separately or in combination, provide most of the diet of mallards and other dabbling ducks wintering in the MAV. Thus, the sum of foods produced in cropland, moist-soil, and bottomland hardwood habitats should be a good index to food resources in the region.

Carrying capacity of food resources in duck-use days (i.e., the quantity of food necessary to feed 1 duck for 1 day) can be estimated with information on food production, metabolizable energy of foods, and daily energy requirements of waterfowl. Here, we use data on the availability and metabolizable energy of foods presented earlier, and estimates of energy requirements from Prince (1979), who suggested that 3 times basal metabolic rate is a reasonable value for the daily energy requirement of mallards at moderate temperatures (0-20 C) typical of the MAV. Thus, the energy requirement of a free-ranging, average-sized mallard (i.e., 1.15 kg [Delnicki and Reinecke 1986]) is about 292 kcal/day (cf. Prince 1979:111). Carrying capacity of food resources in the MAV can be calculated as:

Carrying capacity = Duck use-days$_{cropland}$
    + Duck use-days$_{moist-soil\ areas}$
    + Duck use-days$_{bottomland\ hardwoods}$

where duck use-days for each habitat are calculated as:

Duck use-days =
$$\frac{\text{Food available (g [dry])} \times \text{Metabolizable energy (kcal/g [dry])}}{\text{Daily energy requirement (kcal/day)}}$$

To illustrate use of the equations, we compare 3 hypothetical 50-ha management areas. In each example, we assume that food densities <50 kg/ha are not used by ducks as discussed earlier. For moist-soil impoundments in the MAV, 450 kg/ha is a reasonable estimate of average food production. Consequently, duck-use days are calculated by multiplying the food available (g) in 50 ha (50 ha × [450 kg/ha - 50 kg/ha] × 1,000 g/kg) times the metabolizable energy of moist-soil seeds (about 2.5 kcal/g), and dividing by the daily energy requirement (292 kcal/day). For this example, the result is 171,233 duck use-days.

To evaluate cropland, the type of crop, rate of production, and percentage harvested must be known. Obviously, only crops that receive substantial use by waterfowl would be evaluated. Suppose a 50-ha grain sorghum field on a wildlife management area has been damaged by white-tailed deer (Odocoileus virginianus) and blackbirds, but produces 2,000 kg/ha, which is left unharvested and then flooded for waterfowl. Calculations are similar to those for the moist-soil impoundment, except that metabolizable energy of grain sorghum under field conditions is probably about 3.5 kcal/g, and the resulting duck use-days are 1,168,664.

Tree species composition and flooding characteristics must be known to calculate carrying capacity for bottomland hardwoods. If the food production of a 50-ha GTR, in which 80% of the basal area of large trees is red oaks, averages 71 kg/ha of acorns and 10 kg/ha of invertebrates, and metabolizable energy of acorns and invertebrates is 3.5 kcal/g, then carrying capacity of food resources is 18,579 duck use-days. If a similar site is subject to natural flooding and the area flooded during winter averages 20 ha, then the estimate of duck use-days is 7,432.

Estimating carrying capacity of food resources could provide important information for monitoring habitat protection efforts in the MAV. However, implementation would require refinement of goals of the NAWMP for the MAV. Specifically, guidelines would be needed regarding the (1) minimum or average number of waterfowl to be supported, (2) proportions of food production occurring on public and private lands, and (3) habitat conditions (i.e., dry, average, or wet) under which objectives would be achieved. The proposed monitoring effort would not involve complicated analyses or costly data collection, other than visits to field sites to interview managers.

Determining the Status and Variation of Winter Habitat

No quantitative data are available regarding the current status or annual variation of winter habitat in any land ownership category in the MAV. Habitat protection plans might succeed without this information, but probably would not be very efficient.

Public and Private Lands Managed for Waterfowl.—The current status and annual variation of winter habitat on public lands can be determined by summarizing data from refuges and wildlife management areas. Habitat availability during dry winters can be estimated from areas of management units with controlled water levels. Judgments of local managers will be necessary to determine habitat availability during winters when water conditions are average or wet. Habitat availability on private lands managed for waterfowl varies little from year to year, and can be determined by contacting landowners and managers through agricultural agencies and sportsmen groups. If relatively complete data are obtained for these 2 land ownership categories, carrying capacity of food resources can be estimated with methods described in the preceding section.

Private Lands not Managed for Waterfowl.—Determining the status and variability of winter habitat on private lands that are not managed for waterfowl is complicated because habitat availability depends on the extent of winter flooding. One method for determining habitat availability on unmanaged private land, and on managed public and private land, involves application of remote sensing and geographic information system (GIS) technologies. This approach has considerable potential because presence of surface water is relatively easy to interpret from satellite imagery. However, surface waters must be separated into components relevant to waterfowl-habitat management if satellite imagery is to provide useful information.

Developing a GIS and analyzing several sets of satellite images contrasting water conditions in the MAV between seasons and among winters (Fig. 7) could provide data on the status and variability of habitat in each land ownership category. Imagery taken during late summer would determine the distribution and area of permanent water (Fig. 7). Ideally, this imagery would be taken after irrigated crops have been drained and before crayfish ponds are flooded. Permanent water areas present during summer would include lakes, rivers, sloughs, reservoirs, and aquaculture ponds. Surface water in the MAV increases during fall and winter when moist-soil impoundments, managed and unmanaged agricultural fields, crayfish ponds, and bottomland hardwoods are flooded (Fig. 7). This increase of surface water can be represented as:

$$\text{Surface water}_{winter} = \text{Surface water}_{summer} + \text{Temporary winter flooding}$$

which implies that the area of temporary winter flooding can be calculated as the difference between areas of surface water present during summer and winter. Temporary winter flooding can be classified further using the land ownership and management categories already described:

$$\text{Temporary winter flooding} =$$
$$\text{Managed winter flooding on public land}$$
$$+ \text{Managed winter flooding on private land}$$
$$+ \text{Unmanaged winter flooding on public land}$$
$$+ \text{Unmanaged winter flooding on private land}$$

Combining both expressions yields:

$$\text{Surface water}_{winter} =$$
$$\text{Surface water}_{summer}$$
$$+ \text{Public managed winter flooding}$$
$$+ \text{Private managed winter flooding}$$
$$+ \text{Public unmanaged winter flooding}$$
$$+ \text{Private unmanaged winter flooding}$$

Implications are that, if the area of surface water in summer is subtracted from the area of surface water during a

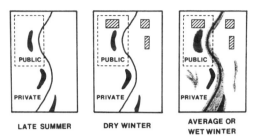

■ PERMANENT WETLANDS AND AQUATIC HABITATS

▨ WINTER HABITAT WITH CONTROLLED WATER LEVELS

▨ WINTER HABITAT THAT FLOODS NATURALLY

LATE SUMMER   DRY WINTER   AVERAGE OR WET WINTER

Fig. 7. Conceptual framework for using remote sensing data to inventory winter habitats of ducks in the Mississippi Alluvial Valley (MAV). See text for explanation.

dry winter, the result will be the area of public and private habitat with managed winter flooding. Furthermore, if the analyses are integrated with a GIS, habitat with managed winter flooding can be separated into private and public components (Fig. 7). If additional imagery is acquired during average or wet winters, areas of naturally flooded habitat can be estimated as the difference between surface water in winter and the sum of surface water in summer and managed winter flooding. Public and private components of naturally flooded habitat could be separated with a GIS as already described (Fig. 7). Accuracy of these analyses would need to be tested with independent data, such as records describing areas of habitat on public lands with managed winter flooding.

Other Research Needs

Research on effects of winter habitat conditions on mallard recruitment (Heitmeyer and Fredrickson 1981, Kaminski and Gluesing 1987) and seasonal survival rates (Reinecke et al. 1987) should be expanded to address possible effects on annual survival rates. Furthermore, effects of winter water conditions on mallard band recovery rates (Blohm et al. 1987) indicate that relationships between availability of winter habitat and hunting

mortality should be studied in greater detail.

Invertebrates are a valuable component of waterfowl diets during winter, and habitats should be managed to ensure their availability. Given the limited data available (White 1985), however, it seems unlikely that invertebrates contribute much to the total biomass of foods available in moist-soil impoundments or bottomland forests. Future studies should emphasize estimation of invertebrate biomass to test this hypothesis.

The low yield and rapid deterioration of soybeans suggest that little food is available in harvested soybean fields, yet many mallards and other dabbling ducks use flooded soybean fields, especially in late winter (J. R. Nassar, unpubl. data). Samples of food availability and collections or observations of feeding ducks are needed to clarify these relationships.

Silvicultural methods needed to maintain or improve the tree species composition of GTRs and other bottomland hardwood stands should be investigated further. In the past, few studies of GTR management have provided true replication of treatments, and results from different study sites sometimes have been inconsistent. Often, data from upland study areas and tree species are used to guide management of bottomland sites. The design of future studies should include long-term data collection and true replication of experimental treatments, perhaps through cooperative studies at several sites. Available data suggest that decreases in the abundance of red oaks and increases of water-tolerant species observed in the understory of GTRs result from differences in growth and survival during seedling and sapling stages. If this hypothesis is true, researchers may be able to develop small experimental GTRs to study effects of water management practices and succession (or shade tolerance) on changes in understory species composition. The ability to transplant seedlings and small saplings would facilitate designing experiments on the growth and survival of various species subjected to different water and light regimes.

Estimates of the number of duck use-days provided by various habitats depend on the untested assumption that food densities <50 kg/ha receive little use by waterfowl. This assumption could be tested by monitoring waterfowl numbers and sampling food densities in several rice and/or soybean fields before, during, and after the main period of field use. Data could be collected with minimal disturbance to the birds by choosing study sites where dabbling ducks feed in flooded fields at night and depart during the day to roost on refuges.

SUMMARY

The MAV is >800 km long, varies from 32-128 km wide, and comprises approximately 10 million ha in 7 states bordering the lower Mississippi River. Historically, the MAV was dominated by forested wetlands and subject to extensive flooding. Today, <20% of the bottomland forests remain, and agriculture is the principal land use. The climate of the MAV is humid subtropical. In southeastern Missouri, the growing season is 210 days, mean annual rainfall is 115 cm, and January minimum and maximum temperatures average -1 and 7 C, respectively. In southeastern Louisiana, the growing season is 270 days, mean annual rainfall is 150 cm, and January minimum and maximum temperatures average 13 and 18 C.

Mallards and wood ducks are the most abundant waterfowl species in the MAV during migration and winter, with the largest numbers of mallards occurring in Arkansas. Black ducks are found primarily in the northeastern MAV, and wood ducks and dabbling ducks other than mallards and black ducks are most abundant in the southern MAV. Canada geese winter primarily in the northern MAV,

and numbers of snow geese are increasing in the central and southern MAV. The distribution and abundance of diving ducks is not well-known, but many lesser scaup and ruddy ducks are found on aquaculture ponds, and canvasbacks and other diving ducks are abundant at traditional wintering areas such as Catahoula Lake, Louisiana.

Although most activities of migrating and wintering waterfowl require foods that are rich in energy, small numbers of invertebrates are found in the diets of most duck species. Dabbling ducks and wood ducks primarily eat agricultural grains, moist-soil seeds, acorns, and invertebrates. Diets of diving ducks include benthic invertebrates, and seeds and tubers of moist-soil and aquatic plants. Geese eat agricultural grains and seeds, rhizomes, tubers, and green vegetation from natural or cultivated plants. Most foraging by dabbling ducks and wood ducks occurs in naturally and artificially flooded croplands, moist-soil areas, and forested wetlands. Forested wetlands also provide mallards and wood ducks with sites for social interaction and protection from disturbance, inclement weather, and predators. Refuges are important for protecting migrating and wintering waterfowl from excessive hunting.

The 3 habitats most frequently managed for waterfowl in the MAV are croplands, moist-soil areas, and forested wetlands. Croplands can be used to reduce exposure of waterfowl to hunting mortality, replace food supplies no longer available from natural systems, and increase the dependability of food resources, but they are expensive to manage and provide little habitat to wildlife other than waterfowl. Moist-soil impoundments produce intermediate quantities of food, are less expensive than farming, and provide habitat for waterfowl and other wildlife. Moist-soil management is an alternative to agriculture on soils with poor drainage, and an alternative to timber management on sites with limited potential for producing waterfowl food. Management of bottomland forests provides natural wetland complexes for waterfowl, habitat for other wildlife, and the ecological benefits of floodplain wetlands. Production of food for waterfowl is relatively low in forested wetlands, however, and acquisition of sites that have a substantial proportion of red oaks should be a high priority. We recommend increased use of moist-soil management on appropriate sites in the MAV, and development of habitat-management complexes comprising cropland, moist-soil impoundments, GTRs, and naturally flooded bottomland forests.

Recognizing 3 categories of land ownership and management provides a framework for understanding the status, trends, and variation of habitat in the MAV. Public and private lands managed for waterfowl, and private lands not actively managed for waterfowl, each provide important migration and winter habitat. Neither the total habitat available nor the proportion of habitat types (i.e., cropland, moist-soil areas, and forested wetlands) is known for any land ownership category, but trends and variation of habitat availability in each category can be described qualitatively. Habitat availability on public land varies annually with food production and water conditions, and has increased appreciably via land acquisition and improved management. On private lands managed for waterfowl, short-term variation and long-term changes in habitat availability have been relatively small. Habitat availability on private lands that are not managed for waterfowl has decreased substantially, and exhibits considerable short-term variation associated with annual flooding.

Past habitat-protection efforts in the MAV can be characterized as an attempt to offset losses of habitat on unmanaged private lands through acquisition and development of public lands. Habitats in the 3 land ownership categories are not completely interchangeable, however. Managers of public lands can increase food production, but cannot meet demands for waterfowl hunting or maintain historic patterns of waterfowl distribution. Thus, complexes of public and private habitat are important on a regional scale. We recommend maintaining traditional efforts to acquire and manage public lands, and initiating innovative programs to protect habitat on private lands.

Among information needs in the MAV are better data regarding the abundance and distribution of winter habitat, and a method for monitoring progress of habitat-protection efforts toward goals of the NAWMP, which seeks to protect an additional 277,624 ha of habitat for dabbling ducks in the MAV by the year 2000. Development of a GIS and analysis of satellite imagery contrasting water conditions in the MAV between seasons and among years is suggested as a means of determining habitat availability in the 3 land ownership categories. Habitat protection and management efforts can be monitored by relating food availability in the 3 primary foraging habitats to food requirements, if the number of waterfowl to be accommodated and habitat conditions are specified.

LITERATURE CITED

Alisauskas, R. T., and C. D. Ankney. 1990. Bioenergetics of breeding waterfowl. *In* B. D. J. Batt, ed. The ecology and management of breeding waterfowl. Univ. Minnesota Press, Minneapolis. In press.

Anderson, D. R., and D. E. Joyner. 1985. Subflocking and winter movements of Canada geese in southern Illinois. J. Wildl. Manage. 49:422-428.

Anderson, J. M., and F. M. Kozlik. 1964. Private duck clubs. Pages 519-526 *in* J. P. Linduska, ed. Waterfowl tomorrow. U.S. Fish and Wildl. Serv., Washington, D.C.

Anderson, M. G., and B. D. J. Batt. 1983. Workshop on the ecology of wintering waterfowl. Wildl. Soc. Bull. 11:22-24.

Anderson, W. L., S. P. Havera, and R. A. Montgomery. 1987. Incidence of ingested shot in waterfowl in the Mississippi Flyway, 1977-79. Wildl. Soc. Bull. 15:181-188.

Armbruster, J. S. 1982. Wood duck displays and pairing chronology. Auk 99:116-122.

Arner, D. H. 1963. Production of duck food in beaver ponds. J. Wildl. Manage. 27:76-81.

———, E. D. Norwood, and B. M. Teels. 1974. Comparison of aquatic ecosystems in two national waterfowl refuges. Proc. Annu. Conf. Southeast. Assoc. Game and Fish Comm. 28:456-467.

Ashley, B. S. 1979. Determining adequacy of regeneration. Pages 18-22 *in* H. A. Holt and B. C. Fischer, eds. Regenerating oaks in upland hardwood forests. Proc. 1979 John S. Wright For. Conf. Purdue Univ., W. Lafayette, Ind.

Baldassarre, G. A., and E. G. Bolen. 1984. Field-feeding ecology of waterfowl wintering on the Southern High Plains of Texas. J. Wildl. Manage. 48:63-71.

———, R. J. Whyte, E. E. Quinlin, and E. G. Bolen. 1983. Dynamics and quality of waste corn available to postbreeding waterfowl in Texas. Wildl. Soc. Bull. 11:25-31.

Bartelt, G. A. 1987. Effects of disturbance and hunting on the behavior of Canada goose family groups in eastcentral Wisconsin. J. Wildl. Manage. 51:517-522.

Bartonek, J. C., R. J. Blohm, R. K. Brace, F. D. Caswell, K. E. Gamble, H. W. Miller, R. S. Pospahala, and M. M. Smith. 1984. Status and needs of the mallard. Trans. North Am. Wildl. and Nat. Resour. Conf. 49:501-518.

Bateman, H. A., T. Joanen, and C. D. Stutzenbaker. 1988. History and status of midcontinent snow geese on their Gulf Coast winter range. Pages 495-515 *in* M. W. Weller, ed. Waterfowl in winter. Univ. Minnesota Press, Minneapolis.

Bell, R. Q., and W. D. Klimstra. 1970. Feeding activities of Canada geese in southern Illinois. Trans. Ill. State Acad. Sci. 63:295-304.

Bellrose, F. C. 1959. Lead poisoning as a mortality factor in waterfowl populations. Ill. Nat. Hist. Surv. Bull. 27:235-288.

———. 1980. Ducks, geese and swans of North America. Third ed. Stackpole Books, Harrisburg, Pa. 540 pp.

Black, R. A. 1984. Water relations of *Quercus palustris*: field measurements on an experimentally flooded stand. Oecologia 64:14-20.

Blohm, R. J., R. E. Reynolds, J. P. Bladen, J. D. Nichols, J. E. Hines, K. H. Pollock, and R. T. Eberhardt. 1987. Mallard mortality rates on key breeding and wintering areas. Trans. North Am. Wildl. and Nat. Resour. Conf. 52:246-257.

Bowers, E. F., and R. B. Hamilton. 1977. Derivation of northern wood ducks harvested in southern states of the Mississippi Flyway. Proc. Annu. Conf. Southeast. Assoc. Fish and Wildl. Agencies 31:90-98.

———, and F. W. Martin. 1975. Managing wood ducks by population units. Trans. North Am. Wildl. and Nat. Resour. Conf. 40:300-324.

Bowling, D. R., and R. C. Kellison. 1983. Bottomland hardwood stand development following clearcutting. South. J. Appl. For. 7:110-116.

Briscoe, C. B. 1961. Germination of cherrybark and Nuttal oak acorns following flooding. Ecology 42:430-431.

Broadfoot, W. M. 1958. Reaction of hardwood timber to shallow-water impoundments. Mississippi State Univ. Agric. Exp. Stn. Inf. Sheet 595, State College. 2 pp.

———. 1967. Shallow-water impoundment increases soil moisture and growth of hardwoods. Soil Sci. Soc. Am. Proc. 31:562-564.

———, and H. L. Williston. 1973. Flooding effects on southern forests. J. For. 71:584-587.

Brock, S. C. 1987. Seed yields of four moist-soil plants on Noxubee National Wildlife Refuge in Mississippi. M.S. Thesis, Mississippi State Univ., Mississippi State. 35 pp.

Brodsky, L. M., and P. J. Weatherhead. 1985. Time and energy constraints on courtship in wintering American black ducks. Condor 87:33-36.

Canadian Wildlife Service and U.S. Fish and Wildlife Service. 1986. North American waterfowl management plan. U.S. Fish and Wildl. Serv., Washington, D.C. 31 pp.

Carney, S. M., M. F. Sorensen, and E. M. Martin. 1975. Distribution in states and counties of waterfowl species harvested during 1961-70 hunting seasons. U.S. Fish and Wildl. Serv. Spec. Sci. Rep. Wildl. 187. 132 pp.

———, ———, and ———. 1983. Distribution of waterfowl species harvested in states and counties during 1971-80 hunting seasons. U.S. Fish and Wildl. Serv. Spec. Sci. Rep. Wildl. 254. 114 pp.

Christopher, M. W. 1985. Wintering waterfowl use of catfish ponds in the Delta region of Mississippi. M.S. Thesis, Mississippi State Univ., Mississippi State. 166 pp.

———, E. P. Hill, and D. E. Steffen. 1988. Use of catfish ponds by waterfowl wintering in Mississippi. Pages 413-418 *in* M. W. Weller, ed. Waterfowl in winter. Univ. Minnesota Press, Minneapolis.

Combs, D. L. 1987. Ecology of male mallards during winter in the upper Mississippi Alluvial Valley. Ph.D. Thesis, Univ. Missouri, Columbia. 223 pp.

Cypert, E., and B. S. Webster. 1948. Yield and use by wildlife of acorns of water and willow oaks. J. Wildl. Manage. 12:227-231.

Davis, J. P., C. H. Thomas, and L. L. Glasgow.

1961. Foods available to waterfowl in fallow rice fields of southwest Louisiana, 1960-61. Proc. Annu. Conf. Southeast. Assoc. Game and Fish Comm. 15:60-66.

Dell, D. A., R. H. Chabreck, P. M. McKenzie, and R. P. Martin. 1987. Wintering waterfowl and their habitats in northeastern Louisiana. La. Agric. Exp. Stn. Res. Rep. 12, Baton Rouge. 40 pp.

Delnicki, D., and K. J. Reinecke. 1986. Mid-winter food use and body weights of mallards and wood ducks in Mississippi. J. Wildl. Manage. 50:43-51.

Denton, D. C. 1987. Food crops for waterfowl. Pages 243-250 in D. E. Wesley and W. G. Leitch, eds. Fireside waterfowler. Fundamentals of duck and goose ecology. Stackpole Books, Harrisburg, Pa.

Dickson, J. G. 1978. Forest bird communities of the bottomland hardwoods. Pages 66-73 in R. M. DeGraff, tech. coord. Proc. workshop management of southern forests for nongame birds. U.S. For. Serv. Gen. Tech. Rep. SE-14.

Drobney, R. D. 1982. Body weight and composition changes and adaptations for breeding in wood ducks. Condor 84:300-305.

DuBarry, A. P., Jr. 1963. Germination of bottomland tree seed while immersed in water. J. For. 61:225-226.

Dubovsky, J. A. 1987. Wintering waterfowl abundance and habitat associations with catfish ponds in the Alluvial Valley region of Mississippi. M.S. Thesis, Mississippi State Univ., Mississippi State. 101 pp.

———, and R. M. Kaminski. 1987a. Estimates and chronology of waterfowl use of Mississippi catfish ponds. Proc. Annu. Conf. Southeast. Assoc. Fish and Wildl. Agencies 41:257-265.

———, and ———. 1987b. Wintering waterfowl abundance and habitat associations with catfish ponds in the Alluvial Valley region of Mississippi. Miss. Dep. Wildl. Conserv., Fed. Aid in Wildl. Restor., Completion Rep. Proj. W-48, Stud. 25, Mississippi State. 100 pp.

Farwick, J. 1987. Arkansas commercial fishery industry survey. Ark. Game and Fish Comm., Fed Aid to Commer. Fish. Proj. 2-371-R-6, Little Rock. 33 pp.

Fleming, W. J., D. R. Clark, Jr., and C. J. Henny. 1983. Organochlorine pesticides and PCB's: a continuing problem for the 1980s. Trans. North Am. Wildl. and Nat. Resour. Conf. 48:186-199.

Forsythe, S. W. 1985. The protection of bottomland hardwood wetlands of the lower Mississippi Valley. Trans. North Am. Wildl. and Nat. Resour. Conf. 50:566-572.

Francis, J. K. 1983. Acorn production and tree growth of Nuttall oak in a green-tree reservoir. U.S. For. Serv. Res. Note SO-289. 3 pp.

Frederick, R. B., and E. E. Klaas. 1982. Resource use

and behavior of migrating snow geese. J. Wildl. Manage. 46:601-614.

Fredrickson, L. H. 1978. Lowland hardwood wetlands: current status and habitat values for wildlife. Pages 296-306 in P. E. Greeson, J. R. Clark, and J. E. Clark, eds. Wetland functions and values: the state of our understanding. Am. Water Resour. Assoc., Minneapolis, Minn.

———. 1979. Floral and faunal changes in lowland hardwood forests in Missouri resulting from channelization, drainage, and impoundment. U.S. Fish and Wildl. Serv. Biol. Serv. Prog. FWS/OBS-78/91. 130 pp.

———. 1985. Managed wetland habitats for wildlife: why are they important? Pages 1-8 in M. D. Knighton, compiler. Proc. water impoundments for wildlife: a habitat management workshop. U.S. For. Serv. Gen. Tech. Rep. NC-100.

———, and M. E. Heitmeyer. 1988. Waterfowl use of forested wetlands of the southern United States: an overview. Pages 307-323 in M. W. Weller, ed. Waterfowl in winter. Univ. Minnesota Press, Minneapolis.

———, and F. A. Reid. 1986. Wetland and riparian habitats: a nongame management overview. Pages 59-96 in J. B. Hale, L. B. Best, and R. L. Clawson, eds. Proc. symp. management of nongame wildlife in the midwest: a developing art. Grand Rapids, Mich.

———, and T. S. Taylor. 1982. Management of seasonally flooded impoundments for wildlife. U.S. Fish and Wildl. Serv. Resour. Publ. 148. 29 pp.

Friend, M., ed. 1987. Field guide to wildlife diseases. Vol. 1. General field procedures and diseases of migratory birds. U.S. Fish and Wildl. Serv. Resour. Publ. 167. 225 pp.

Galloway, G. E., Jr. 1980. Ex-post evaluation of regional water resources development: the case of the Yazoo-Mississippi Delta. U.S. Army Eng. Inst. Water Resour. Rep. IWR-80-D1. 304 pp.

Green, W. E., L. G. MacNamara, and F. M. Uhler. 1964. Water on and off. Pages 557-568 in J. P. Linduska, ed. Waterfowl tomorrow. U.S. Fish and Wildl. Serv., Washington, D.C.

Gysel, L. W. 1956. Measurement of acorn crops. For. Sci. 2:305-313.

Hankla, D. J. 1968. Summary of Canada goose transplant program on nine national wildlife refuges in the southeast, 1953-1965. Pages 105-111 in R. L. Hine and C. Shoenfeld, eds. Canada goose management: current continental problems and programs. Dembar Educ. Res. Serv., Madison, Wis.

———, and R. R. Rudolph. 1967. Changes in the migration and wintering habits of Canada geese in the lower portion of the Atlantic and Mississippi Flyways—with special reference to national wildlife refuges. Proc. Annu. Conf.

Southeast. Assoc. Game and Fish Comm. 21:133-144.

Hanson, H. C., and R. H. Smith. 1950. Canada geese of the Mississippi Flyway with special reference to an Illinois flock. Ill. Nat. Hist. Surv. Bull. 25:67-210.

Harmon, B. G., C. H. Thomas, and L. L. Glasgow. 1960. Waterfowl foods in Louisiana ricefields. Trans. North Am. Wildl. and Nat. Resour. Conf. 25:153-161.

Hawkins, A. S. 1964. Mississippi Flyway. Pages 185-207 *in* J. P. Linduska, ed. Waterfowl tomorrow. U.S. Fish and Wildl. Serv., Washington, D.C.

Heitmeyer, M. E. 1985. Wintering strategies of female mallards related to dynamics of lowland hardwood wetlands in the upper Mississippi Delta. Ph.D. Thesis, Univ. Missouri, Columbia. 378 pp.

———. 1987. The prebasic moult and basic plumage of female mallards (*Anas platyrhynchos*) Can J. Zool. 65:2248-2261.

———. 1988. Protein costs of the prebasic molt of female mallards. Condor 90:263-266.

———, and L. H. Fredrickson. 1981. Do wetland conditions in the Mississippi Delta hardwoods influence mallard recruitment? Trans. North Am. Wildl. and Nat. Resour. Conf. 46:44-57.

Hepp, G. R. 1986. Effects of body weight and age on the time of pairing of American black ducks. Auk 103:477-484.

———, R. J. Blohm, R. E. Reynolds, J. E. Hines and J. D. Nichols. 1986. Physiological condition of autumn-banded mallards and its relationship to hunting vulnerability. J. Wildl. Manage. 50:177-183.

———, and J. D. Hair. 1983. Reproductive behavior and pairing chronology in wintering dabbling ducks. Wilson Bull. 95:675-682.

Hobaugh, W. C. 1984. Habitat use by snow geese wintering in southeast Texas. J. Wildl. Manage. 48:1085-1096.

Hodges, J. D., and G. C. Janzen. 1987. Studies on the biology of cherrybark oak: recommendations for regeneration. Pages 133-139 *in* D. R. Phillips, ed. Proc. 4th Bienn. South. Silvicultural Res. Conf. U.S. For. Serv. Gen. Tech. Rep. SE-42.

———, and G. L. Switzer. 1979. Some aspects of the ecology of southern bottomland hardwoods. Pages 360-365 *in* Proc. 1978 Joint Meet. Soc. Am. For. and Can. Inst. For. Soc. Am. For., Washington, D.C.

Hoffman, R. D., and T. A. Bookhout. 1985. Metabolizable energy of seeds consumed by ducks in Lake Erie marshes. Trans. North Am. Wildl. and Nat. Resour. Conf. 50:557-565.

Hosner, J. F. 1958. The effects of complete inundation upon seedlings of six bottomland tree species. Ecology 39:371-373.

———. 1960. Relative tolerance to complete inundation of fourteen bottomland tree species. For. Sci. 6:246-251.

Hurlbert, S. H. 1984. Pseudoreplication and the design of ecological field experiments. Ecol. Monogr. 54:187-211.

Iverson, G. C., P. A. Vohs, and T. C. Tacha. 1985. Habitat use by sandhill cranes wintering in west Texas. J. Wildl. Manage. 49:1074-1083.

Janzen, G. C., and J. D. Hodges. 1985. Influence of midstory and understory vegetation removal on the establishment and development of oak regeneration. Pages 273-278 *in* E. Shoulders, ed. Proc. 3rd Bienn. South. Silvicultural Res. Conf. U.S. For. Serv. Gen. Tech. Rep. SO-54.

Jemison, E. S., and R. H. Chabreck. 1962. The availability of waterfowl foods in coastal marsh impoundments in Louisiana. Trans. North Am. Wildl. and Nat. Resour. Conf. 27:288-300.

Johnson, R. L. 1975. Natural regeneration and development of Nuttall oak and associated species. U.S. For. Serv. Res. Pap. SO-104. 12 pp.

———, and R. M. Krinard. 1987. Direct seeding of southern oaks—a progress report. Proc. Annu. Hardwood Symp. Hardwood Res. Counc. 15:10-16.

———, and ———. 1988. Development of Nuttall oak following release in a sapling-sized stand. South. J. Appl. For. 12:46-48.

Joyner, D. E., B. N. Jacobson, and R. D. Arthur. 1987. Nutritional characteristics of grains fed to Canada geese. Wildfowl 38:89-93.

Kaminski, R. M., and E. A. Gluesing. 1987. Density- and habitat-related recruitment in mallards. J. Wildl. Manage. 51:141-148.

Kelley, J. R., Jr. 1986. Management and biomass production of selected moist-soil plants. M.S. Thesis, Univ. Missouri, Columbia. 68 pp.

Kennedy, H. E., Jr., and R. L. Johnson. 1984. Silvicultural alternatives in bottomland hardwoods and their impact on stand quality. Pages 6-18 *in* R. W. Gulden, ed. Proc. 14th Annu. South. For. Econ. Workshop, Raleigh, N.C.

Klimas, C. V. 1987. Forest vegetation models for wildlife habitat assessment in the confined floodplain of the lower Mississippi River. Ph.D. Thesis, Univ. Missouri, Columbia. 361 pp.

———. 1988. River regulation effects of floodplain hydrology and ecology. Pages 40-49 *in* D. D. Hook, W. H. McKee, Jr., H. K. Smith, J. Gregory, V. G. Burrell, Jr., M. R. DeVoe, R. E. Sojka, S. Gilbert, R. Banks, L. H. Stolzy, C. Brooks, T. D. Matthews, and T. H. Shear, eds. The ecology and management of wetlands. Vol. 1. Ecology of wetlands. Timber Press, Portland, Oreg.

Kozlowski, T. T., and S. G. Pallardy. 1979. Stomatal responses of *Fraxinus pennsylvanica* seedlings during and after flooding. Physiol. Plant. 46:155-158.

———, and ———. 1984. Effect of flooding on water, carbohydrate, and mineral relations. Pages 165-193 *in* T. T. Kozlowski, ed. Flooding and plant growth. Academic Press, Inc. New York, N.Y.

Krapu, G. L. 1981. The role of nutrient reserves in mallard reproduction. Auk 98:29-38.

———, and H. F. Duebbert. 1989. Prairie wetlands: characteristics, importance to waterfowl, and status. *In* R. R. Sharitz and J. W. Gibbons, eds. Freshwater wetlands and wildlife. Savannah River Ecol. Lab., Aiken, S.C. In press.

———, and K. J. Reinecke. 1990. Foraging ecology and nutrition. *In* B. D. J. Batt, ed. The ecology and management of breeding waterfowl. Univ. Minnesota Press, Minneapolis. In press.

———, and G. A. Swanson. 1975. Some nutritional aspects of reproduction in prairie nesting pintails. J. Wildl. Manage.39:156-162.

Krinard, R. M., and R. L. Johnson. 1981. Flooding, beavers, and hardwood seedling survival. U.S. For. Serv. Res. Note SO-270. 6 pp.

———, and H. E. Kennedy, Jr. 1987. Planted hardwood development on clay soil without weed control through 16 years. U.S. For. Serv. Res. Note SO-343. 4 pp.

Larson, J. S., M. S. Bedinger, C. F. Bryan, S. Brown, R. T. Huffman, E. L. Miller, D. G. Rhodes, and B. A. Touchet. 1981. Transition from wetlands to uplands in southeastern bottomland hardwood forests. Pages 225-273 *in* J. R. Clark and J. Benforado, eds. Wetlands of bottomland hardwood forests. Elsevier Sci. Publ. Co., New York, N.Y.

Lea, R. 1988. Management of eastern United States bottomland hardwood forests. Pages 185-194 *in* D. D. Hook, W. H. McKee, Jr., H. K. Smith, J. Gregory, V. G. Burrell, Jr., M. R. DeVoe, R. E. Sojka, S. Gilbert, R. Banks, L. H. Stolzy, C. Brooks, T. D. Matthews, and T. H. Shear, eds. The ecology and management of wetlands. Vol. 2. Management, use and value of wetlands. Timber Press, Portland, Oreg.

Leslie, J. C. 1983. Population ecology and winter trends of the white-fronted goose in Louisiana. M.S. Thesis, Louisiana State Univ., Baton Rouge. 92 pp.

———, and R. H. Chabreck. 1984. Winter habitat preference of white-fronted geese in Louisiana. Trans. North Am. Wildl. and Nat. Resour. Conf. 49:519-526.

Loesch, C. R. 1988. Weight and body-condition dynamics of captive, wild-strain mallards during winter. M.S. Thesis, Mississippi State Univ., Mississippi State. 62 pp.

Loftis, D. L. 1983. Regenerating southern Appalachian mixed hardwood stands with the shelterwood method. South. J. Appl. For. 7:212-217.

Louisiana Cooperative Extension Service. 1986. Louisiana summary, agricultural and natural resources 1986. Louisiana State Univ. Agric. Cent., Baton Rouge. 200 pp.

Low, J. B., and F. C. Bellrose, Jr. 1944. The seed and vegetative yield of waterfowl food plants in the Illinois River Valley. J. Wildl. Manage. 8:7-22.

Lower Mississippi Region Comprehensive Study Coordinating Committee. 1974a. Regional climatology, hydrology and geology. Vol. I, Appendix C. Lower Mississippi Region comprehensive study. U.S. Army Corps Eng., Vicksburg, Miss. 279 pp.

———. 1974b. Archeological and historical resources. Vol. I, Appendix P. Lower Mississippi Region comprehensive study. U.S. Army Corps Eng., Vicksburg, Miss. 384 pp.

MacDonald, P. O., W. E. Frayer, and J. K. Clauser. 1979. Documentation, chronology, and future projections of bottomland hardwood habitat loss in the lower Mississippi Alluvial Plain. Vol. I. Basic report. U.S. Fish and Wildl. Serv., Vicksburg, Miss. 133 pp.

Marquis, D. A., and J. C. Bjorkhom. 1982. Guidelines for evaluating regeneration before and after clearcutting Allegheny hardwoods. U.S. For. Serv. Res. Note NE-307. 4 pp.

Martin, J. H., W. H. Leonard, and D. L. Stamp. 1976. Principles of field crop production. Third ed. MacMillan Publ. Co., Inc., New York, N.Y. 1118 pp.

Mayeaux, M. M., J. G. Marshall, G. Baskin, and P. R. Vidrine. 1980. Reducing soybean harvest losses. La. Agric. 23(4):18-20.

McKenzie, D. F. 1987. Utilization of rootstocks and browse by waterfowl on moist-soil impoundments in Missouri. M.S. Thesis, Univ. Missouri, Columbia. 93 pp.

McNeal, X. 1950. Effect of combine adjustment on harvest losses of rice. Univ. Arkansas Agric. Exp. Stn. Bull. 500, Fayetteville. 21 pp.

McQuilkin, R. A., and R. A. Musbach. 1977. Pin oak acorn production on green tree reservoirs in southeastern Missouri. J. Wildl. Manage. 41:218-225.

Miller, M. W. 1987. Fall and winter foods of northern pintails in the Sacramento Valley, California. J. Wildl. Manage. 51:405-414.

———, and K. J. Reinecke. 1984. Proper expression of metabolizable energy in avian energetics. Condor 86:396-400.

Minckler, L. S., and D. Janes. 1965. Pin oak acorn production on normal and flooded areas. Univ. Missouri Agric. Exp. Stn. Res. Bull. 898, Columbia. 15 pp.

———, and R. E. McDermott. 1960. Pin oak acorn production and regeneration as affected by stand density, structure and flooding. Univ. Missouri Agric. Exp. Stn. Res. Bull. 750, Columbia. 24 pp.

Mississippi Cooperative Extension Service. 1986a. Estimated costs and returns, soybeans, all areas of Mississippi 1986. Miss. Agric. For. Exp. Stn., Mississippi State. 199 pp.

——. 1986b. Estimated costs and returns, rice, Delta area of Mississippi 1986. Miss. Agric. For. Exp. Stn., Mississippi State. 18 pp.

——. 1986c. Estimated costs and returns, grain sorghum and corn, all areas of Mississippi 1986. Miss. Agric. For. Exp. Sta., Mississippi State. 123 pp.

Mitchell, W. A., and C. J. Newling. 1986. Greentree reservoirs. Sect. 5.5.3, U.S. Army Corps Eng. Wildl. Resour. Manage. Man. Tech. Rep. EL-86-9, Vicksburg, Miss. 22 pp.

Mitsch, W. J., and J. G. Gosselink. 1986. Wetlands. Van Nostrand Reinhold Co., New York, N.Y. 539 pp.

Munro, R. E., and C. F. Kimball. 1982. Population ecology of the mallard. VII. Distribution and derivation of the harvest. U.S. Fish and Wildl. Serv. Resour. Publ. 147. 127 pp.

Nassar, J. R., R. H. Chabreck, and D. C. Hayden. 1988. Experimental plantings for management of crayfish and waterfowl. Pages 427-439 in M. W. Weller, ed. Waterfowl in winter. Univ. Minnesota Press, Minneapolis.

National Research Council. 1977. Nutrient requirements of poultry. Natl. Acad. Sci., Washington, D.C. 62 pp.

Neely, W. W., and V. E. Davison. 1971. Wild ducks on farmland in the South. U.S. Dep. Agric. Farmers' Bull. 2218. 14 pp.

Newling, C. J. 1981. Ecological investigation of a greentree reservoir in the Delta National Forest, Mississippi. U.S. Army Eng. Waterways Exp. Stn. Misc. Pap. EL-81-5, Vicksburg, Miss. 59 pp.

Nichols, J. D., and J. E. Hines. 1987. Population ecology of the mallard. VIII. Winter distribution patterns and survival rates of winter-banded mallards. U.S. Fish and Wildl. Serv. Resour. Publ. 162. 154 pp.

——, K. J. Reinecke, and J. E. Hines. 1983. Factors affecting the distribution of mallards wintering in the Mississippi Alluvial Valley. Auk 100:932-946.

Nix, L. E., J. L. Haymond, and W. G. Woodrum. 1985. Early results of oak enrichment plantings in bottomland hardwoods of South Carolina. Pages 154-158 in E. Shoulders, ed. Proc. 3rd Bienn. South. Silvicultural Res. Conf. U.S. For. Serv. Gen. Tech. Rep. SO-54.

Olinde, M. W., L. S. Perrin, F. Montalbano III, L. L. Rowse, and M. J. Allen. 1985. Smartweed seed production and availability in south central Florida wetlands. Proc. Annu. Conf. Southeast. Assoc. Fish and Wildl. Agencies 39:459-464.

Paulus, S. L. 1980. The winter ecology of the gadwall in Louisiana. M.S. Thesis, Univ. North Dakota, Grand Forks. 357 pp.

——. 1984. Molts and plumages of gadwalls in winter. Auk 101:887-889.

Paxton, K. W., D. R. Lavergne, T. Zacharias, and B. McManus. 1986. Projected costs and returns: cotton, soybeans, rice, corn, milo and wheat, northeast Louisiana, 1986. Dep. Agric. Econ. Res. Rep. 645. La. Agric. Exp. Stn., Baton Rouge. 93 pp.

Pehrsson, O. 1987. Effects of body condition on molting in mallards. Condor 89:329-339.

Pezeshki, S. R., and J. L. Chambers. 1985. Responses of cherrybark oak seedlings to short-term flooding. For. Sci. 31:760-771.

Prevett, J. P., and C. D. MacInnes. 1980. Family and other social groups in snow geese. Wildl. Monogr. 71. 46 pp.

Prince, H. H. 1979. Bioenergetics of postbreeding dabbling ducks. Pages 103-117 in T. A. Bookhout, ed. Waterfowl and wetlands—an integrated review. North Cent. Sect., Wildl. Soc., Madison, Wis.

Purol, D. A. 1975. Metabolizable energy of cellulose, three natural foods and three diets for mallards. M.S. Thesis, Michigan State Univ., East Lansing. 39 pp.

Raveling, D. G. 1969. Social classes of Canada geese in winter. J. Wildl. Manage. 33:304-318.

——, and H. G. Lumsden. 1977. Nesting ecology of Canada geese in the Hudson Bay lowlands: evolution and population regulation. Ont. Ministry Nat. Resour. Fish and Wildl. Res. Rep. 98. 77 pp.

Reeves, H. M., H. H. Dill, and A. S. Hawkins. 1968. A case study in Canada goose management: the Mississippi Valley population. Pages 150-165 in R. L. Hine and C. Schoenfeld, eds. Canada goose management: current continental problems and programs. Dembar Educ. Res. Serv., Madison, Wis.

Reid, F. A. 1983. Aquatic macroinvertebrate response to management of seasonally-flooded wetlands. M.S. Thesis, Univ. Missouri, Columbia. 100 pp.

——, J. R. Kelley, Jr., T. S. Taylor, and L. H. Fredrickson. 1989. Upper Mississippi Valley wetlands—refuges and moist-soil impoundments. Pages 181-202 in L. M. Smith, R. L. Pederson, and R. M. Kaminski, eds. Habitat management for migrating and wintering waterfowl in North America. Texas Tech Univ. Press, Lubbock.

Reinecke, K. J., and G. L. Krapu. 1986. Feeding ecology of sandhill cranes during spring migration in Nebraska. J. Wildl. Manage. 50:71-79.

——, C. D. Ankney, G. L. Krapu, R. B. Owen, Jr., H. H. Prince, and D. G. Raveling. 1988a. Workshop summary: nutrition, condition, and ecophysiology. Pages 299-303 in M. W. Weller, ed. Waterfowl in winter. Univ. Minnesota Press, Minneapolis.

———, R. C. Barkley, and C. K. Baxter. 1988b. Potential effects of changing water conditions on mallards wintering in the Mississippi Alluvial Valley. Pages 325-337 in M. W. Weller, ed. Waterfowl in winter. Univ. Minnesota Press, Minneapolis.

———, C. W. Shaiffer, and D. Delnicki. 1987. Winter survival of female mallards in the Lower Mississippi Valley. Trans. North Am. Wildl. and Nat. Resour. Conf. 52:258-263.

Reynolds, R. E. 1987. Breeding duck population, production and habitat surveys, 1979-85. Trans. North Am. Wildl. and Nat. Resour. Conf. 52:186-205.

Rogers, R., and I. L. Sander. 1989. Flooding, stand structure, and stand density and their effect on pin oak growth in southeastern Missouri. In J. H. Miller, ed. Proc. 5th Bienn. South. Silvicultural Res. Conf. In press.

Rudolph, R. R., and C. G. Hunter. 1964. Green trees and greenheads. Pages 611-618 in J. P. Linduska, ed. Waterfowl tomorrow. U.S. Fish and Wildl. Serv., Washington, D.C.

Rusch, D. H., S. R. Craven, R. E. Trost, J. R. Cary, R. L. Drieslein, J. W. Ellis, and J. Wetzel. 1985. Evaluation of efforts to redistribute Canada geese. Trans. North Am. Wildl. and Nat. Resour. Conf. 50:506-524.

St. Amant, L. S. 1959. Louisiana wildlife inventory and management plan. La. Wildl. and Fish. Comm., Baton Rouge. 329 pp.

Sander, I. L. 1979. Regenerating oaks with the shelterwood system. Pages 54-60 in H. A. Holt and B. C. Fischer, eds. Regenerating oaks in upland hardwood forests. Proc. 1979 John S. Wright For. Conf. Purdue Univ., W. Lafayette, Ind.

———, P. S. Johnson, and R. F. Watt. 1976. A guide for evaluating the adequacy of oak advance reproduction. U.S. For. Serv. Gen. Tech. Rep. NC-23. 7 pp.

Saucier, R. T. 1974. Quaternary geology of the Lower Mississippi Valley. Ark. Archeol. Surv. Res. Ser. 6. 26 pp.

Schlaegel, B. E. 1984. Long-term artificial annual flooding reduces Nuttall oak bole growth. U.S. For. Serv. Res. Note SO-309. 3 pp.

Schmitt, C. J., and P. V. Winger. 1980. Factors controlling the fate of pesticides in rural watersheds of the Lower Mississippi River Alluvial Valley. Trans. North Am. Wildl. and Nat. Resour. Conf. 45:354-375.

Scott, T. G., and C. H. Wasser. 1980. Checklist of North American plants for wildlife biologists. The Wildl. Soc., Washington, D.C. 58 pp.

Shearer, L. A., B. J. Jahn, and L. Lenz. 1969.

Deterioration of duck foods when flooded. J. Wildl. Manage. 33:1012-1015.

Singleton, J. R. 1951. Production and utilization of waterfowl food plants on the east Texas Gulf Coast. J. Wildl. Manage. 15:46-56.

Smith, D. E. 1984. The effects of greentree reservoir management on the development of a basal swelling damage and on the forest dynamics of Missouri's bottomland hardwoods. Ph.D. Thesis, Univ. Missouri, Columbia. 126 pp.

Smith, H. C., L. Della-Bianca, and H. Fleming. 1983. Appalachian mixed hardwoods. Pages 141-144 in R. M. Burns, ed. Silvicultural systems for the major forest types of the United States. U.S. For. Serv. Handb. 445.

Strader, R. W. 1987. South-central Louisiana waterfowl survey. A planning-aid report providing results from the 1986-87 winter survey. U.S. Fish and Wildl. Serv., Lafayette, La. 27 pp.

Sugden, L. G. 1971. Metabolizable energy of small grains for mallards. J. Wildl. Manage. 35:781-785.

Thompson, D. 1973. Feeding ecology of diving ducks on Keokuk Pool, Mississippi River. J. Wildl. Manage. 37:367-381.

Tiner, R. W., Jr. 1984. Wetlands of the United States: current status and recent trends. U.S. Fish and Wildl. Serv., Newton Corner, Mass. 59 pp.

Toth, S. J., F. Tourine, and S. J. Toth, Jr. 1972. Fertilization of smartweed. J. Wildl. Manage. 36:1356-1363.

Trost, R. E., D. H. Rusch, and V. R. Anderson. 1981. Survival and distribution of Canada geese from Ballard County, Kentucky. Proc. Annu. Conf. Southeast. Assoc. Fish and Wildl. Agencies 35:49-58.

———, ———, and D. H. Orr. 1980. Population affiliation of Canada geese from six southern refuges. Proc. Annu. Conf. Southeast. Assoc. Fish and Wildl. Agencies 34:598-606.

U.S. Fish and Wildlife Service. 1988. Final supplemental environmental impact statement: issuance of annual regulations permitting the sport hunting of migratory birds. U.S. Fish and Wildl. Serv., Washington, D.C. 340 pp.

Vaught, R. W., and L. M. Kirsch. 1966. Canada geese of the Eastern Prairie population, with special reference to the Swan Lake flock. Mo. Dep. Conserv. Tech. Bull. 3, Columbia. 91 pp.

Warner, R. E., S. P. Havera, and L. M. David. 1985. Effects of autumn tillage systems on corn and soybean harvest residues in Illinois. J. Wildl. Manage. 49:185-190.

Wellborn, T. L., Jr., M. D. Crosby, R. M. Durborow, and P. W. Taylor. 1987. For fish farmers—status of fish farming in Mississippi—December 1986. Miss. Coop. Ext. Serv. Ref. 87-1. Mississippi State Univ., Mississippi State. 7 pp.

Weller, M. W. 1965. Chronology of pair formation in some nearctic *Aythya* (Anatidae). Auk 82:227-235.

Wells, R. K. 1982. Periodic waterfowl inventories, 1978-82. Miss. Dep. Wildl. Conserv., Fed. Aid in Wildl. Restor. Rep. Proj. W-48, Stud. 1, Job 1, Jackson, Miss. 23 pp.

Wesley, D. E. 1979. Serving up the rice. Ducks Unlimited 43(4):32-33, 35, 37, 39.

White, D. 1985. Lowland hardwood wetland invertebrate community and production in Missouri. Arch. Hydrobiol. 103:509-533.

White, D. H., and D. James. 1978. Differential use of fresh water environments by wintering waterfowl of coastal Texas. Wilson Bull. 90:99-111.

——, W. J. Fleming, and K. L. Ensor. 1988. Pesticide contamination and hatching success of waterbirds in Mississippi. J. Wildl. Manage. 52:724-729.

Wigley, T. B., and T. H. Filer, Jr. 1989. Greentree reservoirs: current management, use and problems. Wildl. Soc. Bull. 17:In press.

Wills, D. 1970. Chufa tuber production and its relationship to waterfowl management on Catahoula Lake, Louisiana. Proc. Annu. Conf. Southeast. Assoc. Game and Fish Comm. 24:146-153.

——. 1971. Food habit study of mallards and pintails on Catahoula Lake, Louisiana, with notes of food habits of other species. Proc. Annu. Conf. Southeast. Assoc. Game and Fish Comm. 25:289-294.

Wright, T. W. 1959. Winter foods of mallards in Arkansas. Proc. Annu. Conf. Southeast. Assoc. Game and Fish Comm. 13:291-296.

Zekor, D. T., and R. M. Kaminski. 1987. Attitudes of Mississippi Delta farmers toward private-land waterfowl management. Wildl. Soc. Bull. 15:346-354.

Zwank, P. J., V. L. Wright, P. M. Shealy, and J. D. Newsom. 1985. Lead toxicosis in waterfowl on two major wintering areas in Louisiana. Wildl. Soc. Bull. 13:17-26.

SOUTHERN COASTAL MARSHES AND LAKES

ROBERT H. CHABRECK, School of Forestry, Wildlife, and Fisheries, Louisiana State University Agricultural Center, Baton Rouge, LA 70803
TED JOANEN, Louisiana Department of Wildlife and Fisheries, Grand Chenier, LA 70643
STUART L. PAULUS, Innovative Research Services, P. O. Box 731, Snoqualmie, WA 98065

The vast southern coastal marshes and lakes in the Mississippi Flyway constitute a unique habitat for wintering waterfowl. Over the centuries, the Mississippi River has transported freshwater and sediments to the Gulf of Mexico to form a large marshy plain well interspersed with ponds, lakes, and bayous. The region is the terminus of the flyway and the destination of many migrant waterfowl not undertaking the long trans-Gulf flights to more southerly habitats. Birds that continue their journey southward make use of the southern coastal marshes and lakes during stopovers in the region while migrating to and from Latin America. The purpose of this paper is to describe waterfowl habitat conditions in southern coastal marshes and lakes of the Mississippi Flyway and to discuss the management programs and research needs for waterfowl in the region.

REGIONAL CHARACTERISTICS

Physiography

The Gulf Coastal Plain gently slopes toward the Gulf of Mexico and forms the coastal regions of Louisiana, Mississippi, and Alabama (Fig. 1). The coastal region is bordered by a broad continental shelf in the Gulf of Mexico and contains relatively shallow water, near shore, which has enhanced development of marshes and barrier islands. Many rivers empty into the Gulf in this region and contain embayments that form highly productive estuarine environments. The coastal zone of the region encompasses >3 million ha of marshes, bays, sounds, lakes, rivers, and other water bodies (Crance 1971, Chabreck 1972, Christmas 1973).

Climate

Climate of the region is temperate with hot summers and mild winters, although several freezes occur annually. The growing season averages about 300 days, and rainfall averages between 140 and 150 cm (Stout 1984). The Gulf Coast is characterized by southerly to southeasterly prevailing winds that are an important source of atmospheric moisture. Hurricanes are common in the region and have had detrimental effects on marshes, beaches, and barrier islands (Chabreck and Palmisano 1973).

Tides

Normal tidal range is between 30 and 60 cm, but the level of individual tides varies with the phase of the moon and direction and velocity of the wind. Lowest tides occur during winter when strong northerly winds are present. Highest tides are associated with hurricanes, with tide levels of 120 to 180 cm in some portion of the region during most years (Marmer 1954).

Water Salinity

Water salinity varies within the region and is largely governed for a particular site by its proximity to the Gulf of Mexico, tide water access, recent rainfall amounts, and river discharge. Salinity in the adjacent Gulf of Mexico usually ranges from 20 to 25 parts per thousand (ppt) and is less saline than normal sea water (36 ppt) (Marmer 1954). As water from the Gulf of Mexico enters adjacent marshes, salinity levels are usually quite high. As Gulf water moves inland by tidal action, it mixes with fresher water

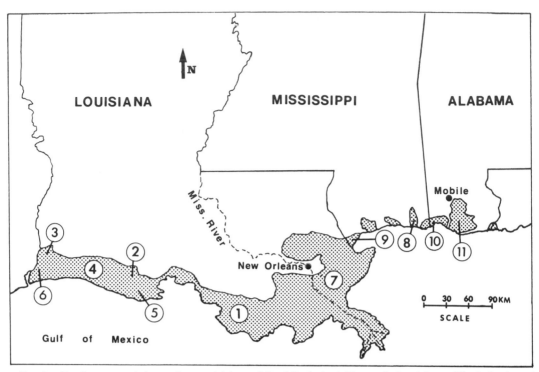

Fig. 1.   Southern coastal marshes and lakes of the Mississippi Flyway in Louisiana, Mississippi, and Alabama. Major waterfowl concentration areas as indicated by numbers are (1) Central Coastal Area, (2) Amoco Marsh, (3) Gum Cove Area, (4) Big Burn, (5) Pecan Island Marsh, (6) Johnson Bayou Marshes, (7) Delacroix Marshes, (8) Pascagoula Marshes, (9) Point Clear Area, (10) Point au Chenes-Grand Bay Area, and (11) Mobile Delta-Mobile Bay.

draining from interior regions toward the Gulf. Consequently, water salinity gradually declines from the coastline to the interior reaches of the coastal marshes.

Geographical Distribution of Coastal Marshes

Southern marshes in the Mississippi Flyway cover >1 million ha and comprise 42% of the total area of coastal marshes in the United States (U.S.), excluding Alaska (Alexander et al. 1986). The coastal marshes of Louisiana comprise 96% of the region (Table 1). The marshes of Louisiana extend inland from the Gulf for distances ranging from 25 to 80 km and consist of the deltaic plain and the chenier plain. The deltaic plain lies in the southeastern part of Louisiana and makes up three-fourths of its coastal region (Chabreck 1970). Marshes of the

deltaic plain were formed from deposition by the Mississippi River and are unstable and in various stages of degradation (Coleman 1966). The marsh is rapidly subsiding and eroding, and being lost at a rate of 100 km² per year (Gagliano et al. 1981). An irregular shoreline, with numerous large embayments, characterizes the area. The deltaic plain has several chains of barrier islands, which represent the outer rim of former deltas of the Mississippi River. Active land building is currently taking place in deltas of the Mississippi River and the Atchafalaya River, a distributary of the Mississippi River.

The chenier plain occupies the coasts of southwestern Louisiana and southeastern Texas. Marshes of the chenier plain were formed from Mississippi River sediment that was discharged into the Gulf of Mexico, carried westward by currents, and

Table 1.   Geographical distribution of marsh types in states[a] along the Northcentral Gulf Coast.

State	Size of marsh types (ha × 100)				
	Salt	Brackish	Intermediate	Fresh	Total
Alabama	28	31	15	28	102 (1%)
Mississippi	75	83	42	78	278 (3%)
Louisiana	2,664	2,960	1,480	2,763	9,867 (96%)
Total	2,767	3,074	1,537	2,869	10,247
	(27%)	(30%)	(15%)	(28%)	

[a]Total area of marsh by state is from Alexander et al. (1986). Distribution of marsh types by state is from Crance (1971) and Chabreck (1972).

deposited against the shoreline. Interruptions in the depositional process resulted in beach formation, and resumption of deposition caused new marshland to form seaward from the beach. This process caused several beach deposits to be stranded in the marshes. The stranded beaches or cheniers represent a major relief feature of the area. Marshes of the chenier plain are underlain by firm clay deposits and will support the weight of levees and spoil deposits, unlike the unstable subsoils of most of the deltaic plain. The chenier plain is bordered by a well-developed beach, which has few openings into the Gulf of Mexico (Russell and Howe 1935).

Mississippi has 3% of the southern marshes of the Mississippi Flyway. The greatest area of marshland is in the southwestern part of the state and forms a section of the deltaic plain (Eleuterius 1973). Marshes along the Alabama coast comprise 1% of the southern marsh area. In Alabama, and adjacent areas of the Mississippi coast, marshes are small, disjunct, and limited to low alluvial deposits along protected bay shores and rivers (West 1977). A series of barrier islands occurs offshore of both states (Crance 1971, Eleuterius 1973).

Marsh Types

Marsh vegetation varies in its tolerance to water salinity, and plants are grouped into communities having similar salinity tolerances and referred to commonly as marsh types. Because water salinity declines along a gradient moving inland

from the Gulf of Mexico, the marsh types generally occur in bands parallel to the shoreline. Four distinct marsh types have been identified in the region and are classified as salt, brackish, intermediate, and fresh (Penfound and Hathaway 1938, Chabreck 1972).

Because the major area of marshland in the region is in Louisiana, most descriptions of marsh types relate to Louisiana. The marsh types contain characteristic associations of plant species (Table 2), hydrological patterns, soils, and fish and wildlife resources.

Salt Marsh.—Salt marsh makes up 27% of the coastal marshes of the North Central Gulf Coast (Table 1). This type generally occupies a narrow zone adjacent to the shoreline of the Gulf of Mexico and many embayments. However, in the deltaic plain, this type is quite extensive because the broken shoreline allows tide water to move far inland.

Salt marsh has the greatest tidal fluctuation of all marsh types and contains a well-developed drainage system. Water salinity averages 18 ppt (range = 8 to 29 ppt), and soils have a lower organic content ($\bar{x}$ = 18%) than fresher types located farther inland (Chabreck 1972). Few species of vegetation occur. Those that do occur are salt-tolerant and dominated by smooth cordgrass (*Spartina alterniflora*), seashore saltgrass (*Distichlis spicata*), and needle rush (*Juncus roemerianus*). Plant nomenclature follows Scott and Wasser (1980).

Brackish Marsh.—Brackish marsh comprises 30% of the marsh area of the region

Table 2. Plant species composition (%) of the marsh types in the Louisiana coastal marshes (Chabreck 1970).

Scientific name	Vegetative type			
	Saline	Brackish	Intermediate	Fresh
Batis maritima	4.41	0	0	0
Distichlis spicata	14.27	13.32	0.36	0.13
Juncus roemerianus	10.10	3.93	0.72	0.60
Spartina alterniflora	62.14	4.77	0.86	0
Eleocharis parvula	0	2.46	0.49	0.54
Ruppia maritima	0	3.83	0.64	0
Scirpus olneyi	0	4.97	3.26	0.45
Scirpus robustus	0.66	1.78	0.68	0
Spartina patens	5.99	55.22	34.01	3.74
Bacopa monnieri	0	0.92	4.75	1.44
Cyperus odoratus	0	0.84	2.18	1.56
Echinochloa walteri	0	0.36	2.72	0.77
Paspalum vaginatum	0	1.38	4.46	0.35
Phragmites communis	0	0.31	6.63	2.54
Alternanthera philoxeroides	0	0	2.47	5.34
Elocharis spp.	0	0.82	3.28	10.74
Hydrocotyle spp.	0	0	0	1.93
Panicum hemitomon	0	0	0.76	25.62
Sagittaria falcata	0	0	6.47	15.15
Other species	2.43	5.09	25.26	29.10
Total	100.00	100.00	100.00	100.00

(Table 1). Although this type lies inland from the salt-marsh type and is farther removed from the influence of highly saline Gulf waters, it is still subjected to daily tidal action. Normal water depths exceed that of salt marsh, and soils contain higher levels of organic matter ($\bar{x}$ = 31%). Water salinity averages 8.2 ppt (range = 1.0 to 18.4 ppt). Brackish marsh contains numerous small bayous and lakes.

Brackish marsh contains greater plant diversity than salt marsh and is dominated by marshhay cordgrass (Spartina patens) and seashore saltgrass. An important wildlife food plant of brackish marsh, Olney bulrush (Scirpus olneyi), grows best in tidal marsh free from excessive flooding, prolonged drought, and drastic salinity changes (O'Neil 1949, Chabreck 1972). Widgeongrass (Ruppia maritima), the dominant submerged aquatic plant of brackish marsh, is a preferred food of ducks and American coots (Fulica americana) (Joanen and Glasgow 1965).

Intermediate Marsh.—The intermediate marsh type lies inland from the brackish type and comprises 15% of the marsh area of the region (Table 1). Intermediate marsh is somewhat influenced by tides, and water salinity averages 3.3 ppt (range = 0.5 to 8.3 ppt). Water levels are slightly higher than in brackish marsh, and soil organic content averages 34%. Plant species diversity is high, and marshhay cordgrass also is dominant in intermediate marsh. Other common marsh plants include common reed (Phragmites australis), narrowleaf arrowhead (Sagittaria lancifolia), and coastal waterhyssop (Bacopa monnieri). Intermediate marsh contains an abundance of submerged aquatics such as pondweeds (Potamogeton spp.) and naiad (Najas quadalupensis).

Freshwater Marsh.—Freshwater marsh makes up 28% of the marsh area of the northcentral Gulf Coast (Table 1). The type occupies the zone between the intermediate marsh and upland terraces or the forested wetlands in the alluvial plain of major river systems. Freshwater marsh is normally free from tidal influence, and water salinity averages only 1.0 ppt (range = 0.1 to 3.4 ppt). Because of slow drainage, water depth and soil organic content ($\overline{x}$ = 52%) are greatest in freshwater marsh. In some freshwater marshes, soil organic matter content exceeds 80% (Chabreck 1972), and the substrate for plant growth is a floating organic mat called flotant (Russell 1942). Freshwater marsh supports the greatest diversity of plants among all marsh types. Dominant plants include maidencane (*Panicum hemitomon*), spikerush (*Eleocharis* spp.), narrowleaf arrowhead, and alligatorweed (*Alternanthera philoxeroides*). This marsh type also contains many submerged and floating-leafed plants. Some floating aquatics, such as water hyacinth (*Eichhornia crassipes*), form dense stands that often block water bodies.

HABITAT IMPORTANCE

Southern coastal marshes in the Mississippi Flyway provide habitat for over 400,000 geese, 4 million ducks, 1.5 million American coots (*Fulica americana*), hundreds of thousands of shorebirds, and other migratory birds that overwinter or pass through on their way to traditional wintering grounds (U.S. Dep. Int. 1982). Louisiana has a greater number of major wintering species of ducks than any other state (Williams and Chabreck 1986). The Louisiana coastal marshes are of great importance to migratory waterfowl and provide winter habitat for more than two-thirds of the entire Mississippi Flyway waterfowl population (Bellrose 1980). Palmisano (1973) noted that one-fourth of the North American dabbling duck population winters in these wetlands, with peak numbers of over 5.5 million in some years. Coastal Louisiana wetlands also support over half of the continental mottled duck (*Anas fulvigula*) population. Nearly 38% of the canvasbacks (*Aythya valisneria*) that winter in the Mississippi Flyway are found in

Louisiana, and Six Mile and Wax lakes of the lower Atchafalaya Basin and Atchafalaya Delta are major concentration areas (Bellrose 1980).

The Louisiana coastal marshes and adjacent agricultural areas have supported 370,000 lesser snow geese (*Chen caerulescens*) and 55,000 white-fronted geese (*Anser albifrons*) in recent years (Fruge 1982). Originally, snow geese wintered mostly in the brackish marshes, but occasionally they ventured short distances into the adjacent wet prairie, particularly after fire removed heavy cover. The coastal tall-grass prairie, which lies inland from the coastal marshes, has been converted to an extensive agricultural area dominated by rice, soybeans, and pasture. Snow geese, subsequently, have extended their winter range to include all of the coastal prairie. Because of these changes, more habitat for snow geese now exists along the Gulf Coast than during historical times (Lynch 1968).

Freshwater marsh represents the most valuable waterfowl habitat and is important to fulvous whistling ducks (*Dendrocygna bicolor*), white-fronted geese, American green-winged teal (*Anas crecca*), mottled ducks, mallards (*A. platyrhynchos*), northern pintails (*A. acuta*), blue-winged teal (*A. discors*), shovelers (*A. clypeata*), gadwalls (*A. strepera*), American wigeons (*A. americana*), canvasbacks, ring-necked ducks (*Aythya collaris*), lesser scaup (*A. affinis*), and hooded mergansers (*Lophodytes cucullatus*). Freshwater marshes provide important year-round habitat for mottled ducks and important pre- and post-breeding habitat for fulvous whistling-ducks (Williams and Chabreck 1986). Intermediate marshes are ranked second to freshwater marsh in their value to waterfowl (Palmisano 1973). Brackish marshes are the most extensive of the coastal marsh zones. They represent the traditional wintering grounds for snow geese and provide year-round habitat for mottled ducks. Brackish marshes are also of high value to gad-walls and lesser scaup. Salt marshes play only a minor role and are generally considered of only low value to waterfowl (Williams and Chabreck 1986).

Major Concentration Areas

Central Coastal Area.—One of the most important waterfowl habitats along the Louisiana coast is the area encompassing some 250,000 ha of the central coastal region between Cote Blanche Bay and Barataria Bay (Fig. 1). This area comprises approximately 70% wetlands with vast freshwater marshes, 29% permanent water, and less than 1% upland. The western part contains the mouth of the Atchafalaya River and Wax Lake Outlet, where active deltaic accretion is occurring. The delta marshes of this area contain numerous natural waterways and ponds, resulting in a uniform mixture of marshes and open water. Several large lakes and bays occur, and provide important winter habitat for diving ducks (U.S. Dep. Int. 1982).

Between 1969 and 1978, these marshes contained approximately 400,000 wintering waterfowl annually. Gadwalls were the most abundant, followed by green-winged teal, shovelers, and mallards. During September and October, these marshes attracted large concentrations of blue-winged teal. Diving ducks were scarce, except during periods of extremely high water. The brackish marshes along the edge of the Atchafalaya Bay support small numbers of snow geese annually. This area also winters a major portion of Louisiana's coot population and a large number of mottled ducks.

This vast wetland complex, the heart of southcentral Louisiana's trapping and commercial fishing industries, affords valuable habitats for furbearing mammals as well as a rich nursery area for marine species. Unfortunately, this habitat is being lost because of saltwater intrusion associated with canal dredging (Fruge

1982). This has resulted in a change in marsh vegetation toward saline vegetative types that are less attractive to waterfowl. Especially noteworthy was the fact that over the 10-year period surveyed, freshwater marsh habitat was overwhelmingly used by the wintering waterfowl and supported 87% of the total population (U.S. Dep. Int. 1982).

Amoco Marsh.—These marshes comprise some 40,000 ha between White Lake and the Intracoastal Waterway in southwestern Louisiana. This area has traditionally wintered >250,000 ducks, including large concentrations of mallards, blue- and green-winged teal, pintails, and gadwalls. These marshes provide important staging areas for fulvous whistling-ducks before their migration to Mexico. Mottled ducks breed extensively on the prairie ridges and concentrate in large numbers during the winter months.

These marshes are currently threatened by the Mermentau River Basin's locking system operated by the U.S. Army Corps of Engineers. When basin water levels are held high to aid water navigation, the production of emergent vegetation is limited, and marsh erosion along lake and pond shores is accelerated.

Gum Cove Area.—The Gum Cove area comprises about 30,000 ha in western Louisiana and extends eastward from Sabine River to the Gum Cove ridge and southward from U.S. Highway 90 to Sabine National Wildlife Refuge (NWR). Intermediate marshes occupy the largest wetland area, followed by brackish and freshwater marshes. Gum Cove probably includes the most diversified wetlands habitat in southwestern Louisiana, with marshes interrupted by several elevated prairie ridges. These ridges and islands also contain bottomland hardwood forests and cypress-tupelo swamps.

This mixed-prairie wetland habitat provides wintering habitat for about 150,000 migratory waterfowl. The major species are gadwall, green-winged teal, pintail, wigeon, mallard, snow geese, and white-fronted geese. During September and October, >20,000 blue-winged teal may use the area, and a large number of mottled ducks nest in the Gum Cove area (U.S. Dep. Int. 1982).

Big Burn.—The Big Burn is in southwestern Louisiana and comprises approximately 24,000 ha. It extends from the Intracoastal Waterway southward to the Little Chenier Ridge and eastward from Louisiana Highway 27 to Grand Lake. Approximately 15% of the Big Burn occurs as intermediate marsh, and 78% occurs as freshwater marsh.

Wintering waterfowl populations contain predominantly gadwall, mallard, green-winged teal, pintail, and wigeon. As many as 20,000 blue-winged teal use the area in early fall. Midwinter waterfowl inventories from 1969-1978 indicated that about 130,000 waterfowl were found within the Big Burn annually (U.S. Dep. Int. 1982).

This area is rapidly deteriorating because of saltwater intrusion from the west via Calcasieu Lake and Grand Bayou. Significant changes in water salinity and vegetation are occurring near Louisiana Highway 27, the western boundary of the Big Burn, and are rapidly progressing eastward.

Pecan Island Marsh.—The Pecan Island Marsh is approximately 40,000 ha and is bordered on the north by the Old Intracoastal Waterway, on the south by the Gulf of Mexico, on the west by the Rockefeller Wildlife Refuge, and on the east by the Bell Isle and Six Mile canals. From 1969-1978, this area contained an average winter population of 107,000 ducks, geese, and coots, annually. Nearly 59% were dabblers, <1% were divers, about 36% were geese, and 5% were coots. Dabblers of greatest importance were mallard, gadwall, green-winged teal, and pintail.

The major threats to the continued productivity of waterfowl habitat in the

Pecan Island area are saltwater intrusion from the south and erosion of the shoreline of White Lake, which is caused by increased water levels in the Mermentau Basin Complex.

Johnson Bayou Marshes.—The marshes of the Johnson Bayou comprise approximately 22,000 ha and extend from the Sabine Pass and Sabine Lake eastward to the Magnolia Vacuum Canal, and from Sabine NWR southward to the Gulf. During 1969-1978, these marshes wintered an estimated 93,000 waterfowl annually. Approximately 51% of the population were dabblers, mostly gadwall, green-winged teal, and pintail. Less than 1% were divers, mostly ring-necked duck, and about 39% were geese, primarily snow geese. Johnson Bayou supports a large breeding and wintering population of mottled ducks, and from September through October, >25,000 blue-winged teal concentrate in the area.

Delacroix Marshes.—These marshes comprise approximately 70,000 ha of marshland and open water and lie east of the Mississippi River and south of the Mississippi River Gulf Outlet. The Delacroix marshes were once considered to be southeast Louisiana's most productive fur and waterfowl marsh habitat, but now the marshes support fewer wintering waterfowl than other major concentration areas in Louisiana. From 1969-1978, this area averaged 20,000 wintering waterfowl annually. The major species of dabblers were gadwall, mottled duck, and mallard; lesser scaup was the only recorded diver species that used the area during the period. The decrease in wintering waterfowl using this area can be attributed to increases in salinity and associated vegetational changes that resulted from construction of the Mississippi River Gulf Outlet, land subsidence, and hurricane damage.

Mississippi Wetlands.—The Mississippi coastal zone extends some 110 km eastward from the Pearl River to the Mississippi-Alabama border. The coast is dissected by four major drainage basins, the largest of which is the Pearl River system. The other three systems are the Pascagoula River system, the Bay St. Louis system, and the Biloxi Bay system. Each system terminates in an estuarine area that contains active sedimentation. The alluvial deposits from the systems form most of the natural marsh habitat.

The estimated 30,000 ha of coastal wetlands in Mississippi are composed of about 15% cypress-tupelo swamp and bottomland forest and 85% marshland. From 1969-1978, about 6,400 waterfowl wintering annually along the Mississippi coast used freshwater and intermediate marshes. Approximately 20,000 redheads (*Aythya americana*) wintered near the Chandeleur Islands off the coast of Mississippi. Species of greatest abundance that occurred within the coastal wetlands were lesser scaup, redhead, ring-necked duck, mallard, wigeon, and gadwall. Diving ducks comprised the majority of the Mississippi winter duck population.

The Pascagoula marshes include some 6,000 ha and span an area between the East Pascagoula and West Pascagoula Rivers. Midwinter inventories during 1969-1978 recorded an average annual population of 2,500 wintering waterfowl in the Pascagoula marshes, 39% of the total wintering waterfowl along the Mississippi coast. With the exception of wood ducks (*Aix sponsa*) that used the swamp areas, the rest of the waterfowl population (two-thirds of which were diving ducks) was found in marsh areas.

The Point Clear area contains about 5,000 ha and winters approximately 1,100 waterfowl annually. Major species using the area are lesser scaup, redhead, ring-necked duck, and green-winged teal. This area also supports a wintering population of snow geese.

The Point aux Chenes-Grand Bay Swamp lies in both Mississippi and Alabama and encompasses some 12,000 ha. This area wintered approximately 1,000 waterfowl annually during 1969 to 1978, with a ratio of about two diving ducks per dabbling duck. Major species were redhead, lesser scaup, wigeon, and mallard. The area also supported a small nesting population of mottled ducks and wood ducks.

Alabama Wetlands.—Wetlands of coastal Alabama extend eastward from the Mississippi-Alabama border to Perdido Bay on the Alabama-Florida border. The most extensive wetlands in Alabama are located in the Mobile River Delta and are essentially freshwater marsh and wooded swamps. Mobile Delta and Mobile Bay are coastal Alabama's primary wintering areas for migratory waterfowl. From 1969 to 1978, nearly 26,000 waterfowl wintered in the Alabama coastal zone annually. Major species included gadwall, redhead, canvasback, pintail, wigeon, lesser scaup, and mallard; dabblers outnumbered divers. One of the Mississippi Flyway's largest wintering canvasback populations, outside of Louisiana, uses Mobile Bay. Small nesting populations of mottled ducks and wood ducks also use the lower Mobile Delta Unit (U.S. Dep. Int. 1982).

HABITAT IMPORTANCE RELATIVE TO WATERFOWL REQUIREMENTS

A number of factors are important in influencing habitat selection by waterfowl during winter, and include the quality and availability of food, water, and shelter (Chabreck 1979). Special requirements, such as grit sites or areas free of disturbance, also are needed. Use of habitats and the distribution of birds are influenced by the ability of individuals to compete with others for resources (Paulus 1983). Habitat selection by waterfowl during winter may primarily reflect average habitat suitability during previous years (Chabreck 1979, Nichols 1982, Paulus 1984*b*). Wetland managers wishing to

Table 3. Time-activity budgets of selected waterfowl in southern coastal marshes and lakes during winter.

Species	Feeding	Resting	Locomoting	Preening	Alert	Agonistic	Courting	Other	N[a]	Reference
Northern pintail	5	70	9	10	6			6	105	Tamisier (1976)[b]
	32	34	10	10	8	1	4		27	Paulus (1986)
Northern shoveler	42	34	9	9	5	<1	<1		71	Paulus (1986)
Green-winged teal	33	45	9	11	<1	<1	<1		430	Rave (1987)[b]
	5	75	9	9				2	162	Tamisier (1976)[b]
	34	34	5	9	8	<1	9		115	Paulus (1986)
Mottled duck	43	36	6	9	7	<1	<1		1188	Paulus (1984b)
Gadwall	64	10	11	5	9	<1	<1		231	Paulus (1984a)

[a]Numbers of hours of observation.
[b]Observations conducted only during daylight hours.

attract waterfowl to an area must recognize that these factors must be provided before habitats are fully occupied by ducks and geese.

Food

Factors Affecting Food Choice.—During winter, waterfowl require energy for a number of physiological and behavioral needs. Upon arrival on southern coastal marshes, most waterfowl replenish lipid and other nutrient stores depleted during migration, and acquire reserves to be used during winter (Paulus 1980, Ankney 1982, Gaston et al. 1985, Hobaugh 1985, Rave 1987). During fall, most species complete the prealternate molt and must have the necessary nutrients to replace feathers (Paulus 1983). Energy also is required for normal metabolic activities of maintenance and for activities such as pair formation, competing for resources, and avoiding harassment from hunting or other disturbances. Although the climate of southern coastal areas is moderate, inclement weather does occur and causes increased energy needs. Finally, waterfowl may require additional food in late winter or early spring to elevate nutrient reserves before migrating northward. Energy demands are high throughout winter, and feeding occupies much of the time of waterfowl (Table 3).

Because nutrient requirements vary seasonally, most species require a variety of foods during winter. Climatic and soil conditions of many southern coastal wetlands allow abundant production of a wide variety of natural and agricultural foods used by waterfowl. However, foods available to waterfowl during winter differ considerably in their nutrient and water content, size, availability, and digestibility (Table 4). For example, agricultural grains tend to contain less fiber, protein, and minerals and more digestible carbohydrates than seeds of native wetland plants. Rhizomes and tubers consumed by geese contain little protein or minerals, but are high in digestible carbohydrates. Submerged aquatic plants contain mostly water and much fibrous material that is difficult to digest. In general, waterfowl tend to select foods that allow the birds to meet their nutrient needs in the shortest amount of time each day (Paulus 1988).

Food choice also reflects the ability of individuals to procure, process, and digest foods. Differences in bill structure and body size influence the types of foods most easily procured by different species. Waterfowl differ in the structure of their digestive system that may allow some species (e.g., gadwalls) to exploit plant foods more efficiently than other species (Miller 1975, Paulus 1982b).

Seasonal Food Habits of Waterfowl.—Diets of dabbling ducks during winter primarily consist of seeds, leafy aquatic vegetation, and some animal matter. Although production of natural seeds per unit area may be similar to that of agricultural foods, ducks will favor agri-

Table 4. Nutritional content (% dry weight) of selected foods used by waterfowl in southern coastal marshes and lakes during winter.

	Protein	Fiber	NFE	Fat	Ash
Agricultural seeds					
Corn	10	5	80	5	2
Rice	9	1	75	2	1
Soybean	42	6	28	19	5
Wheat	26	19	34	4	17
Milo	12	3	80	3	2
Native emergent plants					
Carex spp.	17	26	45	4	8
Cladium jamaicense	7	34	48	2	9
Cyperus esculentus	4	11	69	4	12
Digitaria sanguinalis	14	14	63	2	7
Echinochloa crusgalli	13	9	71	4	3
Echinochloa walteri	16	14	61	4	4
Eleocharis parvula	12	42			
Eleocharis spp.	19	27	44	2	7
Paspalum plicatulum	7	19	65	2	6
Scirpus robustus	8	16	66	3	6
Setaria magna	14	17	64	2	4
Spartina patens	11	32	43	2	11
Rhizomes *(Spartina patens* and *Distichlis spicata)*	4	28	63	2	3
Tubers *(Cyperus* spp., *Scirpus* spp.)	7	12	73	3	5
Submerged aquatic plants					
Algae	14	18			
Ceratophyllum demersum	18	36			
Myriophyllum spicatum	17	50			
Potamogeton spp.	11	20			
Ruppia maritima	17	41			
Animal matter					
Gammarus spp.	48	10	12	8	23

References: Alisauskas et al. (1988), Junca et al. (1962), Linscombe (1972), Mutzar et al. (1976), National Research Council (1971), Paulus (1982*a*), Sugden (1973).

cultural foods such as rice, corn, or soybeans if favorable water depths make these foods accessible, as is often the case in autumn and early winter (Harmon et al. 1960, Palmisano 1973). Agricultural foods may also be favored because they are often of larger size and lower moisture content than natural seeds. These foods enable waterfowl to obtain more nutrients, especially energy, per unit effort and dry weight of food consumed (Baldassarre et al. 1986, Leslie and Zwank 1985, Alisauskas et al. 1988).

Ducks also may select agricultural seeds or natural aquatic vegetation because many types of natural seeds may still be attached to plants standing out of water and are unavailable to ducks until these plants are killed by frosts in winter or made available by flooding (Chabreck 1979). This may explain why mottled ducks were observed consuming leafy aquatic vegetation rather than consuming more nutritious natural seeds in Louisiana in autumn (Paulus 1984*b*). During autumn, the climate is mild, food is readily available in most areas, and ducks spend only moderate amounts of time feeding.

During midwinter, seeds of marsh plants (Fig. 2) are important in the diets of many species of ducks using southern coastal marshes. Agricultural foods are usually less abundant because of consumption by waterfowl during autumn and are of lower quality due to deterioration from moisture or having been killed by frosts (Harmon et al. 1960, Alisauskas

Fig. 2. Annual grasses and sedges produce an abundance of seeds that are important in the diets of many species of ducks using southern coastal marshes.

et al. 1988). Killing frosts and flooding make natural seeds more readily available to ducks (Jemison and Chabreck 1962). In addition, hunting pressure and harassment in agricultural fields may cause ducks to use more secluded natural marshes.

Food habits of species such as gadwall, wigeon, and shoveler, that consume primarily leafy aquatic vegetation or algae, also are influenced by the abundance and quality of vegetation. Wigeongrass is a high-quality aquatic plant and was the primary food chosen by gadwall along coastal Louisiana during autumn (Paulus 1982a). However, gadwall on Marsh Island, Louisiana, mostly consumed Eurasian watermilfoil (*Myriophyllum spicatum*) during fall and early winter. Milfoil was very abundant on the island, but wigeongrass occurred in limited quantities. Although milfoil was less nutritious than wigeongrass, and gadwalls spent nearly all of their time

feeding (80% of the day and night, compared with 40% for wigeongrass), it apparently was advantageous for gadwalls to select milfoil over wigeongrass on Marsh Island.

As more nutritious foods were depleted, gadwalls consumed plants of lower nutrient quality, including dwarf spikerush (*Eleocharis parvula*) and coontail (*Ceratophyllum demersum*), during midwinter (Jemison and Chabreck 1962, Paulus 1982a). As in autumn, ducks primarily used areas where foods were most abundant. However, use of lower-quality foods and increased competition for remaining vegetation among individuals resulted in gadwalls spending more time feeding during midwinter than during autumn to meet their nutritional requirements.

Unlike those for dabbling ducks, the food and habitat requirements of diving ducks wintering in the southern coastal marshes have received little study. Animal foods, including amphipods, decapods, gastropods, and pelycypods, were the primary foods consumed by lesser scaup using both inland and gulf waters in Louisiana (Harmon 1962, Rogers and Korschgen 1966, Afton et al. 1986). Lesser scaup form large rafts on both inland and gulf waters, presumably in areas of greatest food concentration. However, movements of large numbers of lesser scaup between inland and gulf waters have been observed and may reflect changes in food availability and quality in the two areas.

Agricultural grains are important in the diets of geese during fall and early winter in agricultural areas near the southern coastal marshes. Snow geese also congregate in large numbers in areas where marsh vegetation has recently been burned. Burning exposes plant rhizomes and tubers, which are readily consumed by geese, as are new sprouts arising from burned vegetation (Lynch et al. 1947, Alisauskas et al. 1988).

Competition for Foods.—Access to foods is not equal among species or individuals. Several factors, including the species, body size, age, sex, and pair status of the bird may influence which individuals have access to the best foods and food patches (Paulus 1983, Hepp and Hair 1984). In general, when individuals of different species compete for the same resource, larger individuals usually limit use of resources by smaller birds. However, some species are more aggressive than others and are more successful in obtaining desired foods. For example, wigeon are slightly smaller than gadwalls (Bellrose 1980), but often aggressively exclude gadwalls from foods used by both species in Louisiana (Paulus 1980). The degree to which species are associated with specific areas also influences their ability to adapt to changing habitat conditions (Nichols 1982).

Water

Aerial surveys and studies of waterfowl,

using southern coastal marshes and lakes, emphasize the importance of water depth, salinity, and quality, land-water interspersion, and tidal cycles in influencing the distribution of waterfowl during winter (Palmisano 1973, Chabreck et al. 1975, Beshears 1982, Paulus 1984a,b, 1986, Rave 1987). In general, smaller-bodied dabbling ducks (e.g., green-winged teal) forage in shallow water (<15 cm), larger dabbling ducks (e.g., pintail) in habitats with intermediate (15-30 cm) water depths, and diving ducks in habitats with deeper water (>30 cm). Primary factors influencing the range of depths used by waterfowl seem to be food choice and ability of birds to access these foods. Species that consume seeds are limited to depths at which individuals are able to reach seeds on the marsh substrate. Species that feed upon aquatic vegetation (e.g., gadwalls and wigeons) use a greater range of water depths because many aquatic plants are found at and below the surface of the water (Paulus 1982b, 1984a).

Mottled ducks appear unique in that, despite their large body size, they primarily occupy shallow-water habitats (White and James 1978, Paulus 1984b). Seeds, leafy aquatic vegetation, and animal matter appear to be important in the diets of mottled ducks. If mottled ducks consume more animal matter than other dabbling ducks during winter, they may favor shoreline edges and habitats where animal foods are easily procured.

Large areas of open water may be avoided by waterfowl (Chabreck 1979). Large ponds are exposed to wind and wave action, and choppy waters make it difficult for waterfowl to feed and loaf. During severe weather, ducks will usually leave large open-water areas for more secluded marshes (Paulus 1984a). Excessive wave action also has been cited as a major factor responsible for the periodic decline in submerged aquatic plants (Baldwin 1957, Lueth 1963, Beshears 1979).

Habitats under tidal influence are important to many species wintering along the Gulf coast. Green-winged teal, pintail, shoveler, gadwall, wigeon, and snow geese are often observed foraging and loafing in tidal areas. Gadwall and wigeon favor deeper waters and tend to avoid tidal areas during low tides. Other dabbling ducks and geese favor low tides, because these birds forage near the mud-water interface and loaf on mudflats or in shallow water (Paulus 1986, Rave 1987).

Water quality regulates waterfowl use of marsh habitats. Waterfowl are capable of finding food by touch, as well as by sight, as demonstrated by high levels of nocturnal feeding activity (Paulus 1984a, b). However, waterfowl are probably more adept at locating foods during the day where the water is clear. Pollutants, such as oil, may deter waterfowl use of aquatic areas at low levels (Chabreck 1973) but are important mortality factors at higher levels (St. Amant 1971, Chabreck 1979, Paulus 1980). In addition, water turbidity and pollutants inhibit plant growth and waterfowl food production, which in turn reduce waterfowl use of habitats (Baldwin 1957, Duke and Chabreck 1976, Borom 1979, Beshears 1982, Friend et al. 1982).

Protection, Cover, and Disturbance

Southern coastal marshes and lakes not only must provide for foraging, but also must provide for spatial, loafing, and social requirements of waterfowl during winter. In many areas, habitats used by waterfowl for feeding and comfort activities may be spatially distinct. Resting and feeding areas used by a single group of individuals within an area constitute the functional unit for those birds (Tamisier 1976, 1978). In general, use of separate areas for loafing and feeding is most common among ducks that eat seeds, especially agricultural grains. Grazers, including gadwalls, wigeons, and most geese, often are able to meet their forag-

ing and comfort needs in the same area (Paulus 1984a, b).

Loafing and social activities occur most often during the day, and many species spend more time in these activities than feeding during the 24-hr period (Tamisier 1976, Paulus 1986, 1988, Rave 1987). Waterfowl that consume high-energy foods, including agricultural grains, may spend about 60% of their time loafing each day. Thus, habitats that provide for the comfort and social requirements of waterfowl are important.

A wide variety of habitats is used by waterfowl for loafing, but certain characteristics of habitats make them attractive during winter. In general, the largest numbers of birds are found in habitats that have few obstructions and provide good visibility for detection of predators and other disturbances. Waterfowl also favor areas where they can expose themselves to sunlight to lower their cost of thermoregulation.

Many dabbling ducks favor large open-water areas with extended shallow shores (Tamisier 1978, Rave 1987). These areas provide good visibility, shallow-water shorelines, or land upon which ducks can rest, deeper open-water areas for birds to escape predators and other things that disturb them, and sites for social activities. If deeper water is not available, birds avoid landing in shallow water but will fly about until a predator leaves the area. Open-water areas provide little protection from weather, and birds usually move to more secluded marshes during severe weather.

Ducks that feed upon leafy aquatic vegetation in deep water often favor marshes with high land-water interspersion and numerous islands with little cover. Birds loaf both on land and water and often can meet their nutritive, loafing, and social needs in a small area. Because deep water is readily available, birds tend to fly short distances to deeper water when threatened by a predator and remain on the water until it is safe to return. High winds or severe weather are avoided by loafing on the leeward side of islands or shoreline (Paulus 1984a).

Most diving ducks in southern coastal marshes and lakes use deep water ponds, lakes, or bays, or they remain at sea when loafing. Although species using inland areas will move from open-water to more secluded marshes, the activities of ducks at sea during severe weather needs study.

Geese loaf primarily in upland habitats or in shallow water (Leslie and Zwank 1985). By forming large flocks and avoiding dense cover, many individuals keep watch for potential predators. Because of their larger size, geese are less susceptible to avian predators, and thus are not as dependent as ducks for deep open-water areas to avoid avian predation. Also, unlike ducks, geese feed primarily during the day and rest at night when threat of predation or harassment is minimal (Leslie and Chabreck 1984).

Habitats that provide ideal conditions for loafing and are near agricultural fields often contain large numbers of waterfowl. To minimize the threat of predation, waterfowl usually feed at night in shallow-water agricultural fields and move to safer habitats to loaf during the day. By selecting loafing areas near feeding sites, birds can minimize the distance and energy costs of flight that would occur if birds loafed in more distant coastal marshes. An excellent example of this phenomenon occurs at Lacassine NWR, Louisiana, where thousands of ducks spend the day loafing on deep-water pools on the refuge and then fly to agricultural fields at night to feed (Tamisier 1976).

Special Needs

Waterfowl have special habitat requirements during winter that, if met, may enhance their rate of survivorship and use of coastal marshes. If not available locally, waterfowl may travel several km each day to use habitats that provide for these special needs.

Grit.—Although southern coastlines usually contain an abundance of sand or shell that can be used as grit by waterfowl, many interior marshes and agricultural fields contain little grit material (Davis et al. 1961). Because waterfowl may have to fly long distances to obtain grit, birds are attracted to artificial grit sites placed closer to feeding habitats (McIlhenny 1932, Schroer 1974). Artificial deposits of sand and shell have been provided for waterfowl by managers of several refuges along the Gulf Coast. Although greatest use is by geese, large numbers of ducks consume grit at these sites. The fact that most of the grit is consumed within a few years attests to the importance of these sites to waterfowl (D. Richard, pers. commun.).

Open Areas.—Open water within habitats containing dense vegetation or a low land-to-water ratio increases use of an area by ducks and geese. Not only do waterfowl seek open-water habitat to escape predators, but they also use open water for many social activities, especially courting (Paulus 1984a, b). During winter, most ducks form pairs, and courtship displays are an important means by which waterfowl assess the suitability of potential mates (McKinney 1975, Paulus 1983). Open-water areas allow large numbers of birds to participate in courtship activities and readily observe the displays of other participants in the activities.

Refuges.—Federal, state, and private refuges that provide ducks and geese with mostly undisturbed habitats enhance the welfare of waterfowl. Shooting pressure moves many waterfowl to refuges during the day during hunting season (Lueth 1963, Palmisano 1973, Beshears 1979). Ducks on refuges spend more time loafing and less time in energy-costly activities than birds on areas where hunting occurs in Louisiana (Paulus 1984a). High levels of disturbance also may cause geese to abandon areas (Lynch 1941). Nevertheless, waterfowl often select areas where hunting or other disturbances occur, when the quality of habitat is significantly greater than on undisturbed sites. On disturbed sites of high-quality habitat, waterfowl can justify the lower survivorship and extra energy costs of avoiding disturbances (Paulus 1984*a*).

HABITAT MANAGEMENT
Habitat Alteration and Loss

Southern coastal marshes in the Mississippi Flyway are being lost at a rate exceeding 100 km^2/yr (Gagliano et al. 1981). In the deltaic plain of Louisiana, which comprises a major portion of this habitat, annual marsh loss is 2.5% of the total marsh area. Craig et al. (1979) predicted that 50% of the area would be lost during the next 20 years unless drastic measures were taken to reverse the trend.

Much of the current marsh loss is associated with levee construction that occurred along the Mississippi River during the early 20th century for flood control. Before construction of the levees, the river overflowed its banks each spring and allowed vast quantities of freshwater and sediments to filter through the coastal region of Louisiana. This process caused vertical accretion of wetlands and maintained horizontal zonation of marsh types. After completion of the levee system, most freshwater and sediments were discharged directly into the Gulf of Mexico. Thirty percent of the flow of the Mississippi River is diverted down the Atchafalaya River, and new marshland is being built in Atchafalaya Bay in a rapidly expanding delta (Roberts and van Heerden 1982).

Other natural and man-induced factors are contributing to marsh loss, and their effects are accelerated by the loss of freshwater and sediment input from the Mississippi River. Major natural factors causing marsh loss are subsidence, sea-level rise, and hurricanes. Subsidence involves a gradual sinking of the land surface, and losses are more pronounced in former deltas of the Mississippi River (Boesch et al. 1983). Sea levels have begun a gradual rise in recent decades because warming of the earth's atmosphere ("greenhouse effect") has accelerated melting of polar glaciers (Titus et al. 1984). Subsidence and sea-level rise have similar effects, and when combined, are referred to as apparent sea-level rise (Boesch et al. 1983). Because of the flat nature of the coastal region of Louisiana, a 90-cm increase in sea level would flood almost all coastal marshes in the state (Titus et al. 1984). The apparent sea level is predicted to rise 30 cm during the next 30 to 40 years, and between 110 and 215 cm during the next 100 years (Titus 1985). The churning waters and strong currents associated with a hurricane can destroy large areas of marsh in a short time. Severe hurricanes have struck the region in recent decades, and have contributed greatly to marsh loss (Chabreck and Palmisano 1973).

In addition to construction of flood-control levees along the lower Mississippi River, a major man-induced cause of marsh loss is canal dredging. Canals have been dredged for access to oil and gas drilling sites, pipelines, and navigation, and occupy as much as 10% of the land surface in some areas (Craig et al. 1979). Canals cause the greatest damage to coastal marshes when they sever natural tidewater barriers and allow saltwater to encroach inland to low salinity zones. Increased water salinity in coastal marshes destroys established stands of emergent plants and results in formation of large areas of open water (Chabreck 1981). Such changes may temporarily improve the area as habitat for ducks; however, if water salinity and tidal action continue to increase, habitat quality would gradually decline.

Freshwater Diversion

Freshwater diversion from the Mississippi River has been used on a small scale for marsh restoration, but could be used to restore vast portions of the rapidly deteriorating marshes of the deltaic plain. Culverts and siphons are now used to move river water through and over the protection levees at a rate of 7 m^3/sec during flood stages. The idea behind freshwater diversion is to allow water to flow through the marsh, thus adding sediment and nutrients and lowering water salinity in the marsh (Fruge 1982). The added sediment would raise the elevation of the marsh and help offset marsh loss caused by subsidence and sea-level rise. By reducing water salinity and adding nutrients, plant growth and species diversity should increase, and the value of the marsh and adjacent water bodies would improve for fish and wildlife. Habitat for waterfowl would be enhanced by large-scale freshwater diversion. A factor that may reduce the effectiveness of this type of management is a reduction in sediment load carried by the Mississippi River. Dams on upstream tributaries and soil-erosion-control programs are reducing the amount of sediment entering the river. Also, freshwater can be diverted only into marshes in drainage basins adjacent to the river (Gagliano et al. 1973).

The U.S. Army Corps of Engineers, New Orleans District, is conducting studies to determine the feasibility of large-scale controlled diversion of Mississippi River water into adjacent estuarine basins. The studies have indicated that desired fish and wildlife habitat changes could be met for 9 out of 10 years with strategically placed structures of proper size. This would include a 300 m^3/sec diversion structure in the vicinity of Davis Pond in the Barataria Basin (west of river) and a 187 m^3/sec structure at Caernarvon in the Breton Sound Basin (east of river) (Chatry and Chew 1985).

Also, Fruge and Ruelle (1980) recommended use of the existing Bonnet Carre Spillway on a regular basis during flood stages to divert Mississippi River water into the Lake Pontchartrain and Lake Borgne basins.

Management Procedures

Ecological processes in coastal marshes are complex and involve the action and interaction of numerous factors (Chabreck 1981). The objectives of management should be to duplicate these natural processes to produce the desired plant and animal communities. Management may require special projects to accomplish the objective, or it may simply involve habitat protection to maintain present conditions.

Procedures used for management of waterfowl habitat in southern marshes should accomplish several effects. Generally, they should reduce extreme water-level fluctuation, prevent drastic salinity changes, minimize water turbidity, and reduce the rate of tidal exchange. Most importantly, the techniques should produce stands of desirable vegetation in the marsh and marsh ponds and maximize food availability. Techniques that can be applied include manipulating water depth, controlling salinity, burning, creating artificial openings, and controlling undesirable plants with chemicals.

Impoundments.—To regulate or manipulate water depths and salinity, the manager must impound or enclose a marsh with a continuous levee (Chabreck 1960) (Fig. 3). Levee construction is expensive; however, in many areas, much of the necessary levee may already be present and may require only slight modification (Ensminger 1963). Where water-level control is possible, draining the water from fresh marshes during spring or early summer will permit the soil to dry, and grasses, sedges, and other seed-producing annual plants to germinate and grow. The drying process is

Fig. 3. Impoundment of southern coastal marshes provides managers with a system for regulating water depths and salinity to control plant growth and improve feeding and resting habitat for waterfowl.

essential for germination to take place. Reflooding the marsh to a depth of 6 to 50 cm in late summer will make seeds available and will attract ducks. Reflooding may be done within a few weeks after germination, as long as the new plants are not covered with water (Chabreck 1960, Carney and Chabreck 1977). Ponds managed for crayfish (*Procambarus clarkii*) are also handled in this manner, except that reflooding is recommended during fall (LaCaze 1970). Management schemes for ducks and crayfish overlap sufficiently so that an impoundment can be managed for both. Approximately 100,000 ha of shallow water impoundments are managed for crayfish production in southern Louisiana, outside of the coastal marshes, and have greatly increased the area of quality winter habitat for ducks (Nassar 1982).

Fresh- and brackish-water impoundments may also be managed as permanently flooded systems to provide feeding and resting habitat for waterfowl. Because the areas are permanently flooded, the cost of water manipulation is eliminated. Important food plants in freshwater impoundments are white waterlily (*Nymphaea* spp.), watershield (*Brasenia schreberi*), spikerush, and duckweed (*Lemna minor*, *Spirodela polyrhiza*). The major duck food in brackish water impoundments is widgeongrass (Chabreck 1960).

Impoundments have been widely used in Louisiana for waterfowl management. This type of management has been particularly effective in improving marshes for ducks. However, marsh impoundments have certain disadvantages, which at times make it necessary for landowners to use other types of management. First, impoundments are costly to construct and maintain. Also, without facilities for pumping water, years that are unusually wet or dry generally result in poor food production.

A limiting factor in the use of impoundments is location. Impoundments can be built only in areas that will support a continuous levee. In certain areas, such as southeastern Louisiana, impoundment use is limited because of the fluid nature of the subsoil.

Impoundments have been constructed mainly to improve habitat for ducks, but other forms of wildlife and fisheries also have benefited from marsh impoundments (Chabreck 1980). However, impoundment levees that form a barrier to tidal flow also block normal movements of marine organisms and prevent their access to the enclosed marsh and bodies of water. Studies in Louisiana have disclosed that this problem can be partially corrected by opening water-control structures at the proper time to allow passage of marine organisms (Davidson and Chabreck 1983).

Weirs.—The construction of weirs in the drainage systems of a particular area is especially important in marshes that will not support impoundment levees (Chabreck 1968a). Weirs resemble dams and are constructed of steel or wooden sheet piling with the crest about 15 cm below the natural elevation of the marsh (Fig. 4). Weirs do not completely block the flow of water, but prevent drainage of marsh ponds on low tides and reduce the rate of tidal exchange. Ponds behind weirs produce far more aquatic vegetation than do natural ponds (Larrick and Chabreck 1976) and are more attractive to wintering waterfowl (Spiller and Chabreck 1975). Marshes behind weirs maintain permanent water levels and thus facilitate access to the marsh for trapping and hunting; they also improve conditions for furbearing animals as well as waterfowl (Chabreck and Hoffpauer 1962). Hundreds of such structures have been constructed by landowners along the Louisiana coast for the purpose of improving marshlands for wildlife. Weirs may reduce ingress of marine organisms

Fig. 4. Weirs constructed in the drainage systems of southern coastal marshes prevent drainage of marsh ponds on low tides, increase production of aquatic vegetation, and make the marshes more attractive to wintering waterfowl.

in a marsh drainage system; however, this problem can be partially overcome by placing a vertical slot in the weir to allow passage of marine organisms (Rogers et al. 1987).

Potholes and Ditches.—Potholes and ditches have been constructed in marshes to create permanent water areas in dense stands of vegetation. Although such water areas may produce little food, they will attract ducks and also make access easier for trappers and hunters. Ditches and potholes provide permanent water during drought periods, and are particularly important to nesting ducks, furbearing animals, and other wildlife, which help control mosquitoes when marshes are reflooded. Special care should be taken to keep ditches from opening into tidal streams. This may result in salinity changes or excessive drainage of the marshes and damage of wildlife and plant populations (Chabreck 1968a).

Grazing.—Carefully regulated cattle grazing will open up dense stands of vegetation and create conditions favorable for ducks and geese (Chabreck 1968b). Snow geese are attracted to large, wet grasslands where the vegetation is short and the vision of the geese is unobstructed. Not only does grazing tend to reduce certain undesirable perennial plant species in the marsh, but it also favors growth of annual plants. To attract ducks to freshwater or brackish marshes, cattle should be excluded from the marsh during July, August, and September. This will permit desirable grasses and sedges to grow and produce seeds. Also, the marsh should be flooded from October through February, with water ranging from 10-20 cm in depth to make seeds available to waterfowl.

Plantings.—One of the first procedures generally considered to improve marshes for ducks is the planting of vegetation in the marsh to produce food for waterfowl. Thousands of such plantings have been made along the Gulf Coast; however, to date, there is no evidence that any planting was successful in meeting this objective. Usually, the absence of natural food plants in the marsh area is a result of unfavorable soil and water conditions. Consequently, the same conditions will cause the failure of plantings made in the same marsh area. Artificial planting in the marsh should never be considered as a substitute for regulating water levels and salinities to produce natural foods (Chabreck 1975).

Burning.—Burning has been widely used along the Louisiana coast as a marsh-management procedure; however, the value of much of this effort is questionable. Burning may be used in freshwater marsh to prevent encroachment of woody plants. In certain situations, burning also is important for maintaining stands of brackish marsh vegetation (Lynch 1941, O'Neil 1949). Olney bulrush, the choice food of muskrats (*Ondatra zibethicus*) and snow geese, may be replaced by marshhay cordgrass when the two are growing in mixed stands. Burning can be used to favor Olney bulrush; however, burning alone will not maintain Olney bulrush, but should be included along with the necessary water levels (0 to 10 cm) and salinities (5 to 10 ppt) in the management of this species. Burning is important for

removing dense stands of vegetation (Fig. 5) and is widely used for attracting snow geese. Geese are attracted to newly burned areas and frequently remain in the areas until the regrowth is well advanced (Hoffpauer 1968).

Organic matter added to marsh soil by plants is an important source of material for marsh aggregation and, in many areas, is the only land-building material available. In consideration of the rapid marsh loss from subsidence and sea-level rise (Titus 1985), accumulation of organic matter from plant growth should be encouraged. Marsh burning not only destroys the current year's growth but also may destroy organic matter that has accumulated over a period of years if the marsh is burned when dry. Burning in salt marsh should be avoided.

Herbicides.—Chemical control of undesirable plant species in marshes has been used on a limited basis in the past. In the future, the marsh manager will probably place greater emphasis on this method as a tool in marsh management, as more effective herbicides are developed that can be applied to marshes more economically. The manager should consult a specialist in this field before attempting applications of herbicides (Rollings and Warden 1964).

Mineral Development.—Oil and gas developments, pipelines, geophysical operations, and other activities should be closely regulated, and plans for such development carefully studied by persons trained in marsh management. Damage occurring to wildlife and its habitat through the course of mineral developments can be minimized by careful planning. Access to drilling locations, which involves the construction of canals and levees, destroys valuable wetland habitat, but often can benefit marsh wildlife if properly constructed (Chabreck 1975).

Saltwater intrusion and drainage are major problems with canals in tidewater marshes. In salt marshes, canals that are

Fig. 5. Marshes are burned to remove dense stands of vegetation and favor growth of Olney bulrush, a choice food of snow geese.

no longer needed may be back-filled to partially restore the site (Moore et al. 1985). In other marsh types, spoil deposits should be placed so as to form continuous levees along canals that connect to a salt water source. These levees should be carefully constructed, and the company constructing a levee should be responsible for maintenance of levees while operating in the area. By careful placement of canals and levees, water control can be gained over large areas of the marsh at little expense to the landowners. Also, at strategic locations, weirs or other water-control structures should be placed as designated by the manager. Only through careful planning and close supervision can maximum benefits to waterfowl be realized. All developmental activities in wetlands are regulated by the U.S. Army Corps of Engineers under the Clean Water Act. Appropriate permits must be obtained before development is initiated.

Refuges

The Gulf Coast of the Mississippi Flyway has approximately 357,000 ha set aside for wildlife refuges and management areas. Federal ownership includes approximately 100,000 ha, of which 94,000 ha are located in Louisiana. Approximately 228,000 ha are under state ownership or long-term leases by the states. The majority of these lands (225,000 ha) is located in Louisiana (U.S. Dep. Int. 1982). Early management on refuges was directed towards expanding the area of freshwater or brackish marsh by impounding runoff or rainfall behind low dikes along the inner margins of the salt marsh. Such impoundments produced several times the amount of waterfowl food per unit of area as that available in a salt marsh (Gabrielson 1966). Today, marsh-management practices such as diking, creating impoundments, and weir construction are the backbone of the habitat management programs on state- and federally owned properties.

Today, all state and federal refuges are open for public recreation; fishing, bird watching, canoeing, and, in some cases, limited hunting are allowed. There has been an increasing emphasis on developing refuges for use by the public when these activities do not greatly interfere with wildlife use. The overall plan of refuges is to manage areas to maximize wildlife use. As studies are advanced on the basic ecology and life history of various wildlife forms, the management techniques on the refuges are altered using this information to better fit the evergrowing needs and requirements of wildlife populations. Protection, the primary management tool in the early days of the refuge movement, is now incorporated within a multiple-use program of research, development, and public recreation.

Environmental Contaminants and Diseases

The release of chemical pollutants into wetland environments along the Gulf Coast is of great concern to waterfowl managers. Many chemical and industrial complexes are located along the Gulf Coast in close proximity to wetlands used by waterfowl, and the potential for serious mishaps involving waterfowl and pollutants is great. Pollutants may increase waterfowl mortality, affect bird behavior, and ultimately lower reproductive success (Chabreck 1979).

To date, few major losses of waterfowl have been attributed to oil and chemical spills along the Gulf Coast. However, >10 oil spills occur during some years on Mobile Bay (Borom 1979), and Beshears (1979) felt that a major spill could kill much of the flora and fauna of the Mobile Bay Delta. Increased boat traffic along the newly completed Tennessee-Tombigbee Waterway may increase the potential for a major oil spill in Mobile Bay (Stout 1979).

Diving ducks are most affected by oil spills, and >2,000 lesser scaup died from oil contamination caused by a spill on the Mississippi River in 1963 (Anderson and Warner 1969, Chabreck 1979). Water contaminated by oil may deter use by dabbling ducks, although gadwalls have been observed feeding in oil-contaminated waters (Paulus 1980).

Environmental regulations have reduced the threat of a major oil or chemical spill, but low-level, chronic pollution of wetlands remains a serious problem (St. Amant 1971). Leakage of chemicals used in oil exploration, from operating and abandoned well sites, fouls waters used by ducks and geese and inhibits growth of aquatic vegetation. Many desirable aquatic plants used by waterfowl in Mobile Bay have been eradicated by chemical pollutants and have been replaced by less desirable filamentous algae (Borom 1979, Friend et al. 1982).

Lead toxicosis from ingestion of lead shot is a chronic problem in waterfowl. High levels of shot ingestion by ducks and geese is most common in heavily hunted areas and marshlands and flooded agricultural fields with firm bottoms and shallow water (West and Newsom 1979, Paulus 1980). Over 7,000 geese died on Catahoula Lake, Louisiana, in 1953, and 2,000 geese died in rice fields near Lacassine NWR, Louisiana, in 1973 from lead poisoning (Wills and Glasgow 1964, Bateman 1975, Shealy 1982). Recently, over two-thirds of sick or dead waterfowl collected at Catahoula Lake and Lacassine NWR contained high levels of lead in their tissues, and an estimated 31,000 lead pellets/ha were recorded in Catahoula Lake (Smith 1981, Zwank et al. 1985).

Waterfowl feeding in agricultural fields often contain high levels of pesticides in their tissues (Guidry 1977). Pesticides ingested by waterfowl are concentrated in lipid tissue, and as lipids are metabolized during winter, birds may become poisoned. Declines in the number of fulvous whistling ducks during the 1960s and early 1970s were attributed to ingestion of lethal doses of dieldrin and aldrin. Although use of aldrin was prohibited in 1974, the occurrence of aldrin and dieldrin in nearly 50% of adult fulvous whistling ducks collected in rice fields in 1983 suggested that aldrin is still being used illegally in rice fields (Flickinger et al. 1986). Deaths of other waterfowl have been attributed to ingestion of pesticides, and the most critical period occurs when rice is planted in spring (Flickinger and King 1972).

As the amount of wintering habitat available to waterfowl declines, crowding of birds will enhance the spread of contagious and infectious diseases and parasites. Inadequate food supplies and pollutants also may increase disease and parasite problems in the future (Friend 1975, 1981, Hayes and Davidson 1978, Chabreck 1979).

Because of the abundance of high-quality wetland habitat along the Gulf Coast and limited instances of crowding among waterfowl, mortality from disease is infrequent in southern coastal marshes and lakes. Most deaths have been attributed to avian botulism (*Clostridium botulinum* Type C) (Crain and Chabreck 1960, Hayden 1972). High incidence of *Sarcocystis rileyi* was found in pintails (36%), green-winged teal (47%), and shovelers (78%), but was limited to adult birds, and apparently does not adversely affect the host (Chabreck 1965).

CONCLUSIONS
Evaluation of Management Procedures

Controlled diversion of freshwater and sediment from the Mississippi River into the Barataria Bay, Breton Sound, and Lake Pontchartrain basins is recommended for water salinity reduction, nutrient input, and land building. The basins are within the deltaic plain, which provides important wintering habitat for waterfowl but is rapidly deteriorating and being lost because of natural and man-induced causes. Introducing freshwater and sediment from the river will enhance plant growth and improve the region for waterfowl habitat.

Numerous marsh-management programs have been installed in recent years by private landowners. Management efforts were designed mainly to improve habitat for waterfowl and were prompted by deteriorating habitat conditions caused by saltwater intrusion. In most management programs, levees previously constructed for other purposes were used to form management units where water levels and salinities could be controlled to enhance plant growth.

Impoundments offer the most effective means for management of marshes for waterfowl. Various management options are available, and the marsh manager has greater control of the environmental conditions necessary to achieve desired objectives when impoundments are used. However, impoundments are expensive to construct and maintain, and can be constructed only in marshes containing soil that will support a continuous levee system.

Weirs constructed in drainage systems of a marsh stabilize water levels and salinities and enhance growth of aquatic plants. The basin of permanent water held by the structures improves habitat conditions for ducks. However, weirs provide less control of environmental conditions in marshes than impoundments.

In the past, many large landowners across the coast employed a staff of maintenance personnel capable of maintaining isohaline lines in a relatively stable and permanent position. However, since the passage of the Clean Water Act and section 101 permitting process, the majority of this marsh preservation work has stopped. Private landowners are no longer allowed to maintain marshes, as they had in the past, for duck hunting and trapping without obtaining a federal and state coastal use permit.

The purpose of the permitting process was to halt marsh alterations, and only projects with approved management plans that would benefit both fish and wildlife are approved. Projects that allow for ingress and egress of marine organisms also facilitate the continued inland advancement of saline waters. As a result of this decision by the Corps of Engineers, the saline isohaline lines continue to encroach inland each year, and more and more saltwater marshes are being created. The freshwater vegetative type, which provides the best waterfowl habitat, is being reduced in size by the inland advancement of the more saline vegetative type, which provides the poorest waterfowl habitat.

Research Needs

There are currently more environmental resources available to waterfowl using southern coastal marshes than birds to use them (Lynch 1968). However, waterfowl habitat is being lost at an alarming rate because of development, agriculture, and nature. As this trend continues, waterfowl along the Gulf Coast may soon experience many of the same problems, including crowding and higher levels of disease, as those faced by ducks and geese in the Pacific Flyway (Chabreck 1979).

Marsh habitat loss and alteration are often identified as the most important problem facing waterfowl during winter (Table 5). High-quality marshland is rapidly being lost along the Louisiana coastline from erosion, saltwater intrusion, subsidence, channelization, and other factors (Craig et al. 1979, Deegan et al. 1984). Dredging and pollution have increased sedimentation rates and discour-

aged aquatic plant growth in Mobile Bay, Alabama (Stout 1979, Beshears 1982). Wetland managers must make use of available technology to reduce the rate of wetland loss and lessen the impact of exploration and commercial development on marshlands. Research should be directed towards identifying important wetlands used by waterfowl, but more importantly, towards identifying wetland areas preferred by ducks and geese and elements of those habitats crucial to their survival. Because loss of wetlands will continue into the foreseeable future, it is imperative that we understand the needs of waterfowl during winter, and identify and save those wetlands meeting these needs.

Many waterfowl using coastal wetlands spend much of the winter in agricultural fields. These habitats provide an abundance of foods and may compensate for the loss of natural wetland habitat. However, as agricultural harvesting techniques improve or fields are taken out of production for economical reasons, less food may be available to birds dependent upon agricultural grains in their diets (Bellrose 1980). Information is needed on the response of birds to these changes and the impact of changes on survivorship and reproductive output of future generations of waterfowl.

In recent years, there have been several studies that have examined the physical conditions and behaviors of ducks and geese using agricultural habitats or natural wetlands (Jorde 1981, Paulus 1984*b*, Baldassarre et al. 1986, Whyte et al. 1986, Rave 1987). Unfortunately, most research has compared birds at widely different localities, and great differences in climate, habitat structure, hunting pressure, and other factors have made it difficult to interpret the influence of habitat on body composition and survival. Southern coastal wetlands are attractive to researchers because these wetlands provide some of the few remaining areas where birds

Table 5. Waterfowl problems and research priorities for waterfowl in southern coastal wetlands and lakes during winter.

Habitat
Marsh habitat loss or alteration
Inventory marsh resources and maintain updated data base
Habitat use and preference by waterfowl
Response of wintering waterfowl to new or rehabilitated habitats
Evaluate use of islands, grit sites, courting areas, and other special habitats by waterfowl
Estimate total habitat requirements of waterfowl
Waterfowl response to changes in agricultural practices
Need for sanctuaries
Effects of land-use regulations on habitat availability
Impact of agricultural pesticides on wetland habitats
Ecology of offshore habitats
Role of water quality in determining waterfowl use of habitats
Impact of marsh burning on marshes
Impact of crop depredations by waterfowl on landowner attitudes
Impact of improved crop-harvest techniques on waterfowl using agricultural fields
Impact of pest plant species on native species and use by waterfowl
Biology
Relation between physical condition and ecology
Factors influencing migration chronology
Origin of wintering waterfowl
Waterfowl distribution trends over time
Assessment of plant and animal utilization in diets
Importance of native plants and invertebrates in diets of field-feeding waterfowl
Diseases and poisoning
Interactions between migrants and endemic species
Biological needs and special requirements of waterfowl
Philopatry among waterfowl in winter
Sources and magnitude of mortality during winter
Body condition, reproductive potential, and survival rates of waterfowl using agricultural fields and those in
    natural wetlands
Nocturnal behavior and habitat use
Techniques
Habitat rebuilding
Minimize impacts of exploration and development on wetlands
Enhance fallow fields for use by waterfowl during winter
Capture methodologies, especially for species remaining offshore
Upland-wetland inventories
Effects of markers and radio transmitters on survival, behavior, and reproduction
Policy
Refuge management practices
Land-acquisition goals and priorities
Land-use regulations
Distribution of federal funds
Multiple-use policies on refuges
Role of Canada goose satellite flocks
Hunting
Distribution of waterfowl during the hunting season
Additive vs. compensatory mortality
Distribution of hunters
Effects of hunting on behavior and condition of waterfowl
Use of sanctuaries during hunting season
Clarification of baiting regulations
Hunting techniques and technologies
Changes in bag composition over time
Magnitude of illegal kill

References: Bellrose (1980), Beshears (1979, 1982), Hobaugh (1984), Lynch (1968), Paulus (1984c), Rusch (1985), Stout (1979), Woolington (1987), Zwank (1984).

using natural wetlands can be compared with birds in nearby agricultural habitats.

Studies have attempted to determine the impact of hunting, but little is known of the extent of natural factors on waterfowl mortality rates. Because of the expansiveness of coastal marshes, the deaths of most ducks and geese from poisoning, disease, or other factors are rarely observed. Information is needed on the magnitude of nonhunting mortality in waterfowl in southern coastal marshes and lakes.

SUMMARY

Southern coastal marshes and lakes that border the Gulf of Mexico in Louisiana, Mississippi, and Alabama form the lower terminus of the Mississippi Flyway and provide important habitat for wintering, transient, and resident waterfowl. The region comprises >3 million ha that include marshes, bays, sounds, lakes, rivers, and other water bodies. Coastal marshes occupy >1 million ha and comprise 42% of the total area of coastal marshes in the U.S., excluding Alaska. Freshwater, intermediate, and brackish marshes of the region are preferred habitats of waterfowl.

Major waterfowl concentration areas in Louisiana are the Central Coastal area, Amoco Marsh, Gum Cove area, Big Burn, Pecan Island Marsh, Johnson Bayou Marsh, and Delacroix marshes. Major concentration areas in Mississippi are the Pascagoula Marsh and Point Clear area. Mobile Delta and Mobile Bay are major concentration areas in Alabama.

Marshes of the region are rapidly deteriorating and being lost at a rate exceeding 100 km^2/yr. Levee construction along the Mississippi River deprives the marshes of freshwater and sediment that are essential for land building and prevention of saltwater intrusion. A vast network of canals dredged in the marshes further complicates the problem of saltwater intrusion.

Diversion of freshwater from the Mississippi River into the marshes of southeastern Louisiana will be necessary to offset land loss and improve the quality of waterfowl habitat in that area. Management procedures used to improve or maintain favorable habitat conditions for waterfowl include construction of impoundments and weirs to form management units. Burning, creation of artificial openings, chemical control of undesirable plants, control of grazing, regulation of mineral development, and maintenance of refuges are important components of waterfowl-management programs.

Important research needs include information on prevention of marsh loss, improvement of habitat quality, and identification of the biological needs of the many species of waterfowl that use the region.

LITERATURE CITED

Afton, A. D., R. H. Hier, and S. L. Paulus. 1986. Body weights, carcass composition, and foods of lesser scaup during mid-winter in southwestern Louisiana. Minn. Dep. Nat. Resour., Bemidji. 9 pp.

Alexander, C. E., M. A. Boutman, and D. W. Field. 1986. An inventory of coastal wetlands of the USA. U.S. Dep. of Comm., Washington, D.C. 25 pp.

Alisauskas, R. T., C. D. Ankney, and E. E. Klaas. 1988. Winter diets and nutrition of the midcontinental population of lesser snow geese. J. Wildl. Manage. 52:403-414.

Anderson, B. W., and D. W. Warner. 1969. A morphological analysis of a large sample of lesser scaup and ring-necked ducks. Bird Banding 40:85-94.

Ankney, C. D. 1982. Annual cycle of body weight in lesser snow geese. Wildl. Soc. Bull. 10:60-64.

Baldassarre, G. A., R. J. Whyte, and E. G. Bolen. 1986. Body weight and carcass composition of nonbreeding green-winged teal on the Southern High Plains of Texas. J. Wildl. Manage. 50:420-426.

Baldwin, W. P. 1957. An inspection of waterfowl habitats in the Mobile Bay Area. Spec. Rep. 2, Ala. Dep. Conserv., Div. Game and Fish., Montgomery. 41 pp.

Bateman, H. A. 1975. Getting the lead out. La. Conserv. 27:10-14.

Bellrose, F. C. 1980. Ducks, geese and swans of North America. Third ed. Stackpole Books, Harrisburg, Pa. 540 pp.

Beshcars, W. W., Jr. 1979. Waterfowl in the Mobile estuary. Pages 249-263 in H. A. Loyacano, Jr., and J. P. Smith, eds. Symp. on the nat. resour. of the Mobile Estuary, Alabama. U.S. Army Corps of Engineers, Mobile, Ala.

———. 1982. Mobile Delta vegetative study. Ala. Dep. Conserv. Nat. Resour., Proj. W-35, Montgomery. 31 pp.

Boesch, D. F., D. Levin, D. Nummedal, and K. Bowles. 1983. Subsidence in coastal Louisiana: causes, rates, and effects on wetlands. U.S. Fish and Wildl. Serv., FWS/OBS-83/26. Washington, D.C. 30 pp.

Borom, J. L. 1979. Submerged grassbed communities in Mobile Bay, Alabama. Pages 123-132 in H. A. Loyacano, Jr., and J. P. Smith, eds. Symp. on the nat. resour. of the Mobile Estuary, Alabama. U.S. Army Corps of Engineers, Mobile, Ala.

Carney, D. F., and R. H. Chabreck. 1977. An evaluation of spring drawdown as a waterfowl management practice in floating fresh marsh. Proc. Annu. Conf. Southeast. Assoc. Fish and Wildl. Agencies 31:266-271.

Chabreck, R. H. 1960. Coastal marsh impoundments for ducks in Louisiana. Proc. Annu. Conf. Southeast. Assoc. Game and Fish Comm. 14:24-29.

———. 1965. Sarcosporidiosis in ducks in Louisiana. Trans. North Am. Wildl. and Nat. Resour. Conf. 30:174-184.

———. 1968a. Wiers, plugs, and artificial potholes for the management of wildlife in coastal marshes. Pages 178-192 in J. D. Newsom, ed. Proc. of the marsh and estuary manage. symp. Louisiana State Univ., Baton Rouge.

———. 1968b. The relation of cattle and cattle grazing to marsh wildlife and plants in Louisiana. Proc. Annu. Conf. Southeast. Assoc. Fish and Game Comm. 22:55-58.

———. 1970. Marsh zones and vegetative types in the Louisiana coastal marshes. Ph.D. Dissertation, Louisiana State Univ., Baton Rouge. 112 pp.

———. 1972. Vegetation, water and soil characteristics of the Louisiana coastal region. La. Agric. Exp. Stn. Bull. 664. 72 pp.

———. 1973. Bird usage of marsh ponds subjected to oil spills. Proc. La. Acad. Sci. 36:101-110.

———. 1975. Waterfowl management and productivity—Gulf coast habitat. Proc. Int. Waterfowl Symp. 1:64-72.

———. 1979. Winter habitat of dabbling ducks: physical, chemical, and biological aspects. Pages 133-142 in T. A. Bookhout, ed. Waterfowl and wetlands: an integrated review. North Cent. Sect. Wildl. Soc., Madison, Wis.

———. 1980. Effects of marsh impoundments on coastal fish and wildlife resources. Pages 1-16 in P. L. Fore and R. D. Peterson, eds. Proc. of the Gulf of Mexico coastal ecosystems workshop. U.S. Fish and Wildl. Serv. FWS/OBS-80/30. Washington, D.C.

———. 1981. Freshwater inflow and salt water barriers for management of coastal wildlife and plants in Louisiana. Pages 125-138 in R. D. Cross and D. L. Williams, eds. Proc. of the nat. symp. on freshwater inflow to estuaries, Vol. 2. U.S. Fish and Wildl. Serv. FWS/OBS-81/04. Washington, D.C.

———, and C. M. Hoffpauer. 1962. The use of weirs in coastal marsh management in Louisiana. Proc. Annu. Conf. Southeast. Assoc. Fish and Game Comm. 16:103-112.

———, and A. W. Palmisano. 1973. The effects of hurricane Camille on the marshes of the Mississippi River delta. Ecology 54:1118-1123.

———, R. K. Yancey, and L. McNease. 1975. Duck usage of management units in the Louisiana coastal marsh. Proc. Annu. Conf. Southeast. Assoc. Game and Fish Comm. 28:507-516.

Chatry, M., and D. Chew. 1985. Freshwater diversion in coastal Louisiana: recommendations for development of management criteria. Pages 71-84 in C. F. Bryan, P. J. Zwank, and R. H. Chabreck, eds. Proc. of the 4th coastal marsh and estuary manage. symp. Louisiana State Univ., Baton Rouge.

Christmas, J. Y. 1973. Area description. Pages 1-71 in J. Y. Christmas, ed. Cooperative Gulf of Mexico estuarine inventory and study, Mississippi. Gulf Coast Res. Lab., Ocean Springs, Miss.

Coleman, J. M. 1966. Recent coastal sedimentation: central Louisiana Coast. Coastal Studies Ser. No. 17, Louisiana State Univ. Press, Baton Rouge. 73 pp.

Craig, N. J., R. E. Turner, and J. W. Day, Jr. 1979. Land loss in coastal Louisiana (U.S.A.). Environ. Manage. 3:133-144.

Crain, N. W., and R. H. Chabreck. 1960. Waterfowl mortality. 8th Biennial Rep. La. Wildl. and Fish. Comm., New Orleans. 162 pp.

Crance, J. H. 1971. Description of Alabama estuarine areas-cooperative Gulf of Mexico estuarine inventory. Ala. Dep. Conserv., Dauphin Island, Ala. 85 pp.

Davidson, R. B., and R. H. Chabreck. 1983. Fish, wildlife, and recreational values of brackish marsh impoundments. Pages 89-114 in R. J. Varnell, ed. Proc. of the water quality and wetlands manage. conf. La. Environ. Prof. Assoc., New Orleans.

Davis, J. P., C. H. Thomas, and L. L. Glasgow. 1961. Foods available to waterfowl in fallow ricefields of southwest Louisiana, 1960-1961.

Proc. Annu. Conf. Southeast. Assoc. Game and Fish Comm. 15:60-66.

Deegan, L. A., H. M. Kennedy, and C. Neill. 1984. Natural factors and human modifications contributing to marsh loss in Louisiana's Mississippi River deltaic plain. Environ. Manage. 8:519-528.

Duke, R. W., and R. H. Chabreck. 1976. Waterfowl habitat in lakes of the Atchafalaya Basin, Louisiana. Proc. Annu. Conf. Southeast. Assoc. Game and Fish Comm. 29:501-512.

Eleuterius, L. N. 1973. The marshes of Mississippi. Pages 147-190 *in* J. Y. Christmas, ed. Cooperative Gulf of Mexico estuarine inventory and study, Mississippi. Gulf Coast Res. Lab., Ocean Springs, Miss.

Ensminger, A. B. 1963. Construction of levees for impoundments in Louisiana marshes. Proc. Annu. Conf. Southeast. Assoc. Game and Fish Comm. 11:114-119.

Flickinger, E. L., and K. A. King. 1972. Some effects of aldrin-treated rice on Gulf coast wildlife. J. Wildl. Manage. 36:706-727.

————, C. A. Mitchell, and A. J. Krynitsky. 1986. Dieldrin and endrin residues in fulvous whistling-ducks in Texas in 1983. J. Field Ornithol. 57:85-90.

Friend, M. 1975. New dimensions in diseases affecting waterfowl. Proc. Int. Waterfowl Symp. 1:155-162.

————. 1981. Waterfowl management and waterfowl disease: independent or cause and effect relationships? Trans. North Am. and Wildl. Nat. Resour. Conf. 46:94-103.

Friend, J. H., M. Lyon, N. N. Garrett, J. L. Borom, J. Ferguson, and G. G. Lloyd. 1982. Alabama coastal region ecological characterization. Vol. 3. A socioeconomic study. U.S. Fish and Wildl. Serv., Office of Biol. Serv., Washington, D.C. 367 pp.

Fruge, D. W. 1982. Effects of wetland deterioration on the fish and wildlife resources of coastal Louisiana. Pages 99-107 *in* D. F. Boesch, ed. Proc. of the conf. on coastal erosion and modification in Louisiana: causes, consequences, and options. U.S. Fish and Wildl. Serv. FWS/OBS-82/59. Washington, D.C.

————, and R. Ruelle. 1980. A planning aid report on the Mississippi and Louisiana estuarine areas study. U.S. Fish and Wildl. Serv., Lafayette, La. 125 pp.

Gabrielson, I. N. 1966. Wildlife conservation. The Macmillian Co., New York, N.Y. 244 pp.

Gagliano, S. W., P. Light, and R. E. Becker. 1973. Controlled diversion in the Mississippi delta system: an approach to environmental management. Cent. for Wetland Resour. Rep. No. 8, Louisiana State Univ., Baton Rouge. 146 pp.

————, K. J. Meyer-Arendt, and K. M. Wicker. 1981. Land loss in the Mississippi Deltaic Plain. Trans. Annu. Mtg. Gulf Coast Geol. Soc. 31:295-300.

Gaston, G. R., D. Walther, D. Shaheen, and J. D. Felley. 1985. Lipid variations as condition factors in overwintering gadwalls. Final Rep., La. Bd. of Regents Res. and Development Prog., Baton Rouge, 53 pp.

Guidry, K. P. 1977. An analysis of organochlorine pesticide residues and food habits study of the mottled duck in southwest Louisiana. M.S. Thesis, Louisiana State Univ., Baton Rouge. 75 pp.

Harmon, B. G. 1962. Mollusks as food of lesser scaup along the Louisiana coast. Trans. North Am. Wildl. and Nat. Resour. Conf. 27:132-137.

————, C. H. Thomas, and L. Glasgow. 1960. Waterfowl foods in Louisiana ricefields. Trans. North Am. Wildl. and Nat. Resour. Conf. 25:153-161.

Hayden, D. C. 1972. The relationship of certain ecological characteristics of the Louisiana coastal marsh to avian botulism. M.S. Thesis, Louisiana State Univ., Baton Rouge. 315 pp.

Hayes, F. A., and W. R. Davidson. 1978. Waterfowl diseases: status, contributing factors, and control. Proc. Int. Waterfowl Symp. 3:45-58.

Hepp, G. R., and J. D. Hair. 1984. Dominance in wintering waterfowl (Anatini): effects on distribution of sexes. Condor 86:251-257.

Hobaugh, W. C. 1984. Habitat use by snow geese wintering in southwest Texas. J. Wildl. Manage. 48:1085-1096.

————. 1985. Body condition and nutrition of snow geese wintering in southeastern Texas. J. Wildl. Manage. 49:1028-1037.

Hoffpauer, C. M. 1968. Burning for coastal marsh management. Pages 134-139 *in* J. D. Newsom, ed. Proc. of the marsh and estuary manage. symp. Louisiana State Univ., Baton Rouge.

Jemison, E. S., and R. H. Chabreck. 1962. The availability of waterfowl foods in coastal marsh impoundments in Louisiana. Trans. North Am. Wildl. and Nat. Resour. Conf. 27:288-300.

Joanen, T., and L. L. Glasgow. 1965. Factors influencing the establishment of widgeon grass stands in Louisiana. Proc. Annu. Conf. Southeast. Assoc. Game and Fish Comm. 19:102-110.

Jorde, D. G. 1981. Winter and spring staging ecology of mallards in south central Nebraska. M.S. Thesis, Univ. North Dakota, Grand Forks. 116 pp.

Junca, H. A., E. A. Epps, and L. L. Glasgow. 1962. A quantitative study of the nutrient content of food removed from the crops of wild mallards in Louisiana. Trans. North Am. Wildl. and Nat. Resour. Conf. 27:114-121.

LaCaze, C. 1970. Crawfish farming. La. Dep. Wildl. and Fisheries, New Orleans. 6 pp.

Larrick, W. J., Jr., and R. H. Chabreck. 1976. The effects of weirs on aquatic vegetation along the Louisiana coast. Proc. Annu. Conf. Southeast. Assoc. Game and Fish Comm. 30:581-589.

Leslie, J. C., and R. H. Chabreck. 1984. Winter habitat preference of white-fronted geese in Louisiana. Trans. North Am. Wildl. and Nat. Resour. Conf. 49:519-526.

——, and P. J. Zwank. 1985. Habitat suitability index models: lesser snow geese (wintering). U.S. Fish and Wildl. Serv. Biol. Rep. 82. Washington, D.C. 16 pp.

Linscombe, R. G. 1972. Crop damage by waterfowl in southwestern Louisiana. M.S. Thesis, Louisiana State Univ., Baton Rouge. 125 pp.

Lueth, F. X. 1963. Mobile Delta waterfowl and muskrat research. Ala. Dep. Conserv. P. R. Proj. 7-R, Montgomery, Ala. 86 pp.

Lynch, J. J. 1941. The place of burning in management of the Gulf Coast refuges. J. Wildl. Manage. 5:454-458.

——. 1968. Values of the south Atlantic and Gulf coast marshes and estuaries. Pages 51-63 in J. D. Newson, ed. Proc. of the marsh and estuary manage. symp. Louisiana State Univ., Baton Rouge.

——, T. O'Neil, and D. W. Lay. 1947. Management significance of damage by geese and muskrats to Gulf coast marshes. J. Wildl. Manage. 11:50-76.

Marmer, H. A. 1954. Tides and sea level in the Gulf of Mexico. Pages 101-118 in P. S. Galtsoff, ed. Gulf of Mexico: its origin, waters, and marine life. U.S. Fish and Wildl. Serv. Fishery Bull. 89. Washington, D.C.

McIlhenny, E. A. 1932. The blue goose in its winter home. Auk 49:279-306.

McKinney, F. 1975. The evolution of duck displays. Pages 331-357 in G. Baerends, C. Beer, and A. Manning, eds. Function and evolution of behavior. Clarendon Press, Oxford.

Miller, M. R. 1975. Gut morphology of mallards in relation to diet quality. J. Wildl. Manage. 39:168-173.

Moore, D., P. Keney, R. Ruebsamen, and J. Lyon. 1985. National Marine Fisheries Service activities to reduce adverse impacts in Louisiana coastal marshes. Pages 27-48 in C. F. Bryan, P. J. Zwank, and R. H. Chabreck, eds. Proc. of the 4th coastal marsh and estuary manage. symp. Louisiana State Univ., Baton Rouge.

Mutzar, A. J., S. J. Slinger, and J. H. Burton. 1976. Nutritive value of aquatic plants for chicks. Poultry Sci. 55:1917-1922.

Nassar, J. R. 1982. Management of impoundments for crayfish and waterfowl. M.S. Thesis, Louisiana State Univ., Baton Rouge. 112 pp.

National Research Council. 1971. Atlas of nutritional data on United States and Canadian feeds. Natl. Acad. Sci. Washington, D.C. 772 pp.

Nichols, J. D. 1982. Report of the habitat selection discussion group. Pages 6-17 in M. G. Anderson and B. D. J. Batt, eds. Workshop on the ecology of wintering waterfowl. Delta Waterfowl Res. Stn., Portage la Prairie, Manitoba.

O'Neil, T. 1949. The muskrat in the Louisiana coastal marsh. La. Dep. Wildl. and Fish., New Orleans. 152 pp.

Palmisano, A. W. 1973. Habitat preference of waterfowl and fur animals in the northern Gulf Coast marshes. Pages 163-190 in R. H. Chabreck, ed. Proc. of the 2nd coastal marsh and estuary manage. symp. Louisiana State Univ., Baton Rouge.

Paulus, S. L. 1980. The winter ecology of the gadwall in Louisiana. M.S. Thesis, Univ. North Dakota, Grand Forks. 357 pp.

——. 1982a. Feeding ecology of gadwalls in Louisiana in winter. J. Wildl. Manage. 46:71-79.

——. 1982b. Gut morphology of gadwalls in Louisiana in winter. J. Wildl. Manage. 46:483-489.

——. 1983. Dominance relations, resource use, and pairing chronology of gadwalls in winter. Auk 100:947-952.

——. 1984a. Activity budgets of nonbreeding gadwalls in Louisiana. J. Wildl. Manage. 48:371-380.

——. 1984b. Behavior ecology of mottled ducks in Louisiana. Ph.D. Thesis, Auburn Univ., Auburn, Ala. 152 pp.

——. 1984c. Waterfowl-wetland research. La. Dep. Wildl. Fish., Baton Rouge. 6 pp.

——. 1986. Time-activity budgets of waterfowl using different management units on Rockefeller State Wildlife Refuge, Louisiana. La. Dep. Wildl. Fish., Baton Rouge. 24 pp.

——. 1988. Time-activity budgets of nonbreeding anatidae: a review. Pages 135-152. in M. W. Weller, ed. Waterfowl in winter symposium. Univ. Minnesota Press, Minneapolis.

Penfound, W. T., and E. S. Hathaway. 1938. Plant communities in the marshlands of southeastern Louisiana. Ecol. Monogr. 8:1-56.

Rave, D. P. 1987. Carcass composition and time-activity budgets of green-winged teal wintering in Louisiana. M.S. Thesis, Auburn Univ., Auburn, Ala. 65 pp.

Roberts, H. H., and I. L. van Heerden. 1982. Reversal of coastal erosion by rapid sedimentation: the Atchafalaya delta (south-central Louisiana). Pages 214-231 in D. F. Boesch, ed. Proc. of the conf. on coastal erosion and modification in Louisiana: causes, consequences, and options. U.S. Fish and Wildl. Serv. FWS/OBS-82/59. Washington, D.C.

Rogers, B. D., W. H. Herke, and E. E. Knudsen.

1987. Investigation of a weir-design alternative for coastal fisheries benefit. Louisiana State Univ. Agric. Center, Baton Rouge. 98 pp.

Rogers, J. P., and L. J. Korschgen. 1966. Foods of lesser scaups on breeding, migration, and wintering areas. J. Wildl. Manage. 30:258-264.

Rollings, C. T., and R. L. Warden. 1964. Weedkillers and waterfowl. Pages 593-598 in J. P. Linduska, ed. Waterfowl tomorrow. U.S. Fish and Wildl. Serv., Washington, D.C.

Rusch, D. H. 1985. Research studies on winter waterfowl ecology. Wis. Coop. Wildl. Res. Unit, Madison. 7 pp.

Russell, R. J. 1942. Flotant. Geogr. Rev. 32:74-98.

——, and H. V. Howe. 1935. Cheniers of southwestern Louisiana. Geogr. Rev. 25:449-461.

Schroer, J. D. 1974. Flock integrity and movements of snow geese on the Gulf Coast wintering grounds. M.S. Thesis, Louisiana State Univ., Baton Rouge. 108 pp.

Scott, T. G., and C. H. Wasser. 1980. Checklist of North American plants for wildlife biologists. The Wildl. Soc., Washington, D.C. 58 pp.

Shealy, P. M. 1982. A lead toxicity study of waterfowl on Catahoula Lake and Lacassine National Wildlife Refuge. M.S. Thesis, Louisiana State Univ., Baton Rouge. 89 pp.

Smith, C. M. 1981. Duck gizzard collection for examination for ingested lead shot. Completion Rep., W-29, II:4. La. Dep. Wildl. Fish., Baton Rouge. 102 pp.

Spiller, S. F., and R. H. Chabreck. 1975. Wildlife populations in coastal marshes influenced by weirs. Proc. Annu. Conf. Southeast. Assoc. Game and Fish Comm. 29:518-525.

St. Amant, L. S. 1971. Impacts of oil on the Gulf Coast. Trans. North Am. Wildl. and Nat. Resour. Conf. 36:206-219.

Stout, J. P. 1979. Marshes of the Mobile Bay Estuary: status and evaluation. Pages 113-121 in H. A. Loyacano, Jr., and J. P. Smith, eds. Symp. on the nat. resour. of the Mobile Estuary, Alabama. U.S. Army Corps of Engineers, Mobile, Ala.

——. 1984. The ecology of irregularly flooded salt marshes of the northeastern Gulf of Mexico: a community profile. U.S. Fish and Wildl. Serv. Biol. Rep. 85(7.1). Washington, D.C. 98 pp.

Sugden, L. G. 1973. Metabolizable energy of wild duck foods. Can. Wildl. Serv. Prog. Notes 35. 4 pp.

Tamisier, A. 1976. Diurnal activities of green-winged teal and pintail wintering in Louisiana. Wildfowl 27:19-32.

——. 1978. The functional units of wintering ducks: a spatial segregation of their comfort and feeding requirements. Verh. Ornithol. Ges. Bayern 23:229-238.

Titus, J. G. 1985. How to estimate future sea level rise in particular communities. Environ. Prot. Agency, Washington, D.C. 1 pp.

——, M. C. Barth, M. J. Gibbs, J. S. Hoffman, and M. Kennedy. 1984. An overview of the causes and effects of sea level rise. Pages 1-56 in M. Barth and J. Titus, eds. Greenhouse effect and sea level rise: a challenge for this generation. Van Nostrand-Reinhold Co., New York, N.Y.

U.S. Dep. Int. 1982. Category 9—Central Gulf Coast Wetlands. Unpubl. Rep. Washington, D.C. 102 pp.

West, L. D., and J. D. Newsom. 1979. Lead and mercury in lesser snow geese wintering in Louisiana. Proc. Annu. Conf. Southeast. Assoc. Game and Fish Comm. 31:180-187.

West, R. C. 1977. Tidal salt-marsh and mangal formations of Middle and South America. Pages 193-213 in V. J. Chapman, ed. Ecosystems of the world. I. Wet coastal ecosystems. Elsevier Scientific Publ. Co., New York.

White, D. H., and D. James. 1978. Differential use of fresh water environments by wintering waterfowl of coastal Texas. Wilson Bull. 90:99-111.

Whyte, R. J., G. A. Baldassarre, and E. G. Bolen. 1986. Winter condition of mallards on the Southern High Plains of Texas. J. Wildl. Manage. 50:52-57.

Williams, S. O., III, and R. H. Chabreck. 1986. Quantity and quality of waterfowl habitat in Louisiana. Louisiana State Univ. School of For., Wildl., and Fish. Res. Rep. No. 8, Baton Rouge. 84 pp.

Wills, D. W., and J. T. Glasgow. 1964. Lead shot on Catahoula Lake and its management implications. Proc. Annu. Conf. Southeast. Assoc. Game and Fish Comm. 18:90-105.

Woolington, D. 1987. Waterfowl research needs. U.S. Fish and Wildl. Serv., Washington, D.C. 3 pp.

Zwank, P. J. 1984. Winter waterfowl problems. U.S. Fish and Wildl. Serv., La. Coop. Wildl. Res. Unit, Baton Rouge. 2 pp.

——, V. L. Wright, P. M. Shealy, and J. D. Newsom. 1985. Lead toxicosis in waterfowl on two major wintering areas in Louisiana. Wildl. Soc. Bull. 13:26-31.

CENTRAL FLYWAY

Playa with moist-soil development in the foreground, open water in the mid-ground, and crop land in the background, Castro County, Texas (photo by H. W. Miller).

NORTHERN GREAT PLAINS

ROGER L. PEDERSON, Ducks Unlimited Inc., 9823 Old Winery Place, Suite 16, Sacramento, CA 95827
DENNIS G. JORDE, U.S. Fish and Wildlife Service, Patuxent Wildlife Research Center, Laurel, MD 20708
S. GAY SIMPSON[1], South Dakota Department of Game, Fish and Parks, Pierre, SD 57501

The Northern Great Plains (NGP) is an area encompassing portions of 3 Canadian provinces and 4 states in the United States (U.S.) (Fig. 1). The NGP is an important waterfowl breeding area and one of the largest migration corridors in North America, with more than 5-9 million ducks migrating through during autumn and spring (Bellrose 1980). Depending on winter weather, large numbers of waterfowl also may winter in the NGP (U.S. Fish and Wildlife Service 1981).

Our objectives in this chapter are to (1) describe waterfowl populations and habitats in the NGP, (2) relate habitats and habitat management practices to annual cycle requirements of migrating and wintering ducks and geese, and (3) suggest management approaches for wintering and migrating waterfowl. Because habitat management for waterfowl wintering in this region is discussed in Ringleman et al. (1989), we emphasize migration habitat. Many management practices that are designed to benefit breeding waterfowl affect migrating and wintering populations also. Therefore, management techniques described in this chapter include some that traditionally have been thought of as breeding bird management.

REGIONAL CHARACTERISTICS

Biomes

Most of the NGP is located within the Shortgrass Prairie, Tallgrass Prairie, and the Oak-Bluestem Parkland ecoregions (Bailey 1976). After the last glaciation, much of the NGP landscape became dominated by wheatgrasses (*Agropyron*

spp.; plant nomenclature follows Fernald 1950), needlegrasses (*Stipa* spp.), grama grasses (*Bouteloua* spp.), bluestems (*Andropogon* spp.), and fescues (*Festuca* spp.) (Chapman and Sherman 1975). Soils supporting prairie grasslands are generally mollisols with scattered patches of entisols, alfisols, and vertisols (Buckman and Brady 1969). Soils along river floodplains are mosaics of sand, silt, and clays of various combinations and thicknesses (Johnson et al. 1976).

Climate

The climate of the NGP is dry and subhumid with precipitation (often <50 cm/year) substantially lower than potential evapotranspiration (Borchert 1950). Two-thirds of the annual precipitation falls during the growing season, and there is a pronounced decrease in mean annual precipitation from east to west (Fig. 2). The annual wind regime shifts from northwest winds during the winter, to southerly winds during the summer (Johnson et al. 1976). The consistently windy conditions of summer increases evaporation in an already scarce water area and intensifies drought and wind erosion. Summers are hot (July daily mean of 21 C) and winters are quite cold (January daily mean of −12° C); the average frost-free period ranges from <120 days in Canada to 188 days in Nebraska (Chapman and Sherman 1975).

Physiography

The open plains in the western part of the NGP are drained to the southeast by the Missouri River and to the northeast by the Saskatchewan River (Fig. 1). The

[1]Deceased.

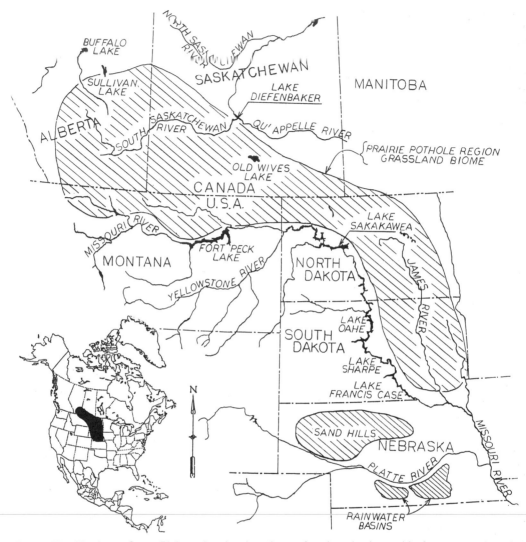

Fig. 1. The Northern Great Plains, showing locations of major physiographic features and wetland regions of importance to waterfowl.

topography of these drainage systems is irregular, with hills, swales, and plateaus that range in elevation from 2,150 m in the Badlands of western South Dakota to 300 m in southeastern Nebraska (Chapman and Sherman 1975).

There are 3 major wetland regions in the NGP (Fig. 1). The glaciated Prairie Pothole Region extends from southcentral Canada to northcentral U.S. and covers about 777,000 km^2 (Tiner 1984). The landscape is pockmarked with millions of pothole depressions, most < 60 cm deep

(Tiner 1984). The Nebraska Sandhills Region is the largest sand dune formation in the western hemisphere, covering approximately 51,000 km^2 (Tiner 1984). Formed primarily by wind action, the Sandhills consist of stabilized sand dunes with groundwater-nourished wetlands in the valleys and perched marshes in sites having poorly drained soils on the upper contours of hills (Tiner 1984). The Rainwater Basin encompasses a 6,720 km^2 drainage area south of the Platte River in southcentral Nebraska (Erickson and Les-

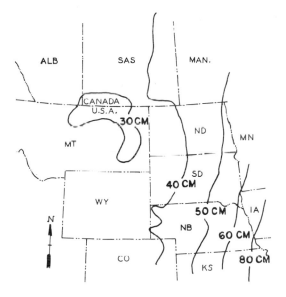

ANNUAL MEAN PRECIPITATION (CM)

Fig. 2. Mean annual precipitation in the Northern Great Plains (data from Chapman and Sherman 1975).

Table 1. A comparison of wetland classes and zones from Stewart and Kantrud's (1971) classification with water regime modifiers from Cowardin et al. (1979).

Class	Zone	Wetland regime modifier
I	Wetland-low prairie	Considered non-wetland
II	Wet meadow	Temporarily flooded
III	Shallow marsh	Seasonally flooded
IV	Deep marsh	Semipermanently flooded Intermittently exposed
V	Permanent open water	Permanently flooded (with mixosaline water)
VI	Intermittent alkali	Intermittently flooded (with saline or hyper-saline water)
VII	Fen	Saturated

lie 1987). Where leaching concentrates clay particles in the subsoils (often forming a 0.1-2.0 m clay layer impervious to water), wetlands develop in sink-like depressions throughout the terrain (Erickson and Leslie 1987). These wetlands are largely dependent on surface runoff and rainfall for water (Erickson and Leslie 1987).

Aquatic Habitats

Vegetation Composition.—Plant communities of NGP wetlands are typically described as distinct bands of vegetation that follow shoreline contours (Stewart and Kantrud 1971, 1972, Cowardin et al., 1979; Table 1). Depending on water permanency, soil and water chemistry, soil characteristics, and land use (Dix and Smeins 1967, Walker and Coupland 1968, 1970, Stewart and Kantrud 1972, Kantrud 1986a, Erickson and Leslie 1987), vegetation often develops into zones characterized as: (1) wetland-low prairie, (2) wet meadow, (3) shallow marsh, (4) deep marsh, (5) permanent open water, (6)

intermittent-alkali, and (7) fen (Stewart and Kantrud 1971, 1972). Plant species typically found in various vegetation zones are listed in Table 2.

Vegetation Dynamics.—Although aquatic vegetation may often appear to form a distinct zonation, this is an oversimplification because aquatic plant populations can be variously distributed along environmental gradients (e.g., water depth, frequency of flooding, soil types, water turbidity, salinity, wave action). The more abrupt the environmental gradient, the more distinct the plant community distribution. As environmental conditions change (e.g., increased frequency of water level changes), some plant populations are eliminated and others become established along new gradients (van der Valk and Davis 1978). This "resorting" of vegetation is a function of recruitment from buried seeds and vegetative propagules, and dispersal of propagules.

During low water periods, wetland soil chemistry changes and buried seeds begin to germinate (Kadlec and Wentz 1974). Spatial differences in buried seed reserves, soil moisture, and chronology of drainage determine the initial species composition. Rising water levels decrease soil aeration and salinity. Seed germination of most species of plants ceases, whereas some emergent plant species continue to vegeta-

Table 2. Plant species commonly found in Northern Great Plains wetlands with different water regimes and salinities (Stewart and Kantrud 1972, Kadlec and Wentz 1974, Fulton et al. 1986, Erickson and Leslie 1987).

Water regime[a]	Abundance[b] in relation to water salinity[c]				
	Fresh	Slightly brackish	Moderately brackish	Brackish	Subsaline
Drained mudflats					
Rayless aster (*Aster brachyactis*)		FC	C	A	
Beggarticks (*Bidens* spp.)	C	C			
Goosefoot (*Chenopodium* spp.)	FC	A	A	A	
Needle spikerush (*Eleocharis acicularis*)	A	A	C		
Wild barley (*Hordeum jubatum*)	FC	C	A	A	
Alkali bulrush (*Scirpus maritimus*)		FC	C	A	A
Kochia (*Kochia scoparia*)	C	A	A	A	C
Marsh ragwort (*Senecio congestus*)	A	S	FC		
Cocklebur (*Xanthium* spp.)	C	C			
Wet-meadow					
Lowland, white aster (*Aster simplex*)	A	A	C	FC	
False aster (*Boltonia latisquama*)	A	FC			
Bluejoint (*Calamagrostis canadensis*)	FC	FC			
Northern reedgrass (*Calamagrostis inexpansa*)	FC	A	A	FC	
Sedge (*Carex* spp.)	A	C	FC		
Saltgrass (*Distichlis stricta*)		FC	C	A	A
Wild barley	C	A	A	A	C
Baltic rush (*Juncus balticus*)	C	A	A	C	FC
Fowl-meadow grass (*Poa palustris*)	A	C	FC		
Prairie cordgrass (*Spartina pectinata*)	C	A	A	FC	
Shallow marsh					
Water plaintain (*Alisma* spp.)	A	A	A	FC	
Sloughgrass (*Beckmannia syzigache*)	A	A	FC		
Sough sedge (*Carex atherodes*)	A	A	C		
Spike rush (*Eleocharis palustris*)	FC	A	A	C	
Tall mannagrass (*Glyceria grandis*)	A	FC			
Reed canarygrass (*Phalaris arundinacea*)	C	FC			
Marsh smartweed (*Polygonum coccineum*)		A	FC		
Alkaligrass (*Puccinellia nuttalliana*)			FC	C	A
Samphire (*Salicornia rubra*)				C	A
Threesquare (*Scirpus americanus*)		FC	C	A	C
Whitetop (*Scolochloa festucacea*)	FC	A	A	FC	
Giant burreed (*Sparganium eurycarpum*)	A	FC			
Deep marsh					
Common reed (*Phragmites australis*)		FC	FC		
Hardstem bulrush (*Scirpus acutus*)	FC	A	A	C	
River bulrush (*Scirpus fluviatilis*)	C	A	FC		
Slender bulrush (*Scirpus heteracheatus*)	A	FC			
Alkali bulrush		FC	C	A	A
Softstem bulrush (*Scirpus validus*)	FC	C			
Narrowleaf cattail (*Typha angustifolia*)		FC	FC	FC	
Hybrid cattail (*Typha glauca*)		A	FC		
Common cattail (*Typha latifolia*)	C	C	FC		
Coontail (*Ceratophyllum demersum*)	C	A	FC		
Muskgrass (*Chara* spp.)	FC	C	A	A	C
Duckweeds (*Lemna* spp.)	A	A	A		
Watermilfoil (*Myriophyllum exalbescens*)	C	A	FC		
Sago pondweed (*Potamogeton pectinatus*)	FC	C	A	A	C
Pondweeds (*Potamogeton* spp.)	A	A	FC		
White water crowfoot (*Ranunculus trichophyllus*)	C		A	C	

Table 2. Continued.

Water regime[a]		Abundance[b] in relation to water salinity[c]				
	Fresh	Slightly brackish	Moderately brackish	Brackish	Subsaline	
Widgeongrass (*Ruppia* spp.)		A	A	C	A	
Common bladderwort (*Utricularia vulgaris*)	A	A	C			
Horned pondweed (*Zannichellia palustris*)		C	A	A	FC	

[a]Mudflats occur in semipermanent ponds and lakes in drought years or when surface water recedes late in the growing season. Temporarily flooded wetlands contain water for only a few weeks in the spring or a few days after heavy rainstorms. Seasonally flooded wetlands typically contain water only through spring and early summer. Semipermanently flooded, intermittently exposed wetlands ordinarily maintain water through spring and summer and frequently into fall and winter.

[b]Relative abundance of species codes as follows: A = abundant, C = common, FC = fairly common.

[c]Salinity categories are defined by mean water conductivities in the following range: fresh ≤ 0.2 mmhos, slightly brackish ≤ 1.0 mmhos, moderately brackish ≤ 2.0 mmhos, brackish ≤ 6.0 mmhos, subsaline ≤ 25.0 mmhos.

tively propagate under water. Depending primarily on the depth and frequency of flooding, water quality, or exposure to waves, wet meadow, shallow marsh, deep marsh or submergent communities will form (Stewart and Kantrud 1972, Kadlec and Wentz 1974, van der Valk and Davis 1978).

Palustrine Wetlands.—Aquatic habitats in the NGP are generally small (<8 ha) and develop in snowmelt and rainwater catch basins or in shallow depressions where groundwater reaches the surface (Stewart and Kantrud 1972). Most "potholes" are considered freshwater, although saline and alkaline types are common in the western NGP (Moore and Mills 1977). In years with little snowfall or spring precipitation, a large percentage of the potholes will dry or will not retain water through summer (Kantrud and Stewart 1977).

Potholes usually occur in complexes of several wetland types in close proximity to each other (Stewart and Kantrud 1973). Tilled basins are the most numerous of all potholes. Of basins not tilled, temporarily and seasonally flooded wetlands are most numerous, whereas seasonally and semipermanently flooded basins encompass the greatest area (Stewart and Kantrud 1973).

A diverse macroinvertebrate fauna is associated with seasonal water conditions and the amount of vegetative structure and detritus of palustrine wetlands (Kan-

trud and Stewart 1977). Temporal patterns of population growth, species composition, and density of macroinvertebrates vary among wetland habitats (Swanson et al. 1974, Serie and Swanson 1976, Nelson and Kadlec 1985).

Lacustrine Wetlands.—Bellrose (1980) lists 213 important waterfowl habitats in the NGP that are >200 ha and that offer substantial benefits to waterfowl. Most of these are located in the drift plain of the northern and eastern part of the NGP. In the western half of the NGP, natural lakes are few because of the well-dissected topography. Numerous reservoirs, however, have been created by the damming of rivers and ephemeral streams. Fort Peck, Lake Sakakawea, and Oahe reservoirs are Missouri River mainstream impoundments and the largest water bodies in the region (see Benson and Cowell [1967] for a review of their physical and chemical variables).

Smaller reservoirs in the NGP are generally shallow, warm-water impoundments. They are frequently well-populated with emergent and submergent aquatic vegetation if fluctuations in water level are not too great (Kadlec and Wentz 1974, Moore and Mills 1977). In lacustrine marshes with shallow water depths, plant communities are often quite similar to those of palustrine wetlands (Stewart and Kantrud 1972, Kadlec and Wentz 1974). In lakes and larger reservoirs, however, aquatic plant communities along shorelines often are limited because of wave action, water turbidity, ice scour, shoreline erosion, drastic water-level fluctuations, and mineral soils (Hutchinson 1975, Keddy 1983).

Riverine Wetlands.—NGP floodplain forests are found along sections of rivers that have not been impounded (Teskey and Hinckley 1978). Stands of cottonwood (*Populus deltoides*), green ash (*Fraxinus pennsylvanica*), boxelder (*Acer negundo*), elms (*Ulmus* spp.), bur oak (*Quercus macrocarpa*), willows (*Salix* spp.), and a number of shrubs and woody vines occupy the floodplain (Weaver 1960, Keammerer et al. 1985). Floodplain forest communities are subject to inundation, severe soil erosion and deposition, and physical damage to trees and understory vegetation from transported debris (Sigafoos 1964). Periodic flooding forms open channels, sand and gravel bars, oxbows, and quiet water areas in the floodplain.

Land Use Changes

Climate, grazing, and fire were once the only major factors affecting the abundance and species composition of vegetation in the NGP (Kantrud 1986a). However, agricultural activities and water resource developments by man have now greatly changed the landscape (Chapman and Sherman 1975, Pendleton and Linder 1984).

In northern and eastern portions of the NGP, native grasslands have been converted to intensively farmed cropland of spring and winter wheat, barley, corn, and alfalfa (Chapman and Sherman 1975). The western portion of the NGP is used extensively as rangeland for cattle, and some areas are being impacted by mining for energy development (Pendleton and Linder 1984).

Agricultural drainage has claimed 60% of the original wetlands in North Dakota, 35% in South Dakota, and 91% in the Rainwater Basin of Nebraska (Tiner 1984). Remaining wetlands also are subjected to a variety of agricultural influences. In dry years, emergent vegetation often is grazed or mowed for forage. Near cropland areas, the wetland low prairie, wet meadow, and shallow marsh zones are cultivated frequently (Weller 1981). Cultivation of wetland basins removes the vegetation detritus that fuels the aquatic food chain when the basin is reflooded (Fig. 3). Tillage of wetland margins also contributes to the salinization of prairie cropland (Prairie Farm Rehabilitation Administration 1983). Sedimentation and herbicide and pesticide loading of wetlands occur, but the effects are not well-understood (Kantrud 1986a).

In response to a cessation of burning and intensive grazing, many wetlands have become overgrown with robust emergent plants. Since the 1920s, cattail has become dominant in wetlands where water salinities range from fresh to slightly brackish (Kantrud 1986a). Purple loosestrife (*Lythrum salicaria*) is another problem plant that is now present in the eastern and northern regions of the NGP (Thompson et al. 1987).

Wetlands often are altered (Fig. 3) to form stock watering ponds or water storage reservoirs for irrigation (Flake 1978). In South Dakota, stock ponds and dugouts now may account for as much as 33% of the small wetland base (Ruwaldt et al. 1979). Stock ponds are located primarily in the western non-glaciated part of the NGP, whereas most dugouts are located in the eastern glaciated area (Flake 1978). Stock ponds now provide open water habitat in large areas of rangeland that previously lacked wetlands (Giron 1981).

Since 1950, numerous impoundments and diversion systems have been developed to control annual flows of NGP rivers for irrigation and other purposes. On the Platte River, approximately 70% of the annual flow now is withdrawn before reaching southcentral Nebraska (Kroonemeyer 1978). This has caused (1)

Fig. 3. A wetland in the Rainwater Basin where a dugout has reduced the littoral zone and permitted cultivation of a portion of the basin.

river channel width to diminish by 90% (Williams 1978), (2) extensive woodlands to become established on much of the former channel area (U.S. Fish and Wildlife Service 1981), and (3) adjoining grasslands to be converted to irrigated agriculture (U.S. Fish and Wildlife Service 1981).

Permanent destruction of riparian habitat on the Missouri River has been caused by federal water development projects (Hoar and Erwin 1985). About 60% of the area flooded by new dams was occupied by woodland-grassland vegetation, and over half the Upper Missouri now must be classified as reservoir rather than as free-flowing river (Hoar and Erwin 1985).

HABITAT IMPORTANCE

During fall and spring, the NGP is a major migration corridor for waterfowl (Bellrose 1980). Depending on winter weather, several hundred thousand mal-

lards (*Anas platyrhynchos*) and Canada geese (*Branta canadensis*) also winter in the region (Bellrose 1980, U.S. Fish and Wildlife Service 1981).

Fall Migration

Chronology.—Autumn migration from the prairies occurs from August through December and varies among and within waterfowl species (Bellrose 1980). Migration usually commences in Canada when high pressure systems and prevailing southerly flows of air occur in late August (Bellrose 1980). Fall migration is generally more prolonged than spring migration and is influenced by the intensity and duration of early winter storms (Bellrose 1980). During years when early winter is characterized by mild weather, several species of waterfowl delay migration until the last week of December or first week of January (Jorde 1981).

Typically, northern pintails (*Anas*

acuta) and blue-winged teal (*A. discors*) are the first to leave staging marshes in mid-August, followed by ruddy ducks (*Oxyura jamaicensis*), northern shovelers (*A. clypeata*), and green-winged teal (*A. crecca*) in late August or early September. The largest number of green-winged teal migrates through eastern areas of the NGP. Gadwalls (*A. strepera*) and American wigeon (*A. americana*) are mid-season fall migrants. The most notable fall concentrations of gadwall occur at LaCreek NWR in South Dakota and Valentine NWR in Nebraska. Canvasbacks (*Aythya valisineria*) and redheads (*Aythya americana*) leave in mid-October, whereas mallards remain until late October. The central NGP is a major migration corridor for redhead, but not for canvasback. Lesser scaup (*Aythya affinis*) arrive at staging marshes late in fall and usually remain until large marshes freeze in early November (Hochbaum 1955).

Generally, adult female and juvenile ducks migrate later than males of the same species (Hochbaum 1944). These within-species differences in migration chronology are due to the timing and energetic costs of growth and molt for juveniles, and nesting activities and molt for females (Hochbaum 1944). Females and juveniles are attracted to large lacustrine marshes with abundant emergent plant cover and submerged aquatic plant beds (Salomonsen 1968).

The pattern of autumn migration in geese and swans is different than among ducks because family bonds hold adults and young together during migration (Bell-rose 1980). White-fronted geese (*Anser albifrons*) are often the first geese to appear on staging areas, with flocks reaching Kindersley, Saskatchewan, as early as August (Bellrose 1980). Lesser snow geese (*Chen caerulescens*) begin to stage in the prairies during the beginning of September, and largest concentrations are present at the end of September with

exodus occurring during October. During mid-autumn, the eastern prairie race of Canada geese migrates through the eastern NGP, whereas the western and tallgrass prairie races migrate through western NGP. Tundra swans (*Cygnus columbianus*) travel through the NGP in early to mid-October and depart in late October or early November.

Shifts in Distribution.—In recent years, shifts in migration distributions of snow geese, mallards, and Canada geese have occurred (Buller 1975). The fall migration of mid-continent lesser snow geese was once a rapid flight from the arctic to the Gulf Coast, with most of the population reaching the coast by mid-November (Bateman et al. 1988). Now, during middle to late November, half of the mid-continent snow goose population is in the midwestern U.S., and large numbers of snow geese overwinter along the Missouri River (Bateman et al. 1988).

This response may be attributable to (1) increased corn acreage in North Dakota and Manitoba (Simpson 1988), (2) arctic breeding range extensions to the west, (3) more fall plowing in the eastern NGP, and (4) increased survival of western and northern migrating populations (less hunting tradition and pressure in these "new" habitats) (Thomas 1983, Bateman et al. 1988). Mallards and Canada geese also have responded to creation of refuges and reservoirs and increases in corn acreage by a gradual northward shift in wintering and migration concentration areas (Bossenmaier and Marshall 1958, Buller 1964, 1975, U.S. Fish and Wildlife Service 1981, Simpson 1988).

Wintering

Concentration Areas.—There are several large populations of waterfowl that winter on the NGP (Table 3). Nebraska winters about 125,000 mallards on the North Platte River, 25,000 on the South Platte River, 50,000 on the Platte River (east of Ogallala), and another 50,000 on

Table 3. Number of waterfowl counted in portions of the Northern Great Plains during the 1987 U.S. Fish and Wildlife Service midwinter inventory (U.S. Fish and Wildlife Service, unpubl. report).

Species	Montana	Nebraska	North Dakota	South Dakota	Total
Mallard	20,200	251,700	5,900	148,100	425,900
Gadwall	500	100			600
American wigeon	500	200			700
Northern pintail	200				200
Lesser scaup	200	100			300
Goldeneye	7,300	9,000	800	100	17,200
(*Bucephala clangula*)					
Bufflehead				100	100
(*B. albeola*)					
Mergansers (*Mergus* spp.)	200	17,800	200	2,400	20.600
Lesser snow goose		51,600			51,600
White-fronted goose		8,700			8,700
Canada goose	8,900	119,300	12,400	174,600	315,200

reservoirs and rivers throughout the southern and central parts of the state (Bellrose 1980, U.S. Fish and Wildlife Service 1981). Mallards also winter along riverine habitats of the South Platte River in Colorado and the North Platte River in Wyoming. In South Dakota, 130,000 mallards winter on reservoirs and 25,000 winter on warm springs near the Black Hills. Montana typically winters <100,000 mallards, with most birds located along the Bighorn, Yellowstone, and Missouri rivers. Wintering Canada geese may number in the hundreds of thousands, with largest concentrations located on the Platte River in Nebraska and Lake Andes and Fort Randall reservoirs in South Dakota. Recently, snow geese have become a frequent winter resident in Nebraska. Goldeneyes, buffleheads, and mergansers winter on the reservoirs and open water discharge areas below dams.

Shifts in Distribution.—The increase in waterfowl on the NGP during winter followed the development of large reservoirs (which provide open water and refuge throughout the winter) and intensified agricultural practices (which provide a high-energy food source in the form of waste grain) (Buller 1964, 1975, Jorde et al. 1983). Also, tradition influen-

ces wintering site fidelity as adult mallards seem to return to areas used during their first winter (Bellrose and Crompton 1970). Subadult waterfowl are more likely to attempt to overwinter as far north as possible when weather conditions are mild at the beginning of winter (Albright et al. 1983).

Spring Migration

Chronology.—Spring migrants arrive at staging areas in Nebraska and South Dakota during early March and continue northward migration during April and early May as winter snow and ice retreat (Bellrose 1980, U.S. Fish and Wildlife Service 1981). Migration chronology of different waterfowl species is essentially the reverse of the autumn migration sequence (Bellrose 1980). However, spring migration is of greater intensity than fall migration, as flocks often become concentrated due to weather and habitat conditions.

Elevation changes from north to south of the NGP create differences in the timing of spring breakup and can significantly affect migration. For example, the Sandhills region of Nebraska is more than 396 m in elevation above the Rainwater Basin area in the southern part of the state (Wright and Bailey 1980).

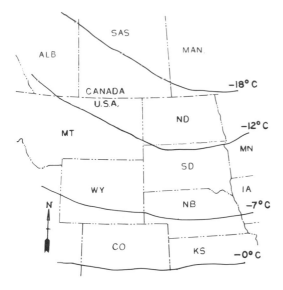

AVERAGE JANUARY TEMPERATURE

Fig. 4. Winter temperature gradients in the Northern Great Plains (data from Chapman and Sherman 1975).

Consequently, the Rainwater Basin and Platte River areas are located along a temperature gradient (Fig. 4) that makes aquatic habitats available to waterfowl earlier than the wetlands in the Sandhills (which thaw at about the same time as wetlands in North Dakota).

Habitat Use

In general, small wetlands are most available to waterfowl during spring and early summer. More permanent aquatic habitats (large marshes, lakes, and reservoirs) and agricultural fields are used by waterfowl during fall migration. Open river channels, warm water canals, tailraces below reservoirs, and agricultural habitats are used during winter.

Riverine Habitats and Reservoirs.—The large size of reservoirs furnishes abundant loafing and resting areas for waterfowl. Large reservoirs also prolong the ice-free period during fall because large volumes of water take longer to freeze. Open water also results from warm freshwater seeps (drainage ditches and sloughs) and areas of rapidly flowing water below reservoirs.

During migration, waterfowl use lake and reservoir shorelines, river oxbows, and impoundments, and quickly deplete food resources (Jorde 1981, Frederick and Klaas 1982). Thereafter, these habitats are used for their sanctuary, shelter characteristics, and proximity to small wetlands (which provide aquatic food resources) or to agricultural fields (which provide grain and browse) (Flake 1978, Frederick and Klaas 1982).

Rivers and streams provide gravel and sandbars that waterfowl use as grit sources and as resting or loafing sites, especially when nearby trees and high river banks provide shelter from adverse weather conditions (U.S. Fish and Wildlife Service 1981, Jorde et al. 1984). Formation of river deltas in upstream ends of reservoirs has provided additional wetland habitat for waterfowl (Stanford 1979). Fluvial sediments are deposited primarily at upstream ends of reservoirs, especially during floods, and after a period of years, much of the delta is colonized by aquatic plants (Stanford 1979). However, because operating guidelines for most reservoirs emphasize flood control or water uses other than wildlife enhancement, delta habitats often are flooded or are otherwise unavailable to migrating waterfowl (Stanford 1979).

NGP wooded floodplains are not major waterfowl habitats during late fall migration and winter because flooding seldom occurs during these seasons. Most flooding occurs during late winter when reservoirs are drawn down to receive anticipated heavy snowmelt, and during spring when melting snow and rain swell rivers beyond their banks. During these conditions, waterfowl often are observed foraging in flooded woodland habitats (U.S. Fish and Wildlife Service 1981).

Lacustrine Wetlands.—Salomonsen (1968) reviewed the literature of migration of waterfowl to large wetlands for molting. Traditionally used lakes or marshes may be valuable to molting waterfowl over a large geographical area (Salomonsen 1968). These lakes and marshes are characterized by abundant food resources (e.g., sago pondweed, widgeon-grass, invertebrates), protected bays with emergent cover, and isolation from human disturbance (Oring 1964, Bergman 1973, Seric and Swanson 1976, Kantrud 1986*b*).

Palustrine Wetlands.—On the NGP, semipermanent, seasonal, and temporary wetlands are most important during spring migration and the breeding season. Palustrine wetlands in the Rainwater Basin in Nebraska are perhaps the most critically important habitat of this type in the NGP (U.S. Fish and Wildlife Service 1981). Tens of thousands of waterfowl congregrate in each basin during the night and forage on waste grain during the day (U.S. Fish and Wildlife Service 1981). These seasonal wetlands also pro-vide plant and invertebrate food resources that supplement the predominantly waste grain diets of many migrating waterfowl species (U.S. Fish and Wildlife Service 1981).

Wet meadow habitats are among the first areas to freeze. Consequently, these areas receive little waterfowl use during middle to late autumn and winter (U.S. Fish and Wildlife Service 1981). However, during spring migration, meadows attract waterfowl (Kantrud and Stewart 1977) especially where snowmelt has created temporary areas of shallow water.

Uplands.—Throughout the year, pas-tures and croplands are important forag-ing habitats, providing high-energy, eas-ily digestible food (Bossenmaier and Marshall 1958, Thomas 1983, Paulus 1988, Simpson 1988). In addition, geese occasionally use cornfields as diurnal loafing areas when aquatic habitats are frozen (U.S. Fish and Wildlife Service 1981).

Waterfowl use of agricultural habitats is related to the proximity of refuges and staging areas and to the type and abun-dance of agricultural grain in the area (Grieb and Bocker 1954, Bossenmaier and

Marshall 1958, Frederick and Klaas 1982, Simpson 1988). Cornfields attract the largest number of waterfowl, although sorghum, soybean, and winter-wheat fields also are used extensively. During spring staging, 75-99% of the diets of mallards and geese is waste corn (U.S. Fish and Wildlife Service 1981, Alisauskas 1988). Seasonally flooded (sheetwater) agricultural ponds that contain stubble or native vegetation also provide important pair-space, foraging areas, and loafing sites (LaGrange and Dinsmore 1988).

In wet autumns, availability of swathed grain increases, and field-feeding species remain longer near northern staging marshes (Sugden 1976). Crop damage in swathed grain fields (principally wheat and barley) on the Canadian prairies is caused by mallards, pintails, and geese (Sugden 1976). Crop damage is greatest near large wetlands used as staging areas by waterfowl, and government payments for depredation are available (Sugden 1976). Crop predation in the U.S. portion of the NGP is less of a problem. Farmers generally assume responsibility for pro-tecting their crops through hazing or selecting crops that are not used by waterfowl (Kittle and Porter 1988).

Disturbance.—Hunting pressure and disturbance often discourage use of pre-ferred habitats by waterfowl. Hunting pressure is variable and specific to local areas (Jessen 1970, Raveling et al. 1972, Koerner et al. 1974, Raveling 1978). Grain harvest and tillage also coincide with waterfowl migration and influence local distribution patterns (Frederick and Klaas 1982, Baldassarre et al. 1983). Similarly, spring plowing disrupts migration patt-erns on southern areas of the NGP (U.S. Fish and Wildlife Service 1981).

During the fall migration, most preda-tor activity is scavenging of waterfowl crippled during the hunting season and of sick or dead birds in areas of disease outbreaks (Lingle and Krapu 1986). Pre-dation during this time period is not believed to be a problem; however, disturbance and mortality associated with predators on wintering areas may be significant..

During winter, waterfowl and predators tend to concentrate around small areas of open water. Raptors commonly perch near concentrations of waterfowl feeding in agricultural fields in South Dakota (Steenhof 1984) and Nebraska (Jorde and Lingle 1988). Disturbance of field-feeding mallards by avian predators can become intense (Jorde and Lingle 1988). The percent of waterfowl in the diet of bald eagles (*Haliaeetus leucocephalus*) increases during severe winters when the availability of open water and fish decreases (Lingle and Krapu 1986). Mallards and Canada geese are major prey in the diet of bald eagles wintering on the High Plains (Lish and Lewis 1975) and the NGP (Lingle and Krapu 1986).

Disease.—Avian botulism (*Clostridium botulinum*) accounts for 90% of the total reported nonhunting waterfowl mortality (Stout and Cornwell 1976). Botulism outbreaks occur primarily in July through September and are typically associated with fluctuating water levels, hot temperatures, and anaerobic water conditions (Locke and Friend 1987). Heavy July or August rains with subsequent hot weather and decreasing water levels seem to start outbreaks. In large marshes or lakes, wind seiches can create the same type of flooding and drying of shoreline zones that trigger bacteria growth.

Duck virus enteritis (DVE) outbreaks have been reported in the NGP (Brand 1987). In 1973, 40% of 100,000 wintering mallards died in a short-lived outbreak at South Dakota's Lake Andes NWR. Severe weather conditions, crowding, and stress were thought to have triggered the die-off.

Crowding in the Rainwater Basins during peak waterfowl migrations in March and April is believed responsible for the avian cholera (*Pasteurella multocida*) epizootics first observed in 1975 (Friend 1987). Avian cholera transmission can occur by bird-to-bird contact and ingestion, and acute infections are common (Friend 1987). Losses can occur at any time of the year, but the focal point in the NGP is the Rainwater Basins in spring. Outbreaks have occurred annually since 1975, killing an estimated 200,000 waterfowl in the area and making an unknown impact on survivors (U.S. Fish and Wildlife Service, unpub. report). During dry springs when birds are concentrated, late winter storms (which may stress the birds) seem to trigger the disease. Species hit hardest are pintails, mallards, white-fronted geese, Canada geese, and lesser snow geese. From the Rainwater Basin area, the disease is spreading northward to western Saskatchewan and the snow goose breeding grounds in the arctic (Friend 1987).

HABITAT IMPORTANCE RELATIVE TO WATERFOWL REQUIREMENTS

Annual Cycle

Because mallards and Canada geese are the only waterfowl species that winter on the NGP in relatively large numbers, our discussion of annual cycle events occurring during migration and winter focuses on these species.

Sex Ratio.—Male mallards dominate winter flocks on the NGP. During a severe winter in Nebraska, adults comprised 72% and males 74% of the wintering mallard population. In a subsequent mild winter, populations contained more juveniles and females (62% adults and 52-61% males) (Ferguson et al. 1981, Jorde et al. 1984).

Pair Status.—The proportion of mallards that pair before arriving at wintering areas on the NGP is not known. Lebret (1961) and Raitasuo (1964) reported that mallards started pairing in late summer and continued courtship throughout fall and winter.

In Nebraska, some mallards arrive on winter areas already paired. Courtship continues throughout winter and during spring staging. Regardless of pair status, gonadal weights of mallards in Nebraska are low during early winter, increase slowly from late January to late March, and thereafter begin rapid development (Jorde 1981).

Young adult geese may take weeks or months to form pair bonds on breeding grounds, whereas adults that have lost mates may form pair bonds in a matter of hours (Bellrose 1980). Data are lacking concerning pairing chronology of geese during winter and spring migration on the NGP.

Pair formation during winter and migration is important because paired waterfowl weigh more (McLandress and Raveling 1981) and are dominant over unpaired birds, especially on foraging areas (Jorde 1981).

Molt.—In Nebraska, the earliest prebasic molt by female mallards during winter was observed in January. Molt continued throughout winter and seemed to be influenced by pair status. Eighty-eight percent of paired females were molting (Jorde, unpubl. data). All females collected after the first week of March were molting (Jorde 1981).

Scheduling of Events.—Because reproduction, molt, and migration are considered energetically expensive events, a trend toward separate scheduling of these activities exists. Bluhm (1988) described 3 general relationships among molt, migration, and reproduction as they relate to waterfowl body size. In larger waterfowl (such as geese), molt, migration, and gonadal growth were completely separate. In medium-sized waterfowl (e.g., mallard), molt, migration, and reproduction are usually separated. However, in unpaired or juvenile females, molt and spring migration may overlap. In smaller-bodied ducks (e.g., blue-winged teal), molt overlaps with both migration and

egg-laying (Bluhm 1988). Habitat influences the ability of a bird to meet requirements for migration, molt, and pairing through seasonal changes in food availability and quality.

In autumn, waterfowl forage intensively to accumulate lipids to use as an energy source for migration and winter maintenance (Jorde 1981), and perhaps to acquire specific nutrients required for molt (Quinlan and Baldassarre 1984). Species that select foods of high-energy content (e.g., agricultural grains) devote the least amount of time to feeding (Paulus 1988).

In winter, waterfowl weight losses (Folk et al. 1966, Jorde 1981) may be associated with an endogenous annual weight cycle and increased catabolism of fat reserves (Johnson et al. 1985) for thermoregulation (Jorde et al. 1984). Energy losses are minimized when birds select thermally favorable microhabitats and spend most of their time resting during the day (Jorde et al. 1984, Paulus 1988). Freedom from harassment by predators, availability of food, and thermally-protected habitats may be critical during this period.

By late winter, feeding increases due to premigratory hyperphagia (Tamisier 1974) and nutrient needs for breeding activities. At this time, increasing air temperatures reduce energy demands for thermoregulation, and increase energy for lipid deposition, molt, courtship, and gonadal development.

Management Implications.—Waterfowl managers are aware of factors which cause direct mortality to waterfowl (e.g., disease, predation, hunting), and have developed programs to address those problems. However, designing a habitat-management program to remedy sublethal effects (e.g., populations with lower body weights because of severe winters) may be more difficult. Because a positive relationship between lipid reserves and clutch size has been shown for various waterfowl species (Ankney and MacInnes 1978, Krapu 1981), failure to meet nutritional needs of waterfowl during winter and spring migration may result in reduced recruitment. Determining when body reserves for breeding are acquired and how fast individuals are able to gain weight helps identify where habitats are needed and what type of management should be provided.

In larger species, such as geese, females are capable of carrying sufficient protein and lipid reserves to enable them to produce eggs (Ankney and MacInnes 1978, Raveling 1979). Most of these reserves are deposited during spring migration (Thomas 1983, Alisauskas 1988), and probably peak just before departure from the last staging area (Raveling 1979).

Smaller-bodied waterfowl, such as ducks, also rely largely on foods (for lipid acquisition) available on spring staging areas (LaGrange and Dinsmore 1988). But these species are more dependent than geese on habitats close to and on breeding areas to supply them with the aquatic invertebrates that provide protein to produce eggs (Krapu 1974, 1981, LaGrange and Dinsmore 1988). Thus, habitats that offer refuge and an abundance and diversity of high-energy and nutritious food need to be available at appropriate locations along spring migration routes.

HABITAT MANAGEMENT
Management Strategies

Land use in the NGP is controlled by climate, water availability, energy costs, farm policies, and commodity prices. Because of this, waterfowl habitat managers can do little to alter land use over broad areas. There are, however, several critical areas that have become focal concentration points during migration (e.g., Rainwater Basin) where management actions have the potential to affect large numbers of birds (Fig. 5). Objectives designed for spring migration seem especially appropriate because waterfowl are in the process of acquiring body reserves necessary for reproduction.

Programs for migrants include (1) developing wetland complexes by restoring drained wetlands, particularly in areas where the habitat base needs to be increased to prevent disease outbreaks; (2) managing native plant communities in large marshes or irrigated drainages to provide waterfowl pair-space, foraging sites, and postbreeding staging marshes; (3) controlling emergent and woody vegetation to provide open water on existing wetlands and river channels; (4) instigating a private-lands program aimed at maintaining sheetwater basins in stubble fields adjacent to staging marshes (Madsen 1986); and (5) managing subimpoundments to provide moist-soil or submerged aquatic vegetation for migrating waterfowl.

Riverine Habitats

Various techniques have been employed to control enroachment of woody vegetation and maintain an open river channel width of at least 150 m for roost sites for migrating cranes and waterfowl (Currier et al. 1985). The tradeoffs of river channel clearing are that certain features of wooded river channels may be lost that provide favorable microsites for wintering waterfowl (i.e., sheltered "cut banks" near open river channels). However, in early spring, open river channels are also the first water habitats open to migrating birds, and availability of these habitats may prevent disease outbreaks (U.S. Fish and Wildlife Service 1981). Inventory of the 2 types of riverine habitats would help in prioritizing and targeting waterfowl wintering versus migration habitat management. Techniques employed in river channel management include (1) river flow maintenance and island leveling, (2) mechanized clearing and burning, and (3) herbicide spraying (Aronson and Ellis 1979).

Fig. 5. Concentration of waterfowl on a frozen wetland in Nebraska's Rainwater Basin.

River flow maintenance (to ensure enough river flow volume to maintain flood scouring) has been the focus of attention for many years; however, due to increasing demands for water, river flows will likely be decreased or maintained at present levels (Aronson and Ellis 1979). Island clearing and leveling involve mechanically clearing (bulldozing) vegetation and then leveling the island to near the base flow in the river. This removes most buried root stalks of fast-growing tree species and promotes flood scouring (low-cost maintenance). Treatment costs are about $1400/ha and Section 404 permits are required (Aronson and Ellis 1979).

Burning removed understory vegetation and small trees, but was relatively ineffective against willows (3-5 m tall). Clearing also was accomplished by pulling various types of machinery over vegetated islands. During periods of minimum river flow in late summer when farm machinery could negotiate the Platte River, large disks (equipped with 92 cm notched disk blades) or rotary mowers (Currier 1984) were used to knock down existing vegetation (Aronson and Ellis 1979). These techniques usually provided only short-term results because new shoots of willow, cottonwoods, and indigo bush (*Amorpha fruticosa*) rapidly developed from remaining stumps. However, repeated treatments (brushhogging and disking) in combination with scouring floods provided good brush control (Currier 1984).

Herbicide spraying (glyphosate) of trees and shrubs was less successful (75% kill) than spraying glyphosate on trees and shrubs that sprouted following rotary mowing (95% kill) (Currier 1984). Tebuthiuron pellets applied at rates of 10-20 kg/ha were effective in killing most tree species (90-95% kill), but were found less effective on willow and dogwood (*Cornus* spp.). Tebuthiuron gave poor results in control of red cedar (*Juniperus virginiana*). Treating trees larger than 22 cm dbh (diameter at breast height) posed a special problem because, once killed, logging techniques were required to remove the trees (Currier 1984). Herbicide management is considered a last resort because of unknown risks of application to aquatic ecosystems.

During severe winters, warm-water seeps and deep drainage channels in protected areas (surrounded by forest) often become concentration areas for wintering mallards. Because of unsuitable soils (usually sand) in these aquatic habitats, food items are relatively scarce and become depleted quickly when birds are forced to concentrate in these small areas. Intensive management for wintering waterfowl could include addition of organic matter (e.g., cattle manure or peat soils) to promote aquatic plant productivity in these critical winter habitats.

Reservoirs, Stock Ponds, and Dugouts

Because of their large size, dynamic water levels, and erodible steep shorelines, reservoirs are not very amenable to specific management practices for waterfowl. One option is the creation of subimpoundments within reservoirs.

In subimpoundments developed for dust abatement in the Canyon Ferry Reservoir, Montana, plantings of sago pondweed and bulrush were made from local sources (Childress and Eng 1979). Plantings were successful when protected from the resident population of Canada geese (which doubled in size due to construction of nesting islands in the impoundments). After impoundment construction, spring and fall use of the reservoir by migrating waterfowl steadily increased to 250,000 ducks and 7,000 snow geese (Childress and Eng 1979). Other management efforts have included establishing vegetation on reservoir shorelines to control erosion (Allen

1978). Hoffman (1977) and Fowler and Hammer (1976) successfully established grasses and emergent hydrophytes on shorelines of Lakes Oahe and Sakakawea. Once established, many of the grasses (reed canary grass, common reed, Garrison creeping foxtail [*Alopecurus arundinaceus*]) spread vegetatively and formed sods. Cattail and bulrush were transplanted successfully as were several tree species (green ash, eastern cottonwood, diamond willow [*Salix rigida*], and white willow [*S. alba*]). Transplanted plants were able to survive periods of inundation in a zone subjected to about 4 m of average annual water fluctuation (Hoffman 1977).

Stock ponds can be improved for migrating waterfowl by (1) making irregular shorelines (e.g., in kidney, "L," or oak-leaf shapes), (2) contouring slopes no steeper than 1:5, and (3) creating basins where water depths generally do not exceed 0.5 m (Poston and Schmidt 1981). In areas subjected to intensive grazing, waterfowl are attracted to ponds containing emergent vegetation. In this case, fencing portions of the pond's shoreline (to at least 16 m from shore) is recommended to encourage use by migrating waterfowl (Hamor et al. 1968).

Ponds near reliable water sources (e.g., wells, storage reservoirs, streams, rivers) can be allowed to dry naturally during summer to encourage development of seed-producing annual plants on mudflats. When flooded shallowly in fall or spring, attractive habitat is created for migratory waterfowl (Hamor et al. 1968).

Building islands, constructing rafts, leveling spoil piles, or intensively grazing selected shorelines will provide waterfowl loafing areas (Hamor et al. 1968, Poston and Schmidt 1981, Kantrud 1986a). Stock ponds and dugouts can be designed with both a sloping shoreline for native plant establishment and a steep-sided shoreline with spoil piles to act as thermal cover (wind protection, south-facing shoreline, open water) for waterfowl.

Lacustrine and Palustrine Wetlands

Constructing Wetlands.—Impoundments (LaRose 1969, Fredrickson and Taylor 1982), irrigation reservoirs (Sankowski et al. 1987), pumping (Nebraska Game and Parks 1972), and altering tile drains have been used to create new seasonal, semipermanent, and permanent wetlands in the NGP. Restoring drained wetlands by removing the drains or installing standpipes on existing drains is a new and exciting technique (Madsen 1986, Piehl 1986).

Water Management for Deep Water Emergents.—Although management objectives vary (Sousa 1987), most water-level management in larger marshes emulates natural hydrologic cycles (Weller 1975, Bishop et al. 1979). This management changes marsh vegetation from "dry" marsh (marshes dewatered through drawdowns or drought and dominated by mudflat vegetation) to "regenerating" marsh (reflooded marshes that are filled with emergent and submergent plants), through "hemi-marsh" (marshes with an equal interspersion of open water and emergent cover), to "lake-marshes" (marshes which are predominantly open water) (Weller and Spatcher 1965).

Water levels in large impounded wetlands often are drained every 3-7 years to maintain hemi-marshes with an interspersion of 50% emergent cover (primarily bulrush or cattail) to 50% open water (Bishop et al. 1979). Generally, interspersed patches (0.1 to 0.2 ha in size) of open water and vegetation are considered ideal (Weller and Spatcher 1965, Weller 1975). "Open water" in this sense is an area sheltered from wind fetch and shallowly flooded (<90 to 120 cm) with water clear enough to support a variety of submersed aquatic plant species (Davis and Brinson 1980, Barko et al. 1986).

Although hemi-marsh management is targeted for breeding waterfowl (Weller 1975), the resulting vegetation structure and composition also are beneficial to migrating and staging birds. Extensive stands of emergents, floating root clumps, sheltered mud bars, and muskrat houses provide storm shelter and loafing areas for molting and staging ducks and geese (McDonald 1955, Kantrud 1986b). Abundant submersed aquatic beds (particularly sago pondweed) and their invertebrate communities (Nelson and Kadlec 1985) are used by molting birds (Fredrickson and Drobney 1979) and migrants (Kantrud 1986b).

Most freshwater wetland soils contain seed reserves that allow recolonization of basins when marshes dry (this is not true for saline wetlands and impounded bays of lakes which have comparatively fewer buried seeds) (Pederson and Smith 1988). Wetland managers have influenced vegetation recruitment from seed banks by altering the timing of drawdowns (Harris and Marshall 1963, Meeks 1969), soil moisture and salinity on drawdown surfaces (Kadlec and Smith 1984), and flooding schedules (Welling et al. 1988).

Seeds of most emergent plant species (e.g., cattail, bulrushes) do not germinate until basin soils are exposed to air and alternating hot and cold temperatures (Harris and Marshall 1963, van der Valk and Davis 1978, Galinato and van der Valk 1986). By exposing only portions of wetland basins, partial drawdowns have been used to restrict cattail establishment in impoundments where cattail cannot be controlled by flooding or increasing soil salinity levels. Early drawdowns (late spring) have been recommended for emergent plant establishment because of the difficulties in completely draining large marshes and to allow emergent seedlings the longest possible growing season.

Seedlings of certain emergent species (e.g., cattail) grow best in saturated soils, whereas seedlings of other emergents (e.g., whitetop) do better in drier substrates (Welling et al. 1988). Because of the water-holding capability of organic or loamy soils, emergent seedlings flourish on these soil types, whereas till, silt, or clay soils are less conducive to plant growth. Irrigation or seepage onto mud-flats can somewhat override the effect of soil type.

Gradual flooding (up to 45-60 cm) in the second year after drawdown stimulates vegetative propagation of emergents if water levels do not exceed depth toleran-ces of seedlings of various species (Kadlec and Wentz 1974). A simple reduction in water levels (without complete drainage) also can promote emergent vegetative growth and stimulate growth and flower-ing of submergent plant species.

In saline basins, "flow-through" and shallow flooding during drawdowns will reduce soil surface salinities, disperse seeds, promote emergent (e.g., alkali bulrush) establishment, and foster sub-merged aquatic tuber and vegetative prop-agule survival (Davis and Brinson 1980, Kadlec and Smith 1984, Barko et al. 1986). Conversely, complete drawdowns that maintain water tables within several cm of the drawdown surface (which allows soil salts to concentrate in the surface soil layer) are an effective plant-control technique (Nelson and Dietz 1966).

Although periodic summer drawdowns in impounded wetlands have been app-lied as a universal formula for hemi-marsh management, many results were disappointing or quite different than desired. This is due to variation in individual wetlands such as (1) local flora (seeds, propagules, and existing plants of various species respond differently to dewatering) (Kadlec and Wentz 1974); (2) basin morphology, hydrologic character-istics, and soil types (basins which dewater quickly become dominated by upland and wet meadow species) (Harris and Marshall 1963); (3) water and soil chemistry (particularly increases in salin-ity that restrict seed germination and seedling recruitment) (Ungar and Reihl

1980, Lieffers and Shay 1982); and (4) plant competition (establishment of unde-sirable species such as purple loosestrife, willow, or excessive stands of cattail and reed canary grass) (Kadlec and Wentz 1974; Weller 1975; Thompson et al. 1987).

Water Management for Seasonally Flooded Emergents.—Throughout the NGP, vegetation found in seasonally-flooded areas is used as cattle forage (Fulton et al. 1986). Ducks Unlimited Canada has developed (Clay and Nelson 1986, Sankowski et al. 1987) "back-flood" projects that involve impounding (LaRose 1969, U.S. Department of Agri-culture 1982) native hay meadows so that spring runoff can be retained until early summer. Back-flood areas provide forag-ing sites and pair-space for migrating and breeding waterfowl.

Ideal sites for back-flood irrigation development include wet meadow and shallow marsh areas (Stewart and Kan-trud 1972) that: (1) are adjacent to large marshes, rivers, or large water bodies which are waterfowl concentration areas; (2) have porous soils so that the root zone will drain after drawdown; and (3) have soil and water salinity levels that do not exceed 1,000 ppm (Ducks Unlimited Can-ada, unpubl. rep.).

Back-flood projects are managed by setting water-control structures to retain water in the fall. Soils are saturated before winter to avoid winter-kill of plant crowns. Either runoff or supplemental pumping is used to flood the area during the following spring so that the root zone is saturated to a 1-m depth (as determined by the ability to push a steel probe to that depth). Depth and duration of flooding are dependent on the water tolerances of plant species (Stewart and Kantrud 1972, Kadlec and Wentz 1974) found in the impoundment, but, generally, flooding should be ≤50 days with water depths ≤30-100 cm (Rumberg and Sawyer 1965, Clay and Nelson 1986). Water is released from impoundments in early summer, and the dewatered basin then furnishes nesting habitat. Harvest of native hay occurs in middle to late summer (Clay and Nelson 1986). Forage biomass production can be 4 times that of unmanaged sites, and vegetation protein levels often can reach 20% (details of the agricultural aspects of back flood management can be found in Neckles et al. 1985, Clay and Nelson 1986, Fulton et al. 1986, Sankowski et al. 1987).

Invertebrate response to back-flood areas is dramatic, and waterfowl are quickly attracted to these areas. Dabbling duck species and geese feed in areas where water depths are <20 cm, whereas divers will use open, deeper-water areas and borrow pits. Flat, low islands created from spoil during impoundment construction, or resulting from undulations in meadow topography, and closely grazed or mowed shorelines are used by waterfowl as loafing sites.

Frequently, waterfowl use will decrease when growing vegetation obscures the birds' vision and they are harassed by predatory birds. With pumping or irrigation capability, water levels can be raised to "keep up" with growing plants in individual units and to prolong waterfowl use. Sequentially flooding different units of a multicelled back-flood project also will extend waterfowl use; however, spring flooding should not occur after early nesting has started (e.g., 15 April in Manitoba). With assured water control and supply, back-flood areas can be periodically burned in fall and reflooded in spring before natural wetlands thaw. This management regime provides habitat for early-arriving migrants.

Water Management for Drawdown Vegetation.—Mudflat species (Table 4) dominate the vegetation on drawdown surfaces during the first year of dewatering and on agriculturally-tilled basins (Harris and Marshall 1963, Stewart and Kantrud 1972). These species are prolific seed-producers, generally do not inhibit

emergent species establishment, and are eliminated during reflooding (Weller and Voights 1983).

Although sheet flooding wetland basins dominated by mudflat vegetation is a technique used frequently for waterfowl management during fall and winter (Burgess 1969, Fredrickson and Taylor 1982), it is only occasionally used in spring in the NGP. Deep wells have been used to supplement spring water levels in some wetlands of the Rainwater Basin. Pumping is done only in the spring, and only when general wetland water conditions are good (to avoid causing extreme concentrations of waterfowl on only a few wetlands during dry years). Often, basins are managed for a more open aspect through light disking or grazing.

Burning.—Dense stands of cattail, common reed, reed canary grass, marsh smartweed, and river bulrush are frequently found in freshwater wetlands that rarely go completely dry and that hold insufficient water during wet years to flood out plant cover. Burning these communities causes short-term changes in vegetation structure (Fig. 6). Schlichtemeier (1967) removed dead stems of common reed and bulrush with a winter burn even though snow covered bases of the plants. Waterfowl use increased on the winter-burned stands the following spring and summer. In the Rainwater Basin of Nebraska, late fall and early winter burning of dense stands of cattail and bulrush opened up large wetland areas for spring migrants (Nebraska Game and Parks 1972).

In general, the composition of herbaceous wetland plant communities is not changed by burning unless the fire penetrates the soil into the root zone (see Fulton et al. 1986 and Kantrud 1986a) (Table 4). Fires have been used to control woody growth in wetlands with best results provided by spring burns (Vogl 1967). Guidelines for prescribed burns in wetlands of the NGP are not as precise as

Table 1. Responses of emergent plant species to grazing, mowing, burning, and tillage (Stewart and Kantrud 1972, Millar 1973, Neckles et al. 1985, Fulton et al. 1986).

Plant species	Grazed			Mowed	Burned	Tilled
	Light	Moderate	Heavy			
Mudflat species						
Beggarticks						I
Cocklebur			I[a]			I
Kochia						I
Goosefoots						I
Pigweeds (*Amarthus* spp.)			D			I
Wild buckwheat (*Polygonum convolvulus*)						I
Smartweeds (*Polygonum* spp.)			P			I
Yellow foxtail (*Setaria glauca*)			I			I
Wet meadow species						
Water plaintain		P	P			P
Blue joint			D			D
Northern reedgrass	D	D				D
Sedges	P,D	D				P
Saltgrass	P,I	P,I	P	P		D
Wildbarley	I	I	I			P
Baltic rush	P,I	I				D
Fowl-meadow grass	D	I,D				D
Prairie cordgrass	I,D	I,D				D
Shallow marsh species						
Sloughgrass	P			P	P	
Slough sedge	P	P,D	P,D	D	P	D
Spike rush	P	P,I	P,I	P	P	D
Tall mannagrass	P	P	P			D
Marsh smartweed		D		P	P,I	P
Three square	P	P				D
Giant burreed		P,I	P			D
Whitetop	P	D	D	I	I,P	D
Deep marsh species						
Common reed	P	P	D	P	P,D	D
Hardstem bulrush		P	I			D
River bulrush	P,I	P	P			P
Alkali bulrush		P	P			P
Softstem bulrush		P	P,I			P
Cattail	P	I	D	D	P,D	D

[a]P (present) indicates the species at least tolerates and may be favored by the disturbance; I (increase) indicates a greater abundance in disturbed than in undisturbed wetlands; D (decrease) indicates a lesser abundance in disturbed than in undisturbed habitats; multiple responses reflect different observations.

specifications for upland burning (Wright and Bailey 1980), but there are general rules (Ward 1968, Linde 1969, Wright and Bailey 1980). Weather conditions suitable for marsh burns are warm (>15 C), sunny days with winds under 25 km/hr (Ward 1968, Linde 1969). Fires do not carry well before the sun has dried the dew or melted the frost off vegetation (Linde 1969). Backfires (burning into the wind) leave shorter stubble than head fires, but are slow and not useful on large areas

(Linde 1969). To increase the area that can be burned in 1 day and to prevent a single head fire from becoming too large, a series of parallel head fires can be started simultaneously. In this way, 120-240 ha can be burned in 1 day by 5 or 6 workers (Linde 1969).

In the absence of water control, burning seasonally flooded wetlands is probably unjustified. Diiro (1982) found that increased early-season productivity of plants and invertebrates in small basins

Fig. 6. Wetland burned in the winter to create an open, shallowly flooded marsh for spring migrants.

(burned the previous fall) was offset by a scarcity of water caused by the reduced snow-trapping ability of burned vegetation. In addition, Kantrud (1986a) felt snow accumulations often crushed the finer-stemmed vegetation in unburned seasonal wetlands, and thus maintained the open or semiopen aspect preferred by migrating waterfowl.

Mowing.—Mowing and haying can temporarily open wetlands and increase waterfowl use, but results generally are short-lived (Table 4). Difficulties in operating machinery in marshes during summer restricts mowing to the seasonally flooded upland fringes of wetlands. Burning dense stands of emergents in winter, followed by shredding the remaining plant stalks with a rotary mower, can effectively control vegetation if the cut stalks are subsequently covered with water for at least 2 weeks in spring (Weller 1975, Murkin and Ward 1980).

Grazing.—Grazing has a variety of effects on wetland vegetation (Table 4), but can be beneficial to waterfowl by opening up wetlands with dense stands of cattails, common reed, or bulrush (Kantrud 1986a). Grazing and trampling at 1.5-2 animal units in river bulrush and cattail marshes in the Rainwater Basin of Nebraska reduced vegetation cover by 25% (Rainwater Basin Wetland Management District, unpubl. rep.). Grazing is most effective in removing emergent vegetation when the site is first burned and livestock then are allowed to graze on newly emerging shoots. Sheep are more efficient than cattle at removing vegetative cover (Ermacoff 1968), whereas horses will eliminate brush and woody vegetation better than cattle or sheep.

Excessive grazing of wetland shoreline vegetation promotes high silt loads entering the wetland basin and is detrimental to wildlife (Olson 1981). During drawdowns or in drought years, livestock trampling in dry basins may change the physical state of soil through compaction (which increases the ability of the basin to retain water), but intense grazing also can impact drawdown vegetation (Ermacoff 1968).

Waterfowl can be used to control emergent plants. At Upper Souris NWR, a cattail impoundment was drawn down in summer, burned, and then flooded with fresh water just before the anticipated arrival of lesser snow geese. The geese foraged in the impoundment, grubbing out and consuming vast amounts of cattail sprouts and rhizomes.

Herbicides.—Herbicides generally are effective, but should be used as a last resort. An August aerial application of glyphosate at 8.5 1/ha was effective in eliminating cattails from Lange Waterfowl Production Area in Nebraska (Rainwater Basin Wetland Management District, unpubl. rep.). The wetland was still open water 2 years after treatment.

Upland

The development of irrigated and dryland farming of small grains (e.g., corn, wheat, barley, milo, winter wheat) has created abundant food resources for field-feeding waterfowl. Little of this land, however, is maintained for waterfowl. Availability of waste grain and green forage is dependent on agricultural markets, government programs, and on climatic factors in the fall which either encourage or discourage fall harvesting and tillage (Frederick and Klaas 1982). Planting crops on refuges, leaving standing corn through winter, and shredding remaining stalks in spring are common techniques to provide food available to waterfowl (Burgess 1969). Upland management in the NGP is covered in more detail by Ringelman et al. (1989).

Refuges

Hunting pressure and disturbance often discourage use of preferred wetlands by migrating waterfowl (Jessen 1970, Raveling et al. 1972, Koerner et al. 1974, Raveling 1978). Closure of hunting in the afternoon has allowed Canada geese to leave refuges and feed unharassed during the evening feeding period in North Dakota. The development of a Waterfowl Rest Area Program (5-year agreements with private landowners) has protected traditional waterfowl staging areas from disturbance. Canada goose closure zones in North Dakota have expanded the range of resident breeding populations of giant Canada geese from 4 NWRs in 1969 to every county in the state.

Each fall during southward migration, thousands of field-feeding waterfowl concentrate on mid-latitude refuges and forage on waste grain in surrounding agricultural land. Refuges are considered necessary for providing sanctuary and adequate food for migrating birds to ensure healthy populations. When large numbers of birds remain on refuges for extended periods, however, hunting pressure may become concentrated, crop damage may develop, and the probability of disease outbreaks may increase. Frederick et al. (1986) developed a simulation model that depicted responses of refuging lesser snow geese at DeSoto NWR. Model results suggested that populations were most sensitive to food density and to the proportion of refuge fields in which food was available. Although the model predicted that additional hunting pressure would increase hunting mortality, the greatest impact of hunting pressure was the disruption of feeding activities and decrease in energy intake (which could cause emigration of geese from the refuge). The utility of modelling efforts is that simulations of management scenarios can be a valuable tool in meeting refuge and waterfowl population objectives.

Disease

The primary objective of the Rainwater Basin Wetland Management District is to provide critical spring staging habitat for waterfowl that arrive annually on their journey north to breeding grounds. (U.S. Fish and Wildlife Service, unpubl. rep.) Management actions to curtail avian cholera outbreaks include rapid collection of carcasses, harassment to encourage the birds to migrate from the region, and intentionally not pumping additional water into wetlands during dry years (again, to encourage the birds to move out of the region). If a reduction occurs in the area of harvested corn and other grains, or if more water is diverted from rivers in spring staging areas, crowding and avian cholera outbreaks would likely increase. Because cholera primarily occurs in stagnant water of wetlands, maintaining adequate flows in nearby rivers may represent the best option for controlling losses to avian cholera (Krapu and Pearson 1981).

CONCLUSIONS

Vegetation composition and structure interact with hydrology and water quality to determine waterfowl values of aquatic habitats (Nelson and Kadlec 1985). Because the successful management of aquatic habitats is primarily the application of ecological principles (e.g., water-level changes, burning, herbivory, decomposition), managers should be proficient in plant ecology and should understand also how to manipulate the physical and biological factors that cause vegetation change. Thus, a well-trained manager can make management prescriptions on the basis of the existing flora and his insight as to what environmental conditions must have occurred to cause the present plant communities (see Knighton [1985] for an example of this approach in northern forested wetlands).

A step in becoming proficient at marsh management is the ability to recognize plants, in adult form and as seedlings. Obtaining regional plant guides (Stuckey 1975) and arranging a field trip with a local taxonomist is a good place to start.

Generally, local and regional plant guides are the easiest keys to use. Most plant taxonomy texts are based on the adult plant in flowering or fruit stages. However, many management practices need to be implemented while plants are seedlings or in a vegetative state. Seedling identification can be accomplished by observing seedling growth and maturity (at which time the plant can be keyed using taxonomic texts). Herbicide companies and extension services are good sources for seedling identification guides because desired plant species of wildlife often are considered highly undesirable for agriculture. Taxonomic guides also are available that distinguish plant species by vegetative characters (see Pederson and Smith 1988).

Life-history information (e.g., seed germination requirements, preferred growth environments, water and salinity tolerances, competitive ability) can be gleaned from the literature (e.g., Kadlec and Wentz 1974, Hutchinson 1975, Thompson et al 1987) and should be supplemented with experience gained through repeated field observations (Fredrickson and Taylor 1982). Armed with this information, managers will be able to make more accurate management prescriptions.

Successful habitat management is accomplished also through cost-accounting and prioritizing various management actions in relation to desired waterfowl response. For the middle and northern latitudes, wildlife response and cost-effectiveness of various management techniques can now be assessed by applying appropriate models to proposed management actions (Frederick et al. 1986, Sousa 1987).

Research Needs

Wintering at northern latitudes influences the physical condition of waterfowl and deserves further research. Also, the need to combat diseases of migratory birds will intensify because of habitat losses. For example, the natural history of avian cholera in waterfowl and other wild birds is poorly understood (Windingstad et al. 1984).

Little is known about practices for restoring agriculturally degraded wetlands. In addition to drainage, cultivation, and siltation, decreased waterfowl use is being caused by the succession of many semipermanent wetlands toward cattail monotypes and the encroachment of woody plants or pest plants like purple loosestrife. Managers often lack information needed (plant life history) to obtain desirable, predictable results from vegetation-control techniques. Studies of various runoff pollutants (i.e., herbicides, pesticides, sediments, and salts) into wetlands should emphasize trophic level interactions.

Riparian areas and many wetlands have been severely degraded or altered, and it may be too late to determine the natural plant associations historically preferred by waterfowl species. Knowledge of the effects of reservoir construction on waterfowl has been limited mainly to post-construction studies. Little information exists regarding the effect on fall and spring staging waterfowl when there is extensive loss of open channels, sandbars, riparian forests, and wetland communities due to water project development.

Finally, habitat management for waterfowl has proceeded in piece-meal fashion because of different jurisdictions of land control (international, federal, state, private) on migratory bird habitat. However, research directed at food availability and carrying capacity (e.g., Klaas et al. 1978, Frederick and Klaas 1982, Frederick et al. 1986) in relation to cross-seasonal waterfowl requirements should aid in designing regional habitat management approaches.

SUMMARY

The NGP encompasses portions of 3 Canadian provinces and 4 U.S. states.

The climate of the NGP is dry and subhumid, with hot summers and severe winters. Precipitation is substantially lower than potential evapotranspiration, with a pronounced decrease in mean annual precipitation from east to west.

Water development projects, wetland drainage, and modern agricultural practices have created a new landscape in the NGP. Adaptable waterfowl species (e.g., mallards, Canada geese, snow geese) have either increased in population and/or exhibited a western and northern expansion of their migratory and winter ranges. Waterfowl species more closely tied to aquatic habitats (e.g., canvasbacks) have exhibited population declines.

Generally, small wetlands that are important to waterfowl during spring and early summer have been affected the most by agriculture. More permanent aquatic habitats (large marshes, lakes, and reservoirs) and agricultural fields are used by waterfowl during fall migration, and open river channels, warm water canals, tailraces below reservoirs, and agricultural habitats are selected during winter.

In autumn, waterfowl forage intensively to accumulate lipids as an energy source for migration and winter maintenance, and perhaps to acquire specific nutrients required for molt. Species that select foods of high-energy content devote the least amount of time to feeding. In winter, waterfowl may lose body weight in response to an endogenous annual weight cycle and increased catabolism of fat reserves. Energy losses are minimized as birds select thermally favorable microhabitats and spend most of their time resting during the day. Freedom from harassment by predators, availability of food, and thermally-protected habitats may be critical during this time period. By late winter, time spent feeding increases due to nutrient needs for upcoming breeding activities.

Most habitat management in the NGP has focused on refuge establishment and planting of upland crops. A variety of techniques (e.g., water-level management, burning, grazing, mechanical methods, herbicides) also have been used in larger marshes to develop an interspersion of emergent cover and open water.

Land use in the NGP is controlled by climate, water availability, energy costs, farm policies, and commodity prices. Waterfowl habitat managers can do little to alter these socioeconomic factors. There are, however, several critical areas that have become concentration points during migration (e.g., Rainwater Basin and the Platte River in Nebraska, Devil's Lake area in North Dakota, NWRs) where management actions have the potential to affect large numbers of birds. Management practices designed for spring migration seem especially appropriate because waterfowl are in the process of acquiring body reserves necessary for reproduction.

Management programs targeted for migrants include (1) developing wetland complexes by restoring drained wetlands, particularly in areas where the habitat base needs to be increased to prevent disease outbreaks; (2) managing native plant communities in large marshes or irrigated drainages to provide waterfowl pair-space, foraging sites, and postbreeding staging marshes; (3) controlling emergent and woody vegetation to provide open water on existing wetlands and river channels; (4) instigating a private lands program aimed at maintaining sheetwater basins in stubble fields adjacent to staging marshes; and (5) managing subimpoundments to provide moist-soil or submerged aquatic vegetation for migrating waterfowl.

LITERATURE CITED

Albright, J. J., R. B. Owen, Jr., and P. O. Borr. 1983. The effects of winter weather on the behavior and energy reserves of black ducks in Maine. Trans. Northeast. Fish and Wildl. Conf. 40:118-128.

Alisauskas, R. T. 1988. Nutrient reserves of lesser snow geese during winter and spring migration.

Ph.D. Thesis, Univ. Western Ontario, London. 188 pp.

Allen, H. H. 1978. Role of wetland plants in erosion control of riparian communities. Pages 403-414 *in* P. E. Greeson, J. R. Clark, and J. E. Clark, eds. Wetland function and values: the state of our understanding. Am. Water Resour. Assoc., Minneapolis, Minn.

Ankney, C. D., and C. C. MacInnes. 1978. Nutrient reserves and reproductive performance of female lesser snow geese. Auk 95:459-471.

Aronson, J. G., and S. L. Ellis. 1979. Monitoring, maintenance, and enhancement of critical whooping crane habitat, Platte River, Nebraska. Pages 168-180 *in* G. A. Swanson, tech. coord. The mitigation symposium: a nat. workshop on mitigating losses of fish and wildl. habitats. USDA Rocky Mountain For. and Range Exp. Stn. Gen. Tech. Rep. RM-65.

Bailey, R. G. 1976. Ecoregions of the United States. USDA Rocky Mountain For. and Range Exp. Stn. U.S. Gov. Print. Off. 777-152.

Baldassarre, G. A., R. J. Whyte, E. E. Quinlan, and E. G. Bolen. 1983. Dynamics and quality of waste corn available to postbreeding waterfowl in Texas. Wildl. Soc. Bull. 11:25-31.

Barko, J. W., M. S. Adams, and N. L. Clesceri. 1986. Environmental factors and their consideration in the management of submersed aquatic vegetation: a review. J. Aquatic Plant Manage. 24:1-10.

Bateman, H. A., T. Joanen, and C. D. Stutzenbaker. 1988. History and status of midcontinent snow geese on their Gulf Coast winter range. Pages 495-515 *in* M. W. Weller, ed. Waterfowl in winter. Univ. Minnesota Press, Minneapolis.

Bellrose, F. C. 1980. Ducks, geese and swans of North America. Third ed. Stackpole Books, Harrisburg, Pa. 540 pp.

———, and R. D. Crompton. 1970. The migration of mallards and black ducks as determined from banding. Ill. Nat. Hist. Surv. Bull. 36:167-234.

Benson, N. G., and B. C. Cowell. 1967. The environment and plankton density in Missouri River reservoirs. Pages 358-373 *in* C. E. Lane, ed. Reservoir fishery resour. symp. Southern District, Am. Fish Soc., Athens, Ga.

Bergman, R. D. 1973. Use of southern boreal lakes by postbreeding canvasbacks and redheads. J. Wildl. Manage. 37:160-170.

Bishop, R. A., R. D. Andrews, and R. J. Bridges. 1979. Marsh management and its relationship to vegetation, waterfowl, and muskrats. Proc. Iowa Acad. Sci. 86:50-56.

Bluhm, C. K. 1988. Temporal patterns of pair formation and reproduction in annual cycles and associated endocrinology in waterfowl. Pages 123-185 *in* R. F. Johnson, ed. Current ornithology, Vol. 5. Plenum Publ. Corp. New York, N.Y.

Borchert, J. R. 1950. The climate of the central North American grassland. Annu. Assoc. Amer. Georgr. 40:1-39.

Bossenmaier, E. F., and W. H. Marshall. 1958. Field-feeding by waterfowl in southwestern Manitoba. Wildl. Monogr. 1. 32 pp.

Brand, C. J. 1987. Duck plaque. Pages 117-127 in M. Friend, ed. Field guide to Wildlife. Diseases. Vol 1. General field procedures and diseases of migratory birds. U.S. Fish and Wildl. Serv. Resour. Publ. 167. 225 pp.

Buckman, H. O., and N. C. Brady. 1969. The nature and properties of soils. Macmillan Co., New York, N.Y. 200 pp.

Buller, R. J. 1964. Central flyway. Pages 209-232 in J. P. Linsuska, ed. Waterfowl tomorrow. U.S. Dep. Int., Washington, D.C.

———. 1975. Redistribution of waterfowl: influence of water, protection, and feed. Int. Waterfowl Symp. 1:143-154.

Burgess, H. H. 1969. Habitat management on a mid-continent waterfowl refuge. J. Wildl. Manage. 33:843-847.

Chapman, J. D., and J. C. Sherman, editors. 1975. Oxford Regional Economic Atlas. The United States and Canada. Oxford Univ. Press. London, England.

Childress, D. A., and R. L. Eng. 1979. Dust abatement project with wildlife enhancement on Canyon Ferry Reservoir, Montana. Pages 282-288 in G. A. Swanson, tech. coord. The mitigation symposium: a nat. workshop on mitigating losses of fish and wildl. habitats. USDA Rocky Mountain For. and Range Exp. Stn. Gen. Tech. Rep. RM-65.

Clay, R. T., and J. W. Nelson. 1986. Waterfowl responses to backflood irrigation management. Colonial Waterbirds 9:203-209.

Cowardin, L. M., V. Carter, F. C. Golet, and E. T. LaRoe. 1979. Classification of wetlands and deepwater habitats of the United States. U.S. Fish and Wildl. Serv. FWS/OBS-79/31. Washington, D.C. 103 pp.

Currier, P. J. 1984. Woody vegetation clearing on the Platte River aids restoration of sandhill crane roosting habitat (Nebraska). Univ. Wisconsin Arboretum, Madison, Restor. and Manage. Notes 2:38.

———, G. R. Lingle, and J. G. VanDerwalker. 1985. Migratory bird habitat on the Platte and North Platte Rivers in Nebraska. The Platte River Whooping Crane Critical Habitat Maintenance Trust, Grand Island, Neb. 177 pp.

Davis, G. J., and M. M. Brinson. 1980. Responses of submersed vascular plant communities to environmental change. U.S. Fish and Wildl. Serv. FWS/OBS-79/33. Washington, D.C. 70 pp.

Diiro, B. W. 1982. Effects of burning and mowing on seasonal whitetop ponds in southern Manitoba, M.S. Thesis, Iowa State Univ., Ames. 48 pp.

Dix, R. L., and F. E. Smeins. 1967. The prairie, meadow and marsh vegetation of Nelson County, North Dakota. Can. J. Bot. 45:21-58.

Erickson, N. W., and D. M. Leslie. 1987. Soil-vegetation correlations in the Sandhills and Rainwater Basin wetlands of Nebraska. U.S. Fish and Wildl. Serv. Biol. Rep. 87(11). 72 pp.

Ermacoff, N. 1968. Marsh and habitat management practices at the Mendota Wildlife Area. Calif. Dep. Fish and Game, Game Manage. Leafl. No. 12. 10 pp.

Ferguson, E. L., D. G. Jorde, and J. L. Sease. 1981. Use of 35 mm color aerial photography to acquire mallard sex ratio data. Photogrammetry Eng. and Remote Sensing 47:823-827.

Fernald, M. L. 1950. Gray's manual of botany. American Book Co., New York, N.Y. 1,632 pp.

Flake, L. D. 1978. Wetland diversity and waterfowl. Pages 312-319 in P. E. Greeson, J. R. Clark, and J. E. Clark, eds. Proc. of the nat. symp. on wetlands. Am. Water Resour. Assoc., Minneapolis, Minn.

Folk, C., K. Hudec, and J. Toufar. 1966. The weight of the mallard, Anas platyrhynchos, and its changes in the course of the year. Zool. Listy. 15:249-260.

Fowler, D. K., and D. A. Hammer. 1976. Techniques for establishing vegetation on reservoir inundation zones. J. Soil Water Conserv. 31:116-118.

Frederick, R. B., W. R. Clark, and E. E. Klaas. 1986. Behavior, energetics, and management of refuging waterfowl: a simulation model. Wildlife Monogr. 96. 35 pp.

———, and E. E. Klaas. 1982. Resource use and behavior of migrating snow geese. J. Wildl. Manage. 46:601-614.

Fredrickson, L. H., and R. D. Drobney. 1979. Habitat utilization by postbreeding waterfowl. Pages 119-131 in T. A. Bookhout, ed. Waterfowl and wetlands—an integrated review. North Cent. Sect., Wildl. Soc., Madison, Wis.

———, and T. S. Taylor. 1982. Management of seasonally flooded impoundments for wildlife. U.S. Fish and Wildl. Serv. Resour. Publ. 148. 27 pp.

Friend, M. 1987. Avian cholera. Pages 69-82 in M. Friend, ed. Field guide to wildlife diseases. Vol. 1. General field procedures and diseases of migratory birds. U.S. Fish and Wildl. Serv. Resour. Publ. 167. 225 pp.

Fulton, G. W., J. L. Richardson, and W. T. Barker. 1986. Wetland soils and vegetation. North Dakota State Univ., Agric. Exp. Stn. Rep. 106, Fargo. 15 pp.

Galinato, M. I., and A. G. van der Valk. 1986. Seed germination traits of annuals and emergents recruited during drawdowns in the Delta Marsh, Manitoba, Canada. Aquatic Bot. 26:89-192.

Giron, B. A. 1981. Wildlife use of man-made wetlands in the Prairie Pothole Region: a selected annotated bibliography. South Dakota State Univ. Coop. Wildl. Res. Unit Tech. Bull. 2, Brookings 29 pp.

Grieb, J. P., and E. L. Boeker. 1954. Waterfowl migration studies and their application to management in Colorado. Trans. North Am. Wildl. and Nat Resour Conf 19:195-210.

Hamor, W. H., H. G. Uhlig, and L. V. Compton. 1968. Ponds and marshes for wild ducks on farms and ranches in the Northern Plains. USDA Farmer's Bull. No. 2234, U.S. Gov. Print. Off., Washington, D.C. 16 pp.

Harris, S. W., and W. H. Marshall. 1963. Ecology of water level manipulations on a northern marsh. Ecology 44:331-343.

Hoar, A. R., and M. J. Erwin. 1985. Relationship between the expansion of agriculture and the reduction of natural riparian habitat in the Missouri River floodplain of northeast Montana, 1938-1982. Pages 250-256 *in* R. R. Johnson, C. D. Ziebell, D. R. Patton, P. F. Ffolliott, and R. H. Hamre, tech. coords. Riparian ecosystems and their management. USDA Rocky Mountain For. and Range Exp. Stn. Gen. Tech. Rep. RM-120.

Hochbaum, H. A. 1944. The canvasback on a prairie marsh. North Am. Wildl. Inst., Washington, D.C. 102 pp.

———. 1955. Travels and traditions of waterfowl. Univ. Minnesota Press, Minneapolis. 301 pp.

Hoffman, G. R. 1977. Artificial establishment of vegetation and effects of fertilizer along shorelines of Lake Oahe and Sakakawea mainstream Missouri River reservoirs. Pages 95-109 *in* Proc. of the workshop on the role of vegetation in stabilization of the Great Lakes shoreline. Great Lakes Basin Comm., Ann Arbor, Mich.

Hutchinson, G. E. 1975. A treatise on limnology. Vol. 3. Limnological botany. John Wiley and Sons, New York, N.Y. 660 pp.

Jessen, R. L. 1970. Mallard population trends and hunting losses in Minnesota. J. Wildl. Manage. 34:93-105.

Johnson, D. H., G. L. Krapu, K. J. Reinecke, and D. G. Jorde. 1985. An evaluation of condition indices for birds. J. Wildl. Manage. 49:569-575.

Johnson, W. C, R. L. Burgess, and W. R. Keammerer. 1976. Forest overstory vegetation and environment on the Missouri River floodplain in North Dakota. Ecol. Monogr. 46:59-84.

Jorde, D. G. 1981. Winter and spring staging ecology of mallards in south central Nebraska. M.S. Thesis, Univ. North Dakota, Grand Forks. 131 pp.

———, G. L. Krapu, and R. D. Crawford. 1983. Feeding ecology of mallards wintering in Nebraska. J. Wildl. Manage. 47:1044-1053.

———, ———, ———, and M. A. Hay. 1984. Effects of weather on habitat selection and behavior of mallards wintering in Nebraska. Condor 86:258-265.

———, and G. R. Lingle. 1988. Kleptoparasitism by bald eagles wintering in south central Nebraska. J. Field Ornithol. 59: 183-188.

Kadlec, J. A., and L. M. Smith. 1984. Marsh plant establishment on newly flooded salt flats. Wildl. Soc. Bull. 12:388-394.

———, and W. A. Wentz. 1974. State of-the-art survey and evaluation of marsh plants establishment techniques: induced and natural. Contract Rep. D-74-9. Vol. I. Report of research. U.S. Army Engineer Waterways Exp. Stn., Vicksburg, Miss. 231 pp.

Kantrud, H. A. 1986a. Effects of vegetation manipulation on breeding waterfowl in prairie wetlands: a literature review. U.S. Fish and Wildl. Serv. Tech. Rep. 3. 15 pp.

———. 1986b. Western Stump Lake, a major canvasback staging area in eastern North Dakota. Prairie Nat. 18:247-253.

———, and R. E. Stewart. 1977. Use of natural basin wetlands by breeding waterfowl in North Dakota. J. Wildl. Manage. 41:243-253.

Keammerer, W. R., W. C. Johnson, and R. L. Burgess. 1985. Floristic analysis of the Missouri River bottomland forests in North Dakota. Can. Field Nat. 89:5-19.

Keddy, P. A. 1983. Shoreline vegetation in Axe Lake, Ontario: effects of exposure on zonation patterns. Ecology 64:331-344.

Kittle, C. E., and R. D. Porter. 1988. Waterfowl damage and control methods in ripening grain: an overview. U.S. Fish and Wildl. Serv. Tech. Rep. 14. 17 pp.

Klaas, E. E., W. H. Anderson, and R. B. Frederick. 1978. Use of landsat imagery for estimating food available to refuging lesser snow geese. Pages 89-94 *in* PECORA IV. Proc. Symp. on application of remote sensing data to wildlife management. Natl. Wildl. Fed., Washington, D.C.

Knighton, M. D. 1985. Water impoundments for wildlife: a habitat management workshop. Gen. Tech. Rep. NC-100. U.S. Dep. Agric., For. Serv., North Cent. For. Exp. Stn., St. Paul, Minn. 136 pp.

Koerner, J. W., T. A. Bookhout, and K. F. Bednarik. 1974. Movements of Canada geese color-marked near southwestern Lake Erie. J. Wildl. Manage. 38:275-289.

Krapu, G. L. 1974. Feeding ecology of pintail hens during reproduction. Auk 91:278-290.

———. 1981. The role of nutrient reserves in mallard reproduction. Auk 98:29-38.

———, and G. L. Pearson. 1981. Susceptibility of the mid-continent population of sandhill cranes to avian cholera in Nebraska—a preliminary report. Pages 7-12 *in* J. C. Lewis, ed. Proc. 1981 crane workshop. Natl. Audobon Soc., Tavenier, Fla.

Kroonemeyer, K. E. 1978. The U.S. Fish and Wildlife Service's Platte River national wildlife study. Pages 29-32 *in* J. C. Lewis, ed. Proc. 1978 crane workshop. Natl. Audubon Soc., Tavenier, Fla.

LaGrange, T. G., and J. J. Dinsmore. 1988. Nutrient reserve dynamics of female mallards during spring migration through central Iowa. Pages 287-297 *in* M. W. Weller, ed. Waterfowl in winter. Univ. Minnesota Press, Minneapolis.

LaRose, M. N. 1969. Engineering limitations on water transfers. Pages 16-20 *in* Saskatoon wetlands seminar. Can. Wildl. Serv. Rep. Ser. No. 6.

Lebret, T. 1961. The pair formation in the annual cycle of the mallard, *Anas platyrhynchos*. Ardea 49:97-158.

Lieffers, V. J., and J. M. Shay. 1982. Distribution and variation in growth of *Scirpus maritimus* var. *paludosus* on the Canadian prairies. Can. J. Bot. 60:1938-1949.

Linde, A. F. 1969. Techniques for wetland management. Wis. Dep. Nat. Resour. Res. Rep. 45. Madison. 156 pp.

Lingle, G. R., and G. L. Krapu. 1986. Winter ecology of bald eagles in southcentral Nebraska. Prairie Nat. 18:65-78.

Lish, J. W., and J. C. Lewis. 1975. Status and ecology of bald eagles wintering in Oklahoma. Proc. Annu. Conf. Southeast Assoc. Game and Fish Comm. 29:415-423.

Locke, L. N., and M. Friend. 1987. Avian botulism. Pages 83-93 *in* M. Friend, ed. Field guide to wildlife diseases. Vol 1. General field procedures and diseases of migratory birds. U.S. Fish and Wildl. Serv. Resour. Publ. 167. 225 pp.

Madsen, C. 1986. Wetland restoration: a pilot project. J. Soil Water Conserv. 41:159-160.

McDonald, M. E. 1955. Causes and effects of a dieoff of emergent vegetation. J. Wildl. Manage. 19:24-35.

McLandress, M. R., and D. G. Raveling. 1981. Changes in diet and body composition of Canada geese before spring migration. Auk 98:65-79.

Meeks, R. L. 1969. The effect of drawdown date on wetland plant succession. J. Wildl. Manage. 33:817-821.

Millar, J. B. 1973. Vegetation changes in shallow marsh wetlands under improving moisture regime. Can. J. Bot. 51:1443-1457.

Moore, R., and T. Mills. 1977. An environmental guide to western surface mining. Part Two: impacts, mitigation, and monitoring. U.S. Fish and Wildl. Serv. Biol. Serv. Program FWS/OBS-78.

Murkin, H. R., and P. Ward. 1980. Early spring cutting to control cattail in a northern marsh. Wildl. Soc. Bull. 8:254-256.

Nebraska Game and Parks. 1972. Survey of habitat Work Plan K-71, Pittman-Robertson Proj. W-13-R-28. Lincoln, Neb. 78 pp.

Neckles, H. A., J. W. Nelson, and R. L. Pederson. 1985. Management of whitetop (*Scolochloa festucacea*) marshes for livestock forage and wildlife. Delta Waterfowl and Wetlands Res. Stn. Tech. Bull. 1, Portage la Prairie, Manit. 12 pp.

Nelson, J. W., and J. A. Kadlec. 1985. A conceptual approach to relating habitat structure and macroinvertebrate production in freshwater wetlands. Trans. North Am. Wildl. and Nat. Resour. Conf. 49:262-270.

Nelson, N. F., and R. H. Dietz. 1966. Cattail control methods in Utah. Utah Dep. Fish and Game Publ. 66-2. 31 pp.

Olson, R. A. 1981. Wetland vegetation, environmental factors, natural wetlands. USDA Rocky Mountain For. and Range Exp. Stn. Gen. Tech. Pap. Rm-85. 19 pp.

Oring, L. W. 1964. Behavior and ecology of certain ducks during the postbreeding period. J. Wildl. Manage. 28:223-233.

Paulus, S. L. 1988. Time-activity budgets of nonbreeding Anatidae: a review. Pages 135-152, *in* M. W. Weller, ed. Waterfowl in winter. Univ. Minnesota Press, Minneapolis.

Pederson, R. L., and L. M. Smith. 1988. Implications of wetland seed bank research: a review of Great Basin and Prairie marsh studies. Pages 81-98 *in* D. A. Wilcox, ed. Indisciplinary approaches to freshwater research. Michigan State Univ. Press., East Lansing.

Pendleton, G. W., and R. L. Linder. 1984. Brood natural habitat regions in the Great Plains. Pages 9A-31A *in* F. R. Henderson, ed. Guidelines for increasing wildlife on farms and ranches. Kansas State Univ. Coop. Ext. Serv., Manhattan.

Piehl, J. P., editor. 1986. Wetland restoration: a techniques workshop. Minnesota Chap. of the Wildl. Soc., Fergus Falls. 48 pp.

Poston, H. J., and R. K. Schmidt. 1981. Wildlife habitat: a handbook for Canada's prairies and parklands. Western and Northern Region, Can. Wildl. Serv. Environ. Canada, Edmonton, Alta. 51 pp.

Prairie Farm Rehabilitation Administration. 1983. Land degradation and soil conservation issues on the Canadian prairies. Soil and Water Conserv. Branch, Agric. Canada. 326 pp.

Quinlan, E. E., and G. A. Baldassarre. 1984. Activity budgets of nonbreeding green-winged teal on playa lakes in Texas. J. Wildl. Manage. 48:838-845.

Raitasuo, K. 1964. Social behavior of the mallard, *Anas platyrhynchos*, in the course of the annual cycle. Pap. Game Res. 24. 72 pp.

Raveling, D. G. 1978. Dynamics of distribution of Canada geese in winter. Trans. North Am. Wildl. and Nat. Resour. Conf.. 43:206-225.

———. 1979. The annual cycle of body composition of Canada geese with special reference to control of reproduction. Auk 96:234-252.

———, W. E. Crews, and W. D. Klimstra. 1972. Activity patterns of Canada geese during winter. Wilson Bull. 84:278-295.

Ringelman, J. K., W. R. Eddleman, and H. W. Miller. 1989. High plains reservoirs and sloughs. Pages 311-340 *in* L. M. Smith, R. L. Pederson, and R. M. Kaminski, eds. Habitat management for migrating and wintering waterfowl in North America. Texas Tech Univ. Press, Lubbock.

Rumberg, C. G., and W. A. Sawyer. 1965. Response of wet-meadow vegetation to length and depth of surface water from wild-flood irrigation. Agron. J. 57:245-247.

Ruwaldt, J. J., Jr., L. D. Flake, and J. M. Gates. 1979. Waterfowl pair use of natural and man-made wetlands in South Dakota. J. Wildl. Manage. 43:375-383.

Salomonsen, F. 1968. The moult migration. Wildfowl 19:5-24.

Sankowski, T. P., K. L. Schmitt, S. J. Guinn, G. R. Stewart, and R. B. Burns. 1987. The Kitsim complex, an example of a small wetland development benefitting waterfowl and cattle production. Pages 189-193 *in* C. D. A. Rubec and R. P. Overend, eds. Proc. wetlands/peatlands symp., Can. Wildl. Serv., Ottawa.

Schildmeieler, C. 1967. Marsh burning for waterfowl. Proc. Tall Timbers Fire Ecol. Conf. 6:41-46.

Serie, J. R., and G. A. Swanson. 1976. Feeding ecology of breeding gadwalls on saline wetlands. J. Wildl. Manage. 40:69-81.

Sigafoos, R. S. 1964. Botanical evidence of floods and flood plain deposition. U.S. Geol. Surv. Prof. Pa. 485-A, U.S. Gov. Print. Off., Washington, D.C. 100 pp.

Simpson, S. G. 1988. Use of the Missouri River in South Dakota by Canada geese in fall and winter, 1953-1984. Pages 529-540 *in* M. W. Weller, ed. Waterfowl in winter. Univ. Minnesota Press, Minneapolis.

Sousa, P. J. 1987. Habitat management models for selected wildlife management practices in the Northern Great Plains. U.S. Dep. Int. Bur. of Reclamation, Off. Environ. Serv. Tech. Rep. REC-ERC 87-11. 100 pp.

Stanford, J. A. 1979. Proliferation of river deltas in reservoirs: a "natural" mitigation process? Pages 193-195 *in* G. A. Swanson, tech. coord. The mitigation symp: a natl. workshop on mitigat-

ing losses of fish and wildlife habitats. USDA Rocky Mountain For. and Range Exp. Stn. Gen. Tech. Rep. RM-65.

Steenhof, K. 1984. Use of an interspecific communal roost by wintering Ferruginous hawks. Wilson Bull. 96:137-138.

Stewart, R. E., and H. A. Kantrud. 1971. Classification of natural ponds and lakes in the glaciated prairie region. U.S. Fish and Wildl. Serv. Resour. Publ. 92, U.S. Gov. Print. Off., Washington, D.C.

———, and ———. 1972. Vegetation of prairie potholes, North Dakota, in relation of quality of water and other environmental factors. U.S. Geol. Surv. Prof. Pap. 585-D, U.S. Gov. Print. Off., Washington, D.C.

———, and ———. 1973. Ecological distribution of breeding waterfowl populations in North Dakota. J. Wildl. Manage. 37:39-50.

Stout, I. J., and G. W. Cornwell. 1976. Nonhunting mortality of fledged North American waterfowl. J. Wildl. Manage. 40:681-693.

Stuckey, R. L. 1975. A bibliography of manuals and checklists of aquatic vascular plants for regions and states in the conterminous United States. Sida 6:24-29.

Sugden, L. G. 1976. Waterfowl damage to Canadian grain: current problem and research needs. Can. Wildl. Serv. Occas. Pap. No. 4. 25 pp.

Swanson, G. A., M. I. Meyer, and J. R. Serie. 1974. Feeding ecology of breeding blue-winged teals. J. Wildl. Manage. 38:396-407.

Tamisier, A. 1974. Etho-ecological studies of teal wintering in the Camargue (Rhone Delta, France). Wildfowl 25:107-117.

Teskey, R. O., and T. M. Hinckley. 1978. Impact of water level changes on woody riparian and wetland communities. Vol. 6. Plains grassland region. U.S. Fish and Wildl. Serv. Biol. Serv. Program FWS/OBS-78/89. 29 pp.

Thomas, V. G. 1983. Spring migration: the prelude to goose reproduction and a review of its implications. Pages 73-81 *in* H. Boyd, ed. Proc. first western hemisphere waterfowl and waterbird symp. Int. Waterfowl Res. Bur., Can. Wildl. Serv., Ottawa.

Thompson, D. Q., R. L. Stuckey, and E. B. Thompson. 1987. Spread, impact, and control of purple loosestrife (*Lythrum salicaria*) in North American wetlands. U.S. Fish and Wildl. Serv. Res. Ser. Publ. No. 2, Washington, D.C. 50 pp.

Tiner, R. W., Jr. 1984. Wetlands of the United States: current status and recent trends. U.S. Fish and Wildl. Serv., Natl. Wetlands Inventory, Washington, D.C. 59 pp.

Ungar, I. A., and T. E. Reihl. 1980. The effect of seed reserves on species composition in zonal halophyte communities. Bot. Gaz. 141:447-452.

U.S. Department of Agriculture. 1982. Ponds—planning, design, construction. Soil Cons. Serv. Ag. Handbook No. 590. 51 pp.

U.S. Fish and Wildlife Service. 1981. The Platte River ecology study special research report. U.S. Fish and Wildl. Serv., Northern Prairie Wildl. Res. Center, Jamestown, N.D. 186 pp.

van der Valk, A. G., and C. B. Davis. 1978. The role of seed banks in the vegetation dynamics of prairie glacial marshes. Ecology 59:322-335.

Vogl, R. J. 1967. Controlled burning for wildlife in Wisconsin. Proc. Tall Timbers Fire Ecol. Conf. 6:47-96.

Walker, B. H., and R. T. Coupland. 1968. An analysis of vegetation-environmental relationships in Saskatchewan sloughs. Can. J. Bot. 46:509-522.

——, and ——. 1970. Herbaceous wetland vegetation in the aspen grove and grassland regions of Saskatchewan. Can. J. Bot. 48:1861-1878.

Ward, P. 1968. Fire in relation to waterfowl habitat of the Delta Marshes. Proc. Tall Timbers Fire Ecol. Conf. 7:255-267.

Weaver, J. E. 1960. Floodplain vegetation of the central Missouri Valley and contacts of woodland with prairie. Ecol. Monogr. 30:37-64.

Weller, M. W. 1975. Studies of cattail in relation to management for marsh wildlife. Iowa State J. Sci. 49:383-412.

——. 1981. Freshwater marshes: ecology and wildlife management. Univ. Minnesota Press, Minneapolis.

——, and C. E. Spatcher. 1965. Role of habitat in the distribution and abundance of marsh birds. Iowa Agric. and Home Econ. Exp. Stn. Spec. Rep. No. 43. 31 pp.

——, and D. K. Voights. 1983. Changes in the vegetation and wildlife use of a small prairie wetland following a drought. Proc. Iowa Acad. Sci. 90:50-54.

Welling, C. H., R. L. Pederson, and A. G. van der Valk. 1988. Recruitment from the seed bank and the development of zonation of emergent vegetation during a drawdown in a prairie wetland. J. Ecol. 76:483-496.

Williams, G. P. 1978. The case of the shrinking channels—the North Platte and Platte Rivers in Nebraska. U.S. Geol. Surv. Circ. 781. 48 pp.

Windingstad, R. M., J. J. Hurt, A. K. Trout, and J. Cary. 1984. Avian cholera in Nebraska's Rainwater Basin. Trans. North Am. Wildl. and Nat. Resour. Conf. 49:576-583.

Wright, H. A., and A. W. Bailey. 1980. Fire ecology and prescribed burning in the Great Plains—a research review. USDA Intermountain For. and Range Exp. Stn. Gen. Tech. Rep. INT-77. 60 pp.

HIGH PLAINS RESERVOIRS AND SLOUGHS

JAMES K. RINGELMAN, Colorado Division of Wildlife, 317 W. Prospect, Fort Collins, CO 80526

WILLIAM R. EDDLEMAN[1], Department of Zoology and Physiology, Box 3166, University Station, Laramie, WY 82071

HARVEY W. MILLER[2], U.S. Fish and Wildlife Service, Office of Migratory Bird Management, 730 Simms, Room 456, Golden, CO 80401

The High Plains is a vast region extending 1,000 km south from the Canadian border to Texas, and 500-800 km east from the Front Range of the Rocky Mountains. Despite climatic extremes, this area still provides attractive habitat for several million migrating and wintering waterfowl. Such was not always the case. An increase in irrigated agriculture following World War II provided new wetlands and abundant food in the form of waste grain. Waterfowl have benefitted from these conditions, especially mallards (*Anas platyrhynchos*) and Canada geese (*Branta canadensis*).

This chapter describes the waterfowl habitats important on the High Plains, then relates habitat use by waterfowl to the nutritional and social requirements of key species. We also provide management practices applicable to highly altered agricultural uplands as well as both natural and man-made wetlands.

CHARACTERISTICS OF THE HIGH PLAINS

Geography and Climate

The Great Plains Province and portions of the Central Lowlands Province (Hunt 1967, Bailey 1978) comprise most of the region commonly referred to as the High Plains (Fig. 1). Much of this region lies west of the 100th meridian. Dominant native vegetation is tall grasses (*Andropogon* spp.) east of the 100th meridian,

Fig. 1. The Great Plains Province and portion of the Central Lowlands Province that correspond to the High Plains Region (hatched region; after Hunt 1967, Bailey 1978). The dashed line denotes the 100th meridian.

and short grasses (*Bouteloua* spp., *Buchloe* spp.) west of the 100th meridian. Plant nomenclature follows that of Scott and Wasser (1980). Trees, especially cottonwoods (*Populus* spp.), occur in valleys and riparian corridors.

The climate of the region is dominated by a north-south cline of temperature and an east-west cline of precipitation (Table 1; Ruffner 1985). Most precipitation (70%-80%) falls during spring and summer. Fall

[1]Present address: Department of Natural Resource Science, University of Rhode Island, Kingston, RI 02881.

[2]Present address: Texas Parks and Wildlife Department, Goddard Building, Texas Tech University, Lubbock, TX 79409.

Table 1.   Selected weather statistics in states of the High Plains (from Ruffner 1985). Temperature and precipitation are reported in C and cm, respectively.

Statistic	Montana, North Dakota, South Dakota, Wyoming		Nebraska, Colorado, Kansas		Oklahoma, Texas, New Mexico	
	$\bar{x}$	Range	$\bar{x}$	Range	$\bar{x}$	Range
Annual temperature	7	5-10	10	8-14	15	12-18
Fall temperature	8	7-11	11	9-14	16	12-18
Winter temperature	−7	−11-−2	−2	−5-−1	4	2- 7
Fall precipitation (% of annual)	18	17-18	19	16-24	24	19-29
Winter precipitation (% of annual)	9	8-10	8	6-11	10	6-16
Number of fall days with maximum temperature <0	6	4- 9	3	1- 5	0	0- 2
Number of fall days with minimum temperature <0	39	32-45	33	16-45	12	6-26
Number of winter days with maximum temperature <0	49	25-65	30	15-76	8	3-12
Number of winter days with minimum temperature <0	88	83-90	84	71-90	66	52-82
Number of fall days with maximum temperature <−18	1	1- 2	0	0- 1	0	
Number of winter days with maximum temperature <−18	29	10-44	11	4-23	1	0- 2
Total precipitation	44	34-56	48	28-85	62	36-99

precipitation (September through November) ranges from 15.5 to 29.0 cm and falls mostly as September thunderstorms. Winter precipitation (December through February, 5.8 to 15.8 cm) falls mainly as snow in the northern portion of the area and as rain or snow in the southern portion. More precipitation falls in the east than in the west.

Mean fall temperatures range from 6.7 to 18.4 C. Maximum daily temperatures <0 C occur in 0 to 9 days in the fall, with colder temperatures in the northern portions of the area. Maximum daily temperatures of <0 C occur for up to 76 days in winter, but vary widely with latitude (Table 1). The largest number of days with a maximum temperature <0 C occurs in North Dakota, Montana, Wyoming, and northern South Dakota. All but the largest reservoirs are frozen over in most years in this portion of the region. Conversely, winter temperatures in New Mexico and Oklahoma are usually warm enough to preclude long-term freezing of reservoirs in most years.

Reservoirs

Reservoirs, which we arbitrarily define as man-made wetlands >200 ha, have markedly affected the distribution and abundance of waterfowl wintering on the High Plains by providing water that formerly was scarce or nonexistent at the onset of winter. Reservoirs are attractive to waterfowl, because they generally are deep enough to remain ice-free well into periods of subfreezing temperatures, and most are large enough to provide relative freedom from disturbance even when open to hunting and fishing. Foods often are available nearby on former rangelands that have been converted to irrigated cropland.

Reservoirs have been constructed in the High Plains area for several uses, including flood control, irrigation, municipal water supplies, power generation, navigation, soil conservation, recreation, and fish and wildlife benefits (Oklahoma Water Resources Board 1980). The reservoirs most important to waterfowl are those constructed for irrigation purposes, because these often are associated with crops. In the face of extensive wetland loss nationally, large reservoirs are one of the few wetlands types to have increased since 1945 (>500,000 ha of increase from the mid-1950s to mid-1970s; Tiner 1984).

A portion of this increase is attributable to transmountain diversions of water from the Colorado River basin through the continental divide into the Missouri River basin (Weaver 1980). The first diversion in Colorado was completed in 1936 (Folk-Williams et al. 1985), and additional projects since that time divert an average of 617 million m^3 of water to eastern Colorado. This represents 15% of the total reservoir storage capacity (Waters 1965), and an even larger fraction of the actual water used, because maximum storage capacities are never achieved region-wide. Thus, "west-slope" water contributes significantly to waterfowl habitat on the High Plains. Development of this water resource coincided with the era of extensive reservoir construction.

From a 1954 inventory, Shaw and Fredine (1956) reported 35,250 ha of "inland fresh open water," including shallow ponds and reservoirs in the "Central Flyway-south" (Colorado, Kansas, New Mexico, Oklahoma, and Texas). A more comprehensive survey by the U.S. Fish and Wildlife Service indicated that in early 1956 there were 1,163 reservoirs comprising 270,000 ha of "high-value" wetlands for waterfowl in these 5 states (Table 2). Most reservoirs deemed high value for waterfowl were in the High Plains; those classified "low value" tended to be in the mountains.

In 1965, Sutherland (1970) reassessed reservoir importance to waterfowl by adjusting estimates reported by Shaw and Fredine (1956) to account for known losses and gains in reservoirs. Because impacts (draining, filling, urbanization) that would destroy or reduce wetlands for waterfowl had been rare in the High Plains, he assumed that any increase in available permanent water reflected construction of reservoirs. Comparing the 1965 estimate of 706,000 ha of permanent water in the southern Central Flyway to the estimated 87,100 ha of inland fresh open water in 1954 (Shaw and Fredine,

Table 2. Numbers and area of reservoirs in states of the recognized wintering-area portion of the Central Flyway, as of 1 January 1956.[a]

State	High-value reservoirs[b]		Low-value reservoirs[b]	
	N	ha	N	ha
Colorado	644	21,477	322	9,754
Kansas	132	14,415	36	474
New Mexico	9	1,929	3	5,466
Oklahoma	76	77,502	92	9,881
Texas	302	154,651	118	26,646
Total	1,163	269,974	571	52,221

[a]Source: U.S. Fish and Wildlife Service, 730 Simms, Golden, CO 80401.
[b]Potential value to waterfowl as per Shaw and Fredine (1956).

1956) suggests nearly a 10-fold increase in the number of High Plains reservoirs during this period.

Recent surveys (Ploskey and Jenkins 1980, Jenkins et al. 1985) show that 171 reservoirs of >200 ha have been constructed in the High Plains (Table 3). Although Oklahoma has the largest number of reservoirs, Kansas has slightly more reservoirs subjectively rated "important" for waterfowl. The total area is heavily inflated by the inclusion of Fort Peck, Garrison, and Francis Case reservoirs (totalling 276,923 ha), which are important wintering areas, but not on a per-unit-area basis.

Construction of large reservoirs has slowed and appears to be nearly halted in the High Plains. The water available for storage in any watershed is limited, and the cost-effective large reservoir sites were the first used. However, large reservoirs are relatively permanent and long-lived. Perhaps the greatest threat of destruction is burgeoning domestic uses, given higher priority than agricultural uses, upstream from reservoirs. On balance, there is no obvious threat to the capacity of reservoirs to accommodate wintering waterfowl on the High Plains.

Rivers and Sloughs

Most reservoirs in the High Plains area are associated with major river systems. Because of this association, reservoirs

Table 3. Number and area of all reservoirs >200 ha and those of importance to waterfowl in the High Plains.

State	All reservoirs[a]		Waterfowl reservoirs[b]		
	N	ha	N	ha	% of total area
Colorado	22	16,750	6	4,239	25
Kansas	21	63,008	16	46,227	73
Montana	7	93,814	2	88,138	94
Nebraska	16	31,879	3	16,437	52
New Mexico	3	7,397	3	7,397	100
North Dakota	5	192,473	1	148,988	77
Oklahoma	61	197,098	14	122,692	62
South Dakota	7	145,713	1	42,105	29
Texas	17	78,388	2	11,012	14
Wyoming	12	24,918	4	7,444	30
Total	171	851,438	52	494,679	58

[a]Sources: Ploskey and Jenkins (1980), Jenkins et al. (1985).
[b]Sources: U.S. Dep. Int. (1955), Buller (1964), Hopper (1968), Bellrose (1976), Heitmeyer (1980).

often are only one component in wetland complexes that include rivers, riverine marshes, side channels, warm-water sloughs, and oxbow lakes. These associated wetlands may be disrupted or absent where extensive dam building or channel alteration have occurred (Heitmeyer and Vohs 1984a). The Missouri River is the major river system in the northern portion of the area, and the one most altered by dams (Buller 1964, Hunt 1967). The North Platte and associated irrigation projects and natural wetlands provide most habitat used by wintering waterfowl in the Wyoming High Plains (U.S. Dep. Int. 1955). Most waterfowl wintering in Nebraska use wetlands associated with the Platte River (Jorde et al. 1983).

River bottoms and associated warm-water sloughs provide reliable open water and thermal protection for waterfowl that winter in association with the South Platte and Arkansas Rivers in Colorado (Hopper 1968, Hopper et al. 1978). The Arkansas and Cimarron River valleys provide most reservoir-associated wintering habitat for waterfowl in western Kansas; the Republican and Smoky Hill

drainages provide some additional habitat (Buller 1964). Reservoir development along the Arkansas, Cimarron, Canadian, and Red rivers in Oklahoma has been extensive (Buller 1964). The Canadian River provides most riverine and reservoir habitat for waterfowl in northeastern New Mexico and the Texas Panhandle (Buller 1964). A few reservoirs also are associated with the Red River in north-central Texas.

Irrigated Agriculture

Cereal-grain farming on the High Plains and use of these foods by waterfowl date back to the advent of irrigated agriculture in the mid-19th century (Steinel 1926). Initially, irrigation water was provided by either gravity flow from water originating in the mountains and transported via ditches, or from High Plains rivers from which water was pumped or diverted into fields adjacent to the river bottoms. This pattern of irrigation created a corridor of grain crops near the Rocky Mountains with "fingers" of irrigated grain extending along river systems. The early distribution of migrating and wintering waterfowl followed this development (Buller 1975).

Modern engineering allowed diversion of water far beyond its former range by creating efficient means to construct dams for small reservoirs, and by providing the technology for pumping water from underground aquifers. The result was a more uniform distribution of migrating and wintering waterfowl, and a buildup of wintering populations at northern latitudes where few birds wintered previously.

HIGH PLAINS WATERFOWL

The number of waterfowl wintering in the High Plains where reservoirs are a major wintering habitat ranges from 1 to 2.5 million ducks and geese, depending on fall population size, severity of winter

Table 4. Yearly mean numbers of ducks and geese estimated from midwinter inventories in the High Plains area, 1979-87.[a] Texas and New Mexico are excluded, because a substantial number of birds winter outside the High Plains area.

State	Ducks		Geese	
	$\bar{x}$	SE	$\bar{x}$	SE
Colorado	169,177	31,264	128,699	13,700
Nebraska	287,527	38,138	57,523	16,307
Kansas	360,989	58,754	112,754	17,580
Oklahoma	176,730	12,749	95,656	10,058
Montana	27,442	3,356	6,830	1,410
Wyoming	57,607	11,191	11,831	1,874
North Dakota	5,919	1,357	5,769	1,954
South Dakota	127,167	25,130	160,582	20,086

[a] Source: Unpubl. file data, U.S. Fish and Wildlife Service, 730 Simms, Golden, CO. 80401.

[b] >90% are mallards in all states, except Montana where goldeneyes comprise the majority of wintering birds. Canada geese are comprised of birds from the Shortgrass Prairie population (*B. c. parvipes*, 50%), Tallgrass Prairie population (*B. c. hutchinsii*, 38%), and Hi-Line population (*B. c. maxima* and *B. c. moffetti*, 12%).

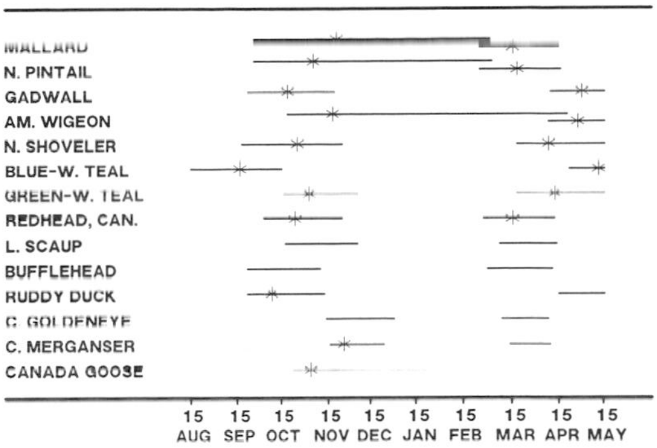

Fig. 2. Chronology of waterfowl migration through the central High Plains. Peak of migration for the most numerous species is denoted with an asterix (after Rutherford 1966).

weather, and available food resources (Table 4). Four classes of migrants use reservoirs in the High Plains, based on their chronology of migration (Fig. 2; Grieb and Boeker 1954, Landes 1961, Eddleman unpubl. data). Blue-winged teal (*Anas discors*) use shallow areas of reservoirs and small natural wetlands and migrate from August to early October (Heitmeyer and Vohs 1984a). Mid-season migrants, including gadwall (*Anas strepera*), northern shoveler (*A. clypeata*), lesser scaup (*Aythya affinis*), redhead (*Aythya americana*), and ruddy duck (*Oxyura jamaicensis*), migrate in September through December, but numbers peak in October (Fig. 2). These species attain local importance in the harvest, because their migration coincides with the opening of waterfowl hunting seasons. Those species that migrate late, peaking in late November and early December, include the common merganser (*Mergus merganser*) and common goldeneye (*Bucephala clangula*). Some species are present throughout the fall, including mallard, American wigeon

(*Anas americana*), green-winged teal (*A. crecca*), and northern pintail (*A. acuta*). The chronology of spring migration is essentially the reverse of fall migration (Fig. 2). The mallard is abundant during all but the early migration period in Colorado (Grieb and Boeker 1954, Landes 1961, Eddleman et al. 1985a).

Mallards and Canada geese comprise the majority of waterfowl wintering on High Plains reservoirs. Over 95% of the dabbling ducks wintering in the area are mallards (Table 5). Important mallard wintering areas include reservoirs on the Missouri (Montana, North and South Dakota), South Platte (Colorado and Nebraska), North Platte (Wyoming), Arkansas (Colorado, Kansas, Oklahoma), and Red rivers (Texas, Oklahoma) (Bellrose 1976). Mallards wintering on the High Plains typically seek open water on large reservoirs (or sheltered areas in severe weather) during the day, then fly to surrounding croplands to feed at night (Grieb and Boeker 1954, Jorde et al. 1983).

Common mergansers winter primarily on reservoirs in Kansas and Oklahoma (Miller 1973). A few hundred to several thousand winter below the dams on the Missouri River (Timkin and Anderson 1969). The northern limit of wintering common mergansers is determined by the availability of open water, because the

Table 5. Yearly mean numbers of ducks and geese counted on midwinter inventories in the Central Flyway, 1978-87.[a]

Species	$\bar{x}$	SE	Range
Ducks			
Mallard	1,431,930	147,241	799,800-2,220,000
Gadwall	155,860	13,750	101,000-258,200
American wigeon	95,770	9,708	76,000-154,400
Green-winged teal	482,731	117,907	195,000-1,201,000
Blue-winged teal	4,380	1,402	1,000-13,800
Northern shoveler	54,630	17,275	33,000-70,300
Northern pintail	713,300	225,565	335,600-1,709,000
Redhead	220,080	69,595	108,000-322,100
Canvasback (Aythya valisneria)	37,700	11,922	16,000-82,200
Lesser scaup	71,520	22,616	29,000-140,300
Ring-necked duck (Aythya collaris)	15,300	4,838	1,500-54,200
Common goldeneye	16,030	5,069	9,100-33,000
Bufflehead (Bucephala albeola)	6,220	1,967	3,300-8,000
Ruddy duck	11,460	3,624	5,200-25,200
Common/red-breasted merganser	117,750	37,236	45,000-291,300
Geese			
Canada goose	642,700	203,240	483,000-844,700
White-fronted goose (Anser albifrons)	127,830	40,423	69,000-194,500
Snow goose (Chen caerulescens)	876,230	277,088	801,000-1,205,000

[a]Source: U.S. Fish and Wildlife Service, 730 Simms, Golden, CO 80401.

birds feed mainly on gizzard shad (*Dorosoma cepedianum*) and other fish (Miller 1973). Southerly shifts in abundance of mergansers often occur in midwinter, when Kansas reservoirs freeze and birds move to Oklahoma and New Mexico. The construction of dams has probably influenced the distributional shift of common mergansers from large rivers to large reservoirs, because areas identified as major habitats in the 1930s presently have smaller numbers of wintering birds. Common goldeneyes winter mostly on rivers in the High Plains, but many also occur on reservoirs (Bellrose 1976). Goldeneyes also depend on the presence of open water, because they feed on small fish and invertebrates.

Three populations of Canada geese, totalling 350,000 to 580,000 birds, winter in the High Plains in association with reservoirs. The Tallgrass Prairie Population of about 150,000 birds winters on several reservoirs in Kansas and western Oklahoma (Bellrose 1976). The Shortgrass Prairie Population of approximately 200,000 birds winters in southern Colo-

rado, western Nebraska, the Texas Panhandle, and northeastern New Mexico. Finally, the Hi-line Plains Population of about 50,000 birds winters mainly in New Mexico, southeastern Wyoming, and along Colorado's Front Range.

HABITAT

Riparian Habitat

Reservoir construction or dewatering for irrigation or other consumptive uses (electrical generation, mining, industrial purposes, municipal supplies, etc.) has occurred in virtually all High Plains streams (Moore and Mills 1977).

Moore and Mills (1977) and Williams and Wolman (1986) summarized reservoir impacts on riparian habitats:

1. Downstream flows are changed in both timing and volume, e.g., flows often are highest during the late spring and summer irrigation season (when flows in unimpounded streams usually are below-average) and lowest to nonexistent at other times. Flooding, common during spring runoff, may be entirely eliminated.

2. Downstream temperatures are substantially lower during the summer irrigation season, but may be higher in winter because discharges usually are from the depths of reservoirs.

3. Annual downstream discharges are reduced because of increased evaporation from reservoirs.

4. Reservoirs slow water-flow, thereby allowing suspended matter to settle out. Evaporation increases the concentration of dissolved constituents. Because of these processes, the water released from a reservoir is seldom similar to the water flowing into it.

5. Because few dissolved salts are removed by plants, irrigation return flows are invariably higher in dissolved constituents than in water applied to the crop. Leaching of nutrients (applied as fertilizer) also increases the dissolved constituents in irrigation return flows. Both conditions may degrade water quality in riparian systems downstream from reservoirs.

6. Downstream discharges usually are diverted into irrigation canals, and flows may be decreased below that diversion. Flows from irrigation back into the stream may augment instream flows and again be diverted farther downstream, resulting in alternating segments of increased and decreased flows during the irrigation season.

Riparian plant communities have undergone dramatic transformations because of the effects of reservoirs described above (Pederson et al. 1988). Crouch (1978) found that from 1961 to 1978, density of cottonwoods along the lower South Platte River in Colorado decreased from 15.5 to 7.1 trees/ha, and from 19.3 to 12.9 trees/ha in grazed and ungrazed sites, respectively. In some years, cottonwood seedlings suffer 98% mortality along this section of river (Snyder 1986). Losses of cottonwoods also have occurred along river bottoms in Nebraska, Kansas, and Oklahoma (Graul 1982). Reproductive

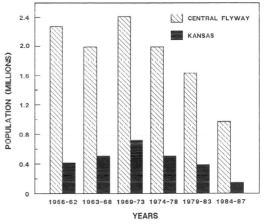

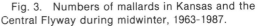

Fig. 3. Numbers of mallards in Kansas and the Central Flyway during midwinter, 1963-1987.

failure, caused by declining or altered stream flows that reduce groundwater levels to below the root zone, is one important factor (Snyder 1986). Livestock grazing is a second major detriment to seedling survival.

Reservoir Use by Waterfowl

Reservoirs can dramatically impact the distribution and abundance of waterfowl. Buller (1975) recorded a nearly linear increase in duck numbers in Kansas (including areas east of the High Plains) from about 100,000 birds in midwinter 1949 (2 reservoirs in existence) to >800,000 in 1973, which coincided with construction of new reservoirs beginning in 1950. Twenty-three large reservoirs exist in Kansas as of 1988 (M. J. Kraft, pers. commun.). Mallards, the species that comprises >90% of Kansas' winter duck population, increased during 1956-68, while the population of Central Flyway mallards declined (Fig. 3). Throughout the 1970s and 1980s, the number of mallards in Kansas during midwinter has declined, but at a rate slower than that of the Central Flyway. This population response is due to attractive habitat, particularly reservoirs, created during the 1960s.

Responses of waterfowl to the creation

of a new reservoir are largely dependent upon location of the reservoir in relation to migration corridors, proximity of the wetland to other wintering areas, and development of agriculture in association with the reservoir. As an example, we highlight Bonny Reservoir, a 825-ha wetland created in 1951 on the South Republican River in east-central Colorado. A 1953 midwinter survey of this reservoir revealed 5,000 ducks (Colo. Div. Wildl., unpubl. data). The population increased rapidly during the late 1950s, and peaked in 1972 during a winter of mild weather and a high mallard population in the Central Flyway (Fig. 4). Generally, high populations were maintained from 1972-82, with annual fluctuations attributable largely to differences in the severity of winter weather. A decline in the winter population began in 1983, perhaps linked to wetland and agricultural changes, as well as a decline in the Central Flyway mallard population.

Case histories of Kansas reservoirs provide evidence that the value of these wetlands to waterfowl declines over time, largely independent of external factors. Focusing on 3 reservoirs cited by Buller (1975), mallard populations fluctuated greatly over time, but changes were unrelated to midwinter mallard populations in either Kansas or the Central Flyway (Table 6). Numbers of mallards using Elk City Reservoir increased during 1974-78 from the 1969-73 period, whereas mallard numbers declined in both Kansas and the Central Flyway between the same periods. Later (1979-83), when Kansas and Central Flyway mallard declines were moderate, this same reservoir experienced a decline. The Cheney Reservoir mallard population declined much more dramatically than either the Kansas or Central Flyway population during 1969-73 through 1979-83, then increased in 1984-87 when Kansas and Central Flyway numbers plummeted. Glen Elder Reservoir experienced an increase in mallards

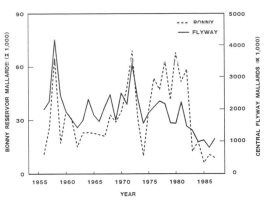

Fig. 4. Numbers of mallards at Bonny Reservoir, Colorado and in the Central Flyway during mid-winter, 1955-87.

during a period in which mallard numbers declined at Cheney and Elk City, reservoirs, as well as throughout Kansas and the Central Flyway.

Apparently, large reservoirs such as these attract waterfowl, particularly mallards, shortly after completion. Thereafter, populations build until the reservoir is 20-30 years old, then mallard use declines sharply. Because most waterfowl do not acquire large amounts of food from reservoirs, the decline in winter use in not likely attributable to a decline in food availability. Rather, it may be caused by changes in the physical structure of inflow and outflow channels, and vegetative succession in these areas and along the margins of the reservoir.

Vegetative succession in newly flooded wetlands, as well as species tolerance of flooding regimes, have been well-documented (Teskey and Hinckley 1978). In the High Plains, willows (*Salix* spp.) are a common pioneer species that are succeeded by a community dominated by cottonwood. As the inflow stream gradient lessens, silt and sand are deposited and water depth decreases, eventually forming sandbars and islands. These provide a substrate for more willows and herbaceous species, such as cattail (*Typha* spp.) and sedge (*Carex* spp.), to invade wetland areas (Fig. 5). Similar responses may occur in shallow or sporadically

Table 6. Average number of mallards at 3 Kansas reservoirs and throughout the Central Flyway during the midwinter inventory 1956-87.

Years	Central Flyway[a] Population	Central Flyway[a] % change between periods	Populations as % of Flyway total Kansas[b] %	Kansas[b] % change between periods	Elk City Reservoir %	Elk City Reservoir % change between periods	Cheney Reservoir %	Cheney Reservoir % change between periods	Glen Elder Reservoir %	Glen Elder Reservoir % change between periods
1956-62	2,271,207		18.2							
1963-68	1,992,049	−12.3	25.2	38.5	2.26		5.25			
1969-73	2,412,551	21.1	29.5	17.1	2.62	15.9	2.31	−56.0	4.77	
1974-78	1,985,162	−17.7	25.5	−13.6	4.47	70.6	1.39	−39.8	4.12	−7.3
1979-83	1,633,410	−17.7	23.6	−7.4	1.22	−72.7	0.52	−62.6	5.14	16.3
1984-87	971,100	−40.5	15.1	−36.0	1.21	−0.8	0.66	26.9	1.63	−68.3

[a]Source: U.S. Fish and Wildlife Service, 730 Simms, Golden, CO 80401.
[b]Source: M. J. Kraft, Kansas Dep. of Wildl. and Parks.

flooded spillway and toe-drain locations. The result is decreased availability of shallow open-water areas where birds loaf and feed. Additionally, because these areas become shallower and water-flow rate decreases, these habitats are more likely to freeze during winter. These changes contribute to an unfavorable pattern of habitat succession that decreases the attractiveness of reservoirs to waterfowl over time.

Agriculture

Without supplemental water, most of the High Plains can naturally support dryland wheat and short-grass prairie pasture grasses. With water, yields of wheat, cotton, and grain sorghum can be increased up to 4-fold from dryland

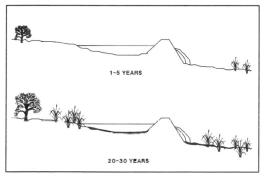

Fig. 5. Diagrammatic (cross-section) representation of vegetative succession on High Plains reservoirs, indicating herbaceous and woody plant growth promoted by sedimentation in the inflow and outlet regions of a typical reservoir.

production. Moreover, water-demanding crops such as corn and sugar beets also will flourish. The agricultural economy of the region is based on both dryland and irrigated agriculture. Because of the reliance of migrating and wintering waterfowl on waste cereal grains for food, the history of agricultural development, present distribution of crop types, and anticipated trends in commodity production are all important considerations for the waterfowl manager.

Much of the irrigation water for the High Plains region is derived from the Ogallala Aquifer. Within this aquifer are approximately 3.7 trillion m^3 of groundwater (High Plains Associates 1982). Extending 1,300 km from Texas to South Dakota, the Ogallala Aquifer underlies not only one of the most intensive agricultural economies in the world, but also some of the most valuable winter waterfowl habitat in the Central Flyway (Fig. 6). Over 94% of the irrigation water in the region is withdrawn from this source; thus, the future of agriculture and waterfowl is closely tied to this aquifer. Unfortunately, the Ogallala Aquifer is being "mined" at a rate that far exceeds the recharge rate.

An era of extensive groundwater irrigation on the High Plains began in 1946, when cheap natural gas became available, natural gas-fired motors were developed, and rural electrification became a reality

320   CENTRAL FLYWAY

Fig. 6. Location of the Ogallala Aquifer in the
High Plains Region.

(Arthur D. Little, Inc. 1982). Total irrigated area in the region overlying the
Ogallala Aquifer expanded from 1.4 million ha in 1950, primarily in Nebraska
and Texas, to >5.7 million ha in 1980.
The increase in feed-grain crops was from
150 million bushels in 1950 to 1.25
billion bushels in 1980 (High Plains
Study Council 1982). On the Texas High
Plains, irrigated cropland exploded from
near 0 to 748,000 ha (nearly 60% of all
available cropland) within 15 years
(Arthur D. Little, Inc. 1982). However,
the thickness of the Ogallala Aquifer
decreases from north to south owing to a
progressively thinner saturated layer
(Arthur D. Little, Inc. 1982), and effects
of groundwater depletion were soon felt
in the southern region. Several southern
Texas counties have been "adjusting" to a
gradual transition back to dryland farm-

ing since the early 1960s, and former 3.2
or 3.9 cm wells have been converted to 0.8
and 1.6 cm systems (Arthur D. Little, Inc.
1982). The 25.9 billion m³ of water
pumped annually from the Ogallala
Aquifer by High Plains farmers cannot be
sustained in the future, yet the use of this
water resource, together with reservoir
development, has allowed production of
the vast quantities of grains that make the
High Plains an important waterfowl
wintering area.

Among the 4 major crops grown on the
High Plains—corn, wheat, cotton, and
grain sorghum—corn is most important
as a waterfowl food. Production of corn
for grain, which was constant from the
late 1920s through the early 1960s, began
a sharp increase in production in 1969
(USDA Agricultural Statistics; Table 7).
In the High Plains states (Fig. 1), corn
production topped 1 billion bushels in
1976, peaking at 1.48 billion bushels in
1979 (U.S. Department of Agriculture
1978, 1981). Much of this increased
production occurred in Colorado, Kansas,
Nebraska, and Texas; the latter of which
increased its corn production from 18.7
million to 186 million bushels from 1967
to 1977. Several factors have been responsible for the increase, including an
increase in irrigated land, improved corn
hybrids, use of insecticides and herbicides, and commodity prices.

Projections of agricultural production
into the year 2020 indicate changes in the
distribution and abundance of grain crops
(Arthur D. Little, Inc. 1982, High Plains
Associates 1982). Most changes will result
from groundwater depletion and rising
energy costs that favor dryland farming.
In Colorado, irrigated farmland will
decrease 41% (95,100 ha) whereas dryland
areas will increase 8% (52,600 ha; High
Plains Associates 1982). Irrigated land in
Texas and Kansas will decline 73% and
17%, respectively; dryland area will
increase 63% and 18%. Nebraska, which
overlays the thicker portion of the Ogal-

Table 7. Mean number of bushels (1,000s) of corn produced annually during selected periods of years in the High Plains states.

State	1927-36	1936-45	1946-55	1957-66	1967-76	1977-84
Colorado	17,039	13,098	13,531	14,071	39,016	80,504
Kansas	94,639	54,852	58,182	60,837	117,789	134,829
Montana	1,362	2,643	2,756	228	575	978
Nebraska	180,280	153,843	207,417	280,970	438,590	702,906
New Mexico	2,909	2,551	1,171	607	2,844	8,273
North Dakota	16,593	21,260	25,202	8,400	7,812	28,192
Oklahoma	40,123	27,644	16,371	4,220	5,680	5,472
South Dakota	64,920	64,525	104,544	104,665	106,416	162,015
Texas	78,002	71,963	43,882	29,774	62,049	131,393
Wyoming	2,112	1,664	1,075	971	1,709	4,337
Total	497,979	414,043	474,131	504,743	782,480	1,267,989

lala Aquifer, will expand irrigated agriculture by 2.74 million ha (144%) at the expense of dryland farming, which will decrease 40%. Irrigated corn will decrease in Colorado, Kansas, and particularly Texas (Bolen et al. 1989). Texas will see corn production decline 93% by the year 2020, to be replaced primarily by cotton (High Plains Associates 1982). Corn production in Nebraska will increase by an estimated 201%. On balance, continued expansion of irrigated agriculture (mainly in Nebraska) and improvements in yields will result in an increase in corn production of slightly over 100%, but the distribution of corn will be much different in the future than it was in 1988.

HABITAT IMPORTANCE RELATIVE TO WATERFOWL REQUIREMENTS

Waterfowl Requirements

The role of habitat in meeting the needs of migrating and wintering waterfowl only can be understood after the physiological requirements of waterfowl during these periods are known. Some ducks are completing the prealternate molt during fall migration and after arrival on the wintering grounds. Completion of this molt and reestablishment of nutrient reserves depleted during breeding, molt, and fall migration may be necessary for courtship and pairing among mallards (Heitmeyer 1985). Court-

ship and pairing are time-consuming and energetically costly events. Moreover, courting birds may be less attentive to their surroundings and more susceptible to avian predators (McKinney 1975, Wishart 1983). Unlike male mallards, which undergo prebasic molt in midsummer and remain in basic plumage only about 2.5 months (Weller 1976), females undergo prebasic molt in midwinter on the High Plains (Jorde 1981) and remain in basic plumage from late winter through the breeding period. As suggested by Heitmeyer (1988), the prebasic molt of female mallards requires that ducks consume substantial quantities of exogenous protein (from invertebrates) for a 6- to 7-week period. As molt nears completion, mallards initiate a rebuilding of endogenous reserves during February-March prior to the onset of spring migration.

Canada geese complete molt prior to migration and do not molt again until after breeding (Hanson 1965). In addition, because adults maintain life-long pair bonds, only subadults and individuals who have lost their mates need to undergo courtship and pairing (Bellrose 1976). Being larger-bodied birds, thermoregulatory costs in geese are relatively lower than in ducks, although cold weather may still limit the winter distribution of some subspecies (LeFebvre and Raveling 1967). Even so, winter is a time of high energy demand for Canada geese as well as mallards, as evidenced by data that indicate low fat reserves in both sexes of geese during midwinter (Raveling 1979).

The term "biological status" might be used to reference these events that occur among migrating and wintering waterfowl. "Social status" could be used to refer to an individual bird's place in the "pecking order" of behavioral interactions. Determinants of social status may include factors independent of biological status, such as age and gender, which may affect food acquisition and energy expenditure (Jorde et al. 1984). Often, however, biological and social events are confounded. Time of nesting, nest success, and date of molt may all impact fall lipid reserves and winter status.

Evidence for cross-seasonal linkage of physiological events (proposed by Heitmeyer [1985] for mallards) is building, although it must be viewed as a hypothesis. Nevertheless, it is a reasonable mechanism to explain the heterogeneity in social and biological status known to exist among waterfowl populations. Although most waterfowl will complete their necessary biological "milestones" during a given season, it is important to recognize that local populations of migrating or wintering waterfowl are comprised of individual birds that differ markedly among each other in their social and biological status. Management of waterfowl during these periods should be tempered with this understanding of population heterogeneity.

Nutrition

Migrating waterfowl consume a diet dominated by plant matter, primarily seeds, from both grain crops and wild plants (see Bellrose 1976). These high-carbohydrate food sources often are available in abundance, and enable waterfowl to deposit fat reserves used during migration or, in the case of birds resident on their wintering grounds, to store energy in the form of fat. Mallards and Canada geese on the High Plains have become highly dependent on agricultural waste grains.

The variety of cereal grains consumed by mallards has been well-documented (McAtee 1918, Martin and Uhler 1939, Stoudt 1944, Bossenmaier and Marshall 1958, Anderson 1959, Wright 1959), but of the grains available on the High Plains (corn, sorghum, barley, wheat), corn is consistently ranked as most important. Corn comprises 50-90% of the winter diet (Gordon 1981, Baldassarre et al. 1983, Jorde et al. 1983).

Corn also is used by Canada geese (Helm 1951, Arthur 1968, Staffon 1976) and snow geese (Frederick et al. 1987). Geese not only rely upon waste grains during migratory and winter periods, but also depend on grain plants in early growth stages as green forage. Winter wheat, barley, rye, and oats are forages consumed by Canada geese (Helm 1951, Taylor 1957, Arthur 1968, Sturdy 1972, Staffon 1976), but winter wheat is the crop most commonly available on the High Plains.

Corn has a high metabolizable energy (Hill et al. 1960), a crude fat content of about 5% (Baldassarre et al. 1983), compared to values of 1-2% for other cereal grains (Sugden 1971), but a lower crude protein content (9.74%; Baldassarre et al. 1983) than other grains (13.2-19.3%; Sugden 1971). Waste corn also is generally plentiful. Depending upon postharvest treatment and several other factors (Baldassarre et al. 1983), waste corn densities on the High Plains range from 50-800 kg/ha, with a mean value of about 350 kg/ha (Jorde 1981, Baldassarre et al. 1983). At this density, mallards can ingest nearly 5 g corn/minute in standing stubble (Colo. Div. Wildl., unpubl. data).

The amount of grain consumed by free-flying ducks is unknown. Captive mallards consume 95 to 115 g/day during early autumn (Sugden 1979). Whyte and

Bolen (1985) found that the amount of ingested corn in mallards following a morning feeding bout ranged from 34-64 g/bird during winter. At this level of consumption, mallards would need to spend only 7-13 minutes/bout or 14-26 minutes/day (assuming morning and evening feeding bouts) to acquire a necessary daily allotment of corn. By capitalizing on an easily obtainable food source with high energy content, such as corn, mallards, and possibly Canada geese, need to spend only about 2-3% of their day field-feeding for grain. This may enable these species to adopt a time-minimization strategy (Schoener 1971) as a means to concentrate energy-costly activities in just 2 periods of the day while minimizing detection by predators, including hunters (Clark et al. 1986).

Corn and other cereal grains are not nutritionally complete. Corn is deficient in the amino acids, lysine, tryptophan, and methionine, as well as the element calcium (Baldassarre et al. 1983), all of which are essential to avian metabolism (Sturkie 1976). On the High Plains, ducks consume a diet dominated by cereal grains but supplemented by lesser but vital amounts of natural plant and animal foods. In Nebraska, duckweed (*Lemna minor*), smartweed (*Polygonum* spp.), and barnyardgrass (*Echinochloa crusgalli*) accounted for most (26%) of the natural vegetative foods consumed by mallards (Jorde et al. 1983). Animal matter, mostly mollusks, accounted for 3% (aggregate to dry weight) of their winter diet. Because these foods typically occur in low densities and often are smaller than corn kernels, search and handling time may be high. As a result, net energy metabolized/unit time is undoubtedly far less than that achieved on a corn diet. The quality of these natural foods is what makes them particularly important in the winter diet of mallards.

In contrast to mallards, Canada geese wintering on the High Plains feed for much of the day. Seasonal changes in nutrient requirements (Raveling 1979) are reflected in dietary changes (Arthur 1968), but weather may influence short-term dietary composition (Staffon 1976). In most locations, Canada geese are opportunistic feeders (Koerner 1971). Nutrients to complement a corn diet are obtained by grazing on green plants. Because the rate of food passage through the alimentary canal is usually <2 h (Ranwell and Downing 1959, Marriott and Forbs 1970, Mattocks 1971, Owen 1975), little cellulose digestion takes place (Mattocks 1971), and geese rely on nutrients from cell solubles released by the mechanical grinding of the gizzard. Although winter wheat is the green forage most often eaten by Canada geese on the High Plains, other green vegetation may be consumed. In urban areas, bluegrass (*Poa pratensis*) is often preferred over other forages. Along the northern portion of Colorado's Front Range, smooth bromegrass (*Bromus inermis*), sedge, alfalfa, and shortawn foxtail (*Alopecurus aequalis*) complement winter wheat and bluegrass as green forage (Staffon 1976). Thus, the feeding strategy of High Plains Canada geese also may be one of reliance on high-energy grains obtained in a relatively short period of time, but supplemented by a variety of green forages consumed in large volumes over extended periods.

Habitat Selection

Habitat selection is a function of biological requirements and habitat availability. Habitat selection, which can incorporate a notion of hierarchal selection (Johnson 1980), is a useful concept for understanding waterfowl-habitat selection on the High Plains and elsewhere. First-order selection (Johnson 1980) can be defined as the winter range of a population. At this level of selection, ducks and geese choose to winter on the High Plains. Second-order selection relates to the local movements made by individuals or social groups. Third-order selection includes that subset of wetland and upland habitats that remain free of ice and snow, and hence available to High Plains waterfowl. Use of these habitats (i.e., fourth-order selection) is a function of several factors including hunting and other disturbances, food requirements, and social status.

Weather.—Winter weather, which regulates the availability of food and open water, influences migratory movements (Flickinger 1981, Eddleman et al. 1985*b*) and the distribution of waterfowl at the first-order level (Pulliainen 1963, Lensink 1964, Nilsson 1973, Nichols et al. 1983). This phenomenon is perhaps nowhere more apparent than on the High Plains, where weather determines not only the winter range of a population but also age and sex ratios, local movements, wetland use, and microhabitat selection. For example, the abundance of waterfowl during midwinter in Colorado decreases during winters with below-average mean temperatures and above-average snowfall (Colo. Div. Wildl., unpubl. data). Similarly, the distribution of Canada geese may be influenced by winter weather conditions (LeFebvre and Raveling 1967).

Second-order selection, the use of habitats on a local scale, is also affected by weather. Precipitation prior to and during winter can have varied effects on waterfowl through its impact on reservoir water levels, turbidity, availability of alternate wetlands, and production of natural and agricultural foods. Reservoir levels must be high enough to provide open water in winter, but not so high as to inundate flats and beaches used by loafing ducks and geese (Rutherford 1970). High pool levels may flood areas used by feeding dabbling ducks during fall and spring migration (Patterson 1982). Turbidity is usually high when reservoir water levels are high or fluctuating, which may eliminate aquatic plants

and invertebrates (Peltier and Welch 1970). Sufficient precipitation to maintain river bottoms and associated warm water sloughs is critical to wintering ducks in the High Plains (Hopper 1968).

Equally important is the manner in which precipitation affects the distribution and amount of available foods, thereby influencing the distribution and number of wintering birds (Rutherford 1970, Owen and Cook 1977). The quantity and distribution of crops are extremely important for refuging geese because a reduction in waste corn can increase movements that result in higher mortality from hunting (Frederick et al. 1987). Continued availability of waste grain throughout winter also may affect subsequent reproduction of Canada geese (Joyner et al. 1984). Mallard body condition and movements also are affected by the availability of waste grain (Owen and Cook 1977).

Unlike some wintering areas such as the Central Valley of California or the Mississippi Alluvial Valley, in which increased rainfall enhances waterfowl feeding opportunities (Miller 1986, Delnicki and Reinecke 1986), winter precipitation on the Northern High Plains generally has detrimental effects (Whyte and Bolen 1984). Low-growing green forage and waste cereal grain quickly become snow covered. Although geese normally can feed under as much as 10 cm of dry snow (Philippona 1966, Sturdy 1972, Newton and Campbell 1973), and ducks can obtain grain under 5 cm of snow, feeding efficiency is reduced. Beyond these depths, grain may become unavailable. Waterfowl then search for patches of food in wind-blown areas, in openings created by cattle (Jorde et al. 1983), or in cattle feedlots (Colo. Div. Wildl., unpubl. data). Unharvested standing grain, as well as natural seed heads, are important under these conditions.

Low temperatures that accompany storm fronts affect third-order selection by freezing wetlands, thereby reducing the amount of available habitat. Shallow wetlands, which frequently harbor aquatic invertebrates, are often the first to freeze. Thus, the quantity and nutritional quality of foods are affected by weather.

Energy expenditures of wintering waterfowl also are influenced by weather. Thermoregulation may be particularly important for ducks. For example, the average high temperature in Texas (11.4 C) is only 1.5 degrees cooler than Mississippi (12.9 C), but the mean low temperature is 6.5 degrees less. Colorado temperatures are considerably lower, averaging 40-50% colder than Texas and 68% (highs) to 120% (lows) colder than Mississippi. Using these temperature data, Ringelman (unpubl. data) developed a computer model to estimate thermoregulatory costs of wintering mallards. He concluded that winter thermoregulatory costs of mallards in Mississippi were 45% less than costs incurred by mallards in Texas. Texas birds had thermoregulatory costs that averaged 31% less than Colorado mallards. Such contrasts in just thermoregulation would seemingly affect regional differences in mallard time and energy budgets.

Emigration in response to weather is a well-known phenomena that drives migrants south during the fall (Bellrose 1957) and also causes long-distance movements of winter "residents" (Bennett and Bolen 1978, Colo. Div. Wildl., unpubl. data). A differential migration by age and sex causes the percentage of males to increase as temperatures decline (Alford and Bolen 1977, Jorde et al. 1984), resulting in northern populations that are comprised mostly of adult males (Anderson and Timkin 1972). Jorde et al. (1984) found that energetically costly activities such as courtship and aggression decreased, whereas field-feeding activity increased, in response to cold weather. In Colorado, mallards generally increase field-feeding time in response to heavy snowfall and moderate cold, but during periods of extreme cold (<-25 C) may cease feeding and flight activity and remain on roost areas in heat-conserving postures (bill tucked under the wing, feet and legs in the plumage, orientation into the wind, etc.; Colo. Div. Wildl., unpubl. data). Similar behavior has been observed among wintering Canada geese (Helm 1951, Hanson 1965, Philippona 1966, Koerner 1971, Raveling et al. 1972).

Lastly, a growing body of data, based largely on qualitative information, indicate that waterfowl, in part, can mitigate the effects of severe weather through selection of appropriate microhabitats (Jorde 1986). Along High Plains riverine areas, mallards often select roost sites in areas sheltered by high banks and trees (Jorde et al. 1984) or in wetlands derived from warm-water sources, such as warm-water sloughs. Such areas are consistently warmer than "ambient" temperatures at other sites (Jorde et al. 1984). Moreover, the other 3 components of microclimate (wind, radiation, and humidity; Gates 1968) also tend to be highly favorable.

Wetlands.—Given, therefore, that weather is a primary factor in wetland selection, what are the characteristics of wetlands selected and what resources are derived from them? To the casual observer, the large reservoirs in the High Plains would appear to be valuable waterfowl wetlands, because it is on these areas that waterfowl often concentrate in large numbers (Fig. 7). Reservoirs afford relatively secure resting locations because the widely fluctuating water levels typical of High Plains reservoirs minimize growth of emergent vegetation, thereby providing open visibility. Following sub-freezing temperatures, waterfowl may continue to use open water areas maintained in reservoirs by underwater currents or by body heat and/or foot movements of the birds. Reservoirs also may serve as information centers for the location of food (Ward and Zahavi 1973, Caccamise and Morrison 1986) and afford

Fig. 7. Extreme water-level fluctuations typical of High Plains reservoirs prohibit the development of emergent plants, thereby creating open shorelines attractive to resting waterfowl. Steep-sided banks and trees adjacent to such areas enhance the thermal qualities of roost sites during winter (photograph by J. K. Ringelman).

a roosting center that may reduce the risks of predation (Hamilton 1971, Weatherhead 1984).

Primary roosts, such as reservoirs, warm-water sloughs, and canals, also serve as courtship arenas for ducks (Colo. Div. Wildl., unpubl. data). After pairing, mallards segregate themselves spatially from unpaired birds (Jorde 1981), probably in an attempt to minimize encounters with conspecific courting drakes (Heitmeyer 1985). Thus, as winter progresses and a higher percentage of birds become paired, large reservoirs may become increasingly dominated by unpaired, courting individuals.

Small man-made and natural wetlands are used by waterfowl to attain their energetic, social, and nutritional needs (Heitmeyer and Vohs 1984b). These habitats are among the most fertile wetlands in the region, and are particularly important as feeding areas during fall. These wetlands are the earliest to freeze and

therefore are largely unavailable to wintering waterfowl in the northern portion of the High Plains. Accordingly, lotic wetlands such as warm-water sloughs, rivers, canals, and ditches provide most of the alternate areas used during winter (Fig. 8). During mild weather, rivers and irrigation canals run freely, affording loafing sites along banks, or in the case of rivers, on islands and sandbars. Generally at temperatures of -7 to -18 C, major rivers form slush ice, which is carried downstream and deposited along bends or behind obstructions. Subsequent cold temperatures may cause these areas to freeze. Some major rivers freeze completely, and the shallow portions always ice-over during winter in the northern High Plains. Regrettably, these areas possess the most suitable water depth for feeding ducks. As discussed by Jorde (1981), considerable yearly variation in ice cover may exist.

Warm-water sloughs are fed by warm-

Fig. 8. Warm-water sloughs, rivers, and canals offer desirable roosting areas that remain unfrozen during much of the winter. Herbaceous aquatic plants provide vegetative foods and substrate for invertebrates (photograph by J. K. Ringelman).

water springs year-round, and therefore never freeze. Their occurrence coincides most often with sandy alluvial soils near major rivers. In Colorado, ducks and some geese retreat to these wetlands in the face of severely cold weather. Vegetative foods, such as watercress (*Nasturtium officinale*) and duckweed, commonly occur in these wetlands. In warm-water sloughs, snails (*Physa* spp.) can attain densities of 0.22 to 0.76 g dry weight/kg wet vegetation (Colo. Div. Wildl., unpubl. data). Ditches, particularly those that serve as drains for nearby reservoirs, share most of the characteristics of warm-water sloughs. Evidence to date indicates that warm-water sloughs and ditches may be the key to maintaining wintering waterfowl on the central High Plains.

Aquatic Vegetation.—Unconsolidated bottoms and frequent wave action inhibit development of submerged macrophytes in reservoirs. As a consequence, waterfowl food plants often are scarce or absent. Some reservoirs that experience minimal water-level fluctuations or that have shal-

low basins may contain large stands of cattail. Without management action, these wetlands quickly become unattractive to waterfowl.

Small, shallow, man-made and natural wetlands, which are available during migration and early winter, often contain high diversities of aquatic vegetation. Bulrush (*Scirpus* spp.) and cattail dominate the upper size range of emergents, whereas rushes (*Eleocharis*, spp., *Juncus*, spp.), barnyardgrass, sedges, smartweed, and dock (*Rumex* spp.) typically dominate the understory. Several varieties of pondweeds (*Potamogeton* spp.), along with coontail (*Ceratophyllum* spp.), buttercup (*Ranunculus* spp.), water milfoil (*Myriophyllum* spp.), and bladderwort (*Utricularia* spp.) occur as common submergent species. These species also serve as a substrate for aquatic macroinvertebrates (Krull 1970).

Riverbed scouring by sand and silt during periods of high flow limits vegetation development in many river systems. Perhaps the most important vegetative components of these areas are tree and shrub vegetation in the floodplain (Fig. 8). Woody species provide thermal cover and shelter from, as well as perch sites for, avian predators. Invasion by woody species has caused changes in the physiognomy and hydrology of the Platte River due to bank and island stabilization (U.S. Fish and Wildlife Service 1981). Declines in the cottonwood communities throughout several High Plains river systems forewarn of radical changes in these riparian systems. Concomitant changes in the macrohabitats and microhabitats available to migrating and wintering waterfowl can be anticipated in the future.

HABITAT MANAGEMENT
Agricultural Grains

Although we have sufficient knowledge to manage grain crops and can make great strides on governmentally-owned land, the vast majority of waterfowl use habitat that is outside of our realm of direct control. Ultimately, agricultural economics, directed by supply and demand and swayed by federal farm subsidies, will determine the abundance and composition of grain crops. Thus, this section should best be viewed as what could be done; a review of the status of our knowledge.

Efforts to manage agricultural grains for waterfowl must concentrate on: (1) increasing the amount of grain available, (2) providing grain that has maximum metabolizable energy, and (3) enhancing the availability of grain through selection of variety and postharvest treatment. The amount of corn remaining after harvest is a function of moisture content of the corn (Baldassarre et al. 1983), harvest operation, slope of the field, insects, and disease. Moisture at the time of harvest is the variable most easily controlled by the manager. Over twice as much waste corn remains in the field when moisture content is 14-21% than when moisture

exceeds 21% (Baldassarre et al. 1983). Additionally, postharvest treatments that reduce ground litter are beneficial, so long as grain density is not reduced appreciably. To a limited extent, disking accomplishes this objective by shattering ears while reducing litter. However, burning corn stubble accomplishes litter reduction without a commensurate decline in grain abundance (Baldassarre et al. 1983), thereby making such fields attractive to feeding waterfowl (Baldassarre and Bolen 1984).

Secondary availability is the accessibility of grain following the immediate postharvest. Snowfall and cattle grazing are the most important components of secondary availability on the High Plains. In Colorado, mallards and Canada geese use standing, unharvested corn during periods of heavy snowfall (Ringelman, pers. data). Cattle grazing in corn stubble generally enhance availability by breaking ears and scattering kernels. Jorde et al. (1983) found that after a snowstorm, cattle expose ground as a result of walking and foraging. Ducks also seek food in cattle feedlots, especially during severe weather. Mallards, in particular, make extensive use of feedlots in Nebraska (Jorde et al. 1983) and Colorado (Colo. Div. Wildl., unpubl. data). Grain stored for cattle, undigested grain in cattle feces, and the feces themselves are consumed.

The growth form of cereal grains may influence its use by waterfowl. Geese prefer to feed in short vegetation and are reluctant to land in standing plants >14 cm high (Kear 1967). Generally, geese will not land in standing corn (Helm 1951, Koerner 1971), but will walk into standing corn or reach for ears from atop snowdrifts. Mallards, however, will land among standing cornstalks and are not reluctant to land in and feed upon unharvested barley (Colo. Div. Wildl., unpubl. data).

Metabolizable energy (ME) of grain

varies by species and even by variety within a species (Sugden 1971). Sugden (1971) proposed that ME should be considered before selecting varieties to plant. Clark et al. (1986) extended this concept to recognize that different grains have inherently different physical structures that influence the rate at which waterfowl can ingest them. Thus, the ME and the morphology of the grain and seed head should be considered in crop selection.

Kernel wastage can be increased by harvesting when moisture content is <21%. Wide swaths of harvested corn should be separated by several rows of unharvested stalks, thereby providing a "snow fence" to enhance the availability of grain on the ground as well as provide a reserve of food that will remain above even the deepest snow. Stubble should be burned, assuming such a practice is compatible with soil erosion considerations. Corn should be planted in blocks of rows running perpendicular to one another. This helps assure that the tops of some rows will be exposed by the prevailing winds during heavy snow. Lastly, in the event of a heavy snowfall, cattle should be allowed to graze in the field to help open up snow cover and increase grain availability.

Natural Foods

Management for natural foods, seeds, and invertebrates usually necessitates manipulation of wetland plant communities. A large body of literature exists on this subject (see Spohrer 1975, Knighton 1982), particularly on the topic of water-level manipulation and its effects on plant composition (Robel 1962, Harris and Marshall 1963, Meeks 1969, Kadlec and Wentz 1974, Fredrickson and Taylor 1982). Management of seasonally-flooded impoundments to encourage the development of moist-soil plants has its origins in high precipitation regions of the U.S. with climates different than those encoun-

tered on the High Plains. Nevertheless, many principles that guide moist-soil management in these areas may be applicable to more arid regions.

Initial development of moist-soil wetlands is expensive, because precise control of water through dikes, water-control structures, and pumps is essential. Details of contruction design and management are available from several sources (Fredrickson and Taylor 1982). Specific vegetative responses to drawdowns are dependent upon the types of seeds present in the soil, the timing, duration, and speed of drawdown, and the age of the wetland. Several plant foods important in the diet of migratory and wintering mallards, such as barnyardgrass and smartweeds (Jorde et al. 1983), respond well to moist-soil management (Fredrickson and Taylor 1982). Aquatic macroinvertebrates typically increase in abundance following reflooding of wetlands.

The expense of water needed to create and maintain man-made wetlands can be prohibitive in some portions of the High Plains. Where ditch water is available along the western edge and river bottoms of the region, costs may range from $4-20/1,000 m^3 (J. Neutze, pers. commun.). Water obtained from underground sources, such as the Ogallala Aquifer, costs from $20-31/1,000 m^3 to pump to the surface (Young et al. 1982). Water costs, as well as initial construction and maintenance expense, should be included in the total price of developing a small waterfowl wetland.

Roost Sites and Microhabitats

Aerators have been used to maintain open water for waterfowl at reservoirs such as Two Buttes in southeastern Colorado. If electrical service is available, this has proven to be a cost-effective technique (Rutherford 1970). Islands in reservoirs or sandbars in rivers also attract waterfowl.

During periods of extreme cold, factors

that slow the flow of water through warm-water sloughs may cause portions of these wetlands to freeze. It therefore may be necessary to periodically remove fallen trees and other debris blocking the waterway. Beaver (*Castor canadensis*) dams are a common problem, and control of beaver is an important practice on these areas. Hopper (1983) recommended trapping beaver and removing their dams beginning at the spring source and continuing downstream until all beavers are eliminated or until the point is reached where even unobstructed flow would cool to the point of freezing. Cattail control may also be necessary to keep water flowing adequately (Pederson et al. 1989).

Management for optimal microhabitats for wintering waterfowl has seldom, if ever, been attempted in any wintering area. Nevertheless, the potential for microhabitat management exists. Wetlands with sheer or steep-sided banks adjacent to broad, gently sloping shoreline areas provide desirable loafing sites because they provide thermal refugia. Creating a long, narrow wetland with the long axis oriented east-west would not only maximize the shoreline-to-surface-area ratio, but also would provide maximum southern shoreline exposure. Undoubtedly, herbaceous vegetation, shrubs, and trees are important components of the thermal environment of riverine and canal roosting ducks. Management of such cover to minimize exposure of waterfowl to prevailing winds and drifting snow could reduce the thermoregulatory costs of birds, although the potential benefits have yet to be quantified.

Recreational Use

Hunting plays an important role in habitat use by waterfowl. Therefore, refuge areas play a vital part in maintaining winter waterfowl populations. On the High Plains, refuge areas are available both spatially and temporally. Urban areas afford spatial protection to thousands of Canada geese wintering along the Front Range of Colorado. Canada geese, in particular, seem to adapt readily to an urban environment that provides abundant bluegrass forage and wetlands. Their abundance in urban areas is a growing problem. A spatial refuge also is effectively maintained by the vast ice surface that surrounds ice holes on large reservoirs, although an increasing number of hunters venture forth onto ice to hunt these areas. In general, however, the open visibility afforded by such a situation enables birds to detect and avoid hunters, and harvest from these wetlands is low. Conventional refuges, posted as "no hunting" areas, also are created by state agencies and private individuals as a means to attract and maintain huntable or viewable waterfowl populations.

Sunset marks the closure of hunting and a decrease in human disturbance at wetlands. Waterfowl respond to this temporal refuge by occupying sites they normally would not use during the day. In Colorado, warm-water sloughs and toe-drains below reservoir dams are used in this manner (Colo. Div. Wildl., unpubl. data). Many private hunting clubs further regulate temporal use of wetlands through club rules that restrict shooting to particular days or hours within days. Several state agencies have imposed similar rules on government-owned management areas. Many High Plains states at middle and low latitudes opt for 2 or 3 hunting periods within the federal season framework. Hunting closures between periods provide waterfowl an opportunity to use wetlands that they previously avoided because of hunting disturbance.

Fishermen, fishing primarily from boats, are in ever-increasing conflict with waterfowl on large reservoirs. Statutes vary among states, but many reservoirs on the High Plains are open to boat fishing until freeze up, and thereafter to ice fishermen. Some agencies have responded by establishing fishing seasons or demarking closed areas of reservoirs with buoy lines or other physical boundary markers.

A conflict exists between the biological needs of wintering waterfowl and the practices of the hunting public. Sportsmen select wetlands to hunt based primarily on their use by waterfowl. These same wetlands, typically palustrine emergent or river streambed classes (Cowardin et al. 1979), often provide ducks the aquatic macroinvertebrates necessary for a balanced diet and provide favorable thermal environments for roosting and pair isolation. The effects of excluding ducks from such wetlands are unknown, because we do not yet recognize the duration, measured in either hours or days, that ducks need access to such areas in order to acquire needed resources. The challenge lies in striking an optimal balance between hunting opportunity and the biological needs of waterfowl.

Diseases and Predation

Avian cholera (*Pasteurella multocida*) is the disease that most consistently kills waterfowl on the High Plains. Traditional "hot spots" are located in northern Texas and south-central Nebraska, but documented losses have occurred in almost every High Plains region (Brand 1984, Friend 1987). Conditions that contribute to avian cholera outbreaks have not been described conclusively (Jensen and Williams 1964, Rosen 1971). Severe winter weather has been linked circumstantially to outbreaks in the Chesapeake Bay (Locke et al. 1970). Overcrowding of waterfowl also is cited as a factor associated with cholera outbreaks (Rosen and Bishchoff 1949, Petrides and Bryant 1951, Klukas and Locke 1970). The stressful winter climate of the High Plains, and the tendency of waterfowl to concentrate in traditional riverine or reservoir roosts,

makes the region a likely host to future cholera die-offs.

Recommended management of avian cholera should focus on frequent monitoring for early detection of sick and dead birds and for rigorous collection of carcasses for incineration or sanitary disposal (Friend 1987). Large bird concentrations should be dispersed. Attempted habitat manipulations to minimize losses to avian cholera have met with mixed success. Temporarily draining wetlands at the focus of the outbreak may redistribute birds to wetlands that are less contaminated. In subfreezing temperatures, eliminating the warm-water source allows the wetland to freeze, thereby producing the same response as draining. The addition of large volumes of fresh water may dilute bacterial concentrations to less dangerous levels. Disinfection of wetlands is also possible, but is generally not practical, and the overall environmental impacts are unknown (Friend 1987).

Aspergillosis (*Aspergillus fumigatus*), a fungal disease, has caused mortalities in Canada geese (McDougle and Vaught 1968) and mallards (Herman 1943, Neff 1955). In the High Plains region, mallards are the most frequent victims. Epornitics involving mallards occurred in north-central Colorado during 1975 and 1976 (Adrian et al. 1978), and again in 1982 (Colo. Div. Wildl., unpubl. data). The spores are widely distributed in nature (Chute 1965), but waterfowl most frequently come in contact with them through moldy grain (McDiarmid 1955). Such contact usually occurs in response to adverse weather such as heavy snowfall, which causes feeding birds to shift from harvested cornfields to ensilage pits or feedlots where moldy grain is consumed (Locke 1987). Epornitics typically begin suddenly and end in <7 days (Adrian et al. 1978). In that brief time, several hundred to thousands of ducks may die. Treatments include disposing of moldy grain or hazing birds from problem areas (Locke 1987). Management of grain fields and supplemental feeding to assure food availability during severe weather may be preventive strategies.

During winter, avian predators such as bald eagles (*Haliaectus leucocephalus*) congregate near waterfowl concentration areas. Eagles frequently are seen feeding on waterfowl carcasses on reservoirs in eastern Colorado (Ringelman, pers. data). Prey availability has a large influence on eagle food habits. When winter is mild and water areas are open, fish are preferred. At the onset of cold weather and restricted fishing opportunity, however, bald eagles switch to waterfowl and small mammals as alternate prey (U.S. Fish and Wildlife Service 1981). Eagles also influence the behavior, and therefore the energy budgets, of wintering birds by causing them to take flight or remain alert (Jorde 1981, Colo. Div. Wildl., unpubl. data), and therefore are important to the survival processes of High Plains waterfowl both directly (through predation) and indirectly (through energy depletion).

Overlap of Management Practices with Other Areas

Problems in the management of large reservoirs for waterfowl are similar in all areas of the country. Waterfowl need (1) open water for resting, (2) aquatic vegetation that provides food and a substrate for invertebrates, (3) loafing areas, (4) nearby feeding sites, and (5) thermal cover (Rutherford 1970, Tamasier 1976, Hobaugh and Teer 1981). Reservoirs possess several attributes in their design and operation that pose special problems for waterfowl managers. These have been discussed previously, and include (1) water-level fluctuations resulting in failure of aquatic plants to become established in shallow water sites, (2) increased turbidity (Peltier and Welch 1970), (3) simplification of invertebrate communities (related to a lack of submerged

aquatic plants) (Driver 1977, Kaster and Jacobi 1978), and (4) flooding of beaches used as loafing sites by geese. In addition, grazing by livestock on lands adjacent to reservoirs (Whyte et al. 1981), shoreline development (Heinzenknecht and Paterson 1978), agriculture, urban pollution, recreational development, and repeated disturbance of loafing birds through uncontrolled hunting (Thomas 1976) are other problems associated with reservoir management.

Techniques to alleviate these effects are sometimes feasible in reservoirs, but often are not instituted because of funding and personnel limitations and difficulties in coordinating management efforts with the primary purposes of individual reservoirs. For example, flood-control lakes are allowed to fill when storage is needed to control downstream flooding, regardless of the needs of wintering waterfowl. Suggested management techniques to improve waterfowl habitat essentially are unchanged from those suggested by White and Malaher (1964). These include establishment of shallowly flooded subimpoundments separate from the main lake, establishment of food plants, properly timed water-level manipulations, refuge status for selected portions of the lake, and control of adjacent agriculture. Additionally, dispersal of birds at major concentration areas may be needed (Rutherford 1970).

Suggested management techniques for providing submerged and emergent plants include seasonal water-level management timed to allow both the establishment of plants and availability to waterfowl. Suggested water-level manipulations include holding pool levels low during January and February, gradually increasing the level from 1 March to 15 May, holding the level high through June, and then abruptly lowering the water level in early July to allow seed germination (Nelson et al. 1978). Reflooding should occur gradually from 1 October to 15 November and be maintained until mid-December to allow access of waterfowl to food plants. Unfortunately, these water-level regimes do not coincide with the normal water-storage patterns of irrigation reservoirs. In most years, reservoir managers begin filling reservoirs in September-November and continue to add water until freeze-up. During winter, pool levels are held constant to minimize the effect of ice action on the face of the dam. With little additional inflow during March-May, pool levels remain fairly constant until the call for irrigation water in June-August, when pool levels decline sharply to low levels.

Additional reservoir-management techniques include (1) fencing selected areas to exclude livestock, (2) seeding disturbed areas with annual grasses to alleviate turbidity problems (Hobaugh and Teer 1981), (3) maintaining adequate plant cover to control soil erosion, (4) providing artificial islands for loafing sites (Mills and MacIver 1964), and (5) planting windbreaks to provide thermal protection for loafing or roosting birds (Bennett and Bolen 1978).

CONCLUSIONS

Management schemes for waterfowl wintering on the High Plains must be tempered with a recognition of the origins of the habitat. Ducks and geese subsist on cereal grains grown as commercial crops and roost primarily on reservoirs and canals built to transport and retain water for agriculture. It is in many respects an artificial habitat with waterfowl as a by-product of human endeavors. Managers can purchase conservation pools of water in reservoirs to assure that a minimum amount of water is retained in a wetland, yet that reservoir will continue to undergo extreme water fluctuations as users draw upon this most valuable western resource. Farm practices might be modified by new technologies that make economic sense and concur-

rently benefit waterfowl, but conservation reserve programs, commodity price supports, and demand will continue to dictate whether a grain crop will be grown. Thus, the "big picture," that of first-order selection, is shaped by forces largely beyond the control of traditional wildlife management. This dependence upon irrigated agriculture suggests that future trends in agriculture should be monitored closely, with an eye towards potential impacts on waterfowl populations.

Unfortunately, federal farm programs, such as the Conservation Reserve Program (CRP) and others, may have minimal or negative impacts on wintering waterfowl on the High Plains. Among other goals, these programs are designed to reduce the abundance of cereal grains that are in surplus, hence contributing to the decline in important winter waterfowl foods. Because reservoirs are secure wetlands that may continue to increase in numbers, "swampbuster" provisions of the CRP and water-bank programs would have little impact on preservation of large water areas. Some benefits may accrue, however, from protection of smaller wetlands used during fall and early winter.

Under projections of rising energy costs and groundwater depletion, corn is the first irrigated crop to become economically unfeasible (Sharp 1979). The least favorable economic models predict the gradual disappearance of irrigated corn from the region overlying the Ogallala Aquifer (which includes much of the High Plains) by as early as 1990 (Young et al. 1982:129). Impacts of groundwater depletion already are being felt in northern Texas and eastern Colorado, where former corn land has been converted to dryland winter wheat or cotton.

Past waterfowl management practices on the High Plains have emphasized regulations, mostly season dates and area closures, to control the distribution and harvest of birds. Habitat management to meet the specific needs of migratory or wintering waterfowl has been minimal. The management practice most often performed is planting grain crops for food, but even these plantings have not been designed to maximize food availability or net energy acquisition. A lack of intensive habitat management is understandable; resources have been plentiful in the past, and little information has been available on management practices that address the needs of waterfowl during this period. But times have changed. Innovative management approaches are going to be necessary to address questions of increased hunting demand and urbanization in the face of a loss in wetland diversity and declines in cereal grain abundance.

One promising approach is to consider waterfowl hunting as an income-producing venture that is a natural complement to agribusiness. Chamberlain (1984) took this approach when analyzing the economic benefits of crop production in concert with fee hunting for waterfowl on the Texas High Plains. She concluded that the supplementary income from waterfowl hunting could help offset economic losses resulting from dwindling water supplies.

RESEARCH NEEDS

The magnitude of mortality experienced by waterfowl during fall and winter and the sources of that mortality are largely undocumented. We know that heterogeneity exists within a population, but the basis for such differences are not understood. Furthermore, the contention that events within a life cycle are "linked," and as such account for "cross-seasonal" effects, remains an untested hypothesis. Despite much research into winter "body condition" of waterfowl, the relationship between condition and reproductive performance is unknown. Investigations of field-feeding behavior

need to be continued, with emphasis on estimating ultimate carrying capacity of an area in relation to efficiency of crop use and weather. Small-scale habitat manipulations down to the level of microhabitat may prove effective in northern wintering areas, but we first must better understand a bird's criteria for selection at the microhabitat level. Finally, we must enhance our knowledge of why ducks and geese use sensitive but key areas such as warm-water sloughs and ditches, and attempt to strike a balance between the needs of waterfowl and hunting opportunity.

Management-research experiments, wherein treatments are evaluated in a research context, would enhance our understanding of waterfowl. Unfortunately, preimpoundment studies of riverine/reservoir wetlands systems are rare. Until comprehensive studies of the use of natural wetlands by waterfowl prior to impoundment are undertaken, the net effects of reservoir construction on waterfowl will remain poorly understood. Related research on impacts of reservoirs on riverine systems also is needed.

SUMMARY

The development of reservoirs and irrigated agriculture has transformed the High Plains region into an important migratory and winter habitat for waterfowl, particularly mallards and Canada geese. Despite severe climatic conditions, especially in the northern portion of the region, waterfowl fulfill their biological requirements by exploiting a diversity of wetland habitats. Case histories indicate a rapid and dramatic response by waterfowl to the creation of new reservoirs, which has resulted in northward shifts in the winter distribution of some species. But reservoirs are not without their costs. Downstream riparian habitats have been severely affected as a result of altered stream-flow volumes, timing of water releases, changes in water quality and temperature, and other factors. Moreover, reservoirs are far from ideal waterfowl habitats. Extreme water-level fluctuations, wave action, and sedimentation are physical conditions that hinder aquatic plant and invertebrate populations. Thus, although valuable as roosting, loafing, and courting areas, reservoirs fall short of meeting the complete habitat needs of waterfowl.

Small, natural wetlands complement the needs of ducks and geese until cold weather freezes these habitats. Thereafter, birds depend on warm-water sloughs, ditches, canals, and rivers in addition to reservoirs. These provide supplemental invertebrate and plant foods, a favorable microclimate, and space for paired individuals to isolate themselves from conspecifics. However, unlike reservoirs, these wetlands often do not afford security from predators, including hunters. Consequently, management of these areas merits special consideration.

Irrigation enabled the cultivation of cereal grains in the arid High Plains. Grains, particularly corn, provide the abundant, high-energy food that is the primary component in the waterfowl diet. Nevertheless, grains cannot meet the complete food needs of birds, because they commonly lack essential amino acids and minerals. Supplementary foods, including aquatic invertebrates and seeds and leafy portions of plants, are consumed by waterfowl in quantities sufficient to balance their nutritional demands.

Some habitat components have a greater potential for management than others. Least manageable are reservoirs, which are constructed and operated to provide water for humans, not for waterfowl. Demands on water and management needs related to dam maintenance are frequently at odds with beneficial waterfowl management practices. Construction of shallowly-flooded subimpoundments, establishment of food plants, properly

timed water-level manipulations, and control of disturbance (especially hunting) have proven effective in some management programs. Smaller wetlands often can be managed effectively by providing desired vegetation structure through mechanical or water-level manipulations, managing moist-soil plants for food, and providing suitable refuge areas. In the northern High Plains, preventing wetlands from freezing by maintaining water flow is important. Control of beaver and emergent vegetation often are enough to accomplish this objective.

Agricultural foods, particularly corn, are easily managed. Combine operation, slope of the field, insects, and disease are all determinants of the amount of waste grain remaining in the field, but corn moisture and postharvest treatment are the most important considerations for managers. Harvesting corn when its moisture content is <21%, then burning the field or otherwise enhancing waste grain availability, are effective techniques. Because snowfall reduces grain availability, some ears should remain on standing stalks, and row orientation should be planned to provide snow-free areas. After a snowfall, cattle enhance corn availability by exposing ears and kernels.

Despite the potential of these and other techniques, important factors remain beyond the control of managers. Groundwater depletion and associated loss of irrigated grain crops could radically alter the future distribution of wintering waterfowl. Weather will affect food resources and energetic/thermoregulatory demand, with concomitant increases in mortality from stress-related diseases such as avian cholera. Hunting and other human disturbance will continue to alter the habitat use of birds. The challenge for managers is to meet the needs of waterfowl in the face of conflicting human desires and anticipated changes in food and wetland resources of the High Plains.

LITERATURE CITED

Adrian, W. J., T. R. Spraker, and R. B. Davies. 1978. Epornitics of aspergillosis in mallards in north central Colorado. J. Wildl. Dis. 14:212-217.

Alford, J. R., and E. G. Bolen. 1977. Influence of winter temperatures on pintail sex ratios in Texas. Southwest. Nat. 21:554-556.

Anderson, B. W., and R. L. Timkin. 1972. Sex and age ratios and weights of common mergansers. J. Wildl. Manage. 36:1127-1133.

Anderson, H. G. 1959. Food habits of migratory ducks in Illinois. Ill. Nat. Hist. Surv. Bull. 27:289-344.

Arthur D. Little, Inc. 1982. Six-state High Plains Ogalalla Aquifer regional resources study. Study element B-9: dryland farming assessment. Arthur D. Little, Inc. Denver, Colo. 299 pp.

Arthur, G. C. 1968. Farming for Canada geese. Pages 113-115 in R. L. Hine and C. Schoenfeld, eds. Canada goose management, current continental problems and programs. Dembar Educ. Res. Serv., Inc., Madison, Wis.

Bailey, R. G. 1978. Description of the ecoregions of the United States. USDA For. Serv., Intermountain Reg., Ogden, Utah. 77 pp.

Baldassarre, G. A., R. J. Whyte, E. E. Quinlan, and E. G. Bolen. 1983. Dynamics and quality of waste corn available to postbreeding waterfowl in Texas. Wildl. Soc. Bull. 11:25-31.

———, and E. G. Bolen. 1984. Field-feeding ecology of waterfowl wintering on the southern High Plains of Texas. J. Wildl. Manage. 48:63-71.

Bellrose, F. C. 1957. A spectacular waterfowl migration through central North America. Ill. Nat. Hist. Surv., Biol. Note No. 36. 24 pp.

———. 1976. Ducks, geese and swans of North America. Second ed. Stackpole Books, Harrisburg, Pa. 543 pp.

Bennett, J. W., and E. G. Bolen. 1978. Stress response in wintering green-winged teal. J. Wildl. Manage. 42:81-86.

Bolen, E. G., G. A. Baldassarre, and F. S. Guthery. 1989. Playa lakes. Pages 341-365 in L. M. Smith, R. L. Pederson, and R. M. Kaminski eds. Habitat management for migrating and wintering waterfowl in North America. Texas Tech Univ. Press, Lubbock.

Bossenmaier, E. F., and W. H. Marshall. 1958. Field-feeding by waterfowl in southwestern Manitoba. Wildl. Monogr. 1. 32 pp.

Brand, C. J. 1984. Avian cholera in the Central and Mississippi flyways during 1979-80. J. Wildl. Manage. 48:399-406.

Buller, R. J. 1964. Central Flyway. Pages 209-232 in J. P. Linduska, ed. Waterfowl tomorrow. U.S. Dep. Int., Fish and Wildl. Serv. Washington, D.C. 770 pp.

———. 1975. Redistribution of waterfowl: influence of water, protection, and feed. Proc. Int. Waterfowl Symp. 1:143-154.

Caccamise, D. F., and D. W. Morrison. 1986. Avian communal roosting: implications of diurnal activity centers. Am. Nat. 128.191-198.

Chamberlain, P. A. 1984. Waterfowl and agriculture—an assessment of wintering waterfowl management and land-use economics on the Texas high plains. Ph.D. Dissertation, Texas Tech Univ., Lubbock, 547 pp.

Chute, H. L. 1965. Diseases caused by fungi. Pages 494-511 in H. E. Biester and L. H. Schwarte, eds. Diseases of poultry. Iowa State Univ. Press, Ames.

Clark, R. G., H. Greenwood, and L. G. Sugden. 1986. Influence of grain characteristics on optimal diet of field-feeding mallards. J. Appl. Ecol. 23:763-771.

Cowardin, L. M., V. Carter, F. C. Golet, and E. T. LaRoe. 1979. Classification of wetlands and deepwater habitats of the United States. U.S. Dept. Int., FWS/OBS-79/31. 103 pp.

Crouch, G. L. 1978. Effects of protection from livestock grazing on a bottomland wildlife habitat in northeastern Colorado. Pages 118-125 in W. D. Graul and S. J. Bissell, coordinators. Lowland river and stream habitat in Colorado: a symposium. Colo. Chapter, The Wildl. Soc. and Colo. Audubon Counc.

Delnicki, D., and K. J. Reinecke. 1986. Mid-winter food use and body weights of mallards and wood ducks in Mississippi. J. Wildl. Manage. 50:43-51.

Driver, E. R. 1977. Chironomid communities in small prairie ponds: some characteristics and controls. Freshwater Biol. 7:121-133.

Eddleman, W. R., C. T. Patterson, and F. L. Knopf. 1985a. Interspecific relationships between American coots and waterfowl during fall migration. Wilson Bull. 97:463-472.

———, F. L. Knopf, and C. T. Patterson. 1985b. Chronology of migration by American coots in Oklahoma. J. Wildl. Manage. 49:241-246.

Flickinger, E. L. 1981. Weather conditions associated with beginning of northward migration departure of snow geese. J. Wildl. Manage. 45:516-520.

Folk-Williams, J. A., S. C. Fry, and L. Hilgendorf. 1985. Water in the west. Vol. 3. Western water flows to the cities. Island Press, Covelo, Calif. 217 pp.

Frederick, R. B., W. R. Clark, and E. E. Klaas. 1987. Behavior, energetics, and management of refuging waterfowl: a simulation model. Wildl. Monogr. 96. 35 pp.

Fredrickson, L. H., and T. S. Taylor. 1982. Management of seasonally flooded impoundments for wildlife. U.S. Dep. Int., Fish and Wildl. Serv. Resour. Publ. No. 148. 27 pp.

Friend, M. 1987. Avian cholera. Pages 69-92 *in* M. Friend, ed. Field guide to wildlife diseases. Vol. 1. General field procedures and diseases of migratory birds. U.S. Dep. Int., Fish and Wildl. Serv. Resour Publ. No. 167.

Gates, D. M. 1968. Energy exchange and ecology. Bioscience 18:90-95.

Gordon, D. H. 1981. Condition, feeding ecology, and behavior of mallards wintering in northcentral Oklahoma. M.S. Thesis, Oklahoma State Univ., Stillwater. 68 pp.

Graul, W. D. 1982. Lowland riparian cottonwood community study. Program Narrative. Colo. Div. Wildl., Fed. Aid Proj. W-136-R and W-124-R, Job 4. Denver. 7 pp.

Grieb, J. R., and E. L. Boeker. 1954. Waterfowl migration studies and their application to management in Colorado. Trans. North Am. Wildl. Conf. 19:195-210.

Hamilton, W. D. 1971. Geometry for the selfish herd. J. Theoretical Biol. 31:295-311.

Hanson, H. C. 1965. The giant Canada goose. Southern Illinois Univ. Press, Carbondale. 226 pp.

Harris, S. W., and W. H. Marshall. 1963. Ecology of water level manipulations on a northern marsh. Ecology 44:331-343.

Heinzenknecht, G. B., and J. R. Paterson. 1978. Effects of large dams and reservoirs on wildlife habitat. Pages 101-147 *in* W. L. Chadwick, ed. Environmental effects of large dams. Am. Soc. Civil Engineers, New York, N.Y. 225 pp.

Heitmeyer, M. E. 1980. Characteristics of wetland habitats and waterfowl populations in Oklahoma. M.S. Thesis, Oklahoma State Univ., Stillwater. 268 pp.

———. 1985. Wintering strategies of female mallards related to dynamics of lowland hardwood wetlands in the upper Mississippi Delta. Ph.D. Thesis, Univ. Missouri, Columbia. 376 pp.

———. 1988. Protein costs of the prebasic molt of female mallards. Condor 90:263-266.

———, and P. A. Vohs, Jr. 1984a. Characteristics of wetlands used by migrant dabbling ducks in Oklahoma, USA. Wildfowl 35:61-70.

———, and———. 1984b. Distribution and habitat use of waterfowl wintering in Oklahoma. J. Wildl. Manage. 48:51-62.

Helm, L. G. 1951. Effects of Canada geese on crops and soils in central Missouri. M.A. Thesis, Univ. Missouri, Columbia. 107 pp.

Herman, C. M. 1943. An outbreak of mycotic pneumonia in mallards. Calif. Fish and Game 29:204.

High Plains Associates. 1982. Six-state High Plains-Ogallala Aquifer regional resources study. Camp Dresser and McKee Inc., Black and Veatch, Arthur D. Little, Inc. Denver, Colo. 453 pp.

High Plains Study Council. 1982. A summary of results of the Ogallala Aquifer regional study, with recommendations to the Secretary of Commerce and Congress. Econ. Dev. Admin., Washington, D.C. 61 pp.

Hill, F. W., D. L. Anderson, R. Renner, and L. B. Carew, Jr. 1960. Studies of the metabolizable energy of grain and grain products for chickens. Poultry Sci. 39:573-579.

Hobaugh, W. C., and J. G. Teer. 1981. Waterfowl use characteristics of flood prevention lakes in north-central Texas. J. Wildl. Manage. 45:16-26.

Hopper, R. M. 1968. Wetlands of Colorado. Colo. Dep. Game, Fish, and Parks Tech. Publ. No. 22. 88 pp.

———. 1983. Management for waterfowl-aquatic ecosystems. Pages 43-45 *in* R. A. Schmidt, Sr., ed. Management of cottonwood-willow riparian associations in Colorado. Colo. Chap., The Wildl. Society, Fort Collins.

———, H. D. Funk, and D. R. Anderson. 1978. Age specificity in mallards banded postseason in eastern Colorado. J. Wildl. Manage. 42:263-270.

Hunt, C. B. 1967. Physiography of the United States. W. H. Freeman and Co., San Francisco, Calif. 480 pp.

Jenkins, R. M., L. R. Aggus, and G. R. Ploskey. 1985. Inventory of U.S. reservoirs. U.S. Fish and Wildl. Serv. Fed. Aid to Fish Restor. Act, Adm. Fund. Washington, D.C. 9 pp.

Jensen, W. I., and C. S. Williams. 1964. Botulism and fowl cholera. Pages 333-341 *in* J. P. Linduska, ed. Waterfowl tomorrow. U.S. Dep. Int., Fish and Wildl. Serv., Washington, D.C.

Johnson, D. H. 1980. The comparison of usage and availability measurements for evaluating resource preference. Ecology 61:65-71.

Jorde, D. G. 1981. Winter and spring staging ecology of mallards in south central Nebraska. M.S. Thesis, Univ. North Dakota, Grand Forks. 116 pp.

———. 1986. Nutritional and thermodynamic aspects of the ecology of black ducks wintering in Maine. Ph.D. Thesis, Univ. Maine, Orono. 113 pp.

———, G. L. Krapu, and R. D. Crawford. 1983. Feeding ecology of mallards wintering in Nebraska. J. Wildl. Manage. 47:1044-1053.

———,———,———, and M. A. Hay. 1984. Effects of weather on habitat selection and behavior of mallards wintering in Nebraska. Condor 86:258-265.

Joyner, D. E., R. D. Authur, and B. N. Jacobson. 1984. Winter weight dynamics, grain consumption, and reproductive potential in Canada geese. Condor 86:275-280.

Kadlec, J. A., and W. A. Wentz. 1974. State-of-the-art survey and evaluation of marsh plant establishment techniques: induced and natural. 2 vols. Natl. Tech. Inf. Serv., Springfield, Va. 229 pp.

Kaster, J. L., and G. Z. Jacobi. 1978. Benthic

macroinvertebrates of a fluctuating reservoir. Freshwater Biol. 8:283-290.

Kear, J. 1967. Feeding habits of the greylag goose (*Anser anser*) in Iceland, with reference to its interaction with agriculture. Proc. Int. Union Game Biol. 7:615-622.

Klukas, R. W., and L. N. Locke. 1970. An outbreak of fowl cholera in Everglades National Park. J. Wildl. Dis. 6:77-79.

Knighton, M. D., compiler. 1982. Water impoundments for wildlife: a habitat management workshop. U.S. For. Ser., North Cent. For. Exp. Stn. Gen. Tech. Rep. NC-100. 140 pp.

Koerner, J. W. 1971. Fall movements of Canada geese near southwestern Lake Erie. M.S. Thesis, Ohio State Univ., Columbus. 139 pp.

Krull, J. M. 1970. Aquatic plant-macroinvertebrate associations and waterfowl. J. Wildl. Manage. 34:707-718.

Landes, R. K. 1961. Phenology and ecology of migratory waterfowl at the Fort Gibson Refuge and vicinity during the season 1960-61. M.S. Thesis, Oklahoma State Univ., Stillwater. 101 pp.

LeFebvre, E. A., and D. G. Raveling. 1967. Distribution of Canada geese in winter as related to heat loss at varying environmental temperatures. J. Wildl. Manage. 31:538-546.

Lensink, C. J. 1964. Distribution of recoveries from bandings of ducklings. U.S. Fish and Wildl. Serv., Spec. Sci. Rep. Wildl. No. 89.

Locke, L. N. 1987. Aspergillosis. Pages 145-150 *in* M. Friend, ed. Field guide to wildlife diseases. Vol. 1. General field procedures and diseases of migratory birds. U.S. Dep. Int., Fish and Wildl. Serv. Resour. Publ. No. 167.

———, V. Stotts, and G. Wolfhard. 1970. An outbreak of fowl cholera in waterfowl on the Chesapeake Bay. J. Wildl. Dis. 6:404-407.

Marriott, R. W., and D. K. Forbes. 1970. The digestion of Lucerne chaff by Cape Barren geese. Aust. J. Zool. 18:257-263.

Martin, A. C., and F. M. Uhler. 1939. Food of game ducks in the United States and Canada. U.S. Dep. Int., Fish and Wildl. Serv. Resour. Rep. No. 30. 308 pp.

Mattocks, J. G. 1971. Goose feeding and cellulose digestion. Wildfowl 22:107-113.

McAtee, W. L. 1918. Food habits of the mallard ducks of the United States. U.S. Dep. Agric. Bull. No. 720. 35 pp.

McDiarmid, A. 1955. Aspergillosis in free living wild birds. J. Comp. Pathol. Therapeutics 65:246-249.

McDougle, H. C., and R. W. Vaught. 1968. An epizootic of aspergillosis in Canada geese. J. Wildl. Manage. 32:415-417.

McKinney, F. 1975. The evolution of duck displays. Pages 331-357 *in* G. Baerends, C. Beer, and A.

Manning, eds. Function and evolution in behavior. Clarendon Press, Oxford.

Meeks, R. L. 1969. The effect of drawdown date on wetland plant succession. J. Wildl. Manage. 33:817-821.

Miller, M. R. 1986. Northern pintail body condition during wet and dry winters in the Sacramento Valley, California. J. Wildl. Manage. 50:189-198.

Miller, S. W. 1973. The common merganser: its wintering distribution and predation in a warm water reservoir. M.S. Thesis, Oklahoma State Univ., Stillwater. 90 pp.

Mills, D., and D. MacIver. 1964. Wildfowl on hydroelectric reservoirs in the Scottish highlands. Annu. Rep. Wildfowl Trust 15:79-84.

Moore, R., and T. Mills. 1977. An environmental guide to western surface mining. Part Two: impacts, mitigation, and monitoring. U.S. Fish and Wildl. Serv., Biol. Serv. Prog., FWS/OBS-78/04. 482 pp.

Neff, J. A. 1955. Outbreak of aspergillosis in mallards. J. Wildl. Manage. 19:415-416.

Nelson, R. W., G. C. Horak, and J. E. Olson. 1978. Western reservoir and stream improvements handbook. U.S. Fish and Wildl. Serv. FWS/OBS-78/56. 250 pp.

Newton, I., and C. R. G. Campbell. 1973. Feeding of geese on farmland in east-central Scotland. J. Appl. Ecol. 10:781-801.

Nichols, J. D., K. J. Reinecke, and J. E. Hines. 1983. Factors affecting the distribution of mallards wintering in the Mississippi Alluvial Valley. Auk 100:932-946.

Nilsson, L. 1973. Annual fluctuations among Swedish mallards (*Anas platyrhynchos*) and their possible causes. Int. Congr. Game Biol. 11:245-248.

Oklahoma Water Resources Board. 1980. Oklahoma comprehensive water plan. Okla. Water Resour. Board Publ. No. 94. 248 pp.

Owen, M. 1975. An assessment of fecal analysis technique in waterfowl feeding studies. J. Wildl. Manage. 39:271-279.

———, and W. R. Cook. 1977. Variations in body weight, wing length, and condition of mallard (*Anas platyrhynchos platyrhynchos*) and their relationship to environmental changes. J. Zool., London 183:377-395.

Patterson, C. T. 1982. Foods of migrating coots (*Fulica americana*) and sympatric ducks during fall and spring in northeastern Oklahoma. M.S. Thesis, Oklahoma State Univ., Stillwater. 31 pp.

Pederson, R. L., D. G. Jorde, and S. G. Simpson. 1989. Northern Great Plains. Pages 281-310 *in* L. M. Smith, R. L. Pederson, and R. M. Kaminski, eds. Habitat management for migrating and wintering waterfowl in North America. Texas Tech Univ. Press, Lubbock.

Peltier, W. H., and E. B. Welch. 1970. Factors affecting growth of rooted aquatic plants in a reservoir. Weed Sci. 18:7-9.

Petrides, G. A., and C. R. Byrant. 1951. An analysis of the 1949-50 fowl cholera epizootic in Texas Panhandle waterfowl. Trans. North Am. Wildl. Conf. 16:193-216.

Philippona, J. 1966. Geese in cold winter weather. Wildfowl 17.95-97.

Ploskey, G. R., and R. M. Jenkins. 1980. Inventory of U.S. reservoirs. U.S. Fish and Wildl. Serv. Natl. Reservoir Res. Prog., Fayetteville, Ark. 40 pp.

Pulliainen, E. 1963. On the history, ecology, and ethology of the mallards (*Anas platyrhynchos*) overwintering in Finland. Ornis. Fennica 40:45-66.

Ranwell, D. S., and B. M. Downing. 1959. Brent goose winter feeding pattern and Zostera resources at Scolt Head Island, Norfolk. Anim. Behav. 7.42-50.

Raveling, D. G. 1979. The annual cycle of body composition of Canada geese with special reference to control of reproduction. Auk 96:234-252.

———, W. E. Crews, and W. D. Klimstra. 1972. Activity patterns of Canada geese in winter. Wilson Bull. 84:278-295.

Robel, R. J. 1962. Changes in submersed vegetation following a change in water level. J. Wildl. Manage. 26:221-224.

Rosen, M. N. 1971. Avian cholera. Pages 59-71 *in* J. W. Davis, R. C. Anderson, L. Karstad, and D. O. Trainer, eds. Infectious and parasitic diseases of wild birds. Iowa State Univ. Press., Ames.

———, and A. I. Bischoff 1949. The 1948-49 outbreak of fowl cholera in birds in the San Francisco Bay area and surrounding counties. Calif. Fish and Game 35:185-192.

Ruffner, J. R. 1985. Climates of the states. Third ed., Gale Res. Co., Detroit, Mich. 1,572 pp.

Rutherford, W. H. 1966. Chronology of waterfowl migration in Colorado. Colo. Div. Wildl., Game Inf. Leafl. No. 40. 2 pp.

———. 1970. The Canada geese of southeastern Colorado. Colo. Div. Game, Fish, and Parks Tech. Publ. No. 26. 65 pp.

Schoener, T. W. 1971. Theory of feeding strategies. Annu. Rev. Ecol. Syst. 2:369-404.

Scott, T. G., and C. H. Wasser. 1980. Checklist of North American plants for wildlife biologists. The Wildlife Society, Washington, D.C. 58 pp.

Sharp, R. L. 1979. Economic adjustments to increasing energy costs for pump irrigation in northeastern Colorado. M.S. Thesis, Colorado State Univ., Fort Collins. 50 pp.

Shaw, S. P., and C. G. Fredine. 1956. Wetlands of the United States. U.S. Dep. Int., Fish and Wildl. Serv. Circ. No. 39. 67 pp.

Snyder, W. D. 1986. Dynamics of cottonwood regeneration. Job Prog. Rep., Colo. Div. Wildl., Wildl. Res. Rep., Fed. Aid Proj. 01-03-045. 10 pp.

Spohrer, M. L. 1975. Marsh management for wildlife. a bibliography with abstracts. La. Coop. Wildl. Res. Unit Spec. Publ. No. 1. Baton Rouge. 55 pp.

Staffon, R. C. 1976. Local movements and food habits of Canada geese wintering in Colorado. M.S. Thesis, Colorado State Univ., Fort Collins. 127 pp.

Steinel, A. T. 1926. History of agriculture in Colorado. State Agric. Coll., Fort Collins, Colo. 72 pp.

Stoudt, J. H. 1944. Food preferences of mallards on the Chippewa National Forest, Minnesota. J. Wildl. Manage. 8:100-112.

Sturdy, J. C. 1972. Production of forage and its utilization at the Salt Plains National Wildlife Refuge. M.S. Thesis, Oklahoma State Univ., Stillwater. 67 pp.

Sturkie, P. D., editor. 1976. Avian physiology. Springer-Verlag, New York. 400 pp.

Sugden, L. G. 1971. Metabolizable energy of small grains for mallards. J. Wildl. Manage. 35:781-785.

———. 1979. Grain consumption by mallards. Wildl. Soc. Bull. 7:35-39.

Sutherland, D. E. 1970. Important migration and wintering waterfowl habitat in the United States, 1985 and 2000, and trends. U.S. Dep. Int., Flyway Habitat Management Unit Proj. Rep. No. 2. 8 pp.

Tamasier, R. 1976. Diurnal activities of green-winged teal and pintail wintering in Louisiana. Wildfowl 27:19-32.

Taylor, W. H. 1957. Utilization, preference, and nutritional value of winter-green agricultural crops for goose food. M.S. Thesis, Virginia Polytechnic Inst., Blacksburg. 125 pp.

Teskey, R. O., and T. M. Hinckley. 1978. Impact of water level changes on woody riparian and wetland communities. Vol. VI. Plains and grassland region. U.S. Fish and Wildl. Serv., FWS/OBS-78/89. 29 pp.

Thomas, G. 1976. Habitat usage of wintering ducks at the Ouse Washes, England. Wildfowl 27:148-152.

Timkin, R. L., and B. W. Anderson. 1969. Food habits of common mergansers in the northcentral United States. J. Wildl. Manage. 33:87-91.

Tiner, R. W. 1984. Wetlands of the United States: current status and recent trends. U.S. Fish and Wildl. Serv., Natl. Wetlands Inventory. 59 pp.

U.S. Department of Agriculture. 1978. Agricultural statistics. U.S. Gov. Print. Off., Washington, D.C. 10 pp.

——. 1981. Agriculture statistics. U.S. Gov. Print. Off., Washington, D.C. 10 pp.

U.S. Department of the Interior. 1955. Inventory of permanent water areas important to waterfowl in Wyoming. Off River Basin Studies, Billings, Mont. 10 pp.

U.S. Fish and Wildlife Service. 1981. The Platte River ecology study. U.S. Dep. Int., Fish and Wildl. Serv., Jamestown, N.D. 187 pp.

Ward, P., and A. Zahavi. 1973. The importance of certain assemblages of birds as "information centres" for food finding. Ibis 115:517-534.

Waters, S. A. 1965. Colorado year book, 1962-1964. Monitor Publications, Inc., Denver, Colo. 1,064 pp.

Weatherhead, P. J. 1984. Two principal strategies in avian communal roosts. Am. Nat. 121:237-243.

Weaver, G. D., editor. 1980. Geography of Colorado. Colorado State Univ., Fort Collins. 244 pp.

Weller, M. W. 1976. Molts and plumages of waterfowl. Pages 34-38 in F. C. Bellrose, ed. Ducks, geese and swans of North America. Second ed. Stackpole Books, Harrisburg, Pa. 543 pp.

White, W. M., and G. W. Malaher. 1964. Reservoirs. Pages 381-389 in J. P. Linduska, ed. Waterfowl tomorrow. U.S. Dep. Int., Fish and Wildl. Serv., Washington, D.C.

Whyte, R. J., and E. G. Bolen. 1984. Impact of winter stress on mallard body composition. Condor 86:477-482.

——, and ——. 1985. Corn consumption by wintering mallards during morning field-flights. Prairie Nat. 17:71-78.

——, N. J. Silvy, and B. W. Cain. 1981. Effects of cattle on duck food plants in south Texas. J. Wildl. Manage. 45:512-515.

Williams, W. G., and M. G. Wolman. 1986. Effects of dams and reservoirs on surface-water hydrology—changes in rivers downstream from dams. Pages 83-88 in D. W. Moody, E. G. Chase, and D. R. Aronson, comp. National water summary 1985—hydrologic events and surface water resources. U.S. Geol. Surv. Water Supply Pap. No. 2300.

Wishart, R. A. 1983. The behavioral ecology of the American wigeon over its annual cycle. Ph.D. Thesis, Univ. Manitoba, Winnipeg. 328 pp.

Wright, T. W. 1959. Winter foods of mallards in Arkansas. Proc. Annu. Conf. Southeast. Assoc. Game and Fish Comm. 13:291-296.

Young, R. A., R. A. Longenbaugh, L. R. Conklin, and R. L. Gardner. 1982. Energy and water scarcity and the irrigated agricultural economy of the Colorado high plains: direct economic-hydrologic impact forecasts (1979-2020). Colorado State Univ. Tech. Rep. No. 34. 362 pp.

PLAYA LAKES

ERIC G. BOLEN,[1] Department of Range and Wildlife Management and the Graduate School, Texas Tech University, Lubbock, TX 79409

GUY A. BALDASSARRE, Environmental and Forest Biology, SUNY College of Environmental Science and Forestry, Syracuse, NY 13210

FRED S. GUTHERY, Caesar Kleberg Wildlife Research Institute, Texas A&I University, Kingsville, TX 78363

The Texas Panhandle coincides with much of the landform known as the Southern High Plains (SHP, Fig. 1). This vast region of 82,000 km², once a short-grass prairie, is now devoted to food and fiber production. The dominant hydrographical features on the SHP are the thousands of shallow wetlands that dot the landscape during years of adequate rainfall (Fig. 2). These are playa lakes— islands of wetland habitat and winter quarters for more than a million waterfowl. Here, we provide an overview of playa ecology and discuss ways that playa lakes might be managed as habitat for waterfowl wintering and migrating in the Central Flyway.

PHYSICAL DESCRIPTION AND SETTING

Playa basins are wind deflated depressions etched on the surface of the SHP during the Pleistocene (Judson 1950, Reeves 1966). Earlier estimates vary, but the most recent study reports about 19,300 playas in Texas, with another 6,000 located in adjacent states (Guthery et al. 1981, Guthery and Bryant 1982). The number of playas per county varies widely, but 450 to 750 basins represent a "working estimate" in those counties where large numbers of waterfowl over-winter (e.g., 621 playas in Castro County). Those playas included in the survey by Guthery et al. (1981) averaged 6.8 ha in surface area, but this parameter

also varied widely (Guthery and Bryant 1982).

The playas annually collect 246,600 to 370,000 ha-m (2-3 million acre-feet) of water (Ward and Huddleston 1970), which is estimated at 89% of all surface runoff (Clyma and Lotspeich 1966). Overall, the playas provide an estimated 93,100 to 101,200 ha of potential aquatic habitat (Sanderson 1976).

In Texas, the basins are lined with Randall clay, and thus differ markedly from the surrounding surface soils (e.g., sandy loams). Randall clays are nearly impermeable, and runoff therefore collects in the basins (Allen et al. 1972). Dvoracek (1981) estimated that percolation provides up to 10% of water loss, thereby indicating that large amounts of water are lost from evapotranspiration (Aronovici et al. 1970). Evaporation may average from 450 m³/ha to more than 1,000 m³/ha (Grubb and Parks 1968, Guthery et al. 1981), which accounts for about 90% of the water deficit in playas where irrigation is not a factor. Precipitation in the region averages about 45 cm, with peaks normally occurring in April and May and in October. Thus, before the current irrigation economy, playas filled during the rainy seasons and dried at other times of the year. There is no evidence of naturally occurring fish populations in playas, although some sites have been stocked with such species as channel catfish (*Ictalurus punctatus*).

Events befalling the southern third of the Ogallala Aquifer greatly influence the hydrological equation for the SHP. During the Pliocene, a network of streams

[1]Present address: Dean of the Graduate School, University of North Carolina at Wilmington, Wilmington, NC 28403.

SOUTHERN HIGH PLAINS

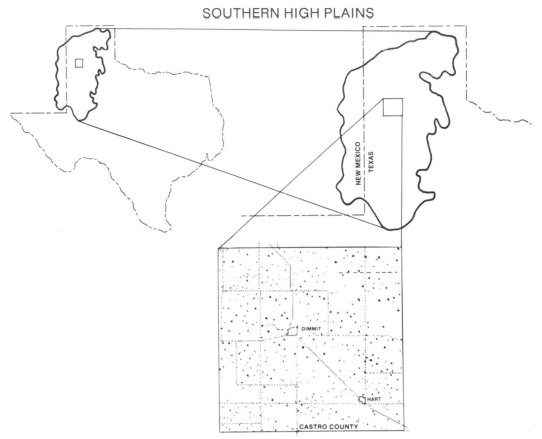

Fig. 1. The Southern High Plains (SHP) occupy a large region of Texas and the eastern fringe of New Mexico. Much of the fieldwork reported herein was conducted on playa lakes near Hart in Castro County (enlarged). Playa locations were determined from the SCS Soils Survey for Castro County (Bruns 1974). The SHP is known regionally as the Llano Estacado, or "Staked Plains," a reflection of the area's Spanish heritage.

and rivers originating in the western cordillera crossed the region. This system deposited a thick stratum of materials— outwash from the Rocky Mountains— which entrapped an immense quantity of water (Frye and Byron 1957). An eolian mantle of Pleistocene sediments eventually buried these deposits, forming the modern landscape (Lotspeich and Coover 1962). Also during the Pleistocene, the SHP became an isolated tableland when the Canadian River captured and diverted the network of streams eastward and, similarly, the Pecos River directed surface drainages to the south. Thus, that part of the Ogallala Aquifer underlying the SHP no longer receives appreciable recharge

and, in effect, pumping mines water from the aquifer. North of the Canadian River, however, the Arkansas, Platte, and numerous other river systems recharge the remainder of the Ogallala, the world's largest aquifer. Because of these geological events, playas on the SHP eventually became the focal point in the management of surface water for agricultural purposes.

Environmental History

Playas have figured prominently in the environmental history of the SHP (Bolen and Flores 1988). Paleoindians of the Folsom Culture (10,900-10,000 BP) supplemented their diet with ducks (*Anas*

Fig. 2. A playa in Castro County, Texas, with good habitat interspersion. The area in the foreground is grazed, whereas the far side of the playa is irrigated cropland, each typical of land use for much of the SHP.

spp.) and muskrats (*Ondatra zibethicus*), and tools of the period were found among bones of elephants (*Mammuthus columbi*) in the bed of an ancient playa (Sellards 1938, Johnson 1983).

Muskrats no longer occur on the SHP, presumably because the lack of suitable aquatic corridors precluded recolonization after extended droughts extirpated earlier populations (Bolen and Flores 1988). At least 2 prolonged droughts gripped the SHP between 6,500 and 4,500 BP (Holliday 1985). In any case, aquatic mammals are absent in the modern playa fauna. The SHP thus never gained importance as a source of fur, notwithstanding optimistic searches for beaver (*Castor canadensis*) in a most unlikely setting (i.e., treeless plains and ephemeral ponds). On finding playas near present-day Lubbock County in 1831-32, Albert Pike noted his despair over the lack of "immense quantities of beaver" promised by a Comanche chieftain (Haley 1968:60).

Playa is the Spanish word for "beach," but why that term was applied to these prairie wetlands remains unknown (i.e., laguito, "little lake," or similar designa-

tions were not adopted). Notations about playas first appear in the records of Coronado's trek across the SHP in 1541: "several lakes . . . round like plates, a stone's throw or more across" (Bolton 1949:254). The vast herds of "cattle" (bison: *Bison bison*) also impressed the conquistadors, which probably began the popular notion that playas originated as "buffalo wallows." Centuries later, in 1841, members of the ill-starred Santa Fe Expedition crossed the SHP and rested their horses near a playa where ". . . large white cranes were standing about," thus suggesting the presence of whooping cranes (*Grus americana*) (Kendall 1847: 167). On venturing onto the SHP late in the summer of 1845, Lt. J. W. Abert found "large shallow pools, covered with flocks of ducks" (Carroll 1941:42). Abert's troops attempted to kill some of the birds, and undoubtedly became the first Anglo duck hunters on the SHP. Abert correctly observed that "these ponds on the open prairie" resulted from heavy rainfall (Carroll 1941:42). Naturalists later visiting the region largely confined their observations to the attractive canyonlands on the

Table 1. Midwinter inventory for 4 species of ducks wintering in northwest Texas, an area including all of the SHP. Data compiled by U.S. Fish and Wildlife Service.[a]

Species	Midwinter inventory—year									
	1977-78	1978-79	1979-80	1980-81	1981-82	1982-83	1983-84	1984-85	1985-86	1986-87
Mallard	76,350	249,500	191,900	166,100	187,300	114,300	75,200	106,300	94,000	92,650
Northern pintail	72,450	20,900	191,600	105,500	207,800	87,600	23,400	71,200	32,400	138,300
Green-winged teal	24,150	4,100	19,600	18,300	15,200	15,100	7,600	35,300	8,800	143,150
American wigeon	12,400	11,400	64,200	42,400	55,000	39,700	5,000	32,800	9,100	8,500

[a]Inventory data in most cases are not "statistical" surveys of established transects, and thus are not accurate enumerations of waterfowl populations. However, midwinter inventories have considerable utility for determining the relative abundance and distribution of waterfowl.

eastern border of the SHP and seldom ventured over the rim onto the flat prairie (McCauley 1877, Strecker 1910).

Bird lists for the SHP were not published until well into the present century (Stevenson 1942, Fischer et al. 1982). In commentary accompanying his checklist, Hawkins (1945:110) emphasized the importance of playas to the regional avifauna: "Fewer than forty kinds of birds use the open plains ... but give the plains a few lakes and it becomes a bird haven, increasing its bird potential by at least eighty species."

HABITAT IMPORTANCE
Species of Waterfowl

Playas are second in importance only to the Gulf Coast as winter habitat for waterfowl in the Central Flyway (Buller 1964). About 30% of all waterfowl wintering in Texas depends on playa environments (Curtis and Beierman 1980). Total numbers, of course, vary yearly, depending on production on the breeding grounds and on water conditions in the playas. Thus, more than 2 million ducks and geese were counted in the 1972 midwinter survey, but the 1978 survey tallied only 232,000 birds. Recent midwinter survey data for selected species appear in Table 1.

At least 20 species of migratory game birds occur on playa lakes in Castro County, Texas (Simpson et al. 1981). Four species of dabbling ducks comprise the majority of waterfowl wintering on playa lakes: green-winged teal (*Anas crecca*), mallard (*A. platyrhynchos*), northern pintail (*A. acuta*), and American wigeon (*A. americana*).

Northern shovelers (*A. clypeata*) and gadwalls (*A. strepera*) overwinter in lesser numbers, and blue-winged teal (*A. discors*) are abundant during migratory periods. Small numbers of cinnamon teal (*A. cyanoptera*) are present regularly in winter. Some species of pochards also occur regularly but in small numbers, including redheads (*Aythya americana*), canvasbacks (*A. valisineria*), and lesser scaup (*A. affinis*). Wood ducks (*Aix sponsa*), ring-necked ducks (*Aythya collaris*), white-winged scoters (*Melanitta fusca*), ruddy ducks (*Oxyura jamaicensis*), buffleheads (*Bucephala albeola*), common mergansers (*Mergus merganser*), and hooded mergansers (*Lophodytes cucullatus*) rarely are encountered.

Canada geese (*Branta canadensis*) overwinter on the playas, but the racial taxonomy of the winter population lacks detailed study. So far as is known, however, the composition is similar or identical to the shortgrass prairie population described by Grieb (1970). Lesser snow geese (*Chen caerulescens*) are less abundant, but the winter population may be increasing gradually. Ross' geese (*C. rossii*) occur in small numbers, and tundra swans (*Cygnus columbianus*) appear infrequently. The playa region of the southwestern Texas Panhandle also overwinters about 360,000 sandhill cranes (*Grus canadensis*) (Iverson et al. 1985).

Relationships with Other Habitat

Banding data for waterfowl on the SHP are not extensive. However, significant differences occur within the mallard population wintering in the Central Flyway (Funk et al. 1971). Of particular importance are those subpopulations wintering west of the 100th meridian, which include mallards associated with playa lakes. Mallards banded on wintering areas showed strong tendencies to return to the same wintering sites in subsequent years. Thus, based on axial-line estimates of mean harvest routes, a track can be made that suggests the migration route for each subpopulation. For those mallards banded on the SHP, the route runs almost due north along the eastern edge of Colorado, across the Nebraska Panhandle, then runs diagonally across the southwestern corner of South Dakota and thereafter traverses northeastern Montana into prairies of western Saskatchewan. Because of this and other features (e.g., low hunting pressure), the SHP is included in the High Plains Mallard Management Unit.

Baldassarre et al. (1988) banded 4,200 green-winged teal on the SHP between October and March in 1980-82, of which 2,410 were marked with patagial tags. Resighting and band-recovery data indicated that many green-winged teal pass through the SHP in early autumn, headed for wintering grounds on the Gulf Coast and in central Mexico. Thus, in addition to providing important winter habitat, playas on the SHP also are major stopping areas during the autumn migration (and presumably during spring migration as well). This study also found that nearly all resightings of marked teal occurred within the original 50-km^2 study area.

In a zoogeographical context, the playas are strategically located for migrating and wintering waterfowl. To the west lie the desert and arid mountains of New Mexico, and southwest is the equally arid area of the Trans-Pecos of Texas. Rivers (e.g., the Red, Brazos, and Colorado rivers) to the east and southeast offer only sparse wetland habitat in the Red Rolling Plains of Texas, whereas immediately south are the rocky hills of the Edwards Plateau. Thus, until the extensive marshes of the Gulf Coast are reached, the playas of the SHP offer the most significant wetland habitat in the southern quarter of the Central Flyway.

Chronology of Playa Use

Breeding species include the mallard, green-winged teal, blue-winged teal, cinnamon teal, northern pintail, redhead, ruddy duck, northern shoveler, and American coot (*Fulica americana*) (Rhodes and Garcia 1981, Simpson et al. 1981). Mallards and teal comprise about 80% of the breeding duck population (Rhodes and Garcia 1981). However, mallards alone comprised 81% of the broods encountered in a 4-year survey of playas in a 12-county area (Traweek 1978). Production is relatively low, however, as the latter survey produced an estimate of only 13,754 ducklings in the best year compared with 3,872 ducklings in the poorest season. Taylor and Guthery (1980) estimated duck nests at a density of 0.80/ha of playa cover, with production at 2.03 ducklings/ha in Castro County, Texas.

Winter populations begin building with the arrival of migrant blue-winged and cinnamon teal in late August (Simpson et al. 1981). By September, the winter population is represented by migrants of the major species—northern pintails, green-winged teal, mallards, and American wigeon, which total about 97% of the wintering population in the south-central Texas Panhandle (Soutiere et al. 1972, Obenberger 1982). Total numbers of win-

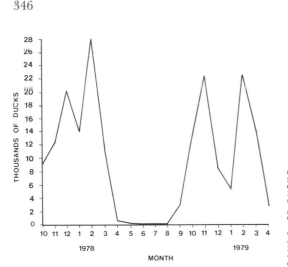

Fig. 3. Mean numbers of ducks observed during replicated monthly censuses of 16 playas in Castro County, Texas, October 1977-April 1979 (Simpson et al. 1981).

tering waterfowl peak during November and February, as do populations for each of the 4 major species (Figs. 3 and 4).

HABITAT IMPORTANCE RELATIVE TO WATERFOWL REQUIREMENTS

Food Habits

Data concerning the foods of waterfowl on the SHP focus entirely on the non-breeding period and indicate that corn is the most heavily used food. For example, corn averages 80-96% volume and 67-91% occurrence in the diets of the 5 most abundant species of ducks wintering on the SHP (Table 2). Moore (1980) collected the largest set of data for duck food habits on the SHP ($n = 647$); the volume of corn in the gullet was 97-100% for mallards, 97-99% for green-winged teal, 100% for American wigeon, and 98-100% for northern pintails. However, Sheeley (1988) noted that these studies were biased because the birds were collected while returning to playas following morning field-feeding flights to cornfields; thus, the proportion of natural foods would be underestimated in the diet. Food habits of geese wintering on the SHP are unstudied, but likely would show great dependence on agricultural foods.

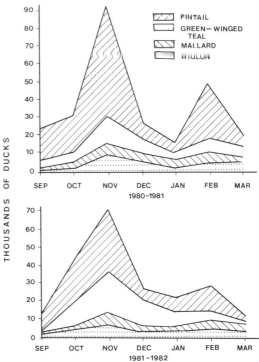

Fig. 4. Temporal trends in numbers and composition of ducks censused on 10 23-km^2 plots on the SHP, September-March 1980-82 (Obenberger 1982).

Despite the dominance of waste grain in the winter diet, ducks may prefer natural plant and animal foods, if available, which seem necessary to offset the nutritional deficiencies of a corn diet (Baldassarre et al. 1983, Quinlan and Baldassarre 1984). Sheeley (1988) noted that the diet of northern pintails collected while feeding in playas contained 80% natural foods. Moore (1980) recorded 52 species of seeds in the diet of waterfowl on the SHP. Of these, pondweeds (*Potamogeton* spp.) occurred most frequently (52%), followed by spikerushes (*Eleocharis* spp., 42%). Barnyardgrass (*Echinochloa crusgalli*) and smartweeds (*Polygonum* spp.) were among the important natural foods (Table 2). (Plant nomenclature follows Gould 1975.) Thus, except for pondweeds, the important natural foods in the diet are "moist-soil" plants (Fredrickson and Taylor 1982), a

Table 2.   Summary of food habits data available for waterfowl wintering on the Southern High Plains of Texas.[a]

Species	n	Agricultural Foods						Natural Foods												Source
		Corn		Wheat		Sorghum		*Echinochloa*		*Polygonum*		*Potamogeton*		*Eleocharis*		Other plants		Animal		
		F	V	F	V	F	V	F	V	F	V	F	V	F	V	F	V	F	V	
Blue-winged teal	11					55	52	73	28	73	1					—	11	64	8	Rollo and Bolen (1969)
	9	11	23					78	75	22	<1	11	<1			—	1	22	1	Sell (1979)
Green-winged teal	16			6	1	25	38	62	3	100	48			6	<1	—	8	31	2	Rollo and Bolen (1969)
	18	67	80	11	6			28	12	22	<1					—	2	6	tr	Sell (1979)
	157	78	95			7	<1	16	1	29	<1	50	<1	56	<1	—	4	27	tr	Moore (1980)
	200	91	96			3	<1	10	2	7	1					—	2	5	<1	Baldassarre (unpubl.)
Mallard	324	72	92			8	2	16	<1	32	<1	60	2	38	<1	—	4	15	tr	Moore (1980)
Northern pintail	106	81	94			6	1	18	<1	29	<1	53	1	44	<1	—	4	16	tr	Moore (1980)
	21[b]	—	90					—	<1	—	<1			—	<1	—	5	—	5	Sheeley (1988)
	26[c]	—	22					—	12	—	8			—	1	—	29	—	27	
American wigeon	60	78	94					13	<1	18	<1	22	<1	23	<1	—	6	13	tr	Moore (1980)

[a] n = sample size; F = frequency of occurrence; V = aggregate volume; except studies by Sheeley (aggregate percent volume, Swanson et al. 1974).

[b] Collected over decoys.

[c] Collected while feeding on playa lakes.

flora favored by the wet-dry hydroperiods characteristic of playa lakes.

The relative importance of animal foods in the diet of waterfowl wintering on the SHP has been reported only for northern pintails. In this case, invertebrates averaged 20% by volume in birds collected after feeding in playas (Sheeley 1988). Few other samples were collected from feeding birds, thus the proportion of easily digestible items (e.g., invertebrates) may be underestimated (Swanson and Bartonek 1970, Swanson et al. 1974). Moore (1980) recorded animal foods that included the insect orders Coleoptera, Diptera, Hemiptera, Homoptera, Hymenoptera, Lepidoptera, Neuroptera, and Odonata, as well as gastropods in the families Planorbidae, Physidae, and Gyralidae. Snails and insects were dominant animal foods in teal collected by Rollo and Bolen (1969). Midge larvae (Chironomidae) were abundant in 6 green-winged teal collected while feeding in playa lakes in Castro County (Quinlan and Baldassarre 1984). Baldassarre and Fischer (1984) reported an average density of $6,175 \pm 671$ midge larvae/m^2 available to shorebirds (and presumably waterfowl) on a playa during September.

Other studies reporting the density and diversity of macroinvertebrates associated with playas include Sublette and Sublette (1967), Richardson (1971), Parks (1975), Merickel and Wangberg (1981), Thompson (1985), and Gray (1986). Gray and Bolen (1987) described the abundance of aquatic invertebrates in playas modified for water storage.

Feeding Ecology

Based on field studies conducted between October and mid-March 1980-82, Baldassarre and Bolen (1984) determined that waterfowl normally participated in 2 field-feeding flights/day (before sunrise and after sunset). Feeding flights between playas and cornfields rarely exceeded 5 km. No flights were observed to harvested sorghum fields or wheat fields; the latter usually is harvested in summer and plowed or replanted before ducks arrive in autumn.

An estimate of corn consumption is available only from birds collected just after returning from the morning feeding flights. Mallards contained 20-64 g corn/bird/flight, with the consumption in late winter reaching 52-64 g (Whyte and Bolen 1985), whereas green-winged teal averaged

13-18 g/bird/flight (Baldassarre et al. 1983).

Most birds (75-90%) in a flock initiated the morning field-feeding flights 11 ± 1.6 minutes before sunrise (Baldassarre and Bolen 1984). All morning flights (except during periods of snowfall, see below) terminated 16.5 ± 1.1 minutes before sunrise, with an average feeding time of 23 ± 1.4 minutes. In contrast, the evening flight began 25 ± 2.0 minutes after sunset, with most birds returning to playa lakes 52 ± 2.8 minutes later. Overall, the average feeding time during evening flights was 37 ± 4.2 minutes from October to March. However, the duration lengthened as winter progressed; the average was 27.1 ± 2.1 minutes from October to December, which differed ($P < 0.05$) from the mean of 53 ± 2.6 minutes from January to March.

Some birds did not participate in the daily feeding flights. Nonparticipants averaged between 5 and 20% of a flock, and at times exceeded 50%. The percentage of nonparticipants was greater in the morning than in the evening flights of the same day, but the percentage decreased markedly as winter progressed, essentially reaching zero when temperatures fell below −7 C during evening flights (Baldassarre and Bolen 1986). The other exception to normal field-feeding behavior was the occurrence of daytime feeding flights during periods of snow accumulation.

Field-feeding waterfowl selected fields in a hierarchy based on the abundance and availability of waste corn, which probably reflected a strategy for minimizing foraging time (Baldassarre and Bolen 1984). For example, because burning removes ground litter and maximizes the availability of waste corn, burned fields always were preferred regardless of the abundance of waste corn. Early in the season (1-15 Oct), however, few fields had been burned and ducks instead selected freshly harvested fields where waste corn

was most abundant (e.g., >700 kg/ha). As winter progressed and fields were disked, ducks then preferred those disked fields with the greatest amounts of corn (e.g., >60 kg/ha). Thus, waste corn resources change dynamically in abundance and availability throughout the winter on the SHP. However, the field-feeding response indicates that corn is not a limited commodity in the diets of waterfowl wintering on playa lakes (Baldassarre and Bolen 1984, Baldassarre et al. 1986).

In addition to their field-feeding behavior, waterfowl forage for natural plant and animal foods associated with playa lakes (Table 2). As mentioned earlier, however, little is known about the importance of natural foods in the diet of waterfowl wintering on the SHP because previous food-habits studies relied on ducks collected after returning from morning field-feeding flights. That collection method biases food-habits data toward corn, whereas the diets of ducks collected in playa lakes contain large amounts of natural foods (Sheeley 1988).

Much of the data concerning natural foods results from indirect evidence (i.e., time budgets), but such information demonstrates that natural foods are used, and even suggests that waterfowl may prefer these to a diet of corn. For example, although green-winged teal regularly participated in field-feeding flights during winter, teal also spent 7-23% of their time foraging in playa basins where the percentage of feeding time was highest (23%) in September and October (Quinlan and Baldassarre 1984). Such observations led to speculation that green-winged teal and other waterfowl may prefer feeding on natural versus agricultural food sources under certain circumstances. Natural wetlands (i.e., playas) satisfy other requirements of wintering waterfowl by providing cover, water, and a variety of foods, whereas cornfields provide only a single kind of food and no cover or water. Heitmeyer and Vohs (1984) noted that waterfowl wintering in Oklahoma preferred natural wetlands in comparison with man-made ponds and reservoirs. Similarly, Rollo and Bolen (1969) determined that teal preferred foods available on unmodified playas compared with playas that were modified for water storage.

Baldassarre and Bolen (1984) observed other evidence that waterfowl prefer the food resources available in playa lakes. During September and October 1980, Castro County received only 6 cm of rainfall. Thus, moist-soil vegetation associated with playas was not available to wintering waterfowl, and field-feeding activity that year began in late August with the arrival of blue-winged teal and northern pintails. Conversely, 17.7 cm of rain fell on the same area during September and October 1981, thereby flooding the available moist-soil communities. In response, most ducks remained on playas and extensive field-feeding did not begin until mid-October.

Relationship of Important Foods to Nutritional Requirements

The nutritional requirements of wintering waterfowl are not well understood in comparison to those of breeding birds (e.g., Krapu and Swanson 1975). Nevertheless, the accumulation of lipid reserves during late autumn remains a common pattern for wintering ducks studied to date (e.g., Whyte et al. 1986). Such reserves are used later in the wintering period during times of food shortage and/or severe weather. There also is evidence that reproductive performance of some waterfowl is influenced by nutrient reserves obtained outside of the nesting areas (Ankney and MacInnes 1978, Raveling 1979, Krapu 1981).

The dynamics of body weight and carcass composition of waterfowl wintering on the SHP have been detailed for green-winged teal (Baldassarre and Bolen 1986, Baldassarre et al. 1986), mallards

(Whyte et al. 1986), and northern pintails (Sheeley 1988). For these species, body weights and lipids were lowest in early autumn, increased to their highest levels by midwinter, declined for the remainder of the winter, but increased again prior to spring migration. In contrast, protein and water content remained relatively unchanged throughout the wintering period.

The high carbohydrate content of corn (80%, Baldassarre et al. 1983) coupled with a high true metabolizable energy (4 kcal/g, Sibbald 1979) provide readily available energy for daily existence activities and facilitate accumulation of lipid reserves. For example, mallards acquired 56-100% of their midwinter lipid reserves from autumn to early winter (Whyte et al. 1986), and the lipid reserves of green-winged teal increased 67-219% (Baldassarre et al. 1986).

During the autumn period of rapid lipid accumulation, mallards consumed 20-45 g corn during morning field-feeding flights (Whyte and Bolen 1985), whereas green-winged teal consumed 13-18 g (Baldassarre et al. 1986). Assuming (1) that green-winged teal require about 100 kcal/day for existence energy on the SHP (Baldassarre et al. 1986) and that mallards require about 300 kcal/day (Whyte and Bolen 1984), and (2) that corn consumption during the evening flight equals the morning flight, then corn provides the teal with 104-144 kcal/day of energy and mallards with 160-360 kcal/day. If these estimates are subtracted from the energy contained in the daily consumption of corn, then mallards potentially could store 6.7 g lipid/day and green-winged teal could store 4.9 g/day (assuming 1 g lipid = 9 kcal energy, Blem 1976). These estimates probably are conservative because food resources also are obtained from playa lakes, and existence requirements were calculated at 0 C (Jan.) when, in fact, autumn temperatures were warmer.

The above calculations demonstrate the

Table 3. Comparative nutritional qualities of waste corn and native plants eaten by waterfowl on the Southern High Plains of Texas (Baldassarre et al. 1983).

| Species[a] | Crude protein | Crude fat | Crude fiber | NFE | Ash | Percent |||| | | | | PPM |||||
						N	S	P	K	Mg	Ca	Na	Fe	Al	Mn	Cn	Zn
Yellow corn	9.74	5.04	3.57	79.68	1.94	1.55	.05	.37	.47	.14	.06	.02	22	43	16	8	17
Pale dock (*Rumex altissimus*)	13.30	2.24	16.90	61.11	6.42	2.12	.08	.38	.92	.52	1.10	.02	171	118	22	35	28
Dock (*Rumex* sp.)	14.32	1.85	17.29	58.99	7.53	2.29	.15	.41	1.06	.49	1.02	.05	191	117	29	45	28
Barnyardgrass (*Echinochloa crusgalli*)	12.53	4.96	22.17	51.40	8.91	2.00	.08	.43	.37	.19	.13	.01	191	149	69	12	34
Johnsongrass (*Sorghum halepense*)	12.51	4.39	17.99	54.82	10.28	2.00	.06	.47	.73	.27	.26	.01	129	107	31	26	33
Curltop smartweed (*Polygonum lapathifolium*)	11.78	3.48	23.64	58.13	2.94	1.88	.07	.46	.74	.22	.22	.01	163	109	36	16	23
Pink smartweed (*Polygonum bicorne*)	9.62	2.44	15.18	69.49	3.25	1.54	.06	.45	.80	.23	.16	.02	98	163	31	13	31
Redroot (*Amaranthus retroflexus*)	22.06	2.66	21.29	43.21	10.75	3.53	.15	.60	2.36	.52	1.72	.01	250	152	35	—	38
Sand dropseed (*Sporobolus cryptandrus*)	15.56	2.14	18.14	55.87	8.26	2.49	.09	.36	.85	.20	.32	.02	—	107	70	15	43
Pondweed (*Potamogeton* sp.)	8.51	3.53	46.48	37.44	4.01	1.36	.05	.32	1.26	.30	.30	.14	211	137	—	12	18

[a]Nomenclature follows Gould (1975).

importance of waste corn in satisfying the energy requirements of waterfowl wintering on the SHP. However, aside from providing readily available amounts of carbohydrates, corn otherwise remains a poor food for waterfowl in comparison with natural foods. Baldassarre et al. (1983) noted several nutritional shortcomings of corn: (1) the average protein content of 9 plant foods used by waterfowl on the SHP was 37% higher than corn (Table 3), (2) the protein content of corn is deficient in the essential amino acids lysine, tryptophan, methionine, and (3) the micro- and macronutrient contents of natural plant foods usually were greater than corn.

The amino acid deficiencies of corn may be especially important when wintering ducks undergo prealternate molt in autumn, and females undergo prebasic molt in spring. The overall protein content of corn also may be too low to satisfy daily maintenance requirements (Quinlan and Baldassarre 1984). Invertebrate foods have not been analyzed on the SHP, but the high quantity and quality of protein in invertebrate foods occurring elsewhere are well-known (Sugden 1973, Reinecke and Owen 1980).

Thus, the exact role of protein in the nutritional requirements of wintering waterfowl is unclear. However, our observations pose strong evidence that the availability of natural plant and animal foods is necessary for the nutritional welfare of waterfowl wintering on the SHP. Accordingly, even though corn provides a rich and readily available source of carbohydrates, waste corn should not be considered a substitute for good quality natural foods.

Management Schedules for Food and Cover Availability

Water Resources.—As might be expected in a semiarid environment, the availability of water is the most important factor affecting duck numbers on the SHP (Guthery et al. 1984). However, depletion of the Ogallala Aquifer in concert with new water-conservation practices (e.g., drip irrigation) currently reduces the amount of irrigation runoff (tailwater) flowing into playa lakes (Bolen and Guthery 1982). Nonetheless, the most widely adopted method for conserving runoff is the excavation of deep, steep-sided pits in playa basins.

Runoff collects in the pits of these "modified playas," thereby storing the water at a favorable surface-area-to-volume ratio, which reduces evaporation and improves pumping efficiency for a second irrigation cycle—that is, significant quantities of stored water can be pumped directly from the pits instead of the more costly operation of pumping from deep wells. Bolen et al. (1979) estimated that 85% of larger playas were modified, but Guthery and Bryant (1982) determined that 69% of 589 playas >4 ha were modified and that 33% of all playas had been modified. Modifications often reduce littoral zones and thus lessen the availability of moist-soil plants and invertebrates (Gray 1986). Pumping from modification pits may completely drain the basins of smaller playas and altogether eliminate moist-soil communities.

Accordingly, acquisition of the larger playas with permanent water represents the most significant management action for assuring quality winter habitat on the SHP. Because winter is a dry season on the SHP (Dec. to Feb. precipitation averages 1 to 1.4 cm/month), most playas are dry or contain little water by midwinter. Ducks concentrate on the remaining playas where water is available. For example, Guthery et al. (1984) noted that 3 relatively permanent water playas with average surface areas of 14 ha received 50% of the duck use on their study area, yet those playas occupied only 2% of available tailwater pits and playa basins. Managed playas should be flooded from late September until November and again in January and February, thereby increasing the attractiveness of the habitat in early autumn and retaining birds on the SHP later in the winter.

The current farm crisis may present the best opportunity in recent years for acquiring or otherwise protecting a strategic core of larger playas. State and federal duck stamp funds spent on relatively small areas of water would benefit large numbers of ducks. Without such a program, the adversities associated with the declining water resources forebode a bleak future for waterfowl wintering on the SHP (Guthery et al. 1984). Indeed, the effects of food shortages, cover requirements, and diseases would be transitory compared to the permanent impact of too little water.

Waste Corn Resources.—The abundance and availability of waste corn on the SHP were measured in Castro County from September to March 1979-82 (Baldassarre et al. 1983). The study area covered 5,000 ha, of which 45% was planted in corn each year. The corn harvest began by 1 September and ended by 14 October during 1980-81, with 70% of the harvest occurring from 15 to 30 September (Baldassarre and Bolen 1984). Additionally, some corn (20% of the study area in 1980) was harvested for ensilage during late August and early September.

Waste corn averaged $3.7 \pm 0.3\%$ ($n = 81$ fields) of the potential crop, with only 6 fields losing more than 10% of the amount harvested; the maximum loss was 2,274 kg/ha (Baldassarre et al. 1983). Average loss per field was 364 ± 12 kg/ha ($n = 202$), of which ears comprised 70% and kernels 30%. The moisture content of the corn at harvest was related inversely to the total amount of waste per field ($r = -0.70$, $P < 0.001$). Overall, fields harvested at 14-21% moisture lost 554 ± 14 kg/ha ($n = 52$), which was more ($P < 0.05$) than twice the corn loss in fields harvested at 22-26% moisture (214 ± 14 kg/ha, $n = 54$) or 27-32% moisture (183 ± 20 kg/ha, $n = 20$). Ensilage fields were not sampled, but probably contained <25 kg waste corn/ha; transient blue-winged teal and early arriving northern pintails fed in these fields (Baldassarre and Bolen 1984).

Declines in the availability of groundwater not only will affect surface water availability, but also will alter the type and amount of crops grown on the SHP. The Texas Department of Water Resources

Table 4. Synopsis of agricultural activities for selected counties on the Southern High Plains of Texas. All data in 1000s of hectares, except percentages shown in parentheses (Texas Agricultural Statistics Service 1985).

Region[a]	County	County size-ha	Planted area-ha (%)[b]	Crop-ha (%)[c]			Irrigated area-ha (%)[d]
				Corn	Cotton	Wheat	
North	Oldham	385	43 (11)	minimum[e]	0 (0)	30 (7)	10 (23)
	Potter	237	28 (12)	0.9 (3)	0 (0)	19 (68)	11 (39)
North-central	Castro	233	131 (56)	39 (30)	22 (17)	45 (34)	109 (83)
	Parmer	229	158 (69)	41 (26)	17 (11)	66 (42)	122 (77)
South-central	Lubbock	233	145 (62)	3 (2)	98 (68)	17 (12)	81 (56)
	Hockley	235	145 (62)	minimum	97 (67)	22 (15)	59 (41)
South	Gaines	390	195 (50)	minimum	122 (63)	31 (16)	101 (52)
	Dawson	234	130 (55)	minimum	91 (70)	7 (5)	14 (11)

[a] Relative position on a north-south axis on Southern High Plains; see Fig. 1.
[b] Percentage of county size.
[c] Percentage of planted area; data for other crops omitted.
[d] Percentage of planted area.
[e] Less than 40 ha.

estimated that of 566,802 ha of corn and irrigated wheat on the SHP in 1977, only 1% will remain by 2020, whereas cotton and dryland wheat will increase concurrently (Bolen and Guthery 1982). Reductions of such a magnitude clearly will affect the ways waste corn is managed for wildlife. We stress, however, that although large numbers of ducks winter in counties where corn is a major crop, water availability is still the major factor affecting duck populations on the SHP (Guthery et al. 1982). Recent statistics indicate the current patterns of agricultural activities on a north-south axis through the SHP (Table 4). In the southern and south-central part of the SHP, cotton is the dominant crop, whereas corn increases in the north-central zone. Farther north, crops of all kinds diminish as rangeland begins dominating the landscape (i.e., ≤12% is planted, mostly winter wheat). The percentage of irrigated land reaches its peak in the SHP "corn belt." Thus, a relatively small area in the north-central SHP presently provides both wetland habitat (i.e., playas) and the potential for large amounts of waste corn.

Baldassarre et al. (1983) provided an estimate based on moisture content of corn at harvest that predicts the amount of waste corn potentially available to waterfowl. The equation: total waste (kg/ha) = 1,544 - 54 (% harvest moisture). Hence, an additional 54 ± 5 kg/ha corn remains as field waste for each 1% decrease in the moisture content of the corn at harvest.

After harvest, waste corn becomes a dynamic food resource for waterfowl as determined by a variety of cultural treatments (Fig. 5). Deep plowing is the most damaging of the several post-harvest treatments of cornfields and should be discouraged in the management plans for wintering waterfowl. Deep plowing turns over soil from depths of 30 to 45 cm, thereby reducing the availability of corn at the surface by 97%. Even light disking (<20 cm depth) reduces the availability of waste corn by 77%. Thus, with diminished irrigation in the years ahead, it seems doubtful that a large waterfowl population could be supported if either of these post-harvest treatments were practiced widely on the vastly reduced acreage of corn projected for the future. Grazing livestock and handpicked salvage removed 84% and 58%, respectively, of the waste grain.

Burning maximizes the availability of waste corn for field-feeding waterfowl; fire removes the stalks and other litter without destroying either the ears or kernels of the residual grain (Baldassarre

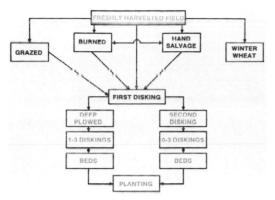

Fig. 5. Flow chart of potential agricultural treatments of freshly harvested cornfields on the SHP.

et al. 1983). The availability of waste corn is so great after burning that ducks can remove nearly all the grain present (Fig. 6). Indeed, field-feeding ducks gleaned all but 2% of the original amounts of waste corn remaining in 2 burned fields.

Thus, waste corn is available when ducks first arrive on the SHP, and many fields averaging >60 kg waste corn/ha are still available by late winter (Baldassarre et al. 1983, Baldassarre and Bolen 1984). Given that the average loss of corn was 3.7% per field (364 ± 12 kg/ha), burning could make nearly the entire amount available to wintering waterfowl, assuming no other post-harvest treatments. Moreover, if mallards consume nearly 100 g corn/day per bird, then a 100-ha field with an average amount of waste corn could feed about 4,000 mallards from December to February. If the entire yield of corn for a 100-ha field was available, 100,000 mallards could be supported for the same period.

Natural Foods.—The production and availability of natural plant and animal foods depend on the water entering playa basins. Farmers cycle tailwater into playa lakes during the growing season; thus many playas develop extensive stands of smartweeds, barnyardgrass, and other moist-soil plants. Later, however, farmers start irrigating with the water stored in playas instead of incurring the greater expense of pumping from the Ogallala Aquifer. Many playas are pumped dry and, lacking autumn rains, the existing moist-soil vegetation is unavailable to waterfowl.

Guthery and Stormer (1984) recommended a management scenario for flooding playas during the autumn and winter months. Periodic flooding during the growing season also was suggested as a means of increasing natural food production. The effects of playa modifications are varied because of the diversity of modification methods (Bolen and Guthery 1982, Guthery et al. 1982). Regardless of modification impacts, autumn-winter flooding of playa basins unquestionably will benefit wintering waterfowl, but the economic feasibility of such management is unknown. Presently, flooding 1 ha to a depth of 30 cm would cost about $85 in pumping costs, but the water may not persist through winter (Gray 1986).

The worst scenario for waterfowl wintering on the SHP will occur if the projections are realized for the declining availability of groundwater, thereby resulting in radically different cropping patterns (i.e., less irrigation). Waterfowl managers must realize that these projections may occur within 20 to 25 years and perhaps sooner if energy prices reach a point where pumping becomes cost prohibitive. The equation is simple: no irrigation = no corn = smaller populations of wintering ducks. It would be enlightening if we could determine how many ducks wintered on the SHP, and how those birds nourished themselves prior to the advent of irrigated agriculture. Under pristine conditions, the carrying capacity of the playas may have been greater than at present (i.e., pits and siltation may have lessened production of aquatic and semiaquatic vegetation). Also, perhaps more playas remained filled for longer periods before irrigation began lowering the watertable.

Fig. 6. Post-harvest appearance of cornfields showing dense litter (upper left). Treatments thereafter include burning (upper right), disking (bottom left), and deep plowing (lower right). Burning maximizes the availability of waste corn for field-feeding waterfowl.

Management Considerations for Other Wildlife

Playas are of significant value to migrant and resident wildlife because they exist as isolated habitats within an area of intensive farming. Guthery (1981) reported a concentration of 186 ring-necked pheasants (*Phasianus colchicus*) on a 12-ha playa during February (15.5 birds/ha). Bolen and Guthery (1982) and Bolen et al. (1979) detailed the abundance and variety of wildlife species associated with playa basins. Larger, open-water playas provide wintering habitat for a large part of the continental population of lesser sandhill cranes, whereas the drier, more heavily vegetated basins provide winter habitat for raptors, especially barn owls (*Tyto alba*), northern harriers (*Circus cyaneus*), and short-eared owls (*Asio flammeus*). Playas also provide significant spring and autumn habitat for migrant shorebirds (Baldassarre and Fischer 1984).

Cottontail rabbits (*Sylvilagus floridanus* and *S. auduboni*) are abundant in playa basins (Scribner 1982). Raccoons (*Procyon lotor*) (Juen 1981) and coyotes (*Canis latrans*) (Whiteside and Guthery 1981) also are major components of the mammalian fauna associated with playas. Small mammal populations, to date, have been surveyed only superficially, but include at least 10 species (Simpson and Bolen 1981).

Guthery and Bryant (1982) surveyed playas in 52 counties in 5 states, and, of these, only 12.6% provided good habitat for pheasants and wintering waterfowl. Seventy-four percent of the playas judged as good wildlife habitat occurred on only 20% of the study area. Forty-four percent of playas receiving irrigation runoff were rated as good habitat, compared to only 10% of those that did not receive tailwater. The primary recommendation was that management efforts focus on the larger playas. Smaller basins—especially those on farmland—are routinely tilled and often grazed, which limit their potential for management. Only 7% of playas <4 ha were assessed as good habitat. Curtailed grazing on farm playas would benefit pheasants during winter and breeding periods (Guthery et al. 1980), and could improve or create wildlife habitat on >60,000 ha.

Because the number of pheasants wintering on a playa is a linear function of the area of cattail (*Typha* sp.) and bulrush (*Scirpus* sp.), playa communities should be managed for emergent plants (Guthery and Whiteside 1984). Guthery and Stormer (1984) noted that creation of cattail and bulrush communities requires large and frequent amounts of water during the growing season. Thus, playas receiving irrigation runoff during summer usually provide good winter habitat for pheasants, which is not necessarily incompatible with habitat management for wintering waterfowl. Ducks, especially mallards, regularly use—and may prefer—playas with dense stands of cattail and bulrush (Moore 1980). These plant communities provide windbreaks, which may reduce stress among waterfowl (Bennett and Bolen 1978).

Disease History

Two major diseases strike waterfowl on the SHP: avian cholera (*Pasteurella multocida*) and avian botulism (*Clostridium botulinum*, Type C). Avian cholera was first documented in North America among wild waterfowl on the SHP near Dimmitt in Castro County (Quortrup et al. 1946, Petrides and Byrant 1951). The disease, perhaps, was introduced from discarded chicken carcasses left where the pathogens could wash into playas. Today, avian cholera claims large numbers of waterfowl throughout the Central Flyway and elsewhere in North America (Brand 1984). The interactions, if any, between playas and other areas with frequent epizootics of avian cholera remain unclear. Because avian cholera is extremely infectious, the high densities of waterfowl concentrating on playas surely contribute to the occurrence of epizootics on the SHP. Nonmigratory species also may be instrumental in maintaining avian cholera in playa environments. Common crows (*Corvus brachyrhynchos*) regularly scavenge duck carcasses on playas, and thus may be among the reservoirs for avian cholera (Taylor and Pence 1981).

Botulism is the second disease striking waterfowl in playa environments. Botulism may occur as early as July on the SHP, but epizootics are not annual events (Thompson 1985). Nonetheless, in some years, botulism and avian cholera together may kill many thousands of ducks and other birds on playa lakes. Moore and Simpson (1980) spot-sampled playas in Castro County, and estimated that the county-wide losses might have reached 35,000 ducks during the winter of 1978-79. Such findings underline the assertion that diseases are major factors among the nonhunting mortality befalling waterfowl populations (Friend 1976, Stout and Cornwell 1976).

As an example of the dynamics of land-use patterns and waterfowl ecology, we point out that castor beans (*Ricinus communis*) once poisoned thousands of waterfowl on the SHP (Jensen and Allen 1981). About 2,000 ducks died from this cause in Castro and Parmer counties in the winter of 1969-70. The primary toxin involved is ricin, a toxalbumin obtained from the direct ingestion of whole beans. Thus, thousands of other deaths in the same area may have been erroneously attributed to botulism (Wallace et al. 1986). In any event, castor beans are not currently part of the agricultural regime on the SHP, but we see in this example how settings can change for wintering waterfowl and their management.

Pesticides are used on the SHP, but Flickinger and Krynitsky (1987) found little evidence of organochlorine residues in ducks from the playas, and only 13% of the samples collected from the upper 6.5 cm of playa sediments contained low (0.05-0.22 ppm) amounts of organochlorines (all were chlordane isomers). The study concluded that agricultural contaminants were an unlikely source of mortality for ducks wintering on the playa lakes.

Significant mortality can occur among ducks and other waterbirds landing in sludge and spillage pits associated with oil fields (Flickinger 1981). The sheen of the oil simulates surface water, and birds landing in the pits quickly succumb in the viscous fluid. Less than 1 g of oil on the plumage of a single duck can cause death (Hunt 1961, Hartung 1967). At a single pit in Texas, Flickinger and Bunck (1987) counted the carcasses of nearly 300 ducks and other birds. At least 735 dead birds, mostly ducks, were counted in a playa used as an open oil-waste-disposal pit in west Texas (Endress and Erskine *in* Flickinger 1981). Similar losses in California have been estimated at 150,000 birds each year (Banks 1979), and a sample of avian mortality at 361 pits led Grover (*in* Flickinger and Bunck 1987) to conclude that 225,000 birds die annually in 5,649 pits in southeastern New Mexico. These estimates are conservative because carcasses sink, and only losses 1 to 3 weeks old can be assessed.

HABITAT MANAGEMENT
Characteristics of Playa Habitat

Most playas of moderate to high value to wildlife are concentrated in the central part of the SHP. Moreover, the density of playas in that area is higher than in other parts of the playa region, including the remainder of the Texas Panhandle, eastern New Mexico, southeastern Colorado, the Oklahoma Panhandle, and southwestern Kansas (Guthery and Bryant 1982). Most studies of playa ecology have

occurred where the high value playas are concentrated, including those cited below.

Fourteen physiognomic habitat types have been identified on playas (Table 5). The types reflect the response of vegetation to more or less natural factors as well as to land-use practices. Land-use practices having major impacts on the floristics and physiognomic communities in playas include (1) livestock grazing, (2) cultivation, (3) modification, i.e., excavation of pits or other means of draining or concentrating water for agricultural uses, and (4) tailwater recovery, i.e., collection of irrigation runoff in playas with or without modifications (according to the High Plains Underground Water Conservation District No. 1 [1977], up to 20% of flood irrigation water may leave farms as tailwater).

In the absence of human disturbances, the physiognomic types on playas often show distinctive, concentric zonation. Guthery et al. (1982:518) stated, "A sequence of community types that can occur from the center of the basin outward is wet meadow, mesic forb, and shortgrass. In drier playas, the wet meadow type is likely to be replaced by the mesic forb type. Some playas (probably those with more frequent and prolonged flooding) contain broadleaved emergent or mudflat types in the center, followed, going outward, by the wet meadow, mesic forb, and shortgrass . . . types. However, depending upon a playa's moisture regime, as influenced by its physical characteristics, tailwater recovery, and modification, intermediate zones may be absent or portions broken and replaced by other types (e.g., the wet meadow zone may be absent in the latter sequence, or the mesic forb type could be replaced by the disturbed forb type)."

The 4 dominant land-use practices have negative, neutral, or positive effects on plant species and physiognomic types important to waterfowl. Grazing reduces the frequencies of midgrasses (potential

Table 6. Names, attributes, and prevalence of physiognomic habitat types on playas (*n* = 101) in the Southern High Plains of Texas (Guthery et al. 1982).

Physiognomic type	Vegetation height (m)	Dominant taxa[a] (feature)	Secondary taxa[a] (feature)	Playas with type (%)
Open water		Pondweed (*Potamogeton* spp.)	Arrowhead (*Sagittaria longiloba*)	28
Broad-leaved emergent	0.5-1.2	Smartweeds (*Polygonum bicorne, P. lapathifolium*)	Barnyardgrass Spikerush	36
Narrow-leaved emergent	1.0-1.5	Cattail (*Typha domingensis*) Bulrush (*Scirpus* spp.)		13
Mesic forb	0.2-1.0	Devilweed (*Aster spinosus*) Gray ragweed (*Ambrosia grayii*)	Smartweeds Barnyardgrass Spikerush	26
Wet meadow	0.2-1.0	Barnyardgrass Red sprangletop (*Leptochloa filiformis*)	Smartweeds Spikerush Devilweed	41
Johnsongrass	0.5-1.5	Johnsongrass (*Sorghum halepense*)		17
Disturbance forb	0.5-1.5	Kochia (*Kochia scoparia*) Blueweed sunflower (*Helianthus ciliaris*)	Horseweed (*Conyza canadensis*) Wild lettuce (*Lactuca* spp.)	9
Cultivation	Variable	Crop		20
Mudflat	<0.5	Absence of vegetation	Barnyardgrass Water-hyssop (*Bacopa rotundifolia*)	16
Spoilbank		Kochia Camphor-weed (*Heterotheca* spp.)	Russianthistle (*Salsola kali*)	1
Midgrass	0.5	Western wheatgrass (*Agropyron smithii*) Vine-mesquite (*Panicum obtusum*)		
Shortgrass	<0.2	Buffalograss (*Buchloe dactyloides*)	Gray ragweed	13
Road-pit[b]	Variable	Absence of vegetation		12
Tree-shrub	Variable	Willow (*Salix nigra*) Saltcedar (*Tamarix gallica*) Chinese elm (*Ulmus pumila*)		21

[a]Dominant taxa were those that were most prevalent in terms of coverage; secondary taxa were those that commonly occurred in a type, but had lower coverage than the dominant taxa. Nomenclature follows Gould (1975).

[b]The road-pit physiognomic type refers to calcereous spoil (caliche) deposited for road fill or excavated from borrow pits in the basin.

nest sites) and cattail, but has neutral effects on foods such as barnyardgrass and smartweed (Table 6). Cultivation obviously reduces the extent of natural communities. Modifications of the drainage patterns in playas (e.g., pits) are associated positively with many desirable features of waterfowl habitat, including the presence of spikesedge, midgrasses, smartweed, arrowhead, pondweed, narrow-leaved cattail, bulrush, and open water. This relationship probably is not a direct result of modification, but instead occurs because 40-60% of modified playas are located in the most heavily irrigated part of the playa region (Guthery and

Bryant 1982). Tailwater recovery, thus, overrides the potential negative effects of modification. Tailwater, by flooding playas, is the most powerful influence on waterfowl habitat in the SHP. Moreover, the influx of tailwater increases the interspersion of physiognomic communities by a factor of 14 (Guthery et al. 1982).

Land-use practices that influence playas usually occur in combinations rather than singly. These interactions have been studied (Guthery et al. 1982, Guthery and Stormer 1984), with the following results:

Voluminous and frequent inputs of tailwater during the growing season fostered wetland situations, regardless of the

Table 6. Effects of playa size and land-use practices on the frequency of occurrence of plant species on playas ($n = 301$) in the Southern High Plains of Texas (Guthery and Stormer 1984). The range of sizes with the highest percentage frequency of occurrence is listed if there were significant ($P < 0.05$) effects. For the land-use practices, $+$ = positive effect, 0 = neutral effect, and $-$ = negative effect ($P < 0.05$).

Species	Overall frequency (%)	Preferred size (ha)	Tailwater	Modification	Grazing	Tillage
Flatspine ragweed						
(*Ambrosia acanthicarpa*)	69	No effect	0	0	0	0
Barnyardgrass	64	No effect	0	0	0	0
Blueweed sunflower	62	No effect	0	0	0	0
Buffalograss	42	>12	+	+	+	−
Lambsquarters						
(*Chenopodium album*)	42	16-20	+	+	0	−
Spikerush						
(*Eleocharis* sp.)	40	>20	+	+	+	−
Belvedere summercypress						
(*Kochia scoparia*)	38	>4	+	+	0	0
Johnsongrass	37	4-16	0	+	−	+
Amaranth						
(*Amaranthus* sp.)	37	No effect	−	0	0	+
Horseweed	31	No effect	+	+	0	0
Devilweed	29	8-16	−	−	0	0
Curltop smartweed	26	20	+	+	+	−
American cocklebur						
(*Xanthium italicum*)	23	12-20	+	+	+	−
Western wheatgrass	23	>16	+	+	−	−
Common sunflower						
(*Helianthus annuus*)	20	8-16	+	+	0	0
Dock						
(*Rumex* spp.)	15	8-12	+	+	0	0
Arrowhead	15	8-20	+	+	0	−
Vine mesquite	13	>8	0	0	−	−
Black willow	12	8-16	+	+	0	0
Chinese elm	11	No effect	+	+	0	0
Pepperwort						
(*Marsilea* sp.)	11	12-20	+	0	0	−
Prickly lettuce						
(*Lactuca serriola*)	9	8-16	0	+	0	+
Pondweed	8	8-20	+	+	0	0
Cattail	7	8-20	+	+	−	0
Bulrush	7	8-20	+	+	0	0
Russianthistle	7	No effect	+	0	0	0
Saltcedar	3	8-12	0	+	0	0

[a]Nomenclature follows Gould (1975).

presence of other land-use practices. Narrow-leaved emergent communities rarely existed without heavy influx of tailwater (Guthery and Bryant 1982).

Heavy spring and summer grazing of large playas, even in the presence of minor modifications, was associated with wet meadow and shortgrass physiognomic types (Table 5).

Cultivation or modification of small playas in the absence of grazing and tailwater influx was associated with disturbance-forb species such as prickly lettuce, horseweed, and lambsquarters or Johnsongrass.

Minor to moderate influx of tailwater during early spring and summer on medium-sized playas surrounded by cropland was associated with dock, curltop smartweed, pepperwort, and some forbs associated with disturbed soil.

Voluminous and persistent influx of

tailwater, in combination with heavy sedimentation and little or no grazing, was associated with tree-shrub physiognomic types, cattail, and disturbance forbs such as common sunflower and lambsquarters.

Low and infrequent influx of tailwater in combination with modification and little or no grazing was associated with disturbance forbs such as Russianthistle and Belvedere summercypress or Johnsongrass.

Frequent tillage on small playas that lack modification, tailwater input, and grazing was associated with disturbance forbs such as redroot amaranth (*Amaranthus retroflexus*), Belvedere summercypress, common sunflower, and lambsquarters.

Experimental Littoral Zones

A management experiment for increasing the production of natural foods employed the construction of artificial littoral zones on pits in modified playa basins. Gray (1986) modified 7 steep-sided pits by adding steplike terraces on 1 side so that shallow, littoral habitats would be available to waterfowl and shorebirds regardless of water depth in the pit (Fig. 7). The pits averaged 73 × 26 m in bottom length and width, and 73 × 54 m in top length and width, and covered a surface area of 0.36 ha. A staircase of 2-5 terraces was constructed on 1 side of the pit; each terrace averaged 68 × 6.7 m in length and width, and 58 cm in height.

Plants on terraces produced more vegetation and 570% more seeds than the opposite steep side of the same pit or on separate control pits. Further, terraced pits provided nearly 3 times more biomass of invertebrates than did control areas. Invertebrate numbers were variable, but often spectacular, as evidenced by densities of $14,000/m^2$ for chironomids and $140,000/m^3$ for cladocerans (*Cladocera* spp.). Waterfowl and shorebirds responded accordingly and used terraced

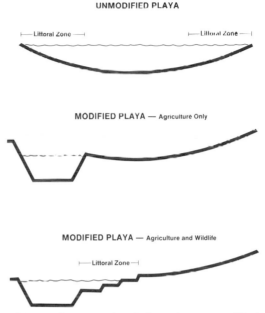

Fig. 7. Cross-sectional view of an unmodified playa basin (top) compared with a basin modified for the storage of water for agricultural uses (middle). Steep-sided pits are common modifications and often drain much of the littoral zones in playa basins. Experimental modification for agriculture and wildlife (bottom) is designed with terraces on one side of the pit so that shallow areas occur at any water depth (Gray 1986, Gray and Bolen 1987). Drawings not to scale.

pits more than controls. Lee (1985) determined that mallards spent 27% of their feeding time in terraced pits versus 9% on unterraced control areas. Terracing probably provided waterfowl with sources of proteinaceous foods that are important nutritional supplements to the staple diet of waste corn.

Given that 33% of the playas observed by Guthery and Bryant (1982) were modified and that there are about 19,300 playas on the SHP in Texas, the potential exists for improving more than 6,300 playas with small-scale management efforts. The cost of constructing terraces on new pits is approximately $1,000, but there are no maintenance costs thereafter (Gray 1986). Indeed, terraced pits may have longer lifespans than steep-sided pits, because vegetation on the terraces entraps much of the silt washing in with the runoff. Lacking silt traps, pits require periodic dredging; otherwise, they are abandoned and replaced with new excavations.

Water volume in the typical unterraced pits averaged 22% of the basin volume (Gray 1986). Because of the reduced surface area, water collecting in the pits often persists for several months (unless pumped for irrigation), and such sites can provide waterfowl with refugia when other areas are dry. Pits also may provide thermally favorable habitats, as they are used heavily by waterfowl during cold weather (Whyte et al. 1986). For example, terraced pits averaged 144 ducks/survey from January to April (Gray 1986) and 1,000 ducks often occur on larger pits. However, steep-sided pits are poor feeding habitat; terraced pits offer a good management alternative relative to the food and cover needs of waterfowl and water storage for agricultural purposes. We caution, however, that pit construction usually produces a high spoil-bank, providing hunters with easy and unseen access to large numbers of ducks. Unscrupulous hunters potentially could kill scores of birds; thus, special construction codes may be necessary to eliminate spoil-banks.

Gray (1986) further suggested that installation of 1-way flip gates on pipes funneling water into pits could create a variety of management scenarios for playa basins. For example, water could be moved from a pit to the surrounding playa basin, thereby increasing waterfowl habitat during winter. In contrast, water could drain into the pit during the summer as a means of increasing the production of moist-soil vegetation in the basin.

Recommendations

We do not yet know how waterfowl wintering on the SHP specifically exploit the playa ecosystem for the full range of their seasonal requirements. Nevertheless, some interaction between water in playas, corn in fields, and natural wetland foods clearly is essential for the welfare of wintering ducks on the SHP. Accordingly, under present conditions, we recommend that managers strive for the following: (1) acquisition or easement of at least 4-5 large (>40 ha), relatively permanent "core" playas per county; (2) construction of terraces on pits excavated in playa basins within 5 km of the core playas; and (3) intensive postharvest management of waste corn on private lands, including planting of fields leased expressly for corn production, within 5 km of the core playas.

CONCLUSIONS
Future Considerations

We emphasize the importance of the relationship between future management opportunities and the participation of private landowners. Except for 2 widely separated national wildlife refuges (Muleshoe and Buffalo Lake), virtually all playas on the SHP and the surrounding lands are held in private ownership. Thus, even with a program of public management (e.g., acquisition of core playas with duck stamp funds), the ultimate welfare of wildlife associated with playa wetlands rests with the private sector. Development of a lease-fee hunting system offers an important incentive for the participation of landowners in long-term habitat management (Chamberlain and Davis 1986).

Bolen and Guthery (1982) discussed the potential importance of hunting fees as farm income considering the forecasts of diminishing groundwater supplies and the associated decrease in dollar returns from dryland crops. For example, by the year 2020, the estimated dollar return from irrigated crop production is $267/ha, whereas the projected value for dryland crops is only $86/ha. Hence, there is potential reduction of $181 for each ha of irrigated cropland reverting to dryland farming These projections indicate that supplemental income in the form of lease-fee hunting would be a welcome—and attainable—option for area farmers Accordingly, the stage is set for actions that will accrue benefits for both farmers and wildlife into the 21st century.

Research Priorities

Disease Control.—Much remains unknown about the epizootiology of many waterfowl diseases, but the extreme virulence of avian cholera makes its control one of the highest priorities for waterfowl management in North America. The matter of disease control is especially crucial on playas and other areas where birds are highly concentrated. Much also needs to be learned about the pathways by which avian cholera moves between playas and other locations in the Central Flyway (e.g., Rainwater Basins in Nebraska). Determination of the ways that avian cholera persists in playa environments seems crucial, as do the associations, if any, between the disease and the wastes discharged from cattle feedlots into nearby playas.

Much more is known about the epizootiology of botulism (Wobeser 1981, Thompson 1985). Moreover, botulism often may be curtailed where water levels can be managed (i.e., rapidly flooding or draining affected habitat). Regrettably, few playas have the potential for such management, and epizootics of botulism remain unchecked on the SHP. Pence (1981) suggested that pits excavated in playas may lessen the occurrence of botulism by reducing fluctuations in water levels. If so, then the management improvements suggested by Gray's (1986) experiments will require additional monitoring. That is, might artificial littoral zones increase epizootics of botulism on managed pits, thereby offsetting gains associated with improved availability of food resources?

Moist-soil Communities and Other

Habitat.—We earlier suggested that the natural foods available in moist-soil communities are important sources of nutrients for waterfowl wintering on the SHP. Plant and animal foods in these communities provide essential proteins and minerals not available in a diet dominated by waste corn. Also, we noted how terraces improved the availability of natural foods in playas where pits have curtailed the normal drainage patterns and reduced the littoral zones and associated moist-soil communities. However, more must be learned about the production and nutritional qualities of moist-soil plants on a larger array of playa types in the SHP and about the selection of these sites by wintering waterfowl.

Overall, a great deal of habitat-oriented research remains, much of which focuses on the dynamic events concerning irrigation and land-use patterns in the years ahead. As mentioned earlier, the reduction of irrigation presents a 2-fold problem for waterfowl management: (1) less corn for food, and (2) less tailwater for the wetland communities in playas. What foods will be available in the future to maintain waterfowl populations at levels of a million or more birds? If irrigation diminishes, then far less water will run into playas. Hence, how can the carrying capacity of playas be improved in a region again dependent on rainfall alone? As an historical aside, we note that bankers early in the current century assessed the water levels of playas as a means of judging rainfall, and hence determined their loans to farmers for the following season (Johnson 1947). In the years ahead, wildlife managers may be making similar assessments for future crops of waterfowl.

SUMMARY

More than 19,000 playa basins dot the SHP in Texas and, in wet years, provide winter habitat for 1-2 million waterfowl. Mallards, green-winged teal, northern pintails, and American wigeon are the principal species. Waste corn dominates the diet of waterfowl wintering on the SHP, but recent evidence indicates that the method of collection overestimates the importance of corn. Further, because corn is deficient in several essential amino acids, the native plant and animal foods in playas provide an important food source for wintering waterfowl.

Nonetheless, waste corn is an important aspect of wintering waterfowl management on the SHP. The amount of waste corn initially available is related to moisture at harvest. Burning field litter maximizes the availability of waste corn for field-feeding waterfowl, whereas disking and plowing reduce availability by 77% to 97%. The enhancement of moist-soil vegetation in playas also is an important management goal. Cultivation, modification (i.e., pits and ditches), grazing, and irrigation runoff are major influences on vegetation associated with playa basins. Playas receiving irrigation runoff offer maximum habitat diversity and provide good habitat for waterfowl and other wildlife. Water-storage pits in playa basins can reduce littoral zones, but construction of terraces in the pits creates new feeding areas.

Recommendations include protection of at least 4 large "core" playas per county in the SHP, construction of terraces in pits within 5 km of the core playas, and intensive management of waste corn. Research priorities center on the control of waterfowl diseases and the influences that changing land-use patterns (e.g., reduced irrigation) will have on waterfowl wintering on the SHP.

LITERATURE CITED

Allen, B. L., B. L. Harris, K. R. Davis, and G. B. Miller. 1972. The mineralogy and chemistry of High Plains playa lake soils and sediments. Water Resour. Cent. Publ. WRC-72-4, Texas Tech Univ., Lubbock. 75 pp.

Ankney, C. D., and C. D. MacInnes. 1978. Nutrient reserves and reproductive performance of female lesser snow geese. Auk 95:459-471.

Aronovici, V. S., A. D. Schneider, and O. R. Jones. 1970. Basin recharging the Ogallala Aquifer through Pleistocene sediments. Pages 182-192 in Ogallala aquifer symp., ICASALS Spec. Rep. 39, Texas Tech Univ., Lubbock.

Baldassarre, G. A., and E. G. Bolen. 1984. Field-feeding ecology of waterfowl wintering on the Southern High Plains of Texas. J. Wildl. Manage. 48:63-71.

————, and ————. 1986. Body weight and aspects of pairing chronology of green-winged teal and northern pintails wintering on the Southern High Plains of Texas. Southwest. Nat. 31:361-366.

————, and D. H. Fischer. 1984. Food habits of fall migrant shorebirds on the Texas High Plains. J. Field Ornithol. 55:220-229.

————, E. E. Quinlan, and E. G. Bolen. 1988. Mobility and site fidelity of green-winged teal wintering in the Southern High Plains of Texas. Pages 483-495 in M. W. Weller, ed. Waterfowl in winter. Univ. Minnesota Press, Minneapolis.

————, R. J. Whyte, and E. G. Bolen. 1986. Body weight and carcass composition of nonbreeding green-winged teal on the Southern High Plains of Texas. J. Wildl. Manage. 50:420-426.

————, R. J. Whyte, E. E. Quinlan, and E. G. Bolen. 1983. Dynamics and quality of waste corn available to postbreeding waterfowl in Texas. Wildl. Soc. Bull. 11:25-31.

Banks, R. C. 1979. Human related mortality of birds in the United States. U.S. Fish and Wildl. Serv., Sci. Rep. Wildl. No. 215:1-16.

Bennett, J. W., and E. G. Bolen. 1978. Stress response in wintering green-winged teal. J. Wildl. Manage. 42:81-86.

Blem, C. R. 1976. Patterns of lipid storage and utilization in birds. Am. Zool. 16:671-684.

Bolen, E. G., and D. L. Flores. 1988. Prairie wetlands of west Texas: the history and ecology of playa lakes. Proc. North Am. Prairie Conf. 10: in press.

————, and F. S. Guthery. 1982. Playas, irrigation, and wildlife in west Texas. Trans. North Am. Wildl. and Nat. Resour. Conf. 47:528-541.

————, C. D. Simpson, and F. A. Stormer. 1979. Playa lakes: threatened wetlands on the southern Great Plains. Pages 23-30 in Riparian and wetland habitats of the Great Plains. Publ. 91, Great Plains Agric. Counc., U.S.D.A. For. Serv., Fort Collins, Colo.

Bolton, H. E. 1949. Coronado, knight of pueblos and plains. Univ. New Mexico Press, Albuquerque. 491 pp.

Brand, C. J. 1984. Avian cholera in the Central and Mississippi flyways during 1979-80. J. Wildl. Manage. 48:399-406.

Bruns, H. E. 1974. Soil survey of Castro County, Texas. Soil Conserv. Serv., Temple, Tex. 41 pp.

Buller, R. J. 1964. Central flyway. Pages 209-232 *in* J. P. Linduska, ed. Waterfowl tomorrow. U.S. Fish and Wildl. Serv., Washington, D.C.

Carroll, H. D., editor. 1941. Journal of Lt. J. W. Abert from Bent's Fort to St. Louis in 1845. Panhandle-Plains Hist. Rev. 14:9-113.

Chamberlain, P. A., and B. Davis. 1986. Marketing waterfowl hunting lease opportunities. Pages 219-225 *in* D. E. Guynn and T. R. Troxel, eds. Proc. 1986 Int. Ranchers Roundup. Texas A&M Univ., Texas Agric. Res. and Extension Center, Uvalde.

Clyma, W., and F. B. Lotspeich. 1966. Water resources in the High Plains of Texas and New Mexico. U.S.D.A. Res. Serv. ARS 41. 114 pp.

Curtis, D., and H. Beierman. 1980. The playa lakes characterization study. U.S. Fish and Wildl. Serv., Austin, Tex. 55 pp.

Dvoracek, M. J. 1981. Modification of playa lakes in the Texas Panhandle. Pages 64-82 *in* J. S. Barclay and W. V. White, eds. Proc. playa lakes symp. U.S. Fish and Wildl. Serv., FWS/OBS-81/07.

Fischer, D. H., M. D. Schibler, R. J. Whyte, and E. G. Bolen. 1982. Checklist of birds from the playa lakes of the southern Texas Panhandle. Bull. Texas Ornithol. Soc. 15:2-7.

Flickinger, E. L. 1981. Wildlife mortality at petroleum pits in Texas. J. Wildl. Manage. 45:560-564.

———, and C. M. Bunck. 1987. Number of oil-killed birds and fate of bird carcasses at crude oil pits in Texas. Southwest. Nat. 32:377-381.

———, and A. J. Krynitsky. 1987. Organochlorine residues in ducks on playa lakes of the Texas Panhandle and Eastern New Mexico. J. Wildl. Dis. 431188 188.

Fredrickson, L. H., and T. S. Taylor. 1982. Management of seasonally flooded impoundments for wildlife. U.S. Fish and Wildl. Serv. Resour. Publ. 18. 29 pp.

Friend, M. 1976. Diseases: a threat to our waterfowl. Ducks Unlimited 40(2):36-37.

Frye, J. C., and L. A. Byron. 1957. Studies of Cenozoic geology along the eastern margin of the Texas High Plains, Armstrong to Howard Counties. Univ. Texas Bur. Econ. Geol. Rep. 32. 60 pp.

Funk, H. D., J. R. Grieb, D. Witt, G. F. Wrakestraw, G. W. Merrill, T. Kuck, D. Timm, T. Logan, and C. D. Stutzenbaker. 1971. Justification of the Central Flyway High Plains Mallard Management Unit. Central Flyway Tech. Comm. Rep. Washington, D.C. 48 pp.

Gould, F. W. 1975. Texas plants—a checklist and ecological summary. Texas Agric. Exp. Stn. Misc. Publ. 585. 121 pp.

Gray, P. N. 1986. Experimental littoral zones in playa lakes as wildlife habitat. M.S. Thesis, Texas Tech Univ., Lubbock. 125 pp.

———, and E. G. Bolen. 1987. Seed reserves in the tailwater pits of playa lakes in relation to waterfowl management. Wetlands 7:11-23.

Grieb, J. R. 1970. The shortgrass prairie Canada goose population. Wildl. Monogr. 22. 49 pp.

Grubb, H. W., and D. L. Parks. 1968. Multipurpose benefits and costs of modifying playa lakes of the Texas High Plains. ICASALS Spec. Rep. 6, Texas Tech Univ., Lubbock. 66 pp.

Guthery, F. S. 1981. Playa basins and resident wildlife in Texas Panhandle. Pages 47-51 *in* J. S. Barclay and W. V. White, eds. Proc. playa lakes symp. U.S. Fish and Wildl. Serv., FWS/OBS-81/07.

———, and F. C. Bryant. 1982. Status of playas in the southern Great Plains. Wildl. Soc. Bull. 10:309-317.

———, J. Custer, and M. Owen. 1980. Texas Panhandle pheasants: their history, habitat needs, habitat development opportunities, and future. U.S.D.A. For. Serv., Gen. Tech. Rep. RM 74. 11 pp.

———, F. C. Bryant, B. Kramer, A. Stoecker, and M. Dvoracek. 1981. Playa assessment study. Water and Power Resour. Serv., Amarillo, Tex. 182 pp.

———, S. M. Obenberger, and F. A. Stormer. 1984. Predictors of site use by ducks on the Texas High Plains. Wildl. Soc. Bull. 12:35-40.

———, J. M. Pates, and F. A. Stormer. 1982. Characterization of playas of the north-central Llano Estacado in Texas. Trans. North Am. Wildl. and Nat. Resour. Conf. 47:516-527.

———, and F. A. Stormer. 1984. Wildlife management scenarios for playa vegetation. Wildl. Soc. Bull. 12:227-234.

———, and R. W. Whitcotte. 1984. Playa important to pheasants on the Texas High Plains. Wildl. Soc. Bull. 12:40-43.

Haley, J. E. 1968. Albert Pike's journeys in the prairie, 1831-1832. Panhandle-Plains Hist. Rev. 41:1-91.

Hartung, R. 1967. Energy metabolism in oil-covered ducks. J. Wildl. Manage. 29:872-874.

Hawkins, A. S. 1945. Bird life in the Texas Panhandle. Panhandle-Plains Hist. Rev. 18:110-150.

Heitmeyer, M. E., and P. A. Vohs, Jr. 1984. Distribution and habitat use of waterfowl wintering in Oklahoma. J. Wildl. Manage. 48:51-62.

High Plains Underground Water Conservation District No. 1. 1977. Guide to irrigation tailwater recovery. High Plains Underground Water Conserv. Dist. No. 1. Rep. 77-01. Lubbock, Tex. 78 pp.

Holliday, V. T. 1985. New data on the stratigraphy and pedology of the Clovis and Plainview sites, Southern High Plains. Quaternary Res. 23:388-402.

Hunt, G. S. 1961. Waterfowl losses on the lower Detroit River due to oil pollution. Pages 10-26 in Proc. 4th conf. on Great Lakes Res. Great Lakes Res. Div., Inst. Sci. and Tech. Publ. 7, Univ. Michigan, Ann Arbor.

Iverson, C. G., P. A. Vohs, and T. C. Tacha. 1985. Distribution and abundance of sandhill cranes wintering in western Texas. J. Wildl. Manage. 49:250-255.

Jensen, W. I., and J. P. Allen. 1981. Naturally occurring and experimentally induced castor bean (Ricinus communis) poisoning in ducks. Avian Dis. 25:184-194.

Johnson, E. 1983. The Lubbock Lake Paleoindian record. Pages 81-105 in V. T. Holliday, ed., Guidebook to the central Llano Estacado. ICASALS and The Museum, Texas Tech Univ., Lubbock.

Johnson, V. 1947. Heaven's tableland, the Dust Bowl story. Farrar, Straus and Co., New York, N.Y. 288 pp.

Judson, S. 1950. Depressions of the northern portion of the Southern High Plains of eastern New Mexico. Bull. Geol. Soc. Am. 61:253-273.

Juen, J. J. 1981. Home range, movements, and denning sites of raccoons on the High Plains of Texas. M.S. Thesis, Texas Tech Univ., Lubbock. 40 pp.

Kendall, G. W. 1847. Narrative of the Texan Santa Fe Expedition. Vol. 1. Washbourne, London. 599 pp.

Krapu, G. L. 1981. The role of nutrient reserves in mallard reproduction. Auk 98:29-38.

——, and G. A. Swanson. 1975. Some nutritional aspects of reproduction in prairie-nesting pintails. J. Wildl. Manage. 39:156-162.

Lee, S. D. 1985. A time budget study of mallards on the Texas High Plains. M.S. Thesis, Texas Tech Univ., Lubbock. 32 pp.

Lotspeich, F. B., and J. R. Coover. 1962. Soil forming factors on the Llano Estacado: parent material, time and topography. Texas J. Sci. 14:7-17.

McCauley, C. A. H. 1877. Notes on the ornithology of the region about the source of the Red River of Texas. U.S. Geol. Geogr. Surv. Territ. 3:655-695.

Merickel, F. W., and J. K. Wangberg. 1981. Species composition and diversity of macroinvertebrates in two playa lakes on the Southern High Plains, Texas. Southwest. Nat. 26:153-158.

Moore, R. L. 1980. Aspects of the ecology and hunting economics of migratory waterfowl on the Texas High Plains. M.S. Thesis, Texas Tech Univ., Lubbock. 80 pp.

——, and C. D. Simpson. 1980. Disease mortality of waterfowl on Texas playa lakes. Southwest. Nat. 25:566-568.

Obenberger, S. M. 1982. Numerical response of wintering waterfowl to macrohabitat in the southern High Plains of Texas. M.S. Thesis, Texas Tech Univ., Lubbock. 43 pp.

Parks, L. H. 1975. Some trends in ecological succession in temporary aquatic ecosystems (playa lakes). Ph.D. Dissertation, Texas Tech Univ., Lubbock. 79 pp.

Pence, D. B. 1981. The effects of modification and environmental contamination of playa lakes on wildlife morbidity and mortality. Pages 83-93 in J. S. Barclay and W. VV. White, eds. Proc. playa lakes symp. U.S. Fish and Wildl. Serv., FWS/OBS-81/07.

Petrides, G. A., and C. R. Byrant. 1951. An analysis of the 1949-50 fowl cholera epizootic in Texas Panhandle waterfowl. Trans. North Am. Wildl. Conf. 16:193-216.

Quinlan, E. E., and G. A. Baldassarre. 1984. Activity budgets of non-breeding green-winged teal on playa lakes in Texas. J. Wildl. Manage. 48:838-845.

Quortrup, E. R., F. B. Queen, and L. J. Merovka. 1946. An outbreak of pasteurellosis in wild ducks. J. Am. Vet. Med. Assoc. 108:94-100.

Raveling, D. G. 1979. The annual cycle of body composition of Canada geese with special reference to control of reproduction. Auk 96:234-252.

Reeves, C. C., Jr. 1966. Pluvial lake basins of west Texas. J. Geol. 74:269-291.

Reinecke, K. J., and R. B. Owen. 1980. Food use and nutrition of black ducks nesting in Maine. J. Wildl. Manage. 44:549-558.

Rhodes, M. J., and J. D. Garcia. 1981. Characteristics of playa lakes related to summer waterfowl use. Southwest. Nat. 26:231-235.

Richardson, L. G. 1971. A sampling study of the macroinvertebrate ecology of a desert playa lake in southwestern New Mexico. M.S. Thesis, Texas Tech Univ., Lubbock. 58 pp.

Rollo, J. D., and E. G. Bolen. 1969. Ecological relationships of blue and green-winged teal on the High Plains of Texas in early fall. Southwest. Nat. 14:171-188.

Sanderson, G. C. 1976. Conservation of waterfowl. Pages 43-58 in F. C. Bellrose, Ducks, geese and swans of North America. Second ed. Stackpole Books, Harrisburg, Pa.

Scribner, K. T. 1982. Population ecology and genetics of the eastern cottontail rabbit on west Texas playa basins. M.S. Thesis, Texas Tech Univ., Lubbock. 46 pp.

Sell, D. L. 1979. Fall foods of teal on the Texas High Plains. Southwest. Nat. 24:373-375.

Sellards, E. H. 1938. Artifacts associated with fossil elephant. Bull. Geol. Soc. Am. 49:999-1,010.

Sheeley, D. G. 1988. Aspects of northern pintail wintering ecology on the Southern High Plains of Texas. M.S. Thesis, Texas Tech Univ., Lubbock. 98 pp.

Sibbald, I. R. 1979. Bioavailable amino acids and true metabolizable energy of cereal grains. Poult. Sci. 58:934-939.

Simpson, C. D., and E. G. Bolen. 1981. Wildlife assessment of playa lakes. Rep. to Southwest Region, Bur. of Reclam., Amarillo, Tex. 159 pp.

———, E. G. Bolen, R. L. Moore, and F. A. Stormer. 1981. Significance of playas to migratory wildlife. Pages 35-45 *in* J. S. Barclay and W. V. White, eds. Proc. playa lakes symp. U.S. Fish and Wildl. Serv. FWS/OBS 81/07.

Soutiere, E. C., H. S. Myrick, and E. G. Bolen. 1972. Chronology and behavior of American wigeon wintering in Texas. J. Wildl. Manage. 36:752-758.

Stevenson, J. O. 1942. Birds of the central panhandle of Texas. Condor 44:108-115.

Stout, I. J., and G. W. Cornwell. 1976. Nonhunting mortality of fledged North American waterfowl. J. Wildl. Manage. 40:681-693.

Strecker, J. K., Jr. 1910. Notes on the fauna of a portion of the canyon region of northwestern Texas. Baylor Univ. Bull. 8:1-33.

Sublette, J. E., and M. S. Sublette. 1967. The limnology of playa lakes on the Llano Estacado, New Mexico and Texas. Southwest. Nat. 12:369-406.

Sugden, L. G. 1973. Feeding ecology of pintail, gadwall, American wigeon and lesser scaup ducklings. Can. Wildl. Serv. Rep. Ser. No. 24. 45 pp.

Swanson, G. A., and J. C. Bartonek. 1970. Bias associated with food analysis in gizzards of blue-winged teal. J. Wildl. Manage. 34:739-746.

———, G. C. Krapu, J. C. Bartonek, J. R. Serie, and D. H. Johnson. 1974. Advantages in mathematically weighing waterfowl food habits data. J. Wildl. Manage. 38:302-307.

Taylor, T. T., and F. S. Guthery. 1980. Use of playa lakes and surrounding cover types for duck nesting. Page 54 *in* R. E. Sosebee and F. S. Guthery, eds. Research highlights Vol. 11. Dep. Range and Wildl. Manage., Texas Tech Univ., Lubbock.

———, and D. B. Pence. 1981. Avian cholera in common crows, *Corvus brachyrhynchos*, from the central Texas Panhandle. J. Wildl. Dis. 17:511-514.

Texas Agricultural Statistics Service. 1985. Texas County Statistics. Texas Dep. Agric. Austin, Tex. 273 pp.

Thompson, G. K. 1985. Factors associated with waterfowl botulism in the Southern High Plains of Texas. M.S. Thesis, Texas Tech Univ., Lubbock. 79 pp.

Traweek, M. S. 1978. Texas waterfowl production survey. Fed. Wildl. Restor. Aid Proj. No. W-106-R-5. Texas Parks and Wildl. Dep., Austin. 17 pp.

Wallace, B. M., D. B. Pence, and E. G. Bolen. 1986. Historical survey of waterfowl diseases in the playa lakes region. Rep. to U.S. Fish and Wildl. Serv., Albuquerque, N.M. 67 pp.

Ward, C. R., and E. W. Huddleston. 1970. Multipurpose modification of playa lakes. Pages 203-286 *in* Playa lakes symposium. ICASALS Publ. No. 4, Texas Tech Univ., Lubbock.

Whiteside, R. W., and F. S. Guthery. 1981. Coyote use of playas in the Texas High Plains. Prairie Nat. 13:42-44.

Whyte, R. J., G. A. Baldassarre, and E. G. Bolen. 1986. Winter condition of mallards on the Southern High Plains of Texas. J. Wildl. Manage. 50:52-57.

———, and E. G. Bolen. 1984. Impact of winter stress on mallard body composition. Condor 86:477-482.

———, and E. G. Bolen. 1985. Corn consumption by wintering mallards during morning field-flights. Prairie Nat. 17:71-78.

Wobeser, G. A. 1981. Diseases of wild waterfowl. Plenum Press, New York, N. Y. 300 pp.

THE RICE PRAIRIES

WILLIAM C. HOBAUGH, Southeast Texas Wildlife Foundation, P. O. Box 666, Columbus, TX 78934
CHARLES D. STUTZENBAKER, Texas Parks and Wildlife Department, 10 Parks and Wildlife Drive, Port Arthur, TX 77640
EDWARD L. FLICKINGER, U.S. Fish and Wildlife Service, Patuxent Wildlife Research Center, P.O. Box 2506, Victoria, TX 77901

In the 1980s, >1 million Central Flyway geese and >1 million ducks have wintered in the coastal marshes and adjacent rice lands of Texas (Larned et al. 1980, Frentress 1986, 1987). Historically, large concentrations of snow geese (*Chen caerulescens*) and other waterfowl wintered along the Gulf Coast in the brackish marshes and wet prairies directly adjacent to these marshes (McIlhenny 1932, Lynch 1975, Bateman et al. 1988). The development of the inland rice industry has altered the wintering areas and habits of these birds. Bellrose (1980) reported that thousands of snow geese have moved out of the coastal areas to new wintering grounds in the rice-producing areas. Winter surveys between 1980 and 1986 show that the rice-producing area southwest of Houston is now the most important goose wintering area in Texas (Stutzenbaker 1980, 1984, Frentress 1987). Over 1.5 million waterfowl now wintering in the rice prairies are dependent on the agricultural practices and land-use patterns associated with rice farming (Hobaugh 1984). Thus, the rice prairies are a vulnerable segment of invaluable wintering habitat for waterfowl. The objectives of this paper are to delineate the current status of waterfowl wintering in the rice prairies of southeast Texas, to describe habitat management techniques that affect migrating and wintering waterfowl there, and to report future management and research needs of waterfowl in this area.

RICE PRAIRIES

Location and Description

"Rice prairies" have been widely used to refer to those former coastal prairies that have been cultivated for rice production. There are 4 major well-known prairies having no distinct boundaries, as well as several smaller ones. The major rice prairies are the Beaumont Prairie east of Houston and, proceeding westward from Houston, the Katy, Lissie, and Garwood prairies, which are separated by bands of timber and wooded areas along the major rivers and creeks (Fig. 1). These rice prairies comprise approximately 9,000 km² in portions of 16 counties.

The Texas rice prairies generally include that area north of the marsh zone extending from Port Lavaca eastward to the Louisiana border (Sabine River) and inland from the coast as much as 125 km. The rice prairies are located in the area normally referred to as the Gulf Coast Prairie vegetational region (Gould 1975). The original plant community in the coastal prairie was mainly tallgrass prairie, with some post oak (*Quercus stellata*) savannah on the upland areas (Gould 1975). Original vegetation was dominated by tall bunchgrasses such as big bluestem (*Andropogon gerardii*), little bluestem (*Schizachyrium scoparium*), indiangrass (*Sorghastrum* spp.), eastern gamagrass (*Tripsacum dactyloides*), and several species of *Panicum* (Gould 1975).

The region is characterized by nearly level to gently sloping topography, with elevations ranging from 10-70 m above sea level. Soils in the rice prairies west of Houston have a surface layer of fine sandy loam above several layers of clay and sandy clay (McEwen and Crout 1974, Westfall 1975). In contrast, soils in the area east of Houston are much heavier, with several layers of clay and sandy clay.

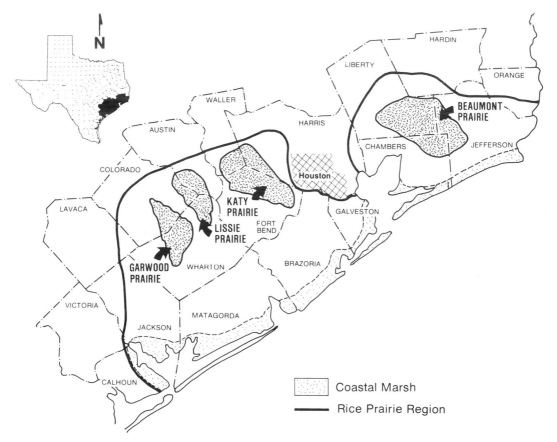

Fig. 1.   The general outline of the rice prairie region of southeast Texas is shown along with the 4 major prairies, the Beaumont, Katy, Lissie, and Garwood Prairies.

The rice prairies have an average annual rainfall of 104 cm (range 90-140 cm), which is fairly evenly distributed throughout the year. The area has a humid climate, with hot summers and mild winters. The growing season averages 270 days per year, and low temperatures in the winter are rarely below −6 C (McEwen and Crout 1974).

Rice Culture

Texas rice culture originated around Beaumont, with the first farming attempts reported in 1850 (Craigmiles 1975). Rice, which was grown with hand labor and without irrigation, was referred to as "providence rice" because the farmers relied on rainwater. Irrigation of rice began in 1891. This venture deve-

loped into the Beaumont Irrigation Company, which was the first water-delivery system on the Texas Gulf Coast (Craigmiles 1975).

Rice production expanded westward across the Gulf Coast Prairie, and the early center of rice production west of Houston was Eagle Lake. Texas had its first large rice crop in 1899, when 3,440 ha of rice were harvested on the Beaumont Prairie and 81 ha were harvested on the Lissie Prairie (Jones et al. 1938).

Until 1935, rice production was dependent primarily on hand labor and animal power and then, to the end of World War II, on steel-wheeled tractors, binders, and threshers (Craigmiles 1975). After World War II, rice production became a highly mechanized operation with the use of large tractors, tandem disk plows, combines, and airplanes. Simultaneously, changes were made in the uses of fertilizers, chemicals for control of weed and insect pests, and the development of new varieties of rice with increased disease resistance and higher yields (Miller 1975). A major advancement occurred in the early 1960s when second-cropping or stubble-cropping became commercially feasible. Second-cropping requires only reflooding of the cut stubble, and fertilizer and herbicide applications (Hottel et al. 1975). Second-cropping became possible with the release of several very early maturing (100-day) varieties of rice (Evatt 1958, Evatt and Beachell 1962, Craigmiles 1975). Nearly 75% of the rice producing area west of Houston is now being second-cropped.

In the mid-1980s, rice farmers in Texas experienced some of the worst economic conditions in decades. Worldwide rice production was good, resulting in large surpluses and low prices. These low prices, combined with the United States Department of Agriculture's (USDA) rice-acreage reduction program, forced many rice farmers out of business. In Texas, rice acreages were reduced by 56%, dropping from 239,000 ha in 1980 to 105,000 ha in 1987 (Texas Agric. Stat. Serv. 1982, 1987). In the top 2 rice-producing counties (Colorado and Wharton), rice acreages have been reduced by over 23,000 ha since 1980. Concurrently, average yields increased from 5,280 to 7,020 kg/ha between 1980 and 1986 (Texas Agric. Stat. Serv. 1987).

Texas rice farmers formerly produced about 25% of all the rice grown in the United States (U.S.) (Hottel et al. 1975). In 1986, 16 upper-coastal Texas counties produced 99% of all Texas rice, but only 13% of the U.S. rice crop (Texas Agric. Stat. Serv. 1987). Texas now ranks fourth in rice production behind Arkansas (40%), California (28%), and Louisiana (15%).

Land Use

Land use in the rice prairies generally can be categorized as either cropland (35%), pasture and rangeland (35%), or woodland (30%) (representative of Colorado and Wharton Counties) (Engstrom et al. 1977). The most important crops in terms of area planted are rice, grain sorghum, soybeans, corn, and cotton (Colorado and Wharton County Agric. Stab. Conserv. Serv. [ASCS] Off., unpubl. data; Texas State ASCS Off. 1980). Most row crops such as cotton, corn, and grain sorghum are grown in cleared bottomland areas near rivers and creeks. Land within the rice prairies is used mainly for rice production, pasture for cattle, rice pasture rotations, and rice-rotation crops (Hobaugh 1984).

Agricultural Practices

The basic requirements for good rice growth include relatively high average temperatures (>20 C) throughout the growing season, level soils with slowly permeable subsoils that prevent seepage loss, a dependable supply of good quality water for irrigation, and a good system for surface drainage. Successful rice production requires intensive land management and the use of "state-of-the-art" techniques. These procedures include proper land and crop rotations, correct land and seedbed preparation, use of appropriate seed varieties, understanding proper seeding methods and rates, and planting within the recommended dates. Furthermore, correct water management (timing of flooding and draining), proper fertilizer application (amounts and timing), and the appropriate use of herbicides and pesticides are vital for maximum yields.

The use of all of the current rice-growing procedures is important to ensure a successful crop. However, only the following practices that are of direct importance to waterfowl will be described: land preparation (which normally occurs while wintering waterfowl are present), rice-rotations (which affect land use), and rice-field weeds (which are important waterfowl foods).

Land Preparation.—Land and seedbed preparation vary geographically with soil type and the farmer. The goals are to prepare a seedbed for the best germination of the rice seed and to control weed growth before planting. In the rice prairies, most farmers practice fall and winter land preparation, which involves fall plowing, disking once or twice during winter, and then leveling the land with large land planes. Rice fields must be as level as possible to ensure uniform irrigation, effective weed control, and proper drainage (Hodges 1975). When land leveling has been completed, contour levees are marked and constructed using a levee disk. The intervals between contour levees generally allow water depths to be maintained between 8-15 cm (Hodges 1975, Smith et al. 1977). Finally, a springtooth harrow is pulled over the land to provide a shallow cultivation before seeding.

Rice Rotations.—Traditionally, continuous rice production on the same land is not practiced because of increased weed problems and decreased soil fertility. The general practice is to rotate rice with cattle pasture or other crops (soybeans or grain sorghum) or to fallow the land. Traditional rice-pasture rotation practices have involved growing rice on the land for 1 or 2 years, and then leaving it idle ("laid out") for 2-5 years before planting rice again (Evers and Craigmiles 1975). The plants (rice field weeds) which respond from the seed bank on the idled land are then grazed by cattle. Cattle grazing aids in reducing the prevalence of weeds and grasses in future rice crops (Craigmiles 1975) and provides an economic return from the fallow land.

A typical 3-year rice-pasture rotation system involves 3 fields. During Oct-Nov,

rice is harvested in 1 field, another field is plowed in preparation for planting rice the next spring, and the third field is being grazed. Another, a common practice is to aerially seed ryegrass onto harvested rice fields, thereby providing winter forage for cattle (Stutzenbaker and Buller 1974, Evers and Craigmiles 1975). Third option is to prepare a seedbed on idled land and then to drill-seed ryegrass or oats for winter forage (Evers and Craigmiles 1975).

Rice-Field Weeds.—One of the most serious problems facing rice producers is the control of weeds. Weeds compete with rice and thus ultimately reduce rice yields. Also, weeds in rice increase the cost of harvesting, drying, and cleaning, hence reducing the market value of the crop. In the U.S., the estimated annual loss to rice producers from weeds and expenditures for their control is approximately $290 million (Smith et al. 1977).

Common weeds found in Texas rice fields also are important waterfowl foods, including barnyardgrass (*Echinochloa crusgalli*), sprangletop (*Leptochloa* spp.), broadleaf signalgrass (*Brachiaria platyphylla*), red rice (*Oryza sativa*), other grasses (*Panicum* spp., *Paspalum* spp.), dayflower (*Commelina* spp.), smartweeds (*Polygonum* spp.), bulrushes (*Scirpus* spp.), spikerushes (*Eleocharis* spp.), nutgrasses (*Cyperus* spp.), and sedges (*Carex* spp.) (Singleton 1951, Harmon et al. 1960, Davis et al. 1961, Horn and Glasgow 1964, Flinchum 1975, Smith et al. 1977, Miller 1987).

HABITAT IMPORTANCE

Waterfowl Use

Historically, geese were rare and puddle ducks were numerous in the rice-prairie region. Thousands of ducks foraged on seeds of native plants and wintered in this region prior to the advent of rice farming. Geese avoided the original tallgrass prairies and wintered in the marshes (McIl-

Fig. 2.   Snow, white-fronted, and Canada geese roosting on a rice prairie rest pond near Garwood, Texas.

henny 1932). After the prairies were cultivated, geese were attracted first to the Beaumont Prairie where they made short flights between the coastal marsh and the new rice fields, directly adjacent to traditional use areas. West of Houston, geese were much slower to use the new rice fields, and most fall migrants continued to winter in the marsh. Ducks quickly responded to the new source of readily available food in the rice fields. Prior to 1935, ducks were considered to be serious pests by many farmers, as the birds fed on the rice before it was threshed.

Canada geese (*Branta canadensis*) and white-fronted geese (*Anser albifrons*) slowly began to use the inland rice prairies, but snow geese were still using the marshes almost exclusively in the mid-1950s. In the late 1950s and early 1960s, snow geese began to take advantage of the roosting water provided by commercial hunting operations and private landowners, and discontinued their flights to the marsh (Fig. 2).

Aerial waterfowl surveys conducted by the Texas Parks and Wildlife Department (TPWD) provide an index to waterfowl populations by broad geographic zone. Due to the configuration of the rice prairies and their juxtaposition to marsh habitat, it is difficult to extract waterfowl population numbers specifically for the rice prairies. However, between 1981 and 1986, the coastal winter aerial survey, which includes the rice prairies region, indicated an average winter population of 1.05 million geese (51%) and 1.00 million ducks (49%), for an average total of 2.05 million waterfowl (Frentress 1987). Snow geese are the most numerous geese, numbering >800,000 birds, followed by an average of 125,000 white-fronted geese and 85,000 Canada geese. Northern pintail (*Anas acuta*) and green-winged teal (*A. crecca*) are the most numerous ducks wintering on the rice prairies (Table 1). These ducks are followed by varying numbers of at least 12 other species of ducks, including northern shovelers (*A. clypeata*), American wigeon (*A. americana*), gadwall (*A. strepera*), mallards (*A. platyrhynchos*), mottled ducks (*A. fulvigula*), blue-winged teal (*A. discors*), and wood ducks (*Aix sponsa*). Mottled ducks are year-round residents of the rice prair-

Table 1. Numbers of common duck species seen during the annual midwinter surveys of the upper and middle Texas Coast, including the Rice Prairies, January 1982-1986.

Species	Year					$\bar{X}$
	1982[a]	1983[b]	1984[c]	1985[d]	1986[e]	
Northern pintail	319,500	199,600	446,600	438,400	230,600	327,000
Green-winged teal	293,700	172,000	213,500	239,300	200,400	223,800
Gadwall	82,200	124,700	145,700	110,200	78,600	108,300
Northern shoveler	50,900	70,400	44,900	45,700	63,200	55,000
Mottled duck	31,000	38,200	50,500	32,100	42,100	38,800
Mallard	42,000	29,200	52,000	17,300	40,000	36,100
American wigeon	10,400	31,400	40,800	8,900	13,900	21,100
Blue-winged teal	600	1,200	2,000	12,300	3,900	4,000
Total	830,300	666,700	996,000	904,200	672,700	814,100

[a] From Stutzenbaker (1983).
[b] From Stutzenbaker (1984).
[c] From Stutzenbaker (1985).
[d] From Frentress (1986).
[e] From Frentress (1987).

ies, although many birds move south to the marshes in the winter. Fulvous (*Dendrocygna bicolor*) and black-bellied whistling ducks (*D. autumnalis*) also are relatively common spring and summer residents.

The continuing expansion of the human population along the Texas coast has created conflicts with respect to the welfare of wintering waterfowl. Of particular concern is the continued westward expansion of the Houston metropolitan area into the Katy Prairie. Land has been purchased to construct an international airport on rice land west of Katy, which will certainly impact an important segment of wintering habitat for waterfowl.

Chronology.—The first migrants to arrive in the rice prairies are blue-winged teal in early August. By early September, large numbers of teal are using the flooded second-crop rice fields. Their numbers increase through the end of September, before many of these birds fly on to wintering grounds in Mexico and in Central and South America. Blue-winged teal are difficult to survey at this time because of visibility problems, but the TPWD has estimated that between 250,000 and 1 million of these birds use the rice prairies each fall, depending on production and habitat conditions.

In late September, the first green-winged teal, shovelers, and pintails arrive, with major influxes in October and November. These are followed by gadwall and wigeon. Mallards generally are the last ducks to arrive in significant numbers, usually in December.

Geese begin to fly over the rice prairies in early September, apparently bound for the Texas coast and northern Mexico. By late September, small flocks of white-fronted geese are using rice fields, but few snow and Canada geese have arrived. During the first 2 weeks of October, thousands of white-fronted geese arrive on the rice prairies and use harvested rice fields almost exclusively (first crop or early second crop) (Hobaugh 1982). From mid-October through November, goose numbers increase daily on the rice prairies. In some years, large numbers of geese arrive in the rice prairies in December as cold weather forces birds down from the midwest. These waterfowl use the rice prairies throughout the winter, but make periodic moves in response to water, food availabilities, and human disturbance.

Puddle ducks are the first to disappear during the spring migration. Pintails and mallards leave in late January and early February, followed by the other puddle duck species. Geese begin to depart from the rice prairies in early March, with the majority generally gone by mid-March.

Fig. 3. Snow and Canada geese in a fallow rice field in late January.

Shovelers are the last of the wintering birds to leave; but before their departure in late March and April, northerly migrating blue-winged teal will have returned. Most blue-winged teal stay until middle to late April before moving north; however, some 500 pairs remain and nest across the coastal zone.

Food Resources and Habitat Use

The importance of rice to wintering waterfowl has long been recognized and documented (Fig. 3) (Glazener 1946, Jordan 1953, Horn and Glasgow 1964, McFarland and George 1966). The greatest amount of rice is readily available to waterfowl in October and November immediately after the second-crop harvest. The mean amount of waste rice left after harvest in second-crop rice fields was 140 kg/ha (range = 73-214 kg/ha) (Hobaugh 1984). By mid-December, the amount of rice present in fields has declined greatly, and almost all of the rice is gone by mid-January, having been consumed by waterfowl and other animals, sprouted, or deteriorated. Similar findings have been reported by Harmon et al. (1960) and McGinn and Glasgow (1963) for Louisiana rice fields.

Soybean fields show a pattern similar to that of rice fields, and almost all of the soybeans are gone by mid-January (Hobaugh 1984). Sprouting forbs and grasses first begin to appear in rice, soybean, and plowed fields in December and early January. Both rice and soybean fields have maximum densities of sprouting green vegetation during March (Hobaugh 1984). In contrast, the density of green vegetation in plowed fields is highest in February and decreases dramatically in March due to spring plowing.

Hobaugh (1982, 1984, 1985) documented the value of the Texas rice prairies to snow, Canada, and white-fronted geese. Foraging geese followed a distinct seasonal pattern of habitat use. Feeding geese were found almost exclusively in rice fields from early October until the end of November. This intensive use of rice fields coincided with the time when the greatest amount of rice was available. Some geese then began to shift to soybean and plowed fields in December as the supply of rice diminished. After the rice was gone, most geese continued to use rice fields through the remainder of the winter, feeding on sprouting green vegetation. Occasionally, thousands of geese were seen in fallow rice fields taking advantage of all available foods (Fig. 3). In fallow rice fields, geese fed on green vegetation, and, during dry cold winters, they fed on seeds of nutgrasses, bulrush, dayflower, smartweed, and panic grasses (Alisauskas et al. 1988). The importance of rice fields and preference for this habitat type also have been documented for white-fronted geese wintering in the rice prairies of southwest Louisiana (Leslie and Chabreck 1984). There whitefronts preferred wet, harvested rice fields over other habitat types, followed by cultivated fields later in winter when green vegetation became available (Leslie and Chabreck 1984). Body condition and nutritional data have shown that the rice prairies provide all of the resources required by snow geese to meet their winter metabolic demands for body maintenance (adults) and growth (juveniles) (Hobaugh 1985).

Ducks also use rice fields extensively throughout the winter. Miller (1987) found that rice was the most important food of pintails wintering in a rice-producing area of California. The waterfowl use of and value of seeds of barnyardgrass, nutgrass, spikerush, smartweeds, and other grasses (e.g., *Panicum* spp.) readily available in harvested and fallow rice fields have been well documented (Singleton 1951, Harmon et al. 1960, Davis et al. 1961, Miller 1987). Miller (1986, 1987) suggested that pintails are probably able to meet their nutritional requirements in rice fields and that they exhibited excellent body condition during normal winters. Flooded, harvested rice fields provide excellent sources of invertebrates for ducks in February and March (Miller 1987).

Water Availability

Several major rivers and numerous creeks flow through the rice prairies in a southeasterly direction; however, waterfowl make little use of these areas. Snow and white-fronted geese seldom use the numerous sandbars along the Colorado, Brazos, and Trinity Rivers, and only about 1,000 Canada geese traditionally use a sandbar on the Colorado River. Duck use of the rivers in the rice prairies is also minimal, except for wood ducks that use adjacent small ponds and oxbows.

The presence of wintering ducks and geese on the rice prairies is largely due to the amount of water available in roost or "rest ponds" (Hobaugh 1984). In the early 1950s, a few large rest ponds were constructed by landowners who had an interest in waterfowl. These ponds were not hunted, and thousands of waterfowl began to use these sanctuaries. Subsequently, commercial hunting interests developed additional water sanctuaries, and now these temporary ponds are the main reason that waterfowl, particularly geese, are able to continue to use the rice prairies in substantial numbers.

Rest ponds range in size from 2-80 ha. Some areas are flooded annually, whereas the locations of other ponds change with rice-field rotation. Water is generally purchased from irrigation companies, pumped from wells or from adjacent creeks in September or early October. Water levels are maintained through winter and supplemented by rainfall. Unfortunately, many of these roosting areas are drained immediately after the hunting season in late January.

Rest ponds are critically important during dry years and may provide most of the surface water available to wintering birds at such times. During wet winters, when practically all rice fields have standing water, the importance of the rest ponds decreases. During dry winters, some rest ponds receive excessive use by thousands of birds, causing poor water quality. The green, bacteria-laden water becomes a concern to wildlife professionals, but, to date, no serious outbreaks of disease have been attributed to the poor water quality.

Annual Harvest

The Texas coast has a strong waterfowl hunting tradition. Around 1900, a number of private hunting clubs were formed around natural lakes, primarily for duck hunting. When large numbers of geese began wintering in the rice prairies in the late 1950s, waterfowl hunters soon followed. Because all rice land was privately owned, commercial hunting operations and clubs were formed to gain access to land where geese could be hunted. Landowners were paid for hunting rights and trespass privileges. Since the early 1960s, there has been a steady trend toward organized commercial hunting in the area (Stutzenbaker and Buller 1974).

Waterfowl hunting is an important part of the rice-prairies economy (Schwartzkopf 1977). Waterfowl hunters bring millions of dollars into the rice prairies as they pay for day-hunting privileges, season leases, food, lodging, gasoline, hunting supplies, and bird processing.

Day-hunting operations are common in the rice prairies. Commonly, the operators of day-hunting clubs obtain the hunting rights to substantial areas of rice land, and then provide "day hunters" with an opportunity to hunt on a price-per-hunt basis. Normally, day-hunting clubs provide their hunters with a field to hunt, white parkas, and a guide who has calls and several hundred white-rag goose decoys. A minimum of 4 hunters is normally required, and most hunts end at noon. Half-day hunting encourages waterfowl to stay in the area by providing them with some undisturbed time each day for feeding and resting.

In the mid-1980s, most available waterfowl habitat was leased to individuals, hunting clubs, or commercial day-hunting operations. The TPWD believes that >95% of all rice prairie habitat in Texas is subject to some form of recreational hunting during the waterfowl season. Hunting pressure is intense, especially during opening weekend and the first several weeks of the hunting season. Hunting pressure subsides as the season progresses, but the actions of >100,000 licensed waterfowl hunters who hunt 5-7 times per year provide some of the most intense waterfowl hunting pressure found in the U.S. (Carney et al. 1983)

Across the rice prairies, waterfowl harvest varies greatly between hunting clubs, day-hunting operations, and individuals. In the late 1970s, a single day-hunting operation reported waterfowl harvests of up to 10,000 birds per year on the Garwood and Lissie prairies. Other operations are not as large or as successful, and harvests range from 100 to several thousand ducks and geese each year.

The average annual Texas state-wide goose harvest between 1971 and 1980 was 180,000 birds (Carney at al. 1983). The average goose harvest in the rice-prairie counties was 156,000, or 87% of the state-wide total. Snow geese generally make up 64% of the total goose harvest, with white-fronted geese accounting for 23%, and Canada geese, 13%. Duck harvest in the rice prairies averaged 166,000 birds annually between 1971 and 1980, which was 46% of the state-wide total. Major species harvested included green-winged teal (22%), mallard (15%), northern pintail (14%), American wigeon (9%), gadwall (9%), blue-winged teal (8%), northern shoveler (5%), and mottled duck (4%).

HABITAT MANAGEMENT
Food Production and Availability

In general, little intentional habitat management, other than water control, is practiced in rice fields for waterfowl.

Fortunately, many of the present agricultural practices associated with rice farming benefit waterfowl due to timing. Specifically, these practices include (1) second-cropping rice, which makes rice available in October and November; (2) fall plowing of fallow land, which produces an ideal seedbed for the germination of forbs and grasses; (3) rotation of rice fields, which allows for growth of native seed producing plants in fallow fields; and (4) planting ryegrass in harvested rice fields or in improved winter pastures. Detrimental agricultural practices include (1) fall plowing of rice stubble, (2) extensive land leveling that eliminates natural ponds, and (3) overgrazing of rice fields, which results in less desirable species composition. All of these practices affect food production and availability.

Rice stubble is certainly the most important habitat type to snow geese and most other waterfowl wintering in the rice prairies. Fall plowing of rice stubble reduces the amount of this valuable habitat that is available to waterfowl. Between 1978 and 1980, nearly 60% of 1.6 million snow geese observed on aerial surveys were seen on rice stubble (Fig. 4) (Hobaugh 1984). Furthermore, rice stubble was the only habitat type on which large numbers of foraging snow and white-fronted geese were consistently seen throughout the October-March period (Hobaugh 1982, 1984).

First-crop rice is normally harvested between mid-July and mid-August in the western rice prairies. The first crop normally accounts for 75-80% of the total rice yield. Nearly 75% of these fields are then second-cropped (Hottel et al. 1975). Second-cropping is beneficial to waterfowl because it makes waste grain available in late October and November versus July-August. Much of the rice left in first-crop fields that are not second-cropped is either consumed by other animals (particularly blackbirds) or sprouts prior to the arrival of waterfowl on the prairies.

McGinn and Glasgow (1963) found that 70% of all rice left on the ground for 60 days deteriorated. Body condition and nutritional data have shown that December was the only difficult month for wintering geese, as little rice remained in the fields, and sprouting forbs and grasses were not yet abundant (Hobaugh 1984, 1985). The later maturing Lemont variety of rice which is currently popular may be alleviating this situation somewhat. The second-crop of Lemont matures in middle to late November versus middle to late October for Labelle and the other rice varieties that were previously popular. This should make substantial amounts of rice available later into December, providing food for the geese until sprouting vegetation becomes available. Nutritionally, rice is high in soluble carbohydrates (NFE = 75%) and energy (GE = 4.2 kcal/g, AME = 3.5 kcal/g), but has only a moderate amount of protein (9.5%) (Hobaugh 1985, Miller 1987).

Many landowners on the rice prairies incorporate livestock grazing into their rice-farming rotation. However, with current rice acreage reductions, it may be more appropriate to say that landowners incorporate rice farming into their grazing program. Many ranchers aerially seed ryegrass into harvested rice fields and others prepare seedbeds in fallow fields for improved winter pasture. Normally, good to excellent stands of ryegrass can be found in these fields by late December, which provide an excellent forage for wintering geese (Stutzenbaker and Buller 1974, Hobaugh 1984). Goose depredation on winter pastures can be locally severe, particularly in dry, cold winters when the growth and density of native forbs and grasses are reduced (Hobaugh 1984).

Wet weather stimulates plant growth and results in an abundance of green vegetation, which is important to wintering geese (Hobaugh 1984, Alisauskas et al. 1988). Wet weather also reduces the

Fig. 4. Snow goose flock on harvested rice field on the Garwood Prairie.

relative attractiveness of improved winter pastures, hence greatly reducing depredation problems (Stutzenbaker and Buller 1974, Hobaugh 1984). Futhermore, wet weather reduces the area that farmers can plow repeatedly during winter, which results in increased plant growth and food availability (Hobaugh 1984). Finally, rainfall and runoff flood numerous new fields during winter, making new food resources (seeds and invertebrates) available to ducks (Miller 1986).

Proper grazing and pasture management are important in maintaining desirable plant species. Overgrazing reduces important seed-producing grasses such as barnyardgrass, sprangletop, and panic grasses, and allows composites (e.g., *Aster* spp., *Bidens* spp., *Xanthocephalum* spp.) that have little value to waterfowl to predominate. Improper pasture management in rice fields also can result in encroachment of undesirable woody plants such as prairie baccharis (*Baccharis* spp.) and chinese tallow (*Sapium sebiferum*).

The planting of supplemental foods for waterfowl, particularly Japanese millet (*Echinochloa crusgalli frumentacea*) has been a successful and widely used management technique. However, the overall impact of supplemental food plantings is minimal in the rice prairies due to the tremendous numbers of waterfowl wintering in the area and the small-scale efforts by landowners and hunting operations. Japanese millet normally matures in 60-70 days, with recommended planting dates between 1 August and 15 September in the rice prairies. Recommended planting rates are 22-33 kg/ha, either broadcasted or drilled shallowly. Staggered planting (2-week intervals) can be an important factor affecting success of millet, particularly those plantings (most) that are dependent on rainfall. Also, staggered planting insures that all of the millet seed does not mature at one time. This is an important consideration where a large concentration of birds can rapidly consume most of the millet in a relatively small area.

Water Control

The Texas rice prairies lie in a 90-140 cm rainfall belt, and despite this relatively high rainfall, water is the key factor in the welfare of waterfowl wintering here. The pioneering success of geese in the rice prairies has been attributed largely to the establishment of numerous roosting sanctuaries across the prairies. The idea behind the rest ponds has been not to hunt or disturb the birds on them, but to hunt the surrounding fields as the ducks and geese come out in the morning to feed. It has been a successful management technique. Currently, all but one of the major rest ponds on the rice prairies are controlled and operated by private interests. The one exception is the roost area recently developed on the Attwater Prairie Chicken National Wildlife Refuge (APCNWR).

The ability to control water is a benefit that comes almost naturally with rice lands due to the intensive water management required in successful rice farming. The series of contour levees, overflows, drainage ditches, water-supply laterals, wells, and irrigation canals makes water control on rice land much easier than on other agricultural lands. Most rest ponds are normally located in the lower portions of rice fields, and levees are constructed and maintained that allow runoff water to collect while holding water pumped in from wells, canal systems, or adjacent creeks. Major roost ponds range greatly in size (2-80 ha), with minimum recommended size of at least 4 ha. Water depth in these ponds rarely exceeds 0.6 m, and the upper ends of the ponds have receding shorelines so that at any water level, shallow water is present. No strategic plans for the location of these temporary rest ponds exist. Instead, these ponds have been developed according to the land controlled by interested landowners, hunters, and commercial hunting operations. Despite lack of planning, the distribution of rest ponds presently does a good job of distributing waterfowl across the prairies except east of Houston on the Beaumont Prairie where rest ponds are limited.

Costs associated with pumping water

on the rice prairies are highly variable. The price for pumping from underground wells can range from $81-$284/ha·m ($10-$35/ac·ft), depending on fuel source (electric, natural gas, diesel) and well depth. Some landowners with producing gas wells have relatively inexpensive sources of fuel, which makes pumping from these wells very practical. Other landowners or farmers are able to purchase the water remaining in rice irrigation canals at reduced prices after the rice irrigation season is finished. This is less costly than purchasing water during the rice irrigation season, which will cost a minimum of $243/ha·m ($30/ac·ft). Pumping water from running streams adjacent to rest ponds is the least expensive alternative, where this is possible. Pumping water to flood large areas can be costly. Furthermore, very dry falls with severe evaporative losses may require additional pumping later in the winter, increasing this cost.

Disease

Diseases in waterfowl have not reached major epidemic proportions on the rice prairies. The first recorded epidemic of diseases in waterfowl occurred in rice fields in Wharton County in October 1973. Avian cholera (*Pasteurella multocida*) was diagnosed as the cause of mortality of >1,000 ducks, primarily green-winged teal, shovelers, and pintails (Traweek 1980). During the winter of 1984-85, a die-off of 200 snow geese from avian cholera occurred on Brazoria NWR (south of the rice prairies) in late December. Minor outbreaks of cholera began to be identified at APCNWR on the Lissie Prairie in early January 1985. The following winter, 61 snow geese and a few ducks died from avian cholera on the APCNWR. Between 1973 and 1984, an outbreak of avian cholera occurred every 5 years on the rice prairies. Since 1984, outbreaks of cholera have occurred annually.

The mode of transmission of avian cholera infections among wild waterfowl populations on the rice prairies is not understood. Furthermore, it is not clear why the occurrence of minor outbreaks of avian cholera has increased since 1984. It is assumed that carriers of the disease spread the infection in dense concentrations of waterfowl that have become susceptible under stress conditions favorable to the disease, such as overcrowding combined with inclement weather (Brand 1984).

The largest number of waterfowl lost in a single disease incident on the rice prairies was from avian botulism (*Clostridium botulinum*). Following the outbreak of cholera in 1973, another epizootic occurred in November in the same rice fields; this outbreak was diagnosed as botulism and involved the loss of 1,800 ducks (Traweek 1980). Over 1,700 of these birds were green-winged teal and shovelers. This is the only recent record of botulism on the rice prairies. In late November 1985, over 600 snow geese and 50 white-fronted geese died from aflatoxicosis in Matagorda County, caused by feeding on waste corn containing high levels of aflatoxin (Lobpries 1986).

Pathological diagnoses of waterfowl die-offs on private land in and near the rice prairies were conducted by several different agencies between 1973 and 1985 including the Texas Veterinary Medical Diagnostic Laboratory, Texas A&M University; Denver Wildlife Research Center, U.S. Fish and Wildlife Service (FWS); and the National Wildlife Health Center (NWHC), FWS. A standardized system for investigating, reporting, and documenting waterfowl losses from disease on the rice prairies was not established until 1985. Then the NWHC established a waterfowl-disease investigation and rapid-response group with a team member assigned to the Central Flyway for early detection and organized response. Personnel of Brazoria and San Bernard NWRs

(the NWR complex with the longest history of waterfowl disease losses on the Texas coast) have developed a waterfowl-disease contingency plan to help reduce losses from disease. In order to detect disease outbreaks at an early stage, weekly surveys for sick or dead waterfowl are conducted in major concentration areas on the NWRs between December and February. The refuge manager immediately notifies designated disease-control specialists of a possible disease outbreak. A disease-control specialist advises the refuge manager on the techniques for collection, preparation, and shipment of specimens immediately to the NWHC for diagnosis and pathogen identification. Records are kept of wildlife losses and other field data. Specific areas are designated for decontamination of personnel and equipment and carcass disposal. All carcasses are collected daily during a disease outbreak and incinerated.

Environmental Contaminants

Pesticides are regularly used in rice farming. Insecticide and fungicide-treated rice seed may be planted as early as late February while many waterfowl are still on the prairies. Aerial applications of insecticides and herbicides to rice fields may occur early enough in spring to affect northward migrating waterfowl.

Between the late 1950s and mid-1970s, acute poisoning of waterfowl from pesticides occurred annually throughout the rice prairies in late winter and early spring. Annual losses may have surpassed 3,000 birds, primarily snow geese. Losses of migrating blue-winged teal may have approached 6,000 birds in some springs from exposure to rice seed treated with toxic, persistent pesticides (Flickinger and King 1972, Flickinger 1979). Weight loss occurred in wintering geese known to have been exposed to pesticides in the 1970s (Flickinger 1979).

Habitat quality for wintering waterfowl was greatly improved on the rice prairies in the mid-1970s after pesticide contamination was reduced. The USDA and the Environmental Protection Agency (EPA) cancelled registrations for toxic, persistent pesticide treatment of rice seed in the early 1970s. Mercury fungicide was cancelled in 1970, and aldrin, an organochlorine (OC) insecticide, was cancelled in 1974. No late-winter mortality of waterfowl due to pesticide poisoning was reported on the rice prairies after 1974 (Flickinger 1979).

Waterfowl migrating through the rice prairies in the spring also benefited from EPA cancellation in 1982 of pesticide-treated rice seed and the cancellation of aerial applications of toxaphene, an OC insecticide. Aerial applications of carbamate (CB) insecticides have been restricted to low rates in spring. Most toxic organophosphate (OP) insecticides are not registered for use on rice. However, in the 1980s, rice seed treated with illegal OC and OP insecticides was found in rice fields, and poisoning mortality of migrating ducks occurred (Flickinger et al. 1984, U.S. Fish and Wildlife Service 1986).

Currently, rice seed is planted without an insecticide treatment in some areas. In other areas, rice seed is planted with legal short-life OP insecticides and fungicides of low toxicity to waterfowl. Aerial applications and rates of insecticides and herbicides are generally of low toxicity to waterfowl, and of short persistence. Mortality of birds is still associated occasionally with some applications of registered OP and CB insecticides. Most of these result from farmers increasing the application rates beyond legal restrictions. Sporadic losses of birds probably will continue to occur in the spring, and the potential for waterfowl losses to insecticides still exists. However, habitat quality for migrating and wintering waterfowl in the rice prairie ecosystem has improved tremendously since the cancellation of the use of toxic-persistent pesticides.

MANAGEMENT RECOMMENDATIONS

Management needs that would benefit waterfowl wintering in the rice prairies of southeast Texas should begin with the development and initiation of a comprehensive management plan that would cooperatively involve federal, state, and private-sector resource managers. The plan should specifically address the following:

1. Ways to encourage landowners to delay until spring or completely eliminate the fall plowing of rice stubble.
2. The potential for leaving small portions of second-crop rice in the field through the use of tax incentives, cash leases, or USDA rice-program modifications.
3. The possibilities and priorities for acquisition of a federal or state waterfowl refuge or several small refuges in the rice prairies where essentially all habitat is privately owned.
4. Ways to encourage landowners and hunting operations to hold water in rest ponds until mid-March instead of draining them in late January.
5. Development of more roosting areas in strategic locations for better distribution of wintering birds throughout the rice prairies (TPWD or FWS involvement through conservation agreements and leases or land acquisition).
6. Development of incentives for landowners to convert temporary water rest ponds into permanent moist-soil management areas in rice land that is now retired from production.
7. Promotion of the proper use of pesticides registered for use on rice and continuation of investigation and elimination of the use of illegal contaminants.
8. Provision of public education on waterfowl diseases to obtain assistance

from landowners and other interested individuals in the documentation and control of waterfowl losses; initiation of immediate remedial action when disease losses become apparent.

9. Monitoring land-use changes, including commercial development that affects waterfowl and threatens remaining habitat.

10. Provision of increased extension wildlife expertise and services to landowners and hunting operations interested in better management of private property.

11. Implementation of innovative annual hunting regulations designed to protect waterfowl populations while offering maximum recreational opportunity (1- to 2-day hunting, zones, and staggered days).

RESEARCH NEEDS

Research designed to answer specific and critical questions is required to assure accurate information on which to base rice-prairie management decisions. Specific topics which need to be addressed include:

1. Determine waterfowl movement patterns within, between, and out of the rice prairies.

2. Determine the extent of year-to-year wintering-ground fidelity in the rice-prairies.

3. Determine the nutritional requirements of key waterfowl species and assess the ability of rice-prairie habitat to provide these resources.

4. Determine the potential of fallow rice fields and retired rice land to produce waterfowl foods under various management regimes (e.g., grazing, nongrazing, seasonal flooding, and burning).

5. Determine the influences of weather, agriculture, and hunting on the survival and distribution of waterfowl in the rice prairies.

SUMMARY

Each year, over 1.5 million waterfowl winter (Oct-Mar) in the rice prairies of southeast Texas. These waterfowl are dependent on agricultural practices and land-use patterns associated with rice farming. Nutritional and body condition data from wintering geese (prior to rice-acreage reductions) have shown that the rice prairies provide the resources geese need for body maintenance. Thus, the rice prairies constitute invaluable wintering habitat.

No federal or state waterfowl refuge is present in the rice prairies; therefore, wintering waterfowl are totally dependent on the wintering habitat provided by private landowners. Currently, the only economic incentive that rice farmers/ landowners have to maintain waterfowl habitat is the money that they derive from hunting leases. The revenue from hunting leases is insufficient to keep a farmer/ landowner in business during bad economic times. However, it can be a factor in determining land-use patterns.

The U.S. Fish and Wildlife Service (1982:15) stated in its National Waterfowl Management Plan that waterfowl habitats in private ownership are critical, because they constitute the greatest share of existing habitat and because they are most vulnerable to loss. This is certainly true in the rice prairies, where there is real concern for the future of rice habitat. Declines in rice acreages (>50%) have already occurred. Furthermore, the continuing expansion of the human population along the Texas coast has created conflicts with respect to the welfare of wintering waterfowl. In the rice prairies, the continued westward expansion of the Houston metropolitan area into the Katy Prairie threatens habitat. Unfortunately, the agricultural productivity of land no longer comes near its value for commercial development. The loss of each piece of habitat causes a decline in the quantity and diversity of habitat available to wintering waterfowl.

Little intentional habitat management, other than water control, is practiced in rice fields for waterfowl. However, many agricultural practices benefit waterfowl, such as second-cropping rice which improves rice availability; fall plowing of fallowland, which enhances germination of forbs and grasses; rotation of rice fields, which allows growth of native plants; and planting of ryegrass pastures. The establishment of sanctuary ponds has promoted goose populations in the area. Future management actions should focus on incentives (farm programs) for the landowner.

LITERATURE CITED

Alisauskas, R. T., C. D. Ankney, and E. E. Klaas. 1988. Winter diets and nutrition of the midcontinent population of lesser snow geese. J. Wildl. Manage. 52:403-414.

Bateman, H. A., T. Joanen, and C. D. Stutzenbaker. 1988. History and status of midcontinent snow geese on their Gulf Coast winter range. Pages 495-515 in M. W. Weller, ed. Waterfowl in winter. Univ. Minnesota Press, Minneapolis.

Bellrose, F. C. 1980. Ducks, geese and swans of North America. Third ed. Stackpole Books, Harrisburg, Pa. 540 pp.

Brand, C. J. 1984. Avian cholera in the Central and Mississippi Flyways during 1979-80. J. Wildl. Manag. 48:349-406.

Carney, S. M., M. F. Sorensen, and E. F. Martin. 1983. Waterfowl harvest and hunter activity in the U.S., 1971-80. U.S. Fish and Wildl. Serv. Sci. Rep. Wildl. 254. 144 pp.

Craigmiles, J. P. 1975. Advances in rice—through research and application. Pages 1-8 in J. E. Miller, ed. Six decades of rice research in Texas. Tex. Agric. Exp. Stn. Res. Monogr. 4. College Station.

Davis, J. P., C. H. Thomas, and L. L. Glasgow. 1961. Foods available to waterfowl in fallow ricefields of southwest Louisiana. Proc. Annu. Conf. Southeast. Assoc. Game and Fish Comm. 15:60-66.

Engstrom, H., H. Sunderman, R. Heinsohn, A. Koehn, and L. Koehl. 1977. Colorado soil and water conservation district program and work plan. Colo. Soil Water Conserv. District, Columbus, Tex. 27 pp.

Evatt, N. S. 1958. Stubble rice production tests, 1956-1957. Tex. Agric. Exp. Stn. Prog. Rep. 2018. College Station. 4 pp.

————, and H. M. Beachell. 1962. Second-crop rice production in Texas. Tex. Agric. Prog. 8(6).25-28.

Evers, G. W., and J. P. Craigmiles. 1975. Rotation-alternate and competitive crops. Pages 70-80 in J. E. Miller, ed. Six decades of rice research in Texas. Tex. Agric. Exp. Stn. Res. Monogr. 4. College Station.

Flickinger, E. L. 1979. Effects of aldrin exposure on snow geese in Texas rice fields. J. Wildl. Manage. 43:94-101.

————, and K. A. King. 1972. Some effects of aldrin-treated rice on Gulf Coast wildlife. J. Wildl. Manage. 36:707-727.

————, D. H. White, C. A. Mitchell, and T. G. Lamont. 1984. Monocrotophos and dicrotophos residues in birds as a result of misuse of organophosphates in Matagorda County, Texas. J. Assoc. Off. Anal. Chem. 67:827-828.

Flinchum, W. T. 1975. Controlling weeds in rice. Pages 51-57 in J. E. Miller, ed. Six decades of rice research in Texas. Tex. Agric. Exp. Stn. Res. Monogr. 4. College Station.

Frentress, C. 1986. Waterfowl harvest recommendations. Tex. Parks and Wildl. Dep. Rep., Pittman-Robertson Proj. W-106-R-12. Austin. 28 pp.

————. 1987. Waterfowl harvest recommendations. Tex. Parks and Wildl. Dep. Rep., Pittman-Robertson Proj. W-106-R-13. Austin. 28 pp.

Glazener, W. C. 1946. Food habits of wild geese on the Gulf Coast of Texas. J. Wildl. Manage. 10:322-329.

Gould, F. W. 1975. Texas plants: a checklist and ecological summary. Texas A&M Univ., College Station. 121 pp.

Harmon, B. G., C. H. Thomas, and L. L. Glasgow. 1960. Waterfowl foods in Louisiana ricefield. Trans. North Am. Wildl. and Nat. Resour. Conf. 25:153-161.

Hobaugh, W. C. 1982. Wintering ecology of geese in the rice prairie area of southeast Texas. Ph.D. Thesis, Texas A&M Univ., College Station. 187 pp.

————. 1984. Habitat use by snow geese wintering in southeast Texas. J. Wildl. Manage. 48:1085-1096.

————. 1985. Body condition and nutrition of snow geese wintering in southeastern Texas. J. Wildl. Manage. 49:1028-1037.

Hodges, R. J. 1975. Putting research into action-decisions and procedures. Pages 115-121 in J. E. Miller, ed. Six decades of rice research in Texas. Tex. Agric. Exp. Stn. Res. Monogr. 4. College Station.

Horn, E. E., and L. L. Glasgow. 1964. Rice and waterfowl. Pages 435-443 in J. P. Linduska, ed. Waterfowl tomorrow. U.S. Gov. Print. Off., Washington, D.C.

Hottel, J. G., R. Stelly, and W. R. Grant. 1975. Economic considerations. Pages 107-114 in J. E.

Miller, ed. Six decades of rice research in Texas. Tex. Agric. Exp. Stn. Res. Monogr. 4. College Station.

Jones, J. W., J. M. Jenkins, R. H. Wyche, and M. Nelson. 1938. Rice culture in the southern states. U.S. Dep. Agric., Farmers Bull. 1808. 28 pp.

Jordan, J. S. 1953. Consumption of cereal grains by migratory waterfowl. J. Wildl. Manage. 17:120-123.

Larned, W. W., S. L. Rhoades, and K. D. Norman. 1980. Waterfowl status report, 1976. U.S. Fish and Wildl. Serv. Sci. Rep. Wildl. 227. 88 pp.

Leslie, J. C., and R. H. Chabreck. 1984. Winter habitat preference of white-fronted geese in Louisiana. Trans. North Am. Wildl. and Nat. Resour. Conf. 49:519-526.

Lobpries, D. S. 1986. Texas waterfowl: seasonal losses of waterfowl. Tex. Parks and Wildl. Dep. Rep., Pittman-Robertson Proj. W-106-R-12. Austin. 11 pp.

Lynch, J. J. 1975. Winter ecology of snow geese on the Gulf Coast, 1925-1975. 37th Midwest Fish and Wildl. Conf., Toronto, Ont. 45 pp.

McEwen, H. F., and J. Crout. 1974. Soil survey of Wharton County, Texas. U.S. Gov. Print. Off., Washington, D.C. 43 pp.

McFarland, L. Z., and H. George. 1966. Preference of selected grains by geese. J. Wildl. Manage. 30:9-13.

McGinn, L. R., and L. L. Glasgow. 1963. Loss of waterfowl foods in rice fields in southwest Louisiana. Proc. Annu. Conf. Southeast. Assoc. Game and Fish Comm. 17:69-79.

McIlhenny, E. A. 1932. The blue goose in its winter home. Auk 49:279-306.

Miller, J. E., editor. 1975. Six decades of rice research in Texas. Tex. Agric. Exp. Sta. Res. Monogr. 4. College Station. 136 pp.

Miller, M. R. 1986. Northern pintail body condition during wet and dry winters in the Sacramento Valley, California. J. Wildl. Manage. 50:189-198.

———. 1987. Fall and winter foods of northern pintails in the Sacramento Valley, California. J. Wildl. Manage. 51:405-414.

Schwartzkopf, C. 1977. "Third cropping" in Texas: conservation and management bring fame to Eagle Lake Rice J. 80:20-21.

Singleton, J. R. 1951. Production and utilization of waterfowl food plants on the east Texas Gulf Coast. J. Wildl. Manage. 15:46-56.

Smith, R. J., Jr., W. T. Flinchum, and D. E. Seaman. 1977. Weed control in U.S. rice production. U.S. Dep. Agric. Res. Serv., Agric. Handbook. 497. 78 pp.

Stutzenbaker, C. D. 1980. Waterfowl harvest recommendations. Tex. Parks and Wildl. Dep. Rep., Pittman-Robertson Proj. W-106-R-6. Austin. 45 pp.

———. 1983. Waterfowl harvest recommendations. Tex. Parks and Wildl. Dep. Rep., Pittman-Robertson Proj. W-106-R-9. Austin. 35 pp.

———. 1984. Waterfowl harvest recommendations. Tex. Parks and Wildl. Dep. Rep., Pittman-Robertson Proj. W-106-R-10. Austin. 47 pp.

———. 1985. Waterfowl harvest recommendations. Tex. Parks and Wildl. Dep. Rep., Pittman-Robertson Proj. W-106-R-11. Austin. 44 pp.

———, and R. J. Buller. 1974. Goose depredation on ryegrass pastures along the Texas Gulf Coast. Tex. Parks and Wildl. Dep. Spec. Rep., Pittman-Robertson Proj. W-106-R. Austin. 13 pp.

Texas Agricultural Statistics Service. 1982. 1981 Texas field crop statistics. U.S. Dep. Agric. Bull. 201. 96 pp.

———. 1987. 1986 Texas field crop statistics. U.S. Dep. Agric. Bull. 237. 100 pp.

Texas State Agricultural Stabilization and Conservation Service Office. 1980. Texas ASCS Annual Report 1979. Tex. State Agric. Stabilization and Conserv. Serv. Off., College Station. 83 pp.

Traweek, M. S., Jr. 1980. Texas waterfowl: seasonal losses of waterfowl. Tex. Parks and Wildl. Dep., Pittman-Robertson Proj. W-106-R-6. Austin. 10 pp.

U.S. Fish and Wildlife Service. 1982. A national waterfowl management plan for the United States. U.S. Fish and Wildl. Serv. Washington, D.C. 49 pp.

———. 1986. Preliminary survey of contaminant issues of concern on national wildlife refuges. Div. of Refuge Manage., U.S. Fish and Wildl. Serv. Washington, D.C. 181 pp.

Westfall, D. G. 1975. Rice soils-properties and characteristics. Pages 22-30 in J. E. Miller, ed. Six decades of rice research in Texas. Tex. Agric. Exp. Stn. Res. Monogr. 4. College Station.

THE TEXAS COAST

CHARLES D. STUTZENBAKER, Wildlife Division, Texas Parks and Wildlife Department, Port Arthur, TX 77640

MILTON W. WELLER, Department of Wildlife and Fisheries Sciences, Texas A&M University, College Station, TX 77843

The Texas Gulf Coast is one of the most important wintering areas for waterfowl in North America. The wet prairies, marshes, and bays of the Gulf of Mexico provide winter habitat for a large number of migratory birds. In addition, these habitats support diverse native freshwater wetland- and marine-dependent animals.

Waterfowl arrive in the fall and winter from most major breeding locations in North America; white-fronted geese (*Anser albifrons*) come from Alaska, and snow geese (*Chen caerulescens*) fly south to the coast from breeding colonies scattered across the Canadian arctic. Northern prairie states and Canadian provinces are the sources of most of the dabbling and diving ducks that use the Texas coast (Bellrose 1980). During the past 10 years (1979-1988), Texas coastal wetland habitat has wintered 83% of all waterfowl surveyed (Jessen 1988) in the state (Table 1). Those same bird numbers made up 52% of the entire Central Flyway waterfowl population as measured by the annual midwinter aerial surveys (Jessen 1988).

The extensive wetland zone of the western Gulf Coast runs from the Pearl River in Mississippi west to the Rio Grande of Texas. Administratively, this area is divided into the Central and Misssissippi flyways with the dividing line adjacent to the Sabine River drainage. This places Texas in the Central Flyway and adjacent Louisiana in the Mississippi Flyway, but similar wetland habitat is located on either side of the flyway boundary, and there are daily exchanges of bird populations.

At some locations, wetland management practices are similar in the 2 flyways, but in some cases, wetland type, management philosophies, species priorities, types of land ownership, leasing arrangements, and land-use priorities provide different management options. This chapter outlines typical field-level management practices currently being used in Texas and also identifies management needs and possibilities.

PHYSICAL, TIDAL, AND CLIMATIC DESCRIPTIONS

The Texas Gulf Coastal Zone stretches for nearly 600 km with about 2,300 km of shoreline along bays, lagoons, and estuaries (Brown et al. 1980). The Coastal Zone, known physiographically as the Gulf Prairies and Marshes (Gould 1975), encompasses parts or all of at least 17 counties and supports one-third of the state's population and economic wealth in about 6% of the land area (Brown et al. 1980). Thus, the intensity of human activity and development conflict directly with major waterfowl habitats. With a national trend toward increasing human activity along coastal zones, problems of wetland loss (Tiner 1984) and subsidence and salinity modification (Gosselink 1984), impacts of humans on waterfowl habitats are likely to increase.

The Texas coastline may represent a more diverse array of climate and wetland diversity than any comparable unit in North America. The coastline is intersected by 7 major and several minor estuarine systems, often derived from several rivers each. These flow from the interior uplands in a southeasterly direction (Fig. 1) and empty into complex bays partially enclosed by barrier islands. Ten

Table 1. Midwinter waterfowl populations (in millions) comparing Texas and the Central Flyway (Jessen 1988).

Year	Total flyway	Texas only	% of flyway total	Texas Gulf Coast	% of total Texas	% of total flyway
1978-79	6.8	4.9	72	4.4	90	64
1979-80	7.1	5.1	71	4.5	88	63
1980-81	6.2	3.2	52	2.4	75	39
1981-82	5.4	3.4	63	2.7	79	50
1982-83	4.8	2.7	56	2.2	81	46
1983-84	4.8	3.4	71	2.9	85	60
1984-85	3.4	3.1	91	2.4	77	71
1985-86	3.9	1.7	44	1.3	77	33
1986-87	5.3	2.2	42	1.6	73	30
1987-88	5.4	3.6	67	3.1	86	57
$\bar{X}$	5.3	3.3	63	2.8	83	52

of the 20 Texas River Authorities are involved in waters that influence these coastal systems, which often include reservoirs and irrigation uses that strongly influence rates of freshwater inflows to the bays. Bay systems are complex and may involve a large outer (primary) bay with moderate (17 parts per thousand [ppt]) to sea-strength (35 ppt) salinities, a secondary bay with brackish (9 ppt) to moderate salinities (17 ppt), and inner or tertiary bays that may be fresh to brackish (Texas Dep. Water Resour. 1984). There also is a rainfall effect from east to west. Rainfall in the Beaumont-Port Arthur area in east Texas exceeds 125 cm annually and declines to less than 77 cm in south Texas (Fig. 2; Texas Dep. Water Resour. 1984). Additionally, the weather is warmer to the west and evaporation greater, which influences mineral concentrations in waters of both bay systems and basin wetlands inland from the coast. In the eastern bays, such as the Trinity River arm of Galveston Bay where freshwater volumes are greater, salinities may be zero to 10 ppt and support predominantly freshwater or intermediate marsh hydrophytes. In the southern coastal area, the barrier islands once were so complete that the Laguna Madre formed one of the largest hypersaline lagoons in the world, with salinities sometimes exceeding 60 ppt (Pulich 1980). The entire coast has been influenced by the Intracoastal Water-

way which is 684 km long, dissects much salt and estuarine marsh, and undoubtedly has modified salinities along its route (James et al. 1977). Additionally, several barrier islands have been cut to create passes for boat access, to modify salinities, and to provide for fishing activities.

The tidal regime in the entire Texas coast is modest, ranging from 31-46 cm at various times of the year, and wind tides often are of greater impact than are lunar tides (Ward et al. 1980). Hence, the regularity of tides common to other parts of the United States (U.S.) coast is lacking. This irregularity influences potential water-management strategies in coastal marsh.

NATURE AND IMPORTANCE OF HABITAT IN THE REGION
Major Regions and Habitat Types

The Coastal Plain is generally <40 m in elevation and varies in width from 80-160 km (Gould 1975). Estuarine wetlands (Cowardin et al. 1979) are more narrow and follow stream and river channels more closely than in the great delta marshes in Louisiana and eastward. In east Texas near the Sabine River, there is a modest amount of chenier marsh that is more extensive in western coastal Louisiana. These ancient and sometimes wooded east-west ridges create elongated

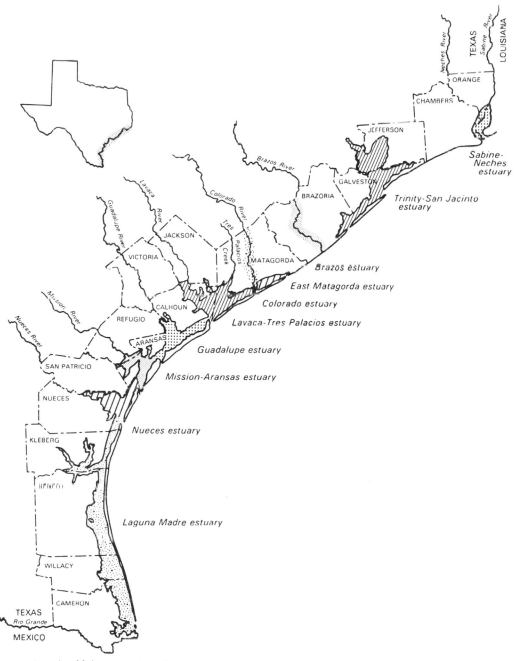

Fig. 1. Major estuaries of the Texas coast (from Texas Dep. Water Resour. 1984).

wetlands that vary from saline near the coast to near-fresh further inland. To the west, marshes are less extensive and restricted to estuarine systems as fringes of emergent grasses and other salt-tolerant herbaceous vegetation. Marshes become smaller and vegetatively less diverse due to the narrower shoreline gradient and the higher salinities in more western and southerly bays and estuaries (Figs. 3-5).

Estuarine Emergent Wetlands.—These wetlands are diverse due to the gradient

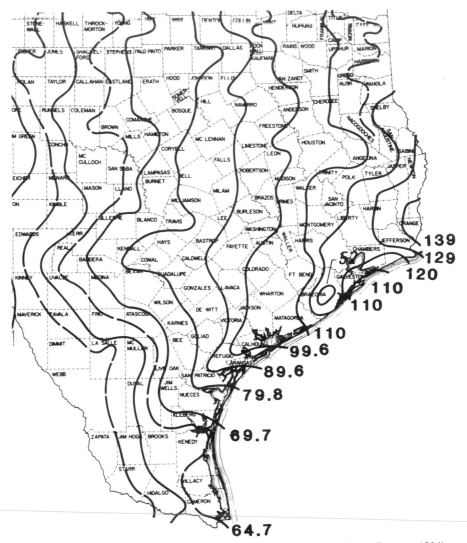

Fig. 2.   Precipitation (cm) in Texas (modified from Texas Dep. Water Resour. 1984).

in salinity and rainfall. The open bays and tidal creeks often are fringed with smooth cordgrass (*Spartina alterniflora*) (plant nomenclature follows Scott and Wasser 1980) where there are water fluctuations essential to this species. Stands are narrow compared to Louisiana and Texas East Coast marshes. Behind this zone may be saltgrass (*Distichlis spicata*), saltwort (*Salicornia* spp.) and sea-oxeye daisy (*Borrichia frutescens*) where drying creates higher salinities. Periodically flooded wetlands with considerable freshwater inflow are characterized by marsh-

hay cordgrass (*Spartina patens*) and Olney bulrush (*Scirpus olneyi*). Both plants may be found with the water-tolerant seashore paspalum (*Paspalum vaginatum*) or longtom (*P. lividum*) in a coastal plant zone termed "intermediate" by Chabreck (1972). The near-freshwater coastal marshes support both marshhay cordgrass and seashore paspalum plus cattails (*Typha* spp.), sedges (*Carex* spp.), beakrushes (*Rhynchosprora* spp.) and bulrushes (*Scirpus* spp.). However, this is a dynamic zone that periodically is flooded in storm surges that may influ-

Fig. 3. The most extensive marsh zone is located along the upper coast from Port Lavaca to Sabine Pass, where the dominant vegetation is marshhay cordgrass.

ence soil salts for long periods. Such coastal wetlands are difficult to classify as they may be fresh enough to be termed palustrine at times but more characteristically would be called estuarine on the basis of salinity (>0.5 ppt) and plant species composition. Some examples of plant distribution were presented by Ward et al. (1980), but there are no published studies correlating plant distribution with environmental factors.

Estuarine Open Water.— This habitat is prominent along the Texas coast and varies in size from small, unvegetated ponds of a few hectares in salt marsh to large shallow bays where wave action limits vegetation to submergents such as widgeongrass (*Ruppia maritima*) and shoalgrass (*Halodule wrightii*). Such open water areas are increasing in Texas as in Louisiana due to subsidence, channelization, and saltwater intrusion into freshwater systems (Gosselink 1984, Tiner 1984, Armstrong 1987).

Tidal Freshwater Marsh.—Tidal freshwater marsh is uncommon in Texas,

perhaps because of the narrowness of the coastal plain and the high stream gradients. Where it exists, it is dominated by emergent plants characteristic of coastal, palustrine wetland such as burhead (*Echinodorus* spp.), pickerelweed (*Pontederia* spp.), sedges, beakrush, cattail, occasionally wildcelery (*Vallisneria americana*), and exotics such as alligatorweed (*Alternanthera philoxeroides*).

Palustrine Wetlands —Freshwater emergent marshes are common in number but are small and seasonal—often ephemeral. They are dominated by moist-soil plants such as sedges, rushes, burhead, and beakrush but also may be surrounded by sennabean (*Sesbania* spp.). In the drier Coastal Bend area south of Corpus Christi, ponds created by blow-outs in sand are numerous but seasonal and secular. Sometimes called "hurricane lakes" because they are filled only after rains associated with tropical depressions, they may occur at densities of 2.2 ponds/ km^2 in wet years but may be virtually absent during other years (Briggs and

Fig. 4.   Marshes from Port Lavaca to Corpus Christi are narrow margins along drainages that enter the bays. Primary vegetation is smooth cordgrass.

Everett 1983, McAdams 1987). During wet periods, plants appear that are rare to absent during dry years, and waterfowl use increases.

Lacustrine Wetlands.—Lacustrine wetlands are those larger freshwater bodies of water >8 ha with <30% areal cover of emergents. They may be termed lacustrine if they are <8 ha when a well-defined shoreline exists and depth is >2 m. They are uncommon along the Texas coast because most of the large basins are shallow and seasonal and dominated by emergent plants. At times, however, the same areas may be open water. Reservoirs and some constructed ponds also fall into this category.

Wet Prairies.—The once extensive wet prairies of the inland coastal plain, often called "rice prairies" because of the current land use, were converted to rice areas by intensive drainage, leveling, and cultivation. Flooded areas hold large numbers of waterfowl during winter (see Hobaugh et al. 1989).

Agricultural Lands.—Crops that influence waterfowl use in winter are rice, soybeans, and milo. Harvested rice fields produce considerable waste grain plus natural moist-soil plants and invertebrates, and are especially attractive when flooded. Although some fields are converted to pasture or other crops during the 2- to 3-year interval between rice crops, many are left fallow and used for livestock grazing. Milo is a dry-land crop that is increasing in coverage throughout South Texas, in particular, and serves as food for species like geese and black-bellied whistling ducks (*Dendrocygna autumnalis*).

Rangelands.—Rangelands include managed and cultivated pastures as well as natural marsh areas, both freshwater and brackish. Many marshes are grazed during the winter when regrowth from early fall fires provides forage, and when mosquitoes are less numerous. Livestock play an important role in reducing surface vegetation and making new shoots and root-

Fig. 5. From Corpus Christi to the Rio Grande, perimeter marshes are narrow or nonexistent, grading abruptly into saline bays where seagrasses are abundant.

stocks more available to grazing and grubbing geese; flooded areas are used by dabbling ducks.

Important Habitats for Waterfowl

Prime wintering habitats for waterfowl on the Texas coast are best grouped according to use by geese, dabbling ducks, inland diving ducks, and seaducks —although there is extensive habitat overlap among species. Geese extensively use the coastal rice-growing areas because of available waste grain and suitable roosting habitat provided by rice reservoirs and water areas managed for hunting (Hobaugh 1985, Bateman et al. 1988). Such areas are most extensive along the upper (i.e., eastern) coast. They also use the traditional brackish marshes, with heaviest use in December and January after rice areas have been exploited. In the marsh, they feed primarily on leafy portions and rootstocks of marshhay cordgrass, Olney bulrush, and seashore paspalum. Geese also use coastal marshes as roosting and feeding sites all along the coast from Port O'Conner to Port Isabel, and may feed in upland crops or use marsh plant rhizomes when available. Availability of disturbance-free, open-water roost sites seems to determine whether an area is used or not (Bateman et al. 1988).

Dabbling ducks use estuarine vegetated wetlands and inland palustrine areas, both natural and constructed. Freshwater impoundments have proven especially attractive all winter to northern pintail (*Anas acuta*), gadwall (*A. strepera*), American wigeon (*A. america*), green-winged teal (*A. crecca*), and northern shovelers (*A. clypeata*), as well as blue-winged teal (*A. discors*) during fall and spring migration. Varying numbers of blue-winged teal and some cinnamon teal (*A. cyanoptera*) winter along the coast. Mallards (*A. platyrhynchos*) are relatively scarce on the upper coast.

Diving ducks are dispersed widely along the coast and are mostly redheads (*Aythya america*), lesser (*A. affinis*) and greater scaups (*A. marila*), ring-necked ducks (*A. collaris*), ruddy ducks (*Oxyura jamaicensis*), and canvasbacks (*A. valisineria*). Many use freshwater ponds and marshes just inland from the coast, but scaup are widely dispersed from Aransas Bay south to Port Isabel in the Laguna Madre. Redheads are most numerous in the Laguna Madre, where over 75% of the U.S. population winters (Weller 1964), but small flocks occur in Christmas, Matagorda, and Aransas bays where widgeongrass and shoalgrass occur in the shallows.

Common goldeneyes (*Bucephala clangula*) and red-breasted mergansers (*Mergus serrator*) are scattered in small groups along the estuaries and open bays of the entire Texas coast, but are more commonly found along the lower coast from Matagorda southward to the Mexican border. These and hooded mergansers (*Lophodytes cucullatus*) also may use freshwater ponds near the coast.

Land Use Patterns and Changes

Although early Spanish and French explorers expressed interest in the Texas coastal zone, and numerous attempts were made to claim the new lands by establishing and maintaining forts and missions, the area remained a wilderness until the early 1800s when the Mexican land-grant system provided large tracts of land for individuals willing to settle. Shortly thereafter, a wave of settlers from the southeastern U.S. crossed the Sabine River to settle the upper and middle Texas coast (Fehrenbach 1985).

In the early to mid-1800s, the major land use was livestock grazing, although some settlers practiced subsistence farming. Prior to the Civil War, a number of plantations were located along the middle coast. Cotton, corn, and sugarcane were the primary agricultural crops, but the majority of the land continued to be used for cattle grazing.

Rice was introduced to the Texas coast in the late 1800s. With the later advent of mechanical farm equipment such as the self-propelled harvester, rice culture accelerated. The surge in the world economy associated with World War II marked significant changes in land use along the Texas coast. The market demand for rice resulted in large-scale cultivation of the original bluestem (*Andropogon* spp.) prairies that lay at elevations slightly above the permanently wet, freshwater to brackish marshes.

By the 1950s, over 525,000 ha of prairie soil had been diverted to rice production (Stutzenbaker and Buller 1974). In the process of providing drainage and irrigation for expanding human population and agriculture, extensive changes were made in natural drainage patterns. The end result was the channelization of most major creeks and bayous and the dredging of the lower portions of practically every major river.

Between 1874 and 1892, the Gulf Intracoastal Waterway was dredged along part of the Texas coast and was completed and widened along the entire coast in the late 1930s and early 1940s (James et al. 1977). This inland waterway traversed wetland habitat for much of its 684 km, and salinity and drainage patterns of extensive areas of the coast were altered.

In the early 1980s, real estate speculators and builders had a greater impact on selected lands than agricultural interests. Human population increase is expected to continue at an accelerated pace at the expense of agricultural lands. Since the 1970s, rice production has declined because of high overhead costs and competition from foreign markets and is not expected to rebound to its former status. Concurrently, low cattle prices have caused many ranchers to drop out of the business. The security of wildlife, and particularly waterfowl, has been tied to large ownerships because cattle and rice production were compatible with wintering waterfowl on the Texas coast. The emerging pattern of continued subdivisions of the larger ranches makes the future welfare of wintering waterfowl less certain.

The demand for recreational access to existing wetland habitat is high, and competition for hunting leases often is great. With a diminishing wetland base in Texas, the demand for hunting recreation and hunting space may result in better management of the wetland areas that remain intact.

Waterfowl

Birds from the central and northern portion of the continent intermingle on the Texas coast to account for an annual game and nongame migratory bird population that must exceed 100 million when both webless and webbed species are considered. Conservation agencies cooperate to survey the major game species, but this involves only 1 goose survey in mid-December and 1 duck survey in early January. Thus, waterfowl population data do not include those birds that migrate through the area in early fall or spring. Records derived from the annual midwinter waterfowl surveys for the most recent 10-year period (1979-1988) showed that totals for all species combined ranged from 1.9 million to 4.5 million with a mean of 2.8 million (Table 1).

Blue-winged teal are the first ducks to arrive in mid-to-late August. By mid-to-late September, a half million or more are present in natural wetlands and flooded, second-growth rice fields. Most blue-winged teal stop only briefly before moving to Central and South America, but many thousands remain through winter during some years. A few thousand early migrating pintails, shovelers, and green-winged teal arrive with blue-wings in September, but major flights of dabbling and diving ducks do not develop until well into October. Although a number of mallards move south to the coast in November, the majority of these birds arrive much later in the year.

Mallard arrival is generally timed with severe, cold weather in the midwestern U.S. During most years, the bulk of the annual fall flight of migratory ducks has been completed by mid-December. During winters 1984-85 to 1986-87, coastal wintering duck populations have averaged 1.2 million birds (Stutzenbaker 1985, Frentress and Lobpries 1988).

The Texas coast is an important wintering area for 3 groups of geese: (1) white-fronted geese, (2) tallgrass Canada geese (*Branta canadensis*), and (3) snow geese. White-fronted geese are the earliest migrants in early September when small groups overfly or stop briefly enroute to northern Mexico. Larger flights of white fronted geese appear on the coast along with snow and Canada geese in late October. By late November, the majority of resident Canada and white-fronted geese has arrived. During some years, snow geese delay their fall migration and assemble in large numbers in the Dakotas, Iowa, and Missouri, and remain until severe weather pushes them south. In recent years, increasing numbers of snow geese have wintered at managed refuges in Missouri. The most recent 3-year average coastal goose population figures for Texas (1984-85 to 1986-87) showed 1 million white-fronted geese, Canada geese, and snow geese (Stutzenbaker 1985).

While on the Texas coast, waterfowl are segregated by habitat preferences. During the early portion of the fall and winter, geese make extensive use of harvested rice fields. In December, as agricultural food is depleted and annual burning makes brackish marshes more attractive to foraging birds, many geese move to the coastal marshes.

Ducks frequent a wider range of habitat than geese. Wood ducks (*Aix sponsa*) use the heavily wooded streams that meander through the coastal prairie. Common dabbling ducks such as northern pintail, green-winged teal, gadwall, American wigeon, northern shoveler, mottled duck (*Anas fulvigula*), and mallard range from marsh to agricultural areas, often making daily forays from one habitat type to another. Large numbers of pintail and lesser numbers of gadwall and wigeon make extensive use of the saline bays, particularly in the area from Port Lavaca south to the Rio Grande. Redheads, scaup, ruddy ducks, and bufflehead (*Bucephala albeola*) make almost exclusive use of shallow, brackish bays and larger marsh lakes. Canvasbacks tend to use large irrigation reservoirs and larger freshwater marshes, especially in east Texas.

By late December and early January, wintering waterfowl populations have become more stable. However, the mobility of individuals in these populations is unknown. In January, minor northward migrations begin. At this time, small numbers of mallards, pintails, and some snow geese leave the coast and fly to the midwestern U.S. However, the bulk of spring migration does not occur until February for ducks, and occurs the first week in March for geese. By mid-March, most wintering ducks and geese have left coastal Texas.

In March and early April, blue-winged teal pass through Texas enroute to northern breeding areas. Blue-winged teal and northern shovelers are the last of the migrants to leave the coast, sometimes remaining until late April or early May. A few remain to nest in years of high rainfall (Cottam and Glazener 1959, McAdams 1987).

Other Species that Influence Waterfowl Management

The estuarine marshes provide vital nursery areas for commercially valuable marine fish and shellfish that are hatched in the Gulf and move into the marshes. They mature there and then return to the open Gulf to complete the annual cycle. The dependence on coastal wetlands by marine species creates a dilemma for waterfowl managers. Waterfowl-habitat management structures may require permits from the U.S. Army Corps of Engineers with approval by National Marine Fisheries Service and the Environmental Protection Agency if water management impedes ingress and egress of marine organisms in saline and brackish marshes (Corps of Engineers 1986).

In addition to marine resources, the brackish marshes produce annual crops of commercially-valuable American alligator (*Alligator mississipiensis*), muskrat (*Ondatra zibethicus*), and nutria (*Myocastor coypu*). Freshwater marshes also produce alligators and furbearers along with extensive crops of crayfish (*Cambarus* spp.), frogs (*Rana* spp.), and fish of several species. Saline and brackish marshes support an extensive commercial and sport fishing industry, whereas the freshwater marshes support an important sport fishing industry.

Although wintering waterbirds far outnumber resident species like the mottled duck, common moorhen (*Gallinula chloropus*), purple gallinules (*Porphyrula martinica*), and clapper rails (*Rallus longirhostris*), the maintenance of viable habitat for these latter species is essential. Hence, it is imperative that management strategies consider the annual cycle of resident species.

IMPORTANCE OF HABITATS TO WATERFOWL REQUIREMENTS

Foods

Although water undoubtedly first attracts waterfowl to an area, food must be present to hold them. Most species of ducks shift from invertebrates during the prebreeding and breeding period to plant foods such as seeds, rhizomes, or delicate leafy foliage such as pondweeds or widgeongrass after breeding (Krapu 1974, Weller 1975). During fall and early winter, geese consume cereal grain and plant materials such as grasses or rhizomes, but in late winter switch plant species and sometimes habitats (i.e., from agricultural areas to brackish marshes) (Bateman et al. 1988).

Important food plants of Texas coastal ducks were studied by Chamberlain (1959) and Singleton (1965), and geese were studied by Glazener (1946). Moist-soil plants such as coast barnyardgrass (*Echinochloa walteri*) and smartweeds (*Polygonum* spp.) are important in fresher sites for dabbling ducks. Fennel leaf pondweed (*Potamogeton pectinatus*), dwarf spikerush (*Eleocharis parvula*), and widgeongrass can be important in fresh to brackish open water. Widgeongrass is most common in brackish water, and shoalgrass occurs in saline or hypersaline areas. Seeds and foliage of widgeongrass are eaten by dabbling ducks, and the foliage is eaten by redheads. Shoalgrass rhizomes are a preferred food of redheads (McMahan 1970, Cornelius 1977). Presumably, scaup, goldeneyes, and buffleheads are feeding on marine invertebrates, and red-breasted mergansers are feeding on fish, but no data are available on the food habits of these species in Texas.

Canada and white-fronted geese eat rice and other field grains, but graze extensively on leafy plant material. Snow geese also eat grains and graze on forbs and grasses in rice fields, but make heavy use of the rhizomes of cordgrass, Olney bulrush, cattail, and seashore paspalum. Forbs of many species also are eaten in spring when other food resources are sparse; these probably are high in plant proteins early in the spring (Hobaugh 1985).

Water for Protection and Roosting

All species vary in their attraction to size and openness of water areas. The more terrestrial geese can feed and loaf in dry uplands where there is food or minimal disturbance, but they invariably roost in shallow-water overnight. Thus,

large, shallow-water areas influence the presence of geese.

Coastal diving ducks like redheads and scaup seem to favor large saline bays for feeding and use nearby freshwater ponds for resting and drinking. Ring-necked ducks and canvasbacks favor more inland freshwater areas; ring-necks in particular will feed in very small ponds (White and James 1978).

Dabbling ducks vary in their choice of water bodies. All species will use small ponds. However, wigeon, gadwall, and pintails like larger areas with extensive submergent growth. Pintails can use extensive sheetwater, including hypersaline shallows.

Loafing Sites

Whereas diving ducks loaf while swimming in water, many dabbling ducks prefer either a dry shoreline or a shallow submerged bar where they can stand, preen, and sun (Ryan 1984). The necessity of these sites is unknown, but favored loafing ponds have these features.

Vegetative Cover for Protection

Vegetative cover has been studied little in Texas or elsewhere as a source of either weather or predator protection. It is clear that most birds seek shelter from the wind in the lee of a ridge, shore, or vegetation windbreak, yet they are cautious to maintain sufficient clearance for escape. Dabbling ducks especially seem to seek cover, whereas diving ducks remain in the open much of the time. However, even redheads that use the open waters of the Laguna Madre seek the wind shelter of landmasses during storms.

Importance of Disease and Contaminants

Very little information is available on losses of waterfowl due to diseases along the coast. Several die-offs due to lead and insecticide poisoning have been reported, and long lists of petrochemicals and toxicants that are potentially harmful have been recorded in Texas coastal waters (Cain 1988).

CURRENT WATERFOWL HABITAT APPROACHES AND METHODS

A relatively small amount of the Texas coast is managed for waterfowl. Management for geese via grazing and burning are the most common methods, but burning for livestock often occurs too early to produce suitable shoots for geese. Water manipulations for waterfowl are more common inland (rice-prairies) than along the coast, except on National Wildlife Refuges and State Wildlife Management Areas.

Wetland management demands effective dewatering techniques. The most productive wetland areas for waterfowl along the coast receive an annual natural- or human-induced spring or summer drawdown each year. The least productive wetland areas are those with stabilized water depth because water is generally too deep for feeding and there is less plant diversity than in drawdown wetlands.

The marsh manager can employ 2 major strategies in waterfowl management on the Texas coast. The first is to manage for desirable submerged and floating aquatic plants and to develop open-water areas. This can be done by long-term flooding and manipulating water depths during the growing season and during the time that wintering waterfowl are present. The second is to manage for nonpersistent emergent vegetation with the emphasis on seed-producing annual grasses. This option necessitates an annual spring drawdown beginning in April or May to allow seed-producing plants to germinate and mature before water is reintroduced in the late summer or early fall. Moist-soil conditions should be the goal during summer, although complete drying helped by extended summer droughts often is desirable. Spring and summer drying aerates the soil, controls undesirable plants such as water hyacinth (*Eichhornia crassipes*) and promotes annual seed-producing plants such as millet. This management technique duplicates natural conditions that occurred in coastal marshes before the disruption in drainage patterns and the development of leveed marshes.

Levees and Structures

Since 1880, drainage has been common among landowners as well as development-oriented county, state, and federal agencies. Oil exploration and development also have modified drainage patterns as a result of the extensive construction of roads, ditches, and access canals. Navigation projects, including dredging of the lower reaches of major rivers and the development of the Intracoastal Canal, have increased drainage effectiveness at practically every wetland location along the Texas coast.

In Texas, the extensive natural marsh is gone. Instead, the deeper marshes that have survived drainage and development are badly cut by canals and levees. Most marshes have a watershed of <1,000 ha. From a practical viewpoint, however, smaller marsh units may allow more effective management than large ones.

Current marsh management mandates that water retention levees be placed at strategic locations to prevent runoff or excessive water accumulation. Heights of levees generally should allow 77 to 123 cm freeboard above normal water levels. To control levee erosion, levees should have as extensive a berm width as is possible, particularly if the levee is adjacent to extensive open water (Fig. 6). Where levees are constructed from materials taken from adjacent borrow ditches, a berm of 10-20 m would be desirable to combat erosion resulting from wave action in the open water of the borrow

Fig. 6. Above is an example of poor levee construction with a narrow berm (2 m) and borrow ditches on both sides. Below, same berm shown 20 years later, showing total erosion by wave action.

ditch. Where possible, construction material should be taken from only 1 side of the levee because maintenance resulting from erosion is significantly more costly where inside and outside borrow ditches exist. A single borrow ditch, whether inside or outside of the levee, provides adequate boat access.

Fig. 7. Weir construction with removable sills to permit manipulation of water levels.

Fig. 8. Flap-gate control structure showing water exiting from wetland into a channel. Flap-gates prevent inflow from the channel to the marsh, and a stop-log structure on the marsh side controls the outflow level.

All levees should be constructed with a smooth and rounded crown to allow for periodic mowing to control the invasion of brush and trees, because grass is a superior soil binder (Fig. 6). Trees shade out herbaceous cover, and when they die or are pushed over by wind, erosion is accelerated.

Effective water-control structures are a necessity for proper vegetation management within leveed areas. Diverse water-control devices are available, but an effective structure is a fixed-crest weir placed on an individual drainage. The fixed-crest weir controls minimum water levels inside the area to be managed. Some weirs have removable sills that allow varying levels of water to be held (Fig. 7). Most weirs in tidal areas feature a bottom or sill height set at 15 cm below prevailing marsh floor. Weir structures are more effective in estuarine areas than dams because they allow ingress and egress of marine species, including brown shrimp (*Penaeus aztecus*) and blue crabs (*Callonectes sapidus*). However, persons with marine interests view weirs with caution, suspecting that impounding structures of any type tend to limit the production of marine species (Rogers and Herke 1985). Waterfowl managers generally subscribe to weir structures, recognizing that some limitations on marine species may be necessary to promote desirable plant communities and to favor other wetland-dependent wildlife.

A second effective water-control structure in tidal influenced areas is a combination stop-log, flap-gate structure (Fig. 8). Stop logs regulate levels on the freshwater side, and flap gates are positioned on the downstream or saltwater side of the culvert to prevent saltwater intrusion into freshwater areas. This system can be used to allow the ingress and egress of saline water and marine organisms by tying the flap gates in a raised position and removing stop logs during desired periods.

Screw-type gates are effective but provide little versatility in water-level management unless they are continually operated by hand. Because screw gates hold water until they are opened, they need constant attention to avoid impounding excessive water during periods of high rainfall. Such structures are most effective in fresh water where marine organisms are not present, or in situations where periodic fluctuation of water levels is less critical. Where screw-type gates have been in place for lengthy periods, changes in plant communities have occurred. Generally, annual seed-producing plants have been eliminated by long-term flooding, and floating and submerged plants eventually dominate the plant association. Management action for wetland areas controlled by screw-type gates should call for an annual or semiannual drawdown.

Marsh managers should be obligated to maintain constant surveillance of plant status to avoid negatively changing the vegetation character of the area under management.

A major problem associated with impounding freshwater behind water-control structures is the eventual development of a sport fish population, primarily largemouth bass (*Micropterus salmoides*). Once a sizable fish population has been developed, sport fishing interests often prohibit a drawdown of sufficient magnitude to positively influence vegetation. The end result is stabilized water levels and deterioration or loss of the original plant associations. Carp (*Cyprinus carpio*) and other rough fish have been introduced in many freshwater wetlands and are a serious problem because they compete with waterfowl for submersed vegetation and invertebrates (Robel 1961).

Flooding by Rainfall and Gravity Flow

Water management depends on annual rainfall, size of the watershed, and the drainage systems impacting the unit. Within tidal zones, wetland-management systems less commonly suffer from lack of water because daily tidal surges are controlled by structures at various points leading into the management unit. Uncontrolled tidal marshes, or marshes with fixed-crest weirs, allow periodic and near complete dewatering during strong winter frontal passages when north winds deflate tides and allow surface water to escape. This is especially true of marshes that are influenced by deep canals tied directly to the Gulf of Mexico.

Some wetland-management units with little or no watershed often can be managed entirely with rainfall. In compartmentalized marshes with effective levees and water-control structures that preclude unintentional water loss, an annual rainfall of >100 cm will provide surplus water beyond plant transpiration and evaporation losses. Along the upper Texas coast, rainfall is generally dependable from September to January so that excess surface water normally will be available in areas where rainfall can be trapped and runoff controlled. In marshes where upstream drainage either courses through or parallels the unit, water structures can be installed to gravity flow or to pump water into the management units. However, protection of that supply from diversion or alternate uses is vital to the continued management of those units. Spring dewatering is accomplished by pumping or gravity flow. On the middle and lower coast, water is usually in short supply, and natural dewatering occurs in midsummer.

Salinity Regulation

Lack of salinity regulation is a major management problem on many wetland areas. Two extremes exist: (1) no regulation of salinities, or (2) the complete prohibition of salt water. The construction of deepwater ports, the Intracoastal Canal, and various oil exploration canals have allowed saline water to penetrate into former freshwater areas (Craig et al 1980). It is not uncommon to see remnant baldcypress (*Taxodium distichum*) stumps in areas where shrimp, redfish (*Sciaenops ocellatus*), and blue crabs (*Callinectes sapidus*) predominate. These areas have lost their original vegetation and have been changed to open water by the scouring effect of tidal action, high salinities, and subsidence. In most of these areas, the degradation is continuing and vegetation is dying along the perimeter of open water. Without remedial action, many of these marshes are destined to become open bays lost forever to the production of emergent aquatic plants. When this point is reached, they will be of value primarily to diving ducks, mergansers, and marine organisms.

A solution to the deterioration of marshes from saltwater intrusion is the establishment of water-control structures designed to allow the upstream to freshen and to be periodically dewatered in the summer to promote the reestablishment of emergent plants.

The second salinity regulation problem is found where levees or water-control structures effectively exclude brackish water. Marshes, which no longer receive periodic inputs of brackish water, quickly become infested with freshwater plants such as water hyacinth, alligatorweed, water-pennywort (*Hydrocotyle* spp.), fragrant water-lily (*Nymphaea odorata*), and cattail. These provide cover but little food for wintering waterfowl. Some of the formerly brackish marshes produce large numbers of alligators and gallinules, however. Appropriate management strategies call for periodic flushes of salt water held sufficiently long to control noxious vegetation and to give salt-tolerant plants a competitive advantage.

Turbidity and Growth of Submergent Vegetation

Salinity and turbidity are factors controlling abundance and distribution of submergent aquatic plants. Salinity generally determines the species present, but their abundance and vigor are more closely tied to water depth and turbidity.

Texas coastal wetlands are perched above nearly impermeable clay subsoils but with varying amounts of accumulated silt which quickly become suspended in open water during times of heavy wind and wave action. Dense turbidity during critical early-growing periods often can limit the growth of submerged aquatics. Conversely, during periods of low wind action and resulting clear water, sunlight penetration can result in dense crops of various submergents.

Widgeongrass is the dominant submerged plant in brackish to saline marshes, whereas freshwater marshes are dominated by hornwort (*Ceratophyllum* spp.), naiad (*Najas* spp.), and fanwort (*Cabomba caroliniana*). Periodic summer partial drawdowns are the best management option for promoting germination of submerged aquatics. Sun-baked sediments shrink, crack, and become firmly bound by drying to the point that fine sediments often are tied up for one or more growing seasons, thus allowing, eventually, for the clearing of the water and sunlight penetration.

Burning

The use of fire is a major management tool in Texas coastal marshes, particularly those marshes where marshhay cordgrass is dominant. Cattle operators and some muskrat trappers favor marsh burns in July and August, whereas most wildlife interests favor burns in September to November or later. Most Texas marsh managers interested in promoting winter waterfowl habitat with fire prefer to set fires on a series of dates beginning late in September and continuing on into late December. This provides burned areas that are in various stages of recovery.

Fall fires remove robust vegetative growths, which encourage cool season sedges (*Scirpus* spp.) valuable as waterfowl food. Fires set by livestock operators are designed to remove dead growth and to promote new growths that emerge within a few days of the fire. This more palatable growth sustains livestock into the spring when they are generally moved to upland pastures to escape mosquitoes and to take advantage of vegetative growth there. Geese have been observed landing in marsh burns that are still smoking to take advantage of the readily available roots and tubers exposed by the fire. As cordgrass, saltmarsh bulrush (*Scirpus maritimus*), and Olney bulrush begin to grow, geese take advantage of the succulent new growth. Ducks (especially pintails) follow goose concentrations into marsh burns. Ducks spend the day feeding and loafing in areas opened by heavy goose-feeding activity, and make use of seeds exposed by the grubbing activities of snow geese.

Ideal burning conditions include low humidities (< 50% and preferably about 25%) and moist soil conditions. Because of dense urban and industrial areas adjacent to many marshes, it is mandatory to burn only with a wind that will keep smoke out of urban areas. The state air quality agency actively monitors marsh fires.

Livestock

Livestock grazing is a major land use in coastal Texas, and practically all privately owned marshes have grazing programs of varying intensities. Decadent marsh vegetation often is too coarse and dense to encourage waterfowl use. Although some ducks, primarily mallards and mottled ducks, use small ponds in heavy emergent vegetation, geese avoid tall standing marsh vegetation and choose open, closely cropped areas for foraging, loafing, and roosting.

Livestock grazing, in concert with burning, reduces the density of cordgrass stands so that ducks and geese can reach seeds and tubers and graze on new growths. Livestock hooves turn the soil, making food items more available and setting back plant succession to a more diverse plant assemblage. Grazing also helps to control the invasion of brush and trees, particularly baccharis (*Baccharis halimifolia*) and chinese tallow (*Sapium sebiferum*).

Nutria and muskrats can open dense marsh through foraging and, in the case of muskrats, lodge building. Both rodents are capable of opening up large areas of dense, emergent stands of reed (*Phragmites communis*), bullwhip (*Scirpus californicus*), and cattail. However, this can be dangerous if other forces like subsidence and salinity create permanent openings.

Mechanical and Chemical Control of Vegetation

Mechanical removal of vegetation has very limited application in wetland management along the Texas coast. Most mechanical removal is limited to mowing dry pastures and levees to control brush and trees. Levee mowing and burning is an important management practice that offers erosion protection to levees and water-control structures. Burning and mowing promote healthy stands of grass such as cordgrass and reed, which bind the levee better than do trees during storms.

Chemical control of noxious vegetation is an important facet of marsh management because of limited alternatives. Where salt water cannot be used to control water hyacinth, water-lettuce (*Pistia stratiotes*), alligatorweed, water-pennywort, and fragrant water-lily, applications of herbicides can be used. Water hyacinth, water-lettuce, and water-penny-wort are considered the most significant aquatic pests in coastal east Texas because they seem to provide little value for wildlife, expand rapidly, and compete with desirable aquatics. Alligatorweed also is considered a noxious plant, but livestock operators favor alligatorweed as forage, and waterfowl use dormant mats in the winter as loafing sites. It is used as food by American coots (*Fulica americana*) and common moorhens, and as nest sites by moorhens.

Planting and Seeding

Hundreds of thousands of dollars have been spent by private hunting interests in attempts to boost waterfowl use through the planting of various seeds and aquatic plants. Many individuals have an optimistic belief that there are plants that can be distributed that will lead to large populations of ducks and geese at specific locations. Unfortunately, few food plantings have been successful. In most cases, the wrong aquatic plant has been planted at the wrong location and time. The best examples of improper techniques continue to be attempts to establish millet in open-water areas where it will not germinate or to plant cultivated rice in marshes with excessive salt.

As a general rule, if conditions are conducive to germination, the seed bank is present and plants will propagate naturally. Some plants, however, do lend themselves to transplanting. Cordgrasses have been transplanted on levees and along water margins to control erosion, and plants like yellow waterlily (*Nymphaea mexicana*) with large roots and tubers can be moved to appropriate sites.

The most common planting involves the seeding of Japanese millet (*Echinochloa crusgalli*) or browntop millet (*Panicum remosum*) to provide an annual crop on prepared fields or drying mudflats. The seeding of Japanese millet onto drying mudflats is suitable only if soil salinity is low and the deposited seeds find adequate moisture levels to germinate. Also, mudflats must remain damp but unflooded until the seeds germinate and become established. After an extensive root system has been established, Japanese millet can tolerate minor flooding (5-15 cm) of fresh water and make a seed crop in less than 60 days. Ideal management calls for shallow (5-15 cm) fresh-water flooding after the seedcrop has matured to make seeds available to migrant waterfowl.

CONCLUSIONS AND RECOMMENDATIONS
Overview of Current Waterfowl Management Activities

There is a real need to reevaluate wetland management on public and privately owned areas in Texas. Poor management usually stems from a lack of expertise or financial and legal restrictions relative to construction of levees and water-control structures. There is, perhaps, too little emphasis on marsh management and too much on road construction and facilities that cater to alternative public uses. Additional effort should be aimed at managing water, fire, and grazing to effectively perpetuate habitat for migratory birds. Only the natural high productivity of wetlands and the adaptability of both plants and waterfowl prevent major catastrophe resulting from inappropriate management.

Trends in Land Use that Influence Management

Three major trends are expected to influence wetland management along the Texas Gulf Coast. First, if the oil-based economy does not return to its former status, the affluence of large land owners will decline. Second, the rapidly expanding human population in coastal Texas, with its accompanying demand for new land on which to develop and the rapidly declining agricultural base, places large and formerly remote wildlife-producing habitats in jeopardy. The demand for urban development areas probably will overwhelm the stability of a rice- and cattle-based agricultural economy that often has been subsidized by oil revenues. Large ranches that have provided secure habitat for waterfowl gradually will be broken into smaller parcels and become subject to development and other uses not beneficial to waterfowl.

The third major trend involves the continuing demand and competition for recreational space by increasing human population. The competition for land and the need for abundant waterfowl populations on those lands could result in increased interest and effort in managing those properties effectively.

Research Needs

A number of research needs should be addressed along the Gulf Coast.

1. Develop new designs for water-con-

trol structures that allow ingress and egress of marine species while modifying water levels and salinity for waterfowl habitat management.

2. Investigate the feasibility of renovating perpetually turbid marsh lakes devoid of aquatic vegetation.

3. Investigate long-term effects of frequent marsh fires in marshhay cordgrass and other species.

4. Determine factors limiting widgeongrass in shallow, brackish marsh ponds.

5. Create wetland areas by (a) restoration of former marshes drained for rice production; (b) management of such areas through water and salinity regulation; and (c) management of dredge-spoil disposal areas to create attractive waterfowl habitats.

6. Develop management schedules for wild millet and other wetland plants useful in marsh restoration and creation.

New Approaches to Creation of Waterfowl Habitat in Texas

The Texas Parks and Wildlife Department (TPWD) has initiated experimental habitat-development work on new spoil sites. Current policies of both TPWD and U.S. Fish and Wildlife Service are to request management sites at newly constructed reservoirs and channelization projects as part of a mitigation plan. Efforts are underway by several agencies in Texas to encourage landowners to develop abandoned or underused areas for wintering waterfowl habitat. This should produce new habitats for waterfowl, which may aid breeding as well as wintering birds.

SUMMARY

The Texas Gulf Coast is a diverse and important wintering waterfowl habitat. Wetlands vary from eastern Texas chenier marshes, which resemble those of western Louisiana, to deltaic marsh fringes along the 7 major estuaries and bay systems. The tidal regime is < 50 cm, and wind tides often influence the flooding regimes. The importance of coastal wetlands as feeding and nursery areas for marine finfish and shellfish complicates the management strategies used at waterfowl areas. Major waterfowl populations of the coast involve large numbers of snow, white-fronted, and Canada geese. In fall and winter, these birds make heavy use of the formerly wet prairies of the upper coast now converted to rice fields; later in winter they move to the brackish marshes where they graze or grub for rhizomes. Although some mallards use the eastern coastal marshes, the bulk of the dabbling ducks that use the estuarine and freshwater coastal wetlands are northern pintails, gadwall, American wigeon and green-winged teal. Redheads concentrate in the hypersaline Laguna Madre. Lesser and greater scaup also are abundant.

Relatively few remaining wetlands are pristine, and are currently being managed for waterfowl and other wildlife. Current waterfowl-management strategies include burning, grazing, and managing water. Burning is used to eliminate dead vegetation and increase accessibility of rhizomes and tubers, as well as to stimulate growth of new vegetation favored by geese in winter and early spring. Livestock also are used to reduce vegetation density and to make seeds and tubers more available.

In freshwater areas, water management often involves diking and water-control structures to hold freshwater for desired plant growth. One common strategy is to hold sufficient water to produce submergent and floating-leaf plants attractive as food directly or as substrates for invertebrates; and another is to drain the water in the spring to encourage the growth of nonpersistent annuals that are excellent seed producers. Seeding and planting are generally unnecessary, as seed banks are suitable when proper germination conditions are provided. Emergent areas are reflooded in the fall to attract feeding waterfowl.

In saline areas, marine interests favor wiers over other types of water-control structures that totally block marine organisms. Wiers are used to attempt to create depths suitable for plant growth or feeding by waterfowl and other migratory birds. However, maintenance of freshwater inflows and installation of combination stop-log and flap-gate structures to hold water are the best current methods of maintaining wetland quality. Use of only freshwater can create problems with excessive plant growth, especially exotics like water hyacinth and alligatorweed. Periodic flushes with brackish water help maintain several plant species like Olney bulrush that are valuable wildlife foods.

Current trends in land management that could be detrimental to maintenance and management of waterfowl areas include the breakup of large ranches, reduction in rice farming, and increased urbanization and recreational demands. New technology for intensive wetland management is needed and should be a goal of future habitat research for wintering waterfowl.

LITERATURE CITED

Armstrong, N. E. 1987. The ecology of open-bay bottoms of Texas: a community profile. U.S. Fish and Wildl. Serv. Biol. Rep. 87(7.12). 104 pp.

Bateman, H. A., T. Joanen, and C. D. Stutzenbaker. 1988. History and status of midcontinent snow geese on their Gulf Coast winter range. Pages 495-515 in M. W. Weller, ed. Waterfowl in winter. Univ. Minnesota Press, Minneapolis.

Bellrose, F. C. 1980. Ducks, geese and swans of North America. Third ed. Stackpole Books, Harrisburg, Pa. 540 pp.

Briggs, R. J., and D. D. Everett. 1983. Avian use of small aquatic habitats. Proc. Annu. Conf. Southeast. Assoc. Fish and Wildl. Agencies 37:86-94.

Brown, L. F., Jr., J. L. Brewton, T. T. Evans, J. H. McGowen, W. A. White, C. G. Groat, and W. L. Fisher. 1980. Environmental geologic atlas of the Texas coastal zone-Brownsville-Harlingen area. Bur. Econ. Geol., Austin, Tex. 140 pp.

Cain, B. W. 1988. Winter waterfowl habitat in Texas: shrinking and contaminated. Pages 583-596 in M. W. Weller, ed. Waterfowl in winter. Univ. Minnesota Press, Minneapolis.

Chabreck, R. H. 1972. Vegetation, water and soil characteristics of the Louisiana Coastal Region. Louisiana State Univ. Agric. Exp. Stn. Bull. No. 644. Baton Rouge. 72 pp.

Chamberlain, J. L. 1959. Gulf coast marsh vegetation as food for wintering waterfowl. J. Wildl. Manage. 23:97-102.

Corps of Engineers. 1986. Regulatory programs of the Corps of Engineers, U.S. Dep. of the Army. Fed. Reg. 51:41205.

Cornelius, S. E. 1977. Food and resource utilization by wintering redheads on lower Laguna Madre. J. Wildl. Manage. 41:374-385.

Cottam, C., and W. C. Glazener. 1959. Late nesting of water birds in south Texas. Trans. North Am. Wildl. Conf. 24: 382-395.

Cowardin, L. M., V. Carter, F. C. Golet, and E. T. LaRoe. 1979. Classification of wetlands and deep water habitats of the United States. U.S. Fish and Wildl. Serv., FWS/OBS-79/31. 103 pp.

Craig, N. J., R. E. Turner, and J. W. Day, Jr. 1980. Wetland losses and their consequences in coastal Louisiana. Z. Geomorph. 34:225-241.

Fehrenbach, T. R. 1985. Lone star: a history of Texas and Texans. Macmillan Co., New York, N.Y. 762 pp.

Frentress, C., and D. Lobpries. 1988. Job progress report. Job 1, W-106-R. Tex. Parks and Wildl. Dep., Austin. 27 pp.

Glazener, W. C. 1946. Food habits of wild geese on the Gulf Coast of Texas. J. Wildl. Manage. 10:322-329.

Gosselink, J. G. 1984. The ecology of delta marshes of coastal Louisiana: a community profile. U.S. Fish and Wildl. Serv. FWS/OBS-84/09. 134 pp.

Gould, F. W. 1975. Texas plants: a checklist and ecological summary. Texas A&M Univ., College Station. 112 pp.

Hobaugh, W. C. 1985. Body condition and nutrition of snow geese wintering in southeastern Texas. J. Wildl. Manage. 49:1028-1037.

——, C. D. Stutzenbaker, and E. L. Flickinger. 1989. The rice prairies. Pages 367-383 in L. M. Smith, R. L. Pederson, and R. M. Kaminski, eds. Habitat management for migrating and wintering waterfowl in North America. Texas Tech Univ. Press, Lubbock.

James, W. P., S. Giesler, R. DeOtte, and M. Inoue. 1977. Environmental considerations relating to operation and maintenance of the Texas Gulf Intracoastal Waterway. Sea Grant Prog. Publ. No. SG-78-204. Texas A&M Univ., College Station. 227 pp.

Jessen, R. 1988. Job progress report. Job 1, WE-106-R. Tex. Parks and Wildl. Dep., Austin, in press.

Krapu, G. L. 1974. Feeding ecology of pintail hens during reproduction. Auk 91:278-290.

McAdams, M. S. 1987. Classification and waterfowl use of ponds in south Texas. M.S. Thesis, Texas A&M Univ., College Station. 112 pp.

McMahan, C. A. 1970. Food habits of ducks wintering on Laguna Madre, Texas. J. Wildl. Manage. 34:946-949.

Pulich, W. Jr. 1980. Ecology of a hypersaline lagoon: the Laguna Madre. Pages 103-122 *in* P. L. Fore and R. D. Peterson, eds. Proc. Gulf of Mexico coastal ecosystems workshop. U.S. Fish and Wildl. Serv., FWS/OBS-80/30. 214 pp.

Robel, R. J. 1961. The effect of carp populations on the production of waterfowl food plants on a western waterfowl marsh. Trans. North Am. Wildl. Conf. 26:147- 159.

Rogers, B. D., and W. H. Herke. 1985. Estuarine-dependent fish and crustacean movements and weir management. Pages 201-219 *in* C. F. Bryan, P. J. Zwank, and R. H. Chabreck, eds. Proc. fourth coastal marsh and estuary manage. symp. Baton Rouge, La. 241 pp.

Ryan, C. J. A. 1984. Analysis of behavior of selected dabbling ducks wintering near Seadrift, TX. M.S. Thesis, Texas A&M Univ., College Station. 88 pp.

Scott, T. G., and C. H. Wasser. 1980. Checklist of North American plants for wildlife biologists. The Wildl. Soc., Washington, D.C. 58 pp.

Singleton, J. R. 1965. Waterfowl habitat management in Texas. Tex. Parks and Wildl. Dep. Bull. 47. 68 pp.

Stutzenbaker, C. D. 1985. Job progress report. Job 1, W-106-R. Tex. Parks and Wildl. Dep., Austin. 44 pp.

——, and R. J. Buller. 1974. Goose depredation on ryegrass pastures along the Texas coast. Tex. Parks and Wildl. Dep. Spec. Rep. Austin. 13 pp.

Texas Department of Water Resources. 1984. Water for Texas. Tex. Dep. of Water Resour., GP-4-1, GG72. Austin. 53 pp.

Tiner, R. W., Jr. 1984. Wetlands of the United States: current status and recent trends. U.S. Fish and Wildl. Serv., Washington, D.C. 59 pp.

Ward, G. H. Jr., N. E. Armstrong, and the Matagorda Bay Project Teams. 1980. Matagorda Bay, Texas: its hydrography, ecology and fishery resources. U.S. Fish and Wildl. Serv., D.C. FWS/OBS-81/52. 290 pp.

Weller, M. W. 1964. Distribution and migration of the redhead. J. Wildl. Manage. 34:946-949.

——. 1975. Migratory waterfowl: a hemispheric perspective. Publ. Biol. Inst. Invest. Cienc. 1:89-130.

White, D. H., and D. James. 1978. Differential use of fresh water environments by wintering waterfowl of coastal Texas. Wilson Bull. 90:99-111.

THE EAST COAST OF MEXICO

GUY A. BALDASSARRE, Environmental and Forest Biology, SUNY College of Environmental Science and Forestry, Syracuse, NY 13210
ARTHUR R. BRAZDA, U.S. Fish and Wildlife Service, 210 John Glenn Road, Lafayette, LA 70608
EMILIO HANGEL WOODYARD, Ducks Unlimited de Mexico, A.C., Monterrey, N.L., Mexico

Associated with the 2,970-km shoreline along the east coast of Mexico are important yet poorly known habitats used by Nearctic wintering waterfowl. Indeed, within this area are some of the largest undisturbed wetland complexes in the Western Hemisphere. This region, also known as the Gulf and Caribbean Coastal Zone (Saunders and Saunders 1981), contains the states of Tamaulipas, Veracruz, Tabasco, Campeche, Yucatan, and Quintana Roo (Fig. 1). The other major wintering waterfowl areas in Mexico are the wetland systems of the Pacific Coastal Zone and the Interior Highlands Zone.

Reconnaissance of wetlands, waterfowl, and other flora and fauna in Mexico began in 1892 (Goldman 1951). Additional historical data are in Leopold (1959), and some habitats in the Interior Highlands are treated by Arellano and Rojas (1956). Most quantitative data concerning wintering waterfowl populations began with the aerial flights of the U.S. Fish and Wildlife Service that were initiated in Mexico in 1938 as part of the midwinter waterfowl inventory; formal flights began on the east coast in 1948.

Saunders and Saunders (1981) summarized data from aerial and ground surveys in Mexico from 1937-64, and this represents the definitive source of information on waterfowl and wetlands in Mexico for that period. Their accounts of ground studies are largely qualitative, but nonetheless are invaluable from ecological and management perspectives. Detailed ground investigations are rare, excepting some notable work in the Pacific Coastal Zone (Smith and Jensen 1970, Kramer 1976, Scott 1983, Kramer and Euliss 1986, Mora et al. 1987). Overall, data from

Mexico are embryonic in comparison to other waterfowl habitats in North America.

Despite such limited information, however, the east coast of Mexico is of major importance to wintering waterfowl from the Central and Mississippi Flyways. For example, midwinter aerial surveys from 1948-62 have averaged 926,000 ducks and 11,000 geese, with highs being about 1.9 million ducks in 1948 and 23,000 geese in 1959 (Saunders and Saunders 1981). From 1970-88, the total number of ducks surveyed on the east coast has ranged from 642,745-1,861,380, and averaged 1,135,691 (Table 1).

Saunders and Saunders (1981) identified 17 waterfowl wintering areas associated with the east coast of Mexico, which together constitute more waterfowl habitat than the Pacific Coastal Zone and Interior Highlands Zone combined. Currently, there are 7 survey units along the east coast: (1) the Rio Grande Delta, Tamaulipas; (2) the Lower Laguna Madre-Tamaulipas lagoons, Tamaulipas; (3) the Tamesi and Panuco river deltas (Tampico lagoons) in Tamaulipas, Veracruz, and San Luis Potosi; (4) Tamiahua Lagoon south to Veracruz, Veracruz; (5) the Alvarado lagoons, Veracruz; (6) the Tabasco lagoons, Tabasco; and (7) the Campeche-Yucatan lagoons, Campeche and Yucatan. An additional unit on the Caribbean side of Quintana Roo was surveyed a few years but was abandoned because of sparse waterfowl populations.

Our objectives were to summarize (by survey unit) the information obtained during the midwinter aerial surveys conducted from 1970-88, and to review new ground studies and developments in

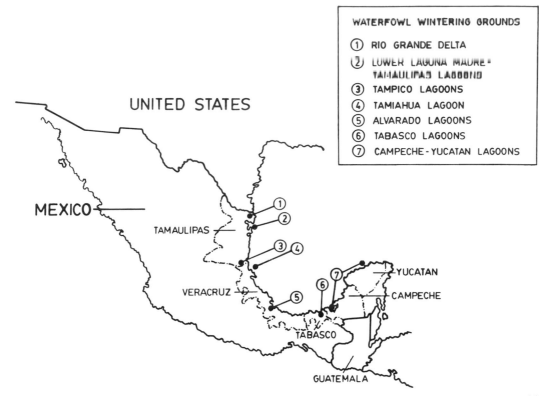

Fig. 1. Location of 7 wetland areas surveyed by the U.S. Fish and Wildlife Service during the mid-winter waterfowl inventory on the east coast of Mexico from 1970-88.

wetland conservation-management that have occurred on the east coast of Mexico during this period. The comparative importance of each unit as wintering waterfowl habitat then was ranked using the criteria of average duck numbers and habitat conditions per unit from 1970-88.

We chose 1970 as a starting point because surveys from 1965-69 either were not conducted (1968 and 1969), were partial (1965 and 1966), or were conducted by inexperienced observers (1967). Beginning in 1970, nearly all surveys covered the entire east coast, and data variability was reduced because surveys were coordinated by the same biologist (A.R. Brazda). Surveys were not conducted from 1971-74, and in 1976, 1983, 1984, 1986, and 1987.

Plant nomenclature follows Fassett (1957) and Hotchkiss (1972) except for some strictly tropical species, which were listed as reported by Saunders and Saund-

ers (1981). Waterfowl recorded during the surveys were fulvous whistling duck (*Dedrocygna bicolor*), black-bellied whistling duck (*D. autumnalis*), mallard (*Anas platyrhynchos*), mottled duck (*A. fulvigula*), gadwall (*A. strepera*), American wigeon (*A. americana*), green-winged teal (*A. crecca*), blue-winged teal (*A. discors*), northern shoveler (*A. clypeata*), canvasback (*Aythya valisineria*), redhead (*Aythya americana*), lesser scaup (*Aythya affinis*), greater scaup (*Aythya marila*), ring-necked duck (*Aythya collaris*), common goldeneye (*Bucephala clangula*), bufflehead (*B. albeola*), ruddy duck (*Oxyura jamaicensis*), common merganser (*Mergus merganser*), red-breasted merganser (*M. serrator*), Canada goose (*Branta canadensis*), white-fronted goose (*Anser albifrons*), snow goose (*Chen caerulescens*), as well as American coot (*Fulica americana*).

Table 1. Estimated numbers of ducks seen in survey units on the east coast of Mexico, January 1970-88.

Survey unit	1970	1975	1977	1978	1979	1980	1981	1982	1985	1988
Rio Grande Delta	84,325	61,375	253,855	113,525	147,390	166,350	138,765	111,740	108,950	25,240
Lower Laguna Madre	58,686	114,170	956,770	463,685	430,615	405,380	865,795	373,950	355,450	373,145
Tampico Lagoons	45,024	31,830	23,210	56,000	30,280	197,400	143,460	21,205	28,215	35,005
Tamiahua Lagoon	23,300	16,370	46,620	90,015	81,010	47,085	65,090	70,310	27,285	27,380
Alvarado Lagoons	130,925	147,620	113,875	101,910	184,550	83,175	89,675	62,800	122,845	57,850
Tabasco Lagoons	215,310	153,900	220,150	211,385	334,320	297,885	227,345	155,330	[a]	211,150
Campeche-Yucatan Lagoons	147,280	143,025	246,900	220,125	320,325	235,405	178,575	43,930	[a]	54,120
Total	704,850	668,290	1,861,380	1,256,645	1,528,490	1,362,650	1,708,705	839,265	642,745	783,890

[a] Unit was not surveyed.

GENERAL HABITAT DESCRIPTION

Rainfall increases from north to south along the east coast of Mexico but becomes variable on the Yucatan Peninsula. For example, annual average rainfall is 68 cm at Brownsville, Texas; 114 cm in Tampico, Tamaulipas; 156 cm in Veracruz, Veracruz; and 288 cm in Minatitlan, Veracruz. In Yucatan, however, the average is 397 at Teapa (near the southern edge of the marshes) but is only 88 cm at Merida, which is in the interior (Saunders and Saunders 1981).

Published data on specific wetland soil types are lacking, excepting some survey maps. Saunders and Saunders (1981) provide general descriptions of water salinity regimes and associated wetland vegetation along the east coast. Their early descriptions of waterfowl habitat associated with survey units on the east coast of Mexico are relatively thorough.

HABITAT IMPORTANCE

Lower Laguna Madre and Tamaulipas Lagoons

Although Saunders and Saunders (1981) discussed several areas within the Lower Laguna Madre of Mexico, these sites were incorporated into a single unit in 1962 (Fig. 2). This unit is noted for its concentrations of redheads and northern pintails, which comprised 49% and 23%, respectively, of the ducks using the laguna (Table 2). Overall, this unit winters 98% of the redheads and 61% of the northern pintails surveyed on the east coast (Table 3). These species largely use the laguna proper, whereas other ducks use inland lakes and ponds (the Tamaulipas lagoons).

The basin of the Lower Laguna Madre begins about 55 km south of the mouth of the Rio Grande and extends about 160 km, covering an area of approximately 2,030 km^2 (Saunders and Saunders 1981). The laguna is widest at the northern end (about 30 km) and becomes increasingly narrower southward; water depth averages 1.3-1.6 m. The principal waterfowl food plant is shoalgrass (*Halodule* sp.), which is most abundant in the deeper, northern end. Cornelius (1977) reported that shoalgrass was the dominant plant and the principal food of redheads wintering in the Laguna Madre in the United States (U.S.). Dominant mollusks were *Tellina* sp., *Cumingia tellinoides*, and *Tagelus plebeius*, but these were not major foods of redheads. There is no comparable study of the Laguna Madre in Mexico.

The hydrology of this unit and its attractiveness to wintering waterfowl depends on 2 factors: (1) the number and size of channels or passes that extend through the barrier dune system into the Gulf of Mexico, and (2) the influx of freshwater from the mainland. From 1909-1960 the laguna reportedly had 1 or more such connecting channels to the Gulf whereby salinity approximated sea water. However, because of shifting sands, the major pass in the Lower

Fig. 2.   The Lower Laguna Madre in Tamaulipas.

Laguna Madre (Eighth Pass) nearly was closed by 1960. This closure created hypersaline conditions (>50% above sea water) in the laguna as entrapped salt-water evaporated and decimated most shoalgrass, mollusks, and other waterfowl foods. These conditions caused a near disappearance of wintering waterfowl in

the laguna as evidenced by the 1966 survey that reported no open passes to the gulf and no waterfowl present.

Habitat conditions began recovering in 1967 when Hurricane Beulah opened many passes to the Gulf of Mexico. Redhead populations subsequently increased from 3,045 (5% of all ducks) in

Table 2.   Percent species composition of ducks wintering within survey units on the east coast of Mexico 1970-88, compared with survey reports (1948-64) of Saunders and Saunders (1981) (in parentheses).

				Survey unit			
Species	Rio Grande Delta	Lower Laguna Madre	Tampico Lagoons	Tamiahua Lagoon	Alvarado Lagoons	Tabasco Lagoons	Campeche-Yucatan Lagoons
Whistling ducks	3 (<1)	0 (<1)	17 (2)	0 (<1)	12 (3)	9 (9)	0 (<1)
Mallard	0 (<1)	0 (<1)	0	0	0	0	0
Mottled duck	2 (<1)	0 (<1)	0 (<1)	0 (<1)	0	0	0
Gadwall	10 (9)	2 (1)	10 (19)	6 (5)	4 (12)	1 (1)	0 (1)
American wigeon	17 (6)	10 (3)	8 (8)	15 (4)	11 (13)	4 (17)	5 (18)
Green-winged teal	16 (9)	1 (<1)	14 (10)	3 (<1)	1 (2)	0 (<1)	0 (<1)
Blue-winged teal	2 (5)	0 (<1)	12 (10)	13 (2)	48 (22)	70 (33)	54 (20)
Northern shoveler	19 (11)	1 (<1)	6 (4)	4 (1)	4 (2)	7 (<1)	3 (<1)
Northern pintail	25 (47)	23 (22)	13 (27)	13 (4)	8 (31)	4 (16)	3 (16)
Canvasback	1 (<1)	1 (<1)	1 (2)	3 (3)	1 (<1)	0 (<1)	0 (<1)
Redhead	0 (<1)	49 (62)	0 (<1)	10 (<1)	0 (<1)	0 (<1)	0 (<1)
Scaup	1 (1)	10 (5)	14 (13)	31 (77)	6 (11)	3 (18)	25 (43)
Ring-necked duck	0 (<1)	0 (<1)	0 (2)	0 (<1)	3 (<1)	2 (2)	10 (1)
Common goldeneye	0	0	0	0	0	0	0
Bufflehead	0	0	0	0	0	0	0
Ruddy duck	4 (<1)	1 (<1)	2 (2)	2 (<1)	1 (<1)	0 (<1)	0 (<1)
Mergansers	1 (<1)	0	0	0	0	0	0

Table 3. Percent species composition of waterfowl wintering among the survey units on the east coast of Mexico, 1970-88.

Species	Rio Grande Delta	Lower Laguna Madre	Tampico Lagoons	Tamiahua Lagoon	Alvarado Lagoons	Tabasco Lagoons	Campeche-Yucatan Lagoons	Total
Whistling ducks	8.7	0.1	20.2	0.4	30.3	40.1	0.1	446,933
Mallard	93.2	6.8	0.0	0.0	0.0	0.0	0.0	1,395
Mottled duck	64.4	26.7	5.4	0.4	2.6	0.5	0.0	28,456
Gadwall	33.4	28.2	15.0	7.8	11.1	3.7	0.8	363,683
American wigeon	19.8	42.8	4.0	6.8	11.9	6.8	7.9	1,046,129
Green-winged teal	56.7	13.4	21.3	4.0	3.7	0.8	0.1	345,183
Blue-winged teal	0.6	0.4	2.2	2.2	17.8	47.9	28.9	2,972,911
Northern shoveler	40.5	9.4	6.1	3.4	8.2	25.0	7.5	553,386
Northern pintail	18.2	61.1	4.3	3.9	5.0	4.8	2.7	1,684,406
Redhead	0.1	97.5	0.0	2.1	0.0	0.0	0.2	2,199,735
Canvasback	11.4	55.2	7.9	17.7	7.5	0.1	0.2	86,734
Scaup	1.1	36.7	6.3	12.7	5.6	5.4	32.2	1,224,627
Common goldeneye	89.6	10.4	0.0	0.0	0.0	0.0	0.0	720
Ring-necked duck	1.1	2.9	1.9	0.3	14.4	17.5	62.0	253,157
Bufflehead	39.7	29.7	17.2	4.6	0.0	8.7	0.0	4,580
Ruddy duck	31.8	33.8	14.9	7.2	7.5	4.9	0.0	132,530
Mergansers	62.7	32.8	0.2	0.1	4.1	0.0	0.1	12,345
Canada goose	68.0	27.3	4.7	0.0	0.0	0.0	0.0	42,425
White-fronted goose	60.7	28.6	6.6	4.1	0.0	0.0	0.0	173,479
Snow goose	68.4	21.2	0.0	10.4	0.0	0.0	0.0	157,037
American coot	12.7	11.7	16.0	13.9	13.5	7.0	25.2	5,297,843

1970 to 281,450 (75%) birds in 1988 (Table 4). Current habitat conditions within the laguna are considered good, because 2-3 natural passes have remained open to the gulf since 1970. Four passes were observed in January 1988, 3 of which are maintained for small craft moving between the laguna and the gulf.

In addition to the Laguna Madre proper, this unit also contains numerous freshwater and brackish ponds to the west (the Tamaulipas lagoons), as well as some additional ponds on the barrier ridge separating the unit from the gulf. Saunders and Saunders (1981) reported that many of the Tamaulipas lagoons supported aquatic vegetation including widgeongrass (*Ruppia maritima*), muskgrass (*Chara* spp.), naiad (*Najas* spp.), dwarf spikerush (*Eleocharis parvula*), and bulrush (*Scirpus* spp.). The few ponds on the barrier islands did not contain valuable waterfowl foods. Nonetheless, the Tamaulipas lagoons comprise an important component of the habitat in this unit and

are used especially when poor habitat conditions exist within the laguna.

Since 1970, this unit has contained 39% of the ducks surveyed on the east coast of Mexico as compared to only 17% from 1948-64 (Table 5). Average duck populations since 1970 have been 439,765 (39% dabbling ducks and 61% diving ducks) (Table 4). The most abundant species has been the redhead (49%), followed by northern pintail (23%), scaup (mostly lesser scaup) (10%), and American wigeon (10%) (Table 2). These rankings of abundance are similar to Saunders and Saunders (1981). However, the proportion of redheads wintering in the unit has decreased from 62% of all ducks to 49%, whereas the proportion of scaup and American wigeon has increased; the proportion of pintails was nearly equal between the 2 survey periods (Table 2). This unit ranks second to the Rio Grande Delta in numbers of wintering geese (Table 3).

The maintenance of the man-made

Table 4. Numbers of waterfowl in the Lower Laguna Madre and Tamaulipas lagoons, Tamaulipas, Mexico, January 1970-88.

Species	1970	1975	1977	1978	1979	1980	1981	1982	1985	1988
Dabbling ducks										
Whistling ducks	0	75	0	0	0	0	0	200	0	0
Mallard	0	0	0	0	5	0	90	0	0	0
Mottled ducks	726	70	150	255	95	640	4,105	240	270	1,050
Gadwall	12,285	4,180	13,340	7,320	7,800	17,620	14,385	8,310	7,350	10,000
American wigeon	6,870	15,470	83,950	58,150	35,885	79,550	124,740	25,090	10,450	7,300
Green-winged teal	3,405	1,705	3,580	1,885	3,900	4,310	7,590	2,970	6,780	10,025
Blue-winged teal	0	210	1,960	70	150	970	6,870	260	1,080	375
Northern shoveler	855	1,665	4,795	15,000	4,515	6,280	9,000	2,320	2,370	5,200
Northern pintail	13,905	8,705	297,515	99,045	117,170	91,570	280,020	51,970	27,830	40,650
Subtotal	38,046	32,080	405,290	181,725	169,520	200,940	446,800	91,360	56,130	74,600
Diving ducks										
Redhead	3,045	74,500	265,895	266,790	192,150	192,300	340,105	265,820	263,720	281,450
Canvasback	1,065	465	950	3,970	8,950	3,910	24,465	2,420	520	1,200
Scaup	11,856	3,195	276,860	5,795	53,450	3,840	50,595	7,030	26,120	11,200
Ring-necked duck	3,645	980	1,065	580	290	340	65	80	200	0
Common goldeneye	0	0	0	0	0	0	75	0	0	0
Bufflehead	60	35	100	20	240	120	210	70	230	275
Ruddy duck	945	2,775	6,520	4,485	5,190	3,710	3,420	6,720	7,720	3,295
Mergansers	15	140	90	320	825	220	60	450	810	1,125
Subtotal	20,640	82,090	551,480	281,960	261,095	204,440	418,995	282,590	299,320	298,545
Total ducks	58,686	114,170	956,770	463,685	430,615	405,380	865,795	373,950	355,450	373,145
Geese										
Canada	1,725	50	0	0	150	3,445	4,600	390	400	815
White-fronted	555	125	235	550	1,500	7,940	23,240	2,150	9,265	4,035
Snow	12	50	0	0	0	4,600	22,575	4,250	1,100	775
Total geese	2,292	225	235	550	1,650	15,985	50,415	6,790	10,765	5,625
American coot	26,550	46,365	82,150	53,740	77,205	65,220	76,605	80,690	61,400	49,075

openings and the occurrence of natural openings to the gulf should keep salinity levels in the laguna within a range conducive to growth of important plant and animal food resources. Maintenance of these openings should be a major management objective. Of additional concern is contaminant run-off associated with nearby agricultural operations, as well as regular monitoring of petrochemical activity. However, current habitat conditions in the unit are near optimum, whereby we would rank this area the number 1 wintering waterfowl habitat on the east coast of Mexico (Table 5).

Tabasco Lagoons

The Tabasco lagoons encompass about 10,000 km². These wetlands result primarily from sediment deposition and flooding by the Grijalva and Usumacinta rivers as well as flooding by several smaller rivers that empty into the region surrounding Villahermosa, Tabasco (Scott and Carbonell 1986). These delta wetlands extend into Campeche state to form a wetland complex of about 20,000 km², which is the largest and commercially most important wetland resource in Mexico (Fig. 3). Indeed, the Tabasco-Campeche wetlands are among the largest in

Table 5. The average percentage of ducks seen per survey area on the east coast of Mexico from 1970-88 compared with percentages reported in Saunders and Saunders (1981).

Time period	Survey area						
	Rio Grande Delta	Lower Laguna Madre	Tampico Lagoons	Tamiahua Lagoon	Alvarado Lagoons	Tabasco Lagoons	Campeche-Yucatan Lagoons
1948-64	3.3	17.2	22.6	7.8	14.0	11.6	23.5
1970-88	10.7	38.7	4.8	4.4	9.6	17.8	14.0
Importance ranking	5	1	6	7	3	2	4

Fig. 3.   The Tabasco lagoons constitute the largest complex of wetlands in Mexico.

the world. The wetland systems are freshwater, excepting tidewater lagoons near the gulf. The system is not subject to drought because annual rainfall averages 152-305 cm (Saunders and Saunders 1981).

Scott and Carbonell (1986) list principal habitat types in these wetlands as follows: (1) beach communities; (2) forests of black mangrove (*Avicennia germinans*), red mangrove (*Rhizophora mangle*), and white mangrove *(Laguncularia racemosa)*; (3) thickets of botoncillo (*Conocarpus erectus*) and hibiscus *(Hibiscus* sp.); (4) shrub marsh; (5) grass, sedge, and forb marsh with cattail (*Typha latifolia*), common reed (*Phragmites communis*), sedges (*Cyperus* spp.), and other plants; (6) lakes and ponds; (7) brackish lagoons; (8) savannas; and (9) gallery forest along streams and channels. This unit also includes the largest mangrove forest in Mexico (1,100 km^2), which is located around the Laguna de Terminos in Campeche. The western part of Tabasco contains dense swamp forest and

heavily vegetated marshes characterized by little open water. Consequently, most waterfowl use occurs in the eastern sector of the unit, as this area includes the Usumacinta and Grijalva river deltas, which contain most of the lagoons in the state. The area north of Villahermosa (toward Laguna de Terminos) was vegetated densely in 1988 and received almost no use by waterfowl.

The vastness of this wetland complex and its associated habitat diversity render the area to be of extreme importance to waterfowl and other wetland species. Ducks do not occur in large flocks, thus total numbers probably are underestimated because aerial coverage of the survey unit usually ranges from 4-10%. The population of wading birds was estimated at 250,000 in May 1977 and included the largest colony (10,000 breeding pairs) of wood storks (*Mycteria americana*) known in North and Central America (Sprunt and Knoder 1980). This area also contains the northernmost

Table 6. Numbers of waterfowl in the Tabasco lagoons, Tabasco, Mexico, January 1970-88.

Species	1970	1975	1977	1978	1979	1980	1981	1982	1985[a]	1988
Dabbling ducks										
Whistling ducks	14,900	40,700	18,380	13,790	24,280	3,900	8,133	20,490		23,200
Mallard	0	0	0	0	0	0	0	0		0
Mottled ducks	0	0	0	140	0	0	0	0		0
Gadwall	1,700	1,950	2,420	1,345	1,900	850	1,350	1,930		100
American wigeon	7,375	20,650	3,900	2,015	6,300	4,850	17,875	7,440		650
Green-winged teal	125	600	0	1,600	0	0	255	0		50
Blue-winged teal	127,300	60,700	159,560	135,235	262,540	265,750	172,785	71,930		167,350
Northern shoveler	20,460	5,750	8,400	21,205	32,400	8,750	14,240	22,510		4,700
Northern pintail	25,950	13,700	6,610	9,750	1,800	11,105	5,350	2,900		4,400
Subtotal	197,810	144,050	199,250	185,080	329,220	294,805	220,570	132,620		206,450
Diving ducks										
Redhead	0	0	0	0	0	0	0	0		0
Canvasback	0	0	0	80	0	0	0	0		0
Scaup	0	7,850	13,400	19,900	2,200	2,700	4,125	12,500		3,000
Ring-necked duck	17,500	2,000	6,000	2,325	2,900	350	2,250	9,300		1,600
Common goldeneye	0	0	0	0	0	0	0	0		0
Bufflehead	0	0	0	0	0	0	400	0		0
Ruddy duck	0	0	1,500	4,000	0	0	0	860		100
Mergansers	0	0	0	0	0	0	0	0		0
Subtotal	17,500	9,850	20,900	26,305	5,100	3,050	7,635	22,710		4,700
Total ducks	215,310	153,900	220,150	211,385	334,320	297,855	227,345	155,330		211,150
Geese										
Canada	0	0	0	0	0	0	0	0		0
White-fronted	0	0	0	0	10	0	20	0		0
Snow	0	0	0	0	0	0	0	0		0
Total geese	0	0	0	0	10	0	20	0		0
American coot	10,850	99,100	24,200	45,575	59,900	11,000	65,480	19,800		33,050

[a]Not surveyed in 1985.

breeding population of Jabiru storks (*Jabiru mycteria*), an endangered species in Central America. The nutrient-rich waters also support major commercial fisheries in inshore waters and provide a nursery for the largest shrimp fishery in Mexico. This unit supports the most diverse flora and fauna of all the wetland units along the east coast of Mexico.

In addition to the high wildlife value of this unit, these aquatic systems also are unique in being the only area on the east coast (except Yucatan) where a planned wetland conservation program is in progress. The Instituto Nacional de Investigaciones sobre Recursos Bioticos (INIREB) completed a plan in December 1986 which proposed a 2,920 km^2 Biosphere Reserve (The Reserva de los Pantanos de Centla) to be protected within these wetlands.

From 1970-88, winter duck populations in the Tabasco lagoons averaged 225,194 (Table 6). The unit primarily winters dabbling ducks (94%), of which blue-winged teal predominate (70%); no other duck species comprises >10% of the total (Table 2). Since 1970, the unit has contained 18% of the ducks surveyed on the east coast (Table 5), including 48% of the blue-winged teal (Table 3). The large size and habitat diversity of this unit make aerial survey difficult; thus, population estimates are minimal. Nevertheless, owing to the size and near pristine condition of the habitat, we would rank the Tabasco lagoons second in importance as wintering waterfowl habitat on the east coast (Table 5).

This wetland complex is considered by most wetland experts to be pristine. Any habitat degradation likely will result from petrochemical activities because the largest known oil reserves in Mexico exist beneath these wetlands. PEMEX (the national petroleum company of Mexico) aggressively extracts oil and gas in western Tabasco, whereas little oil activity has occurred in eastern Tabasco and Campeche. These activities have resulted in some serious pollution problems, most notably near the cities of Minatitlan,

Coatzacoalcos, and Villahermosa. The most serious spill to date was the IXTOC I blowout in the early 1980s that spilled thousands of barrels of oil into surrounding wetlands. Another industrial threat is the large sulphur plant at Minatitlan, which dumps wastes into nearby wetlands.

Other threats include proposed dam projects on the Usumacinta River and the expansion of road systems within the delta; both could alter the system's hydrology. International banks and government agencies recently have become involved in large-scale agricultural development projects that seriously have affected these wetlands. In 1986, for example, Mexico's Ministry of Agriculture and Hydrologic Resources headed a project clearing 100 km² of lowland wet forest for rice culture along the southern edge of Laguna de Terminos. Future plans are to expand this project to 500 km². Other threats include harvest of the mangroves for timber and disturbance from fishing and other human activities.

A strong step toward conservation of this system would be the establishment of the Centla Biosphere Reserve. Additionally, appropriate U.S. agencies (e.g., National Park Service, Fish and Wildlife Service) as well as private international groups (i.e., National Audubon Society, Conservation International, Ducks Unlimited) should seek ways to work with PEMEX in relation to oil extraction procedures that would minimize impacts in this fragile wetland complex. Habitat quality for waterfowl could be enhanced directly by burning the large areas of closed marsh that exist within this unit, which should open water areas for growth of more desirable waterfowl foods.

Alvarado Lagoons, Veracruz

The Alvarado lagoons complex is a delta and coastal lowlands system that spreads over about 5,380 km² located mostly south of Alvarado, Veracruz (Fig.

4). There are about 2,500 km² of wetlands associated with the area (Scott and Carbonell 1986), which result from the confluence of several major river systems of which the most notable are the Papaloapan and San Juan. Laguna Alvarado (18 km long and 5-6 km wide) is the only major wetland in the unit that is saltwater, because it is connected to the Gulf of Mexico at Boca de Alvarado. The remaining lagoons in the unit are freshwater except after tidal surges associated with tropical storms and hurricanes. The other major wetland in this unit is Laguna Camaronera, which also is freshwater.

Pineapple and sugar-cane production have caused some habitat loss, but it is the growth of undesirable aquatics that has reduced the attractiveness of many areas to waterfowl. Principal undesirable plants are water hyacinth (*Eichornia crassipes*), water velvet (*Azolla* sp.), and duckweeds (*Lemna* spp.), which form a continuous mat over many of the smaller ponds and lagoons. However, wetland areas not dominated by pest plants contain several desirable waterfowl foods such as spikerushes (*Eleocharis* spp.), smartweeds (*Polygonum* spp.), bulrushes, arrowhead (*Sagittaria* sp.), and waterstargrass (*Heteranthera dubia*). Insect larvae and small gastropods also are abundant (Saunders and Saunders 1981, Scott and Carbonell 1986). This unit also has been impacted by the construction of several dams on the major rivers (the Papaloapan Project), which have reduced the flushing action that formerly removed tons of pest plants from the system.

Laguna Alvarado is primarily a mangrove swamp with freshwater lagoons extending landward for many kilometers. Widgeongrass grows in much of the laguna, and mollusks are abundant in the sand substrate and on plants; less is known about Laguna Camaronera.

Waterfowl use has declined from an estimated 500,000 ducks in 1947 to 53,000

Fig. 4. The Alvarado lagoons complex in Veracruz results primarily from overbank flooding and deposition of several major river systems.

in 1965 (Saunders and Saunders 1981), but has averaged 109,523 since 1970; no geese have been recorded since 1975 (Table 7). Overall, the Alvarado Lagoons currently winter 10% of the ducks surveyed on the east coast (Table 5).

The unit primarily winters dabbling ducks (89%), with the most abundant species being blue-winged teal (48%), followed by whistling ducks (12%), and American wigeon (11%) (Table 2). This distribution reflects a dramatic shift in the proportional occurrence of these species as compared to the surveys from 1948-64. For example, whistling duck composition has increased from 3-12%, and blue-winged teal from 22-48%. The unit ranks second to the Tabasco lagoons as a site for whistling ducks since 1970 (30%) and third in numbers of blue-winged teal (18%) (Table 3).

Some oil and industrial pollution has been observed during surveys in the 1980s, but it has not yet seriously impacted wetland habitats. Habitat loss due to agricultural expansion and con-tinued upriver water diversion and impoundment pose much more serious threats than those from oil or industrial pollution. Nevertheless, because of the size and habitat diversity of the unit, we rank it third in importance along the east coast and estimate that the unit could accommodate many more waterfowl than it presently does.

The Campeche-Yucatan Lagoons

Saunders and Saunders (1981) treat the Campeche and Yucatan lagoons as separate units, but few waterfowl use the associated wetlands in Campeche state. Both these areas have been surveyed as a combined unit since 1965, but an estimated 90% of the ducks occur in Yucatan.

The main body of water in Campeche is Laguna de Terminos, which is a 3,000 km^2 brackish lagoon with a water depth usually <1 m. The major rivers entering the Laguna are the Palizada, Champan, and Candelaria (Scott and Carbonell 1986). Currently, Laguna de Terminos appears to be of minor importance to

Table 7. Numbers of waterfowl in the Alvarado lagoons, Veracruz, Mexico, January 1970-88.

Species	1970	1975	1977	1978	1979	1980	1981	1982	1985	1988
Dabbling ducks										
Whistling ducks	26,500	2,900	2,850	1,255	39,850	3,300	21,400	3,900	30,985	2,575
Mallard	0	0	0	0	0	0	0	0	0	0
Mottled ducks	0	400	300	40	0	0	0	0	0	0
Gadwall	17,725	1,300	1,125	3,295	4,590	4,625	110	2,150	3,420	2,025
American wigeon	23,305	30,070	21,975	11,640	6,950	6,025	2,460	3,900	12,100	6,425
Green-winged teal	750	1,250	0	0	500	3,750	3,585	0	0	3,050
Blue-winged teal	25,265	75,050	54,825	57,070	88,400	35,775	60,185	45,850	61,050	24,950
Northern shoveler	7,200	6,200	2,500	8,410	10,270	2,150	1,180	250	1,170	5,875
Northern pintail	20,615	13,800	6,250	1,990	9,870	14,275	110	1,200	12,270	4,175
Subtotal	121,360	130,970	89,825	83,700	160,430	69,900	88,980	57,250	120,995	49,075
Diving ducks										
Redhead	10	0	0	0	0	0	0	0	350	0
Canvasback	1,685	250	225	150	100	4,125	0	0	0	0
Scaup	4,095	13,550	17,175	6,435	16,870	4,700	695	550	1,000	3,775
Ring-necked duck	3,150	1,750	6,400	11,325	4,350	2,125	0	3,500	500	3,425
Common goldeneye	0	0	0	0	0	0	0	0	0	0
Bufflehead	0	0	0	0	0	0	0	0	0	0
Ruddy duck	625	850	0	300	2,800	2,325	0	1,500	0	1,575
Mergansers	0	250	250	0	0	0	0	0	0	0
Subtotal	9,565	16,650	24,050	18,210	24,120	13,275	695	5,550	1,850	8,775
Total ducks	130,925	147,620	113,875	101,910	184,550	83,175	89,675	62,800	122,845	57,850
Geese										
Canada	0	0	0	0	0	0	0	0	0	0
White-fronted	20	0	0	0	0	0	0	0	0	0
Snow	0	0	0	0	0	0	0	0	0	0
Total geese	20	0	0	0	0	0	0	0	0	0
American coot	97,390	135,050	99,625	44,895	91,800	34,450	137,600	18,900	12,650	45,375

wintering waterfowl. The laguna does contain extensive beds of widgeongrass and muskgrass, but the area harbors more wading birds, shorebirds, gulls, brown pelicans (*Pelecanus occidentalis*), and associated species than it does waterfowl. Many coastal lagoons within Campeche state were destroyed by hurricanes in the 1930s, which still is evidenced by the dead mangroves that occur over much of the area; few waterfowl use these habitats.

The wetlands of Yucatan differ from other survey units in being limited to the immediate coast. This occurs because the entire Yucatan Peninsula is a limestone formation; thus, most drainage occurs underground and no surface water exists except for scattered sinkholes (cenotes). The 2 major wetland types in this area are (1) long, narrow open water wetlands inside the beach ridge and parallel to the gulf (i.e., Laguna de Celestun); and (2) mangrove swamp lagoons. Underground water flow provides a great influx of freshwater, but the proximity to the coast renders these wetlands brackish to some degree. These wetlands span the coastline,

but the most important areas for wintering waterfowl extend from the Laguna de Celestun to the city of Progreso. Beyond Progreso there is little use by waterfowl, because water areas are larger and deeper and submergent plants are lacking. This habitat condition probably occurs because of the sand substrate and apparent scouring action by the wind. In contrast, the lagoons from Celestun to Progreso are brackish to saline and support extensive beds of widgeongrass and muskgrass. Other stands of aquatic vegetation (probably shoalgrass) lie close offshore in many areas, and probably are used by lesser scaup and other ducks.

Saunders and Saunders (1981) reported an average of 256,000 ducks in this unit, which accounted for 24% of the east coast total (Table 5). This contrasts with an average of 176,632 ducks from 1970-88, which was 14% of the east coast total (Tables 3, 8). Survey totals from 1970-88 consisted of 65% dabbling ducks and 35% diving ducks, of which blue-winged teal were most abundant (54%), followed by lesser scaup (25%) (Table 2). Thus, this

Table 8. Numbers of waterfowl in the Campeche-Yucatan lagoons, Mexico, January 1970-88.

Species	1970	1975	1977	1978	1979	1980	1981	1982	1985[a]	1988
Dabbling ducks										
Whistling ducks	0	0	20	500	0	0	0	0		0
Muscovy ducks	0	0	0	0	0	0	0	0		0
Mottled ducks	0	0	0	0	0	0	0	0		0
Gadwall	100	105	1,260	135	500	500	0	90		100
American wigeon	8,350	1,845	10,700	9,550	9,485	11,680	29,170	575		875
Green-winged teal	100	0	50	165	0	0	0	0		0
Blue-winged teal	16,325	114,240	95,180	85,780	217,480	179,950	105,245	14,875		31,550
Northern shoveler	8,945	4,080	1,910	7,335	1,420	6,375	5,350	3,650		2,490
Northern pintail	15,275	810	1,370	1,055	11,405	6,795	6,400	1,560		1,605
Subtotal	49,095	121,080	110,490	104,520	240,290	205,300	146,165	20,750		36,620
Diving ducks										
Redhead	3,525	0	0	0	0	250	400	0		0
Canvasback	0	105	0	0	35	0	0	0		0
Scaup	12,660	11,610	112,990	109,870	69,500	26,420	26,450	23,180		1,500
Ring-necked duck	82,000	10,215	23,420	5,735	10,500	3,435	5,560	0		16,000
Common goldeneye	0	0	0	0	0	0	0	0		0
Bufflehead	0	0	0	0	0	0	0	0		0
Ruddy duck	0	0	0	0	0	0	0	0		0
Mergansers	0	15	0	0	0	0	0	0		0
Subtotal	98,185	21,945	136,410	115,605	80,035	30,105	32,410	23,180		17,500
Total ducks	147,280	143,025	246,900	220,125	320,325	235,405	178,575	43,930		54,120
Geese										
Canada	0	0	0	0	0	0	0	0		0
White-fronted	0	0	0	0	0	0	0	0		0
Snow	0	0	0	0	0	0	0	0		0
Total geese	0	0	0	0	0	0	0	0		0
American coot	190,220	73,440	78,070	220,435	227,160	160,450	275,315	62,470		48,440

[a]Not surveyed in 1985.

unit ranked second for these species in the total percentage wintering on the east coast. The unit ranked first (62%) in numbers of ring-necked ducks (Table 3).

The current species composition in this unit (Tables 2, 3) contrasts strongly with the proportions reported by Saunders and Saunders (1981), as blue-winged teal increased from 20% to 54%, whereas scaup decreased from 43% to 24%. American coot populations have averaged 148,444 since 1970 which is 25% of the east coast total (Tables 3, 8).

The Yucatan lagoons may be an important staging area during migration of blue-winged teal and other species because the lagoons are the first good waterfowl habitat encountered in Mexico. Local hunters interviewed from 1986-88 reported the best blue-winged teal hunting occurred in March. Thus, because of duck numbers within the unit, habitat quality, and geographical position, we rank this area fourth in importance to waterfowl on the east coast (Table 5).

This unit also winters the only popula-tion of Caribbean flamingos (*Phoeni-copterus ruber ruber*) in Mexico. The specific breeding location varies annually, but is within the Rio Lagartos Estuary of Yucatan; the primary wintering site is the Laguna de Celestun. The Laguna de Celestun was designated a national park in 1979, which makes this area the only officially protected wetland (59,130 ha) on the east coast of Mexico. Hunting is prohibited within the refuge.

There has been some encroachment and industrial development into these wetlands in the Progreso area, but from Celestun to Sisal the wetland systems are nearly pristine. In the late 1970s and early 1980s, development around Progreso has modified salinity patterns, which resulted in destruction of about 20,000 ha of mangrove swamp. Loss of mangroves appears to be spreading from Progreso toward Sisal; thus, a comprehensive study of the hydrology of these wetlands is an important research priority.

A significant feature within this unit is the Ducks Unlimited de Mexico, A.C.

(DUMAC) wildlife investigation center, which was constructed in Celestun in 1986. The purpose of the center is to provide a base for students and scientists to study surrounding wetland systems as well as other fish and wildlife. Several studies were initiated in 1986 and should begin to provide a needed base of research information on the estuary and nearby areas.

Rio Grande Delta

Saunders and Saunders (1981) described this system as a 2,000 km^2 area extending from the mouth of the Rio Grande south to Laguna Madre, of which about 360 km^2 are intermittently or permanently flooded basins of varying salinity. This unit then extends westward approximately 56 km inland from the Gulf of Mexico. Waterfowl use of the delta probably was most extensive before 1930, when annual flooding inundated the marshes and lagoons of the delta. Since then, floodwaters have been reduced by construction of several major upriver reservoirs (Falcon, El Azucar, El Culebron), flood control levees, and water diversion projects for irrigated cropland along both sides of the border in the Rio Grande Valley.

These changes mean that flooding of wetlands in the delta depends more on local rainfall than upriver waterflow. Even with frequent flooding, however, there are few freshwater lagoons in this unit. The largest and most important area is Laguna de San Juan, which is usually about 800 ha and located 25 km east of Matamoros. Principal waterfowl food plants in the lagoon are widgeongrass, muskgrass, and dwarf spikerush (Saunders and Saunders 1981). Permanent freshwater areas are more numerous near the Rio Grande than the delta proper, and usually are the result of old river oxbows and former river channels.

Hundreds of other small basins dot this unit, but most hold water only in wet years. Common emergent vegetation includes saltwort (*Batis maritima*), spike-rushes, saltgrass (*Distichlis spicata*), sea oxeye (*Borrichia frutescens*), tomatillo (*Lycium carolinianum*), and glasswort (*Salicornia* spp.); submergents include widgeongrass and muskgrass (Saunders and Saunders 1981).

Even under pristine conditions, the natural hydroperiod and upriver flooding rendered the Rio Grande Delta highly variable relative to use by wintering waterfowl. For example, in wet years of the 1930s and 1940s, this unit sometimes held 500,000 wintering ducks and 50,000 geese; whereas in dry years, only 50,000 ducks and 8,500 geese were recorded (Saunders and Saunders 1981). Overall, however, the pattern of human activities related to water use has "reduced the district from one of the finest waterfowl wintering grounds in North America to one of minor rank and highly variable carrying capacity" (Saunders and Saunders 1981:10). Nevertheless, duck use of this unit rises dramatically when the area remains wet for 2-3 years and aquatic foods can develop. Since 1970, duck numbers have averaged 121,115 (Table 9).

This unit primarily winters dabbling ducks, which have averaged 93% of all ducks since 1970 (Table 9). During this period, northern pintails have averaged 25%, followed by northern shoveler (19%), American wigeon (17%), and green-winged teal (16%) (Table 2). Overall, the Rio Grande Delta has wintered 11% of all ducks surveyed along the east coast of Mexico from 1970-88 (Table 5).

The Rio Grande Delta winters more geese than any other unit along the east coast of Mexico (Table 3). The total goose population since 1970 has averaged 24,145, with 44% being white-fronted geese, 44% being snow geese, and 12% being Canada geese (Table 9). Goose populations have increased markedly since early surveys, partially because of better coverage but also because, since

Table 9. Numbers of waterfowl in the Rio Grande Delta, Tamaulipas, Mexico, January 1970-88.

Species	1970	1975	1977[a]	1978[a]	1979[a]	1980[b]	1981[b]	1982[b]	1985	1988
Dabbling ducks										
Whistling ducks	0	700	3,180	8,230	10,425	12,910	0	3,000	0	0
Mallard	30	90	840	5	85	45	680	10	90	0
Mottled ducks	1,090	1,590	1,450	2,830	2,040	1,575	5,980	540	995	240
Gadwall	11,310	4,840	12,380	8,230	17,875	20,790	13,595	9,050	17,155	6,240
American wigeon	20,245	19,895	24,190	27,500	19,865	38,515	24,645	14,080	15,060	2,940
Green-winged teal	15,950	7,975	82,975	3,830	25,575	19,715	11,085	4,580	23,040	900
Blue-winged teal	1,980	1,625	5,995	1,440	155	430	4,870	90	2,150	80
Northern shoveler	22,400	7,710	54,415	10,130	23,665	21,025	47,920	16,990	11,940	7,740
Northern pintail	7,785	14,640	62,605	34,500	46,835	40,205	27,585	38,560	27,520	5,720
Subtotal	80,785	58,995	247,530	96,695	146,520	154,810	136,360	87,700	97,950	23,860
Diving ducks										
Redhead	30	0	85	690	5	840	120	0	100	0
Canvasback	90	575	40	1,210	0	2,850	100	4,440	440	120
Scaup	105	25	170	5,330	215	425	0	3,690	3,490	40
Ring-necked duck	195	800	0	1,020	80	150	60	40	320	120
Common goldeneye	0	0	0	0	0	0	645	0	0	0
Bufflehead	275	95	90	150	25	165	545	310	45	120
Ruddy duck	2,745	835	645	7,830	345	6,705	300	15,220	6,605	860
Mergansers	100	50	5,295	600	200	405	635	340	0	120
Subtotal	3,540	2,380	6,325	16,830	870	11,540	2,405	24,040	11,000	1,380
Total ducks	84,325	61,375	253,855	113,525	147,390	166,350	138,765	111,740	108,950	25,240
Geese										
Canada	1,560	6,900	1,530	3,900	2,885	1,830	4,705	3,710	1,230	600
White-fronted	11,875	28,455	7,150	7,800	30,480	7,920	2,485	1,040	6,855	1,200
Snow	1,125	29,650	115	23,860	16,070	5,610	5,130	11,010	5,690	9,075
Total geese	14,560	65,005	8,795	35,560	49,435	15,360	12,320	15,760	13,775	10,875
American coot	88,715	60,520	179,610	20,120	33,550	159,750	39,960	17,710	61,005	9,440

[a]Does not include Don Martin Reservoir.

[b]Does not include Don Martin and Falcon reservoirs.

1950, large areas of brush country in Tamaulipas have been converted to grain sorghum. Sorghum attracted populations of wintering geese, but also may have "short-stopped" some white-fronted geese formerly wintering in the Interior Highlands (Saunders and Saunders 1981). Currently (1970-88), goose populations have averaged 17% of all waterfowl surveyed in the unit, whereas the average prior to 1964 was about 9% (Saunders and Saunders 1981). The unit also contains the most mottled ducks and mallards on the east coast (Table 3).

Major waterfowl-management programs focusing on the Rio Grande Delta appear difficult at this time as agriculture continues to expand in the region. This unit has been affected by continual agricultural development south of Matamoros toward the northwest edge of Laguna Madre. The accompanying wetland drainage in the delta proper, coupled with irrigation systems upriver, will further degrade habitat conditions within this unit and should be monitored closely. Also, the Culebron and Ensenada reservoirs west of Matamoros were drained for agricultural purposes during the 1980s.

The overall decline in habitat quality is evidenced by the 1988 survey where numbers of ducks tallied were 79% below the 1970-88 average. However, the expanding sorghum industry appears to be providing alternate foraging opportunities, and during years of high precipitation the delta itself can attract substantial numbers of ducks and geese. Continued midwinter inventory seems the only viable management activity at present. Based on the percentage of ducks using this unit, and given the existing and future potential habitat conditions, we rank this area fifth in importance to waterfowl wintering on the east coast (Table 5).

Tamesi River and Panuco River Delta (Tampico Lagoons)

The Tamesi and Panuco rivers drain an

extensive area that spans parts of Tamaulipas, San Luis Potosi, and Veracruz. This unit contains about 4,035 km² of potential waterfowl habitat, of which >540 km² exists as lagoons and marshes during years of favorable water conditions (Saunders and Saunders 1981). Hydrologically, the habitat conditions within the unit depend more on the extent of rain in the upper portions of the watershed rather than local rainfall in the river deltas. The frequency and extent of flooding, however, were greater before development of upriver impoundments and diversions for agricultural irrigation.

Saunders and Saunders (1981) described this area as very diverse relative to the abundance and availability of waterfowl foods that included dwarf spikerush, widgeongrass, smartweed, banana water-lily (*Nymphaea mexicana*), and others. Scott and Carbonell (1986) noted that this area contained "extensive marshes" of bulrush and cattail, and lakes and ponds characterized by floating beds of water hyacinth and floating heart (*Nymphoides* sp.). Because of differences in watershed size, flooding frequency, and siltation, the 2 river deltas vary annually relative to quality of waterfowl habitat.

Historically, oil extraction activities seriously have impacted the waterfowl habitat within this unit. Prior to development of pipeline systems (pre-1920), diked reservoirs were built to hold extracted oil and these areas often attracted and killed large numbers of waterfowl. Indeed, Saunders and Saunders (1981) documented an instance where a series of such reservoirs killed several hundred thousand ducks. One particular mishap killed so many birds that the oil was deemed unusable because of the volume of accumulated feathers and carcasses. This method of storing oil has been stopped, but other forms of oil and industrial pollution have been noted in the area during recent surveys. Oil pollution is particularly acute in the vicinity of Ebano

and in the Guzman Marsh (Laguna de Tamoa). This environmental degradation has rendered the Tampico lagoons much reduced in their capacity as a quality wintering habitat.

Evidence of the habitat deterioration in this unit is suggested by comparing the midwinter surveys of Saunders and Saunders (1981) with survey results since 1970. For example, this unit formerly wintered an average of 247,000 ducks or 23% of the east coast total; however, the average from 1961-65 was only 89,000 ducks (Saunders and Saunders 1981). The 1970-88 average was 54,163, which is only 5% of the ducks surveyed on the east coast (Table 5). Since 1970, the number of ducks has exceeded 60,000 only twice (1979, 1980); and for the 1982, 1985, and 1988 surveys, the total count was ≤30,000 (Table 10). However, the unit has wintered >100,000 ducks as recently as 1980-81.

The Tampico lagoons primarily winter whistling ducks (17%) and dabbling ducks (63%; Table 2). The most common species are black-bellied whistling ducks and fulvous whistling ducks, followed nearly equally (10-14%) by lesser scaup, northern pintail, green-winged teal, blue-winged teal, and gadwall (Table 2). These proportions contrast somewhat with Saunders and Saunders (1981), particularly the increase in whistling ducks (2-17%) and the decrease in pintails (27-13%). This unit also is important as a breeding area for an estimated 20,000 pairs of wading birds (Scott and Carbonell 1986).

We rate the Tampico lagoons sixth in importance for wintering waterfowl on the east coast of Mexico because of habitat deterioration and low numbers of waterfowl. Three theories advanced for the decline in waterfowl use of the area are (1) the general reduction in continental waterfowl populations, especially northern pintails; (2) the concurrent improvement of habitat conditions northward at Laguna Madre; and/or (3) the

Table 10. Numbers of waterfowl in the Tamesi River and Panuco River Deltas (Tampico lagoons), Tamaulipas-Veracruz, Mexico, January 1970-88.

Species	1970	1975	1977	1978	1979	1980	1981	1982	1985	1988
Dabbling ducks										
Whistling ducks	14,919	6,600	900	11,900	6,600	100,000	10,000	8,000	6,000	1,000
Mallard	0	0	0	0	0	0	0	0	0	0
Mottled ducks	10	50	130	240	55	140	585	175	50	90
Gadwall	7,173	9,800	5,530	9,140	5,315	7,780	1,800	3,165	2,025	2,715
American wigeon	4,034	3,520	4,180	6,375	4,570	8,920	1,065	3,540	4,290	1,455
Green-winged teal	2,613	910	1,970	4,075	1,200	24,240	31,530	210	960	5,985
Blue-winged teal	2,611	2,220	4,290	7,565	5,595	7,860	18,975	1,800	8,500	4,545
Northern shoveler	2,171	2,590	1,570	9,055	1,620	7,900	3,135	1,335	670	3,630
Northern pintail	3,936	3,100	470	1,085	1,360	37,480	18,120	4,305	1,020	1,680
Subtotal	35,861	28,740	18,490	49,485	26,265	115,200	93,330	18,835	22,965	23,100
Diving ducks										
Redhead	45	0	10	0	0	20	165	0	0	30
Canvasback	424	190	2,030	490	560	2,100	660	45	110	210
Scaup	2,462	1,270	2,280	4,495	2,230	4,820	47,070	2,280	2,500	7,650
Ring-necked duck	477	860	140	1,020	635	380	135	45	110	900
Common goldeneye	0	0	0	0	0	0	0	0	0	0
Bufflehead	760	0	0	20	0	0	0	0	0	10
Ruddy duck	4,995	770	260	470	590	4,880	2,100	0	2,530	3,105
Mergansers	0	0	0	20	0	0	0	0	0	0
Subtotal	9,163	3,090	4,720	6,515	4,015	12,200	50,130	2,370	5,250	11,905
Total ducks	45,024	31,830	23,210	56,000	30,280	127,400	143,460	21,205	28,215	35,005
Geese										
Canada	0	0	0	300	0	1,700	0	0	0	0
White-fronted	1,364	240	480	300	355	7,990	0	110	350	290
Snow	0	0	0	0	0	0	0	0	0	0
Total geese	1,364	240	480	600	355	9,690	0	110	350	290
American coot	48,513	69,970	90,060	69,190	109,280	94,400	179,445	63,900	74,740	48,495

reduction in habitat quality because of oil and industrial pollution and reduced water flow resulting from upriver water diversion for agricultural purposes. Surveys since 1970 indicate that pollution is probably the most serious problem in this area and that such activity must be reduced for the unit to improve as wintering waterfowl habitat (Table 5).

Tamiahua Lagoon

The Tamiahua Lagoon is a 1,050 km² coastal laguna that begins near Tampico Alto and extends southward about 100 km to its only opening to the Gulf of Mexico. The lagoon is shallow (usually <2.5 m) and normally brackish, although the water occasionally is nearly fresh if inflow is sufficient. The bottom is sandy, with the few marsh habitats located near the southern end. Tamiahua Lagoon lacks a large influx of freshwater and siltation because no large rivers or streams flow into the lagoon. This variable hydroperiod makes the laguna unpredictable relative to food plant development, which can be extensive when freshwater influx is sufficient (Saunders and Saunders 1981). This unit also includes some narrow bands of pastureland, but nearly all waterfowl use occurs in the lagoon proper except during extremely wet years.

Oil pollution has impacted this area more seriously than any other along the east coast of Mexico. Major damage occurred during the Dos Bocas well blowout in 1909, which spilled an estimated 100,000 barrels/day and eventually covered the entire lagoon with oil; an eyewitness reported "hundreds of thousands and probably millions of dead ducks" (Saunders and Saunders 1981; 21). However, the lagoon did recover from the 1909 spill, because 300,000 ducks and 1,700,000 American coots occurred on the lagoon in 1939 (Saunders and Saunders 1981). Other events that have caused severe habitat damage include blowouts, pipeline breaks, the pumping of oil sludge into the laguna, and the recent serious spills in 1981 and 1982.

Table 11. Numbers of waterfowl in the Tamiahua Lagoon and coastal area south to Veracruz, Mexico, January 1970-88.

Species	1970	1975	1977	1978	1979	1980	1981	1982	1985	1988
Dabbling ducks										
Whistling ducks	0	110	0	0	400	165	780	0	500	0
Mallard	0	0	0	0	0	0	0	0	0	0
Mottled ducks	10	0	0	5	10	0	0	0	35	60
Gadwall	1,185	1,990	2,620	1,035	8,055	3,700	3,800	4,070	1,010	1,020
American wigeon	1,525	4,350	10,520	4,395	15,235	11,580	5,950	10,470	2,390	5,240
Green-winged teal	440	450	100	45	2,640	2,380	4,140	1,970	120	1,600
Blue-winged teal	2,015	2,160	4,750	985	9,290	6,980	13,200	13,360	3,025	10,280
Northern shoveler	1,045	1,010	1,340	885	1,050	5,100	1,120	5,120	550	1,380
Northern pintail	2,770	2,660	6,700	2,960	30,720	6,080	7,250	3,560	860	1,560
Subtotal	8,990	12,730	26,030	10,310	67,400	35,985	36,240	38,550	8,490	21,140
Diving ducks										
Redhead	6,640	550	130	1,070	6,790	2,140	2,140	17,370	5,775	4,680
Canvasback	1,625	490	1,120	3,505	1,630	4,920	1,540	170	380	0
Scaup	5,230	2,120	15,300	74,390	3,030	3,600	23,530	14,120	12,520	1,540
Ring-necked duck	280	20	0	210	160	140	0	0	0	0
Common goldeneye	0	0	0	0	0	0	0	0	0	0
Bufflehead	110	0	0	0	0	0	100	0	0	0
Ruddy duck	415	460	4,040	530	2,000	300	1,510	100	120	20
Mergansers	10	0	0	0	0	0	0	0	0	0
Subtotal	14,310	3,640	20,590	79,705	13,610	11,100	28,850	31,760	18,795	6,240
Total ducks	23,300	16,370	46,620	90,015	81,010	47,085	65,090	70,310	27,285	27,380
Geese										
Canada	0	0	0	0	0	0	0	0	0	0
White-fronted	40	480	555	900	820	1,025	390	490	1,920	495
Snow	750	270	350	1,815	1,410	3,000	2,760	1,720	1,745	2,500
Total geese	790	750	905	2,715	2,230	4,025	3,150	2,210	3,665	2,995
American coot	10,935	135,520	121,890	175,885	215,800	30,780	12,270	16,530	15,130	3,040

Duck numbers in this unit are divided nearly equally between dabblers (54%) and divers (46%) (Tables 2, 11). In the late 1930s, the laguna wintered as many as 50,000 canvasbacks, which apparently were attracted to the area when populations of clams (*Macoma* sp.) were high. The lagoon wintered 18% of the canvasbacks on the east coast from 1970-88 (Table 3).

The great annual variability in habitat quality within the lagoon, coupled with impacts of oil pollution and resultant low numbers of wintering waterfowl, render this unit lowest in importance along the east coast in providing habitat for wintering waterfowl. Indeed, from 1970-88, Tamiahua Lagoon has wintered an average of 49,447 ducks (4% of the east coast total), which was the lowest percentage among all survey units (Table 5). A detailed ground survey would be necessary to determine the extent of pollution-induced degradation in the lagoon, but available evidence suggests that this area may not recover in the foreseeable future.

CONCLUSIONS AND RECOMMENDATIONS

The wetland complexes along the east coast of Mexico represent some of the last areas of basically undisturbed wintering habitat for North American waterfowl. However, the potential exists for considerable alteration and destruction of these wetlands through agricultural development, sedimentation, water diversion projects, and industrial and urban encroachment, as well as petrochemical and other forms of pollution. Significant habitat damage already has occurred (e.g., Tamiahua Lagoon and Tampico lagoons), but most of the 7 survey units are relatively pristine. We emphasize, however, that techniques for wetland conservation and management that are successful in the U.S. and Canada may not work in Mexico. In the face of an ever-expanding human population and the associated staggering need for economic development, it is unrealistic to assume that wetland conservation in Mexico will become a priority where it competes with agricultural expansion, urban development, and petrochemical activities. Nevertheless, where it can be demonstrated that quality wetland habitats are linked closely to the human condition (e.g., Tabasco), it is realistic to assume that significant programs of wetland conservation can be achieved in Mexico. Certainly the Ria de Celestun Reserve, where flamingos, ducks, and other wildlife co-exist with the fishermen, is an outstanding example of the potential conservation programs that can be achieved. We further emphasize, however, that the grassroots movement for wildlife conservation in Mexico must originate within the country. The need for outside assistance is great, but only the Mexican people themselves will ultimately see this goal to fruition.

Because of the size and undisturbed condition of most wetlands, management should be extensive and focus on surveys, preservation, and conservation. An important goal would be interaction with appropriate conservation agencies with national or international interests (i.e., World Bank, Agency for International Development) that finance or otherwise support agricultural or water development projects in Mexico. Certainly, the proposed dam projects in several of these systems pose potential catastrophic impacts on the associated wetlands. Accordingly, agencies involved should be encouraged and aided in assessing environmental impacts of such projects.

The future importance of the wetlands along the east coast of Mexico, relative to wintering waterfowl, is speculative. Since 1970, duck populations have averaged about 1.1 million, whereas geese averaged about 39,000. However, the importance of these wetlands likely will increase, particularly if wetland habitat loss continues to accelerate along the Gulf Coast of the United States. Accordingly, action is necessary now to work cooperatively and to seek innovative ways to protect these valuable wetland habitats.

Research Needs

All units are in need of a detailed ground inventory that should include the major elements of flora and fauna, documentation of the associated hydroperiod, and mapping of existing wetlands. Floral and faunal surveys may be especially important because presence of unique elements, rather than large numbers of waterfowl, may lead to conservation of significant areas of habitat (e.g., the flamingo reserve at Celestun). More habitat studies over the entire wintering period are essential if the role of Neotropical wetlands, relative to the welfare of Nearctic waterfowl, is to be understood. Essentially, most knowledge of wintering waterfowl in Mexico stems from the midwinter aerial surveys and short ground inspections. Initial research efforts should include patterns of habitat use, feeding ecology, and time budget studies. These studies then could guide habitat manipulations within the units. A harvest survey also would be beneficial because the hunter kill in Mexico has only been estimated. The composition of the harvest may be especially important where it involves species whose populations are currently low (e.g., redheads and northern pintails).

SUMMARY

Wintering waterfowl and associated wetland habitats along the east coast of Mexico are important yet studied poorly in relation to other wetland complexes in North America. The U.S. Fish and Wildlife Service has been conducting midwinter aerial surveys on the east coast since 1948. There are 7 survey units for which we summarize the results of the midwinter surveys from 1970-88 and detail recent changes in wetland habitats. Each unit was ranked in importance to wintering waterfowl based on (1) the percentage of all ducks surveyed along the east coast that occurred in each unit, and (2) habitat quality within each unit.

Rankings of units in descending order of importance were (1) Lower Laguna Madre, (2) Tabasco lagoons, (3) Alvarado lagoons, (4) Yucatan lagoons, (5) Rio Grande Delta, (6) Tampico lagoons, and (7) Tamiahua Lagoon.

Total duck numbers surveyed along the east coast have averaged 1.1 million from 1970-88; geese have averaged 39,000. For some duck species in North America currently experiencing sharp population declines, the Lower Laguna Madre is an especially important habitat because it winters 97% of the redheads and 61% of the northern pintails that occur on the east coast of Mexico during winter.

Research needs within the survey units should focus on basic patterns of habitat use, floral and faunal surveys, feeding ecology, time-activity budgets, and harvest surveys. Management on a large scale most probably will be extensive in nature and must seek compatible ways to conserve wetlands in concert with current and future land use practices. The importance of these wetlands to waterfowl wintering on the east coast of Mexico likely will increase in the 21st century.

LITERATURE CITED

Arellano, M., and P. Rojas. 1956. Aves acuaticas migratorias en Mexico. Inst. Mex. de Recursos Naturales Renovables. Mexico, D.F. 270 pp.

Cornelius, S. F. 1977. Food resource utilization by wintering redheads on Lower Laguna Madre. J. Wildl. Manage. 41:374-385.

Fassett, N.C. 1957. A manual of aquatic plants. Univ. Wisconsin Press, Madison. 405 pp.

Goldman, E. A. 1951. Biological investigations in Mexico. Smithsonian Inst. Misc. Coll. 115. 476 pp.

Hotchkiss, N. 1972. Common marsh plants of the United States and Canada. Dover Publ., Inc., New York.

Kramer, G. W. 1976. Winter ecology of black brant at San Quintin Bay, Baja California, Mexico. M.S. Thesis, Humbolt State Univ., Arcata, Calif. 79 pp.

——, and N. H. Euliss. 1986. Winter foods of black-bellied whistling ducks in northwestern Mexico. J. Wildl. Manage. 50:413-416.

Leopold, A. S. 1959. Wildlife of Mexico, the game birds and mammals. Univ. California Press, Berkeley. 568 pp.

Mora, M. A., D. W. Anderson, and M. E. Mount. 1987. Seasonal variation of body condition and organochlorines in wild ducks from California and Mexico. J. Wildl. Manage. 51:132-141.

Saunders, G. B., and D. C. Saunders. 1981. Waterfowl and their wintering grounds in Mexico, 1937-64. U.S. Fish and Wildl. Serv., Resour. Publ. 138. 151 pp.

Scott, D. A., and M. Carbonell (Compilers). 1986. A directory of neotropical wetlands. IUCN and IWRB, Slimbridge, England. 684 pp.

Scott, J. N., Jr. 1983. The biology of the resident ducks of the Marismas Nacionales, Mexico and adjacent areas, and recommendations for their management. Final rep. U.S. Fish and Wildl. Serv., Denver, Colo. 25 pp.

Smith, R. H., and G. H. Jensen. 1970. Black brant on the mainland coast of Mexico. Trans. North Am. Wildl. and Nat. Resour. Conf. 35:227-241.

Sprunt, A., and C. E. Knoder. 1980. Populations of wading birds and other colonial nesting species on the Gulf and Caribbean coasts of Mexico. Pages 3-16 in P. P. Schaeffer and S. M. Ehlers, eds. The birds of Mexico. Their ecology and conservation. Proc. Natl. Audubon Soc. Symp., New York, N.Y.

PACIFIC FLYWAY

Contour furrows constructed to promote establishment of emergent vegetation at Bear River Migratory Bird Refuge, Utah (photo by J. A. Kadlec).

NORTHWEST RIVERINE AND PACIFIC COAST

I. JOSEPH BALL, U.S. Fish and Wildlife Service, Montana Cooperative Wildlife Research Unit, University of Montana, Missoula, MT 59812
RICHARD D. BAUER, U.S. Fish and Wildlife Service, 500 N.E. Multnomah Street, Suite 1692, Portland, OR 97232
KEES VERMEER, Canadian Wildlife Service, P.O. Box 340, Delta, British Columbia, Canada V4K 3Y3
MICHAEL J. RABENBERG, U.S. Fish and Wildlife Service, Long Lake National Wildlife Refuge, Moffit, ND 58560

The Northwest Riverine and Pacific Coast Region is diverse in climate, topography, and agricultural practices. Aquatic habitats important to waterfowl are dominated by rivers, lakes, irrigation reservoirs, estuaries, and marine environments (Table 1). Production of plant and animal foods for waterfowl tends to be low in many of the freshwater habitats because of depth, current velocity, coarse substrates, or the dramatic fluctuations in water levels that usually accompany irrigation and the production of hydroelectric power. Our objectives are to describe how populations of migrating and wintering waterfowl relate to these environmental variables and to examine the associated habitat management opportunities. We divided the region into subareas (Fig. 1) based on political boundaries, primarily because winter waterfowl survey data were available in that format. In many cases the political boundaries also coincided reasonably well with ecological differences.

Information on waterfowl numbers and distribution within the region were summarized from 1980-1987 Pacific Flyway Midwinter Waterfowl Surveys. Plant nomenclature follows Hitchcock and Cronquist (1973).

Waterfowl habitats in southern Idaho consist primarily of the Snake River and associated impoundments, bordered by agricultural lands in most areas. In northern Idaho, bays of large lakes such as Pend Oreille, Coeur d'Alene, and Priest provide scattered areas of waterfowl habitat among a largely mountainous and forested landscape; agricultural lands are scattered and relatively rare. The Pacific Flyway portion of Montana east of the continental divide includes the Missouri River, its tributaries, several remnant glacial lakes (Benton and Freezeout lakes), and vast expanses of grain fields. West of the divide, important winter waterfowl habitat is provided by several bays of Flathead Lake and by the Flathead, Bitterroot, and Clark Fork rivers. Most of the area is mountainous and forested. Most of the important winter waterfowl habitats of eastern Washington and eastern Oregon are associated with the Columbia and Snake rivers and their related impoundments and irrigation projects. Western Oregon, western Washington, and coastal British Columbia provide winter waterfowl habitat in river valleys, estuaries, straits, and fjords. We arbitrarily established Prince Rupert as the northern limit of the region; several million waterfowl winter to the north and west, but difficult survey conditions have hampered the gathering of winter inventory data.

Midwinter surveys of waterfowl populations in the United States (U.S.) portion of the region between 1980 and 1987 averaged 1.8 million birds or about 30% of U.S. Pacific Flyway totals (Table 2). Overall, the region supported >10% of Pacific Flyway midwinter populations of 15 species or species groups as follows: brant (92%), trumpeter swans (91%), redheads (87%), goldeneyes (85%), mallards (67%), Canada geese (62%), scoters (60%), buffleheads (59%), mergansers (54%), scaups (37%), ring-necked ducks (33%), American wigeon (22%), canvasbacks

429

Table 1. Winter weather[a] and major waterfowl habitats within the Northwest Riverine and Pacific Coast Region.

Area	Weather station	$\bar{x}$ J temp (C)	$\bar{x}$ J days <0C[b]	$\bar{x}$ annual $\bar{x}$ precip (cm)	Major waterfowl habitats
Southeast Idaho	American Falls	−3.8	13	26.4	Rivers, irrigation reservoirs
Southwest Idaho	Caldwell	−1.0	8	27.7	Rivers, irrigation reservoirs
Northern Idaho	Coeur d'Alene	−2.1	11	65.5	Large lakes, rivers
Western Montana					
East of Divide	Fairfield	−6.8	15	31.8	Remnant glacial lakes, rivers
West of Divide	Kalispell	−5.4	16	39.1	Large lakes, rivers, irrigation reservoirs
Eastern of Oregon	Hermiston	0.0	8	22.6	Large rivers, irrigation reservoirs
Western Oregon	Corvallis	+3.9	2	108.2	Winter-flooded pastures, large rivers, estuarine and marine areas
Eastern Washington	Moses Lake	−3.1	13	19.6	Large rivers, irrigation reservoirs, seep lakes
Western Washington	Bellingham	+2.6	4	89.7	Winter-flooded pastures, large rivers, estuarine and marine areas
Southwest British Columbia	Vancouver	+2.5	3	111.2	Estuarine and marine areas
Westcentral British Columbia	Prince Rupert	−3.7	6	250.2	Estuarine and marine areas

[a]U.S. weather data from Ruffner (1985). Canadian data from Canadian Climate Center, Winnipeg, Manitoba. All means are for 1951-1980.
[b]Daily maximum temperature ≤0C.

Fig. 1. The Northwest Riverine and Pacific Coast Region. 1 = western Oregon, 2, = eastern Oregon, 3 = southwestern Idaho, 4 = southeastern Idaho, 5 = western Montana, 6 = northern Idaho, 7 = eastern Washington, 8 = western Washington, and 9 = coastal British Columbia.

(18%), tundra swans (12%), and green-winged teal (11%).

KEY SPECIES AND HABITATS
Dabbling Ducks (Anatini)

About 1.1 million mallards winter in the region, making up roughly 80% of all wintering dabbling ducks and 60% of all wintering waterfowl present. Eastern Washington, eastern Oregon, and southwestern Idaho account for >80% of the regional total. The most important water areas are the Columbia and Snake rivers, which are impounded along most of their lengths. Irrigated croplands, especially corn, provide the staple winter food resource in the major concentration areas. American wigeon rank second in abundance ($\bar{x}$ = 126,000). About half of these birds occur in western Washington where they are generally associated with pasture lands, portions of which flood during winter rains; similar habitats in western

Table 2. Summary of winter population surveys and distribution of waterfowl within the Northwest Riverine and Pacific Coast Region during 1980-1987. Data are from Pacific Flyway Midwinter Waterfowl Surveys, and exclude Mexico, Canada, and Alaska.

	SE Idaho	SW Idaho	N Idaho	W Mont	E Oregon	W Oregon	E Wash	W Wash	Total	% of Pacific Flyway Total
	Mean annual midwinter count by area									
Mallard (*Anas platyrhynchos*)	39,800	163,666	1,310	40,076	261,967	46,652	466,868	57,776	1,078,115	67
Gadwall (*A. strepera*)	161	86	154	29	128	699	2,174	1,129	4,560	9
American wigeon (*A. americana*)	2,421	2,804	1,079	562	6,053	31,170	22,829	59,143	126,061	22
Green-winged teal (*A. crecca*)	59	610	1	187	1,389	11,994	6,148	7,832	28,250	11
Blue-winged and cinnamon teals (*A. discors* and *A. cyanoptera*)	1	0	0	0	0	t	2	101	104	3
Northern shoveler (*A. clypeata*)	0	62	0	0	30	1,364	656	1,490	3,602	1
Northern pintail (*A. acuta*)	1,024	1,344	137	145	14,652	42,486	14,571	30,605	104,964	6
Wood duck (*Aix sponsa*)	0	56	0	1	4	74	51	30	216	t
Total dabblers	43,466	168,658	2,681	41,000	284,223	134,438	513,298	158,106	1,345,872	28
Redhead (*Aythya americana*)	37	318	10,709	2,982	163	252	5,480	92	20,033	87
Canvasback (*A. valisineria*)	12	132	503	463	243	2,466	3,433	3,326	10,578	18
Greater and lesser scaups (*A. marila* and *A. affinis*)	52	1,398	2,935	338	1,361	7,124	7,420	29,350	49,978	37
Ring-necked duck (*A. collaris*)	0	650	148	208	258	995	1,136	558	3,962	33
Common and Barrow's goldeneyes (*Bucephala clangula* and *B. islandica*)	4,585	4,166	306	2,309	639	193	1,528	16,143	29,869	85
Bufflehead (*B. albeola*)	63	83	84	106	268	2,466	670	19,445	23,185	59
Common, red-breasted, and hooded mergansers (*Mergus merganser, M. serrator,* and *Lophodytes cucullatus*)	690	733	1,699	958	640	995	2,016	8,372	16,103	54
Black, surf, and white-winged scoters (*Melanitta nigra, M. perspicillata,* and *M. fusca*)	0	0	0	0	0	1,796	0	52,334	54,130	60
Ruddy duck (*Oxyura jamaicensis*)	3	173	2	0	139	1,869	241	4,731	7,158	6
Unidentified ducks	735	677	226	0	571	5,156	132	4,438	11,935	34
Total ducks	49,643	176,997	19,293	48,364	288,505	157,759	535,355	297,276	1,573,192	30
American coot (*Fulica americana*)	289	4,081	6,237	3,848	1,996	13,764	17,678	9,223	57,116	20
Canada goose (*Branta canadensis*)	18,553	10,910	2,192	3,554	23,688	61,281	49,559	14,983	184,720	62
Brant (*B. bernicula*)	0	0	0	0	0	1,004	0	9,063	10,067	92
Snow goose (*Chen caerulescens*)	3	1	0	t	8	1,407	t	25,520	26,939	6
Greater white-fronted goose (*Anser albifrons*)	0	0	0	0	6	6	0	25	37	t
Tundra swan (*Cygnus columbianus*)	26	31	121	33	56	3,313	84	4,503	8,167	12
Trumpeter swan (*C. buccinator*)	118	0	0	199	t	1	0	947	963	91
Total Waterfowl	69,032	192,020	27,843	55,998	314,259	238,535	602,678	360,836	1,861,201	30

Oregon support 31,000 wintering wigeon. About 29,000 wigeon winter in eastern Washington and eastern Oregon, associated with the agricultural fields and wetland habitats of the Columbia Basin Irrigation Project. Green-winged teal ($\bar{x}$ = 28,000) winter mainly in western Washington and western Oregon. Northern pintail populations average about 105,000, with western Washington and western Oregon accounting for 70% of the total, although this percentage comprises only 6% of the Pacific Flyway total.

The Fraser River Delta of British Columbia is not surveyed during the U.S. midwinter waterfowl surveys, but it winters 25,000-30,000 ducks, about 40% mallards and 25% wigeon (Vermeer and Levings 1977).

Diving Ducks (Aythyini and Mergini)

A few localized areas within the region support a greater proportion of Pacific Flyway redheads than any other duck species. Northern Idaho, particularly bays of Lake Pend Oreille and associated river mouths, averaged 10,700 wintering redheads during the 1980s, with 18,200 present in January of 1987. Thus, nearly half of the redheads wintering in the Pacific Flyway occur in northern Idaho, and the number appears to be increasing. The middle Columbia River of eastern

Washington represents another area especially important to redheads, canvasbacks,
lesser scaup and ring-necked ducks. A
wide segment of the Columbia River near
Bridgeport Bar in Washington is the
major concentration area. About 3,000
redheads also use bays of Flathead Lake
in western Montana.

Buffleheads and common and Barrow's
goldeneyes concentrate mostly in western
Washington, particularly on the numerous bays and inlets of Puget Sound. Open
water along the Snake River in southern
Idaho attracts about 9,000 goldeneyes, or
30% of the regional total.

About 90,000 scoters were counted
annually during midwinter counts in the
U.S. portion of the Pacific Flyway, with
over half occurring in western Washington. However, Vermeer (1981) estimated
700,000 scoters along the British Columbia coast in March and 200,000 in
midwinter; about 85% of these birds were
surf scoters. Obviously, only a small
proportion of these populations are
accounted for during U.S. midwinter
surveys. A similar situation exists for
eiders (Somateria spp., Polysticta stelleri),
harlequin ducks (Histrionicus histrionicus), and oldsquaws (Clangula hyemalis).

Canada Geese

Canada geese of several races and
populations winter throughout the
region, comprising 62% of the flyway
total. Slightly over 18,000 western Canada
geese (B. c. moffitti) of the Rocky Mountain Population (Krohn and Bizeau 1980)
winter in southeastern Idaho, with most
depending on American Falls Reservoir
and its surrounding mudflats and grainfields. Southwestern Idaho winters about
11,000 western Canada geese, mostly birds
from northern segments of the Pacific
population. Relatively few Canada geese
(2,200-3,500) winter in northern Idaho
and western Montana, although during
most years almost all of the relatively
sedentary local breeding populations are
present.

Eastern Washington and eastern
Oregon, particularly the Columbia Basin
portion, winter about 73,000 Canada
geese. Racial composition has not been
quantified; Taverner's (B. c. taverneri) and
lessers (B. c. parvipes) predominate, but
western Canada geese also occur.

Western Washington and Oregon winter about 76,000 Canada geese, with the
Willamette Valley and lower Columbia
River as key areas. Numbers are increasing, and the racial affinities are changing
(Simpson and Jarvis 1979, Cornely et al.
1985, Jarvis and Cornely 1988). Nearly all
dusky Canada geese (B. c. occidentalis)
winter in the area. In recent years the
flock has numbered 10,000-12,000 birds.
Taverner's Canada geese make up most of
the remainder, but lesser, western, Vancouver (B. c. fulva), and an increasing
number (10,000 in 1987) of cackling
Canada geese (B. c. minima) also are
present.

Other Waterfowl

Snow geese winter on the Skagit Delta
in Washington (33,000 in 1987) and the
Fraser River Delta in British Columbia
(6,000 in 1987). Together, these 2 areas
winter about 25% of the snow goose
breeding population from Wrangel
Island. A major southward shift in the
wintering grounds of black brant has
occurred since the 1950s (Bellrose 1976,
Bartonek 1986), with U.S. portions of the
flyway commonly wintering 50,000-80,000
brant prior to 1958, but fewer than 10,000
during most years from 1972 onward.
Over 90% of Pacific Flyway brant populations ($\bar{x}$ = 120,000) now winter in Mexico,
although U.S. counts of 14,000 in 1986
and 16,000 in 1987 provide tentative hints
that a reversal of the long-term trend may
have begun. Concentration areas include
Boundary Bay in British Columbia;
Skagit, Padilla, and Willapa bays in
Washington; and Coos and Tillamook
bays in Oregon. California typically wintered 20,000-60,000 brant prior to 1958,
but <1,000 annually since 1969.

Trumpeter swans of 2 populations winter in the region. The Rocky Mountain Population (1,600 in 1987) winters mainly in the Tristate region near Yellowstone Park, and is treated in the chapter on Great Basin and Intermountain Marshes (Kadlec and Smith 1989). Nearly 10,000 trumpeters of the Pacific Coast Population breed in Alaska and winter at scattered locations in coastal British Columbia, Puget Sound, and Washington and Oregon estuaries. Tundra swans wintering in the region average about 8,000, concentrated mostly in western Washington and Oregon along the lower Columbia River.

AQUATIC HABITAT CONDITIONS

Absolute amounts of aquatic habitats important to waterfowl are relatively low within the region, although only crude comparisons can be made. Of the U.S. wetland areas tallied by Shaw and Fredine (1956), the region contained only about 3% of all wetland area ranked as having high or moderate values to waterfowl. Both inland and coastal areas of the region tend to have relatively steep topography, so that zones of rooted vegetation along upland-aquatic borders tend to be narrow. Many of the rivers flow across high gradients, a situation that minimizes development of vegetated riverine wetland habitat. Furthermore, virtually all of the major rivers in the region have been impounded along most of their length, further reducing the amount and value of wetland habitats.

Aquatic plant communities vary markedly across the region, so much so that broad-scale regional descriptions seem pointless. However, examples of aquatic plant species/water depth relationships at various locations within the region are presented in Table 3. Common wetland plant species in the region are listed in Environmental Laboratory (1987).

HABITAT CHANGE

The most dramatic change in the region, with respect to wintering waterfowl habitat and populations, relates to the spectacular response of mallards to development of impoundments and irrigated agriculture in the Columbia Basin along the Snake River and the Columbia River in southcentral Washington and northcentral Oregon. This area wintered <200,000 mallards in the early 1950s but midwinter populations peaked at just over 1 million in the early 1960s, dropped below 350,000 during the late 1970s, and peaked again at nearly 1 million in 1982 and 1983 (Fig. 2).

Because increased mallard numbers in the northern Columbia Basin during the 1950s and the southern Columbia Basin in the 1980s paralleled increases in field corn acreage, much emphasis has been placed on corn's role in determining midwinter mallard populations (Lauckhart 1961, Galbreath 1962, Anonymous 1986). However, the relationship between corn acreage in the Columbia Basin and number of mallards wintering there seems neither simple nor necessarily one of direct cause and effect. Between 1952 and 1980, mallard numbers in the northern Columbia Basin showed no correlation with corn acreage. Indeed, when mallard populations peaked in 1964, corn acreage was 32% below the long-term average (Rabenberg 1982).

Periods of increasing mallard numbers in the Columbia Basin have generally corresponded with years of severe drought in the Prairie Pothole Region. Buller (1975) suggested that displacement of mallards by drought may be related to increases in wintering mallard populations in the basin. Hansen and McKnight (1964) and Pospahala et al. (1974) provided evidence that drought-displaced ducks migrated from the prairies to northern Alberta, Alaska, and the Northwest Territories. Breeding ground

Table 3. Examples of common aquatic plant distributions in the region. Species are roughly arranged from xeric to hydric conditions within areas.

Oregon and Washington Tidal Marshes (Seliskar and Gallagher 1983)
1. gutul (*Gnadiln.i ni. sp.*)
2. silverweed (*Potentilla pacifica*)
3. redtop bentgrass (*Agrostis alba*)
4. tufted hairgrass (*Deschampsia cespitosa*)
5. Lyngby's sedge (*Carex lyngbyei*)

6. saltgrass (*Distichlis spicata*)
7. pickleweed (*Salicornia virginica*)
8. jaumea (*Jaumea carnosa*)
9. arrow-grass (*Triglochin maritima*)
10. eelgrass (*Zostera marina*)

Oregon and Washington—Columbia River Sloughs (Tabor 1976)
1. cheat grass (*Bromus tectorum*)
2. filago (*Filago arvensis*)
3. swainsona (*Swainsona salsula*)
4. prickly lettuce (*Lactuca serriola*)
5. western centaury (*Centaurium exaltatum*)
6. common cattail (*Typha latifolia*)

7. sprangletop (*Leptochloa fascicularis*)
8. flatsedge (*Cyperus erythrorohizos*)
9. water pimpernel (*Veronica anagallis-aquatica*)
10. softstem bulrush (*Scirpus validus*)

Central Washington—Sand Dune Potholes (Harris 1954)
1. willow (*Salix* spp.)
2. saltgrass (*Distichlis stricta*)
3. Nevada rush (*Juncus nevadensis*)
4. Baltic rush (*J. balticus*)
5. Torry's rush (*J. torreyi*)
6. Douglas sedge (*Carex douglasii*)
7. woolly sedge (*C. lanuginosa*)
8. American bulrush (*Scirpus americana*)

9. common spike-rush (*Eleocharis palustris*)
10. common cattail
11. hardstem bulrush (*Scirpus acutus*)
12. fennel-leaved pondweed (*Potamogeton pectinatus*)
13. coontail (*Ceratophyllum demersum*)
14. muskgrass (*Chara vulgaris*)
15. bladderwort (*Utricularia vulgaris*)
16. ditch-grass (*Ruppia maritima*)

Western Montana—Lake and River (Mackey et al. 1987)
1. willow (*Salix longifolia, S. bebbiana*)
2. mugwort (*Artemisia lindleyana*)
3. hemp dogbane (*Apocynum cannabinum*)
4. field mint (*Mentha arvensis*)
5. tufted hairgrass
6. compressed bluegrass (*Poa compressa*)
7. fowl bluegrass (*P. palustris*)
8. redtop bentgrass
9. tickseed (*Coreopsis atkinsoniana*)
10. curly dock (*Rumex crispus*)
11. slender spike-rush (*Eleocharis acicularis*)
12. common spike-rush
13. jointed rush (*Juncus articulatus*)
14. Nevada rush
15. Baltic rush
16. blister sedge (*Carex vesicaria*)

17. Nebraska rush (*C. nebraskensis*)
18. reed canarygrass (*Phalaris arundinacea*)
19. water horsetail (*Equisetum fluviatile*)
20. arumleaf arrowroot (*Sagittaria cuneata*)
21. beaked sedge (*Carex rostrata*)
22. marestail (*Hippuris vulgaris*)
23. flowering-rush (*Butomus umbellatus*)
24. common cattail
25. hardstem bulrush
26. muskgrass
27. fennel-leaved pondweed
28. Richardson pondweed (*Potamogeton richardsonii*)
29. small pondweed (*P. pusillus*)
30. grass-leaved pondweed (*P. gramineus*)
31. waterweed (*Elodea canadensis, E. nuttallii*)
32. spiked water-milfoil (*Myriophyllum spicatum*)

reference areas in Alaska, British Columbia, the Mackenzie District, and northern Alberta (Anderson and Henny 1972) supply 50-60% of the mallards harvested in Washington and Oregon, and probably an even greater proportion of the birds present there during early January when the midwinter surveys are flown (Munro and Kimball 1982).

Rabenberg (1982) examined relationships between midwinter mallard populations in the northern Columbia Basin and numerous variables. Estimated mallard breeding populations in southwest Alberta were negatively correlated with those in Alaska and the Yukon. Wintering mallard populations in the northern Columbia Basin were negatively correlated with breeding populations the previous spring in southwest Alberta. In addition, midwinter mallard numbers in the basin were positively associated with warmer temperatures in November and negatively associated with snow cover in

Fig. 2. Results of midwinter surveys of mallards in Washington and Oregon. Counts in the Columbia Basin portion of the 2 states are represented by the solid line and those in the remainders of the 2 states by a dashed line. Solid triangles along the horizontal axis designate years when the estimated continental breeding population was <7.5 million.

January. We conclude that, although corn is responsible for attracting large numbers of wintering mallards to the basin and is necessary to sustain these populations, other factors are important also. The size of the mallard population remaining in the basin during early January seems to depend partly upon distribution of birds on breeding grounds the previous spring and partly upon the influences of early-winter weather patterns on mallard arrival dates, rates of southward migration, chronology of the corn harvest, and snow or ice cover.

Development of the irrigation projects influenced not only field-feeding opportunities for mallards and geese, but also the presence, characteristics, and habitat values of water bodies. Impoundment and subsequent manipulation of water levels on the Snake and Columbia rivers provided mixed benefits and negative impacts. Historically, strong currents in the rivers would have made flocking on open water a difficult strategy for avoiding hunting in the unimpounded system, but rafting on open water or reliance upon refuge areas are dominant strategies today. Rivers widened by impoundment provide increased security, although waterfowl may be exposed to rough water during windy weather.

Waterfowl often loaf on islands or roost on calm water in the lee of islands. Both strategies presumably provide thermal advantage. Impoundments usually destroy most of the islands on rivers. New islands created by impoundments often are eroded by waves (Ball et al. 1981).

In Grant County, Washington, approximately 400 ha of potholes (Harris 1954) were lost to development of the Columbia Basin Irrigation Project. However, project development also created Potholes Reservoir (11,000 ha), 2 unchannelized irrigation flowages (2,000 ha), and numerous seep wetlands and lakes (Fig. 3). Most of these developments were on nonirrigable lands (generally, steep topography or poor soils) and have been relatively permanent. In contrast, wetlands on irrigable lands are generally shallower and richer with more gradual contours. Wetlands of this type peaked at about 4,000 ha in the mid-1960s, but over 160 km of drains were constructed annually during the late 1960s and early 1970s. Nearly complete elimination of this class of wetlands was projected to occur by 1990 (U.S. Bureau Reclamation 1976).

A 570-ha cooling reservoir for a coal-fired electrical generating plant began operation during 1982 near Umatilla, Oregon adjacent to the Columbia River. Warm water, several thousand hectares of nearby cornfields, and almost complete protection from hunting or other disturbance proved overwhelmingly attractive to mallards, and up to 700,000 birds were surveyed there at times. This development accompanied, and may have caused, a shift in mallards from more northerly portions of the Columbia Basin. That shift did not reverse itself when the powerplant was closed during 1986 and 1987 because of a power surplus (Anonymous 1986).

In the relatively few situations on the impounded Columbia River, where water depths are shallow enough to support submerged macrophytes but deep enough

Fig. 3. Wintering mallards at Columbia NWR near Othello, Washington. Steep terrain, narrow emergent zones, and coarse bottom substrates minimize the development of aquatic food resources for waterfowl in many portions of the region.

to avoid regular desiccation, stands of pondweeds and spiked water-milfoil have developed. These attract migrating and wintering redheads, lesser scaup, canvasbacks, and ring-necked ducks. Certainly, this sort of habitat would have been extremely rare in the unimpounded system, so its creation is considered a net gain. However, the benefit is vulnerable to loss from changes in river water-level regimes for hydroelectric production. In fact, a drawdown was conducted in 1984 on the middle Columbia (Wells Pool, Bridgeport Bar) specifically to reduce submerged aquatics that were breaking loose from the bottom and clogging intake screens on the dam. An additional and probably greater threat is that power-peaking flows or other hydroelectric strategies could alter water level on a more permanent basis, making survival of the submerged aquatics unlikely.

Development of irrigated agriculture in southwestern Idaho resulted in increased mallard wintering populations parallel in many respects to the situation in the Columbia Basin of Washington and Oregon. However, declines in wintering mallard numbers have been severe and generally unreversed in southwestern Idaho. This trend may have resulted partly from declines in mallard populations and from reduced availability of corn. However, urban sprawl westward from Boise, Idaho toward the Oregon border has consumed many of the fields that formerly provided feeding sites in the Deer Flat National Wildlife Refuge (NWR) area.

Wetland habitat changes in western Washington and western Oregon have been clearly detrimental to wintering and migrating waterfowl. In 11 Puget Sound estuaries, loss of wetland area was 69% by the mid-1970s (Bortleson et al. 1980). This loss resulted from: (1) flood control, (2) pasture diking, (3) filling for urban or industrial development, (4) dredging, (5) shell fishing, and (6) development of marinas. The introduction of 3 species of cordgrass (*Spartina alterniflora, S. patens,* and *S. townsendii*) involves serious and potentially widespread threats to waterfowl habitat. Cordgrass invades open intertidal areas and competes with native plants of value to waterfowl (*Carex* spp., *Salicornia* spp., *Triglochin* spp., and *Scirpus* spp.).

Most of the wetlands in the Willamette Valley have been lost to agricultural drainage and urban sprawl. This loss continues today and probably has had more negative impacts on ducks than on geese. Principal crops in the valley are ryegrass and fescues for seed production; these provide abundant forage for geese.

In western Montana, significant changes in habitat values for migrating and wintering waterfowl have accompanied manipulation of water levels for hydroelectric power production, irrigation, flood control, and recreational purposes. Losses of about 1,200 ha of wet meadow and marsh habitat around Flathead Lake in Montana were caused by the construction and operation of Kerr Dam at the lake's outlet (Casey and Wood 1987, Mackey et al. 1987). The overall magnitude of annual fluctuations in water levels changed relatively little with creation of the dam in 1938, but the duration of high water was changed from an early-summer peak to peak levels all summer followed by a late-fall drawdown that is maintained through March. Under the current regime, native emergent vegetation survives primarily as dense stands of common cattail, and these stands appear to be associated with perched water tables near the high water mark. During winter and spring, the cattail stands are separated from open water by mudflats 200-1,000 m wide. Stands of flowering-rush have become established in parts of the seasonally dewatered zone (Casey and Wood 1987). This exotic species may be better adapted to the unnatural water regime than are any of the native emergents. Shallow portions of the lake support submergents such as muskgrass, pondweeds, waterweed, bladderwort, and water-milfoil. However, availability of these plants as midwinter food resources appears to be limited by the drawdown regime.

Pablo and Ninepipe reservoirs (also in the Flathead Valley) provide important migration and wintering habitat until freeze-up, usually in late November. Both

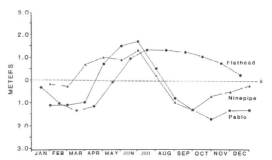

Fig. 4. Average monthly water levels in Flathead Lake, Ninepipe Reservoir and Pablo Reservoir, 1976-1985. The average variability of water levels within months over the 10 year period was 1.0 m on Flathead Lake, 1.9 m on Ninepipe Reservoir, and 3.9 m on Pablo Reservoir.

reservoirs are managed as waterfowl refuges, but water levels are manipulated primarily for irrigation purposes. The total range in amplitude of water-level fluctuations is similar among Pablo, Ninepipe, and Flathead Lake (Fig. 4), but differences in seasonal regimes result in widely differing responses by aquatic vegetation. Water levels in Pablo vary the most on an annual basis, rise later in the spring than at Ninepipe, drop lower in the fall, and vary the most between years. This regime inhibits development of nearly all aquatic vegetation, although sparse stands of goosefoot (*Chenopodium* spp.) and other annuals develop on dewatered areas. A more moderate drawdown regime at Ninepipe results in reasonably good development of emergents, submergents, and moist-soil species such as smartweed (*Polygonum coccineum*) and slender spike-rush. During years when extensive mudflats surround Ninepipe because of drawdown, geese and wigeon use them consistently. Craighead and Stockstad (1956) noted that geese seldom left the reservoirs after the first few days of hunting season during low-water years, and believed that vulnerability of the birds to hunting was relatively high when the reservoirs were full.

Little information is available about habitat conditions or change in northern Idaho. Agricultural development is less

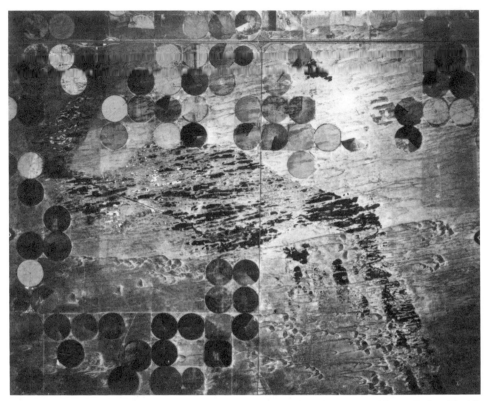

Fig. 5. Aerial view of Winchester Wasteway in the Columbia Basin near Moses Lake, Washington. Irrigation water routed through shifting sand dunes created the wasteway (center) in the 1950s, and center-pivot irrigation circles soon provided field-feeding opportunities for waterfowl. Purple loosestrife invaded the wasteway in the 1970s and 1980s.

than in most other areas of the region, and numbers of wintering mallards and geese reflect this characteristic. Lake Pend Oreille undergoes a 3-m winter drawdown for power production, but the effects on waterfowl habitat are poorly understood. Wild rice (*Zizania aquatica*) was introduced to the Coeur d'Alene system in the 1930s, is well established, and is used heavily by ducks.

Purple loosestrife (*Lythrum salicaria*) has become established in at least 15 locations around the region (Thompson et al. 1987). Infestations in the Columbia Basin of Washington escaped from plantings established by a beekeeper adjacent to flowages of the Columbia Basin Irrigation Project (Fig. 5). In approximately 20 years, loosestrife expanded to dominate 30-60% of the emergent vegetation zone on >2,000 ha of wetlands in 3 drainage

systems of the project. A more recent introduction occurred in the Flathead Valley of western Montana, where loosestrife currently affects <100 ha. This infestation is also associated with an irrigation project, and hence it has the potential for rapid spread throughout the system.

HABITAT IMPORTANCE RELATIVE TO WATERFOWL REQUIREMENTS

Food Resources

Agricultural crops are the dominant food resource for Canada geese and dabbling ducks, particularly mallards and wigeon, throughout the region. Furthermore, we conclude that the vast majority of agricultural crops consumed by ducks and geese are produced on private land

Table 4. Characteristics of mallard field feeding locations in the Columbia Basin, Nov-Feb 1978-79 and 1979-80[a].

Crop type	Field condition	N	% observations	% land-use[b]	X^2
Corn	Stubble	187	83.6	9.1	1962.20[c]
	Disked stubble	13	5.8	5.2	0.16
	Chopped (silage)	5	2.2	1.9	0.13
	Unharvested	2	0.9	0.2	5.30[d]
	Plowed	2	0.9	0.1	14.08[c]
	Unidentified	3	1.3		
Corn subtotal		212	94.6		
Small grain	Stubble	9	4.0	2.4	2.44
	Green winter wheat	1	0.5		
Small grain subtotal		10	4.5		
Feed lot		1	0.4		
Unidentified		1	0.4		
Other		0	0.0		
Total		224	100.0	100.0	

[a]From Rabenberg (1982).
[b]Availability based on weighted late November land-use transect results (1979).
[c]$P < 0.001$.
[d]$P < 0.05$.

instead of on lands dedicated to waterfowl management. Thus, the production and availability of most of the food consumed by perhaps 75% of all waterfowl wintering in the region depend upon cropping patterns and other forces beyond the control of waterfowl managers.

Although mallards feed in wheat and barley-stubble fields throughout the region, corn proves most attractive to mallards wherever it is grown. In the northern Columbia Basin of Washington, cornfields comprised <17% of total land use but supported 95% of 224 mallard field feeding sites used between late November and early February (Table 4). Most (187/212) of the feeding sites were in corn-stubble (i.e., fields picked by combines) rather than in those chopped for silage. Mallards fed mostly in corn-stubble fields ungrazed by livestock, except when crusted snow conditions forced them to rely on cattle to provide access to the corn. Average distance between roosting areas and field feeding sites was 8.3 km (SE = 0.24).

Studies of mallard food habits in the Columbia Basin of Washington also emphasized the dominance of corn during fall and early winter (Fig. 6). Food habits were most diverse in mid-October when aquatic and moist-soil seeds (primarily bulrush, smartweed, and barnyard-grass [*Echinochloa crusgalli*]) comprised up to 25% (aggregate volume) of the diet. Invertebrates and aquatic vegetation (primarily pondweed tubers and duckweeds [*Lemna* spp.]) each made up less than 1% of the diet but were found in 70% of the males and 46% of the females sampled. Wheat and barley also were important early, but mallards switched almost exclusively to corn soon after the harvest began. A nearly pure corn diet was established by mid-November and was maintained through late January with the exception of a small but consistent increase in consumption of small grain after mid-December. Despite the high use of waste grain, over 40 genera of plants and 10 families of invertebrates were represented in the diet. A more detailed food habits analysis can be found in Rabenberg (1982).

Although corn is the dietary staple for wintering Columbia Basin mallards, the small proportions of other foods consumed must be important to the birds' overall nutritional condition. Corn is deficient in protein (particularly the

MALES

FEMALES

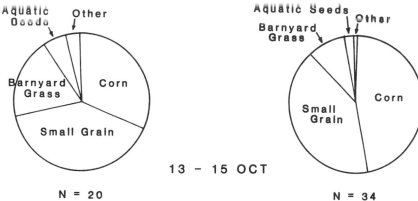

13 – 15 OCT

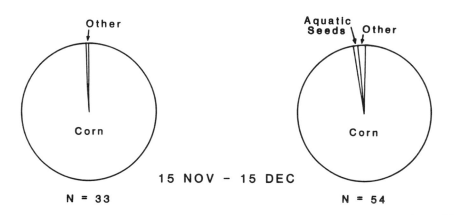

15 NOV – 15 DEC

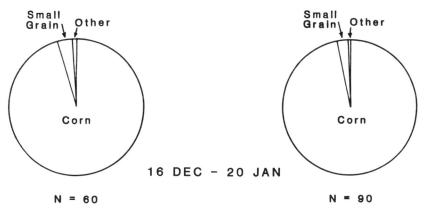

16 DEC – 20 JAN

Fig. 6. Fall and winter food habits (% volume) of mallards in the Columbia Basin of Washington (1979-80) as determined from esophageal contents of hunter-killed birds (Rabenberg 1982).

essential amino acids lysine and trypto phan) and calcium (Rommel and Vedder 1915, Morrison 1936, National Research Council 1977). The value of corn as an easily attainable, high-energy food to fuel continued migration or to underwrite the metabolic costs of wintering in a cold environment are obvious. However, selecting a nearly exclusive corn diet can eventually become a nutritional drain rather than a benefit (Labisky and Anderson 1973). Consequently, the small amounts of animal matter and aquatic and terrestrial seeds and vegetation may be critical during winter and are certain to become so as spring approaches (Krapu 1981).

Observations of Canada geese in several parts of the region suggest that agricultural crops provide most of their winter food supply. We also have observed a seasonal progression in use of different crops. Wheat or barley stubble appear to receive the most use early, followed by corn stubble during midwinter (particularly during periods of snow and cold). Finally, green winter wheat seems to become more important during milder periods of late winter and early spring. Similar patterns of a seasonal shift from grains early to sprouted vegetation later were noted by Leslie and Chabreck (1984) in white-fronted geese and by Hobaugh (1982) in snow geese.

Winter rains in the Columbia Basin of Washington promote the green-up of cheat grass, and these areas are commonly grazed by western Canada geese even among stands of big sagebrush (*Artemisia tridentata*). Also, Canada geese of all races seem strongly attracted to cheat grass or grass-sage areas where recent range fires have promoted green-up and reduced visual obstruction.

Closely cropped pastures and grass fields used for seed production provide much of the food resource for Canada geese and American wigeon in western Oregon and western Washington. In the Willamette Valley of western Oregon, fields of fescues and annual and perennial ryegrasses are burned during late summer and early fall to reduce litter buildup and inhibit fungal development. This practice presumably increases the value of the fields to geese by reducing vegetation height and improving forage quality.

Mallards, pintails, and green-winged teal on the Fraser River Delta fed primarily on the seeds of Lyngby's sedge and bulrush (*Scirpus validus, S. americanus*) (Burgess 1970, Vermeer and Levings 1977). Wigeon and gadwall on the Fraser used these foods plus algae (e.g., *Ulva* spp., *Enteromorpha* spp., *Lola lubrica*). Algae comprised 93% of food eaten by greater scaup in winter, with bivalves (5%) and gastropods (3%) making up the remainder.

Habitat selection and distribution of seaducks within the region appears closely linked to food resources of the various species (Table 5). Water depths and substrates influence distribution of prey items, which subsequently influences the distribution of the duck species. For example, common goldeneyes and buffleheads inhabit shallow, inshore waters with a variety of bottom substrates, where they consume mostly gastropods and crustaceans. Conversely, Barrow's goldeneyes and surf scoters often concentrate in deep, rocky fjords where mussels are a staple food resource (Vermeer 1982).

Water Areas and Sanctuaries

The need for sanctuaries and opportunities for providing them vary widely across the region. The preponderance of rivers as roosting areas is perhaps the most important distinction between this region and most others. Hunters in many parts of the region do not hunt in open water away from shoreline vegetation. The paucity of offshore hunting, in conjunction with an abundance of large bodies of open water over much of the region, provides an abundance of "de

Table 5. Percentage wet weight of food items in the esophagi and gizzards of seaducks from fall or winter samples.

Duck species	Bivalves	Gastropods	Chitons	Crustaceans	Echinoderms	Polychaetes	Insects	Fish/eggs	Plants	Unidentified[a]	Source
Bufflehead	3	25		40				7	3	21	Vermeer (1982)
	26	10		30	1	1	4	17	3	7	Erskine (1972)
Barrow's goldeneye	99	t[b]		1						1	Vermeer (1982)
Common goldeneye	7	8		83				t	2		Vermeer (1982)
	16	7		61						16	Vermeer and Levings (1977)[c]
White-winged scoter	60	14		26					t	t	Vermeer and Bourne (1982)
	53	36		9					1	2	Vermeer and Levings (1977)
Black scoter	60	t		4	21				4	11	Vermeer and Levings (1977)[c]
Surf scoter	84			8	4	t			t	t	Vermeer (1981)
	81	3		1		6			1	8	Vermeer and Levings (1977)
Harlequin	t	24	15	19	t			26	9	6	Vermeer (1983)
	t	51	11	21						16	Gaines and Fitzner (1987)[d]
Oldsquaw	59	37		4							Vermeer and Levings (1977)

[a]Mostly digested animal matter.
[b]t = <0.5%.
[c]Includes winter, spring, and summer samples.
[d]Data are % volume.

facto" refuges for species that can adapt to these conditions. Mallards and Canada geese seem to benefit most (or suffer least). Conversely, species such as green-winged teal or northern shovelers that must feed in shallow wetlands may be unable to adapt to these conditions and must either suffer unacceptable hunting pressure or disperse. Perhaps the prime example of a species sensitive to hunting disturbance is the brant. Hunting at key concentration areas, sometimes in conjunction with disturbance by fishermen or boaters, can force brant to leave estuaries to raft on the ocean (Murrell 1962), and this displacement may presage displacement from the area (Kramer et al. 1979).

The effectiveness of de facto refuges consisting of large bodies of open water often depends upon weather conditions, particularly wind. In the southern Columbia Basin mallards commonly adopt feeding and roosting patterns that make them nearly immune to hunting except when high winds force them to forsake expanses of open water or when cold and snowy weather promotes field-feeding during legal shooting hours. Geese adopt similar patterns except that they seem more likely to feed during daylight hours even during mild weather.

Concern over shifting midwinter distributions of mallards to the southern portions of the Columbia Basin resulted in an attempt to redistribute the birds by creating 2,100 ha of sanctuaries in the northern portion, and reducing closures near Umatilla, Oregon (Anonymous 1986). Although the northern closures resulted in some birds being held in northern areas, other factors such as de facto refuges, relatively cold winter temperatures, and increasing availability of corn in the southern areas apparently overwhelmed any major response.

Geese in the Flathead Valley of western Montana congregate on Ninepipe and Pablo NWRs before the hunting season opens and use these areas for roosting until freeze-up in late November. Then the birds move to the nearby Flathead River, which remains open most years. Concern about overharvest on the river, harassment by hunters in jet boats, and the feeling that the geese were being forced to migrate southward led to a hunting closure on geese beginning on the Monday following Thanksgiving. The large concentrations of diving ducks on the lower Pend Oreille River and bay near Sandpoint, Idaho receive some protection from a partial closure on the major concentration area. The closure was initiated to reduce conflicts between hunters and residents of shoreline dwellings. Waters <180 m from shore are closed to hunting, and few hunters attempt to hunt the open water.

Statutory refuges are probably more important to waterfowl in the Willamette Valley and lower Columbia River Valley than elsewhere in the region. Potential de facto refuges are of limited value because hunting activities, swift river currents, boat traffic, and hazing to prevent crop damage limit waterfowl use during most of the winter. An extensive system of federal and state refuges, in conjunction with conservative goose harvests, was designed to aid the dusky Canada goose population (Chapman et al. 1969). However, dusky Canada geese are approximately twice as vulnerable to harvest as Taverner's and lesser Canada geese (Simpson and Jarvis 1979, Cornely et al. 1985, Jarvis and Cornely 1988). Large increases in the numbers of the latter 2 races and cackling Canada geese wintering in the area have greatly complicated attempts to reduce harvest of duskies and cacklers while maintaining or increasing pressure on Taverner's and lesser Canada geese.

Contaminant and Disease Problems

Mortalities from contaminants or diseases have been observed in most major waterfowl concentration areas of the region, but losses to date have been relatively light in comparison to other western regions. Spring losses to avian cholera in the Mud and Market lakes area of southeastern Idaho have occurred every few years (>8,100 birds were lost in 1980). Cholera outbreaks have been rare in the Willamette Valley and lower Columbia River, but about 1,500 ducks died in 1976. Chronic but light losses to botulism occur during most years in the Sauvie Island area, particularly at Smith and Bybee lakes. Outbreaks occur prior to fall rains, and annual losses of up to 650 birds have been documented. Botulism losses of up to 20,000 birds occurred historically at

Benton Lake NWR in western Montana, but annual losses in the last decade have been low (<2,000 birds), apparently as a result of intensive sanitation activities when outbreaks first occur. One component of this program is to lower water levels rapidly in affected units so that dead birds are not overlooked in emergent vegetation.

Direct losses to pesticides have been observed at many locations in the region and typically have killed <200 birds per incident. Examples include rodenticides at orchards and grain elevators, insecticides on golf courses, and avicides intended for starlings (*Sternus vulgaris*) at feedlots. Reduced productivity and heavy mortality of adult western Canada geese occurred near Umatilla, Oregon when the birds consumed wheat seed treated with heptachlor epoxide, an insecticide used to control wireworms (Blus et al. 1979).

Contamination of waterfowl by lead and other residues of mining and smelting operations has been documented in western Montana and northern Idaho (Chupp and Dalke 1964, Benson et al. 1976). Elevated levels of silver, mercury, lead, zinc, and copper occurred in greater scaup and surf scoters near a sewer outfall on the Fraser River Delta in British Columbia (Vermeer and Peakall 1979). Elevated levels of selenium have been detected in sediments and biological samples from Benton Lake NWR and Freezeout Lake in Montana (Knapton et al. 1988). The highest concentrations occurred in association with saline seep areas. Lead poisoning from ingested shotgun pellets was a serious problem in the Sauvie Island area of Oregon, but was alleviated with the mandatory use of steel shot. Most major waterfowl concentration and hunting areas in the region have made the conversion to steel shot, and all are scheduled to do so by 1991.

HABITAT MANAGEMENT

Most waterfowl management areas

within the region suffer from one of two limitations relative to managing aquatic systems. On many areas opportunities for controlling water levels are limited or absent. Secondly, the production of hydroelectric power and the delivery of irrigation water usually take precedence over waterfowl habitat concerns even where control is possible.

In areas with the capability to manipulate water levels, managers most often use water management to influence abundance and distribution of submergent and emergent vegetation. We were unable to document the extent of active, planned management programs with prescribed treatments and defined goals.

Moist-soil management (e.g., Fredrickson and Taylor 1982) is rare in the region, probably because of the previously mentioned constraints in availability of water and facilities for controlling water levels. Also, the waterfowl objectives for most management areas include waterfowl production, and many managers avoid using drawdowns at any time during the breeding season. Finally, we suspect that the practice rarely is used here partly because the tradition to do so is lacking and there is little expertise locally to guide initial efforts.

Although moist-soil plant species are no doubt used by waterfowl at many locations in the region, we learned of only 4 locations where the value seemed to be recognized. In 2 instances, the responsible water regime is an inadvertent byproduct of drawdowns for irrigation purposes. One of these, Ninepipe NWR (Montana), has been described previously in this chapter. The second, at Deer Flat NWR in Idaho, also involves a summer drawdown for irrigation, which results in extensive stands of smartweeds and other moist-soil species. Increasing water levels during the fall flood these stands and ducks are attracted.

At Benton Lake NWR in Montana, a system for delivery of water was completed in 1964, and diking and pumping facilities to improve internal control have been developed since then. Pumping costs can be high and there are concerns over water quality in the irrigation-return flows that provide the major water source. However, the system provides one of the most manageable wetland units in the region. Reduced water levels provide shallow-water habitats for shorebirds and promote invasion of alkalai bulrush (*Scirpus paludosus*) into open-water impoundments. Dewatered zones develop moist-soil plant communities, and species composition appears to be largely a function of drawdown timing. Zones dewatered in spring generally develop relatively monotypic stands of foxtail barley (*Hordeum jubatum*). Areas drained later usually develop mixed stands of goosefoot and kochia (*Kochia* spp.). Virtually all drawdown areas at Benton Lake become attractive to waterfowl when reflooded in late summer or fall, but the goosefoot-kochia stands are used more than foxtail stands. Previously, we mentioned perceived conflicts between spring-summer drawdowns and waterfowl production objectives. Units at Benton Lake probably are in partial or complete drawdown more often than other management areas in the region. However, duck production also is among the highest we have observed in the region or elsewhere (e.g., about 7 ducklings were produced/ha or 11/wetland ha in 1987).

Moist-soil management at Ridgefield NWR in Washington has been practiced only for a few years, but initial responses have been encouraging. Water levels are maintained high through the spring to minimize development of reed canarygrass (*Phalaris arundinacea*), which would otherwise become dominant. Drawdowns are conducted in late May or June. Smartweeds and beggar-ticks (*Bidens* spp.) are produced, and the reflooded stands attract migrating waterfowl.

Production of agricultural crops for use

by migrating and wintering waterfowl is a common practice in the region. The majority of management areas conduct some farming operations, often under sharecropping arrangements. For 25 areas with farming operations, total area of regularly tilled cropland is 3,490 ha. Crops grown include wheat or barley (19 areas/1,896 ha), corn (13/639 ha), alfalfa (8/581 ha), proso millet (1/192 ha), Sudan grass (1/32 ha) and other crops (3/150 ha) including beans, potatoes, and red clover. The last category and alfalfa are most often grown as part of a crop rotation system.

Improved pastures for waterfowl occur on fewer areas than tillage agriculture but account for more total area (8 areas/3,911 ha). Grass species include ryegrasses, fescues, and native grasses. Pastures usually are harvested for seed, then burned, fertilized, or mowed.

Because irrigation is such a dominant activity throughout the region, improved management of water levels in irrigation reservoirs offers potential for improving habitat. Issues of water rights and economics make progress difficult, and the key seems to be in managers being able to envision and help design systems that accomplish waterfowl habitat goals with minimal impacts on irrigation. An example of this type of situation occurred at Pablo NWR in western Montana where shallow arms of Pablo Reservoir provided little waterfowl habitat because they were dry most of the year. The volume of water necessary to flood these areas was of little concern to irrigation interests, but the system could not be managed to provide the levels needed for waterfowl habitat while still providing for irrigation demands. However, agreements were reached to make the needed improvements, and Ducks Unlimited designed and constructed dikes, control structures, and a delivery canal. The system provided 91 ha of habitat in 5 impoundments. Water can be delivered in most years either before or after the irrigation season. We believe that many similar opportunities exist throughout irrigated portions of the region. Recognizing these opportunities and pursuing the essential negotiations should become a priority for managers.

RESEARCH AND MANAGEMENT NEEDS

Improving our knowledge about the ecology of diving ducks in northern Idaho, eastern Washington, and western Montana should be considered a priority. In particular, research should focus on relationships between the species present and the available food resources. Information also is badly needed on the present impacts of fluctuating water levels on food resources and the potential impacts of foreseeable water regimes that may be desired for power production or other uses. Conflicts are virtually certain to arise, and realistic assessments of risks and alternatives will be impossible unless the necessary research is completed (or at least initiated) in advance.

Our general impression is that waterfowl species diversity within the region is largely a function of the diversity and richness of aquatic habitats. The relationship could be considered self-evident. Alternatively, it could be formally evaluated using detailed wetland inventory data and fall-winter waterfowl survey data. The issue is important from a management perspective because one could argue that (except for the coastal areas) the region primarily attracts mallards and Canada geese, so most management activities should focus on the agricultural crops important to these species. The obvious alternative argument is that the region attracts mostly mallards and Canada geese because the habitat needs of other species are not met. Under this interpretation management activities should emphasize development of diverse aquatic habitats.

We suggest that special efforts be made to document responses of vegetation and invertebrates on the management areas within the region where planned manipulation of water levels have been used most intensively. Currently, detailed information on these responses in the region is lacking. Similarly, on those areas where drawdowns occur because of power production or flood-control activities, we suggest that managers evaluate whether altering water regimes within the constraints imposed by other demands may improve conditions for waterfowl. Managers cannot realistically hope to gain complete control over water levels in many systems, but major gains probably could be made with acceptable costs to primary water users. In systems with little current flexibility in water regimes, careful consideration of economic and waterfowl needs may find alternatives based on additional diking or other construction activities. These activities could be funded by public or private waterfowl management interests and would be supported by irrigation or hydroelectric interests if real or perceived conflicts could be minimized.

Altering bottom contours within irrigation reservoirs may allow the development of moist-soil plants with acceptable costs to irrigators, although this approach has not been tested. Depending on normal water regimes, current bottom contours, and soil types, low berms could be constructed to slow the dewatering process in summer irrigation drawdowns. Another approach might be to construct low islands that would emerge to mudflat status at normal summer low-water levels. Identifying and pursuing opportunities to improve irrigation reservoirs for waterfowl is an important priority for the region.

A final management need involves planning and continuing education relative to waterfowl habitat management. Development of water management plans is occurring on many management areas, and this effort could be aided greatly by a regional workshop on wetland habitat management. Suitable topics would include agricultural crop production versus moist-soil management and the resolution of conflicts between habitat management for fall-winter benefits and breeding season benefits.

SUMMARY

The Northwest Riverine and Pacific Coast Region exhibits substantial variation in climate, wetland types, and upland habitat. Large, deep rivers and lakes comprise much of the available wintering habitat, and diversity and richness of aquatic habitats is low with the exception of some coastal wetlands and the most aggressively managed impoundments. Diversity of wintering waterfowl species also is low, likely resulting from habitat conditions dominated by large, deep water areas and adjacent agricultural lands. Although most management areas provide agricultural crops for waterfowl, private agricultural lands provide the vast majority of food consumed by wintering waterfowl in the region.

Habitat change in the region has included both positive and negative aspects. In the Columbia Basin of Washington and Oregon, development of irrigated agriculture and adjacent impoundments provided habitat for large numbers of mallards and Canada geese where few wintered before development. Deep water components of these developments have been relatively permanent, but many of the shallower and richer wetlands were drained soon after they developed. Recurring buildups and declines of mallard wintering populations in the area have been influenced by weather patterns and distribution of breeding birds as well as by habitat conditions in the basin. At a few locations in the basin, impoundment of the Columbia River resulted in development of habitat suitable for diving ducks, although these areas are at continual risk to loss from changing water management regimes for hydroelectric production.

Throughout much of the region, fluctuations in water levels caused by irrigation demands or production of hydroelectric power are dominant influences on wintering waterfowl habitat quality, although the impacts of these fluctuations are poorly understood. In several situations, drawdowns coincidently produce conditions beneficial to waterfowl, and the potential exists for improvements within the constraints of irrigation or power interests.

Although food habits of mallards in the Columbia Basin are strongly dominated by corn as soon as harvest begins, relatively small amounts of diverse natural foods may be extremely important in providing nutrients lacking in corn. In addition, private agricultural lands probably provide adequate opportunities for field-feeding by mallards and geese in many areas. These considerations, in addition to the fact that most waterfowl species do not feed in fields, emphasize the importance of protecting, creating, and managing wetland habitat for waterfowl food production.

The importance of refuges to waterfowl in the region varies substantially geographically and by species. Mallards and Canada geese appear to need few legislated closed areas where large water areas are common and a rafting strategy can be followed under most weather conditions. Conversely, species such as brant and ducks that are ecologically dependent on wetland food resources can derive little benefit from de facto sanctuaries.

The most common intensive management activity for migrating or wintering waterfowl within the region is the production of agricultural crops (25 areas, 3,490 ha) and the provision of burned, mowed, or fertilized grasslands (8 areas, 3,911 ha). Management of aquatic habitats in most parts of the region is

hampered because managers often do not have the legal or physical capability to control water levels. Moist-soil management is rare, occurring at only 2 known locations. Research and management needs include (1) development of a basic understanding of the relationships between diving ducks and their food resources as influenced by water regimes, (2) improved documentation of habitat responses to planned and inadvertent drawdowns, (3) a comprehensive review of opportunities for improving habitat conditions on irrigation reservoirs, and (4) a regional workshop on managing habitat for migrating and wintering waterfowl.

LITERATURE CITED

Anderson, D. R., and C. J. Henny. 1972. Population ecology of the mallard: I. A review of previous studies and the distribution and migration from breeding areas. U.S. Fish and Wildl. Serv. Resour. Publ. 105. 166 pp.

Anonymous. 1986. Columbia Basin waterfowl redistribution plan evaluation of 1983-84, 1984-85, and 1986-87 seasons. Wash. Dep. Wildl., Olympia. 31 pp.

Ball, I. J., E. L. Bowhay, and C. F. Yocom. 1981. Ecology and management of the western Canada goose in Washington. Wash. Dep. Game, Biol. Bull. 17. Olympia. 67 pp.

Bartonek, J. C., compiler. 1986. Pacific Flyway midwinter waterfowl survey. U.S. Fish and Wildl. Serv., Portland, Oreg. 12 pp.

Bellrose, F. C. 1976. Ducks, geese and swans of North America. Second ed. Stackpole Books, Harrisburg, Pa. 543 pp.

Benson, W. W., D. W. Brock, J. Gabica, and M. Loomis. 1976. Swan mortality due to certain heavy metals in the Mission Lake area, Idaho. Bull. Environ. Contam. Toxicol. 15:171-180.

Blus, L. J., C. J. Henny, D. J. Lenhart, and E. Cromartie. 1979. Effects of heptachlor-treated cereal grains on Canada geese, Umatilla, Washington. Pages 105-116 in R. L. Jarvis and J. C. Bartonek, eds. Management and biology of Pacific Flyway geese. Oregon State Univ. Bookstores, Inc., Corvallis.

Bortleson, G. L., M. J. Chrzastowski, and A. K. Helgerson. 1980. Historical changes of shoreline and wetlands at 11 major deltas in the Puget Sound region, Washington. Hydrologic investigations atlas HA-612. U.S. Geol. Surv., Denver, Colo. 11 pp.

Buller, R. J. 1975. Redistribution of waterfowl, influence of water, protection, and feed. Int. Waterfowl Symp. 1:143-154.

Burgess, T. E. 1970. Foods and habitat of four anatids wintering on the Fraser Delta tidal marshes. M.S. Thesis, Univ. British Columbia, Vancouver. 124 pp.

Casey, D., and M. Wood. 1987. Effects of water levels on productivity of Canada geese in the northern Flathead Valley. U.S. Dep. Energy, Bonneville Power Adm., Portland, Ore. 132 pp.

Chapman, J. A., C. J. Henny, and H. M. Wight. 1969. The status, population dynamics, and harvest of the dusky Canada goose. Wildl. Monogr. 18. 48 pp.

Chupp, N. R., and P. D. Dalke. 1964. Waterfowl mortality in the Coeur d'Alene River Valley, Idaho. J. Wildl. Manage. 28:692-702.

Cornely, J. E., B. H. Campbell, and R. L. Jarvis. 1985. Productivity, mortality and population status of dusky Canada geese. Trans. North Am. Wildl. and Nat. Resour. Conf. 50:540-548.

Craighead, J. J., and D. S. Stockstad. 1956. Measuring hunting pressure on Canada geese in the Flathead Valley. Trans. North Am. Wildl. Conf. 21:210-238.

Environmental Laboratory. 1987. Corps of engineers wetlands delineation manual. Technical Rep. Y-87-1, U.S. Army Eng. Waterways Exp. Stn., Vicksburg, Miss. 100 pp. + appendices.

Erskine, A. J. 1972. Buffleheads. Can. Wildl. Serv., Monogr. Ser. 4. Ottawa, Ontario. 240 pp.

Fredrickson, L. H., and T. S. Taylor. 1982. Management of seasonally flooded impoundments for wildlife. U.S. Fish and Wildl. Serv. Resour. Publ. 148. 29 pp.

Gaines, W. L., and R. E. Fitzner. 1987. Winter diet of the Harlequin duck at Sequim Bay, Puget Sound, Washington. Northwest Sci. 61:213-215.

Galbreath, D. S. 1962. Waterfowl population increase in the Columbia Basin. Wash. Game Bull. 14:6-7.

Hansen, H. A., and D. E. McKnight. 1964. Emigration of drought-displaced ducks to the Arctic. Trans. North Am. Wildl. and Nat. Resour. Conf. 29:119-127.

Harris, S. W. 1954. An ecological study of waterfowl of the Potholes Area, Grant County, Washington. Am. Midl. Nat. 52:403-433.

Hitchcock, C. L., and A. Cronquist. 1973. Flora of the Pacific Northwest. Univ. Washington Press, Seattle. 730 pp.

Hobaugh, W. C. 1982. Winter ecology of geese in the rice prairie area of southeast Texas. Ph.D. Dissertation, Texas A&M Univ., College Station. 187 pp.

Jarvis, R. L., and J. E. Cornely. 1988. Recent changes in wintering populations of Canada geese in western Oregon and southwestern Washington. Pages 517-528 in M. W. Weller, ed. Waterfowl in winter. Univ. Minnesota Press, Minneapolis

Kadlec, J. A., and L. M. Smith. 1989. The Great Basin marshes. Pages 451-474 in L. M. Smith, R. L. Pederson, and R. M. Kaminski, eds. Habitat management for migrating and wintering waterfowl in North America. Texas Tech Univ. Press, Lubbock.

Knapton, J. R., W. E. Jones, and J. W. Sutphin. 1988. Reconnaissance investigation of water quality, bottom sediment, and biota associated with irrigation drainage in the Sun River area, west-central Montana, 1986-87. U.S. Geol. Surv., Water Resour. Invest. Rep. 87-4244. 78 pp.

Kramer, G. W., L. R. Rauen, and S. W. Harris. 1979. Populations, hunting mortality and habitat use of black brant at San Quintin Bay, Baja California, Mexico. Pages 242-254 in R. L. Jarvis and J. C. Bartonek, eds. Management and biology of Pacific Flyway geese. Oregon State Univ. Bookstores, Inc., Corvallis.

Krapu, G. L. 1981. The role of nutrient reserves in mallard reproduction. Auk 98:29-38.

Krohn, W. B., and E. G. Bizeau. 1980. The Rocky Mountain population of the western Canada goose: its distribution, habitats, and management. U.S. Fish and Wildl. Serv. Spec. Sci. Rep.—Wildl. 229. 93 pp.

Labisky, R. F., and W. L. Anderson. 1973. Nutritional responses of pheasants to corn, with special reference to high-lysine corn. Ill. Nat. Hist. Surv. Bull. 31:86-112.

Lauckhart, J. B. 1961. Waterfowl population changes. Proc. Annu. Conf. West. Assoc. State Game and Fish Comm. 40:157-160.

Leslie, J. C., and R. H. Chabreck. 1984. Winter habitat preference of white-fronted geese in Louisiana. Trans. North Am. Wildl. and Nat. Resour. Conf. 49:519-526.

Mackey, D. L., S. K. Gregory, W. C. Matthews, Jr., J. J. Claar, and I. J. Ball. 1987. Impacts of water levels on breeding Canada geese and methods for mitigation and management in the southern Flathead Valley, Montana. U.S. Dep. Energy, Bonneville Power Adm., Portland, Ore. 162 pp.

Morrison, F. B. 1936. Feeds and feeding: a handbook for the student and stockman. 20th ed. Morrison Publishing Co., Ithaca, N.Y. 1050 pp.

Munro, R. E., and C. F. Kimball. 1982. Population ecology of the mallard: VII. Distribution and derivation of the harvest. U.S. Fish and Wildl. Serv. Resour. Publ. 147. 127 pp.

Murrell, S. L. 1962. A study of crippling loss, kill and aging techniques of black brant (Branta nigricans) at Humboldt Bay, California. M.S. Thesis, Humboldt State Coll., Arcata. 56 pp.

National Research Council. 1977. Nutrient requirements of poultry. Seventh ed. Natl. Acad. Sci., Washington, D.C. 62 pp.

Pospahala, R. S., D. R. Anderson, and G. J. Henny 1974. Population ecology of the mallard: II. Breeding habitat conditions, size of the breeding populations, and production indices. U.S. Fish and Wildl. Serv. Resour. Publ. 115. 73 pp.

Rabenberg, M. J. 1982. Ecology and population dynamics of mallards wintering in the Columbia Basin. M.S. Thesis, Washington State Univ., Pullman. 135 pp.

Rommel, G. M., and E. B. Vedder. 1915. Beri-beri and cottonseed poisoning in pigs. U.S. Dep. Agric., J. Agric. Res. 5:489-493.

Ruffner, J. A. 1985. Climates of the states. Third ed. Gale Research Co., Detroit, Mich. 1572 pp.

Seliskar, D. M., and J. L. Gallagher. 1983. The ecology of tidal marshes of the Pacific Northwest coast: a community profile. U.S. Fish and Wildl. Serv., Div. of Biol. Serv., Washington, D.C. FWS/OBS-82/32.

Shaw, S. P., and C. G. Fredine. 1956. Wetlands of the United States. U.S. Fish and Wildl. Serv. Circ. 39. 67 pp.

Simpson, S. G., and R. L. Jarvis. 1979. Comparative ecology of several subspecies of Canada geese during winter in western Oregon. Pages 223-241 *in* R. L. Jarvis and J. C. Bartonek, eds. Management and biology of Pacific Flyway geese. Oregon State Univ. Bookstores, Inc., Corvallis.

Tabor, J. E. 1976. Inventory of riparian habitats and associated wildlife along the Columbia River. Vol. II A. Report to U.S. Army Corps of Engineers. Oreg. Coop. Wildl. Res. Unit, Corvallis. 861 pp.

Thompson, D. Q., R. L. Stuckey, and E. B. Thompson, 1987. Spread, impact, and control of purple loosestrife (*Lythrum salicaria*) in North American wetlands. U.S. Fish and Wildl. Serv., Fish Wildl. Res. 2. 55 pp.

U.S. Bureau Reclamation. 1976. Columbia Basin Irrigation Project. Final Environ. Impact Statement. Boise, Idaho. 376 pp.

Vermeer K. 1981. Food and populations of surf scoters in British Columbia. Wildfowl 32:107-116.

———. 1982. Food and distribution of three *Bucephala* species in British Columbia waters. Wildfowl 33:22-30.

———. 1983. Diet of the harlequin duck in the Strait of Georgia, British Columbia. Murrelet 64:54-57.

———, and N. Bourne. 1982. The white-winged scoter diet in British Columbia waters: resource partitioning with other scoters. Pages 30-38 *in* D. N. Nettleship, G. A. Sanger, and P. F. Springer, eds. Marine birds: their feeding ecology and commercial fisheries relationship. Proc. Pacific Seabird Group Symp. Can. Wildl. Serv. Spec. Publ., Ottawa, Ontario.

——— and C. D. Levings. 1977. Populations, biomass and food habits of ducks on the Fraser River Delta intertidal area, British Columbia. Wildfowl 28:49-60.

——— and D. B. Peakall. 1979. Trace metals in seaducks of the Fraser River Delta intertidal area, British Columbia. Mar. Pollut. Bull. 10:189-193.

THE GREAT BASIN MARSHES

JOHN A. KADLEC, Department of Fisheries and Wildlife, Utah State University, Logan, UT 84322-5210
LOREN M. SMITH, Department of Range and Wildlife Management, Texas Tech University, Lubbock, TX 79409

According to Sanderson (1980), there are about 1.2 million ha of waterfowl habitat in the Intermountain Region of the United States (U.S.), and 1.6 million if California valleys are included. Most of Sanderson's discussion, and indeed most of the literature about waterfowl in this region, concern waterfowl production. Yet some of the best marshes and concentration areas in this area host millions of waterfowl during winter and migration. For example, Tule Lake National Wildlife Refuge (NWR) in the Klamath Basin (Fig. 1), California, may attract >5 million waterfowl during migration, and is often considered the single most important waterfowl refuge in the U.S. (Gilmer et al. 1986). The complex of marshes on the east and north sides of Great Salt Lake in Utah also hold >1 million waterfowl in fall (Nelson 1966). In contrast to the perception that the Great Basin is a "desert" of little value to waterfowl, the reality is that the marshes and wetlands are of higher value to waterfowl than are many areas in wetter regions. In fact, the very rarity of marshes in a dry region adds to their value.

The region west of the Rocky Mountain crest to the Sierra and Cascade Mountains is geomorphically diverse. There are 4 major subregions (Fig. 1): (1) Columbia Plain, (2) Snake River Plains, (3) Colorado Plateau, and (4) Basin and Range Region of which the Great Basin is a major part (Graff 1987). Precipitation ranges from >130 cm/year on the western slopes of the Rockies to <15 cm/year in the deserts. Mountain ranges are interspersed with valleys, some of which are broad and flat. Even the valley floors are quite high, especially in the northern part of the region. The floor of the Great Salt Lake desert and salt flats is >1300 m above sea level.

In the high mountains, there are lakes, often of glacial origin, and wet meadows that have value for breeding waterfowl, but are little used for migration (Peterson 1969, Brown 1985). Streams draining these high altitude wetlands often have steep gradients in their upper reaches and have little value for waterfowl, unless dammed by beaver. In general, there is not much important migration habitat and essentially no winter habitat in the upper levels of the mountain ranges.

At lower elevations, the rivers have broader valleys, and may meander considerably in some valleys. Because of the importance of water for irrigation and water power, damming of rivers and streams is widespread. Some of these reservoirs are important for waterfowl; many are not, because of steep banks and large annual fluctuations in water levels.

Natural lakes occur in a few locations at lower elevations, and most are directly or indirectly important to waterfowl. Some are periodically dry because inflowing water has been diverted for irrigation (e.g., Sevier Lake in Utah [Platts and Jensen 1986]).

The Columbia Plain encompasses about 260,000 km^2 in the northern part of the Intermountain Region (Platts and Jensen 1986). It includes much of Idaho, Oregon, and Washington north of the Great Basin. The Snake and Columbia rivers and associated reservoirs and wetlands are prominent. In western Washington is a pothole region (Harris 1954) with 800-1,000 permanent and ephemeral wetlands in Grant County

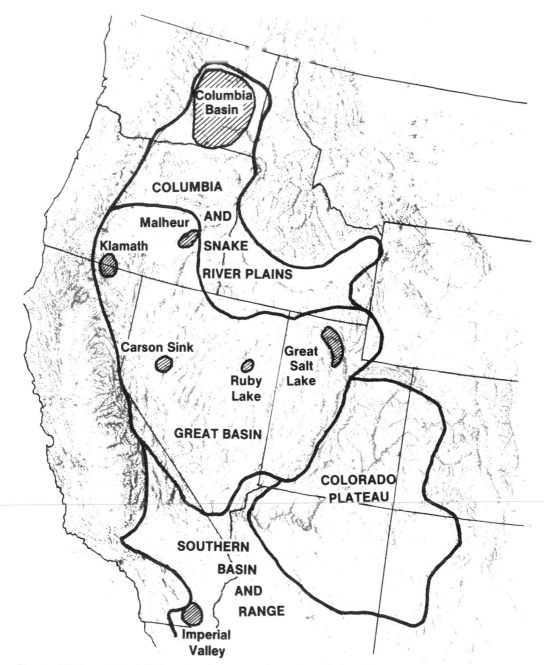

Fig. 1. Western United States, showing approximate boundaries of major geomorphic regions and locations of important areas for waterfowl.

(Harris 1954). Spring-fed wetlands are common; some are warm springs.

The Great Basin part of the Basin and Range Province extends south from the Columbia Plain to the Colorado Basin. It is unique in that all drainage is internal;

there are no outlets to the sea. Topographically, it is marked by many small- to moderate-sized north-south mountain ranges separated by broad level valleys (Platts and Jensen 1986). Valleys are dominated by alluvial flats and playas.

Shrubs such as sagebrush (*Artemisia* spp.), saltbush (*Atriplex nuttallii*), and greasewood (*Sarcobatus vermiculatus*) dominate the upland vegetation. Plant nomenclature follows Cronquist et al. (1977). Major lakes occur on the east (Great Salt Lake, Utah Lake) and west (Pyramid Lake) flanks of the Basin. Most streams and rivers start in mountains, often relying heavily on snowmelt for water supply, and flow into closed basins such as Great Salt Lake.

Wetlands in the Great Basin are generally associated either with the rivers and lakes or with the abundant springs. Important marshes include the Great Salt Lake complex, Utah, Ruby Lake NWR (spring fed) and Carson Sink, Nevada, Malheur NWR (stream-fed, closed basin), Oregon, and the Klamath Basin in Oregon and California (Fig. 1). Many of these areas have been greatly impacted by man's activities, especially drainage for agriculture and diversion of water for irrigation or other uses.

The Colorado Plateau lies in the southeastern part of the Intermountain Region in Utah, Colorado, Arizona, and New Mexico (Fig. 1). High rugged terrain (25% rock outcrop), hot dry summers, and cold winters make this region inhospitable to waterfowl. Most of the wetlands are associated with rivers and streams. Good waterfowl habitat is scarce and often the result of impoundments. Some spring-fed marshes also are present. The southern deserts have little waterfowl habitat, except for a few spring-fed areas and some riverine wetlands along the lower Colorado River (Brown 1985).

The climate of the Intermountain Region varies from cool (<0 C) in the north to hot (>25 C) in the south, and from semiarid to arid. Snowfall on mountains (up to 6 m) is an important source of water. Summers are dry in the north, but in the south, summer thunderstorms are an important component of the total annual precipitation.

The Great Basin and associated sections of the Intermountain Region are too cold in the high and/or northern sections for waterfowl to winter except in association with flowing waters or warm springs. In a few cases where springs or flowing waters contain or are adjacent to food supplies, large numbers of mallards (*Anas playtrhynchos*) and Canada geese (*Branta canadensis*) winter. The entire Rocky Mountain population of trumpeter swans (*Cygnus buccinator*) winters in the so-called Tristate region where Idaho, Montana, and Wyoming meet near Yellowstone National Park. The southern sections of the Intermountain Region are generally too dry and lack habitat attractive to wintering waterfowl. However, a substantial fraction of Pacific Flyway waterfowl pass through the central and northern Great Basin on migration. In general, there are 2 major paths from the breeding grounds to the wintering grounds in the Pacific Flyway—1 coastal and 1 interior (Bellrose 1980). Many prairie-nesting species, for example, migrate southwest across the northern part of the Intermountain Region on their way to California wintering areas.

To complicate fall migration patterns over the Great Basin, some waterfowl migrate southeasterly to the Texas coast and eastern Central America. Thus, areas such as the Great Salt Lake marshes are at the crossroads of several migration patterns used by great numbers of waterfowl. With many birds and few stopover areas, spectacular concentrations often are found on suitable areas (Chattin 1964).

The Intermountain West shares problems of water supply and competition for water from other uses (e.g., municipal, agricultural, and industrial) with western prairies and California valleys. Western water-law appropriates water from stream or river channels or lake basins for out-of-channel use, giving priority to "beneficial" uses such as agricultural irrigation. Rights to volumes of water are bought

Table 1. Estimates of fall and winter populations of waterfowl in the Pacific Flyway and the Great Basin. Numbers in thousands except Fall 1981-83 index.

Species	Fall population[a] in flyway	Migrants through Great Basin	Minimum of winter population (UT, ID, NV, AZ[b])	Flyway[c]	Fall 1981-1983 index for UT, ID, NV[d]
Trumpeter swan[e]	1.6		1.6	1.2	
Tundra swan (*Cygnus columbianus*)	123	35-40	3.8	63.2	
Lesser snow goose (*Chen caerulescens*)	500	160	2.3	412	
Canada goose	100	100	69	300	
American wigeon (*Anas americana*)	700	700	3.8	652	531
Gadwall (*A. strepera*)	900	130	3.7	51	516
American green-winged teal (*A. crecca*)	1,000	500	10.4	280	842
Mallard	2,000	1,500	134	1,551	2,976
Northern pintail (*A. acuta*)	3,000	2,000	13	2,023	872
Cinnamon teal (*A. cyanoptera*)	300	300	0	3.8	78
Northern shoveler (*A. clypeata*)	500	500	10	432	—
Canvasback (*Aythya valisneria*)	100	50	3.5	58	508
Redhead (*Aythya americana*)	100	200	12.5	21	402
Scaup (*Aythya* spp.)	300	50-100	6.4	136	120
Ruddy duck (*Oxyura jamaicensis*)	175	175	2.7	103	

[a]Interpreted from Bellrose (1980).

[b]Average 1986-88, calculated from Pacific Flyway reports.

[c]1978-1988 average, calculated from Bartonek (1988).

[d]Based on indices reported in Canadian Wildlife Service and U.S. Fish and Wildlife Service (1987). Average of peak month (not necessarily the same each year) for October-January 1981-82, 1982-83, 1983-84. Index is average population density on all NWRs in state expanded by area of habitat in state.

[e]Data from Gale et al. 1987 for Rocky Mountain population.

and sold, but even purchase of water rights for wildlife does not guarantee a supply in dry years.

Another problem shared among western marsh managers is natural salinity or alkalinity. In the closed drainages common to the Great Basin, California, and western prairies, water loss from the basins is largely or entirely by evaporation. All salts brought to the basins by surface and subsurface flows collect in the basins, often leading to ionic concentrations equal to or greater than seawater. Consequently, some plants in western marshes are the same as or are closely related to species that occur in tidal salt marshes. Therefore, management in the Great Basin shares some aspects of coastal marsh management. Many of the impounded, managed marshes are nearly fresh, and management techniques in these areas should be similar to methods used in freshwater marshes elsewhere.

HABITAT IMPORTANCE
Waterfowl Use

According to Bellrose's (1980) migration maps, major rivers and marshes in the Great Basin and closely associated areas in the Columbia Plain are vital stopovers for a significant part of Pacific Flyway waterfowl populations (Table 1). For comparison, Table 1 also lists average winter populations for 1986-88 and an index of Oct-Jan (fall migration) populations based on data compiled for the analysis of stabilized hunting regulations (Canadian Wildlife Service and U.S. Fish and Wildlife Service 1987). Data were available for the periods Oct-Jan 1981-82, 1982-83, and 1983-84. The peak indices for each species in each of these 3 periods were averaged to facilitate comparison with Bellrose (1980) and the winter counts. A certain amount of agreement in the numbers is expected because some

Table 2. Peak population indices for October–January periods, 1981–1984, by state and species (from Canadian Wildlife Service and U.S. Fish and Wildlife Service, 1987).

Species	AZ	CA	ID	NV	NM	OR	UT	WA	ID, NV, and UT combined[a]
Mallard	3.3	4,755.2	2,492.4	183.1	210.9	4,391.1	300.5	5,988.1	2,976
Gadwall	2.3	301.7	65.9	365.2	27.6	85.2	333.8	97.5	765
American wigeon	4.0	4,734.6	55.9	289.0	124.7	187.3	219.3	1,614.7	564
Green-winged teal	1.7	2,449.0	52.7	649.4	7.4	141.9	302.5	352.0	1005
Blue-winged or Cinnamon teal	2.3	118.7	4.1	54.4	9.9	9.5	9.1	11.1	78
Northern pintail	3.2	13,294.4	97.7	360.6	80.4	414.6	613.5	936.9	1072
Redhead	1.1	71.6	64.4	329.2	13.1	13.5	62.1	27.4	456
Canvasback	0.1	199.5	34.4	453.0	2.5	21.3	60.6	37.9	548
Lesser scaup	1.9	71.4	68.7	21.3	8.0	30.4	9.8	77.3	100
Ring-necked duck	0.5	122.0	9.8	20.4	0.4	3.5	4.1	29.8	34
All ducks	25	27,100	2,782	2,077	36.3	5,024	1,915	8,541	6,879

[a]Rounded.

counts are common to all the data sets. Nevertheless, several key points emerge (1) only mallards, Canada geese, and trumpeter swans winter in the interior in significant numbers; (2) a substantial portion of the winter populations of all species passes through the interior; and (3) diving ducks occur in relatively low numbers except for Nevada. A composite 3 state index for Idaho, Nevada, and Utah (Tables 1 and 2) for Oct-Jan populations reflects these migration patterns. The low index for northern pintails relative to mallards may reflect a decrease in the interior pintail migration in the early 1980s. Cinnamon teal are under-represented in the index because many leave the region before October. The mallard index (Table 2) is quite high, but does not include the huge populations in western Washington.

The habitat in 1982-1985 was wet in the Great Basin. Great Salt Lake rose to unprecedented levels (Smith and Kadlec 1986), the Malheur Basin flooded, and the Carson Sink, dry in drought years, became a huge lake. Many playa basins were flooded. Established waterfowl marshes became lakes, but new marshes began to appear where none had previously existed. Although local observers have noted great differences in local

waterfowl concentrations, the events are too recent for definitive data to be compiled. One interesting comparison is the Utah peak-fall population indices (Table 3) with estimates made in the 1950s for Great Salt Lake marshes (Nelson 1966). These data suggest a relative increase in mallards and gadwalls. However, aerial surveys have shown a dramatically reduced duck population, down from 0.5-1.0 million prior to the 1980s to about 300,000 (J. D. Huener, pers. commun.), after the marshes were inundated. Presumably, there have been major shifts in concentration areas and, perhaps, even the migration corridors in recent years, but these are difficult to infer without detailed data. One dramatic change, which may be indicative of the extent of shifting patterns, was the near total abandonment of the deeply flooded Great Salt Lake marshes by tundra swans. Prior to 1983, 15,000-25,000 (high of 60,000 in 1982, J. D. Huener, pers. commun.) swans stayed on these marshes in November, and up to 3,000 (Bellrose 1980) wintered there in mild years. Now there are only 1,000-3,000 birds, and there are more frequent reports of tundra swans scattered throughout adjacent marshes in Utah, Idaho, and Nevada, suggesting that the birds have dispersed into available

Table 3. Comparison of 2 measures of species composition of peak duck population (%) in Utah.

	Great Salt Lake Area[a]	Indices[b] Based on NWRs
Gadwall	40,000 (4.3)	334 (16.8)
Green-winged teal	250,000 (27.0)	302 (15.2)
Mallard	50,000 (5.4)	300 (15.1)
Northern pintail	500,000 (54.1)	937 (47.2)
Cinnamon teal	15,000 (1.6)	11 (0.6)
Canvasback	40,000 (4.3)	38 (1.9)
Redhead	30,000 (3.2)	62 (3.1)

[a]From Nelson (1966).

[b]From Canadian Wildlife Service and U.S. Fish and Wildlife Service (1987).

habitats. Unfortunately, the vast changes in region-wide habitat have been coupled with drastic population changes due to drought of the breeding grounds (Canadian Wildlife Service and U.S. Fish and Wildlife Service 1987) making it impossible to trace population responses to habitat change.

Actual wintering of waterfowl is not very important in the Intermountain Region, with 3 major exceptions: Canada geese, mallards, and trumpeter swans. The Great Basin Canada goose (*B. c. moffitti*) is only partially migratory and will winter wherever there is open water and fields for feeding that are not covered deeply with snow (Rienecker 1985). Although small populations winter in many areas, the Snake River in southern Idaho may winter 12,000; 20,000 may stay in the Columbia Basin; 10,000 in the Harney Basin, Oregon; and 6,000 in Carson Sink, Nevada (Bellrose 1980). Those same areas also hold wintering mallards: for example, up to 730,000 in the Columbia Basin and 350,000 near Boise, Idaho, along the Snake River. Again, the recent high water in the Great Basin has produced some changes, but less dramatic than in migration patterns. For example, tundra swans and some ducks (e.g., northern shovelers) formerly wintered on Great Salt Lake. The lake now is fresh enough to freeze completely, and only a few ducks winter near the mouths of inflowing springs, streams, and rivers.

The entire Rocky Mountain population of about 1,600 trumpeter swans winters in ice-free springs and flowing waters of the Tristate region (Gale et al., 1987). Geothermal activity helps maintain open water in 2 ponds on the Red Rock Lakes NWR in Montana. The Henry's Fork of the Snake River below Island Park Dam in Idaho is the main wintering area, if enough water is released from the dam to prevent ice cover. Other wintering areas include sections of the Yellowstone and Madison Rivers in Yellowstone National Park, the Madison River and ice-free areas of Hegben Lake in Montana, the Snake River in Jackson Hole, Wyoming, the Teton River in Idaho, and several smaller areas in the region that remain ice-free.

For most of the major habitat areas in the Great Basin, periods of the year without some migratory waterfowl can be very short. Some fall migrants linger well into December, conditions permitting. Spring migration begins in late February around Great Salt Lake. However, <100 km away, the marshes of the Bear Lake NWR in southern Idaho are mostly frozen from late October or early November until April. The difference is elevation. Great Salt Lake is about 1,283 m and Bear Lake is 1,830 m above mean sea level. Fall migration also begins early. There is a molt migration of northern pintails, mostly drakes, into the Great Basin and especially into Great Salt Lake in late June or early July, in which birds banded earlier the same year in Alaska have been recovered (Nelson 1966). Up to 20,000 gadwalls and 50,000 mallards also stage in Great Salt Lake marshes by early August (Nelson 1966).

Two major habitats seem to provide the requisites of large numbers of migrants, staging birds, and wintering populations. For those species that field-feed, reservoirs or rivers that remain ice-free in association with nearby winter-wheat, rye, or corn fields are an important habitat. Second, large shallow lakes with abundant sago pondweed (*Potamogeton pectinatus*) or widgeon grass (*Ruppia maritima*) attract large numbers of ducks, as well as swans and geese (Hamilton et al. 1986, Kantrud 1986). Presumably the seeds, foliage, and tubers are all sought as high-energy foods. Pondweed beds also harbor invertebrates (Huener 1984), so that a high-protein food supply also is available.

Land-Use Change

The major impact of man on migratory and wintering waterfowl in the Great Basin and associated areas has been the development of water resources for energy, agricultural, industrial, and domestic use. Irrigation accounts for about 90% of the freshwater used in the 17 western states (National Research Council [NRC] 1982). However, irrigated land is not increasing substantially in area (Table 4). Similarly, projected demands for irrigation remain stable. For example, in the Great Basin in 1975, about 26 million m^3/day of water were used in irrigation; by 2030, the amount is expected to be 21 million m^3/day (NRC 1982). Although the total is decreasing, this does not mean that no new land is being irrigated; rather, it reflects more land going out of production than new land being irrigated. Water formerly used for irrigation is being increasingly diverted for domestic and industrial use. For example, in Utah, the construction of a large coal-fired power plant was contingent in part upon the ability of the company to buy water from agricultural users who owned the water rights. Consequently, the water was not available for irrigation, and land went out of production. Similarly, the human population is growing rapidly, especially in the southern part of the region, and domestic water demands are resulting in less water for irrigation. It is simply a matter of economics—cities and industries can pay more for water than can agriculture. The recent economic difficulties in agriculture have exacer-

Table 4. Irrigated area (ha × 10^3) in the Great Basin states from 1944-1974 (NRC 1982).

State	1944	1954	1964	1974
Idaho	820	940	1,134	1,157
Oregon	457	603	651	632
Utah	455	434	442	393
Nevada	273	229	334	315
Total	2,005	2,206	2,561	2,497

bated the shift, because farmers cannot afford the increasing price of water.

The shift in water use from agriculture to urban and domestic demands has had mixed impacts on waterfowl habitats. Before the rise of Great Salt Lake, the volume of water available for waterfowl-management areas along the eastern shore of the lake was actually increasing. However, the water showed indications of decreasing quality because of increased urban runoff. The flooding of Great Salt Lake, and probably other closed basins in the region, would have been worse without the irrigation demands. Great Salt Lake levels might have been 1.5 m higher in the absence of irrigation (Arnow 1984).

Water use for agricultural, industrial, and domestic purposes is partially a misnomer. Much of it is used only temporarily, then is returned to some kind of receiving channel or basin. These "return flows" often carry substantial contaminants (e.g., silt, nutrients, heavy metals, insecticides). In the West, water tends to be used over and over again, usually with progressive deterioration in quality. Because many of the major waterfowl areas in this region are the last in the line of users, water quality can be a serious problem.

The seasonal impact of water diversion for irrigation and urban use can be detrimental to late-summer early-fall staging and migration areas. In dry years, all of the water may be diverted before reaching the marshes, which then dry up at the time they are needed by the birds (Christiansen and Low 1970).

Most of the large rivers in the region have been impounded to some degree.

Some impoundments have some benefit to waterfowl, especially in their upper reaches, if water levels do not fluctuate excessively. Some impoundments also are used as fall concentration areas by Canada geese and by field-feeding mallards. In the northern part of the region, impoundments freeze, and the late migrants and wintering waterfowl use free-flowing rivers.

In the terminal sinks and playas, the existence of the high-value marshes (e.g., Carson Sink, Klamath Basin) depends on the degree to which water is diverted and used for other purposes. Increasing pressures for diversion may threaten the very existence of these marshes.

Other land uses also affect waterfowl habitat in the Great Basin, notably livestock grazing. Grazing may be directly detrimental to breeding waterfowl (Kadlec and Smith 1989), but the impacts on migration and winter habitat are more subtle. Excessive grazing increases runoff and especially erosion, resulting in excessive siltation, which can destroy valuable shallow-water habitat.

HABITAT IMPORTANCE RELATIVE TO WATERFOWL REQUIREMENTS

Plants

Compared with other major wintering and migrating regions in the U.S., very little is known about the requirements of waterfowl in the Great Basin relative to the available habitat. Many of the waterfowl species that occur in the Great Basin, however, are ubiquitous throughout North America, and studies from other regions can be consulted for body condition and nutritional requirements. Although we will refer to studies from other regions, the reader is directed to those chapters for details on individual species that occur in this area.

Staging and winter-habitat management in the region has centered on meeting the food and water requirements of waterfowl. Increases in body weight and condition following arrival, maintenance throughout winter, and proper condition for subsequent breeding (e.g., Whyte and Bolen 1984, Miller 1986, Sheeley and Smith 1989) are thought to be met by the provision of food from certain plant communities. Sago pondweed, alkali bulrush (*Scirpus maritimus*), Olney three-square (*S. americanus*), hardstem bulrush (*S. acutus*), pickleweed (*Salicornia* spp.), widgeon grass, and horned pondweed (*Zannichellia palustris*) are the primary species managed for migratory birds. To a lesser extent, certain moist-soil plants such as red goosefoot (*Chenopodium rubrum*) and smartweed (*Polygonum* spp.) are promoted but meet with salinity problems.

Sago pondweed probably is considered the most important plant species for diving and dabbling ducks in the region. In the Malheur-Harney lakes basin of Oregon, habitat models for diving and dabbling ducks relied mainly on the surface area of sago pondweed available to predict waterfowl use-days (Hamilton et al. 1986). Also, prior to high water levels, tundra swan use of Great Salt Lake marshes was probably related to available sago pondweed (Sherwood 1960). Trumpeter swans and a few tundra swans that winter on rivers and springs in the Tristate area seem to rely heavily on submersed aquatic plants. Water weed (*Elodea canadensis*) and sago pondweed apparently are important species, but Richardson's pondweed (*Potomogeton richardsonii*), water buttercup (*Ranunculus aquatilis*), and milfoil (*Myriophyllum spicatum*) often are abundant in these areas as well. Food habits and herbivory relationships are not well-known in these wintering areas (Gale et al. 1987).

Nutrition

Dabbling ducks and geese field-feed on agricultural crops. Potential nutritional problems associated with a diet dominated by agricultural grains have been suggested (Baldassarre et al. 1983). Wheat and barley are the primary crops used by field-feeding waterfowl, because they are the most commonly planted crops. Although a diet dominated solely by cultivated grains may cause nutritional deficiencies, the problem is probably not widespread. Data derived from most studies on wintering waterfowl diets have been obtained from hunters. These birds have not been observed feeding prior to collection; therefore, subsequent analyses may have overestimated the importance of agricultural grains in the diet (Sheeley and Smith 1989). Few studies exist on wintering waterfowl diets in the Great Basin marshes.

Waterfowl feeding on agricultural grains, natural wetland seeds, natural vegetative material, and invertebrates likely will meet their requirements if the foods are available in sufficient quantity. Although not often considered in winter-habitat management, invertebrates are high in energy, protein, and essential nutrients, and have been found to occur in high percentages in diets of some wintering birds (Miller 1987, Sheeley and Smith 1989). Seeds of many wetland plants also are higher in protein, minerals, metabolizable energy, and amino acids (Baldassarre et al. 1983, Miller 1987) than many cultivated grains. Wheat, however, is high in crude protein, ranging from 15-19%, and has a metabolizable energy of about 3.5 kcal/g (Sugden 1971). Clark et al. (1986) suggested that the rate of energy intake, rather than energy content, was more important in determining cereal grain choice by mallards. In the Sacramento Valley, California, Miller (1987) noted that alkali bulrush seeds made up a small proportion and were underrepresented (relative to availability) in the diet of northern pintails. Alkali bulrush seeds were relatively high in apparent metabolizable energy (3.24 kcal/

g), but were low in crude protein (9%) (Miller 1987). Pederson and Pederson (1983) also found that digestability of alkali bulrush seeds was low compared to other natural foods. These results emphasize the need for data concerning waterfowl feeding ecology and nutritive quality of marsh plants in the Great Basin. If subsequent studies substantiate the California results for a broad group of waterfowl species in the Great Basin, managers should reevaluate plans that include promotion of alkali bulrush stands for wintering and migrating waterfowl. This would need to be weighed against the perception by many managers that alkali bulrush stands are important over-water nesting cover for redheads. Miller (1984) noted that waterfowl adapt readily to foods of variable quality by adjusting consumption rates; but the higher quality of the food, the more rapidly waterfowl can recover from weight losses.

Few data are available on the nutritive quality of separate sago pondweed plant parts (seeds, tubers, and foliage). Values for mixed aboveground sago plant parts range from 11% to 17% crude protein (Riemer and Toth 1969, Linn et al. 1975a, b). As with any of the vegetation types noted, it is difficult to judge the nutritional value of a plant species alone to waterfowl without also considering its associated invertebrate fauna.

Water Supplies

The availability and quality of water largely determine the plant and invertebrate populations that will be present; therefore, water dictates the abundance and species composition of waterfowl. Many of the marshes in the Great Basin region depend on snowmelt from adjacent mountain ranges for water (Duebbert 1969, Christiansen and Low 1970).

In years of average precipitation, plant communities are readily managed in marshes that have water-control structures. In marshes without control structures, plants exist that are adapted to local conditions. When precipitation is below normal, many areas become dry in summer and fall because much of the water is taken from the inflowing rivers for agricultural purposes (Christiansen and Low 1970, Turner 1980). Because of water demands, western Nevada has lost 12,000 of the 50,000 ha of available wetlands (Nevada Chapter, The Wildlife Society 1980). In many Great Basin marshes salinity increases dramatically in the sediments following drying conditions (Kadlec 1982). Marshes in this region exist only where there is a water source other than rainfall.

When precipitation is above normal, marshes with water-control structures generally can be manipulated for the desired plant communities and waterfowl species. However, as noted earlier, recent above-average precipitation has resulted in new historic high-water levels in many of the Great Basin marshes (e.g., Malheur NWR; Great Salt Lake). Most of the major marshes in the Great Basin are closed, having no outflows, and high water has caused losses of plant communities from either depth of inundation or saline water intrusion (Smith and Kadlec 1986). In the Great Salt Lake marshes, > 160,000 ha of habitat have been lost (Smith and Kadlec 1986), and at Malheur Lake NWR, 19,700 ha of habitat have been deeply flooded (Hamilton et al. 1986). High-water levels also have caused a decline in invertebrate resources (Smith and Kadlec 1986). Subsequently, waterfowl use of these areas has declined, and many birds now bypass the area. In addition, the large open water areas now are subject to wave action, reducing establishment of vegetation (Pederson in Hamilton et al. 1986).

Snowfall covering fields and frozen freshwater areas often occur in mid-winter, forcing birds out of the area unless they inhabit the few hotspring or river marshes that occur in the area. Extended cold weather and snow cover cause waterfowl to lose weight and lipid reserves (Whyte and Bolen 1984). Also, the costs of flight by birds moving from these areas are high (Prince 1979).

Disturbance

Waterfowl generally use areas relatively free from human disturbance (Kantrud 1986). The large, open units closed to public use at Bear River Bird Refuge, for example, had larger concentrations of staging waterfowl than units that experienced higher human activity. One suspected reason that the Henry's Fork River in Idaho holds wintering swans is that human disturbance is controlled because it is within Harriman State Park (Gale et al. 1987). As noted earlier, the energetic cost of flight by waterfowl disturbed from areas is relatively high (Prince 1979). Vegetative cover can reduce the impacts of human disturbance as well as provide a more favorable microclimate for waterfowl. Human disturbance also can affect waterfowl by inadvertently impacting vegetation. Boat action in Ruby Lake NWR resulted in a loss of approximately 80% of the submerged vegetation compared to non-use areas (Bouffard 1982). Erosion and siltation also were evident. Although the immediate impacts were related to breeding waterfowl, the loss of submerged vegetation also could be expected to cause lower use by migrating and wintering birds.

Disease

Avian botulism (*Clostridium botulinum* Type C) is the most prevalent disease in the Great Basin marshes. Indeed, botulism provided the impetus for establishment and construction of many Great Basin marshes (Smith and Kadlec 1986). An estimated 250,000 ducks died of botulism in the Great Salt Lake alone in 1932 (Jensen and Williams 1964).

Waterfowl losses to botulism usually occur in this region from August to October, although winter outbreaks occur in thermally polluted areas. Environmental conditions (warm water >20 C, alkaline pH, abundant invertebrates, and oxygen depletion) that promote botulism outbreaks are commonly found during these months (Wobeser 1981). The effects of botulism are probably most dramatic on residents and early migrants because of the timing of outbreaks. Other diseases, such as avian cholera (*Pasteurella multocida*) and lead poisoning, have occurred with less frequency than botulism; however, the extent and cumulative effects of these losses relative to the population at large are unknown.

The effects of predation on wintering populations also are unknown for this region. Avian predation probably accounts for the majority of these types of losses.

Environmental Contaminants

Few data are available on water contaminants for the Great Basin. Creating chemical disposal ponds causes potential problems for waterfowl. For example, it was determined that ammonium chloride (NH$_4$Cl) disposal ponds along the eastern shore of the Great Salt Lake created hazards for waterfowl (Ernst 1982). Dispersal techniques were recommended to minimize impacts (Ernst 1982).

The now infamous selenium contamination problem at Kesterson NWR (Di Silvestro 1985) is probably a worst-case example of the kind of water-quality problem that is widespread. Use and re-use of water, high natural levels of heavy metals (selenium, arsenic, etc.) plus contaminants added by human use, and evaporative concentration set the stage for problems with toxic chemicals. After Kesterson, surveys were initiated throughout the west, and problems subsequently were found in many places (Lee 1986). For example, selenium and boron, in excess of U.S. Environmental Protection Agency standards for freshwater aquatic life, have been found in irrigation return flows entering the Stewart Lake Waterfowl Management Area (WMA) in Utah (D. James, pers. commun.). High levels of heavy metals have been found in sediments of the Farmington Bay WMA near the outlet of the Salt Lake City sewage effluent disposal canal. These metals are associated with oil deposits that are not recent, suggesting an origin of untreated oil refinery water in the 1950s.

HABITAT MANAGEMENT

Marshes in the Great Basin are managed on the basis of whether the underlying sediments are fresh or saline. For many of the marshes in the western portion of the Great Basin and Great Salt Lake, marshes exist only where freshwater inflows have caused sediments to become less saline. Where the salinity in the sediments has been lowered, vascular plants have become established. To create a larger marsh area from those marshes existing only at the mouths of rivers, impoundments have been constructed around freshwater inflows, spreading the water across salt flats (Smith and Kadlec 1986). Sediment salinity then decreases in the upper layers and permits establishment of aquatic macrophytes (Kadlec 1982). Sago, curly-leaved pondweed (*Potomogeton crispus*), horned pondweed, muskgrass (*Chara* spp.), and widgeon grass respond on sites with slightly higher water levels (45-60 cm) (Fig. 2). The more shallow areas are dominated by alkali bulrush, Baltic rush (*Juncus balticus*), hardstem bulrush, cattail (*Typha* spp.), Olney three-square, and salt grass (*Distichlis spicata*) (Fig. 3). Sediment moisture and salinity effects are confounded. Figures 2 and 3 show examples of increasing moisture levels with concomitant decreases in salinity levels as plant communities typically change with water-level management. In the less saline

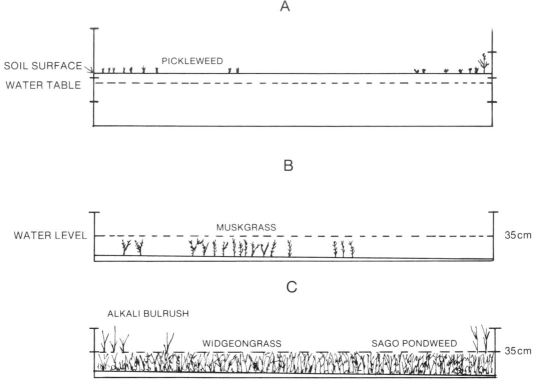

Fig. 2. Typical plant development and water management for submersed aquatic plants in the Great Basin marshes: (a) salt flat with little vegetation and high soil salinities, (b) intermediate stage following flooding, (c) final stage with dense submersed aquatics and low soil salinities.

marshes, these same species occur, but plants such as alkali bulrush and salt grass occur to a lesser extent and many moist-soil species such as smartweeds and red goosefoot become prevalent. A more complete list of important marsh plant species occurring in these areas can be found in McCabe (1982), Smith and Kadlec (1983), Duebbert (1969), and Bolen (1964).

Understanding the life-history characteristics of the marsh plants (van der Valk 1981), including seed reserves and dispersal mechanisms, permits the manager to manipulate the composition of the marsh with only fair success (Smith and Kadlec 1985a). Available models (van der Valk 1981) work well only in a general sense because plants rarely respond on a discrete scale to environmental conditions, as allowed for in the model, but instead respond on a continuum of environmen-

tal factors. Unfortunately, complete life-history data exist only for the most common species. Seed bank studies are useful in determining the species present and their basic life-history characters (van der Valk 1981). Numerous sources of life-history data exist, and a literature review will save a manager time in the field.

Any marsh that is maintained in the same condition over many years will likely show a decline in productivity. For example, simply impounding water year after year resulted in lower productivity in terms of waterfowl use in some Great Salt Lake marshes. Periodic disturbance is natural and essential for long-term productivity and wildlife use of managed marshes (Smith and Kadlec 1986). Disturbances, such as drawdown and fire, are commonly used to manipulate plant communities that favor waterfowl use. Some type of disturbance every 5 years

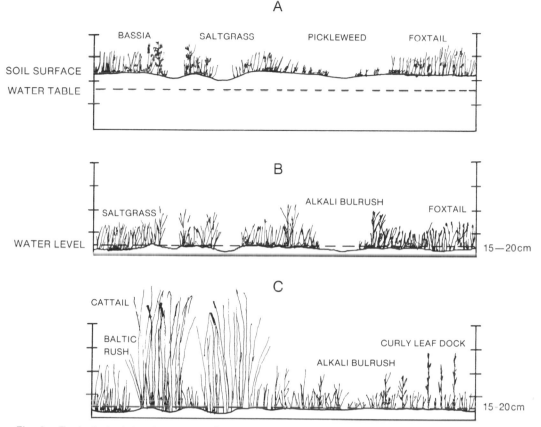

Fig. 3. Typical plant development and water management for emergent aquatic plants in the Great Basin marshes: (a) upland site with vegetation adapted to high soil salinities, (b) intermediate stage with fluctuating water, 0-20 cm, (c) long-term (> 6 years) effects of flooding (0-20 cm) and lowered soil salinities.

would probably be beneficial. However, marshes that were not constructed or do not have water-level control structures are subject to natural disturbances (e.g., drought, flooding), thus maintaining high productivity. For example, some unmanaged areas on the east side of Great Salt Lake maintained high productivity apparently because of natural water-level fluctuations (J. D. Huener, pers. commun.). Indeed, it was recommended that Malheur Lake NWR not be modified with water-control structures, such as dikes, because the natural high- and low-water events maintained the marsh in a productive state with wildlife well adapted to these fluctuations (Duebbert 1969, U.S. Fish and Wildlife Service 1980). Carp problems and cross-diking

have recently made this type of management difficult. Certainly a "no-management" scheme is viable for some marshes that are subjected to natural disturbances. However, in most instances, manipulations are necessary to maintain high animal and plant productivity.

Water-Level Manipulation

In saline marshes, freshwater (0.5-1.0 mmhos/cm conductivity) flooding of saline sediments decreases the interstitial water conductivity in the rhizosphere, allowing marsh plants to become established in all but totally stagnant situations (Smith and Kadlec 1985a). Deep flooding pushes salts down into the sediments (Kadlec 1982). Managers easily can obtain an estimate of salinity levels by measuring conductivity (which is closely related to salinity) with commercially available equipment. As areas are drained, sediment salinity increases rapidly, preventing management of most moist-soil plant species that require exposed sediments and freshwater conditions to germinate and survive. Periodic flooding and drying cause salts to return to the surface via capillary action.

Pickleweed and salt cedar (*Tamarix pentandra*) can germinate and survive under conditions of high conductivity (> 25 mmhos) if the soil stays moist. Salt cedar is difficult to control, once established. Therefore, drawdowns that maintain just a few centimeters of water are recommended, because they keep salinities low, prevent establishment of salt cedar, and allow many preferred species such as hardstem and alkali bulrush to germinate (Smith and Kadlec 1983). Water requirements to meet these needs depend on evapotranspiration requirements, water quality (primarily salinity), and precipitation. Christiansen and Low (1970) provide detailed guidelines for calculation of management-area water needs.

Most emergent (cattail, alkali bulrush, hardstem bulrush) and submergent species (sago pondweed, widgeon grass) studied to date germinate best with freshwater (0.25 mmhos) conditions (Teeter 1965, Christiansen and Low 1970, Mayer and Low 1970). Drawdown and reflooding generally do not cause changes in seed densities in marsh sediments (Smith and Kadlec (1985*b*). However, if few seeds are present, as is often the case for submergent plants in open-water zones, water level manipulations alone may do little to change the species composition of the site (Smith and Kadlec 1983, 1985*b*).

Plant growth also is generally optimum under freshwater conditions. However, different species exhibit adaptations to a wide range of salinity conditions. Kau-

shik (1963) considered alkali bulrush most tolerant to elevated salinity levels, with hardstem bulrush being intermediate in tolerance, and cattail least tolerant. For example, cattail had little growth at 9.6 mmhos, hardstem bulrush made substantial growth at this level, and alkali bulrush still showed good growth at 12.8 mmhos. Plant zones can be distinguished in the field (Fig. 4) on the basis of their tolerance to salinity (Nelson 1954, Bolen 1964, Ungar et al. 1979).

Manipulation of water levels can be used to change salinity levels favoring particular plant species. For example, Figure 5 illustrates a specific schedule for alkali bulrush management. Nelson and Dietz (1966) found that by drawing down water in existing areas of vegetation and increasing salinity levels, cattail could be controlled and replaced by alkali bulrush. Cattail may be more susceptible to fungal attacks under salinity stress (Anderson 1977). Alkali bulrush is generally dominant at sediment salinity levels of 10-25 mmhos.

Sago pondweed produces well in areas of slightly lower salinity that can be provided immediately upon reflooding drawdown areas. Teeter (1965) noted that seed germination of sago pondweed was reduced by any increases in salinity, but that tuber growth and production peaked at approximately 3,000 ppm of sodium chloride. In areas previously dominated by sago pondweed, regrowth following winter die-off is mainly from tubers (Yeo 1965). Tubers can be found in sediments down to 45 cm and can survive freezing temperatures when insulated by sediments (Yeo 1965).

In areas where sago pondweed is colonizing, such as a newly flooded salt flat, establishment is generally from seed, therefore, the less saline the water, the higher the germination (Teeter 1965). In the Great Basin marshes, the availability of freshwater is highest in spring (Kadlec 1982) when seeds germinate in newly

Fig. 4.   Aerial view of plant zonation patterns as affected by salinity. Emergent plants are present in the foreground where freshwater inflows are present; higher plants are absent from the background due to high salinity levels.

colonized areas. As the summer progresses, the water increases in salinity, but vegetative growth is not greatly affected until salinity reaches 9,000-11,000 ppm (Teeter 1965).

Robel (1962) found that standing crops of sago pondweed increased up to 46 cm water depth. Anderson (1978) suggested that standing crops would decrease when water depths exceeded 60 cm. Many of the Great Salt Lake marshes dominated by sago pondweed were drained annually in midwinter to prevent ice damage to dikes, to consolidate the sediments, and to control carp. Drainage appeared to have a negligible impact on the subsequent production of sago pondweed, because production ensued from tubers upon reflooding in spring. However, this practice likely reduces the availability of invertebrates to early migrating waterfowl (Huener 1984).

Smith and Kadlec (1986) noted that many of the more preferred species, such as sago pondweed and alkali bulrush, can tolerate moderate salinity levels. Conductivities of around 18 mmhos generally will permit growth of these desired plant species, but will discourage competition from undesirable plants. Maintaining continuous flooding over a wide range of flow rates allows sediments to become fresh, giving the competitive advantage to reed (*Phragmites australis*) and cattail. Therefore, by fluctuating water levels, a manager can achieve a desired salinity level (e.g., 18 mmhos) and then can adjust water depths to promote either submergent or emergent species. Water depths of about 45-60 cm will promote sago pondweed, whereas lower levels will allow emergents to flourish. Cattail and hardstem bulrush are more tolerant of flooding 30-45 cm in depth than is alkali bulrush. Frequency of water-level fluctuation would depend on monitoring the plant species present and monitoring salinity levels in sediments and water. In

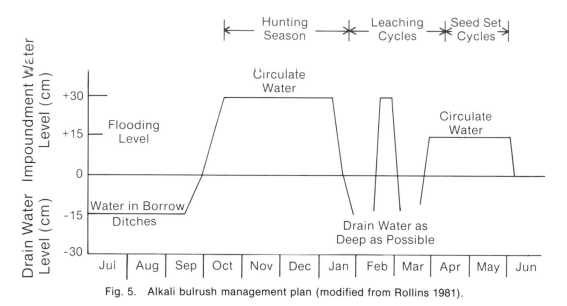

Fig. 5.   Alkali bulrush management plan (modified from Rollins 1981).

saline marshes, moist-soil plants such as red goosefoot and smartweeds only grow where freshwater seepage keeps sediments moist, but cattail often dominates in these situations if levels are maintained for > 1 year (Nelson 1954).

In the freshwater marshes (< 8 mmhos sediment conductivity during drawdown) of the Great Basin, drawdowns that promote moist-soil plants are successful. Procedures are similar to those used in the Mississippi and Central flyways. Sediments at Klamath Basin NWR are not as saline as those in the Great Salt Lake, and drawdowns for moist-soil plant establishment have met with success (E. H. McCollum, pers. commun.). Drawdowns in March have stimulated germination of red goosefoot, smartweed, and summer cypress (*Kochia scoparia*) on exposed mudflats.

Burning and Mowing

Burning and mowing are commonly used as methods to control undesirable or overly dense stands of emergent marsh plants, such as cattail, in an effort to establish more desirable plant communities (Fig. 6). Nelson and Dietz (1966) found that cattail could be controlled by

mowing or burning if water was promptly restored to a sufficient depth. We (Smith and Kadlec 1985c) studied the effects of burning and mowing on alkali bulrush, cattail, hardstem bulrush, and salt grass. Cutting and burning produced similar results, in that salt grass was controlled with 10 cm water coverage following treatment, but other species were not affected. Usually, > 20 cm water coverage is required to control these other emergent plant species. Deep flooding is required because heat penetration into the sediments from fires is generally insufficient to cause below-ground plant mortality (Smith and Kadlec 1985c). When plant shoots are flooded rapidly following burning or mowing treatment, or are cut below the water surface, oxygen in the submerged plant parts is consumed rapidly, causing decay of the submerged plant material and lowering regenerative capabilities (Sale and Wetzel 1983).

If sediments are dry and there is a surface layer of high organic content available, burning may cause below-ground plant mortality. Fires sometimes continue to burn in the organic layer for extended periods of time. These types of fires can cause changes in plant composi-

Fig. 6.   Prescribed burning of wet meadow vegetation (*Carex* spp., *Juncus* spp.) at Malheur National Wildlife Refuge (Photo by Carlton M. Britton).

tion without prompt reflooding (e.g., Fish Springs NWR). However, they are not common because of the unique conditions they require. Following control, it is necessary to provide good growing conditions for more desirable plants. Few data exist, but burning does not appear to affect the seed bank by improving or hindering germination (Smith and Kadlec 1985c). Following growing season, sediment temperatures may be elevated relative to unburned areas (Smith and Kadlec 1985b), stimulating germination of some species.

Control of emergent marsh plants is not the only beneficial aspect of burning. Even though plants may not be controlled without sufficient water depths, the nutritive quality of the plants may be improved compared to plants prior to the fire (Smith et al. 1984). Herbivory by waterfowl and muskrats (*Ondatra zibethicus*) may be higher on marsh plant communities following burning (Smith and Kadlec 1985d), suggesting some potential for biological control of plant species. Whether waterfowl or muskrats select vegetation in previously burned areas on the basis of nutritive quality, or merely because burned sites provided improved foraging (i.e., less litter) is unknown. Nevertheless, burning can improve the quality of forage for herbivores.

Cutting or haying also can be used to attract geese in winter. Burning or mowing of cheat grass (*Bromus tectorum*) is often used to attract Canada geese (J. D. Huener, pers. commun.). Owen (1975) noted that cutting and fertilizing grasslands increased numbers of white-fronted geese (*Anser albifrons*). Increased use of these areas was related to (1) increased nutritive quality of the vegetation, (2) better visibility afforded to geese, (3) ease of movement, and (4) feeding efficiency.

Haying is common in the Great Basin on upland portions of state and federal waterfowl management areas.

Establishment of Native Plants

Many managers of the NWRs and WMAs in the Great Basin plant crops (primarily wheat) for migrating ducks and geese. Planting native food and cover species is not as common as planting annual farm crops. Generally, if water conditions are adequate, plant species adapted to the region will be present. However, if high water levels occur over an area for several years, such as occurred at Malheur NWR and the Great Salt Lake marshes, planting of native vegetation may be justified when water levels return to normal. High water levels not only eliminate existing vegetation but also cause seed-bank loss through sedimentation, and/or cause water currents that flush seeds from sediments (Smith and Kadlec 1986).

Creating natural or artificial barriers to seed dispersal also can enhance vegetation establishment. The relatively low numbers of emergent seeds available in open water and submerged plant zones have been related to seed dispersal (Smith and Kadlec 1985c). Seeds transported by water and wind continue to move across these relatively open sites until a barrier to dispersal is reached. This may be the reason emergent plant zones with dense vegetative cover have relatively large seed banks. In addition, by elevating the soil surface, as with contour furrows, emergent plant seeds can be trapped in areas that previously had few seeds or had a seed bank dominated by submergent species (Kadlec and Smith 1984).

Livestock Grazing

Livestock grazing occurs on many waterfowl management areas, but its effect on wintering waterfowl habitat has received little study. Although grazing is generally thought to impact nesting waterfowl negatively (Molini 1977), grazing might be used to provide low plant structure that is preferred by geese feeding during winter. Pintails and American wigeon in British Columbia used pastures in preference to other upland land-use types (Hirst and Easthope 1981). In the Klamath Basin, heavily grazed areas that are flooded provide attractive habitat for dabbling ducks and geese, presumably because of the new vegetative growth (E. H. McCollum, pers. commun.). Whyte and Cain (1981) also noted that cattle grazing could be used in limited instances to improve waterfowl use of stock ponds, if carefully controlled. By fencing shallow areas of the ponds to protect vegetation, but allowing cattle to reduce dense emergents such as cattail, these ponds can be of value to cattle and waterfowl.

Carp Management

Carp (*Cyprinus carpio*) are considered a major problem in the Great Basin marshes (Robel 1961, U.S. Fish and Wildlife Service 1980, Berry 1982). Carp negatively impact submergent vegetation. Submerged plants are consumed and also dislodged by carp as they forage for invertebrates in the sediments (Berry 1982). The diet of carp at Bear River Bird Refuge was 15% plant matter and 85% invertebrates (Sigler 1958). Carp, therefore, also cause a direct loss of invertebrates through feeding and cause increased turbidity. The net result is a decreased food resource for waterfowl.

In Utah (J. D. Huener, pers. commun.), carp control is often a winter project whereby carp are concentrated using drawdowns. They then are killed, using chlorine and rotenone, or are harvested commercially with seines. At Bear River Bird Refuge, carp overwintered in deep pools and canals. Berry (1982) recommended that carp be poisoned with rotenone in these areas prior to their movements back into the marsh proper. Rotenone will kill aquatic inver-

Fig. 7. A screen over inflow structure to prevent carp entry.

tebrates, but invertebrate populations will recover in a short time. Also, by placing bar screens (Fig. 7) over inflow structures, large carp were prevented from reinfesting management units. Numbers of small fish increased at Bear River Bird Refuge after control of the larger carp, and were of forage size for fish-eating birds (Berry 1982). At Malheur NWR, the U.S. Fish and Wildlife Service (1980) recommended that rotenone be used to kill carp and that fish screens be placed over intake structures to further control infestations. They also suggested the possibility of biologically controlling carp with intro-ductions of predatory fish.

Disease Management

Disease management in the Great Basin marshes often overshadows other manage ment strategies because of the enormous losses of waterfowl that can occur. In this region, most efforts center on decreasing avian botulism by controlling the envir-onmental factors that promote the disease. Therefore, most preventative management plans are available for marshes that have water-control structures (Wobeser 1981).

Rosen (1971) suggested the following methods to prevent outbreaks from occur-ring: (1) Newly constructed management units should have steep shorelines and be permanently flooded to prevent seasonal water fluctuations associated with inverte-brate die-offs; (2) These units should be relatively deep (45-60 cm) to minimize effects of water fluctuations; (3) in areas flooded periodically, flooding should be conducted later in the year (i.e. November) when water temperatures are lower; (4) vegetation should be controlled through disking or burning to decrease the substrate available for invertebrates. Also, an intensive monitoring program should be used to detect waterfowl mor-tality and to detect a continuation of outbreaks from waterfowl feeding on maggots from dead birds. Obviously, many of these suggestions are not com-patible with practices that promote estab-lishment of most emergent or moist-soil vegetation types. The potential loss of birds from botulism should be carefully weighed against promoting increased waterfowl use. If the decision is made to manage for increased waterfowl use, an effective monitoring and sanitation program is needed.

Once outbreaks are detected, Hunter et al. (1970) recommended that the area be drained quickly to prevent bird use or flooded rapidly to make the toxic substrate unavailable (Wobeser 1981). Generally, water availability in early fall is low, when outbreaks occur, and therefore drainage is recommended most often. Pickup and disposal of dead and dying birds are recommended to reduce maggot populations. Finally, bird-scaring techniques are recommended to prevent birds from using the area after an outbreak has started.

Management and the Public

Most WMAs and NWRs have zones that are open to the public for fishing, boating, wildlife observation, and hunting. These same areas also have zones that restrict public access. Although public-use problems may be less than in other flyways because of the relatively sparse human populations, public-access problems do exist in Great Basin marshes. The U.S. Fish and Wildlife Service accommodates recreational use of NWRs only when compatible with wildlife objectives (Bouffard 1982). For example, after a lawsuit filed by the Defenders of Wildlife, regulations at Ruby Lake NWR prohibited using gas-powered boats and water-skiing during the waterfowl breeding season. During August through December, outboard motors < 10 hp are allowed. Not only will this help breeding waterfowl, but also it will protect vegetation important to migrating and wintering birds against wave and erosion damage caused by larger powerboats. Even tour routes are likely to affect use by wintering birds. Restricting public use to observation blinds during peak-use periods may alleviate some of these effects.

Heavily hunted areas also experience less waterfowl use when compared to restricted areas (e.g., Ogden Bay WMA,

Utah; V. Bachmann, pers. commun.). Rest-rotation schedules of hunting activities may reduce the impacts. Restricting hunting to certain weekdays and/or times during the day is plausible.

RESEARCH AND MANAGEMENT NEEDS

Few data are available that relate management of waterfowl food sources in the Great Basin to waterfowl physiological requirements. Studies are needed that relate availability and nutritive quality of foods to waterfowl use and the efficiency of that use. We believe that this is the first step needed to justify or alter many current management plans. In addition, the importance of invertebrates in the winter diet of waterfowl needs investigation. Whether or not a particular vegetation type should be promoted should not be based solely on its particular use or nutritive quality but also on its associated invertebrate fauna.

Secondly, basic ecological studies are needed on plant and invertebrate species life histories. For example, an understanding of the mechanisms affecting community structure can be reached with autoecological data on plant species (Verhoeven et al. 1982). This type of data is required to predict, more accurately, species occurrences and abundance as a result of management practices (Smith and Kadlec 1985a). Specifics include water requirements, salinity tolerance, and temperature and light requirements. These studies would allow investigations concerning the management of these factors to affect changes in the community. The manipulation of sediment salinity levels to change species composition is an example of this approach.

Another area in need of study is the impact of disturbance caused by human activity on staging and wintering concentrations. The suggestion from anecdotal observation is that even low levels of human activity (e.g., bird watching) cause ducks and geese to disperse. On the other hand, the urbanization of Canada geese and mallards suggests that those species, and perhaps others, can become habituated to non-threatening human activity. One hypothesis might be that the birds' behavior patterns are such that low levels of human activity are least tolerated. Another potential management question is whether patterns of emergent vegetation and open water can reduce the impact of human activity on non-breeding waterfowl. The mediating effects of cover on waterfowl physiological requirements need investigation. Additional studies regarding recreational use of important wintering areas would provide much needed data necessary to manage this increasing demand.

Research also is needed on methods of managing upland habitat in arid or semi-arid regions where soils are often saline or alkaline. Although many crops and grasses can be grown if irrigated, water supplies often do not permit such an approach. We suspect that a good deal of practical knowledge of upland management for crops and pasture exists, but is not readily available to the waterfowl manager. Consulting with range managers may provide much needed expertise. Further, there may well be native species of plants even better suited for such sites, but, in general, we do not know the best methods for favoring such species.

SUMMARY

Because good migration and winter habitat are scattered in the Great Basin, existing areas are used heavily. Most of the valuable marshes are in the central and northern part of the region, often in basins with no outlet. Salinity and marginal water supplies are a common problem, even though flooding in the recent years has caused lower waterfowl use.

Migration corridors over the northern part of the region commonly lead southwesterly toward the wintering areas in California and the western part of Mexico. Another major pathway is southeast to the Gulf coast of Texas and Mexico. The extent of waterfowl wintering in the Great Basin depends on lack of ice and snow. If the birds can find ice-free water and snow-free crop fields, mallards and Canada geese will winter in large numbers. The entire Rocky Mountain population of trumpeter swans winters in the Tristate region, primarily on Henry's Fork of the Snake River in Harriman State Park, Idaho.

The development of water for human use has been, and will continue to be, the major land use impacting habitats for migrating and wintering waterfowl. Although agricultural demands for irrigation water are projected to decline in the foreseeable future, domestic and industrial uses will more than make up the difference. Water is precious in the Great Basin, and is used and re-used. Waterfowl marshes are near the bottom of the priority of use. These areas receive water after it has been used by other interests. Therefore, marshes often receive water unfit for any other use. Indeed, in some cases, the water is not fit for waterfowl, as the Kesterson example has shown.

Sago pondweed, alkali bulrush, hardstem bulrush, Olney three-square, and, to a lesser extent, moist-soil plants are the primary vegetation managed for waterfowl in Great Basin marshes. However, little is known about these plants in terms of actually meeting the physiological and behavioral requirements of wintering waterfowl in the region. Marshes maintained under the same conditions year after year decline in productivity, and some type of disturbance (e.g., drawdown, fire) is required to maintain high waterfowl use. An understanding of plant life histories and responses to habitat manipulations is essential in predicting results of management actions.

Sediment salinity in many marshes decreases the success of moist-soil plant management. Salinity increases during drawdowns, preventing establishment of moist-soil plants that require exposed sediments and freshwater conditions. Therefore, in saline areas, drawdowns that maintain a thin layer of freshwater (4 cm) will keep sediment salinities low and still will allow establishment of many plant species. On exposed sediments in freshwater areas, smartweed and red goosefoot establishment is successful. Salinity manipulations can be used to change the species composition of established adult plants.

Burning and mowing can be used to control dense undesirable plants such as cattail if water of sufficient depth is flooded rapidly over treated areas. Nutritive quality of marsh plants usually is improved following burning, and waterfowl consume these plants preferentially to plants in unburned areas. Artificially establishing native plants by creating barriers to seed dispersal, such as contour furrows, also has been successful.

Carp are a major management concern because they impact sago pondweed and invertebrates. Carp are controlled primarily with rotenone while they are concentrated in small areas and prevented from immediate reinfestation with the use of fish barriers. Avian botulism is a major disease problem in the area, primarily affecting early-migratory waterfowl. Botulism is controlled by managing the environmental factors associated with outbreaks. Management of botulism may not be compatible with habitat management designed to increase waterfowl use.

Research is needed to determine the relationships of managed vegetation types and waterfowl physiological requirements. Life-history data on plant and invertebrate species also are needed to better predict the results of management practices.

LITERATURE CITED

Anderson, C. M. 1977. Cattail decline at Farmington Bay Wildlife Management Area. Great Basin Nat. 37:24-34.

Anderson, M. G. 1978. Distribution and production of sago pondweed (*Potamogeton pectinatus* L.) on a northern prairie marsh. Ecology 59:154-160.

Arnow, T. 1984. Water-level and water-quality changes in Great Salt Lake, Utah, 1847-1983. U.S. Geol. Surv., Circ. 913. 22 pp.

Baldassarre, G. A., R. J. Whyte, E. .E. Quinlan, and E. G. Bolen. 1983. Dynamics of waste corn available to postbreeding waterfowl in Texas. Wildl. Soc. Bull. 11:25-31.

Bartonek, J. C. 1988. Pacific flyway midwinter waterfowl survey-1988. Rep. to Pacific Flyway Council. Corvallis, Ore. 10 pp.

Bellrose, F. C. 1980. Ducks, geese, and swans of North America. Third ed. Stackpole Books, Harrisburg, Pa. 540 pp.

Berry, C. R., Jr. 1982. Behavior and ecology of carp in the Bear River Migratory Bird Refuge. Final Completion Rep. Utah State Univ., Logan. 48 pp.

Bolen, E. G. 1964. Plant ecology of spring-fed salt marshes in western Utah. Ecol. Monogr. 34:143-166.

Bouffard, S. H. 1982. Wildlife values versus human recreation: Ruby Lake National Wildlife Refuge. Trans. North Am. Wildl. and Nat. Resour. Conf. 47:553-558.

Brown, D. E. 1985. Arizona wetlands and waterfowl. Univ. Arizona Press, Tucson. 169 pp.

Canadian Wildlife Service and U.S. Fish and Wildlife Service. 1987. Stabilized duck hunting regulations evaluations. Mimeogr. 274 pp.

Chattin, J. E. 1964. Pacific Flyway. Pages 233-252 *in* J. P. Linduska, ed. Waterfowl tomorrow. U.S. Gov. Print. Off., Washington, D.C.

Christiansen, J. E., and J. B. Low. 1970. Water requirements of waterfowl marshlands in northern Utah. Utah Div. Fish and Game Publ. 69-123. Salt Lake City. 108 pp.

Clark, R. G., H. Greenwood, and L. G. Sugden. 1986. Influence of grain characteristics on optimal diet of field-feeding mallards *Anas platyrhynchos*. J. Appl. Ecol. 23:763-771.

Cronquist, A., A. H. Holmgren, N. H. Holmgren, J. L. Reveal, and P. K.Holmgren. 1977. Intermountain flora. Vol. 6. Columbia Univ. Press, New York. 584 pp.

Di Silvestro, R. L., editor. 1985. Audubon wildlife report 1985. Nat. Audubon Soc., New York, N.Y. 671 pp.

Duebbert, H. F. 1969. The ecology of Malheur Lake and management implications. Bur. Sports Fish. Wildl. Refuge Leafl. 412. 24 pp.

Ernst, R. P. 1982. Impact of chemical waste evaporation ponds on waterfowl and potential mitigation. Utah Dep. Nat. Resour., Salt Lake City. 45 pp.

Gale, R. S., I. J. Ball, and E. O. Garton. 1987. The ecology and management of the Rocky Mountain population of trumpeter swans. Bozeman, Mont. 261 pp.

Gilmer, D. S., J.M. Hicks, J. C. Bartonek, and E. H. McCollum. 1986. Waterfowl harvest at Tule Lake National Wildlife Refuge. 1936-41. Calif. Fish and Game 72:132-143.

Graff, W. L., editor. 1987. Geomorphic systems of North America. Geol. Soc. America, Inc., Boulder, Colo. 643 pp.

Hamilton, D. B., G. T. Auble, R. A. Ellison, and J. E. Roelle. 1986. Effects of flood control alternatives on the hydrology, vegetation, and wildlife resources of the Malheur-Harney Lake Basin. U.S. Fish and Wildlife Serv., Nat. Ecol. Center, Fort Collins, Colo. NEC-86/20. 85 pp.

Harris, S. W. 1954. An ecological study of the waterfowl of the potholes area, Grant County, Washington. Am. Midl. Nat. 52:405-432.

Hirst, S. M., and C. A. Easthope. 1981. Use of agricultural lands by waterfowl in southwestern British Columbia. J. Wildl. Manage. 45:454-462.

Huener, J. D. 1984. Macroinvertebrate response to marsh management. M.S. Thesis, Utah State Univ., Logan. 85 pp.

Hunter, B.F., W. E. Clark, P. J. Perkins, and P. R. Coleman. 1970. Applied botulism research including management recommendations. Prog. Rep. Calif. Dep. Fish and Game. Sacramento. 87 pp.

Jensen, W. I., and C. Williams. 1964. Botulism and fowl cholera. Pages 333-341 *in* J. P. Linduska, ed. Waterfowl tomorrow. U.S. Gov. Print. Off., Washington, D.C.

Kadlec, J. A. 1982. Mechanisms affecting salinity of Great Salt Lake marshes. Am. Midl. Nat. 107:82-94.

———, and L. M. Smith. 1984. Marsh plant establishment on newly flooded salt flats. Wildl. Soc. Bull. 12:388-394.

———, and ———. 1989. Habitat management for waterfowl in breeding areas. In press, *in* B. D. J. Batt, ed. The ecology and management of breeding waterfowl. Univ. Minnesota Press, Minneapolis.

Kantrud, H. A. 1986. Western Stump Lake, a major canvasback staging area in eastern North Dakota. Prairie Nat. 18:247-253.

Kaushik, I. K. 1963. The influence of salinity on the growth and reproduction of marsh plants. Ph.D. Thesis, Utah State Univ., Logan. 123 pp.

Lee, W. S. 1986. The National Wildlife Refuge system. Pages 413-456 *in* R. L. Di Silvestro, ed. Audubon wildlife report 1986. Natl. Audubon Soc., N.Y.

Linn, J. G., R. D. Goodrich, D. E. Otterby, J. C. Meiske, and E. J. Staba. 1975a. Nutritive value of dried and ensiled aquatic plants. II. Digestibility by sheep. J. Anim. Sci. 41:610-615.

———, E. J. Staba, R. D. Goodrich, J. C. Meiska, and D. E. Otterby. 1975b. Nutritive value of dried or ensiled aquatic plants. I. Chemical composition. J. Anim. Sci. 41:601-609.

Mayer, F. L., Jr., and J. B. Low. 1970. The effect of salinity on widgeongrass. J. Wildl. Manage. 34:658-661.

McCabe, T. R. 1982. Muskrat population levels and vegetation utilization: a basis for an index. Ph.D. Thesis, Utah State Univ., Logan. 111 pp.

Miller, M. R. 1984. Comparative ability of northern pintails, gadwalls, and northern shovelers to metabolize foods. J. Wildl. Manage. 48:362-370.

———. 1986. Northern pintail body condition during wet or dry winters in the Sacramento Valley, California. J. Wildl. Manage. 59:189-198.

———. 1987. Fall and winter foods of northern pintails in the Sacramento Valley, California. J. Wildl. Manage. 51:405-414.

Molini, W. A. 1977. Livestock interactions with upland game, nongame, and waterfowl in the Great Basin. A workshop synopsis. Cal.-Neva. Wildl. Trans. 1977:97-103.

National Research Council. 1982. Impacts of emerging agricultural trends on fish and wildlife habitat. Natl. Acad. Press, Washington, D.C. 303 pp.

Nelson, N. F. 1954. Factors in the development and restoration of waterfowl habitat at Ogden Bay Refuge, Weber County, Utah. Utah Div. Fish and Game Publ., Salt Lake City. 87 pp.

———. 1966. Waterfowl hunting in Utah. Utah Dep. Fish and Game Publ. No. 66-10, Salt Lake City. 100 pp.

———, and R. H. Dietz. 1966. Cattail control methods in Utah. Utah State Dep. of Fish and Game Publ. 66-2. Salt Lake City. 31 pp.

Nevada Chapter, The Wildlife Society. 1980. Position statement: the maintenance and management of wetlands on public lands for public benefit in Lahontan Valley, Nevada. Nev. Chap., Wildl. Soc., Reno. 12 pp.

Owen, M. 1975. Cutting and fertilizing grassland for winter goose management. J. Wildl. Manage. 39:163-167.

Pederson, G. B., and R. L. Pederson. 1983. Feeding ecology of pintails and mallards on Lower Klamath marshes. Humboldt State University Found. Rep., Humboldt State Univ., Humboldt, Calif. 89 pp.

Peterson, S. R. 1969. Waterfowl ecology and utilization of Uinta Mountain water areas. M.S. Thesis, Utah State Univ., Logan. 58 pp.

Platts, W. S., and S. Jensen. 1986. Wetland/riparian ecosystems of the Great Basin/desert and montane region: an overview. Pages 5-316 *in* J. H. Sather and J. B. Low, eds. Proc. workshop on Great Basin/Desert and Montana regional wetland functions. Salt Lake City, Utah.

Prince, H. H. 1979. Bioenergetics of postbreeding

dabbling ducks. Pages 103-117 in T. A. Book-hout, ed. Waterfowl and wetlands—an inter-grated review. North Cent. Sect., Wildl. Soc., Madison, Wis.

Riemer, D. N., and S. J. Toth. 1969. A survey of the chemical composition of *Potamogeton* and *Myriophyllum* in New Jersey. Weed Sci. 17:219-223.

Rienecker, W. C. 1985. Temporal distribution of breeding and non-breeding Canada geese from northeastern California. Calif. Fish and Game 71:196-209.

Robel, R. J. 1961. The effects of carp populations on the production of waterfowl food plants on a western waterfowl marsh. Trans. North Am. Wildl. and Nat. Resour. Conf. 26:147-159.

———. 1962. Changes in submersed vegetation following a change in water level. J. Wildl. Manage. 26:221-224.

Rollins, G. L. 1981. A guide to waterfowl habitat management in Suisun Marsh. Calif. Dep. Fish and Game, The Resources Agency, Sacramento. 109 pp.

Rosen, M. N. 1971. Botulism. Pages 100-117 in J. W. Davis, R. C. Anderson, L. Karstad, and D. O. Trainer, eds. Infectious and parasitic diseases of wild birds. Iowa State Univ. Press, Ames.

Sale, P. J. M., and R. G. Wetzel. 1983. Growth and metabolism of *Typha* species in relation to cutting treatments. Aquatic Bot. 15:321-334.

Sanderson, G. C. 1980. Conservation of waterfowl. Pages 43-58 in F. C. Bellrose, ed. Ducks, geese and swans of North America. Third ed. Stack-pole Books, Harrisburg, Pa.

Sheeley, D. G., and L. M. Smith. 1989. Diet and condition bias associated with hunter-killed northern pintails. J. Wildl. Manage. 53:765-769.

Sherwood, G. A. 1960. The whistling swan in the west with particular reference to Great Salt Lake Valley, Utah. Condor 62:370-377.

Sigler, W. F. 1958. The ecology and use of carp in Utah. Agric. Exp. Stn. Bull. 405. Utah State Univ., Logan.

Smith, L. M., and J. A. Kadlec. 1983. Seed banks and their role during drawdown of a North American marsh. J. Appl. Ecol. 20:673-684.

———, and ———. 1985a. Predictions of vegetation change following fire in a Great Salt Lake marsh. Aquatic Bot. 21:43-51.

———, and ———. 1985b. Comparisons of prescribed burning and cutting of Utah marsh plants. Great Basin Nat. 45:462-466.

———, and ———. 1985c. The effects of disturbance on marsh seed banks. Can. J. Bot. 63:2133-2137.

———, and ———. 1985d. Fire and herbivory in a Great Salt Lake marsh. Ecology 66:259-265.

———, and ———. 1986. Habitat management for wildlife in marshes of Great Salt Lake. Trans. North Am. Wildl. and Nat. Resour. Conf. 51:222-231.

———, ———, and P. V. Fonnesbeck. 1984. Effects of prescribed burning on the nutritive quality of marsh plants in Utah. J. Wildl. Manage. 48:285-288.

Sugden, L. G. 1971. Metabolizable energy of small grains for mallards. J. Wildl. Manage. 35:781-785.

Teeter, J. W. 1965. Effects of sodium chloride on the growth and reproduction of sago pondweed. J. Wildl. Manage. 29:838-845.

Turner, R. J. 1980. The status of nongame values of Carson Lake, Nevada. Cal.-Neva. Wildl. Trans. 1980:6-10.

Ungar, I. A., D. K. Benner, and D. C. McGraw. 1979. The distribution and growth of *Salicornia europaea* on an inland salt pan. Ecology 60:329-336.

U.S. Fish and Wildlife Service. 1980. Future man-agement of Malheur Lake Marsh: recommenda-tions of the technical advisory committee. U.S. Fish and Wildl. Serv., Portland, Oreg. 85 pp.

van der Valk, A. G. 1981. Succession in wetlands: a Gleasonian approach. Ecology 62:688-696.

Verhoeven, J. T. A., P. P. W. M. Jacobs, and W. Van Vierssen. 1982. Life-strategies of aquatic plants: some critical notes and recommendations for further research. Pages 158-164 in J. Y. Symoens, S. S. Hooper, and P. Compere, eds. Studies on aquatic vascular plants. Royal Bot. Soc. of Belgium, Brussels.

Whyte, R. J., and E. G. Bolen. 1984. Impact of winter stress on mallard body composition. Condor 86:477-482.

———, and B. W. Cain. 1981. Wildlife habitat on grazed or ungrazed small pond shorelines in south Texas. J. Range Manage. 34:64-68.

Wobeser, G. A. 1981. Diseases of wild waterfowl. Plenum Press, N.Y. 300 pp.

Yeo, R. R. 1965. Life history of sago pondweed. Weeds 13:314-321.

THE CENTRAL, IMPERIAL, AND COACHELLA VALLEYS OF CALIFORNIA

MICKEY E. HEITMEYER[1], Department of Wildlife and Fisheries Biology, University of California, Davis, CA 95616

DANIEL P. CONNELLY, California Department of Fish and Game, 1416 Ninth Street, Sacramento, CA 95814

ROGER L. PEDERSON[2], Delta Waterfowl and Wetlands Research Station, RR1, Portage la Prairie, Manitoba, Canada R1N 3A1

Wetlands in California historically have hosted one of the largest concentrations of wintering waterfowl in the world. In the mid-1800s, an estimated 2 million ha of wetlands were present in California, and early explorers reported vast concentrations of waterfowl and other marsh and shore birds (California Department of Fish and Game 1983). As recently as the 1970s, an estimated 10-12 million ducks, geese, and swans wintered in, or migrated through, California (U.S. Fish and Wildlife Service 1978).

Wetlands in California occurred primarily in the Central Valley (Fig. 1), as did most waterfowl. Other significant waterfowl habitat was present in the Modoc Plateau, Klamath Basin, Big Valley, Honey Lake, Surprise Valley, coastal salt marshes (particularly Humboldt and San Francisco Bays), Owens Valley, Colorado River drainage, and the Imperial and Coachella valleys.

More than 95% of the historic wetland area in California has been destroyed or modified (Gilmer et al. 1982). Of the 115,000 ha of wetlands that remain in the Central Valley (U.S. Fish and Wildlife Service 1987a; Fig. 1), two-thirds are privately owned and managed for duck hunting; the remaining one-third is divided between state and federal ownership and managed by the California Department of Fish and Game (CDFG) as wildlife management areas (WMA) or by the U.S. Fish and Wildlife Service (USFWS) as national wildlife refuges (NWR) (Gilmer et al. 1982). Most of these wetlands are intensively managed; the cost for management may exceed that for any other wetland area in North America.

The purpose of this paper is to review existing information on the management of wetlands for waterfowl within the Central, Imperial, and Coachella valleys of California. These areas contain the majority of wetlands and wintering waterfowl in California. We describe historical and present wetlands; the evolution of management goals and strategies; current management goals relative to the nutritional and social requirements of waterfowl; and economic, political, and physical problems impeding management. Finally, we suggest needs for future research and information.

HABITAT CHARACTERISTICS

The Central Valley of California averages 64 km wide by 644 km long and is comprised of 2 lesser valleys (Sacramento in the north, San Joaquin in the south) and a delta where the two drainages meet (the Sacramento-San Joaquin River Delta [referred to as the Delta], Fig. 1). The Imperial and Coachella valleys adjoin the Salton Sea in southern California on the south and north, respectively (Fig. 1). The Central, Imperial, and Coachella valleys stretch over 7 degrees latitude and encompass a great diversity of geology, physiognomy, and climate. Because of this diversity, hydrology and plant com-

[1]Present address: California Waterfowl Association, 3840 Rosin Court, Suite 200, Sacramento, CA 95834.

[2]Present address: Ducks Unlimited, Inc., 9823 Old Winery Place, Suite 16, Sacramento, CA 95827.

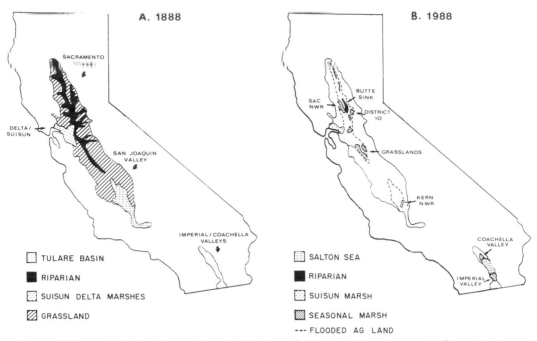

Fig. 1. Valleys of California and the distribution of historic (A) and current (B) wetlands and grasslands. Adapted from Roberts et al. (1977), U.S. Fish and Wildlife Service (1978), Madrone Associates (1980), and Barry (1981).

munities vary regionally and impose different constraints on wetland management. Hence, this paper describes characteristics of, and discusses management activities within, each region separately (i.e., Sacramento Valley, San Joaquin Valley, Sacramento-San Joaquin River Delta and Suisun Marsh, Imperial and Coachella valleys).

Sacramento Valley

The climate of the Sacramento Valley is typically mediterranean with cool, wet winters and hot, dry summers. Average annual rainfall is 50.8 cm, falling mostly between November and February (U.S. Department of Commerce 1986). Temperatures average 5 C in January and 23 C in July, the coldest and hottest months, respectively. Annually, there are <15 days of below-freezing temperatures.

The Sacramento Valley is drained by the Sacramento River and its tributaries and is bounded by the Klamath Mountain Range to the north, the Sierra Nevada to

the east, and the Coast Range to the west. Peak runoff and discharges down the Sacramento River occur in March (Kahrl 1979). With the exception of the lower reaches of the Mississippi River and certain areas of the Columbia and Ohio rivers, flood waters of the Sacramento River are greater than any other river in the United States (U.S.) (Scott and Marquiss 1984).

Historically, many small creeks and sloughs were braided throughout the Sacramento Valley floor. Some creeks ended in lower depressed "sinks" and did not join the main network of the Sacramento River except during floods (Thompson 1961, Scott and Marquiss 1984). Sedimentation and scouring associated with frequent flooding created mosaics of natural levees, abandoned channels, sinks, lowland swamps, and hummocks over the otherwise relatively flat floodplains (Lapham et al. 1909, Keller 1977, Scott and Marquiss 1984). The extent of these floodplains varied

Table 1. Area (ha) of wetland habitat (percentage of wetland area in parentheses) managed for permanently flooded-summer water (PSW), seasonally flooded-tule (SF-T), seasonally flooded moist soil (SF-MS), watergrass (Echinochloa spp.) (WG), riparian (RIP), and upland (UP) habitat types on private duck clubs and public waterfowl areas in California during 1986-87.

Habitat type	Sacramento[a] Valley		San Joaquin[b] Valley		Imperial and Coachella valleys[c]		Delta and Suisun Marsh[d]	
	Private	Public	Private	Public	Private	Public	Private	Public
PSW	1,296 (5.4)	725 (9.3)	2,512 (12.9)	209 (4.4)	553 (28.8)	324 (18.4)	4,212 (24.5)	1,849 (34.1)[e]
SF-T	11,077 (45.8)	8,931 (50.5)	5,470 (28.2)	1,306 (27.3)	526 (27.4)	381 (21.6)	4,900 (28.5)	1,620 (30.0)
SF-MS	8,505 (35.1)	2,204 (28.3)	11,321 (58.2)	2,618 (54.6)	810 (42.1)	389 (22.1)	7,006 (40.8)	1,742 (32.2)
WG	2,268 (9.4)	908 (11.7)	122 (0.6)	243 (5.1)	34 (1.8)	666 (37.8)	101 (0.6)	61 (1.1)
RIP	1,053 (4.4)	16 (0.2)	20 (0.1)	415 (8.7)	2,005[f]	111[f]	972 (5.7)	134 (2.5)
UP	1,822	2,754	7,554	2,779	526	676	2,714	1,215

[a]Data adapted from Sacramento Valley Waterfowl Habitat Management Committee 1984; Sacramento NWR Complex unpublished reports; Heitmeyer, unpublished data.

[b]Only west grasslands. Data adapted from 1979 Soil Conservation Service wetland vegetative survey; unpublished California Dep. Fish and Game (CDFG) reports provided by J. Beam; and U.S. Fish and Wildlife Service (USFWS) records supplied by G. Zahm.

[c]Data adapted from Fredrickson (1980); CDFG aerial survey estimates, Oct-Mar 1984-87; USFWS records supplied by G. Kramer; CDFG estimates provided by B. Henry; and Imperial Irrigation District estimates provided by C. Holmes.

[d]Combined Delta Suisun area. Data for the Suisun Marsh from Miller et al. (1975) with adjustments provided by F. Wernett. Data for the Delta provided by F. Wernett.

[e]Primarily on Sherman Island WMA.

[f]Mostly salt cedar tamarisk (Tamarix pentandra).

from a few hundred meters to several kilometers wide (Thompson 1961, Katibah 1984).

The extent of wetlands in the Sacramento Valley in the mid-1800s is not entirely known, but probably exceeded 600,000 ha (Fig. 1). Riparian forests and semipermanently flooded tule marshes composed >75% of these wetlands (Thompson 1961, Katibah 1984). At present only 32,000 ha of wetlands remain; these are dominated by semipermanently flooded tule marshes (Table 1). Most wetlands have been drained for agriculture or have been altered by land leveling and construction of levees, removal of riparian forests, and controlled water regimes. Approximately 65%, 26%, and 9% of remaining wetlands are in private, federal, and state ownership, respectively.

Riparian forests formerly were present adjacent to rivers and creeks. Sloughs, oxbows, and meander scars were interspersed within riparian forests. Riparian forests were flooded by river overflow waters during periods of increased precipitation and runoff in winter, and from snowmelt runoff from surrounding mountains in spring. Floods also occasionally occurred in fall (U.S. Department of Commerce 1986). As high

water receded in late spring and summer, water drained from riparian forests but became trapped in low depressions behind natural levees and created permanently or semipermanently flooded marshes.

Plant communities in permanently and semipermanently flooded wetlands were dominated by dense emergents, whereas those in seasonally and ephemerally flooded wetlands were dominated by moist-soil annual and perennial plants (Table 2). Grassland communities were located on alkaline soils at higher elevations of seasonal wetlands and supported extensive saltgrass flats dotted with vernal pools (Crampton 1976). These grasslands often were flooded by late winter and spring rains and occasionally were flooded from river overflows in wet winters.

Presently, 162,000 ha of agricultural lands in the Sacramento Valley are subject to flooding from river overflows and local runoff during wet winters. More than 32,000 ha of harvested rice fields are intentionally flooded for waterfowl hunting during fall and winter (California Department of Fish and Game 1979). Also, 2 major flood-control bypasses adjoin the Sacramento River and flood up

Table 2. Plant species commonly occurring in wetland habitat types in the Sacramento Valley (SAC), San Joaquin Valley (SJ), Suisun Marsh (SU), and Imperial-Coachella valleys (IC)[a]

Habitat type[b] and common species	Region			
	SAC	SJ	SU	IC
Riparian Forest				
Boxelder (*Acer negundo*)	+	+		
Alder (*Alnus* spp.)	+			
Buttonwillow (*Cephalanthus occidentalis*)	+	+		
Dogwoods (*Cornus* spp.)	+			
Oregon ash (*Fraxinus latifolia*)	+			
Fremont's cottonwood (*Populus Fremontii*)	+	+		
California sycamore (*Platanus racemosa*)	+	+		
Valley oak (*Quercus lobata*)	+	+		
Poison oak (*Rhus diversiloba*)	+			
Wildrose (*Rosa californica*)	+	+		
Blackberries (*Rubus* spp.)	+	+		
Willows (*Salix* spp.)	+	+		
Elderberry (*Sambucus* spp.)	+			
Salt cedar tamarisk				+
Wild grape (*Vitis californica*)	+	+		
Permanent/summer marsh				
Water fern (*Azolla* spp.)	+	+		
Water hyssops (*Bacopa* spp.)	+	+		
Muskgrass (*Chara* spp.)		+	+	+
Marsh pennywort (*Hydrocotyle* spp.)	+			
Water primrose (*Jussiaea californica*)	+	+	+	+
Duckweeds (*Lemna* spp.)	+	+		
Frog fruit (*Lippia* spp.)	+	+		
Water-horehound (*Lycopus* spp.)	+	+		
Marsilea (*Marsilea mucronata*)	+			
Milfoils (*Myriophyllum* spp.)	+			
Water nymphs (*Najas* spp.)	+	+		
Common reed (*Phragmites communis*)			+	
Pond weeds (*Potamogeton* spp.)	+	+		+
Widgeon grass (*Ruppia maritima*)			+	+
Arrowheads (*Sagittaria* spp.)	+	+		
Tule bulrush (*Scirpus acutus*)	+	+	+	
California bulrush (*Scirpus californica*)			+	
Olney bulrush (*Scirpus olneyi*)			+	
Alkali bulrush (*Scirpus robustus*)	+	+		+
Cattails (*Typha* spp.)	+	+	+	+
Vervains (*Verbena* spp.)	+	+		
Seasonal Marsh				
Horned pondweed (*Zannichellia palustris*)		+	+	+
Iodine bush (*Allenrolfea occidentalis*)			+	
Ammania (*Ammania* spp.)	+	+		
Fathen (*Atriplex patula*)			+	
Carex sedges (*Carex* spp.)	+	+	+	+
Centromedia (*Centromedia pungens*)		+		
Brass buttons (*Cotula cornopifolia*)			+	
Pricklegrass (*Crypsis niliaca*)	+	+	+	+
Bermuda grass (*Cynodon dactylon*)	+	+	+	+
Nutgrasses (*Cyperus* spp.)	+	+	+	+
Saltgrass (*Distichilis spicata*)	+	+	+	+
Watergrass	+	+	+	+
Spikerushes (*Eleocharis* spp.)	+	+	+	+
Gumplant (*Grindelia* spp.)	+			
Swamp timothy (*Heleochloa schenoides*)	+		+	+
Rushes (*Juncus* spp.)	+	+	+	+
Baltic rush (*Juncus balticus*)			+	+
Smartweeds (*Polygonum* spp.)	+	+	+	+
Docks (*Rumex* spp.)	+	+	+	+
Tule bulrush	+	+	+	+
Alkali bulrush	+	+	+	+
Alkali mallow (*Sida hederacea*)	+	+		
Cattails	+	+	+	+
Cocklebur (*Xanthium* spp.)	+	+	+	+
Grasslands/vernal pools				
Allocarya (*Allocarya* spp.)	+	+		
Soft chess (*Bromus mollis*)	+	+		
Carex sedges	+	+		
Pricklegrass	+	+		
Saltgrass	+	+		
Downingia (*Downingia* spp.)	+	+		
Frankenia (*Frankenia grandifoliz*)	+	+		
Swamp timothy (*Heleocloa schenoides*)	+	+		

[a] Plant nomenclature follows Mason (1957) and Munz and Keck (1975). Data are from Jepson (1893), Lapham (1909), Bryant (1914), Strahorn et al. (1914), Hoover (1935), Crampton (1959, 1976), Thompson (1961), Arkley (1962), Mall (1969), Gill and Buckman (1974), Miller et al. (1975), Conard et al. (1977), Keller (1977), Mac Donald (1977), Madrone Associates (1980), Zedler et al. (1982), Josselyn (1983), and Katibah (1984).

[b] Riparian forests are habitats dominated by woody growth occurring immediately adjacent to natural water courses; permanent/summer marsh are wetlands dominated by emergent vegetation and containing water for most, or all, of the year; seasonal marsh are wetlands dominated by short-stature annual and perennial vegetation and flooded from 1-8 months annually, typically from early fall through early spring; grassland/vernal pools are upland and emphemerally flooded depressions dominated by grasses or annual vegetation, typically flooded for < 2 months in late winter and early spring.

to 26,000 ha in an average of 3 of every 5 winters (Kahrl 1979). Lands within the bypasses are mostly farmed for rice and row crops, but idle lands, ditches, pasturelands, and some marshes are also present. Reservoirs constructed on the Sacramento River and its tributaries also provide some sanctuary habitat.

San Joaquin Valley

The climate of the San Joaquin Valley is arid; mean annual rainfall is <23 cm and occurs primarily from October-February (U.S. Department of Commerce 1986). Temperatures average 6 C in January and 25 C in July. Typically, there are few, if any, days with below-freezing temperatures.

The San Joaquin Valley is bounded by the Delta to the north, the Tehachapi Mountains to the south, the Sierra Nevada to the east, and the Coast Range to the west. It is divided into 2 distinct basins: the San Joaquin (northern two-thirds) and the Tulare (southern one-third). The San Joaquin River and its tributaries drain the San Joaquin Basin. The Tulare Basin, is separated from the San Joaquin Basin by an elevational uplift created by the merging alluvial fans of the Kings River and the Los Gatos Creek. Historically, waters from tributary rivers flowed into the Tulare Basin, which had no outlet to the sea. During long-term "wet cycles," Tulare Lake in the Tulare Basin filled to a depth of 27 m and diverted water from the Kings River and the Tulare Basin into the San Joaquin River.

Peak water flows and associated river overflows are lower (Fig. 2) and later in the San Joaquin Valley than in the Sacramento Valley (Kahrl 1979). Consequently, deposition of sediments and formation of natural levees and floodplains were less extensive (<81,000 ha) in the San Joaquin Valley (Strahorn et al. 1914, Arkley 1962), and riparian wetlands were generally confined to narrow strips immediately adjacent to tributaries (Katibah 1984).

Although water flows were low in the San Joaquin Basin, when flooding did

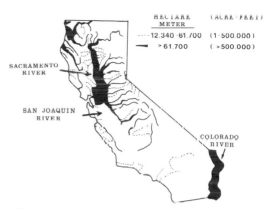

Fig. 2. Average annual streamflows in major streams and rivers in California (from Warner and Hendrix 1985).

occur, waters easily breached low natural levees and spread over extensive areas of the relatively flat valley floor. Depressions behind natural levees or in old meander scars held water until early summer and supported dense stands of cattail and tules (Table 2). Higher elevations usually became flooded only for short periods during late winter or spring, and historically supported a variety of herbaceous plants, sedges, and grasses tolerant of the highly alkaline soils (Table 1, Wester 1981). Vernal pools were also common at higher elevations and were usually inundated from December-February (Crampton 1959, Holland and Griggs 1976). The historical extent of wetlands in the San Joaquin Basin probably exceeded 400,000 ha, most of which was seasonally flooded grasslands (Fig. 1).

Wetlands within the Tulare Basin were historically confined to Tulare, Kern, Goose, and Buena Vista lakes, which covered 253,000 ha and were flooded for most of the year, except during extreme drought (U.S. Fish and Wildlife Service 1978). These lakes received most of their annual water input in spring from snowmelt from the Sierra Nevada. Following winters with heavy snows, the basins of all of these lakes were connected by sloughs. Derby (in Dasmann 1966:154-55) described these lakes in 1849-50 as large bodies of shallow open water surrounded by wide bands of dense tule marsh, sometimes up to 16 km wide. Seasonally flooded grasslands were also present on the south side of Tulare Lake.

At present, <51,000 ha of wetlands remain in the San Joaquin Valley (Table 1); most of these are seasonally flooded ponds in the San Joaquin Basin (Grassland Water District 1987). In late spring and summer, evapotranspiration can be as high as 1.5 cm per day. Where a wetland is supplied with water during summer, the transition zone between marsh and desert is usually only a few meters.

The majority of the once vast marshes of the Tulare Basin have been drained and converted to agricultural croplands (U.S. Fish and Wildlife Service 1978). Crops, especially barley, in the Tulare Basin often are flooded for a few weeks following harvest and prior to planting another crop (referred to as preirrigation); this shallow flooding provides some habitat for ducks in early fall (Jones and Stokes Associates 1988). Ponds used for evaporation of irrigation drain water are also present. Lakes on tributaries of the San Joaquin River provide some waterfowl habitat, mostly used as loafing areas. Ownership of San Joaquin Valley wetlands is 63% private, 25% federal, and 13% state.

Sacramento-San Joaquin River Delta and Suisun Marsh

Temperatures in the Delta and Suisun Marsh average 8 C in January and 22 C in July. Mean precipitation is 20 cm and occurs mostly between November and March (U.S. Department of Commerce 1986).

Delta.— The delta is an inland 284,000-ha network of sloughs and islands that formed at the confluence of the Sacramento, San Joaquin, Mokelumne, and Consumnes rivers. Historically, the delta was comprised of nearly 100 islands separated by a labyrinth of sloughs and

channels. Tidal freshwater marshes covered most of the islands (Thompson 1957, Atwater 1970, Madrone Associates 1980). These marshes ranged from dense tule marshes immediately behind alluvial levees to riparian forests at higher inland elevations (Madrone Associates 1980). Most lands in the delta were close to mean sea level (MSL), with highest points only 4.5 m above MSL. When flood and runoff waters reached the delta from December-May, the entire area was inundated (Basye 1981).

Of the original 284,000 ha of wetlands in the delta, only 7,290 ha remain (Fig. 1). Beginning as early as 1852, levees were constructed, wetlands drained, and lands farmed on delta islands (Thompson 1957). Currently, all islands except Frank's Tract and portions of Mildrid and Sherman islands are protected by large levees; the elevation of many of the islands is >4.5 m below MSL. Lands in the delta are farmed for corn, wheat, rice, safflower, and milo (Smith 1979). About 8,100 ha of these croplands are flooded each winter for waterfowl hunting, or to leach soil salts, and to provide some seasonal wetland habitat (California Department of Fish and Game 1979). Levee breaks and floods also have inundated some islands in recent years and created additional temporary wetland habitat.

Suisun Marsh.—The Suisun Marsh is an estuarine wetland created 6,000-7,000 BP when sea levels rose and expanded into San Pablo and Suisun bays (Atwater et al. 1977, Josselyn 1983). The Suisun Marsh was then comprised of 12 tidally flooded islands and inland areas, interwoven by numerous sloughs and the Sacramento River.

Historically, most of the Suisun Marsh was brackish (Josselyn 1983). A gradient of tidal influence, salinities, elevations, and marsh vegetation existed from Suisun Bay inland to the surrounding hills. Below mean low-tide level, vegetation was dominated by California bulrush.

Between the mean low-tide and mean high-water levels, a mixture of cattails, California bulrush, tule bulrush, Olney bulrush, and alkali bulrush was present. Above the high-water level, a varied group of halophytes occurred. Where salinities were high, pickleweed, saltgrass, fathen, and gumplant were found. In areas where salinity was lower, brass buttons and baltic rush were common.

Currently, tide gates and levees protect most of the Suisun Marsh from flooding. Salinities have gradually increased in the marsh as waters have been diverted from the Sacramento and San Joaquin rivers (Mall 1969). Attempts to farm many of the diked lands in the Suisun Marsh were made in the 1920s-50s; however, high soil and water salinities precluded most crop production, and lands now are maintained as wetlands and managed as duck clubs. Vegetation in the Suisun Marsh is presently dominated by relatively salt-tolerant robust emergents (Table 2). Pickleweed, brass buttons, and fathen occur near high tide level, and saltgrass, baltic rush, and common reed occur above the high tide level.

The current wetland area in the Suisun Marsh (22,000 ha) is only slightly reduced from the historic area (24,300 ha) (U.S. Fish and Wildlife Service 1978). Urban expansion and agricultural development destroyed some marsh lands, but creation of private duck clubs has been primarily responsible for saving these wetlands. The Suisun Marsh Protection Act of 1977 and the 1987 "Suisun Marsh Preservation Agreement" currently provide adequate water quality in tidal sloughs. This water quality is maintained by large salinity control gates at the east end of Montezuma Slough—the principal water course into the marsh. Ownership of Suisun Marsh wetlands is 84% private and 16% state.

Imperial and Coachella Valleys

The climate of the Imperial and Coachella valleys is arid. Average annual rainfall is <5 cm and temperatures average 10 C in January and 32 C in July.

The Imperial and Coachella valleys and the Cahuilla Basin (the present Salton Sea) were created along the San Andreas fault and represented an extension of the Gulf of California (Carpelan 1961). During the Pleistocene, the Colorado River created a fanlike delta separating the valleys from the ocean, and as the river flowed over the almost flat delta, it sometimes flowed southward into the Gulf of California and at other times northward into the Imperial and Coachella valleys. When northward flows occurred, a large, inland freshwater lake (the Salton Sink) was created. At other times, the extremely arid climate of the region dried existing wetlands and maintained a desert ecosystem.

The last known historical flow of the Colorado River into the Imperial and Coachella valleys occurred in 1891 and created a lake of 40,000 ha (Carpelan 1961). When this lake water evaporated, a short-lived inland salt marsh was created. It subsequently dried, leaving behind huge salt deposits. In 1901, Colorado River water was diverted into the Imperial Valley through an old river channel to supply irrigation water. In 1905, this diversion faltered and water from the Colorado River flowed into the Imperial Valley, creating the present Salton Sea.

Since 1907, waters of the Colorado River that enter Salton Sea have been controlled by an elaborate irrigation system originating near Yuma, Arizona. In the early 1900s, the permanent water in the Salton Sea and scattered wetlands on the Colorado River Delta attracted migrating and wintering waterfowl to the Imperial and Coachella valleys for longer periods than in previous years (Fredrickson 1980). This increased waterfowl population subsequently encouraged private groups to flood lands and create freshwater ponds for waterfowl hunting. These artificial marshes, which total 3,683 ha at present (Table 1), created "new" wetlands in an otherwise dry, desert environment. Private duck clubs compose 52%, and public lands compose 48%, of these wetlands. Vegetation present in these "new" wetlands consists mostly of salt-grass, alkali bulrush, swamp timothy, bermuda grass, smartweeds, and dock (Table 2). In areas where water is fresher and more permanent, cattail and common reed occur. Levees are often overgrown with salt cedar tamarisk and arrow-weed (*Pluchea sericea*).

HABITAT IMPORTANCE RELATIVE TO WATERFOWL REQUIREMENTS

Abundance, Chronology, and Distribution of Waterfowl

Some waterfowl are present in the Central, Imperial, and Coachella valleys year-round. Mallards (*Anas platyrhynchos*) are the most common breeding waterfowl. Other species that commonly nest in California include Great Basin Canada geese (*Branta canadensis moffitti*), cinnamon teal (*A. cyanoptera*), gadwall (*A. strepera*), northern shoveler (*A. clypeata*), wood duck (*Aix sponsa*), redhead (*Aythya americana*), ruddy duck (*Oxyura jamaicensis*) and, in some locations, northern pintail (*A. acuta*) and American wigeon (*A. americana*). Post-breeding dispersals of breeding adults and young concentrate several hundred thousand ducks, especially mallards, in the Klamath Basin and Sacramento Valley in late summer and early fall.

Waterfowl concentrations are greatest in California during fall and winter when migrants from northern latitudes join locally breeding or produced birds (Kozlik 1975, Bellrose 1980). The Central, Imperial, and Coachella valleys wintered 3.5 million ducks, and 0.5 million geese and swans, annually during 1978-87 (Table 3). This represents >60% of all waterfowl (excluding sea ducks) wintering in the Pacific Flyway, and about 20% of those wintering in the entire U.S. Of special importance, California wintered >20% of all mallards, wigeon, green-winged teal, shovelers, canvasbacks, and ruddy ducks; >30% of all lesser snow geese and tundra swans; >50% of all pintails, white-fronted geese, and Ross' geese; >80% of all cackling and Great Basin Canada geese; and 100% of the Aleutian Canada and tule geese in the U.S.

Migrants begin arriving in the Central Valley in early August (Bellrose 1980). Early migrants are mainly adult male pintails and most concentrate in the Sacramento Valley (also, formerly in the Tulare Basin) (Miller 1985). By October, large numbers of female and young pintails, and all sexes and ages of wigeon, shovelers, gadwalls, green-winged teal, and ruddy ducks have arrived. In contrast, most locally nesting cinnamon teal have migrated south into the Imperial and Coachella valleys and Mexico by mid-October. Tundra swans and most geese arrive in the Sacramento Valley by mid-November; however, many may remain in the Klamath Basin in some years. White-fronted geese arrive earlier than other geese and swans. Smaller numbers of ring-necked ducks, buffleheads, redheads, and canvasbacks also arrive in November. Peak numbers of most species occur in mid-December.

Most mallards, tule geese, snow geese, large Canada geese, wood ducks, and wigeons winter in the Sacramento Valley; but most shovelers, green-winged teal, and gadwalls winter in the San Joaquin Valley (Table 3). Ross' geese, cackling Canada geese, Aleutian Canada geese, tundra swans, and white-fronted geese traditionally begin the winter in the Sacramento Valley, but by late winter, most have moved to the Delta or the San Joaquin Valley (Rienecker 1965, McLandress 1979, Woolington et al. 1979). Dabbling ducks, especially pintails, move

Table 3. Mean number of waterfowl counted in the Central, Imperial, and Coachella valleys of California during U.S. Fish and Wildlife Service mid-winter inventories, 1978-87.

Species	Region				Imperial-Coachella valleys	% of Pacific Flyway 1977-86 Ave.
	Sacramento Valley	San Joaquin Valley	Suisun Marsh	Delta		
Mallard	314,712	30,438	15,221	4,667	389	24
Gadwall	11,698	23,137	602	25	465	83
American wigeon	403,038	10,913	9,318	847	5,623	64
Green-winged teal (*Anas crecca*)	16,336	90,479	6,913	961	3,092	89
Cinnamon teal	131	2,541	42	2	242	74
Northern shoveler	122,557	209,142	28,456	3,022	12,670	77
Northern pintail	1,429,698	238,191	60,347	141,190	14,091	79
Wood duck	1,062	15				76
Redhead	84	87	81		336	3
Canvasback (*Aythya valisineria*)	11,735	2,036	3,446	7,065	1,691	39
Scaup (*A. affinis* and *A. marila*)	217	368	1,711	960	1,760	4
Ring-necked Duck (*A. collaris*)	3,896	717	404	85	110	56
Bufflehead (*Bucephala albeola*)	99	173	54	81	49	1
Ruddy Duck	16,361	15,985	2,558	2,184	16,269	49
Canada geese[a]	3,807	4,802	586	448	3,296	[b]
White fronted geese (*Anser albifrons*)	20,092	4,884	6,491	20,768		83
Snow and Ross' geese (*Chen caerulescens* and *C. rossii*)	304,310	35,397	82	19,278	16,835	86
Cackling Canada geese (*Branta canadensis minima*)	10,792	4,128	2,520	830		80
Aleutian Canada geese (*B. c. leucopareia*)	360	1,035	72	59		100
Tundra swan (*Cygnus columbianus*)	21,283	357	4	19,999		66

[a]Mostly Great Basin Canada geese.
[b]Percentages of Pacific Flyway totals are not calculated because of varying populations present.

among valley areas during winter (Rienecker 1976, 1987); movements are erratic depending on disturbance, food availability, and wetland conditions.

Shifts in the winter distribution of many species have probably occurred since the late-1800s in response to habitat and land-use changes. For example, market hunting records indicate that large numbers of snow and Ross' geese were present in wetlands surrounding San Francisco Bay in the late 1800s (Stine 1980). With the large increase in small-grain production in the Sacramento Valley and major losses of coastal wetlands, snow geese are now nearly absent from San Francisco Bay and Suisun marshes, but abundant in the Sacramento Valley. The abundance of small grains, and habitat loss in other areas, have probably also attracted and held larger numbers of

pintails, mallards, green-winged teal, wigeons, and small Canada geese in the Sacramento Valley in recent years.

Pintails are the first ducks to begin migrating out of the Central Valley in spring; major movements northward begin in mid-February (Bellrose 1980). By March, most pintails have left, and large numbers of wigeons and geese have migrated northward into the Klamath Basin, the Modoc Plateau, and the Willamette Valley of Oregon. By mid-April, most shovelers, gadwalls, ruddy ducks, green-winged teal, and buffleheads have migrated northward, whereas cinnamon teal have returned to the Central Valley.

Resource Requirements and Availability

Waterfowl undergo several biologically important and nutritionally costly processes throughout the year (e.g., molt, migration, pairing, nesting, and brood rooring) These physiologic and behavioral events require different quantities and qualities of nutrients, and impose different social and behavioral constraints on individuals (e.g., Weller 1975, Raveling 1979, Heitmeyer 1985, McKinney 1986, Fredrickson and Heitmeyer 1988). Species meet these requirements by varying habitat use, food consumption, flocking structures, and daily activities mediated by morphological and behavioral adaptations. The chronology and number of annual events that occur in California vary among species, and within species by sex and age, and in relation to habitat and climatic conditions (Heitmeyer 1985, 1987, Miller 1986).

Although most waterfowl have similar requirements during each annual event (e.g., all species have increased protein requirements during egg laying and molt), strategies exhibited by species to meet these requirements are different. Historically, the abundance and wide diversity of wetland habitat types present in California provided large quantities of foods and habitats necessary to support large numbers of waterfowl throughout the year.

The resources needed by waterfowl during annual events in California are provided in different habitat types (Table 4). Permanently and semipermanently flooded habitats such as tule marshes and backwater sloughs provide tubers from plants such as arrowheads, abundant floating and submergent plants, aquatic insects and their larvae, snails, and zooplankton (Usinger 1956, Josselyn 1983, Reid 1985, Murkin and Kadlec 1986). Permanently flooded habitats provide dense emergent cover used for protection by wintering birds from winds, rains, and predators. These habitats also provide nest sites for over-water nesters such as redheads, and escape cover for broods and flightless adults.

Seasonally flooded marshes range from those that support an interspersion of scattered cattails and tules (referred to as tule mix habitats) to those that primarily support annual plants such as watergrass, swamp timothy, pricklegrass, alkali bulrush, and smartweeds (collectively referred to as moist-soil habitats). Seasonally flooded habitats usually provide abundant seeds, tubers, and aquatic insects and their larvae (Table 4). Terrestrial invertebrates also are available when wetlands are first inundated. Abundance, biomass, and types of invertebrates in seasonal marshes depend on plant species composition, length of flooding, detrital material, and decomposition rates of dominant plants (Grodhaus 1980, Murkin et al. 1982, Nelson and Kadlec 1984, Reid 1985, Murkin and Kadlec 1986). Stems and leaves of sedges, bulrushes, and grasses provide forage for geese and wigeons. Dense stands of annual wetland plants also provide nest sites to ducks during drawdown stages (McLandress and Yarris 1987, McLandress et al. 1987).

Uplands, sedge meadows, and vernal pools provide forage for geese and wigeons, and when flooded, these uplands and vernal pools also provide seeds, terrestrial insects, earthworms, and spiders (Alexander 1976, Holland and Jain 1977). Uplands also provide nest sites for many waterfowl, especially where spring vegetation is dense (McLandress and Yarris 1987).

Riparian forests provide acorns, samaras, berries, moist-soil seeds, benthic crustaceans, and fingernail clams (Pisidium spp.) (Table 4, Batema et al. 1985, White 1985, Fredrickson and Heitmeyer 1988). Riparian forests also supply nesting and roost sites to wood ducks (Parr et al. 1979, Bellrose 1980), and courtship and pairing habitat for mallards and wood ducks (Armbruster 1982, Heitmeyer 1985).

Croplands supply residual and waste grains that are especially attractive to

Table 4. Resources provided in various wetland habitat types present in California. Number of plus signs denotes relative quantities of available resources.

Habitat[a]	Small grains	Moist-soil seeds	Acorns	Tubers	Graze	Aquatic plants	Invertebrates	Thermal cover	Nest sites
PSW				+	+	+++	++	+++	+[b]
Seasonal									
Tule mix		++		++	+	+	++	+++	+[bc]
Watergrass		+++		+			+	++	
Moist-soil		+++		++	+	+	+++	+	+[c]
Alkali bulrush		++		++	+		+	++	+[c]
Pickleweed		+			+		++		
Uplands		+[d]		+	+++		+		+++
Riparian		+	+++	+		+	+++	++	+[c]
Cropland	+++	+			+		+		+

[a]PSW = permanently flooded and summer water; Seasonal = seasonally flooded and dominated by cattails and tules (Tule Mix), watergrass, moist-soil plants, alkali bulrush, and pickleweed.
[b]For species that nest over water.
[c]If water is not present.
[d]When flooded.

dabbling ducks when shallowly flooded. Some moist-soil "weeds" (e.g., watergrass) also commonly grow in croplands, especially in rice. Common invertebrates in rice fields include adult and larval insects (especially Chironomidae) and spiders (Araneae) (Darby 1962). Flooded rice fields are used by adult mallards during prelaying and laying periods, and by newly hatched broods. In early spring, crops such as winter wheat, barley, and alfalfa (*Medicago sativa*) provide forage for geese and wigeons, and, later in spring, they provide nesting sites to locally nesting ducks.

The existence requirements of waterfowl wintering in the Central, Imperial, and Coachella valleys of California can be estimated and compared to estimates of food provided in existing wetlands. An average of 75 million use-days by geese and swans and 500 million use-days by ducks occurs from September through March in the Central, Imperial, and Coachella valleys (calculated from chronology and survey data in Table 3, Bellrose 1980). The basal metabolic energy requirements (BMR) (calculated using the equation of Aschoff and Pohl 1970) of these waterfowl are 35.6×10^9 kcal for geese and swans and 100×10^9 kcal for ducks. If natural foods have an apparent metabolizable energy of 2.5-3.5 kcal/g (Miller 1987), then an average of 237 kg of available food/ha must be provided on the 120,000 ha of wetlands (excluding rice areas) remaining in the valleys of California just to satisfy requirements. Productive processes such as molt, migration, and reproduction of waterfowl are usually several times the cost of BMR, however, and when daily flight time is also considered, the food production on wetlands necessary to support current wintering and local breeding populations is estimated at 700-950 kg/ha. We emphasize that waterfowl numbers were much greater in years previous to the last 10; therefore, food requirements were also greater during these earlier years.

Impacts of Habitat Alteration

Several examples illustrate the impact of habitat loss or alteration on waterfowl in California. First, the large reduction of permanently flooded freshwater wetlands has reduced the amount of habitat available for nesting sites for over-water nesters such as ruddy ducks and redheads. The reduction of these wetlands also has reduced cover and food for broods of all species that nest locally, and aquatic plant foods needed by breeding and wintering canvasbacks, redheads, wigeon, and gadwalls. Loss of permanent wetlands has reduced nesting attempts and local production by all waterfowl.

Second, the destruction of >95% of riparian wetlands in California has reduced habitats needed by wood ducks throughout the year and by mallards and tule geese in winter. Wood duck and tule goose numbers presently are low in California. Mallards have adapted to the loss of riparian habitats by switching to waste grains to supply high-energy foods in midwinter. Protein is available to mallards from the invertebrates found in remnant riparian areas, in seasonally flooded marshes, and in rice fields. As mallards have switched to modified habitats to acquire resources, they must compete with many other species of dabbling ducks for invertebrates in marshes, be exposed to unknown biomagnification of pesticides from invertebrates consumed in rice fields, and face possible nutrient deficiencies because small grains lack adequate protein, minerals, and vitamins. The Butte Sink (Fig. 3), which contains the largest remaining area of riparian habitat in the Central Valley, supports large numbers of mallards and wood ducks in winter. Further reduction of this habitat in the Butte Sink could be devastating for these species.

Finally, changes in water quality from increased contaminants or salinity have changed plant and invertebrate communities, and thus have directly affected waterfowl populations in several areas of California. Increases in salinity in the Suisun Marsh have resulted in lower seed production of waterfowl food plants and caused a shift in plant species composition toward more salt-tolerant species (Mall 1969). Similarly, increased contamination by natural salts has occurred in the San Joaquin, Imperial, and Coachella valleys (Fredrickson 1980, Grasslands Water District 1987). Selenium contamination in the San Joaquin Valley has reduced or contaminated invertebrates and seeds needed by wintering and breeding waterfowl and created mutational deformities in embryos (Ohlendorf et al. 1986a, Zahm 1986). These changes in food resources may have been partly responsible for reduced waterfowl populations in the Suisun Marsh, San Joaquin, Imperial, and Coachella valleys in recent years.

HABITAT MANAGEMENT

Historical Development

The management of wetlands for waterfowl in California has a long and varied history. We consider this management as occurring in 4 eras: (1) 1880-1935: early decline of waterfowl populations, mosquito abatement, establishment of duck clubs; (2) 1936-1960: crop depredations, establishment of refuges; (3) 1960-1980: stabilized duck populations, enhancement of food production; (4) 1980-present: decline of waterfowl populations, management of marsh complexes, enhancement of breeding efforts.

1880-1935.—Sport hunting of waterfowl first became a common activity in California in the 1840s and 1850s (DeWitt 1910, Exley 1931, Stine 1980). The first duck club in California was established in 1879 in the Suisun Marsh (McAllister 1930, Stoner 1937). Market and some sport hunting were also common in the Delta (Stine 1980), Sacramento Valley (McGowan 1961), and San Joaquin Valley (Exley 1931) in the late 1800s and early 1900s, but establishment of duck clubs and eventual management of wetlands in these areas were later than in south San Francisco Bay, Napa, and Suisun marshes.

Reductions in waterfowl numbers (apparently because of market hunting and decreased wetland habitats) were noted throughout California as early as the 1870s. One of the first game laws in California outlawed shooting of wood ducks (Grinnell and Bryant 1914), and Lake Merritt in Oakland was established

Fig. 3. Seasonally flooded emergent wetland typical on private duck clubs in the Butte Sink of the Sacramento Valley. Emergent vegetation is primarily cattail and tules; trees are mostly black willow (*Salix nigra*). Water is generally present from September through May or June.

as the first state waterfowl refuge in 1870 (Richards 1916). In 1913, the California legislature passed the Flint-Cary Law outlawing market hunting. This law was overturned in 1914, and it was not until the 1918 enactment of the Migratory Bird Treaty Act and the 1923 passage of legislation by the California legislature that it became illegal to sell wild waterfowl.

Drought in the Canadian prairies further reduced duck numbers in North America during the late 1920s and early 1930s (Farrington 1945). Wetlands continued to be drained in the 1920s, and by 1926, much of the remaining wetland habitat was in duck clubs (California Department of Fish and Game 1983). Because of concern over the lack of wetlands and sanctuaries, 4 state waterfowl refuges were purchased from 1929-31 (Table 5).

In the 1910s and 1920s, mosquitos and the diseases they carried became a concern

for growing urban populations, many of which were located near historic wetlands (Elbright et al. 1916). Mosquito abatement districts became established and enforced regulations prohibiting the fluctuation of water levels in wetlands from spring through fall. Additionally, ditches were constructed to drain many wetland areas, and pesticides such as DDT were commonly used to control mosquitos.

1936-1960.— In the late 1930s and early 1940s, Canadian prairies became wet again, and waterfowl populations increased dramatically (Farrington 1945). As many as 50 million ducks and geese may have wintered in California in the 1940s (Arend 1967); however, wetland area in California had been reduced to <400,000 ha by that time. By 1945, 97,200 ha of rice were grown in California. The combination of increased waterfowl populations, decreased wetland area, shortage of ammunition during World War II, and wet weather that delayed crop harvesting

Table 5. Chronology of waterfowl habitat acquisition[a] by the U.S. Fish and Wildlife Service (NWR) and the California Department of Fish and Game (WMA) in California.

Area	Year established	Additions	Total area (ha)	Wetland area (ha)
Sacramento Valley				
Gray Lodge WMA	1931	1952-71	3,483	1,822
Sacramento NWR	1937	1971	4,371	2,491
Sutter NWR	1944	1953-56	1,049	1,011
Colusa NWR	1945	1949-53	1,636	1,040
Delevan NWR	1962		2,281	1,258
Butte Sink NWR	1980	1987	292	270
San Joaquin Valley				
Los Banos WMA	1929	1965	1,299	972
Merced NWR	1951		1,038	620
Mendota WMA	1954	1955-56	3,825	2,632
Kern NWR	1960		4,300	1,296
Volta WMA	1965		1,094	1,053
San Luis NWR	1967	1970	2,973	1,080
Kesterson NWR	1970		2,390	1,059
Imperial-Coachella Valley				
Salton Sea NWR	1930	1948	15,073	115
Imperial WMA	1931	1954	3,169	1,539
Delta-Suisun Marsh				
Joice Island WMA	1931		764	726
Grizzly Island WMA	1950		3,556	2,481
Sherman Island WMA	1965		1,256	688

[a]Ownership by fee title.

created large crop depredations by waterfowl in the Sacramento, San Joaquin, Imperial, and Coachella valleys in the 1940s. Crop damages caused by waterfowl peaked at $1.75 million during 1943 (Horn 1949, Biehn 1951). Sacramento NWR was established in 1937 to help alleviate depredations with funds from the Emergency Conservation Fund Act of 1933 and with funds from Emergency Relief Appropriations from the Department of Agriculture during 1935-38.

Waterfowl management committees recommended increased farming on refuges, leasing of farmlands in the Colusa Trough and Sutter Basin, and feeding of grains on flooded areas, especially in the Imperial and San Joaquin valleys to help alleviate crop depredations (California Department of Fish and Game 1983). Passage of the Lea Act of 1948 authorized the acquisition and development of management areas in California solely for the purpose of alleviating crop damage. Subsequently, Colusa and Sutter NWRs were purchased, and the Salton Sea NWR was enlarged. A management plan to protect waterfowl and agriculture was developed in 1950 (Gordon 1950), and shortly thereafter, the Grizzly Island and Mendota WMAs and Merced and Kern NWRs were created (Table 5).

During the 1940s, pressure to relieve crop depredations stimulated the beginning of moist-soil management for waterfowl food production. Large stands of volunteer annual plants, especially watergrass, occurred in croplands, and managers gradually managed ponds for both watergrass and grains. Management emphasis gradually switched to watergrass because its production required only half as much water as production of rice during summer when water was limited. Summer irrigations were used to increase watergrass yields, but these irrigations also encouraged cattails and tules, which often became dense within a few years. Consequently, pond management gradually incorporated rotational planting systems and burning, mowing, or disking to control dense emergents.

A consequence of large waterfowl concentrations, drainage of native marshes, and irrigation of agricultural crops was the death of several hundred thousand waterfowl caused by avian botulism (Clostridium botulinum Type C) in the Tulare Basin in summer and fall 1938-41 (McLean 1946). Flooding and heavy rains in 1937 and 1938 broke many levees and flooded thousands of hectares of farmland in the Tulare Basin. These flooded croplands attracted up to 4 million ducks, and as waters were pumped or receded from croplands, large expanses of mudflats and decaying vegetation occurred and facilitated botulism outbreaks. Water-fowl continued to be attracted to this area in summer and fall 1939-41, when farmers irrigated croplands following harvest in late summer, and held water on lands for up to several months. These hot, shallow conditions facilitated further botulism outbreaks, peaking with the loss of 250,000 birds in 1941. Efforts were undertaken to control these losses by CDFG, and these efforts initiated a precedent for disease control in California. Control methods included picking up dead and dying ducks, placing sick birds in pens where shade and fresh water were supplied, and giving birds potassium permanganate (Mays 1911). In 1942, new pre-irrigation practices were initiated in the Tulare Basin. This pre-irrigation consisted of flooding lands only until soils were saturated and then draining water to other fields. This practice decreased the attractiveness of the area to ducks and also decreased stagnation that facilitated botulism outbreaks.

In addition to crop depredation and disease problems, procurement of water to flood and manage wetlands became difficult in the 1940s and 1950s. In the Sacramento, Imperial, and Coachella valleys, irrigation waters were made available to refuges and duck clubs to help reduce crop depredation (Gordon 1950, Arend 1967). In the San Joaquin Valley, however, where water shortages were critical largely because of overdrafting of groundwater tables, water for wetland management was often limited to unpredictable surpluses (U.S. Department of the Interior 1950). Through the efforts of private duck clubs, the Grassland Water Bill (PL 674, 68 Stat. 879) authorized the Secretary of the Interior to deliver some Central Valley Project (CVP) water, mainly surpluses, to the grasslands beginning in 1953. The definition of "surplus" water was never fully reconciled; however, the delivery of 61 million m^3 of CVP water each fall was established and has since been maintained.

Breeding by many species of waterfowl in California had long been recognized (Bryant 1914), and efforts to investigate the numbers, distribution, habitat use, and success of nesting were initiated in the late 1940s and early 1950s (Hunt and Naylor 1955, Mayhew 1955, Anderson 1956, 1957, 1960, Rienecker and Anderson 1960). These studies concluded that production was greatest in northeastern California and was often limited in the Central Valley. These findings caused administrators to place primary emphasis on managing habitats in California for wintering rather than breeding waterfowl.

1960-1980.—The acquisition of wetlands in California by the USFWS and CDFG in the 1940s and 1950s, and the increased water supplied to the San Joaquin Basin each fall, alleviated much of the depredation problems. Biologists subsequently turned to developing improved techniques to maximize food production. A marsh management project was established by CDFG in 1956 and continued to some degree until 1979 (Miller and Arend 1960, George 1963, Ermacoff 1969, Connelly 1979).

Wintering waterfowl populations remained relatively stable in California from 1960 to 1980 (LeDonne 1980). Management continued to emphasize small-grain production on public lands and shallow flooding during hunting seasons on duck clubs. The high price of water, land, and levee repair frequently discouraged intensive management, and some clubs converted existing wetlands into rice fields in an effort to offset costs while providing hunting. This conversion destroyed an additional 10,000 ha of wetlands in the 1970s.

Attempts to acquire additional public wetlands in California for waterfowl management in the 1960s-70s were largely unsuccessful. High land costs, government programs that encouraged agricultural production, and the perceived lack of need because of adequate waterfowl populations precluded public acquisitions of wetlands in the 1960s and 1970s. Exceptions were the purchase of the San Luis NWR and additions to Gray Lodge and Los Banos WMAs (Table 5). Also, the U.S. Department of Agriculture established a Water Bank Program in California in the early 1970s. In California, the Water Bank Program was used to encourage private landowners to protect and improve important wetlands. The emphasis in 1988 of the Water Bank in California was to provide pair and brood habitat, and required that at least 20% of the wetland area remain flooded until 15 July each year.

1980-1988.—The laissez-faire attitude of wetland management in California during the 1960s and 1970s ended in the late 1970s. The primary stimulus for change was a decline in waterfowl numbers, particularly pintails and arctic-nesting geese (U.S. Fish and Wildlife Service 1978, Raveling 1984, U.S Fish and Wildlife Service and Canadian Wildlife Service 1986). Reduced numbers of birds made hunters less successful, especially on poorly managed or marginal properties such as reflooded rice lands. Duck clubs began seeking information on how to manage to attract more ducks, and the USFWS and CDFG intensified management for natural foods. Concern over the destruction of wetlands peaked when the relationship between winter habitat quantity and quality, and waterfowl recruitment was demonstrated (Heitmeyer and Fredrickson 1981).

Efforts to secure and protect more wetlands were accelerated in the 1980s. Important implementation programs included a conservation easement program by the USFWS under the authority of the Migratory Bird Conservation Act; recategorizing Central Valley wetlands as the top priority for waterfowl habitat preservation in the U.S. by the USFWS; and the passage by California voters of Proposition 19, a $60-million bond issue passed for wetland acquisition and management. Additionally, increased support,

both financially and legislatively, from the private duck hunting sector of California, primarily through the California Waterfowl Association (CWA); increased research on wetlands and waterfowl by private, university, and government sectors; and development of wetland projects in California by Ducks Unlimited and CWA accelerated wetland protection.

Two additional developments stimulated increased interest in wetland management in California in the 1980s. First, was the "rediscovery" of large nesting populations of some waterfowl, especially mallards, in the Central Valley. Research documented that nesting success was high, local production accounted for a large portion of the mallard harvest in California, and management of upland nesting cover and freshwater wetland in spring could increase recruitment (McLandress et al. 1987). Second, was the recognition that duck hunting was better on well-managed wetlands than on flooded rice fields, and that rice lands could readily be converted back to wetland habitats. Rice lands are especially easy to convert because most exist on former wetland soils, water-control structures and delivery systems are already in place, and moist-soil seed banks are already present. The potential conversion of rice lands into wetlands is currently facilitated by the low price supports and general poor economy of rice farming, the reduced value of lands for rice production but increased values for waterfowl hunting, and current Agriculture Stabilization and Conservation Service farm programs which remove a proportion (25-35% in recent years) of existing rice lands from production.

SPECIFIC MANAGEMENT APPROACHES AND CONCERNS
Sacramento Valley

Active management of wetlands in the Sacramento Valley began during the 1920s by private managers and consisted primarily of flooding ponds immediately prior to hunting seasons, and then draining them immediately after the seasons (Sacramento Valley Waterfowl Habitat Management Committee 1984). Small areas of wetlands were naturally subject to prolonged flooding and were often left permanently flooded (Arend 1967).

At present, most wetlands are managed as permanently flooded, summer water, and seasonally flooded habitats (Table 1). In the past, these habitats have been rotated with rice production on public areas. In general, soil saturation and standing water occur for longer periods of the year in the Sacramento Valley than in other areas of the state because of greater winter precipitation and more regular river overflows. These hydrological characteristics often encourage tule bulrush and cattail growth even when water is not managed, and has led to a preponderance of these emergent habitat types (Table 1).

In permanently flooded ponds, water is held year-round at depths up to 2-3 m. Many managers drain these ponds every 5-10 years to control the dense stands of cattail or tules that develop. Burning, mowing, and disking are the methods most often used to open up dense emergent stands.

In summer water management, ponds are flooded from June through February or March. Drawdowns in March encourage some germination of moist-soil annuals; however, these summer water ponds usually develop dense stands of cattail or tules within 5 years. As with permanently flooded ponds, summer water habitats usually require control of emergent plants within 5 years.

Seasonally flooded habitats are flooded from early fall (usually just prior to waterfowl hunting seasons) through late winter or spring. Late-winter or early-spring drawdowns (January-March) encourage germination of dock, slender aster (*Aster exilis*), and smartweeds (Fig. 4). Drawdowns in April and May encour-

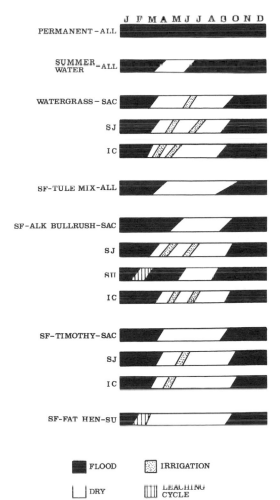

Fig. 4. Flooding and draining schedules of management for various wetland habitat types in California. Descriptions of habitat types and associated plant species are in the text. Diagonal lines represent the chronological range of flooding or drying. ALL = all valley regions, SAC = Sacramento Valley, SJ = San Joaquin Valley, SU = Suisun Marsh, IC = Imperial-Coachella valleys, SF = Seasonally Flooded. Irrigations consist of saturating soils for 1-2 weeks, leaching consists of repeatedly flooding and drying ponds with each inundation lasting up to 1 week

age germination of pricklegrass, swamp timothy, and watergrass. Drawdowns in May and June encourage tule and cattail growth and germination of cockleburs or alkali bulrush (Fig. 4). Seasonally flooded ponds are usually flooded 10-30 cm deep in early fall.

Ponds managed for watergrass are typically flooded from October to mid-spring and are irrigated at least once during summer (Fig. 4). Some watergrass units are not irrigated during summer, but are flooded in early August; however, seed production is lower in unirrigated than in summer-irrigated units. Watergrass habitats on public lands were historically flooded in September or October to provide foods for early fall migrants and to deter potential depredation. Depredations have been minimal in recent years because of low waterfowl populations, presence of flooded high-energy foods on refuges, and early maturing varieties of rice. As a result, flooding of many watergrass fields on public lands has recently been delayed until November.

Although management has tended to emphasize plant production, interest in managing for invertebrates has increased (Euliss and Grodhaus 1987). Invertebrate management is still in its infancy, but flooding small ponds in late summer several weeks prior to marsh flood-up in fall may provide brood stock ponds for invertebrates and increase biomass (Euliss and Grodhaus 1987). This early flooding (i.e., September) of brood stock ponds is generally consistent with mosquito-control practices that limit water fluctuations from March through September (Garcia and Des Rochers 1985).

Providing a combination of the above habitats plus managed uplands is often a goal on public management areas. Resources in this complex of habitat types provide an abundance of moist-soil seeds, invertebrates, forage, tubers, and nesting and brood-rearing habitats (Table 4).

In contrast to public lands, most private duck clubs flood their ponds 1-2 weeks before hunting season, and drain ponds within 3 weeks following the close of hunting seasons. However, recent interest in providing pair and brood-rearing habitats to locally breeding mallards, and in providing late-winter habitat for migrants, has influenced this management. Some managers now hold water in ponds through spring. Additionally, private clubs managed under the USDA Water Bank Program are required to be flooded from 1 January through 15 July. Water to flood most private wetlands is primarily available during early fall when rice fields are drained. At other times, waters often are limited to irrigation surpluses, local runoff, and floods.

In permanently flooded wetlands, water is often circulated from August through October to avoid stagnant water conditions conducive to avian botulism (Sacramento Valley Waterfowl Habitat Management Committee 1984). When botulism outbreaks do occur, dead and dying birds are removed and water is either drained or flushed (Rosen 1965). Actions used to control avian cholera include the above methods plus hazing birds from an area and treating contaminated ponds with copper sulfate (Hunter et al. 1970, Titche 1979).

Management of uplands in the Sacramento Valley has generally been neglected. Small areas of upland habitat are, however, managed as grazing areas for geese or as dense nesting cover for ducks. Burning most commonly is used to enhance new growth of upland grasses and sedges (Sacramento Valley Waterfowl Habitat Management Committee 1984, Mensik 1986). Little direct seeding of annual grasses or legumes occurs, although winter wheat, barley, clover (*Trifolium* spp.), and alfalfa have been sown on a few areas. Uplands managed for nesting cover are sometimes seeded to tall wheatgrass (*Agropyron elongatum*), vetch (*Vicia* spp.), or ryegrass (*Lolium* spp.), but usually naturally occurring vegetation is simply allowed to grow undisturbed.

Production of rice provides considerable habitat for waterfowl. Rice fields are generally laser-leveled and diked with contour levees. Seed beds are prepared in late spring or early summer (Mar-May) by disking or plowing, applying fertilizers, herbicides, and pesticides, and by flooding fields 5-10 cm deep (Rutger and Brandon 1981). Rice seed is treated with a fungicide and applied aerially. Water is added to rice fields during summer to reduce evapotranspiration losses. Pesticides such as parathion, copper sulfate, and carbamate (and formerly, furadan) are applied to control rice water weevils (*Lissorhoptrus oryzophilus*), tadpole shrimp (*Triops longicandatus*), and crayfish (*Procambarus* spp.); and thiocarbamate and phenoxy herbicides are applied to control watergrass and sprangletop. Most currently planted rice varieties mature in 120-140 days, and water is drained from fields 20-30 days before harvest. Harvest generally is initiated when the grain has a <24% content of moisture. After harvest, most fields are burned to destroy straw that harbors the fungus *Sclerotium oryzae* that causes stem rot. Because of recent concerns with air pollution, stubble is sometimes left standing, disked, or rolled instead of being burned. Flooded rice fields provide significant habitat for breeding waterfowl and broods; however, the effects of pesticide biomagnification in food chains are not well-known. Harvested rice fields provide winter foods and habitats to waterfowl, especially if they are shallowly flooded after harvest. Some duck clubs leave fields unburned in fall and mow or disk areas around blinds; others flood burned fields only during hunting seasons.

Wild rice also is planted in California (in 1988, 10,000 ha). Methods of growing wild rice are similar to regular rice production except that fields are planted and flooded in late March. Therefore, these fields may be especially important as early brood habitat.

San Joaquin Valley

The earliest wetland management in the San Joaquin Valley occurred in the 1880s when the Miller and Lux Corporation irrigated large tracts of grassland habitat (Exley 1931). These irrigations shallowly flooded grasslands on floodplains that were normally dry during summer, and encouraged vegetation that provided abundant moist-soil seeds, forage, and invertebrates used as food by wintering ducks and geese. Early winter rains further stimulated growth of grasses and sedges and provided forage for waterfowl. In 1926, Miller and Lux sold much of its land, but retained water rights, to individuals who operated the land as shooting clubs and/or cattle ranches (U.S. Department of the Interior 1950). Miller and Lux eventually sold the water rights for this land to the U.S. Bureau of Reclamation, but the bureau had no place to sell the water from 1939 until the Friant-Kern Canal was completed in 1952. During this period, the bureau let clubs and ranchers have water at the previous low rate, and water was mostly managed by the Grasslands Mutual Water Association (U.S. Department of the Interior 1950). Since 1953, the previously mentioned Grasslands Water Bill has made provisions for supplying CVP water to San Joaquin wetlands. Most wetlands owned by duck clubs were grazed by cattle until early fall when lands were flooded for duck hunting. However, heavy grazing reduced biomass and seed production of desirable moist-soil plants. Many clubs no longer allow cattle to graze wetlands.

In the 1970s, attempts were renewed to increase food production from native marsh plants, and new techniques to grow swamp timothy and spikerush were developed (Connelly 1979). Most wetlands in the San Joaquin Valley are currently managed as seasonally flooded habitats (Table 1). Most ponds are drained in early spring to stimulate germination of swamp timothy and pricklegrass, and typically at least 1 irrigation is made in midsummer to increase seed production (Fig. 4). This irrigation is usually done when swamp timothy leaves start to show necrosis and when plants are flowering, thus preventing infertile seed heads. Some ponds are drained in late spring to enhance production of watergrass and alkali bulrush. Newly created or planted stands of watergrass and alkali bulrush usually need 2 summer irrigations to stimulate growth and seed production; however, existing stands usually require only 1 irrigation. Some wetlands also are permanently flooded to provide brood and pair habitat. These wetlands quickly become dominated with cattails and tules, however, and must be drawn down and thinned at least once every 5 years. Disking, burning, prolonged drying, grazing by sheep and cattle, and mowing are used to control undesirable cattails and tules (Ermacoff 1969).

Many duck clubs in the San Joaquin Valley manage almost exclusively for short annual vegetation such as swamp timothy or pricklegrass. This management is highly attractive to pintails and also reduces the demand for water, which is often unavailable, of poor quality, or expensive. Clubs frequently mow any emergent growth that stands above 20-30 cm, thus creating a shallow "sheet water" appearance that is desired for pintail hunting. These sheet water-timothy habitats provide abundant seeds in early fall and invertebrates in spring (Severson 1987). Disease outbreaks in the San Joaquin Valley, with the exception of major die-offs from botulism in the Tulare Basin, have not been as great as in the Sacramento Valley. When disease outbreaks occur, the disease control techniques previously described are used.

Availability of good water quantity and quality remains a problem in the San Joaquin Valley. Agricultural crops require large amounts of irrigation water; however, salts accumulate in the surface soil as a result of evaporation and must be removed by leaching. Percolation of water into aquifers and deeper soil layers is inhibited by impermeable clay layers, and soils becomes waterlogged or laden with salts, thus inhibiting plant growth. Subsurface drains have been constructed throughout much of this agricultural land to alleviate the problem (Letey et al. 1986).

The potential for using agricultural drainage water for wetland management was suggested in the 1940s and 1950s (Leach 1960, Jones and Stokes Associates 1977, Letey et al. 1986). The Grasslands Water District began accepting drainage water for flooding of wetlands with the stipulation that it contain <3,000 ppm salt, feeling that the salt could be adequately diluted with the CVP water they received each fall. This worked successfully as long as the accumulating salts were flushed from wetlands each winter. However, toxicity problems became acute in the early 1980s when reservoir ponds on the Kesterson NWR were turned into terminal evaporation sumps rather than holding or regulating reservoirs as originally intended (Letey et al. 1986, Zahm 1986). Since drain waters began flowing into Kesterson in 1978, the extreme toxicity of drain waters, particularly from naturally occurring selenium, has been recognized (Hamilton et al. 1986, Ohlendorf et al. 1986a, b). Since 1985, use of drain waters to flood private and public lands has been reduced. Litigation and proposals to dispose drain waters, prevent contamination of wetlands and ground water, and provide "good quality" alternate water sources (such as more CVP water) were pending in 1989.

Sacramento-San Joaquin River Delta and Suisun Marsh

Management of wetland habitat in the delta area is mostly restricted to the Suisun Marsh. In the delta, approximately 4,900 ha are flooded for duck hunting, but >80% of these lands are harvested corn, milo, sunflower, and rice fields. Flooding of these croplands usually occurs from October-February; little additional management occurs. Wheat is also grown in the delta and provides forage for geese and swans. The small area of marsh that exists in duck clubs in the delta is mostly managed for seasonally flooded tule habitats, but a few permanently flooded ponds exist. Water management regimes and emergent plant control are similar to those used in the Sacramento Valley.

Early (1900-1925) management of wetlands in the Suisun Marsh consisted of placing low levees around ponds and controlling water levels with tide gates (Moffitt 1938). "Overflow" lands within leveed areas were flooded from September to February; only subsoil moisture was provided in summer. This water management initially encouraged growth of desirable plants, but when this "dry" water regime management was continued over many years without adequate flushing, seasonally flooded ponds became saline and acidic, and only the most salt-tolerant plants such as saltgrass and pickleweed survived. Some duck clubs impounded freshwater that flowed into the delta during May and June, and later added this water to more saline bay waters for flooding of ponds (Moffitt 1938). Some areas were permanently flooded and equipped with gates that continually circulated water through the ponds to keep them as fresh as possible. These ponds contained abundant sago pondweed, water nymph, and widgeongrass until carp (*Cyprinus carpio*) populations became excessive. Experimentation on the Joice Island Duck Club ponds during the late 1950s proved that draining the ponds completely in February and then re-flooding them in March controlled the carp problem. Pickleweed was considered undesirable by most clubs and was discouraged by disking and flooding (Moffitt 1938). Many duck clubs allowed cattle to graze on marsh vegetation during summer. Attempts were made to farm

lands within the Suisun Marsh from 1900 to 1930; however, increases in soil salinity, low pH, and 3 major floods in the early 1900s virtually eliminated the growing of crops by the early 1930s, except on Grizzly Island (Mall 1969, Miller et al. 1975).

During the 1950s and 1960s, techniques were developed within the constraints of mosquito abatement regulations to decrease soil salinity and increase production of alkali bulrush, fathen, and brass buttons (George et al. 1965, Mall 1969, Miller et al. 1975, Rollins 1981). Managers were encouraged to repeatedly flood and dry marshes from the end of duck season to the first of April to leach salts. The length of these leaching cycles controlled the vegetation composition (Fig. 4, Rollins 1973). By maintaining dry conditions in pond bottoms during summer, cattail and tule growth was restricted and heavy equipment could be used to disk pond bottoms for vegetation control. Stands of saltgrass were frequently burned to prevent dense matting, which allowed it to outcompete more desirable plants such as brass buttons and fathen. Alkali bulrush was encouraged because it was tolerant of saline soils and considered to be a desirable duck food (George 1963, Mall 1969, Mall and Rollins 1972, Rollins 1981).

Managers and biologists now recognize that maintaining extremely dry soil conditions throughout summer on the cat clay soils that underlay much of the Suisun Marsh can drastically alter soil and water chemistries (Neely 1958, 1962, Lynn 1963, Crapuchettes 1987), and that alkali bulrush seeds are poorly metabolized by waterfowl (Swanson and Bartonek 1970). Interest in managing for invertebrates has also increased (e.g., Connelly and Chesemore 1980, Euliss and Harris 1987, Miller 1987), and some managers now encourage pickleweed, which was formerly considered undesirable (Moffitt 1938).

Soils and vegetation within the Suisun Marsh evolved under tidally flooded regimes and high soil moistures. Completely drying soils causes accelerated decomposition of marsh litter, subsidence, oxidation of soils, and drastically lowered pH (Neely 1958, 1962, Lynn 1963). When alkaline waters inundate these low pH soils, dissolved iron becomes suspended and eventually precipitates as ferric hydroxide (causing "red water," which is toxic to some plants and invertebrates) (Lynn 1963, Crapuchettes 1987). Red water conditions can be avoided by flooding ponds throughout the year, by rotating flooding and drying ponds in alternate summers, and by maintaining high soil moisture throughout the year by holding water at higher levels (i.e., <10 cm from the soil surface) in water delivery ditches. Maintaining high soil moisture and more permanent water regimes increases growth of alkali bulrush, tules, and cattail, and these must be controlled if undesired. Consequently, alternate yearly flooding and drying may provide the best management strategy by reducing acidity and permitting managers to control undesired vegetation during dry periods.

Mallards nest in the Suisun Marsh. Managers in 1988 provided permanently flooded wetlands for pairs and broods, maintained dense upland cover for nesting, and grew watergrass as high-energy food (McLandress et al. 1987). These habitats combined with traditional winter seasonally flooded marshes provide the complex of habitats necessary to support both breeding and wintering waterfowl.

Imperial and Coachella Valleys

Early attempts at wetland management in the Imperial and Coachella valleys consisted primarily of flooding diked ponds from October through March (Fredrickson 1980). A rise in the level of Salton Sea inundated most of Salton Sea NWR in the 1940s, and by 1950,

extremely saline conditions (35 ppt) were present. Widgeongrass grew along the south shore of the Salton Sea, where dilution kept salinities at <24 ppt until 1956; however, fluctuating water levels of the Salton Sea, coupled with meandering tendencies of the New and Alamo rivers, precluded most management from 1930 to 1950, and the Salton Sea NWR became primarily an open water refuge area. Shoalgrass (Halodule wrightii) was introduced in the Salton Sea as early as 1957, and several truckloads of sod were transplanted from the Laguna Madre in Texas in the early 1960s. Shoalgrass persisted for a few years, but rapidly rising water and lack of tidal currents eventually eliminated it. The Imperial WMA was originally managed as a sanctuary, and no hunting was allowed. Here, water was held on ponds until early summer, and dense stands of tules and cattails developed (California Department of Fish and Game 1983).

Crop depredation problems in the Imperial and Coachella valleys in the early 1940s encouraged the USFWS and CDFG to plant crops on their own or leased lands. In 1948, the Imperial Irrigation District leased up to 9,800 ha within the Salton Sea Reserve to the USFWS and CDFG for waterfowl management, primarily for the provision of row crops (Gordon 1950). These lands were leveed to protect them from flooding by the rising water levels of the Salton Sea.

In 1947, the USFWS began placing feed on refuge lands to discourage crop depredations. This feeding program continued through 1978. In 1953, the CDFG adopted regulations to permit duck clubs to feed waterfowl on their lands during the waterfowl hunting season to help alleviate depredations. This feeding program was suspended in 1958, but was reinstituted in 1959 and continues to the present. Feeding is currently restricted to 9 southern California counties (Fredrickson 1980). The legality of the California

Feeding Program has been challenged by the USFWS since 1981, and controversies continued in 1989.

Depredation problems in the Imperial and Coachella valleys have been minimal in recent years; feeding programs have apparently done little to minimize depredations, and harvest does not seem to be affected by feeding, but rather by effective marsh management that provides abundant natural foods (Fredrickson 1980). As a result, many managers now expend more effort in managing ponds for natural plants than in the continuance of "feeding". However, the high cost of water, the salinity of soils and agricultural drain water, and evaporation rates make management costly and difficult. Club managers that have access to artesian waters in the Coachella Valley can flood and circulate water more easily and cheaply, and therefore grow more moist-soil plants than most clubs in the Imperial Valley (U.S. Fish and Wildlife Service 1987*b*).

Managers promoting moist-soil plants usually flood ponds from September to March (Fig. 4). When water is available, salinity is decreased by circulating water through ponds. This regime encourages swamp timothy, pricklegrass, dock, and sprangletop. Watergrass and Japanese millet are grown on a few clubs; however, watergrass production requires summer flooding which increases soil salinity and encourages growth of cattails, salt cedar, tules, and sesbania (*Sesbania* spp.), which are often considered undesirable. Dense emergents and salt cedar are controlled primarily by burning, disking, and mowing. Some permanently flooded ponds are present near the Salton Sea where the sea precludes drainage, but fresh water must be added periodically to maintain low salinities. Presently, the Salton Sea is much saltier than the ocean (i.e., >40 ppt).

CONCLUSION

Wetlands and agricultural lands in the Central, Imperial, and Coachella valleys of California support 20% of all (and > 50% of several species) wintering waterfowl in North America. No other area in North America is as important for wintering waterfowl, yet paradoxically, no other wintering area has experienced as great a wetland loss. The obvious question is: will the limited wetland base that remains be adequate to support current and desired future populations?

Wetlands are among the most productive (biomass/area) ecosystems in the world (Mitsch and Gosselink 1986), but food production on California's highly modified wetlands varies widely depending on location and management activities. Provision of an average of 750-950 kg/ha of food (calculated earlier as the amount necessary to support current waterfowl populations) in all wetlands in California of the seasonal quality necessary to meet requirements of waterfowl annual cycle events seems unlikely. Some intensively managed wetland complexes may exceed this theoretical need, but most do not. Hunting probably restricts waterfowl use of many private wetlands and hunting areas on public lands during hunting seasons. Because of limited wetland resources, it is apparent why the large waterfowl populations that were present prior to the 1980s readily supplemented foods obtained in wetlands with waste agricultural grains. We doubt that the large waterfowl populations wintering in California in the 1940s-1970s could have been maintained without large areas of small-grain crops. Although most waste grains are good sources of energy, many lack essential nutrients. Consequently, foods provided in wetlands that have proper complements of amino acids, fatty acids, minerals, and vitamins are crucial to survival and reproduction of waterfowl. We suspect that the availability of foods in wetlands was possibly limiting to waterfowl populations during years or seasons of drought, even as recently as the mid-1970s. The quantity and quality of foods on both wetlands and agricultural lands increase when precipitation and associated river overflows are high in winter. Correspondingly, greater availability of resources in wet winters allows birds to attain better physiological condition (Miller 1986), proceed through annual cycle events more rapidly (Heitmeyer 1985, 1987), and survive and reproduce more successfully (Raveling and Heitmeyer 1988).

Consideration of the requirements of waterfowl must not be limited to nutritional needs or to diurnal periods. Social systems vary among species (Kear 1970, McKinney 1986), and consequently, habitat use, flocking structure, and philopatric tendencies also vary. Maintenance of wintering and breeding traditions to specific areas is dependent upon the availability of refuges where waterfowl have freedom from disturbance, mortality, and predation (Raveling 1978, Cowardin et al. 1985). Waterfowl also commonly use different habitats and have different activities during the day and night (e.g., Euliss and Harris 1987). Some habitats used at night may provide food for certain species (e.g., green-winged teal), but only provide thermal cover or protection from nocturnal predators for others (e.g., wood ducks, mallards). Consequently, provision of adequate resources and habitats may often require a diversity unappreciated solely by daytime observation.

The above considerations lead us to believe that management of wetland complexes, where sanctuaries also are provided, is essential and exhibits the greatest potential for maintaining waterfowl populations in California. By managing wetland complexes where a variety of foods and habitats are available adjacent to existing private agricultural lands, the annual cycle requirements of many species can be met. The "magic" size of areas where all habitats must be present is poorly understood. If all habitats can be provided within an area, such as a large (>200 ha) duck club, we feel the response by waterfowl would be especially noticeable, biologically valuable, and financially justifiable.

Attainment of wetlands that provide adequate resources to waterfowl will require knowledge of annual cycle requirements and will require intensified management of existing private and public wetlands. Private and public lands often have different priorities and constraints, thus management should not necessarily be the same on lands of different ownership; management that complements values on adjacent lands is especially desirable. Managers of public lands often have the flexibility to provide resources that are absent or limited on private lands. Techniques and conceptual strategies for management of breeding (McLandress et al. 1987, McLandress and Yarris 1987) and wintering (Heitmeyer 1985) waterfowl in California are available, but transfer of information among managers and researchers is currently insufficient.

The diverse climate, topography, geology, and water quantity and quality available within California require different management strategies within regions. Management is often most successful when it attempts to emulate natural, hydrologic conditions. Valuable lessons were learned from attempts to manage wetlands in a way that varies considerably from natural flooding regimes (e.g., prolonged drying of Suisun Marsh soils, which increases soil acidity and reduces productivity).

For wetland management to be successful, the natural structure and function of wetlands must be maintained. Because wetlands are dynamic and complex ecosystems, management should make provisions for periodic change (such as occasional drawdowns) to alter nutrient dynamics, vegetation communities, soil and water chemistry, and associated biological productivity. Ecological studies of wetlands in California have been neglected. Integrated investigations of nutrient, plant, invertebrate, and chemical aspects of wetlands and the effects of management will be productive avenues for research.

Wetland management in California is currently reaching a new level of sophistication, but is also faced with problems. Increased urban populations in California and worldwide demands for agricultural commodities will accelerate demands on already limited water supplies. Although provisions for water to flood managed wetlands have been made in the past, litigation and compromise have been required and likely will be necessary in the future. Problems related to water quality have recently been brought to the forefront, as exemplified by selenium contamination at the Kesterson NWR. Water that is contaminated with pesticides, heavy metals, salts, or that contains extremely high nitrogen and phosphorus or low oxygen concentrations may exacerbate failures of reproduction, reduced survival, and disease outbreaks among waterfowl. Disease outbreaks and their impacts on waterfowl, and their relation to wetland management, remain poorly studied.

Reduced waterfowl populations result in poorer hunting, which discourage many hunters. As hunter numbers decline, wetland and waterfowl preservation in California likely will suffer. Without the considerable financial and political support of waterfowl hunters, it seems doubtful that wetlands of value to waterfowl will remain. On the positive side, reduced waterfowl numbers also often raise the consciousness and resolve of both private and public groups to protect and increase wetland habitats upon which waterfowl populations depend. In this light, financial and political support from the private sector

and state and federal governments in California has recently increased. Recognition of biological requirements of waterfowl and the promise that this understanding offers to better management also are currently reaching an all-time high in California.

Also, the North American Waterfowl Management Plan (NAWMP) calls for action to improve, protect, and restore wetland habitats in the Central Valley of California (Canadian Wildlife Service and U.S. Fish and Wildlife Service 1986). A Central Valley Habitat Joint Venture of the NAWMP was initiated in February 1988 and adopted the following objectives: (1) protect an additional 32,400 ha of existing wetlands through fee or perpetual easement acquisition; (2) secure an incremental firm 50 million m^3 (410,050 acre-ft) of water; (3) secure CVP power for NWRs, WMAs, and the Grassland Resource Conservation District; (4) increase wetland area by 48,600 ha; (5) enhance wetland habitats on 117,450 ha of public and private lands; and 6) enhance habitat on 182,250 ha of agricultural lands.

SUMMARY

Wetlands in the Central, Imperial, and Coachella valleys of California provide resources that support the largest concentration of wintering waterfowl in North America. Despite the importance of these wetlands, only 115,000 ha remain; most are privately owned and managed for duck hunting.

Wetlands in the Sacramento Valley total 32,000 ha. These wetlands occur primarily in floodplains of the Sacramento River and its tributaries and typically flood more permanently than wetlands elsewhere in California. Management of wetlands in the Sacramento Valley has evolved from primarily flooding during waterfowl hunting seasons and attempting to discourage crop depredations in the early and mid-1900s, to providing a complex of flooding regimes and habitat types in the 1980s. Harvested rice fields in the Sacramento Valley provide waste grain to waterfowl and 162,000 ha of farmlands are subject to flooding in winter. Additionally, 32,000 ha of rice lands are intentionally flooded for waterfowl hunting each fall.

Wetlands in the Sacramento-San Joaquin River Delta have mostly been destroyed; only 7,290 ha remain. Delta wetlands are managed similar to those in the Sacramento Valley. About 8,100 ha of croplands are flooded each winter for waterfowl hunting or to leach soil salts. The Suisun Marsh is a tidally influenced estuarine wetland complex that encompasses 22,000 ha; 84% is privately owned. Techniques have been developed in the Suisun Marsh to decrease soil salinity and increase production of alkali bulrush, fathen, and brass buttons. Repeatedly flushing wetlands in late winter and early spring created effective leaching cycles, and the timing of these flushes controls vegetation composition.

Wetlands in the San Joaquin Valley occur in the northern San Joaquin Basin (49,000 ha) and the southern Tulare Basin (2,000 ha). Most wetlands in the San Joaquin Valley are seasonally flooded, are often alkaline, and support less emergent, but more annual grassland plants than in the Sacramento Valley. This is because of the more arid (<23 cm of annual precipitation) climate in the San Joaquin Valley than in the Sacramento Valley. The arid climate has encouraged management that conserves water and encourages annual vegetation. When flooded, these wetlands have a shallow sheet water appearance that is attractive to pintails.

Wetlands in the Imperial and Coachella valleys were mostly created by man in the early 1900s after Salton Sea was created. The extremely arid (<5 cm of annual precipitation) climate and saline soils of the area often preclude marsh management, and many wetlands are simply flooded during waterfowl hunting seasons.

If numbers of wintering waterfowl in California return to mid-1970s levels, management of wetlands will have to increase production and quality of resources to meet waterfowl requirements. Breeding mallards in California also bring responsibility and the challenge to manage existing wetlands and uplands for both breeding and wintering waterfowl.

Many problems impede effective management in California; these include increased urban populations and development, inadequate quantity and quality of water, disease outbreaks and resource limitations imposed by increasing concentrations of waterfowl on reduced habitat bases, and reduced hunter numbers and incentives for privately owned wetland preservation. Despite these problems, financial and political support from the private sector remains high. The Central Valley Habitat Joint Venture of the NAWMP seeks to impact over 400,000 ha of wetlands, uplands, and agricultural lands for the benefit of waterfowl.

Future research avenues that seem most productive include identification of specific resource requirements of waterfowl species during annual cycle events, and integrated studies of nutrient, plant, invertebrate, and chemical aspects of wetlands.

LITERATURE CITED

Alexander, D. G. 1976. Ecological aspects of the temporary annual pool fauna. Pages 32-36 in S. Jain, ed. Vernal pools—their ecology and conservation. Inst. of Ecol. Publ. 9, Univ. California, Davis.

Anderson, W. 1956. A waterfowl nesting study on the grasslands, Merced County, California. Calif. Fish and Game 42:117-130.

———. 1957. A waterfowl nesting study in the Sacramento Valley, California, 1955. Calif. Fish and Game 43:71-90.

———. 1960. A study of waterfowl nesting in the Suisun Marsh. Calif. Fish and Game 46:217-226.

Arend, P. H. 1967. Water requirements for the waterfowl of Butte Basin, California. Calif.

Dep. Fish and Game, Water Projects Branch Rep. 6, Sacramento, Calif. 73 pp.

Arkley, R. J. 1962. Soil survey of Merced area, California. U.S. Soil Conserv. Serv. and Calif. Agric. Exp. Stn, U.S. Gov, Print Off, Washington, D.C. 10 pp.

Armbruster, J. S. 1982. Wood duck displays and pairing chronology. Auk 99:116-122.

Aschoff, J., and H. Pohl. 1970. Der rueheumasatz von vogeln als funktion der tageszeit and der korpergrosse. J. Ornithol. 111:38-47.

Atwater, B. F. 1979. Ancient processes at the site of southern San Francisco Bay: movement of the crust and changes in sea level. Pages 143-174 *in* T. J. Conomos, ed. San Francisco Bay: the urbanized estuary. Pacific Div. Am. Assoc. Adv. Sci., San Francisco, Calif.

———, C. W. Hedel, and E. J. Helley. 1977. Late quaternary depositional history, Holocene sea-level changes, and vertical crustal movement, southern San Francisco Bay, California. U.S. Geol. Survey, Professional Pap. 1014. 15 pp.

Barry, W. J. 1981. Map of California native grasslands then and now. Fremontia 9:18.

Basye, G. 1981. The Sacramento-San Joaquin Delta—an historical perspective. Pages 6-15 *in* A. Sands, ed. The future of the Delta. Inst. Gov. Affairs and Univ. Calif. Extension, Davis.

Batema, D. L., G. S. Henderson, and L. H. Fredrickson. 1985. Wetland invertebrate distribution in bottomland hardwoods as influenced by forest type and flooding regimes. Pages 196-202 *in* J. O. Dawson and K. A. Majerus, eds. Proc. 5th Cent. Hardwood For. Conf. Dep. For., Univ. Illinois, Urbana.

Bellrose, F. C. 1980. Ducks, geese and swans of North America. Third ed. Stackpole Books, Harrisburg, Pa. 540 pp.

Bielm, E. R. 1951. Crop damage by wildlife in California with special emphasis on deer and waterfowl. Calif. Dep. Fish and Game, Game Bull. 5, Sacramento. 71 pp.

Bryant, H. C. 1914. A survey of the breeding grounds of ducks in California in 1914. Condor 16:217-239.

California Department of Fish and Game. 1979. Duck club survey. Project W-30R-26 to W-30R-31. Calif. Dep. Fish and Game, Sacramento. 5 pp.

———. 1983. A plan for protecting, enhancing, and increasing California's wetlands for waterfowl. Calif. Dep. Fish and Game, Sacramento. 59 pp.

Canadian Wildlife Service and U.S. Fish and Wildlife Service. 1986. North American Waterfowl Management Plan. Environment Canada and U.S. Dep. Interior, Washington, D.C. 33 pp.

Carpelan, L. H. 1961. History of the Salton Sea. Pages 15-98 *in* B. W. Walker, ed. The ecology of

the Salton Sea, California, in relation to the sport fishery. Calif. Dep. Fish and Game, Fish Bull. 113, Sacramento.

Conard, S. G., R. L. MacDonald, and R. F. Holland. 1977. Riparian vegetation and flora of the Sacramento Valley. Pages 47-56 *in* A. Sands, ed. Riparian forests in California, their ecology and conservation. Inst. of Ecol. Publ. 15, Univ. California, Davis.

Connelly, D. P. 1979. Propagation of selected native marsh plants in the San Joaquin Valley. Calif. Dep. Fish and Game Wildl. Manage. Leafl. 15, Sacramento. 13 pp.

———, and D. L. Chesemore. 1980. Food habits of pintails, *Anas acuta*, wintering on seasonally flooded wetlands in the northern San Joaquin Valley, California. Calif. Fish and Game 66: 233-237.

Cowardin, L. M., D. S. Gilmer, and C. W. Shaiffer. 1985. Mallard recruitment in the agricultural environment of North Dakota. Wildl. Monogr. 92. 37 pp.

Crampton, B. 1959. The grass genera *Orcuttia* and *Neostapfia*: a study in habitat and morphological specialization. Madrono 15: 97-110.

———. 1976. A historical perspective on the botany of the vernal pools in California. Pages 5-11 *in* S. Jain, ed. Vernal pools—their ecology and conservation. Inst. of Ecol. Publ. 9, Univ. California, Davis.

Crapuchettes, P. W. 1987. An hypothesis regarding poor duck use of the Suisun Marsh. Univ. California, Davis. 8 pp.

Darby, R. E. 1962. Midges associated with California rice fields, with special reference to their ecology. Hilgardia 32:1 206.

Dasmann, R. F. 1966. The destruction of California. MacMillan Co., New York, N.Y. 247 pp.

DeWitt, J. 1910. Duck shooting in California. Overland Monthly 56:439 444.

Elbright, J., R. L. Wibur, W. B. Herms, K. F. Meyers, and G. H. Whipple. 1916. The malaria problem. Trans. Commonwealth Club of Calif., San Francisco 11:1-6.

Ermacoff, N. 1969. Marsh and habitat management at the Mendota wildlife area. Calif. Dep. Fish and Game, Game Manage. Leafl. 12, Sacramento. 10 pp.

Euliss, N H., Jr., and G. Grodhaus. 1987. Management of midges and other invertebrates for waterfowl wintering in California. Calif. Fish and Game 73:242 247.

———, and S. W. Harris. 1987. Feeding ecology of northern pintails and green-winged teal wintering in California. J. Wildl. Manage. 51:724-732.

Exley, J. 1931. Notes of John Exley. Calif. Fish and Game 17:66-68.

Farrington, S. K. 1945. The ducks came back. Coward-McCann Inc., New York, N.Y. 138 pp.

Fredrickson, L. H. 1980. An evaluation of the role of feeding in waterfowl management in southern California. Final rep. for U.S. Fish and Wildl. Serv., Office of Migratory Bird Manage. Washington, D.C. 177 pp.

——, and M. E. Heitmeyer. 1988. Waterfowl use of forested wetlands in the southeastern United States—an overview. Pages 307-323 in M. W. Weller, ed. Waterfowl in winter—a symposium and workshop. Univ. Minnesota Press, Minneapolis.

Garcia, R., and B. Des Rochers. 1985. Towards an integrated mosquito control for Gray Lodge Wildlife Refuge with emphasis on the floodwater species: *Aedes melanimon* and *A. nigromaculus*. Proc. Conf. Calif. Mosquito and Vector Control Assoc. 52:173-180.

George, H. A. 1963. Planting alkali bulrush for waterfowl food. Calif. Dep. Fish and Game, Game Manage. Leafl. 9, Sacramento. 9 pp.

——, W. Anderson, and H. McKinnie. 1965. An evaluation of the Suisun Marsh as a waterfowl area. Calif. Dep. Fish and Game Admin. Rep., Sacramento. 20 pp.

Gill, R., and A. R. Buckman. 1974. The natural resources of Suisun Marsh, their status and future. Calif. Dep. Fish and Game, Coastal Wetlands Ser. 9, Sacramento. 152 pp.

Gilmer, D. S., M. R. Miller, R. D. Bauer, and J. R. LeDonne. 1982. California's Central Valley wintering waterfowl: concerns and challenges. Trans. North Am. Wildl. and Nat. Resour. Conf. 47:441-452.

Gordon, S. 1950. California's fish and game program. Rep. to the Wildl. Conserv. Board and Calif. Legislature Assembly, Sacramento. 246 pp.

Grassland Water District. 1987. A report of the economic impacts of selenium contamination of agricultural drainage water on the grasslands area of Merced County. Rep. for Calif. State Water Resour. Control Board, Los Banos. 18 pp.

Grinnell, J., and H. C. Bryant. 1914. The wood duck in California. Calif. Fish and Game 1:49-52.

Grodhaus, G. 1980. Aestivating chironomid larvae associated with vernal pools. Pages 315-322 in D. A. Murray, ed. Chironomidae: ecology, systematics, cytology, and physiology. Pergamon Press, New York, N.Y.

Hamilton, S. J., A. N. Palmisano, G. A. Wedmeyer, and W. T. Yasutake. 1986. Impacts of selenium on early life stages and smoltification of fall chinook salmon. Trans. North Am. Wildl. and Nat. Resour. Conf. 51:343-356.

Heitmeyer, M. E. 1985. Wintering strategies of female mallards related to dynamics of lowland hardwood wetlands in the Upper Mississippi Delta. Ph.D. Dissertation, Univ. Missouri, Columbia. 378 pp.

——. 1987. The prebasic moult and basic plumage of female mallards. Can. J. Zool. 65:2248-2261.

——, and L. H. Fredrickson. 1981. Do wetland conditions in the Mississippi Delta hardwoods influence mallard recruitment? Trans. North Am. Wildl. and Nat. Resour. Conf. 46:44-57.

Holland, R. F., and F. T. Griggs. 1976. A unique habitat—California's vernal pools. Fremontia 4: 3-6.

——, and S. K. Jain. 1977. Vernal pools. Pages 515-536 in M. G. Barbour and J. Major, eds. Terrestrial vegetation of California. John Wiley and Sons, New York, N.Y..

Hoover, R. F. 1935. Primitive vegetation of the San Joaquin Valley. M.S. Thesis, Univ. California, Berkeley. 10 pp.

Horn, E. E. 1949. Waterfowl damage to agricultural crops and it's control. Trans. North Am. Wildl. Conf. 14: 577-585.

Hunt, E. G., and A. E. Naylor. 1955. Nesting studies of ducks and coots in Honeylake Valley. Calif. Fish and Game 41: 295-314.

Hunter, B. F., W. E. Clark, P. J. Perkins, and P. R. Coleman. 1970. Applied botulism research including management recommendations. Calif. Dep. Fish and Game, Wildl. Manage. Prog. Rep., Sacramento. 87 pp.

Jepson, W. L. 1893. The riparian botany of the lower Sacramento. Ethyreal 1: 238-246.

Jones and Stokes Associates. 1977. An evaluation of the feasibility of utilizing agricultural tile drainage water for marsh management in the San Joaquin Valley, California. U.S. Fish and Wildl. Serv., Washington, D.C. 172 pp.

——. 1988. Private wetlands in the Kern-Tulare Basin, California: their status, values, protection, and enhancement. Final rep. prepared for the Calif. Dep. Fish and Game and Calif. Waterfowl Assoc., Sacramento. 160 pp.

Josselyn, M. N. 1983. The ecology of San Francisco Bay tidal marshes: a community profile. U.S. Fish and Wildl. Serv., Div. Biol. Sci., Washington, D.C. FWS/OBS-83/23. 102 pp.

Kahrl, W. L. 1979. The California water atlas. Calif. Governor's Off. of Planning and Res. and Calif. Dep. Water Resour., Los Altos. 118 pp.

Katibah, E. F. 1984. A brief history of riparian forests in the Central Valley of California. Pages 23-29 in R. E. Warner and K. M. Hendrix, eds. California riparian systems. Univ. California Press, Berkeley.

Kear, J. 1970. The adaptive radiation of parental care in waterfowl. Pages 357-392 in J. H. Crook, ed. Social behaviour in birds and mammals. Academic Press, London.

Keller, E. A. 1977. The fluvial system: selected observations. Pages 39-46 in A. Sands, ed.

Riparian forests in California, their ecology and conservation. Inst. Ecol. Publ. 15, Univ. California, Davis.

Kozlik, F. M. 1975. Management and production—west coast habitat. Proc. Int. Waterfowl Symp. 1:88-91.

Lapham, M. H., A. T. Sweet, A. T. Strahorn, and L. C. Holmes. 1909. Soil survey of the Colusa area, California. U.S. Dep. Agric., U.S. Gov. Print. Off. 10 pp.

Leach, H. R. 1960. Wildlife and fishery resources in relation to drainage disposal problems in the San Joaquin Valley. Calif. Dep. Fish and Game Final Rep. 127 pp.

LeDonne, J. R. 1980. California Pacific Flyway report. Pages 43-113 in J. C. Bartonek, comp. Pacific Flyway Waterfowl Rep. Pacific Flyway Study Committee, Portland, Ore.

Letey, J., C. Roberts, M. Penberth, and C. Vasek. 1986. An agriculture dilemma: drainage water and toxics disposal in the San Joaquin Valley. Univ. of California, Div. of Agric. and Nat. Resour., Agric. Exp. Stn. Special. Publ. 3319, Davis. 56 pp.

Lynn, W. C. 1963. A study of chemical and biological processes operative in reclaimed and unreclaimed tidal marsh sediments. Ph.D. Dissertation, Univ. California, Davis. 254 pp.

MacDonald, K. B. 1977. Coastal salt marsh. Pages 263-294 in M. G. Barbour and J. Major, eds. Terrestrial vegetation of California. John Wiley and Sons, New York, N.Y.

Madrone Associates. 1980. Sacramento/San Joaquin Delta wildlife habitat protection and restoration plan. Calif. Dep. Fish and Game and U.S. Fish and Wildl. Serv., Washington, D.C. 10 pp.

Mall, R. E. 1969. Soil-water-salt relationships of waterfowl food plants in the Suisun Marsh of California. Calif. Dep. Fish and Game, Wildl. Bull. 1, Sacramento. 59 pp.

———, and G. Rollins. 1972. Wildlife resource requirements, waterfowl and the Suisun Marsh. Pages 60-68 in J. E. Skinner, Comp. Ecological studies of the Sacramento-San Joaquin estuary. Delta Fish and Wildl. Protection Study Rep. 8. Calif. Dep. Fish and Game, Sacramento.

Mason, H. L. 1957. A flora of the marshes of California. Univ. California Press, Berkeley. 878 pp.

Mayhew, W. W. 1955. Spring rainfall in relation to mallard production in the Sacramento Valley, California. J. Wildl. Manage. 19:36-47.

Mays, A. S. 1941. Observations on duck disease at Tulare Lake Basin, 1940. Calif. Fish and Game 27:154-163.

McAllister, M. H. 1930. The early history of duck clubs in California. Calif. Fish and Game 16:281-285.

McGowan, J. A. 1961. History of the Sacramento

Valley Vol. I. Lewis Hist. Publ. Co., New York, N.Y. 430 pp.

McKinney, F. 1986. Ecological factors influencing the social systems of migratory dabbling ducks. Pages 153-171 in D. I. Rubenstein and R. W. Wrangham, eds. Ecological aspects of social evolution. Princeton Univ. Press, Princeton, N.J.

McLandress, M. R. 1979. Status of Ross' geese in California. Pages 255-265 in R. L. Jarvis and J. C. Bartonek, eds. Management and biology of Pacific Flyway geese. Oregon State Univ. Bookstores, Corvallis.

———, and G. S. Yarris. 1987. An evaluation of California duck production. Prog. Rep. 30 June 1987. Rep. to Calif. Fish and Game, Sacramento. 44 pp.

———, ———, and A. E. H. Perkins. 1987. An evaluation of California duck production. Prog. Rep. 30 Sept. 1987. Rep. to Calif. Fish and Game, Sacramento. 32 pp.

McLean, D. D. 1946. Duck disease at Tulare Lake. Calif. Fish and Game 32:71-80.

Mensik, G. 1986. Marsh management—"Fed style." Calif. Waterfowl Assoc. Q. Newsletter 12(4):10-11.

Miller, A. W., R. S. Miller, H. C. Cohen, and R. F. Schultze. 1975. Suisun marsh study—Solano County, California. U.S. Soil Conserv. Serv., Davis, Calif. 186 pp.

———, and P. H. Arend. 1960. How to grow watergrass for ducks in California. Calif. Dep. Fish and Game, Game Manage. Leafl. No. 1, Sacramento. 16 pp.

Miller, M. R. 1985. Time budgets of northern pintails wintering in the Sacramento Valley, California. Wildfowl 36:53-64.

———. 1986. Northern pintail body condition during wet and dry winters in the Sacramento Valley, California. J. Wildl. Manage. 50:189-198.

———. 1987. Fall and winter foods of northern pintails in the Sacramento Valley, California. J. Wildl. Manage. 51:405-414.

Mitsch, W. J., and J. G. Gosselink. 1986. Wetlands. Van Nostrand Reinhold Co., New York, N.Y. 539 pp.

Moffitt, J. 1938. Environmental factors affecting waterfowl in the Suisun area, California. Condor 40:76-84.

Munz, P. A., and D. D. Keck. 1975. A California flora and supplement. Univ. California Press, Berkeley. 1,681 pp.

Murkin, H. R., R. M. Kaminski, and R. D. Titman. 1982. Responses by dabbling ducks and aquatic invertebrates to an experimentally manipulated cattail marsh. Can. J. Zool. 60:2324-2332.

———, and J. A. Kadlec. 1986. Responses by benthic macroinvertebrates to prolonged flooding of marsh habitat. Can. J. Zool. 64:65-72.

Neely, W. W. 1958. Irreversible drainage—a new factor in wildlife management. Trans. North Am. Wildl. and Nat. Resour. Conf. 23:342-348.

——. 1962. Saline soils and brackish waters in the management of wildlife, fish, and shrimp. Trans. North Am. Wildl. Conf. 27: 321-335.

Nelson, J. W., and J. A. Kadlec. 1984. A conceptual approach to relating habitat structure and macroinvertebrate production in freshwater wetlands. Trans. North Am. Wildl. and Nat. Resour. Conf. 49:262-270.

Ohlendorf, H. M., D. J. Hoffman, M. K. Saiki, and T. W. Aldrich. 1986a. Embryonic mortality and abnormalities of aquatic birds: apparent impacts by selenium from irrigation drainwater. Sci. Total Environ. 52:49-63.

——, R. L. Hothem, C. M. Bunck, T. W. Aldrich, and J. F. Moore. 1986b. Relationships between selenium concentrations and avian reproduction. Trans. North Am. Wildl. and Nat. Resour. Conf. 51:330-342.

Parr, D. E., M. D. Scott, and D. D. Kennedy. 1979. Autumn movements and habitat use by wood ducks in southern Illinois. J. Wildl. Manage. 43:102-108.

Raveling, D. G. 1978. Dynamics of distribution of Canada geese in winter. Trans. North Am. Wildl. and Nat. Resour. Conf. 43:206-225.

——. 1979. The annual cycle of body composition of Canada geese with special reference to control of reproduction. Auk 96:234-252.

——. 1984. Geese and hunters of Alaska's Yukon Delta: management problems and political dilemmas. Trans. North Am. Wildl. and Nat. Resour. Conf. 49:555-575.

——, and M. E. Heitmeyer. 1988. Relationships of population size and recruitment of pintails to habitat conditions and harvest by hunters in the United States. Univ. California, Davis. 52 pp.

Reid, F. A. 1985. Wetland invertebrates in relation to hydrology and water chemistry. Pages 72-79 in M. D. Knighton, ed. Water impoundments for wildlife: a habitat management workshop. U.S. For. Serv., St. Paul, Minn.

Richards, W. W. 1916. Lake Merritt—a refuge for waterfowl. Calif. Fish and Game 3:133-136.

Rienecker, W. C. 1965. A summary of band returns from lesser snow geese (Chen hyperborea) of the Pacific Flyway. Calif. Fish and Game. 51:132-146.

——. 1976. Distribution, harvest, and survival of American wigeon banded in California. Calif. Fish and Game 62:141-153.

——. 1987. Migration and distribution of northern pintails banded in California. Calif. Fish and Game 73:139-155.

——, and W. Anderson. 1960. A waterfowl nesting study on Tule Lake and Lower Klamath National Wildlife Refuges, 1957. Calif. Fish and Game 46:481-506.

Roberts, W. G., J. G. Howe, and J. Major. 1977. A survey of riparian forest flora and fauna in California. Pages 3-20 in A. Sands, ed. Riparian forests in California, their ecology and conservation. Inst. Ecol. Publ. No. 15, Univ. California, Davis.

Rollins, G. L. 1973. Relationships between soil salinity and the salinity of applied water in the Suisun Marsh of California. Calif. Fish and Game 59:5-35.

——. 1981. A guide to waterfowl habitat management in Suisun Marsh. Calif. Dep. Fish and Game Publ., Sacramento. 109 pp.

Rosen, M. N. 1965. Control of waterfowl botulism. Calif. Dep. Fish and Game, Game Manage. Leafl. No. 10, Sacramento. 6 pp.

Rutger, J. N., and D. M. Brandon. 1981. California rice culture. Sci. 244:42-51.

Sacramento Valley Waterfowl Habitat Management Committee. 1984. Pacific Flyway waterfowl in California's Sacramento Valley wetlands—an analysis of habitat . . . a plan for protection. Calif. Waterfowl Assoc., Redwood City. 259 pp.

Scott, L. B., and S. K. Marquiss. 1984. A historical overview of the Sacramento River. Pages 51-57 in R. E. Warner and K. M. Hendrix, eds. California riparian systems. Univ. California Press, Berkeley.

Severson, D. J. 1987. Macroinvertebrate populations in seasonally flooded marshes in the San Joaquin Valley of California. M.S. Thesis, Humboldt State Univ., Arcata, Calif. 113 pp.

Smith, F. E. 1979. Discussional and background material, waterfowl-agriculture data input. Rep. for Adaptive Environ. Assessment Workshop, Calif. Water Policy Center and U.S. Fish and Wildl. Serv., Sacramento. 175 pp.

Stine, S. W. 1980. Hunting and the faunal landscape subsistence and commercial venery in early California. M.S. Thesis, Univ. California, Berkeley. 50 pp.

Stoner, E. A. 1937. A record of twenty-five years of wildfowl shooting on the Suisun Marsh, California. Condor 39:242-248.

Strahorn, A. T., J. W. Nelson, L. C. Holmes, and E. C. Eckmann. 1914. Soil survey of the Fresno area, California. U.S. Dep. Agric., U.S. Gov. Print. Off., Washington D.C. 50 pp.

Swanson, G. A., and J. C. Bartonek. 1970. Bias associated with food analysis in gizzards of blue-winged teal. J. Wildl. Manage. 34:739-746.

Thompson, J. 1957. The settlement and geography of the Sacramento-San Joaquin Delta, California. Ph.D. Dissertation, Stanford Univ, Palo Alto, Calif. 50 pp.

Thompson, K. 1961. Riparian forests of the Sacramento Valley, California. Ann. Assoc. Am. Geogr. 51:294-315.

Titche, A. R. 1979. Avian cholera in California. Calif. Dep. Fish and Game Adm. Rep. 79-2, Sacramento. 49 pp.

U.S. Department of Commerce. 1986. Climatological data, California, Vol. 90. Natl. Oceanic and Atmos. Admin., Natl. Climate Center, Asheville, N.C. 10 pp.

U.S. Department of the Interior. 1950. Waterfowl conservation in the lower San Joaquin Valley. U.S. Fish and Wildl. Serv., Washington, D.C. 123 pp.

U.S. Fish and Wildlife Service. 1978. Concept plan for waterfowl wintering habitat preservation, Central Valley, California. U.S. Fish and Wildl. Serv., Region 1, Portland, Oreg. 116 pp.

———. 1987a. Draft concept plan for waterfowl wintering habitat preservation—an update, Central Valley. U.S. Dep. Int., U.S. Fish and Wildl. Serv., Region 1, Portland, Oreg. 17 pp.

———. 1987b. A report on the feasibility of growing marsh plants in the Imperial and Coachella Valleys of California. U.S. Fish and Wildl. Serv., Region 1, Portland, Oreg. 16 pp.

———, and Canadian Wildlife Service. 1986. 1986 status of waterfowl and fall flight forecast. U.S. Fish and Wildl. Serv., Washington, D.C. 38 pp.

Usinger, R. L., editor. 1956. Aquatic insects of California Univ. California Press, Berkeley. 508 pp.

Warner, R. F., and K. M. Hendrix. 1985. Riparian resources of the Central Valley and California desert. Calif. Dep. of Fish and Game, Sacramento. 10 pp.

Weller, M. W. 1975. Migratory waterfowl: a hemispheric perspective. Publ. Biol. Inst. de Invest. Cienc. U.A.N.L. 1:89-130.

Wester, L. 1981. Composition of native grasslands in the San Joaquin Valley, California. Madrono 28:231-241.

White, D. C. 1985. Lowland hardwood wetland invertebrate community and production in Missouri. Arch. Hydrobiol. 103:509-533.

Woolington, D. W., P. F. Springer, and D. R. Yparraguirre. 1979. Migration and wintering distribution of Aleutian Canada geese. Pages 299-309 *in* R. L. Jarvis and J. C. Bartonek, eds. Management and biology of Pacific Flyway geese. Orgeon State Univ. Bookstores, Corvallis.

Zahm, G. R. 1986. Kesterson reservoir and Kesterson National Wildlife Refuge: history, current problems and management alternatives. Trans. North Am. Wildl. and Nat. Resour. Conf. 51:324-329.

Zedler, J. B., M. N. Josselyn, and C. Onuf. 1982. Restoration techniques, research, and monitoring: vegetation. Pages 63-72 *in* M. N. Josselyn, ed. Wetland restoration and enhancement in California. Calif. Sea Grant College Prog. Rep. T-CSGCP-007. La Jolla.

THE PACIFIC COAST OF MEXICO

GARY W. KRAMER, U.S. Fish and Wildlife Service, P.O. Box 120, Calipatria, CA 92233
RODRIGO MIGOYA[1], Direccion de Flora y Fauna Silvestres, Rio Elba No. 20, 16 piso, Mexico, D.F.

Wintering waterfowl in Mexico average 4.7 million or 8% of North America's total waterfowl population (U.S. Fish and Wildlife Service 1981). In 1985, 48% of the ducks, geese, and American coots (*Fulica americana*) in Mexico occupied the Pacific Coast marshes, making it the most important waterfowl habitat in the Republic. This region wintered from 1 to 1.5 million waterfowl from 1976 to 1985 (U.S. Fish and Wildlife Service 1976-85).

The Pacific Coast region of Mexico, for the purpose of this paper, includes mostly coastal marshes in the states of Baja California Norte, Baja California Sur, Sonora, Sinaloa, and Nayarit (Fig. 1). Additional, less important wetlands are located farther south on the Pacific Coast. Because <5% of the region's waterfowl population occurs there, these areas will not be addressed.

Waterfowl and wetland conservation efforts in Mexico have only recently been initiated. However, Mexico has not experienced wetland losses of comparable magnitude to that documented for California (Gilmer et al. 1982) and other major wintering grounds in the Pacific Flyway. Many of Mexico's Pacific Coast wetlands are still relatively pristine. Although habitat destruction has been minimal, some habitat changes have occurred. Construction of irrigation reservoirs and resulting agricultural expansions in Sonora and Sinaloa in recent decades have changed cropping patterns, created habitat alterations (Saunders and Saunders 1981), and caused potential contaminant situations (Mora et al. 1987). The increase in agriculture has enhanced food resources for some waterfowl species (Kramer and Euliss 1986), but the effects on other species are largely unknown. Research and management efforts in Mexico have been minimal compared to other wintering grounds in North America.

In this paper, we review the available data on waterfowl use and the management of wetlands on the Pacific Coast of Mexico.

HABITAT CHARACTERISTICS

The Pacific Coast of Mexico is extensive, covering more than 4,000 km. It can be divided into 2 main physiographic regions: the Baja California Peninsula and the Mainland West Coast (Fig. 1). Because the 2 regions are different in climate, topography, plant communities, and hydrological characteristics, they are discussed separately.

Major Wintering Regions and Important Wetlands

Baja California.—The Baja California Peninsula is a 50 to 250 km-wide finger of land extending 1,500 km southward from the United States (U.S.) border. The climate, rainfall, and vegetation of Baja California are highly varied. Distinctive areas and conditions include the coniferous forests of the San Pedro Martir, where freezing temperatures and snow are frequent, to the Vizcaino Desert, where years may pass without measurable precipitation (Wiggins 1980, Wilbur 1987). However, the majority of the Peninsula's waterfowl habitat areas are found in the bays and estuaries of the Pacific Coast and in the Rio Colorado Delta (Fig. 1); therefore, only these areas are addressed.

The climate is arid to semiarid; annual rainfall in the major waterfowl habitat areas of Baja California ranges from 4 to

[1]Present Address: Department of Zoology and Wildlife Sciences, 331 Funchess Hall, Auburn University, AL 36849.

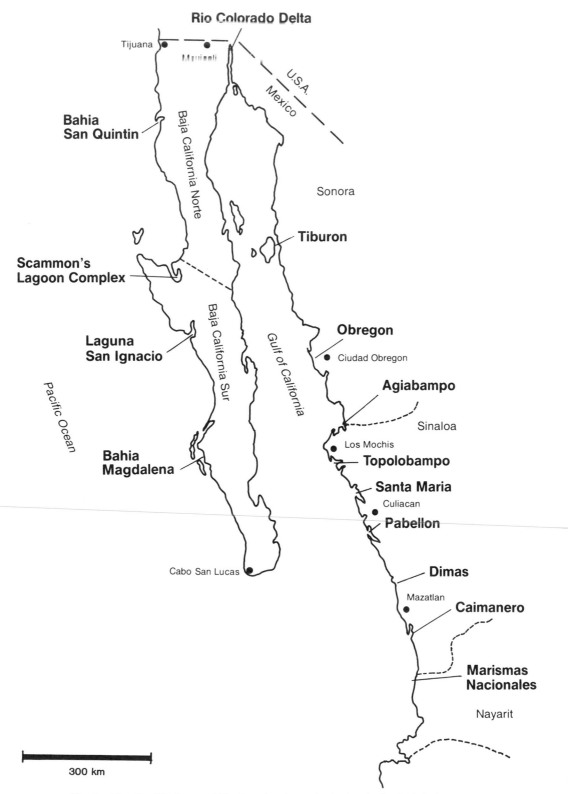

Fig. 1. The Pacific Coast of Mexico showing principal waterfowl wintering areas.

Table 1. Important wetlands of Baja California, Mexico.

Area	Size km²	Type	Waterfowl habitats	References
Bahia San Quintin	43	tidal estuary	eelgrass	Dawson (1962)
			open water	Kramer (1976)
			salt marsh	
Scammons Lagoon Complex		tidal estuaries	eelgrass	Phleger and
Laguna Ojo de Liebre	210		open water	Ewing (1962)
Laguna Guerrero Negro	70		salt marsh	Saunders and
Laguna Manuela	15			Saunders (1981)
Laguna San Ignacio Complex		tidal estuaries	eelgrass	Saunders and
Laguna San Ignacio	175		open water	Saunders (1981)
Estero la Bocana	12		salt marsh	Wilbur (1987)
Laguna Escondido	15		mangroves	
Bahia Magdalena	240	tidal lagoons	eelgrass	Saunders and
		protected by	open water	Saunders (1981)
		barrier islands	salt marsh	Wilbur (1987)
			mangroves	
Rio Colorado Delta	100	riverine marsh	cattail-bulrush marsh	Saunders and
			riparian	Saunders (1981)
			agricultural land	Wilbur (1987)

39 cm (Phleger and Ewing 1962). In the northwest, rainfall is light but frequent between October and March. Farther south, and in the Rio Colorado Delta, the climate is more tropical, and most of the precipitation occurs from July to October (Wilbur 1987).

The Pacific Coast of the Baja California Peninsula is characterized by large, shallow coastal lagoons (Table 1), which are influenced by tidal movements (Scott and Carbonell 1986). The majority of these lagoons are hypersaline due to the lack of freshwater inflow, the high degree of evaporation caused by constant winds, and high solar radiation (Postma 1965, Alvarado et al. 1986). Water temperatures inside the lagoons vary seasonally, with a low of 18 C in winter and a high of 22 C in summer.

Bahia San Quintin, 250 km south of Tijuana (Fig. 1), is a tidal lagoon protected on the west and south by sand spits. The bay has an average depth of 1.8 m during high tides (Kramer 1976).

Major waterfowl habitats at Bahia San Quintin consist of extensive beds of eelgrass (*Zostera marina*) in the open waters of the bay and intertidal salt marshes dominated by cordgrass (*Spartina*

foliosa) and pickleweed (*Salicornia* spp.) (Dawson 1962, Kramer et al. 1979) (Table 1). Ecology of these plant communities can be found in Zedler (1982) and Boone and Hoeppl (1976).

The Scammon's Lagoon complex, 850 km south of Tijuana (Fig. 1), comprises 3 lagoons: the largest, Laguna Ojo de Liebre, is at the south end, Laguna Guerrero Negro lies in the center, and the smallest, Laguna Manuela, is the most northerly. Laguna Ojo de Liebre extends inland about 40 km and is separated from Laguna Guerrero by a low land-bridge. A second land-bridge separates Laguna Guerrero Negro from Laguna Manuela. (Phleger and Ewing 1962).

All 3 lagoons support extensive eelgrass beds. Rocky areas support sea lettuce (*Ulva lactuca*) and other algae (Foster and Schiel 1985). Most shorelines and uplands support sparse halophytic desert vegetation. Some shorelines support salt marshes of cordgrass and pickleweed (Table 1) (Saunders and Saunders 1981, Wilbur 1987). Extensive areas of the Laguna Ojo de Liebre have been converted to salt evaporation ponds.

Laguna San Ignacio, 1,150 km south of Tijuana (Fig. 1), is a broad saline tidal lagoon with eelgrass, widgeongrass (*Ruppia maritima*), and algae as its principal marine vegetation (Saunders and Saunders 1981, Ward 1983). Red mangrove (*Rhizophora mangle*), black mangrove (*Avicennia germinans*), and salt marshes of cordgrass, pickleweed, and saltgrass (*Distichlis spicata*) occur along many shoreline areas (Table 1) (Wilbur 1987). Most of the shoreline and the entire adjacent uplands are dominated by Agave-Ambrosia desert (Wilbur 1987). Similar vegetative communities are found at two smaller lagoons, Laguna Escondido and Estero la Bocana, lying to the north of San Ignacio.

The Bahia Magdalena region, 400 km northwest of Cabo San Lucas, is actually a series of coastal lagoons extending a distance of more than 200 km (Fig. 1). These saline waters are protected by a chain of barrier islands, which are separated by several passes to the Pacific Ocean (Saunders and Saunders 1981).

Bahia Magdalena contains extensive mangrove swamps and salt marshes that make up only a small part of the shoreline vegetation. Eelgrass and several species of algae are common in the bays (Table 1). Uplands are dominated by arid desert (Wilbur 1987).

The only significant freshwater habitat on the Baja California Peninsula occurs in the Rio Colorado Delta (Table 1). The delta encompasses more than 80 km of the lower Colorado River as that river flows from the U.S. border to the Gulf of California (Fig. 1). Many areas of the delta are not as rich in waterfowl habitat as they were historically, but some riverine areas, nearby flooded agricultural fields, and backwater sloughs and marshes still provide suitable waterfowl habitat.

Mainland West Coast.—The region contains 9 important wetland areas for wintering waterfowl. It is most convenient to discuss these areas according to U.S. Fish and Wildlife Service survey unit terminology (Saunders and Saunders 1981, U.S. Fish and Wildlife Service 1985).

The region consists of a long, narrow coastal plain bordered by shallow coastal lagoons which receive variable amounts of fresh water from rivers and agricultural irrigation channels. The largest waterfowl populations wintering in this area are generally associated with excess irrigation water, especially where it flows into salt flats or tidal basins creating fresh to brackish conditions. Rice, wheat, and other small grains provide abundant foods for field-feeding ducks and geese (Saunders and Saunders 1981, Scott 1983, Kramer and Euliss 1986).

The most northerly area along the Mainland West Coast is the Tiburon unit (Fig. 1). Of major importance to waterfowl is the Canal del Infiernillo lying between Isla Tiburon and the mainland. Although these waters are subject to extreme tidal fluctuations and high winds, they support extensive stands of eelgrass (Table 2).

The Obregon unit (Fig. 1) includes the agricultural district adjacent to Ciudad Obregon, Oviachi Reservoir, the Rio Yaqui Delta, and several nearby coastal lagoons including Bahia Lobos, Bahia Tobari, Bahia Santa Barbara, and Bahia Yavaros (Table 2) (Saunders and Saunders 1981, U.S. Fish and Wildlife Service 1985). The freshwater marshes are dominated by cattail (*Typha* spp.) and bulrush (*Scirpus* spp.), whereas widgeongrass and horned pondweed (*Zanichellia palustris*) are found in brackish areas (Saunders and Saunders 1981).

The agricultural district of Obregon was created by clearing a large area of thorn forest on the coastal plain from Ciudad Obregon southwest to the Pacific shore. As early as 1930, some areas were cultivated. Agriculture increased with the construction of several reservoirs in the 1940s, and, by 1950, 141,750 ha of irrigated croplands were present (Saunders and Saunders 1981).

Laguna Agiabampo and Estero Bacore-

Table 2. Important wetlands of the Mainland West Coast of Mexico[a].

Area[b]	Size km[2]	Type	Waterfowl habitats
Tiburon	960	tidal channel	eelgrass, open water
Obregon	600	tidal estuaries freshwater marshes brackish marshes	eelgrass, open water, salt marsh, cattail-bulrush marsh, agricultural land
Agiabampo	300	tidal estuaries freshwater marshes brackish marshes	eelgrass, open water, salt marsh, cattail-bulrush marsh, agricultural land, mangroves
Topolobampo	400	tidal estuaries freshwater marshes brackish marshes	eelgrass, open water, salt marsh, cattail-bulrush marsh, agricultural land, mangroves
Santa Maria	1,330	tidal estuaries freshwater marshes brackish marshes	eelgrass, open water, salt marsh, cattail-bulrush marsh, agricultural land, mangroves
Pabellon	800	tidal estuaries freshwater marshes brackish marshes	open water, salt marsh, cattail-bulrush marsh, agricultural land, mangroves
Dimas	120	tidal estuaries freshwater marshes brackish marshes	open water, salt marsh, cattail-bulrush marsh, agricultural land, mangroves
Caimanero	300	tidal estuaries freshwater marshes brackish marshes	open water, salt marsh, cattail-bulrush marsh, mangroves
Marismas Nationales	1920	tidal estuaries freshwater marshes brackish marshes	open water, salt marsh, cattail-bulrush marsh, mangroves

[a]Data derived from U.S. Fish and Wildlife Service (1948-87) and Saunders and Saunders (1981).
[b]Areas are those described as survey units by U.S. Fish and Wildlife Service (1948-87).

huis, both tidal lagoons, make up the coastal habitats of the Agiabampo unit, which lies on the boundary between Sonora and Sinaloa (Fig. 1). The area is 38 km long and includes 70,000 ha of irrigated cropland near Navojoa and Mocuzari Reservoir. Saunders and Saunders (1981) believed these lagoons supported submerged aquatic vegetation, probably widgeongrass and marine algae. In 1985, Kramer (unpubl. data) found eelgrass growing in Laguna Agiabampo (Table 2).

The Topolobampo unit (Fig. 1) comprises large brackish lagoons and shallow saltwater bays with little aquatic vegetation (Scott and Carbonell 1986). Major areas include Bahia San Esteban, located just south of the mouth of the Rio Fuerte, Bahia de Santa Maria, Bahia Topolobampo, and Bahia Navachiste (Table 2). This survey unit also includes the agricultural lands near Los Mochis. The principal reservoir in the area is the

Presa el Majon on the Rio Fuerte (Saunders and Saunders 1981).

The principal wetlands of the Santa Maria unit are adjacent to Bahia de Santa Maria, near the mouth of the Rio Mocorito (Fig. 1). The bay parallels the coast for about 74 km. Altamura Island (42 km long) separates the bay from the ocean. The bay contains an abundance of eelgrass and widgeongrass (Table 2) (Saunders and Saunders 1981).

The principal feature of the Pabellon unit is Ensenada del Pabellon, a large tidal lagoon (Fig. 1). Most of its freshwater comes from the Rio Culiacan. Adjacent to the lagoon are salt flats, tidal pools, and mangrove swamps (Table 2). The large, shallow southern lobe of Pabellon becomes very turbid during high winds and has large mudflats exposed at low tides.

Saunders and Saunders (1981) found little aquatic vegetation in Ensenada del Pabellon other than algae, but abundant populations of small mollusks were used by diving ducks. Small lagoons on the mainland contained mostly widgeongrass, some muskgrass (*Chara* spp.), and other algae. Extensive irrigated lands supporting rice and wheat extend from northwest of Culiacan southward for 40 km. Two large reservoirs, Presa El Humaya and Presa Sanalona, lie nearby (Saunders and Saunders 1981).

The Dimas unit is a series of lagoons between Ensenada del Pabellon and Mazatlan (Fig. 1). The most northerly lagoon extends about 60 km from the mouth of the Rio San Lorenzo to near the Rio Elota. When water conditions are favorable, these lagoons provide good habitat with an abundance of widgeongrass (Table 2), but in years of low runoff, many of the basins are dry and waterfowl use is correspondingly light (Saunders and Saunders 1981).

The estuaries between Mazatlan and the Rio Baluarte constitute the Caimanero unit (Fig. 1). The principal waterfowl area is Laguna del Caimanero, which begins 24 km southeast of Mazatlan and lies between the deltas of the Rio del Presidio and Rio del Baluarte. Caimanero Lagoon is shallow and varies greatly in size, seasonally, depending on the amount of runoff from the adjacent foothills. In the 1950s, the principal waterfowl food was widgeongrass, which thrived in the brackish-to-saline waters of the northern end (Table 2). Green algae and mollusks of several species also were present (Saunders and Saunders 1981).

The Marismas Nacionales unit comprises a series of marshy lagoons (Fig. 1) extending from the delta of the Rio del Baluarte to the delta of the Rio San Pedro. The principal source of freshwater is the Rio de Acaponeta and several smaller streams. Surface water varies greatly between years, depending on rainfall and runoff. Waterfowl habitats include broad, shallow, saline lagoons, fairly deep mangrove-bordered pools, and vast marshes and mudflats (Table 2) (Saunders and Saunders 1981).

Waterfowl Populations

A total of 38 species of ducks, geese, and swans have been recorded on Mexico's Pacific Coast, and 24 species have been recorded with regularity (Table 3) (Leopold 1959, Bellrose 1980, Saunders and Saunders 1981, Wilbur 1987). Population data used here were derived from aerial waterfowl surveys conducted once a year, usually in January (U.S. Fish and Wildlife Service 1948-87). This midwinter survey provides only indexes of waterfowl numbers, with an unknown degree of precision (B. Conant, pers. commun.).

The primary emphasis of the survey is to obtain black brant population estimates. Every third year, a more comprehensive survey is conducted to count all waterfowl. The most recent comprehensive survey occurred in January 1985 (U.S. Fish and Wildlife Service 1948-87). Because the emphasis is on brant, even in years when other species are estimated, little survey work occurs away from coastal areas. Large numbers of ducks may be found in some wetlands that lie between the coast and the mountains (J. Voelzer, pers. commun.).

The number of white-fronted geese counted during the midwinter inventory is probably significantly lower than actual population levels. Geese, other than brant, are estimated only on an opportunistic basis. Inland areas are not surveyed, and estimates are included only when geese are seen near coastal areas (B. Conant, pers. commun.).

Baja California.—Baja California is primarily a wintering area. Only localized nesting of small numbers of mallards, cinnamon teal, and ruddy ducks has been documented (Grinnell 1928, Wilbur 1987). The actual number of waterfowl produced in Baja California is unknown, but based on the extent of suitable breeding habitat, it is probably insignificant.

Table 3.   Waterfowl of Mexico's Pacific Coast

Common name	Scientific name	Breeding	Wintering
Tundra swan[a]	*Cygnus columbianus*		X
White-fronted goose	*Anser albifrons*		X
Snow goose	*Chen caerulescens*		X
Ross goose[a]	*Chen rossii*		X
Canada goose	*Branta canadensis*		X
Aleutian Canada goose[a]	*B. c. leucopareia*		
Black brant	*Bernicla nigricans*		X
Light-bellied brant[a]	*B. b. hrota*		
Mallard	*Anas platyrhynchos*	X	X
Gadwall	*A. strepera*		
Green-winged teal	*A. crecca*		X
American wigeon	*A. americana*		X
Eurasian wigeon[a]	*A. penelope*		
Northern pintail	*A. acuta*		X
Northern shoveler	*A. clypeata*		X
Blue-winged teal	*A. discors*		X
Cinnamon teal	*A. cyanoptera*	X	X
Ruddy duck	*Oxyura jamaicensis*	X	X
Masked duck[a]	*O. dominica*	X	X
Fulvous whistling-duck	*Dendrocygna bicolor*	X	X
Black-bellied whistling-duck	*D. autumnalis*	X	X
Wood duck[a]	*Aix sponsa*		X
Canvasback	*Aythya valisineria*		X
Redhead	*A. americana*		X
Ring-necked duck	*A. collaris*		X
Greater scaup[a]	*A. marila*		X
Lesser scaup	*A. affinis*		X
White-winged scoter	*Melanitta fusca*		X
Black scoter[a]	*M. nigra*		X
Surf scoter	*M. perspicillata*		X
Oldsquaw[a]	*Clangula hyemalis*		X
Common goldeneye	*Bucephala clangula*		X
Barrow's goldeneye[a]	*B. islandica*		X
Bufflehead	*B. albeola*		X
Common merganser[a]	*Mergus merganser*		X
Red-breasted merganser	*M. serrator*		X
Hooded merganser[a]	*Lophodytes cucullatus*		X
Muscovy duck[a]	*Cairina moschata*	X	X

[a]Has been recorded but occurs infrequently.

Although most important as wintering grounds, virtually all of Baja California's waterfowl areas also are used by migrants. The Rio Colorado Delta is used in September by early migrant northern pintails and cinnamon teal. Concentrations of northern shovelers, cinnamon teal, and green-winged teal occur there in spring.

Between 1980 and 1985, an average of 45,000 ducks, 200 geese, and 99,000 brant wintered in the Baja California segment of the Pacific Coast. This represents 4% of

all ducks, <1% of the geese, and 76% of the brant found on Mexico's Pacific Coast in winter (U.S. Fish and Wildlife Service 1980-85).

About 65% of Baja California's ducks, including the majority of its puddle ducks, are found in the Rio Colorado Delta, but most of the diving ducks occur in the saltwater bays of the Pacific Coast. Northern shoveler, green-winged teal, and northern pintail were the most numerous species in the Rio Colorado Delta between 1948 and 1962 (Saunders and

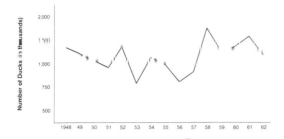

Fig. 2. Number of ducks observed on the Mainland West Coast, Mexico, during U.S. Fish and Wildlife Service midwinter (generally January) waterfowl surveys, 1948-62.

Saunders 1981). During more recent surveys, pintails have been the most numerous species (U.S. Fish and Wildlife Service 1985). The most common diving ducks in Baja California are lesser scaup and redheads.

Mainland West Coast.—Although the Mainland West Coast is used primarily by wintering and migrant birds, up to 6 species of ducks have been reported breeding there (Table 3). The most numerous nesting species are black-bellied whistling ducks and fulvous whistling ducks. Low numbers of ruddy ducks, cinnamon teal, and masked ducks also nest in the area. Wild muscovy ducks were reported to be present during the early 1980s by local observers in the interior of the Marismas Nacionales (Scott 1983).

The Mainland West Coast receives birds primarily from the Pacific Flyway, with smaller numbers of waterfowl originating in the Central Flyway (Saunders and

Saunders 1981), and wintered an average of 1.3 million ducks from 1948 to 1962 (Fig. 2). More recently, an average of 1.1 million ducks (Table 1), 5,500 geese, and 30,100 brant wintered along the Mainland West Coast. The marshes and lagoons of the Mainland West Coast are of special importance to certain species of ducks; >10% of all pintails, >20% of the green-winged teal, >30% of the shovelers, lesser scaup, ruddy ducks and redheads, >95% of the cinnamon teal, and >99% of all whistling ducks in the Pacific Flyway are found there in winter.

Pintails, cinnamon teal, and shovelers begin arriving in Sonora and Sinaloa by early September. By October, these are joined by more pintails, cinnamon teal, green-winged teal, shovelers, ruddy ducks, and American wigeon. By then, the black-bellied and fulvous whistling ducks gather from widely scattered breeding areas and are present in the marshes and lagoons from southern Sonora southward to the Guatemala border (Leopold 1959). Later arrivals include lesser scaup, redheads, and gadwall. Populations of all species build to peak numbers in December (Velazquez-Nogueron et al. 1972).

Of the 9 survey regions on the Mainland West Coast, the highest average number of ducks counted from 1976-85, in descending order, were found at Pabellon, Topolobampo, Marismas Nacionales, and Obregon (Table 4). However, all of the survey units were important to certain species, whereas some regions like Topo-

Table 4. Number of ducks counted by survey unit for the Mainland West Coast, Mexico, 1976-85[a].

Survey unit	1976	1977	1978	1979	1980	1981	1982	1983	1984	1985	Average
Tiburon	31,070	55,160	27,980	91,340	50,110	14,210	37,060	41,270	23,240	23,780	39,520
Obregon	447,100	142,030	155,500	71,680	154,310	43,210	142,380	86,150	187,980	131,520	156,190
Agiabampo	69,540	90,460	32,890	77,770	57,340	65,800	79,760	133,540	118,330	70,900	79,630
Topolobampo	276,510	372,640	180,560	344,670	335,330	160,150	213,920	233,330	415,240	305,020	283,740
Santa Maria	94,000	26,730	122,740	43,780	52,210	24,910	90,430	19,290	83,190	13,000	57,030
Pabellon	527,750	83,560	549,600	576,430	283,730	213,150	391,450	371,500	246,210	332,690	357,610
Dimas		90,500	381,480	59,380	132,500	140,710	61,910			7,150	124,800
Caimanero		78,770	86,640	40,960	70,640	51,620	124,540			94,860	78,290
Marismas Nacionales		182,130	199,910	144,010	103,410	197,710	245,020			139,200	173,060
Total	1,445,970	1,121,980	1,737,300	1,450,020	1,239,580	911,470	1,386,470	885,080	1,074,190	1,118,120	

[a]Data derived from U.S. Fish and Wildlife Service midwinter (generally January) waterfowl surveys.

Table 5. Average duck use of Mexico's Mainland West Coast survey units, 1979-85[a].

Species	Survey units								
	Tiburon[e]	Obregon	Agiabampo	Topolobampo	Santa Maria	Pabellon	Dimas	Caimanero	M. Nacionales
Gadwall						x[b]			x
American wigeon	x	x	x			x		x	x
Green-winged teal	x	x	xx	x		x	x		x
Cinnamon teal[c]			xx			xx	x		x
Northern-shoveler		x	x	x		x		x	x
Northern pintail	x	x	xx	x		xxx	xx	x	x
Whistling ducks[d]						x			x
Redhead			x	x					
Lesser scaup	x	x	x					x	
Ruddy duck								x	x

[a]Data derived from U.S. Fish and Wildlife Service midwinter (generally January) waterfowl surveys.
[b]Number of x's denotes magnitude of use: x = 5,000-50,000; xx = 50,001-100,000; xxx = >100,000.
[c]Includes small numbers of blue-winged teal.
[d]Includes both black-bellied and fulvous whistling ducks.
[e]<5,000 were observed for each species.

lobampo not only hosted large numbers of individuals but also hosted many species (Table 5).

Species of Special Concern.—Saunders and Saunders (1981) found an average of 11,000 geese, excluding brant, along the Mainland West Coast from 1948 to 1962. From 1980 to 1985, an average of only 5,500 geese were found. Ninety-five percent of the geese counted in this region were white-fronted geese. The Pacific white-fronted goose population has experienced a general population decline in recent years, from an estimated 500,000 in 1967 to 73,100 in November 1979 (O'Neil 1979, U.S. Fish and Wildlife Service 1979).

The Mainland West Coast white-fronted goose population has only averaged 5,000 birds in recent years, and this represents about 8% of the total Pacific Flyway population. Some additional Pacific Flyway white-fronted geese are known to winter in the eastern neighboring states of Durango and Chihuahua (Lensink 1986)—outside the area considered in this paper.

The first migrant white-fronted geese pass through California's Imperial Valley in early September (W. Henry, pers. commun.), and arrive in Sonora and northern Sinaloa in mid-September. The winter population is well-distributed along the Mainland West Coast by early October. Few data are available on the chronology of the spring migration. Velazquez-Nogueron et al. (1972) observed a decline in white-fronted goose numbers beginning in early February.

The most important area for white-fronted geese on the Mainland West Coast was the Obregon district, where about 50% of the white-fronted geese were counted between 1948 and 1962. Beginning in the early 1960s, these geese began to use newly developed rice- and wheat-growing regions in the Topolobampo and Pabellon units. Between 1961 and 1965, only 8% of the white-fronted geese were counted in the Obregon unit, whereas 40% and 30% were counted in the Topolobampo and Pabellon units, respectively (Saunders and Saunders 1981). Since the late 1960s, the geese have shifted even farther south. Between 1979 and 1985, the Obregon unit held 8% of all white-fronted geese, 10% were at Topolobampo, 32% at Pabellon, and 50% in the Dimas unit (U.S. Fish and Wildlife Service 1979-85). Reasons for the most recent shift in use areas are unknown.

A second species of concern is black brant. Mexico's Pacific Coast is the primary wintering region for brant. Between 1977 and 1986, the bays and lagoons in Baja California wintered 70%

of all black brant in the Pacific Flyway; 22% were found along the Mainland West Coast of Mexico, and only 8% wintered in the U.S. (Fig. 3) (U.S. Fish and Wildlife Service 1977-86). An unmeasured, but minor, percentage also winter annually in British Columbia and Alaska.

Formerly, a large proportion of the brant population wintered along the coasts of Washington, Oregon, and California (Chattin 1970, Bellrose 1980). However, a shift in the late 1950s from wintering grounds in the U.S. to Mexico was detected (Smith and Jensen 1970). The trend has continued, and the U.S. population of black brant declined from 44% of the total population in 1957 to 7% in 1975 (Fig. 3) (Kramer et al. 1979). The reasons for the decline in U.S. populations are speculative, but are believed to be a result of human harassment and disturbance (Chattin 1970, Smith and Jensen 1970, Kramer et al. 1979).

In Baja California, brant occur in the 4 major bays on the Pacific Coast. Between 1977 and 1986, the Scammon's Lagoon Complex hosted winter populations averaging 36,000, and Laguna San Ignacio wintered 32,000 brant. Bahia Magdalena held an average of 22,100, and Bahia San Quintin held an average of 8,200 (Table 6).

After the initial southward migration from Alaska to the Baja California wintering grounds in late October or early November (Jones 1973), there apparently is little movement between wintering areas. Kramer et al. (1979) found a stable winter population of 8,000-9,000 brant at Bahia San Quintin from early November to mid-January. The lengthy spring migration period at Bahia San Quintin began in mid-January and continued until late April. Peak numbers were observed in late March (Kramer et al. 1979).

The first black brant along the Mainland West Coast were found in 1958, even though aerial surveys had been conducted

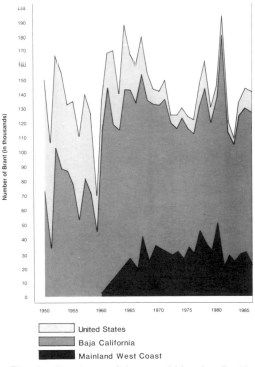

Fig. 3. Numbers of brant within the Pacific Flyway (excluding Alaska and British Columbia) as measured by U.S. Fish and Wildlife Service midwinter (generally January) waterfowl surveys, 1950-86.

regularly for the previous 10 years. In 1958, 4 brant were observed at Laguna Agiabampo (Smith and Jensen 1970). In 1959, 1,700 were recorded in several locations, and by 1963, the wintering population was 13,200. Between 1964 and 1976, an average of 29,995 were tallied on the Mainland West Coast, and from 1977 to 1986, brant numbers averaged 31,550.

Of the 9 survey regions on the Mainland West Coast, black brant have been found only at the 5 northernmost units (Fig. 1). They have not been recorded south of Bahia Santa Maria, which also is believed to be the southern limit of eelgrass. From 1969 to 1977, the Santa Maria unit wintered the highest average number of brant, followed by Tiburon and Topolobampo. More recently (1977 to 1986), the Tiburon unit wintered 43% of the Mainland West Coast population, and

Table 6. Number of black brant counted by survey unit for the Pacific Coast of Mexico, 1977-86[a].

Survey unit	1977	1978	1979	1980	1981	1982	1983	1984	1985	1986	Average
Tiburon	23,790	13,020	6,480	24,020	5,670	13,500	13,190	10,540	11,970	13,860	13,530
Obregon	3,910	910	4,970	2,310	790	1,340	1,430	630	1,570	1,750	1,960
Agiabampo	1,250	550	5,270	1,150	2,330	1,420	4,350	2,620	3,540	1,670	2,420
Topolobampo	5,290	6,060	5,730	7,250	3,030	5,850	1,760	8,140	8,550	2,150	5,440
Santa Maria	9,360	16,120	9,760	13,130	9,380	6,190	2,429	7,610	5,240	2,750	8,200
Magdalena	28,890	23,630	23,550	34,410	50,130	18,310	19,960	6,720	6,380	9,180	22,120
San Ignacio	20,580	30,660	26,140	23,740	45,770	34,340	26,460	32,370	57,450	26,590	32,410
Scammon's	32,030	41,780	34,480	28,350	59,030	23,430	22,310	11,150	32,070	45,680	36,030
San Quintin	5,040	10,410	3,690	3,160	5,630	9,040	13,030	14,940	5,510	11,090	8,200
Total	130,140	143,140	120,070	137,550	181,760	113,120	105,919	124,720	131,580	114,720	

[a]Data derived from U.S. Fish and Wildlife Service midwinter (generally January) waterfowl surveys.

Santa Maria wintered 26% (Table 6). Topolobampo was the third most important area, wintering 17% of the population during both time periods.

The chronology and routes of migration for the mainland segment of Mexico's brant population are unknown. Because brant seldom fly overland while on the wintering grounds, it is unlikely that they fly over the Baja California Peninsula to reach the Mainland West Coast. They probably fly around the tip of the Peninsula and then east and northeast to the mainland wintering grounds.

Land-Use Changes

Baja California. The most significant event to affect the natural resources of Baja California was the December 1973 completion of the transpeninsular highway (Mexico 1). The 1,600-km highway linked Tijuana to Cabo San Lucas at the tip of the Baja California Peninsula (Fig. 1). The paved highway allowed easy travel by passenger cars and heavy trucks. Before construction of the highway, travel over the dirt road was restricted to high-clearance or 4 wheel-drive vehicles (Kramer 1976). The new highway provided access for tourists, sport fishermen, hunters, whale watchers, and commercial trucks. Since the highway opened, tourism has increased 500%, sport fishing 400%, hunting 100%, whale watching 100%, and commercial trucking 600% (S. Miller, pers. commun.). This increase in human use of Baja California has impacted waterfowl resources in some areas.

Hunting in Baja California has increased, but at Bahia San Quintin, the increase was only 15% in the 10 years between 1974 and 1984 (Eldridge and Kramer 1985, SEDUE 1985). Even this modest increase has been sufficient to drive brant from Bahia San Quintin to the ocean, and precluded brant use of the bays' waters at high tide.

At Laguna Ojo de Liebre and Bahia San Ignacio, whale-watching activity has increased and is most popular in winter, coinciding with the use period for brant and other waterfowl. The disturbance of brant by boat traffic associated with whale watching is probably highest at Laguana Ojo de Liebre. The impact of this activity on brant and other waterfowl is not known. San Ignacio also supports a whale-watching industry with little impact on gray whales (*Eschrichtius robustus*) or brant (Swartz and Jones 1978, 1981). The U.S. Fish and Wildlife Service (1979) reported that tourism continues to be the major threat to waterfowl habitat in Baja California. Whale watchers and fishermen who operate boats near the eelgrass beds cause brant to move to other areas of the bays. However, as of 1979, tourist disturbance had not caused brant to leave any specific areas permanently.

The most significantly altered wetlands along Baja California's Pacific Coast are at Laguna Ojo de Liebre, where the world's largest saline works (20,000 ha)

Fig. 4.   Salt evaporation ponds constructed in saltmarsh habitat at Laguna Ojo de Liebre.

have been built (Fig. 4). Before development of the salt works, the area was occupied primarily by saltmarsh and salt flats subject to periodic tidal inundation (Nelson 1921). Boat traffic inside Ojo de Liebre occurs from the salt works to a port offshore at Isla de Cedros, where salt is exported to Japan. So far, no disturbance to brant from this boat traffic has been reported (J. Bremer, pers. commun.). At Bahia Magdalena, a phosphoric rock extraction plant has been constructed and is operational, but its impact on wildlife is unknown.

Striking changes in Baja California wetland habitat have occurred in the Rio Colorado Delta. Diking, upstream storage, and diversion of water for irrigation, after 1900, allowed settlement and cultivation of an area that had supported riverine marshes, riparian habitat, and desert. These practices allowed Mexicali to grow from a community of about 500 in 1910 (Nelson 1921) to the second largest population center in Baja California, with a population of 500,000 (Wilbur 1987). The Rio Colorado Delta today is subjected to both flooding and drought conditions even though upstream dams control river flows. As a result of these factors, in times of high water, great volumes of water are released downstream, causing flooding in the delta; but during periods of low water, virtually no instream flow is maintained. In pristine times, spring floods recharged marshes and maintained waterfowl habitat. The current water regime is so altered that wetland habitat in the Rio Colorado Delta is now of only moderate to poor quality.

Mainland West Coast.—Along the Mainland West Coast, the major land-use change has been the clearing of native thorn forest and large-scale conversion to agriculture. Construction of reservoirs, primarily for irrigation and secondarily for flood control, began in the 1940s in the Obregon area, and in the late 1950s and early 1960s in the Los Mochis and Culiacan areas. Several irrigation reservoirs were completed in Sinaloa as recently as 1981.

Three major agricultural districts were created when reservoirs were built on almost every major river in southern Sonora and Sinaloa. Previously, these areas contained family farms where small areas were cultivated by hand, or with horses or antiquated tractors. Before the irrigated agriculture period, crops were corn, beans, milo, cotton, and vegetables. Only small quantities of rice and wheat were produced (J. Cerritos, pers. commun.).

By 1950, after the construction of reservoirs on the Rio Yaqui and its tributaries, there were over 140,000 ha of irrigated cropland in the Obregon district. Delta and riparian areas downstream from reservoirs were adversely affected after stream flows were controlled, but waste agricultural waters created some new habitat. Excess agricultural water created new brackish areas along the coast, and the irrigated small grains enhanced food resources for some ducks and geese. Geese and pintails responded to the availability of rice and winter wheat by increasing their use of this region. Peak waterfowl populations were present in the Obregon region during the 1950s (Saunders and Saunders 1981).

In the 1960s, after construction of reservoirs on the Rio Fuerte, Rio Sinaloa, Rio Culiacan, and others, new agricultural districts were developed in the Los Mochis area and near Culiacan. Waterfowl populations shifted from the Obregon district to these areas in response to the production of rice, wheat, milo, and soybeans. The estimated total number of ducks in the Los Mochis area (Topolobampo unit) increased from 21,000 in 1951 before agricultural development to 743,000 in 1963. Ducks at Los Mochis are mostly pintails that feed chiefly in the

fields near Culiacan (Pabellon unit), as agricultural land and wastewater areas were created, waterfowl populations increased from 197,000 in 1951 to 510,000 in 1965 (Saunders and Saunders 1981).

HABITAT IMPORTANCE RELATIVE TO WATERFOWL REQUIREMENTS
Important Food Resources

Important waterfowl resources vary from wetland to wetland, and particularly between physiographic regions. The lagoons of Baja California support abundant eelgrass beds, the most important winter food for black brant. Besides vegetable nutrients contained within every plant, eelgrass also provides substrate for small snails (Gastropoda), clams (Pelecypoda), and other invertebrates, which may be important protein sources for waterfowl (Smith and Jensen 1970, Saunders and Saunders 1981).

Invertebrates in the soft bottoms of Baja California's coastal areas are important foods for diving ducks, particularly surf scoters, lesser scaup, and buffleheads (Saunders and Saunders 1981). However, dabbling duck foods apparently are scarce. Although there are few data available (Dawson 1962, Kramer 1976, Ward 1983), the low numbers of dabblers and the absence of field feeding observations in western Baja California suggest the low availability of such foods.

Eelgrass beds along the Mainland West Coast are less extensive than in the lagoons of Baja California, and extend only as far south as Bahia Santa Maria (Fig. 1). Before the agricultural development of the Mainland West Coast, river deltas, saltwater bays, and their associated freshwater and brackish marshes provided wild foods for waterfowl. Overall, the most important natural foods for waterfowl are widgeongrass, spikerush (*Eleocharis* spp.), junglerice barnyardgrass (*Echinochloa colonum*), ragweed (*Ambrosia* spp.), and snails (Table 7)

Table 7. Percent volume of food items consumed by waterfowl on the Pacific Coast of Mexico.[a]

Food items

Waterfowl Species	Bulrush	Softstem bulrush (Scirpus validus)	Widgeongrass	Pepperwort (Marsilea spp.)	Spikerush	Water hyssop (Gratiola spp.)	Sedge (Carex spp.)	Ragweed	Lippia (Lippia spp.)	Spiny naiad (Najas spp.)	Anelema (Anelema spp.)	Dodder (Cuscuta spp.)	Junglerice barnyard-grass	Waterlily (Nymphaea odorata)	Floating heart (Nymphoides spp.)	Shoalgrass (Halodule wrightii)	Mesquite (Prosopis spp.)	Heliotrope (Heliotropum spp.)	Bindweed (Convolvulus spp.)	Eelgrass	Rice	Corn	Wheat	Unidentified plant	Beetles (Coleoptera)	Snails	Clams	Water boatmen (Læmiptera)	Midges (Chironomidae)	Crabs (Crustacea)	Unidentified animal
Mallard		14.2		9.9																	51.3				0.9	0.3	0.3				
Gadwall			22.1		9.0	14.2	14.2		14.2												18.3			13.2	tr[b]	tr	tr				
American wigeon					18.5					17.6											20.8			7.6	1.6						
Green-winged teal											11.5		26.6								26.6				4.7					tr	
Cinnamon teal					9.8			5.3													41.5					17.4	2.1	3.8			
Northern shoveler												4.7									82.2			5.2	tr	17.2		tr			
Northern pintail																							5.5								3.5
Black-bellied whistling duck	30		10											15	10							10		15							
Fulvous whistling duck															99	8.3															
Redhead			59.8																		7.8			7.5	tr	10.4		tr	4.6		
Canvasback																	6.5							86							
Lesser scaup			8.4					15.7										5.5						3.8		tr	8.6		10.0	4.5	
Bufflehead				56				38											6							26.6	tr				
Ruddy duck																								7		10			83		
Black brant																				99											
White-fronted geese																					55		29.3								

[a]Derived from Saunders and Saunders 1981.

[b]tr ≤ 0.10%.

Note: Data summarize only the principal items found; therefore, percentages generally do not total 100.

(Saunders and Saunders 1981, Kramer and Euliss 1986).

In modern times, vast agricultural areas on the Mainland West Coast have attracted hundreds of thousands of dabblers. Rice, corn, and wheat are the most important foods eaten by field-feeding ducks and geese in these areas (Saunders and Saunders 1981, Kramer and Euliss 1986) (Table 7).

Relationship of Important Foods to Nutritional Requirements

Caloric values of plant seeds eaten by birds have been reported as low for Gramineae, somewhat higher for Leguminosae and Malvaceae, and relatively high for Umbelliferae and Compositae. However, it is possible that the seeds with high gross-energy values may not have much greater metabolizable energy than the seeds of low gross-energy (Kendeigh and West 1965).

Natural foods, if available, may be preferred over agricultural foods, due to differences in nutritional content (Quinlan and Baldassarre 1984). Common agricultural foods used by waterfowl rate high in caloric content, but low in general nutrition compared to natural foods. Proteins of agricultural crops are deficient in several amino acids, and the micro- and macronutrient content of natural plant foods is usually greater than in crops (Baldassarre et al 1983).

Many wintering waterfowl, particularly geese, accumulate lipid reserves during late fall for use during periods of food shortage or severe weather conditions (Ankney and MacInnes 1978, Raveling 1979). Although no research has been done in Mexico, accumulation of lipid reserves to cope with cold weather would not appear to be as critical for waterfowl wintering on Mexico's Mainland West Coast as for those in areas farther north. Even during December and January, air temperatures are high in this region.

At Bahía San Quintín, on the Baja California coast, brant spent 78% of the daylight hours feeding. They also spent a greater percentage of time foraging in spring than in fall. The increased foraging time in spring may be related to a need to build energy reserves for migration and the need to develop body reserves for egg production (Kramer 1976, Vangilder et al. 1986).

The long period spent foraging daily by brant may be explained from a dietary point of view, because eelgrass has a high water-and-fiber and low protein content. Considerable amounts of eelgrass must be consumed to satisfy minimal nutritional requirements (Vangilder et al. 1986). The vast eelgrass beds along the Baja California coast appear to be adequate to support present brant populations.

Exposure to relatively low atmospheric temperatures and continuous winds occurs more frequently in Baja California than on the Mainland West Coast. This suggests that a greater need for lipid reserve accumulations to cope with cold weather during the winter may be necessary in Baja California.

Water Availability

Wetlands in the Rio Colorado Delta and coastal areas of the Mainland West Coast are influenced by variations in rainfall. Generally, wintering waterfowl populations increase in years of high rainfall (Saunders and Saunders 1981), but the extent to which rainfall influences habitat use by waterfowl has not been studied.

Environmental Contaminants

The major environmental contaminant concerns along the Mainland West Coast are the accumulated effects of heavy and often unregulated pesticide, herbicide, and fertilizer use in the agricultural districts of Sonora and Sinaloa. Most agricultural drainage water reaches the coast, where contaminants are deposited in the lower coastal-plain marshes. Studies in western Mexico, to document the level of contamination in waterbirds, are few (Mora 1984, Henny and Blus 1986, Mora et al. 1987).

Mora (1984) studied organochlorine residues in pintails during the breeding season in northern California, and residues in pintails and whistling ducks on wintering areas in southern California and northern Mexico. He found a higher accumulation of DDE residues on the wintering grounds than in breeding areas. However, accumulation levels of the main contaminants, DDE and DDT, declined toward the south. Mora et al. (1987) concluded that overall organochlorine levels in the waterfowl studied were below those known to have an adverse effect on reproduction and survival. Hexachlorobenzene (HCB) and benzene hexachloride (BHC) were higher in mid-latitude wintering areas (Salton Sea, San Quintin, and Culiacan) than at far northern (Klamath Basin) or far southern (Lerma) marshes. Residue levels in pintails and gadwalls were similar to those in resident whistling ducks near Culiacan. However, dieldrin was present in a greater number of samples from near Culiacan than in the other areas studied (especially in resident whistling ducks), suggesting that accumulation occurred in that area (Mora 1984).

The level of concern in Mexico for wildlife in general and environmental contamination is relatively low by comparison to that in the U.S. Numerous situations are reported that involve intentional dumping of agricultural chemicals into waterways.

HABITAT MANAGEMENT

Many U.S. wetlands have, for decades, been managed for waterfowl (Moffett 1938). Great strides have occurred in the development and application of the techniques needed to manage these habitats (Connelly 1979, Frazer and Kramer 1984). In contrast, no wetland habitat improvements or maintenance activities have occurred on Mexico's Pacific Coast. Perhaps one reason for the lack of wetland management in Mexico is that the rate of wetland loss there has not been as severe as in the U.S. Many wetland areas along the Mainland West Coast are at tidewater and in areas not suitable for farming. Inland, few areas have been drained. In most coastal bays and estuaries, traditional fishing techniques and lack of heavy industry have not yet stimulated dredging and marina construction.

As the major agricultural areas along the Mainland West Coast were developed, food resources for some waterfowl were enhanced. Also, the quality and quantity of waterfowl habitat in some areas have improved. The mixing of saltwater and irrigation drainage water formed brackish marshes on former barren salt flats. In other areas, the continual flow of agricultural runoff has changed the character of existing brackish and freshwater marshes. In portions of Laguna Chiricahueto, heavy agricultural drainage flows containing concentrations of fertilizer have changed an open brackish marsh that attracted many waterfowl to a less attractive freshwater cattail monoculture (J. Voelzer, pers. commun.).

Actual habitat-management activities along Mexico's Pacific Coast are restricted to 2 feasibility studies concerning water control and a nest box program. These projects are being conducted with funding and personnel provided by Ducks Unlimited de Mexico (DUMAC). The feasibility studies deal with the design and construction of water-control facilities to maintain suitable water levels for waterfowl near Mazatlan, Sinaloa, and in the Rio Colorado Delta. Both studies are progressing and, by the end of 1988, water-control structures should be installed.

Since the nest box construction and

installation project began in 1986, more than 1,000 nest boxes designed for black-bellied whistling ducks and muscovy ducks have been installed. The nest boxes are scattered throughout the marshes of Sinaloa and Nayarit, where whistling duck populations are stable but muscovy populations are dangerously low.

In addition to DUMAC, other private organizations have shown some interest in wetland management. Private outfitters who lease hunting rights from the federal government (most of Mexico's interior wetlands and all coastal wetlands are owned by the federal government) have considered installation of control structures to regulate water levels (P. Salomon, pers. commun.), but no structures have yet been installed.

Because Mexico's Pacific Coast wetlands are extensive and relatively undisturbed, large-scale wetland management programs may be unnecessary. Therefore, the major effort in terms of habitat management should be preservation. Secondly, habitat management should occur in areas where wetland degradation has taken place. Where open marshes have become cattail monocultures, prescribed burning and/or application of herbicides may be appropriate management activities. In other locations, wetlands could be improved by installing culverts to restore tidal flows or water-control structures to regulate water flows. Many wetland habitat-management techniques used in the U.S. could be applied to areas on Mexico's Pacific Coast.

Although habitat management activities are few, efforts to protect wildlife and their habitats by laws, treaties, and cooperative agreements have been successful. The first protective legislation intended specifically for the conservation of Mexican wildlife was passed in 1894. The law, aimed at forest conservation, included regulations concerning the taking of wild game and penalties for infractions (Leopold 1959). The most

important wildlife conservation measure was the Migratory Bird Treaty between Mexico and the U.S., implemented in 1936 and expanded in 1972. The treaty covers most species migrating between the two countries, and prohibits the killing of insectivorous birds, except under permit, and regulates the taking of game species (Wilbur 1987).

In 1964, Isla Raza became the first area on Mexico's Pacific Coast to be set aside for the protection of wildlife. The island in the Gulf of California was established primarily for the protection of nesting seabirds (Anderson et al. 1976). Forty-seven other islands in the Gulf of California were declared wildlife reserves in 1978 (Anderson 1980).

As an outgrowth of the 1972 modifications to the Migratory Bird Treaty, the first reserve of significant value to waterfowl was established. In 1972, by presidential decree, Laguna Ojo de Liebre became the first wildlife refuge in Baja California. Hunting was prohibited on the new refuge; it is particularly valuable to brant, diving ducks, and several species of waterbirds.

In 1979, Laguna San Ignacio was declared a refuge for gray whales and other wildlife. The protection of areas along Baja California's Pacific Coast continued, and in March 1980, the protection afforded to Laguna Ojo de Liebre was extended to include the entire Scammon's Lagoon complex, which includes Lagunas Ojo de Liebre, Guerrero Negro, and Manuela. Now that the Scammon's Lagoon complex and Laguna San Ignacio are refuges, about 50% of the Pacific Flyway black brant population winters in protected areas.

The most recent cooperative agreement was entered into by Mexico and the U.S. in 1975. Among the waterfowl projects made possible by the joint agreement are the continuation of midwinter waterfowl surveys in Mexico, black brant harvest surveys, habitat monitoring on the Pacific

Coast, and snow goose wintering ecology studies in Chihuahua and Durango.

CONCLUSIONS AND RECOMMENDATIONS

Waterfowl populations in the U.S. portion of the Pacific Flyway have declined in recent years. In contrast, populations along Mexico's Pacific Coast have remained relatively stable (U.S. Fish and Wildlife Service 1980-87). During the last complete midwinter inventory in January 1985, 22% of the ducks in the Pacific Flyway were found on the Pacific Coast of Mexico. Particularly high percentages of gadwall, green-winged teal, northern shoveler, and northern pintail populations were found throughout the flyway.

Because California has lost most of its original wetlands (Gilmer et al. 1982, California Department of Fish and Game 1983), Mexican wintering areas have taken on an increased significance to Pacific Flyway waterfowl. Gilmer et al. (1982) estimated that populations of waterfowl wintering in the Central Valley of California peak at about 5.6 million, but 10-12 million may winter or pass through the area. Thus, 4 million or more waterfowl could be wintering in western Mexico. Even though midwinter aerial surveys do not indicate this magnitude of use, the wintering grounds on Mexico's Pacific Coast are probably more important than is currently believed (Johnsgard 1975).

With these factors in mind, it becomes important to promote the conservation and protection of Mexico's wetland resources. Even though wetland losses have been minimal on the Pacific Coast, significant wetland loss and degradation have occurred in the marshes of the interior highlands (Leopold 1959, Saunders and Saunders 1981). Conservation and habitat-management efforts are inherently more difficult to achieve in countries that do not enjoy the standard of living found in the U.S. Only with some degree of affluence can government officials and the general public turn their energy and efforts from obtaining food, shelter, and economic security to habitat conservation and management.

To successfully protect and manage a natural resource in a developing country, whether it be wetlands for waterfowl or the breeding grounds of the gray whale, several elements must be in place. First, there must be support both from government officials, and in a democratic republic like Mexico, a reasonable majority of the people. Some component of the conservation effort must generate revenue, or become a point of national pride, or both. Further, the conservation efforts must be well-publicized and understood. Lastly, there must be some concern for the welfare of the resource for it to be protected and managed.

Efforts to protect and manage wetlands are progressing slowly. Governmental support is good now, but public support is nonexistent except in rare cases. Some revenue is generated from wetlands, mostly from hunting, but there is no sense of national pride connected with wetlands. The need to conserve and manage wetlands is not publicized and most people still consider wetlands as muddy, mosquito-infested areas that are often in the way. Until education efforts are initiated and the conservation ethic becomes more widespread, wetland protection, and later management, will occur in painfully small increments.

A first step toward the protection and wise use of wetlands on Mexico's Pacific Coast should be the continuation and expansion of Mexico's Wildlife Reserve System. Two areas have been protected in Baja California. Similar designations should be given to at least three areas on the Mainland West Coast. These should include Canal del Infiernillo to protect important black brant habitat. Portions of Bahia Topolobampo and Bahia Nava-

Fig. 5. An aerial view of Marismas Nacionales, the most pristine wetland area on the Pacific Coast of Mexico.

chiste should be designated wildlife reserves for preservation of important waterfowl use areas. The Marismas Nacionales also should be protected (Fig. 5). It represents the most pristine wetland area on the Pacific Coast, and possibly the only habitat still used by muscovy ducks in western Mexico.

After designation as wildlife reserves, these areas should be staffed with professional wildlife managers and biologists. Managers should then be charged with the stewardship of the areas, and where appropriate, conduct habitat-improvement and restoration activities. Technical assistance for such an endeavor could be provided to Mexico under the provisions of the current U.S.-Mexico joint committee for wildlife conservation. The North American Waterfowl Management Plan should also help in this regard.

Management and research needs are endless, but most important are several baseline studies including a complete wetland inventory, accurate waterfowl population and harvest estimates, monitoring of contaminant levels, food habits studies, a catalogue of wetland plants, in depth ecological studies of the muscovy duck, and general ecological studies of major regional wetlands.

SUMMARY

In 1985, 48% of the ducks, geese, swans, and coots in Mexico were counted on the Pacific Coast, making it the most important wintering region in the Republic. This region winters from 1 to 1.5 million waterfowl. The Pacific Coast region of Mexico includes Baja California Norte, Baja California Sur, Sonora, Sinaloa, and Nayarit. The Pacific Coast of Mexico covers more than 4,000 km and can be divided into two main physiographic regions: the Baja California Peninsula and the Mainland West Coast.

The Pacific Coast of the Baja California Peninsula is characterized by large, shallow, intertidal coastal lagoons. The only significant freshwater habitat on the Baja California Peninsula is in the Rio Colorado Delta.

The Mainland West Coast region consists of a long, narrow, coastal plain bordered by shallow coastal lagoons, which receive a variable amount of freshwater inflow from rivers and agricultural irrigation channels. The largest waterfowl populations wintering in this area are generally associated with agricultural lands and excess irrigation water, especially where it flows into saltwater and creates freshwater to brackish marshes.

Baja California has relatively low numbers of ducks, but high numbers of black brant. Between 1980 and 1985, an average of 45,000 ducks, 200 geese, and 99,000 brant were found in Baja California during midwinter surveys. The Mainland West Coast had an average 1.1 million ducks, 5,500 geese, and 30,100 brant during the same period. Marshes and lagoons of the Mainland West Coast are of special importance to pintails, green-winged teal, shovelers, lesser scaup, ruddy ducks, redheads, cinnamon teal, and whistling ducks.

The Pacific Coast region of Mexico winters approximately 18% of all ducks, <1% of the geese, and 92% of the brant found in the Pacific Flyway. During the period 1948 to 1962, an average of 11,000 geese, other than brant, wintered along the Mainland West Coast. More recent aerial surveys (1980-85) have shown only 5,500 geese, but because of recent declines in the Pacific population of white-fronted geese, about 8% of the population is found along the Mainland West Coast in winter. Black brant were first observed on the Mainland West Coast in January 1958, and by 1963, the wintering population had increased to 13,200. Between 1977 and 1985, an average of 31,549 brant was recorded along the Mainland West Coast.

The 1973 completion of the Baja California transpeninsular highway resulted in an increase in human uses of the area. The increased use poses potential threats to the waterfowl and wetlands of the area. In the Rio Colorado Delta, diking, upstream storage, and diversion of water for irrigation, since 1900, have allowed settlement and cultivation of former river-plain forests and desert. Large areas of the Mainland West Coast have been cleared and devoted to irrigated agriculture, complete with the development of numerous water-storage reservoirs. Agricultural expansions near Obregon, Los Mochis, and Culiacan created food supplies that attracted increased waterfowl populations to the areas. The estimated total number of ducks in the Los Mochis area (Topolobampo unit) increased from 21,000 in 1951 to 743,000 in 1963. Similar increases were noted near Culiacan (Pabellon unit). The majority of ducks using the agricultural areas are pintails and wigeon.

Important food resources vary among wetlands, and particularly between physiographic regions. Areas on the Baja California Pacific Coast have abundant eelgrass beds, the most important food for brant. Coastal wetlands on the Mainland West Coast have less extensive eelgrass beds, and these extend only as far south as Bahia Santa Maria. Overall, the most important natural foods along the Mainland West Coast are widgeongrass, various moist-soil plants, and snails.

The major environmental contaminant concern along the Mainland West Coast is the accumulated effect of heavy and often unregulated pesticide, herbicide, and fertilizer use in the major agricultural districts. Most of the agricultural drainage water in these regions eventually reaches the coastline, where contaminants are deposited in the lower coastal-plain marshes.

For decades, wetland areas in the U.S. have been managed for waterfowl. In contrast, essentially no wetland habitat-

improvement of maintenance activities
have occurred on Mexico's Pacific Coast.
Actual habitat-management activities
along Mexico's Pacific Coast are restricted
to 2 feasibility studies concerning water
control, and a nest box program. All are
being conducted with funding and manpower provided by DUMAC.

Although actual habitat-management
activities are few, efforts to protect wildlife and their habitats by laws, treaties,
and cooperative agreements have been
more progressive. In 1972, Laguna Ojo de
Liebre became the first reserve for migratory aquatic birds and other wildlife. The
protection of areas along Baja California's Pacific Coast continued, and in July
1979, Laguna San Ignacio was declared a
refuge for gray whales and other wildlife.
However, similar wildlife reserves do not
yet exist on the Mainland West Coast.

Gilmer et al. (1982) estimated that
populations of waterfowl wintering in the
Central Valley of California peak at about
5.6 million, but 10-12 million winter or
pass through the area. Thus, 4 million or
more waterfowl could be wintering in
western Mexico. Even though midwinter
aerial surveys do not indicate this magnitude of use, the wintering grounds on
Mexico's Pacific Coast are probably more
important than is generally believed.

LITERATURE CITED

Alvarado, J., J. Galindo, M. Iwadare, R. Migoya,
and M. Vazquez. 1986. Evaluecion de los
parametros ambientales y su relacion con la
distribucion y movimientos de la ballena gris
(*Eschrichtius robustus*) Lilljeborg en la Laguna
Ojo de Liebre, B.C.S., Mexico. Cienc Pesquera
5:33-49.

Anderson, D.W. 1980. Islands; seabirds and man:
Conservation in the Gulf of California. pages
27-37 *in* P. P. Schaefter and S. M. Ehlers, eds.
The Birds of Mexico, their ecology and conservation. Natl. Audubon Society, Tiburon, Calif.

———, J.E. Mendoza, and J.O. Keith. 1976. Seabirds
in the Gulf of California, a vulnerable international resource. Nat. Resour. J. 16:489-505.

Ankney, C.D., and C.D. MacInness. 1978. Nutrient
reserves and reproductive performance of female
lesser snow geese. Auk 95:459-471.

Baldassarre, G.A., R.J. Whyte, E.E. Quinlan, and

E.G. Bolen. 1983. Dynamics and quality of
waste corn available to post-breeding waterfowl
in Texas. Wildl. Soc. Bull. 11:25-31.

Bellrose, F.C. 1980. Ducks, geese and swans of North
America. Third ed. Stackpole Books. Harrisburg, Pa. 540 pp.

Boone, C.G., and R.E. Hoeppl. 1976. Feasibility of
transplantation, revegetation, and restoration of
eelgrass in San Diego Bay, California. U.S.
Army Corps of Eng. Waterways Exp. St.,
Vicksburg, Miss. Misc. Paper Y-76-2. 42 pp.

California Dep. of Fish and Game. 1983. A plan for
protecting, enhancing and increasing California's wetlands for waterfowl. Calif. Dep. Fish
and Game. Rep. SCR-28, Sacramento. 53 pp.

Chattin, J.E. 1970. Some uses of estuaries by
waterfowl and other migratory birds. pages 108-
118 *in* Proc. N.W. Estuarine Coast. Zone Symp.,
Portland, Ore.

Connelly, D.P. 1979. Propagation of selected native
marsh plants in the San Joaquin Valley. Calif.
Dep. Fish and Game; Wildl. Manage. Leaflet
15, Sacramento. 12 pp.

Dawson, E.Y. 1962. Benthic marine exploration of
Bahia de San Quintin, Baja California, 1960-61,
marine and marsh vegetation. Pacific Nat.
3:275-281.

Eldridge, W.D., and G.W. Kramer. 1985. Sport harvest of brant in Mexico during the 1984/85
hunting season. Unpub. Rep. U.S. Fish and
Wildl. Serv., Calipatria, Calif. 21 pp.

Foster, M.S., and D.R. Schiel. 1985. The ecology of
giant kelp forests in California: a community
profile. U.S. Fish and Wildlife Serv., Washington, D.C. FWS/OBS-85/7.2. 152 pp.

Frazer, S.E., and G.W. Kramer. 1984. Assisting
private landowners with wetland habitat developments in California. Cal-Neva Wildl. Trans.
1984:33-38.

Gilmer, D.S., M.R. Miller, R.D. Bauer, and J.R.
LeDonne. 1982. California's Central Valley
wintering waterfowl: concerns and challenges.
Trans. North Am. Wildl. and Nat. Resour.
Conf. 47:441-452.

Grinnell, J. 1928. A distributional summation of the
ornithology of Lower California. Univ. California Publ. Zool. 32. 300 pp.

Henny, C.J., and L.J. Blus. 1986. Radiotelemetry
locates wintering grounds of DDE-contaminated
black-crowned night herons. Wildl. Soc. Bull.
14:236-241.

Johnsgard, P.A. 1975. Waterfowl of North America.
Indiana Univ. Press, Bloomington. 575 pp.

Jones, R.D., Jr. 1973. A method for appraisal of
annual reproductive success in the black brant
population. M.S. Thesis, Univ. Alaska, Fair-
banks. 117 pp.

Kendeigh, C.S., and G.C. West. 1965. Caloric values
of plant seeds eaten by birds. Ecology 46:553-
555.

Kramer, G.W. 1976. Winter ecology of black brant at San Quintin Bay, Baja California, Mexico. M.S. Thesis, Humboldt State Univ., Arcata, Calif. 79 pp.

——, and N.H. Euliss. 1986. Winter foods of black-bellied whistling ducks in northwestern Mexico. J. Wildl. Manage. 50:413-416.

——, L.R. Rauen, and S.W. Harris. 1979. Populations, hunting mortality and habitat use of black brant at San Quintin Bay, Baja California, Mexico. Pages 242-254 in R.L. Jarvis and J.C. Bartonek, eds. Management and biology of Pacific Flyway geese. Oregon State Univ. Book Stores, Corvallis.

Lensink, C.J. 1986. Recoveries of Alaska banded white-fronted geese in Mexico. U.S. Fish and Wildl. Serv. Res. Inf. Bull. Anchorage, Alaska. 2 pp.

Leopold, A.S. 1959. Wildlife of Mexico—the game birds and mammals. Univ. of California Press, Berkeley. 568 pp.

Moffett, J. 1938. Environmental factors affecting waterfowl in the Suisun area, California. Condor 40:76-84.

Mora, M.A. 1984. Seasonal and geographic variation of organochlorines in waterfowl from California and Mexico. M.S. Thesis, Univ. California, Davis. 46 pp.

——, D.W. Anderson, and M.M. Mount. 1987. Seasonal variation of body condition and organochlorines in wild ducks from California and Mexico. J. Wildl. Manage. 51:132-141.

Nelson, E.W. 1921. Lower California and its natural resources. Natl. Acad. Sci. 16, First Mem. 194 pp.

O'Neil, E.J. 1979. Fourteen years of goose populations and trends at Klamath Basin Refuges. Pages 316-321 in R.L. Jarvis and L.S. Bartonek, eds. Management and biology of Pacific Flyway geese. Oregon State Univ. Book Stores, Corvallis.

Phleger, F.B., and G.C. Ewing. 1962. Sedimentology and oceanography of coastal lagoons in Baja California, Mexico. Bull. Geol. Soc. Am. 73:145-182.

Postma, H. 1965. Water circulation and suspended matter in Baja California lagoons. Netherlands J. Sea Res. 2:566-604.

Quinlan, E.E., and G.A. Baldassarre. 1984. Activity budgets of non-breeding green-winged teal on playa lakes in Texas. J. Wildl. Manage. 48:838-845.

Raveling, D.G. 1979. The annual cycle of body composition of Canada geese with special reference to control of reproduction. Auk 96:234-252.

Saunders, G.B., and D.C. Saunders. 1981. Waterfowl and their wintering grounds in Mexico, 1937-64. U.S. Fish and Wildl. Serv. Res. Publ. 138. 151 pp.

Scott, D.A., and M. Carbonell. 1986. A directory of neotropical wetlands. IUCN Cambridge and IWRB Slimbridge. 79 pp.

Scott, J.N., Jr. 1983. The biology of the resident ducks of the Marismas Nacionales, Mexico and adjacent areas, and recommendations for their management. Final Rep. U.S. Fish and Wildl. Serv., Denver Wildl. Res. Cent., Denver, Colo. 25 pp.

SEDUE. 1985. Estudio cinegetico y ecologico sobre la poblacion invernante de la branta negra (Branta bernicla nigricans) en la Bahia de San Quintin, B.C. durante la temporada de caza 1984-85. Direccion General de Flora y Fauna Silvestres. Direccion de Area de Flora y Fauna Acuaticas. Depto. de Fauna Acuatica. Mexico, D.F. 55 pp.

Smith, R.H., and G.H. Jensen. 1970. Black brant on the mainland coast of Mexico. Trans. North Am. Wildl. and Nat. Resour. Conf. 35:227-241.

Swartz, S., and M.L. Jones. 1978. The evaluation of human activities on gray whales (Eschrichtius robustus), in Laguna San Ignacio, Baja California, Mexico. Final Rep. to U.S. Marine Mammal Comm. Contract MM5AC11, Natl. Tech. Information System. Washington, D.C.

——, and M.S. Jones. 1981. Demographic studies and habitat assessment of gray whales, Eschrichtius robustus, in Laguna San Ignacio, B.C. Mexico, Cet. Res. Assoc. 56 pp.

U.S. Fish and Wildlife Service. 1948-87. Winter waterfowl survey, Mexico west coast and Baja California. U.S. Fish and Wildl. Serv., Portland, Oreg. 80 pp.

Vangilder, L.D., L.M. Smith, and R.K. Lawrence. 1986. Nutrient resources of premigratory brant during spring. Auk 103:237-241.

Velazquez-Nogueron, V., V. Aguilar, and H. Ortega. 1972. Programa de aves acuaticas en Marismas Nacionales. Sin. Informe 1972, DGFS. Mexico D.F. 41 pp.

Ward, D.H. 1983. The relationship of two seagrasses: Zostera marina and Ruppia maritima to black brant, Branta bernicla nigricans, San Ignacio Lagoon, Baja California, Mexico. M.S. Thesis, Univ. of Oregon, Eugene. 57 pp.

Wiggins, I.L. 1980. Flora of Baja California. Stanford Univ. Press, Stanford, Calif. 1025 pp.

Wilbur, S.R. 1987. Birds of Baja California. Univ. California Press, Berkeley. 235 pp.

Zedler, J.B. 1982. The ecology of southern California coastal salt marshes: a community profile. U.S. Fish and Wildl. Serv., Washington, D.C. FWS/OBS-81/54. 110 pp.

BIOPOLITICAL STRATEGIES

Cleared, former lowland hardwood area regenerated in Pennsylvania smartweed (pink flowers) and other moist soil, waterfowl food plants, Yazoo National Wildlife Refuge, Mississippi (photo by R. M. Kaminski).

BIOPOLITICAL STRATEGIES FOR WATERFOWL HABITAT PRESERVATION AND ENHANCEMENT

ROLLIN D. SPARROWE, U.S. Fish and Wildlife Service, Washington, D.C. 20240
THOMAS J. DWYER, U.S. Fish and Wildlife Service, Washington, D.C. 20240
PETER G. POULOS, U.S. Fish and Wildlife Service, Washington, D.C. 20240
LAURENCE R. JAHN, Wildlife Management Institute, 1101 14th Street, N.W., Washington, D.C. 20005
DAVID M. SMITH, U.S. Fish and Wildlife Service, Washington, D.C. 20240
ROBERT J. MISSO, U.S. Fish and Wildlife Service, Washington, D.C. 20240

The purpose of this paper is to present an overview of waterfowl migration and wintering habitats in North America, to describe the biopolitical strategies utilized to preserve and reclaim these habitats, and to address long-term habitat needs. Other papers have discussed specific migrational and/or wintering habitats in each of the 4 recognized waterfowl flyways. Our treatment of waterfowl habitats focuses on broader continental needs.

The focus on migrating and wintering waterfowl shifts our attention from the northern portions of North American waterfowl habitat (northern United States, Canada, and Alaska) to the southern portions of North America (United States, Mexico, Central America, and the Caribbean). As such, much of the discussion is concentrated on the status of wetland habitat and strategies employed to maintain, enhance, and reclaim this habitat in the United States (U.S.). Equal attention could not be devoted to Mexico, unfortunately, because information and/or mechanisms were not in place to permit an in-depth analysis of this region. Perhaps this effort can at least serve to identify the critical importance Mexico plays in maintaining a viable North American waterfowl population.

Wetland habitat is discussed as it relates to waterfowl (Family Anatidae). However, multiple values of wetlands are acknowledged as productive ecosystems that support a wide range of species, and are acknowledged also for their value in contributing to water quality, flood control, and outdoor recreation. Within the Family Anatidae, 45 species are common to the U.S., Canada, and Mexico, and are protected by various treaties and, therefore, are subject to federal regulation. Twenty-four of these species are shared among the U.S., Canada, and Mexico; 12 species with the U.S. and Canada; 3 species with the U.S. and Mexico; and 6 species are within U.S. jurisdiction only (Table 1).

First, information is presented on the status of wetland habitats in North America, including a brief mention of upland production habitats in northern areas. This is followed by a discussion of key migration and wintering habitats and ongoing habitat-protection programs that support migrating and wintering waterfowl habitat. This section focuses almost exclusively on the U.S. Finally, future needs are discussed. How can government programs be realigned to more effectively preserve waterfowl nonbreeding habitats? How can private organizations join with governments to accelerate habitat-preservation efforts? Lastly, how can Mexico, Central America, and the Caribbean be incorporated into the cooperative effort initiated by Canada and the U.S. with the North American Waterfowl Management Plan, so that the title of that document accurately reflects North American waterfowl management activities?

STATUS OF WETLAND HABITATS

Many published sources and many authors of this volume have implicated loss and degradation of habitat as a primary waterfowl management problem

531

Table 1. List of North American waterfowl species, Family Anatidae, common to the U.S.,
Mexico, and Canada.

Table 1. Continued

Hawaiian duck (*Anas wyvilliana*)
Laysan duck (*Anas laysanensis*)
Geese
Emperor goose (*Chen canagica*)
Hawaiian goose (*Nesochen sandvicensis*)

Canada, United States, and Mexico
  Ducks
    American wigeon (*Anas americana*)
    Blue-winged teal (*Anas discors*)
    Bufflehead (*Bucephala albeola*)
    Canvasback (*Aythya valisineria*)
    Cinnamon teal (*Anas cyanoptera*)
    Common goldeneye (*Bucephala clangula*)
    Common merganser (*Mergus merganser*)
    Gadwall (*Anas strepera*)
    Greater scaup (*Aythya marila*)
    Green-winged teal (*Anas crecca*)
    Lesser scaup (*Aythya affinis*)
    Mallard (*Anas platyrhynchos*)
    Northern pintail (*Anas acuta*)
    Northern shoveler (*Anas clypeata*)
    Red-breasted merganser (*Mergus serrator*)
    Redhead (*Aythya americana*)
    Ring-necked duck (*Aythya collaris*)
    Ruddy duck (*Oxyura jamaicensis*)
    Surf scoter (*Melanitta perspicillata*)
    White-winged scoter (*Melanitta fusca*)
  Geese
    Canada goose (*Branta canadensis*)
    Greater white-fronted goose (*Anser albifrons*)
    Snow goose (*Chen caerulescens*)
  Brant
    Brant (*Branta bernicla*)
Canada and United States
  Ducks
    American black duck (*Anas rubripes*)
    Barrow's goldeneye (*Bucephala islandica*)
    Black scoter (*Melanitta nigra*)
    Common eider (*Somateria mollissima*)
    Harlequin duck (*Histrionicus histrionicus*)
    Hooded merganser (*Lophodytes cucullatus*)
    King eider (*Somateria spectabilis*)
    Oldsquaw (*Clangula hyemalis*)
    Wood duck (*Aix sponsa*)
  Geese
    Ross goose(*Chen rossii*)
  Swan
    Trumpeter swan (*Cygnus buccinator*)
    Tundra swan (*Cygnus columbianus*)
United States and Mexico
  Ducks
    Mottled duck (*Anas fulvigula*)
    Black-bellied whistling-duck (*Dendrocygna autumnalis*)
    Fulvous whistling-duck (*Dendrocygna bicolor*)
United States
  Ducks
    Spectacled eider (*Somateria fischeri*)
    Steller's eider (*Polysticta stelleri*)

in the U.S. In the U.S., there is good information on losses of the 2 key wetland systems most important to wintering waterfowl: the estuarine system and the palustrine system. Tiner (1984) and Frayer et al. (1983) provide the most up-to-date information on losses to palustrine emergent, palustrine scrub-shrub, palustrine forested, and estuarine wetlands between the 1950s and the 1970s (Fig. 1). Major findings are summarized briefly:

1. For estuarine wetlands there has been a net loss of 82,559 ha of estuarine intertidal emergent wetlands (74,894 ha loss in Louisiana, 6,070 ha loss in Florida) and a net loss of 150,548 ha of estuarine vegetated wetlands (Louisiana and Florida accounted for most of the loss).

2. For palustrine wetlands there has been a net gain of 930,810 ha of palustrine nonvegetated wetland (mainly due to construction of farm ponds in the Mississippi and Central flyways) and a net loss of 4,451,700 ha of palustrine vegetated wetland; 2,428,200 ha palustrine forested wetland, mainly in the lower Mississippi river valley; 1,902,090 ha of palustrine emergent wetland, primarily in the Central Flyway and California.

Unfortunately, no complete estimates comparable to Tiner (1984) and Frayer et al. (1983) exist for losses of wetlands in Canada, Mexico, and Central America. However, various qualitative and quantitative estimates have been made for Canada. A general picture of wetland destruction is evident. Since earliest settlement, more than 65% of maritime salt marshes, 70% of southern Ontario and St. Lawrence Valley wetlands, 40% of prairie

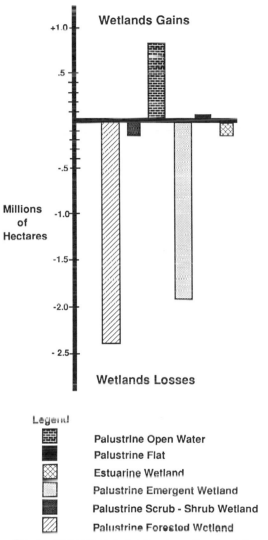

Wetlands Gains

Wetlands Losses

Millions of Hectares

+1.0
.5
-.5
-1.0
-1.5
-2.0
-2.5

Legend

Palustrine Open Water
Palustrine Flat
Estuarine Wetland
Palustrine Emergent Wetland
Palustrine Scrub - Shrub Wetland
Palustrine Forested Wetland

Fig. 1. Net losses and gains in wetlands of the conterminous U.S. between the mid-50s and mid-70s (from Frayer et al. 1983).

wetlands, and up to 70% of Pacific estuaries have been converted to other uses (Wildlife Habitat Canada 1986). However, in several Canadian regions, specific estimates have been made:

1. Some 60% of the St. Lawrence estuarine marshes have been destroyed (Wildlife Habitat Canada 1986).

2. Over 3,000 ha of wetlands have been lost due to expansion of Montreal, Trois-Rivieres, and Quebec City between 1945 and 1976 (Wildlife Habitat Canada 1986).

3. Southern Ontario wetlands are being lost at an annual rate of 1-2%, and most recent estimates suggest that 70-80% of southern Ontario wetlands have been severely altered (Wildlife Habitat Canada 1986).

4. Forty-one percent of the natural wetlands of the southwestern Fraser River lowlands were lost between 1967-82 (Wildlife Habitat Canada 1986).

5. Sixty-five percent of maritime salt marshes have been diked for agricultural purposes (Wildlife Habitat Canada 1986).

6. Losses of 70% and 61% of the prairie potholes have been reported for parts of Manitoba (Rakowski and Chabot 1983) and Alberta (Schick 1972), respectively.

In Mexico, wintering waterfowl surveys have been conducted since 1937. Saunders and Saunders (1981) provided a detailed description of all waterfowl wintering grounds in Mexico for the period of 1937-64. More recently, Brazda (1986) summarized wintering waterfowl populations and habitat conditions along the east coast of Mexico. His work divides the east coast of Mexico into 7 survey units from the U.S. border to the northeast tip of the state of Yucatan

Habitats in only 3 of the units (Rio Grande Delta, Laguna Madre-Tamaulipas lagoons, and Compeche-Yucatan lagoons) show considerable variation from extreme drought to completely wet. Habitat in the remaining rain-forest units has remained relatively stable (Brazda 1986).

The Rio Grande Delta rates high as a site of potential habitat destruction (Brazda 1986). Extensive drainage and irrigation systems may be built in the area for agricultural purposes. Several of the areas are continually subjected to oil pollution, with the Tanesi and Panuco rivers and Tamishua Lagoon and coastal area to Veracruz being most impacted (Baldassarre et al. 1988).

The most comprehensive treatment of Central American wetlands is found in Scott and Carbonell (1986). This publication is a series of reports by country covering Central America, South America, and the Caribbean. Most reports include an inventory of wetlands thought to be most important to waterfowl, using the Ramsar definition (Ramsar 1987) of waterfowl as birds ecologically dependent on wetlands. The Scott and Carbonell (1986) study is not an inventory of wetland loss and does not present information similar to that available for Canada or the U.S. However, it does contain information on major threats to wetlands in each country. These threats involve drainage of lakes and marshes, diversion of rivers and changes in patterns of flooding, and pollution (both industrial and human).

STATUS OF UPLAND PRODUCTION HABITATS

This volume examines primarily the management needs of migrating and wintering waterfowl, and as such, is concerned with the status of migrating and wintering habitat used by these species. Although Canadian and north central U.S. habitat-management practices are the primary components in enhancing waterfowl production habitats, wintering habitat concerns force us to shift our emphasis to the U.S. and Mexico. However, before focusing on the southern wintering habitats (recognizing of course, the importance of Alaskan and Canadian habitats in the initial stages of migration), a brief review of production habitat reveals the importance of breeding-production areas in supplying birds for migration and wintering areas.

The prairie-pothole region of North America is recognized as the principal duck production area (Crissey 1969, Pospahala et al. 1974). Comprising only about 10% of the continental duck breeding area, it normally produces close to 50% of the fall flight of ducks. This prairie and prairie-parkland area in the U.S. and Canada supports over 40% of the breeding mallard population. About two-thirds of this region occurs in Canada.

Historically duck productivity in this region was regulated mainly by the abundance of wetlands (Pospahala et al. 1974). During the last decade, managers have become increasingly aware that the effects of intensive agriculture can severely affect dabbling duck production in the presence of an adequate wetland base. Studies in North Dakota (Higgins 1977) show that where more than 85% of the landscape has been tilled, waterfowl are not capable of sustaining their populations. Mallard-nest success rate in much of the prairie-pothole region of the U.S. is below the rate believed necessary for mallard populations to be self-sustaining (Cowardin et al. 1985).

During the past 30 years in the U.S., the trend has been toward more intensive agriculture with more powerful equipment (Duebbert and Kantrud 1987), while wetland drainage rates continue to average from 1-5% per year (Harmon 1979). From 1965 to 1975, in the best duck production area in North Dakota, over 50% of the remaining grassland was converted to cropland (Tiner 1984).

Recent studies (Turner et al. 1987, Greenwood et al. 1987) show the same trends for the prairie-parkland areas of Canada. Although rates of annual wetland drainage are lower than in the U.S., high degradation rates of both wetland margins and basins are common (Turner et al. 1987). Between 1981 and 1985, almost 80% of the 10,000 wetlands margins monitored were degraded by agriculture (Turner et al. 1987).

Areas of uncultivated grassland and parkland in Canadian prairies are declining at a rapid rate. Rowe and Coupland (1984) estimate that 80% of the presettled area of aspen parkland has been altered or destroyed. Miller (1986) investigated the extent of conversion to agriculture on 65 sites across Canadian prairies and found the following proportion of uncultivated habitats remaining; tall-grass prairie, 3.4%; short-grass prairie, 12.2%; mixed-grass prairie, 18.2%; and aspen parkland, 15.1%.

Concurrently, Greenwood et al. (1987) showed that highest duck-nest success rates in prairie Canada were associated with large blocks of native pasture containing brush. Marginal farming practices (Boyd 1985) are presently a serious threat to duck populations in the prairie-pothole region of Canada, because most of the best habitats already have been altered.

MIGRATING AND WINTERING HABITATS

Because waterfowl constitute an international resource, most large-scale planning for habitat preservation has been done by national governments. Before 1986, the Canadian and U.S. Governments had National Waterfowl Management Plans that set general goals and strategies for maintenance of waterfowl populations, including strategies for habitat preservation. The governments of Mexico and other Central American countries generally do not have such specific national plans for waterfowl.

In 1985, the U.S. Fish and Wildlife Service (FWS) adopted a 10-Year Waterfowl Habitat Acquisition Plan to attain habitat objectives for 9 species of ducks and geese. The species were mallard, canvasback, redhead, American black duck, black brant, white-fronted goose, cackling Canada goose, wood duck, and northern pintail. These species were selected for a variety of administrative and biological reasons. It was recognized that attainment of habitat goals for these 9 species likely would result in tremendous benefit to the remaining dabbling and diving duck and goose populations using the U.S. areas. The plan identified 11 areas of concern and established acreage goals for preservation of upland and wetland habitats. Nine of 11 areas are

important wholly or in part as wintering areas for waterfowl. All are used by migrating waterfowl.

In 1986, the Canadian Minister of Environment and the U.S. Secretary of the Interior signed the North American Waterfowl Management Plan (NAWMP), which outlines strategies for cooperative efforts to protect waterfowl habitat, builds up declining waterfowl populations, and enhances waterfowl research and management. As drought has persisted and land-use changes have taken place on many important breeding areas and on migrating and wintering areas farther south, populations of important waterfowl species have declined at an alarming rate. The plan outlines far-reaching efforts that must be taken in both countries to return waterfowl populations to levels that meet public demand.

The NAWMP may be best described as a series of goals with a strategy for achieving them. The plan recognizes that more than 75% of the ducks are produced in Canada, yet more than 75% of the demand is in the U.S. Overall, the existing successful programs, such as wetland acquisition in the U.S. with duck stamp revenues and Ducks Unlimited wetland protection efforts in Canada, have not been able to provide nesting and wintering areas sufficient to maintain abundant waterfowl. The plan does not propose a federal program, but rather acknowledges that the national governments of the two countries cannot carry out an effort of this scope without assistance. It calls for participation of state, provincial, territorial, and local governments; private conservation groups; businesses; and individual citizens. It describes what needs to be done on behalf of waterfowl by those interested in them, whether hunters, naturalists, landowners, or subsistence users. Specifically, the plan has the following major components through which it:

1. Establishes population goals for

ducks, geese, and swans to be met by the year 2000;

2. Establishes habitat-protection goals for the U.S. and Canada to sustain duck populations consistent with population goals;

3. Recommends joint ventures between private and government entities to attain major objectives, such as for Canadian prairie habitat, black duck management, and management of arctic breeding geese;

4. Calls for a variety of approaches to protect and manage wetlands and associated uplands which benefit breeding waterfowl;

5. Proposes research and further development of surveys and data bases on specific waterfowl populations to enhance management;

6. Establishes a NAWMP Committee composed of Canadian and U.S. representatives to guide implementation of the plan.

The NAWMP identifies 34 waterfowl habitat areas of major concern in the U.S. and Canada (Fig. 2). These areas form the most comprehensive and recent identification of key habitats in North America for breeding, migrating, and wintering waterfowl.

Canada

The primary migration and wintering areas identified in the NAWMP for Canada are as follows:

Arctic Areas.—Thirteen Canadian Arctic and subarctic areas are identified in the NAWMP (Fig. 2). The most pressing needs for these areas are to balance conflicts between geese/brant and native ownership and/or control. Native claims have been settled in parts of Quebec and the Northwest Territories; settlement is pending in the rest of the Northwest Territories which hosts a major portion of molting snow geese, brant, and white-fronted geese. Important goose-habitat areas, sensitive periods of time, and

detrimental activities must be identified and communicated to native peoples. Natives must be involved in the planning and execution of waterfowl-management activities in the future.

James Bay is a large marine inlet of Hudson Bay bounded on the east by northern Quebec and on the west by northern Ontario (Fig. 2). Plans exist to develop hydropower resources in the area and convert James Bay to a freshwater reservoir. Canada lacks a strong environmental review process; no consideration of cumulative effects or alternatives is required. The hydropower development proposed for this region would lead to damming or diversion of all major rivers entering James Bay from the east. There is a critical need to define the habitat impacts to staging and migrating North American waterfowl from this project.

Coastal Areas.—Both the upper Pacific and Atlantic coasts of Canada are identified by the NAWMP as important waterfowl areas (Fig. 2). A target goal for preservation of 4,000 additional ha of coastal black duck migration and wintering habitat is suggested for the Atlantic coast. Brant, canvasbacks, scaup, scoters, buffleheads, goldeneyes, and other sea ducks use the Canadian upper Pacific coast. The province of British Columbia, Ducks Unlimited (Canada), Wildlife Habitat Canada, and The Nature Trust of British Columbia have identified 12 critical areas totaling almost 52,000 ha. Most of this area is wetland whose preservation will enhance waterfowl populations.

Lower Great Lakes-St. Lawrence Basin.—Protection of 24,282 ha of breeding and migration habitat for black ducks and mallards is recommended in the Great Lakes-St. Lawrence Lowlands of Canada. The work here should focus on maintaining farm ponds and marshes for all ducks in the western part of the area and preserving natural nesting habitat and marshes, primarily for black ducks, in the eastern portion of the basin.

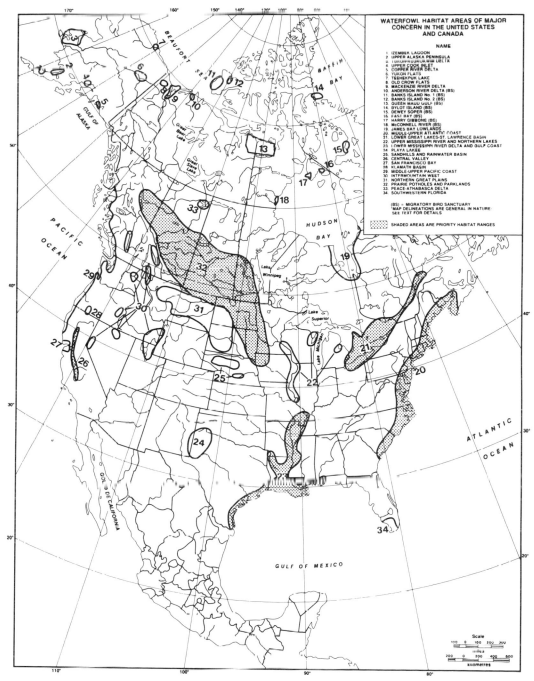

Fig. 2. Waterfowl habitat areas of major concern in Canada and the U.S.

United States

Detailed planning was undertaken by the U.S. FWS in development of its 10-Year Waterfowl Habitat Acquisition Plan released in 1985. The NAWMP adopted this set of recommendations for the 11 areas entirely in the U.S. and added a twelfth area, the Lower Great Lakes-St. Lawrence Basin. Migration and wintering habitat descriptions and habitat-preservation goals are taken from the 10-Year Plan and the NAWMP. Acreage goals outlined in the NAWMP are intended to be flexible and to best represent minimum amounts necessary to restore waterfowl populations to the level of the 1970s.

Alaska.—Seven areas have been identified as needing some form of preservation or management to enhance waterfowl populations (Fig. 2). Four of these, Izembek Lagoon, the Upper Alaska Peninsula, Upper Cook Inlet, and the Cooper River Delta are critical areas for staging and migrating ducks, geese, brant, and swans.

Izembek Lagoon consists of about 38,445 ha of submerged land currently owned by the state of Alaska and designated as a waterfowl refuge. It contains the largest known eelgrass beds in the world. Uplands surrounding it are owned by U.S. FWS as part of Izembek National Wildlife Refuge (NWR). The eelgrass beds of the lagoon are vital to brant because essentially the entire population stages there each fall for 6-9 weeks before its 1,800 km transoceanic, nonstop migration to the coasts of California and Mexico. The lagoon also is used as a spring staging area for up to 25,000 brant for 3-6 weeks. Also, the majority of the world population of emperor geese and up to 100,000 lesser Canada geese stage on the lagoon during fall migration. The major threats to the lagoon and brant population are the high potential for oil contamination of the critical eelgrass beds and the disturbance of staging brant by substantial increase in ground, fixed-wing, and helicopter traffic associated with oil development, production, and transportation.

Two estuarine areas on the north side of the Upper Alaska Peninsula are heavily used by several waterfowl species of concern. The areas include the mouth of the Cinder River and Pilot Point, collectively less than 80,940 ha. Most of the 2 areas are submerged tidelands owned by

the State of Alaska and classified as important habitat. Some privately owned (native) lands occur in the area. Other estuarine areas in the upper Peninsula, of somewhat lesser importance, are the Ugashik Tidelands and Naknek and Egegik river flats. Over 95% of the cackling goose population stages in the Pilot Point-Cinder River area during fall prior to migration to the next major staging area in northern California. Some 25,000 or more use the area for staging in spring as they prepare for nesting on the Yukon-Kuskokwim Delta to the north. This could represent up to 20% of the spring population. An unknown number use the area during fall migration. In addition, black brant use these estuarine habitats as stopovers during their fall migration from nesting and molting areas to the primary fall staging area of Izembek Lagoon. Offshore and onshore oil-gas exploration, development, and transportation pose the most significant threats to this staging habitat. A possible approach to further protection and preservation of this area would be to add key areas such as Pilot Point and Cinder River staging areas to the Alaska Peninsula NWR through land exchanges.

Upper Cook Inlet is bordered by a series of tidal marshes, including Susitna Flats, Palmer Hay Flats, Trading Bay, Redoubt Bay, Chickaloon Flats, Potters Marsh, Kenai and Kasilof river deltas, and Kalgin Island, which are of major importance to many waterfowl species as spring or fall staging habitat. Cackling Canada geese use the Upper Cook Inlet tidal marshes as a spring staging area prior to moving to the Yukon-Kuskokwim Delta nesting grounds. Some 10,000 or more cackling geese stage there in spring, where they build up fat and protein reserves needed for nesting. At least 20,000 Pacific white-fronted geese use the tidal marshes during spring and fall. Chickaloon, Susitna, and Palmer Hay flats and Trading Bay are the most important areas used by these birds. This area, Redoubt Bay in particular, is also the only known breeding ground of the tule white-fronted goose, which numbered 4,000-5,000 in 1982. All of the important bays and marshes are state-owned tidal and submerged lands and most are classified as state refuges or important habitat, except Redoubt Bay. Onshore and offshore oil-gas exploration, urbanization, and coal and hydroelectric development are major threats. Efforts to have Redoubt Bay designated as a critical area or waterfowl refuge should be increased.

The Copper River Delta's prime importance is as a spring and fall staging area. Peak populations during spring are estimated to be up to 500,000 ducks, 125,000 geese, 15,000 tundra swans, and 2,500 trumpeter swans. Fall populations peak at up to 600,000 ducks, 130,000 geese, 30,000 tundra swans and 3,000 trumpeter swans. Cackling Canada geese use the area in unknown numbers during spring migration. Pacific white-fronted geese stage there in spring and fall, peaking at up to 100,000 birds (the majority of the population). The area is within the Chugach National Forest, and is administered by the U.S. Forest Service. Potential threats are coal development by native corporations in the Bering River coal fields, increased recreational use of the area, and oil-spills associated with Port Valdez (terminus of the Trans-Alaska Pipeline). Cooperative agreements with the U.S. Forest Service and native corporations for management of the delta for waterfowl seem to be the most promising protective measures.

Central Valley of California.—This valley winters about 60% of the Pacific Flyway populations of waterfowl, including nearly the entire population of cackling Canada geese and Pacific white-fronted geese. Only 4% of the original wetlands of the Central Valley remain (less than 120,000 ha, compared to 1,600,000 ha in the late 1800s). The most intensive forms of agriculture in North America are practiced here. Soon, the only remaining wetlands will be those dedicated specifically to waterfowl and other wildlife and those created by waters drained from agricultural lands. The latter are of uncertain value to waterfowl, and studies are in progress to determine their future use in waterfowl management. The recommended action is to acquire easements on 28,392 ha of waterfowl habitat in the Central Valley and to acquire fee title on an additional 4,047 ha.

Lower Mississippi River and Gulf Coast.—The lower Mississippi River delta area is the most important wintering area for mallards and wood ducks. The average annual conversion from forest to cropland in the lower Mississippi River category is 105,220 ha per year. In addition, existing cropland areas that currently provide some waterfowl values are being subjected to improved drainage, with a resultant reduction in waterfowl values. As these habitats are drained and cleared, waterfowl become more restricted in their distribution. This increases their vulnerability to disease, possible over-harvest, and other forms of stress. There is evidence that decreased wetland habitat during winter influences productivity of mallards, although our understanding of this phenomenon is incomplete. The recommended action is to preserve 121,410 ha.

The Gulf Coast area winters millions of waterfowl, including 87% of the mid-continent flocks of lesser snow geese, 59% of the midcontinent population of white-fronted geese, and 70% of the North American population of redheads. The Gulf Coast is the most rapidly developing industrial area in the U.S. Oil refineries, petrochemical plants, and an array of related industries have resulted in power plants, pipelines, waste-disposal sites, loading docks, canals, houses, and recreation facilities which destroy coastal wetlands. In the eastern portion of this category, habitat is being lost to erosion, subsidence, and saltwater intrusion due to navigation and flood-control projects. The recommended action is to (1) preserve 34,804 ha in fee title and 80,940 ha in perpetual easements along the Texas coast, and (2) in the central and eastern portions of this category, preserve 12,141 ha in fee title and 28,329 ha in perpetual easements.

Middle Upper Atlantic Coast.—This category contains over 404,700 ha of habitat that have been identified as important to wintering populations of black ducks. Chesapeake Bay and North Carolina coastal areas are major wintering grounds for canvasbacks. Forty-five percent of this area is in private ownership and not considered adequately protected. Water quality in many canvasback habitats has declined, forcing changes in their distribution and diets. The long-term consequences of this are only partially understood. The recommended action is to acquire 20,235 ha of wetlands important to wintering black ducks. Purchases may include both fee title and conservation easements.

Intermountain West.—Scattered wetlands between the Cascades-Sierra Nevada and the Rocky Mountains are important for the production of redheads, mallards, canvasbacks, pintails, and wintering mallards. Approximately 80% of the U.S. breeding population of redheads occurs here, and 1.5 million mallards winter in this area. These wetlands are being drained or filled for a variety of economic reasons. The recommended action is to acquire perpetual easements on 14,164 ha.

Playa Lakes.—Located primarily in the panhandles of Texas and Oklahoma, perhaps as many as 50% of the pintails that winter south of the U.S. migrate through this area, and hundreds of thousands of pintails and mallards winter there. Development of irrigated agricul-

ture, largely since World War II, made the Playa Lakes regions one of the most intensively farmed regions in North America. The main source of water, the Ogallala aquifer, is being depleted. As a result, playas increasingly are being used as sumps to capture return flows and serve as reservoirs for temporary storage of well water pumped during off-peak periods. Pits, often with drainage ditches to collect water from the rest of the basin or dikes, are constructed to concentrate the water, thereby reducing the surface exposed to evaporation, making it more accessible to pumps. Surrounding basins of modified playas usually are dry or have substantially less water surface area with little littoral zone. The recommended action is to protect 19,426 ha of selected playas near recognized disease hot spots. These will serve as alternate wetlands when disease outbreaks occur.

Klamath Basin.—This area is critical to cackling Canada geese and Pacific white-fronted geese as 80-90% of these populations migrate through it. Pintail numbers often reach 1 million in fall and spring. Habitat continues to decrease in the Klamath Basin. Due to the low overall waterfowl population levels in the Pacific Flyway in recent years, and sharp declines in cackling Canada goose and white-fronted goose numbers, the current conditions in the basin are adequate to support present populations. However, increases in these populations to levels identified as management objectives would probably force waterfowl out of this area and into the Central Valley of California, where habitat conditions would not be adequate to support them. The recommended action is to obtain conservation easements on 607 ha.

Middle-Upper Pacific Coast.—This large coastal zone is important to migrating and wintering mallards, pintails, canvasbacks, and Pacific brant. Major habitat losses are occurring in the middle Upper Pacific Coast due to diking of estuaries and river floodplains, dredging, commercial shellfishing, log storage, and marine development. The recommended action is to purchase in fee title, 20,235 ha of selected high-quality wetlands in areas such as Port Susan Bay, Padilla Bay, Gray's Harbor, Willapa Bay, Columbia River, Tillamook Bay, Yaquina Bay, and Coos Bay.

San Francisco Bay.—This bay is the major wintering area for the western population of canvasbacks. It also winters major numbers of pintails. Diking and filling of shallow marsh and tidal flats have reduced the bay by 50%. Original marsh areas have been reduced by 80%. Lower water quality from upstream agricultural and industrial uses threatens canvasback habitat. The recommended action is to acquire in fee title, 1,214 ha of key wetlands.

Other U.S. Areas of Concern.—Four other areas (Sandhills and Rainwater Basin, Northern Great Plains, Upper Mississippi River, and Northern Lakes and Southwest Florida) also are identified by the NAWMP. These areas have not yet undergone extensive acquisition or preservation planning efforts by waterfowl managers, but some waterfowl habitat has been acquired over the past several decades. Nonetheless, they are important waterfowl migration and wintering areas in the U.S.

Mexico

Information on Mexico is not as extensive as that for the U.S. and Canada. Additionally, government activity in Mexico has not focused on wetland/waterfowl preservation as a priority issue. Consequently, private organizations have taken the lead in wetland enhancement and protection efforts, specifically Ducks Unlimited of Mexico (DUMAC), which sponsors many of the current programs in Mexico. However, a full-scale, successful wetland protection program can only occur with active government participation.

The U.S. FWS has been conducting aerial waterfowl surveys in Mexico since 1947. Although these surveys are used in conjunction with the winter survey in the U.S. to determine the winter distribution and relative abundance of various North American waterfowl, survey personnel are simultaneously observing habitat, and, as a result, are providing the best overall information on the status of Mexico's wetland habitats. U.S. FWS survey efforts in Mexico are discussed in greater detail by Voelzer (1985), Baldassarre et al. (1988), and Kramer and Migoya (1988).

Based on the data compiled through many years of surveys, the U.S. FWS has identified 29 areas that are considered critical to the maintenance of wintering waterfowl populations in Mexico. These areas are listed (Table 2) with the observations made (species number and habitat status) in the 1985 survey (Fig.3). Continuation of these efforts and the cooperation of the Mexican government are needed for resolving habitat degradation problems. The value of Mexican habitats to North American waterfowl is obvious. Without protection of these wintering areas, waterfowl production efforts in Canada and the U.S. will be ineffective.

International

The Convention on Wetlands of International Importance especially as Waterfowl Habitat, known as the Ramsar Convention, is an international treaty that provides the framework for establishing a world list of important wetlands to be naturally preserved. This includes a pledge by member nations to make wise use of all wetlands. There are 45 contracting parties; they include, from this hemisphere, Canada, U.S., Mexico, Suriname, Uruguay, and Chile.

Canada, a member nation since 1981, has 17 wetland sites identified under the Ramsar Convention totaling approximately 10,117,500 ha, almost half the total Ramsar acreage, and has nominated 11 additional sites. The U.S. only recently

Table 2. Mexico's critical wintering habitat sites (see Fig. 3 for geographical locations).

(1)	Lower Laguna Madre
	Extremely important to several species of ducks and up to 40,000 geese (snows and white-fronts). Primary concern would be redheads (200,000-300,000), pintails, and American wigeon. Some development in the form of new ocean channels and oil-drilling activity. Considerable amount of low-key commercial fishing.
(2)	Laguna Tamiahua
	10,000-20,000 redheads, plus gadwall and wigeon. Several forms of pollution possible: small industry, oil, and human.
(3)	Alvarado Lagoon
	Primary: blue-winged teal, wigeon, gadwall, fulvous and black bellied tree ducks, roseate spoonbills. Concern: industrial and oil pollution.
(4)&(5)	Minatitlan Lagoons
	Primary: Extremely large blue-winged teal concentrations 100,000+. Unit 4 is the most critical as pollution, a sulphur plant, and possibly oil development are encroaching steadily. Unit 5 has a great amount of oil development involved.
(6)	Tabasco Lagoons
	Primary: large concentrations of blue-winged teal, both tree ducks, some gadwall and wigeon. Considerable amount of oil development with corresponding pollution in certain areas.
(7)	Celestin Lagoon
	Primary: scaup concentration up to 100,000, plus large numbers of gadwall and American coot (100,000). Also 3,000-5,000 American flamingo and some brown pelicans. Concern would be oil pollution and industrial development.
(8)	Mangrove Swamp
	Primary: Large concentrations of blue-winged teal, white and brown pelicans, and literally untold numbers of shore birds. No immediate concern; area is subjected to periodic drying but the town of Progreso is developing as a seaport. Brown pelicans all along coast.
(9)	Rio Lagartos, El Cuyo, Islan Holbox
	Primary: American flamingos, brown pelicans, and blue-winged teal. No concern at present, but human encroachment should be monitored.
(10)	Lago de Cuitzeo
	Important wintering area for northern shoveler (400,000), blue-winged teal, gadwall, ruddy duck, and canvasback (75,000).
(11)	Lago de Chapala (east end)
	Wetlands on the east end would make a good sanctuary. Important area for wigeon, pintail, and scaup.
(12)	Marismas Nacional
	Concentration area for numerous species of wading birds plus northern shoveler, blue-winged teal, and cinnamon teal.
(13)	Laguna de Santiaguillo (north end)
	Wintering waterfowl concentrate on this end because of permanent water. Important for snow geese, white-fronted geese, and dabbling ducks. Would be a good refuge.
(14)	Laguna de Santiaguillo (south end)
	Normally dry. In years of plentiful water, it serves as a feeding and loafing area for ducks. Sandhill cranes use the extreme southern portion.
(15)	Victoria
	A small lake that can be important for snow geese (8,000-10,000) and white-fronted geese (8,000-10,000).
(16)	Ensenada del Pabellon
	Probably the most important wintering area in Mexico for pintails. Usually 150,000 to 500,000 use this area. Area hunted from Pichihuile Club.
(17)	Bahia Santa Maria
	Area winters about 100,000 ducks. Important for green-winged teal and brant (6,000+).
(18)	Topolobampo South (Isla San Ignacio)
	A few brant and scaup.
(19)	Topolobampo North (Bahia Ohuira)
	The wetlands in the northeast part of this bay constitute a very important sanctuary for teal, wigeon, shoveler, pintail, whistling ducks, and scaup. This is the most important area in western Mexico for these species. Up to 10,000 brant can be found in the main bay.

Table 2. Continued

(20)	Laguna de los Mexicanos
	A popular area for wintering snow geese and white fronted geese. A natural basin surrounded by grain farming. Also used by 3,000-5,000 sandhill cranes and 20,000+ pintails. This area especially important when other parts of the northern highlands are dry.
(21)	Laguna Bustillos
	A migration stopover for dabbling ducks and snow geese. Several bald eagles winter here. Pollution on the south end from some form of industry threatens to destroy the water quality in the entire reservoir.
(22)	San Jose de Bavicora
	A very important highland wintering area for pintail, teal, and shoveler plus snow and white-fronted geese. Area has been drying up in recent years due to diversion of natural inflow plus drought. This area is unique and would be an important ecosystem to preserve. Very important for sandhill cranes.
(23)	Nuevo Casas Grandes
	A migration stop for snow geese and sandhill cranes.
(24)	Ascension
	Up to 25,000 ducks and 15,000 snow geese. Whooping cranes from the Grey's Lake foster parent flock have been known to use this area.
(25)	Colorado River Delta
	Rather unimportant as a waterfowl wintering area until the high water of the recent past; a unique ecosystem.
(26)	Bahia San Quintin
	Popular wintering area for up to 15,000 brant. Also serves as a migration stop for brant both north and southbound. Traditional brant hunting area.
(27)	Laguna de Scammon (Laguna Ojo de Liebre)
	Already set aside by Mexico as a sanctuary. A major wintering area for brant and whales.
(28)	Laguna San Ignacio
	A major wintering area for brant. Already set aside by Mexico as a sanctuary.
(29)	Bahia Magdalena
	A very important secondary wintering area for brant if food conditions are not sufficient at (28) or (27).

(April 1987) ratified the convention, and consequently, has 4 designated wetland sites (Izembek NWR, Ash Meadows NWR, Forsythe NWR, and Okefenokee Swamp) and 2 nominations (Chesapeake Bay and the Everglades). The Ramsar wetland designation does not place additional responsibilities or restrictions on Canada or the U.S., but instead conforms with already applicable laws and treaties.

There are basically 3 obligations for parties under the Ramsar Convention. First, member nations are encouraged to include wetland conservation coordination within their land-use planning. Secondly, they are encouraged to promote the conservation of wetlands through the establishment of nature reserves. Thirdly, they are obligated to designate wetlands for inclusion in a "List of Wetlands of International Importance" (Ramsar 1987).

The International Waterfowl and Wetlands Research Bureau (IWRB) is an international nongovernment body that serves as a scientific advisory group to the Ramsar Convention. The IWRB is composed of research groups that, in addition to conducting international waterfowl counts, inventory wetlands of international importance.

The Ramsar Convention uses a general definition for the term wetlands and consequently incorporates a wide range of habitat types that can include rivers, coastal areas, and coral reefs (Ramsar 1987). However, given all these factors that extend the scope of wetland protection beyond the wintering-migrating waterfowl habitat addressed in this volume, Ramsar does heighten awareness of important wetland sites. This could serve as an impetus for Latin American

Fig. 3.   Mexico's critical wintering habitat sites.

countries to become more actively involved in wetland protection-management issues.

HABITAT PROTECTION PROGRAMS

U.S. Federal Efforts

The majority of significant waterfowl habitat under federal control is adminis-

tered as part of the National Wildlife Refuge System (NWRS). Currently, there are 437 refuges in 49 states (none in West Virginia), Puerto Rico, the Virgin Islands, and the Pacific Trust Territories, comprising about 35,775,480 ha. The Alaska National Interest Lands Conservation Act of 1980 set aside vast wetland acreages in Alaska as part of the NWRS. The 16 national wildlife refuges in Alaska encompass over 31,161,900 ha and include much important waterfowl habitat. In addition, there are Waterfowl Production Areas (WPAs) in 150 counties in the previously glaciated regions of Michigan, Minnesota, Montana, Iowa, Nebraska, North Dakota, South Dakota, and Wisconsin. These areas, which total about 687,990 ha, are small natural wetlands preserved primarily to benefit nesting ducks, but which also serve as migration habitat. Finally, over 485,000 ha of wetlands are preserved by perpetual conservation easements in this area. Total wetland area in the NWRS is estimated at 13,557,450 ha, with about 1,861,620 ha of this located in the lower 48 states.

Although northern freshwater wetlands are primary waterfowl nesting areas in spring and summer, wetlands in all parts of the U.S. are used for feeding and cover during migration and winter. The status and trends of wetlands and deepwater habitats in the conterminous U.S. were reviewed by Tiner (1984) and the National Wetlands Inventory Group (1985). They reported that 40,065,300 ha of wetlands remain in the lower 48 states; this represents about 46% of the area existing at the time of the nation's settlement. (Estimates of Alaska's wetland resource vary, but about 89 million ha probably remain.) Net wetland losses in the lower 48 states between the mid-1950s and the mid-1970s averaged 185,352 ha annually. Important waterfowl habitat that has been lost includes portions of the Prairie-Pothole region, California's Central Valley, and the Lower Mississippi River Valley. Arkansas, California, Illinois, Nebraska, the Dakotas, the Atlantic, Gulf Coast, and Great Lakes states experienced the greatest wetland losses. Waterfowl habitat protection is accomplished by acquisition of priority wetlands by federal, state, local, and private entities, and legal and administrative processes that regulate wetland uses.

The Migratory Bird Hunting and Conservation Stamp Act of 1934, as amended, requires the purchase of "duck stamps" by waterfowl hunters aged 16 years and older (nonhunters also may buy stamps). Revenue generated by the sale of duck stamps is used by the FWS to protect migratory bird habitat, either by land purchase or through long-term easements with landowners. Easements prevent wetlands from being drained, burned, leveled, or filled. Between 1934 and 1986, approximately 91.7 million duck stamps were sold, raising $313 million for waterfowl habitat protection.

The Migratory Bird Conservation Fund (MBCF), administered by the U.S. FWS, finances 2 land acquisition programs. The first, involving the purchase of major areas for migratory birds, is carried out under the authority of the Migratory Bird Conservation Act of 1929, as amended, and requires consideration and approval by the Migratory Bird Conservation Commission. The second involves the acquisition of WPAs and perpetual conservation easements that are acquired under the authority of the Migratory Bird Hunting and Conservation Stamp Act and do not require approval of the commission. All MBCF acquisitions become part of the NWRS. Through 30 September 1987, $361 million from the MBCF had been expended for the purchase of easements and fee title of 1,515,492 ha of land for migratory birds.

The U.S. Department of Agriculture (USDA) administers several programs that preserve waterfowl habitat. The Water Bank Act of 1970 authorized USDA to make payments under 10-year leases to private landowners and operators who agree not to drain, fill, level, burn, or otherwise destroy wetlands, and who agree to maintain grassy cover on adjacent land. The designated acreage must provide essential habitat for waterfowl. Participation has been mostly in prime nesting areas in Minnesota and the Dakotas. However, significant amounts of wintering habitat in Arkansas, California, Louisiana, and Mississippi have been preserved with this program. Under the Water Bank Program, through 1986, the USDA paid approximately $8.9 million annually to protect some 226,632 ha of wetlands and adjacent uplands in 12 states. Over 55,039 ha preserved with this program benefited wintering waterfowl in the 4 states identified above.

In the west, the Bureau of Reclamation (BOR) plays a major role in water-resource management. In the Central Valley of California, for example, BOR is the most active federal agency. There are 20 dams and reservoirs, 8 hydroelectric plants, 2 pumping generating plants, 54 pumping plants along the 2,313 km of aqueducts, and 309 km of drains, all of which comprise the Central Valley Project, the largest undertaking in BOR's history (U.S. Department of the Interior [USDI] 1988). BOR has 16 billion m^3 of storage and about 25 billion m^3 of water rights associated with the Central Valley Project, and water from the project fully irrigates 46,536 ha, partially irrigates 1 million ha, and supplies water for municipal and industrial use (USDI 1988). Consequently, by providing water for agriculture, BOR has a major impact on the maintenance of wetland habitats and, ultimately, on waterfowl use in the Central Valley.

In addition to the artificial manipulation of the water supporting this habitat is the subsequent impact of contamination resulting from drain water. This is exemplified by the degradation of waterfowl habitat at the Kesterson NWR. BOR has estimated that cleanup of the Kesterson site will cost between $10 million and $150 million, depending on the alternative selected (USDI 1988).

Three major BOR projects in the planning stage could result in additional threats to this habitat. The first is the Auburn-Folsom South Unit, comprising a 2.8 billion m^3 reservoir and a 99 km canal. It was authorized in 1965 to provide increased power and flood protection to the Sacramento area. The second is the San Jaoquin Valley, and the last is the San Louis Unit, consisting of a distribution and wastewater drainage system. This last project would provide supplemental water to 236,000 ha and 32 million m^3 for municipal and industrial use and provide some flood control and recreational benefits (USDI 1988).

Irrigation water users are heavily subsidized by the U.S. government, but in recent years, steps have been taken to reduce this level of subsidy. For example, the Reclamation Reform Act of 1982 has imposed higher water prices on owned or leased lands that are larger than 388 ha. Also, water districts seeking to increase water supplies must amend their BOR contracts to pay full operation and maintenance costs. In addition, BOR has adopted a new rate-setting policy that sets annually adjustable water rates to eliminate the problems stemming from fixed-rate contracts.

Several laws provide important protection to waterfowl habitat by regulating certain uses of wetlands. The foundation of federal wetland regulations is Section 10 of the Rivers and Harbors Act of 1899 and Section 404 of the Federal Water Pollution Control Act of 1972 (later amended as the Clean Water Act of 1977), which requires the U.S. Army Corps of Engineers to have permits for dredging, filling, and for other types of construction activities in wetlands (Tiner 1984). Under the Fish and Wildlife Coordination Act of 1934, as amended, the FWS reviews these permit applications and makes recommendations based on environmental considerations. However, most agricultural and silvicultural activities, including drainage, clearing, and flooding, are exempt. The Coordination Act also requires federal water resource agencies to give full consideration to the need to acquire habitat, including mitigation lands, specifically for the conservation and enhancement of fish and wildlife.

Wetlands and other waterfowl habitat also receive regulatory protection under more general federal statutes, including the National Environmental Policy Act of 1969, Endangered Species Act of 1973 (as amended), Coastal Zone Management Act of 1972 (as amended), Coastal Barriers Resources Act of 1982, and Water Resources Development Act of 1986. These laws restrict federal agencies from undertaking or funding activities that would have adverse environmental impacts. Executive Orders 11988 and 11990, promulgated in 1977, require federal agencies to take actions to minimize the destruction, loss, and degradation of wetlands.

Although not all federal policies provide protection for wetlands, 3 laws recently passed promise to offer a major opportunity for protection and enhancement of wetland habitats. This legislation is the 1985 Food Security Act (P.L. 99-198), the Emergency Wetland Resources Act of 1985 (P.L. 99-645), and the Water Resources Development Act of 1986 (P.L. 99-662).

1985 Food Security Act (Farm Act).—In the U.S., agricultural practices have had a greater impact on waterfowl habitat than other human activities. Habitats have been converted to grain and forage crops resulting in outright destruction of wetlands, with the secondary impact of increases in erosion and sedimentation further threatening remaining wetlands. In the U.S., 87% of all wetland loss is attributed to agriculture (National Wetland Inventory Group 1986a). When it is recognized that between 70 and 75% of the remaining wetlands are in private ownership (Heimlich and Langner 1986, National Wetland Inventory Group 1986b), the magnitude of this impact can be realized. The Farm Act provides new avenues to address this wetland loss problem.

The Farm Act contains a special wetland conservation section commonly referred to as the Swampbuster Provision. Under Swampbuster, any person who produces an agricultural commodity on wetlands converted to such agricultural production after 23 December 1985 becomes ineligible for most agricultural subsidies. The restriction applies to the year such production occurs and to all lands, including nonwetlands, under control of that person. The intent of Swampbuster is to reduce agricultural surplus production by reducing the amount of new land being brought into production, and to protect wetlands from conversion to agricultural production.

A second major provision of the Farm Act that indirectly benefits wetlands is the Conservation Reserve Program (CRP). Under this program, approximately 18 million ha of predominantly highly erodible croplands are to be placed in a not-less-than-10-year Set-Aside status. Once in the program, an annual payment is made to the landowner and a 50% federal cost-sharing of vegetative cover establishment is provided. Although the CRP focuses upon predominantly highly erodible lands, it offers tremendous wetland benefits as well. Many of the highly erodible land areas contain interspersed wetlands. These wetlands thus become a part of the Set-Aside efforts and are approved as a cost-sharing practice by the Department of Agriculture. The CRP can serve as a means to protect existing wetlands as well as to provide an avenue through which drained wetland basins may be restored. Uplands, in proximity to such wetland basins that receive erosion stabilization attention in the form of vegetative cover establishment, provide vital nesting cover for waterfowl and protect the wetland basins from siltation (Fig. 4).

A third aspect of the Farm Act, one just now beginning to emerge in terms of potential wetland conservation significance, involves the Farm Loan Program of the Farmers Home Administration (FmHA). The FmHA is widely recognized as the lender of last resort. When an eligible borrower, such as a family farmer, cannot secure adequate financing

Fig. 4. Permanent upland cover being established under the Conservation Reserve Program will reduce sediments and pollutants entering wetlands and improve nesting habitat.

from another lending institution, he may qualify for a FmHA loan. By the very nature of this lending process, many of the FmHA loans involve marginal lands. Because the lands in question are frequently marginal, the rate of farm failure is much greater than normally would be expected. Many of the FmHA borrowers are facing serious debt crises, and many others already have voluntarily conveyed their lands to the FmHA. Foreclosure proceedings are resulting in still other lands being placed into the inventory of the FmHA.

Several wetland conservation opportunities associated with the Farm Loan Program of the FmHA are available as a primary result of the Farm Bill. The Farm Debt Restructure and Conservation Set-Aside Provision (Section 1318) would allow the Secretary of Agriculture to grant partial debt relief to a present borrower in exchange for not less than a 50-year easement, for conservation purposes, to selected lands held by the borrower. Another provision (Section 1314) allows the secretary to grant or sell easements, restrictions, development rights, or the equivalent thereof, for conservation purposes, to a unit of local or state government or a private nonprofit organization before resale. This provision applies to lands that are in the FmHA inventory.

The Farm Debt Restructure and Conservation Set-Aside Provision (Section 1318) is intended to help borrowers in debt to the FmHA regain a positive cash flow by allowing them to place selected lands in a conservation easement status while continuing to farm better lands. The duration of the easement cannot be for less than 50 years. The intent of the easements is for conservation, wildlife, and recreational purposes. Selection of suitable lands, formulation of terms and conditions of the easements, and enforcement are the responsibility of the Secretary of Agriculture in consultation with the Director of the U.S. FWS. Implementation of this provision is discretionary.

Section 1314, allowing the Secretary of

Agriculture to grant or sell an easement to a unit of local or state government, applies to land that is held by the FmHA in its inventory. In principle, the provision could allow a state fish and wildlife agency or private conservation entity to secure, at no cost, development rights to lands containing important wetlands. Transfer authority of inventory lands has recently been enacted that allows the Secretary of Agriculture to transfer to any federal or state agency, for conservation purposes, any real property that has marginal value for agricultural production, is environmentally sensitive, and has special management importance.

The greatest wetlands conservation potential inherent in the Farm Loan Program occurs as a result of the willingness of FmHA to place protective deed restrictions on wetlands before resale of inventory farm properties. Under authority of Executive Order 11990-Protection of Wetlands, the FmHA has concluded that it has an affirmative responsibility to protect and enhance wetlands in conjunction with property disposal. Consequently, the U.S. FWS has been provided the opportunity, by a recently enacted Memorandum of Understanding, to assist with wetlands preservation and enhancement efforts.

The Memorandum of Understanding calls on the U.S. FWS, in close coordination with the respective state fish and wildlife agency, to (1) screen inventory lands, (2) identify important wetland protection opportunities, and (3) formulate or sponsor the implementation by a third party of mutually acceptable plans for wetlands preservation and enhancement. Deed restrictions that either protect existing productive wetlands from future disturbance or provide for the restoration or enhancement of previously impacted wetlands are appropriate for recommendation. The deed restrictions are perpetual in duration and may provide for ingress and egress rights for the opera-

tion, maintenance, management, and replacement of facilities and habitat conditions (e.g., water-control structure operation and vegetative manipulation). Deed restrictions may (1) include designated buffer areas; (2) provide for waterfowl, migratory bird or wildlife sanctuary status designation; and (3) identify a state or private conservation entity as an appropriate entity to be involved in subsequent on-site wetland activities.

With approximately 700,000 ha of property in the FmHA inventory, and with the inventory expected to include several million additional hectares in the next few years, the scope and magnitude of this opportunity are significant.

1986 Emergency Wetlands Resources Act.—The Emergency Wetlands Resources Act (EWRA) provides authority for the federal government to strengthen wetland efforts in close coordination with state governments. It calls for the establishment of a National Wetlands Priority Conservation Plan (currently under development by the U.S. FWS) that identifies locations of wetland projects and types of wetlands that should receive priority consideration for federal and state acquisition. This legislation also amends the Land and Water Conservation Fund Act (LWCF) to authorize the use of LWCF for migratory birds.

The EWRA authorizes the use of entrance fees for designated units of the NWRS, with 70% of those receipts being paid into the Migratory Bird Conservation Fund (MBCF), and authorizes an increase in duck stamp prices with a resulting increase in revenues for the MBCF. A third funding increase for the MBCF will include a yearly transfer of funds equal to the import duties on arms and ammunitions.

This legislation extends the Wetlands Loan Act for 2 years and excuses the $200 million advanced by Congress to fund wetland acquisition under the Wetlands Loan Act. Had this repayment not been excused, the U.S. FWS would have been required to use 75% of annual duck stamp receipts to make repayment.

The U.S. FWS now is authorized to continue its National Wetlands Inventory Project, and a schedule has been established for the completion of inventory maps. Reports on the status of wetlands must be submitted periodically to Congress and must include information on factors responsible for wetland destruction, federal expenditures related to wetlands, and trends or patterns in ownership of wetlands.

1986 Water Resources Development Act (Water Bill).—The U.S. Army Corps of Engineers (Corps) is the principal federal agency for flood-control and navigation projects. Corps projects influence, both directly and indirectly, the quality and quantity of wetlands associated with inland rivers and lakes and coastal waters of the U.S. Traditionally, the focus of water project authorities has been narrow, confined largely to navigation and flood control. Until now, the Corps has not been asked to broaden its scope to assure that management of water and wetlands is supported by sound principles of natural resource management. This has changed with passage of the Water Resources Development Act of 1986 (Water Bill).

For a sense of the potential impact this legislation can have on waterfowl habitat protection and enhancement, consider this quote from the Congressional Record: "Until now, mitigation for land turned over to water development projects came about on a hit-or-miss basis. For the first time, mitigation will have to go forward with the project requiring the mitigation, not afterward. This Act requires that the Corps develop mitigation plans for each and every new project, or tell the American people why such work is not justified. In addition, this section establishes a new continuing authority, funded at $30 million annu-

ally. This authority will allow the Corps to go back and repair the fish and wildlife damage that its existing projects have produced" (Senator Robert Stafford as Chairman of the Senate Committee on Environment and Public Works).

The Lower Mississippi River Valley provides an excellent case history of a resource of major importance to wintering waterfowl. It demonstrates the traditional approach to water projects and the role that Congress can play to reverse the process. Superimposed on this 8 million ha floodplain is the world's largest flood-control/drainage project, the Mississippi River and Tributaries Project (MRT). In 1928, Congress authorized the MRT to promote and protect regional development of the area by protecting the Lower Mississippi River Valley from catastrophic flooding. Subsequent amendments stimulated the drainage and conversion of large segments of the forested wetland complex of this floodplain to agricultural uses, and also stimulated the deterioration of the vast coastal marshes of Louisiana.

Although the MRT has provided great benefits to the nation, the lack of a broader multipurpose perspective has led to unforeseen impacts from inappropriate conversion of wetlands, degradation of water quality, and erosion of coastal marshes. The Water Act now offers the opportunity to reverse this trend. Section 1135 authorized $2 million for each of 3 fiscal years (1987-89) for the Corps, in coordination with the Departments of Interior and Commerce and appropriate state agencies, to "develop and implement projects for the creation, protection, restoration, and enhancement of wetlands in conjunction with authorized projects for navigation and flood control in the Lower Mississippi Valley."

Additionally, Section 1135 authorized a review of projects constructed before enactment of the Water Act to assess the need to modify structures and operations of water resources projects to improve the quality of the environment in the public interest. A $25-million funding level is authorized for a 2-year demonstration program. Within 2 years after enactment of the Water Act, the Corps was required to transmit to Congress a report on the results of the review of projects and on the demonstration program. The Secretary of the Army also was required to recommend in his report whether the program required modification.

Section 1135 also can be a vehicle for restoring wetlands on certain lands that should never have been farmed. The rate of farm failure in the Lower Mississippi River Valley has been higher than average because of pressures to produce soybeans on lands too frequently flooded to sustain agriculture. The Farm Act contains some key provisions that form a bridge to build on opportunities in the Water Act. More than 100,000 ha of abandoned farmlands are administered in the Lower Mississippi River Valley by the FmHA or other elements of the farm credit system. Many wetland restoration opportunities on these lands can be realized by the Corps through simple modification of project operations or through implementation of low-cost structural modifications (e.g., dikes, water-control structures, etc.).

Section 704 directs the Secretary of the Army to investigate the feasibility of using Corps expertise to conserve fish and wildlife (including their habitats). The projected scope of these studies includes the use of engineering or construction capabilities to improve, enlarge, develop, or otherwise beneficially modify existing habitats of such fish and wildlife. Of major significance in this section is the specific concern expressed for habitat.

Section 906 requires that project-induced losses of bottomland hardwood wetlands be replaced in-kind to whatever extent possible.

Historically, mitigation features have not received attention until after project construction was well underway or com-pleted. At this point, the Corps usually turned its attention to the next construction project on its list. Thus, mitigation rarely became a reality. Now, however, Congress requires that mitigation for losses to fish and wildlife, including acquisition of the land or interests, shall be acquired before construction of the project commences, or acquired concurrently with lands and interests in land for project purposes. This procedure, in effect, becomes a contractual agreement between the Corps and their appropriations committees. In other words, Congress will continue to pay the bills as long as the Corps makes satisfactory progress on all project components.

Finally, after consulting with appropriate federal and nonfederal agencies, the Secretary of the Army is authorized to mitigate damages for fish and wildlife resulting from any water resources project under his jurisdiction, whether completed, under construction, or to be constructed. This is the section referred to by Senator Stafford as allowing the Corps to "go back and repair the fish and wildlife damage that its existing projects have produced." Retrofit mitigation features for previously authorized and constructed projects costing up to $7.5 million, or 10% of total project cost, may be implemented without further specific reports to Congress. Up to $30 million can be budgeted each year for this purpose. The Water Bill goes even further by authorizing acquisition, primarily of wetlands, at 15 specific projects. Two of the larger projects are in the Lower Mississippi River Valley. The Atchafalaya Basin, Louisiana, and the Yazoo Backwater Area, Mississippi, provide for easements or fee title acquisition of more than 161,880 ha of mitigation lands.

In summary, the Water Act requires the Corps to (1) mitigate for project-induced losses of fish, wildlife, and their habitats; (2) modify structures or operations of their projects; (3) improve the environment; and (4) provide the broad authority needed to create, protect, restore, and enhance wetlands in the Lower Mississippi River Valley

The linchpin for coordinating these efforts may well be the Water Quality Act of 1987, a bill which reauthorized and amended the Clean Water Act of 1972. The control of nonpoint source pollution has been one of the emerging national environmental issues of the eighties. Cleanup of Chesapeake Bay and other important estuaries has been initiated through recognition that nonpoint source pollution is a major degrader of water quality and needs to be controlled. The amended legislation creates a new program for the control of nonpoint source pollution that addresses problems in a more focused manner than before. Funding by the Environmental Protection Agency will favor states that have developed comprehensive regional programs. It follows that groups of states (such as Louisiana, Mississippi, Arkansas, Tennessee, Kentucky, Missouri, and Illinois) will be more effective in competing for these federal dollars collectively than they would as individual states.

State Efforts

Inasmuch as no single federal agency or department can act alone in providing a comprehensive mechanism to protect all the nation's wetland resources, federal agencies acting collectively require the cooperation and assistance of state agencies to play a significant role in this effort. This was recognized over 30 years ago as increased state participation demanded a greater voice in setting waterfowl regulations. In 1947, the FWS divided the U.S. into flyways for the purpose of setting hunting regulations. By 1952, the states had organized by flyways and had formed flyway councils (Hawkins et al. 1984).

In addition to assisting in the development of hunting regulations, states develop wildlife refuges, protect unique habitats, and establish management areas. As described previously, the EWRA requires the U.S. FWS to coordinate with the states in amending their statewide comprehensive outdoor recreation plans to identify wetlands for acquisition. If outdoor recreation plans are not used, the states are required to develop wetland concept plans listing priority wetland sites. The wetlands identified in the state concept plans would then be eligible for funding by the LWCF grant-in-aid program administered by the National Park Service.

The Federal Aid in Fish and Wildlife Restoration Program is administered by the U.S. FWS as a national effort to strengthen the abilities of states to preserve, protect, and enhance fish and wildlife resources. These grant-in-aid programs are a product of the Federal Aid in Wildlife Restoration Act (Pittman-Robertson Act) and the Federal Aid in Sport Fish Restoration Act (Dingell-Johnson Act).

The Pittman-Robertson Act was enacted in 1937 and created a "Federal Aid to Wildlife Restoration program" to provide a secure funding source for allocation to the states. Today, this fund consists of revenue collected by manufacturers from excise taxes on sale of sporting arms and ammunition, archery equipment, and handguns. To be eligible to participate in the program, states were required to pass legislation that includes a prohibition against the diversion of hunting license fees for any purpose other than the administration of the state fish and wildlife agencies.

The states are able to use the Pittman-Robertson funding (75%/25% federal/state cost share) to provide for restoration and management of wildlife habitats. To access these funds, state fish and wildlife agencies select the projects to be funded, then submit proposals to the U.S. FWS for review and approval. Each project must address a need and be designed to meet that need. Extensive habitat for waterfowl, totaling 640,000 ha in 47 states, has been purchased since 1938 (Table 3).

States also provide their own funding in support of habitat protection and restoration efforts. These taxation programs can give an advantage to the individual by reduction of property tax or income tax as incentives for wetland protection, or can be used to increase revenues through sales of state duck stamps, sales taxes, or voluntary nongame state income tax checkoff contributions. The following state taxation programs were compiled by the U.S. Environmental Protection Agency, Office of Wetland Protection (Cowles et al. 1986), and represent some of the mechanisms used by the states to increase revenues for wetland protection. An Open Space protection tax incentive is found in Connecticut, Delaware, Maine, New Hampshire, North Carolina, Rhode Island, Tennessee, Vermont, and Virginia, and wetlands often comprise a major portion of the land protected under open space programs. Iowa, Minnesota, and New Hampshire offer tax abatement specifically for retaining wetlands in their natural condition. Some programs in Connecticut, Maine, New Hampshire, Rhode Island, Tennessee, and Virginia discourage landowners from changing the undeveloped state of their property by levying a substantial penalty. When landowners grant conservation easement, they can obtain property tax reductions (Delaware, Maryland, New Jersey, Rhode Island, South Carolina). New York offers a reduction in property tax to landowners who have been denied permission to develop wetlands. Thirty-two states have checkoff programs that supply funding to protect areas, including wetlands (Alabama, Delaware, Illinois, Kentucky, Massachusetts, Mississippi, South Carolina) and to fund acquisitions of wetlands along with other natural areas (Iowa, Louisiana, New Mexico, Ohio, Oregon, West Virginia). A

Table 3. Area of habitat acquired for migratory birds by states using Pittman-Robertson federal-aid funds, 1937-1984.

State	Ha	Cost ($)
Alabama	6,611	64,164
Alaska	100	119,175
Arizona	1,144	295,034
Arkansas	15,357	1,982,535
California	2,650	304,173
Colorado	6,166	596,885
Connecticut	3,796	1,983,027
Delaware	3,035	727,531
Florida	21,503	9,962
Georgia	10,769	134,041
Idaho	7,442	816,450
Illinois	10,435	1,489,806
Indiana	19,501	3,805,850
Iowa	13,236	2,898,547
Kansas	10,096	1,217,608
Kentucky	5,377	531,850
Maine	4,913	207,165
Maryland	18,294	390,858
Massachusetts	2,011	38,868
Michigan	34,652	4,942,371
Minnesota	130,903	11,872,094
Mississippi	6,310	245,473
Missouri	13,899	6,576,222
Montana	7,901	439,019
Nebraska	3,588	1,140,588
Nevada	28,246	954,274
New Hampshire	1,255	224,374
New Jersey	8,718	1,079,842
New Mexico	3,365	1,599,924
New York	11,788	3,505,852
North Carolina	8,578	22,428
North Dakota	11,494	316,410
Ohio	16,750	2,861,193
Oklahoma	2,553	22,207
Oregon	7,968	894,142
Pennsylvania	4,288	693,227
Rhode Island	1,265	600,937
South Carolina	7,478	173,884
South Dakota	21,188	878,680
Tennessee	1,290	72,428
Texas	4,416	441,236
Utah	7,359	232,346
Vermont	2,833	355,319
Virginia	5,017	129,751
Washington	8,173	330,939
Wisconsin	109,247	8,350,782
Wyoming	1,253	109,732
Total	639,809	66,672,283

[a]Funds shown are federal share only.

percentage of the sales tax in Missouri is used for the acquisition of property, including wetlands.

Private Efforts

An extensive examination of the effort of private organizations is not addressed in this chapter. We wish only to reiterate the importance that these organizations play in the protection and enhancement of waterfowl habitat. Of the private organizations involved in waterfowl protection issues, Ducks Unlimited (DU), The Nature Conservancy (TNC), and the National Audubon Society (NAS) are the most prominent.

DU celebrated its 50th anniversary in 1987. Since its inception, it has acquired, under easement or reservation, up to 1,618,800 ha of waterfowl habitat, constructed over 3,000 wetland projects, and established more than 10,000 km of nesting shoreline (Campbell 1987). In addition, the development of a state grant program, Matching Aid to Restore States' Habitats (MARSH), can only further enhance the impact of DU on wetland issues (Table 4).

The Nature Conservancy and the NAS also control land that provides valuable habitat for waterfowl. In early 1983, TNC began a 5-year effort called the National Wetland Conservation Project that focuses on protecting endangered aquatic and wetland ecosystems of the U.S. (Fenwick 1985). This continues TNC efforts, which have included 3,500 projects, 48% of which have been wetland or aquatic related. These projects include over 40,470 ha of bottomland hardwoods along Gulf Coast rivers from Florida to Louisiana, and over 12,141 ha of Virginia coastal barrier islands (Fenwick 1985). Much of TNC holdings are eventually sold or donated to the U.S. FWS or other federal and state agencies. In addition, TNC has helped establish over 40 state Natural Heritage Programs. These programs often are useful in raising funds for acquisition and providing for management of acquired lands. The NAS owns, operates, or maintains 29 sanctuaries, with 41,469 ha in 15 states, that have significant

Table 4. The number of projects and the developed and/or reserved area implemented by Ducks Unlimited.

State	Completed projects	Management area (ha)	Wetland area (ha)
Alaska	2	3,116	905
California	5	5,520	1,986
Minnesota	18	16,747	3,106
Montana	11	10,212	4,650
North Dakota	35	21,336	13,535
South Dakota	11	2,358	28,300
Total	82	59,289	27,013

[a]Ducks Unlimited, Inc., letter to Office of Migratory Bird Management, 12 March 1987.

wetland habitat attractive to waterfowl. One final component, and probably the most important, is that private waterfowl hunting clubs control, through ownership or lease, a substantial but unknown amount of waterfowl habitat. Braun (1965) reported that 11,000 hunting clubs controlled a minimum of 2,104,440 ha of land. Some 68% of this was located in wintering areas of Arkansas, California, Louisiana, and Texas.

FUTURE NEEDS
Federal Programs

Several new federal laws (e.g., the 1985 Farm Act and the 1986 Water Act, in particular) need the fullest support of the conservation community to be effective in maintaining and enhancing wintering waterfowl habitat.

The effectiveness of field implementation of the Swampbuster provision of the Farm Act continues to be the subject of debate. Principal entities charged with field implementation are the Agricultural Stabilization and Conservation Service (ASCS) and the Soil Conservation Service (SCS). Field personnel of the 2 agricultural agencies are being asked to place wetlands conservation above their traditional agricultural missions. This transition will not be easy. It is imperative that field activities include the active participation of U.S. FWS personnel as a means of balancing the essentially prodrainage tradition of many ASCS and SCS personnel. Only with a great deal of conservation, community scrutiny, and subsequent congressional support will Swampbuster ultimately become an effective deterrent to further wetland destruction.

Some improvements in the CRP are warranted. Where the cost of wetland restoration exceeds the basic cost associated with establishment of vegetative cover, it may be necessary to provide supplemental funding to encourage involved landowners to agree to the wetland restoration option in lieu of the frequently less expensive vegetation establishment option. Funds could be used to restore wetlands on CRP lands where the landowner agrees to such action. The landowner potentially saves his share of the cost of cover establishment, otherwise required if vegetative cover was being established, and the U.S. FWS, state, or private entities could gain access to restorable wetland basins. The only land costs involved would be payments made by the Department of Agriculture to the landowner for overall participation in the CRP. This approach to restoring valuable wetland habitat should be given priority consideration and support. A greatly expanded effort may be needed.

In some cases, it may be appropriate to make supplemental payments simply to ensure that a landowner with potentially valuable habitat for waterfowl or other important wildlife is encouraged to enroll a particular tract of land in the CRP. In other cases, supplemental payments can be used to acquire management rights on lands already in the CRP. The FWS is participating, to a limited extent, in such a supplemental payment program in the prairie-pothole region. It is referred to as the "Piggyback Agreement" effort. These agreements are designed to compensate landowners for wildlife management practices that will be beneficial to wildlife, generally, and, in this case, to

breeding ducks. Approximately 25,000 ha are presently involved. The benefits that result from the Piggyback Agreement approach warrant close attention. Expansion of the effort may be needed, especially in key wintering areas.

The Farm Debt Restructure and Conservation Set-Aside provision of the Farm Act should be completed as soon as possible. Interim regulations to implement the program were published on Sept. 14, 1988 in the Federal Register, but final regulations are pending. This important Farm Act provision should be implemented to the fullest extent possible. The opportunity to assist indebted farmers while securing valuable conservation easement must be maximized. Significant wetland conservation benefits will be one result of this provision in key wintering areas such as the lower Mississippi delta.

As identified in previous sections, the FmHA inventory-land disposal program currently includes approximately 687,990 ha, with the potential to include several million additional hectares in the next few years. The opportunity exists to implement important wetland protection and restoration projects through this FmHA program and the CRP. For the FWS, funds and personnel are needed to support the general site-review efforts, to identify wetlands, and to develop and negotiate wetland protection and management to be included in the property deeds. Funds and personnel to support the actual implementation of restoration projects, and the necessary management and monitoring inherent in these programs, will also be needed.

Finally, Title XII of the 1985 Farm Act would allow inclusion of lands in the CRP if those lands ". . . pose an off-farm environmental threat or . . . pose a threat of continued degradation of productivity due to soil salinity . . . ." Off-farm contaminant problems have degraded wintering waterfowl habitat in many parts of the country; the Central Valley of California, the Gulf Coast, and the Chesapeake Bay are notable examples. The USDA should be encouraged to identify erodable, contaminant-contributing lands for inclusion in the CRP. This action could reduce sedimentation, contain contaminants, and result in higher quality wintering waterfowl habitat. The USDA has begun to address this problem by providing incentives for greater cover and tree planting on areas designated as "filter strips" adjacent to water bodies.

In 1970, Congress authorized $10 million/year for preservation of waterfowl habitat under the Water Bank Act. In 1980, Congress showed interest in expanding this program by authorizing $30 million/year. However, no more than $8.9 million has ever been appropriated. Increasing this program in specific wintering waterfowl areas could be a significant step in the preservation of habitats.

The Corps must be encouraged to pursue the wetlands creation, restoration, and development aspects of the 1986 Water Act. The critical need now is for the Corps to be vigorously encouraged to pursue this opportunity to take a new look at its projects. Federal and state agencies and local interests must help in this regard by pointing to those opportunities with the biggest payoff in wetlands protection or creation and by keeping the public informed. Building and maintaining public and congressional support are crucial to the success of these efforts.

The Corps is not likely, at first, to champion these new imperatives with the same enthusiasm that it demonstrates for more traditional pursuits. In fact, its upcoming budget priorities almost certainly will focus on the construction and development aspects of its program. However, Congress has recognized that the enormous and rapid changes imposed in the last few decades by water resource projects in the Lower Mississippi River

Valley, and elsewhere, have exacted too great a cost in the wetland values of this public trust. An informed public, working in conjunction with a coordinated conservation community and the Congress, can have a positive impact. Wintering waterfowl habitat will surely benefit.

For a number of years, the Department of Interior has worked toward an Interior Wetland Policy. The Department of Interior (in reality, the FWS) should complete this process in coordination with other federal agencies. The next step would be development of a national wetland policy. The authority for this effort is the Fish and Wildlife Coordination Act (1956). A national policy should strive toward a "no-net-loss" goal (Wentz 1987). Another policy that could benefit waterfowl tremendously would be large-scale restoration of wetlands. As a national policy evolves, we should see the eventual termination of wetland drainage and, ultimately, a reversal of the process (Wentz 1987).

The stage may be set for a change in Canadian federal water policies. For the first time, recommendations have been made to adopt consistent criteria for evaluating water-development projects that consider direct and indirect costs, assess all implications of irreversible actions, consider all alternatives, and monitor impacts after construction (Pearse et al. 1985). Adoption of these operating procedures will help preserve migration and wintering habitats in Canada. The support of the international conservation community is needed, however.

Legislation

Congress may be ready to give a potentially giant boost to wetland preservation programs from energy resource development revenues. The Arctic NWR is one of the largest wildlife refuges in the world. If Congress determines that exploration and extraction of oil and gas are in the U.S. best interests, several conservation groups have suggested that the resulting revenues should contribute to fish and wildlife conservation. Specifically, suggestions have been made to establish a special trust fund in the MBCA which would receive 40% of the revenues. Fifty percent of this trust would be dedicated to implementing the NAWMP, including use of some of these funds in Canada. Several pieces of introduced legislation address these issues, and a concerted effort is needed to ensure passage of an acceptable bill.

As a result of the passage of the Agriculture Credit Act of 1987, FmHA now has the authority to transfer real property, without reimbursement or interest therein, to federal and state agencies for conservation purposes. Lands that are either marginal for agricultural production, environmentally sensitive, or that have management value to the requesting agency may be eligible for such transfer. Interim regulations were published on Sept. 14, 1988, in the Federal Register but final regulations are pending. The U.S. FWS and state conservation agencies should take advantage of this act to protect, in perpetuity, lands important to North American waterfowl.

Joint Ventures

The previous discussion of future needs identified several diverse ways that government agencies and Congress could improve programs to the betterment of wintering waterfowl and their habitats. What has been lacking, however, is some way to bring all these programs and the private sector together in an organized effort to accomplish stated NAWMP goals. The individuals preparing the NAWMP realized that problem, and developed the concept of joint ventures to attain major objectives. Joint ventures might best be described as a pooling of resources by federal, state, provincial government entities, and the private sector to achieve the habitat protection and

enhancement goals identified in the NAWMP.

The NAWMP suggests initial joint ventures for Canadian prairie habitats, black duck, and arctic goose management. All are progressing with various agencies and groups participating. The Canadian Prairie Habitat Joint Venture is the largest undertaking. In its efforts to change land-use practices on 1,456,920 ha in Canadian prairies to benefit breeding ducks, it serves as a good model from which to develop other habitat-based joint ventures in the U.S. It involves federal agencies (FWS, Canadian Wildlife Service, Canadian Prairie Farm Rehabilitation Agency) and state, provincial, and private entities (DU, Wildlife Habitat Canada, National Fish and Wildlife Foundation, and Delta Waterfowl and Wetlands Research Station).

As a means of launching efforts for the Canadian Prairie Habitat Joint Venture, the concept of a First Step Project was developed by the International Association of Fish and Wildlife Agencies. In this one-time First Step Project, up to $1 million would be committed by state wildlife agencies, to be matched by Ducks Unlimited, Inc. The $2 million combined funding would be presented to the National Fish and Wildlife Foundation for an additional $2 million match by Congressional appropriation. The $4 million total U.S. contribution would then be used to implement the First Step Project in Canada. In the interest of building momentum to implement the NAWMP, Canada agreed to match the $4 million.

Twelve states committed $1 million during 1987, and DU agreed to match that amount. The National Fish and Wildlife Foundation was successful in securing amendment of its authorizing legislation to allow international activities under the NAWMP, and was successful in obtaining the $2 million Congressional match.

The primary focus of the First Step

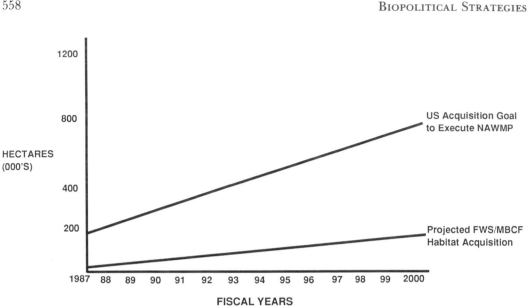

Fig. 5. Comparison of U.S. waterfowl habitat acquisition goals and projected FWS Migratory Bird Conservation Fund acquisition.

Project is the Quill Lakes area of Saskatchewan, which has biological and historical importance as a staging area for a half million ducks and a quarter million geese each fall. The nearby Touchwood Hills are a prime pothole area. Most wetlands remain, but much of the upland habitat has been modified by agriculture. Funds will be allocated to secure and manage uplands surrounding the wetlands in the Touchwood Hills.

The FWS is developing habitat-based joint ventures for 7 areas in the U.S. Four of these (Central Valley of California, Lower Mississippi River Valley, Gulf Coast, and Middle Upper Atlantic Coast) are the most important wintering areas for waterfowl in the U.S.

Total FWS commitments to habitat preservation under the NAWMP will not accomplish the preservation goals for U.S. areas by the year 2000 (Fig. 5). The shortfall must be made up by cooperative federal/state and private activities. Certainly, federal/state acquisition efforts should continue to increase the amount of publicly managed land available for waterfowl. In many parts of the country, however, the key to achieving NAWMP goals lies with private land. By far the largest percentage of land occurs in the private unmanaged category. Activities on these lands can and should be made more compatible with waterfowl and other wildlife. Joint ventures involving public and private sector integrated programs are the key to success.

SUMMARY

Calls for action to perpetuate migratory birds are based on long-standing migratory bird treaties among countries, as well as the 1986 NAWMP. Accumulated experiences show that the U.S. Congress, as well as the Canadian Parliament, must be provided with additional well-designed proposals for new approaches to integrate migratory-bird-benefiting features into tax laws, agricultural programs, water developments, and other land/water authorities, programs, and practices.

The desire for new approaches to eliminate inconsistencies among national program elements was exemplified by the 1986 U.S. tax code reform approved by Congress. The tax code reform eliminated fast write-off of wetland drainage costs, a change that signaled hope for helping to curtail the 87% of annual wetland loss of approximately 185,000 ha associated with agricultural land uses (despite an excessive supply of many agricultural commodities).

Regrettably, past U.S. federal program systems too frequently have encouraged grassroots decisions that moved uses of land away from, rather than toward, an integrated commodity/conservation program. Such inappropriate systems must be realigned to avoid exploitation of the resource base and to reduce taxpayer costs for the multibillion dollar agricultural programs, for example. Needed is broad installation of an integrated conservation/commodity program to place agricultural land use on a sustainable basis that includes benefits for waterfowl and other wildlife. What agricultural program elements can be designed that are attractive to landowners and helpful in meeting specific objectives of each of the joint ventures in the NAWMP? What incentives are needed to interest landowners in such multi-beneficial programs? Attention must be focused to obtain multiple benefits from use of taxpayer funds in agriculture.

The biopolitical strategies suggested by the title of this paper are emerging through efforts to blend agricultural business and conservation programs, and to develop joint ventures under the NAWMP. Such activities focus different interest groups on independent and collective actions with common goals, only in the broadest sense. They can achieve an overall purpose of providing the matrix of habitats necessary to sustain a strong and diverse waterfowl population in North America. Those primarily interested in ducks, geese, and their habitats have realized that they cannot afford to do the job alone, and they are moving quickly to involve a wide array of forces needed to get that job done.

Finally, a pressing need is to convince Mexico to support the habitat protection principles of the NAWMP. Once this occurs, both the U.S. and Canada can begin to arrange joint ventures with the Mexican government. One of the first ventures should be refined identification of critical wintering areas and methods to preserve them within the Mexican political process.

LITERATURE CITED

Baldassarre, G. A., A. R. Brazda, and E. Rangel Woodyard. 1989. The east coast of Mexico. Pages 407-425 *in* L. M. Smith, R. L. Pederson, and R.M. Kaminski, eds. Habitat management for migrating and wintering waterfowl in North America. Texas Tech Univ. Press, Lubbock.

Boyd, H. 1985. The large-scale impact of agriculture on ducks in the prairie provinces, 1956-81. Can. Wildl. Serv. Prog. Notes 149. 13 pp.

Braun, C. E. 1965. A survey of land directly attributed to waterfowl within the contiguous U.S. M.S. Thesis. Montana State Univ., Bozeman. 132 pp.

Brazda, A. R. 1986. Winter waterfowl populations and habitat evaluation, aerial surveys east coast of Mexico. Unpubl. Rep. U.S. Fish and Wildl. Serv., Lafayette, La. 26 pp.

Campbell, H. K. 1987. The president's report. Ducks Unlimited Magazine 51:34-36.

Cowardin, L. M., D. S. Gilmer, and C. W. Shaiffer. 1985. Mallard recruitment in the agricultural environment of North Dakota. Wildl. Monogr. 92. 37 pp.

Cowles, C. D., L. B. Haas, G. J. Akins, W. Britt, T. Hoffman, and A. Wing. 1986. State wetland protection programs—status and recommendations. U.S. Environ. Protect. Agency, Off. of Wetland Prot., Washington, D.C. 101 pp.

Crissey, W. F. 1969. Prairie potholes from a continental viewpoint. Saskatoon Wetlands Seminar. Can. Wildl. Serv. Rep. Ser. 6:161-171.

Duebbert, H. F., and H. A. Kantrud. 1987. Use of no-till winter wheat by nesting ducks in North Dakota. J. Soil and Water Conserv. 42:50-53.

Fenwick, G. H. 1985. The Nature Conservancy's national wetlands conservation project. Nat. Wetlands Newsletter 7:12-15.

Frayer, W. E., T. J. Monahan, D. C. Bowden, and F. A. Graybill. 1983. Status and trends of wetlands and deepwater habitats in the conterminous United States, 1950's to 1970's. Colorado State Univ., Fort Collins. 32 pp.

Greenwood, R. L., A. B. Sargeant, D. H. Johnson, L. M. Cowardin, and T. L. Shaffer. 1987. Mallard nest success and recruitment in prairie Canada. Trans. North Am. Wildl. and Nat. Resour. Conf. 52:298-309.

Harmon, K. W. 1979. Mitigating losses of private wetlands: the North Dakota situation. Pages 157 168 in The Mitigation Symp. U.S. For. Serv. GTR RM-65.

Hawkins, A. S., R. C. Hanson, H. K. Nelson, and H. M. Reeves, editors. 1984. Flyways, pioneering waterfowl management in North America. U.S. Fish and Wildl. Serv.. Washington, D.C. 517 pp.

Heimlich R. E., and L. L. Langner. 1986. Swampbusting: wetland conversion and farm programs. U.S. Dep. Agric., Econ. Res. Serv. Agric. Econ. Rep. No. 551. Washington, D.C. 34 pp.

Higgins, K. F. 1977. Duck nesting in intensively farmed areas of North Dakota. J. Wildl. Manage. 41:232-242.

Kramer, G. W., and R. Migoya. 1989. The Pacific coast of Mexico. Page 507-528 in L. M. Smith, R. L. Pederson, and R. M. Kaminski, eds. Habitat management for migrating and wintering waterfowl in North America. Texas Tech Univ. Press, Lubbock.

Miller, J. B. 1986. Estimates of habitat distribution in the settled portions of the prairie provinces in 1982. Can. Wildl. Serv. Unpubl. Rep. Saskatoon, Saskatchewan. 41 pp.

National Wetlands Inventory Group. 1985. Status and trends of wetlands and deepwater habitats in the conterminous United States, 1950's to 1970's. Trans. North Am. Wildl. and Nat. Resour. Conf. 50:440-448.

———. 1986a. Wetland status report. U.S. Fish and Wildl. Serv. Washington, D.C. 3 pp.

———. 1986b. Quantification of private/public owned wetlands. U.S. Fish and Wildl. Serv., Washington, D.C. 2 pp.

Pearse, P. H., F. Bertrand, and J. W. MacLaren. 1985. Currents of change, final report, inquiry on federal water policy. Ottawa, Ontario. 222 pp.

Pospahala, R. S., D. R. Anderson, and C. J. Henny. 1974. Population ecology of the mallard II. Breeding habitat conditions, size of the breeding populations and production indices. U.S. Fish and Wildl. Serv. Resour. Publ. 115. 73 pp.

Rakowski, P. W., and B. P. Chabot. 1983. Changes in land use in the Minnedosa district of southwestern Manitoba; an update on the Kiel-Hawkins transects. Can. Wildl. Serv. Unpubl. Rep., Winnipeg, Manitoba. 10 pp.

Ramsar Convention Edition 1987. 1987. Convention on wetlands of international importance especially as waterfowl habitat. Internat. Union for Conserv. Nature and Nat. Resour., Switzerland 13 pp.

Rowe, J. S., and R. T. Coupland. 1984. Vegetation of the Canadian plains. Prairie Forum 9:231-248.

Saunders, G. B., and D. C. Saunders. 1981. Waterfowl and their wintering grounds in Mexico, 1937-64. U.S. Fish and Wildl. Serv. Resour. Publ. 138. 151 pp.

Schick, C. D. 1972. A documentation and analysis of wetland drainage in the Alberta parkland. Can. Wildl. Serv. Unpubl. Rep., Edmonton, Alberta. 15 pp.

Scott, D. A., and M. Carbonell, compilers. 1986. A directory of neotropical wetlands. IUCN Cambridge and IWRB Slimbridge. 684 pp.

Tiner, R. W., Jr. 1984. Wetlands of the United States: current status and recent trends. Natl. Wetlands Inventory. U.S. Fish and Wildl. Serv. 59 pp.

Turner, B. C., G. S. Hochbaun, F. D. Caswell, and D. J. Nieman. 1987. Agricultural impacts on wetland habitats on the Canadian prairies, 1981-85. Trans. North Am. Wildl. and Nat. Resour. Conf. 52:206-215.

U.S. Dep. Int. 1988. Report to Congress on the impact of federal programs on wetlands (draft). Washington, D.C. 10 pp.

Voelzer, J. F. 1985. Mexico winter waterfowl survey, 1985. U.S. Fish and Wildl. Serv. Portland, Oreg. 42 pp.

Wentz, W. A. 1987. Functional status of the nation's wetlands. In press. In D. D. Hook, ed. The ecology and management of wetlands. Croom Helm Ltd., London.

Wildlife Habitat Canada. 1986. The status of wildlife habitat in Canada, problems, issues, and opportunities. Ottawa, Canada. 72 pp.